encyclopedia of the
DOCUMENTARY FILM

encyclopedia of the
DOCUMENTARY FILM

Volume 3
P–Z
INDEX

Ian Aitken

editor

Routledge
Taylor & Francis Group
New York London

Published in 2006 by
Routledge
Taylor & Francis Group
270 Madison Avenue
New York, NY 10016

Published in Great Britain by
Routledge
Taylor & Francis Group
2 Park Square
Milton Park, Abingdon
Oxon OX14 4RN

Printed in the United States of America on acid-free paper
10 9 8 7 6 5 4 3 2 1

International Standard Book Number-10: 1-57958-445-4 (Hardcover)
International Standard Book Number-13: 978-1-57958-445-0 (Hardcover)
Library of Congress Card Number 2005046519

Library of Congress Cataloging-in-Publication Data

Encyclopedia of the documentary film / edited by Ian Aitken.
    p. cm.
Includes bibliographical references and index.
ISBN 1-57958-445-4 (set : alk. paper) -- ISBN 0-415-97637-5 (v. 1 : alk paper) -- ISBN 0-415-97638-3 (v. 2 : alk. paper) -- ISBN 0-415-97639-1 (v. 3 : alk. paper)
    1. Documentary films--Encyclopedias. I. Aitken, Ian.

PN1995.9.D6E53 2005
070.1'8--dc 22   2005046519

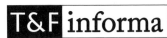

Taylor & Francis Group is the Academic Division of T&F Informa plc.

Visit the Taylor & Francis Web site at
http://www.taylorandfrancis.com

and the Routledge Web site at
http://www.routledge-ny.com

BOARD OF ADVISERS

LIST OF CONTRIBUTORS

Angela Aguayo
University of Texas at Austin

Ian Aitken
De Montfort University, and Hong Kong
Baptist University

Jae Alexander
University of Southern Mississippi

Jessica Allen
Independent Scholar

Samara Allsop
Independent Scholar

Joshua Amberg
University of California, Los Angeles

Carolyn Anderson
University of Massachusetts, Amherst

Kevin Anderson
University of Massachusetts, Amherst

Richard Armstrong
British Film Institute

Isabel Arredondo
State University of New York, Plattsburgh

Michael B. Baker
Independent Scholar

Kees Bakker
Independent Producer of Documentaries

Charles Bane
Louisiana State University

Ilisa Barbash
Harvard University

Elke Bartel
Middle Tennessee State University

Stefano Baschiera
National University of Ireland, Cork

Gerd Bayer
University of Wisconsin, Whitewater

Philip Bell
University of New South Wales, Australia

Nitzan Ben-Shaul
Tel-Aviv University

Jeff Bergin
Independent Producer

Ina Bertrand
University of Melbourne

Robert Beveridge
Napier University

Daniel Biltereyst
Universiteit Gent, Belgium

Mira Binford
Quinnipiac University

Elizabeth Bishop
University of Texas at Austin

Jennifer Bottinelli
Kutztown University

Brett Bowles
Iowa State University

Melissa Bromley
British Film Institute National Film &
Television Archive

LIST OF CONTRIBUTORS

John Burgan
Documentary Filmmaker

Andrew Burke
University of Winnipeg

Marina Burke
University College Dublin

Alan Burton
De Montfort University

Andreas Busche
Film Critic and Film Archivist

Lou Buttino
University of North Carolina, Wilmington

Jose Cabeza San Deogracias
Complutense University, Madrid

Michael S. Casey
Graceland University

Catalina Ceron
Independent Director and Producer of
Documentaries

Michael Chanan
University of the West of England

David Chapman
University of East London

Stephen Charbonneau
University of California, Los Angeles

Thomas Cohen
Rhodes College

Kathleen Collins
Indpendent Scholar

John Cook
Glasgow Caledonian University

Pat A. Cook
Brunel University

Sarah Cooper
University of Cambridge

John Corner
University of Liverpool

Kirwan Cox
Concordia University, Canada

Sean Cubitt
University of Waikato, New Zealand

Jacobia Dahm
Johannes Gutenberg-University, Germany and
Columbia University

Fergus Daly
University College Dublin

Jill Daniels
University of East London

Amy Darnell
Southern Illinois University, Carbondale

Jonathan Dawson
Griffith University

Rafael De Espana
University of Barcelona

Maria Elena De las Carreras-Kuntz
University of California, Los Angeles, and
California State University, Northridge

Annette Deeken
University of Trier, Germany

David Diffrient
University of California, Los Angeles

Caroline Dover
CAMRI (Communication & Media Research
Institute), University of Westminster

Dean Duncan
Brigham Young University

Sarah Easen
British Universities Film & Video Council

Suzanne Eisenhut
San Francisco State University

Jack Ellis
Northwestern University (emeritus)

Robert Emmons
Rutgers University, Camden

Leo Enticknap
University of Teesside, Middlesbrough, UK

Dino Everett
UCLA Film & Television Archive

Kirsty Fairclough
University of Salford

Tamara Falicov
University of Kansas

Seth Feldman
York University, Canada

Ramona Fotiade
University of Glasgow

Steven Foxon
Independent Scholar

Hugo Frey
University College, Chichester

Hideaki Fujiki
Nagoya University

Oliver Gaycken
University of Chicago

Jeff Geiger
University of Essex

Aaron Gerow
Yale University

Hal Gladfelder
University of Rochester

Paul Gleed
State University of New York at Buffalo

Marcy Goldberg
University of Zurich

Annie Goldson
Writer and Documentary Filmmaker

Ian Goode
University of Glasgow

Barry Keith Grant
Brock University, Canada

Leger Grindon
Middlebury College

Tom Grochowski
Queens College, City University of New York

Sapna Gupta
University of Calgary

Roger Hallas
Syracuse University

Ben Halligan
York St. John College, University of Leeds

Martin Halliwell
University of Leicester

Britta Hartmann
Universität der Künste Berlin

Vinzenz Hediger
Ruhr University, Bochum, Germany

Gillian Helfield
York University, Toronto, Canada

Walter Hess
Independent Scholar

Jeremy Hicks
Queen Mary College, University of London

Christine Hilger
University of Texas at Dallas

Jim Hillier
University of Reading

Roger Hillman
Australian National University

Lisa Hinrichsen
Boston University

Kay Hoffman
Haus des Dokumentarfilms, Germany

David Hogarth
York University, Canada

Bert Hogenkamp
Netherlands Institute for Sound and Vision /
Utrecht University

Bruce Horsfield
University of Southern Queensland

Kerr Houston
Maryland Institute College of Art

Amanda Howell
Griffith University

Robert Hunt
Webster University

LIST OF CONTRIBUTORS

Katherine Ince
University of Birmingham, UK

Michael Ingham
Lingnan University

Dina Iordanova
University of Leicester

Jeffrey Isaacs
University of Chicago

Gunnar Iversen
Trondheim University, Norway

D. B. Jones
Drexel University

Chris Jordan
Pennsylvania State University

Verónica Jordana
Independent Scholar

Uli Jung
University of Trier, Germany

Brett Kashmere
Concordia University, Canada

Alexander Kaufman
Purdue University

Misha Kavka
University of Auckland, New Zealand

Tammy A. Kinsey
University of Toledo

Michael Kogge
Fulbright Scholar in Iceland, 2000-2001

Yves Laberge
Film historian and Series Editor, Cinema et société, Les Presses de l'Université Laval

Suzanne Langlois
York University, Canada

Maximilian Le Cain
Independent Filmmaker and Writer

Charles Lee
St. Martin's College

Peter Lee-Wright
Southampton Institute

Neil Lerner
Davidson College

Jacquie L'Etang
University of Stirling, UK

Melinda C. Levin
University of North Texas

Jean-Luc Lioult
Université de Provence

André Loiselle
Carleton University

Alice Lovejoy
Yale University

David Lugowski
Manhattanville College

Catherine Lupton
Roehampton University of Surrey

Theresa C. Lynch
University of New Hampshire

David MacDougall
Australian National University

Misha MacLaird
Writer and Editorial Contractor

Wendy Maier
Oakton Community College

Joshua Malitsky
Northwestern University

Sunil Manghani
York St. John College, University of Leeds

Starr Marcello
Independent Scholar

Gina Marchetti
University of Hong Kong

Harriet Margolis
Victoria University of Wellington, New Zealand

Susan McFarlane-Alvarez
Georgia State University

Heather McIntosh
Pennsylvania State University

Luke McKernan
British Universities Film & Video Council

Tom McSorley
Canadian Film Institute and Carleton
University

Dhugal Meachem
Independent Scholar

Chris Meir
Concordia University, Canada

Martin Mhando
Murdoch University, Western Australia

Paul Miller
Davidson College

Ángel Miquel
Universidad Autónoma del Estado de Morelos,
Mexico

Akira Mizuta Lippit
University of California, Irvine

Julio Montero
Complutense University, Madrid

Albert Moran
Griffith University

James Moran
Emerson College, Los Angeles

Patrick Murphy
Independent Scholar, and York St. John
College, University of Leeds (emeritus)

Justine Nagan
University of Chicago

Caryn Neumann
Ohio State University

Abe Markus Nornes
University of Michigan

Harvey O'Brien
University College Dublin

Jules Odendahl-James
Southwestern Missouri State University

Tony Osborne
Gonzaga University

Derek Paget
University of Reading

Andreas Pagoulatos
Independent Scholar

Silke Panse
University of Kent

María Antonia Paz Rebollo
Complutense University, Madrid

Geraldene Peters
University of Auckland, New Zealand

Rod Phillips
Michigan State University, James Madison College

Shira Pinson
London Film School

Carl R. Plantinga
Calvin College

Wendy Pojmann
Johnson County Community College

Reza Poudeh
Texas Southern University

Jason Price
New York University

Paula Rabinowitz
University of Minnesota, Twin Cities

Charles Ramirez-Berg
University of Texas at Austin

Fernão Pessoa Ramos
Universidade de São Paulo

Laura Rascaroli
National University of Ireland, Cork

Richard Raskin
University of Aarhus, Denmark

Kokila Ravi
Atlanta Metropolitan College

Ramón Reichert
University of Art and Industrial Design, Linz,
Austria

Robert C. Reimer
University of North Carolina, Charlotte

John Riley
British Universities Film and Video Council

Churchill Roberts
University of Florida

Michael Robinson
Doc Films, Chicago

MJ Robinson
New York University

Jane Roscoe
Griffith University

Tom Ruffles
National Extension College, Cambridge, UK

Theresa Scandiffio
University of Chicago

Frank Scheide
University of Arkansas

Ralf Schenk
Film Historian

Paige Schilt
University of Texas at Austin

Jesse Schlotterbeck
University of Iowa

Alexandra Schneider
The Free University, Berlin

Steven Schneider
New York University

Danielle Schwartz
McGill University

Rada Sesic
International Documentary Film Festival
Amsterdam, and International Film Festival
Rotterdam

Jamie Sexton
University of Wales Aberystwyth

Sharon Shelton-Colangelo
Northwest Vista College

Kevin Sherman
San Francisco State University

Philip Simpson
Brevard Community College, Palm Bay Campus

James Skinner
University of Victoria, Canada

Belinda Smaill
Monash University

Ryan Smith
Clatsop Community College, Oregon

Beretta E. Smith-Shomade
University of Arizona

Gustavo Soranz
Independent Scholar

Pierre Sorlin
University of Paris, Sorbonne

Nicholas Stabakis
Independent Scholar

Eva M. Stadler
Fordham University

Sunny Stalter
Rutgers University

Cecile Starr
Film reviewer and film critic

D. Bruno Starrs
University of Melbourne

Matthias Steinle
Marburg University, Germany

Tracy Stephenson
Louisiana State University

Julianne Stewart
University of Southern Queensland

Martin Stollery
Southampton Institute

Dan Streible
University of South Carolina

Thomas Stubblefield
University of Illinois, Chicago

Richard Suchenski
Princeton University

Catherine Summerhayes
Australian National University

Yvan Tardy
De Montfort University

Thomas Tode
Independent scholar

Peter Urquhart
University of Nottingham

Trudi Van Dyke
William Paterson University & Rutgers
University

Roel Vande Winkel
Sint-Lukas Hogeschool, Belgium

Jennifer VanderBurgh
York University

Cristina Vatulescu
Society of Fellows, Harvard University

Joe Wagner
University of North Carolina, Greensboro

Alistair Wardill
Harrow College, UK

Charles Warren
Harvard University and Boston University

Gerlinde Waz
Filmmuseum Berlin

Mark Westmoreland
University of Texas at Austin

Catherine Wheatley
St. John's College, University of Oxford, UK

Helen Wheatley
University of Reading

Diane Wiener
University of Arizona

Danielle Williams
Auburn University

Deane Williams
Monash University

Gordon Williams
University of Wales, Lampeter

Keith Williams
University of Dundee

Ronald Wilson
University of Kansas

Sheena Wilson
University of Alberta, Canada

J. Emmett Winn
Auburn University

Mark J. P. Wolf
Concordia University, Wisconsin

Charles C. Wolfe
University of California, Santa Barbara

Alan Wright
University of Canterbury, New Zealand

John Young
University of Nottingham

CONTENTS

LIST OF ENTRIES A TO Z

THEMATIC LIST OF ENTRIES

Films

Abel Gance: Yesterday and Tomorrow
Act of God
Adolescents, The
American Family, An
Anais Nin Observed
Angela: Portrait of a Revolutionary
Ark, The
Ascent of Man
Aubervilliers

Back of Beyond, The
Basic Training
Bataille du Rail, La
Battle for Our Soviet Ukraine, The
Battle of Chile, The
Battle of China, The
Battle of Midway
Battle of Russia, The
Battle of San Pietro, The
Battle of the Somme
BBC: The Voice of Britain
Berlin: The Symphony of a Great City
Beruf: Neonazi
Black Box BRD
Blue Eyed
Bridge, The
Bronx Morning, A
Bumming in Beijing
Burden of Dreams
Burma Victory

Camera Natura
Canada Carries On
Cane Toads: An Unnatural History
Cathy Come Home
Chair, The
Chang
Chelsea Girls
Children at School

China!
Chronique d'un été
Chulas Fronteras
Churchill's Island
City, The
City of Gold
Close-Up
Coal Face
Comizi d'Amore
Contact
Cuba, Si!
Culloden

Dead Birds
Death of a Princess
December 7
Del Mero Corazón
Desert Victory
Diary for Timothy, A
Dinner Party, The
Divided World, A
Divine Horsemen
Dockers
Don't Look Back
Drifters

Eiffel Tower, The
Enough to Eat?
Enthusiasm
Eternity
Être et Avoir
Every Day Except Christmas
Exile and the Kingdom

Fall of the Romanov Dynasty, The
Family Portrait
Far from Vietnam
Farrebique
Finding Christa
Fires Were Started
First Love

THEMATIC LIST OF ENTRIES

Individuals: Directors and Producers

THEMATIC LIST OF ENTRIES

THEMATIC LIST OF ENTRIES

Countries and Regions

Scandinavia
Scotland
Southeast Asia
Spain
Switzerland

Underground/ Activist Documentary: Australasia/
   Oceania
Underground/Activist Documentary: Chile
United Kingdom
United Kingdom: Documentary Drama

West Indies and Caribbean

Yugoslavia (former)

General Topics and Concepts

Activist Filmmaking
Autobiography and documentary

Chicano Tradition
Cinemagazine

Docusoap

Globalization and Documentary Film

Mocumentary

News Magazines and Television Current Affairs
   Programming

Publicity and Public Relations

Realism, Philosophy and the Documentary Film
Reality Television
Reflexivity

Third Cinema

Video

Styles, Techniques, and Technical Issues

Acting
Animation

Camera Technology
Cinema Novo
Compilation
Computer Imaging

Computer Simulation
Digital video
Digitization
Distribution and Exhibition

Editing Techniques
Editing Technology

Film Stock
Found Footage

IMAX
Indexicality
Interactivity

Multimedia
Music

Narration

Production Processes

Sound
Spoken Commentary ("Voice of God")
Subjunctive Documentary

Videotape

Themes, Issues, and Representations

Aesthetics and Documentary Film: Poetics

Bosnian Documentary Movement

Deconstruction, Documentary Film and

Ethnographic Documentary Film

Falklands War
Fascist Italy
Fascist Spain
Feminism: Africa
Feminism: Critical Overview
Feminism: North America
Feminism: United Kingdom

Hitler and National Socialist Party
Homosexuality and Documentary Film
Human Rights and Documentary Film

Marxism
Modernism: Avant-garde and Experimental Early
   Silent European Documentary

INTRODUCTION

The documentary film can be regarded as the first genre of the cinema. During the 1890s, when the cinema came into existence, most viewers saw some kind of 'actuality' film. These early documentaries were often simple, single-shot affairs, showing newsworthy events, scenes from foreign lands, or everyday events. However, more fictional (or 'staged') actualities also began to be produced from the earliest years of the cinema, based on the special effects capacity of the cinema. An example here might be the Lumière brothers' *Arroseur arrose*, which appeared as early as 1895, but perhaps the most well known is Georges Melies' *A Trip to the Moon* (1902). Between 1895 and 1905 a number of identifiable genres of documentary film emerged, including 'topicals', 'travelogues', 'scenics', 'industrials', sports films, 'trick' films, 'fantsy' films, and films that used fictional reconstruction or staging in a variety of ways. These early genres of documentary film were quickly assimilated into existing modes of popular culture and entertainment and initially appeared in venues that used other, non-filmic, forms of performance such as acrobatics, song, and dance.

However, from quite early on, the value of documentary film as a form of promotion and persuasion was also recognised. For example, the 'industrials' were usually made by corporate businesses in order to promote their image. Examples include English 'industrials' such as *The Story of a Piece of Slate* (1904). Such films were primarily descriptive and expressed little if any opinion on the industrial processes they represented.

Later, the value of the documentary film as a form of social and political critique, ideology, and propaganda was quickly recognised, particularly so during World War I. During the war, all the participating countries embarked upon major programmes of propaganda production involving the use of the documentary film. The documentary moved out of the province of entertainment and private sponsorship and into the service of the state. Initially, government services were antipathetic and suspicious about this new medium that had emerged from the working classes and appeared to possess the worrying ability to show things that governments would prefer to keep well hidden, or, at least, maintain as the preserve of minority elites. As a consequence, strict controls were placed on documentary filmmaking during the war. For example, upon the outbreak of war, the War Office in England allowed cameramen to accompany the British Expeditionary Force (BEF) into France. A decisive victory had been expected, but when the BEF was forced to retreat from Mons and Ypres in late 1914, all newsreel permits were withdrawn and a blanket censorship was imposed. Nevertheless, important films were made during the war in all the participating countries. Perhaps the most important of these was the British film *Battle of the Somme* (1916). This film, striking for its images of life on the front line, had a considerable impact on its audience. Nevertheless, it was produced within the constraints of an extensive censorship system and would not have appeared if its representations were not acceptable to that system.

The documentary film did not really come into its own as a major and significant form of filmmaking until the 1920s. Before 1920, documentary films were largely 'un-authored', so to speak, and often rather simple in both form and aspiration. Despite the appearance of *Battle of the Somme*, few large-scale documentaries were made before 1920, and fewer of these can be regarded as historically, aesthetically, or politically important. However, the inter-war period in Europe was an age of ideology, and documentary film was soon put to the service of political promotion as well as artistic accomplishment.

One of the most important films in the history of the documentary film also appeared as early as 1922. It is difficult to exaggerate the historical impact of Robert Flaherty's *Nanook of the North*. Set in the far north of Canada, *Nanook of the North* presents compelling images of Eskimo life and reveals the startling potential of the documentary film for bringing the everyday world to life. This potential was not lost on early film theorists, who soon began to see documentary film as the principal means through which a genuine form of film art could be created, against the background of the accelerating domination of the medium by the mass-produced Hollywood feature film. Thus, André Sauvage regarded *Nanook of the North* as an example of 'pure cinema', by which he meant that Flaherty's film foregrounded the raw, visual naturalism that Sauvage believed to be at the heart of the aesthetic specificity of the medium.

Nanook was also an inspiration for the emergence of a number of hybrid documentaries that appeared in France and Germany during the 1920s. These films, which combined documentary with modernist form, include *Rien que les heures* (Alberto Cavalcanti, 1926) and *Berlin: die Symphonie der Grossstadt* (Walter Ruttmann, 1929). In addition to these films, *Nanook* also made it possible for Schoedsack and Coopers' *Grass* (1925) and *Chang* (1928) to appear, with their respective accounts of the tribulations of Iranian and Siamese peasant life and, less directly, Victor Turin's *Turksib* (1929), with its epic story of the building of the trans-Siberian railway. It was also in the Soviet Union that the second most important documentary film of the 1895–1945 period emerged: Dziga Vertov's *Man With a Movie Camera* (1929). As with *Nanook of the North*, it is difficult to exaggerate the importance this film has had, both in terms of the documentary film and in terms of film theory.

The 1930–1945 period marked another stage in the historical development of the documentary film, when individual authors began to emerge and documentary was put to increasing social and political use. In the United States, the Workers' Film and Photo League was formed, and committed (or socially concerned) films such as *Native Land* (Paul Strand and Leo Hurwitz, 1942) appeared. Similar organisations sprang up in Europe, and committed documentary filmmakers such as Joris Ivens, Henri Storck, Pare Lorentz, and Ivor Montagu also came to prominence. In Britain, John Grierson's documentary film movement made important films such as *Drifters* (1929) throughout the 1930s and 1940s and cultivated important filmmakers, such as Paul Rotha, Alberto Cavalcanti, Basil Wright, and Humphrey Jennings. Wright's *Song of Ceylon* (1934) and Grierson's *Drifters* remain impressive today for their command of aesthetic form and visual beauty. During the war the documentary film movement also played a role in developing a new genre: the dramatised documentary, exemplified by Jennings' *Fires Were Started* (1943).

After 1945, documentary film developed in a number of different directions. More clearly 'authored' but still socially concerned films began to appear, by such directors as Frederic Rossif, Karel Reisz, Lindsay Anderson, Georges Franju, and Alain Resnais. Of particular note is Resnais' *Nuit et brouillard* (1957, *Night and Fog*), with its stark and uncompromising portrayal of the Nazi death camps. Documentary genres were also developed further during this period. Chris Marker produced philosophical travelogues such as *Letter from Siberia* (1958), while the ethnographic film was taken to a new level of importance by Robert Gardner in *The Hunters* (1956) and *Dead Birds* (1963). Even more important in this respect was Jean Rouch, particularly his ground-breaking, reflexive *Chronicle of a Summer* (1961). The films of French filmmakers such as Rouch also influenced the development of the North American *cinéma vérité* movement and the films of Robert Drew, Richard Leacock, the Maysle Brothers, and others. Their work, in turn, influenced the filmmaking of Frederick Wiseman. Interview-based films, such as Marcel Ophuls' *The Sorrow and the Pity* (1970) and the British TV series *The World at War* (1974–1975) also made important advances within the field by tapping into historical experience in an often profoundly moving and discomforting manner. *The World at War* also broke new ground in telling the story of World War II from the perspective of ordinary people, rather than from the perspectives of the great and good.

During the period from the 1980s to the present, important documentary films and filmmakers continued to emerge. Important filmmakers of this period include Claude Lanzmann, Michael Moore, Errol Morris, Chris Marker, Jill Godmilow, Trinh T. Minh-ha, Barbara Kopple, Julia Reichert, Nick Broomfield, Molly Dineen, Peter Watkins, and many others too numerous to mention.

Perhaps the most significant development during this period was the gradual reemergence of the documentary film as a mainstream cultural form and the creation of new, popular genres. Today, genres such as the docusoap, reality TV, the 'mockumentary', and others receive widespread broadcast coverage around the world and significantly increase the audience for the documentary film, turning it from the preserve of intellectuals and activists into yet another form of mass entertainment. Nevertheless, the recent success of a film such as *Farenheit 9/11* bucks this trend and returns documentary to its subversive roots. *Farenheit 9/11* also exemplifies a characteristic common to much recent documentary filmmaking: a tendency to indulge in a postmodern bricolage of technique, ranging from straight interview to fanciful reconstruction. Moore's film also illustrates another issue often set before documentary filmmakers: the issue of the impact of this genre of highly realistic and apparently persuasive cinema. Yet, despite its controversial character and public exposure, *Farenheit 9/11* did not derail George W. Bush's reelection campaign.

To some extent, documentary film theory has reflected more general trends within film theory. Early written attempts to assess the role and importance of the documentary film tended to focus on questions of realism, authorship, and social representation, reflecting the concerns of much so-called classical film theory. These include the work of Paul Rotha, Erik Barnouw, John Grierson, Basil Wright, and others. Later work by André Bazin and Siegfried Kracauer in the field of film theory also contained a strong documentary dimension.

However, from the 1970s onward, documentary film theory tended to adopt the concerns and intellectual orientations of theorists within the semiotic, structuralist, poststructuralist, and postmodernist camps of film theory. Perhaps it was inevitable that a medium such as documentary film would become a subject of criticism, on account of its supposed 'realism', given the 'antirealist' orientation of 'screen theory' and its derivatives. Given the general tendency of the period to dispense with 'master narratives' and a 'metaphysics of being', it was not surprising to find documentary film theory becoming increasingly preoccupied with the rhetoric and discursive patterns, the codes and interest-based practices of the documentary film, rather than more abstract questions of realism. Bill Nichols was something of a pioneer here, but he was quickly followed by others. This approach to understanding the 'rhetoric' of the documentary film also dominated documentary film theory in the 1980s and 1990s, often giving such theory a pronounced poststructuralist, postmodern, or relativist orientation. Within these approaches, it is the practical impact that documentary film and theory can have on behalf of the minority, or way in which documentary film deploys a post-colonialist, patriarchal, or heterosexist rhetoric, which is of particular import.

Since the early 1990s, however, the field of documentary film theory has broadened, reflecting the spirit of 'post-theory' in film theory. One crucial question affecting documentary film is the representation of history. Historical work on the documentary film has continued, and includes the work of Ian Aitken, Jack C. Ellis, Lewis Jacobs, Deane Williams, Thomas Waugh, and others. Questions of documentary film theory and history are also explored in the work of Charles Warren, Aitken, Derek Paget, William Rothman, Bert Hogenkamp, Philip Rosen, Vivian Sobchack, Michael Renov, and others. Questions of realism and reality in relation to the documentary film are also explored in works by Rosen, Renov, Winston, Anna Grimshaw, and Linda Williams. However, the issue of documentary film and its relation to questions of truth-value, objectivity and reference are rarely considered, though Winston has done so to some extent, and Aitken does in this Encyclopedia. Many of these writers, together with others such as Julia Lesage, Carl Plantinga, Bill Nichols and Trinh T. Minh-ha and Anna M Lopez, also continue to work in a framework informed by gender and postmodern theory.

Structure of the Encyclopedia

In attempting to achieve the requisite degree of comprehensiveness, the goal of this encyclopedia has been to encompass a wide range of different classificatory categories. The most common categories to appear in this work are those of individual films and filmmakers. Entries here range from short (500-word) pieces to much longer accounts of important films and filmmakers, such as *Nanook of the North* and Dziga Vertov.

In addition to this category, the encyclopedia also attempts to assess more broad-based documentary filmmaking traditions within nations and regions, or within historical periods. These are, in general, much longer pieces, ranging from 2,000 words to 7,000 words. Such entries attempt to sum up the most important developments in the documentary film in respective nations, regions, or historical periods. These entries may also prove to be particularly important in bringing to light new material and insights and in providing a rich source of information for future research.

These volumes also encompass a variety of theoretical areas such as deconstruction and feminism. Finally, a number of categories relating to style, technique, technology, production, distribution, exhibition, and other factors are included. All of these entries have a pronounced critical dimension: contributors have been encouraged to think hard about their entries and to interpret them insightfully. All entries also contain detailed empirical sections, such as biographies, bibliographies, and filmographies. Many of these are extensive and the product of considerable research.

INTRODUCTION

This encyclopedia provides a much-needed infrastructural support for the field of documentary film studies, and the material that it contains should provide the basis for many future research projects. The encyclopedia also enables the field to be considered, and even eventually theorised, as a totality. It is now, and for the first time, possible to make comparative studies of different national and regional documentary film traditions, and to create an overall 'map' of the field. This will prove an invaluable aid to future research.

Another function of the encyclopedia is to bring neglected authors, films, and geographical areas of production back into the light of analysis. English-speaking readers will, for example, discover here the names and details of many little-known documentary filmmakers from countries such as India, Bosnia, and China. In this respect, the encyclopedia will also play a particularly important role in bringing attention to bear on films and filmmakers from the former Soviet bloc of eastern European countries. Still another achievement of the Encyclopedia is to provide the opportunity for many contributors to write about the documentary film.

Many contributors to the encyclopedia are eminent scholars. Others are less well known, the representatives of a new generation of writers in the field. Many have produced admirably well-thought and well-researched entries. A smaller group of contributors are nonacademic, but bring their own personal experience to bear on the subject.

The field of documentary film studies is becoming an increasingly important area of study. Since the 1980s, a growing number of publications have appeared on the subject, and that subject has also begun to enjoy a greater presence within the academy. Standing conferences such as Visible Evidence and others also provide regular international forums for interested scholars to exchange ideas and research findings. The encyclopedia will aid this process of consolidation and advancement by making available a substantial corpus of critical writing and data that colleagues can draw upon.

Finally, I wish to thank the Board of Advisors of the encyclopedia for their generous help and advice during the course of this project.

IAN AITKEN

P

PARER, DAMIEN

Damien Parer is Australia's most respected war photographer. His "moment" was World War II, when he filmed the experiences of the ordinary soldier close to or in contact with the enemy in North Africa, New Guinea, and the South-West Pacific. He won Australia's first Academy Award for his *Kokoda Front Line,* documenting the grim jungle war against the Japanese in Papua New Guinea. Parer grew up during the Great Depression in the milieu of Australian Irish Catholic anti-British feeling and the ideological struggles in 1930s Europe, becoming a committed Catholic, political liberal, and social egalitarian. Both by temperament and as a keen member of the Catholic Campion Society, Parer was staunchly anticommunist, anti-Nazi, and anti-Fascist, intensely patriotic, and, until he visited what was then Palestine in World War II , anti-Semitic (McDonald, 1994: 42).

He was self-taught as a stills photographer, moving into cinematography as camera operator on the feature films of Australian director Charles Chauvel. Parer not only taught himself professional camera skills such as lighting, aperture setting, and selecting and framing the shot, but—unusual for an Australian professional photographer—he also evolved informed ideas about European film theory. Parer was a serious intellectual in his approach to film, and he studied foreign films such as Eisenstein's *Battleship Potemkin* and *October.* Parer also engaged critically with film theory debates of this period. For example, he disagreed with Pudovkin that the single shot and the single word are equivalent, and his main theoretic influence was Vladimir Nilsen's *The Cinema as Graphic Art,* which arose from the montage controversies in 1920s revolutionary Russia (McDonald, 1994: 13–14). Parer agreed with Nilsen that technique without purpose was vacuous, and he shared Ruskin's conviction that "art is the definition of an idea through a form," a dictum where form and idea coalesce (Brennan, 1994: 47). Parer read avant-garde film journals addressing European and Russian film theory, and he was influenced by John Grierson, whose definition of documentary, "the creative treatment of actuality," was displayed in Parer's workroom (McDonald, 1994: 14). He became convinced of the central importance of narrative structuring in film, even in newsreels and stills news photographs.

Appointed as an official stills and movie war photographer in January 1940, Parer had already identified his mission: to apply his skills and theories to recording truths of the Australian soldier at war and to explain the war and its contexts to the Australian public and the world. At his best when applying the style of the pictorial and still photographers to film (p. 32), he moved resolutely from one theater of war to another, always looking for opportunities to express truth as he saw it with artistry, freshness, and vitality. His training and commitment gave him a sense of compositional discipline and artistic orientation, even during the frequent unnerving moments when he was with troops under fire. He invariably sought a profound honesty and penetration below mere appearances, eschewing wherever possible simulations and re-enactments and seeking pictures expressive of an Australian identity and self-definition that would enhance the national culture and self-reliance of what was then a minor British colony. Although there was clearly powerful war propaganda potential in his striking frontline material, Parer scorned what he regarded as the mere surface realities of propaganda footage, insisting on the transcendent value of the truthful pictorial statement. He was adept at filming soldiers—unnoticed by them—at their most intense moments of perception or reaction but would not press them if they were reluctant to be filmed. Filming the soldier's spontaneous personal responses to his war experiences became an ideal that often drove Parer to position himself out in front of advancing soldiers to capture faces, eyes, and gestures. This insistence on a rear-facing camera position in "no man's land" led directly to his death in 1944.

Although he was a noncombatant, Parer's stamina, professionalism, and empathy earned him the respect of fighting soldiers wherever he worked. He carried his cumbersome camera gear across the debilitating Kokoda Track in New Guinea, a gruelling system of high ridges, braving knee-deep mud, rain, cold, malaria, tropical ulcer, dysentery, and a host of diseases that drastically reduced in numbers whole fighting battalions. The gloomy jungle was useless for filming, and action shots were restricted to the jungle clearings. With film stock always in short supply, Parer carefully filmed the fighting and suffering around him, editing in camera and selecting his shots sparingly. He was technically proficient enough to maintain his cameras and to improvise when they broke down.

Parer's Papua New Guinea films were also driven by his deep concern that, although the Japanese Army was on Australia's doorstep, the Australian people seemed to lack a sense of urgency about the war and were ignorant about the hardship their soldiers were undergoing in Papua New Guinea. This concern gave his documentary aesthetic a further significance, and he sent back unsettling, disturbing footage of the chaos, confusion, mismanagement, official neglect, and exhausted soldiers during the Australian retreat from the Japanese along the Kokoda Track. But despite the appalling conditions along Kokoda, and Parer's increasing fatigue, he kept firmly to his production ethic.

Parer's nationalism caused him to react against the public relations media material emanating from General Douglas McArthur's headquarters in Australia. Although Australian forces in New Guinea inflicted on the Japanese their first defeat of the war, McArthur continued to minimise Australian successes in his press releases, while inflating the achievements of American troops. Parer hoped that his coverage of Australians would correct this slight by giving the Australians their fair share of public recognition.

Parer's best-known war films include *Sons of the Anzac* (documentary), *Assault on Salamaua, Bismarck Convoy Smashed, Kokoda Front Line, Men of Timor, Salamaua Frontline,* and *War on the Roof of New Guinea* (newsreels).

BRUCE HORSFIELD

Biography

Born Melbourne, Australia, August 1, 1912, into a staunch Catholic family of Spanish ancestry. After school, became a highly skilled photographer before joining Charles Chauvel's movie production of *Heritage* as a camera assistant. Filmed several features before joining the Department of Commerce as a camera operator and stills photographer. With the outbreak of World War II in 1939, his department was absorbed by the Department of Information, and Parer became a war photographer of the Australian forces. From 1940 until late 1943, filmed Australian troops, often in fierce battles, in Palestine, North Africa, Greece, the Middle East, and Papua New Guinea. In 1943, *Kokoda Front Line* won an Academy Award for Parer and Ken Hall jointly. After a series of disagreements with management, resigned from the Department of Information and joined U.S. Paramount News covering the American thrust through the South-West Pacific in Tarawa, New Britain, the Admiralty Islands, Hollandia, and Guam. In September 1944, was killed by Japanese machine gun fire on Peleliu Island in the Palau Group.

Further Reading

Brennan, Niall, *Damien Parer, Cameraman*, Melbourne: Melbourne University Press, 1994.
The Chester Wilmot Files, Australian Archives (SP 300/4).
The Department of Information Files, Australian Archives (SP 109/1).
Legg, Frank, *The Eyes of Damien Parer*, Adelaide: Rigby Ltd, 1963.
McDonald, Neil, "Damien Parer and Chester Wilmot at Tobruk," in *Quadrant*, 44(7/8), July–August, 1986.

————, *War Cameraman: The Story of Damien Parer*, Melbourne: Lothian, 1994.

McDonald, Neil, and Brune, Peter, *200 Shots: Damien Parer, George Silk and Australians at War in New Guinea*, Sydney: Allen and Unwin, 1998.

The Parer Papers, Mitchell Library, Sydney (MLMSS 197/1–4).

Routt, William D., "Review of *Damien Parer: Cameraman* by Niall Brennan and *My Friend Parer* by Maslyn Williams," in *Metro*, 101, 1995, 85–86.

PARIS 1900

(France, Nicole Védrès, 1948)

Although rarely given more than a passing mention in surveys of French cinema and documentary film, *Paris 1900* was in its time a much-loved popular success and a significant landmark in the development of the compilation film. Composed of footage drawn from over 700 actualités, newsreels, and fiction films from the 1900–1914 period, the film offers a panorama of the events, pastimes, and personalities of Belle Epoque France. It is unashamedly rose-tinted in its nostalgic evocation of this lost epoch, and it is not difficult to imagine its appeal to French audiences still reeling from the impact of war and occupation. Yet it conveys too the potent and unexpected freshness of discovering a forgotten past preserved in celluloid. Much of the continuing fascination of *Paris 1900* lies in seeing such legendary figures as Sarah Bernhardt, Auguste Renoir, and a young Maurice Chevalier captured on film (and on records), but the film also catches and reflects on the poignancy of contemporary celebrities who were not so well remembered by posterity.

Paris 1900 was the product of a collaborative effort. Its producer, Pierre Braunberger, had the original idea for the film before World War II. He wrote a complete treatment with Marc Allégret in 1941, while staying with Allégret in Cannes. Braunberger had originally approached Henri Langlois to plan *Paris 1900*, but he found that despite the latter's prodigious memory of films and their content, Langlois did not possess the necessary creative skills to shape the project. Upon returning to Paris after the war, Braunberger pursued his plans for *Paris 1900*, hiring Nicole Védrès to write the commentary and direct the film, and a young Alain Resnais as her assistant.

Braunberger claims that he and the editor Myriam Borsoutzky were the true directors of the film, creating together its overall shape and its key innovations in montage. Other commentators have given more weight to Védrès's input. Jay Leyda emphasises the importance of her rediscovery of early French cinema through Langlois's screenings at the Cinémathèque Française, and the extraordinary montage book of photographs, *Images du cinéma français* (1946), that she compiled in the wake of this experience—a work that anticipates the achievement of *Paris 1900* in creating a persuasive formal and thematic cohesion out of radically disparate source materials.

Paris 1900 opens with actualité street scenes of Paris as a background to key events and icons heralding the new century: the *Exposition Universelle*, the Eiffel Tower, and the first *métro*. It ends in 1914 with the first mobilization and the affecting image of a troop train pulling away from the camera, packed with conscripts waving goodbye to the viewers. Between these two historical turning points, the film is organized into loose thematic clusters that compress and rearrange chronological events but are composed overall to convey a sense of change and historical momentum. One early sequence begins with a lighthearted survey of women's fashions in the 1900s, and then considers how the handicap of long skirts impeding women's participation in sport led to the "scandal" of women wearing trousers. Symbolically empowered by the new garments, if not actually shown wearing them, women appear doing traditionally male jobs such as driving a tram. This leads to accounts of the later women's suffrage campaigns, then back on a lighter note to examine the tyrannies of the corset.

Paris 1900, 1948.
[*Still courtesy of the British Film Institute*]

Such effective blending of topical novelty with larger social and historical transformations is typical of the way *Paris 1900* handles its different themes, integrating a concern for the minutiae of everyday life and the ephemeral forms of popular culture into a wider narrative of the flowering and fading of the Belle Epoque.

Paris 1900 carries echoes of the city symphony films of the 1920s. It loosely follows their "day in the life" pattern of beginning at dawn—with footage of the market traders in Les Halles—and closing with night falling and a new dawn, as a symbolic shot of an electric street light going out is linked to the declaration of war. It also adopts the city symphony films' presentation of social microcosms by ranging thematically through urban rituals, fashion, leisure, popular entertainment, theatre, art, politics, sports, and topical events. The vision of France that dominates much of *Paris 1900* is of an

eternal summer holiday of social contentment, leisure, and relaxation. It is only in the last quarter of the film, heralded by a visit to the squalor and poverty of the Zone, that the tone and emphasis shift to examine political unrest and the negative consequences of modernization for the labour force. This move in turn opens up a widening geographical and political focus as the film rapidly traces the international events leading to the outbreak of World War I.

As Jay Leyda notes, the successful compilation film relies on sensitivity to the formal qualities of its archival sources and on the ability to use montage to create graphic associations between disparate pieces of film that will shape and carry the meanings of the compilation work. *Paris 1900* is exemplary in this respect, because it is able to achieve a smooth integration even between actualité and fiction footage, by capitalizing on similarities of composition and content. Discussing her working methods (in

Leyda, 1964: 79), Védrès also emphasises the importance of what she calls the second meanings of filmed images, dominant moods or feelings that may have little connection to their manifest content. Such feelings are often precisely the product of historical distance from the original sources, or, more specifically, the benefit of hindsight. Thus the brief shot of a "sinister" bearded man used to create a disquieting mood, appropriate to the growing shadow of war, works effectively by making emotions appear to come from the original material itself, as well as by evoking the distance between past and present knowledge.

The sense of historical distance also inflects the seemingly random associations made by the commentary, as one theme or idea triggers another in a deceptively effortless flow, creating a movement akin to the digressive processes of human memory. As the film images appear in response or in parallel to the commentary, the effect is of their being spontaneously remembered. André Bazin registers this effect in finding the achievement of *Paris 1900* to be its forging of a collective memory that, although it does not belong to individual spectators, is experienced as powerfully as if it did.

Ultimately, if unconsciously, *Paris 1900* attests to the role of film itself as a specific medium through which the past reaches us. It offers a compendium of the techniques and developing conventions of early cinema, from the spontaneous charm of people glancing and smiling at the camera in the earliest actualités, through the sets and performance conventions of early narrative melodramas and filmed plays, to the inventory of newsreel parades and political meetings that close the film. It even holds a mirror up to its own medium, with a fantasy short shown as a film-within-a-film and preceded by a delightfully ironic reminder of those days when, some thought, cinema was an invention without a future.

CATHERINE LUPTON

Paris 1900 (Fr, 1948, 79 min.). Pantheon Productions. Produced by Pierre Braunberger. Directed and researched by Nicole Védrès. Scenario and commentary by Nicole Védrès. Production supervision by Claude Hauser. Assistant supervision and research by Alain Resnais. Edited by Myriam Borsoutzky, assisted by Yannick Bellon. Music by Guy Bernard. Sound engineered by Claude Carrère.

Further Reading

Bazin, André, "Nicole Védrès," in *Le Cinéma français de la Libération à la nouvelle vague, 1945–58*, Paris: Cahiers du Cinéma / Éditions de l'Étoile, 1983: 166–69.
Braunberger, Pierre, *Cinémamémoire*, Paris: Centre Georges Pompidou / Centre nationale de la cinématographie, 1987.
Leyda, Jay, *Films Beget Films*, London: Allen and Unwin, 1964.

PARIS IS BURNING

(US, Livingstone, 1991)

Jennie Livingston's first feature documentary focuses on a two-year period in the lives of a group of black and Latino gay men who take part in the drag balls of Harlem, New York City. Filmed between 1987 and 1989, *Paris Is Burning* is as valuable a socio-historical document of this aspect of the ball circuit and street life in gay New York as it is a film that questions the boundary between realness and its imitation in this North American late-1980s context. Thus, although this documentary is conventionally shot, its partici-pants challenge the very reality such convention takes as its foundation. The film allows its performers to take centre stage without calling attention to itself or its filmmaker (Livingston's presence is largely unobtrusive but acknowledged aurally), letting their imitative fantasies question the performance and definition of what it means to be "real."

Cynthia Fuchs states that this documentary takes the problematic of reality per se as its focus, creating the ambivalent flow between fact

Paris Is Burning, 1990.
[*Courtesy of the Everett Collection*]

and fiction that Trinh T. Minh-ha associates with a documentary aware of its own artifice. Fuchs's work on Livingston's film is one in a long line of varied critical responses to *Paris Is Burning* that question the extent to which the performances at the balls trouble our understanding of authenticity through more or less subversive imitations of the world beyond the ballroom. The Paris of the title of the film comes to signify the high-fashion world of designer labels, fame, and fortune to which the performers at the balls wish to belong. For these men, to imitate is to be. At the balls they compete with each other in dressing up to see who can appear more real. The visual images of the film are interspersed periodically with terminology related to the ball circuit—in upper-case white writing on a black screen—that requires definition and explanation for those who do not engage in this activity. One such category is "Realness," which is defined, as other categories are, by the performers and spectators at the balls; their commentary sometimes takes the form of a voice-over, sometimes the form of on-screen responses to questions asked by Livingston in numerous interviews. Realness is the look that each participant is striving to achieve in a competitive and at times viciously critical arena whose backdrop is the straight, white world of the economically privileged classes of America. Being real is associated in this context with looking like one's straight counterpart, and the balls provide the forum for the participants to act out their longing to be someone other than who they are. Indeed, pas-

sing for someone they are not becomes a matter of survival beyond the ball space, because many of the participants live out these performances beyond the circuit as well as within it.

The film charts the varied fates of some of the participants we encounter, introducing them to us in the first part, filmed in 1987, and then taking us back to some of them in 1989. Each of the performers belongs to a "house" with a "mother" who looks after her "children." These houses become points of contact and support networks for those who are long since distanced from their original families. The ball circuit we see seems a safe space in which fantasies can be enacted freely, but the arena and its surrounding redefinition of family life cannot protect all of its children all of the time. By 1989 Willi Ninja, mother of the House of Ninja and the most talented of the vogue street artists featured in the film, has been catapulted toward the fame and fortune that most of the other participants in the film covet. His dream came true in a way that nobody else's did during the course of filming. In striking contrast, Venus Xtravaganza, a pre-operative male-to-female transsexual, was murdered during the course of filming.

The performers act out positions that they cannot occupy in the idealized view they have of the "real world," yet the power of this film lies in its ability to turn the real and the imagined inside out. The ball circuit enables these men to enter into another world, described by one of them as

Paris Is Burning, 1990.
[*Courtesy of the Everett Collection*]

like passing through the looking glass and being able to feel comfortable in a way that they never do in the world at large. In their varied imitations of straight, white, wealthy America, they attempt to erase their difference, without explicitly questioning the privileged status of the models they are imitating. On the contrary, they idolize the objects of their imitation uncritically. However, Livingston's filming beyond the ball circuit introduces more critical leverage on this point. The documentary is structured such that scenes from the world the performers emulate and wish to belong to are juxtaposed with the imitations of this world enacted at the balls. Livingston films people walking down the street, going about their daily business unaware that they are being filmed. These shots, coupled with a scattering of images from fashion or high-society magazines, set up the idealized models that are desired and copied by the ball attendees, but they also reflect on the status of the idealized society. Judith Butler's reading of the film emphasizes its subversive aspects, even as she cautions against seeing the film as solely subversive. If looking like one's straight counterpart is seen as the equivalent of being straight, then attending to the formation of the drag queen or the transsexual's identity as a series of imitative performances calls into question the privileged status of the straight model. This critically transgressive aspect of the film is not enough, however, to give any of its participants what they want. While *Paris Is Burning* gives itself over to their dreams and desires, it can confer a modicum of international fame on its subjects, but only for its rather fleeting duration.

SARAH COOPER

Paris Is Burning (US, Off White Productions, 1990, 71 min.). Distributed by Academy Entertainment and Off White Productions. Produced by Richard Dooley, Jennie Livingston, and Barry Swimar. Directed by Jennie Livingston. Cinematography by Paul Gibson. Music by Lynn Geller. Editing by Jonathan Oppenheim. Filmed in New York.

Further Reading

Bruzzi, Stella, *New Documentary: A Critical Introduction*, London: Routledge, 2000.
Butler, Judith, "Gender Is Burning: Questions of Appropriation and Subversion," in *Bodies That Matter*, New York: Routledge, 1993.
Fuchs, Cynthia, "'Hard to Believe': Reality Anxieties in *Without You I'm Nothing*, *Paris Is Burning*, 'Dunyementaries,'" in *Between the Sheets, In the Streets: Queer, Lesbian, Gay Documentary*, edited by Chris Holmlund and Cynthia Fuchs, Minneapolis: University of Minnesota Press, 1997.
Goldsby, Jackie, "Queens of Language: *Paris Is Burning*," in *Queer Looks: Perspectives on Lesbian and Gay Film and Video*, edited by Martha Gever, John Greyson, and Pratibha Parmar, New York: Routledge, 1993.
Hooks, Bell, "Is Paris Burning?" in *Black Looks: Race and Representation*, Boston: South End Press, 1992.

PATHÉ (UK)

The main significance of Pathé's UK operation lies in the fact that it produced the earliest and longest-lasting newsreel to be regularly released in British cinemas. There were also a number of cinemagazine series and individual nonfiction films made by Pathé's UK unit.

The Pathé company has its origins in the two decades between the Lumière brothers' Paris screening on December 28, 1895 (believed to be the first successful projection of moving images to a paying audience) and World War I, during which France dominated the global film industry. The entrepreneur Charles Pathé had been dealing in film-related equipment (notably pirated versions of Edison's Kinetoscope) since 1895, but the birth of the Pathé empire proper occurred in December 1897, when he formed a partnership with a wealthy French industrialist and began manufacturing film stock. Along with the other corporate giants of French cinema—Gaumont and Éclair—Pathé generated most of its revenue from hardware sales and laboratory services during the first decade of its existence. However, all three firms gradually moved into film production, and in 1908 the *Pathé Fait-Divers* began to be released; it is believed to have been the world's first newsreel, in the generally accepted sense of the word.

Pathé had sold his products and services in Britain since the early part of the decade, and in 1910 he decided to export the newsreel too. He established an office in London and took on a team of cameramen and editors, and in February 1910 the *Pathé Animated Gazette* released its first issue. In the period before World War I, the average length of a typical newsreel was 300 feet (approximately five minutes) and issues were released weekly. This had risen to 700-foot biweekly editions by the early 1920s, a format that became established as the industry norm for the remainder of the newsreel's life as a mass medium.

Early Pathé cameramen, notably Jock Gemmell and Jack Cotter, who later became key figures in the "newsreel wars" of the 1930s, quickly established a reputation for delivering high-quality location footage from a range of topical events and issues. World War I saw the infrastructures of all the major newsreel companies pooled under the auspices of the War Office Cinematograph Committee (between October 1915 and February 1919), with footage taken at the European fronts being made available to the newsreel companies and government filmmakers. After the war the "Animated" was removed from Pathé's title, making it simply the *Pathé Gazette*, a title that would remain until the newsreel's next relaunch in January 1946. In addition to its core newsreel, other Pathé releases included the cinemagazines *Pathé Pictorial* (1918–1969) and *Eve's Film Review* (1921–1933), the latter marketed specifically to female audiences. Pathé was also the only newsreel to regularly include colour footage during the silent period, releasing a number of fashion- and sport-related items in the *Pictorial* using the Pathécolor stencil process.

The conversion to sound saw the British newsreel industry consolidate into five major production companies, with many of the smaller ones (most notably *Topical Budget*) being forced out of business by the increased costs. Those that remained at the middle of the decade were Pathé, Gaumont-British, British Movietone (owned or controlled by British film or print media interests), British Paramount, and Universal Talking News (offshoots of their respective U.S. operations). The 1930s saw intense competition between them over the speed and exclusivity with which footage was released, especially coverage of prominent sporting and ceremonial events. The decade was also characterised by extensive and wide-ranging political censorship of practically everything shown in British cinemas. Although newsreels were the only films that did not have to be vetted by the British Board of Film Censors (BBFC), the Home Office maintained an effective system of informal control, and the two most widely shown newsreels (Gaumont-British and Movietone) also had close links to the political establishment. The result is that newsreels rarely covered politically or ideologically contentious issues and virtually never criticised the government of the day. The bulk of their output consisted of royal appearances, sports, and other events that roughly fitted the definition of current affairs but met cinema exhibitors' and the government's insistence upon apolitical entertainment.

World War II once again saw the newsreel industry being semi-nationalised, this time under the auspices of the Ministry of Information. A rota system was introduced for allocating cameramen to be attached to units of the armed forces, while the Ministry's Films Division was responsible for footage pooling and censorship. The role of the newsreel within the British mass media also underwent a fundamental change, arising largely from their role as a public information provider on the progress of the war. This process reached its climax in April 1945, when all five newsreel producers independently made the decision to devote an entire issue to footage taken shortly after the liberation of the Bergen-Belsen concentration camp.

In the aftermath of World War II, Pathé's producer, Howard Thomas, made the decision to avoid a return to what he perceived as the banality of the 1930s and to follow the lead of the Documentary Movement, promoting a more discursive approach and encouraging the expression of political viewpoints. (This put him directly at odds with Sir Gerald Sanger of Movietone, who sought an immediate return to the prewar model and even argued against covering the 1945 general election at all.) To this end, the *Gazette* was relaunched as *Pathé News* at the beginning of 1946. Typical of what Thomas had in mind is issue 46/60 (July 29, 1946), *Germany's Food—The Truth*, which examined arguments for and against Great Britain continuing to commit a significant proportion of her GDP to maintaining occupied Germany. Thomas also founded the Pathé Documentary Unit, which produced a significant output of educational films for schools during the 1950s.

The 1950s and 1960s witnessed the gradual decline of the British newsreel, as current affairs coverage shifted gradually to television, and declining cinema audiences eroded the newsreels' income. Pathé was the next to last of the "big five" to cease production, releasing its last national newsreel to cinemas on February 26, 1970. However, the company remained in existence for three more decades, exploiting its 60-year archive by licensing footage to broadcasters and TV documentary producers. In 2002, almost a century after Pathé launched the first regular newsreel in Britain, the company achieved another "first," publishing its entire surviving output as streamed digital video available via the Internet. It was taken over the following year by ITN Archives, which continues to commercially exploit the Pathé material.

LEO ENTICKNAP

See also **Ministry of Information; Newsreel Series: UK**

Further Reading

Abel, Richard, *The Ciné Goes to Town: French Cinema, 1896–1914*, Berkeley and Los Angeles, University of California Press, 1994.
Aldgate, Anthony, *Cinema and History: British Newsreels and the Spanish Civil War*, London: Scolar Press, 1979.
Ballantyne, James (ed.), *Researchers' Guide to British Newsreels*, vol.1, London: British Universities' Film and Video Council (1983).
———, vol. 2, 1988.
———, vol. 3, 1993.
Hammerton, Jenny, *For Ladies Only? Eve's Film Review, 1921–33*, Hastings: The Projection Box, 2001.
Huret, Marcel, *Ciné actualités: Histoire de la presse filmée*, Paris: Éditions Henri Veyrier, 1984.
Pronay, Nicholas, "British Newsreels in the 1930s—Audience and Producers," in *History*, 56, October 1971, 411–418.
Smither, Roger, and Wolfgang Klaue (eds.), *Newsreels in Film Archives*, Trowbridge: Flicks Books, 1996.

PELECHIAN, ARTAVAZD

Armenian filmmaker Artavazd Pelechian remains shamefully neglected among the world's great documentary filmmakers. Creator of an astounding series of montage-based short films that were for many years shelved by the Soviet authorities, he has worked little in recent years, despite support in the West, as a consequence of the challenging nature of his experimental work. His latest completed films are the companion pieces *Konec* (1992) / *End* and *Zizn'* (1993) / *Life*, which run for eight and seven minutes, respectively.

It's impossible to ignore the legacy of Eisenstein's thinking in the work of the Armenian. Since the late 1960s Pelechian, an important theorist as well as practitioner, has situated his work within the problematic of 1920s Soviet Montage theory and practice.

His main aim has been to extend Montage theory—in particular the more radical aspects of Eisensteinian thought—to capture the movement of life on a cosmic scale. In line with recent developments in both science and the arts (for example, musical aesthetics), Pelechian's "montage at a distance" concentrates on the material reality of the work, seeking to emphasise and exploit the shot's nonrepresentational features. It is a concept of abstraction and a use of the medium that presuppose in the

filmic material the persistence of connections that exceed its sense and signification from a spectatorial viewpoint. Pelechian writes,

> The fundamental elements, the principal detonator of contrapuntal montage, exercise a reciprocal action on all the other elements according to a law and fulfill a function that one can qualify as nuclear. This involves a double contrapuntal link with every or any other point of the film according to vectorial lines. They provoke a bilateral chain reaction amongst all the subordinate links, first descending, then ascending.

Pelechian's position is as much influenced by the post-68 Godardian version of Montage theory (and in turn his *Natchalo, Nacalo* or *Skisb* (1967) / *In the Beginning* will be a model for Godard's masterpiece *Histoire(s) du Cinéma* [1988–1998]), and as much by the radical formal innovations of American Underground artists such as Brakhage and Conner, as it is by Eisenstein.

Pelechian's relation to Eisenstein can be summarised in the following terms.

Through inflecting Eisensteinian Montage theory in the direction of more broadly cosmic concerns, Pelechian can relativise the historical/ Historicist perspective of Eisenstein. Pelechian's pits the David of little Armenia against the Goliath of Eisenstein's Soviet Union. *Menk* or *My* (1969) / *Us,* his most overtly political film, uses material from the Central State Archives and the Documentary archives of Yerevan studios to remember this lost people of history, its culture, and its landscape. *Tarva Yeghanaknere* or *Vremena goda* (1972) /*The Seasons* presents images of the human fully immersed in nature, carried along on its waves, no longer its master as in the Western, Cartesian tradition, but forming one energetic element in the grand turbulent system of life. Whether he uses images of crowds or of flocks of birds (as he did in *Obitateli* or *Bnakitchnere* (1970) / *The Inhabitants*), historical footage or material staged in the present, his cinema constitutes a kind of rhythm-analysis whereby Pelechian seeks to express all of the forms of movement and all of the dimensions of reality. In forcing the cinema to "acquire other dimensions," the Armenian invents a contrapuntal method emphasizing what he calls the "pitches of expressivity" whereby, as in the philosophical notion of Univocity, the world sings of itself. This Univocal tendency (the work's ontological facet that on occasion can allow the mood to veer unproblematically, with a mere shift in intensity, from tragedy to burlesque) is in line with Pelechian's immanent methodology, a criteria of selection of and placement of shots whereby no external necessity dictates the logic of cutting and assembly, lending each work a unique rhythm and temporality. There is no belief in transcendence; religion is merely a social fact and progress a ruse (see Pelechian's answer to Kubrick's *2001 A Space Odyssey, Nas vek* or *Mer dare* (1982) / *Our Century* or *Cosmos*). His fascination with the science of complexity, in particular the physics of clouds, has led the effect on the viewer of his unique method of selecting and ordering shots to be compared to the Butterfly Effect; that is, the "fluttering" of a single shot can produce turbulence in all the other shots.

Whereas Eisenstein's dialectical thinking rests on a sensorimotor unity of man and nature, and therefore, in Deleuzian terms (and it has largely been within this conceptual frame of reference that the Armenian's work has been considered by critics), remains a cinema of movement-images, Pelechian's Univocal philosophy has led him to produce genuine time-images, and in *The Seasons* the complete lack of spatiotemporal coordinates and sociocultural landmarks has given rise to an abstract and cosmic vision of life as aberrant movement (in which the human is merely one rhythmic force among others) in fusion with the enveloping "chaosmosis" of torrential nature.

Following from this, I would suggest that there is a new logic of thought inPelechian, one that perhaps moves him furthest away from Eisenstein's position. If there is a certain sense of impenetrability (but one that accounts for the films' incredible intensity) about Pelechian's montages, it is an essential element of this new thought; we can no longer sanction the all-powerful thought of Dialectics and the Grand Narratives it gave rise to. To think the Cosmos is to recognise the void at the heart of thought that no logical succession or associative chain (and no *Aufhebung*) can fill. Montage at a distance can express what is unthought in our manners of being, seeing, and doing. Against the Eisensteinian organic Totality wherein all oppositions are overcome according to the laws of Dialectics, the whole for Pelechian is a nontotalizing Becoming governed by a dissociative force—the Force of Time, an Interstitial universe ceaselessly emitting incommensurable series.

In line with Deleuze's account of the Neo-Baroque times we live in, there are no harmonic resolutions in Pelechian, only dissonant tunings. In manipulating found or staged footage through acceleration, slow-motion photography, repetition, inversion, or running images backwards, Pelechian rejects what he calls, in his influential text Contrapuntal Editing, "the classical rules of montage: exposition, development, resolution," in favour of an ever-increasing turbulence, without beginning or end.

FERGUS DALY

Biography

Born in Leninakan, Armenia, in 1938. In the 1960s , studied cinema at the VGIK (Cinematic Institute of Moscow). Made his first film in 1964. Although his films were suppressed under Soviet rule, he has since achieved a measure of acclaim worldwide and received the Scam Prize for Television in 2000.

Selected Films

1964 *Gornyj patrul* / *Mountain Patrol*
1967 *Natchalo, Nacalo* or *Skisb* / *In the Beginning*
1969 *Menk* or *My* / *Us*
1970 *Obitateli* or *Bnakitchnere* / *The Inhabitants*
1972 *Tarva Yeghanaknere* or *Vremena goda* / *The Seasons*
1982 *Nas vek* or *Mer dare* / *Our Century*
1992 *Konec* / *End*
1993 *Zizn'* / *Life*

Further Reading

Cazals, Patrick, and Danielou, Laurent, "The Galaxy Pelechian: Interview with Pelechiam," in *Discourse*, January 22, 2001.

Godard, Jean-Luc, "Un Language d'avant Babel, conversation entre Arthur Pelechian et J-L Godard," in *Le Monde*, April 2 1992.

Niney, Francois, "Montage with Images That Don't Exist: Interview with A. Pelechian," *Discourse*, January 22, 2001.

Pelechian, Artavazd, "Le montage à contrepoint, ou la théorie de la distance," in *Trafic*, 2 spring 1992.

Pelechian, Artavazd, "Time Against Me, My Cinema Against Time," in *Discourse*, January 22, 2001.

Pigoullié, Jean-Francois, "Pelechian: Le montage-mouvement," in *Cahiers du Cinéma*, 454, April 1992.

PENNEBAKER, D.A.

A pioneer in the cinema verité movement in the United States, D.A. Pennebaker has brought his observational style to music and politics since the 1960s and continues his practice today.

After completing several short works, he traveled to Moscow and made *Opening in Moscow* (1959) with the help of Albert Maysles, though the sponsors refused to pay for the film. That same year he joined Drew Associates, where he helped develop the first portable, synchronized 16mm camera and sound system.

With Drew Associates, Pennebaker worked on a variety of landmark films that helped define the cinema verité movement in America, including *Primary* (1960), *On the Pole* (1960), *David* (1961), *Jane* (1962), and *Crisis: Behind a Presidential Commitment* (1963). A new style emerged in the making of these films, noted primarily for their eschewing of traditional documentary conventions, such as reenactments and voice-over narration, in favor of seemingly pure observation. The mobility of the newly developed equipment facilitated unprecedented access to private situations, creating the illusion of the camera operator acting like a "fly on the wall." It is this style that Pennebaker continued in his own films after leaving Drew Associates in 1963 and starting his own company with Richard Leacock.

Pennebaker first made a name for himself with *Dont Look Back* (1967), a prototypical concert film that set the standard for others to follow, and that incorporated much of the cinema verité traditions started in the Time-Drew Associates films. Begun on just a handshake and without funding, the film followed Bob Dylan on his 1965 British concert tour and became a classic document of the counterculture movement. *Dont Look Back* refuses to paint a realistic portrait of the enigmatic Dylan, instead opting toward as much irreverence toward its subject as its subject had for the world. Pennebaker captures Dylan's duality in his personality through the musician's disrespect for the press on the one hand and through his charisma with his fawning fans on the other. Numerous concert film conventions (some of them derivatives of cinema verité conventions) begin in this film, including the informal backstage jams with Donovan and other artists, interaction with British fans, travel time, press conferences and interviews, and, of course, on-stage performances before enraptured audiences.

In this film Pennebaker also celebrates his level of access into private spaces and moments. He highlights the behind-the-scenes planning performed by manager Albert Grossman through his extensive telephone negotiations. He follows Dylan down a long hallway to the stage (a convention often featured in other concert films and even spoofed in *This Is Spinal Tap* [1984]). During one of Dylan's concerts, the sound system fails, and Pennebaker keeps us backstage with the crew members as they frantically scramble to get the correct cables plugged in and the sound working again. All of these work to provide a greater sense of intimacy with the subject, a key characteristic of many of Pennebaker's works.

After his success with *Dont Look Back*, Pennebaker continued to make documentaries in cinema verité style about music, musicians, and music festivals. *Monterey Pop* (1968) and *Sweet Toronto* (*Keep on Rockin'*, 1972) chronicle two rock festivals. Both films favor the long take and attempt to maintain a fidelity to the festivals' happenings. In some ways this fidelity creates complications in *Ziggy Stardust and the Spiders from Mars*, a 1973 film of David Bowie's final performance as

PENNEBAKER, D.A.

Ziggy Stardust. This work focuses primarily on onstage events, although critics of the camera work complain about the lack of framing on Bowie himself. Critics also complain about the poor sound quality and lack of backstage access, something flaunted in *Dont Look Back*. Another music-subject film from this time by Pennebaker is *Company—The Original Cast Album* (1970).

In 1977, Pennebaker met and began working with Chris Hegedus. Their first films together took on political subjects such as the proposal to deregulate natural gas in *Energy War* (1978). The pair's best-known collaboration is probably *The War Room* (1993). In keeping with the cinema verité tradition, the film follows Bill Clinton's 1992 campaign staff, including the fiery James Carville and the staid George Stephanopoulos. From the New Hampshire primary to the election night victory, it chronicles the pitfalls that mired the campaign, including Gennifer Flower's allegations of sexual misconduct, draft-dodging accusations, and other mud-slinging. The film earned an Oscar nomination for Best Documentary Feature and won the D.W. Griffith Award for Best Documentary of the Year.

The War Room (which refers to the Clinton campaign headquarters in Little Rock, Arkansas) also demonstrates the risk involved in this type of documentary filmmaking. In pursuing real life in real life contexts with as little interference as possible, there is little guarantee of the outcome. If Clinton had lost the election, there would not have been much in terms of a sellable film.

But music remains the primary passion for these collaborators, and their titles cover a wide variety of music genres. *Depeche Mode 101* (1989) features the 1980s pop group's massive concert at the Rose Bowl Stadium in Pasadena, California, and a group of fans who travel cross-country to witness it. *The Music Tells You* (1992) is a portrait of jazz saxophonist Branford Marsalis. *Down from the Mountain* (2001) returns Pennebaker to his concert film origins, though this time in bluegrass music, not rock; *Only the Strong Survive* (2002) is a who's who of soul, including Wilson Pickett, Carla Thomas, Mary Wilson, and the Chi-Lights.

Pennebaker and Hegedus married in 1982 and run Pennebaker Hegedus Films, based in New York City. Their most recent film is the Emmy-award winning *Elaine Stritch at Liberty* (2004), a portrait of the Tony-winning Broadway legend. A project in progress includes a piece on political satirist Al Franken (with Nick Doob).

HEATHER MCINTOSH

See also **Dont Look Back**; **Drew Associates; Hegedus, Chris; Leacock, Richard;** *Primary*

Biography

Born in 1925 in Evanston, Illinois. Earned a degree in mechanical engineering from Yale in 1947 and spent a year studying naval architecture at the Massachusetts Institute of Technology before joining the Navy for two years. Then held a variety of odd jobs in New York City, and during this time began experimenting with and making films. Joined Drew Associates in 1959. Left Drew Associates in 1963 to start his own company with Richard Leacock. In 1977, met and began working with Chris Hegedus. Married Hegedus in 1982. Currently runs Pennebaker Hegedus Films, based in New York City.

Selected Films

1959 *Opening in Moscow*
1960 *Primary*: cinematographer, editor
1963 *Crisis: Behind a Presidential Commitment*: cinematographer
1967 *Dont Look Back*
1968 *Monterey Pop*
1970 *Company—The Original Cast Album*
1970 *Sweet Toronto (Keep on Rockin')*
1973 *Ziggy Stardust and the Spiders from Mars*
1978 *Energy War* (with Chris Hegedus)
1989 *Depeche Mode 101* (with Chris Hegedus and David Dawkins)
1992 *Branford Marsalis: The Music Tells You* (with Chris Hegedus)
1993 *The War Room* (with Chris Hegedus)
2001 *Down from the Mountain* (with Nick Doob and Chris Hegedus)
2002 *Only the Strong Survive* (with Chris Hegedus)
2004 *Elaine Stritch at Liberty* (with Nick Doob and Chris Hegedus)

Further Reading

Levin, G. Roy, "Donn Alan Pennebaker," in *Documentary Explorations: 15 Interviews with Film-makers*, Garden City, NY: Doubleday and Company, 1971, 223–270.
Mamber, Stephen, *Cinéma vérité in America: Studies in Uncontrolled Documentary*, Cambridge: The MIT Press, 1974.
Pennebaker Hegedus Films, http://www.phfilms.com/index.php.
Rosenthal, Alan, "*Don't Look Back* and *Monterey Pop*: Don Alan Pennebaker," in *The New Documentary in Action: A Casebook in Filmmaking*, Berkeley and Los Angeles: University of California Press, 1971, 189–198.
Stubbs, Liz, "D.A. Pennebaker and Chris Hegedus: Engineering Nonfiction Cinema," in *Documentary Filmmakers Speak*, New York: Allworth, 2002, 41–68.
Swift, Lauren Lowenthal, "Pennebaker: D. A. Makes 'em Dance," in *Film Comment*, 24, 6, November 1988, 44–49.

PEOPLE'S CENTURY

(UK, BBC/WGBH, 1997)

An ambitious documentary project, *People's Century* was four years in the making. The series, co-produced by the BBC and WGBH Boston, aimed to chronicle the major themes and events that shaped the world in the twentieth century.

The epic 26-part documentary, broadcast on PBS in the United States and the BBC in the UK between 1995 and 1999, was recognised as a significant development in the history of documentary making. Winner of numerous awards, including an International Emmy and a George Foster Peabody Award, the series is widely considered one of themost boldly envisaged and painstakingly researched television documentaries ever created.

People's Century was the product of a large collaborative team from the United States and the UK, overseen by the executive producer for WGBH, Zvi Dor-Ner, and by Peter Pagnamenta as executive producer for the BBC. Most of the 26 episodes of the series comprise newsreel footage, industrial or commercial film footage, and propaganda film footage, much of which had previously never been broadcast on television. Interspersed are personal testimonies of members of the public who witnessed major historical events.

The series intended to present a global perspective, and the producers' commitment to presenting major historical events through the eyes of the people who experienced them is commendable. The vast subject matter is not consistently organised in strict chronological order. Using extensive research material, each of the 26 episodes is devoted to a focus year, while also covering a wide range of issues over a period of years. The series begins with "The Age of Hope," an examination of the optimism of a new century, and continues in a roughly chronological manner, occasionally weaving back and forth in time to illustrate a particular point.

The series addresses a number of key historical events and trends, including the First World War and the failed attempts to prevent another, the rise of Nazism and World War II, the Cold War, and the atomic bomb and its repercussions.

A number of episodes consider political transformations, including the Russian Revolution, the demise of colonialism in Africa and Asia, the American civil rights movement; the anti-apartheid movement in South Africa, and the collapse of Soviet communism. Economic and social developments are also addressed in episodes focused on the rise of mass industrialisation and the difficulties related to unionisation, the Great Depression, the postwar baby boom, the rise of Asian economies, public health issues, the environmental movement, and the influence of film and television on societies. The series concludes with "Fast Forward," which examines the development of the global economy and the widening economic and cultural divides at the end of the twentieth century.

Visually engaging and skilfully edited, *People's Century* is effective in producing snapshots of the major events of the century. The series is narrated by John Forsythe and Alfred Woodward. The overall tone is appropriately sombre and uplifting in equal measure.

The series is a valuable resource, but nonetheless there are some glaring omissions. For example, in the early episodes there is a notable absence of any reference to South American history. Although it is clear that the producers have worked diligently to present a range of perspectives, the complexity of a particular subject and the time limitations of the episode can leave gaps in the historical narrative. There is an undeniable Western perspective, and this can be frustrating at times, but the producers have created a commendable and important documentary series that chronicles the highs and lows of a century of change.

For example, Episode 5, "On the Line," explores the development and effects of a consumer society boosted by mass production. There is a discussion of the influence of the assembly line method of manufacturing as a catalyst for increased production, immigration, and greater access to consumer goods. However, the narration pays scant attention to the fact that many people did not benefit from the increased access to consumer goods, and this theme is not developed throughout the episode. But overall, the series largely succeeds in meeting its challenging goal of representing the disparate cultures, groups, and ideologies active in twentieth-century social and political history.

Much of the early archival footage is remarkable, and the researchers have clearly benefited from related events at the start and end of the century. Indeed, the rise of totalitarian government and the eventual disintegration of the Soviet bloc have allowed much of the previously unseen film clips and archival material to become available. Included is not only footage of the more momentous events at the start of the twentieth century, but also fascinating images of the everyday lives of ordinary people, who are seen at work and at play. The producers have commendably travelled as necessary to interview centenarians who experienced such events. Interviews with a *Titanic* survivor, a man who recalls when Japan decided to open its doors to the "barbarian" West, and an English woman who speaks of voting for the first time, among others, add weight and poignancy to the overall narrative thread of the series.

The series as a whole provides "snapshots" of the major events of the century rather than a unified narrative. Although it undeniably offers a Western perspective on the history of the past hundred years, it nevertheless imparts an enthralling insight into the evolution of a changing world.

KIRSTY FAIRCLOUGH

People's Century: 1900–1999 (UK, US, BBC/WGBH, 60 min, 26 episodes) Produced by Zvi Dor-Ner, executive producer; David Espar, producer; and Peter Pagnamenta, executive producer. Various directors. Narrated by John Forsythe. Graphic designers Alfred Woodard and Iain Macdonald. Research led by Christine Whittaker.

Further Reading

Hodgson, G., *People's Century: From the Dawn of the Century to the Start of the Cold War*, London: BBC Books, 1995.
Purcell, Hugh, (1995) *People's Century, History Today*, www.pbs.org/wgbh/peoplescentury.

PERIES, LESTER JAMES

Lester James Peries, founder of indigenous Sinhala cinema, laid the foundations for a serious national cinema in Sri Lanka and played a pivotal role in shaping a vigorous film culture in the island from the mid-1950s to the present.

Influenced by his early training as a documentary filmmaker, Peries was the first to take the camera outside the confines of the cardboard houses built in South Indian film studios and shoot on location in natural light, with amateur actors. His first feature film, *Rekawa / Line of Destiny* (1956), was the first Sinhalese movie to portray people, their environment, and their culture in a realistic way.

From 1939 to 1952, Peries led a bohemian existence in London. Although he had gone there to start his career as a writer, that period in Britain was crucial to his formation in a different way. London was then the centre of a vigorous documentary film tradition associated with the British Post Office, the GPO Film Unit formed by Grierson, Cavalcanti, and Wright, among others. One of the most popular of these films was *Night Mail* (Wright, Watt, Cavalcanti, and others, 1936), a film about the functioning of the mail trains that transported the post all over Britain.

It was this vigorous tradition of the documentary cinema that Peries inherited when, in 1952, he returned to Colombo to work for the Government Film Unit as assistant to the British chief producer Ralph Keene and began churning out several documentaries on several subjects, including malaria and vehicle traffic.

The Government Film Unit (GFU) was established in 1948 to produce newsreels and documentaries to educate people about their newly won independence. Noted for its "creative treatment of actuality" and high filmmaking standards, it became the nursery from which many of Sri Lanka's future eminent filmmakers emerged. One of them was James Lester Peries. (Varma, 1997).

In the beginning the GFU was headed by Guido Petroni and Federico Serra, two Italian filmmakers influenced by the neorealism movement who brought elements of it into their Sri Lankan films, though Serra's film *Royal Mail,* about the country's postal service, showed that the British influence was also in the air.

However, it was under the stewardship of Ralph Keene that the GFU—with films such as *Kandy Perahera* (George Wickramasinghe), *Rhythms of the People (*Pragnasoma Hetiaracchchi), *Makers, Motifs and Materials* (Pragnasoma Hettiaracchchi), and *Conquest of the Dry Zone* (Lester James Peries, 1954), a 14-minute film on the eradication of malaria from the North Central Province of Ceylon that was awarded a diploma of honour at the Venice Film festival in 1954—radically changed the style of documentary filmmaking in Ceylon. (Dissanayake and Ratnavibhushana, 2000).

In those years, Peries and his colleagues were being trained in the finest traditions of British documentary (Peries, 2001). At that time he also assisted Keene with *Heritage of Lanka* (1953) and the prize-winning film *Nelugama* (1953), depicting the life of a fishing community, and made many documentaries for numerous private-sector firms and organizations. For the Ceylon Tobacco Company (CTC) he shot at least two. One was on Navajeevana, CTC's 500-acre farm in Mahiyangana where the company settled sixty farmer families and opened a new chapter in farming, introducing new crops such as soya and maize. The other was on another of CTC's diversified projects: the sugarcane cultivation and manufacture of jaggery at a time when sugar was a scare commodity due to foreign exchange shortage.

In 1955, when he had just finished a film on road safety, *Be Safe or Be Sorry* (1955), and had been asked to make a film on venereal diseases, Peries's second cousin suggested starting a company to produce Sinhala films. Bored with the subject matter of the GFU films, and more interested in fiction, characters, and human beings, Peries resigned from the Government Film Unit and embarked on the shooting of his first feature film, *Rekawa / Line of Destiny* and his subsequent film career.

Peries developed a personal film style, the twin hallmarks of which were the stylistic construction of narrative and his ability to capture and project actualities in a realistic manner. It was his documentary experience and his literary background that made this possible. Peries succeeded in portraying the existential realities and nuances of rural Sri Lanka and its ontological veneer. (Jeyaraj, 2001).

Even after resigning from the GFU and enjoying international success with his feature films, Peries continued to make documentaries, including *Too Many Too Soon* (1961), a documentary for the Family Planning Association; *Home from the Sea* (1962), on the lives of fishermen and their faith in St. Anthony; and *Steel* (1969), a documentary record of the construction and working of a steel-rolling mill at Oruwela, for the National Steel Corporation.

VERÓNICA JORDANA

See also **General Post Office Film Unit; Grierson, John;** *Night Mail***; Wright, Basil**

Biography

Born on April 5, 1919 in Dehiwela, a suburb of Colombo, Sri Lanka. Studied at St Peter's College in Colombo. At the age of 17, left school to pursue a career as a journalist and to escape from his teachers' intention that he become a priest. Wrote for the *Kesari,* a cultural newspaper, and worked as a broadcaster for Radio Ceylon reviewing books, 1939. Left for London, where he led a bohemian life and worked as a correspondent for the *Times of Ceylon,* 1940–1954. Shot and finished *Soliloquy,* his first short film, which won an award for artistic and technical merit from the Institute of Amateur and Research filmmakers of Great Britain in 1951. Returned to Sri Lanka and joined the Government Film Unit, where he shot several documentaries, 1952–1957. Resigned from the GFU and, with cameraman Willie Blake and Titus Thotawatte, made *Rekawa / Line of Destiny,* his first feature film. A member of the Legion of Honour (Republic of France), he received the Lifetime Achievement Award at the International Film Festival of India in January 2000. Received UNESCO's Fellini Gold Medal at the Cannes Festival, 2003.

Selected Films

1952 *Nelugama:* assistant director
1953 *Heritage of Lanka:* assistant director
1954 *Conquest of the Dry Zone*: director, writer
1955 *Be Safe or Be Sorry:* director, writer
1956 *Rekawa / Line of Destiny:* director, writer
1961 *Too Many Too Soon:* director, writer
1962 *Home from the Sea:* director, writer
1969 *Steel:* director, writer

Further Reading

Ariyadasa, Edwin, "The History of Sinhala Cinema," in *Framework: The Journal of Cinema and Media*, 37, 1989.
Asian Film Center, *A Brief History of Sri Lanka Cinema*, Sri Lanka: 1999.

Dissanayake, Wimal, and Ratnavibhushana, Ashley, *Profiling Sri Lankan Cinema*, Sri Lanka: Asian Film Centre, 2000.

Peries, Lester James, "Pragnasoma Hettiarachchi: A Personal Tribute," in *Sunday Observer*, October 7, 2001.

Jeyaraj, D. B. S., "Sinhala Film's Line of Destiny," in *The Sunday Leader*, March 12, 2000.

Varma, Mitu, "Historical Perspective: Films in Search of a Movement," in *Himal Magazine*, December 1997.

PERRAULT, PIERRE

Pierre Perrault practiced law for two years in Montreal before he found a job with the Canadian Broadcasting Corporation (CBC), producing programs on the rural areas of Québec, in 1956.

He was hired by the National Film Board of Canada (NFB) in 1962 to work with Michel Brault on a project on the people of Île-aux-Coudres, an island in the St. Lawrence River. The resulting film was *Pour la suite du monde / The Moontrap* (1963), the first Canadian feature documentary shown at the Cannes Film Festival and generally recognized as marking the high point of the direct cinema movement in Québec. At the core of the film are a group of middle-aged men who try to resuscitate the traditional beluga whale hunt that their fathers practiced forty years earlier. The revival of the whale hunt was in fact initiated by the filmmakers themselves, as means both to recapture a disappearing way of life and to provide a unique opportunity to record the voices and faces of the men and women of Île-aux-Coudres as they came together to reanimate their past. While Brault was primarily responsible for the splendid images of the film, Perrault focused on collecting the words of these people by spending extended periods of time with them to establish a genuine dialogue. Perrault directed two other films on Île-aux-Coudres: *Le régne du jour /The Reign of the Day* (1966) and *Les voitures d'eau / The Water Cars* (1968); both are imbued with the rustic poetry of his subjects.

Some of his films are explicitly political, such as *Un pays sans bon sens! / Wake Up, Mes Bons Amis* (1970) and *L'Acadie, l'Acadie!?! / Acadia, Acadia?!?* (1971). But most are concerned less with politics per se than with the people who make up the nation of Québec. In the 1970s, Perrault concentrated his energy on two ambitious series or cycles of films, one on the Abitibi region of northwest Québec (four films), and the other on the native peoples of Northern Québec (three films). In the 1980s, Perrault abandoned his cycles to direct a few seemingly heterogeneous films, all of which, however, reflect his fascination with the land. *La bête lumineuse / The Shimmering Beast* (1982) follows a group of men on a moose-hunting trip. *Les voiles bas et en travers / Lower the Sails* (1984) and *La grande allure / Sailing at Great Speed* (1985) examine the life of French explorer Jacques Cartier and his role as the forefather of Québec culture. His last two films, *L'oumigmag ou l'objectif documentaire / Oumigmag or the Documentary Objective* (1993) and *Cournouailles / Icewarrior* (1994) were shot in Québec's far north and are at once visual poems on the musk ox and evocative reflections on the very act of filming wilderness.

Pierre Perrault holds a unique place in the history of Québec cinema. One of the very few filmmakers of his generation who never made mainstream fiction films, he is also one of the few who have found a place within the high-brow discourse of French film theory, especially in the work of Gilles Deleuze. Deleuze, in *Cinéma 2* (1985), is especially interested in how Perrault creates temporal shifts among past, present, and future with individuals and groups who generate "la suite du monde" (the future of the world) through a present-tense narrative of their past. Perrault was also a prolific writer, publishing commentaries on his films, poems, and other creative works. Jean-Daniel Lafond's film *Les traces du rêve* (1986) documents Perrault's life.

ANDRÉ LOISELLE

See also **Brault, Michel; Canadian Broadcasting Corporation; National Film Board of Canada**

Biography

Born June 29, 1927, into an upper-class family. Studied law in Montréal, Toronto, and Paris. Practiced law for two years in Montréal. Hired by the Canadian Broadcasting Corporation (CBC) in 1956. Hired by the National Film Board of Canada (NFB) in 1962 to work with Michel Brault on a project on the people of Île-aux-Coudres. Died June 24, 1999.

Selected Films

1963 *Pour la suite du monde | The Moontrap*
1967 *Le Règne du jour | Reign of the Day*
1968 *Le Beau Plaisir | Beluga Days*
1968 *Les Voitures d'eau | The Water Cars*
1970 *Un pays sans bon sens! | Wake Up, Mes Bons Amis*
1971 *L'Acadie, l'Acadie?!? | Acadia, Acadia?!?*
1975 *Un royaume vous attend | A Kingdom Is Waiting for You*
1976 *Le Retour à la terre | Back to the Land*
1977 *C'était un Québécois en Bretagne, Madame! | He Was a Québecker in Brittany, Lady!*
1977 *Le Goût de la farine | The Taste of Flour*
1980 *Gens d'Abitibi | People of Abitibi*
1980 *Le Pays de la Terre sans arbre ou le Mouchouânipi | The Land Without Trees or Mouchouanipi*
1982 *La Bête lumineuse | The Shimmering Beast*
1983 *Les Voiles bas et en travers | Lower the Sails*
1985 *La Grande Allure (1re partie) | Sailing at Great Speed I*
1985 *La Grande Allure (2e partie) | Sailing at Great Speed II*
1993 *L'Oumigmag ou l'Objectif documentaire | Oumigmag or the Documentary Objective*
1994 *Cornouailles | Icewarrior*

Further Reading

Brûlé, Michel, *Pierre Perrault ou un cinéma national*, Montréal: Presses de l'Université de Montréal, 1974.
Deleuze, Gilles, *Cinéma 2, L'Image-Temps*, Paris: Les Éditions de Minuit, 1985.
Écriture de Pierre Perrault, Montréal: Cinémathèque québécoise, 1983.
Warren, Paul, *Cinéaste de la parole*, Montréal: Hexagone, 1996.
Waugh, Tom, *To Wake the Heart and the Will: Pierre Perrault and Cinéma-Direct in Québec, 1956–1971*, Ph. D. dissertation, Columbia University, 1974.

PHANTOM INDIA

(France, Malle, 1969)

By the mid-1960s, the prominent French director Louis Malle was profoundly bored with working in the mainstream film industry. Partly to make a break with France, he accepted a cultural mission to India to promote New Wave cinema in film clubs and other Indian cultural centres. On his arrival in India, Malle was immediately fascinated by the nation. Symbolism and spiritualism seemed to infuse every aspect of Indian social life. Accompanied by his sound man Jean-Claude Laureux and his photographer Etienne Becker, Malle returned to shoot documentary material. It was out of this quasi-instantaneous set of encounters that Malle would edit together two substantial pieces, the film *Calcutta* (1969) and the better-known seven-part television series *Phantom India* (1969).

Malle's decision to focus so intently on India marked a significant turning point in his career. The films were the first substantial documentaries that he had made since working as an assistant director to Jacques Cousteau in the mid-1950s on *The Silent World* (1956). Therefore, the Indian films reignited the director's interest in a form that would prove vital to his career. With the benefit of historical hindsight, one can also interpret Malle's Indian experience as a quintessentially 1960s episode. Rejecting Western European sociopolitical values, Malle, like many members of his generation, was attracted to the alternative model perceived to have been provided by India.

Phantom India is a free-flowing travelog. It is a self-reflexive work in which Malle is frequently seen on screen and heard via voice-over. Appropriately, everything that Malle shows through his camera is offered as exclusively his own vision. It is for this reason that the films can be interpreted as a treatise on a Westerner's awe-struck encounter with India, rather than as a dissection of that nation per se. Many passages from the series of films are moving and visually impressive. At its

Phantom India, 1969.
[*Still courtesy of the British Film Institute*]

best, *Phantom India* demonstrates both its director's passion for India and that country's rich cultural variety.

Malle identified his films as an exercise in the free-flowing direct cinema form that he would hone further in *Place de la République* (1974). However, as American critic Todd Gitlin noted as early as 1974, parts of the films are very troubling. Malle's enthusiasm for the people and groups that he encountered tends to lack any moral or ethical centre. Thus, when Malle visits a tribe in which women are indoctrinated to worship men, to literally kiss their feet, the director describes this group as a Utopian society. Such comments are unnerving. In part, they are indicative of Malle's increased fascination with the politics and provocation of sexual freedom, later also played out in fictional exercises such as *Le Souffle au coeur* (1971) and *Pretty Baby* (1978). Nevertheless, in light of such statements, the viewer is left suspicious of Malle's numerous tracking shots of beautiful young Indian women, his camera endlessly exploring their social space, seemingly without much regard to their viewpoint or concern with their consent.

Other aspects of the films are also unsettling, not least Malle's commentary on the Indian Jewish community, which he describes as decadent. However, it was neither because of these remarks nor because of explicit and implicit sexism that the films proved controversial upon their initial release. Purchased by the British Broadcasting Company (BBC), the films were shown on British and French television. The reaction to the series was especially intense in Britain and India. The British Indian community felt that Malle had shown an exclusively one-sided picture that concentrated on an impoverished and backward India, rather than on a modernizing nation. The Indian government felt similarly insulted, and a diplomatic incident quickly ensued. The Indian authorities were so irritated by Malle's work that they challenged the BBC to cease broadcasting it or face severe penalties. The BBC stood by Malle and was indeed briefly ordered to leave its New Delhi bureau. This telling postcolonial incident has long since been forgotten. It deserves renewed historical research.

HUGO FREY

Phantom India (*L'Inde fantôme*, 1968) Produced by Nouvelles Editions de Films (Paris). Directed by Louis Malle. Photography by Etienne Becker and Louis Malle. Sound by Jean-Claude Laureux. Edited by Suzanne Baron. Narration by Louis Malle.

Further Reading

Billard, Pierre, *Louis Malle: le Rebelle solitaire*, Paris: Plon, 2003.

French, Philip (ed.), *Malle on Malle*, London: Faber, 1993.

Frey, Hugo, *Louis Malle*, Manchester: Manchester University Press, 2004.

Gitlin, Todd, "Phantom India," in *Film Quarterly* 27(4), 1974, 57–60.

Malle, Louis, *Malle sur Malle*, Paris: Editions de l'Athanor, 1978. Includes published extracts from Malle's India diaries.

Malle, Louis, "Louis Malle," *Cinéma du réel*, edited by C. Devarrieux and M.-C. De Navacelle, Paris: Autrement, 1988, pp. 22–31.

PHILIPPINES

See **Southeast Asia**

PHILOSOPHY

See **Realism, Philosophy and the Documentary Film**

PICTURES OF THE OLD WORLD

(Slovakia, Hanak, 1972)

Dušan Hanák's *Pictures of the Old World* (*Obrazy Star ho Sveta*) was not widely seen when it was completed in 1972, but more than fifteen years after it was suppressed by communist censors, this Slovakian film won awards at film festivals around the world and made a name for its director. Even though Hanák made mostly feature films, his only documentaries, *Pictures of the Old World* and *Paper Heads* (1995), have earned him the most attention.

As indicated by the title, *Pictures of the Old World* is about people who live in the modern world yet adhere to more traditional, modest means of subsistence. Filming the inhabitants of

Pictures of the Old World, 1972.
[*Still courtesy of the British Film Institute*]

rural communities in the remote Tatra Mountains, Hanák captures the everyday facts of their existence while the subjects provide free-form commentary. The men he profiles often comment on their inclusion in the project. One subject informs the director that his profile had better be funny, because "one is interested in what is funny." In a unique move, Hanák includes a series of still and filmed photographs for each subject, who often comment on the pictures in synch with their appearance on the film. Inverting the more conventional documentary style, where a carefully composed script is read over the filmed material, Hanák allows the subjects' commentary to overlay the images whenever simultaneously recorded sound is not present. Although the director is virtually absent from the sight and sound of the film, his hand is evident in the structure of the work.

Pictures of the Old World features a series of nine self-contained portraits, all of poor, rural people living alone. With few exceptions—two women and one younger man—Hanák profiles only elderly men. (A sequence where numerous respondents take on "what is most important in life" shows that Hanák probably conducted extensive interviews with a broader range of subjects before deciding to focus almost exclusively on older men.) One could be critical of Hanák for so limiting his subjects, but even though the men featured in the film are from the same generation, they express a wide range of views. The range of experiences accounted for is, perhaps, made all the more remarkable by the similarity of the sampled demographic. Each subject appears free to comment on his life however he sees fit, and accordingly, the final cut includes contrasting responses. While leading similar lives as poor, agricultural workers, these men view their experiences in fundamentally different ways. Some find gratification in their labor; others find solace only in the promise of an afterlife. Some find simplicity and satisfaction in their modest way of life. (One man says, "You city people will get hard and dried on asphalt. Your heart is made of cement. I live on a proud bunk." Another remarks that "Whoever's got some wants more, whoever's got nothing, got a grand time"). A third, however, finds similar conditions inhumane. He says, "A man puts up with more than an animal." (The ubiquity of alcohol is the only absolutely consistent element through every profile.) Still, the film is most intriguing when the profiled subject possesses a singular interest. One old man is still consumed by memories of his stint in the army, and another spends his time making elaborate mobiles. The sixth man featured stands out as the most exceptional. He speaks a few sentences in passing of his work (for another farmer) and his partner's (selling newspapers) but is otherwise monomaniacally obsessed with space exploration. His face lit with glee, this man lists one astronomical fact after another as Hanák, in a rare move, splices appropriate footage of space exploration alongside his commentary.

Although the title of the film, *Pictures of the Old World*, and the quote that opens it ("These are the stories of people rooted in the soil they came from. Replanted they would perish.") imply the possibility of sentimentalizing or romanticizing the lives of these elderly villagers, the film proceeds to work conscientiously against this tendency. The range of statements both in opposition to and in endorsement of this style of life show a filmmaker more interested in exploring the ambiguity of his subjects than motivated to produce a piece with a particular argument. It is clear from the material on display in this cut that Hanák, had he wanted, could have crafted a piece about the bucolic simplicity of village life or, conversely, about the forbidding harshness of it. He chose, instead, to include both sides.

The style of *Pictures of the Old World* is similarly two-sided, as Alojz Hanúsek and Martin Martincek shift between unselfconscious, straightforward means of filming with a single, handheld camera and more stylized sequences. In one instance, the camera focuses on a subject's feet and then moves up his body at a horizontal angle before turning upright at the man's face. The film-

makers also appear fond of the extreme close-up, although it is not clear whether this was a conscious decision or they simply chose to indulge subjects who wanted to be inordinately close to the camera. Still, in accordance with conventional documentary style, the film tends more toward straightforward shooting than toward stylized sequences. In the context of a primarily observational documentary, it is notable that the stylized sequences are present at all.

The use of a single handheld camera, black-and-white film, and the usually unadorned style of Hanák's picture could lead to comparisons with the direct cinema approach, but the director deliberately breaks the transparency of the film on numerous occasions. He includes shots that emphasize the making of the picture. In one sequence, a bashful elderly couple awkwardly pass a microphone back and forth, uncertain what to say. Hanák also shows a woman who shouts her answers into the mike, evidently unsure how well such devices work. Although the director could have coached his subjects into being more conventional interviewees, he chose, instead, to include their tentative early encounters with the filmmaking process. These scenes effectively portray the villagers' lack of familiarity with modern technology, in addition to emphasizing the construction of the picture. Using another hallmark technique of self-reflexive documentaries, Hanák sometimes includes sound clips of himself asking the interviewees questions. More often, documentarians erase their questions from the final cut to create the illusion of a single, coherent monologue from the subject's point of view.

The use of music in *Pictures of the Old World* is also notable. It ranges from naturalistic, sometimes simulated, on-location sounds and folk songs sung by the subjects to an expressive but minimal classical score and strange, high-frequency synthetic noises.

Following *Pictures of the Old World*'s release in 1988, Hanák earned a Special Mention at the European Film Awards in 1989 and was given an award for a lifetime's achievement in cinema at the first National Free Festival of Czech and Slovak films the following year.

JESSE SCHLOTTERBECK

Pictures of the Old World | Obrazy starého sveta (Slovakia, Slovak Film Institute, 1972, 64 min.). Written and directed by Dušan Hanák. Original music by Václav Hálek and Jozef Malovec. Nonoriginal music by Georg Friedrich Händel. Cinematography by Alojz Hanúsek and Martin Martincek. Film editing by Alfréd Bencic. Sound by Andrej Polomský.

PILGER, JOHN

Australian-born television documentary maker John Pilger is first and foremost a journalist. He made his first television documentary in 1970 (*The Quiet Mutiny*), which revealed the rejection of the Vietnam War by large numbers of U.S. conscripts. Pilger's print journalism output is prolific (it includes a regular column in the *New Statesman*), and he has published numerous books and a play, as well as more than fifty television documentaries, always on controversial political issues. He is an accredited war correspondent and has reported from conflicts in Vietnam, Cambodia, Bangladesh, Biafra, and the Middle East.

Pilger's film style is direct, and some have called it "polemical," whereby he confronts the objects of his criticism in a direct and uncompromising manner. He is said to have a knack for getting people in authority to make statements on camera that they would not normally make. He has said that he "grew up in Sydney in a very political household, where we were all for the underdog" (Barsamian, 2002). However, although they critique the wrongs of society and present the voice of the powerless, his films stop short of offering the viewer any alternatives. He says, "I am not going to offer anything in its place. I am saying that people should be aware of it and identify it and then they have the power of that knowledge to do something about it if they want to" (*Sydney Morning Herald*, April 11, 1998).

One of his best-known documentaries is *In Search of Truth in Wartime*, which critically scrutinizes the role of the war correspondent in conflicts ranging from Crimea to Vietnam. Impressively structured, the film begins with the famous black-and-white footage of the little Vietnamese girl running terrified from the flames of napalm during the Vietnam War, to illustrate immediately where Pilger's strongest sympathies lie in any conflict—with its innocent victims. In reflecting on the role of the journalist in war, he suggests that many reporters wittingly or unwittingly serve the state in sanitizing and rationalizing war, exemplified by the images they send to their media organizations back home, such as those of the soldiers' coffins draped respectfully in flags as they are met at airports by dignitaries and family. It is unusual for journalists to criticize their own profession, but to Pilger nobody is exempt from his critical gaze if it means an opportunity to bring to light unjust practices or institutions.

Pilger calmly informs us (direct to camera from a domestic interior) of the press collusion in the British government's conspiracy to hide the futility and extent of the carnage of World War I. The complicity of the journalists having been established, we are shown newsreel after newsreel, revealed by Pilger to the contemporary viewer as clear propaganda, but not seen as such at the time. With more recent wars, we move to Pilger's interviews with some of the journalists who covered the conflicts. In these interviews, more cases of collusion between government and the press are revealed, including stories fabricated by the U.S. government of barbaric "official" North Korean press releases and the CIA's staging of the filmed "invasion" of South Vietnam by the North, needed to justify the commencement of U.S. aerial bombing of North Vietnam.

Controversial as always, Pilger refutes the myth that the media affected the outcome of the Vietnam War, either positively or negatively, except that free media access during this conflict prompted the subsequent decision by the British Ministry of Defence never to give cameras the same freedom in any future war. This fact is then illustrated by news footage of the Falklands War (1982), in which a former correspondent from that war states that the British government allowed only a few hand-picked British journalists to cover the conflict.

Pilger made two documentaries titled *Palestine Is Still the Issue* (1974 and 2002), the first of which was one of his most widely viewed films. These documentaries comment on the irony that the Palestinians have become for the Israelis the displaced people that the Jews were for the Europeans before the creation of the state of Israel. Interviews take place with people on both sides of the conflict, most of whom express a strong desire for peace and cannot see war as the solution. In the sequel Pilger addresses the camera: "If we're to speak of the great injustice here, nothing has changed. What has changed is that the Palestinians have fought back."

In some films, Pilger is not afraid to implicate himself among those he attacks. In *The Secret Country* (1985), about the systematic but officially unacknowledged mistreatment by white Australian settlers of Aboriginal people (made during the period leading up to the Bicentenary of European settlement in that country), Pilger locates a cottage built by his own father on the site of a 100-year struggle between Aboriginals and settlers. He also talks of the sanitization of the "encounters" between Europeans and Aboriginals "when I learned history at school" in his native Sydney. Pilger is not a "holier-than-thou" journalist, morally separated from the objects of his critique; rather, his is the concerned, serious voice of someone deeply troubled by what his career has led him to witness and what his astute mind, impeccable training, and political consciousness have driven him to expose.

Pilger's films are didactic and ideologically motivated. Numerous accusations of bias have been leveled at him by the establishment, because his films confront power cliques and hegemonic interests, including governments and the media. He lives in an era when few documentary makers consistently critique such interests, and his films have frequently been refused screenings in the United States. He has been described by the right as "a left-wing polemicist"("Editor Falls Victim to Iraq 'Scoop,'"*Sunday Mirror*, May 16, 2004) and a "professional conspiracy theorist"("Truth Is Pilgered," *The Australian*, Features, February 17, 2003: 10). His documentary on Israel-Palestine conflict was even denounced as "one-sided . . . factually incorrect, historically incorrect" by his own producer at Carlton Television ("Pilger Biased, Says TV Boss," *The Times*, Overseas News, September 20, 2002: 15). Auberon Waugh, right-wing journalist and staunch critic of Pilger, joked that "Pilger" was a verb that meant "to seek to arouse indignation by inflated or absurd propositions" and that to "Pilgerise" meant "to distort in a tendentious way."

On the other hand, Phillip Knightly, a journalist supporter of Pilger, provided his own definition of the "verb"*to Pilger* as "to regard with insight, compassion and sympathy, coined as a tribute to the work of one John Pilger, a well-known huma-

nitarian journalist who wrote about the world's underprivileged" (Ricketson: M15).

Pilger continues to be a prolific writer and documentary film producer, whose most recent production is *Breaking the Silence: Truth and Lies in the War on Terror* (2003), about the U.S. and British prosecution of their "war on terror"in Iraq. Here Pilger uses his trademark archival footage accompanied by interviews with human rights activists, members of the White House staff, and former intelligence analysts to make his case that Bush used the September 11 terrorism as an excuse to activate plans to assert control over Iraq's oil. Pilger again juxtaposes benign footage of Bush and Blair arguing that war in Iraq is moral and just with interviews and images which that suggest the opposite. Conservative criticism of his journalistic stance has clearly not diminished the volume of his documentary output, nor has it softened his confronting style. Pilger has received numerous awards for his journalism in Britain, in the United States, and from the United Nations.

JULIANNE STEWART

Further Reading

Arnove, Anthony, "Cautionary Tales: Documentaries on the UN Sanctions and War with Iraq," in *Cinéaste*, 28 (2), spring 2003.
Barsamian, David, "The Progressive Interview: John Pilger," in *The Progressive*, 66(11), November 2002. Online at http://www.progressive.org/nov02/intv1102.html. Accessed May 23, 2004.
Hayward, Anthony, *In the Name of Justice: The Television Reporting of John Pilger*, Bloomsbury: London, 2001.
ITV.COM, *Biography of John Pilger*. Online at http://www.google.com.au/search?q=cache:hhLm3cGwW2MJ:pilger.carlton.com/home/biography+%22biography+of+John+Pilger%22+&hl=en (cached). Accessed May 23, 2004.
Sweeney, Brian, "Siding with the Enemy," in *The Weekend Australian*, Features, July 5, 2003, 26.

PINCUS, EDWARD

With *Diaries (1971–1976)* (1980), Ed Pincus made an extraordinary breakthrough in the realm of the film about one's own life, shot as it is happening. This film, along with Pincus's teaching at the Massachusetts Institute of Technology Film/Video

Section in the 1970s, helped shape the work of a generation of autobiographical filmmakers—Joel DeMott, Ross McElwee, Rob Moss, Mark Rance, Ann Schaetzel, and others. Pincus's work is not as well known or as much discussed as it deserves to be, because he retired young from film-making, and his films have not been promoted or widely distributed (one must contact him personally to obtain a print, and nothing is available on videotape or DVD).

Pincus became active in the American Civil Rights movement of the early 1960s and began making films at that time in the cinema verité or direct cinema mode established by Robert Drew, Richard Leacock, Albert and David Maysles, D. A. Pennebaker, and others. Pincus's *Black Natchez* (1966) is an exemplary film of this kind, a sixty-minute, strictly observational account of the Mississippi city and its black population's struggles to organize political protest in the face of white violence. Pincus, working with David Neuman, shoots here with handheld camera and synchronous sound recording. He has clearly won the confidence of people and made himself inconspicuous enough so that he gets remarkable footage of everyday life, political meetings, a secret society, and infighting. The film is a complex portrait of political debate and movement toward decisive action at a time of great tension.

Shot at the same time in Natchez, but completed only later, *Panola* (1970) is a different kind of film. Here the 35-year-old black man named in the title addresses the camera, talks about his hard life and his aspirations, engages the filmmakers in interplay, invites them into his house in the black slums, appears drunk at one point, behaves histrionically. However truthful a report on black life in the South and on the state of mind of one charismatic, disturbed, ordinary man, the film is nevertheless a performance, a display of speech and action offered with full consciousness of the camera, a display made *for* the camera by one who can command it.

Diaries (1971–1976) comes to rest after its three hours and twenty minutes, on a hilltop in Vermont on the holy day of Yom Kippur. And indeed, this film is a work of atonement, bringing together what is in conflict, working toward peace in a process of moral growth. The film centers on Pincus, his wife Jane, and their small children, as the couple come to deepen their commitment to each other, ultimately deciding to move to a new home in a new place. The world of the film takes in the Cambridge, Massachusetts, filmmaking scene, Pincus's and Jane's extramarital affairs, anti-Vietnam-War politics, the Women's Movement of the 1970s, rural Vermont, and trips to New York, the American Southwest, and California. Pincus's lovers, friends, and professional associates become major characters. Pincus films life as it evolves, not knowing where it will go, often turning the camera on himself. He gets remarkably intimate—even painful—encounters on film, and of course he also elicits self-consciousness, performance, even melodramatics, all of which has its way of being revealing. The film is alive with the possibilities of sex and of political and social change. The shaping of the material into the finished work is at one with Ed and Jane's process of coming to understand themselves better and to make decisions about their family life and future.

Diaries has a curious double quality. On the one hand it seems raw, as if abundant life is caught awkwardly on film and assembled into a simple chronology. This in itself is fascinating. But the film is artistically masterful. Every shot and the structuring seem deeply well judged. The camera is always in the right place. In the many conversations in cars, the interior lines of the vehicle, and what passes in the window, slowly, quickly, or in a blur, seem to define the state of mind of the speaker. The images of a trip to the Grand Canyon, Las Vegas, and elsewhere seem mental, indicating an expansion of spirit, an irresponsible lark that is a contribution to growth. The film moves more quickly, changing places and acknowledging diverse actions, when Ed and Jane are in creative turmoil, thinking, forming a new plan for life. *Diaries* draws on and realizes that basic power of documentary film, and of film in general, to capture to some extent what is vital and uncontrollable, and to transfigure life into an art shape or art structure that amounts to understanding.

CHARLES WARREN

Biography

Born in Brooklyn, New York, July, 6, 1939. Graduated from Brown University in 1960. Studied philosophy at the graduate level at Harvard University, 1961–1963. Established the Film/Video Section at the Massachusetts Institute of Technology in 1969, brought in Richard Leacock, Steven Ascher, and others to teach, and taught there himself until 1980. Taught filmmaking at Harvard, 1980–1983. Co-authored *The Filmmaker's Handbook* with Steven Ascher, 1984. At that time, gave up filmmaking to work as a cut-flower farmer in Vermont.

Further Reading

Lane, Jim, "The Career and Influence of Ed Pincus," in *The Journal of Film and Video*, 49(4), 1997, 3–17.
———, *The Autobiographical Documentary in America*, Madison: University of Wisconsin Press, 2002.
Levin, G. Roy, *Documentary Explorations: 15 Interviews with Filmmakers*, Garden City, NY: Doubleday, 1971.

Pincus, Ed, "New Possibilities in Film and the University," in *Quarterly Review of Film Studies*, 2(2), 1977, 159–78.

Rothman, William, "Looking Back and Turning Inward: American Documentary Films of the Seventies," in *Lost Illusions: American Cinema in the Age of Watergate and Vietnam, 1970–1980*, edited by David Cook, vol. 9 of *Scribner's History of the American Cinema*, New York: Scribner's, 1999.

PLOW THAT BROKE THE PLAINS, THE

(US, Lorentz, 1936)

Pare Lorentz's first film, *The Plow That Broke the Plains,* marked a significant point in the history of documentary film in the United States. It was the most widely publicized peacetime attempt by the federal government to communicate to its entire citizenry through a motion picture, and its elaborately synchronized soundtrack was groundbreaking. It was the first film to be placed in congressional archives, and President Franklin Roosevelt wanted it to be shown before a joint session of Congress, which would have happened had the Capitol chambers been equipped to present a sound film. The film had been produced under the sponsorship of the Resettlement Administration (RA), a New Deal agency directed by Rexford Tugwell (one of Roosevelt's "brain trusters"). The RA's mission was to find relief for the chronic rural poverty in the central part of the United States then known as the Dust Bowl, and its recuperative strategies included providing housing, financial, medical, and educational aid to the displaced families, as well as finding ways to restore and conserve the environment. Property interests among the middle and upper classes feared the loss of cheap labor and the undermining of rental rates that could occur as a result of government assistance.

Several factors, not the least being the perceived "socialist" bent of the RA, conspired to hinder the film's distribution. For one, its length (around half an hour) was deemed awkward—too short to fill a feature-length slot, but too long to be a newsreel. The timing of the film's release (May 1936) coincided with a particularly sensitive moment in U.S. partisan politics, as Roosevelt and the reforms of the Democratic Party's New Deal were facing a major reelection campaign in November of 1936.

For that reason, Republicans widely criticized the film, although a number of Democratic elected officials, especially those from the states depicted in a negative light, also took issue with *The Plow's* images of devastation and poverty (an Oklahoma Democrat publicly threatened to punch Tugwell in the nose over the film). Real estate interests from the Plains states bemoaned the negative representations. Finally, the distribution of a government-produced film through the established commercial channels was perceived by the film industry as a competitive threat, so the film was denied bookings through the major theater chains. Despite that opposition, and because of the efforts of RA staff to promote the film through the Midwest in the summer of 1936, *Plow* was shown through independent theater chains, at an estimated 3,000 of the approximately 14,000 commercial theaters in the United States at that time. The experiment of the state-produced film of persuasion could probably not be declared an unqualified success as an effective new mode of disseminating information, although it did lead to a handful of further films produced by the U.S. government (*The River, The Fight for Life,* and the uncompleted *Ecce Homo!*) and to a short-lived United States Film Service run by Lorentz (1938–1940).

Sometimes compared to Grierson, Lorentz is one of the great pioneers in U.S. documentary film history. His blending of the visual (shot composition, *mise-en-scène,* editing), the musical (with noted composers Virgil Thomson and Louis Gruenberg), and the poetic (his narration for *The River* was praised by James Joyce as the "most beautiful prose" he had heard in ten years) created a kind of cinematic *Gesamtkunstwerke,* or "total

The Plow That Broke the Plains, 1936.
[*Still courtesy of the British Film Institute*]

work of art," intended here not for an elite Aryan audience but rather for mainstream media consumption in the United States. Lorentz was purported not to have liked the term *documentary*, preferring instead the somewhat immodest term *film of merit*; he used the terms *documentary musical picture* and *melodrama of nature* to describe *The Plow That Broke the Plains* in his own review of his film. Lorentz began working with the RA in the summer of 1935, not long before the Information Division of the RA started documenting its activities and the state of rural living by assembling a team of still photographers that included Dorothea Lange and Arthur Rothstein, both of whom would have connections to *The Plow*: Lange, skilled at posing subjects, assisted Lorentz in filming the California migration sequence, and Rothstein's famous steer skull photos were probably influenced by Lorentz's imagery in *Plow*. In addition to still photographs, radio programs, and pamphlets, the RA in 1935 decided to add motion pictures as a way of dramatizing the violence of dust storms.

With experience only as a film critic, Lorentz was a novice filmmaker when he began work on *The Plow That Broke the Plains*. He hired a group of experienced cameramen (Leo Hurwitz, Ralph Stei-

ner, and Paul Strand) who were involved with the left-wing Film and Photo League and later the filmmaking collectives known as Nykino and Frontier Films. Some of the greatest drama associated with *Plow* would take place off camera, as the photographers found their ideological and professional differences with Lorentz increasingly intolerable. Lorentz envisioned a fantasy sequence where presumably wealthy men in top hats would walk across a field, mount tractors, and plow up the land—just one example from a flimsy script that Strand found unfilmable. The three cameramen went "on strike," as reported in *Variety*, and offered Lorentz an alternative script that infuriated him. After they filmed what he needed—Lorentz sent Hurwitz and Strand off to film dust storms while he and Steiner teamed up to shoot, among other things, the top hat sequence—Lorentz released his crew (the fact that he did not hold all the cameramean in equal esteem is reflected in their nonalphabetical listing in the credits). Lorentz then went to California to purchase stock footage and to film the final sequence at a roadside migrant camp on U.S. Highway 99. He was able to purchase stock footage only through the insider assistance of his Hollywood friend King Vidor (whose 1934 film

Our Daily Bread may have provided some visual inspiration for *Plow*). And filming of the final sequence was facilitated by a fourth cameraman, Paul Ivano, and Dorothea Lange, on loan from Roy Stryker's Historical Section of the RA.

The film follows a chronological arc that attempts to explain how the Plains became the Dust Bowl, ostensibly tracing a history of the place and people, yet as a historical document the narrative is incomplete, and as a piece of rhetoric, the argument is perhaps too subtle, because Lorentz tends to focus more on elemental forces at the expense of political and economic ones. The excised epilogue contains the only direct narrational references to the government programs offering relief. A similar historical narrative and several key phrases appeared earlier in a 1935 *Fortune* story by Archibald MacLeish called "Grasslands," which may have provided a framework for Lorentz. In place of dialogue and identified characters, Lorentz wrote a script for Thomas Chalmer's godlike narration. Beginning with an animated map of the entire United States, the affected regions called "the Plains" are traced out and exaggerated with dotted lines; the words "625,000 sq miles" and "400 million acres" appear before an image of waving grasslands fills the area within the dotted lines, and then the region's borderlines wipe outward so that the landscape fills the entire frame. If nothing else, the film works powerfully to create a national issue out of a regional problem. Sweeping panoramic shots of lush grasslands are next followed by the introduction of cattle grazing and by the massive homesteading and settlement of the region. After a sequence depicting early drought problems, a montage showing the necessity of wheat during World War I suggests that overproduction led to further misuse of the soil, culminating in dust storms and families fleeing the devastation. One of the most vexing issues surrounding this famous documentary is the fact that two versions exist: a three-minute epilogue explaining the RA's role was screened for some audiences in 1936 (most initial reviews refer to it) but was then, for reasons still only speculative, removed. The Museum of Modern Art preserved the copy with the epilogue, but the version that was shown through the summer of 1936, as well as the version re-released by the Department of Agriculture in 1962, lacked the epilogue. The epilogue's narration overtly stated what had only been implied up to that point: irresponsible and shortsighted use of the soil led to the creation of a disaster area, and government intervention was now required. Images of "model farms in Nebraska" may have borne too close a similarity to Soviet communal farms, particularly given the Republican cries of "New Deal propaganda" that preceded the 1936 fall elections.

The film's musical accompaniment, written by Thomson (famous at that time for *Four Saints in Three Acts*), was called "the finest musical score of any American film" in a 1936 review, and it accounts for much of the film's power. Partly borrowed—including, for example, cowboy songs and a Protestant hymn ("Old Hundred")—and partly original material, Thomson's underscoring employs considerably more dissonance than was allowed in Hollywood's music at that time, although it did rely on certain stock musical conventions, such as pounding tom-toms supporting melodies in parallel fourths as a code for "Indians" (although "Indians" are mentioned only once in Lorentz's narration, the music provides multiple invocations of those earlier inhabitants who managed to live on the land for centuries without driving it into dust). Once hoping to work as a music critic, Lorentz provided several articulate and detailed sets of instructions for Thomson. He interviewed eleven other composers before settling on Thomson. Lorentz showed his rough edit to Thomson, who composed a score that Lorentz then used to re-edit his final cut. Thomson converted the entire score into a suite for concert performance, where it has become a recognized part of the twentieth-century musical canon, and parts of its style (such as its fondness for open intervals) were quickly absorbed into Hollywood's musical codes for "Americana."

Throughout *The Plow That Broke the Plains*, music and images rely on repetition and dialectic. Lorentz calculatedly contrasted scenes of fecundity with drought. Pan shots of lush grasslands are matched later in the film with a succession of still images showing cow skulls and abandoned farm equipment resting on cracked, baked-out soil; Thomson underscored the pastoral idyll with a theme in a major key that returns for the drought scenes in a minor key, reorchestrated for saxophone. In sequences meant to depict the overproduction of wheat during World War I, Lorentz's images alternate rapidly between tractors and tanks, bayonets and plow blades, cannons and grain chutes. Their rapid juxtaposition, together with the narration ("Wheat will win the war!"), suggests that wheat became a weapon for the allies. Thomson matches the visual cross-cutting by alternating the famous World War I melody "Mademoiselle from Armentières" between major and minor keys. The 1920s are set up as a period of economic, ecological, and social excesses through Thomson's jazz-inflected score and images of an African-American jazz musician, all culminating in the stock market crash, which is metonymically signaled by a stock ticker breaking on the ground. Moments of the score, such as the cattle sequences accompanied by cowboy songs, are genuinely ebullient, but Thomson occasionally slips in ironic commentary. In one scene showing a home overpowered by a dust storm, we see the dust swirling through the living room as we hear a harmonium play "Old Hundred," a hymn whose words refer to a divine bounty that is notably absent. The most puzzling musical-visual juxtaposition occurs with the shots of migrant workers driving into California camps, as Thomson transforms a melody from earlier in the film into a haunting tango whose associations with upper-class leisure are asynchronous with the images of impoverished domestic life and ecological disruption. Both score and film indulge in melodramatic excesses: the narrative cueing is overstated, and its emotional ranges are limited to extremes. Particularly without the epilogue, *The Plow That Broke the Plains* is "agit" without the "prop": its images and sounds are powerfully affecting, but they only hint at the larger structural causes of the Dust Bowl and make no explicit mention of the federal relief programs in existence.

NEIL LERNER

See also **Lorentz, Pare**

The Plow That Broke the Plains (US, 35mm b & w, mono sound, Resettlement Administration, 1936, 25 min; a 3-minute epilogue was shown to some audiences in 1936). Written and directed by Pare Lorentz. Photographed by Leo T. Hurwitz, Paul Ivano, Ralph Steiner, and Paul Strand. Music composed by Virgil Thomson, orchestrated by Henry Brant, and conducted by Alexander Smallens. Narrator, Thomas Chalmers. Research editor, John Franklin Carter, Jr. Editor, Leo Zochling. Sound technician, Joseph Kane. Filmed in Montana, Wyoming, Colorado, Kansas, Texas, and California. Starring Bam White (others unnamed). Budget of $6,000 grew to $19,260.

Further Reading

Alexander, William, *Film on the Left: American Documentary Film from 1931 to 1942*, Princeton, NJ: Princeton University Press, 1981.

Allan, Blaine, "Canada's *Heritage* (1939) and America's *The Plow That Broke the Plains* (1936)," in *Historical Journal of Film, Radio and Television*, April 19, 1999, 439–72.

Curtis, James, *Mind's Eye, Mind's Truth: FSA Photography Reconsidered*, Philadelphia: Temple University Press, 1989.

Lorentz, Pare, *Movies 1927 to 1941: Lorentz on Film*, New York: Hopkinson and Blake, 1975.

MacCann, Richard D., *The People's Films: A Political History of U.S. Government Motion Pictures*, New York: Hastings House, 1973.

Snyder, Robert L., *Pare Lorentz and the Documentary Film*, Norman: University of Oklahoma Press, 1968.

Thomson, Virgil, *Virgil Thomson*, New York: Dutton, 1966.

O'Connor, John E., "Case Study: *The Plow That Broke the Plains*," in *Images as Artifact: The Historical Analysis of Film and Television*, edited by John E. O'Connor, Malabar, FL: Robert E. Krieger Publishing Company, 1990.

Rabinowitz, Paula, *They Must Be Represented: The Politics of Documentary*, London and New York: Verso, 1994.

Van Dyke, Willard, "Letters from *The River*," in *Film Comment*, 1965, 38–56.

PODNIEKS, JURIS

Juris Podnieks, best known as a chronicler of the decline of the Soviet Union, was part of a new wave of documentary filmmaking that emerged in the wake of Mikhail Gorbachev's *perestroika* and corresponding attempts at *glasnost*, begun in 1985. As these forces began to take hold in the film industry, the first reaction to the new situation came from the documentary cinema. The renaissance of documentary was evident across the Soviet Union, in the studios of the Ukraine, Belarus, the Urals, and Siberia, as well as Juris Podnieks's native Latvia. The documentary emerged as one of the most active expressions of *glasnost*, as documentarists addressed a series of formerly taboo subjects linked to social and political problems in the Soviet Union.

Podnieks's *Is It Easy to Be Young?* (1986) was one of the first and most distinguished of these hard-hitting documentaries. The film opens with a rock concert in Riga, in July 1985—images that in themselves are an important statement about the increasing significance of pop music in Soviet youth culture—and follows its young subjects (not all of whom were present at the concert) over a period of almost two years. The film addresses juvenile delinquency, teenage suicide, and drugs, topics that were to assume a vital role in a number of subsequent documentaries. From a portrayal of youth lost in crime, suicide, and drugs, the documentary turns, for the first time on a Soviet screen, to the war in Afghanistan, adding to the picture of a lost generation new political and moral dimensions. Podnieks depicts a widespread sense of confusion, disappointment, and antisocial feeling with startling honesty, in a characteristically rhythmic and startling juxtaposition of images punctuated by increasingly disturbing interviews and held together by an edgy electronic soundtrack. Not surprisingly, the film broke box office records in the Soviet Union and later enjoyed a wide international distribution.

As the Soviet Union crumbled, Podnieks's collaborations with Central Television and Channel 4 added up to a haunting collective portrait of a society disintegrating morally, physically, and socially. The five-part series transmitted as *Hello, Do You Hear Us?* (1990) ranges over diverse topics and portrays a wide variety of individuals all over the Soviet Union, in a kaleidoscope of rapidly edited images drawn from personal interviews, newsreel, and found film footage, and amateur videotape. As in *Is It Easy to Be Young?*, there is a question mark at the end of the series's title, suggesting a tentative investigation rather than any ready or easy answers.

Homeland (1991), also made for Central Television, is a powerfully lyrical portrait of the emergent Baltic republics, structured around the 20th Latvian Song Festival. The songs and music provide an evocative soundtrack for Podnieks's highly accomplished cinematography and more muted polemics, and make this one of his most coherent and powerful films.

His final film, *(A Portrait of an) Unfinished Business* (1993), was completed by his crew after his untimely death. It depicts the slow and painful rebirth of three former Soviet republics through the central linking device of a Trans-Siberian train journey. Uncharacteristically, the film adds an intermittent voice-over to the scenes from daily life, based on Podnieks's filming notebook. The speculative tone of the commentary, together withtestimonies from various crew members, leaves us with a sense of a man firmly in the tradition of "spiritual" cinema in the Soviet sense of a preoccupation with serious matters of the human mind and spirit.

Formally, Podnieks's documentaries are distinguished by their powerful images and rhythmic editing, and by a detached narrative style that eschews voice-over and relies on a mixture of interviews, music, and archive footage—a style described by Horton as "expressionistic cinema verité" (Horton, 1992: 75). In all of his films, it is the faces and voices of ordinary people caught in the fall-out from the disintegration of the Soviet empire that give them their haunting poetic density. Encouraged by the unobtrusive off-camera questioning, people reveal themselves with extraordinary openness. At times, however, as Julia Neuberger points out, Podnieks's passionate empathy can result in a loss of the ambivalence that is so revealing throughout his films and slip into a "heroic onesideness," favouring some ethic groups over others. (Neuberger, 1994: 297).

MARINA BURKE

See also **Russia/Soviet Union**

Biography

Born in Riga, Latvia, in 1950. Graduated from the cinematography faculty of VGIK, the State Film Institute in Moscow, in 1975. Went to work at the Riga Film Studio, first as assistant cameraman, then as cameraman, before finally becoming a director in 1979. His first production, *The Cradle*, won a prize at the Leipzig Festival, and *The Kokar Brothers* took first prize at the Kiev Youth Festival in 1981. In the same year, won widespread recognition both inside and outside the Soviet Union for his film *Constellation of Rifleman,* which won honours at the 17th All State Festival in Leningrad' and also the Latvia Komsomol prize. The film that first won international recognition was *Is It Easy to Be Young?* (1986), which exploded many popular myths about Soviet youth. Subsequently, commissioned by Central Television to make the series of documentaries about the Soviet Union at the end of the 1980s that were transmitted on Channel 4 in 1990 as *Hello, Do You Hear Us?* While filming the follow-up to Homeland (1991), two members of Podnieks's film crew were killed after coming under sniper fire during the Soviet coup in Riga. Podniek himself died in a freak diving accident on June 23, 1992.

Selected Films

1982 *Constellation of Rifleman* (Strelnieku Zvaigznajs)
1985 *The Stone of Sisyphus* (Vel Sizifs Akmen)
1986 *Is It Easy to Be Young?* (Legko li byt' molodym?)
1990 *Hello, Do You Hear Us?*
1991 *Homeland* (Krestyni put')
1991 *End of Empire*
1993 *Unfinished Business*

Further Reading

Graffy, Julian, "Juris Podnieks," *Sight and Sound*, 3(2), February 1993, 30–31.

Horton, Andrew, and Brashinsky, Michael, *The Zero Hour: Glasnost and Soviet Cinema in Transition*, Princeton, NJ: Princeton University Press, 1992.

Horton, Andrew, "Nothing Worth Living For: Soviet Youth and the Documentary Movement," in *Wide Angle*, 12(4), October 1990, 38–47.

Neuberger, Julia, "Soviets," *Russian Review*, 53(2), April 1994, 296–97.

Plakhov, Andrei, "Soviet Cinema into the 90s," in *Sight and Sound*, 58, Spring 1989, 53–57.

POETICS

See **Aesthetics and Documentary Film: Poetics**

POIRIER, ANNE CLAIRE

Anne Claire Poirier, who joined the National Film Board of Canada (NFB) in 1960, spent a few years working as assistant editor and assistant director in the shadow of her male colleagues, who included Claude Jutra, Michel Brault, and Gilles Groulx. In 1963, she was commissioned to direct a documentary on the actor Christopher Plummer, (*30 Minutes, Mister Plummer*) and, the following year, wrote and directed her first fiction short, *La Fin des étés / The end of Summers* (1964), starring Geneviève Bujold. Poirier is credited with initiating feminist filmmaking in Québec in 1967 with her landmark feature-length documentary *De mère en fille / Mother-to-Be*. A personal as well as political reflection on pregnancy and maternity, *De mère en fille* was the first feature film ever directed by a French Canadian woman.

A few years later, as part of her proposal to the NFB for the establishment of a production program coordinated by women, Poirier, along with Jeanne Morazain Boucher, published the text *En tant que Femmes: Rapport de recherches / As Women: Research Report* (1971). This veritable manifesto for the creation of an interventionist feminist cinema in Québec would break the isolation of women and educate men on the female condition. It led to the production of the "En tant que femmes" film series, the first significant wave of activist documentaries and docudramas created by women at the NFB. While head of the "En tant que femmes" program, from 1972 to 1974 Poirier produced four films by female directors, as well as directing two films of her own: *Les Filles du Roy / They Called Us "Les Filles du Roy"* (1974), a history of Québec women's traditional roles as servants, mothers, and wives, which employed an effective mixture of historical reconstruction and personal commentary to paint a vibrant picture of a subject systematically ignored by male cinéastes; and *Le Temps de l'avant / Before the Time Comes*, 1975), a straightforward dramatic feature aimed primarily at sensitizing men to the issue of abortion.

In 1979, Poirier achieved full recognition as a major filmmaker with the release of her strikingly innovative and daring docudrama on rape, *Mourir à tue-tête / A Scream from Silence*. In this uncompromising look at the individual and collective brutalization of women's bodies, Poirier adopts a radical feminist perspective that blends documentary and fiction to criticize society and institutions for failing to provide victims with the support to which they are entitled. The film's graphic depiction of rape and its putative suggestion that all men are potential rapists raised a storm of debate seldom seen in the history of Canadian film.

A cry of rage that still echoes today, *Mourir à tue-tête* is certainly the most controversial production of Poirier's career. In contrast, her fiction films, *La Quarantaine / Forty Something* (1982), and *Salut Victor! / Hi Victor!* (1988) are accessible, traditional dramas on how friendship can transcend time and differences. Her most recent documentary film, *Tu as crié Let Me Go! / You Screamed, Let Me Go!* (1997), returns to the violent theme of *Mourir à tue-tête*. But the explicit political agenda of the 1979 production is replaced here by a highly personal outlook on the corruption of contemporary society, as Poirier reflects, with a mixture of pain and serenity, on the murder of her own daughter in October 1992 in a drug-related dispute. In 1989, for the fiftieth anniversary of the NFB, she made a documentary on the representation of women in dozens of NFB films: *Il y a longtemps que je t'aime / I've Loved You for a Long Time.*

ANDRÉ LOISELLE

Biography

Born June 6, 1932 in Montréal. Studied law before switching to drama. Worked at the Société Radio-Canada. Joined the National Film Board of Canada (NFB) in 1960. Made her first feature-length film, *De mère en fille / Mother-to-Be,* in 1967.

Selected Films

1963 *Mister Plummer:* director, script, editing
1965 *Les Ludions / Players:* director
1968 *De mère en fille / Mother-to-Be:* director, script
1974 *Les Filles du Roy / They Called Us "Les Filles du Roy":* producer, director, script
1979 *Mourir à tue-tête / A Scream from Silence:* producer, director, script
1989 *Il y a longtemps que je t'aime /I've Loved You for a Long Time:* director
1997 *Tu as crié Let Me Go!:* director, script

Further Reading

Special issue on Anne Claire Poirier, *Copie Zéro*, 23, Montréal: Cinémathèque québécoise, 1985.
Loiselle, André. *Mourir à tue-tête / Scream from Silence,* Trowbridge, England: Flicks Books, 2000.

POIRIER, LÉON

Although Léon Poirier has been largely forgotten by contemporary cinema scholars, he was among the most popular and technically ambitious French filmmakers of the 1920s and 1930s. A versatile director, writer, and producer, he set new quality standards for on-location shooting in standard documentary and historical reconstruction, or docudrama. The success of *La Croisière noire/The Black Journey* (1926), *Verdun, visions d'histoire/ Verdun, Visions of History,* (1928), *L'Appel du silence/The Call* (1936), and *Brazza, ou l'épopée du Congo/Brazza, or the Saga of the Congo* (1940) helped integrate both genres into the commercial mainstream and had a lasting impact on the form and practice of documentary cinema. In his films, Poirier critiqued the decadence and materialism of modern Western civilization, positing spirituality, patriotic self-sacrifice, and contact with "primitive" cultures as antidotes to the identity crisis that Europe confronted in the wake of World War I.

Poirier began his career as a theatre manager, producer, and owner in Paris. He came to cinema after suffering serious burns in an automobile fire that led to his bankruptcy and a temporary job making short entertainment films for Gaumont just before World War I. After his demobilization in 1919, Poirier returned to the profession full-time, directing several critically acclaimed literary adaptations (*Jocelyn*, 1922; *Geneviève*, 1923; *La Brière/ The Salt Marsh*, 1924) whose outdoor shooting in rugged rural environments created a unique painterly depth, pictorial realism, and documentary feel.

In 1924, automobile manufacturer André Citroën hired Poirier and assistant Georges Specht to film a 20,000 kilometre, seven-month expedition across Africa. Simultaneously a grandiose marketing tool and a suspense-filled adventure story that dramatized man and machine conquering some of the harshest terrain on earth (including the Sahara desert, dense rain forests, raging rivers, and vast savannahs), *La Croisière noire* was also an unabashed tribute to colonialism that symbolically unified French possessions in North, West, and Central Africa. In the spirit of newly instituted associationist colonial policy that encouraged respect for rather than erasure of native cultures, Poirier crafted a well-intentioned, though methodologically naïve ethnographic study in the picturesque and the exotic. His footage of collective rituals and distinctive physical characteristics is consistently charged with an unselfconscious voyeurism that betrays a European fear of decadence and desire for renewal by appropriating the uncorrupted vitality of "primitive" African cultures.

Released in late 1926, *La Croisière noire* was a critical and commercial mega-hit that elevated documentary to the level of feature film. More important, it paved the way for subsequent ethnographic documentaries (including Marc Allégret's *Voyage au Congo*, 1927) and established representational conventions that would inform colonial cinema and popular perceptions of Africa throughout the interwar period. For Poirier, the experience was a personal revelation that decisively influenced his conception of documentary. As he wrote in the July 1926 issue of *Ciné-Miroir*:

> An exotic film is not a script that one carries in one's luggage; it is a work of art that one shapes along the way with the landscapes that one encounters, the human characteristics that one analyzes, and the incidents that one records. By virtue of his sensitivity, the cinematographer must extract the poetry, joy, and pain directly from the lives he discovers, then fashion a work of art capable of making others feel what he himself felt.

Verdun, visions d'histoire applied this approach to reconstructing the bloody 1916 battle in which Poirier had fought. Shot on location in France and Germany with actual veterans playing all but a few roles, the film echoed Abel Gance's classic *J'accuse/I Accuse* (1919) in its pacifist denunciation of war and internationalist plea for reconciliation among the belligerent nations. Stylistically *Verdun* was a striking mix of expressionist allegory and documentary realism that integrated universal type characters such as the Mother, the Son, the Husband, the Wife, the Peasant, and the Intellectual with graphic reenactments of combat, death, and the soldiers' psychological agony. Poirier further amplified this realism by editing several segments of authentic newsreel footage into the military scenes—the first time such a technique had been used in a film about the Great War. Like *La Croisière noire*, *Verdun* drew international acclaim and performed well at the box-office, thereby solidifying the director's reputation in the French film industry.

Yet like many directors of his generation Poirier found the transition to sound cinema difficult. After releasing two mediocre fiction films set in eastern Africa (*Caïn, aventures des mers exotiques/Cain*,

1930; *La Voie sans disque/The Unmarked Track*, 1933) and an overblown remake titled *Verdun: Memories of History* (1931), he undertook a cinematic biography of Charles de Foucauld, an obscure soldier turned Catholic missionary who had been killed in 1916 during an anti-French uprising. *L'Appel du silence*, which brought together the themes of Western decadence, spiritual regeneration, pacifism, and patriotic martyrdom present in Poirier's previous work, marked the crowning achievement of his career and made Foucauld an instant national hero.

Financed by Poirier himself and small public donations collected during a two-year fundraising tour, the film was shot primarily on location at Foucauld's isolated retreat in the Algerian Sahara. In addition to winning the 1936 Grand Prize of French Cinema, it was the top box-office draw of the year, selling nearly a million tickets in Paris and ranking among the five biggest successes of the entire decade. French conservatives seized on *L'Appel du silence* to validate their agenda and discredit the socialist-led Popular Front government that had recently taken power, but the film contains no clear endorsement of any party, instead portraying all politics as corrupt. As for moral regeneration and colonialism, at the time both were broadly pan-ideological values—hence the film's extraordinary popularity. Nevertheless, cinema historians have often retrospectively cast Poirier as an apologist for the Right.

Poirier's next project, *Brazza, ou l'épopée du Congo*, focused on the late-nineteenth-century exploration of Equatorial Africa by Pierre Savorgnan de Brazza, who, like Foucauld, is presented as a visionary Christ figure seeking to revitalize France spiritually and culturally through benevolent colonialism. Shooting in the rain forests of Gabon and the Belgian Congo was an enormous logistical challenge that required specially modified film and sound equipment, as well as a production team of two hundred native labourers, a half dozen French engineers, and a small fleet of boats. Though its technical quality and thematic appeal equalled that of *L'Appel du silence*, *Brazza* was overshadowed by World War II, its run cut short by the German invasion.

Poirier remained in France during war, but maintained a low profile to preserve his independence in an industry that was tightly regulated by Vichy French and German authorities. He made only one film during the Occupation, a melodrama titled *Jeannou*, whose proruralist message led to postwar suspicions of Pétainism but no formal indictment or sanctions like those levied against so many of his peers. In 1947, Poirier made his

POIRIER, LÉON

final film, *La Route inconnue/The Unknown Road*, about Charles de Foucauld's early-life adventures in Morocco and spiritual awakening. Its failure to resonate with postwar audiences pushed him into retirement, bringing an otherwise distinguished career to an abrupt and anticlimactic end.

BRETT BOWLES

Biography

Born in Paris, 25 August 1884, nephew of Impressionist painter Berthe Morisot. Successful theatre manager, producer, and owner, 1906–1913. Served in artillery unit during the Great War, 1914–1918. Fiction film director and producer at Gaumont, 1919–1924. Transition to documentary with hits *The Black Journey* and *Verdun: Visions of History*, 1924–1928. Brief return to fiction film and experimentation with sound cinema, 1929–1933. Made *The Call* and *Brazza, or the Saga of the Congo*, 1935–1939. Virtual inactivity during World War II, 1940–1945. Researched and shot *The Unknown Road*, 1946–1948. Retired to Urval-le-Buisson, France, became mayor, and published memoirs, 1949–1953. Died in Urval, June 26, 1968.

Selected Films

1926 *La Croisière noire/The Black Journey*: director
1928 *Verdun, visions d'histoire/Verdun, Visions of History*: director, writer, producer
1931 *Verdun, souvenirs d'histoire/Verdun, Memories of History*: director, writer, producer
1934 *La Croisière jaune/The Yellow Journey* (André Sauvage): editor

1936 *L'Appel du silence/The Call*: director, writer, producer
1940 *Brazza, ou l'épopée du Congo/Brazza, or the Saga of the Congo*: director, writer, producer
1948 *La Route inconnue: Charles de Foucauld au Maroc/The Unknown Road: Charles de Foucauld in Morocco*: director, writer, producer

Further Reading

Abel, Richard, *French Cinema: The First Wave, 1915–1929*, Princeton: Princeton University Press, 1984.
Boulanger, Pierre, *Le Cinéma colonial de "L'Atlantide" à "Lawrence d'Arabie,"* Paris: Seghers, 1975.
Haardt, Georges-Marie, and Louis Audouin-Dubreuil, *La Croisière noire: expédition Citroën Centre-Afrique*, Paris: Plon, 1927.
Leprohon, Pierre, *L'Exotisme et le cinema: les chasseurs d'images à la conquête du monde*, Paris: J. Susse, 1945.
Levine, Alison J., "Film and Colonial Memory: *La Croisière Noire*, 1924–2004," in *Memory, Empire, and Postcolonialism: Legacies of French Colonialism*, edited by Alec Hargreaves, Lexington: Lexington Books, 2005.
Piault, Marc Henri, "L'exotisme et le cinéma ethnographique: la rupture de *La Croisière noire*," in *Journal of Film Preservation*, 63, 2001, 6–16.
Poirier, Léon, *Vingt-quatre images à la seconde: du studio au désert*, Tours: Maison Mamé, 1953.
———. *A la recherché d'autre chose*, Bruges: Desclée de Brouwer, 1968.
Slavin, David, *Colonial Cinema and Imperial France, 1919–1939*, Baltimore: Johns Hopkins University Press, 2001.
Ungar, Steven, "Léon Poirier's *L'Appel du silence* and the Cult of Imperial France," in *Journal of Film Preservation*, 63, 2001, 41–46.

POLAND

Short documentary films first appeared in Poland in the years before World War II. They were a means by which ideas that would otherwise have remained suppressed in the communist nation could be discreetly presented for interpretation by viewers. At the time, Polish documentaries either focused mainly on social themes or were "avant-garde and experimental films created by artists closely connected with avant-garde circles in painting and poetry" (Fuksiewicz, 1973: 58). Studios and films were subsidized by the state (Kornatowska, 1992: 47). Shorts had to be produced in such a way that the government would approve of

them and see them as being of educational value to the nation. The type of subject matter covered by documentaries was limited.

It was after World War II that a reorganization of Polish cinematography occurred, as the young generation began taking over and working with shorts. This new generation turned to documentaries as a means to explore their creativity and their new ideas. "During the war, photographs and other materials were collected and later used to produce documentaries on the Polish contribution to the victory over Nazism" (Fuksiewicz, 1973: 58). This led to a sense of nationalism among the Polish and helped unite them during war. The first short films to be made in Poland after liberation were Jerzy Bossak's *Bitwa O Kolobrzeg* (1945, *The Battle for Kolobrzeg*) and *Zaglada Berlina* (1945, *The Annihilation of Berlin*). "Antoni Bohdziewicz's *Ostatni Parteitag W Norymberdze* [1946, *The Last Parteitag in Nuremburg*] was an attempt at a complete settlement of accounts with Nazi war crimes" (Fuksiewicz, 1973: 59).

During and after the war, the devastation and rebuilding of Poland were a central theme of documentary. One of the most popular works on this theme remains Tadeusz Makarczynski's *Suite Varsovienne* (1946, *Warsaw Suite*).

Throughout the postwar period, Polish cinematography began developing at a much faster pace. An increase in films led to an increase in the range of subject matter being depicted and accepted by the public. As the film industry expanded, the number of filmmakers in Poland grew.

In the 1950s, four main influences led to the increasing numbers of documentaries and short films in Poland. The first was the expansion of the film industry, which led to an expansion of production studios, greater willingness to take risks, enhanced creativity, and the exploration of a variety of new ideas. The second factor to play an important role in the increased production of documentaries in Poland was the emergence of young directors newly graduated from the Higher State Film School. The third major influence was the change in the political and social climate that took place in the mid-1950s. And finally, there was the founding of The Warsaw Documentary Film Studio, the main place where documentaries began being made.

In 1955, with the introduction of so-called Black documentaries, a new atmosphere emerged in Poland. "The term 'Black series' bracketed those films which attacked problems that were not supposed to exist" (Bren, 1986: 48). W. I. Borowik's film *Paragraf Zero* (1957, *Paragraph Zero*) is one such film; it depicts the life of prostitutes. Another such film is Jerzy Hoffman and Edward Skorzewski's *Uwaga Chuligani* (1955, *Watch Out! Thugs!*), dealt with the growing problem of juvenile delinquency in Poland. At this point, filmmakers started intertwining fiction with reality in order to produce documentaries. The documentaries were grounded in fact, but the filmmakers used fictional means to create their characters. It was these "Black" films that made the public more aware of the documentary genre.

As their atmosphere and surroundings changed, directors relied on documentaries to illustrate the economic and social changes taking place in Poland. Changes such as the growth and expansion of industry, the variety of career paths becoming available to the younger generation, and the everyday working life of the nation were themes that dominated the documentaries. Following the theme of transformations emerging in Polish life, Witold Lesiewicz's *Wesola II* (1952, *Vesola II*) traces the opening of a coal mine.

In the late 1950s, two key elements further transformed documentaries: the intimate way of perceiving work and the remarkable way that individuals were being portrayed. Between 1956 and 1957, documentaries began further reporting the various kinds of negligence and social ills that accompanied rapid industrial development. Films such as Hoffman and Skorzewski's *Dzieci Oskarzaja* (1955, *The Children Accuse*) revolve around themes such as alcoholism invading lives and the backwardness of regions untouched by new development. Films helped remind Polish audiences of difficult, complex social problems, while giving them glimpses of positive changes in the community. Documentaries mimicked reality, which forced individuals to face issues directly. As documentaries continued developing and evolving, direct sound recording soon became a basic element in their production. While realist documentaries gained popularity, there also began to emerge "philosophic shorts," which were polar opposites of realist documentaries in that they gave means freer rein to creativity and personal interpretation of new ideas. Films such as these often exposed the disturbances in our modern world, such as human ruthlessness, cruelty, and egotism. Roman Polanski's *Dwaj Ludzie Z Szafa* (1958, *Two Men and a Wardrobe*) is one of the better known of these films.

In the following years, filmmakers began focusing less on immediate problems and more on the individual. Interest in social themes remained, but producers stopped singling out specific Polish affairs and adopted a wider, calmer perspective. Issues of national crisis and war became less prevalent, as social issues such as gambling, alcoholism, childhood, and the intimacy of human life took over. This trend continued and developed in the years that followed, as more experienced documentary film producers moved on to making feature films and the younger generation continued exploring the world of shorts (Fuksiewicz, 1973: 65). One of the more popular shorts produced at this time was Jerzy Hoffman and Edward Skorzewski's film *Gangsterzy I Filantropi* (1962, *Gangsters and Philanthropists*).

In 1961, The Short Film Festival took place in Krakow. It was the first Polish film festival to be held in the country. By 1964, it had evolved into an international festival, and the majority of the productions shown were documentaries. The grand prize of the first Krakow Festival was awarded to

Muzykanci (1960, *Musicians*), a classic documentary made by Kazimierz Karabasz. It was Karabasz, along with another film producer, Jerzy Bossak, who gave rise to the documentary approach of marrying ethics with aesthetics in the course of production.

By the second half of the 1960s, World War II was being examined by documentary filmmakers. A great deal of historical material became newly available to filmmakers, material that depicted Nazi crimes and Poland's struggle throughout the war.

By the late 1970s and early 1980s, many changes being made in Polish society affected the documentary film industry. For instance, in 1978 the Film and Television School at Katowice was founded. This film school taught students a documentary-oriented style of production and was seen as a direct competitor of the National Film School at Lodz (one of the first film schools to be founded in Poland). Up until the 1980s, Polish documentary films were seen merely as additions that would precede feature films. In the late 1980s, it became obvious that the "additions" were competing with the feature films in terms of aesthetics. It did not take long for documentaries to be viewed independently, apart from any other type of film. Clearly, they were a means by which views that would otherwise be opposed to by communist authorities could be "smuggled in."

The year 1989 brought great change to the film industry in Poland, because it was during this year that Polish society made the transition from a Communist regime to a democracy. Following the 1989 "Freedom Shock," the state-controlled and state-owned industry was transformed into independent studios and companies, which were free to make their own financial and production decisions. "The relationship between the state and the artist, as well as between the artist and its audience had been modified dramatically. . . . The idea was to create a new system in which state patronage co-exists with private initiatives" (Haltof, 1995: 137, 139).

One year later, in 1990, there was yet another drastic alteration to the Polish film industry: censorship was abolished. Film producers and directors suddenly were responsible for both the successes and the failures of their products. "As a consequence of these recent political transformations, hidden archives and victimized dissidents no longer constituted the Polish film landscape" (Haltof, 1995: 15). Filmmaking quickly shifted from a national and social mission to a strictly professional endeavor. Suddenly, filmmakers were held accountable for their own productions. They had their films as a defense, rather than the state as well. It was now up to the producer to decide what was to be censored and what was to be portrayed to the audiences. This movement granted film producers much more liberty, but it also led some to feel an immense, sometimes unbearable sense of responsibility. This post-communist period attempted to deviate from issues of politics and history, because the Polish audiences had grown tired of these central themes.

In the late twentieth century, many social, economic, and political problems arose as a result of Poland's transition to a market economy. In order to keep film production numbers up and steady, three government funding bodies were introduced in 1991: the Script Agency, the Film Production Agency, and the Film Distribution Agency. The Script Agency (Agencja Scenariuszowa) was established in order to ensure the existence of a prominent market for film scripts in Poland. The funds available through the Script Agency are used to support script development and pre-production work. The Film Production Agency (Agencja Produkcji Filmowej) was founded as a means of collecting funds used mostly for the production of projects that are seen as having "cultural value," such as documentaries and educational films. Finally, the Film Distribution Agency (Agencja Dystrybucji Filmowej) was initiated to ensure the distribution of important cultural and national films.

The future of Polish cinema is uncertain. Today, there are many foreign and international filmmakers entering Poland. Polish filmmakers are worried that their national cinema runs the risk of undergoing commercialization by Western distributors entering the Polish market. In 1992, for example, "more than seventy percent of the Polish repertoire consisted of American films; Polish films made up only thirteen percent" (Haltof, 1995: 141). Although movie directors such as Steven Spielberg are traveling to Polish soil to film productions such as *Schindler's List* (1993), the demand for Polish productions is waning. It is important to support co-productions, but it is equally important that Polish theaters not become filled with American movies. Needless to say, Polish critics are insisting that the influx of films needs to be controlled in order to preserve the Polish film industry.

Despite the turbulence and uncertainty that the Polish film industry has faced since the 1989 "Freedom Shock," Polish documentary film continues to thrive. Today, between 150 and 200 documentary films are produced each year in Poland. The majority of these are broadcast on television and have attracted the attention of worldwide audiences. One of the most popular documentary series that airs on television in Poland is *Czas Na Dokument* (*Time for a Documentary*). Other documentaries, such as Maciej Drygas's *Uslyszcie Moj Krzyk* (1991, *Hear*

My Cry)]; Marcel Lozinski's *89 MM Od Europy* (1993, *89 MM from Europe*); Dariusz Jablonski's *FotoAmateur* (1998, *Amateur Photographer*); and Wojciech Staron's *Syberyjska Lekcja* (1998, *Syberian Lesson*) have all earned great critical acclaim and have received awards at international film festivals.

Present-day Polish documentaries, and those of the 1990s, can be divided into four main categories. The first two categories are named in honor of two famous Polish documentary makers, Marcel Lozinski and Andrzej Fidyk. The last two categories are consist of historical documentaries and biographical documentaries. The four different types of shorts are more thoroughly summarized below.

Lozinski documentaries are documentaries in which the producer's main interest lies in the everyday life of the everyday individual. There is much mystery found in getting to the absolute essence of the ordinary life being lived by the ordinary person. The producer feels a great sense of responsibility in depicting the life of the individual, and the individual himself or herself, as accurately as possible. Films such as Lozinski's *Wizyta* (1974, *A Visit*) and Marcin Latalla's *Slad* (1996, *Trace*) are world-renowned documentaries that fall in this category.

Fidyk documentaries are similar to Lozinski documentaries, but they are less interested in everyday life and more committed to making contemporary issues as attractive as issues depicted in Hollywood productions. The Fidyk documentary deals with contemporary problems and present-day changes in customs and morals. However, it is produced in such an ingenious way that rather than getting bored, contemporary audiences are naturally drawn in. Included in this genre are Fidyks's *Defilada* (1989, *Parade*), Sladkowski's *Szwedzkie Tango* (1999, *Swedish Tango*), and Piotr Morawski's *Tata, I Love You* (1998, *Daddy, I Love You*). Such films are known for "attracting the most interest but, at the same time, arousing the most controversy and disputes" (Lubelski, 2004: 10).

The third type of documentary prevalent today consists of historical documentaries. A great majority of them were produced in the early 1990s, right after the communist regime collapsed in Poland. Historical documentaries were produced more as a duty to the country than anything else. Filmmakers believed that they owed it not only their nation, but also to the community, to produce films that continued documenting Polish history. This was critical then, because with the abolition of censorship, filmmakers had an opportunity to retell history accurately, without interference. Thanks to unlimited access to historical archives, Marek Drazkiewicz's documentary *Zdrada* (1991, *Treason*) is one such

film in which "there is a new approach presented to the history of Polish foreign policy in the period between the two world wars" (Lubelski, 2004: 12). Historical documentaries aim to discover the truth behind history and to uncover all the distortion that characterized postwar "history."

The final group of short films consists of biographies. These films trace the lives of politicians, scientists, and artists, offering educational value to the nation. Films such as Jadwiga Zajicek's *Zycie Jak Film* (1994, *A Life Like a Film*) and Andrzej Wajda's *Idac, Spotykajac* (1999, *Going, Meeting*) not only educate audiences but also show how famous individuals, including leading filmmakers, got to where they are today.

In the past, Polish producers had to face the challenge of producing documentaries that accurately represented reality but at the same time appealed to both the Polish audience and the communist authorities. As the years progressed, and Poland entered a postwar era that transformed the economy into a democracy, the major challenge for film producers was to uncover the truths that remained hidden. Although today the state has no say in what type of film an artist decides to produce, the filmmaker has just as big a challenge to face as ever before. The challenge is no longer to please a state, a government, or a body of authorities but, rather, to attract an audience that has disintegrated into numerous entities. With democracy comes freedom, and with freedom comes the liberty to voice countless opinions on countless subjects. The challenge facing the present-day filmmaker in Poland is significant: to produce documentaries that will be accepted and praised by audience members of varying tastes both at home and around the globe.

SAPNA GUPTA

See also **Bossak, Jerzy; Karabasz, Kazimierz; Lozinski, Marcel**

Further Reading

Bren, Frank, *World Cinema 1: Poland*, London: Flicks Books, 1986.
Dowell, Pat, "The Man Who Put Poland on the Post-War Map of Cinema: An Interview with Andrzej Wajda," in *Cineaste*, 19, fall 1992, 51–54.
Fuksiewicz, Jacek, *Polish Cinema*, Poland: Interpress Publishers, 1973.
Haltof, Marek, "A Fistful of Dollars: Polish Cinema after the 1989 Freedom Shock," in *Film Quarterly*, 48, spring 1995, 15–25.
Haltof, Marek, "Everything for Sale: Polish National Cinema After 1989," in *Canadian Slavonic Papers*, 39, March–June 1997, 137–53.
Kornatowska, Maria, "Polish Cinema," in *Cineaste*, 19, fall 1992, 47–51.

Lubelski, Tadeusz, "Polish Contemporary Documentary Film: Essays on Polish Culture," in *Culture.pl*, August 25, 2004, <http://www.culture.pl/en/culture/artykuly/es_film_dokumentalny>.

Michalek, Boleslaw, and Turaj, Frank, *The Modern Cinema of Poland*, Bloomington: Indiana University Press, 1988.

Rogerson, Edward, "Polish Cinema: An Internal Exile?" in *Sight & Sound*, 55, summer 1986, 195–97.

Sosnowski, Alexandra, "Cinema in Transition: The Polish Film Today," in *Journal of Popular Film and Television*, 24, spring 1996, 10–16.

Warchol, Tomasz, "Polish Cinema: The End of a Beginning," in *Sight & Sound*, 55, summer 1986, 190–94.

POLIZEISTAATSBESUCH, DER

(Germany, Brodmann, 1967)

Der Polizeistaatsbesuch is a German documentary by Roman Brodmann in the direct cinema style that was especially popular in the 1960s. The film acutely illustrates the inherent impact and power of film. *Der Polizeistaatsbesuch* follows the visit of the shah of Iran to Germany in 1967, focusing particularly on the efforts of the German state to protect the official guest. In the middle of the film, it changes its position from that of an ironic spectator of the official visit to that of the student protest against the shah. In Berlin, a student is shot by the police, and the TV team is very close to that accident. Hence the film documents the beginnings of the student movement, which changed German society fundamentally from 1968 on. Therefore, it is regarded as the most important film of the documentary department of the SDR, which was called the "Stuttgarter Schule."

Initially, the concept of the film was quite different. The choice of the visit of the shah and his wife was a coincidence. The film was intended to show the luxury of such a visit and the subservience of the German host. Thus not the shah, but the details of the ceremony of such an official act, were to be the focus of the film. The preparation of the different places that the shah visits is unmasked in a very ironic way—for example, the welcoming ritual at the airport, the fresh painting of the Rothenburg central station or the Thyssen manufacturing plant half an hour before the delegation arrives, and how a hotel owner in Rothenburg rehearses welcoming the highest guest (the commentator notes that she also once offered an apple to Adolf Hitler). Roman Brodmann exposes the satirical aspects of such a real event as a sign of the times and as typical for such an official visit.

The film was shot with two teams on 16mm film. Director Roman Brodmann, cameraman Franz Brandeis, and soundman Klaus Schuhmacher went to Rothenburg ob der Tauber to concentrate on the preparations there: the rehearsal of the police and of the music and dance groups, the street repairs, decoration of buildings, and so on. The second team, with Brodmann's assistant Rainer C. M. Wagner, cameraman Michael Busse, his assistant Heinz Rexer, and soundman Rainer Bosch, concentrated on following the official route of the visit. Included were the welcoming ceremonies at the airport, the reception by the German president, a meeting with the chancellor, and sightseeing visits to companies and technical points of interest such as the atomic energy research site in Jülich. After five days of shooting, the two teams met in Rothenburg. The four other cities visited (Munich, Berlin, Hamburg, and Lübeck) were to be only an appendix. But then Brodmann heard about the student protests in Berlin and decided to go there with his team. Soon he changed the concept of the film, in which Rothenburg was no longer the highlight. In Berlin, he decided that the film should concentrate on two perspectives: the official visit on the one hand, and the protest against it on the other hand. Instead of following the delegation to the opera, the team (still in their tuxedos) went on the streets to shoot the demonstrations and the brutal police reactions. On the soundtrack they documented the shot that killed the student Benno Ohnesorg. The dynamic sequences that they filmed would have been possible only with handheld cameras and synchronised sound. The team was able to get only one press pass for the German president's reception at the Bühl castle.

Therefore, cameraman Michael Busse was equipped as a one-man team with a reflector and a microphone mounted directly on the camera. His shots are not always sharp, but they infused a new style of authenticity into documentary filmmaking. The same is true for the shooting of the demonstrations in Berlin. On the other hand, some sequences had to be shot silent in order that they be filmed from different perspectives.

In the final film, the increasing gravity of the situation in Berlin is cleverly prepared, as the police actions and the attempts to protect the guest became the central theme of the film. The title was changed from *Der Staatsbesuch / The State Visit* to *Der Polizeistaatsbesuch / Visit in a Police State*. The commentary states that often there were more policemen on the street than citizens welcoming the shah. All in all, 30,000 policemen and security services were activated for that visit. Highways were closed, and we see a policeman every few hundred meters along the route. When the commentary mentions that thousands of people were controlled, the image shows a police dog with a muzzle. This kind of ironic association is very typical for the style of the Stuttgart documentary department, which developed editing to mastery. Another remarkable sequence is the welcome at the airport, where every handshake of the shah and his wife is undercut with the salute shots of the cannons, making it appear grotesque.

The station received around 200 letters in reaction to the program. They were mainly positive and thanked Brodmann for his democratic courage with that film. A survey after the broadcast shows that 22 percent found the film excellent, 42 percent good, 18 percent satisfactory, 13 percent moderate, and 5 percent very bad. Also, the commentary in the press was overwhelmingly positive. But some viewers and journalists of the conservative press viewed the film as communist propaganda in Goebbels's style or complained that it was not objective. Heinz Huber, head of the department, responded very vigorously. The charge of bias surprised him, because live coverage of several hours on German television had shown only the positive aspects. Therefore, a 45-minute more critical report should be acceptable in a democratic TV program. Der Polzeistaatsbesuch won the highest TV prize in Germany (Adolf-Grimme-Preis) in silver and many other prizes. The film is regularly broadcast on German television.

KAY HOFFMAN

See also **Brodmann, Roman**

Der Polizeistaatsbesuch. Beobachtungen unter deutschen Gastgebern (Germany, Süddeutscher Rundfunk, 1967, 45 min.). From the series: Zeichen der Zeit. Director, script: Roman Brodmann. Assistant: Rainer C. M. Wagner. Camera: Franz Brandeis, Michael Busse. Sound: Rainer Bosch, Klaus Schumacher. Editing: Dorrit Wintterlin. Narration: Alwin Michael Rueffer.

Further Reading

Althoff, Burkhard, *Der Dokumentarfilmer Roman Brodmann – Werkübersicht und Analyse des satirischen Stils*, M.A. thesis, University of Erlangen-Nürnberg 1993.

Böhm, Frauke, *Zeitkritischer Dokumentarfilm im Spannungsfeld zwischen Fernsehjournalismus und Autorenfilm: Roman Brodmann*, Ph.D. thesis, University of Marburg, 2000.

Busse, Michael, *Die Gewalt hinter dem Operettencharme*, in Süddeutsche Zeitung, March 13, 1990.

Hoffmann, Kay, *Zeichen der Zeit. Zur Geschichte der Stuttgarter Schule*, Munich, 1996.

Müller, Jürgen K., *Zeichen der Zeit. Eine Fernseh-Dokumentationsreihe des Süddeutschen Rundfunks (1957–1973). Sechs Filmanalysen,* M.A. thesis, University of Tübingen, 1991.

Prümm, Karl, *Klassizität, die nicht einschüchtert*, in: epd - Kirche und Rundfunk, 21.3.1990.

Steinmetz, Rüdiger, and Helfried Spitra (eds.), *Dokumentarfilm als, "Zeichen der Zeit." Vom Ansehen der Wirklichkeit im Fernsehen*, Munich, 1992.

PORTILLO, LOURDES

Lourdes Portillo is a Mexican-born, Chicana-identified documentary filmmaker. Her work has centered primarily on gendered Latin American and Chicano/Latino themes. She was part of a Marxist film collective in the 1970s called CineManifest, and later founded the oldest Latino film organization, Cine Acción, which operates to this day in San Francisco. After receiving her MFA at the San Francisco Art Institute, she began working on her first documentary, *After the Earthquake* (*Despues del terremoto*, 1979), a piece about a Nicaraguan immigrant who flees his native country and settles in the Bay Area.

Her 1985 film, *Las Madres: The Mothers of the May Plaza*, which she co-directed with Susana Muñoz, was nominated for an Academy Award for Best Documentary. It describes the heroic efforts made by the mothers of the *desaparicidos* or "disappeared" children who were kidnapped and killed during Argentina's Dirty War, a dictatorship which lasted from 1976–1983.

Portillo has focused her work in documenting the role of women within the Chicano/Latino/Latin American community and related issues of identity, politics, and culture in a contemporary setting. Her documentaries have ranged from Argentine "maternal" activists, Mexican practices of the "Day of the Dead" ritual celebration, a portrait of the Tejana singer Selena and her fan base in Corpus Christi, Texas, her familial probe into the death of her favorite uncle Oscar in Mexico, to the unresolved case of over 200 young women murdered in the maquiladora town of Juárez, Mexico.

Rosa Linda Fregoso, Portillo's foremost biographer and critic, sums up Portillo's aesthetic sensibility in the following manner: "While her work conforms to the realist aesthetics of cinema, Portillo has created a genuinely hybrid style of filmmaking insofar as she crosses the border of multiple styles and playfully blends aesthetic traditions." (Fregoso 2000: 100). In films such as *The Devil Never Sleeps,* for instance, she mixes the traditional documentary mode of interviews with beautiful and stylized shots of images such as tomatoes, toy tractors, and family photographs suspended on rippling water.

In her documentary, *La ofrenda: Days of the Dead*, Portillo connects common themes between the Mexican and Mexican-American experiences of the Day of the Dead ceremony. She examines the traditional ritual in small Mexican villages, but then shifts to a more modern rendition in the gay Latino community of San Francisco. Her idea is to trace parallels between the Mexican religious ritual and the altars made in the United States to honor the deaths caused by AIDS. By making these connections, Portillo is making radical claims about the Latino diaspora and the collective identity of Latinos that is ultimately deterritorialized, but remains unified by cultural and religious ritual. By bridging the gap between Latin Americans, Chicanos/as and U.S. Latino/as, she is acting in political ways to stress commonalities and linkages between these geographically separated groups.

Portillo's strengths in her documentaries have been the uses of unorthodox or "non-legitimate" sources of knowledge, such as rumor, folktales, telenovela clips, *dichos* (proverbs) and other forms of popular culture (they are often "feminized" practices such as gossip) to examine how knowledge is constructed in Mexico and in the United States. Her films often share themes of border crossing, the nature of truth, and the filmmaker's self-reflexivity in story telling. Fregoso states that *The Devil Never Sleeps* also "sketches the permeable borders between nations, genres, and the political/familial identities" (Fregoso, 2000: 90). Portillo has deemed this film a *melodocumystery* due to its form of crossing genres, borders, and styles of filmmaking. Her aim was to infuse the traditional U.S. documentary form with some elements of melodrama, a narrative device often utilized in Latin America, but oftentimes disliked by Americans. In an interview she states that "in traditional documentaries, there's a sense of objectivity in documentary where you are not supposed to feel strong feelings. And that's what melodrama is about, the exaggeration of drama" (Portillo in Fregoso, 1999: 324).

Humor is also an important device used in Portillo's films. In 1993, to commemorate and contest Columbus's "discovery" of America, Portillo teamed up with the Chicano comedy troupe, Culture Clash, to create the eighteen-minute piece *Columbus on Trial* whereby the main character, a Native American named Stormcloud (Richard Montoya) charges Columbus with genocide in a comedic parody of courtroom dramas. This piece utilizes an inventive use of blue screen, whereby you can see Portillo's hand in placing "exotic backdrops" to illustrate the various voyages that Columbus made. While it appeals to the viewer's sense of humor, it simultaneously engages the audience to critically rethink Columbus' legacy from the point of view of oppressed citizens.

Señorita Extraviada (Missing Young Woman) tells the haunting story of the more than 200 kidnapped, raped, and murdered young women of Cuidad Juárez, Mexico from 1993 to the present. The majority have come to the border city from the rural villages to work in the maquiladoras. Portillo spent three years in Juárez, meeting with human-rights groups and speaking with the family members of the victims, who became the protagonists of the film. This documentary could be considered part of the Latin American literary/film genre the *testimonio,* whereby silenced or marginalized people are given a space to speak of their traumatic experiences. These stories, in the words of Portillo, "spoke to me and became the heart of my film. These voices were the most important because they rang true and demanded justice" (Portillo, 2003: 230).

The film tries to outline some of the possible murder suspects by describing a tangled web involving police complicity, government corruption, and a powerful group of drug traffickers in Juárez. Portillo's film worked as a consciousness-raising tool and a call to action. Portillo, along with Mexican filmmaker María Nováro organized both indoor and outdoor film screenings in Mexico to educate the public about this group of unsolved murders. The film helped to galvanize discussion, and soon various human-rights and women's groups visibly organized around this issue (232).

Although Portillo tackles difficult and sometimes taboo subjects in her native Mexico (e.g., questions of homosexuality, adultery, rape, and political corruption) she is able to gain entré into this society due to her Northern Mexican roots, but also because of her special status as an outside observer coming from the United States. Her dual subject positions as a Mexicana and Chicana allows her to straddle two worlds: she takes the critical distance needed to see the problems of Mexican society from an outsider's point of view, while intimately understanding the nuances of the people and the culture she has such an interest in comprehending.

TAMARA L. FALICOV

See also **Chicano Tradition**

Biography

Born in Chihuahua, Mexico, Portillo was raised in Los Angeles from the age of 13. In 1978, after graduating from the San Francisco Art Institute, Portillo was awarded the American Film Institute (AFI) Independent Filmmaker Award to create an internationally acclaimed narrative film, *After the Earthquake / Despues del terremoto*, about a Nicaraguan refugee living in San Francisco. In 1985 Portillo won an Academy Award nomination in the Best Documentary category for *Las Madres: The Mothers of the Plaza de Mayo*. This film won twenty awards and positioned her to obtain PBS funding to complete her next film, *La Ofrenda: The Days of the Dead*, in 1989. In 1992, in connection with commemorattion of Columbus's "discovery" of America, Portillo won an NEA Inter-Arts

grant to produce a performance piece called "Columbus on Trial," featuring the Chicago comedy troupe Culture Clash. It screened at the London and Sundance film festivals. This film was selected for the 1993 Whitney Biennial. In 1994 she was awarded a Guggenheim fellowship in recognition of her achievements in filmmaking. Continuing with Mexican and Mexican-American themes, she next created a film about border crossing and family secrets in Mexico called *The Devil Never Sleeps / El diablo nunca duerme*. In 1999 she directed the documentary *Corpus: A Home Movie for Selena* about the impact that the Tejana singer Selena Quintanilla had on young Chicanas in Texas. Her most recent film, *Señorita Extraviada*, is a grim story of the 300 murdered young women of Juarez, Mexico. The filmmaker poetically investigates the circumstances of the murders and the horror, fear, and courage of the families whose children have been taken.

Selected Films

1979 *After the Earthquake / Después del terremoto*
1986 *Las Madres: The Mothers of the Plaza de Mayo*
1988 *La Ofrenda: The Days of the Dead*
1992 *Columbus on Trial*
1994 *The Devil Never Sleeps/El diablo nunca duerme*
1999 *Corpus: A Home Movie for Selena*
2001 *Señorita Extraviada/Missing Young Woman*

Further Reading

Fregoso, Rosa Linda, *Lourdes Portillo: The Devil Never Sleeps and Other Films*, Austin: University of Texas Press, 2001.
———, "Sacando los trapos al sol (airing dirty laundry) in Lourdes Portillo's Melodocumystery, The Devil Never Sleeps," in *Redirecting the Gaze: Gender, Theory and Cinema in the Third World*, edited by Duana Robin and Ira Jaffe, New York: SUNY Press, 1999, 307–29.
Fusco, Coco, "Las Madres de la Plaza de Mayo: An Interview with Susana Muñoz and Lourdes Portillo," in *Cineaste*, 15(1), 1986, 22–25.
González, Rita, "The Said and the Unsaid: Lourdes Portillo Tracks Down Ghosts in Señorita Extraviada," in *Aztlan: A Journal of Chicano Studies*, 28(2), fall 2003, 235–40.
Portillo, Lourdes, "Filming Señorita Extraviada," in *Aztlan: A Journal of Chicano Studies*, 28(2), fall 2003, 229–35.

PORTUGAL

The first Portuguese documentaries were a series of short films produced in 1896 by the film pioneer Aurélio da Paz dos Reis (1852–1931). Obviously influenced by the Lumière brothers, the films depicted scenes of daily life in Portugal—cattle markets, firemen at work, arrival of trains, and a very typical *Saída do Pessoal Operario da Fabrica Confiança* (*Worker's Exit From the Confiança Shirt Factory*). Although Paz dos Reis can be considered the first filmmaker of the Iberian peninsula, his career was extremely brief. When a screening of his films in Brazil in 1897 failed, he lost all interest in filmmaking.

During the first twenty-five years of cinema in Portugal, the documentary was reduced to the filming of newsreel scenes, which led to the curious fact that all films of more or less "documentary" condition were generically defined as *actualidades*, or newsreels. It was not until the end of the silent cinema that the influence of foreign filmmakers, and the critical commercial success of works by Flaherty, Ruttmann, and Vertov, marked a turning point in Portuguese documentary filmmaking. This turning point was marked by the release of three important films: *Nazaré, Praia de Pescadores/The Fishers of Nazaré* (1929), *Alfama, Velha Lisboa/Alfama, the Oldest Lisbon* (1929), and *Douro, Faina Fluvial/Working at the Douro* (1931).

Filmed in 1928, *Nazaré* was photographed and produced by Artur Costa de Macedo (the only name in the credits when it was first released) and directed by José Leitão de Barros. According to its title, it shows the daily life in that fishermen's village, with great attention to atmospheric detail. The critics hailed the superb photography and handsome editing, and soon it was classified as a milestone of Portuguese cinema. Unfortunately, the prints preserved are fragmentary. In the two following decades, Leitão de Barros (1896–1967) became one of the major Portuguese filmmakers, although not in the documentary genre. He directed such epics as the first "talkie," *A Severa* (1931, filmed in Paris), *Bocage* (1936), and *Camões* (1946).

Alfama, Velha Lisboa is forgotten today, but in 1929 it was warmly received. Because its credited director was an amateur, a medical student named João de Almeida e Sá, the merits of the film are usually attributed to its cinematographer, again Artur Costa de Macedo.

Douro Faina Fluvial is the most accomplished of these three films, in part because of the name of its director, the now nonagenarian and still active Manoel de Oliveira (born 1908), but also because of its modern, avant-garde cinematic language that was probably one of the reasons for its weak critical and commercial reception. In 1934, the film was re-released in a new version, which had been slightly reedited by Oliveira and had an added soundtrack, as a companion to the successful feature *Gado Bravo/Brave Bulls*, directed by Oliveira's former assistant António Lopes Ribeiro. *Douro Faina Fluvial* was reevaluated by critics and is now considered a classic.

Between 1933 and 1974, and after the military coup of 1926, Portugal lived under an authoritarian regime called Estado Novo. António de Oliveira Salazar, professor of economics at the University of Coimbra, was the leader of this dictatorship, which was based on the political clichés of religion, family, and authority, with the addition of light Fascist elements and a solid friendship with one democratic power, Great Britain, which actually was the main supporter of Salazar's regime until its very last years. Cinema was not one of the priorities of the new regime's politics; in fact, the Portuguese film industry was practically nonexistent, and theatres only showed foreign films, but Salazar knew that control of every medium was necessary.

Because the number of fiction films being produced was minimal, all efforts were concentrated on documentaries. In 1933, a propaganda office called the Secretariado da Propaganda Nacional (SPN) was created to oversee the ideological messages circulated by newspapers, radio, and cinema (in 1944, the name was subtly changed to *Secretariado Nacional da Informação, Cultura Popular e Turismo*: SNI). The main collaborator among cinema people was António Lopes Ribeiro (1908–1995), who was responsible for the most important cinematic projects of Salazarism. One of them was related to the colonies: during nine months of 1938, the SPN organized an expedition to Portuguese Africa ("Missão Cinegráfica às Colónias de África"), led by Ribeiro, to shoot enough material to edit a series of films of variable length. The results led to an 80-minute documentary, *Viagem de Sua Exª. O Presidente da República a Angola/Journey of His Excellency the President To Angola* (released 1939), some short subjects like *Guiné, Berço do Império/Guinea, Birth of Empire* (1940, 20 minutes), *Aspectos de Moçambique/Vistas of Mozambique* (1941, 12 minutes), or *Angola, a Nova Lusitánia/Angola, a New Lusitania* (1944, 30 minutes), and a feature film with actors, *Feitiço do Império/The Enchantment of Empire* (1940). Ribeiro continued his service to Salazar until 1974.

In 1956, Manoel de Oliveira, retired from filmmaking since 1942, presented a 30-minute documentary entitled *O Pintor e A Cidade/The Painter and the City*, a tribute to his native city, Porto (like the earlier *Douro Faina Fluvial*) as well as to the painter António Ruiz. The release of this film acted as the prelude to the most productive period of Portuguese documentary—paradoxically the result of a negative factor.

In the mid-1950s, film production in Portugal collapsed as a result of several factors. The weak domestic market contributed to the problem, as did the lack of markets for export reduce the production of newsreels and documentaries, most of them shot inexpensively using 16mm equipment and black-and-white photography. This is not the case for *Rapsódia Portuguesa/Portuguese Rhapsody* (1958, directed by João Mendes), a 35mm, colour, handsomely mounted travelog produced by the SNI for strictly touristic purposes; but it does characterize *A Almadraba Atuneira/The Tunny-Fishery* (1961), film debut of the best documentarist filmmaker of Portugal, António Campos (1922–1999). Campos's innovative and courageous work is largely unknown, even in Portugal, and merits attention. He generally writes and shoots his own films, and receives production support from cultural institutions, mainly the Gulbenkian Foundation, where he was a civil servant for years. His films are little masterpieces of ethnographic cinema. To name only a few from a filmography of almost fifty titles, we can select two medium-length works, *Vilarinho das Furnas* (1971) and *Falamos de Rio de Onor/Talking About Rio de Onor* (1974), both clever studies of primitive rural societies.

Apart from the films of Campos, marked by their ethnographic approach, the documentaries produced during the 1960s can be classified by subject. The less interesting are those made to promote tourism, some of them edited only in English versions, like José Fonseca e Costa's (later a noted feature director) *The Pearl of the Atlantic* (about Madeira, 1969) and *Golf in the Algarve* (1972).

Another subject was figures of Portuguese culture, living or dead. Among the writers profiled, the best examples are the tributes to poet *Sophia de Mello Breyner Andresen* (1968, released 1972) by João César Santos (later known as Monteiro), and to novelist *Fernando Namora* (1969) by Manuel Guimarães. Both films were produced by Ricardo Malheiro, who, along with, Francisco de Castro, was one of the most enterprising producers of those years. Malheiro was also the sponsor of *27 Minutos con Fernando Lopes-Graça/27 Minutes with Fernando Lopes-Graça* (shot 1968–1969, released 1971), directed without credit with another future great filmmaker, António Pedro Vasconcelos (Lopes-Graça was a musician), and Castro produced *Almada Negreiros Vivo, Hoje/Almada Negreiros Live, Today* (1969), homage to this painter by Antonio de Macedo, which was one of the most celebrated titles of this series. Manuel Guimarães produced and directed *Carta a Mestre Dórdio Gomes/A Letter For Mr Dórdio Gomes* (1971, about a painter) and *Areia, Mar – Mar, Areia/Sand, Sea – Sea, Sand* (1973, about

sculptor Martins Correia). Distinguished documentary specialist Faria de Almeida (born in Mozambique in 1934) provided one of the most ambitious "biographic" films about a living writer: *Vida e Obra de Ferreira de Castro/Life and Works of Ferreira de Castro* (1971, released 1974), which included scenes of the character's childhood, testimonies of colleagues like Jorge Amado, and excerpts from amateur films. It was produced by Telecine-Moro, a company specializing in commercial filmlets, that contributed to the production of documentaries and newsreels. A more conservative approach was given by veteran Lopes Ribeiro in his *Gil Vicente e o Seu Teatro/Gil Vicente and His Theatre* (1965), an official SNI production for the Fifth Centennial of the famed playwright.

The most accomplished film about a living character was *Belarmino* (1964), directed by Fernando Lopes (born 1935) and produced by António da Cunha Telles, based on the remembrances of Belarmino Fragoso, a former box champion. An incisive portrait of a man and a city (Lisbon), this testimonial documentary is justly remembered today as one of the landmarks of the "New Portuguese Cinema" and one of the few films of this period with a real social concern, only comparable to another Lopes title, *Nacionalidade: Português/Nationality: Portuguese* (1972, released 1974), a slightly softened exposé of the hard conditions of the life of Portuguese workers in Paris.

Indicative of the strange situation of film industry during this period is a series of documentary shorts with diverse sponsors. For example, Francisco de Castro produced for the National Tobacco Factory the politically incorrect (by the standards of the time) *Nicotiana* (1963). This film marked the beginning of a ten-year collaboration with the director António de Macedo (born 1931), probably the main specialist of "industrial" films, among them, *História Breve da Madeira Aglomerada/A Short History of Agglomerate Wood* (1970), a surprisingly good management of the subject. The other great director in this field was Faria de Almeida, who, with *Faça Segundo a Arte/Make It As You Know* (1965), produced by the Indústria Portuguesa de Especialidades Farmacêuticas, succeeded in making the process of manufacturing medical drugs entertaining.

Glorification of empire persisted, despite the increasing unrest in colonial territories. Some films with propaganda goals were sufficiently ambiguous to arouse censorship suspicions. The most flagrant case was that of Faria de Almeida's *Catembe* (1965), about daily life in Mozambique, which, after a semi-clandestine preview, was cut from eighty-seven to forty-five minutes. The most impressive effort in colonialist propaganda was *Angola na Guerra e no Progresso/Angola: War and Progress* (1971), a widescreen, colour blockbuster produced by the SIPFA (*Serviço de Informação Pública das Forças Armadas*) and directed by Quirino Simões, an Air Force officer who was also an accomplished filmmaker. Simões (born 1931) is the author of another accomplished work of propaganda, *Guiné, A Caminho do Futuro/Guinea, The Road to the Future* (1971), a tribute to Gen. António de Spinola, then Governor of Guinea, as well as two fiction films (shot in 1967 and 1991).

The Carnations's Revolution of April 25, 1974 changed Portugal's political landscape, which was reflected by film. Cinema and television documentaries were conceived as propaganda weapons. The first report of the Revolution (and an impressive depiction of its time) was *As Armas e o Povo/Arms and the People* (shot 1974, edited 1975), which, as with many of the titles produced during this period, was presented without directorial credit, as a production of a group calling themselves "Trabalhadores da Actividade Cinematográfica." Among these "workers" were such noted filmmakers as Luis Galvão Teles (one of the main animators of this militant cinema), Fernando Lopes, Alberto Seixas Santos, António de Macedo, António de Cunha Telles, António Pedro Vasconcelos, José Fonseca e Costa, and Brazilian talent Glauber Rocha. The other important piece of militant cinema was *Deus, Patria, Autoridade/God, Country, Authority* (1975) by Rui Simões. If the earlier film was the first cinematic portrait of revolutionary days, the second was the first critical approach to the forty years of Salazar's dictatorship. Co-produced by the newly formed IPC (Instituto Português de Cinema) and the RTP (Portuguese Television), its message sounds today a little partisan, but it was a phenomenal success.

One of the most active filmmaker cooperatives of this period was the Grupo Zero, responsible for two documentaries on agrarian reform made in 1976: *A Lei da Terra/The Law of the Earth*; also know as *Alentejo 76*), mainly directed by Alberto Seixas Santos, and *A Luta do Povo/The People in Arms*, which according to the most credible sources was directed by Swedish-born Solveig Nordlund. Nordlund was the editor of Alberto Seixas Santos's curious experiment on Estado Novo, *Brandos Costumes/Sweet Habits*, 1975, a mix of documentary and fiction elements filmed in part before April 25, 1974 and later completed with archive material. Another important purveyor of militant films was Cinequanon, a company founded by Luis Galvão Teles. Among its titles were *O Outro Teatro/The Other Theatre* (1976)

by António de Macedo, about the staging of politically nonconformist plays, and *Colonia e Vilões/Colonies and Villages* (1977) by Leonel Brito, about political and religious repression on the island of Madeira. The most elaborate and widely known piece on agrarian reform was a co-production with West Germany about a people's cooperative, *Torre Bela* (1977), directed by Thomas Harlan, son of that Veit Harlan famous (or infamous) for his cinematic contributions to Nazi propaganda. The independence of African territories was another political subject for documentaries, Fernando Matos Silva's *Acto dos Feitos da Guiné/History of the Events of Guinea* (1980) being one of the most accurate. The cycle of political documentaries ended in the late 1970s, with Rui Simões' *Bom Povo Português/Good Portuguese People* (1981) standing as a sort of summary of the illusions and disappointments of the revolutionary period.

Despite the increasing presence of political messages in documentaries, some of them managed to follow the lines established before 1974. In the ethnographic category, we have a masterpiece by António Campos, *Gente da Praia da Vieira/People from Praia da Vieira* (1975), a tribute to this fishermen's village where he directed one of his first amateur films, *Um Tesouro/A Treasury* (1958). The impoverished villages of the northeast of Portugal were the subject of *Máscaras/Maks* (1975) by Noémia Delgado and the superb *Trás–os–Montes* (1976) by António Reis and Margarida Martins Cordeiro. The daily life of women in the village of Lanheses was beautifully portrayed by Manuela Serra in *O Movimento das Coisas/Things in Motion* (1985).

Among biographical films, one of the best is *Ma Femme Chamada Bicho/Ma Femme Called Bicho* (1976), produced by the Gulbenkian Foundation and directed by José Álvaro Morais, about the painting couple Maria Helena Vieira da Silva and Arpád Szenes. An original approach was that of Lauro António's *Prefácio a Vergílio Ferreira* (1975), which was a sort of preface to a later adaptation by António of one of the most celebrated novels by Ferreira, *Manhã Submersa/Hidden Dawn* (1979). A little disappointing were *Herculano*, filmed in 1978 by João Matos Silva for the centennial of one of the great Portuguese writers, and *Maranos* (1978) by Dórdio Guimarães, about poet Teixeira de Pascoaes, produced by IPC and the Ministry of Culture. But the most original work of this category appeared some years later: *A Ilha de Moraes* (1984) by Paul Rocha, a study of Wenceslaus de Moraes, a nineteenth-century writer enchanted by Japanese culture. De Moraes had previously been the hero of Rocha's time-consuming feature film, *A Ilha dos Amores*, which was shot with great difficulties in Japan between 1979 and 1982.

The mid-1980s marked the collapse of documentary production, or, to be exact, of those films intended to be shown in a theater. An audience who turned increasingly toward television and away from the cinema, an increase in costs, and a decrease in state sponsorship were the main causes of the decline in film production.

In the early 1990s, however, a slight revival took place because of two factors. One was exclusively technical: The increased use of video stock, which was less expensive and easy to edit, decreased costs. The increased participation of national institutions like the ICAM [Instituto de Cinematografia, Audiovisuais e Multimédia, known as IPACA until 1999] and, especially, Portuguese Television [RTP] in filmmaking also helped.

The points of view were, curiously, generally the same as in earlier years. For example, the ethnographic approach was apparent in the depiction of the rural areas of Portugal in Fernando Matos Silva's *Alentejo—As Quatro Estações/Alentejo—The Four Seasons* (1994) and *A Luz Submersa/The Obscured Light* (2001), as well as *Rabo de Pexe/Isinglass Island* (2000) by Joaquim Pinto and Nuno Leonel; the African and Asian immigrants to Portugal in *Afro Lisboa/Afro Lisbon* (1996) by Ariel de Bigault, *Kulandakilu* (1998) by Margarida Leitão, or *Swagatam/Bemvindos* (*Swagatam/Welcome* (1998) by Catarina Alves Costa. Current life in the former colonies was portrayed in *O Homem da Bicicleta/The Bycicle Man* (1997) by Ivo M. Ferreira and António Pedro, *Céu Aberto/Open Sky* (1998) by Graça Castanheira, *A Dama de Chandor/The Lady from Chandor* (1998) by Catarina Mourao, *Com Quase Nada/Brincar em Cabo Verde/With Near Nothing, or How Children Play in Cabo Verde* (2000) by Carlos Barroco and Margarida Correia. The team Pinto-Leonel produced some titles about Brazil such as *Surfavela/Poor Man's Surf* (1996) and *Moleque da Rua/Children of the Streets* (1998).

Another important approach of previous decades, the biographical portrayal, was represented by *Aurélio da Paz dos Reis* (1995) by veteran Faria de Almeida; *Táxi Lisboa* (1996) by the Bavarian Wolf Gaudlitz, about and made with the writer Vergílio Ferreira; *Vencer a Sombra/Fighting with Shadows* (1996) by Paulo Ares and Pedro Madeira, about an aged boxer, a sort of sequel to Fernando Lopes's *Belarmino*; *As Escolhidas/The Elected Women* (1997) by Margarida Gil, about painter Graça Morais; *Joaquim Bravo* (1999) by Jorge

Silva Melo, about this painter; *No Quarto da Vanda/In Vanda's Room* (2000) by Pedro Costa, a 160-minute mix of reality and fiction on the daily life of Vanda Duarte, former actress of Costa's *Ossos* (*Bones*, 1997), in Fountainhas, the caboverdians' quarter of Lisbon; *Ilusíada—A Minha Vida Dava Um Filme/The Illusitans or My Life Would Be a Movie* (2001) by Leonor Areal, about four unknown characters whose modest lives reflected fifty years of Portuguese history, which was presented theatrically as a 135-minute film and in three fifty-eight-minute chapters for television; and *Agostinho Neto* (2001) by Orlando de Fortunato, about the Angolese leader. Bruno de Almeida's *A Arte de Amália/The Art of Amália* (2000) was a tribute to legendary fado singer Amália Rodrigues, which used footage from the 1920s until her death in 1999, including live clips from her concerts.

The designation of Lisbon and Portugal as "European Cultural Capitals" in 1994 and 2001 encouraged the production of the following documentaries by prestigious filmmakers: Joaquim Leitão's *A Cidade Qualquer/Just Another City* (1994) opted for an experimental, pseudo-impressionistic approach, and Manoel de Oliveira's *Porto da Minha Infância/Port of My Childhood* (2001) used Fellini-like fictionalized sequences for a nostalgic trip to a city that he had depicted cinematically on other occasions, for example in his early masterpiece *Douro, Faina Fluvial*.

RAFAEL DE ESPAÑA

See also **Newsreel Series: Spain/Portugal**

Further Reading

Le cinéma portugais, Paris: Centre Georges Pompidou, 1982.

Cinema Novo Português, 1960–1974, Lisbon: Cinemateca Portuguesa, 1985.

de España, Rafael, *Directory of Spanish and Portuguese Filmmakers and Films*, Westport, CT: Greenwood Press, 1994

de Matos-Cruz, José, *Anos de Abril (Cinema Português 1974–1982)*, Lisbon: Instituto Português do Cinema, 1982

———. *Prontuario do Cinema Português 1896–1988*, Lisbon: Cinemateca Portuguesa, 1989.

———. *O Cais do Olhar. O Cinema Português de Lungametragem e a Ficção Muda*, Lisbon: Cinemateca Portuguesa, 1999.

Paulo, Heloísa Paulo, "Documentarismo e Propaganda. As Imagens e os Sons do Regime," in Luís Reis Torgal (ed.), *O Cinema Sob o Olhar de Salazar*. Lisbon: Temas e Debates, 2001.

de Pina, Luís, *Documentarismo Português*, Lisbon: Instituto Português do Cinema, 1977.

Ramos, Jorge Leitão, *Dicionário do Cinema Português 1962–1988*, Lisbon: Caminho, 1989.

PRAYER

(Cuba, Trujillo, 1983)

Prayer, directed by Cuban filmmaker Marisol Trujillo, is a short documentary film in the tradition of the aesthetic and political experimental work associated with Third Cinema practitioners. The film embodies a Third Cinema aesthetic in its commitment to "an imperfect cinema" that challenges First Cinema practices and seeks to address audiences at a political level (Chanan, 1985: 251). Trujillo's hard-hitting film harks back to an exceptional period of experimentation in radical political film in the 1960s and 1970s associated with the Cuban Institute of Cinematographic Art and Industry (ICIAC). Representative works include Santiago Alvarez's *Now!* (1965), which offers a powerful exposition of institutionalised racism in America, and *LBJ* (1968), which delivers a stinging critique of American political life through a montage of found images that associatively link Lyndon B Johnston with political corruption.

Throughout *Prayer,* Trujillo draws on the traditions of Soviet montage filmmaking and employs montage editing techniques to juxtapose still and film footage of found images, with music, and poetic dialogue. These elements function cumulatively to mount a powerful Marxist critique of the ideological structures and institutions of Western capitalism, in a visual style similar to that of her fellow Cuban filmmaker Alvarez.

Trujillo was one of several female Cuban filmmakers who worked under the auspices of ICAIC. *Prayer* embodies a strong Marxist-feminist aesthetic in the way images of Marilyn Monroe's life are juxtaposed with political events of the time. For much of the film, the spoken verse of Ernesto Cardenal's poem *Oración por Marilyn Monroe (Prayer for Marilyn Monroe)* is superimposed over the visuals, presenting a catalogue of abuse associated with Marilyn Monroe, from child rape, through her time as a product of the "Hollywood Dream Factory," to her early suicide.

Trujillo's selection of found images of Marilyn Monroe emphasizes the way the female body is objectified by mainstream media conventions and would seem to directly reference the work of film theorist Laura Mulvey (1975) on "the male gaze." The film includes many promotional "glamour shots" of Marilyn Monroe as media celebrity and film footage of her in her many roles as screen goddess, posed suggestively in revealing costume, while the camera, by lingering on parts of her body, fragments and dehumanises the woman into "body parts": breasts, legs, or open yielding mouth. These striking visual sequences represent Marilyn as the object of the male gaze and illustrate the way in which the female body is exploited as a mere spectacle for male pleasure.

Marilyn's "glamour shots" and other images of fetishised female "body parts" are juxtaposed with conflicting images from the latter part of Marilyn's troubled career, clearly interpreting her as a hunted victim of media intrusion. Archive photographic material from Marilyn's childhood and youth are also included with a spoken dialogue, which refers to her long-standing history of abuse and domination prior to her celebrity status and entrance into the Hollywood Studio system. Throughout *Prayer,* Marilyn's image functions as a cinematic metaphor for patriarchal oppression.

Through the use of associative montage, the film's thematic concern with Marilyn's exploitation within a patriarchal system shifts to a more direct critique of political regimes and the ideological structures that oppress their people. There are many startling and repetitive motifs throughout the film that link Marilyn's exploitation and death with that of "innocents" throughout the world. The overriding thematic concern with Marilyn is interspersed with stills and film footage from around the world (hunger marches, political rallies, children living on the street, child prostitutes) and juxtaposed with images of state violence, police beatings, and military hardware. In one sequence, images of Marilyn's softly yielding mouth are juxtaposed with startling images of an open-mouthed starving child from the Third World: in another, pictures of the headless bodies and the decapitated heads of political victims echo the "body parts" imagery of earlier visuals of Marilyn. The film constructs strong links between global capitalism and Third World oppression.

Throughout the film, in spoken dialogue and imagery, the ideological practices of Western media are critiqued. Twentieth Century Fox in particular is singled out as representative of the exploitive practices of global capitalism and is associatively linked to the oppression, violence, and poverty experienced by many people living in the Third World. *Prayer* offers its audience a harrowing visual catalogue of brutality and exploitation, which is reinforced by Cardenal's poetic dialogue.

Nevertheless, the film ends on a note of optimism. As it reaches its climax, Cardenal's dialogue is overlaid with Blake's *Jerusalem,* which rises to a crescendo as, in a rapid montage sequence, edited images of "people empowerment" flash across the screen. The pace picks up pace as the film shifts from cataloguing injustice throughout the world to images of revolutionary militancy. Transcultural motifs of arms raised in power salutes are interspersed with iconic images of Che Guevara and of heavily armed young revolutionaries, male and female "brothers" in arms, who are represented as having literally taken up arms in their determination to protect "the innocent." There would seem to be no place for patriarchal oppression within the revolution (an optimistic if conflicting statement on female empowerment within Cuban society, given

that *machismo* remained a powerful influence in Cuban society after the revolution). The film ends with a long take on the static image of a small child of indeterminate sex, smiling with arms outstretched in exuberance, happy and at peace. The screen fades to black as the audience is left to contemplate this lasting image of carefree childhood, a powerful visual statement on moral obligation.

In addition to *Prayer,* Trujillo made several other documentaries under the auspices of ICIAC, focusing on Cuban culture and famous Cuban artists. *Motivations* (1988) profiled the Cuban painter and sculptor Manuel Mendive and explored the sources for his art. *Encounter* (1981) documented the meeting between the Cuban prima ballerina Alicia Alonso and the Soviet dancer Vladimir Vasiliev when they met in preparation for their duet in *Giselle. Woman Before the Mirror* (1983) profiled the Cuban dancer Rosario Suarez.

PAT A. COOK

See also **Alvarez, Santiago; *LBJ*; *Now!***

Further Reading

Chanan, Michael, *The Cuban Image*, London: BFI, 1985.
Pines, Jim, and Paul Willemen, *Questions of Third Cinema*, London: BFI, 1989.
Wayne, Michael, *Political Film: The Dialectics of Third Cinema*, London: Pluto Press, 2001.

PRELORÁN, JORGE

Jorge Prelorán, a native of Argentina, is the most widely recognized and prolific ethnographic filmmaker of Latin America. His films generally focus on the folkways of individual subjects within a rural or natural environment. The majority of his work explores the various indigenous tribes throughout the provinces of Argentina, but it includes portraits of indigenous people and communities in countries such as Venezuela and Ecuador. He has also worked as the co-director and co-producer on a film that one of his former UCLA students made about a poet, philosopher, and cabin builder in Oregon, USA, entitled *Luther Metke at 94* (1979). This film was nominated for an Academy Award the following year.

Preferring the term ethnobiographer to ethnographer, Prelorán tends to focus on one man's life experiences and perspectives, which become emblematic of a tribe or people typically living on the margins. To achieve a strong rapport with his subject, he would spend long stretches of time with his subject before turning on a film camera. After a comfort level was achieved, Prelorán would record an audio track with his subject and would later intertwine the subject's voice with silent camera footage recorded later. Prelorán has produced over seventy films, in which he has worked as the director, cameraman, soundman, and editor. Many times he will complete a film, only to go back months later to recut the film into a different version. Over a span of years, a work may have multiple incarnations. Just as culture is constantly in flux, so too are Prelorán's films.

His style has been compared to Flaherty's depictions of the harmony between man and nature. However, in an interview, Jorge Prelorán has stated that although he identifies with Flaherty's humanism, he has been influenced the most by the Italian neorealists of the 1950s. His interest focuses primarily on documenting indigenous culture in Latin America as a way to preserve the folk traditions and rituals, while simultaneously elevating the importance of these cultures, which are too often marginalized and threatened with extinction in the Americas. Despite the fact that Prelorán's work is widely recognized and studied by visual anthropology scholars, he prefers to categorize his films as simply "human documents." Because his interviews are in Spanish, a language he can understand, Prelorán labels his films as folkloric, rather than ethnographic. In this way, he believes that "the magic of his human documents is the sensitivity with which many of the things shot were achieved. . . ." (Sherman, 1985).

His best-known film, *Hermógenes Cayo* (*Imaginero*) (1969), features Cayo, a deeply spiritual and religious icon carver in the province of Santiago del Estero. As Sharon Sherman (one of Prelorán's former students), explains, "his early films look at single events which place the protagonists in their environments, but the rituals themselves, rather than the participants, are the central focus." Prelorán, while interviewing subjects such as Hermógenes and others, excises his questions out of the voice-over narration to avoid calling attention to himself as a main narrative framing agent for the film. With the exception of the film on the Warao, a Venezuelan tribe, all of Prelorán's films since 1967 have used the subjects' voices to describe their own lives. In this way, according to Sharon Sherman, he has chosen a group of characters who represent a culture. Documenting their quotidian activities alongside their religious and cultural traditions, Prelorán tries to be an invisible filmmaker, much in the style of traditional documentarians. However, this does not rule out what he calls the "subjective" or "artistic" focus in which filmmaking can be an art—that is, whereby the language of cinema and the dramatic structure of fictional film are used (Prelorán, 1995). According to filmmaker Ron Norman, Prelorán's films "have the humanism of Jean Renoir and Akira Kurosawa, the inner or personal life of Ingmar Bergman, and the revelations of Robert Flaherty and Satyajit Ray." (Taquini, 1994).

Politically, he is committed to eliminating any trace of his own ideology from his films: "I do not want to impose my own ideas. This means that my films are not political or ideological. I have no intention to use my film as a vehicle for my ideas rather than [those of] the protagonists. I try to listen to people and convert this into a film." Although he may not be overtly adopting a political agenda, it is clear that he aims to empower these communities that are often excluded from Latin American public sphere by making them visible. He has shared some of the money made in film screenings and sales with his films' protagonists. It is clear that Prelorán's self-described "apolitical" work has been aimed at bettering the life of rural people in Argentina, and this could have had dangerous consequences after a military junta seized power in 1976. Fleeing in exile to the United States, Prelorán and his wife Mabel, also a filmmaker, left their country definitively in search of better working conditions.

Prelorán lives in Los Angeles, where he is professor emeritus of ethnographic film at UCLA's School of Film and Television. His work has been recognized widely in ethnographic film festivals, but otherwise, it is not readily accessible. Always working outside of the studio system in Argentina and the United States, he has generally worked solo or with his wife to produce and promote his films. Only one film, *Mi Tia Nora*, filmed in Ecuador, was a fictional film based on a true story and was produced as a feature-length commercial release.

TAMARA L. FALICOV

Biography

Born May 28, 1933, in Buenos Aires, Argentina. Studied architecture at the Universidad Nacional de Buenos Aires but left to attend the University of California, Los Angeles, where he finished film school in 1961. Awarded a Tinker Foundation Grant to direct four films on Argentine gauchos in 1963. Funded by the National University of Tucumán (an Argentine provincial city) in 1967 to document various folkloric traditions in Argentina. In 1976 he fled Argentina and began living in exile in the United States. He lives in Los Angeles, where he is professor emeritus in the Ethnographic Film program in the School of Film and Television at the University of California, Los Angeles. He has produced more than seventy films over a period of twenty years.

Selected Films

The Argentine Gaucho Today (*El gaucho argentino, hoy*): Director
1966–1971 *Araucanos of the Ruca Choroy* (*Araucanos de Ruca Choroy*): Director
The Image Maker (*Hermógenes Cayo Imaginero*): Director
1973 *Ona People* (*Los ona: Vida y muerte en Tierra del Fuego*): Director
1975 *Cochengo Miranda*: Director
Zerda's Children (*Los hijos de Zerda*): Director

Luther Metke at 94: Co-director (with Steve Raymen), co-producer (with Richard Hawkins)
1982 *Zulay Confronts the Twentieth Century* (*Zulay frente al siglo XX*): Director
My Aunt Nora (*Mi tia Nora*): Director

Further Reading

Ardévol, Elisenda, and Luis Pérez Tolón, eds., *Imagen y cultura: perspectivas del cine ethnográfico*, Bibioteca de etnología 3, Granada, Spain: Publicaciones del diputación provincial de Granada, 1995.
Barnard, Timothy, "Hermógenes Cayo (Imaginero)," in Timothy Barnard and Peter Rist, eds., *South American Cinema: A Critical Filmography, 1915–1994*, Austin: University of Texas Press, 1996, 50–52.
Chicello, Rubén D., "*Jorge Prelorán: The Documentary as Poetry*," in *Américas*, 34(6) November–December 1982, 55.
Devereaux, Leslie, and Roger Hillman, eds., *Fields of Vision: Essays in Film Studies, Visual Anthropology, and Antropology*, Berkeley: University of California Press, 1995.
Kriger, Clara, and Paraná Sendrós, "Jorge Prelorán" in Clara Kriger and Alejandra Portela, eds., *Diccionario de realizadores*, Buenos Aires: Ediciones del jilguero, 1997, 128–29.
MacDougall, David, *Transcultural Cinema*, Princeton, NJ: Princeton University Press, 1998.
Mathieu, Agustin, *Breve historia del cine nacional*, Buenos Aires: Alzamor Editores, 1974.
Prelorán, Jorge, "Conceptos éticos y estéticos en el cine etnográfico," in Elisenda Ardévol and Luis Pérez Tolón, eds., *Imagen y cultura: perspectivas del cine ethnográfico*, Bibioteca de etnología, 3, Granada, Spain: Publicaciones del diputación provincial de Granada, 1995, 123–60.
Sherman, Sharon R., "Human Documents: Folklore and the Films of Jorge Prelorán," in *Southwest Folklore* 6(1), 1985, 17–61.
———, *Documenting Ourselves: Film, Video, and Culture*, Lexington: University of Kentucky Press, 1998.
Taquini, Graciela, *Jorge Prelorán*, Buenos Aires: Centro Editor de América Latina, 1994.

PRESTON, GAYLENE

Gaylene Preston, director and producer of both documentaries and fiction films, is one of Aotearoa New Zealand's senior filmmakers, a status earned through the quality of her own productions and her efforts at all levels—from education to funding—to help other local filmmakers with their work. Preston's interest in telling local stories for local audiences has tied her to Aotearoa New Zealand, although she has often wished for bigger budgets and more consistent funding for her projects. (The advantage of accepting local budgetary restraints has been total control of all her projects.) In keeping with her understanding of film as an important part of its local community, she acknowledges film's collaborative nature and refers to her "creative team." She has played, and continues to play, an important role in developing creative talent and practical skills among a large and varied group of protégées, through hiring them to assist her; through producing their early efforts; through mentoring via Women in Film and Television, the New Zealand Film Commission, and the Film School; and through her efforts to attract local and national government support for the New Zealand film and television industries. An active filmmaker who made the second feature-length fiction film directed by a woman in Aotearoa New Zealand (a gender-bender thriller entitled *Mr. Wrong* [1984]), she has recently been honored as film laureate for the country. She is currently working on her first feature-length fiction film to be made from a script by her alone, starring Sam Neill.

Although Preston has made several successful fiction films (including a comic satire, *Ruby and Rata* [1990], that deals with ethnic, gender, and class stereotypes, and *Bread and Roses* [1994], a television miniseries/feature film docudrama based on the autobiography of nurse, social activist, and eventually MP Sonja Davies), the bulk of her work has taken the form of documentaries about extraordinary individuals as seen through Preston's eyes. Her favorite film, she says, is one of her earliest, *Learning Fast* (1981), about a group of small-town teenagers whom she and her camera track over approximately a year of their lives as they make the transition from school to unemployment. The teenagers start with high hopes and confidence, but the town's lack of employment opportunities wears them down. Typically, this film sympathizes with the individual's point of view at the same time that it situates the individual's dilemma within an acute analysis of the social context.

The best example of Preston's ability to draw attention to systemic frameworks for individual dissatisfactions comes at the close of *Married* (1993), Preston's contribution to a series of TV dramas made by women in honor of the centenary of women's suffrage in Aotearoa New Zealand. Having established that the married couple in question have their own joys and troubles, Preston ends her film with the frustrated wife sitting on the back steps; the camera pulls away to show a long row of similar houses in the dawn light, each with its own, presumably similar story to tell of husbands and wives boxed in by economic limitations. According to Preston, *Married* is her "most unpopular film" because it is done "in doco-realism," a style that doesn't let audiences "off the hook."

If a group of unemployed teenagers might not seem particularly extraordinary, Preston's first documentary subject was more obviously unusual. Bruce Burgess, incapacitated by cerebral palsy, wanted to get to the top of Mount Ruapehu, one of Aotearoa New Zealand's active volcanoes. *All the Way Up There* (1978), which documents his successful ascent (accomplished with the aid of committed expert climbers), was a financial success for Preston (Encyclopaedia Brittanica bought it) as well as a *succès d'estime* that won Preston international prizes and some local recognition. Her next film, *Hold-Up* (1981), is a docudrama in the sense that it combines a dramatized scene of a hold-up witnessed by three disabled bystanders with interview material about the players' own responses as disabled persons to the idea that their testimony would have no credibility because of their disabilities.

Although *Making Utu* (1982) is about Geoff Murphy's second complete feature film, it is not a "making of" movie, partly because of Preston's experience dealing with similar issues while contributing extensively to Merata Mita's *Patu!* (1983), a politicized documentary about the 1981 Springbok rugby tour. Like later Preston documentaries, *Making Utu* is more evocative than denotative. During the 1980s, while working on projects expressive of her political convictions, Preston also worked in advertising and in music videos.

The success of *All the Way Up There* meant that Preston attended the Cannes market, one result of which was that she and Robin Laing formed a professional partnership as director and producer that has lasted nearly twenty years. In 1995 they produced *War Stories Our Mothers Never Told Us*, a feature-length opportunity for seven women (including Preston's own mother) to talk about their experiences during World War II—the embodiment of Preston's desire to get her subjects "to relive the moment of past experience." A mix of simple presentation and engrossing storytelling, *War Stories* has achieved international recognition and has played to record domestic audiences for a feature-length documentary.

Preston calls *Kai Purakau* (1987) and *No Other Lips* (1997) her "bookends," because they are television documentaries about New Zealand writers: Booker Prize winner Keri Hulme and poet Hone Tuwhare. The former was made for Thames Television to be broadcast in Britain, the latter for Greenstone Pictures and New Zealand television. Preston comes from the same part of the country as Hulme, which has figured in responses to criticism that a Maori should have made the film about Hulme, who identifies as Maori. Despite similar criticism a decade later, Hone Tuwhare himself invited her to direct the film about him, and the warm feeling between subject and documentarist, as well as Preston's characteristic appreciation of humor, pervades the film.

Working increasingly as a producer, Preston also co-directed *Getting to Our Place* (1999), a "fly-on-the-wall documentary" about meetings—specifically, the meetings involved in constructing Te Papa, the country's new national museum that has become internationally influential. Simultaneously, Preston produced *Punitive Damage* (1999), a documentary focusing on a New Zealand mother's grief over the loss of her son in civil unrest involving the East Timorese and Indonesians.

Finally, in *Titless Wonders* (2001), Preston presents stories of breast cancer survivors and of friends who have succumbed to the disease. It is her most specifically local film, despite the universality of its topic. Her ability once again to bring a joyous humor to a painful subject—her ability to celebrate life—is the hallmark of a Preston film.

HARRIET MARGOLIS

See also **Aesthetics and Documentary Film: Rhetoric and Documentary; Feminism: Critical Overview of, and Documentary Film; Human Rights and Documentary Film**

Biography

Born in 1947 in Greymouth, on the West Coast of the South Island, Aotearoa New Zealand. Attended boarding school in Nelson and art school in Christchurch. Received Dip Art Therapy, St Albans School of Fine Arts, England, 1974. While using art therapy to help psychiatric patients, made first short films. Returned to Aotearoa New Zealand (1976) and worked for six months at John O'Shea's Pacific Films. Served on New Zealand Film Commission (1979–1985). With Robin Laing, formed Preston*Laing Productions (1984). One child, a daughter, born in 1987. Board member of New Zealand On Air and of Creative Film Fund. Turned down Centenary of Suffrage medal (1993) because of political disagreements with the then prime minister. Named a Laureate of New Zealand, 2001. Received a Media Peace Award, 2001, for *Titless Wonders*. Honored as an officer of the New Zealand Order of Merit for services to the New Zealand film industry, 2001.

Further Reading

Ahuriri, Monika, "Stubborn Bloody Mindedness," in *Newsreel* (The New Zealand Film Archive) 48, November 2001, 3.

Beattie, Keith, "First Say and Last Cut," in *Media Studies Journal* (Massey University), 1996, 4–16.

"The Benefits Outweigh the Compromise," in *The Business of Film* (New Zealand Special Issue), May 2001, 85.

Benjamin, Julie, and Alison Maclean, "Revolving Clotheslines and Morris Minors: A Discussion of New Zealand Film Making with Gaylene Preston," in *Alternative Cinema*, 11(4), summer 1983–1984, 21–24.

Dennis, Jonathan, "Reflecting on Reality: An Interview with Gaylene Preston," edited by Jonathan Dennis and Jan Bieringa, in *Film in Aotearoa New Zealand*, Wellington: Victoria University Press, 1992, 161–72.

Hardy, Ann, "Gaylene Preston," edited by Annette Kuhn and Susannah Radstone, in *The Women's Companion to International Film*, London: Virago, 1990, 325–26.

Horrocks, Roger, "Gaylene Preston," in *New Zealand Film Makers at the Auckland City Art Gallery*, part 5, November 1984.

Johnson, Stephanie, "Through Women's Eyes," in *Quote Unquote*, June 1995, 14–17.

Shepard, Deborah, "Gaylene Preston," edited by Christina Barton and Deborah Lawler-Dormer, in *alter/image: Feminism and Representation in Recent New Zealand Art*, Wellington: City Gallery, 1993, 99, 115–16.

Shepard, Deborah, *Reframing Women: A History of New Zealand Film*, Auckland: HarperCollins, 2000.

PRIESTLEY, J. B.

John Boynton Priestley was a prolific British novelist, essayist, dramatist, scenarist, and broadcaster. His *English Journey* (1934) was one of the most important reportages on the state of the nation during the Depression. It greatly influenced other documentary texts, such as Orwell's *The Road to Wigan Pier* (1937) and Jack Hilton's *English Ways* (1940) and the photography of Bill Brandt, especially *The English at Home* (1936).

Priestley anticipated and/or reflected many of the concerns of cultural intellectuals and filmmakers in more vernacular forms, which could be effective without being patronising. He was equally at home on the BBC, scripting for Gracie Fields, and chairing the 1941 Committee (the unofficial "Brains Trust" linked with campaigning photomagazine *Picture Post's* "Plan for Britain"). Most important, Priestley catalysed the reformist mood of the "People's War" and, in particular, helped forge what Angus Calder calls the Myth of the Blitz. He was instrumental in infusing wartime filmmaking with a more populist, left-of-centre agenda and "middlebrow" sensibility.

Priestley had been involved with documentary film in the mid-1930s, although he recalled discussions for projects ranging from "the steel industry to Beethoven's Ninth Symphony" (Priestley, 1962) that were unfortunately never realised. He did, however, script a commentary for John Grierson, from residual footage about the Swiss Post Office—a narrative written in reverse, as he put it. The result, *We Live in Two Worlds* (1937), illustrated, rather optimistically, how national barriers were supposedly undermined by the "new internationalism" of modern transport and communications. Priestley attributed its modest success to Cavalcanti's able direction, while dismissing his own appearance as an "apopletic frog talking with a broad Yorkshire accent" (Priestley, 1939).

However, Priestley also used the title as a metaphor for the dissociation between 1930s documentary and commercial features. British documentarists were "leading the world" technically, in films such as *Drifters, Song of Ceylon, Night Mail,* and *Voice of Britain*. Although Priestley found their theorising slightly priggish, he felt Britain's national cinema would never evolve aesthetically, or increase in social texture, without learning from them. Nonetheless, Priestley was sceptical about documentary being more "nakedly" veracious about ordinary life than other modes. Ironically, its realism, no matter how conscientiously observed, was in fact "romantic heightening," because it was not raw actuality "but the treatment that counts." Artful editing and synchronisation with music and/or verse meant that "What the documentary film producer is really saying is . . .'Oh, you think the steel industry or life in a fishing village dull, do you? Well, now you'll see!'"

Despite such misgivings, Priestley was chosen by Paul Rotha to present a showcase of British documentaries at New York's Metropolitan Museum of Modern Art in autumn 1937. However, like his literary contemporary Graham Greene, his critical influence on the medium was greater than his limited direct involvements might suggest. This was particularly the case in wartime film policy. Priestley fronted the initial struggle with the Ministry of Information's failure to enlist creative talent and its mandarin contempt for the masses: "The truth is the people in power have not yet fully understood that this war depends more on public opinion and morale than anything else" (letter quoted in Cook, 1997). His determination not to serve up patriotic propaganda or ignore social reforms led Priestley into sharp differences of opinion with successive Conservative heads of the MOI: "[A] lot of people were fighting the war to keep Britain exactly as it had been—not possible, anyhow—but none of them lived in back-to-back houses mostly on tea, bread and margarine" (Priestley, 1962).

Priestley's warm Yorkshire voice, made famous by his BBC *Postscript* commentaries (from the fall of France to the onset of the Blitz), was a real sign of the demotic shift in wartime culture. Reputedly as widely recognised as Churchill's, it made Priestley a kind of alternative national figurehead. (He recalled his profile wryly: "I found myself tied, like a man to a gigantic balloon, to one of those bogus reputations that only the mass media know how to inflate" [Priestley, 1962].) His ideas were elaborated in *Out of the People* (1941) and undoubtedly established an attitude toward current events that filmmakers built on to reconstruct the nation's self-image, especially by identifying class privilege as an obstacle to efficient resistance, stamping a template for socialist patriotism instead.

The *Postscripts* first played a major part in mythologising Dunkirk, converting abject defeat into collective heroism by ordinary people. Symptomatic of their influence was the GPO's eight-minute short *Britain at Bay*, a rapidly improvised cinematic analogue, directed by Harry Watt, for which Priestley wrote and spoke the commentary in July 1940. Its opening shots of pastoral landscapes, contrasted with grimmer Northern ones, set a pattern for projecting the image of the nation that people should be fighting for. Britain's "blackest cities" could still be changed, but the Nazi war machine necessitated "the expense of all the decencies and amenities of civilised life." The climax was synchronised with cliffs as natural fortifications: "The future of the whole civilised world rests on the defence of Britain," not just on conventional armed forces, "but on all of us." *Britain at Bay* demanded a "citizens' army" of essential workers, of both sexes. It also promoted the recently formed LDV, showing lunch-break manoeuvres, even though the government was still suspicious of what would become the Home Guard.

Priestley called for an impregnable citadel of "free people." However, like much wartime filmmaking, *Britain at Bay* begged the question of the Empire, asking only for "fair dealing among nations and an end to murderous treachery." Footage of dominion troops "from the ends of the earth" featured no blacks. Priestley ended by quoting Churchill's "fight them on the beaches" speech, over matching footage of guarded landing grounds, streets, hills, and the like, literally translating the P.M.'s sentiments into his own audiovisual register.

After the onset of the Blitz, the logical follow-up was *Britain Can Take It* (1940), with Priestley's commentary accompanying the domestic release. Although Priestley did not work with Watt and Jennings again (he played a minor role in Donald Taylor's *Battle for Music* [1943], making a witty speech showing that neither Hitler nor the government could suppress public performance in Britain), he nonetheless left a permanent imprint on the style and subject matter of subsequent Home Front documentaries. Priestley did, however, collaborate with Cavalcanti again, in 1941, on *The Foreman Went to France*, dramatising the real incident of a Welsh machinist's sabotage mission. It was, in effect, typical wartime fruit of Priestley's advocacy of creative liaison between documentary and topical features. His 1945 MOI pamphlet *Letter to a Returning Serviceman*, about "wining the peace" also has parallels with documentaries considering the postwar world, such as John's Eldridge's *Our Country* and Jennings's *Diary for Timothy*. Clearly, Priestley's influence on the documentary mode continued well beyond his practical involvement in it.

KEITH WILLIAMS

See also **Britain; Grierson, John; Ministry of Information: World War II**

Biography

Born in 1894 in Bradford, Yorkshire, England, UK. Studied at Belle Vue Grammar School. Worked as a junior clerk at Helm & Co., a wool company, 1910–1914. Served in World War I in Flanders, Germany. Took a B.A. degree from Cambridge University, 1921. Worked as a journalist in London. Married the archaeologist Jacquetta Hawkes, 1953. Offered a knighthood, which he refused. Accepted the Order of Merit, 1977. Died August 14, 1984, in Stratford-Upon-Avon, England, UK.

Further Reading

Aldgate, Anthony, and Jeffrey Richards, *Britain Can Take It: The British Cinema in the Second World War*, 2nd ed., Edinburgh: Edinburgh University Press, 1994.

Calder, Angus, *The Myth of the Blitz*, London: Jonathan Cape, 1991.

———, *The People's War: Britain 1939–45*, London: Jonathan Cape, 1969.

Cook, Judith, *Priestley*, London: Bloomsbury, 1997.

Coultass, Clive, *Images for Battle: British Film and the Second World War 1939–1945*, London, Toronto, and Newark, Delaware: Associated University Presses and University of Delaware Press, 1989.

Maclaine, Ian, *Ministry of Morale: Home Front Morale and the Ministry of Information in World War II*, London: Allen and Unwin, 1979.

Priestley, J. B., *English Journey*, London: Heinemann, 1934.

———, *Midnight on the Desert: A Chapter of Autobiography*, London: Heinemann, 1937.

———, *Rain Upon Godshill: A Further Chapter of Autobiography*, London: Heinemann, 1939.

———, *Margin Released: A Writers Reminiscences and Reflections*, London: Heinemann, 1962.

Neil Rattigan, *British Film and the People's War, 1939–1945*, London: Associated University Presses, 2001.

Williams, Keith, *British Writers and the Media 1930–45*, Houndmills: Macmillan, 1996.

PRIMARY

(US, Drew, 1960)

Primary is a landmark in the development of direct cinema as an aesthetic and journalistic movement, both because it exemplifies the work done by the seminal television documentary team of Drew Associates and because it provides access to aspects of the political campaign process inaccessible before and since. As a hybrid of traditional and direct cinema styles, *Primary* bears traces of a struggle between pretelevision documentary's reliance on voice-over narration and classic Hollywood conventions and an emerging style of mobile reportage further developed by Drew Associates alumni Richard Leacock, Donn Alan Pennebaker, and Albert and David Maysles. *Primary*'s own reliance on editing and sound-image matching to mold reality into dramatic form belies its claim of objectivity, but its success in stripping away accumulated conventions through direct cinema techniques was rightfully hailed as a leap forward in documentary filmmaking's quest to capture "truth."

Primary's style of detached observation is strikingly different from Jean Rouch's *Chronicle of a Summer* (1961), a cinema verité documentary released one year later that continually reminds both the on-camera participants and the audience watching it that a film is being made. Like *Chronicle*, however, *Primary* pursues a subject ripe with social, cultural, and political insights waiting to divulge itself: the 1960 Wisconsin presidential primary between senators John F. Kennedy and Hubert Humphrey. As narrator Joseph Julian intones in a low-key voice-over heavy-handed by today's standards, "Now, traveling along with them, hot on the heels of two fast-moving presidential hopefuls, you are about to see a candidate's view of this frantic process, and an intimate view of the candidates themselves."

The film's delivery on this promise proved groundbreaking in its capture of intimate details of candidate behavior. Humphrey, for example, flips to *The Red Skelton Show* as he seeks diversion from disappointing voter returns, and an atypically nervous Kennedy paces the floor of his hotel suite while anxiously dragging on cigarettes. *Primary* also delights in exposing through this backstage form of reportage the subjective limitations of newspapers, photography, and radio in their interpretations of the candidates as people and politicians.

During a sitting for a campaign poster, for example, Kennedy sits in a small portrait studio encircled by spotlights opposite a photographer and his camera. Catching himself after offering up a glad-handing grin for the camera, Kennedy acknowledges to the photographer (who has just tinkered with his equipment and adjusted the candidate's shirtsleeve cuffs), "It's not time to smile yet, Wally." A cut that juxtaposes the perfectly coiffed and stiff-backed Kennedy posing for the portrait with a campaign poster of a smiling Humphrey on the back of a bus overlays the image of Kennedy's rival with the photographer's request to "swing your body a little bit more to the camera." Recalling Robert Drew's observation that the studio portrait session was a "ritual in many small towns," the juxtaposition of the photographer's instructions with the paper image of a smiling Humphrey implies that the campaign posters that pervade *Primary* are a painstakingly staged construction of personhood that cannot compete with the raw veracity of direct cinema's handheld shots, synchronous sound, and (often) poorly lit passages of footage.

In a reversal of the cut from the photo session to Humphrey's campaign poster, *Primary* juxtaposes Humphrey's behind-the-scenes preparation for a television call-in show with a video image of Kennedy on a television screen. Staking out a position in the television studio behind a TV camera, Humphrey supplies the show's host with the first question to be asked of him, instructs the camera operator where to focus, and informs his wife Muriel that she has 30 seconds of air time to summarize for viewers how she has spent the day. The cut from Humphrey to Kennedy reminds the audience that the latter's erudite television image is also the product of technical preparation and planning.

The filmmakers arrange these scenes in symmetrical bookend fashion in order to suggest that they have taken great pains to remain value-neutral in their presentation of the candidates. Furthermore, both scenes remind us that the Drew team avoids both directing the subjects (as the photographer directs Kennedy in the studio) and being directed by them (as Humphrey directs the camera operator in the television studio).

Conversely, *Primary* fails to acknowledge the visual and aural sleights of hand that characterize its own reportage. In one of the most celebrated sequences of the film, Albert Maysles's camera follows Kennedy's arrival at a rally in Milwaukee, snaking down a long corridor, up a stairway,

through a doorway, and out onto a stage where a cheering crowd greets both camera and candidate. The claustrophobia of the narrow path, the anticipation of the crowd, and the burst of blinding light and applause that accompanies Kennedy's arrival onstage deliver a riveting example of narrator Julian's opening promise. Subsequent shots of the rally, however, subjectively frame the panoply of events by carefully isolating details, overlapping sound and image, and using matches-on-action to establish cause-and-effect relationships between discrete bits of footage.

As the ever-poised Jacqueline Kennedy addresses the crowd, for example, a close-up reveals her white-gloved hands fidgeting nervously behind her back. Students of direct cinema objected to the use of a cut (rather than a zoom) to the close-up, arguing that the filmmakers juxtapose the steady and confident sound of Mrs. Kennedy's voice with the image of her hands in a way that achieves verisimilitude without being real. Other instances of this imposition of form on raw footage appear throughout the film, revealing the subjectivity inherent in direct cinema's claim of ostensible objectivity.

The rising cost of television network air time during the 1970s led Drew to lament the replacement of single-subject documentaries such as *Primary* by multi-subject television news magazines such as *60 Minutes*, which he derided as "entrapment journalism" because of their reliance on hidden cameras and ambush interview techniques. (1988: 401) Even though *Primary* also fell short in its effort to capture filmic truth, its pursuit of this goal proved an invaluable contribution to documentary filmmaking.

CHRIS JORDAN

See also **Drew Associates; Leacock, Richard; Maysles, Albert; Pennebaker, D.A.**

Primary (1960, 53 min.). Distributed by Direct Cinema. Produced by Robert Drew. Photographed by Richard Leacock, Donn Alan Pennebaker, Terence Macartney-Filgate, and Albert Maysles. Written by Robert Drew. Edited by Robert Drew, Richard Leacock, Donn Alan Pennebaker, and Terence Macartney-Filgate.

Further Reading

Bluem, A. William, *Documentary in American Television*, New York: Hastings House Publishers,1965.
Bruzzi, Stella, *New Documentary: A Critical Introduction*, New York: Routledge, 2000.
Drew, Robert, "An Independent with the Networks," in *New Challenges for Documentary*, edited by Alan Rosenthal, Berkeley: University of California Press, 1988.
Hall, Jeanne, "Realism as a Style in Cinema Verité: A Critical Analysis of *Primary*,"*Cinema Journal* 39(4), summer 1991, 38–45.

Hammond, Charles Montgomery, *The Image Decade: Television Documentary 1965–1975*, New York: Hastings House, 1981.

Nicols, Bill, *Representing Reality: Issues and Concepts in Documentary*, Bloomington: Indiana University Press, 1991.

O'Connell, P. J. *Robert Drew and the Development of Cinema Verité in America*, Carbondale: Southern Illinois University Press, 1992.

PRODUCTION PROCESSES

Documentary producers first generate, then manage. They research and draft proposals, then secure funds by lining up investors. They establish a budget for the film, then ensure that the budget is adhered to; they present detailed plans for the four stages of moviemaking, then deal with any glitches that arise during development, preproduction, production, and postproduction. They coordinate the formation of the crew, then supervise their activities. They choose specific methods of distribution, then confirm that the films are exhibited according to these specifications.

On larger documentaries, such as *Fahrenheit 9/11* (Moore, 2004), with a production budget of $6 million, an executive producer might delegate some or all of the aforementioned duties to a staff member—for instance, a line producer, responsible for making sure that the production stays within its financial confines; a production manager, responsible for the production board (a detailed catalogue of cast, shots, scenes, and locations); or a production coordinator, responsible for the day-to-day logistics of cast, equipment, and crew. On smaller sets, such as *SuperSize Me* (Spurlock, 2004), with a $65,000 budget, the producer might by necessity also be the writer, narrator, and/or director.

Just as every documentary film, regardless of its size, employs a producer, every film passes through the four filmmaking stages. The first, development, is perhaps the most nebulous, if only because an idea might languish here for years before it moves into the next stage. During this time, the writer or producer develops a core concept into a proposal, which outlines the work's central themes and target audience, and which helps it raise funds and obtain distribution. *Hoop Dreams* (1994) entered development in 1986 when filmmakers Peter Gilbert, Steve James, and Frederick Marx approached the production company Kartemquin Films about the possibility of making a short centered on Chicago basketball players; seven years and 250 hours of footage later, the movie won the audience award for best documentary at the Sundance Film Festival.

Once the documentary has financial backers, whether individual investors or a studio, it moves into preproduction, at which point the writer, producer, and director finalize a shooting script, a shot-by-shot breakdown of the movie, and the budget, which now itemizes above-the-line and below-the-line costs. The former category includes salaries for the director, writer, and any talent, or actors, as well as the fee for any story rights or materials used in the film. The latter lists salaries for the crew, any equipment or lab fees, insurance, travel costs, and a contingency fund for emergencies (usually 10 to 30 percent of the estimated budget). In addition to weighing in on technical decisions, such as whether to use single or multiple cameras and whether to shoot using film stock or digital video, the production staff hires the crew, including the director of photography (also known as the cinematographer) and camera operator(s); the production accountant to handle all financial transactions incurred during production; the electrical department (whose members are sometimes referred to as gaffers) to prepare, light, and shoot scenes; the grip department to break down and transport equipment; the design department to "dress" the sets and handle any props or costumes; and the sound department to "mike" scenes, as well as to mix and record the audio.

The decisions made during preproduction affect the quality of the results obtained during shooting. *Hearts of Darkness: A Filmmaker's Apocalypse* (Bahr, 1991), a documentary cobbled together from Eleanor Coppola's surreptitious recordings, depicts the problems that plagued the making of her husband's *Apocalypse Now* (1979). During production, the producer recedes into the background as the director advances into the foreground: It is the director who now controls the documentary. She or he dictates interview styles, locations, lighting, shots, lenses, and camera positions. Each day the director watches that day's footage, called dailies or rushes, along with the cinematographer and the picture editor. Together, they shape the film's structure and style by controlling pacing, identifying emerging themes, emphasizing cause-and-effect relationships, or determining expository characters or events.

Through this daily collaboration, production blends into postproduction, or the editing stage, because the editor begins altering the footage as the director continues to shoot. Editors generally compose three versions of the film: the assembly cut, a very rough ordering of the best shots according to the shooting script; the rough cut, a more focused collation in which a structure or narrative handle begins to emerge; and the final cut, the finished negative printed by the lab and distributed as the completed documentary. Although many directors still shoot using traditional film stock, editors usually rely on nonlinear digital technology to cut and paste clips, or the smallest units that can be edited (usually a clip consists of a single continuous recording, or take). As the picture editor concentrates on the visuals, the mixer, or head technician, collates the audio clips, including any narration or voice-overs, as well as the music-and-effects (M&E) track.

A film's ultimate purpose, along with its creators and backers, determines the exact processes of production. Some documentarians, such as Ken Burns, who acted as music director, co-writer, chief cinematographer, director, producer, and executive producer on both *Baseball* (1994) and *The Civil War* (1990), prefer a systematic production style. Other contemporary filmmakers employ a "shoot now, shape later" strategy akin to the cinema verité, or direct cinema, aesthetics of the 1960s, which emphasized the spontaneous capture of key moments and minimalized the role of the director, producer, and script. For example, as Andrew Jarecki began researching popular children's clowns, he realized there was a far more interesting story behind one particular red nose: *Capturing the Friedmans* (2003) documents the dissolution of a family as two of its members face allegations of child molestation. Although the way documentaries tell stories has changed, the essential features of production have not and, in all likelihood, willnot.

JESSICA ALLEN

See also **Burns, Ken; Drew Associates; Moore, Michael; Pennebaker, D.A.**

Further Reading

Barnouw, Eric, *Documentary: A History of the Non-Fiction Film*, 2d ed., New York: Oxford University Press, 1993.

Ellis, Jack C., *The Documentary Idea: A Critical History of English-Language Documentary Film and Video*, Englewood Cliffs, NJ: Prentice-Hall, 1989.

Kindem, Gorham, and Robert B. Musburger (eds.), *Introduction to Media Production*, 2d ed., Boston, MA: Focal Press, 2001.

Kochberg, Searle (ed.), *Introduction to Documentary Production*, London: Wallflower Press, 2002.

Rosenthal, Alan, *Writing, Directing, and Producing Documentary Films*, 3d ed., Carbondale: Southern Illinois University Press, 1990.

PROGRESSIVE FILM INSTITUTE

A series of left-wing film organisations flourished in Britain in the 1930s, and one of the best known was the Progressive Film Institute. Set up in 1935, it initially operated as a distribution company before moving into production. It became less active after the end of the Spanish Civil War and disbanded in 1941.

Given the widely recognised effectiveness of Soviet propaganda films, it is surprising that the established parties of the British Left often failed to capitalise on, or even recognise, cinema's agitational potential or its power to counter the politically timorous newsreels. This meant that many left-wing filmmakers, rejecting John Grierson's view of the state as a potential supporter but without large-scale sympathetic backers, had to rely largely on themselves. Moreover, no single left-wing body attracted enough support to finance fulfilling all of cinema's proposed roles, so a plethora of organisations emerged to serve different parts of a fragmented "market." But most of these failed relatively quickly. Unmourned at the time and with personalities in common (or in conflict) and ad hoc unreported agreements between them, these enterprises constitute an aspect of British cinema that can prove confusing.

The moving spirit behind many of these organisations was the communist aristocrat Ivor Montagu. His left-wing credentials were clear, but his experience in the film industry, including working with Hitchcock and Eisenstein, gave his views on cinema a particular authority. In 1925 Montagu had helped found the Film Society to show films under club conditions, including titles banned by the BBFC. In 1933 he co-founded Kino (later transmogrified into the Workers' Film and Photo League, before dropping the first word of its new name) to import and distribute similar films. Kino distributed 16mm prints, and in March 1935 the Progressive Film Institute was set up as a parallel 35mm distributor.

Some titles shown by the Film Society were re-edited by Montagu, and such reworkings became a regular feature of the PFI's output, blurring the line between original productions and distribution of other organisation's films. In July 1935 it released its first film, *Free Thaelmann!*, a documentary about the German communist leader who was imprisoned despite winning a substantial popular vote. This was actually a shortened version of *Ernst Thaelmann—Fighter Against Fascism* (USA, 1934). The PFI also arranged a promotional screening of *Blow, Bugles, Blow* (1934), the Socialist Film Council's accomplished fiction film showing how two ordinary couples print pamphlets and help organise a Franco-British strike to avert war. Despite this support, it was only in 1938 that the film was finally released, by the Independent Labour Party.

But it was with the outbreak of the Spanish Civil War that the PFI found its real place and developed into a production/distribution company, many of its films aimed at raising both awareness and funds as well as lending footage to other organisations, including Victor Saville's Realist Film Unit. *The Defence of Madrid* (1936), contrasting life before and after an air raid, was directed by Montagu and filmed by Norman McLaren. Though silent, it was an ambitious production, which they managed to release relatively quickly on December 28, 1936. It proved enormously popular and successful, so much so that the British Communist Party began to claim to have been involved in its production; it is still one of the highpoints of the PFI's output.

In 1937 the company got into its stride and released several films, either its own productions or remodellings of others' work, including re-editing episodes of the Republican government's newsreels *Spain Today, News from Spain,* and *Madrid Today.* PFI productions proper included *Sunlight in Shadow,* on caring for children made homeless by the war. Also in that year the PFI produced *International Brigade* and *Crime Against Madrid.* Turning away from Spain but staying on an anti-Fascist, anti-imperialist theme, *The Birth of an Empire* attacks Italy's invasion of Abyssinia. On a completely different track are two shorts on music competitions, both clearly modelled on Soviet cultural documentaries: *Violin Virtuosos* (the Ysaye Competition) and *Piano Prodigies* (the Chopin Competition).

In 1938 the leading lights of the PFI went to Spain again, and although they were unable to make the three films they had planned, completing only *Spanish ABC* on the literacy campaign, they shot enough to make other films. The desire to show German and Italian involvement in the civil war led to *Behind the Spanish Lines* and two related films: *Prisoners Prove Intervention in Spain,* which was later expanded as *Testimony on Non-Intervention.* The PFI also began to turn more attention to home affairs; *XVth Congress* records the Communist Party congress, culminating with the leader Harry Pollitt appearing in colour, according to Montagu to avoid his speech being too boring. But the PFI returned to Spain as a subject with *Britain Expects* (1938), which examines British-Spanish trade, and *Mr. Attlee in Spain.*

The PFI's last important film, and its best, was *Peace and Plenty* (1939), a stinging rebuke and very personal attack on Chamberlain, using stock footage and a model of the prime minister equipped with his ubiquitous umbrella, made by Elsa Lanchester's mother.

With the outbreak of World War II, most left-wing film organisations, including the PFI, found themselves without access to international films for distribution and prey to Ministry of Information censorship. Moreover, many were confused about how to respond to the coalitionist Labour Party and the shifting Soviet position, and only the Workers Film Association survived. After distributing the Soviet anti-Nazi feature *Professor Mamlock* (1938), the PFI crafted its last production. *War Songs of China* (1940) was a self-explanatory sing-along documentary complete with a bouncing ball over the lyrics. The PFI ceased operations in 1941, and ten years later its cameras and equipment went to New Era, while its films, along with a small sum of money, went to Plato (later to become ETV). Ernest Lindgren was also keen to acquire PFI material for the National Film Library: "It has always seemed to me that the films made of the Spanish Civil War form, for some reason, a particularly impressive record; . . . I have been anxious that we should have as many as possible." He happily accepted Montagu's offer to deposit some prints, which have since been joined in the National Film and Television Archive by the ETV Collection.

JOHN RILEY

See also **Montagu, Ivor;** *Testimony on Non-Intervention*

Selected Films

1935 *Free Thaelmann!* [re-edited from *Ernst Thaelmann—Fighter Against Fascism* (USA)]
1936 *The Defence of Madrid*
1936 *Government of Spain* (part of *Spain Today* series)
1936 *Here Is Fascism's Work* (part of *Spain Today* series)
1937 *News from Spain*
1937 *International Brigade* (also known as *International Column*)
1937 *Crime Against Madrid*
1937 *Madrid Today*
1937 *Piano Prodigies*
1937 *Violin Virtuosos*
1937 *The Birth of an Empire*
1937 *Sunlight in Shadow*
1938 *Prisoners Prove Intervention in Spain*
1938 *Behind the Spanish Lines*
1938 *Spanish ABC*
1938 *Testimony on Non-Intervention*
1938 *XVth Congress Film*
1938 *Britain Expects*
1938 *Mr Attlee in Spain*
1939 *Peace and Plenty*
1940 *War Songs of China*

Further Reading

Hogenkamp, B., *Deadly Parallels: Film and the Left in Britain, 1929–1939*, London: Lawrence and Wishart, 1986.
Jones. S. D., *The British Labour Movement and Film, 1918–1939*, London: Routledge and Kegan Paul, 1987.
Low, R., *The History of the British Film 1939–1939: Films of Comment and Persuasion*, London: George Allen and Unwin, 1979.
MacPherson, D., and P. Willemen, *Traditions of Independence: British Cinema in the Thirties*, London: British Film Institute, 1980.

PROKINO

Prokino (Proletarian Film League of Japan) was the filmmaking arm of Japan's proletarian arts movement. It was active making films; publishing journals, books, and a newspaper; and exhibiting films from its official inception in 1929 until 1934. Even before that, however, a number of leftist groups, many of them affiliated with labor unions, several within the film industry itself, were already beginning to make use of film and criticism. Thus the proletarian film movement has no single point of origin. Prokino's activities must be seen against the historical backdrop of a tremendous increase in social action during the decade that followed the end of World War I and the series of "Rice Riots" that rocked nearly every area of Japan in 1918.

Among the voices contending for leadership of the burgeoning Prokino movement, some sided with strict theoretical orthodoxy while others opted for immediate political action—a split echoed in communist groups in Japan and around the world. The filmmaking activities of Prokino first coalesced around a young Tokyo University French literature student, Sasa Genju, who began as a member of the proletarian theater troupe known as Trunk Theater. In June of 1928 Sasa published an impassioned article in one of the Proletarian Arts Movement's journals, *Senki* In "Camera—Toy/Weapon," proclaiming the potential for film produced with a Pathé Baby 9.5mm camera, Sasa wrote about turning a plaything of the well-to-do into a weapon of class struggle. With the means of production thus within reach, he had already made four films, including one of the 1927 Tokyo May Day parade and one of the activities of striking workers at Kikkôman production plants in Noda and had screened them to rousing receptions. All of these films have been lost. Sasa's essay proved to be a manifesto of sorts for a film movement that would soon make an enthusiastic contribution to film journalism and would lead to open experimentation in political filmmaking.

The group's journals include writings about similar groups in Korea, Taiwan, and in Europe and hence were a rare and valuable source of information. Prokino's filmmaking activities included not only documentation of its own activities but also animation, dramatic features, educational films, experimental pieces, and films aimed at children. Prokino produced 48 films, mostly in 9.5mm and 16mm formats; eleven newsreels, twelve documentaries, nineteen "incident" films, two dramatic pieces, two agitprops, an animated film, and another that mixed animation and live action (Namiki, 1986.) Iwasaki Akira, who headed Prokino for several years, is one of Japan's boldest and most original film theorists; had his Prokino film *Asufaruto no michi* (1930, *Asphalt Road*) survived, it might well have been a milestone in prewar Japanese avant-garde filmmaking. Prokino affiliate groups appeared in cities around Japan, although the Tokyo group made the lion's share of the films. As part of the group's activities, traveling exhibition teams went to small towns and villages, providing, for some spectators, their first ever direct experience of cinema.

The group's very success, however, also hastened its downfall. Prokino was closed down by heavy-handed police action over several years that increased in intensity in 1932 and worsened through 1934, when the group was completely banned. Most members served time in prison, where they were pressured to renounce their views—an action known as *tenkô* (forced political apotheosis.) Alumni of the movement, however, went on to populate every aspect of film culture in Japan for the next half century. This is especially true in documentary production and in film criticism. Prokino also had many supporters who never joined its full-time ranks. In 1930, for instance, it published a list of intellectuals, authors, and sympathizers from the film world who were members of Friends of Prokino. This impressive list that includes Mizoguchi Kenji, Ito Daisuke, Hasegawa Nyozekan, Oya Soichi, Kataoka Teppei, Takeda Rintaro, Ushihara Kiyohiko, Miki Kiyoshi, Hijikata Yoshi, Suzuki Shigeyoshi, and Suzuki Denmei. Over the five or so years of its existence, the organization's emphasis shifted from critique to publishing to film production and exhibition and then to a bolshevization of its membership. Because of its size, scope, theoretical and tactical sophistication, and reach, Prokino is probably the era's most successful leftist film movement of its kind, which helps explain why similar movements in New York and Germany apparently looked to Prokino for inspiration and ideas (Senda, 1931; Hogenkamp, 1984).

JEFFREY ISAACS

Selected Films

1928 *Noda sogi* / *The Noda Strike*, made before the founding of Prokino
1929 *Yamamoto Senji kokubetsushiki* / *Yamamoto Senji's Farewell Ceremony*
1929 *Yamasen Watamasa rônôsô* / *Yamamoto Senji Watanabe Masanosuke Worker-Farmer Funeral*
1929 *Yamasen rônôsô* /*Yamamoto Senji's Worker-Farmer Funeral*
1930 *Prokino news*, number 1
1930 *Sumidagawa* / *Sumida River*
1930 *Asufaruto no michi* / *Asphalt Road*
1930 *Kodomo*/ *Children*
1931 *Dai jyûnikai Tokyo Mê dê* / *The Twelfth Tokyo May Day*
1931 *Dorei sensô* / *Slave War*
1931 *Sports*
1931 *Tochi* / *The Land*
1931 *Kyôsakuchi no nômin o sukui e* / *Toward the Relief of Farmers Whose Croplands Have Failed*
1931 *Zensen* / *The Front Lines*
1932 *Dai jyûsankai no Tokyo Mê Dê* / *The Thirteenth Tokyo May Day*
1932 *Prokino news*, numbers 6, 7, 8, and 9
1932 *Yokohama Prokino News*
1932 *1932 Sapporo Mê Dé* / *1932 Sapporo May Day*

Further Reading

"Documentarists of Japan, No. 5: Prokino," interview of Komori Shizuo and Noto Setsuo by Makino Mamoru and Aaron Gerow, translated by Alan Christy, *Documentary Box* No. 5, Tokyo: Yamagata International Documentary Film Festival Organizing Committee, September, 1994, http://www.city.yamagata.yamagata.jp/yidff/docbox/5/box5-2-e.html.
Hogenkamp, Bert, "Workers' Newsreels in Germany, the Netherlands and Japan During the Twenties and Thirties," in *"Show Us Life:" Toward a History and Aesthetics of the Committed Documentary*, edited by Thomas Waugh, Metuchen, NJ: Scarecrow, 1984.
Iwasaki, Akira, *Nihon eiga shishi* (*A Personal History of Japan's Cinema*) Tokyo: Asahi shimbun sha, 1977.
Makino, Mamoru, "Rethinking the Emergence of the Proletarian Film League of Japan," translated by Abé Mark Nornes in *In Praise of Film Studies: Essays in Honor of Makino Mamoru*, edited by Aaron Gerow and Abé Mark Nornes, Yokohama, Ann Arbor: Kinema Club, 2001.
———, "Shinkô eiga, Purorotaria eiga, Purokino, Dainiji purokino oyobi eiga kurabu: Kaisetsu, kaidai" ("Shinkô eiga, Proletarian Film, Prokino, the Second Prokino and Film Club: Commentary and Bibliography"), in *Shôwa shoki sayoku eiga zasshi: Bekkan* (*Early Shôwa Left-wing Film Journals: Supplement*), Tokyo: Senki Fukkokuban Gyokai, 1981.
Namiki, Shinsaku, *Nihon puroretaria eiga dômei (purokino) zenshi* (*A Complete History of the Japan Proletarian Film League – Prokino*), Tokyo: Godo Shuppan, 1986.
Nornes, Abé Mark, *Japanese Documentary Film: The Meiji Era Through Hiroshima*, Minneapolis: University of Minnesota Press, 2003.
———, ed., *Prewar Proletarian Film Movements Collection*, Ann Arbor, MI: Center for Japanese Studies Press, 2004. An online, digital reprint series containing most of the

movements' journals, monographs, and films. http://www.umich.edu/~iinet/cjs/pubs/cjsfaculty/filmseries.html.

Senda, Koreya, "Proletarische Film-Bewegung in Japan," in *Arbeiterbuehne und Film* 18(2), February 1931, 26–27.

Tanikawa, Yoshio, *Dokyumentari eiga no genten: sono shisô to hôhô* (*The Origins of Documentary: Thought and Method*), Tokyo: Futôsha, 1977.

PUBLICITY AND PUBLIC RELATIONS

Public relations is a complex and controversial subject that continues to provoke its critics, often located in journalism, or media sociology. This article seeks to clarify the following aspects: basic definitions of contemporary public relations practice; origins and historical developments focusing on the UK; conceptual frameworks; the role of the British documentary film movement in the emergence of public relations; the development of the academic discipline, its architecture, and its links to media sociology, journalism, marketing, and management.

Contemporary public relations practice

Public relations is the organisational function responsible for presenting an organisation's purpose and activities to a range of stakeholders (shareholders, consumers, employees, clients, competitors, suppliers, local and central government, the local community) and to the media. It is responsible for an organisation's public identity and for justifying or defending organisational position and reputation and can be usefully described as "organisational diplomacy." Public relations practitioners seek to develop and enhance important relationships and to monitor and interpret public opinion and the developing issues of the day.

Public relations has the complex tasks of researching, analysing, and articulating organisational culture and strategy; understanding internal and external organisational relationships; and facilitating communication between an organisation and its publics with the intention of enhancing organisational position. Public relations work may be informational, educational, persuasive, argumentative, defensive, or aggressive. In this sense, the work is akin to that of an organisational advocate or lawyer.

Public relations has both a strategic and a technical dimension, supporting managerial position and communicating with stakeholders. It comprises corporate-level public relations, which establishes the aims of public relations and identifies how communication strategies and tactics can support organisational vision and mission, and the technical production of communication products (promotional brochures, press releases, and web pages). Thus public relations necessitates both qualitative and quantitative research and analysis into organisations, organisational relationships (communication audits), and public opinion on issues relevant to the organisation, as well as intervention in public debate.

Although much of the work is representational, the focus on relationships does imply the need to engage in dialogue, a concept of considerable importance to both practitioners and academics. Nevertheless, it would be wrong to underplay the practical and sociopolitical consequences of the media relations aspect of public relations in terms of distortion of communicative action and the implications for the public sphere. The fact that major institutions in society (including government, finance, corporations, multinationals, cultural industries, think tanks, and political parties of all persuasions) sponsor such activities has considerable implications for the shaping of communicative space. Even apparently resource-poor groups and activist organisations and charities have developed the necessary expertise in media relations and lobbying.

Public relations is associated with democracies as a consequence of historical developments outlined below. The occupation exists internationally, although forms of practice vary somewhat with history and culture. For example, in some countries, public relations tends to be limited to straightforward publicity on behalf of interest groups, rather than the research-driven occupation it is in others. Nevertheless, public relations can be seen as a feature, or even a driver, of globalisation, even though effective practice has to be highly sensitive to cultural differences.

Public relations intersects all aspects of contemporary developed societies in the competition for ideas, markets, and resources. Public relations practitioners are discourse workers acting as interpreters, communicators, and orators and are engaged in both identity construction and argumentation. They contribute to public communication discourse about contemporary issues, including sport, science, health, and tourism, as well as the more obvious areas of politics and economics. In other words, public relations is part of the architecture of contemporary society.

Of particular interest to critical scholars is the relationship between public relations and the media. For some, public relations is an outgrowth of capitalism and the expansion of the mass media. Media sociologists in particular have focused on the hidden influence of public relations sources on media content; the apparently increasing tendency of journalists to rely on public relations sources uncritically, and the potential impact of public relations practice on the erosion of the public sphere. Particularly strong criticism has emerged in relation to the public relations specialty of lobbying. Interestingly, the currently fashionable denigration of "spin doctors" is commonplace in a political context but less so in the corporate and activist contexts.

Origins and historical developments focusing on the UK

Considerably more is known about the development of public relations in the United States than elsewhere. Indeed, such is the imbalance in our current knowledge that some writers seem to assume that public relations was invented in the United States and then exported to the rest of the world. For example, it is not uncommon for U.S. texts to present the American experience as "the history of PR" or for non-American English-language texts to recount historical developments in the United States alone.

In the U.S. context there have been some very important contributions that elucidate developments: Stuart Ewen's *PR! A Social History of Spin* clearly links developments of the practice to the response to progressivism and fears of social unrest as articulated by Lippman and of mob rule as delineated by Le Bon; Roland Marchand's *Creating the Corporate Soul* explores the corporate quest for social and moral legitimacy and the internal unseen struggles to define organisational image; Scott Cutlip's two books recount key biographical

and organisational histories (including consultancies and those in-house) and attempt to retrace retrospectively what might be seen as public relations work prior to the emergence of the term in the late nineteenth century. Thus any activities that attempted to influence popular opinion or the public will in Greece or Rome; or efforts to educate populations, such as the farm bulletins in Iran in 1800 BC; or publicity to extol the rulers of ancient Egypt; or religious promotion by the Catholic Church is defined restrospectively by Cutlip as embryonic public relations. Despite mentioning these interesting examples, his books nevertheless, concentrate on the American experience of promotion from the initial hype for the colonies onward.

There is one other distinctive and rather influential approach taken to the emergence of public relations. This proposes that public relations has passed through four stages of development, the first two of which—publicity and public information—are seen as one-way communication in contrast to the later stages—asymmetrical and symmetrical communication—which are seen as two-way communication. The framework is promoted both as historical explanation and as a typology of practice that has become a somewhat culturally monolithic model within academic public relations. Initial research into developments in the UK suggests a somewhat different trajectory.

The major driver for the development of public relations as a discrete occupation in the UK was local and central governments in the early twentieth century during a particularly turbulent era of European and world history. Prior to this period, advertising had existed in a form we would recognise since the early nineteenth century. However, historians of advertising, like historians of public relations, have pointed out that publicity was established practice in Greek and Roman times, which suggests that promotion and persuasive communication are indeed intrinsic to human society. Nevitt records a range of significant developments, such as the spread of printing in the latter part of the fifteenth century; the set of rules for the clergy that was accompanied by the phrase *supplico stet cedula,* which he loosely translates as "Pray do not pull down this advertisement" (p. 7); the development of newspapers and press advertising; the introduction of publications devoted entirely to advertisements; posters and the increasing complexity of urban life, which meant that word of mouth was no longer effective. However, it was not until the twentieth century that the slightly different occupation of public relations began to emerge before World War I. Naturally, its development was confusing to many, for who could distinguish at that time the differences among advertising, publicity, and public relations? There was some overlap in interests; for example, one of the dominant figures in advertising who advised several government departments before and after World War I, Charles Higham, had tremendous enthusiasm for the use of film for community education and government propaganda and thus appears to have anticipated many of the ideas of the Scottish documentarist John Grierson.

The question of the distinction between public relations and publicity was especially confusing and was raised in early meetings of the Institute of Public Relations (IPR) in the late 1940s and early 1950s when criteria for membership were being established. Advertising by then had a poor reputation for puffery and unethical practices, so it was important for those seeking to establish the legitimacy of public relations to distinguish it as a separate occupation. Separating publicity from public relations was particularly difficult and was poorly articulated in the official journals and papers of the Institute. Public relations was seen as having greater concern with the important issues of the day and as being a means for organisations to influence public policy but also to take into account public opinion and the views of important interest groups. In other words, it had more to do with negotiation and less to do with the simple statement or promotion of organisational position. Nevertheless, these distinctions are still arguable to the present day, even though publicity is usually seen as part of the tactics of public relations rather than as its main purpose.

There is a final, even more problematic distinction that continues to dog public relations: that of its relationship to propaganda. The history of public relations in the UK illustrates well this dilemma: government communication in wartime is usually referred to as propaganda (though governments tend to describe it as "information." But what of government peacetime efforts such as the Empire Marketing Board or the British Council? A number of people worked during World Wars I and II in government propaganda and then proceeded to have civilian careers in public relations, a development that was apparently considered quite unproblematic at the time.

Public relations in Britain clearly emerged from major changes in the political, economic, cultural, and technological spheres and cannot be attributed solely to the creativity of a few individuals, even though some important figures can be identified. The influence of wartime propaganda has been

mentioned and in some ways is unremarkable; in a democratic society public opinion needs to be managed, and governments censor information likely to affect morale on the home front.

Economic policies were also important. The creation of the Empire Marketing Board in the mid-1920s to promote imperial preference was one example. It also facilitated the career development of civil servant Sir Stephen Tallents, who not only wrote the blueprint for The British Council but also worked closely with Scottish documentarist John Grierson. Other important economic stimuli for the growth of public relations included the government policies of nationalisation and de-nationalisation (privatisation), which stimulated the development of corporate and trade union opposition and required specialist communicators and lobbyists. Likewise, the era of de-colonisation affected government and corporations alike and provided a stimulus for the development of public relations in those countries affected. Companies had to look ahead to the forthcoming era of independence and try to protect their economic interests by developing and maintaining good relations with the indigenous opinion formers; government had to deal with insurgency and counter-propaganda, while at the same time trying to maintain the best possible diplomatic relations for the future benefit of Britain.

The contribution of local government to the intellectual and professional development of public relations was crucial. Local government officials were coming to occupy high-profile positions in an increasingly de-centralised system. They were responsible for communicating policies and legislation to local communities, and as key lynchpins in democratic practice, they were forced to consider the relationship between themselves and the publics they served. The consequence was a number of extremely thought-provoking and sophisticated articles in *Public Administration* that explained public relations as relations with the public and as a vital tool in achieving smooth administration. Other complementary activities were those of "intelligence," which was defined as information gathering and analysis in order to keep up to date with policy developments with a view to being able to influence that policy; and "publicity," which in that context was seen as the specific medium for techniques used to promote particular ideas. Local government officials contributed not only this multilayered notion of public relations but also a notion of public service that has remained an important part of public relations ideology. Furthermore, they possessed the practical administrative skills to set up the

Institute of Public Relations in 1948 and were the driving force behind its establishment.

The role of the British documentary film movement

The British Documentary Movement was an important strand in the history of public relations in the UK. There was a fortuitous collaboration between senior civil servant Sir Stephen Tallents (who served as president of the Institute of Public Relations 1948–1949 and 1952–1953) and John Grierson, whom Tallents engaged to run his film unit. Tallents claimed to be the first person appointed to a post titled "public relations officer" and had a passion for "national projection," which he believed to be vital for Britain's trade relations, tourism, and sense of national identity. The worsening international situation meant that his ideas fell on fertile ground and made the notion of peace-time propaganda more widely acceptable than might otherwise have been the case. Grierson's passion for democratic education was not restricted to the tactical use of film. He wrote many articles and speeches exalting the role of public relations and arguing for a more ambitious role for practitioners in society and the "art of public persuasion." At least partly as a consequence of his connection with Tallents, Grierson associated with a range of influential practitioners with backgrounds in the BBC, the Ministry of Information, the Post Office, and the Inter-Departmental Coordinating Committee on Government Publicity in the late 1930s. Grierson's understanding of public relations was not limited to theoretical musings or technical production: after leaving the Canadian Film Board, he became UNESCO's first Director of Mass Communications and Public Information (although he left after a year, disillusioned by the practical problems that often plague bureaucracies).

Grierson's vision of public relations had some influence within Institute of Public Relations circles, thanks to a speech made to that body in 1950, which received wide circulation and was subsequently either directly quoted or paraphrased many times. A comparative analysis of Grierson's extensive archive of writings reveals a number of themes in common with those discussed in the IPR's journal. He seemed to see public relations and propaganda as linked practices that could overcome societal fragmentation through education, and his evangelism appealed to public relations practitioners who were seeking to establish their occupation as a respectable profession.

The development of the academic discipline: conceptual frameworks

At present there are still relatively few academic researchers specialising in public relations outside the United States. Thus the dominant paradigms are still American, liberal pluralist and have tended to be based on management, psychological, or marketing frameworks and methodologies. In particular, the most widely known model promotes public relations as supporting democratic practice (in terms of facilitating debate in the marketplace of ideas rather than the Griersonian notion of civilian education), facilitating communication and dialogue between organisations and publics. The public relations academic Ron Pearson was the first to use Habermas's theory of communicative action as way of understanding public relations practice in terms of critical communicative processes and effects.

Much academic work in the United States has been functional, directed toward managerial concerns of excellence and effectiveness. Thus the field has applied positivist methodologies, and there is still a dearth of reflective work in the field. Much research is based on the dominant U.S. typology of public relations practice and systems theory and is based on the assumption that consensus should be the major outcome of public relations work. In the early 1990s the potential for a new paradigm—that of rhetoric—was articulated, but many of those writing in this tradition still tend to work toward the ideal of consensus.

One major research theme has been that of gender, but most of this work has concentrated on the career ambitions of American middle-class women. Interestingly, although men are in a minority in public relations practice, they have not received any attention. Other major themes include professionalism, professionalisation, ethics, and education—interests that reflect practitioner concerns over the status of their occupation. Critical work has begun to emerge in the last decade, particularly from New Zealand and Scotland, but is still a tiny proportion of the work published. And such work as there is has sometimes not been well received within the field.

Academically, public relations is in a curiously isolated and rather vulnerable position. Media sociologists tend to be interested only in the media relations and lobbying aspects of the practice and to ignore aspects such as employee and community relations. Likewise they rarely, if ever, seem to acquaint themselves with the literature or arguments within public relations literature. And for their part, marketing academics tend to be interested only in publicity and consumers. There is considerable work relevant to public relations in organisational communication, culture, and climate, but academics in these fields seem rarely to address public relations. Public relations academics themselves are often overly introspective, thus contributing to a situation in which a major social practice is still rather poorly understood.

JACQUIE L'ETANG

See also **Empire Marketing Board Film Unit; Grierson, John; Tallents, Stephen**

Further Reading

Bernays, Edward L., *The Later Years: Public Relations Insights 1956–1986*, London: H&M Publishers, 1986.

Bromley, Dennis Basil, *Reputation, Image and Impression Management*, New York: Wiley, 1986.

Cutlip, Scott M., *The Unseen Power: Public Relations*, Mahwah, NJ: Lawrence Erlbaum, 1994.

Cutlip, Scott M., *Public Relations History: From the 17th to the 20th Century*, Mahwah, NJ: Lawrence Erlbaum, 1995.

Elwood, William N., *Public Relations Inquiry as Rhetorical Criticism: Case Studies of Corporate Discourse and Social Influence*, Praegar Series in Political Communication, Westport, CT: Praeger, 1995.

Ewen, Stuart, *PR! A Social History of Spin*, New York: BasicBooks, HarperCollins, 1996.

Davis, Aeron, *Public Relations Democracy: Public Relations, Politics and the Mass Media in Britain*, Manchester: Manchester University Press, 2002.

Grant, Mariel, *Propaganda and the Role of the State in Inter-war Britain*, Oxford: Clarendon Press, 1994.

Heath, Robert (ed.), *Handbook of Public Relations*, London: Sage, 2001.

Kilborn, Richard, "A Marriage Made in Heaven or Hell?: Relations Between Documentary Film Makers and PR Practitioners," in *Public Relations and Contemporary Practice*, edited by Jacquie L'Etang and Magda Pieczka, Mahwah, NJ: Lawrence Erlbaum, forthcoming 2005.

L'Etang, Jacquie, "Grierson and the Public Relations Industry in Britain," in *From Grierson to the Docusoap: Breaking the Boundaries*, edited by John Izod, Richard Kilborn, and Matthew Hibberd, University of Luton Press, 2000.

———, *Public Relations in Britain: A History of Professional Practice in the Twentieth Century*, Mahwah, NJ: Lawrence Erlbaum 2004.

L'Etang, Jacquie, and Magda Pieczka (eds.), *Critical Perspectives in Public Relations*, New York: Routledge, 1996.

———, *Public Relations and Contemporary Practice*, Mahwah, NJ: Lawrence Erlbaum, forthcoming 2005.

Marchand, Roland, *Creating the Corporate Soul: The Rise of Public Relations and Corporate Imagery in American Big Business*, Berkeley: University of California Press, 1998.

Mickey, Thomas J., *Deconstructing Public Relations: Public Relations Criticism*, Mahwah, NJ: Lawrence Erlbaum, 2003.

Nevett, T. R., *Advertising in Britain: A History*, London: William Collins & Sons, 1982.

Olasky, Marvin N., *Corporate Public Relations: A New Historical Perspective*, Mahwah, NJ: Lawrence Erlbaum, 1987.

Tedlow, Richard S., *Keeping the Corporate Image: Public Relations and Business 1900–1950*, JAI Press, 1979.

Tilson, Donn, and Alozie, E. (eds.), *Toward the Common Good: Perspectives in International Public Relations*, Boston, MA: Allyn & Bacon, 2004.

Van Ruler, Betteke, and Vercic, Dejan (eds.) *Public Relations in Europe—a Nation-by-Nation Introduction to Public Relations Theory and Practice*, Walter de Gruyter, 2004.

PULL MY DAISY

(US, Frank and Leslie, 1959)

Part documentary, part dada-esque farce, Robert Frank and Alfred Leslie's short film *Pull My Daisy* stands, along with films such as John Cassavetes's *Shadows* (1959), as one of the most important cinematic statements of the postwar Beat Movement. Based loosely on the third act of Jack Kerouac's unproduced stage play *The Beat Generation*, the film provides a brief glimpse into the lives of bohemian artists and writers of 1950s New York City.

The play was adapted for the screen by Frank and Leslie, who changed the title to *Pull My Daisy* after learning that MGM was planning to produce a Beat exploitation film titled *The Beat Generation*. The new title came from a whimsical 1949 poem by Kerouac and Allen Ginsberg—a poem that, when set to music by David Amram, provided the film's theme song and set the tone for the film's eccentric action.

Both Robert Frank (1924–) and his co-director, contemporary realist painter Alfred Leslie (1927–), were members of The Group, a small collective of American independent filmmakers formed in 1960 with loose ties to Free Cinema in England and to as the *Nouvelle Vague* in France. Frank had been best known as a still photographer prior to the release of *Pull My Daisy* in 1959. His still photographs, such as those published in *The Americans* (1959), a collection of more than eighty photos bluntly chronicling life in postwar America, pioneered the "snapshot aesthetic" in which the documentary image is rendered starkly with a minimum of conscious artistry. It was a visual aesthetic well matched to the Beat Movement's embrace of literary spontaneity to capture experience, once described briefly by poet Allen Ginsberg as "First thought, best thought." Not surprisingly, Frank's first motion picture shares the same stark imagery and spontaneous feel of both his earlier photographs and much of the poetry and prose produced by writers of the Beat Movement.

Filmed silently in black and white, with an over-dubbed narration, *Pull My Daisy* documents a single day in the lives of a small circle of bohemian poets and artists in a dingy loft apartment on New York's Lower East Side. The cast is made up of some of the Beat Movement's most important artists. Poets Allen Ginsberg, Peter Orlovsky, and Gregory Corso appear as themselves. Composer/musician David Amram plays the role of jazz musician Mezz McGillicuddy, and painter Larry Rivers appears as Milo, the workingclass poet at the center of the film's story line (a character whose life bears a strong resemblance to Kerouac's friend Neal Cassady). Although Kerouac does not make an appearance in the film, he acts as the narrator and supplies all of the voices for the film's characters (the only exception is the voice of a small boy, probably provided by Robert Franks's son Pablo).

Much of the film is concerned with the tension between the routine life of work, family, and home and the less constrained and more spontaneous life offered by the Beat Movement. The film begins with a peaceful domestic scene typical of the period; a young woman (identified in the credits only as "Milo's wife") readies her son for school while she awaits the return of her husband Milo from his job as a railroad brakeman. The morning's calm is broken, however, as poets Ginsberg and Corso arrive, quickly making themselves at home with wine, marijuana, and an animated discussion of poetics. When Milo arrives home from work a few hours later, accompanied by Peter Orlovsky, he tells the assembled poets that a bishop will be

paying the household a visit that evening and warns them to be on their best behavior. As the bishop arrives for what Milo's wife hopes will be a pleasant visit, accompanied by his sister and his very proper mother, the scene quickly turns into an uncomfortable evening of increasingly bizarre and intoxicated antics, as the poets ask the cleric strange yet pointed questions about the spiritual realm. Despite Milo's wife's best efforts to control the tone of the event, the evening further disintegrates with the arrival of jazz musician Mezz McGillicuddy, who turns the apartment into the scene of a jam session, as the bishop and his family look on in quiet shock. The film ends with Milo's wife in tears, as the bishop and his party leave abruptly, and Milo is jubilantly led out of the apartment by his bohemian friends for an adventurous night on the town.

Pull My Daisy documents a moment of interaction between two worlds: the mundane, proper, and feminized life of the mainstream (exemplified by Milo's wife, the bishop, and his mother and sister), and the wild, joyous, and very masculine life of "kicks" to be found among the bohemian artists of the Bowery (exemplified by Milo, Ginsberg, Orlovsky, and McGillicuddy). Contemporary viewers will no doubt be troubled by the irresponsible and, at times, seemingly sexist actions presented by the film's subjects and may find themselves in agreement with Beat scholar Joyce Johnson, who has suggested that the film is "about the right to remain children." Nonetheless, the work provides a striking visual representation of the Beat Movement and its struggle with the stifling conformity of the 1950s.

ROD PHILLIPS

Pull My Daisy (USA, G-String Productions, 1959, 20 min.). Produced and directed by Robert Frank and Alfred Leslie. Cinematography by Robert Frank and Alfred Leslie. Written and narrated by Jack Kerouac. Featuring David Amram, Beltiane (Delphine Serig), Gregory Corso, Pablo Frank, Allen Ginsberg, Sally Gross, Alice Neal, Denise Parker, Mooney Peebles (Richard Bellamy), Peter Orlovsky, and Larry Rivers. Editing by Leon Prochnik, Robert Frank, and Alfred Leslie. Music by David Amram. Filmed in New York City.

Further Reading

Allen, Blaine, "The Making (and Unmaking) of *Pull My Daisy*," in *Film History* 2, 1988, 185–205.

Frank, Robert, *The Americans*, Millerton: Aperture, 1959.

Sargeant, Jack, *Naked Lens: Beat Cinema (Creation Cinema Collection #7)*, London: Creation Books, 2002.

Sterritt, David, *Mad to Be Saved: The Beats, the '50s, and Film*, Carbondale: Southern Illinois University Press, 1998.

Tyler, Parker, "For *Shadows*, Against *Pull My Daisy*," in *Film Culture* 24, 1962, 28–33.

PUMPING IRON

(US, Fiore and Butler, 1976)

Pumping Iron generated intense public interest in bodybuilding, an activity that theretofore lacked credibility as a legitimate sport or art form. It also started Arnold Schwarzenegger on his rise to superstardom, catapulting him into public consciousness in a way that his previous films, *The Long Goodbye* (1973) and *Stay Hungry* (1976), had failed to do. At almost every level, the film was a collaborative effort. Based on the book of the same name, written by Charles Gaines and George Butler, *Pumping Iron* as a film project was carried from conception to completion by the efforts of Butler. Butler co-produced the film with Jerome Gary and co-directed with Robert Fiore. Larry Silk and Geof Bartz handled editing. Michael Small oversaw music throughout and wrote the title song for the film.

From the opening credits, featuring quaint clips of old-time muscle men and backed by Small's engaging, humorous score, the film never takes itself too seriously. When the viewer is then faced with a compelling human drama, it comes as unexpected delight. Filmed across the United States and culminating in South Africa, *Pumping Iron* follows the workouts and preliminary competitions through which the world's top bodybuilders must pass to become "Mister Olympia," the ultimate glory for the bodybuilding community. Success, each contestant understands, involves more than approximating bodily perfection. To become Mister Olympia ultimately requires besting the dominating international presence in the sport—Schwarzenegger.

Unlike its sequel, *Pumping Iron II: The Women* (1985), this low-budget, intimate film foregoes contrived dramatic elements and lets contestants speak for themselves through word and deed. With minimal narration and only occasional interviews to "flesh out" main characters, Butler and Fiore gently offer the viewer the chance to love or hate each of the Mister Olympia hopefuls, though there is little doubt that only "Arnold! Arnold!" (as his mesmerized fans chant) will win the title. In a film replete with people literally larger than life, Schwarzenegger stands head and shoulders above his peers physically and mentally, while demonstrating a depth of personality and psyche that few in Hollywood can match on camera. A smash box office success, and available on the shelves of video rental stores ever since because of Schwarzenegger's popularity, *Pumping Iron* remains one of the most financially successful American documentaries.

MICHAEL S. CASEY

See also **Sport: Critical Overview of**

Pumping Iron (USA, White Mountain Films, 1976, 85 min., color). Distributed by Cinema 5 Distributing. Produced by George Butler and Jerome Gary. Directed by George Butler and Robert Fiore. Cinematography by Robert Fiore. Music by Michael Small. Editing by Larry Silk and Geof Bartz. Sound by Harry Lapham. Lighting by Michael Lesser. Titles by Martin S. Moskof. Narration by Charles Gaines. Peter Davis and Charles Gaines served as consultants. Filmed in New York; Los Angeles; San Francisco; Holyoke, Massachusetts; and South Africa.

Pumping Iron, 1976.
[*Still courtesy of the British Film Institute*]

Further Reading

Butler, George, *Arnold Schwarzenegger: A Portrait*, New York: Simon & Schuster, 1990.
Gaines, Charles, *Pumping Iron: The Art and Sport of Bodybuilding*, New York: Simon & Schuster, 1982.
Nowell-Smith, Geoffrey, *The Oxford History of World Cinema*. London: Oxford University Press, 1996.
Schwarzenegger, Arnold, and Douglas Kent Hall (contributor), *Arnold: The Education of a Bodybuilder* (reprint edition), New York: Fireside, 1983.

Q

¡QUE VIVA MÉXICO!

(USSR and South America, Eisenstein, 1931)

¡Que viva México! is the name Sergei M. Eisenstein gave to an unfinished project on which he worked between December 1930 and January 1932, assisted by Grigori Alexandrov and cinematographer Eduard Tissé. This project, financed by American producers headed by writer Upton Sinclair, was born when Eisenstein's negotiations to film a movie in Hollywood fell through. It was originally planned, in a very vague fashion, in the form of an apolitical travelog that was to portray Mexico through its people, its culture, and its natural environment. But once in the country, Eisenstein changed his mind and wrote a script for a semihistorical and political fiction film based on a narrative that took advantage of the fact that in Mexico, between 1910 and 1917, a popular revolution similar to that which occurred in Russia had taken place.

Eisenstein's script revealed a Marxist conception according to which the history of the country would have developed dialectically in a number of stages: an indigenous origin, pure though primitive; a *mestizo* stage characterized both by the advantages of a superior social development and by the miseries of exploitation; and finally, a third stage,

that was initiated by a revolution against the old order and was about to culminate in a society in which classes and races would be reconciled. According to this plan, the film would consist of six sections. The first was to be a brief prologue about the pre-Hispanic civilization. This was to be followed by a group of four longer episodes located in the immediate past. The first, "Zandunga," was to depict moments of everyday life in an indigenous area still untouched by the injustice of modern civilization. The second story, "Maguey," would illustrate a conflict between peasants and landowners in a more modern region of the country, around 1900, during the dictatorship of Porfirio Díaz. It was taken for granted that this conflict was the result of centuries of Spanish conquest and domination, which nevertheless had also had positive results, particularly in the areas of the religious and the festive. The third story, "Fiesta," would focus on these positive contributions. Then the plan was to include "Soldadera," an episode located in the time of the revolution in which the people in arms triumphed over the despotic government of Porfirio Díaz. The film was to end with an

¡Que Viva México!, uncompleted film by Sergei Eisenstein. Released re-edited as Thunder Over Mexico, 1933.
[*Courtesy Glenn Loney/Everett Collection, Courtesy of the Everett Collection*]

epilogue focused on the cultural, artistic, and industrial achievements of contemporary Mexico, culminating with the ancestral celebration of Día de Muertos, where not only the present would be linked to the past, but also, in an implicit way, the triumph of the revolution would be associated with the triumph of life over death.

The script (which was written after a substantial amount of the film had been shot) called for the inclusion of ethnographic documentary scenes such as dances in honor of the Virgin of Guadalupe, the process for making the popular alcoholic beverage *pulque* from the maguey plant, and the activities that take place in an indigenous market. Also, in Eisenstein's characteristic way, the film was not to include professional actors or set shots. But it was obvious that all these documentary characteristics were to be integrated into a fiction film located almost entirely in the past.

The transformation of the original travelog into this more complex structure prolonged the shooting, and by the end of 1931, more than a year after the project got going, the producers stopped sending money. At the beginning of 1932 Eisenstein returned to the Soviet Union, trusting that the negatives, then in the hands of the producers in Hollywood, would be sent to him. He would not make the script's film but an alternative version, because he had lacked the time to film the "Soldadera" episode. Unfortunately, the producers decided to sever relations with Eisenstein and to use his materials to edit *Thunder over Mexico* (Sol Lesser, 1933) and other minor films. Eisenstein never saw his Mexican material again. Nearly fifty years later, when he was already dead, his old assistant Alexandrov recovered a considerable part of what they had filmed

and, following the structure of the script and indications given by Eisenstein's drawings, edited a personal version of *¡Que viva México!*

The first noticeable thing about this film is the beauty of at least two different groups of images. On the one hand, there are the images that reproduce nature (nopales, magueyes, big clouds), the local customs, and popular faces, which all together suggest the atemporal spirit of the land. On the other, there are Eisenstein's famous symbolic shots, prepared to create metaphoric effects like that of a maguey with bullet holes in it from which flows the juice of the plant resembling blood, or to allude to universal symbols such as the three rebel peasants about to be sacrificed whose figures are organized formally according to the pictorial tradition of the Crucifixion. The aesthetic impact of all these images is so powerful that a considerable amount of later Mexican cinema was inspired by them.

Notwithstanding this film's photographic beauty, it is obvious that Eisenstein's guiding hand is missing in the montage. Repeatedly the narrative is subordinated to the visual, and this makes the film somewhat static. The script talks about *¡Que viva México!* as a "film symphony," and it is this musical aspect—above all the well-proportioned rhythmic combination of lyricism and dramatic intensity, which we find in other Eisenstein works, such as *Battleship Potemkin*—that is lacking in Alexandrov's version.

The most obvious failure of *¡Que viva México!* is its sound track. As in other productions of the transition period in which it was filmed, Eisenstein had planned a sound film with music but no dialogue. In Alexandrov's version there is a very poor sample of musical motifs, which frequently contrasts in an irritating way with the beauty of the

¡Que Viva México!, uncompleted film by Sergei Eisenstein. Released re-edited as Thunder Over Mexico, 1933.
[*Courtesy Glenn Loney/Everett Collection, Courtesy of the Everett Collection*]

images. And instead of the dialogue inter-titles of a silent movie, a voice often takes charge of the narration and the spatio-temporal identification of the story. Two scenes of Alexandrov himself talking to the camera, explaining, with the help of archive materials such as drawings and still photographs, how Eisenstein's *¡Que viva México!* was conceived, filmed, and then aborted, makes this film, in a broader sense, also a documentary.

During Eisenstein's stay in Mexico he filmed two documentaries with the aim of obtaining extra resources for *¡Que viva México!* One of these films, which was a propaganda production for the Partido Nacional Revolucionario then in power, apparently has not survived. The other, a fifteen-minute newsreel about an earthquake in the province of Oaxaca, shows images of destroyed houses and churches, with shots that bear testimony once again to cinematographer Tissé's virtuosity and to Eisenstein's search of beauty even in the midst of pain and suffering.

ÁNGEL MIQUEL

See also **Sinclair, Upton**

¡Que viva México! (USSR, 1931–1979, 90 min). Produced by Grigori Alexandro and N. Orlov. Mosfilm-Gosfilmofond. Directed by Sergei Eisenstein and Grigori Alexandrov.

Script by Sergei Eisenstein. Cinematography in black and white by Eduard Tissé. Music by Eduard Artemiev. Editing by Grigori Alexandrov and Esfir Tobak. Filmed in Yucatán, Oaxaca, Puebla, Hidalgo, and Distrito Federal, Mexico.

Further Reading

Bergan, Ronald, *Sergei Eisenstein: A Life in Conflict*, New York: The Overlook Press, 1999.

Christie, Ian, and David Elliott, (eds.), *Eisenstein at Ninety*, Oxford: Museum of Modern Art, 1988.

De la Vega, Eduardo, *Del muro a la pantalla. S. M. Eisenstein y el arte pictórico mexicano*, Mexico City: Imcine / Canal 22 / Instituto Mexiquense de Cultura, 1997.

Eisenstein, Sergei, *Immoral Memories: An Autobiography*, Boston: Houghton Mifflin, 1983.

Eisenstein, Sergei, *¡Que viva México!*, New York: Arno Press / New York Times, 1972.

Geduld, Harry M., and Ronald Gottesman (eds.), *Sergei Eisenstein and Upton Sinclair: The Making and Unmaking of* ¡Que viva México!, Bloomington: Indiana University Press, 1970.

Karetnikova, Inga, and Leon Steinmetz, *Mexico According to Eisenstein*, Albuquerque: University of New Mexico Press, 1991.

Seton, Marié, *Sergei Eisenstein*, New York: Wyn, 1952.

R

RAIN

(Holland, Ivens, 1929)

With the premier of *Rain* at the Filmliga (Film League) in Amsterdam in 1929, Joris Ivens established his reputation as a serious director. His previous film, *The Bridge* (1928), had been well received, particularly among followers of the avant-garde, but *Rain* was hailed as a *cinépoem* by French critics (Ivens, 1969), an ideal synthesis of thematic and formal elements communicated through moving images.

As Bill Nichols suggests, *Rain* could be seen as operating within the modernist "poetic mode" of documentary: a style that goes against the standards of continuity editing to explore associations and patterns that arise out of "temporal rhythms and spatial juxtapositions" (Nichols, 2001). Indeed at this point in his career, Ivens was closely aligned with the ideological and aesthetic aims of Amsterdam's Film League, a group founded in 1927 to promote the screening of avant-garde films and that associated mainstream cinema with the masses, with "the commercial regime, America, kitsch" (Stufkens, 1999). Ivens served as the Film League's technical advisor and agreed that films should offer an alternative to the monolithic cinema industry that produced low entertainments and seduced the public "by adapting to the public's bad taste" (Stufkens, 1999). *Rain* does go against many of the common practices of silent continuity editing, but does not go so far as to dispense with narrative entirely. Instead, a narrative unfolds that dramatizes the rhythms of a natural event, a single rain shower, which in turn gestures toward larger existential and aesthetic concerns. In *Rain*, the built urban environment is utterly transformed not only by the natural event but also, perhaps more important, by the steady gaze of the camera, which can capture those fleeting visual patterns produced by everyday movements that might be missed by the naked eye.

In his autobiography, Ivens recalls that he and an assistant, Chang Fai, shot *Rain* over several months in 1928, using two 35mm amateur hand cameras. In all, however, the twelve-minute film took almost two years to complete. The story, based on a scenario by Mannus Franken, is straightforward: A bright day in the city gives way to a darkening sky, wind, the first drops of a rain shower, and then a deluge that increases in

Rain, 1929.
[*Still courtesy of the British Film Institute*]

force until it finally ebbs away, the weakened daylight returning to a drenched landscape. Within this slight narrative frame, other more abstract impressions are communicated through the camera's meditation on movements, patterns, and forms. Changing light effects are highlighted through the interplay of sun and shadow in the early scenes; reflections produced in pools, puddles, and rain-slicked streets are emphasized in later scenes. The film rarely focuses on human actions, which are subordinate to those of the primary player, the rain. With the exception of an obviously staged shot of a man holding out his hand to feel for raindrops, then turning up his collar and rushing for cover, people are primarily shot from behind or overhead. Human figures, although integral to the mise-en-scène, remain wholly anonymous. Still, these shots are not deployed to produce sterile, carefully composed scenes surveyed from a safe distance; instead they work with other moments in the film that align the spectator's eye more closely with the camera's lens. *Rain* conspires to make viewers experience the rainstorm firsthand. Ivens wanted audiences to feel "damp" after watching his "super-wet" images (Ivens, 1969).

Many critics have noted the influence of Walter Ruttmann's *Berlin: Symphony of a Great City*, which Ivens saw when he met the director in 1927, though years later Ivens would distance himself from that film, suggesting that "a city film with human interest and content could be done without Ruttmann's virtuosity and superficial effects" (Ivens, 1969). *Rain*'s emphasis on the formal composition of shots and on the juxtaposition of different movements, shot scales, and camera angles also suggests an affinity with the contemporary montage experiments of Sergei Eisenstein and

Dziga Vertov, whom Ivens met while working with the Film League. What sets Ivens's film apart, however, is its sustained focus on a single event, its formal unity and coherence, and its ability to capture kinetic images that are imbued with the singularity and compositional intensity of still photographs. Patterns produced by juxtaposing movement and stasis are revealed in images such as a boat traveling under a bridge, while the steady shadow of the bridge's iron railing cuts across the movement of the boat beneath it. The recurring motif of raindrops falling into water further suggests a dialectic of motion and stillness: a seemingly stable aesthetic form both produces, and is produced out of, the force of multiple, fragmented movements and events.

One of the film's most striking sequences begins with a street scene framed by the arch of an umbrella, which cuts to a traveling shot of a man under an umbrella. Further images of groups of people holding umbrellas cut to raindrops falling into a puddle, and then several arresting overhead shots of a street scene appear in succession, in which groups of umbrellas form a recognizable, yet somewhat surreal, shuddering mass. The sequence is tied up when the final shot fades to black, a technique used only sparingly in the film. Although the images might appear simply to indulge in aesthetically pleasing forms, they also indirectly articulate the relationship between the modern city dweller and the anonymous masses, suggesting the constant interplay between the individual and the social organism, the whole and its innumerable parts.

Rain preceded Ivens's more openly political phase, generally considered to have begun after 1929. He would later see his early films as failed attempts to fight bourgeois ideology through formalist revolutionary strategies, labeling his late-1920s work as fundamentally apolitical and "parochial" (Stufkens, 1999). But *Rain* was clearly a foundational film for Ivens and a defining moment in the modernist avant-garde. The subtleties of *Rain*'s camera work—capturing images both banal and arresting, like the street filmed through the streaming windows of a moving tram—are typical of an attention to documentary aesthetics that would persist throughout Ivens's long career.

JEFFREY GEIGER

See also **Aesthetics and Documentary Film: Poetics; Ivens, Joris**

Rain (Netherlands, 1929, 12 min, silent). Produced, directed, and written by Joris Ivens and Mannus Franken.

Photographed and edited by Joris Ivens. Music composed by Lou Lichtveld (1932) and Hanns Eisler (1941). Production company, CAPI Amsterdam. Filmed in Amsterdam.

Further Reading

Heller, Berndt, "The Reconstruction of Eisler's Film Music: Opus III, *Regen*, and *The Circus*," in *Historical Journal of Film, Radio, and Television*, 18, October 1998, 541–560.

Ivens, Joris, *The Camera and I*, Berlin: Seven Seas Publishers, 1969.
Leyda, Jay, and Sidney Meyers, "Joris Ivens: Artist in Documentary," in *The Documentary Tradition*, edited by Lewis Jacobs, New York: Norton, 1979.
Nichols, Bill, *Introduction to Documentary*, Bloomington: Indiana University Press, 2001.
Stufkens, André, "The Song of Movement: Joris Ivens's First Films and the Cycle of the Avant-garde," in *Joris Ivens and the Documentary Context*, edited by Kees Bakker, Amsterdam: Amsterdam University Press, 1999.

RAY, SATYAJIT

Indian filmmaker Satyajit Ray, highly acclaimed and assiduously studied by aspiring film professionals, has left a lasting impression on audiences and film professionals alike. Ray's first film, *Pather Panchali* (1955), which later became the first of the celebrated Apu trilogy, is based on a novel by Bengali writer Bibhutibhushan Banerji, and chronicles the life of a young boy Apu, his growth and maturation. Although anchored in late nineteenth and early twentieth century Bengal, the film achieves universality with its soul-stirring celebration of the wonder of life and the eternal courage of the human soul. In *Aparajito* (1957), his second film of the Apu trilogy, Ray provides social commentary of a profoundly changing culture of Bengal, which is seen through the protagonist's (Apu's) dilemma between traditional and modern education, and in his decision to abandon his ancestral path in search of his uncertain destiny in Calcutta. Drawing symbolic meaning from the road as a metaphor of life's journey, *Apu Sansar* (1959), the concluding movie of the trilogy, shows Apu on the road once again, but this time not leaving anywhere, but going home. The complexity of meaning, economy in expression, and the precision in the choice of expressions to evoke the finer shades of meaning and thought, characterize the Apu trilogy and define Ray's humanism and universal appeal.

Three generations of Ray's work have been nurtured by the city of Calcutta with its ever-changing social and political mores. In *Devi* (1960), Ray uses the motif of window bars, darkness and shadows, and veils and curtains, and depicts the pervasive feeling of confinement, oppression, and ignorance within the household, which in turn reflects the destructive power of ignorance and superstition in a decadent and selfish society devoid of logic and progressive thought. In the opening scene of *Devi*, Ray depicts the adornment of the Kali statue that figuratively foreshadows the inevitable fate of the naïve and trusting character Doya, who too is manipulated and transformed into the image of goddess Kali.

His next film, *Mahanagar* (1963), offers an insightful examination of modern society, presenting the obsolescence of cultural tradition and the changing role of women in the financial instability of an emerging economy. Subrata and Arati, the two principal characters, in an early scene in the film are seen having breakfast together hurriedly before leaving for work; Arati does not serve her husband first, as is customary in the traditional family. Through clever use of close-ups, Ray portrays the rocky road women sometimes tread on their way to independence and self-identity.

Using heavy Victorian furniture, costumes, wallpaper, and the typography of the journal run by Charulata's husband, Ray recreates the Victorian era in *Charulata* (1964), set in the Calcutta of 1879, and thus captures the essential spirit of the Bengal renaissance. The opening scene of this movie communicates Charulata's boredom by showing her wandering aimlessly around the house speaking just one line of dialogue in seven minutes.

Agantuk (1991), his last film and one of only a few color films, is provocatively insightful and probes the nature of humanity and human relationships through the use of static interior shots that subtly reflect the characters' self-imposed entrapment, which arises as a result of their conformity to civilized behavior and societal norms. Manmohan (the stranger) amusingly evaluates the contribution of civilization through the use of the longest word in the first edition of the Oxford English Dictionary—*floccinauccinihilipilification*, a jest word meaning to render something of little or no value, which essentially describes his own existence as it comes a full circle. Seeking to refine his art studies, Manmohan realizes the innate beauty in primitive cave paintings. Traveling to the West to advance his knowledge of civilization, he discovers that the essence of humanity resides in the customs of ancient tribes. Here, Ray epitomizes the need for the reconciliation between cultural legacy and the spontaneity of humanity, the inevitable marriage of savagery and civilization, tradition, and westernization.

KOKILA RAVI

Biography

Satyajit Ray was born in 1920 to a Bengali family in India. Educated at Rabindranath Tagore's open university, Shanti Niketan, where he observed nature, studied fine art, and became interested in graphic design. Returning to Calcutta in 1943, worked with D.J. Keymer, a British-owned advertising company in India, as a visualizer. Profoundly influenced and encouraged by Jean Renoir, who visited Kolkata to choose locations for his film, *The River* (1950), Ray was also inspired by Vittorio de Sica's *Bicycle Thief* (1949). After three decades of filmmaking, because of ill health in the 1980s, had to pause and finally resumed artistic endeavors in 1988. In 1992, received honorary Academy Award for Lifetime Achievement "in recognition of his rare mastery of the art of motion pictures and for his profound humanitarian outlook, which has had an indelible influence on filmmakers and audiences throughout the world." Died April 23, 1992.

Selected Films

The Apu Trilogy:
1955 *Pather Panchali* ("Song of the Road")
1956 *Aparajito* ("The Unvanquished")
1960 *Apur Sansar* ("The World of Apu")
1958 *Jalsaghar* ("The Music Room")
1958 *Devi* ("The Goddess")
1961 *Rabindranath Tagore* (Documentary)
1963 *Mahanagar* ("The Big City")
1964 *Charulata*
1968 *Goopy Gyne Bagha Byne*: a children's film
1970 *Pratidwandi* ("The Adversary")

Further Reading

Dasgupta, Chidananda, *The Cinema of Satyajit Ray*, New Delhi: Vikas, 1980.
Ray, Satyajit, *Our Films, Their Films*, 1st U.S. ed. New York: Hyperion Books, 1994/Bombay: Orient Longman, 1976.
———, *The Apu Trilogy: Pather Panchali, Aparajito, Apur Sansar*. Calcutta: Seagull Books, 1985.
Seton, Marie, *Portrait of a Director: Satyajit Ray*. Bloomington: Indiana University Press, 1971.

REALISM, PHILOSOPHY, AND THE DOCUMENTARY FILM

The question of the relationship between documentary film and the representation of reality has always been central to discussions and assumptions concerning the medium. Early film, and the prehistory of the medium, was, after all, often preoccupied with the ability of film to reproduce reality in terms of perceptual visual experience. This approach—what André Bazin referred to as the "resemblance complex"—actually conforms to a naïve realist epistemological position, in which it is assumed that a direct relationship may exist between representation and reality. Such assumptions, which we now believe to be philosophically untenable, could be said to have driven the development of very early documentary, though, in such films, the naïve realist desire to create a "window on the world" is also combined with more generic, rhetorical forms. Despite the intrinsic realistic, or naturalistic, tendencies of the medium, however, no theorist of note has attempted to develop a naïve realist position on the documentary film, and, on the contrary, most theorists have attempted to theorise documentary realism in other than naïve realist terms, both epistemologically and ontologically. What is undeniably the case, though, is that, how ever the matter is addressed, documentary film cannot evade the question of realism.

The term "documentary film" was initially probably derived from the French term *documentaire*, one coined by French critics to distinguish serious travel and expedition films from more superficial, generic travelogs. From the beginning, therefore, documentary was regarded as more serious, authoritative, or significant than other filmic genres more closely related to "entertainment"; and the source of that sense of greater import was thought to lie in documentary's relationship with reality. The first use of the term *documentary* in English was probably by John Grierson in 1926. In developing his notion of documentary film, however, Grierson did not draw on naïve realist premises, but on the highly un-naïve realist philosophical idealism of Kant, Hegel and Bradley. In taking up the Hegelian notion of zeitgeist, and the Kantian distinction between noumena and phenomena, for example, Grierson argued that the documentary film should strive to represent an underlying reality, or what he called the "continuing reality," or "matrix of interdependence," as opposed to the surface events of reality. Here, documentary realism is defined in idealist rather than naïve realist or perceptual naturalist terms. In addition, the imperative to represent an underlying reality also takes Griesonian documentary realism away from a naturalist position and means that, for Grierson, in order to be realistic, documentary could actually adopt a markedly non-naturalistic style. Grierson was quite clear about this, arguing that, in some cases, a modernist or formalist approach might be better suited to capturing what he called "the real" than documentary naturalism. For example, Grierson was opposed to a cinema verité approach to the documentary film, and his own film, *Drifters* (1929), can be defined as an example of documentary-realist modernism, modeled on idealist premises. Griersonian documentary realism, therefore, can be defined as a form of abstract "representational realism" (see later), rather than direct realism, or naturalism.

Although Griersonian documentary realism was based on an imperative to represent abstract, noumenal realities, for Grierson, as for many other early theorists of the documentary film, the empirical was also the principal means through which such abstract realities could be indicated. For

such theorists, this also meant that the documentary film was superior to the fiction film because of its inherent ability to display the phenomenal world. Whether superior or not, however, the dialectic between documentary's ability to reproduce perceptual reality and its use of film form to depict more abstract realities—or just "signify"—was a central concern of many early theorists of the documentary film. Such theorists also placed differing weight on the importance of the naturalistic and formative potentials of documentary film. Grierson's ideas were, for example, influenced by those of the Austrian theorist Béla Balázs. In his *Theory of Film* (1930), Balázs was at pains to argue that film technique should be used to substantially restructure actuality footage and that the use of film form should be foregrounded as part of this project. Implicit in this is also the idea that a naturalistic documentary approach is inferior to a more modernist one because it is overbased on the naturalism of the image and denies the role of the constructing process. This view also reflects the key Marxist distinction between naturalism and realism, one that Balázs, as a Marxist, was also influenced by. Here, naturalism is regarded as inferior to realism because of its inability to indicate the deeper structures of reality, though, rather than because it disguises the formative processes of textual construction.

In addition to the desire to foreground technique and avoid the vicissitudes of naturalism, however, Balázs's position was also influenced by a desire, common at the time, to focus on the philosophical and formal aesthetic specificity of the documentary film. This imperative is apparent, for example, in the approach taken by another early theorist, Rudolph Arnheim, who argued that film should demonstrate its reality as a signifying structure by refocusing attention from the object represented to the specific characteristics and conventions of the medium. This clearly rules out an excessively naturalistic approach and also led Arnheim to consider documentary as inferior to the fiction film, because documentary was inherently unable to utilise the full range of aesthetically specific forms available to the film in general. In terms of the idea of cinematic aesthetic specificity, therefore, documentary is regarded here as a lesser, or subsidiary cinematic genre.

Arnheim's concern with the aesthetic specificity of the cinema stemmed from a formalist tradition that also influenced two other influential early Russian formalist theorists and filmmakers: Sergei Eisenstein and Dziga Vertov. One central feature of Russian cinematic formalism, as perhaps with any species of formalist aesthetics, was a desire to uncover the underlying structure of film form, and principles of construction that were specifically "cinematic." This imperative to establish the specific interior principles of representation of the medium played an important role in influencing the development of the Soviet montage cinema of the 1920s, and, also, Eisenstein's first theory of montage: the "montage of attractions." Russian formalism, however, was also influenced by yet another fundamental notion, and one that was to influence Dziga Vertov far more than Eisenstein: the idea of *ostranenie,* an idea initially derived from kantian aesthetics, and particularly from the Kantian notion of *Naturschöne.* Both these tendencies also make clear that, within the terms of this particular formalist approach to film form, the relationship between internal formal structures is more important than the question of the relationship between documentary film and reality. Even though, at one level, the relationship of film to reality was *supposed* to be a central concern of these Marxist filmmakers, in practice their alignment with formalist modernism led them away from the issue and toward a stance that was at odds with the official, more directly "realist" position derived from Engelsian Marxist aesthetics.

Ostranenie, or to "make strange," was initially advocated by the Russian formalist theorist Viktor Shklovsky. In contradistinction to the formalist imperative to seek underlying forms and principles, an essentially reductive exercise, *ostranenie* emphasises the need to complicate representation as it is experienced by a spectator, and so stretch out and problematise the process of aesthetic experience. Shklovsky believed, following Kant, that, in an "instrumental" modern world, art had a particularly important role to play in creating the conditions that would enable a free subjectivity to flourish. *Ostranenie* was one of the means through which art could attempt to carry out such a vocation. Following Shklovsky, Vertov embodied something like the principle of *ostranenie* in his *The Man with a Movie Camera* (1929), one of the most important documentary films in the history of the medium. The contrast between the two previously mentioned central principles of formalism, however, also led to a dispute between Eisenstein and Vertov over the character and import of documentary film. In *The Man with a Movie Camera,* for example, Vertov assembles what he refers to as "cine-facts" (actuality shots) so as to build up an impressionist account of a day in the life of Moscow. Here, Vertov rejects all preexisting literary, theatrical, and filmic conventions that had their origins in bourgeois culture and argues that film should capture the new life of the Soviet era "as it exists." The documentary film should seek to capture "life caught unaware," through the use of the "film eye," and should then seek to organise examples of "life caught unaware" into a work of "film-facts." The result is *The Man with the Movie Camera.* Vertov's conception of such an "unstaged" documentary film, however, led him into dispute with Eisenstein, over the latter's reliance on literary and theatrical forms. Vertov, and others associated with the journal *Novy Lef,* accused Eisenstein of excessively transforming reality in films such as his *October* (1928). Eisenstein, in turn, criticised Vertov for making ambiguous, impressionistic films and countered Vertov's notion of the *ostranenie*-like "film-eye" with the more directive notion of the "film-fist." What is really at issue here, however, in terms of issues of documentary and realism, is the relationship that should be adopted between documentary as a form of perceptual naturalism, and as an aesthetic construct; and, also—something far more politically controversial—the relationship that should be declared between documentary as an absolutely original aesthetic form, and one that still bears the traces of preexisting aesthetic positions. Here, the question is not just whether or not documentary film is an aesthetically *specific* cultural form, but also an aesthetically *new* one. And as with formalist modernism, however, the adoption of the latter avant-gardist stance was at odds with the recuperative-realist stance taken by officials such as Anatole Lunacharsky, the Commissar for Culture, when he asserted in 1923 that "I am a great protagonist of the renaissance of realism . . . classical realism."

Unlike this "official" position on philosophical aesthetics, Eisenstein, Arnheim, and Vertov also believed that film form should be foregrounded. Unlike Eisenstein and Arnheim, however, Vertov also places considerable emphasis on the importance of the naturalistic potential of documentary and its ability to display the phenomenal world in all its indeterminate complexity. In this respect, Vertov's position can be associated with Husserl's philosophical idea of the *Lebenswelt,* which will be discussed later, as well as with notions such as *ostranenie* and *Naturschöne.* Given this, we can provisionally define Vertov's position, in philosophical aesthetic terms, as a form of modernist naïve documentary realism (naïve, given Vertov's advocacy of the "ciné-fact") pemised on an intuitionist model of knowledge.

As mentioned earlier, Balázs' *Theory of Film* embodied the more formative approach to film associated with the ideas of Eisenstein and Arnheim. In his earlier *Der Sichtbare Mensch oder Der Kultur des Films* (1924), however, Balázs was, as with Vertov, both more sympathetic to the empirical aspect of the documentary film and also more wedded to an indeterminate intuitionist model of knowledge. For Balázs, like Grierson, it is the ability of the documentary image to express a nonrational truth or reality, through its evocative portrayal of the visual world, which is important. Grierson's adoption of an intuitionist model of knowledge stemmed from his influence by American mass communication theory in the 1920s, and this influence led him to argue that the evocative form and content of the documentary film could communicate to the masses in a generalised, impressionistic way and may also be consumed in the same manner. Though not influenced by scientific naturalist mass communication models, Balázs, like Shklovsky, was also influenced by a kantian critique of modernist rationality, and this led him, as Grierson, to adopt intuitionism instead of rationalism. Here, in his 1924 piece, Balázs endorses a primarily visual and noncognitive aesthetic, which, in emphasising the importance of empirical observation, also implies an advocacy for the latent inherent consequence of the documentary film.

This idea—that the documentary image was able to portray abstract forms of reality in an intuitive manner—influenced much theory to emerge in France and Germany during the 1920s and 1930s. In the case of both countries, notions of the inherent importance of documentary were also based on intuitionist, rather than empiricist or rationalist, models of knowledge. In Germany, for example, the belief that language was inscribed within dominant and oppressive forms of "instrumental rationality" and ideology led to the emergence of a notion that visual experience constituted an alternative domain of potential freedom from linguistic, rational determination. The visual was seen as embodying a primal and underlying mode of communication, which offered the possibility of a return to sensory contact, and, consequently, to a more valid form of human experience. In this sense, the visual is both primordial and *new*, as it was for Vertov. Whilst Vertov looked to the visual for evidence of the existence of a new era, Balázs looked to the visual for traces of the premodern. This emphasis on a return to the primordial visual and concrete as redemptive, clearly, once more, signals the particular importance that might be ascribed to documentary, and was also, again, influenced by two crucial philosophical ideas

already discussed: Kant's concept of *Naturschöne* and Husserl's notion of the *Lebenswelt*. Both these ideas imply a form of aesthetic experience that is rich in empirical detail, and both conform to, or allow one to theorise, a particular form of aesthetic documentary representation.

In France, this irrationalist, intuitionist approach to documentary film led to the emergence of a belief in the particular importance of documentary over the feature film. A key influence here was the impact of another seminal documentary film: Robert Flaherty's *Nanook of the North* (1923). After watching Flaherty's film, for example, André Sauvage argued that documentary film was the highest expression of "pure cinema." Here, Sauvage means that documentary, through its ability to render the natural world in terms of it own natural expressive beauty, is able to reveal and communicate significant knowledge about reality. Again, as with Balázs and Weimar film theory, what we find here is an intuitionist model of knowledge, one that is concerned with the expressive potential, and aesthetic experience, of the documentary film. Here also, however, Sauvage and others hint at the interpretation of the documentary film through the perspective of something approaching the kantian sublime. Flaherty's film, and particularly its depiction of the natural environment, was often discussed in such terms at the time. The elevation of the aesthetic is also apparent here, and such elevation has its roots in a French romantic and symbolist tradition that also influenced French cinematic impressionism and pictorialist naturalism, in films such as André Antoine's *La Terre* (1921).

Although the film theories of Bazin and Siegfried Kracauer was not specifically oriented toward the documentary film, they were, nonetheless, still based on the documentary capacities of the film image. Both theorists, for example, emphasised the importance of film's ability to reproduce perceptual reality, and, like Grierson, both theorists also saw this ability as a profoundly redemptive one for the human condition within modernity. Kracauer's work was strongly influenced by the ides of Max Weber and the Frankfurt School, and he was particularly influenced by their view that, in modernity, the experience of subjectivity has become a "disenchanted" and "abstract" one. Although accepting this, however, Kracauer also argued that a return to the concrete and particular through experience of the realistic film image was able to counter such abstraction. Such a position clearly suggests that, as part of such a return, the documentary film would have an important role to play. Using terminology derived from Alfred

North Whitehead's *Science and the Modern World* (1925), for example, which Kracauer discusses briefly in his own *Theory of Film*, Kracauer argues that the solution to the problem of modernity lies in a return to the concrete labyrinth of the *Lebenswelt*, in order to experience things in all their "poignancy," "preciousness," and "concreteness." Later, in *Theory of Film*, Kracauer quotes Whitehead more fully to expand on what the latter might mean by such a return to the "poignancy preciousness and concreteness" of immediate experience:

> When you understand all about the sun and all about the atmosphere and all about the rotation of the earth, you may still miss the radiance of the sunset. There is no substitute for the direct perception of the concrete achievement of a thing in its actuality. We want concrete fact with a high light thrown on what is relevant to its preciousness.

In addition to Kracauer, this same approach to the importance of the empirical can also be found in the ideas of André Bazin, although he was more influenced by the phenomenology of Bergson and existentialism of Sartre than by Kant, Weber, or Husserl.

All the positions referred to previously can be loosely defined in philosophical terms as forms of "representational realism." Here, representation can be thought of as linked to reality, but not in a direct way, as it is in forms of naïve realism. In representational realism, it is assumed that representation can, at least in principle, "converge" with some sort of reality, although that reality may be both an abstract one, and one that remains largely out of reach, because it exists beyond our conceptual schemes and representations. A representational realist position also accepts that a documentary representation is a constructed, signifying article, and that this means that such a representation can never converge totally with reality, or the truth. A representational realist position contains within it the propensity to slip into conceptual idealism: the notion that representations do not represent reality in any substantial way at all, but primarily mobilise concepts, ideas, and forms of rhetorical discourse. Such an approach takes us away from the approach to documentary representation discussed so far, and into a more recent realm of thought, in which the documentary is regarded mainly as a structure of semantic and syntactic conventions. Such a "conventionalist" approach to documentary epistemologically is at odds with a philosophical realist approach and with representational realism of Balázs, Grierson, Bazin, and Kracauer, because it is not premised on the idea that representation can converge with reality. The "screen theory" approach of the 1970s is based on this idea. For example, Bill Nichols argues, in *Screen*, in 1976, that:

> We need to examine the formal structures of the documentary film, the codes and units which are involved, in order to re-see documentary, not as a kind of reality frozen in the amber of the photographic image a la Bazin, but as a semiotic system which generates meaning by the succession of choices between differences, the continuous selection of pertinent features. Despite the denunciation of various cinematic realisms this work has scarcely begun with documentary.

(Nichols 1976)

The difference of tone here, when compared to the quotation from *Theory of Film*, is particularly marked, and also betrays a different aesthetic position on the documentary film.

Nichols's quote sums up the approach of screen theory, and the professed need to mount a "denunciation of various cinematic realisms" is emblematic of the position that screen theory adopted in relation to the question of realism and the documentary film. The object, in terms of screen theory, was to understand documentary as a signifying structure, rather than as something that could be said to represent reality. The paradigmatic shift from utopian representation in *Theory of Film* to critical deconstruction of signification here was based on the presumed need to understand how representations, such as documentary, mobilise ideological configurations, and, how the idea of "reality" was often used to naturalise dominant ideology. After Nichols, most critical studies on documentary to appear in the 1970s and 1980s under the overall umbrella of a post-Saussurian, screen theory stance, also adopted this approach. The concept of reality, and of the ability of documentary to represent reality, was, in turn, marginalised, as critical study focused on how documentary film mobilised forms of rhetoric to create the so-called "impression of reality." In the 1980s, this approach was also reinforced by a postmodern-pragmatist turn, strongly influenced by Foucault, Derrida, and others, which tended to regard documentary representation as connected to ideology and the priorities of interest groups. Here, documentary was primarily seen as a player in a political struggle, either on behalf of dominant groups or minorities.

Yet, at hardly any point did such theorists stop to ponder on the philosophical implications of the position they were promoting. This position was, essentially, a conceptual idealist, relativist, pragmatist one, which rejected ideas of objectivity, truth, and warranted best model. Such a position is fraught with obvious difficulty, because it implies that documentary film does not, in fact, represent reality at all and is unable to achieve any kind of truth or objectivity. But if that is the case, then documentary film's presumptions concerning its explanatory potential is a delusion, and the medium is just as much a "fictional" one as is the Hollywood feature film. In effect, the idea that documentary film is little more than a self-interested rhetorical structure removes part of the value from the medium, and we have come a long way indeed from the ideas of Grierson, Balázs, Kracauer, and Bazin. The question of convergence remained an important one for documentary film, however, because most lay people still assume that documentary film is able to be more than just a form of conventional rhetoric, and that it is able, in some way, to represent reality well, or fairly, or "truthfully." Given this, it could be argued that a defense of documentary film in terms of realism is necessary to stop what Trigg calls "the chill winds of relativism blowing ever stronger." What will be attempted now, therefore, will be an endeavor to, necessarily schematically, theorise documentary film in relation to conceptions of convergence, reference, and truth value at the philosophical level. The chill winds of relativism may blow elsewhere across the field of the documentary film, but, in these final pages, the warming rays of realism as an absolute will be brought to bear.

The issue of realism and documentary film will be theorised here in two related ways: in terms of the importance of the empirical, and in terms of the relation between the empirical and theory. One attempt, within the philosophy of science, to show how the empirical (and as will be argued later, for our purposes, the documentary film) can be theorised as the basis for the convergence between reality and representation can be associated with the ideas of the analytical philosopher, Mary Hesse. Hesse draws on the ideas of three other analytical philosophers, F. Duhem, Hilary Putnam, and W. V. O. Quine, to develop what she calls a "machine analogy" for perception, in which she argues that there is a constant and invariant relationship between data reaching us from the external world and our cognitive and perceptual processing mechanisms. This invariant relationship enables realism to hypothesise a symbolic equivalent between conceptual schemes and forces and phenomena in the external world. It is, then, the invariant interface between external data and internal coding principles, and the cumulative information that results from this, which enables the possibility of postulating an indirect symbolic equivalence between external reality and conceptual schemes (and therefore, as will be argued later, between external reality and documentary represen-

tation). Empirical experience may be the product of symbolic transformation, as perceptual data is transformed into what Hesse calls "coded input," but it is also the phenomenal manifestation of the invariant factors involved in the interaction between our faculties and the external world. This appears to give the empirical (and an empirically based form of film such as the documentary) an important status.

Hesse's notion provides a philosophical model of how our documentary "projections" might be thought to "converge" with reality. Such a model, however, cannot be explored much further here, given constraints of wordage. What will be attempted instead will be something more targeted: an analysis of documentary realism in terms of yet another philosophical realist principle (though, one that is also shared with philosophical pragmatism), that of "warranted assertibility," particularly in relation to the use of theory and evidence. In addition to the brief account of the relation between projection and convergence just given, therefore, it will be argued here that an enhanced account of documentary realism can also be theorised through exploring the documentary film in relation to the issue of truth-value and warranted assertibility in the use of evidence and theory. It is also admitted, however, that such an enterprise elides important distinctions that should be made between representational realism and pragmatism.

There are, of course, many different types of documentary film. For the purpose of this exercise, however, one type only will be considered here: what Nichols refers to as the classical "expository" documentary. Documentary films tend to appear in this form on a day-to-day basis, and this is the staple form of the genre, one that millions of people rely on to give them "the facts" about the world around them, or at least, interpret those facts plausibly soundly. The object here, therefore, in this final section of this essay, is to discuss the issue of documentary realism, not in terms of conventionalised rhetoric or discursive formations (such terms are the basis of most critical work on documentary film and do not need to be repeated here), but in terms of the way a documentary film may be seen to utilise theory and evidence in a "warranted" manner to portray reality. This is not to underplay the importance of investigations into the rhetoric and discourse of the documentary film, but to emphasise that here, we are principally concerned with documentary and realism in terms of questions of warranted assertability, theory, and evidence.

One model that can be drawn on in this respect is the "network" theory of meaning, which is derived from philosophers such as Hesse, Quinn, Putnam, and Duhem. Here, a theory is regarded as consisting of a network of theoretical categories, ranging from the abstract to the intermediate to the particular and formed around a set of core concepts internal to that particular theory. The most abstract categories constitute the centre of the theory. These abstract concepts both generate and imply a network of associated and dependent intermediate theoretical categories, which contain a greater degree of reference to observable, empirical phenomena. Ideally, this theoretical network is then applied to a subject of enquiry, which is conceived of as problematic in some respect, and some initial, provisional hypotheses are proposed, based largely on the internal categories of the theoretical network, and their assumed a priori ability to explain the subject of enquiry. The theoretical network is then brought into conjunction with a more extensive network of observable empirical information, whose function is to qualify the theoretical network, and its account of the object of enquiry. This empirical information is not theory neutral, but consists of "empirical concepts," which are derived from observable phenomena, but which are also constituted and influenced by the theoretical network. There is, therefore, no theory neutral empirical data that can "test" the truth of interpretation in any direct sense, either in relation to the subject of enquiry or in relation to other theories. The primary function of the empirical material is to modify and affect terms and relations within the theoretical network, leading to a realignment of theoretical categories and relations, and therefore to a modification of the theory's explanation of the subject of enquiry.

This process of qualification is necessarily influenced by the fact that the empirical material is always constituted in terms of the determining theoretical framework in the first place, but it nevertheless also provides a catalyst through which theoretical categories can potentially be affected. This is because empirical material inevitably, and always, contains a quantity and diversity of terms and relations that are more extensive than those contained within a theoretical network, and this acts as a catalyst, which impels the network to adapt its internal terms and relations to accommodate the material. Whereas, in some cases, this may be primarily an act of assimilation, designed to verify the core internal categories of the theory, it may also generate a process of qualification and internal inquiry that leads to radical alterations within the theoretical network. For example, those interpretations whose postulates conflict increasingly with the empirical will, or at least ought to, undergo a more extensive reevaluation of their central imperatives and evolve into new paradigms. Theories should be capable of rational critique based on both logical coherence criteria and the empirical, and, if empirical categories are not used, a theory will tend to evolve only in relation to the coherence logic implied by its core postulates.

Whilst the preceding can function as a generalised model of the use of evidence and theory in interpretation within the philosophy of science, it also indicates how the documentary film, as an expository aesthetic form, might use theory and evidence to produce accounts of the world. For example, a "classical," "expository," documentary film may consist of one or more systems of theoretical categories, ranging from the abstract to the intermediate to the particular, and organised around one or more sets of core concepts, which are applied to an object of enquiry. The object of enquiry is first conceived of as problematic and as requiring interpretation. A number of alternative formats are possible at this stage. Either the documentary could present a number of theoretical paradigms on a comparative basis, or one might be used and then elaborated at length. The first approach may tend toward a "centrist" explanation, or relatively exterior analysis of the subject; in the second approach, there may also be less ability for prevailing paradigms of interpretation to be effectively countered, given that the alternatives postulated would be given only marginal representation. Of course, the second approach could lead to a radical challenge to prevailing paradigms if it mobilised an oppositional theoretical network. But we are dealing here with the dominant, staple, and institutional form of the expositional documentary film, and, in this respect, deployment of the second approach referred to previously is more likely to legitimate, rather than challenge, the dominant paradigm.

Which ever format is used, however, the same process and deployment of empirical and theoretical categories would, in an ideal situation, take place as follows. First, a network of theoretical categories provide descriptions of the subject as problematic and also provides provisional accounts of causality, effects, and solutions to the problematic. At this stage of the process, the role of the empirical is mainly to provide an a priori substantiation for the theories being used to scrutinise the subject of enquiry. These provisionally substantiated theories, however, would then be brought into conjunction with a more extensive range of observable empirical material relating to the object of enquiry. Each encounter with a complex empirical situation presents a theory with a range of alternative potential explanations, and empirical information presents a degree of richness that both resists absorption and, at the same time, suggests antithetical paradigms. Antithesis will also be suggested by the abstract terms and relations of the theory, as these cannot be rationally formulated without reference to their antithesis in the first place. But it is at the empirical level that the antithesis is most apparent, because, even though the empirical is absorbed into concepts within the network, the richness of empirical material and attendant ability to suggest additional structures of causality and content, resists complete absorption. The greater the range of empirical material encountered, the more likely it will also be for alternatives to be generated.

This model of warranted assertibility in the use of theory and evidence suggests how a certain type of documentary film: The standard expository film (which, of course, may not exist in any pure sense) can be understood in terms of one of the principles of philosophical realism. Of course, there are both other types of documentary film and other philosophical realist principles that could be applied to them. It also remains to apply the model described previously to specific examples of the documentary film. Nevertheless, it should be apparent that the model of warranted assertibility in the use of theory and evidence set out here can be applied to scrutiny of the sort of documentary film, or news report, that we see on our screens everyday, and would provide a better model than the semi-theorised ones currently used by professional broadcasters and journalists. Finally, this account of documentary film and realism is meant to be a guide for structuring the classical expository documentary film to achieve best model status in the use of theory and evidence. This does not necessarily mean, however, that such models can be said to be "true," and discussions concerning documentary representations and the correspondence theory of truth and truth-values are found elsewhere.

IAN AITKEN

Further Reading

Aitken, Ian, "John Grierson, Idealism and the Inter-war Period," in *Historical Journal of Film, Radio and Television*, 9, 3, 1989.
———, "Distraction and Redemption: Kracauer, Surrealism and Phenomenology," in *Screen*, 39, 2, summer 1998.
———, *European Film Theory and Cinema, a Critical Introduction*, Edinburgh: Edinburgh University Press, 2001.
———, *Film and Reform: John Grierson and the Documentary Film Movement*, London: Routledge, 1990, 1992.
———, "The Documentary Film Movement," in *The British Cinema Book*, edited by Robert Murphy, London: BFI, 2001.
———, *Realist Film Theory and Cinema*, Manchester: Manchester University Press, 2005.
Allen, Richard, and Smith, Murray (eds.), *Film Theory and Philosophy*, Oxford: Clarendon Press, 1997.
Arnheim, Rudolph, *Film*, London: Faber and Faber, 1933.
Balázs, Béla, *Der sichtbare Mensche oder Der Kultur Des Films*, Vienna and Leipzig: Deutsch-Osterreichischer Verlag, 1924.
Bazin, André, *What Is Cinema?* Volume 1, Berkeley and Los Angeles: University of California Press, 1967.
———, *What Is Cinema?* Volume II, Berkeley and Los Angeles: University of California Press, 1972.
Furst, Lilian, R. (ed.), *Realism*, London and New York: Longman, 1992.
Hake, Sabine, (ed.), *The Cinema's Third Machine: Writing on Film in Germany 1907–1933*, London, Lincoln: University of Nebraska Press, 1993.
Harré, Rom, *The Philosophies of Science, An Introductory Survey*, Oxford, New York: Oxford University Press, 1972.
———, *Varieties of Realism*, Oxford: Blackwell, 1996.
Kracauer, Siegfried, *The Mass Ornament, Weimar Essays*, Cambridge, MA, London: Harvard University Press, 1995.
———, *Theory of Film, The Redemption of Physical Reality*, Princeton, NJ: Princeton University Press, 1997.
MacCabe, Colin, "Realism and the Cinema: Notes on Some Brechtian Theses," in *Screen*, 15, 2, summer 1974.
Putnam, Hilary, *Representation and Reality*, Cambridge, MA, London: The MIT Press, 1991.
Winston, Brian, *Claiming the Real: The Documentary Film Revisited*, London: BFI, 1995.

REALITY TELEVISION

Reality television is a product of the 1990s, arising from structural changes to the television industry in the 1980s, coalescing in the early 1990s with real-crime/emergency service programmes, and developing by the end of the decade into the worldwide sweep of *Big Brother*. Ten years after its beginnings, the real-crime series *Cops* (US/Fox network) has become a television institution (Mitchell, 2002), *Big Brother* has spawned forty different versions and *Popstars* twenty-two series around the world. Reality television formats are diversifying into a staggering range of subgenres.

Despite being regularly condemned as cheap programming and "trash TV," reality television has changed the television landscape, challenging the dominance of sitcoms and dramas, edging out news magazines, and influencing the shape and address of TV documentaries.

By the mid-1990s, critical responses to reality TV had crystallized into three positions, which Jon Dovey has named the "trash TV," "empowerment," and "nightmare" approaches (Dovey, 2000: 83). The "trash TV" position is an extension of the Frankfurt School critique of mass culture and sees reality television as the product of market-led tabloidisation and the "dumbing down" of audiences. In this perspective, producers are constantly looking for ways to minimize costs and maximize ratings, on the basis that audiences will gravitate to anything that offers thrills and is not too intellectually demanding.

The "empowerment" position, by contrast, celebrates reality television for providing everyday voices with access to public media and "fostering interactive participation in social space" (Dovey, 2000: 83). From this perspective, reality television counteracts the paternalism of traditional public-service television by giving voice to people's very real anxieties, concerns, and behaviours (Glynn, 2000).

The "nightmare" position takes reality television to be an inevitable product of the postmodern culture of simulacra, where referentiality has been displaced by simulation, dissolving into "the non-being and nothingness of TV" (Nichols, 1994: 52). To these three critical positions must be added at least one other, which concerns itself with the relations between reality television cameras and power. Such an approach covers issues of public surveillance, the production of celebrity, and the voyeuristic appeal of reality programming.

As with any evolving form, reality television defies easy definition. Programmes that fall into this genre, however, share three basic characteristics: they use nonactors, are nonscripted, and hence fall into the zone of nonfiction. In more loaded terms, reality television is an example of "factual programming," which uses "ordinary people" who act, react, and interact before cameras without scripts. As a genre of factual programming, reality television shares certain similarities with information/news programming on the one hand and documentary on the other, but should be differentiated from both. Unlike news programmes, reality television shows rely heavily on postproduction techniques such as editing and music to incorporate elements of narrative and even melodrama. This leads some critics to say that its strongest generic affinity is with soap opera (Roscoe, 2001: 480f). Indeed, like the soap opera, reality television shows (sometimes referred to as "docusoaps") highlight personal and emotional issues through an emphasis on the conflictual interactions of individuals. It is thus perhaps best to categorize reality television as factual entertainment, in recognition of its hybrid mix of "fact and fiction, drama and documentary," reality and artifice (Roscoe, 2001).

Unlike documentaries, which reflect on sociohistorical contexts to educate or inform the public, reality television is about individuals without historical subjectivity, who are placed in an ever-present temporality (Nichols, 1994). The main focus of reality television is not to document lived reality but to capture individuals in a situation of "heightened reality." Such a situation may well be constructed, particularly in those programmes that follow the *Big Brother* model of creating artificial living environments for participants. Rather than assuming that reality television dupes audiences into mistaking the artificial for the real, however, it is important to consider that producers and audiences alike recognize the constructed aspects of the shows (Roscoe, 2001: 479). The "undocumentary" ways in which reality television shows draw attention to the camera highlight emotional conflict and set up situations for maximum dramatic effect have in turn begun to influence documentary-making (see John Corner on "postdocumentary," 2002).

While the relation of reality television to documented history is the subject of often critical speculation (Nichols, 1994), the history of reality television itself can be stated with some certainty. Reality television traces its history in large part to caught-on-tape TV, going as far back as *Candid Camera* (1959–1967), through versions of practical-joke programmes, natural disaster footage, talent-search series, and amateur-video shows. These programmes, seen in various local forms throughout the 1980s and into the 1990s, in each case involve some element of the reality television mix; they use either ordinary people, hidden or portable camera technology, and/or affect-inducing footage, from laughter to thrills (cf. the "When Tornadoes Strike" genre). In addition to this specific television history, larger social forces have influenced the growth of reality TV, such as the tendency toward a breakdown of distinct private and public zones (van Zoonen, 2001), which is often manifested in the "personalization" of the public-interest sphere (Macdonald, 2000), as well as the move toward greater inclusion of minority or marginalized voices in the media (Holland, 2001: 85f). As Jon

Dovey points out, reality television in the United Kingdom can be said to have roots in Social Action Broadcasting, developed in the 1970s with the aim of providing people access to appearing on television (Dovey, 2000: 86f).

The beginnings of reality TV in the United States were signaled with *Unsolved Mysteries* (NBC, 1987) followed by *America's Most Wanted* (Fox, 1988), both of which used dramatic reconstructions as an emotional backdrop for soliciting aid from viewers to catch criminals. In its ethos of public appeal and faith in the state juridical system, *America's Most Wanted* is not unlike *Crimewatch UK* (BBC), which began in 1984. By 1990, the public-appeal reconstruction programme was supplemented by the ride-along programme, where a camera-person accompanies the police or detective team as they go out on calls. The exemplar of the ride-along programme, and its longest-running series, is *Cops* (Fox, 1990), a half-hour show consisting of three segments, each centred on police officers from different areas of the United States, who frame their particular segment with reflections on the city and the "nab" in voice-over.

The first-generation reality television programmes, dominated by police and emergency services, produced a staggering number of derivatives in the mid-1990s. The American *Rescue 911*, for instance, ran in Britain as *Emergency 999*, in Australia as *Emergency 000*, in Germany as *Notruf*, and in Spain as *Lines 900*. In the United States, this generation included shows such as *American Detective, Top Cops*, and *Code 3*; in Britain the BBC's *Crimewatch* and *Emergency 999* was rivaled by ITV's *Police Camera Action* and *Blues and Twos*.

Second-generation reality television, which places people in a challenging situation and usually pits them against each other, can be traced to the first series of *Big Brother*, originating in Holland in late 1999. Though the Dutch producers of *Big Brother*, Endemol, are generally credited with the reality television turn from criminal-catching to social experimentation with a houseful of strangers, the rise of this second phase goes back earlier, to MTV's long-running series *The Real World* (1992), Sweden's proto-*Survivor* programme *Expedition Robinson* (1997), and even the radical endurance-and-embarrassment game shows in Japan, which involve challenging contestants to complete potentially dangerous acts. (For example, a man, code-named "Nasubi," was locked into an empty apartment and allowed to use nothing but winnings from magazine contests to feed and clothe himself [McNett, 2000]). Nonetheless, it was the massive

ratings and financial success of *Big Brother* that changed the face of reality TV programming.

From Holland *Big Brother* spread within a few months to Germany and on to the rest of Europe, including the United Kingdom and Poland, and then to the United States (CBS)—the only country where it received average ratings—and overseas to Argentina and Australia. Not everyone commissioned the format, but *Big Brother* derivatives still appeared, such as *Taxi Orange* in Austria and *Loft Story* in France. In many countries, the format caused public outcry, such as in Germany, where there were protests by the regional government, in France, where *Loft Story* met with intellectual opprobrium, and in Portugal, where the Church protested (see Mathijs and Jones, 2004).

The idea of isolating a group of strangers, carefully chosen to represent a social demographic on the one hand and to inspire intense interactions on the other, has since spawned various subgenres: the dating/relationship category (for example, *Temptation Island, Perfect Match*, and the long-running *Bachelor/Bachelorette* series), the challenge category (most notoriously *Survivor*, but also travel-and-discovery shows such as *The Mole* and *The Amazing Race*), and the talent category (*Popstars* followed by *Pop Idol*, but also extending to proto-models, proto-chefs, and even proto-enterpreneurs, as in *The Apprentice*). Notably, all of these programmes provide a rationale for the participants in the form of cash or fame (or both), as well as an incentive to viewer engagement in the form of regular expulsions of participants. Many of them also draw on media convergence, supporting television with Internet and mobile phone platforms, as conceived in the original *Big Brother* format. Recently, the makeover show, which began its life with neighbours doing over one another's bedroom or lounge in *Changing Rooms*, has expanded from property to people, engaging not only builders but also designers and cosmetic surgeons in a form of consumer therapy that involves making houses and people beautiful.

The transportability of reality television formats, resulting in large part from the globalization of media forms, is a basic facet of reality TV. Yet reality television is not an example of full-scale globalization. The format may be global, but the content is always local. This applies not only to local production teams and nationally chosen participants, but also to the popularity of certain shows. Not every format works in every country, indicating that reality TV formats hit up against marked differences in cultural formations. *Big Brother*, for instance, has been a ratings failure in the United States relative to the ongoing success of the *Survivor* series (in the second series of *Big Brother* on CBS, a producer was hired to make the show more competitive, more strategy-oriented—in other words, more like *Survivor*). In the United Kingdom and Australia, on the other hand, *Big Brother* has been highly popular, especially in the coveted 18 to 49 age group, whereas *Survivor* caused barely a blip on the television radar in either country. Similarly, *Temptation Island* has proved popular in Romania but not India. This indicates that reality TV formats are not as mobile and translatable as globalism may suggest, but rather that these programmes circulate within, and help define, deeply ingrained cultural discourses and modes of collective self-understanding.

While media commentators in 2001–2002 were predicting the demise of reality television, the third series of *Big Brother* in the United Kingdom achieved unheard-of ratings for Channel 4, the U.S. Fox network received huge ratings for the first series of *American Idol* (remade from the UK *Pop Idol*), and MTV signed the Osbournes to a lucrative second season of the real-family series. Reality TV, it would appear, will not quietly pass into television history; rather, it continues to evolve, producing new subgenres and influencing other genres of media culture. The highbrow dismissiveness of the "trash TV" position jostles with attempts to take more seriously the popular appeal of reality television, from the opportunity it provides for viewer interactivity (Roscoe, 2001), to its fulfillment of a "widely shared desire for everyday recognizability" (van Zoonen, 2001), to the more general role played by television in a shifting "ethos of engagement or relationality" (Hawkins, 2001). The media convergence of television with Internet, telephone, and print journalism is helping to position reality television in the midst of this "ethos of engagement," as manifested by viewer interactions, call-in voting,

and in some cases chat rooms with the participants themselves. Reality television thus suggests the burgeoning of a rather different, and hotly contested, participatory "public" within media culture.

MISHA KAVKA

See also **Television Documentary: Critical Overview of**

Further Reading

Andrejevic, Mark, *Reality TV: The Work of Being Watched*, Lanham, MD: Rowman & Littlefield, 2004.

Corner, John, "Performing the Real: Documentary Diversions," in *Television & New Media*, 3, 3, 2002, 255–270.

Dovey, Jon, *Freakshow: First Person Media and Factual Television*, London: Pluto Press, 2000.

Fetveit, Arild, "Reality TV in the Digital Era: A Paradox in Visual Culture?" in *Media, Culture and Society*, 21, 1999, 787–804.

Fishman, Mark, and Gray Cavender (eds.), *Entertaining Crime: Television Reality Programs*, New York: Aldine de Gruyter, 1998.

Glynn, Kevin, *Tabloid Culture: Trash Taste, Popular Power, and the Transformation of American Television*, Durham, NC: Duke University Press, 2000.

Hawkins, Gay, "The Ethics of Television," in *International Journal of Cultural Studies*, 4, 4, 2001, 412–426.

Hill, Annette, and Gareth Palmer (eds.), Special Issue on *Big Brother* in *Television and New Media*, 3, 3, 2002.

McNett, "The Wacky World of Television," Salon.com, 13 March 2000.

Mathijs, Ernest, and Janet Jones (eds.), *Big Brother International: Formats, Critics and Publics*, London: Wallflower Press, 2004.

Mitchell, Elvis, "The Movies Can Credit a Cop Show," *New York Times*, June 30, 2002.

Nichols, Bill, *Blurred Boundaries: Questions of Meaning in Contemporary Culture*, Bloomington, IN: Indiana University Press, 1994.

Roscoe, Jane, "*Big Brother* Australia: Performing the 'Real' Twenty-four-seven," in *International Journal of Cultural Studies*, 4, 4, 2001, 473–488.

van Zoonen, Liesbet, "Desire and Resistance: *Big Brother* and the Recognition of Everyday Life," in *Media, Culture and Society*, 23, 2001, 669–677.

REEVES, JOSEPH

Joseph Reeves made a significant contribution to workers' cinema in Britain from the 1920s through the 1940s. He was also influential in developing youth work, workers' travel, leisure and education,

and pursuing politics and propaganda to effect social change.

As education secretary, Reeves was responsible for introducing film work at the Royal Arsenal

Co-operative Society after World War I. Commencing in 1920, film records of the Society's trading and cultural activities were taken, with the democratic aim of informing the working-class members about the collective business. Film shows were provided to children "for the purpose of counteracting the effect of the sensational film" (Reeves quoted in Burton, 1994), and late in the 1920s a suitably equipped hall was put at the disposal of the nascent London Workers' Film Society. Reeves was unusually prepared to work with the radical left and was an active Council Member with Kino and on the Directorial Board of the Progressive Film Institute, organisations close to the Communist Party of Great Britain. From the former was obtained a copy of Eisenstein's *The General Line* (1929), hired for a twelve-month period in 1934 and touring the Society's trading district in more than one hundred screenings.

In the mid-1930s, Reeves's experience in film propaganda was put to the wider advantage of the labour movement. At a Co-op conference in 1936 he proposed a national scheme for Co-operative education by film, and although the official body of the Co-operative Union did not take up the idea, the National Association of Co-operative Education Committees (NACECS) launched a National Film Society. This brought programmes of progressive films, on the cheaper 16mm format, to local Co-op members and was the stimulus to film work for the Trades Union Congress (TUC) and Labour Party, which sought to modernise their political publicity. Reeves was instrumental in the formation of the Workers' Film Association (WFA) in the autumn of 1938, and this brought together the three wings of the labour movement, the co-ops being represented initially by the NACECS. Reeves left the RACS to assume the post of Secretary-Organiser of the WFA and set about making the labour movement "film conscious."

The TUC and Labour Party had to be convinced of the value of film publicity, so Reeves used his influence and contacts in the cooperative movement to undertake a programme of cinema propaganda. With finance provided by the London Co-operative Societies' Joint Education Committee a "Five Year Film Plan" was commenced, the inaugural film being *Advance Democracy* (1938). This was an impressive blend of documentary and fiction, produced by the Realist Film Unit under the supervision of Film Centre. Reeves was an advocate of the social responsibility preached within the British documentary movement and

was keen to gain credibility through association and to take advantage of its professionalism in film production. Only one further film was realised in the Five Year Plan as war intervened in the production schedule. *The Voice of the People* (1939) was a film "which expressed in pictorial form the struggles of the workers to obtain their present important place in the state" (Reeves, 1944). The influence of Reeves and the WFA was evident over this production, which was financed by cooperative societies but took the broader labour movement, its struggles and aspirations, as its theme.

With these films Reeves sought to encourage the unions and Labour parties to become active in film propaganda. He wrote at the time:

> I would like to see the Railway Unions providing a film on the life of a railway man, the Transport Workers Union one on the risks a motor driver takes from day to day providing transport for people and goods; indeed the life of the great army of the workers, builders, miners, seamen, printers, electricians and others should be dramatised because their lives and work are the stuff of which life is made.

(Quoted in Burton, 1994)

Film commissions were slow to materialise, however, and just a handful of modest productions were completed. A WFA newsreel was commenced in 1939, but only appears to have run to a single issue, probably a consequence of the outbreak of war. The problems of the Association were further compounded when Reeves was appointed to the Films Division of the Ministry of Information in the spring of 1940. Although nominally the representative of the National Council of Labour, he seems to have experienced difficulties at the MOI and was active again at the WFA after a little over a year. The Association was eventually successful with film distribution and education. A film library and road show service was maintained throughout the war and a number of film schools attracted high profile lecturers like Michael Balcon, Basil Wright, Paul Rotha, Edgar Anstey, Artur Elton, and, of course, Joe Reeves.

After the war the WFA was replaced with a National Film Association to which Reeves acted as adviser. But this again existed largely on the generosity of the cooperative movement and was wound up in 1953 having failed to generate much interest in film publicity among the unions or Labour Party branches.

Reeves believed passionately in education for social change. For him the broader cultural activities sponsored by the labour movement played their part in "preparing its members for their growing social responsibilities in a society undergoing radical changes" (Reeves, 1944). The cinema was a potent modern means of mass education and Joe Reeves worked tirelessly to bring the cinema to the aid of the workers' movement.

ALAN BURTON

See also **Anstey, Edgar; Balcon, Michael; Elton, Arthur; Film Centre (UK); Rotha, Paul; Workers' Film Association; Wright, Basil**

Biography

Born in Camberwell, South London, January 28, 1888, the son of a printer. Apprenticed as a ticket and show card writer, before going into business as a sign writer and illuminator. At sixteen joined the Independent Labour Party and unsuccessfully stood for election in Camberwell in 1909. Secretary of the Christian Socialist Fellowship and assistant editor of the *Christian Socialist*. A conscientious objector during World War I. 1918–1938, Education Secretary Royal Arsenal Co-operative Society. 1938–1946, Secretary-Organiser, Workers' Film Association. Unsuccessfully contested the 1931 and 1936 Elections as a Labour-Co-operative candidate. 1945–1959, MP for Greenwich. 1946–1956, co-operative representative on the National Executive of the Labour Party. Served on numerous labour movement bodies and committees. Died on March 8, 1969 in Eastbourne, England.

Further Reading

Attfield, John *With Light of Knowledge: A Hundred Years of Education in the Royal Arsenal Co-operative Society, 1877–1977*, London, West Nyack: RACS/Journeyman Press, 1981.

Burton, Alan, *The People's Cinema. Film and the Co-operative Movement*, London: NFT, 1994.

———, *The British Co-operative Film Movement Film Catalogue*, Trowbridge: Flicks Books, 1997.

———, *The British Consumer Co-operative Movement and Film, 1890s to 1960s*, Manchester: MUP, 2005.

Reeves, Joseph, *The Film and Education*, Stoke: NACECS, 1936.

———, *Education for Social Change*, Manchester: Co-op Union, 1936.

———, *A Century of Rochdale Co-operation 1844–1944*, London: Lawrence and Wishart, 1944.

REFLEXIVITY

Reflexive and *reflexivity* are pivotal terms in contemporary documentary theory because they condense salient aspects of debates about documentary truth claims. Consequently, there are various definitions and uses of these terms. Brian Winston, for example, contrasts a realist tradition, consisting of the griersonian documentary and direct cinema, to an equally long-standing, albeit more marginalized, reflexive tradition encompassing any documentary that in some way reveals, rather than conceals, its processes of construction (Winston, 1995). Thus for Winston the reflexive tradition incorporates *Man with a Movie Camera* (Dziga Vertov, 1929), which makes explicit its makers' analytical organisation and interrogation of documentary footage in pursuit of a "higher mathematics of facts," beyond surface appearances. It also includes *Chronicle of a Summer* (Jean Rouch and Edgar Morin, 1961). In this film, the film makers' presence is overtly acknowledged. The truth produced by the film is situated as the result of interactions around and performances for the camera, which can nevertheless be profoundly revealing.

Bill Nichols, in an influential discussion of this topic, offers a narrower definition (Nichols, 1991). For Nichols, films in what he calls the reflexive mode of documentary utilise diverse strategies designed to unsettle any assumption on the part of the viewer that documentary provides some kind of straightforward access to truth. Reflexive documentaries are as much (or more) about their own construction as they are about their ostensible subject matter. They problematise not only the filmmaker's relationship to his or her filmed subjects but also the spectator's position within the basic processes of documentary representation. Some of the examples Nichols cites include *Of Great Events and Ordinary People* (Raul Ruiz, 1979), *Far From Poland* (Jill Godmilow, 1984), and *The Thin Blue Line* (Errol Morris, 1987).

Nichols links the emergence of a reflexive mode of documentary in the 1970s and 1980s to the skepticism inherent in poststructuralist and postmodernist critiques of the possibility of producing neutral, objective knowledge. This contemporary reflexivity is less epistemologically confident than earlier examples like *Man with a Movie Camera*. Yet even within Nichols's definition, different tendencies can be identified. One of these is explicitly political, although it does not deal in political certainties. A number of reflexive documentaries produced by radical leftist filmmakers in the late 1960s and 1970s were influenced by Louis Althusser's reformulation of the concept of ideology. Particularly significant was his notion that one of the basic functions of ideology was the interpellation of the subject into an imaginary position of coherence and unity in relation to social processes.

From this perspective the "impression of reality" produced by dominant forms of documentary had to be countered by a thoroughgoing reflexivity that unsettled any fixed position in relation to the representation of the social world. The imaginary coherence of bourgeois subjectivity would be fragmented, and this would encourage a more critical attitude on the part of the spectator. An active, critical attitude would also be fostered by setting different, even contradictory discourses into play without ultimately privileging one over the others. The documentaries produced by Jean-Luc Godard and his collaborators during the late 1960s and early 1970s belong to this tendency (MacCabe, 1980). *The Nightcleaners* (Berwick Street Collective, 1975) is a British example of political documentary reflexivity. Rather than inviting the adoption of a straightforwardly committed position, this film challenges the spectator to analyse the complexities of a unionisation campaign by a group of women nightcleaners. It also acknowledges some of the complexities of making a film about this topic (Johnston and Willemen, 1984).

Reassemblage (Trinh T. Minh-Ha, 1982) is an example of a slightly different reflexive tendency. This film, produced by a filmmaker thoroughly versed in contemporary critical theory, is a postmodernist critique of conventional anthropological documentary. *Reassemblage* seeks to emphasise the instability and mutability of the identities of both the observer and the observed. It strives to open up other, supposedly less authoritarian, ways of knowing and experiencing that are more attuned to cultural hybridity, heterogeneity, and contingency. *Reassemblage*'s reflexivity is far more comprehensive than *Chronicle of a Summer*'s references to the filmmakers' presence as a guarantee of honesty (Minh-Ha, 1991).

Shot in rural Senegal, *Reassemblage* has no central thematic focus and does not deliver conventional anthropological knowledge. The director's voice-over says it is "A film about Senegal; but what in Senegal?" *Reassemblage* uses decentred shot compositions and camera movements, which rarely come to rest in a secure framing. Jump cuts present alternate takes exploring what different camera positions reveal (Minh-Ha, 1992). The soundtrack stops and starts abruptly and the voice-over meditates at a tangent to the images. These strategies are designed to make explicit the film's materiality and to draw attention to choices and processes usually left implicit. *Reassemblage* does not arrive at a definitive, secure position on its subject matter. It attempts to leave the process of making meaning and responding to the film radically open rather than directing the viewer toward a fixed end point.

Debates about the value and effectiveness of both tendencies encompassed by Nichols's definition of the reflexive mode have been widely rehearsed within contemporary documentary theory. Contrary to what subsequent commentators such as Carl Plantinga and Stella Bruzzi have suggested, Nichols does not necessarily endorse the reflexive mode as superior to all others (Plantinga 1997; Bruzzi, 2000). One of the dangers he associates with this mode is that a preoccupation with problems of representation may overwhelm everything else. The reflexive documentary may become about nothing other than itself. The paramount issue for Nichols is political reflexivity; whether or not a documentary questions dominant ideology and contributes to the production of an alternative, progressive social consciousness on the part of its viewers. Films in the reflexive mode may serve this purpose in certain contexts, but formal reflexivity does not in itself guarantee this.

If reflexive documentary is considered in relation to concrete exhibition contexts and socially differentiated audiences, rather than just as an isolated text operating on an abstract spectator, a number of further issues come to the fore. It has been argued that a reflexive stance on the part of documentary filmmakers or theorists runs the risk of underestimating the critical acumen of audiences (Plantinga, 1997). It has also been pointed out that reflexive documentaries have traditionally been produced and exhibited within the independent film sector, rather than via mainstream broadcast institutions (Corner, 1996). Some documentary theorists have suggested that conditions of television viewing are not conducive to the active, critical questioning reflexivity demands (Kilborn and Izod,

1997). Alternatively, it can be argued, extrapolating from Pierre Bourdieu's sociology of taste, that reflexive documentary is generally avoided or rejected by popular audiences because of its association with the elitist "pure gaze," which prioritises form and detached contemplation over more utilitarian functions (Bourdieu, 1984).

MARTIN STOLLERY

See also *Chronicle of a Summer; Man With a Movie Camera; Thin Blue Line, The*

Further Reading

Bourdieu, Pierre, *Distinction: A Social Critique of the Judgement of Taste*, London: Routledge, 1984.
Bruzzi, Stella, *New Documentary: A Critical Introduction*, London: Routledge, 2000.
Corner, John, *The Art of Record*, Manchester: Manchester University Press, 1996.
Johnston, Claire, and Paul Willemen, "Brecht in Britain: *The Nightcleaners* and the Independent Political Film," in *Show Us Life*, edited by Thomas Waugh, Metuchen, NJ: Scarecrow Press, 1984, 192–211.
Kilborn, Richard, and John Izod, *An Introduction to Television Documentary*, Manchester: Manchester University Press, 1997.
Minh-Ha, Trinh T., *Framer Framed*, London: Routledge, 1992.
———, *When the Moon Waxes Red*, London: Routledge, 1991.
Nichols, Bill, *Representing Reality*, Bloomington and Indianapolis: Indiana University Press, 1991.
Plantinga, Carl, *Rhetoric and Representation in Nonfiction Film*, Cambridge: Cambridge University Press, 1997.
Winston, Brian, *Claiming the Real*, London: BFI, 1995.

REICHERT, JULIA

Julia Reichert was a prominent producer and director in the social issue documentary movement the 1970s and early 1980s. Of particular note are four documentaries she co-directed with James Klein. *Growing Up Female* (1971), the first documentary study of the American societal forces that mold female identities, influenced subsequent feminist documentaries through its combination of interviews, advertisements, and popular music. *Methadone: An American Way of Dealing* (1975) critiques the use of methadone as a method of combating drug addiction. Her next two documentaries were Oscar-nominated. *Union Maids* (1976) blends feminist and labor history through oral interviews of three women who played roles in the unionization drives in the United States during the 1930s. *Seeing Red: Stories of American Communists* (1983) records the personal oral histories of American Communist Party members from the 1930s to the 1950s.

After 1983, Reichert began working on dramatic films, although the subject of one of those films, *Emma and Elvis* (1992), is a middle-aged countercultural documentary filmmaker. She has recently returned to documentary filmmaking. She worked as a creative consultant on *Welcome to Warren* (2003), which examines the relationship of inmates and guards at the Warren Correctional Institution in Warren, Ohio, and she was a collaborator on *A People's History: Dayton's People's History, Twenty Years Later* (2003). In 1997, Reichert began work on *A Lion in the House*, which marks her return to directing. The film, scheduled to air on PBS in 2005, uses the subject of adolescent cancer patients as a context to discuss larger social issues such as health care, race, and poverty.

Like many social issue documentarians, Reichert is motivated by a particular political activism. Her primary interests are gender and working-class life, and she approaches them from a socialist perspective. But her activism is not limited to the choice and treatment of these subjects. Though her early films are not technically innovative, she pioneered novel approaches to production, marketing, and distribution. In the early 1970s, Reichert was a founding member of New Day Films, which was originally created to promote the Women's Movement. New Day was the first American cooperative distribution company operated entirely by and for filmmakers (the company is still active today, and distributes the work of over fifty filmmakers: see http://www.newday.com).

Many of her films are made for particular working class audiences, and are distributed to them directly through a variety of political institutions and organizations such as unions, schools, YMCAs, and health care providers. Because of this control, Reichert can focus on her explicit goal of promoting discussion and social change. To that end her films are often accompanied by discussions or meetings and include complementary handouts and discussion questions. *Methadone* incorporates a midway break for discussion, and some of her work is so audience-specific that it is produced for particular working class neighborhoods and never distributed beyond them. She has written a book on film distribution, *Doing It Yourself*, devoted to the dissemination of this model.

Reichert also attempts to incorporate her socialist, nonhierarchical politics into the production and structure of her documentaries. Her collaborative models, such as co-directing many of her films with James Klein, undermine common hierarchical structures in film production. In *Union Maids*, for example, she and Klein chose to work with video, despite the compromised quality, because video allowed more extended, collaborative interviews, and because it allowed them to work with less experienced students. Video not only allowed more shooting, but also allowed them to direct inexperienced cinematographers by intercom while watching on a monitor. *Union Maids* also exemplifies Reichert's aversion to heroic figures. Reichert has argued in interviews that focusing on individuals and aggrandizing their actions leads the audience to believe that such people are unusually gifted and unique, and that they drive history. She wishes, rather, to forward a model of collective agency. Consequently, *Union Maids* mixes the testimonies of three women of different ethnicities to demonstrate the wide range of people who collaborated in the cause of unionizing American industry.

Reichert's focus on agency led to an early shift in her filmmaking. Her first major film, *Growing Up Female,* depicts the problem of gender roles in the United States, but does not develop possible responses to the problem. Her next film, *Methadone,* begins in a similar vein with a critique of the societal response to drug addiction, but the second half of the film explores possible solutions to the problem. In her subsequent documentaries, Reichert incorporates positive role models and opportunities for agency.

Critical reception of Reichert's documentary films has focused on her use of direct cinema techniques. Because Reichert's documentaries generally eschew voice-over narration and use oral interviews

extensively, they are less able to develop the broader context of the topics they explore. Further, despite Reichert's aversion to portrayals of individual heroism, critics have claimed that her films aggrandize the few people interviewed. *Union Maids* and *Seeing Red*, for example, are criticized for oversimplifying social relations by giving an incomplete, uncontested story primarily through oral interviews of small numbers of like-minded people. Such an approach can be read as a legitimate form of counter-history, and recent critics have argued for the recuperation of such direct cinema techniques for the creation of counter-histories that dispute conventional representations of authority and give more heteroglossic alternatives (see entry on *Union Maids*). Other critics, however, have argued that Reichert tends to present oral histories as independent arguments and not as primary source material in need of a broader explanatory frame. The lack of such a frame, it is claimed, can make her films appear naïve—an endorsement of a partial, self-protective history rather than a meta-critical response to previous histories (Nichols, 252).

DEREK LOH AND PAUL MILLER

See also **Klein, James;** *Union Maids*

Biography

Graduated from Antioch College in 1970 with a degree in documentary arts. Co-founded New Day Films in 1971. Co-founded the Film Fund, a foundation to promote social issue films, 1977. Published *Doing It Yourself: A Handbook of Independent Film Distribution*, 1977. *Union Maids* nominated for Academy Award for Best Documentary Feature, 1978. Named Artist of the Year by the Ohio Arts Council (with James Klein), 1983. *Seeing Red* nominated for Academy Award for Best Documentary Feature, 1984. Named by the American Film Institute as one of nineteen artists who influenced the decade in film, 1985. Appointed to the Ohio Humanities Council by Governor Celeste, 1986. Reichert is currently vice-president of Ohio Valley Regional Media Arts Coalition and professor in the Department of Theater Arts and the School of Medicine at Wright State University.

Selected Films

1970 *Growing Up Female*: co-director
1975 *Methadone: An American Way of Dealing*: co-director
1975 *Men's Lives*: co-producer
1976 *Union Maids*: co-director, editor
1983 *Seeing Red: Stories of American Communists*: co-director
1992 *Emma and Elvis*: director, co-writer, co-producer
2003 *Welcome to Warren*: creative consultant
2003 *A People's History: Dayton's People's History, Twenty Years Later*: co-writer, co-producer

Further Reading

Kleinhaus, Chuck, "Julia Reichert and Jim Klein," In *Jump Cut* 5, 1975, 11–12.

Nichols, Bill, *Representing Reality*, Bloomington: Indian University Press, 1991.

Reichert, Julia, *Doing It Yourself: A Handbook on Independent Film Distribution*, New York: Association of Independent Film and Video Makers, 1977.

———, "Feminist Film Comes of Age," in *With Both Eyes Open: Seeing Beyond Gender*, edited by Patricia A. Johnson & Janet Kalven, New York: Pilgrim Press, 1988.

Rosenthal, Alan, "Union Maids," in *Documentary Conscience*, edited by Alan Rosenthal, Berkeley: University of California Press, 1980.

———, (ed.), *New Challenges for Documentary*, Berkeley: University of California Press, 1988.

Rubenstein, Lenny, "Who's Who in Filmmaking: Julia Reichert and James Klein," In *Sightlines* 20, 2, 1986–1987, 22–25.

Waldman, Diane and Janet Walker (eds.), *Feminism and Documentary*, Minneapolis: University of Minnesota Press, 1999.

REISZ, KAREL

The film director and producer Karel Reisz was a prominent member of the Free Cinema movement (1956–1959), an informal group of young artists that also included Lindsay Anderson, Tony Richardson, and the cameraman Walter Lassally. Free Cinema was concerned with the relationship between art and society, and the need for the film *auteur* to be free from the commercial constraints of mainstream cinema, so that committed artists might make films that offered significant commentary on contemporary society.

Reisz chose initially to work in documentary film, but was outspoken about his antipathy to what he considered the legacy of the 1930s British Documentary Film Movement, and a tendency to make documentaries about, "the Lake District, Stirling Moss, old trams and the beauties of spring" (Lovell, 1977: 138). He did acknowledge, however, the strong influence of Humphrey Jennings's poetic realism on the Free Cinema practitioners and referred to Jennings's film *Fires Were Started* (1943) as "the source film for Free Cinema" (Orbanz, 1977: 57).

The Free Cinema movement was substantially six programmes of films presented at the National Film Theatre between 1956 and 1959, and a series of critical articles in journals, such as *Sequence,* which Reisz co-founded in 1947 with Lindsay Anderson, and *Sight and Sound,* in which they set out the broad themes of the group. Reizs's short documentary film, *Momma Don't Allow* (1955), co-directed with Tony Richardson and funded by the BFI Experimental Film Fund, was screened at the first Free Cinema programme in September 1956.

We are the Lambeth Boys (1959) directed by Reisz, was part of the *Last Free Cinema* programme in 1959. Both films embody the low budget production style and the attitude of Free Cinema in capturing the mood of the late 1950s by focusing on the working class and an emerging youth culture in a sympathetic manner.

Reisz, along with Anderson and Richardson, went on to achieve critical acclaim in mainstream cinema and became prominent figures in the British New Wave of socially concerned realist films, popular between 1959 and 1963. Focusing on working class experience, their work included *Saturday Night and Sunday Morning* (Karel, Reisz, 1960), *A Taste of Honey* (Tony Richardson, 1962), and *This Sporting Life* (Lyndsey Anderson, 1963). Given their Oxbridge background, however, their representations of working class life have been called into question (Armes, 1978: 2–5).

PAT A. COOK

See also **Anderson, Lindsay;** *Fires Were Started***; Jennings, Humphrey;** *Momma Don't Allow***;** *We Are the Lambeth Boys*

Biography

Born in Ostrava, Czechoslovakia in 1926. Immigrated to Britain as a young man and joined the Royal Air Force towards the end of World War II. After the war, studied Natural Sciences at Emmanuel College, Cambridge. Worked for three years as the Programmes Officer at The National Film Theatre. In 1956, became head of the Ford Motor Company's TV and Film Programme. Co-authored, with Gavin Miller, *Techniques of Film Editing* (1953). Died in London in 2002.

Selected Films (Director)

1955 *Momma Don't Allow* (UK)
1958 *We Are the Lambeth Boys* (UK)
1960 *Saturday Night and Sunday Morning* (UK)
1964 *Night Must Fall* (UK)
1966 *Morgan: A Suitable Case for Treatment* (UK)
1968 *Isadora* (UK)
1974 *The Gambler* (US)
1978 *Who'll Stop the Rain* (UK)
1981 *French Lieutenant's Woman* (UK)
1985 *Sweet Dreams* (US)
1990 *Everybody Wins* (US)
2000 *Act Without Words 1* (UK) BBC Television.

Further Reading

Armes, Roy *A Critical History of British Cinema*, London, 1978, 2–5.
Barsam, Richard, *Non Fiction Film: A Critical History*, Indianapolis: Indiana University Press, 1992, 249–254.
Films and Filming, 25, 4, January 1979 12–17.
Lovell, Alan, and Jim Hillier, *Studies in Documentary*, London: Secker and Warburg, 1977, 133–172.
Murphy, Robert, *Sixties British Cinema*, London: BFI, 1972, 18–21, 73–74, 271–272.
Orbanz, Eva, *Journey to a Legend and Back: The British Realistic Film*, Berlin: Volker Speiss, 1977, 53–63.
Stills, 1, 4, winter 1982, 7–15.

RENOV, MICHAEL

Michael Renov, a professor of critical studies in the School of Cinema-Television at the University of Southern California, is a key figure in the current theoretical debates surrounding documentary film, specifically the demystification of the dictum that documentary film is an objective conveyor of "reality." Along with Bill Nichols, Renov paved the way for a decidedly critical and multifaceted consideration of documentary film in academic film studies. The bulk of Renov's theoretical direction is informed by the notion that subjectivity is prevalent to all forms of documentary, whether the subjectivity in question is that of the filmmaker, the ideological influences that consciously and unconsciously influence the subject matter and its rendition, or the viewer's own processes of making sense/meaning of documentary film. Subjectivity—which assumes the mediated nature of any visual representation—is thus a *sine qua non* of documentary film.

Michael Renov's post-structuralist heuristic comes out of a literary theory tradition greatly informed by such thinkers and works as Roland Barthes and his seminal *S/Z*, the theories of Jacques Derrida, and the psychoanalytic views of Freud and Lacan, among others. Such a diverse range of conceptual frameworks is detailed and illustrated by an equally varied choice of visual and filmic texts. More specifically, in addition to analyzing the hegemonic representations produced during World War II of women and the Japanese threat to America in

Hollywood film and advertising, the theorist has focused on the political dimensions of 1960s American Newsreel, as well as Vietnam and its representation in documentaries from that same decade. For the last ten years, Michael Renov has contributed to scholarship aimed at autobiographical practices in documentary film/video and New Media, including the Internet.

Interrogating and questioning the ideologically assumed status of the documentary as a vehicle for "truth" claims, Renov argues for bridging the divide between aesthetics/politics and fiction/nonfiction. By asserting reciprocity between the terms of each dyad, Renov infers an ideological dimension to all filmic art and disagrees with the occlusion of the fictive and creative as elements endemic to the nonfiction or documentary text. In other words, fiction and nonfiction are not disparate but "enmeshed." One of the theorist's most oft-cited contributions to documentary analysis is his poetics of the documentary. His "four functions as modalities of desire" break the film mode into the following tendencies: (1) to record or reveal or preserve, (2) to persuade or promote, (3) to analyze or interrogate, and (4) to express (Renov, 1993b). Examples include home movies, ethnographic film, and the experimental or essayistic—though Renov opines that all documentaries have a persuasive function.

Brief mention should be made of the essayistic, which the theorist explores in conjunction with visual media, such as autobiography. Michel de Montaigne, Roland Barthes, and Theodore Adorno are several writers/critics whose essayistic work Renov refers to as the type of inquiry documentary film engages with. Renov explains, "I privilege a writing practice that couples a documentary impulse—an outward gaze upon the world—with an equally forceful reflex of interrogation" (Renov, 2004: 105). Documentary films that the theorist considers in conjunction with the framework of the essayistic include Jonas Mekas's *Lost, Lost, Lost* (1975), Ilene Segalove's *My Puberty* (1987), and Lynn Hershman's *First Person Plural* (1988). Moreover, Renov's areas of interest with regard to self-inscription in visual media include gay and lesbian film/video, first-person confessional video, the avant-garde, and the personal web site. Bridging the personal and autobiographic in visual media with the essayistic makes implicit the reciprocal relationship between the work and its creator. For Renov the dichotomized and yet dependent relationship between writer/filmmaker and subject echoes Jacques Lacan's theories on the connection between the self and Other. The self exits and is able to self-identity only because of the presence of and its relation to the Other. Thus, Renov has a keen interest in the function of the psychoanalytical in documentary film production and analysis and has devoted significant attention to what he judges to be the neglected ties between documentary work and psychoanalysis.

Operating against the perceived assumption that documentary or nonfiction is tied to the conscious, and that fiction has a privileged relationship to the unconscious, Renov argues that the documentary gaze is more than what Bill Nichols describes as epistephilic, or knowledge-driven curiosity. The gaze is as equally motivated by the "ecstatic" or pleasurable. In post-structuralist fashion, Renov considers the documentary film to be "constitutively multiform" and its content as well as form to be founded on difference rather than reassuringly stable or fixed binaries and representations—a collection of and references to signifiers instead of signifieds.

Regarding documentary texts, Renov supports his theories and assertions with examples drawn from the world of independent cinema. Many of the documentary film and video examples he cites are low budget, marginal, and truly outside the realm of mainstream documentary film/video. The theorist devotes critical attention to, for instance, Marlon Riggs's *Tongues Untied* (1989), the collective Newsreel's *Columbia Revolt* (1968), Haskell

Wexler's super self-reflexive *Medium Cool* (1969), and independent video projects, such as Wendy Clarke's *The Love Tapes* and *L.A. Link* (1978–1994)—a collaborative project among Renov, Wendy Clarke, and Marita Sturken. Michael Renov supports and celebrates the politically subversive potential of documentary visual media, devoting substantial academic space to parsing those counter-hegemonic discourses and texts that defy mainstream notions and representations of race, class, and gender.

JENNIFER BOTTINELLI

See also **Aesthetics and Documentary Film: Poetics**

Biography

Graduated in 1982 with a Ph.D. in Motion Pictures/Television from UCLA. Professor of critical studies and Associate Dean of Academic Affairs in the School of Cinema-Television at USC. Co-founder of the international documentary studies conference, "Visible Evidence: Strategies and Practices in Documentary Film and Video." Founder of the public forum "Eye & Thou: Jewish Autobiography in Film and Video;" Los Angeles, 1998; New York, 2001. Member of the Editorial Board of *Cinema Journal*, 1997–2002. Member of the advisory board of the Pew Trust Center for Religion and Media, NYU, 2003 to present. Most recent critical project is *The Subject of Documentary* (2004)—a series of his essays that originally appeared in previously collected volumes of essays by a variety of writers on documentary film/video edited and co-edited by Renov, including *Theorizing Documentary, Collecting Visible Evidence,* and *Resolutions: Contemporary Video Practices*. Other pieces have appeared in the collection *Feminism and Documentary* (edited by Diane Waldman and Janet Walker) and the journals *Afterimage* and *Wide Angle*.

Further Reading

Renov, Michael, "Documentary Horizons: An Afterward," in *Collecting Visible Evidence*, edited by Jane M. Gaines and Michael Renov, Minneapolis: University of Minnesota Press, 1999.
———, *Hollywood's Wartime Women: Representation and Ideology*. Ann Arbor: UMI Research Press, 1988.
———, "Introduction: Resolving Video," in *Resolutions: Contemporary Video Practices*, edited by Michael Renov and Erika Suderberg, Minneapolis: University of Minnesota Press, 1996.
———, "Introduction: The Truth About Non-Fiction," in *Theorizing Documentary*, edited by Michael Renov, New York: Routledge, 1993a.
———, "Rethinking Documentary: A Taxonomy of Mediation," in *Wide Angle*, 8, 3–4, 1986, 71–77.
———, *The Subject of Documentary*. Minneapolis: University of Minneapolis Press, 2004.
———, "Toward a Poetics of Documentary," in *Theorizing Documentary*, edited by Michael Renov, New York: Routledge, 1993b.

RESNAIS, ALAIN

"If the short film had not existed, Resnais would surely have invented it," Jean-Luc Godard wrote in praise of Resnais's documentaries in 1959, the miraculous year when the French New Wave was born and Resnais had just made his first feature, *Hiroshima mon amour*. Godard added that without Resnais's work "the new young French cinema would not exist."

Between 1946 and 1948, Resnais made a number of 16mm films including a series of "Visits" to contemporary artists. These films were not released, but prints are in the archives of the Centre Pompidou in Paris. From 1947 to 1958, Resnais worked as editor on six films made by others. His own career as a professional documentary filmmaker, which lasted for ten years, also began in 1948 with his 35mm *Van Gogh.*

Resnais's eight short documentaries, generally commissioned works, focus not on people but on things and places. Three are art films; three, including *Nuit et brouillard/Night and Fog*, are works that focus on places charged with memories, and the last two are explorations of issues surrounding contemporary industrialization. They constitute an important body of work in the history of short film and also served as a testing ground for techniques and themes that have contributed to making Resnais's feature films among the most important works of twentieth-century cinema.

In the documentaries, Resnais shows his lack of interest in the so-called realist cinema and his commitment to raising formal questions and confronting difficult, enigmatic contemporary philosophical and social issues. "I want to make films that are experiments. All experiments are interesting," he told an interviewer in 1961 (cited by Armes, 1968).

Resnais's training and work as a film editor have had a marked impact on all his films. Except for *Nuit et brouillard* and *Le Mystère de l'Atelier Quinze*, Resnais was both director and editor of all his documentary films. For him the crucial stage in the making of a film is the editing, not only the montage of the images but also sound editing and mixing. The musical score establishes rhythms, punctuates patterns of montage, and plays a central role in the films.

Ghislain Cloquet, who was cinematographer for *Les Statues meurent aussi, Nuit et brouillard*, and *Toute la mémoire du monde,* comments on the impact of this focus on sound and rhythm on the cameraman. Cloquet sees a development from what he calls "normal" camera movements or pans in the first documentaries to dolly shots in *Night and Fog* and shots that allow a fuller exploration of three dimensions in *Toute la mémoire du monde.* He writes that Resnais opened his eyes by his patient and careful observation of objects (Pingaud, 1990). The resulting long tracking shots are characteristic of Resnais's style. The camera moves into the subject whether it is a painting by Picasso, the camp at Auschwitz, or the French National library to find traces of the past, to learn, to explore.

Memory and closed worlds are recurrent themes. It has been suggested that by editing his tracking shots, Resnais has created a form that allows one to see and to feel the strange and disturbing resemblance between many seemingly disparate sites of modern life. "Resnais's short films show the vast imprisonment which controls our lives and our fear of death in a world from which we are separated," Neyrat has noted. He goes on to underscore, however, that "against this imprisonment the films also bring a power of liberation—the aesthetic power of the cinema, its power of redeeming the contingent through form and beauty."

In *Van Gogh* (1948), which won the Academy Award Oscar for Best Foreign Short Subject in 1950, Resnais takes the camera on a "voyage into painting." We are shown only images from the paintings; there are no photographs of real landscapes. Resnais treats "the whole of the artist's output as one large painting over which the camera has wandered as freely as in any ordinary documentary" (Bazin, 1967). The camera tracks into the paintings, selects and fuses. The material selected serves neither art criticism nor biography but allows the filmmaker to find out, as Resnais stated after finishing the film in 1948, "whether painted trees, painted people, painted houses could, thanks to the editing, fulfill the role of real objects and whether, in this case, it was possible to substitute for the spectator and almost without his knowing it, the interior world of the artist in place of the world as it is revealed by photography" (Armes, 1968). The film is shot in black and white and this reveals hidden potentialities of the paintings and allows the filmmaker more freedom to explore space and create links between the canvases. The musical score by Jacques Besse plays a predominant role in structuring the shots. "It is no longer there to 'to accompany the images' but to create the very backbone of the film," Resnais wrote in 1948 (Armes, 1968).

Gauguin (1950) is a much shorter film tracing the journey of the painter, Paul Gauguin, from his native Brittany to Tahiti. It is told in much the same way as *Van Gogh*, using the paintings and, this time, a musical score by Darius Milhaud and commentary drawn from the writings of Gauguin. Economic circumstances rather than aesthetic choice forced Resnais to shoot this film in black and white; however, the paintings of the great colorist were not suited for this approach and Resnais, in a 1960 interview, spoke of this film as a failure.

Resnais's third art film, *Guernica,* also made in 1950, takes Picasso's fresco as subject for another black-and-white documentary. Picasso's "Guernica," painted in black, white, and tones of gray, is well suited for this approach. The filmmaker dismantles the spatial arrangement of the painting and rearranges the pieces along with other Picasso paintings and sculptures, as well as photographs of the ruined Spanish town, newspaper headlines, and graffiti in a new pattern focusing on the destruction and suffering caused by war. Over images of death and desolation the voice of the actress Maria Casarès recites a text written by the poet Paul Eluard. "Stylistically . . . *Guernica* represents for the director the first totally successful fusion of all the elements on which his mature style is based. Fragments of photographs, painting and sculpture are welded into a visual rhythm and set against an aural rhythm of music and verbal poetry bound together in a tone that combines documentary realism with pure lyricism," Armes has written. "I was very moved by the massacre at Guernica because it seemed to me like the prelude to all the massacres which were to follow," Resnais recalled in 1983 (Fleischer, 1983).

Les Statues meurent aussi/Statues Also Die (1950–1953), co-directed with Chris Marker, is a tribute to African art and a rebuke of the colonizer who negated its value, took it out of its context, treated it as folklore, and thus contributed to its decline. The documentary also serves to recall the European efforts to shape Africa in its own image: "All this is dominated by the White Man who sees everything from his position and raises himself above the contradictions of reality," the voice of Marker's commentary reminds the viewer (cited by Gauthier, 1995). The film, which was awarded the Prix Jean-Vigo in 1954, was banned by the French government for more than ten years.

Nuit et brouillard/Night and Fog, shot in 1955 in a mix of black and white and color, is no doubt Resnais's finest and best-known documentary. In this thirty-one-minute film dealing with the Holocaust, the filmmaker undertook the challenge of presenting a reality that seems impossible to document. The film is narrated from the perspective of ten years after the end of World War II and opens on a long take of a seemingly peaceful countryside shot in muted color. Then the camera tilts up, moves through torn barbed wire, and tracks slowly through the remains of what was the camp at Auschwitz—the empty buildings, the factories, the latrines, the gas chambers. Intercut with this probing inquisition by the camera, archival footage, in black and white, alternates to show the past and the horror of the camps: the construction of the sites, the rounding up of people all over Europe, the cattle trains, the naked and emaciated prisoners, the massed bodies of the dead. Photographs of piles of eyeglasses, combs, shoes, shorn hair, and endless lists of names bear silent witness to the enormity of the carnage. The camera searches to understand. "We can only show the surface," the voice-over comments in a low-key, almost neutral tone, which itself seems to question our ability to grasp what is being described. Language seems paralyzed before the moral outrage. Jean Cayrol, the author of the commentary who had himself been deported during the Holocaust, wrote that he and Resnais wanted the film to reach a wide audience not only to have people remember but also to sound a warning against all future nights and fogs (Raskin, 1987). The magnificent musical score by Hanns Eisler adds to the profound meaning of the film. In an essay accompanying the DVD release of the film, Philip Lopate has noted that this didactic work against war and violence, this very personal examination of the meaning of memory and forgetfulness, anticipates the modern documentary genre of the essay-film.

In *Toute la mémoire du monde/All the Memory of the World,* a film about the French National Library made in 1956, Resnais invites the viewer to penetrate the memories that reside in books. Treasures from the past are presented by the camera's eye along with present day works: the Maya Codex alongside the comic strip of *Mandrake the Magician.* Who knows, the commentary asks, which will bear more authentic witness of our civilization? The film is technically striking as the camera tracks back and forth through corridors and passageways. Cloquet recalls that "Resnais wanted us to move through the National Library as if in a rocket, like a fish through water" (cited by Pingaud, 1990).

Resnais and Remo Forlani, who wrote the script for *Toute la mémoire du monde*, projected a series of forty short films centered on the subject of "The Organization of Work." This project was unrealized though a 35mm documentary, *Le Mystère de l'atelier quinze/The Mystery of Workshop Fifteen*, related to the project, was made in 1957 and co-directed by Resnais. It is the least known of Resnais's documentaries and focuses on the case of a workman who falls ill for no apparent reason. The commentary was written by Chris Marker and the film, though entirely planned by Resnais, was actually directed by his former assistant, André Heinrich.

Resnais's last documentary, *Le Chant du Styrène/The Song of Styrene*, was commissioned by Péchiney Industries in 1958 to show the complex transformation of materials in the manufacture of polystyrene plastic, an entirely manufactured product. Resnais handled the assignment in a surprising manner and in a 1962 interview explained that this film is "far less an industrial documentary than a synthesis of verbal abstraction and lyricism" (cited by Kreidl, 1977).The commentary, written by the novelist and poet Raymond Queneau in alexandrine verse, serves as a humorous and informative accompaniment to the patterns created by wide-screen shots of pipes and machines in brilliant, often unrealistic color. In its use of musical rhythms, *Le Chant du Styrène* can be seen to prefigure Resnais's later "musical" films (Fleischer, 1998).

Jean-Luc Godard called *Le Chant du Styrène* "an Olympian film, a serious film without equal." Just a few months later, Resnais released his first feature *Hiroshima mon amour,* a film that won the International Critics Prize at Cannes in 1959 and worldwide acclaim for the director.

Hiroshima mon amour grew out of a commission to make a documentary on the effects of the atomic bomb. Marguerite Duras, author of the script, calls Resnais's first feature "a false documentary," and, indeed, one of the themes of this structurally complex love story revolves around memory and the impossibility of documenting the events that had occurred at Hiroshima.

A number of critics writing about Alain Resnais's feature films since 1959 have underscored the importance of the short documentaries in developing the formal and thematic issues central to his work as a whole. Bounoure, Armes, and Monaco have drawn

actual parallels between individual documentaries and later feature films. The importance of the work of Alain Resnais as a documentarist cannot be overestimated either in its impact on the filmmaker's later work or, as Neyrat has observed, "as an extended meditation on modernity, on the changes of man and art in the age of technology and aesthetics."

EVA MARIA STADLER

See also **Night and Fog**

Biography

Born in Brittany on June 3, 1922. A few years older than Godard and the other young filmmakers associated with the *Cahiers du cinéma* and the New Wave. As a boy, showed great interest in comics and movies, asked for the gift of an 8mm camera, and began a number of film projects. In 1940, went to Paris, first to study acting and two years later filmmaking/editing.

Selected Films

1948 *Van Gogh* (20 min. b&w)
1950 *Gauguin* (11 min. b&w)
1950 *Guernica* (12 min. b&w)
1950–1953 *Les Statues meurent aussi* (30 min. b&w)
1955 *Nuit et brouillard* (32 min. b&w and Eastmancolor)
1956 *Toute la mémoire du monde* (21 min. b&w)
1957 *Le Mystère de l'atelier quinze* (18 min. b&w)
1958 *Le Chant du Styrène* (14 min. CinemaScope/Eastmancolor)

Further Reading

Armes, Roy, *The Cinema of Alain Resnais*, London: A. Zwemmer Limited and New York: A.S. Barnes & Noble, 1968.
Bazin, André, "Painting and Cinema," in *What Is Cinema?* Translated by Hugh Gray, Berkeley & Los Angeles: University of California, 1967.
Bounoure, Gaston, *Alain Resnais*, Paris: Seghers, 1962.
Burch, Noel, "A Conversation with Alain Resnais," in *Film Quarterly*, spring 1960.
———, "Four Documentaries," in *Film Quarterly*, Fall 1959.
Fleischer, Alain, *L'Art d'Alain Resnais* Paris: Centre Pompidou, 1998.
Gauthier, Guy, *Le Documentaire—un autre cinéma*, Paris: Nathan, 1995.
Godard, Jean-Luc, "Chacun son tour," *Cahiers du Cinéma* 92, February 1959.
Kreidl, John Francis, *Alain Resnais*, Boston: Twayne, 1977.
Marcorelles, Louis, "Rebel with a Camera," in *Sight and Sound*, winter 1960.
Monaco, James, *Alain Resnais: The Role of Imagination*, New York: Oxford UP, 1979.
Neyrat, Cyril, "Horreur/bonheur: métamorphose," in *Alain Resnais—Anthologie*, edited by Stéphane Goudet, Paris: Gallimard, 2002, 47–54.
Pingaud, Bernard and &Pierre Samson, *Alain Resnais ou la créations au cinéma. "L'Arc,"* Paris: Duponchelle, 1990.
Raskin, Richard, *Nuit et brouillard by Alain Resnais*, Denmark: Aarhus UP, 1987.

RETOUR, LE

(France, Cartier-Bresson and Banks, 1946)

Le Retour is a thirty-two-minute documentary film depicting the return home of prisoners of war, deportees, and refugees from camps in Germany and former German-occupied territories at the end of World War II. The film was produced by the Office of War Information (U.S.), at the request of the French Ministère des Prisonniers, Déportés et Rapatriés, and it premiered in Paris in January 1946. As its scriptwriter, editor, and technical consultant, French photographer and filmmaker Henri Cartier-Bresson worked with two officers from the U.S. Army Signal Corps.

During World War II, the Signal Corps had documented every major military campaign (film and photographs) and gathered visual evidence of the Nazi atrocities on the European Theater of Operations. This material was used in films presenting war crimes, such as *Nazi Concentration camps* (George Stevens, United States, 1945) or reeducation films such as *Die Todesmühlen/Death Mills* (Hanuš Burger, United States/Germany, 1945). *Le Retour* also made use of this material, and it added segments about displaced persons and prisoners returning home in 1945.

World War II resulted in destruction and human suffering on an unprecedented scale. *Le Retour* documents a singular moment in the war, when the arms fall silent and the gigantic task of repatriating millions of displaced persons across the continent began: Allied soldiers liberated from prisoners of war camps; civilian deportees who survived detention in concentration camps; millions of others brought to Germany as slave labor. All wanted to go home. The immediate needs were enormous—clothing, medicine, transportation—and the chaotic return demanded military organization and Soviet-American cooperation. On the last leg of the journey, the camera witnesses the emotional minutes when former French prisoners get off the train in Paris and look at anxious awaiting relatives and friends. On both sides there was apprehension, hope, and restrained joy.

Henri Cartier-Bresson (1908–2004) was internationally known as a photographer and a reporter. On the Left of French politics, he became interested in film during a visit to the United States in 1935. Afterwards, he became assistant filmmaker to Jean Renoir, and a film director in his own right, in the polarized political context of the Spanish civil war (*Victoire de la vie*, 1937 and *L'Espagne vivra*, 1938). Having been a prisoner of war from 1940 until his escape in February 1943, he brings sensibility to this film. As with his documentaries on Spain, he envisioned *Le Retour* as a testimony to human resilience in time of war. Cartier-Bresson mastered composition and always tried to capture the "decisive moment" defined by a person or an event. As a way of life, he strove "to place head, heart and eye along the same line of sight."

The thematic filmography on deportation developed slowly and did not initially identify the specificities of persecutions against particular groups. Films were made in different countries and languages. *Le Retour* is one of the most well-known documentary films; it focuses on repatriation and the moment of reunion with loved ones. Its timeframe is the present and its theme opens the future.

Le Retour presented prisoners of war and deportees in the same breath without differentiating them; this problematic interpretation was supported by the French authorities of 1945 who emphasized national unity. Soldiers became prisoners because of the defeat of the French army in 1940; other prisoners were civilians, arrested and deported for political or racial reasons. The first group were combatants, the latter victims. They were not in the same camps, they were not treated the same way, but the film blurs this distinction by mixing together images from the military camps and the concentration camps. As the title indicates, *Le Retour* was all about the return and causes were minimally addressed. People had been taken away by the war, victory allowed their return. At the time, it was not possible to ask the painful question: why were these civilians (resisters, political militants, Jews) deported from France? The Vichy government had collaborated with the German occupation forces and therefore shared responsibility for the criminal internment of deportees from France.

The very name of the Ministry responsible for prisoners and deportees only aggravated the confusion. It was an ambiguous subject for filmmakers. The defeated soldiers of 1940 and racial deportees were not heroes. Apart from *Le Retour*, this theme was absent from French cinematography until the end of the 1940s. In *Retour à la vie* (1949), four of five short stories are about prisoners of war. Only *Le retour d'Emma*, by André Cayatte, was about the return of a deportee. Both *Le Retour* and *Retour à la vie* focus on the return as the central event, without venturing into the causes.

It was several years before the necessary distinctions were made and the difficult questions asked. Even then, censorship was watching, as demonstrated by the controversy about the documentary film *Nuit et brouillard/Night and Fog* (Alain Resnais, France, 1955–1956). The film had been commissioned to commemorate the tenth anniversary of the liberation of the camps. Nonetheless, state collaboration was still taboo in French films and Resnais had to camouflage the *képi* of a French *gendarme* guarding an internment camp in France in order to break the visual link between the French authorities and deportation.

Before they were screened, films were examined by a Commission de contrôle des films cinématographiques (the film censorship board) and filtered through a system of mandatory visas for internal and export markets. National interest was one of the principal concern of the state. The military struggle took precedence over the ideological conflicts of World War II. This less contentious interpretation of the war was favored by the government and included in *Le Retour*. In film, just as in official commemorations, the fate and the wartime experience of racial and political deportees were ignored.

SUZANNE LANGLOIS

Le Retour (France/USA, Services américains d'information/ Office of War Information, 35mm, black & white, 1944–1946, 32 min.). Produced by the Office of War Information; producer Noma Ratner. Directed by Henri Cartier-Bresson; co-directors Richard Banks and Jerrold Krimsky from the U.S. Army Signal Corps. Scriptwriter and technical consultant: Henri Cartier-Bresson. On-screen commentary: Claude Roy. Cinematography by U.S. Army Signal Corps, Henri Cartier-Bresson and Claude Renoir. Editing by Henri Cartier-Bresson and Richard Banks. Music by Robert Lannoy. Archival material from the last months of the war, American troops in Germany, Dachau concentration camp, Elbe river, aerial views of Paris, Gare d'Orsay. A nineteen-minute version, *Reunion* (1946), was adapted from *Le Retour* by the U.S. Army Pictorial Service.

Further Reading

Butler, Margaret, *Film and Community in Britain and France: From* La Règle du jeu *to* Room at the Top, London: I.B. Tauris Publishers, 2004.

Cartier-Bresson, Henri, *Henri Cartier-Bresson: Photographer*, Boston: Little, Brown and Co., 1992 *De qui s'agit-il? Henri Cartier-Bresson*, Paris: Fondation Henri Cartier-Bresson/Gallimard and Bibliothèque nationale de France, 2003.

Langlois, Suzanne, *La Résistance dans le cinéma français 1944-1994. De* La Libération de Paris *à* Libera me, Paris: L'Harmattan, 2001.

Lindeperg, Sylvie, *Les Écrans de l'ombre. La Seconde Guerre mondiale dans le cinéma français (1944-1969)*, Paris: CNRS Éditions, 1997.

Namer, Gérard, *Batailles pour la mémoire. La commémoration en France de 1945 à nos jours*, Paris: Papyrus, 1983.

Rousso, Henry, *The Vichy Syndrome: History and Memory in France since 1944*, Cambridge: Harvard University Press, 1994.

Thompson, George Raynor, *The Signal Corps: The Outcome (mid-1943 through 1945)*, Washington: Office of the Chief of Military History, U.S. Army, 1966.

RIEFENSTAHL, LENI

Leni Riefenstahl is generally regarded as one of the most brilliant and controversial filmmakers in the history of cinema. Though she preferred fiction, in which she excelled as an actress, writer, and director, she will be forever linked to nonfiction on the strength of two classic documentaries—*Triumph Des Willens/Triumph of the Will* (1935) and *Olympia/Olympia* (1938).

Trained in classical ballet, Leni Riefenstahl displayed an early interest in and talent for the visual arts and music. She often choreographed her own dance routines, selected the music, and designed her costumes. An injury forced her to suspend dancing, and during recovery, she happened to see a film that changed her life. *Berg des Schicksals/Mountain of Destiny* (1924*)*, a film by Dr. Arnold Fanck, was shot in the Dolomite Mountains in northern Italy. The realistic setting, with images of angular rocks and clouds and alpine slopes, made such an impression that she boldly set out to meet the star of the film, Luis Tenker, and the director, Franck, and to offer her services as an actress. The ploy worked, and soon Leni Riefenstahl was starring in mountain films herself. In the first such film, *Der Heilige Berg/The Holy Mountain* (1926), Leni played the role of a dancer, Diotima, caught in a love triangle. She went on to star in other mountain films such as *Der Grosse Sprung/The Great Leap* (1927), *Die Weisse Hölle Vom Piz Palu/The White Hell of Pitz Palu* (1929), and *Stürme Über Dem Montblanc/Storm over Mont*

Blanc (1930), her first film with sound. The films required Riefenstahl to master mountain climbing and barefoot rock climbing, and to endure the hardships of freezing temperatures and blizzardlike conditions. All the while she was performing as an actress, Riefenstahl was studying and mastering the techniques of cinema.

By the time she directed her first film, the fairy-tale *Das Blaue Licht/The Blue Light* (1932), Riefenstahl was already one of Germany's best-known actresses. With her directing debut, she became world famous. *The Blue Light*, in which she produced, collaborated on the screenplay, starred in, directed, and edited, tells the story of Junta, a young mountain girl accused by nearby villagers of being a witch and causing the deaths of young men who perished in their attempts to climb Monte Cristallo on nights when a full moon cast a shimmering blue light over the mountain. Junta inadvertently allows her lover to discover the source of the blue light, a crystal grotto that villagers find out

Leni Riefenstahl filming during the 1936 Olympics for *Olympiad* (released 1938).
[*Courtesy of the Everett Collection*]

about and loot. Junta, believing she has been betrayed, leaps to her death. *The Blue Light* was filmed on location in the village of Ticino and the Dolomites. With a perfectionist's eye, Riefenstahl calculated every lens setting and focal length before shooting, and even ordered a special lens and more sensitive film stock to achieve a nightlike effect.

In 1932, Riefenstahl met Adolph Hitler, soon to be named Chancellor of Germany. The leader of the National Socialist German Workers Party, or Nazis, Hitler was a spellbinding orator whose message of German nationalism and strength resonated with a population beset by unemployment and the still lingering humiliation of defeat in World War I. Like many other Germans, Riefenstahl was attracted to the worldview that Hitler promoted. Hitler in turn admired Riefenstahl's films, particularly *The Holy Mountain* and *The Blue Light*. In her autobiography she quotes Hitler as saying, "Once we come to power, you must make my films." Despite an apolitical nature, Riefenstahl agreed to make a film about the annual party rally in Nuremberg. Hastily put together, the short film *Sieg Des Glaubens/Victory of Faith* (1933), contained only seeds of what would become the next year the most famous propaganda film of all time, *Triumph Des Willens/Triumph of the Will* (1935).

The timing of *Triumph of the Will* could not have been more important. Hitler had come to power in January 1933 and had begun immediately to suspend civil liberties and issue anti-Jewish degrees. In August of the next year, the president of Germany, the revered World War I leader Field Marshall Paul von Hindenburg, died, enabling Hitler to combine the office of chancellor and president. A few months before, to appease the military, Hitler had ordered a purge of his own party, assassinating the leader of the SA (Stürmabteilung or "brown shirts"), Ernst Röhm.

With the world press raising questions about Germany's direction, and party stalwarts uneasy about their own fates, a film promoting party solidarity and German unity would be a public relations coup. On this score, Riefenstahl delivered a masterpiece of propaganda, a 114-minute film that would solidify Hitler's role as Führer and forever brand Leni Riefenstahl as a Nazi sympathizer. Ostensibly, *Triumph of the Will* is an account of the Sixth National Socialist Party Rally held in Nuremberg in September of 1934. Financed and distributed by the German film studio UFA, whose largest shareholder, Alfred Hugenberg, was a supporter of Hitler, *Triumph of the Will* had a crew of eighteen camerapersons. The documentary is chock-full of speeches, rallies, ceremonies, par-

ades, and ritual. But it is made with such artistry and such an understanding of German values and needs that it rises above the typical propaganda film. *Triumph* begins with Hitler's arrival in Nuremberg as his plane descends from the clouds and glides above the spires of the ancient city. The mystical quality of the arrival is enhanced by the anticipation of the crowd, straining on tiptoes to catch a glimpse of the Führer. After a motorcade into the city and a welcome rally, Riefenstahl changes the pace of the film, which she likens to the changes in the rhythm of a musical composition. The viewer sees Nuremberg at daybreak, still asleep, the absence of people a prelude to the activity that follows. The pace quickens as the camera captures a tent city of young soldiers and workers—shaving, cooking, playing games, and always smiling and laughing. Next, the viewer is treated to a folk parade in honor of the Führer. After inspecting a group of flag bearers, Hitler boards his open Mercedes limousine and, surrounded by other party leaders, disappears. Riefenstahl allows the camera to lose focus, thereby adding to the mysticism of the moment. For the opening of the Party Congress, Riefenstahl features short clips of speeches by Party leaders. Perhaps the most important of the Hitler speeches is his address to the SA. It is the only time Hitler refers to the purge several months before. "Men of the SA and the SS. A few months ago, a black shadow spread over the movement. Neither the SA, nor any other institution of the party, had anything to do with this shadow." Ever mindful of the importance of symbols, Riefenstahl makes full use of them and the many symbolic acts carried out—a solemn wreath-laying ceremony, a flag consecration, parades of swastika flags, jack-booted SS troops marching in unison, and always, endless salutes and tributes to the Führer. Nuremberg itself was filled with historic symbolism, its Imperial Castle and medieval walls a reminder of the first so-called Reich, The Holy Roman Empire. Music in *Triumph* was likewise symbolic. Scored by Herbert Windt, it made liberal use of the Party anthem, the Horst Wessel song, composed by an early martyr of the Nazi Party. Windt also included German folk music and German marches as well as music of Hitler's favorite composer, Richard Wagner. The film premiered in Berlin in March 1935. After complaints by the German army that it had been slighted in *Triumph*, Riefenstahl agreed to make a short film of the next Party Conference, focusing on military maneuvers. The result was a twenty-eight-minute film, *Tag Der Freiheit!—Unsere Wehrmacht!/Day of Freedom!—Our Armed Forces!* (1935).

Riefenstahl claimed that one of the most difficult aspects of making the Party films was working with the propaganda minister Joseph Goebbels. A notorious womanizer who worshipped Hitler and saw Riefenstahl as a rival for the Führer's affections, Goebbels controlled the film industry during the Third Reich and resented competition from Riefenstahl, who at one point earned the unofficial title of "Film Expert to the National Socialist Party." Throughout her life, Riefenstahl has maintained that her relationship with Goebbels was anything but cordial, a result of Goebbels's failure to interest her romantically. Nevertheless, in a 1993 documentary, *The Wonderful, Horrible Life of Leni Riefenstahl*, director Ray Müller confronted Riefenstahl with excerpts from Goebbels's 1933 diary suggesting that he and Riefenstahl visited one another socially.

Some critics question whether *Triumph* was really a documentary. Siegfried Kracauer believed the rally was staged for the camera, though, in fact, Nazi Party rallies had been held in Nuremberg since 1927. David Hinton argued that editing *Triumph* in the chronological order in which events occurred was of little importance to Riefenstahl—that the guiding principle was a "deliberately conceived sense of rhythm." Lotte Eisner and Susan Sontag condemned Riefenstahl as a pawn of Hitler. Despite the many criticisms of *Triumph* as pure propaganda—an ode to fascism or paean to Hitler—Richard Barsam said it fused art and politics and was "a masterful blend of the four basic elements of cinema—light, darkness, sound, and silence—but it is not just an achievement in cinematic form, for it has other essential elements—thematic, psychological, mythological, narrative, and visual interest—and it is in the working of these elements that Riefenstahl transcends the limitations of the documentary film and the propaganda film genres."

Leni Riefenstahl's other major contribution to documentary film was *Olympia: Fest Der Völker/Olympia: Festival of the People* and *Olympia: Fest Der Shöenheit/Olympia: Festival of Beauty* (1938), and a two-part film of the 1936 Berlin Olympics hosted by Germany. The first great sports film ever made, it featured staged prologues, innovative camera techniques, and a fluid editing style that elevated it far above the typical sporting events film. Sanctioned by the International Olympics Committee as the official film of the 1936 Olympics, and financed and distributed by the German film company TOBIS, *Olympia* begins with a reverential tribute to the origin of the games—ancient Greece. The camera tracks through smoky, silhouetted statues and ruins of ancient temples. Suddenly one of the statues is transformed into a human being—a discus thrower. A dance scene that includes Riefenstahl herself precedes the lighting of the Olympic torch and a symbolic journey from ancient Greece to modern Berlin. The first part of *Olympia* features the many track and field events. Riefenstahl always thought in terms of the most artistically composed shot, so for the pole-vaulting sequence, she had pits dug to capture the athletes catapulted across the sky. In slow motion, their graceful bodies seem to defy gravity. Throughout both parts of the film, Riefenstahl used balloons, dollies, catapults, telescopic lenses, any means she could use to convey the pain and ecstasy of competition. For the diving competition, Riefenstahl used underwater cameras to follow the divers below, as well as above the surface of the water. Perhaps the most famous sequence is the high diving competition in part two of *Olympia*. The sequence begins with a series of fast-paced dives that gradually become more silhouetted as the sky darkens. Projected in slow motion, the balletlike acrobatics of the divers framed against a cloud-laced sky appear almost super human. In fact, one of the criticisms of *Olympia* is that Riefenstahl 's seemingly cultlike obsession with beauty, particularly the beauty of the human body, reflected a fascist aesthetic consistent with the ideals of the Nazi Party. This argument is undermined, however, by the fact that the star of the 1936 Olympics was an African-American athlete, Jesse Owens, who received prominent attention in the film and contradicted Nazi notions of a superior Aryan race. *Olympia* premiered in 1938 at the UFA-Palast am Zoo in Berlin and was later shown throughout Europe. It won numerous awards, including the Grand Prize at the International Film Festival in Venice. In 1956, American directors designated it one of the ten best films of all time.

In 1938, Riefenstahl traveled to the United States to promote *Olympia*, but her visit was marred by anti-Nazi sentiment that followed Germany's Crystal Night, a night of terror in which Jewish synagogues, homes, and businesses were wrecked, burned, and looted, and more than 30,000 Jews were arrested. Hitler biographer John Toland noted: "The reaction from abroad was immediate and the acts of brutality were given an unforgettable name—inspired by the multitude of smashed windows—Crystal Night. On all sides Germany was assailed as a barbarous nation." Despite a friendly visit in Chicago with automobile tycoon Henry Ford, the film world by and large shunned her. Gary Cooper cancelled an invitation to meet her, and Walt Disney declined an offer to screen *Olympia*. Later, he told the press he really didn't know who Leni Riefenstahl was.

During World War II Riefenstahl served for a brief time as a war photographer and worked whenever possible on a feature film she directed and starred in, *Tiefland/Tiefland* (1954), begun in 1934 but not completed until after the war. At the close of World War II she was arrested by U.S. authorities and then released. The U.S. Army concluded that she may not have been aware of what went on in Nazi Germany and that her sin was one of omission, "which appears all the more serious due to the fact that she, more than any person, had the opportunity to get to the truth. She is a product of the moral corruption which characterizes the regime. But it would be false to picture her as an ambitious female who wanted to attain fame and wealth on the NSDAP bandwagon. She is certainly no fanatical National Socialist who had sold her soul to the regime. Admiration for Hitler had closed her eyes to all that his regime meant for Germany. His protecting hand insured her artistic activities—contrary to those of so many others. His hand offered protection from the political clutches, and built a dream-world for her in which she could live with 'her art'. . . . If her statements are sincere, she has never grasped, and still does not grasp, the fact that she, by dedicating her life to art, has given expression to a gruesome regime and contributed to its glorification." The French military was less forgiving. Shortly after being released by the U.S. Army, Riefenstahl was arrested by French police and remained in custody until 1947. In 1949, she was officially de-Nazified by a French tribunal. The Baden State Cammisariat classified her as a "fellow traveler."

Eventually, most of the films that had been confiscated from her were returned, either by government or court action. Though she attempted to resume her career as a filmmaker, press coverage of her activities made financing impossible to obtain. Riefenstahl claimed that Jewish organizations and not the German government were to blame. In the 1950s and 1960s, Riefenstahl began traveling to Africa, at first to make a film, but later to take still photographs of tribes in the southern Sudan. The result was her first book of still photographs, published in English as *The Last of the Nuba* (1974). About the same time, Riefenstahl learned to dive and became an accomplished underwater photographer, using both still and motion picture cameras. With her companion, Horst Kettner, she organized diving expeditions to the Red Sea, Honduras, the Caribbean, the Indian Ocean, and elsewhere to capture the undersea world. In 1976, a second book of Africa photographs was published, *The People of Kao*, followed two years later by a book of underwater photographs, *Coral Garden* (1978). She wrote the text and composed the layout for a fourth book, *Leni Riefenstahl's Africa* (1982). Her autobiography, *Leni Riefenstahl: A Memoir*, was published in 1987 and another book of still photographs, *Wonders under Water*, in 1991. The last of her publications, *Leni Riefenstahl: Five Lives*, appeared in 2000. The "five lives" refers to her many careers—as a dancer, actress, director, photographer, and diver.

CHURCHILL ROBERTS

See also **Olympia; Hitler and National Socialist Party: Critical Overview of; Triumph of the Will**

Biography

Born in Berlin, August 22, 1902. Showed an early interest in gymnastics, music, poetry, and dance. Finished schooling at the Kollmorgen Lyceum in Berlin in 1918, then attended the Grimm-Reiter Dance School and later the Jutta Klamt School and the dance school of Dresden. In 1923, gave first solo dance performance. In 1924, met actor Luis Trenker and director Arnold Fanck and soon starred in her first film, *The Holy Mountain*. In 1932, directed *The Blue Light*, followed by *Triumph of the Will* (1935) and *Olympia* (1938). War photographer in 1939, worked intermittently on a feature film, *Tiefland*, completed in 1954. Arrested in 1945 and released in 1947. Made the first of many trips to Africa in 1956 and in 1973 passed a diving test. First of five books of still photographs published in 1973. Photographed the 1972 Olympics for the *Sunday Times Magazine* and was guest of honor at the summer Olympics in Montreal in 1976. In 1982, awarded a gold cup by the International Olympic Committee for *Olympia*. Died in 2003 at the age of 101.

Selected Films

1926 *The Holy Mountain*: actress
1929 *The White Hell of Pitz Palu*: actress
1930 *Storm over Mont Blanc*: actress
1932 *The Blue Light*: actress, director, editor
1933 *Victory of Faith*: director, editor
1933 *SOS Iceberg*: actress
1935 *Triumph of the Will*: director, editor
1935 *Day of Freedom!—Our Armed Forces!*: director, editor
1938 *Olympia Part I: Festival of the People*: director, editor
1938 *Olympia Part II. Festival of Beauty*: director, editor
1954 *Tiefland*: director, actress, editor

Further Reading

Barsam, Richard M., *Film Guide to Triumph of the Will*, Bloomington: Indiana University Press, 1975.

Berg-Pan, Renata, *Leni Riefenstahl*, Boston: Twayne Publishers, 1980.

Fanck, Arnold, *Er führte Regie mit Gletschern, Stürem, Lawinen*, Munich: Nymphenburger Verlagshandlung, 1973.

Ford, Charles, *Leni Riefenstahl*, Paris: La Table Ronde, 1978.

Hinton, David B., *The Films of Leni Riefenstahl*, 3rd edition, Lanhan, MD: Scarecrow Press, 2000.

Hull, David Stewart, *Film in the Third Reich*, New York: Simon and Schuster, 1973.

Infield, Glen B., *Leni Riefenstahl: The Fallen Film Goddess*, New York: Thomas Y. Crowell Company, 1976.

Riefenstahl, Leni *Leni Riefenstahl: A Memoir*, New York: Picador USA, 1995.

———, *Leni Riefenstahl: Five Lives*, Cologne: Taschen, 2000.

Rother, Rainer, *Leni Riefenstahl: The Seduction of Genius*, London: Continuum. 2002.

Salkeld, Audrey, *A Portrait of Leni Riefenstahl*, London: Pimlico, 1997.

RIEN QUE LES HEURES

(France, Cavalcanti, 1926)

Rien que les heures was Alberto Cavalcanti's first directed film. The film was produced by Pierre Braunberger, an enlightened entrepreneur, committed to the enhancement of French independent film culture, who also produced films for other independent filmmakers during the 1920s.

Rien que les heures opens with an inter-title stating that "this film does not need a story, it is no more than a series of impressions on time passing." Nevertheless, the film does contain a story, concerning a day in the life of the city of Paris, although, unlike other "city symphony" films of the period, such as Joris Ivens's *Regan* (1929), chronology is neither linear nor logical in the film. No explanation is given, either, for these odd discrepancies. The primary function of the characters in the film is also to reinforce the central thesis of *Rien que les heures*, which is that, underlying the apparent civilised façade of bourgeois society, there exists a darker reality marked by violence, inequality, and brutality. This thesis, which is represented metaphorically in various sections of the film, is given particular substance in the film's subplot of criminality, violence, and victimisation.

One of the characters in the film is an old woman. Unconnected to the narrative causality of the film's story, she seems to function as a symbol, and metaphorical victim, of the degenerate urban world around her. Although a sense of irony pervades much of *Rien que les heures*, particularly in the way in which playful juxtapositions and modernist special effects are used, the sequences involving the old woman appear strikingly harsh and harrowing, and the last time she is seen, sitting down in an abandoned rubbish yard, could be interpreted as signifying her impending death.

At a retrospective of his work mounted at the National Film Theatre in 1977, Cavalcanti chose, rather surprisingly, to select a number of light Parisian songs to accompany a screening of *Rien que les heures*. This apparently had the effect of making the film appear largely ironic and even comic in parts, and of making the figure of the old woman appear paradoxic rather than tragic. The reasons for Cavalcanti's decision to use popular songs to accompany the film are unclear, but it is difficult to imagine how the old lame woman in the film

Rien que les heures, 1926.
[*Still courtesy of the British Film Institute*]

could have been rendered comic by such treatment. Whatever Cavalcanti's motives were in 1977, a careful viewing of the film suggests that this character is to be read realistically, rather than paradoxically.

The use of modernist devices in *Rien que les heures*, such as wipes, dissolves, and superimpositions, also serves to emphasise the authorial source of the critique of bourgeois norms mounted within the film, and the vision of the filmmaker is foregrounded here through the application of these explicitly modernist devices. *Rien que les heures* does not use these modernist devices for merely experimental purposes, but to demystify conventional forms of representation in order to critique bourgeois society. The film, therefore, can be said to possess a subversive intent.

Underlying *Rien que les heures* is also a notion of reality as masked, and the film uses juxtapositions to render the impression that a gradual unmasking process is taking place as the film unfolds. The film also uses a binary oppositional structure as part of this unmasking process, as conventional images based on clichéd perceptions of Parisian life repeatedly give way to others that subvert or contradict them. One example of this is a scene in which shots of food in a marketplace are followed by glimpses of rubbish in a bin. Again, the underlying idea is that, beneath the civilised façade, something far more primal and animalistic lurks.

Rien que les heures undoubtedly cemented Cavalcanti's reputation as an important avantgarde director. It is difficult, however, to compare the film with others of the period. Although Siegfried Kracauer has compared the film to Ivens's *Regan*, the two films are not really comparable. The anarchistic modernism of *Rien que les heures* also means that the film cannot really be compared with French cinematic impressionism, or the cinema pur. The use of melodramatic characterisation in the film also means that it cannot be easily compared to the "city symphony" genre. Perhaps the easiest association is with René Clair's *Entr' acte* (1924), although Cavlcanti's film still lacks the overtly Dadaist aspirations of Clair's film. Cavalcanti drew on many influences in making *Rien que les heures*, and the film is best regarded as a distillation of these influences, rather than a film that can be closely associated with others of the period. *Rien que les heures* was also the first, and almost the last high-modernist film made by Cavalcanti, and he was only to return to this type of filmmaking once more during the course of his career, with the collaborative project of *Coal Face* in 1935.

IAN AITKEN

See also Cavalcanti, Alberto

Rien que les heures (1926). Directed and edited by Alberto Cavalcanti. Produced by Pierre Braunberger and Neo-Films.

Further Reading

Aitken, Ian, *Alberto Cavalcanti, Realism, Surealism and National Cinemas*, London: Flicks Books, 2001.
———. *Film and Reform*, London: Routledge, 1990.
———. *The Documentary Film Movement, An Anthology*, Edinburgh: Edinburgh University Press, 1998.
Cavalcanti, Alberto, *Filme e Realidade*, Rio de Janeiro: Editora Artenova, in collaboration with Empresa Brasiliera de Filmes – Embrafilme, 1977.
Ghali, Noureddine, *L'Avant-Garde Cinématographique en France dans les Anées Vingt*, Paris: Editions Paris Experimental, 1995.
Pellizari, Lorenzo, and Claudio M. Valentinetti (eds.), *Alberto Cavalcanti*, Locarno: Éditions du Festival international du films de Locarno, 1988.
Sussex, Elizabeth, "Cavalcanti in England," in *Sight and Sound*, 44, 4, autumn, 1975.

RIGGS, MARLON

The filmmaker Marlon T. Riggs used film as a means to inform mainstream America of the complexities of African-American gay life, and to deconstruct black visual representation. In terms of focus, Riggs followed in the tradition of documentarians such as William Greaves and alongside filmmakers such as Henry Hampton, both of whom believed in the power and viability of the media to convey important social concerns regarding African Americans. Riggs's worked throughout the 1980s and early 1990s, during the presidencies of Ronald Reagan and George H.

W. Bush. At that time, the United States enjoyed tremendous financial gains, while simultaneously undermining and eliminating social services for the poor and people of color. The much-touted "cultural wars" shaped the artistic landscape. The culmination of enhanced commerce and communication advances led to an explosion of visual opportunities, especially via cable.

In his work, Riggs emphasized both commonalities and differences between the black gay community and black communities at large. He calls into question black spirituality, African heritage, black duality, and black humanity. He distinguishes a radical black aesthetic while pushing the boundaries of black aesthetics in general. Riggs's works addressing black gay life include *Tongues Untied* (1989), *Affirmations* (1990), *Anthem* (1991), and *Non, Je Ne Regrete Rien/No, I Regret Nothing* (1992).

The self-reflexive stance in Riggs's works offers an important commentary on African Americans specifically and others more generally. His confrontational approach of examining black homosexuality locates dialogue discrepancies within black communities. Because his work advocates change, his productions incited critical and popular debate.

Tongues Untied became Riggs's most controversial and celebrated work. Appearing on the national public television series *P.O.V.* in 1989, the documentary received the Best Documentary Award at the Berlin Film Festival and awards at other film festivals. It later became the center of a heated debate involving funding for the National Endowment for the Arts (NEA) and the Corporation for Public Broadcasting. Criticizing the film as vulgar and amoral, the Christian Coalition edited a sensationalized clip of the film and distributed it to every member of Congress. Republican Patrick Buchanan re-edited a twenty-second clip from the film to use in an attack on the NEA during the 1992 presidential primary. Riggs responded with an op-ed piece in the *New York Times* entitled "Meet the New Willie Horton."

Tongues Untied centers on the realties of black, male homosexual love. This was the first televised frank discussion of black homosexuality. In interviews Riggs said that he drew on his own personal experience in creating the documentary. He wanted to speak loudly about the painful experiences of being gay and black. *Tongues Untied* contemplates the nuances of self-definition, and the pressures and demands of an attempt to define oneself via multiple identities.

In *Tongues Untied*, the audience is directly addressed through the multilayering of both sounds and images. Alone and in concert with other voices, Riggs juxtaposes words, music, and sound to accost his audience. This cacophonous musical tradition plays very much into African-American sensibilities. Black music and oral traditions unify because they confront individuals with the truth of black existence. This same usage of music occurs in his film short *Anthem*. For example, Blackberri's rendition of the song "America" is positioned subversively to illuminate its irony for blacks and gays. Riggs uses rhythmic African drumbeats throughout *Tongues Untied* and *Anthem* to draw a line of continuity between the present and the past. Through Riggs's positioning of music in the background, as well as in the narrative of his films, he addresses gay and heterosexual African Americans in ways that transcend sexuality and race.

Not all of his projects take this combative, highly personal approach. *Ethnic Notions* (1987), his first major project, traced the evolution of racial stereotypes. It received an Emmy Award and has become a core text in college courses across the United States. *Color Adjustment* (1991) takes on television representations of blacks. For its insightfulness and creativity, it received one of television's highest accolades, the George Foster Peabody Award. These documentaries offer more traditional approaches to African-American representation in the commodified world of television and film. They use "voice-of-God" narration, scholarly experts, and multilayered images of blacks depicted over the span of seventy years in film and television. While in some ways Riggs's use of the prevailing techniques of majority aesthetics seem to give credence to them, it serves more usefully to undermine those same techniques by presenting subject matter rarely seen.

In his final work, *Black Is . . . Black Ain't* (1995), Riggs tackled the complex inner workings of black identity. Through his creative production methods, use of black aesthetics, and inclusion of his dying body as a template, Riggs's art functions as a foundation for critical examinations of African-American relations as a whole. Overall, Marlon Riggs's documentaries provide a road map for collective introspection and progress.

BERETTA E. SMITH-SHOMADE

Biography

Born in Fort Worth, Texas, February 3, 1957. Graduated *magna cum laude* from Harvard University and received Masters' degree from the University of California, Berkeley. Appointed a professor in Berkeley's Graduate

School of Journalism. At the age of 37, died of AIDS on April 5, 1994. His final film, *Black Is . . . Black Ain't*, was completed by his co-producer Nicole Atkinson and editor/co-director Christiane Badgely from the footage shot previously and notes left by Riggs.

Selected Films

1987 *Ethnic Notions*
1989 *Tongues Untied*
1990 *Affirmations*
1991 *Anthem*
1991 *Color Adjustment*
1992 *Non, Je Ne Regrete Rien/No, I Regret Nothing*
1995 *Black Is . . . Black Ain't*

Further Reading

Becquer, Marcos, "Snap!thology and Other Discursive Practices in Tongues Untied," in *Wide Angle*, 13, 2, April 1991, 6–17.
Datcher, Michael, "Pride and Prejudice: Ground-breaking Filmmaker Marlon Riggs Explores Two of Today's Most Controversial Issues: Race and Sexuality," in *San Francisco Focus*, February 1994, 38–43.
Grundmann, Roy, "New Agendas in Black Filmmaking: An Interview with Marlon Riggs," *Cineaste*, 19, 2–3, 1992, 52–54.
Riggs, Marlon, "Black Macho Revisited: Reflections of a Snap! Queen," in *The Independent*, April 1991, 32–4.

RIKLI, MARTIN

Before he got involved in filmmaking, Martin Rikli contributed largely to the development of camera equipment, most notably in the construction of the lightweight Kinamo, which revolutionized documentary filmmaking. He worked on contraptions that enabled slow motion, time lapse, and vibration-free microscopic photography. In his early films he combined his interest in aviation (he was a pioneering pilot) and aerial photography. Later on he applied microscopic and time-lapse photography to educational purposes in films.

Rikli's work can be subdivided into three groups: first are his expedition films for which he traveled to Africa and Asia (*Heia Safari*, 1928; *Am Rande der Sahara*, 1930; *Filmtagebuch vom Krieg in China*, 1932; *So ist China*, 1932; *Abessinien von heute – Blickpunkt der Welt*, 1935; and others) Around these films Rikli usually edited short features and also published news reports and books, thus always using his material in more than one medium. In this group of work Rikli's experience as a pilot was also visible, as they incorporate more than once aerial photography.

The second group consists of educational films in the field of chemistry and physics (*An der Schwelle des Lebens*, 1924; *Werden und Vergehen. Entstehung von Bakterien und Milben*, 1929–1930; *Unsichtbare Wolken*, 1932; *Strömungen und Wirbel*, 1934; *Röntgenstrahlen*, 1937; *Kalt, kälter, am kältesten*, 1937; and others). These films catered to Rikli's interest in the technological aspect of filmmaking. They gave him ample opportunity to apply microscopic and time-lapse photography. Customarily he mixed in touches of humor and entertainment.

The third group consists of films that were more or less in line with Nazi visions on the world. Still, he managed to apply a fresh style that was only peripherally "adorned" with Nazi rhetoric. *Strassen ohne Hindernisse* (1934), for example, records the construction of the German highway system in a fairly matter-of-fact way. Assessments by Fritz Todt and Adolf Hitler appear rather foreign in this discourse. *Wir erobern Land* (1937), on the other hand, praises the achievements of the Reichsarbeitsdienst and ends on images from the 1937 party rally and excerpts of Hitler's address. Likewise, *Flieger, Funker, Kanoniere* (1938) is an ode to the German air force and was made under the auspices of the Reich Ministry of Aviation.

With the beginning of the war, Rikli made *Wissenschaft weist neue Wege* (1939), which takes up the issue of the shortage of supply. *Schiessen und Treffen* (1940) applies extreme time-lapse photography to explain the trajectories and the impact of bomb shells. By the end of 1940, Rikli was commissioned to cover the German campaign in Norway. Although he was handed over the entire material of the official German war reporters, no film materialized.

Rikli resided to films on aerodynamics (*Windige Probleme*, 1941) and geological phenomena (*Erdbeben und Vulkane*, 1942), made in color. He also made a film on color photography (*Die Welt in Farben*, 1943). After the war he managed to achieve only a few short features on phenomena of the clouds.

There has been a discussion as to whether it is justifiable to call Rikli the Nazis's ready propagandistic war reporter. While Jürgen Brandt and Ursula von Keitz maintain that he made Nazi propaganda early on (even before their ascend to power), Kerstin Stutterheim points out that some of his pre-Nazi films were later adjusted to Nazi demands. His *Land ohne Schatten* (1929), which does look at Arab people from a European point of view, was recut into *Am Rande der Sahara* (1930) in which Rikli's material was incorporated, and which carried nationalistic and racist elements which already anticipated Nazi ideology. Moreover his assignment to the Norway project in 1940 did not materialize despite the large-scale support of the German army.

Biography

Born on January 19, 1898, in Zürich. Studied chemistry and earned doctoral degree with a dissertation on "*Die Abhängigkeit der Entflammbarkeit photographischer Zellulosefilme vom chemischen Alter*" (*The Inflammability of Photographic Celluloid Film and Its Dependence on Its Chemical Age, 1923)* Before then, turned to aviation and was one of the founders of the Akademische Gesellschaft für Flugwesen (Academic Society for Aviation) in Zürich. 1923 research department of Zeiss-Ikon in Dresden hired him as engineer. Published widely and gave lectures on the technology of film and cinematography. 1927 took leave to participate as a camera operator on an expedition to Africa during which he shot *Heia Safari*, which turned out to be such a commercial success that Ufa hired him for its Kulturabteilung. Films made during his tenure at Ufa are in line with the company's aim to popularize science and technology. With the rise of the Nazis, turned to subject matters more clearly ideological, conveying the "modernity" of Nazi and military institutions. In 1944, sensing the impending fall of the Nazis, returned to Switzerland. Founded the Institut für Farbenfotografie (Institute for Color Photography). Turned to the production of educational films. Nazi past made it difficult for him to find a firm footing in the film industry. In 1949, made his five last short feature documentaries. Until his death, lectured on color photography, wrote, and worked as a photographer for magazines. Died April 7, 1969 in Zürich.

Selected Films

1925 *Ägypten, das Land der Pyramiden*
1926 *An der Schwelle des Lebens*
1928 *Heia Safari!*
1929–1930 *Land ohne Schatten. Durch Nordafrikas Steppenländer*
1930 *Am Rande der Sahara* (with Rudolf Biebrach)
1931 *Das geheimnisvolle Schiff*
1932 *Unsichtbare Wolken. Ein Film über die Sichtbarmachung warmer Luft*
1932 *Filmtagebuch vom Krieg in China*
1934 *Als man anfing zu filmen* (with Wilhelm Prager)
1934 *F.P. 1 wird Wirklichkeit*
1934 *Gorch Fock. Bilder vom Leben und der Arbeit auf dem Segel-Schulschiff der deutschen Reichsmarine*
1935 *Straßen ohne Hindernisse. Ein Film über die Reichsautobahnen*
1935 *Abessinien von heute – Blickpunkt der Welt/ Abessinien*
1936 *Unendlicher Weltenraum*
1936 *Husaren der See. Deutsche Torpedoboote im Manöver*
1936 *Vom Schießen und Treffen*
1937 *Röntgenstrahlen*
1937 *Kalt . . . , kälter . . . , am kältesten . . .*
1937 *Achtung! Asien marschiert!*
1937 *Flieger, Funker, Kanoniere. Ein Querschnitt aus der Aufbauzeit der deutschen Luftwaffe*
1938 *Arbeitsmaiden helfen*
1939 *Flieger zur See*
1939 *Wissenschaft weist neue Wege*
1940 *Radium*
1940 *Jugend fliege*
1940 *Schießen und Treffen*
1942 *Erdbeben und Vulkane*
1943 *Volksleben am Rande der Sahara*
1943 *Wolkenspiel*
1943 *Die Welt in Farben*
1947 *Wolken als Wetterpropheten*
1949 *Kabel verlegen*
1949 *Trolleybus*

Further Reading

Brandt, Hans-Jürgen, "Porträt Martin Rikli," in *Filmfaust*, 36, Oktober/November 1983, 45–55.
Rikli, Martin, *Am Rande der Sahara*, Berlin: Hobbing, 1930.
———, *Wie ich Abessinien sah*, Berlin: Scherl 1935.
———, *Flieger, Funker, Kanoniere. Ein Querschnitt durch die deutsche Luftwaffe. Hg. von Dr. Martin Rikli*, Berlin: Schützen, 1938.
———, *Ich filmte für Millionen. Fahrten, Abenteuer und Erinnerungen eines Filmberichters*, Berlin: Schützen, 1942.
———, *Seltsames Abessinien. Als Filmberichter am Hof des Negus*, Zürich: Interverlag, 1947.
Rikli, Martin, and Roland Strunk. *Achtung! Asien marschiert! Ein Tatsachenbericht*, Berlin: Drei Masken, 1934.
1977 *Shatranj Ke Khiladi* ("The Chess Players").
1991 *Agantuk* ("The Stranger").

RIVER, THE

(US, Lorentz, 1937)

Pare Lorentz's follow-up film to *The Plow That Broke the Plains* (1936), *The River*, tells a story of the economic and ecological changes experienced along the Mississippi River and its tributaries. Its goal was to inform U.S. citizens about the problems posed by the rivers and their abuse, as well as to promote the solutions offered by a number of President Franklin Roosevelt's New Deal agencies, chiefly the Tennessee Valley Authority but also the Farm Security Administration (FSA) and the Civilian Conservation Corps (the Resettlement Administration, the agency behind *Plow* and *The River*, ceased to exist and many of its missions were absorbed within the FSA). Although it was first screened only to southern U.S. audiences, *The River* was intended for national distribution, which it eventually got through the assistance of Paramount Pictures. Considered to be Lorentz's greatest achievement, it beat seventy other films (including Leni Riefenstahl's *Olympia*) when it became the first U.S. film honored as the best documentary film at the Venice International Film Festival.

The film uses a documentary paradigm familiar in the 1930s: an initial situation is described (the Mississippi region was beautiful and held economic value), a problem is revealed (misuse of the land has led to soil erosion and flooding), and finally a solution is recommended (a variety of government agencies can restore the region to its original state). "Conservation," as suggested in *The River*, only implied the TVA's policies of flooding vast valleys to create dams and cheap hydroelectric power. Surrounding these federally funded dams were controversial issues including the government creation of electrical power, afforestation, reforestation, and the relocation of farmers from flooded lands to less productive areas in the hills. It was a project that would have massive political, economic, and ecological repercussions for the entire region. A film explaining this project would be representing and advocating many New Deal policies and agencies, and thus Roosevelt was willing to provide a much larger budget for *The River* than *Plow*, which was filmed in five states while *The River* was filmed in fourteen.

Lorentz filmed along the Mississippi River and its tributaries in late 1936, thinking he would use stock footage of floods and flooding as he finished his initial shooting in January 1937. Photographer Willard Van Dyke, whose letters written during the filming provide an important source of information on Lorentz's shooting process, estimated that Lorentz took one hundred thousand feet of film for a final product that would only total three thousand feet. The devastating floods of early 1937 allowed him the rare chance to capture shots of the flooded Mississippi and Ohio Rivers; the fresh memories of that natural disaster must have played a powerful role in the film's critical and popular reception. Furthermore, in contrast to the bleak ending in *Plow*, which ended, in the more widely shown version without its epilogue, with dust storms and displaced families heading off to an uncertain future, *The River* has a far more hopeful conclusion, showing images of ecological and economic regrowth: majestic shots of hydroelectric dams and power cables, of workers restoring fields. Its remarkably optimistic tone was popular among politicians, critics, and especially audiences, many of whom were reported to have cheered and applauded at the screenings. The initial four-reel version was shortened to a three-reel version where it enjoyed widespread distribution for many years among schools.

The collaboration between Lorentz and composer Virgil Thomson rivals that of Eisenstein and Prokofiev in their tight coordination between the visual and audible parts of the film. Dialectical gestures involving image and music, such as the alternating major-minor mode contrasts showing fertile and barren soil in *Plow*, return in *The River*, where Thomson instead contrasts diatonic and chromatic versions of a trumpet melody to underscore the distinction between lush and abused nature scenes. In addition to recycling

The River, 1937.
[*Still courtesy of the British Film Institute*]

parts of his earlier *Symphony on a Hymn Tune* (1928), Thomson wrote original cues based on a study of southern Protestant hymns and regional folk songs. Thomson's music for the log sequences includes quick-paced arrangements of popular songs like "Hot Time in the Old Town Tonight" as we see log after log shoot off the sluices into the water. The music accompanying the flood sequence is based on the hymn named "Mississippi" whose (unheard) lyrics describe an apocalyptic scene, and Thomson's treatment of this musical material builds synergistically with the imagery. As the flood on the image track builds up from dripping icicles to an overpowering deluge, the music grows from a single line stating the hymn melody into a thick fugue, finally culminating in the original harmonization of the hymn as found in the shape-note books. Visuals—long aerial shots of the bloated river and submerged houses—and music climax at this

moment. Parts of *The River's* score were reused in Nicholas Meyer's ABC-TV movie about nuclear bombings, *The Day After* (1983).

The River has been widely praised for its careful and effective blending of image, word, and music. Lorentz's narration, which has been compared to the poetry of Walt Whitman, and which James Joyce reportedly called the most beautiful prose he had heard in ten years, was not written until after the score had been composed and the film edited into its final form. Epic catalogues of river names and towns are repeated, as are key phrases. Parts of Lorentz's argument in *The River* have been criticized for being overly subtle, hyperbolic, and obtuse. He perhaps overemphasizes the connection between deforestation and flooding. As in *Plow*, Lorentz sought to encourage national identification with a regional problem and he again exaggerates the amount of territory in question; the rivers in Lorentz's maps take on Brobdagnigian proportions, although without any swiftian irony. His focus on larger natural and national forces tends to diminish the individuals and their reactions to adversity, although *The River* contains memorable images of intense human suffering, such as the shots of the faces of flood victims and migrant farmers.

NEIL LERNER

See also **Lorentz, Pare;** *Plow That Broke the Plains, The*

The River (U.S.A., black and white; Western Electric Mirrophonic Recording; Farm Security Administration; 1937, 35 mm, 36 min.; 16 mm, 27 min.). Released Oct. 29, 1937, premiering in New Orleans, Louisiana; Memphis, TN, November 1, 1937; St. Louis, November 10; Washington, DC, December 7. Distributed by Paramount Pictures. Written and directed by Pare Lorentz. Photographed by Floyd Crosby, Stacy Woodard, Horace Woodard, and Willard Van Dyke. Music composed by Virgil Thomson, orchestrated by Henry Brant, and conducted by Alexander Smallens. Narrator: Thomas Chalmers. Editing: Lloyd Nosler; Leo Zochling. Research editor: A. A. Mercey. Sound: Al Dillinger. Filmed along the Mississippi River Valley from October 1936 through March 1, 1937. Cost: ca. $50,000.

Further Reading

Alexander, William, *Film on the Left: American Documentary Film from 1931 to 1942*, Princeton: Princeton University Press, 1981.

Barsam, Richard M., *Non-Fiction Film: A Critical History*, Revised and expanded edition, Bloomington and Indianapolis: Indiana: Indiana University Press, 1992.

Lerner, Neil, "Damming Virgil Thomson's Music for *The River*," in *Collecting Visible Evidence*, edited by Jane M. Gaines and Michael Renov, Minneapolis and London: University of Minnesota Press, 1999.

MacCann, Richard D., *The People's Films: A Political History of U.S. Government Motion Pictures*, New York: Hastings House, 1973.

Rabinowitz, Paula, *They Must Be Represented: The Politics of Documentary*, London and New York: Verso, 1994.

Rollins, Peter C., "Ideology and Film Rhetoric: Three Documentaries of the New Deal Era," in *The Journal of Popular Film*, 5, 2, 1976, 126–145.

Snyder, Robert L., *Pare Lorentz and the Documentary Film*, Norman: University of Oklahoma Press, 1968.

Thomson, Virgil, *Virgil Thomson*, New York: Dutton, 1966.

Tommasini, Anthony, *Virgil Thomson: Composer on the Aisle*, New York and London, Norton, 1997.

Van Dyke, Willard, "Letters from *The River*," in *Film Comment*, 1965, 38–56.

Widgery, Claudia Joan, *The Kinetic and Temporal Interaction of Music and Film: Three Documentaries of 1930's America*, Ph.D. dissertation, University of Maryland, 1990.

ROBERT FLAHERTY FILM SEMINAR, THE

Having provided fifty years of service to the field of independent film, the Robert Flaherty Film Seminar is a unique institution that inspires, encourages, and challenges filmmakers and other artists to explore and contemplate the creative aspect of the moving image and its potential to illuminate the human spirit. Through screenings, discussion, and debate, the seminar provides an intensive inquiry into the state of independent film and other media forms, with an emphasis on the art and practice of documentary.

Robert Flaherty (1884–1951), an engineer, explorer, and writer, was a pioneer in the field of documentary film. Between 1913 and 1951, he acted as a producer, director, writer, editor, cinematographer, and narrator and was involved in the making of nineteen films. Many of the fourteen

films he directed are considered to be innovative, artistic, and legendary classics and include *Nanook of the North* (1922), *Moana* (1926), *Man of Aran* (1934), *Elephant Boy* (1937), *The Land* (1941), and *Louisiana Story* (1948). Flaherty was unique in his understanding of the artistic potential inherent in film, in his goal of seeing and representing the human condition, and in his development and implementation of an innovative filmmaking style.

In 1954, three years after Flaherty's death at the age of 67, his widow and frequent collaborator, Frances, and his brother, David, who was also a documentary filmmaker, invited a small group of filmmakers and students to meet together informally in the "Barn" at the Flaherty farm in Vermont. The group viewed Flaherty's films, reflected on his vision of a humanistic cinema, and discussed their own work in relation to his films and vision. The informal gathering was such a success that Francis and David decided to renew it annually so that they could keep Flaherty's films and vision alive.

In 1955, Francis formed the Robert Flaherty Foundation to administer the annual seminar, which came to be known as "the Flaherty Experience," as well as to encourage the study of "the Flaherty method" of filmmaking, to provide information and advice to young directors, and to ensure the continued availability of Flaherty's films. Francis maintained that Flaherty's "name and spirit . . . can only be perpetuated as he would wish it by an institution whose prime purpose is to help new talent to explore further and further into the possibilities of a medium so immense and so unknown." The first formal Robert Flaherty Film Seminar was held that year at the Flaherty farm.

In 1960, the Foundation was absorbed by International Film Seminars Inc. (IFS), a New York–based nonprofit organization. Over time, IFS has developed into an established and respected media arts institution, and, although the seminar remains its central and defining activity, it is recognized as a leader in its dedication to the global advancement and development of independent films, videos, and other moving-image arts.

Since its intimate and informal beginnings, the seminar has developed into a unique forum. It has moved beyond its initial focus of Flaherty's own films and has been expanded from one weekend to seven days, but the seminar does continue be faithful to its original design, which was to allow participants to become immersed in the process of exploration and discovery that was such a distinguishing factor in Flaherty's life and films.

Today, every June, the seminar brings together more than one hundred participants, including worldwide film and media artists, scholars, critics, archivists, programmers, curators, librarians, students, and enthusiasts of film and video, and provides them with an unparalleled opportunity to carry on Flaherty's work. Participants continue to explore the creative process; to discover, reveal, and illuminate the ways of life in different cultures around the world; and to reaffirm the freedom of the independent artist to extend the form and content of moving images beyond their existing limitations.

In a relaxed retreat environment, participants view a rich mixture of works of exceptional artistic quality from around the world (including documentary, narrative, experimental, avant-garde, animated, and new media works) and then participate in intense and productive discussion sessions about the films with their respective directors. To ensure that participants are able to experience the three films screened each day from a fresh perspective, the programmers do not reveal the identity of any of the films until they are actually screened.

Seminar participants reside in the same location and are encouraged to attend all screenings, discussion sessions, and meals together so that they can build a sense of community and have a common basis for engaging in the overall discourse that develops throughout the week. Experienced and respected programmers have the complete discretion to select the films that will be screened at the seminar, and the flexibility to revise the viewing schedule as the week progresses so they can accommodate the overall trajectory of the discussions as various issues, ideas, and themes surface and develop. Each year after a seminar has ended, a selection of the films presented at that seminar is screened at the Museum of Modern Art in New York.

Over the years, the seminar has addressed many interesting and diverse topics, including "Essays, Experiments and Excavations," "Out-Takes Are History," "Investigating the Real," "Gender Dichotomies and Social Spectacles," "Animated Images and Exploration of Multicultural Talents," "Exploration in Memory and Modernity," "Documenting the Community," "Passin' It On: The Documentary Across Generations," "Landscapes and Place," "The Camera Reframed: Technology and Interpretation," and "Cinema and History." The seminar also has had the privilege of hosting a number of diverse and distinguished guests and programmers, including Eric Barnow, Shirley Clarke, Joris Ivens, Louis Malle, Chris Marker, Trinh T. Minh-Ha, D. A. Pennebaker, Satyajit Ray, Marlon Riggs, Michael Renov, Jean Rouch, Susan Sontag, Peter Watkins, and Frederick Wiseman. The seminar is based, produced, and usually held in New York, but in recent years, it also has been held in California, Connecticut, Israel, Latvia, Minnesota, Ohio, Puerto Rico, Massachusetts, North Carolina, and Vermont. Regional and international seminars also are presented on an occasional basis.

Directors who screen their films at the seminar, as well as participants who attend it, universally find the seminar to be an invaluable experience. One director noted that the seminar is "the toughest, most valuable, most stimulating arena in which a filmmaker can present his/her work. . . . If one is lucky enough to exhibit one's work, while putting ego and defense in cold storage (at least during the seminar), one will emerge from it with a treasure trove of helpful hints, insights, and much durable and invaluable commentary on one's work." One participant pointed out that the seminar "is truly a unique experience. A group of people from various parts of the world, with diverse outlooks on film, . . . [is] brought together for one week of intensive screenings and discussion. Our link to one another is our serious devotion to film as a means of communicating something about the human condition . . . although the discussions sometimes became heated . . . [the] two way communication between film-maker and audience was, for me, the most important part of the learning process."

The IFS Web site has the most up-to-date and complete information about the seminar and its history (the contents of certain portions of the web site have been summarized in this entry).

SUZANNE EISENHUT

See also **Flaherty, Robert**

Further Reading

International Film Seminars, Inc. Website: http://www.flahertyseminar.org.

ROCHEMONT, LOUIS DE

Best known and remembered as creative head of *The March of Time* series, Louis de Rochemont was an innovator in other types of filmmaking that were also influential and imitated, all of which featured a certain emphasis on realist technique and style. His early (begun in adolescence) and extensive background was as a newsreel cameraman and director.

In 1934, he created *The March of Time* (*MOT*) with Roy Larson of *Time* magazine (its first issue was February 1935) and remained its head until 1943. *The MOT* was a twenty-minute monthly news magazine of one to three stories. De Rochemont called it "pictorial journalism," and it made use of interviews, newsreel footage, and recreations of actual events. In 1940, *March of Time* released a feature-length compilation entitled *The Ramparts We Watch*, which summarized the European situation after the outbreak of World War II.

From 1943 to 1946, de Rochemont was a producer at 20th Century-Fox (which was distributing *March of Time*). His work included the feature-length Technicolor documentary *The Fighting Lady* (1944), about the final phase of the war in the Pacific. (The title refers to an aircraft carrier, the Yorktown in this case.) It was directed by famed still photographer Edward Steichen and narrated by movie star Robert Taylor, both then in the Navy. (De Rochemont had himself been a naval officer from 1917 to 1923.)

At Fox he began production of semi-documentary features based on actuality: *The House on 92nd Street* (1945) was about the FBI exposure of a German espionage ring; *13 Rue Madeleine* (1947) focused on the training and a mission of Office of Strategic Services (OSS) agents during the war; and *Boomerang!* (1947) was based on events in the life of Homer Cummings, who became Attorney General under Franklin Roosevelt. Although these films do not otherwise seem to have much in common with the British wartime semi-documentaries, they share the same characteristic documentary concentration on how things are done. But most pointedly, they use a Voice-of-Time style narration over their openings and subsequently to provide explanations and transitions, and to imply their authenticity.

After leaving Fox in 1948, he established Louis de Rochemont Associates. This firm continued to make occasional semi-documentary theatrical features (*Lost Boundaries*, 1949; *The Whistle at Eaton Falls*, 1951), sponsored films for advertising and public relations use, and classroom films. His major educational project was *The Earth and Its Peoples* series of thirty-six films, each about twenty minutes long, containing such titles as *Eskimo Hunters*, *Highlands of the Andes*,

Horsemen of the Pampas, *Farmers of India*, and *On Mediterranean Shores*.

As far as documentary film is concerned, de Rochemont remains a peripheral, if highly influential, producer. *March of Time* set off a succession of similar series. John Grierson and members of his group were involved with it in England and New York, and Grierson carried its conception with him to Canada as the model for the National Film Board's *World in Action* series. In the United States there were several imitative competing series including *Pathé News* and *Paramount News*. The influence of *The March of Time*, and perhaps most especially the compilation feature coming out of it, *The Ramparts We Watch*, is very evident in the U.S. Armed Forces *Why We Fight* series supervised by Frank Capra. *MOT* influence even carried over recognizably into television in the Murrow/Friendly *See It Now* (1951–1958), and *60 Minutes* (1968–). De Rochemont's semi-documentaries established precedents for subsequent theatrical features based on fact, including *The China Syndrome* (1979), about the possible meltdown of a nuclear reactor, and *Missing* (1982), about the disappearance and death of an American writer in Chile.

But de Rochemont, while never exactly part of the Hollywood filmmaking community, was not at home among the documentarians working in New York City and Washington, DC.

He is best categorized as on the edge of the theatrical film industry, with his early experience in newsreels remaining a continuing central influence.

JACK C. ELLIS

See also **March of Time**

Biography

Born in Chelsea, Massachusetts, January 13, 1899. Attended Massachusetts Institute of Technology; Naval Aviation School; Harvard Naval Cadet School. Served in British Military Intelligence, 1916–1917. Officer in United States Navy, 1917–1923. Cameraman for International, and for Pathé News; director of short film program, 20th Century-Fox (*Adventures of a Newsreel Cameraman* and *Magic Carpets of Movietone* series), 1923–1929. Created, with Roy E. Larson, the *March of Time* series, 1934. Creative head of *March of Time*, 1935–1951. Producer, 20th Century-Fox, 1943–1946. Founded Louis de Rochemont Associates, 1948. Produced *The Earth and Its Peoples* educational series, and films in Cinerama and other wide-screen processes. Received Special Academy Award for *The March of Time*, 1936. Died December 23, 1978.

Further Reading

Fielding, Raymond, *The March of Time: 1935–1951*, New York: Oxford University Press, 1978.
Lafferty, William, "de Rochemont, Louis," *International Dictionary of Films and Filmmakers*, Detroit: St. James Press, 1993, vol. 4, 211–213.

RODRÍGUEZ, MARTA AND JORGE SILVA

The Columbian team of Marta Rodríguez and Jorge Silva began to make their mark with their first film together, the remarkable *Chircales/Brickworkers*, a portrait of a family of workers in the brickyards on the outskirts of Bogotá. The film was completed in 1972 after five years of work. It was immediately recognised internationally for its originality and beauty as a quite exceptional fusion of politics, visual poetry, and ethnographic documentary.

Marta Rodríguez came to documentary through sociology and anthropology, Jorge Silva, the cinematographer of the pair, through journalism, photography, and the film club movement. Their collaboration, which ended in 1987 with Silva's early death, was a harmonious union in which the two were entirely complementary. It also conjoined the lyricism of Silva's camerawork with the new radical sociology associated with Camilo Torres, and the new thinking about visual anthropology of Jean Rouch, with both of whom Rodríguez studied in Bogotá and Paris, respectively. As she explained in a 1974 interview, "When you combine the social sciences with a mass medium like film, you are challenging the uses to which both are put by the privileged class while simultaneously putting them at the service of the working class. In contrast to the kind of hermetic treatise that only five initiates can read, this is a way to use anthropology or sociology so that the working class can put it to use analyzing their particular situation."

This approach explains the time they took to make *Chircales* and subsequent films. The methodology required extensive periods of field work, using stills photography and tape recordings; then the elaboration of a script, followed by filming and then editing, all the while allowing time for the subjects of the film to participate in the process at each stage. The result is to draw the discourse of documentary into the subjects' own subjectivity without losing a sociopolitical perspective. In thus uncovering the whys and wherefores of everyday life among the most marginalised victims of social "progress" in the Third World, their work also exemplified the aims of the new documentary then emerging across Latin America.

Planas, testimonio de un Genocidio/Planas: Testimony About Ethnocide (1970) was made rather more rapidly, while *Chircales* was still being completed. This is a denunciatory film that documents the genocide of the Guajibo people of the Amazon region and explores the economic and social causes of the slaughter. Then in 1976, they completed *Campesinos/Peasants*, which turns to questions of popular memory, reconstructing the peasant struggles for land of the 1930s through the recollection of the older generation. For the next five years they worked with an indigenous group in the region of Cauca on *Nuestra Voz De Tierra, Memoria Y Futuro/Our Voice of Land, Memory and Future* (1981), which takes the discourse of documentary further into the interior spaces of social identity and ideology. In telling the story of the creation of the Regional Indigenous Council of Cauca (CRIC), the film uses enactment to visualise an old legend about a landowner who makes a pact with the devil to rob the peasants of their land and labour. But this is a long way from the docudrama conventions of British or American television, both in style and intent. Here, the social subjectivity of myth and legend is seen as a living metaphor of exploitation, the symbolic expression of the process of extraction of surplus value.

Before *Nuestra Voz . . .* was completed, they again interrupted their work to make another film of denunciation, *La voz de los sobrevivientes/The Voice of the Survivors* (1980), made at the request of the CRIC to condemn the assassination of a number of peasant leaders. Then followed *Amor, Mujeres Y Flores/Love, Women and Flowers* (completed 1989 by Rodríguez after Silva's death), an investigation of the Columbian flower industry—the country's second largest export industry at the time—and its use of pesticides, made by companies like Bayer, which are banned at home but freely exported to the Third World. There they are used, as in this case, to produce perishable consumer goods that are whisked back to Europe to be sold, leaving the women who sort the flowers with damaged health, and their children born with genetic defects. A multilayered film told from the point of view of the men and particularly women who work within it, the film unfolds a graceful metaphor that brings women and flowers together, intertwining the process of production with the cycle of life and death—the life and death of the flowers against the life and death of the workers. The film refrains from explicit denunciation of responsibility, but critics at home, when it was shown on television, worried that it would damage Columbian flower sales abroad, while one of its foreign funders, the U.S. Interamerican Foundation, was so upset that they took their name off the credits.

After Silva's death, Rodríguez made one more documentary on film, *Nacer de nuevo/Born Again* (1987), a reflection on death, solitude, and love told by two aged survivors of the eruption of the Nevado del Ruiz, before she turned to video, working with indigenous groups in workshops she helped to set up in 1992, which have joined the indigenous video movement that began in Brazil and has subsequently spread through the countries of the Andes.

MICHAEL CHANAN

Biography

Marta Rodríguez. Born 1938 in Bogotá, Colombia. Jorge Silva. Born 1941. Died 1988.

Selected Films

1971 *Planas: testimonio de un etnocidio*: co-directors
1972 *Chircales*: co-directors

RODRÍGUEZ, MARTA AND JORGE SILVA

1975 *Campesinos*: co-directors
1980 *La voz de los sobrevivientes*: co-directors
1981 *Nuestra voz de tierra: memoria y futuro*: co-directors
1987 *Nacer de Nuevo*: Marta Rodríguez, director
1988 *Amor, mujeres y flores*: co-directors
1992 *Memoria vida*: Marta Rodríguez, director

Further Reading

Burton, Julianne (ed.), *Cinema and Social Change in Latin America: Conversations with Filmmakers*, Austin: University of Texas Press, 1986.
Paranagua, Paulo Antonio (ed.), *Cine Documental en America Latina*, Madrid: Editorial Catedra, 2003, Jump Cut No.38.

ROGER & ME

(US, Moore, 1989)

Roger & Me was the debut film of radical journalist Michael Moore and an immediate critical and, rare for a nonfiction film, commercial success. It has attracted endless criticism for its formal inventiveness and complex rhetoric, and an equal measure of controversy regarding the filmmaker's supposed violation of the documentary code of ethics. The result, according to one critic, is "an extraordinary film which is likely to be regarded as a major landmark in contemporary documentary" (Corner, 1996: 156).

The film traces the industrial decline of Flint, Michigan, the "company town" of General Motors (GM) and home to Michael Moore. The filmmaker sets off in search of Roger Smith, GM chairman, to confront him about the factory closures and the plight of the town in the 1980s. Moore draws on a panoply of interactive and reflexive techniques to construct his film; home movies, promotional videos, news sources and interviews combine to produce an hilarious but telling critique of the postindustrial corporate system and the shallowness of public discourses in dealing with the consequences of industrial change.

The production cost about $160,000, paid for by Moore, donations, product placement, and various fund-raising events. It played to enthusiastic screenings at film festivals and, in one of the saga's many ironies, was acquired for distribution for an unprecedented $3 million by the world's then-largest media corporation, Time-Warner. Initially, influential critics like Roger Ebert and Vincent Canby praised the film highly, but accusations of bad practice surfaced in a published interview with Moore in *Film Comment*, which doubted the validity of the film's depicted chronology; Pauline Kael endorsed this view at the *New Yorker* and furthermore questioned the derogatory treatment of some of the respondents in the film and its presumed moral superiority. Some radicals were put off by the film's whimsicality. Many were quick to defend the filmmaker, however, and a wide-ranging debate now surrounds *Roger & Me*, Moore's populism, and his unconventional style and legacy.

Juxtaposition and contrast are the principal characteristics of the film. These are evident in the fundamental opposition of Moore's personal, biographical and hence subjective placement in the text, and his objective responsibility as an investigative journalist in exposing the "truth" about

Roger & Me, Michael Moore, 1989.
[*Courtesy of the Everett Collection*]

Roger & Me, Michael Moore, with Rhonda Britton (Flints Bunny Lady) and Fred Ross (Repo Man) in front of a Buick ad, 1989.
[*Courtesy of the Everett Collection*]

economic and social conditions in Flint. Moore brilliantly extends this approach to his film style. The local officials' pathetic attempts to talk up the virtues of the town and develop its tourism are stood against a seemingly endless series of evictions of families from their homes. While the wealthy and secure, at their garden parties and golf clubs, harp on about opportunities that await those with the right positive attitude, we meet laid off workers queuing to sell their blood for a few dollars or forlornly shooting hoop at the local mental health clinic. The callousness of the "better classes" are further exposed in their thoughtless enjoyment of an opening night party at a newly commissioned jail, which Moore revisits when it is full of disillusioned and criminalized ex-car workers, presided over by former colleagues now forced to work for a much lower hourly rate. The film culminates in a masterly intercut sequence between Roger Smith delivering his annual Christmas message to GM

workers and stockholders, and the eviction in the snow of a poor black family. While Smith mouths his platitudes, a little child looks on in dismay as the sheriff's men dump Christmas presents on the sidewalk. Throughout, Moore retains a keen eye for the quirky and bizarre: the self-styled Captain Dada, come to rescue Flint in its hour of need, is summarily shot by a nervous police force; the inability of U-Haul to keep any trucks in Flint due to the exodus of people out of the luckless town; and the sudden blackening of a *Nightline* broadcast on the factory closures following the theft of the OB truck by a disgruntled local citizen.

It is widely assumed that the backlash of negative criticism cost *Roger & Me* the Oscar for Best Documentary. GM was quick to circulate copies of Kael's scathing review. Moore's manipulations of chronological sequence to heighten thematic and narrative effect seriously undermined the integrity of the film for some, but for supporters these are mere trifles when compared to the larger issues of unemployment, poverty and the abuse of corporate responsibility. After all, no one can dispute the fact of the plant closures and their effects. Adopting this line, Miles Orvell argues that Moore sacrifices historical accuracy for satiric fiction and "what Moore delivers is not the 'straight' truth of documentary but the oblique truth of satire" (Orvell, 1994–1995). From such a position, the film's radical credentials are not undermined.

The film grossed $7 million on its initial North American run, and was followed up in 1992 with the short *Pets or Meat*, which updated the story of the earlier film's leading characters, Deputy Fred and the Bunny Lady. Moore has continued to produce popular, commercial, and controversial documentaries, notably with *Bowling for Columbine* (2002) and *Fahrenheit 9/11* (2004); the latter is likely to become the most successful documentary film of all time.

ALAN BURTON

See also **Moore, Michael**

Further Reading

Corner, John, *The Art of Record. A Critical Introduction to Documentary*, Manchester: MUP, 1996.
Jacobson, Harlan, "Michael and Me," in *Film Comment*, November–December, 1989, 16–26.
Orvell, Miles, "Documentary Film and the Power of Interrogation. *American Dream & Roger and Me*," in *Film Quarterly*, winter, 1994–1995, 10–18.
Pierson, John, *Spike, Mike, Slackers and Dykes. A Guided Tour across a Decade of Independent American Cinema*, London: Faber and Faber, 1996.

ROGOSIN, LIONEL

Lionel Rogosin, the controversial director initially recognized by the free cinema movement in the mid-1950s, rejected traditional documentary style and technique. Rogosin emphasized a focused and personal approach toward storytelling. With postwar optimism competing against Cold War paranoia, Rogosin directed his attention to the individual problems that existed against such a politicocultural backdrop.

By the time Rogosin had entered the film world, the development of lightweight equipment, coupled with the advent of magnetic sound tape, allowed the cameraman and film director more freedom of mobility. Suddenly filmmakers were able to easily venture forth, into a variety of environments. Rogosin used this new technology on his first film, *On the Bowery* (1957), which focused on the inhabitants of New York's skid row. Rogosin took his camera to the streets where the homeless congregated, capturing the uninterrupted daily exchanges of those living the life of the downtrodden. The images captured in these shots are not only indicative of his work in general, but more often prove to be the key aspect of his work's influence on subsequent filmmakers and critics.

In his work, the long take is valued for its expansive and atmospheric qualities, rather than as an instrument of pure voyeurism. The direct cinema movement argued that such emphasis on capturing life from a "fly on the wall" perspective was key to the entire documentary enterprise. Many, however, considered this a controversial stance, and questioned whether the camera was picking up life uninterrupted, or was inherently interpreting what was recorded, from the perspective of the director's point of view.

Rogosin often presented his documentary films as the temporal progression of a loosely scripted narrative. Rather than writing a lengthy script and then contracting actors to portray the characters, however, Rogosin and his crew found real individuals who embodied the characters of his vision.

There are elements of compassion in the mise-en-scène of Rogosin's work, that at times elevates his films beyond others of the time. Part of this can be attributed to Rogosin's ability to never fully align himself with just one theoretical approach—he was influenced by Robert Flaherty, as well as John Grierson and others. *On the Bowery* was recognized for its honest portrayal of the gritty underside of human existence, while maintaining an aversion to melodrama. As significant as his films are, however, they were also criticized for the elements of staging that occurred, a controversial aesthetic that would follow throughout Rogosin's career, but one that Rogosin himself defended as necessary.

Rogosin's next film, *Come Back, Africa* (1960), was received with mixed reviews. It was as if to review the film one had to acknowledge it as two separate films in one. Many seemed to recognize the emotional power of the documentary segments, especially given the difficulty Rogosin faced in obtaining the footage. At the time of filming, government control forbade depictions of apartheid, and Rogosin's crew obtained visas to film in South Africa only under the false guise of an innocuous musical about mine workers. As bogus dailies of the musical were given to the government for approval, the real documentary footage of widespread repression and poverty was smuggled out of the country in suitcase lining.

As important a feat as it was for Rogosin to make *Come Back, Africa* and as powerful as the clandestine footage was, those are only some aspects of the film, not the complete work. As with many of his films, the dialogue sequences proved confusing and left many to ponder the value of their inclusion in the film, and to question Rogosin's decision to include such staged material in what was otherwise a well-constructed documentary. In one particular sequence there is a fifteen-minute roundtable discussion, half improvisational, half scripted, that is broken up only by a musical number from Miriam Makeba. A dialogue sequence of this length would seem somewhat excessive in most pictures, and to many reviewers it appeared especially so with such amateur actors. Rogosin always stuck by the merits of his nonactors and continued to use them in similar socially conscious films for the next two decades.

Rogosin's theories on the documentary were often as controversial as his films. He seemed to support the use of nonfiction almost as a scientific base to help project his interpretations into the mind of the viewer, to create an alternate reality for that viewer. When one takes into account his background in chemical engineering it seems to make sense, if one considers the friction he created by juxtaposing raw realist footage diegetic narratives, for example.

DINO EVERETT

See also **On the Bowery**

Biography

Born the son of a wealthy industrialist in New York City, January 22, 1924. Studied chemistry at Yale University before leaving to serve as an engineer during World War II on a U.S. Navy minesweeper. After the war, returned to school and graduated from Yale with a degree in chemical engineering before turning his focus toward film in his early 1930s. Hired by United Nations to direct a public information film in 1956. In 1958 won the grand prize for a documentary from the Venice Film Festival, a British Film Academy award, and was nominated for an Oscar for his first independently produced feature, *On the Bowery* (1957). From 1960–1974, was owner of the Bleeker Street Cinema in Greenwich Village, an important venue for independent films. In 1966, along with Shirley Clarke and Jonas Mekas, was one of the founding partners in the Film-Maker's Distribution Center, a nonprofit releasing venture that sought to spread the films of the avant-garde. Continued to make socially conscious films throughout the late 1960s and 1970s while lecturing on college campuses. Father of producer/director Daniel Rogosin. Died December 8, 2000, in Los Angeles of a heart attack.

Selected Films

1956 *Out*: cinematographer
1957 *On the Bowery* (Sufrin): producer, co-director, cinematographer, co-writer
1960 *Come Back, Africa a.k.a. An African Story*: director, co-writer
1966 *Good Times, Wonderful Times*: director
1972 *Black Fantasy*: director
1973 *Woodcutters of the Deep South*: director

Further Reading

Davis, Peter, "Rogosin and Documentary," in *Film Culture*, 24, spring 1962, 25–28.
Dickinson, Thorold, "A Note on Out," in *Sight and Sound*, spring 1957, 174.
Hey, Kenneth R., "Come Back Africa (1959): Another Look," in *Film & History*, X, 3, September 1980, 61–66.
James, David E., *To Free The Cinema*, Princeton, NJ: Princeton University Press, 1992.
Rogosin, Lionel, "Interpreting Reality (Notes on the Esthetics and Practices of Improvisational Acting)," in *Film Culture*, 21, summer 1960, 20–28.
Sufrin, Mark, "Filming A Skid Row," in *Sight and Sound*, winter 1955–1956, 133–139.

ROMANIA

Only five months after its world premiere in Paris, the cinematograph arrived in Bucharest (Romania), on May 27, 1896, brought along by a team of the Lumière Company, led by Edwin Schurmann. The first projections took place inside the building of the French-language newspaper, *L'Indépendance roumaine*, which had been printed in Bucharest since 1876. Schurmann's team showed a number of early *ciné-vérité* productions including: *A Dinner-Party, Cycling Lessons, The Conservatory, Parishioners Leaving the Church, Breakfast Picnic, Place de l'Opéra, The Buffet*, as well as the legendary *Arrival of a Train in the Ciotat Station*. The first film made in Romania was a newsreel recording of the Royal Parade in Bucharest on May 10, 1897, shot by the Lumière cameraman, Paul Menu (1876–1973). Within two months, sixteen other similar newsreels on various topics followed: *The Moshilor Fair, The Hippodrome and the Races at Băneasa, The Terrace of the Capşa Café, The Flood in Galatzi, The Training of Terrestrial Marines, The Ships of the Danube Fleet*, and others. Paul Menu became known as a Romanian filmmaker during his stay in the country. His camera was later bought by Dr. Gheorghe Marinescu (1863–1938), who used it for his research in neurology, and who eventually completed the first scientific film in the world (*Walking Disturbances of the Physical Paresis*, 1898), together with the Romanian cameraman, Constantin M. Popescu. The same year, Prof. M. Benko introduced audiences from Transylvania to the cinematograph, at a time when the region was still part of the Austro-Hungarian Empire. This accounts for the independent manner in which the cinematographic industry developed across the Romanian territory during the first two decades of its existence (that is, before Transylvania joined the other two provinces, Moldavia and Valachia, in 1918). One of the important figures of this early period was the Hungarian-born filmmaker Eugen (Jeno) Janovics, who made several documentaries about Romania (for productions companies based in Cluj), before contributing to some of the first Hungarian fiction films (such as *A sarga csiko*, 1913), as co-producer alongside Pathé.

The first photographers (turned filmmakers) born in the Balkans region, however, were the Romanian-Macedonian brothers Ienake Manaki (1878–1954) and Miltiade Manaki (1882–1964), who captured still images of a popular uprising in 1903 for the Romanian newspaper *Universul*. Before them, the Romanian painter, Carol Popp de Szathmary (1812–1888), became the first war correspondent in the world, taking photographs of the Crimean War in the 1850s. The Manaki brothers successfully exhibited their work at the 1906 International Exhibition in Bucharest, where they saw the cinematographic camera for the first time. The two bought a Bioscope 300 camera from the Charles Urban & Co firm during a trip that took them from Paris to London, thanks to a grant from King Karol I. The same year they made a documentary film, *Household Traditions of the Romanian-Macedonian Women from Pind*, soon followed by several other productions showing popular dances, religious rituals, weddings, and funerals of the same region, which can be considered among the first, if not the first ever, ethnographic films in the world. The Manakia brothers also pioneered the longer newsreel film by recording the visits of Sultan Mehmed Rashid V to Salonika and Bitola in 1911. Less than two decades later, in 1928, Prof. Dimitrie Gusti and his team of trained sociologists started making the first sociological documentaries: *Romanian Folkloric Traditions* (1928, directed by Mihail Vulpescu), *Drăguş—Life in a Romanian Village* (1929, directed by Paul Sterian, Nicolae Argintescu-Amza), *A Village in Bessarabia—Cornova* (1931, directed by Henri Stahl, Anton Golopenţia), and *Traditions from Bucovina* (1937, directed by Henri Stahl, Constantin Brăiloiu).

As in most other countries, the documentary as a genre predated fiction films in Romania. The earliest Romanian feature production (*Amor Fatal*) dates from 1911, shortly followed by the

first historical production, *The Independence of Romania* in 1912. During World War I, the Romanian government was relocated to Iaşi (in Northern Moldavia), where the Cinematographic Service of the Romanian Army came into existence in December 1916. It was one of the earliest state-run production companies in the world that specialised in documentary films. A number of cameramen, such as Constantin Ivanovici, Tudor Posmantir, Georges Ercole, and Nicolae Barbelian, started their careers in this company, making newsreel films during the war. The Cinematographic Service was endowed with its own studio in 1937, a year before the company became independent. A constant production of newsreels on Romanian and foreign current affairs marked the activity of the newly founded National Office for Cinematography during the 1930s. Other topics dealt with in subsisting newsreels of the period included cultural and sports events, natural disasters, religious services, demonstrations, as well as installments of the serialised documentary, *Get to Know Your Country* (which presented picturesque places in Romania).

During World War II, several Romanian documentaries were awarded prizes at the Venice Festival: *The Motzilor County* (1939, directed by Paul Călinescu, with a commentary by the novelist, Mihail Sadoveanu), which disclosed the survival of traditions dating back to the Middle Ages in a remote mountainous community; *Romania and the Fight against Bolshevism* (1941, directed by Paul Călinescu), a film based on newsreel recordings from the Eastern Front; and *We* (1942, directed by Ion Cantacuzino), which presented an outline of Romanian history.

The first dedicated studio for documentary films, Sahia, was founded in 1949. At its height, the studio reached a maximum turnaround of one hundred films per year. As in the case of other Eastern Europe communist countries, a proportion of these productions represented commissioned propaganda, touristic, or scientific films, but a significant number of documentaries have maintained their interest despite the passage of time. The wave of postwar documentary filmmakers in Romania gained international recognition during the 1960s and 1970s, when an important corpus of films was produced. Mirel Ilieşu won the Palme d'Or at Cannes in 1969, with *The Renaissance Songs*, a film about the Romanian choir, *Madrigal*. In 1962, Dumitru Done and Sergiu Nicolaescu co-directed *Ordinary Spring*, which was awarded the First Prize at the International Documentary Film Festival in Prague. The next year, Sergiu Nicolaescu completed *The Memory of the Rose*, a short film that used spectacular slow-motion photography and soundtrack as part of a metaphorical reflection on the transitory nature of beauty, confronted with the violence of barbed wire and machine guns. After winning the Grand Prize at Edinburgh and getting into the official selection at Cannes in 1963, *The Memory of the Rose* was awarded the Silver Medal at Trieste (1965). The same year, Eric Nussbaum's art documentary, *Ciucurencu*, won a prize at the Film Festival in Venice. Dona Barta's *Ephemerae* (1968), which provided a refined visual meditation on the short-lived existence of insects, won a medal at the Buenos Aires Film Festival. The evolution of the scientific documentary genre in Romania, starting with Dr. Gheorghe Marinescu's early experiments with Marey's chronophotographic camera at the Salpêtrière Hospital in 1889, was marked by the activity of a number of exceptional filmmakers during the 1960s and 1970s, such as Dona Barta (*The Quiet Swamp*, 1967; *The Silk Moth*, 1975; *Diatoms, the Jewels of Nature*, 1976), Mircea Popescu (*The 14th Element, Silicon*, 1969), and Ion Bostan (*Under the Eagle's Wing*, 1964; *The Flooded Forest*, 1973; *Impressions from the Delta*, 1978). One of the founding fathers of the Romanian documentary and the author of an impressive filmography, Ion Bostan remains associated with an exceptional series of documentaries on the Danube Delta, *The Sanctuary of Nature*, which collected thirteen episodes, spanning several years of shooting and totalling 169 minutes of screening time. His outstanding achievement was matched only by Titus Meszaros's *Reeds* (1966), a memorable feature-length documentary on the harsh life of manual workers in the Danube Delta. It is significant that Ion Bostan's earlier productions included equally compelling explorations of the art world: *The Painter Nicolae Grigorescu* (1955), *The Slaying of the Infants* (1957), and *Bach—El Greco* (1970).

Many filmmakers turned to ethnographic and natural life documentaries during the 1960s and 1970s, in an attempt to escape censorship and the increasing ideological pressure of the Communist government. Slavomir Popovici, who started off as a remarkable analyst of social phenomena (*The Factory*, 1964, and *Harsh Romances*, 1966), later adopted less controversial topics, relating either to artistic creation or ethnography (*The Black Sun*, 1968; *The Chronicle of Hrib*, 1974). Among those who chose to pursue their career in exile, Paul Barbăneagră, came to prominence in the early 1960s, with films such as *The Conductor* (1964), and then settled in Paris, where his visual essays on art achieved wider recognition (for example,

Sacred Architecture and Geography, Mircea Eliade and the Re-discovery of the Sacred), earning him a mention in Georges Sadoul's *History of World Cinema from Its Origins to the Present*. Conversely, Nina Behar's outstanding art documentaries were quickly forgotten after the author left Romania for Israel, then France, in the 1970s. Two decades passed before her work was rediscovered and celebrated alongside that of major filmmakers, such as Alain Resnais, at the *Biennale internationale du film d'art* in Paris, in 1996. Nina Behar's early experiments, such as *Luchian*, 1958; *An Artist Accuses the World*, 1964; *Monumental Art*, 1966; *The Painter's Hands*, 1967; *Looking at a Painting*, 1972; and *Pătraşcu*, 1973, can still be said to provide some of the finest examples of the rapidly evolving montage and mise-en-scène techniques during the 1960s and 1970s.

The ethnographic documentary genre was given a new impetus at the time by directors who either endeavoured to perfect the art of the cinematographic poem (such as in Paula Popescu Doreanu's work: *Head Ornaments*, 1967; *Căluşarii*, 1968; *The Nieces' Celebration*, 1973), or strove to emphasise the scientific aspect of the commentary (for example, Ion Bostan's productions of the 1950s, such as *The Song of the Olt River*, which foreshadowed his landmark series of films on the Danube Delta, *The Sanctuary of Nature*). In a slightly different vein, Iancu Moscu's *The Eternal Feminine* (1970) won a prestigious prize at the Film Festival in Melbourne, although the author was mostly known in his own country for propaganda works commissioned by the communist government (for example, *Romania, a Country without Arms* and *Romania—Songs of Praise*). The output of several other talented documentary filmmakers displayed a similar tension between their aesthetic explorations (for example, Ioniţă Octav's *Rhythms*, 1972), and their commissioned works (for example, Ioniţă Octav's *Romania, My Country*, 1972; *Romania Today*, 1974; and *Sweet Romania*, 1975).

In the area of the *cine-vérité* productions, Florica Holban, the first woman-cameraman at Sahia, directed a number of compelling "cinematic reports" or newsreel documentaries on daily life: *Whose Fault Is It?* (1965) (which dealt with the situation in Romanian orphanages, and included children's testimonies), *Children, Yet Again* (1966), *Where Can We Play?* (1968), and others. Along the same lines, Alexandru Boiangiu's films captured social and psychological aspects of the interaction between individuals and the communities they live in: *Our Beautiful House* (1963) (which disclosed the contradictions between a

GP's professional discourse on hygiene and her lifestyle) and *Mr. D's Case* (1966) (an analysis of the situation of old people in residential care).

At the beginning of the 1970s, one film in particular seemed destined to become the manifesto of a new generation of documentary filmmakers. *Water Like a Black Buffalo* (1971) recounted the devastating effects of large-scale flooding in Romania, as well as the fight for survival and rescue operations that took place in remote areas of the country. Seven young directors took part in the filming and contributed to its unique blend of poetic images and objective presentation of events: Dan Piţa, Mircea Veroiu, Petre Bokor, Iosif Demian, Stere Gulea, Dinu Tănase, and Andrei Cătălin Băleanu. Even if none of the major documentary authors that emerged later in the 1970s (that is, Constantin Vaeni, Nicolae Cabel, Ada Pistiner, and Felicia Cernăianu) were involved in this film, *Water Like a Black Buffalo* had an undeniable impact on the work of celebrated fiction filmmakers such as Dan Piţa (*Philip the Good*, 1974) or Stere Gulea (*The Green Grass from Home*, 1977), while continuing to inform the stylistic and thematic concerns of the documentary directors during the 1980s. Ada Pistiner's films, for example, *And One . . .* (1978), *A Team of Young People and the Others* (1976), *A Community Arts Centre* (1977), can be said to represent the pinnacle of the documentary production during the 1970s. Nevertheless, a number of Constantin Vaeni's social studies, in particular, *And Then the City was Born* (1972), which displays strong similarities with *Water Like a Black Buffalo*, also marked a decisive departure from the restrictive ideological framework of the time and managed to provide, alongside Nicoale Cabel's similar explorations into a poetics of visual language (*The Earth Like a Beautiful Gift*, 1979; *George Bacovia, Tomorrow's Poem*, 1983; and *The Morning Horses*, 1986), the trademark for the most recent stylistic experimentation at the borderline between documentary and fiction films.

During the 1980s, a more introspective approach came to the fore, although many young directors also started to privilege the narrative and dramatic potential of the social reality they observed. A significant number of documentaries focused on their protagonists' feelings, or on their reactions to an idea or to a given situation: the wish-fulfilment reasoning of children in Tereza Barta's witty and light-hearted *If I Were a Fairy* (1980), the feeling of solitude of an international competition athlete in Ovidiu Bose Paştina's *And as for Emotion: A Crystal* (1987), the unhappiness of construction workers in Sabina Pop's *What's a Builder's Life Like, Ion?* (1983), the isolation of displaced workers from rural communities in Adrian Sârbu's *I'm in Good Health and Doing Well* (1982), the anxieties of waiting and the nature of hope in Ioana Holban's *If There Was No Love* (1983), and Copel Moscu's *Evening Classes* (1982). Among the more recent productions of the same generation, Sabina Pop's prize-winning *Panc* (1990), which won important distinctions in Oberhausen, Bordeaux, Zlatibor, Uppsala, and Kaliningrad, followed the tribulations of an amateur theatre group from a deprived, remote village in Romania where the passion for artistic expression manages to transform people's lives.

The popular uprising that toppled the communist government in December 1989 inspired a number of documentaries, starting with the well-known *Free Diary/The Romanian Revolution of 1989* (1990), to which a great number of filmmakers contributed: Adrian Sârbu, Sabina Pop, Horia Bolboceanu, Tiberiu Lazăr, Ovidiu Miculescu, Cornel Mihalache, Cătălina Fernoagă, Anita Gârbea, Doru Spătaru, and others. The same intention of capturing the overwhelming emotional charge of the moment, while nevertheless providing an accurate account of events, guided Ovidiu Bose Paştina's directorial vision in *Timişoara—December 1989* (1991). The stylistic unity of this film, and its perceptive comments on individual and collective responses to an unprecedented violent upheaval, earned the author a prize at Neubrandenburg, and placed him among the twenty best documentary filmmakers to be included in the official selection at Tokyo in 1992. Two other documentary productions made intelligent use of reel-footage (captured on amateur or professional cameras) to reflect on the significance of recent political events: *The Shortest Day* by Ştefan Gladin, retraced the presidential couple's movements during the last day before their capture in December 1989, while *On Christmas Day We Had Our Share of Freedom* (scripted and directed by two students in cinematography, Cătălina Fernoagă and Cornel Mihalache) described the euphoria of the early postrevolution days. The film that had the greatest impact in Romania, however, was Stere Gulea's *The University Square—Romania* (1991), which, at times, adopted the style of a news report or live commentary of events.

A number of dedicated production companies and studios for documentary films opened after the demise of the communist regime in Romania: Editura Video, FAV (The Visual Arts Foundation), Astra Film Studio, and Video Dialog. This enabled young filmmakers, such as Sorin Ilieşiu, to complete an impressive number of political documentaries in the early 1990s (for example, *The Monarchy Saves Romania*, 1992; *We'll Die and We'll Be Free*, 1992; and *Liberation*, 1993). Another strand in recent years can be said to gather those who, like Viorel Branea, have a background in television and have started to investigate the long-term effects of social and economic neglect on certain categories of the population during the Communist era. As early as 1990, Viorel Branea's shattering documentaries, *Apocalips '90* and *Our Working-Class Goes to Heaven*, disclosed the poverty, humiliation and large-scale ecological disaster in Copşa Mică and Valea Jiului, two of the most deprived mining regions of Romania. The director of the Astra Film Studio, based in Sibiu, Dumitru Budrală, authored, scripted, or produced an impressive number of documentaries, which renewed the tradition of ethnographic films in Romania: *Transylvanian Winter* (1996); *On the Road* (1998), which won the Silver Medal at the Kalamata International Festival in 2000, and was a finalist in the Cinéma du Réel competition in Paris, in 1999; *Village of the Watermills* (2001); *Traditions in Festival* (2002); and *Zina, the Story of a Village in the Carpathians* (2004).

Other filmmakers, such as Alexandru Solomon and Radu Igaszag, successfully pursued more formal explorations in the art documentary genre (for example, *Duet for Paoloncello and Petronome*, 1994; *Via Regis*, 1995). In recent years, Alexandru Solomon also directed a feature-length political documentary, *The Great Communist Train Robbery* (2004), which aired on BBC4. He had previously been awarded twice the prize for the best documentary in the Dakino Film Festival for *The Man with*

a Thousand Eyes (2001) and *A Dog's Life* (1999). In 1993, he won the prize for the best experimental film at the "Mediawave" Festival in Hungary for *Shriek into the Ear-Drum* (1993). The same year, Cornel Mihalache directed an equally memorable docudrama, entitled *The Sculpturor* (1993), and inspired by the life and work of the Romanian artist, Constantin Brancusi.

The Visual Anthropology Foundation, which was set up in 1995 as a production company and nonprofit, nongovernmental organisation, runs a biennial documentary film festival (the Astra Film Festival). At its seventh edition in 2004, the Astra Festival had already attracted large numbers of filmmakers, students, and scholars in visual anthropology from across Europe. Another noteworthy initiative concerns the activity of the Visual Arts Foundation, which teamed up with the Swiss Foundation for Culture, Pro-Helvetica, in 1999, and launched The Centre for Audiovisual Memory, with the aim of creating a multimedia archive, based on ethnographic and cultural research into the Romanian rural civilisation. A CD-ROM encyclopedia of Romanian traditions is currently being developed as part of this collaborative project.

RAMONA FOTIADE

Further Reading

Cernat, Manuela Cernat, *A Concise History of the Romanian Film*, Bucharest: Editura Enciclopedică, 1983.

Damian, Laurenţiu Damian, *Filmul documentar. Despre documentar . . . încă ceva în plus*, Bucureşti: Editura Tehnică, 2003.

Sadoul, Georges *Histoire du cinéma mondial des origines à nos jours*, Paris: Flammarion, 1998.

ROMM, MIKHAIL

After gaining prominence with his much-praised directorial debut, *Boule de Suif* (1934), Mikhail Romm continued to make films that were both narratively engaging and politically tendentious. His transposing of John Ford's *The Lost Patrol* to the Russian Civil War as *The Thirteen* (1936) is typical. These qualities are also present in Romm's first attempts to use nonfiction material:

the historical dramas *Lenin in October* (1937) and *Lenin in 1918* (1939). These are gross distortions of the historical facts of the Revolution and Civil War years where Trotsky is excised and Bukharin vilified. Lenin becomes an incarnation of perfect justice who all but appoints Stalin his successor.

Romm's first use of documentary film, *Vladimir Il'ich Lenin* (1949), articulates the same vision of

history by combining documentary footage and
genuine photographs with paintings incorrectly
showing Stalin to have been Lenin's closest confi-
dante from 1905 on and to have played the pivotal role in the Revolution. Moreover, despite the
film's title, this chronologically constructed narrative reaches 1924, the year of Lenin's death five
reels from the end. As a result, over a third of the
film stresses Stalin's continuation of his cause
through industrialisation, World War II, and postwar reconstruction.

Romm's next documentary project, *Living Lenin*
(1958), was made after the death of Stalin had
precipitated something of a conversion to a humanistic vision of socialism and seems to be an
attempt to atone for the excesses of *Vladimir Il'ich
Lenin*, in that it is entirely composed of authentic
newsreel footage of Lenin shot during his lifetime.
Yet where the voice-over in the earlier film at times
possessed a polemical bite, Romm's concern in this
film is solely to corroborate the authenticity of the
material and consequently it lacks dynamism.

His next documentary project, *Ordinary Fascism*
(1965), effectively combines a highly expressive
voice-over spoken by Romm himself, with a concern for authenticity. It is his most celebrated work
and along with his factional film about Soviet
nuclear scientists, *Nine Days of a Year* (1961), one
of the Russian films of the period that had the
greatest impact.

Romm's final documentary project, *Yet I
Still Believe* (1975), about young people, was completed posthumously.

JEREMY HICKS

See also **Ordinary Fascism**

Biography

Born January 24, 1901 in Butyriatiia, Siberia. Served in the
Red Army during Russian Civil War, 1918–1921. Completed Moscow Higher Institute of Art and Crafts in
sculpture, 1925. Worked as a screenwriter and assistant
director from 1931. Directorial debut *Boule de Suif*
(1934) won a prize at the Venice Film Festival after
which made a series of highly commended films. Member
of Communist Party from 1939, decorated with the People's Artist of the USSR 1950. From 1949 onward,
taught at State Film Institute (VGIK), becoming a professor in 1958, where he taught Andrei Tarkovskii and
numerous others. Became a liberal figurehead after his
denunciation of Soviet anti-Semitism in 1962, for which
he was publicly rebuked by Khushchev in 1963. Died
November 1, 1971.

Selected Films

1949 *Vladimir Il'ich Lenin*: co-director
1958 *Zhivoi Lenin/Living Lenin*: co-director
1965 *Obyknovennyi fashizm/Ordinary Fascism*: co-author,
    director, voice-over
1975 *I vse-taki ia veriu/Yet I Still Believe*: co-author and
    director

Further Reading

Romm, Mikhail, *Izbrannye proizvedeniia*, 3 vols, Moscow:
    Iskusstvo, 1980–1982.
Woll, Josephine, *Real Images: Soviet Cinema and the Thaw*,
    London: IB Tauris, 2000.
Zak, Mark, *Mikhail Romm i ego fil'my*, Moscow: Iskusstvo,
    1988.

ROOS, JØRGEN

Jørgen Roos, one of the most important Danish
documentary filmmakers of the postwar period,
combined work for different government agencies
with experimental avant-garde films. His work is
in some ways typical of the independent filmmakers in Scandinavia. Roos made many films,
around one hundred documentaries, both films of
information and more artistic films, and one of
the characteristic features of his work is that he
handles a broad spectrum of themes and genres.

Jørgen Roos started as a camera assistant in the
Danish company Minerva Film in Copenhagen in
1939, and his first assignment was photographing
the documentary filmmaker Theodor Christensen
leaving for England to visit John Grierson. Roos
has been categorized as a documentary filmmaker
in the griersonian tradition of social critique, information, and public enlightenment. His first films as
a director, however, were the first experimental
films in Denmark. *Flugten/The Escape* (1942),

with the artist Albert Merz, and *Spiste Horisonter/ Eaten Horizons* (1950) were among his early experimental films.

Roos worked as a photographer and editor for Theodor Christensen, and his first documentaries were influenced by Christensen and his work. Roos made many short films about cultural history and specialized in portraits of places, cities, and people. His *En by ved navn København/ A City Called Copenhagen* (1960) was disliked by the municipal experts who commisioned the film, and was shelved for two years, but was finally released to great acclaim. The success of this beautiful portrait of Denmark's capital resulted in assignments in other countries, but after *Jørgen Roos zeigt Hamburg/Jørgen Roos Shows Hamburg* (1962) and *Oslo/Oslo* (1963), he turned down all other offers to make films about cities.

Roos has made his mark on the genre of the portrait. Often he made portraits of artists, like *Johannes V. Jensen—Grundtanken i mit forfatterskap/Johannes V. Jensen—The Core of My Authorship* (1947) or *Carl Th. Dreyer/Carl Th. Dreyer* (1966), but he has also made portraits of inventors or explorers. His award-winning portrait of the Danish expert on Greenland, Knud Rasmussen; *Knud/Knud* (1966) is one of his best portraits, and with this film he also started a series of films on Greenland. He made travelogs and portraits of people from Greenland, as well as educational films on language and history. Most often Roos has depicted modern life in Greenland, and he has often been critical of Denmark's treatment of the Greenlanders, but he has also shown national pride in Denmark's presence in Greenland. His many films about life on Geenland, like *17 minutter Grønland/17 Minutes on Greenland* (1967) or *Kaláliuvit? (Er du Grønlænder?)/ Kaláliuvit? (Are You from Greenland?)* (1970), have been shown extensively in the schools in Denmark, so Roos has heavily influenced several generations of Danes and contributed to their image of Greenland.

Among his most famous films are his film-essays about bacon production, *Den strømlinede Gris/The Streamlined Pig* (1952), and noise, *Støj/Noise* (1965). In films like these, Roos is a committed social critic examining the dysfunctional aspects of modern society. These films inspired a new generation of Danish filmmakers in the late 1960s and early 1970s.

In addition to directing nearly one hundred documentaries, Roos worked as a photographer or editor on many films by other directors. He covered all sorts of issues and themes, from films about cultural history; *Historien om et slot/History of a Castle* (1951) to depictions of an urban slum; *Slum/ Slum* (1952), from a film about the photographs made of the writer H. C. Andersen; *Andersen hos fotografen/Andersen Visiting the Photographer* (1975), to a three-part film about the history of documentary filmmaking in Denmark; *Den levende virkelighed/The Living Reality* (1989). He even made a feature fiction film; *Seksdagesløpe/The Six Day Race* (1958).

Roos was regarded as one of the most important European documentary filmmakers, especially in the 1960s, and several of his films received awards at international film festivals. *A City Called Copenhagen* received second prize in Cannes in 1960, and was nominated for an Academy Award. His portrait of the explorer and expert on Greenland, *Knud*, received the Golden Bear at the Berlin Film Festival in 1966.

The documentaries made by Roos is characterized by a combination of warmth and sober detachment. His often ironic cutting, with great emphasis on details and rhythm, marks him as a personal and committed filmmaker. He is perhaps the most important Danish documentary filmmaker, and his work has influenced many Scandinavian documentary filmmakers.

GUNNAR IVERSEN

See also **Scandinavia**

Biography

Born in Gilleleje, Denmark, in 1922. Worked as camera assistant, and later cameraman and director for the company Minerva Film from 1939. Freelance photographer, editor, writer, and director. One of the founders of Association Internationale des Documentaristes in 1964. Became a Fellow of the Royal Society of Arts in Denmark in 1965. Died in 1998 at the age of 76.

Selected Films

1942 *Flugten/The Escape*
1947 *Johannes V. Jensen—Grundtanken i mit forfatterskap/ Johannes V. Jensen—The Core of My Authorship*
1950 *Spiste Horisonter/Eaten Horizons*
1951 *Historien om et slot/History of a Castle*
1952 *Den strømlinede Gris/The Streamlined Pig*
1952 *Slum*
1958 *Seksdagesløpet/The Six Day Race*
1960 *En by ved navn København/A City Called Copenhagen*
1962 *Jørgen Roos zeigt Hamburg/Jørgen Roos Shows Hamburg*
1963 *Oslo*
1965 *Støj/Noise*
1966 *Carl Th. Dreyer*

1966 *Knud*
1967 *17 minutter Grønland/17 Minutes on Greenland*
1970 *Kaláliuvit? (Er du Grønlænder?)/Kaláliuvit? (Are You from Greenland?)*
1975 *Andersen hos fotografen/Andersen Visiting the Photographer*
1989 *Den levende virkelighed/The Living Reality*

Further Reading

Bang, Hans V. (ed.), *Jørgen Roos—et liv som dokumentarist*, Haderslev: Dok Film Akademiet & Det Danske Filminstitut/Videoværkstedet, 1998.
Birkvad, Søren, and Jan Anders Diesen, *Autentiske Inntrykk*, Oslo: Samlaget, 1994.

ROSSIF, FRÉDÉRIC

Frédéric Rossif, the French director who began his career in the 1950s, was known primarily for his television work on such varied subjects as wildlife, luminaries of the entertainment world, and historical events. Rossif was responsible for several successful French television series, and his historical and political documentary films also met with acclaim. His compilation films were considered both creative and controversial. The combination of his World War II experiences (being of Jewish ancestry, he fled his home in Yugoslavia) with his residence in a postwar country gave his political films a strong, sometimes unsettling presence.

Rossif's documentary work generally displays a realist aesthetic and an observational approach. In television programs on wildlife, Rossif presented his subjects in natural environments, but often adjusted the temporal aspects to heighten the meaning. At times the speed and strength of an animal would be conveyed through quick editing, slow motion, or collision montage, similar to that used by Eisenstein. By using such techniques, Rossif developed a relationship that takes the viewer beyond the observational into a more psychological meditation on humankind's relation animals.

Rossif's work was generally praised, but at times he was criticized for his extensive use of editing. At a time when the genre was moving away from the influential aesthetic of Vertov, Rossif rarely used the long take, which was gaining favor. In the case of a film such as *Brel* (1982), his homage to the Belgian-born singer, this contributed to the criticism. Throughout the film, which is rooted in Brel's live performances, Rossif is careful to never let the viewer become too absorbed in the performance of a song. Brel's song performances are broken up, and intercut with elements such as newsreel footage, historical events, and landscape scenes. Rossif collides the various images, runs the clips backwards, and toys with the composition to make some scenes almost unrecognizable. Thus the director toys with the passivity of the documentary viewer.

When focusing on historical topics, Rossif made compilation films similar to those of Vertov, by assembling found footage from national archives; however, he enhanced the films through aesthetic manipulations, such as sound editing. In these films, he often addressed painful historical topics, forcing the viewer to confront difficult and unsettling events. These films met with praise and critical acclaim, most notably *Mourir a Madrid /To Die in Madrid* (1963). As a result, in 1967 Rossif's crew was the first Western film unit allowed to film extensively in the Soviet Union. Rossif was also given access to the Soviet film archives, with permission to reproduce any footage he wished. The resulting film, *Revolution d' Octobre/October Revolution* (1967), was composed from original footage shot by Rossif, as well as a great amount of archival footage, including segments from Vertov's *Chelovek s Kinoapparatom/Man with a Movie Camera* (1929).

Rossif was recognized primarily for his overtly political films; however, the bulk of his work was made for television. Ultimately, he contributed to more than 300 programs. He made one fiction film, *Aussi Loin que l'amour/As Far as Love Can Go* (1971), but it was unsuccessful, and he returned to the documentary genre.

Rossif's film career ended on the same subject it began: World War II. That conflict brought Rossif to France to begin his film career, so it seemed appropriate that his career conclude with an exposé of the atrocities of war criminals—the types of crimes that forced him to flee his homeland. Released posthumously, *De Nuremberg a' Nuremberg/From Nuremberg to Nuremberg* (1989) uses a more traditional approach than much of his work. Nevertheless, it remains shocking and effective.

DINO EVERETT

See also **Man With a Movie Camera; To Die in Madrid; Vertov, Dziga**

Biography

Born in Centinje, Montenegro, Yugoslavia, August 14, 1922. Being of Jewish ancestry, fled Yugoslavia in 1941, stopping for a time in Athens, Greece, and then Katerni, avoiding the Germans, until finally arriving in France. Served in the French Foreign legion until the end of World War II. After the war, worked for many years as a draftsman for Renault and Citroen. Worked for the Cinematheque Francaise in the 1950s. Directed his first programs for French TV, including *Cinepanorama* in 1956 and the news program *Cinq Colonnes a' la Une* in 1959. Awarded the Prix Jean Vigo in 1963. Nominated for an Oscar in 1966. Won both the British Academy of Film and Television Arts (BAFTA) Flaherty Documentary Award and the Berlin International Film Festival Golden Berlin Bear in 1968. Began a twenty-year collaboration with the composer Vangelis in 1972. Continued to alternate between film and television work and appeared as an actor in a cameo role in Etienne Chatieliez's 1990 feature *Tatie Danielle*. Died April 18, 1990 of a heart attack in Paris. His final film, the two part, *De Nuremberg a' Nuremberg,* was released posthumously.

Selected Films

1956 *Cine'panorama/Cinema Panorama* (TV): director, producer
1959 *Cinq Colonnes a' la Une/Five Columns on the Front Page*(TV): director
1961 *Le Temps du Ghetto/The Witnesses*: director, co-writer
1963 *Mourir a' Madrid/To Die in Madrid*: director, writer; *Les Animaux/The Animals*: director
1967 *Re'volution d'Octobre/October Revolution*: director, writer
1970 *Un mur a' Jerusalem/A Wall in Jerusalem*: director
1976 *La Fe'te Sauvage/The Wilderness Party*: director
1982 *Brel*: director, writer
1989 *De Nuremberg a' Nuremberg/From Nuremberg to Nuremberg*: director

Further Reading

Chapsel Madeleine, *Mourir a Madrid. Film de Frederic Rossif*, Paris: Seghers, 1963.
Colombat, Andre, *The Holocaust in French Film*, Metuchen, NJ: Scarecrow Press, 1993.
Landy, Marcia(ed.), *The Historical Film: History and Memory in Media*, New Brunswick, NJ: Rutgers University Press, 2001.
Payne, Stanley G., *The Spanish Civil War, the Soviet Union and Communism*, New Haven: Yale University Press, 2004.
Rossif, Frederic, *Revolution d'octobre*, Paris: Hachette, 1967.
Rubenstein, Leonard, "Facism Revisted," in *Film Society Review*, February 6, 1971, 41–46.
———. "Facism Revisted," in *Film Society Review*, December 4, 1970, 43–47.
Vertov, Dziga, *Kino-Eye: The Writings of Dziga Vertov*, Los Angeles: University of California Press, 1995.

ROTHA, PAUL

Paul Rotha, a filmmaker and critic who helped found the British documentary film movement, played an instrumental role in the development of British film culture during the 1930s and 1940s. His theories about film were shaped by the rise of the Soviet Union, the failed economic system apparent in the Great Depression, and the promise offered by the post-World War II world. In this period, questions about the impact of free enterprise on the individual and the proper relationship of the state to the economy became the focus of sharp debate. Heavily influenced by John Grierson's view of the artist as a person of social and political action, Rotha held that filmmakers had an obligation to serve the nation by combining social criticism with art and that the government had a responsibility to its citizens to sponsor domestic film production. Personally apolitical and a determined nonconformist, Rotha can best be understood as social-democratic reformer rather than a communist or socialist theorist.

Rotha's theory of documentary film revolved around the materialist problems of the first half of the twentieth century and rested on the belief that documentary film could serve as a method of clarifying and coordinating modern thought to achieve a full analysis of world problems that would lead to definite conclusions. His work was influenced by John Grierson's belief that film could be used to promote communication between the various elements of society, as well as by the example of the heavily politicized films of the Soviet Union. To Rotha, serious social analysis constituted the best use of the filmic medium.

Film appealed to Rotha in large part because of its expressive possibilities, and in 1931 he began his film career by joining the Empire Marketing Board (EMB) under John Grierson. It was during his time at EMB that Rotha wrote *Celluloid: The Film Today* and began to formulate his theory of the documentary film. A prolific contributor to *Cinema Quarterly*, as well as a frequent speaker before a multitude of groups, Rotha's steady stream of articles and lectures about documentary film helped the British movement gain its excellent critical reputation. The documentaries that Rotha directed for EMB were very low-budget Poster films: endless loops shot on a hand-turned Debrie on subjects like Scottish tomatoes and Australian wine. After a few months of learning to make films on a shoestring, Rotha lost his job at EMB after a conflict with Grierson.

Grierson eventually became a close friend, and his influence on Rotha is reflected in the latter's attitude toward documentaries. Rotha believed that a greater and more sophisticated appreciation of the art of documentary filmmaking would have a positive impact on the British film industry, but he also argued that art should be in service to social problems. He criticized many of the French and German directors of the 1920s and 1930s for their obsession with abstract aestheticism that led to the production of films that had no value to civilization. Although these films used interesting techniques and tricks, no essential aim lay behind the pretty pictures making these works failures in the cinema. As Rotha would repeatedly insist, one of the first aims of a documentary should be to examine the problem of the place of people in society. Rather than seeing the documentary as a work of art, in the manner of the French and Germans, it should be seen as a useful document containing artistic aspects.

After a year of scattered employment, Rotha found work with the publicity department of the oil giant Shell-Mex. His first documentary, *Contact,* financed by Shell, focused on the overseas routes of Imperial Airways to show the close communication between people made possible by air travel and airmail. Typical of the Rotha films, it is not a mere travelog but instead blends visual beauty with social criticism. A Venice Film Festival gold medal winner, it would be the first full-length British documentary film to have a wide commercial release.

To be successful, Rotha held, documentaries had to be persuasive and this involved engaging the emotions of viewers. He praised the Soviets for being the first to develop a fully expressive cinema by creating fictionalized documentaries. The Russian documentaries were not completely accurate because the compromises necessary for dramatic impact precluded truthfulness. Robert Flaherty, another Rotha influence and a co-worker at EMB, used a similar approach with his material. *Nanook of the North* and *Louisiana Story.* Both used faked shots and fictionalized situations to create poetically evocative films, with Rotha later citing both films as examples of basic documentary technique. Staged scenes and actions helped filmmakers to persuade the audience to a point of view. Documentaries were not instructional films filled only with pictorial views of people and places, Rotha held. Dramatization served as a requirement of the genre.

When he began to cut *Contact*, Rotha relied heavily on techniques that he had acquired from the Soviets. To further their propagandistic aims, the Soviet directors had become masters of editing, a skill that Rotha especially admired and duplicated. He argued that even a plain statement of fact demanded a dramatic interpretation to bring it alive on the screen. The Soviets had learned to dramatize expressions of editorial opinions by analytical cutting methods, and they saw individual shots as building blocks to be blended into a montage to create a concept. Rotha embraced Vsevolod Pudovkin's belief that editing formed the essence of documentary film and learned aspects of montage from the Film Society lectures given by one of his favorite filmmakers, Sergei Eisenstein. The films of Eisenstein came alive on screen with montage used to make particular points. Rotha would copy Eisenstein's style and incorporate montage into many of his own films in a similar effort to dramatize the material.

During 1934–1935, Rotha continued to write film criticism while making four documentaries for GB-Instructional. The first one, *Rising Tide*, involved footage shot by another director of a new quay and dock at Southampton. Rotha helped develop the film's theme, which touched on unemployment, industry in the North of Britain, and the economic relationship between the Empire and the nation. A documentary to Rotha had to reflect the problems and realities of the present. Not especially impressed by American films, he saw Europe as the vanguard of film and viewed the Soviets as the first to fully realize the potential of documentary films because they were the pioneers in portraying reality. Soviet films of the 1920s, unlike those made by many of the American and British directors, reflected the social conditions of the period. To interpret individual motivations on film, the Russians had to find a way to interpret an individual's attitude toward the government, as well as incorporating into the documentary the economic and social relationships that affected the subject. The Soviet films all had political purposes with the duties of the Russian directors seen by Rotha as expressing those purposes as clearly, powerfully, and vividly as possible.

Rotha's theory of documentary film envisaged the documentary as the voice of the people. While driving to Lancashire to make his second major documentary, *Shipyard*, Rotha passed abandoned factories, ugly slums, filthy canals, and out-of-work men being harassed by the police. Angered by comments in the press that industry had recovered from the depression and that Britain again led the world in industrial production, Rotha aimed to show the true situation of the working people. *Shipyard* reflected some of this tragedy, with a final scene showing shipbuilders triumphantly watching a completed ship as it goes down the slipway then turning despairingly and jobless, hands jammed in pockets, to walk to the Employment Exchange. While Rotha illuminated Britain's problems but did not propose a solution in *Shipyard*, his next film offered a plan for rebuilding Britain on a firm and well-organized economic basis. *The Face of Britain* focused on the possibilities of replanning Britain, both rural and industrial, based on the flexible power of the national electricity grid that was under construction in 1934. Radically different from the travelog type of film that had become the standard British documentary, both *Shipyard* and *The Face of Britain* ran into distribution problems that prevented them from being widely seen.

Few people saw Rotha's films, but many read his theories of film. In his seminal 1936 work, *Documentary Film*, he pushed for the humanization of films to appeal to a wide audience. The documentary had materialized as the result of sociological, political, and educational requirements and it must be accessible to the people. Rotha attacked as dangerous to the documentary form an increasing return to theatricality that removed the characters in a film from the realm of believability. For a documentary to be persuasive, the audience needed to be provided with familiar figures with which they could relate, because the characters must be able to convey their thoughts to the audience. The establishment and development of characters should lead to the growth of ideas in the minds of the characters, allowing the audience to grow with the characters. In *Documentary Film* Rotha also expressed his reservations about the advent of sound films, fearing that the introduction of the human voice would relieve directors of their obligation to convey meaning visually. Documentaries required a range of perception wider than that of descriptive films because propaganda demands persuasive statements and implications that sink deeply into the national conscience. Rotha saw dialogue films as the equivalent of stage productions and spoke for the moral superiority of documentary to fiction. Hollywood-type films, unlike documentaries, deliberately kept people from analyzing the state of the nation.

In 1935, Rotha became Director of Productions for Strand Films and assumed the role of a catalyst. Bearing full financial and artistic responsibility for Strand's films, Rotha also became involved in the economics of the documentary movement. As the most powerful means of social expression available and Britain's major contribution to the film world, he believed that documentary film deserved some type of arms-length government support. Filmmakers had struggled to find sponsorship while providing an essential public service. As the most accessible of all the mediums, film had the ability to raise questions and search for answers, but its fault lay in its potential to reconstruct reality. This connection led many directors to abandon film as an expressive art in favor of film as an imitation of life, a practice that had been exacerbated by the conservatism of British distributors and exhibitors who were unwilling to financially risk showing art films. Rotha would repeat a call that he had first issued in 1931 for a London-based national repertory film theatre programmed by an expert advisory committee and connected to a regional network of film societies specifically to solve the problem of documentary film distribution and showing. Many of Rotha's ideas, including a magazine dealing with the development of film and a cinema museum with a film archive, would be incorporated into the British Film Institute.

To help develop an American documentary movement based on public service using progressive social purposes, Rotha joined the newly established Film Library in New York for six months in 1937–1938. On his return to Britain, he again directed films and would eventually make more than 250 during his career, but the problem of financing continued to plague the documentary movement. After World War II as Britain began to nationalize industries, Rotha offered two film financing proposals to the government. In 1945 "The Government and the Film Industry" suggested that Britain establish a film corporation to finance and produce independent British features and documentaries as a means of combating American dominance in film. Two years later, Rotha proposed improvements to the National Film Finance Corporation in line with his original vision to give filmmakers more creative control.

Part of a generation influenced by the development of an intellectual film culture in the 1920s, Rotha had a commitment to a politically and socially progressive cinema that never abated during his lifetime. Determined to solve the problems of the world through film's power to educate and inform, he remained passionate about the need for a vibrant British film culture and film industry.

CARYN E. NEUMANN

See also **Contact;** *EMB Film Unit; Grierson, John*

Biography

Born Paul Treeve Fawcett Thompson in Wealdstone, England, UK June 3, 1907. Attended thirteen schools, some of them boarding, and left the last one at sixteen. Attended Slade School of Art 1924–1925 and won the students' prize for theatre costume design at the International Theatre Exhibition in Paris in 1925. Changed surname to Rotha, after the title of an Edwardian book, upon being advised that a foreign-sounding name would help him succeed in theatre design in 1926. Rotha would become his legal name after his father's 1942 death. Having failed to find any design work, joined Elstree Studio art department as a prop supplier in 1928. Fired for criticizing British art directors in *Film Weekly* article "Technique of the Art Director," 1928. Married Margaret Louise Lee, 1930–1939. A director at Empire Marketing Board Film Unit, 1931. Director of Production at Strand

Films, 1935–1937. Lecturer, Film Library in New York City, 1937–1938. Producer, Realist Films 1939–1941. Volunteer in East End canteen during the German air raid Blitz of World War II, 1940. Establishes Paul Rotha Productions, 1941–1944. Producer, Films of Fact, 1944–1948. Married Margot Rose Perkins, 1944–1960. Head of Documentary Film for the British Broadcasting Corporation's television service, 1953–1955, producing more than seventy-five films. Married Constance Rose Smith, 1961–1981. Died March 7, 1984.

Selected Films

1933 *Contact*: director, writer, editor, producer
1933 *Roadworks*: director, writer, editor, producer
1934 *Rising Tide*: director, writer, editor
1935 *Shipyard*: director, writer, editor, producer
1935 *The Face of Britain*: director, writer, editor, producer
1936 *Death on the Road*: director, writer, editor, producer
1936 *Peace of Britain*: director, co-writer, editor, producer
1938 *New Worlds for Old*: director, writer, editor, producer
1940 *The Fourth Estate*: director, writer, editor, producer
1940 *Mr. Borland Thinks Again*: director, writer, editor, producer
1943 *World of Plenty*: director, co-writer, editor, producer
1945 *Total War in Britain*: director, editor, producer
1946 *A City Speaks*: director, co-writer, editor, producer
1947 *The World Is Rich*: director, editor, producer
1953 *World Without End*: co-director, editor, producer
1961 *The Life of Adolf Hitler*: director, co-writer, editor

Further Reading

Low, Rachael, *Documentary and Educational Films of the 1930s*, London: Allen and Unwin, 1979.
Marris, Paul(ed.), *Paul Rotha: BFI Dossier 16*, London: BFI, 1982.
Orbanz, Eva, *Journey to a Legend and Back: The British Realistic Film*, West Berlin: Volker Apeiss, 1977.
Perkins, V.F., *Film as Film*, Harmonsworth: Penguin, 1972.
Petrie, Duncan, and Robert Kruger (eds.), *A Paul Rotha Reader*, Exeter: University of Exeter Press, 1999.
Rotha, Paul, *Celluloid: The Film Today*, London: Longman's Green, 1931.
———, *Documentary Diary: An Informal History of the British Documentary Film, 1928-1939*, London: Secker and Warburg, 1973.
———, *Documentary Film*, London: Faber, 1935.
———, *The Film Till Now*, London: Jonathan Cape, 1930.
———, *Movie Parade: A Pictorial Survey of the Cinema*, London: Studio, 1936.
———, *Robert J. Flaherty: A Biography*, Philadelphia: University of Pennsylvania Press, 1983.
———, *Rotha on the Film*, London: Faber, 1958.
———, *World of Plenty: Book of the Film*, London: Nicholson and Watson, 1945.
Sussex, Elizabeth, *The Rise and Fall of the British Documentary*, Berkeley: University of California Press, 1975.

ROUCH, JEAN

Jean Rouch is a significant figure in ethnographic film, the stylistic development of cinema verité, and he inspired the young filmmakers of the *nouvelle vague*. His career spans more than fifty years and more than 120 films. He is best known for his earlier documentary works, but he continued to make films until 2003. More than a documentary filmmaker, Rouch was an ethnographer and cinematic innovator and is often referred to as the Father of African Cinema. He is credited for coining the term cinema verité and for developing it with sociologist Edgar Morin. Rouch is responsible for elevating the use of the handheld camera style and natural lighting to a respectable position in the art of cinema. Proponents of the style and techniques of cinema verité argue that his stylistic developments allow filmmakers to capture reality.

Cinema verité is both a philosophy and a style of filmmaking. The fundamental concept of "cinema truth" is explored, developed, and demonstrated in Rouch's many ethnographic films. His best known documentary films are focused on the Songhay people and traditions of the West African state of Niger. Having first gone to Africa as a civil engineer in the early 1940s, Rouch was struck by African culture and belief. His drive to document and understand what he saw inspired him to film this region and its people over the course of many years. This pursuit to capture what he experienced on celluloid has become know as "visual anthropology." Yet in doing so, Rouch was careful not to oversimplify, dismiss, or evaluate in his films. His goal was to document and in that pursuit he invited his subjects to participate in the filmmaking process, thus making important strides in developing participatory ethnography. His techniques and cinematic experiments were not universally accepted, and he was criticized by some traditional ethnographers and academics. His movies are thematically centered on racism, cultural interaction, colonialism, the poor, migration of young Africans from traditional homelands to populated coastal cities, and materialism.

During the Nazi occupation of France, Rouch was active in the Resistance. In 1941, however, he left France for Niger where he could work as a civil engineer. He began his civil service career building a road in the isolated town of Niamey. During construction, Rouch became friends with Damoré Zike, a Nigerian road foreman. Zike introduced Rouch to the mysterious spirituality of the Songhay people and would aid him in the making of several films. Damoré's grandmother was a high priestess of the Naimey and initiated Rouch into the world of Songhay magic and possession. Rouch became fascinated by the surreal ceremonies that he attended. As ethnographer Paul Stoller (1992) explains "Rouch had entered a truly surreal world. . . . At that moment Rouch may have realized that film was the best way to capture the dream he was living" (31). Rouch began documenting the ceremonies in ethnographic writing and photos that he sent to Marcel Griaule in Paris. Griaule introduced Rouch's work to the *Institute Française d'Afrique Noire*, which took an interest in Rouch. In the early 1940s, Rouch presented his first paper on Africa via an IFAN seminar. In 1943, Rouch joined the Free French Army Corps of Engineers and was able to go back to Paris after it was liberated. There he once again returned to his studies with Griaule and held an entry level position at the *Institute Française d'Afrique Noire*.

In 1946, Rouch returned to Africa with two French colleagues to travel the length of the Niger River in a dugout canoe. The trip was financed by stories the three wrote for the *Agence France Press* before and during the trip and by a financial gift from the AFP once they were in Niger and in need of money. Rouch took a war surplus 16mm camera on the expedition and for nine months they traversed the river. Thus Rouch began his filmmaking career in 1947 with *Au pays des mages noirs/In the Land of the Black Seers*. The film recounts Rouch's trip down the Niger to the ocean. During the trip Rouch was asked to photograph a hippopotamus hunt by the local people. Because of an accident, Rouch was unable to use a tripod and decided to shoot the footage by holding the camera in his hand. Thus he adopted one of his most cherished techniques, the handheld camera. Most of the footage of the trip was stolen along with the bulk of the troupe's possessions, but the hippopotamus hunt and some of the other footage survived and comprises the documentary with the addition of added stock footage. In 1949, Rouch received the Grand Prix du Documentaire at the Biarritz Film Festival organized by Henri Langlois, the founder of the Cinémathèque Française. Rouch was awarded the top prize for his films *La circoncision/The Circumcision* (1948–1949) and *Initiation a la danse des possesedes/Initiation to the Dance of the Possessed* (1948–1949). Both these films and *Les magicians de Wanzerbe* were shot from 1947–1948 when Rouch returned to Niger to complete his ethnographic field work for his thesis. As Stoller (1992) explains "the bulk of Rouch's work . . . concentrates on Songhay possession. There are cinematic interviews with possession priests . . . and a score of short films on Songhay *yenaandi* ceremonies, the possession rites during which spirits are asked to bring rain" (6).

Les magicians de Wanzerbe is one of Rouch's less seen works. It is a portrait of the priests' incantations, medicinal plants, and magician's dance, and this short film introduces the audience to the wizards of Wanzerbe and their rituals. Perhaps the most important aspect of the film is the magician's dance during a purification ceremony. The magician dances for hours and is joined by his son. Both seem to be in trances. At one point he jolts and vomits a magic chain, which hangs from the end of his tongue and is then swallowed again where he will continue to carry the enchanted power chain until he dies. The film also contains footage of the annual ceremony in which a cow is sacrificed and butchered to ensure a healthy and bountiful year. The film provoked critics to accuse Rouch of African exoticism, and Stroller (1992) reported that even the people of Wanzerbe complained of misrepresentation; however, the documentary stands as an important ethnographic recording of these riveting ceremonies.

In the mid-1950s, Rouch released *Les maîtres fous/The Mad Masters*. The film is a cinematic study of the possession rituals of a group of Songhay known as the Hauka. The ritual is reportedly a means in which the Hauka contact the spirits of their former colonial "masters." In the ritual, entranced participants behave as the members of the colonial military and then act out a violent ceremony in which a dog is sacrificed, boiled, and eaten. They also cut a chicken's throat and spill the blood on an already blood-stained alter. In their trances they act out military marches and conferences. Afterward, the Hauka people are shown carrying on with their normal daily routines. The Hauka sect became very popular in the region and despite the attempts of government officials, the group grew in numbers. Rouch described the popularity of the group as a way for the people to show defiance toward colonial oppression. He punctuates this belief cinematically by adding scenes of the British colonial military with the scenes of the Hauka ritual. Rouch filmed the ceremony at the request of the leaders of the Hauka sect. The film was controversial and was banned in the region. Some African and French intellectuals rejected the film as reinforcing Black stereotypes and for lacking objectivity; others objected to Africans presenting such violent representations of Europeans. Yet the film was awarded the Venice Festival Grand Prix in 1957 and remains a fascinating view of this ritual that combines elements of traditional spiritual trance and possession ceremonies with modernized spirits in the form of colonial military personnel. In this way the film symbolically represents the clash of traditional African cultures with the enforced modernization brought on by colonialism. This cinematic ideological comment was probably the reason for the film's popularity throughout Europe.

Rouch's *La chasse au lion à l'arc/The Lion Hunters* (1957–1964) follows Songhay hunters as they track and kill a group of dangerous lions with only bows and arrows. The movie presents the viewer with the African bush, a wild and seemingly dangerous place for humans. Then the film juxtaposes the bush with the cultivated land of the hunters, known as the Gow, a subgroup of the Songhay. The hunters must track and kill a lion that is attacking and killing domestic animals of the Fulan people. The lion is not eating its victims, so the hunters know that it is the same lion making all the kills. The film presents many details of the hunt, but its focus is on the rituals that are performed in the course of the expedition. It took Rouch seven years to complete the film, beginning in 1957 and concluding in 1964. Because of delays with the hunt, Rouch had to make several trips to Africa during this time period to film different aspects of the hunt and the related ceremonies such as the making of the poison for the arrows, and the killing of the lions trapped in the Gow hunters' iron leg traps. The hunters first trap and kill a young lion and kill it with their poison arrows. Next they trap a lioness, but she is able to free herself and attack one of the herdsmen before she is killed by the hunters. Interestingly, Rouch was unable to film the complete attack, but his sound person captured the frightening incident and so the entire episode is presented in the film. The film was a critical success and was awarded the Golden Lion prize at the Venice Film Festival. Critics praised this film as Rouch's masterpiece and suggested that it elevated him to the elite group of French filmmakers. Stoller (1992) argued that the film successfully demonstrates the inseparable union of the Songhay people's mundane and sacred lives. Further, Stoller explains that Rouch has dialectically linked film and ethnography but suggests that Rouch crosses the boundary between reality and fictional narrative many times.

Rouch's first feature film, *Moi, un noir/I, a Black* (1957) combines documentary and fiction. The film was shot fairly objectively in the Ivory Coast in a slum of Abidjan. It follows the daily life of a stevedore, Oumarou Ganda (who calls himself Edward G. Robinson) and two friends. Ganda then records the voice-over narration of the film, filling in his hopes and aspirations as a backdrop to the 16mm cinematography. Later, Ganda became a leading figure in African filmmaking as a director in Niger. The film was banned by the government of the Ivory Coast. Critics of cinema verité argue that the move into fictionalized cinema demonstrates that cinema verité is no more than a style of filmmaking, where handheld 16mm cameras and natural lighting are the accepted conventions, much like high production values and beautiful cinematic shots are conventions of classic narrative cinema. Rouch followed in 1959 with *La Pyramide humaine*, which used a fictional story to explore the interaction of black and white teenage students at an Abidjan school, the *Lycée d'Abidjan*. The film was shot silent and Rouch attempted to have the students revoice the commentary in voice-overs, but this did not work out well, as the students were unable to relive their spontaneous conversations after the fact. Proponents of the film argue that it is an important text that seeks to explore racism and segregation in an innovative and stylistically interesting manner.

Before the early 1960s, most documentary film was shot silent, with music, narration, and other sound effects added in after production. This condition resulted from the lack of sound equipment that was portable enough to use effectively and efficiently in the field. The advent of light weight and reliable portable tape recording equipment with 16mm camera synchronization became widely available in the late 1950s. The availability of the equipment revolutionized the making of documentary film. This was especially true in France, where Rouch led the revolution by using the new technology in the cinema verité movement. Rouch was central in the development of cinema verité and used it in the style and form of his films in controversial ways. In his *Chronique d'un été/Chronicle of Summer* (1960), Rouch and Edgar Morin explored French culture just after the Algerian War from the streets of Paris. Rouch uses the same approach that used in his African documentaries. The film is partly an answer to critics who accused him of only filming in exotic locales and the first film to be self-consciously cinema verité. The film is unique in that it incorporates some of the responses of the people interviewed to their own footage, thus undermining some of the "objective distance" of the documentary. The use of handheld cameras and diegetic sound and a denunciation of the objective narrator were indicative of Rouch's larger rejection of earlier documentary filmmaking style and classic narrative film conventions. Reliance on a classic cinematic style that emphasized beautiful shots and compelling stories was cast aside as an obstacle to filmic truth. From this initial interest in transforming documentary, cinema verité moved to a focus on developing innovative narrative film styles. *Chronique d'un été* was not a commercial success, but Rouch followed it up with *La Punition/The Punishment*. Although the film was shot very quickly and in the innovative style of cinema verité, the unrehearsed actors and improvised scenes about a young woman who is sent home from school and spends the day looking for something to do, preferably with a male, is criticized for being too aimless. Although the cinema verité movement was influential to the directors of the French New Wave, these two Rouch films are most significant for what they suggest about the relationship of film to reality rather than as testaments to the success of the style.

Jaguar (1967) is a further development of Rouch's hybrid between documentary and fiction. Some scholars use the term *ethnofiction* to describe this type of filmmaking. Unlike the docudrama, ethnofiction relies on the basic tenets of ethnographic filmmaking. The film follows the lives of three young Songhay men who migrate from their tribal homes to the Gold Coast of West Africa in a quest of discovery and experience, and who return changed men. Rouch's ethnographic writings on this theme explore the history of this migration and its cultural significance. The film marks a movement away from Rouch's earlier focus on the mystical Songhay world of magic and ritual by concentrating on the social, or mundane, aspects of these men's lives and their reasons for taking part in the migration. Thus the title of film is not about the animal; for these men being a jaguar means that they are successful and that they look and behave cool. Eventually, the men return home with stories and material goods before the seasonal rains begin. The idea for *Jaguar* was conceived in 1954. The film was shot silently, primarily in 1957. Later, Rouch had the principals do the voice-over commentary as they watched the film. Thus their improvisation is driven by the images locked in the celluloid. The entire commentary was completed in a single day in a sound studio in Ghana. The film was shown at different times before its final release in 1967. In the film we see the men make the long journey to the Gold Coast on foot through the grasslands and mountains. There they meet the Somba, "primitive others," whose male members wear only penis sheaths. Once they arrive at the coast they split up, and the film cross-cuts from one to another as they establish their daily lives and work. The men are able to achieve jaguar status, the condition of being "with it" and "cool" but eventually decide it is time to return to their homes and their old lives. Once they return, they give away all the material possessions that they bring with them and settle back into their former lives and roles. Stoller (1992) suggested that this ethnofiction film exemplifies Rouch's *pourquoi pas* (why not?) method of research and filmmaking, and this lends the film a sense of play. Some critics feel that the film stands as Rouch's anti-colonial testament and brings to light several problems brought on by modernization facing West Africans at the time.

Rouch wrote many ethnographic books and articles with a wealth of thick description and photographs of the Songhay people and their spiritual artifacts. His written works are more detailed and ethnographically informative than his films. Rouch's "why not?" method of filmmaking does little to answer the questions that his movies ask. The films themselves are often visually exotic, provocative, and challenging, thus leaving his viewers shocked and interested but confused as to context and explanation.

Rouch was killed in an automobile crash in Niger on February 18, 2004. He had returned once more to Africa to attend a film festival.

J. EMMETT WINN

See also **Chronique d'un été**

Biography

Born May 31, 1917 in Paris. His father was a naval scientist and meteorologist who instilled a scientific interest in Jean as the family traveled extensively. In the late 1920s, they lived in Morocco where his father was the director of the Oceanographic Museum. There Rouch first experienced Africa and its peoples. At school in Paris, in the 1930s, became very interested in surrealism. Also developed into avid film enthusiast, often attending the programs at the Cinémathèque Française. Studied civil engineering at *L'Ecole des Ponts et Chausseés*. Active in the Resistance during the Nazi occupation of France. In 1941, left France for Niger to work as a civil engineer. Served as the Director of Research at the *Central National de la Recherche Scientifique* from 1966–1986 and was the General Secretary of the Cinémathèque Française from 1985–1986, after which he was its Director from 1987 to 1991. Rouch was married twice. The first time to Jane George in 1952, and his second marriage was to Jocelyne Lamothe in 2002. Killed in an automobile crash in Niger on February 18, 2004.

Selected Films

1946–1947 *Au pays des mages noirs*: director
1948–1949 *Les magiciens de Wanzerbe*: director, cinematographer, producer
1948–1949 *Initiation à la danse des possédés*: director, cinematographer, producer
1948–1949 *La circoncision*: director, cinematographer, producer
1953–1954 *Les maîtres fous*: director, cinematographer
1954–1967 *Jaguar*: director
1957 *Moi, un noir*: director, writer
1957–1964 *La chasse au lion à l'arc*: director, cinematographer
1958–1959 *La pyramide humaine*: director, writer
1960 *Chronique d'un été*: director (with Edgar Morin)
1960 *La punition*: director, writer
2003 *Le rêve plus fort que la mort*: director

Further Reading

Adams, John W., and John Marshall, "John Rouch Talks About His Films to John Marshall and John W. Adams," in *American Anthropologist*, 80, 1978, 1005–1022.

Armes, Roy, *French Cinema*, New York: Oxford UP, 1985.

DeBouzek, J., "The Ethnographic Surrealism of Jean Rouch, in *Visual Anthropology*, 2, 1989, 301–317.

Eaton's Mick (ed.), *Anthropology — Reality — Cinema: The Films of Jean Rouch*, London: British Film Institute, 1979.

Feld, Steven, "Themes in the Cinema of Jean Rouch," in *Visual Anthropology*, 2, 1989, 223–249.

Lanzoni, Rémi Fournier, *French Cinema: From Its Beginnings to the Present*, New York: Continuum, 2002.

Ruby, Jay (ed.), *The Cinema of Jean Rouch*, London: Harwood Academic Publishers, 1989.

Stoller, Paul, *The Cinematic Griot: The Ethnography of Jean Rouch*, Chicago: Chicago UP, 1992.

Williams, Alan, *Republic of Images: A History of French Filmmaking*, Cambridge: Harvard UP, 1992.

ROUQUIER, GEORGES

As a teenager, Georges Rouquier already admired the great directors of his time. Having obtained his *certificat d'études*, he took a job as an apprentice typographer in Montpellier. He gradually learned how to operate the linotype and, at the age of 16, he left for Paris and found employment as a skilled linotypist. He dedicated his spare time to the cinema, frequenting such film societies as l'Etoile's and the famous Studio 28 movie theatre.

It was on account of these visits that he met director Eugen Deslaw, who had just completed *La Marche des Machines* (1928) with relatively little money. Following Deslaw's advice, he bought a second-hand Debrie Sept 35mm camera and learned how to operate it, even taking it apart for better understanding and mastery. He devoted his next holiday to making his first motion picture, *Vendanges* (1929), about the grape harvest near Lunel. The film was later destroyed. Rouquier then completed his military service before going back to work as a linotypist.

At this point Rouquier was little more than a cultivated, film-loving linotypist. Thirteen years after *Vendanges*, however, he met the producer Etienne Lallier, who agreed to back the making of a short, *Le Tonnelier/The Cooper* (1942). The resulting composition focuses on the two-day labour process required for the production of one barrel (a *demi-muid*) by an elderly artisan and his apprentice, under the supervision of the master cooper. The film was once again shot in Lunel and displays great maturity and harmony. Though derived of ambient sound, it magnifies handicraft, dexterity, and know-how, depicting the craftsmen's traditional techniques in a way that would inspire many other films, including some of Rouquier's own. The next year it was awarded a Grand Prix at the Premier Congrès du Film Documentaire in Paris alongside Marcel Ichac's *A l'Assaut des Aiguilles du Diable* and René Lucot's *Rodin*.

Now determined to become a filmmaker, Rouquier directed three commissioned films in 1943. *Le Charron* could in some ways be compared with *Le Tonnelier, La Part de l'Enfant,* and *L'Economie des Métaux* are much less personal.

Lallier subsequently suggested Rouquier direct a feature film about peasant life. This came to be *Farrebique*, often compared with Storck's *Symphonie Paysanne*, which follows a similar outline. *Farrebique* succeeds thanks to its feeling of authenticity, which the documentary mise en scène method respects. Although rewarded several times, this once controversial film, the filmmaker's most famous opus, did not guarantee the director's success.

Rouquier continued to make shorts on commission, addressing diverse subjects. *L'Oeuvre Scientifique de Pasteur* (1947) was co-directed by Jean Painlevé. *Le Chaudronnier* (1949), a "handicraft film" again depicts how the artisan technique of the coppersmith had to adapt itself to industrial times. *Le Sel de la Terre* (1950), "a documentary western" (Auzel), is an apology for the fertilization plan to the area of the Camargue, albeit an original, lyrical, and aesthetic one.

In 1955, Rouquier produced his young assistant Jacques Demy's first film, *Le Sabotier du Val de Loire*. In the mid-1950s he also tried his hand at fiction, with two feature films. *Sang et Lumière* was the first French film to use the Eastmancolor process. A Spanish version was made currently. The results are far from convincing. *S.O.S. Noronha* (1957), inspired by reality, drew a parallel between the uprising of political prisoners in Brazil and an accident involving the pilot Mermoz, both events perceived from a radio guiding station. This Franco-German-Italian production is no achievement either. More convincing were Rouquier's various performances in a dozen French feature films, among which was Costa-Gavras' *Z* (1969).

As a filmmaker, Rouquier showed a preference for documentary. His curious *Lourdes et ses Miracles* (1955) was produced by a Catholic corporation, a religious adviser appearing in its credits. The subject matter is that of the allegedly miraculous recoveries of pilgrims. Rouquier endeavoured to present an objective standpoint, maintaining, "it is up to the spectator to conclude." Having no facility to record direct synchronous sound outdoors, he nonetheless used authentic (ambient) sound material to full advantage. The way in which Rouquier appears on-screen to introduce and conclude the film prefigures to some extent the "performative" documentary mode (Nichols) to come.

Rouquier's career came to a close with two films that echoed his first two. *Le Maréchal Ferrant* (1979) is the portrait of a craftsman, which inevitably recalls *Le Tonnelier*; however, it situates the main character and his trade in a rural world altered by modernisation, and questions the issue of transmitting artisan know-how. *Biquefarre* (1983) is the sequel to *Farrebique* that the filmmaker had wished to make for nearly forty years.

The enthusiasm of American scholars and a subsidy from the National Endowment for the Humanities enabled Rouquier to elaborate the script. Two French producers then managed to convince the Crédit Agricole de l'Aveyron to get involved in the project. Rouquier was to depict what his family's farm—and subsistence farming in general—had become. He essentially used the same method as he had done in 1946 (real characters, documentary mise en scène). The story, however, displays a finer type of coherence. It intertwines sociopolitical (and ecological) issues with the individual's destiny to demonstrate in a bittersweet mood how a whole world is coming to its end. It remains the testimony of a man who constantly paid tribute to the humble.

JEAN-LUC LIOULT

Biography

Born 1909. Descended from peasants on his father's side. Worked on the family farm as a youth. Having obtained his *certificat d'études*, returned to the farm for a short while before beginning his job as an apprentice typographer in Montpellier. Left for Paris at age 16 and found employment as a linotypist. Worked nights, learned the new sound techniques in filmmaking during the day. Called up to military service in 1939 and served as an artilleryman until the end of World War II. Died in 1989.

Selected Films

1942 *Le Tonnelier*: director, writer, narrator
1946 *Farrebique*: director, writer, narrator
1949 *Le Chaudronnier*: director
1955 *Lourdes et ses Miracles*: director, narrator
1979 *Le Maréchal Ferrant*: director, writer, narrator
1983 *Biquefarre*: director, writer, narrator

Further Reading

Auzel, Dominique, *Georges Rouquier, de Farrebique à Biquefarre*, Paris: Petite Bibliothèque des Cahiers du Cinéma, 2002.
Gauthier, Guy, *Le Documentaire, un autre cinéma*, Paris: Nathan Université, 1995.
Piault, Marc-Henri, "Changer sans changements: résister à l'histoire avec Georges Rouquier," in: *Anthropologie et cinéma*, Paris: Nathan Cinéma, 2000.

RUBBO, MICHAEL

Michael Rubbo is an Australian filmmaker who first made his mark at the National Film Board of Canada where he wrote and directed some its most memorable documentaries—*Sad Song of Yellow Skin* (1969), *Wet Earth and Warm People* (1971), *Waiting for Fidel* (1973), *Solzhenitsyn's Children . . . Are Making a Lot of Noise in Paris* (1978), *Daisy: Story of a Facelift* (1984)—and many more. Rubbo is known for a very personal style of filmmaking that takes the viewer on a journey or exploration and allows the person to experience the subject matter through the thoughts, observances, and feelings of the filmmaker. His on-screen interventions make his films as much about him as about his subjects. Author and filmmaker Alan Rosenthal cites other distinctive aspects of Rubbo's films—a diary form of storytelling and an avoidance of the expected.

These characteristics are especially apparent in *Waiting for Fidel* (1973) in which Rubbo is one of the major characters. The other two are former Newfoundland premier Joey Smallwood and radio and television tycoon Geoff Stirling. The supposed purpose of the film is to follow Smallwood and Stirling as they visit Cuba and talk to Fidel Castro about socialism, admired by

Smallwood but disparaged by Stirling. As they await the meeting with Castro, the camera records their discussions at a protocol house where they are staying and at schools and hospitals they visit. Instead of being a background figure, Rubbo is very much in the foreground, posing questions, getting into arguments, particularly with Stirling, the film's underwriter, and through narration, giving the audience a diary-like impression of what he is witnessing. The title of the film is taken from Samuel Beckett's play, *Waiting for Godot*, and as in the play, Fidel (Godot) never shows up, so the film turns out to be about Rubbo's encounters with Smallwood and Stirling.

In a number of films, Rubbo comes across as a curious, sensitive outsider/amateur observer trying to understand or unravel a foreign culture or a complex personality or an unresolved mystery. Film professor Joan Nicks says "Rubbo's on-screen persona foregrounds the inexpert 'self,' the out-of-place NFB filmmaker acting and improvising his way through the shooting. . . . The impulse that propelled Rubbo to 'dig in' culturally as an inexpert persona, in the guise of a footloose documentary filmmaker displaced from the Board and Canada (and his native Australia), ultimately mocks the imperialist bias of most Western documentaries about exotic others."

A good example of Rubbo's tendency to "dig in" culturally is *Sad Song of Yellow Skin* (1970), a look at how the Vietnam War and the American presence in Vietnam affected the lives of Vietnamese in Saigon. The film is seen through the eyes of three journalists/peace activists from the United States who, along with Rubbo, are outsiders trying to understand the people and their culture. One journalist lives on a monk's island of peace in the Mekong River. Another seeks to befriend people in a seedy, isolated part of town called the cemetery. And a third provides a home, or semblance of a home, for street kids—shoe shine boys who pimp and steal on the side. Rubbo is along to observe and to tell the viewer what he is observing—street-smart kids who use and are used by American soldiers, young girls turned prostitutes, children laughing and playing in the midst of filth and poverty, the burial arrangements for an old, opium-addicted cabaret performer and mistress whose heyday was during the French occupation. Throughout the film, Rubbo intersperses sounds and images of the United States: popular music, Richard Nixon on television, GIs looking for a good time, and an American Forces weathercast featuring a dancing weather woman billed as a "bubbling bundle of barometric brilliance." These sounds and images, along with Rubbo's quiet but pointed commentary about Americans (they believe all Vietnamese are gooks—some good gooks, some bad gooks, but all gooks), about what the Vietnamese think of Americans (Americans either kill or give), and about what he sees as American influence (GIs came looking for girls and marijuana, now all that remains are the babies they left behind), paint a picture of a culture being corrupted by American dollars and American values.

In *Wet Earth and Warm People* (1971) Rubbo is again the outsider trying to understand another culture, this time Indonesia. "Watching Indonesia," Rubbo observes, "is like watching a snake shed skins." The skins refer to past influences, particularly Dutch influence. In this film Rubbo tries to understand Indonesia's struggle to modernize. He follows Jakarta's chief of police (who is also a singer with his own television program) and also the driver of a Pedi cab or becak (Indonesia's traditional means of transportation, often regarded as a symbol of its backwardness) and travels to a small village to experience the true Indonesia, with its puppet plays and agrarian practices. The reflexive nature of Rubbo's documentaries is most apparent in *Wet Earth and Warm People* (1971). In diary-like form, Rubbo accounts for some of the problems and possible resentment the crew has encountered: the cameraman looks like a colonialist, the sound man (making his first trip outside North America) appears to be on a tropical trip, and his (Rubbo's) correspondent's suit is mistaken for military. These revelations take the viewer backstage, as well as on stage, and make the process of filmmaking an integral part of the story.

Rubbo's interventionist style is also at the forefront of *Daisy: The Story of a Facelift*. In part the story of a feisty middle-aged woman (and fellow employee of the NFB) determined to turn back time, it is also the story of a twentieth-century cultural phenomenon—society's preoccupation with physical appearance. Rubbo explores the underlying motives for cosmetic surgery (breast enlargements, tummy tucks, nose jobs, and the like), and follows Daisy on her personal odyssey as she discusses her youth, marriages, growing old, and fears and expectations. The close, personal relationship between filmmaker and subject is apparent in the banter between Rubbo and Daisy and in Rubbo's provocations of Daisy, at one point pushing Daisy to ask a total stranger (in a patient waiting room) what he was doing there. Nicks believes the film "assumes the character of a parody of male voyeurism in Rubbo's obsession with what drives Daisy's pursuit of a more youthful face to recapture a romantic past."

In *Much Ado about Something* (2002), commissioned by the Australian Broadcasting Corporation, Rubbo tries to unravel the authorship of William Shakespeare's plays and sonnets. Following some colorful characters known as Marlovians, all of whom are convinced Christopher Marlowe was the hidden hand behind Shakespeare, Rubbo tests their ideas against what is known—or not known—about Shakespeare and Marlowe. Presented as a kind of tongue-in-cheek, who-done-it murder mystery (literally in the case of Marlowe's death), *Much Ado about Something* (2002) features Rubbo as chief detective and provocateur, a role he has played in previous films. What is different about *Much Ado* is that Rubbo also did most of the camera work, using an inexpensive, lightweight, digital camera.

CHURCHILL ROBERTS

See also **National Film Board of Canada; *Sad Song of Yellow Skin; Waiting for Fidel***

Biography

Born in Melbourne, Australia. Studied anthropology at Sydney University and completed a master's degree in film at Stanford University. In 1965, went to work for the National Film Board of Canada where he wrote and directed more than thirty-five films. From 1980 to 1990 wrote and directed feature films for children, among them *The Peanut Butter Solution* (1984), *Tommy Tricker and the Stamp Traveler* (1986), and *Vincent and Me* (1990). Returned to his native Australia in 1995 and headed the documentary division and special projects of ABC TV. At ABC developed the series *Race Around the World* and produced and direc-

ted *Little Box That Sings* (1999) and *The Man Who Is Still Going* (1999), an update of a 1973 NFB film. Has lectured widely on documentary and has taught at the Australian Film Television and Radio School and Harvard University. Is currently an independent filmmaker and painter residing in Avoca Beach, Australia.

Selected Films

1970 *Sad Song of the Yellow Skin*: writer, director
1971 *Wet Earth and Warm People*: writer, director
1974 *Waiting for Fidel*: director, editor
1978 *Solzhenitsyn's Children . . . Are Making a Lot of Noise in Paris*: writer, director
1982 *Daisy: The Story of a Facelift*: director, editor
1984 *Margaret Atwood: Once in August*: writer, director
1984 *The Peanut Butter Solution*: writer, director
1988 *Tommy Tricker and the Stamp Traveler*: writer, director
1991 *Vincent and Me*: writer, director
1998 *The Little Box That Sings*: writer, director
2002 *Much Ado about Something*: writer, director

Further Reading

Ellis, Jack, *The Documentary Idea: A Critical History of English-Language Documentary Film and Video*, Englewood Cliffs, NJ: Prentice Hall, 1989.

Nichols, Bill, *Introduction to Documentary*, Bloomington: Indiana University Press, 2001.

Nicks, Joan, "The Documentary of Displaced Persona: Michael Rubbo's *Daisy: Portrait of a Facelift*, in *Documenting the Documentary: Close Readings of Documentary Film and Video*, edited by Barry Keith Grant and Jeannette Sloniowski, Detroit: Wayne State University Press, 1998, 302–317.

Rosenthal, Alan, "*Sad Song of the Yellow Skin*" and "*Waiting for Fidel*": Michael Rubbo," in *The Documentary Conscience: A Casebook in Film Making*, Berkeley: University of California Press, 1980, 232–244.

———, *Writing, Directing, and Producing Documentary Films and Video, revised edition*, Carbondale: Southern Illinois University Press, 1996.

RUSPOLI, MARIO

Jean Ruspoli was in some respects a dilettante, working as a writer, a painter, and a musician. Although he did not devote himself exclusively to documentary cinema, he is noted for a few landmarks in the history of direct film.

Initially involved in the popular "Connaissance du Monde" lecture-and-film tours, he suggested to his former schoolmate, the famous producer Anatole Dauman (Argos Films), that he adapt his first work, *Les Hommes de la Baleine,* for movie theatre distribution. Dauman borrowed some money from Aristotle Onassis and hired Henri Colpi and Chris Marker to edit and narrate a short version of the film, which premiered with Marker's *Lettre de Sibérie*.

Ruspoli then directed two films, *Campagne Romaine* (1958), and *Ombre et Lumière de Rome* (1959). His next two films, both shot in Lozère (where Ruspoli was from), displayed the characteristics of direct cinema in their attempts to penetrate a specific milieu and seize on genuine situations. *Les Inconnus de la Terre* (1961) paints a picture of the conditions of the life of small farmers. Dauman brought in cinematographer Michel Brault and the Coutant camera prototype (both of which had been involved in *Chronique d'un Eté*). Ruspoli applied an empathic, participative way of filmmaking. *Regard sur la Folie* (1962), about the pioneering approach to mental illness of Dr. Tosquelles at Saint Alban hospital, can be considered the first modern film on its subject matter and the precursor of numerous works to come.

In some of his writings, Ruspoli developed and formulated the concept of direct cinema, regarding it in its relationship with the use of 16mm synchronous equipment, and contextualizing it with a social, humanist view. He insisted that "associating the words cinema and vérité is a nonsense," the Kino-Pravda idea was "not the aim in itself, but the means," and suggested using the phrase "Cinéma Direct." He advocated the filmmaker's "greatest sincerity, highest self-effacement in facing the events he is filming, and which he never must provoke." In filming practice, according to Ruspoli's view, "the sound must rule the picture," as speech is irreplaceable, unlike the image—in fact, a sign of his concern with the relationship between people. Likewise, a film crew has to be a united team, "of a high moral level based on a broad mutual confidence." The crew at work "is living a filmed adventure, plunging collectively into the audiovisual reality."

Ruspoli also made *Petite Ville* (1963) and *Chaval* (1970), the latter a tribute to the caricaturist. Before he died, he completed a set of four TV programs and a book about the prehistoric paintings of Lascaux.

JEAN LIOULT

See also **Brault, Michel; Marker, Chris**

Biography

Born June 17, 1925, in Rome. Studied at the Ecole du Louvre. Died June 13, 1986, in Villepinte, Seine-Saint-Denis, France.

Further Reading

Gerber, Jacques (Préf. Elia Kazan), *Souvenir-écran : Anatole Dauman, Argos Films*, Paris: Centre Georges Pompidou, 1989.
———. "Le groupe synchrone cinématographique léger," Rapport UNESCO, Octobre 1963.
Ruspoli, Mario, "L'équipe synchrone audiovisuelle," Revue, in *Image et Son*, 173, Mai 1964, 34–37.

RUSSIA/SOVIET UNION

Russia has been extremely influential in the development of documentary film. From early newsreels to avant-garde experimentations to multi-part television series, Russian filmmakers have captivated the world for nearly a century. Supported by a government who not only saw film as an effective tool for reaching the masses but also went so far as to open a state supported film school, Russian filmmakers have, from the beginning, remained in the forefront of technology and technique.

Shortly after the revolution of 1917, the Union of Soviet Socialist Republics began to recognize the power of cinema. According to the head of the People's Commissariat of Education, Anatoli Lunacharsky, Lenin considered cinema to be the most important of all the arts for the newly formed republic. During this time, Denis Arkadievich Kaufman (1896–1954), the son of a librarian, was in Petrograd (St. Petersburg) studying medicine and psychology. Influenced by the futurist poet Vladimir Mayakovsky, Kaufman began writing his own poetry, rejecting traditional syntax in favor of word montages. Like most futurists, he reveled in the clamor and rhythm of machines in a world quickly becoming industrialized. He created an audio laboratory where he would create sound montages and changed his name to Dziga Vertov, a name that denotes turning or revolving, signaling that he would become a driving force in the new cinematic movement.

In October 1917, Vertov volunteered to serve on the Cinema Committee in Moscow and was appointed editor of its newsreel *Kino-nedeyia/ Cinema Week*. For three years, Vertov's job was to take all incoming bits of film, which included fragments of struggle, crisis, disaster, and victory, and assemble them into a meaningful structure before sending them out again for viewing by the public. His mission was to unite the people by keeping them informed of the ups and downs of the struggle. While compiling the newsreels, Vertov began to reuse footage, stringing it together to create features that provided a much broader context than was possible in the newsreels. Three of the most important of these early full-length features are *Godovchina revoljutsii/Anniversary of the Revolution* (1919), *La Bataille de Tsaritsyne/The Battle of Tsaritsyne* (1920), and *Istoriya grazhdanskoj vojny/History of the Civil War* (1922). Vertov felt that these films played an increasingly important role in the struggles of the new Soviet Republic.

Soon after the struggle ended, film stock was scarce and new projects sat waiting to be produced. Fiction films returned to theaters and Vertov found himself editing footage supplied by other filmmakers. From 1920–1922, he began to write manifestos that attacked the current state of film in the Soviet Union, which he saw as "movie dramas garbed in splendid technological dressing" and called for a new breed of filmmakers to rise to the challenge of creating a new Soviet Cinema by "experiment[ing] with this dying organism." Vertov saw fiction film as "opium for the people" and wanted the new Soviet Cinema to document socialist reality (Barnouw, 1993: 54).

With his wife, Yelizaveta Svilova, as editor and his brother, Mikhail Kaufman, as cameraman, Vertov formed the Council of the Three and began to produce a series of monthly newsreels entitled *Kino-pravda/Cinema Truth* (1922–1925). During its three-year run, twenty-three issues of the series appeared. Running approximately twenty minutes and generally covering three separate topics, each issue focused on everyday experiences in the marketplace, bars, and schools. Vertov rarely asked permission to film and usually used a hidden camera to capture the hidden truth of socialist reality. The cinematography is simple, functional, and minimalistic. The issues included non-narrative vignettes and exposés: the renovation of a trolley system, the organization of farmers into communes, and starvation in the emerging Marxist state. Although the issues of *Kino-pravda* rarely included reenactments or stagings, one notable exception is a segment about the trial of the Social Revolutionaries in which Vertov staged several scenes including newspapers being sold on the streets and read in the trolley. Vertov's tendency toward propaganda is also present. One issue runs the subtitle: "Tanks on the labor front," as the former Tsar's tanks help to prepare the foundation for a new airport. Although the series continued to run, it had become so experimental after half its issues that critics began to dismiss Vertov's work as "insane." This did not deter Vertov who, at the end of the final episode, encouraged his audience to contact him with interesting stories for future projects.

While producing *Kino-pravda*, Vertov continued his practice of providing context by expanding shorter pieces into features. The result was *Kinoglaz/Kino-Eye: Life Caught Unawares* (1924), a documentary that examines the joys of life in a small Soviet village. Some of its various segments are interesting; some are not. One segment focuses on the activities of the "Young Pioneers," children who spend their days pasting propaganda posters on walls, passing out pamphlets, and encouraging everyone to buy from the cooperative. Other segments highlight a Chinese magician who performs tricks for bread, a cocaine addict, and a murdered factory worker. The three most interesting and experimental portions of the film focus on the slaughter of a bull, the baking of bread, and a series of dives. Each of these segments begins with the final frame and then reverses, showing respectively the entrails moving back into the bull, the skin closing, the bull standing up, walking backwards onto a train car, and rejoining the herd; the bread coming out of the oven, reversing from dough to batter, and eventually from batter to its original ingredients; and divers going into and then coming back out of the water. *Kinoglaz* also includes one animated segment. The film ends in a mental health hospital. Although there is no structured narrative of any sort—all the images are simply ones captured unaware by the camera eye—*Kinoglaz* is interesting for its cinematography and techniques. The reverse segments are the first of their kind and are only now beginning to be used in contemporary documentary and fiction films.

Drastic ninety-degree angles capture views of the countryside, city, and people in interesting ways. Ultimately the film is important as a document of a way of life that no longer exists and for Vertov's experimental techniques.

Five years later, Vertov completed his masterpiece, *Chelovek s kinoapparatom/Man with a Movie Camera* (1929. Like *Kinoglaz*, this film is experimental, but is much more cohesive. It is a silent documentary film about filmmaking. Vertov follows a cameraman, his brother Mikhail Kaufman, around various cities. The film intercuts Kaufman's footage with Vertov's footage of Kaufman filming and footage of Yelizaveta Svilova editing. The film introduces a number of innovative cinematic techniques: double exposure, fast and slow motion, freeze-frame, jump cuts, split screens, Dutch angles, extreme close-ups, and tracking shots. The self-reflexive storyline is also the first example of a meta-documentary. Vertov superimposes a shot of Kaufman setting up his camera atop a second camera and later inside a glass. Although at the time cameras were large and noisy, Vertov was sending a message about the prevalence and unobtrusiveness of film and again encouraging Soviet filmmakers to capture life unawares. Claiming that "we cannot improve our eyes but we can always improve the camera," Vertov ends his film by animating the camera and letting it walk away from Kaufman, no longer reliant on human control. Again critics attacked Vertov and his film for a few obvious stagings and its drastic experimentation, but the film has since become a classic of the genre and was released on DVD in 1996 with a new soundtrack performed by the Alloy Orchestra. Based on notes left by Vertov, the soundtrack incorporates sound effects including sirens, babies crying, and crowd noise.

Over the years, Vertov frequently debated film theory and philosophy with his colleague, Sergei Mikhailovich Eisenstein (1898–1948), known mainly for his fact-based historical dramas. Vertov championed the unobtrusive *kino-eye*, but Eisenstein argued that the Soviet Republic needed a *kino-fist* to impress on people the message of socialism. Although they differed in their ideas of film construction, they both agreed on the importance of editing to the finished product and the illusion of reality. Although Eisenstein's films were scripted fictions based on historical fact, they often took the form of newsreels and documentaries. In fact, the single most important technique pioneered by Eisenstein that is still used by documentary filmmakers today is *montage*. Montage stresses the fragmentation of events by rearranging them and juxtaposing shots that do not "naturally" go together. By using montage techniques, the filmmaker constructs new impressions and insights, creating a visual metaphor that comments on the camera's subject. Eisenstein believed that through cinema, filmmakers were not simply documenting reality, but creating a new reality:

> Is this not exactly what we of the cinema do . . . when we cause a monstrous disproportion of the parts of a normally flowing event, and suddenly dismember the event into "close-up of clutching hands," "medium shot of the struggle," and "extreme close-up of bulging eyes," in making a montage disintegration of the event in various planes? In making an eye twice as large as a man's full figure! By combining these monstrous incongruities, we newly collect the disintegrated event into one whole, but in *our* aspect. According to the treatment of our relation to the event.

(Donald, 1999: 34)

Bronenosets Potyomkin/Battleship Potemkin (1925) glorifies the 1905 mutiny against oppressive officers on a battleship. Using the form of a newsreel, Eisenstein carefully crafts his propaganda film by painstakingly editing it in a way that would manipulate the audience and produce the strongest emotional response possible. This subtly crafted montage encourages the viewer to sympathize with the rebellious sailors and despise the cruel officers. The most famous scene from the movie is the Odessa Steps Massacre in which ruthless soldiers of the Tsar, like machines, march rhythmically down an endless flight of stairs and slaughter a crowd of innocents who are attempting to flee. The scene has been imitated and parodied over the years and still has an emotional impact on audiences who travel to the country to see the Odessa Steps. Interestingly enough, the entire scene is fictitious and scripted, a testament to the power of filmed "reality."

Two years later, Eisenstein created the first mockumentary with *Oktyabr/October: Ten Days That Shook the World* (1927). Commissioned by the Soviet government to honor the tenth anniversary of the 1917 October Revolution, Eisenstein used the film to advance what he saw as the further development of his theories of montage, using a concept he described as "intellectual montage." The film was not as successful or influential as *Bronenosets Potyomkin*, and Eisenstein's metaphorical experiments met with official disapproval. Eisenstein was ordered to reedit the work to expurgate negative references to Trotsky and to make it more accessible to the masses. In recent years, however, the film has come to be considered a historical epic and powerful representation of Eisenstein's genius and artistry. Eisenstein's theories and techniques continue to influence documentary filmmakers, both in Russia and internationally, as montage laid the groundwork for the pioneering compilation documentaries of Esfir Shub and the didactic emphasis that John Grierson gave to documentary in the Great Britain of the 1930s.

While Eisenstein and Vertov argued and debated, Esfir Shub (1894–1959), a young female filmmaker, diligently worked on her own documentaries. Although she is not as well known as either of her colleagues, her methods and techniques have proven to be more influential to Soviet cinema than either of the other two directors. Born into a family of landowners, Shub studied literature in Moscow before attending classes at the Institute for Women's Higher Education. She joined the State Commissariat of Education and was appointed as Theatre Officer, a job that allowed her to work closely with Vsevolod Meyerhold, a famous avant-garde theatre director. After leaving the Commissariat, Shub joined the Goskino film company where she met Vertov. Although they maintained a lifelong professional friendship, it was often stormy because of their theoretical disagreements. Shub shared Vertov's belief in the intrinsic power of film to reveal the hidden aspects of reality. But she differed from Vertov in that she believed that film could be used in the representation and interpretation of history, not simply as a document of the contemporary world.

She learned the art of editing by recutting "approved" versions of imported films such as D. W. Griffith's *Intolerance* (1916) and Fritz Lang's *Dr. Mabuse, der Spieler/Dr. Mabuse, King of Crime* (1922). When the film stock shortage slowed down the production of new projects, Shub did not wait for stock to become available or recoat existing stock. Rather, she sifted through archival footage in search of material that could be edited and interpreted for the masses. She was so diligent in her work that she was given access to the Tsar's personal film library. The footage she found and compiled enabled her to produce a trilogy of documentary films: *Padeniye dinastij Romanovykh/The Fall of the Romanov Dynasty* (1927), *Velikij put/The Great Way* (*Road*) (1927), and *Rossiya Nikolaya II i Lev Tolstoy/Leo Tolstoy and the Russia of Nicholas II* (1928). While making the trilogy, Shub was faced with two major problems: finding the "right" footage and compensating for damaged or missing footage. Once she collected the most valuable existing footage, she "replaced"

any relevant damaged footage with new footage. By doing so, she provided a contemporary context for the archival footage. *Padeniye dinastij Romanovykh*, the first part of the trilogy, has had the most lasting resonance. It follows the sequence of events in Russia from the first Russian revolution in 1905 to the second revolution in October 1917. Shub introduces leaders of the Duma, gentry and peasants, soldiers and sailors, the bourgeoisie, and the Tsar. In May 1913, Europe's crowned heads come to Petrograd to celebrate 300 years of Romanov rule, even as most of them prepare for war. With great skill and care Shub produced a dramatic account of events as they were actually happening. The result is a film that still has an emotional impact when viewed today.

Unknowingly, Shub created a completely new genre: the historical compilation film. She later claimed that she simply wanted to create newsreels with an editorial slant. Both critics and colleagues admired Shub's work. She had successfully found a balance between narrative and documentary forms. Although she remained quiet and out of the spotlight, working sporadically, she did return to the documentary form with a collaboration with Vsevolod Pudovkin (1893–1953) entitled *Kino za XX let/Twenty Years of Soviet Cinema* (1940). After this successful film, Shub left Goskino to become chief editor for Moscow's central studio for documentary film, where she spent her final years confined to editing duties. Although Vertov and Eisenstein helped to define avant-garde filmmaking and theory, Esfir Shub's style and technique have survived as the most prominent form in modern documentary filmmaking. In addition, her scholarly achievement in researching and locating valuable archival footage helped to encourage the development and maintenance of film archives.

The year 1928 brought about yet another change in Soviet cinema, with the publication of Alexei Gan's essay "Constructivism in the Cinema." Like Vertov before him, Gan called for a new type of cinema that, though rooted in reality, was poetic and expressed the mark of the filmmaker.

It is not enough to link, by means of montage, individual moments of episodic phenomena of life, united under a more or less successful title. The most unexpected accidents, occurrences, and events are always linked organically with the fundamental root of social reality. While apprehending them with the shell of their outer manifestations, one should be able to expose their inner essence by a series of other scenes. Only on such a basis can one build a vivid film of concrete, active reality, gradually departing from the newsreel, from whose material this new ciné form is developing (130).

This essay addresses the issue of film form, specifically the assembly of shots into a pattern that affirms the voice of the filmmaker, by calling for a new style that moves beyond simply showing "attractions" or making unobtrusive scientific observations. Gan, like Eisentstein, was calling on filmmakers not only to document but also to comment on their subjects. Two filmmakers who quickly answered the call were Victor Turin (1895–1945) and Mikheil Kalatozishvili, more commonly known as Mikhail Kalatozov (1903–1973).

Victor Turin's *Turksib* (1929) documented the construction of a railroad linking Turkestan and Siberia through the harshest region of the central Asian desert. The end of the film, showing a locomotive looming in the horizon under a blast of thick black smoke, signals the triumph of modern technology. Turin's organization of his huge project, and his success in giving it innovative dramatic impact, won wide admiration and influenced documentary filmmakers throughout the world. A memorable sequence, introduced with the simple title "Strangers . . . ," shows people in a remote Turkestan desert village watching the arrival of surveyors. This scene sets the stage for a later climactic sequence in which an engine arrives on the new track for the first time. Some men on horseback ride up and cautiously inspect the new contraption as it stands at rest, puffing quietly. As the engine starts up, the terror of the horses and men and their temporary retreat provide fascinatingly authentic moments. Later we see them joyfully racing the engine across vast plains. One major innovation of Turin's film is the incorporation of lengthy subtitles that seem to anticipate spoken commentary.

Born Mikhail Kalatozishvili in Tiflis, Kalatozov originally studied to be an economist. In 1925, however, he began working as an actor in the Georgian studios. Shortly after this, he began to learn the art of shooting and editing film, which led him to create his first short documentary *Mati samepo/Their Empire* in 1928. Two years later he created an amazingly beautiful, stark, and blunt chronicle of life in post-Revolutionary Russia with *Jim Shvante (marili svanets)/Salt for Svanetia* (1930). The film focuses on a starkly isolated mountain community between the Black and Caspian Seas that has been deprived of an essential mineral: salt. The villagers and animals all suffer and go to any lengths necessary to find the precious commodity. Kalatozov shows the viewer a farmer lying down in his field to rest from his labor. As he does so, a cow comes to lick the

sweat from his brow. After the farmer urinates, the cattle lick his urine. Whenever a baby is born, dogs lick the placental fluid from its body. Kalatozov's film sends out the message that the people are not only suffering from a lack of salt, but also from their cultural isolation from the progress of the new Republic. The villagers retain their primitive beliefs by adhering to their religion and giving what little money they have to the Church that is powerless to help. The climax of the film comes as a Soviet-built road is constructed, and thanks to Soviet progress, Svanetia is saved by a shipment of salt.

The Stalin regime felt that the film was unbalanced and unfair to Svanetia and that Kalatozov was far too fascinated by the backwardness and superstition of Svanetia, and too overtly pushed the socialist solution. Kalatozov had allowed his voice to sound too loudly in the film as opposed to simply documenting the reality. Kalatozov followed *Jim Shvante* with *Lursmani cheqmashi/Nail in the Boot* (1931), a film that received more of the same criticism and was ultimately banned. Kalatozov was then assigned to strictly administrative duties within the film industry. During World War II, he was appointed to the office of Chief Administrator of Soviet Feature Film Production. During this time, he sometimes worked in Los Angeles as the Soviet cultural representative. After the war, Kalatozov received an appointment as Deputy Minister of Film Production and was allowed to resume his directing career. Twenty-seven years after making *Jim Shvante*, Kalatozov received the Palme d'Or at the Cannes Film Festival for *Letjat zhuravli/The Cranes Are Flying* (1957), a wartime romantic drama. Unfortunately, he left no other documentaries in his short but impressive catalogue.

The Soviet films of this early period helped to develop modern documentary filmmaking style and techniques. Their focus on the modern world, politics, and historical contexts sought to agitate viewers and move audiences to action. Unfortunately, the artistic peak of this early phase of Soviet cinema was short-lived. As Stalin's regime grew stronger and more paranoid in the 1930s, more and more documentaries were censored or outright banned and the voices of their creators silenced. Still, their influence survives in worldwide documentary filmmaking today, even as new voices in Russia are emerging.

Having written, directed, and starred in more than thirty films, Eldar Ryazanov (1927–) has established himself as one of Russia's most formidable filmmakers. His films are distinctly Russian in nature, as he himself says that he can inhabit no other country than his own and embraces his native climate, culture, and language. Ryazanov tends to work in the area of comedic fiction, but he still attempts to capture the reality of Russian life by focusing on stories about ordinary people and unforgettable situations. He believes the most important element of the film director's profession is a carefully balanced combination of tenderness and toughness. He tries to capture the raw reality of life in the most cinematically beautiful way possible. It is this combination that he brings to his four part documentary series on the Russian bard Vladimir Vysotsky, *Chetyre vechera s Vladimirom Vysotskim/Four Meetings with Vladimir Vysotsky* (1987). In the documentary, Ryazanov acts as director, writer, and commentator as he explores the life of Vysotsky through four stages. The first part deals with Vysotsky's early life, the second with his career as an actor in the theater, the third with his career as a film actor, and the final installment with his career as Russia's preeminent poet, singer, and musician.

Using archival footage and providing his own modern commentary, Ryazanov beautifully captures the hard-living, hard-drinking actor who was admired by virtually all circles of Soviet society. Through his music Vysotsky was a voice of dissent who was often banned, but through his films he was a simple entertainer. Although he was "discovered" while playing Hamlet on stage, his most memorable role was captured on Russian television as he took on the role of tough homicide detective Gleb Zheglov in the series *Mesto vstrechi imenit nelzya/Can't Change the Meeting Place* (1979). With this documentary, Ryazanov in many ways returns to Vertov by making a film about film and its power. Unlike Vertov, however, Ryazanov is not promoting the government through propaganda. Rather he is criticizing it by creating a testament to one of Russia's greatest critics. Although Vysotsky held no office, he did play an important political role by condemning the system under which he was born. Throughout his lifetime, the government was able to silence and control his criticism, but through Ryazanov's film, Vysotsky's voice has been captured. This marks a major departure from the Stalinist regime that all but destroyed the documentary tradition in Russia.

In the 1990s, Stanislav Govorukhin (1936–) emerged as the dominant documentary filmmaker of Russia. A member of the Duma, the lower house of the Russian parliament, Govorukhin is not only one of the most favorite directors, but also a politician whose opinions are listened to and respected. He is known for making emotionally charged speeches that motivate some listeners and enrage others. With many reforms beginning to take place in his country in the early 1990s, Govorukhin create documentaries with a definitive political slant. His films lash out at emerging criminal elements including corruption and white collar crime. When criticized for mixing his politics with his art, he replied, "This is a creative process . . . I don't see much difference between politics and directing." His films are as up front and daring as his speeches and the titles make no attempt to sanitize the director's opinions. *Tak zhit nelzya/You Can't Live Like That* (1990), *Rossiya, kotoruyu my poteryali/Russia That We've Lost* (1992), and *Velikaya kriminal'naya revolyutsiya/Great Criminal Revolution* (1994) make up a trilogy that provides Govorukhin's view of historical and contemporary events in Russia, tracing its context and consequences from the final years before the 1917 revolution, its public and economic life, the Bolshevik rule that turned out fatal for the people to the fate of Russia, complete with its historical role and prospects for the future. According to Govorukhin in the films, "A pessimist is a well-informed optimist. . . . What I know suggests that things are pretty bad. Nevertheless, I do hope that life in Russia will gradually improve." Govorukhin is reluctant to discuss the future. But he often talks nostalgically of the past, stating that his time is the nineteenth century and that it is a pity that he was not born a century earlier. Although he has recently turned to narrative fiction, his most recent documentary project is a filmed interview with the famous writer, Alexander Solzhenitsyn. The film includes narration about Solzhenitsyn's life and work in America, his family, his dreams, and intentions. The as yet unreleased film is simply entitled *Alexander Solzhenitsyn* (1994). In 2003, Govorukhin released *Blagoslovite zhenshchinu/Bless the Woman*, another narrative drama that focuses on a tiny Soviet village in the years before World War II. Still productive, Govorukhin hopes to return to the documentary form soon.

Beginning in 1993, the Krupny Plan Motion Picture and Video Association teamed with Castle Communications and Eastern Light Productions to produce documentaries that would reflect the lost footage and films of the Stalin era. By using the talents of a number of directors, including Aizenberg, M. K. Kaufman, and Zolotukhin, *Rossiya: zabytie gody/Russia: The Forgotten Years* covers such diverse historical topics as the Revolution and the final years of Romanov rule, as well as cultural topics including the Russian ballet and histories of the naval fleet, aviation squadron, and the space race. *Istoriya grazhdanskoi voiny/ The History of the Civil War* (1993) covers the period from 1918–1922 and informs the viewer of the most significant events on the eve of the civil war through its opening stages. There is a considerable amount of archival footage and newsreels that has been made available for the first time. One of the most interesting segments documents the creation of the Red Army and its vital role in maintaining central Russia and achieving crucial victories on all fronts despite desperate resistance from the White forces. The beautiful cinematography and clever editing capture the suppression of the Kronstadt uprising in 1921 and the final expulsion of Japanese forces from Vladivostok in late 1922, marking the end of five years of conflict and establishing the Soviet Union as a major power.

Velikaya otechestvennaya voina/The Eastern Front a.k.a. *The Great Patriotic War* (1993) makes up three films in the series as the filmmakers use various newsreels to recreate a grandiose picture of the 1941–1945 battle with its magnificent victories and enormous losses. The trilogy begins with Hitler's invasion of the Soviet Union in June 1941, possibly the most dramatic campaign of World War II, and follows the war through the anticipated Blitzkrieg on the Eastern Front, and the Wermacht's first major defeat at Moscow. The film then dramatically captures the battle at Stalingrad, where the Russian troops fiercely held their ground against overwhelming forces and the momentous tank battle at Kursk. This segment, documenting the epic actions that turned the tide of World War II, could take their place alongside the great war films of history. The trilogy concludes with Operation Bagration, the destruction of the Wermacht in Byelorussia. The filmmakers do not hide the fact that the Red Army's thrust to Germany's border turned into a fierce and costly campaign, but show both the horrors and triumphs as Zhukov's two-million man force crushes Hitler's last defenses in Berlin.

Istoriya krasnoi armii/The History of the Red Army (1994) further explores one of the world's most powerful fighting forces. Emerging in 1918 under the control of Lev Trotsky, the Red Army was initially made up of 300,000 soldiers, but within two years had grown to more than 5 million. This documentary traces the first twenty years of its history from the civil war through its battles in World War II. The film strongly criticizes Stalin who had purged the forces, leaving them decimated as they entered the most important war of their history. Although the footage of the army's victory over the Nazi forces is impressive, the most impressive segments deal with the campaigns against the Japanese in Manchuria, the Finnish, and of the army's later involvement in Hungary, Czechoslovakia, and Afghanistan. Editing together unique and unseen archival footage, the documentary reaches high drama at many points.

One final important film of the *Forgotten Years* series is *Chekisty/The Story of the KGB* (1994). The film is divided into two parts, with part one covering the period 1917–1933, the beginnings of the KGB, and part two focusing on the professional police force active from 1934–1953. Having perfected the art of espionage, political assassinations, and rigged trials under the guidance of Feliks Dzerzhinsky, under Stalin the KGB became the ultimate tool for maintaining control over the country. During the 1930s and 1940s, the secret police force orchestrated mass purges and consolidated immense resources and political power and permeated every aspect of Soviet reality. This film in the series again uses archival footage mixed with contemporary commentary to create a great dramatic thriller while representing the reality of the Soviet people.

All of the films in the *Forgotten Years* series hearken back to the style created by Esfir Shub, taking existing footage and arranging it in a way to provide an interpretation for a new audience. Since Vertov, Russian cinema has pushed the boundaries of possibility with film. Ever striving for new styles and techniques, Russian filmmakers all seem to the share one bond: the voice of the filmmaker must be heard. Although many critics argue that documentary filmmakers should not be explicit in their views and, like Vertov, should simply attempt to capture "life unawares," the modern Russian filmmaker is more in line with Eisenstein's *kino-fist*. The events should not be staged, they should be natural, but in the editing process they should be arranged in a way to achieve the proper response from the audience. After many silent years, Russian cinema is back in the forefront, searching the archives of the past to move forward into the future.

CHARLES BANE

See also **Fall of the Romanov Dynasty, The; Man with a Movie Camera**; Shub, Esther; Turin Victor; **Turksib;** Vertov, Dziga

Further Reading

Barnouw, Erik, *Documentary: A History of the Non-Fiction Film*, 2nd revised edition, Oxford: Oxford UP, 1993.

Bordwell, David, and Kristin Thompson, *Film Art: An Introduction*, 6th edition, New York: Mcgraw-Hill, 2001.

Donald, James et al. (eds.), *Close Up 1927–1933: Cinema and Modernism*, Princeton: Princeton UP, 1999.

Gan, Alexi, "Constructivism and the Cinema," in *The Tradition of Constructivism*, edited by Stephen Bann, New York: Viking, 1974.

Grant, Barry Keith, and Jeannette Sloniowski (eds.), *Documenting the Documentary: Close Readings of Documentary Film and Video*, Detroit: Wayne State UP, 1998.

Jacobs, Lewis, *The Documentary Tradition*, 2nd edition, New York: Norton, 1979.

Mouratov, Sergei, "The Unknown Cinema: Documentary Screen, Glasnost Era," in *Journal of Film and Video*, 44, 1–2, 1992, 9–18.

Nichols, Bill, *Introduction to Documentary*, Bloomington: Indiana University Press, 2001.

Roberts, Graham, *Forward Soviet!: History and Non-Fiction Film in the USSR*, New York: I.B. Tauris, 1999.

———, *The Man with the Movie Camera*, New York: I.B. Tauris, 2001.

Vertov, Dziga. *Kino-Eye: The Writings of Dziga Vertov*, Translated by Kevin O'Brien, Berkeley: University of California Press, 1995.

Zimmermann P. R., "Reconstructing Vertov: Soviet Film Theory and American Radical Documentary," in *Journal of Film and Video*, 44, 1–2, 1992, 80–90.

S

SAD SONG OF YELLOW SKIN

(Canada, Rubbo, 1970)

Sad Song of Yellow Skin, directed by Michael Rubbo, is one of the most enduring films to emerge from the Vietnam War. The film is representative of the then-recent ascendancy of the director's role at the National Film Board (NFB) of Canada and marks a significant development toward what would become Rubbo's signature style. It also stands apart from more conventional documentary treatments of the war.

In the early 1960s, the NFB was organized into production units headed by executive producers. The units functioned in varying degrees autocratically, and filmmakers generally were subordinate to producers. In 1964–1965, rebellious filmmakers forced a dismantling of the unit system and the adoption of a "pool" system that gave directors the power often to propose subjects, initiate projects, and choose producers. As a result, a spate of films representing the personal or political interests of the filmmakers emerged in the latter part of the 1960s and continued into subsequent decades.

Rubbo entered the National Film Board in 1966 and for several years made sponsored films as well as children's films. As the Vietnam War dragged on, he proposed making a film about the war. An overtly antiwar film would not have been permitted at that time, and the NFB had a policy that each of its films had to have "Canadian content." Rubbo's proposed film would be centered on the work of a Canadian-sponsored foster parents program in Vietnam. Once in Vietnam, however, he discovered that the program offered meager filmic possibilities. He wired the NFB and got permission from his producer, Tom Daly, to focus on three idealistic young Americans in Saigon who were working against the war and its effects.

Rubbo's change of focus proved pivotal in several ways. *Sad Song of Yellow Skin* became the NFB's first significant documentary without any Canadian content (with the exception of some NFB films sponsored by the United Nations). By using the three likeable Americans as his guide, Rubbo avoided simplistic anti-Americanism. Most important, the opportunity enabled Rubbo to make a film that did not pretend to project the knowledge he did not have.

Rubbo, who narrates the film off-camera, explores Saigon through the three Americans and their work, and the audience discovers Saigon through his search. The film is structured such that Rubbo's initial disorientation in a hectic foreign city is represented in a fast-moving series of images of exotic bustle; our gradual if ultimately limited familiarity with Saigon follows Rubbo's own.

Except for details, the knowledge we ultimately gain is essentially the knowledge of mystery. One of the most moving scenes in the film is the funeral of an opium addict Rubbo had met through one of the Americans. The woman had been a highly admired dancer; she died in wretched destitution. Her tearful older daughter holds the baby sister she must now care for alone while neighbors arrange her mother's corpse in a primitive wooden coffin lined with sawdust. The film ends on the "Island of Peace," a serene Buddhist colony headed by a withered old priest on an island in the Mekong River. The priest, educated in Europe as an engineer, hopes to bring peace to Vietnam by symbolic means: his daily trek from Hanoi to Saigon on a wooden platform shaped and painted to resemble a map of Vietnam. The film's conclusion in death and spiritual quest is at once strange and familiar. As if Rubbo is aware that he has strayed far from the subject of war, the last sounds we hear are bursts of machine gun fire laid in over the final credits.

Sad Song of Yellow Skin was dismissed by some for its apparent lack of political analysis. The film is devoid of the anger of such Vietnam-era films as *Hearts and Minds* (1974) and *Interviews with My Lai Veterans* (1971) or the battle content of *The Anderson Platoon* (1967). Its only direct representation of military presence is the occasional shot of a U.S. soldier in Saigon and those bursts of machine gun fire; the latter seem like less a reminder than an afterthought. Some critics sensed a patronizing tone to the film. When it was shown to a group of Cuban filmmakers, for instance, Rubbo was asked why the camera seemed to always be looking down at the Vietnamese—which it does, but largely because the American subjects were tall and the cameraman was six feet, four inches tall. Rubbo's reliance on U.S. guides has also been questioned, but there is an honesty in the way it shows the film's sources on screen. And some people were put off by Rubbo's first-person narration, which he delivers in an almost matter-of-fact, sometimes hesitant, groping style. The Canadian Broadcasting Corporation refused to air the film because of its personal, nonobjective point of view.

Although they were perceived by some as shortcomings, Rubbo developed these aspects of *Sad Song of Yellow Skin* into a distinctive style. Beginning with his next film, *Wet Earth and Warm People* (1971), Rubbo didn't just personally narrate; he stepped in front of the camera to engage with the material as another character. He would often use intermediaries as guides to the subject of his inquiries, as in *Solzhenitsyn's Children . . . Are Making a Lot of Noise in Paris* (1978). He would treat his villains gently, as in *Persistent and Finagling* (1971). The quintessential Rubbo film, where the various components of his approach mesh together most effectively, is *Waiting for Fidel* (1974).

D.B. JONES

See also **Daly, Tom; Documentary Film: Canada; Grierson, John;** *Hearts and Minds;* **National Film Board of Canada; Rubbo, Michael;** *Waiting for Fidel;* **War: Vietnam**

Sad Song of Yellow Skin (Canada, National Film Board, 1970, 58 mins.). Distributed by the National Film Board of Canada. Produced by Tom Daly. Directed by Michael Rubbo. Cinematography by Martin Duckworth and Pierre Letarte. Sound by George Croll, Michel Descombes, Les Halman, and Pierre Letarte. Edited by Torben Schioler and Michael Rubbo. Narration written and spoken by Michael Rubbo.

Further Reading

Dobi, Steve, "Michael Rubbo" (interview), *Sightlines*, Fall 1975, 17–20.

Handling, Piers, "The Diary Films of Mike Rubbo," in *Take Two*, edited by Seth Feldman, Toronto: Irwin Publishing, 1984.

Hughes, John, "Michael Rubbo: Hiding behind the 'I'" (interview), *Cinema Papers*, January/February 1981, 41–45, 89.

Jones, D. B., *Movies and Memoranda*, Ottawa: Deneau, 1982.

Jones, D. B., *The Best Butler in the Business: Tom Daly of the National Film Board of Canada*, Toronto, University of Toronto Press, 1996.

Rosenthal, Alan, "*Sad Song of Yellow Skin* and *Waiting for Fidel*" (interview with Michael Rubbo), in *The Documentary Conscience: A Casebook in Film Making*, Berkeley: University of California Press, 1980.

SADNESS: A MONOLOGUE BY WILLIAM YANG

(Australia, Ayres, 1999)

Sadness: A Monologue by William Yang is one of the most innovative documentaries to be produced in Australia in the late 1990s. *Sadness* existed as a highly acclaimed performance piece by Australian photographer and performance artist, William Yang, before it was adapted to the screen by writer and director, Tony Ayres, in 1999. It is the combination of performance, documentary, and Yang's evocative monologue that marks *Sadness* as a unique Australian documentary.

Funded by SBS Independent and Film Australia's National Interest Program initiative, *Sadness* weaves together a number of different narratives in such a way as to construct a commentary on identity, community, and nationhood. These many narratives represent aspects of Yang's experience that function, for him, as sites of mourning. Following the death of his mother, Yang travels through Australia's northeastern state, Queensland, in order to discover the truth about the murder of his uncle, William Fang Yuen, which occurred in the 1920s. He visits family and other witnesses, and while the accounts he collects are conflicting, everyone agrees that the misconducted murder trial represented the authorities' lack of regard for the Chinese-Australian community.

These scenes concerning family, past and present, are interspersed with sequences devoted to a number of friends Yang lost to AIDS in Sydney's gay community. Yang describes his relationship with Scotty, David, Nicholas, and others, as their physical decline becomes apparent on screen. Through juxtaposing the two discourses of family and gay identity, *Sadness* problematises the way they are often considered mutually exclusive. As a documentary, *Sadness* can be understood within a tradition of essayist filmmaking in the sense that the self-consciously subjective and performed nature of the narrative allows for the productive juxtaposition of seemingly divergent discourses.

This bricolage across the different aspects of Yang's experience works to displace the construction of a centre and a margin, or the "Australian" identity and the "ethnic" identity, while also denying the possibility of a singular notion of identity.

In *Sadness*, Yang himself presents his monologue in a type of stage-set environment and his photography is either projected in this space or shown in cutaways. It is through this still photography that the audience is given access to the different characters that inhabit the stories. The differing versions of the murder and Yang's journey are portrayed through reenactments and employ the technique of back-projection, lending a highly stylised aspect to these sequences. The trace of the earlier staged performance piece is present in the documentary in ways that extend and render visible the authored and performative aspect of all documentary. As is the case with many examples of reflexive documentary, in *Sadness,* realism and documentary truth are rethought in order to privilege a more subjective approach that questions the production of meaning and the relationship between history and experience and identity and cultural stereotypes. Through a personal engagement with narratives of mourning, *Sadness* works to explore the complexity of a gay Chinese Australian subjectivity. These political and thematic concerns can also be found in Ayres's earlier documentary, *China Dolls* (1997).

BELINDA SMAILL

Sadness: A Monologue by William Yang (Australia, Film Australia, 1999, 52 mins.). Distributed by Film Australia. Produced by Michael McMahaon and Megan McMurchy. Directed by Tony Ayres. Based on the original work *Sadness* by William Yang. Script by Tony Ayres. Script consultant William Yang. Cinematography by Tristan Milani. Edited by Riva Childs. Sound by Pat Fiske, Livia Ruzic and Peter Walker.

Further Reading

Chan, Dean, "The Dim Sum vs. the Meat Pie: On the Rhetoric of Becoming an In-Between Asian Australian Artist," in *Alter/Asians: Asian-Australian Identities in Art, Media and Popular Culture*, edited by Ien Ang et al. Sydney: Pluto Press, 2000, 141–151.

Khoo, Tseen, "Re-siting Australian Identity: Configuring the Chinese Citizen in Diana Giese's *Astronauts, Lost Souls and Dragons* and William Yang's *Sadness*," in *Bastard Moon: Essays on Chinese Australian Writing*, edited by Wenche Ommundsen, Melbourne: *Otherland Journal*, 2001, 95–109.

Smaill, Belinda, "Disorientations: *Sadness*, Mourning and the Unhomely," in *The Journal of Australian Studies*, 73, 2002, 161–169.

Yang, William, *Sadness*, Sydney: Allen and Unwin, 1996.

SALESMAN

(US, Maysles, 1969)

Salesman is a landmark film of the American Direct Cinema Movement of the 1960s and 1970s. In the documentary, the camera accompanies four Bible salesmen over the course of six weeks as they advance from door-to-door, trying to sell Bibles for the Mid-American Bible Company, first in the greater Boson area and later in the suburbs of Miami. The film is striking for its mixture of humor and melancholia. It is equally striking for its form: filmed and packaged as a documentary, yet generating drama and tension as it documents the decline of a profession.

Salesman, as is the case for many Direct Cinema films, is shot in black and white, reflecting the origins of new style in photojournalism. The film is one of many collaborations between director and cameraman Albert Maysles and his brother David, his long-standing editor and sound engineer. Until 1961, both had been part of Drew Associates, a group of innovative young filmmakers developing a new documentary film style with journalist and filmmaker Robert Drew.

The technological innovations of the decade before *Salesman*—faster and more light-sensitive 16mm film stock, portable (and hence less intrusive) wireless cameras, and synchronous sound—had made unobtrusive filmmaking possible. It was henceforth feasible for the camera, as illustrated by *Salesman*, to follow people into their private spaces, without involving complex planning or, supposedly, resulting in the loss of spontaneity of the subjects. The camera was able to catch people as they were, directly.

It has been argued that, despite their various claims of filming authentic experience, and unlike their French contemporaries participating in *cinema verité*, the practitioners of Direct Cinema did not always observe life at its most ordinary.

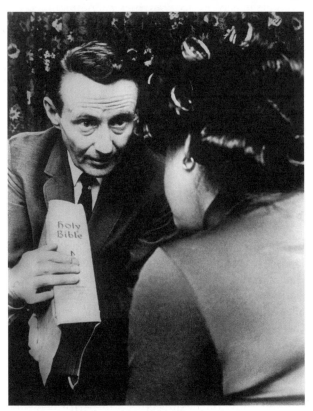

Salesman, 1969.
[*Courtesy of the Everett Collection*]

Earlier Direct Cinema films revolved around celebrities such as John F. Kennedy (Robert Drew, *Crisis*, 1963) and Jane Fonda (D. A. Pennebaker, *Jane*, 1962). These films were able to rely on the "natural" attraction of their subjects to keep audiences engaged (Rosenthal, 1988: 127, 128). *Salesman* stands out because it concerns itself with ordinary people.

Salesman portrays four real-life, middle-aged Bible salesmen, their frustrations, and the hardship that accompanies a life on the road and a job where competition is tough, where few get rich, and where many fall by the wayside. The settings alternate between sparse motel rooms, often poor and small homes and constrained lifestyles, and the cars in which the salesmen drive to prospective customers.

The film starts out with the main protagonist, 56-year-old Paul Brennan, confidently explaining (over a screenshot of the Bible with "Holy Bible" in lavish print across the cover): *"The best seller in the world is the Bible. For one reason. It's the greatest piece of literature of all time."* Paul will never again sound so reassured, as the audience watches him move from one failed sales pitch to another. His colleagues—Raymond "The Bull" Martos, Charlie "The Gipper" McDevitt, and James "The Rabbit" Baker (all nicknamed after their sales strategies)—are both pals and rivals, and as time goes by, Paul's decline, and his resulting anger and frustration, leave him increasingly isolated from these friends. Slowly it becomes clear that Paul is not going to catch up on his subscriptions and will likely lose his job.

Although one of Direct Cinema's self-declared approaches to documentary was observing, rather than narrating, it is clear from early on that *Salesman* is a carefully edited film. In fact, the film follows a suspense dramaturgy. The tension is set up just a few minutes into the film, when the manager announces that the company has to "eliminate a few men." The audience has already witnessed that Paul is having difficulties meeting the sales requirements, and now they know what is at stake. Paul's situation singles him out among his three colleagues and serves as the structuring point of the narrative.

While "unscripted and unrehearsed" (Barsam, 1973: 302), *Salesman* uses a range of techniques to maintain the flow of the narrative. When Paul is on a train to the Chicago sales meeting and quietly looks out the window, the off-voice of manager Ken fades in, giving one of his bullying speeches. This technique is more specific to fiction than to documentary storytelling. In blending the image of

Paul and the voice of Ken, the filmmakers move beyond what can be known through direct observation alone. *Salesman* also uses nondiegetic sound, as can be seen later in the film, as the Beatles song "Yesterday" accompanies Raymond "The Bull" Martos as he leaves another successful sale. Even more striking is how the protagonist Paul is at one point given control over the narrative. While driving in Miami, he describes his pals and their different sales approaches. Laughing and talking, he looks directly into the camera and his words trigger a string of sequences, illustrating his stories about the sales styles of the Gipper, the Rabbit, and the Bull.

Ultimately, the film's drama is anchored in the sales pitches themselves. The sales pitches provide the moments of tension, with the success of the salesmen depending on their skill in manipulating the prospective buyers—however impoverished—into enough guilt so they end up buying. Moreover, the absurdity of many of the sales pitches provide comical scenes that are interspersed through the film, as the men try to reconcile the materialistic with the religious aspects of their enterprise, and the desperation of their economic conditions.

JACOBIA DAHM

See also **Drew Associates; Maysles, Albert**

Salesman (US, 1968, 91 mins., black and white). Directed by Albert and David Maysles and Charlotte Zwerin. Produced by Albert and David Maysles. Cinematography by Albert Maysles. Edited by David Maysles and Charlotte Zwerin. Contributing film editor: Ellen Giffard. Assistant editor: Barbara Jarvis. Sound mixer: Dick Vorisek. Filmed in Boston, Chicago, and Miami.

Further Reading

Allen, Robert C., and Douglas Gomery, *Film History. Theory and Practice*, New York, London: McGraw-Hill, 1985.

Barnouw, Erik, *Documentary: A History of the Non-fiction Film*, Oxford, New York: Oxford University Press, 1993.

Barsam, Richard M., *Nonfiction Film. A Critical History*, Bloomington: Indiana University Press, 1973.

Breitrose, Henry, "On the Search for the Real Nitty-Gritty: Problems & Possibilities in Cinéma Vérité," *Film Quarterly*, 17.4 (Summer 1964), Berkeley: University of California Press, 1964, 36–40.

Bruzzi, Stella, *New Documentary: A Critical Introduction*, London, New York: Routledge, 2000.

Kolker, Robert Philip, "Circumstantial Evidence. An Interview with David and Albert Maysles," *Sight and Sound*, 40.4 (Autumn 1971), 183–186.

Levin, G. Roy, *Documentary Explorations. 15 Interviews with Film-Makers*, New York: Anchor Press, 1971.

Macdonald, Kevin, and Mark Cousins, *Imagining Reality. The Faber Book of the Documentary*, London, Boston: Faber and Faber, 1996.

Mamber, Stephen, *Cinema Verité in America*, Cambridge, MA: MIT Press, 1974.

Nichols, Bill, R*epresenting Reality. Issues and Concepts in Documentary*, Bloomington:, Indiana University Press, 1991.

Rosenthal, Allan (ed.), *New Challenges for Documentary*, Berkeley, Los Angeles, London: University of California Press, 1988.

Stubbs, Liz, *Documentary Filmmakers Speak*, New York: Allworth Press, 2002.

Warren, Charles (ed.), *Beyond Document. Essays on Nonfiction Film*, Hanover, London: Wesleyan University Press, 1996.

Young, Colin, "Cinema of Common Sense," *Film Quarterly*, 17.4 (Summer 1964), Berkeley: University of California Press, 1964, 26–29.

SALT OF THE EARTH

(US, Biberman, 1954)

Salt of the Earth is often recognized as one of the only blacklisted U.S. films from the McCarthyism days of the early 1950s. Although other labor-referent films dating back to the 1920s dealt with their share of opposition, that which surrounded Herbert Biberman's film and its participants stands out in some ways due to the fact the film was made in the face of political and industry opposition. The film continues to find an audience in spite of its original exhibitive difficulties. In many ways it is the film's reliance on telling the story as a bio-fictional fantasy-type narrative, rather than that of a realist documentary, that gives the film its strength and applicable longevity.

Salt of the Earth was made not only at a time of great political upheaval in the Hollywood film industry but also from those with first-hand experience. The idea for the film originated with blacklisted screenwriters Paul Jarrico and Academy Award–winner Michael Wilson, who developed the story from a labor dispute unfolding in Grant County, New Mexico, and presented it to their partner, director Herbert Biberman. Biberman had recently spent time in jail as one of the infamous "Hollywood Ten" for refusing to discuss his political affiliations after being named as a Communist by Budd Schulberg in one of the HUAC hearings. The trio had been looking for a film project to develop of exactly this sort, and set about making the film in direct collaboration with the subjects they would be portraying.

The story in *Salt of the Earth* focuses on a fair wages and conditions strike between the Mexican American members of the International Union of Mine, Mill and Smelters Workers Local #890, and Empire Zinc. For legitimacy, many of the miners portrayed in the film were members of the Local #890, including one of the main characters, Ramon Quintero, portrayed by Juan Chacon, on whom the character was based. As the strike wears on unsuccessfully, the story unfolds with many of the wives of the strikers (spearheaded by Esperanza Quintero [Rosaura Revueltas], a character based on Chacon's wife Virginia) overcoming their initial sociopatriarchal positioning to join the fight on the front lines, while the men stay at home with the families. Such social reversals took the narrative beyond the labor-capitalist models developed in the silent era and allowed the film enough ambiguity to stand in for oppression of all sorts. This approach, coupled with some early, suggested changes in the script from union members, allowed the film to avoid the typical racial and sexual stereotyping of the times. In tandem, this provided the film with less polemics to date the fight than bits of optimism, allowing future viewers to apply the struggle to multiple social and political interpretations.

The entire production and exhibition process of *Salt of the Earth* was met with resistance

Salt of the Earth, Rosaura Revueltas, Juan Chacon, 1954.
[*Courtesy of the Everett Collection*]

because the film was made by individuals black-listed in the industry and was being labeled as narratively relative to certain Communist ideology. This obstacle manifested itself not only in the reluctance of Hollywood unions to allow production workers be hired on the film but also in postproduction, as labs and editing houses were threatened not to participate or be faced with repercussions of their own. Opponents as influential as RKO's Howard Hughes and Californian Congressman Donald Jackson labeled the film as anti-American propaganda and broadened the call to stop its production. The fact that a crew was assembled and even did so by breaking with certain industry Jim Crowisms only added to the importance the film has garnered over the years. Lead actress Revueltas even had a run-in with immigration and was deported and blacklisted from the United States. Her remaining scenes and emotional narration had to be completed in Mexico, away from Biberman and the principal production, with film being smuggled back and forth across the border. Revueltas, who was one of the few

trained actors in the film, and a successful one, eventually found her career somewhat stifled because of the film, finding only occasional work after *Salt of the Earth,* such as a short stint in Berlin as part of Bertolt Brecht's company.

Completed in 1954, *Salt of the Earth* became an enigma of sorts, as initial exhibition was, at best, sparse. The film did manage to run in a few metropolitan areas, such as Los Angeles and New York, but even those were cut short due to continued pressure on the theaters, this time including projectionist unions. In some regard, the conservatives appeared to have won; although they were unable to stop the film entirely, they were certainly able of suppressing the film from the majority of the 1950s audience. It wasn't until many years later when politically active students rediscovered the film and recognized the ongoing relevance of not only the struggle depicted onscreen but the one that occurred in bringing the story to the screen, that the film finally received the widespread exhibition it had always deserved. In 1969, the film began

Salt of the Earth, Rosaura Revueltas, 1954.
[*Courtesy of the Everett Collection*]

regular showings on university campuses around the United States, at times even accompanied by lectures from Biberman. The dissention resulting from the students' protests resembled all too closely that which was experienced by Biberman, and diegetically by the Quintero characters.

Aesthetically speaking, *Salt of the Earth* is a decent film, and one that requires no real concessions for any of its shortcomings. The majority of actors who worked on the film were not professionals, to which Biberman acknowledges in the closing credits. Although the performances may come across as rudimentary, perhaps they compensate for the overtly picturesque cinematography, keeping the film somewhat grounded in realism, while the visuals maintain an aura of fantasy. Biberman's style is more that of classical Hollywood than a utilization of documentary conventions, providing more ambiguity in the film's message than the iconoclastic subversiveness of which the film was accused. As with many controversial entities, *Salt of the Earth* fails to deliver in the way of sensationalism, but its political and social relevance will continue to be recognized for generations to come.

DINO EVERETT

Salt of the Earth (USA, Independent Productions Corporation, 1954, 94 mins.). Distributed by Independent Productions Corporation. Produced by Paul Jarrico, Adolfo Barela, and Sonja Dahl Biberman. Directed by Herbert J. Biberman. Written by Michael Wilson, additional writing by Michael Biberman. Cinematography by Stanley Meredith and Leonard Stark. Music by Sol Kaplan. Editing by Joan Laird and Ed Spiegel. Filmed in Grant County, New Mexico, and parts of Mexico.

Further Reading

Kael, Pauline, "Morality Plays Right and Left," in *Sight and Sound*, 24, no. 2, October/December 1954, 67–73.

Lorence, James J., *The Suppression of* Salt of the Earth, Albuquerque: The University of New Mexico Press, 1999.

Miller, Tom, "*Salt of the Earth* Revisited," in *Cineaste*, XIII, no. 3, 1984, 31–36.

Ross, Steven J., *Working Class Hollywood*, Princeton, NJ: Princeton University Press, 1998.

Trumbo, Dalton, *The Time of the Toad: A Study of Inquisition in America*, New York: Harper & Row, 1972.

Wilson, Michael, and Deborah Silverton Rosenfelt, *Salt of the Earth*, Old Westbury, NY: The Feminist Press, 1978.

SANDER, HELKE

Helke Sander belongs to the first generation of political filmmakers who emerged from the leftist milieu of the 1960s in Germany. Widely labeled as the "The New German Film," this movement had ultimately withdrawn from the misguided development of postwar German cinema with the conception of the "Oberhausener Manifest," a pamphlet published in 1962 by a collective of 26 filmmakers (among them Alexander Kluge and Edgar Reitz). The declaration constituted a clear breach with the commodities and conventions of the films produced within the German industry after the Second World War, a quixotic mixture of kitschy *heimatfilms* and artless comedies.

As a matter of principle, Helke Sander—as well as her contemporaries Ulrike Öttinger, Helma Sanders-Brahms, and Margarethe von Trotta—must be seen in the context of this so-called German New Wave, although Sander soon opposed the authoritative position of her male colleagues, criticizing that their manifesto had not accounted for one single female opinion. Her own films were a radical move away from the predominantly paternalistic practice of political filmmaking in the 1960s and 1970s, which culpably dismissed women as an active political subject. Returning from Finland in 1965 where she had directed a number of television and theater productions, Sander became one of the first female students who graduated from the newly founded Deutsche Film und Fernsehakademie Berlin (DFFB).

Sander's notion of filmmaking as a political practice shaped not only the first generation of female filmmakers and media workers in Germany but also resonated in the steadily growing women's liberation movement of the early 1970s. Her claim for a radical shift of the social paradigm within German society corresponded with current debates about equal rights, abortion laws, and the economical status of women within the domestic work sphere. Films such as *Brecht die Macht der manipulateure* (*Break the Power of the Manipulators*, 1967/1968), *Eine Prämie für Irene* (*A Bonus for Irene*, 1971), and *Die allseitig reduzierte Persönlichkeit–Redupers* (*The All-Sided Reduced Personality*, 1977) addressed a variety of social and political issues that directly affected women's everyday lives.

By the early 1970s, Sander had realised that the women's emancipation as societal subjects was likely to fail as long as the means of production remained distributed disproportionately. In November 1973, her conception of a collectively political practice culminated in the Internationale Frauenfilmseminar in Berlin, which established a network of female filmmakers from all over the world and entailed the foundation of the self-published journal *Frauen und Film*. However, Sander did not succeed in elaborating on a coherent practical framework of feminist filmmaking; rather, she provided a fundamental critique of the *patriarchal* control mechanisms in western societies. Considering her inadequate labour conditions, it is no surprise that Sander never accomplished such a practical foundation of her work. Throughout her career many projects had collapsed due to resentments and a lack of funding, which left considerable gaps in her body of work.

Whether Helke Sander's complete work is divided into two categories—the fiction, or rather fictitious, film with biographical and historiographical elements and the classical documentary—one characteristic distinguishes all of her films: her treatment of content over form. Aesthetical issues were never a concern of her. Far from being ideological, Sander's films struggle with the disavowal of female subjectivity in a broader cultural sense and the difficulty of political articulation with a predominantly male terminology. Her "fictitious" films of the 1960s and 1970s featured playful and ironic approaches to these structural problems and made her a key figure among feminist filmmakers in Germany. But it was primarily the documentary, *Befreier und Befreite* (1991/92), a critical account on the war crimes of Russian soldiers toward German women during the Second World War, that finally put her name on the landscape of internationally acclaimed documentary filmmakers.

ANDREAS BUSCHE

Biography

Born in Berlin, Germany, January 31, 1937. Studied German Language/Literature and Psychology at the University Helsinki, Finland, 1960–1962. Directed productions for Finish Television, 1964/1965. Return to Berlin, 1965. Student at the Deutsche Film und Fernsehakademie Berlin, 1966–1969. Foundation of the women's collective "Brot und Rosen," in 1972. Coorganized the Internationale Frauenfilmseminar in Berlin, 1973. One year later, founded the journal *Frauen und Film*, published and edited by Sander until 1982. Teaching position at the School for Plastic Arts in Hamburg, 1975. In 1992, her documentary film, *Befreier und Befreite*, caused a controversy in the United States. Professorship at the School for Plastic Arts in Hamburg, 1981–2001. From 1989 to 1993, co-director of the Bremer Institut Film/Fernsehen.

Selected Films

1967/1968 *Brecht die Macht der Manipulateure*: director, writer
1971 *Eine Prämie für Irene*: director, writer
1977 *Die allseitig reduzierte Persönlichkeit*: director, writer
1981 *Der subjektive Faktor*: producer, director, writer
1983 *Der Beginn aller Schrecken ist Liebe*: co-producer, director, writer
1989 *Die Deutschen und ihre Männer*: producer, director, writer
1992 *Befreier und Befreite*: co-producer, director, writer

Further Reading

Elsaesser, Thomas, *New German Cinema—A History*, Houndsmill, New Brunswick, NJ: MacMillan/Rutgers University Press, 1989.
Hansen, Miriam, "Frauen und Film and Feminist Film Culture in West Germany," in *Gender and German Cinema: Feminist Interventions*, Vol. 2, edited by Sandra Frieden, Richard W. McCormick, Vibeke R. Petersen, and Laurie Melissa Vegelsang, Providence: Oxford, 1993.
Knight, Julia, *Women and the New German Cinema*, London, New York: Verso Books, 1992.
Mohrmann, Renate, *Die Frau mit der Kamera*, Munchen, Wien: Hanser Verlad, 1980.
Silverman, Kaja, *Helke Sander and the Will to Change*, in Discourse No. 6, Berkeley, 1983.

SANG DES BÊTES, LE

(France, Franju, 1949)

Le Sang des Bêtes (The Blood of the Beasts), the first of Georges Franju's documentaries, is among the most beautiful and upsetting of films: for Franju, the two attributes were inseparable. In interviews he observed that "in my short films, when I could choose the subject, I was always drawn to themes that I didn't want to touch because they frightened me," and that he had chosen to make a film about slaughterhouses "because I love animals" (Milne, 1975). No film before or after *Le Sang des Bêtes* has administered such concentrated doses of pity and terror; yet in defiance of Aristotle's canons of tragedy, Franju offers the viewer no catharsis. Shifting abruptly from surrealist disorientation to misty lyricism to matter-of-fact horrors so extreme as to elicit laughter, *Le Sang des Bêtes* is both indelible and utterly resistant to interpretation. Franju's most famous short film, it is also, at moments, almost unwatchable: a contradiction emblematic of its director's conflicted relationship to documentary.

According to Franju, the subject came first: "I never wanted to be a filmmaker at all. . . . I wanted to investigate a particular subject" (Levin, 1971). Thirty-seven years old when *Le Sang des Bêtes* was made, he had been involved with film for more than a decade as an archivist and administrator when the slaughterhouse idea came to him. For a first film, *Le Sang des Bêtes* is extraordinarily accomplished, due in large part to Franju's astute choice of collaborators: the cinematographer Marcel Fradetal (who had worked on Dreyer's *Vampyr*), the composer Joseph Kosma (who had worked regularly with Renoir and Carné on such films as *La Régle du Jeu* and *Les Enfants du Paradis*), and Franju's colleague at the Institut de Cinématographie Scientifique, Jean Painlevé, maker of documentaries on vampire bats and sea urchins, among other creatures, and author of the voice-over commentary to *Le Sang des Bêtes*.

With the exception of Painlevé, Franju's collaborators did not come from a documentary background, and this accounts (in part) for the film's disconcertingly elegant visual and aural textures, its likeness to the work of such directors as Lang and Murnau. For Franju, in documentary "you endow what's natural with an aspect of the artificial . . . some of the skies that I waited for in *Le Sang des Bêtes* seem almost to be studio skies" (Levin, 1971). As with all his subsequent documentaries, Franju had scripted and planned the editing of *Le Sang des Bêtes* before he began shooting. Yet far from allowing us to feel a comfortable aesthetic distance from the violence the film depicts, Franju's careful deployment of artifice only brings the reality of the slaughterhouse more painfully, because more deliberately, to light— to light, that is, in a literal as well as a metaphorical sense. Franju later explained that "the choice of the month of November for shooting the interiors was dictated by the fact that at this season of the year the animals are slaughtered by electric light, and the blood steaming in the glacial cold of the scalding bays allowed us, despite all the technical problems, to compose our images" (Durgnat, 1967). The animals' blood becomes, perhaps cruelly, an aesthetic means, but a means for revealing, precisely, the horror of bloodshed.

One could describe *Le Sang des Bêtes* as a work composed of a prologue and four movements or episodes, followed by a coda. In the prologue, which Gabriel Vialle has called a "surrealist overture" (Vialle, 1968), we are shown a series of views, from panoramic shots to extreme close-ups, of a wasteland on the outskirts of Paris with scattered high-rises, a bare tree, and, incongruously, bits of a flea market: a chandelier hanging from a branch, a man sitting alone at a huge Louis XV table, and, juxtaposed in one shot, a nude armless

Le Sang des Bêtes, 1949.
[*Still courtesy of the British Film Institute*]

female mannequin, a phonograph horn, and the line of a train in the distance cutting across the screen. A young woman's voice describes the scene in a lyrical voice-over; a young couple kiss; and Franju cuts to an off-kilter medium shot of a train and a slagheap. The voice-over resumes: At the Porte of Vanves, there are also the abattoirs of Vaugirard; these specialize in the slaughter of horses. A man's voice now takes over, enumerating the different tools of the abattoir as we see a close-up of a hand picking up each in turn: poleaxes, spikes, stun guns. A white horse is led up to the slaughter-house door. The first movement, then, shows the slaughter of horses; the second, of cattle (another white beast); the third, of calves for veal (whiteness again: "for the white meat of veal, total blood drainage by decapitation is necessary"); the fourth, of sheep.

The voice-over names each new location, introduces some of the men who work there, and describes the procedures in a scrupulously neutral tone. No outrage is voiced. It is the film's aesthetic composure, in fact, that imprints the horror it reveals so indelibly. Franju does not overwhelm us with gore or use cinematic shock tactics (amplified animal cries, fast cutting, extreme close-ups, weird angles) to augment the violence. Rather, the film's visual style—the dif-

fuse light registered in carefully modulated greys, the use of mainly medium and long shots at eye level, the lucid but unemphatic *mise-en-scéne*—is designed not to hector but to let us see. This is why all the reassuring interpretative claims made for *Le Sang des Bêtes*—the idea, for example, that as we watch, "a sense of reconciliation floods the screen" (Milne, 1980); the idea that the film condemns animal slaughter; the idea that it *doesn't* condemn animal slaughter; the idea that slaughter stands allegorically for the Holocaust—ring so false. Simply by looking, Franju uncovers the *insolite*, the strange, in the everyday. A long shot of twelve headless sheep lying on a conveyor belt, their legs still kicking, looks like a dance number out of Busby Berkeley; another shot of six pure white flayed veal carcasses laid out on six workstands, a mist rising off them, evokes nineteenth-century spirit photographs. Such moments of violence are, in Franju's phrase, "lyrical explosions" that shock us into seeing. But *Le Sang des Bêtes* does not make our judgments for us.

HAL GLADFELDER

See also **Franju, Georges**

Le Sang des Bêtes/The Blood of the Beasts (France, 1949, 22 mins.). Directed by Georges Franju. Assistant directed by André Joseph and Julien Bonardier. Script by Franju. Commentary by Jean Painlevé, spoken by Nicole Ladmiral and Georges Hubert. Cinematography by Marcel Fradetal, assisted by Henri Champion. Edited by André Joseph. Music by Joseph Kosma. Sound by Raymond Verchère. Produced by Forces et Voix de France.

Further Reading

Durgnat, Raymond, *Franju*, London: Studio Vista, 1967.
Franju, Georges, *Le Sang des Bêtes* [shooting script], in *L'Avant-Scéne du Cinéma*, 41, 1964, 46–50.
Levin, G. Roy, "Georges Franju" [interview], in *Documentary Explorations*, edited by G. Roy Levin, 1971, 113–129.
Milne, Tom, "Georges Franju: The Haunted Void" [interview], *Sight and Sound*, 44.2, 1975, 68–71.
———, "Georges Franju," in *Cinema: A Critical Dictionary*, edited by Richard Roud, New York: Viking, 1980, 387–393.
Sloniowski, Jeannette, "'It Was an Atrocious Film': Georges Franju's *Blood of the Beasts*," in *Documenting the Documentary: Close Readings of Documentary Film and Video*, edited by Barry Keith Grant and Jeannette Sloniowski, Detroit, MI: Wayne State University Press, 1998.
Vialle, Gabriel, *Georges Franju*, Paris, Editions Seghers, 1968.

SANS SOLEIL

(France, Marker, 1982)

Like many of his other films, Chris Marker's *Sans Soleil* (*Sunless*) might be described as an imaginary documentary made of real documents—or is it, as the voice that narrates the film repeatedly asks, the other way around? As a work that continually calls into question the status and significance of its own representations, *Sans Soleil* has been classified as "an instance of postmodernism" (Branigan, 1992), but its closest affinity may rather be with a work like Laurence Sterne's *Tristram Shandy*, written over 200 years earlier. Like Sterne's novel, Marker's film is an invented autobiography of often breathtaking digressiveness, complexity, poignancy, and wit, which unfolds not according to a linear chronology or argument but across a network of associations, echoes, and resemblances—both a meditation on history and memory and a disenchanted interrogation of its own form.

Marker has described the "story" of *Sans Soleil* in these terms:

> An unknown woman reads and comments upon the letters she receives from a friend—a freelance cameraman who travels around the world and is particularly attached to those "two extreme poles of survival"—Japan and Africa, represented here by two of its poorest and most forgotten countries, even though they played an historical role: Guinea Bissau and the Cape Verde Islands. The cameraman wonders (as cameramen do, at least those you see in movies) about the meaning of this representation of the world in which he is the instrument, and about the role of memory he helps to create. A Japanese pal of his, who clearly has some bats in the belfry (Japanese bats, in the form of electrons) gives his answer by attacking the images of memory, by breaking them up on the synthesizer. A filmmaker grabs hold of this situation and makes a fiction of it, but rather than present the characters and show their relationships, real or supposed, he prefers to put forward the elements of the dossier in the fashion of a musical composition, with recurrent themes, counterpoints, and mirror-like fugues: the letters, the comments, the images gathered, the images created, together with some images borrowed. In this way, out of these juxtaposed memories is born a fictional memory . . .

(Marker, 1983)

The narrative structure Marker outlines here is like that of another film he made twenty-five years before, *Letter from Siberia* (1957), whose opening voiceover—"Je vous écris d'un pays lointain" ("I'm writing you from a faraway country")—could stand as the epigraph to his whole career as a filmmaker. And as with others of Marker's works, it is unclear where collaboration ends and mythomania begins. According to an end credit, "Sandor Krasna's letters were read by Alexandra Stewart" (Florence Delay in the French version), but Sandor Krasna, the cameraman, seems to be a fictional surrogate for Marker himself, notwithstanding the straight-faced biography included in the film's publicity materials; certainly his letters are unmistakably Markerian in their language, their obsessions, their speculative improvisations on the themes of memory and time. In which case Sandor's brother, Michel Krasna, credited with the film's electronic sound, is presumably yet another of the filmmaker's fictional personae. The "Japanese pal," Hayao Yamaneko, credited with the synthesized manipulation of the cameraman's images—a key element in the film's provocatively antirealistic visual texture—is perhaps real, but in fact the very uncertainty Marker creates by listing elusive, untraceable collaborators as coauthors of this intensely personal film is precisely the point: Personal identity is rooted in memory-narratives that are unstable, impersonal, and endlessly vulnerable to manipulation and decay.

Sans Soleil is typical of Marker's work in the prominence—indeed, the shaping role—of its voice-over commentary. Although there are certainly visual continuities created through the recurrence and transformation of certain motifs (cats, emus, dreaming passengers on ferries and trains, neighborhood festivals, political demonstrations, video games, women in a marketplace), it is the commentary that links the disparate elements of the film together and articulates its principal themes. In part, this could be seen as a response to the practical problem of assembling a single coherent film out of footage accumulated

Sans Soleil, 1982.
[*Still courtesy of the British Film Institute*]

over fifteen or more years from extremely far-flung locales: Iceland, Japan, Guinea-Bissau and Cape Verde, Ile-de-France, Netherlands, Okinawa, San Francisco, the island of Sal, and perhaps others. But of course this "problem" was of Marker's own invention. There was no outward necessity to bring these particular materials together, so the decision to do so through the device of a (partly) fictional commentary suggests that the film's real subject is disparateness itself, the myriad forms of temporal, geographical, historical, and social distance that travel and all the varieties of information technology (not least, film itself), far from repairing, only multiply.

The juxtaposition of commentary, documentary image (much of the footage filmed vérité-style with handheld cameras), and electronic manipulations of both sound and image allows Marker to comment in passing on an extraordinary range of philosophical, political, and aesthetic issues. Those most directly relevant to the subject of documentary film involve the fraught relationship between images and different sorts of truth, the image as a repository of cultural and historical memory. Late in the film, half a world away from Japan, the speaker reads these words: "I remember that month of January in Tokyo. Or rather I remember the images I filmed of the month of January in Tokyo. They have substituted themselves for my memory—they are my memory. I wonder how people remember things who don't film, don't photograph, don't tape." In this passage, the writer both affirms the efficacy of the mechanically reproduced image in making memory possible and registers a sense of loss: He no longer has the capacity to remember within himself, independent of technological mediation. But perhaps he never had that capacity. If Marker seems sometimes to lament his

and our dependence on mechanical forms of memory, at other moments—such as during his account of the revolutionary struggles in Guinea-Bissau that led to the overthrow of the Portuguese dictatorship—the documentary image enables memory to outlast or circumvent historical oblivion. By isolating and reflecting on the images out of which it is made, *Sunless* places itself in the same relation to documentary as *Tristram Shandy* occupies in relation to the novel: at once the most singular and, as Viktor Shklovsky contended, "the most typical" of its kind.

HAL GLADFELDER

See also **Marker, Chris**

Sans Soleil/(Sunless) (France, 1982, 100 mins.). Distributed by Argos Films. Conception and editing by Chris Marker. Assistant direction by Pierre Camus. Editorial assistance by Anne-Marie L'Hôte and Catherine Adda. Commentary read by Alexandra Stewart (English version) and Florence Delay (French version). Electronic sound by Michel Krasna and Isao Tomita. Music by M. Moussorgski, J. Sibelius (treated by Isao Tomita); song by Arielle Dombasle. Sound mix by Antoine Bonfanti and Paul Bertault. Special effects by Hayao Yamaneko. Film extracts from Sana na N'hada (Carnival in Bissau), Jean-Michel Humeau (Ranks ceremony), Mario Marret and Eugenio Bentivoglio (Guerilla in Bissau), Daniéle Tessier (Death of a giraffe), and Haroun Tazieff (Iceland 1970). Still photography by Martin Boschet and Roger Grange.

Further Reading

Branigan, Edward, *Narrative Comprehension and Film*, London: Routledge, 1992.

Casebier, Allan, "A Deconstructive Documentary," *Journal of Film and Video*, 40.1, 1988, 34–39.

Howe, Susan, "Sorting Facts; or, Nineteen Ways of Looking at Marker," in *Beyond Document: Essays on Nonfiction Film*, edited by Charles Warren, Hanover: Wesleyan University Press, 295–343.

Lopate, Philip, "In Search of the Centaur: The Essay Film," in *Beyond Document: Essays on Nonfiction Film*, edited by Charles Warren, Hanover: Wesleyan University Press, 243–270.

Marchessault, Janine, "Sans Soleil," *CineAction!* 5, 1986, 2–6.

Marker, Chris, unpublished publicity materials for New Yorker Films' press kit for the American release of *Sunless/Sans Soleil*, 1983, from Pacific Film Archives (Berkeley, California) CineFiles website, www.mip.Berkeley.edu/cinefiles/

———, "Sunless," *Semiotext(e)*, 4.3, 1984, 33–40.

Rafferty, Terrence, "Marker Changes Trains," *Sight and Sound*, 53.4, 1984, 284–288.

Russell, Catherine, *Experimental Ethnography: The Work of Film in the Age of Video*, Durham: Duke University Press, 1999.

Walsh, Michael, "Around the World, Across All Frontiers: *Sans Soleil* as *Dépays*," *CineAction!* 18, 1989, 29–36.

SARAJEVO'S DOCUMENTARY FILM SCHOOL

See **Bosnian Documentary Movement**

SAUVAGE, ANDRÉ

André Sauvage (1891–1975) was one of the most talented filmmakers to emerge in Paris during the 1920s. He figures among the small group of avant-garde cinematographers who were passionate about this new form of expression and who actively explored the medium's formal and social potential. Film historians qualify the short period of European cinema between 1927 and 1933 as the "Nouvelle Vague documentaire" (the Documentary New Wave of 1928), which ensured the transition between silent and sound film. That brief period was the most important time for André Sauvage's "poetic modernist documentary films" (Aitken, 2001).

The 1920s were years of exciting developments in documentary film. The camera, ever more mobile, was a part of the renewed discovery the world, near or far. The profound human quality of *Nanook of the North* (Robert Flaherty, 1923), the Swedish avant-garde interest for nature as an autonomous film subject, and the dynamism of the formal experimentation of the Soviet montage techniques captured the imagination of a generation. Human adventure, the perpetual motion of people in time and space and the technological challenges of his time became André Sauvage's major cinematographic themes. The loose narrative structure of his films, combined with his mastery of film technique and careful imagery, transformed his work into visual poetry. This is especially true for his films on Paris and Greece. He often worked alone (shooting and editing) with limited funding and equipment, or with very small crews. He created his own production company, Les Films André Sauvage, more to suit his independent personality than as a venue for his commercial abilities.

André Sauvage turned his camera on mountain climbers (*La Traversée du Grépon*, 1923); on the urban environment as the ideal microcosm of modernity and on ordinary Parisians working and strolling in their city (*Études sur Paris*, 1927); on Greece past and present, deftly depicting the archeological sites, the fishing villages, country roads, and peasants (*Portrait de la Gréce,* 1927); on his own children playing in the garden of his house [*Rue du Pré-aux-Clercs (les Sauvages)*, 1930]; and on the trying but extraordinary car expedition across Central Asia between Beirut and Peking (*La Croisiére jaune*, 1934). André Sauvage did not like to categorize film in genres. N. Ghali wrote that Sauvage may have been afraid of marginalizing documentary films, whereas his artistic aims were to couple truth and reality without excluding imagination. This is what is implied in the expression "creative documentary" (Jeancolas, 1989).

His best-known films are the series of five short cinematographic studies on Paris, *Études sur Paris* (1928), an evocative urban journey through the diverse activities of the city, quietly observed using subdued lighting: *Nord-Sud; Paris-Port; Petite Ceinture; Les Iles de Paris;* and *De la Tour Saint-Jacques à la Montagne Sainte-Geneviéve.* They reflect his intimate knowledge of the city's rhythms and his fascination with movement. He introduced impressionist and sometimes mysterious images of the less well-known parts of Paris, such as the barges slowly passing through the underground section of the Canal Saint-Martin. Some shots take the viewer out to the city's limits, along the old line of fortification, where the rag-pickers in *La Zone. Au pays des chiffonniers* lived and toiled (Georges Lacombe, 1928), or recall sequences of other city films such as Walther Ruttmann's *Berlin. Die Sinfonie der Großstadt (Berlin. Symphony of a Great City,* Germany, 1927).

The 1931/1932 film work for *La Croisiére jaune* confirmed his talent. This feature-length documentary film was financed by the French car manufacturer André Citroën to display Sauvage's versatile half-tracks. André Sauvage disavowed the film that premiered in March 1934, much delayed by serious postproduction problems and the sponsor's decision to seize the film stock and hire another filmmaker, Léon Poirier, to do the final cut. Sauvage believed that the editing, the music score, and the commentary had destroyed his film beyond recognition. But enough of the extraordinary images remain of men and machines progressing through magnificent scenery, combined with his mastery of light, his empathy towards ordinary people—local guides and carriers recruited along the way between Persia and China—who made the adventure possible. There are also segments of direct sound—traditional music or brief conversations and messages—recorded by pioneering sound technician Robert William Sivel.

André Sauvage had a keen eye, a sensitive approach to his subjects, and a wonderful sense of humor. In what is left of his films, his empathy is expressed in his choice of characters and how he discreetly captured the social contrasts of his time, whether he was filming workers in Paris or servants in British India. During the Citroën expedition, he did not shy away from filming the political violence inflicted on the Chinese people by warlords, as their country moved toward disintegration. In his cinematography he combined the eye of the painter with the eye of the social observer.

At age 43, disgusted by the take-over of his film material of the Central Asia expedition—which, according to Philippe Esnault, amounted to 150,000 metres of negatives, positives, images, and sounds—André Sauvage abandoned filmmaking altogether.

SUZANNE LANGLOIS

Biography

Born July 1891 to a middle-class merchant family from the Bordeaux region in southwestern France. Upon his father's death, he quit his graduate studies and in 1917 went to Paris. There, he met a group of young writers and poets and was attracted to artistic work. He began to write, but soon became more interested in painting, before being seduced by film. Sauvage started a career in filmmaking in the early 1920s, but ended it abruptly in 1934, following the sad ending of the *Croisiére jaune* expedition. Although he lived to be age 84, he never returned to filmmaking, preferring farming and painting.

Selected Films

1923 *La Traversée du Grépon*: director
1927 *Portrait de la Gréce*: director, producer
1928 *Études sur Paris: Nord-Sud; Paris-Port; Petite Ceinture; Les Iles de Paris; De la Tour Saint-Jacques à la Montagne Sainte-Geneviéve*: director, editor, producer
1930 *Rue du Pré aux Clercs (les Sauvages)*: director, producer
1934 *La Croisiére jaune*: cinematographer

Further Reading

Abel, Richard, *French Cinema: The First Wave 1915–1929*, Princeton, NJ: Princeton University Press, 1984.
Aitken, Ian, *European Film Theory and Cinema. A Critical Introduction*, Bloomington: Indiana University Press, 2001.
Comes, Philippe de, and Michel Marmin (eds.), *Le cinéma français 1930–1960*, Paris: Editions Atlas, 1984.
Dictionnaire du cinéma français des années vingt, edited by François Albera and Jean A. Gili, in *1895 Revue de l'Association française de recherche sur l'histoire du cinéma*, 33, June 2001.
Esnault, Philippe, "André Sauvage, cinéaste maudit," *La Revue du cinéma*, 394, May 1984, 92–94.
Gauthier, Guy, *Le Documentaire. Un autre cinéma*, Paris: Nathan/VUEF, 2003.
Ghali, Noureddine, *L'Avant-garde cinématographique en France dans les années vingt*, Paris: Éditions Paris Expérimental, 1995.
Jeancolas, Jean-Pierre, "N.V.D. 28, appel à témoins," *100 Années Lumiére*, Paris: AFAA Intermedia, 1989, 20–27.

SCANDINAVIA

In Scandinavia, the documentary film is highly respected, and documentaries are popular on television and at the cinemas. They play an important role in public debates, and state funding supports the production of shorts and feature-length documentaries. Recently there have been two documentaries with successful commercial releases in the theatres: *Heftig og begeistret* (*Cool and Crazy,* 2001), about a male choir in a small fishing village in the northern part of the country, and *Alt om min far* (*All about My Father,* 2002), about a family dealing with a father who is a transvestite. In Sweden and Denmark, important directors such as Stefan Jarl, Eric M. Nilsson, PeÅ Holmquist, Lennart Nilsson, Jørgen Leth, Jon Bang Carlsen, Sami Saif, and Anne Wivel produce groundbreaking films.

Local actualities were produced in Scandinavia by the late 1890s, and out of the most popular types two documentary genres evolved in the 1920s: the travelogue and the "nation-film." The most popular early documentary genre in Scandinavia was the travelogue, and especially the expedition film. In Sweden, directors such as Prince Wilhelm and Oscar Olsson traveled to Africa, and the exotic *Bland vildar och vilda djur* (*Among Savages and Wild Animals,* 1921) became a huge success. In Denmark and Norway, the camera-expeditions looked mostly to colder territories. Knud Rasmussen and Roald Amundsen always made films as a part of their expeditions. The four feature-length documentaries Amundsen's cameramen made in the 1920s were very popular in Scandinavia, and even made an international impact. Unlike a film such as *Nanook of the North,* the documentaries produced by Amundsen employed a more "primitive" view and aesthetic quality, resembling a series of magnificent slides, but always looking at the foreign cultures from outside. These expedition films were often marked by a nationalistic pathos, especially when exploring unknown territories.

Scandinavian filmmakers also explored their own countries, in a genre called "nation-films." In Sweden, the director Ragnar Ring produced different types of documentaries for the industry or for tourist promotion. In 1924 he made a feature-length film about Sweden, *Sverige, vårt vackra land* (*Sweden, Our Beautiful Country*). With this film a new genre was born, and after Ring's poetic homage to his country, several long documentaries were made that explored both countryside and cities. These films were very popular, since most people did not have the means or opportunities to travel, even in their own country. Some of these films from Norway and Sweden were also intended for the population of Scandinavians in the United States—for example, *Se Norge* (*Norway Today*) by Gustav Lund in 1924. This genre remained popular in the early 1930s, and *Norge, vårt Norge—i toner og billeder* (*Our Norway, in Music and Pictures*) by Lyder Selvig also became a success in Sweden in 1930.

While the Swedish and Norwegian "nation-films" were tourist-like and idyllic in their images of their countries, some of the Danish films were more critical, and employed a degree of social commentary. The film *Danmark* (*Denmark,* 1935), made by the Danish architect and writer Poul Henningsen, was heavily criticized in Denmark. This film has a more poetic form, and marks the beginning of a more ambitious documentary tradition in Scandinavia, both in terms of style and social criticism.

Documentaries in Scandinavia both before and after World War II were seldom concerned with social issues. Another important genre that was popular especially in Sweden and Norway was the nature and wildlife film. The Swedish director Bengt Berg's films about wild birds were popular in the early 1920s, and in Norway, the director Per Høst made his first long documentaries in the late 1930s.

In Sweden, Stig Wesslén and Arne Sucksdorff are the most important names in documentary film. Wesslén's wildlife films often use the year cycle as a way to organize his filmic observations of wildlife. A film such as *I lapplandsbjörnens rike* (*The Realm of the Lapp-Bear,* 1940) depicts a wealth of animal life, but also makes points about the importance of defending the country. Arne Sucksdorff is one of the biggest names in Scandinavian documentary history, and his wildlife films were international hits. He started out making shorts, depicting nature and animals in the films *En Sommarsaga* (*A Summer Saga,* 1940) and *Trut!* (*Seagull!,* 1944), but also the city symphony, as in *Människor i Stad* (*City People,* 1947). Sucksdorff often criticized civilization, but he was himself often criticized for using tame animals and having an anthropomorphic perspective on animals. This is clear in his first feature-length documentary, *Det stora Äventyret* (*The Big Adventure,* 1953), in which animals sometimes seemingly think and act like people.

Like many other wildlife filmmakers, Sucksdorff turned to a more ethnographic perspective in the late 1950s. His next feature, *En Djungelsaga* (*A Jungle Saga,* 1957), was a portrait of the Muria tribe in India. In his last features, *Pojken i trädet* (*The Boy in the Tree,* 1961) and *Mitt hem är Copacabana* (*My Home Is Copacabana,* 1965), he presents fully realized portraits of young people who are alienated by society. His social consciousness is important, and in the 1960s he became the mentor of Stefan Jarl, the most important modern documentarist in Sweden.

Other documentarists in the 1950s turned from wildlife to ethnography. In Norway, the most popular documentary filmmaker was Per Høst. He was a zoologist, but turned to filmmaking, and produced a wealth of short films from the 1940s throughout the1960s. His most famous film, *Same Jakki* (*The Laplanders,* 1957), was an ethnographic study of the Lapps in northern Norway and their relationship to nature.

The most famous Scandinavian documentary film in the 1950s was *Kon-Tiki,* which won an Oscar in 1952. The film was a joint Swedish-Norwegian venture, produced by the Swedish company Artfilm and directed by Olle Nordemar, but based on the 16mm material that the archaeologist and adventurer Thor Heyerdahl filmed when he traveled from Peru to the Polynesian islands on a balsa raft in 1947. This expedition film gave the audience a new and sensuous feeling. The low quality of the filmic material helped convey a sensation of actually being on the raft, due to the fluid and trembling images. This was a new aspect of expedition films or wildlife films in the 1950s. Films no longer merely presented the world, but tried to re-create the experience of being in the represented moment with the filmmaker.

The 1950s was a golden age of documentary in Scandinavia. Short films accompanied most features, and a large number of feature-length documentaries were produced. The introduction of television to Denmark in 1954, Sweden in 1956, and Norway in 1960 brought this golden age of short films to a close. The newsreels disappeared and were replaced by television news. Both short films and full-length documentaries nearly disappeared from the screens during the 1960s. Many filmmakers got jobs in the national television organizations, making programs in the same genres as before—biographies, travelogues, portraits, and so on—but it became harder to produce documentaries outside of the television organizations, and even harder to produce documentaries not intended for television.

Some documentary filmmakers managed to produce short films. In Denmark, Theodor Christensen and Jørgen Roos are among the most important. Theodor Christensen met John Grierson in 1939. During and after the World War II he made several outstanding shorts, including *Skoven* (*The Wood,* 1941) and *Det gælder din frihed* (*It's about Your Freedom,* 1946), with Karl Roos. Like most other independent directors, Christensen made shorts for different government agencies, but he managed to turn out films that not only informed the citizens about issues, but he commented on these issues as well, often in an ironic way. Christensen also made important contributions to the documentary film in Denmark when he worked at the new State Film School in the 1960s.

In Norway, the director Erik Løchen had an equal position. He started the production company ABC-Film with friends, and this company produced over 100 shorts over the course of twenty years. They made films for different government and municipal agencies, but were also pioneers in creating the "free artistic short film." Erik Løchen, and friends and colleagues Erik Borge and Carsten Munch, were tired of making pure information films. They wanted most of all to make documentaries without a voice-over, and succeeded in getting the government to support the production of more artistic and poetic meditations, the first being *Nedfall* (*Fallout,* 1963) by Erik Borge. This film was a poetic impression of village life, but emphasizing its vulnerability in case of atomic fallout. Løchen made several influential modernist documentary shorts, most famous *Søring Nordover* (*Southerner Going North,* 1976), on the differences between south and north in Norway.

Many documentaries produced in Denmark after World War II were journalistic or informational in character, but there were also strong connections between the documentary filmmakers and the avant-garde movement. These connections were stronger than in Norway, and the director Jørgen Roos made some of the earliest experimental films in Denmark with *Flugten* (*Flugten,* 1942), with Albert Mertz, and *Spiste Horisonter* (*Eaten Horizons,* 1950). Jørgen Roos is one of the most important Danish documentary filmmakers, and his work is in some ways typical of the independent filmmakers in Scandinavia. Roos made many films—films of information as well as more artistic films—and one of the characteristic features of his work is the fact that he handles a broad spectrum of themes and genres. He has made portraits of famous people and cities, travelogues, and even a three-part film about documentary filmmaking in Denmark, *Den levende virkelighed* (*The Living Reality,* 1989). At the same time, he has made film-essays about bacon production, *Den strømlinjede gris* (*The Streamlined Pig.* 1952), and noise, *Støj* (*Noise,* 1965).

Few Scandinavian documentaries made before the late 1960s were overtly political or discussed social issues, but later in the decade this changed. Suddenly a new generation of filmmakers turned to the political documentary, using filmmaking as a weapon in the fight for radical societal changes. In Sweden, the novelist and painter Peter Weiss, another avant-garde artist turning to filmmaking, made the first controversial social documentaries with *Ansikten i skugga* (*Faces in the Shadows,* 1956) and *Enligt Lag* (*By Law,* 1957). These portraits of outcasts in the welfare society, made without the use of voice-over, marked the beginning of a new type of social documentaries in Scandinavia, focused on attacking the wrongs perpetuated in and by welfare society.

In the late 1960s and the early 1970s, a wave of political radicalism swept through the arts in Scandinavia, leaving its mark on documentary film production. A new, angry generation of filmmakers emerged. Most important of these new filmmakers was the Swedish director Stefan Jarl. He helped establish the organisation Film-Centrum in 1968, which was an important base for the new radical filmmakers, but he is best known for his "Mods Trilogy"—three full-length films that follow two members of Sweden's underclass, and their children, over several decades. The first two films, *Dom kallar oss Mods* (*They Call Us Misfits,* 1968) and *Ett Anständigt Liv* (*A Decent Life,* 1979), made an enormous impact on Scandinavian documentary and society. The second film was shown in all schools in Sweden and Norway as part of a project to inform schoolchildren about the dangers of narcotics. Jarl's films are frightening, showing how the youngsters Kenta and Stoffe change from happy-go-lucky boys in opposition to the bourgeois society to drug addicts. Although often criticized for his methods, Jarl shows absolute solidarity with the boys. The death of Stoffe gives *Ett Anständigt Liv* a tragic dimension. In his third film, *Det Sociala Arvet* (*The Social Heritage,* 1993), Jarl follows the children of Kenta and Stoffe, who, surprisingly, are relatively prosperous and successful. In this film Jarl includes himself to a larger degree, making a reflexive, even performative, auto-critique of his own film practice.

Stefan Jarl is mostly known for his angry social documentaries, which inspired many Scandinavian filmmakers, but also for his nature documentaries, particularly those dealing with Lapps. His film *Hotet* (*The Threat,* 1987) dealt with Chernobyl's effect on the Lapps, and the short *Jåvna, Renskötare år 2000* (*Jåvna: Reindeer Herdsman in the Year 2000,* 1991) is a portrait of a young boy with a difficult future, squeezed between two cultures. He also made the angry ecological film *Naturens Hämnd* (*The Revenge of Nature,* 1983) about the havoc wreaked by chemical fertilizers on agricultural cycles. Jarl's attention to detail, interest in regional cultures, and careful integration of the landscape makes him a cinematic poet, a true heir to Arne Sucksdorff.

The nature poet Sucksdorff has also been Jan Troell's inspiration. He switches successfully between documentary and fiction film, like many Scandinavian directors, and has made many short poetic documentaries. Troell is kinder and milder in his artistic temperament. His major documentary is the three-hour *Sagolandet* (*Land of Dreams,* 1988), which is an essayistic reflection on life in a welfare society, where the state takes care of its citizens from birth to death.

In Denmark, some radical films were made in the 1970s, attacking the smug bourgeoisie, but the most important director, Jørgen Leth, was an experimental modernist that kept an ironic distance to any specific trend. He started out making stylistic and ironic commentaries on life and people in Denmark, with films such as *Det Perfekte Menneske* (*The Perfect Man,* 1967) and *Livet i Danmark* (*Life in Denmark,* 1971), but turned to making sport films and personal portraits or travelogues. Among his essayistic travel films are the highly original *66 scener fra Amerika* (*66 Scenes from America,* 1981) and *Haiti—uden Titel* (*Haiti—Without Title,* 1996). His most famous films are his cycling documentaries, his full-length film about Giro d'Italia, *Stjernerne og Vandbæreren* (*The Stars and the Water-Carriers,*

1973), and *En Forårsdag i Helvede* (*Springtime in Hell*, 1976).

Norwegian documentary changed drastically in 1972, when the young filmmaker Oddvar Einarson made the first documentary attack on the government, focusing on the close connections between the Norwegian government and U.S. businesses in *Kampen om Mardøla* (*The Fight for Mardøla*, 1972). The film depicted the clash between environmentalists and the police, and Einarson used every means available to criticize or ridicule the government, resulting in a fierce debate in society.

The most important modern Norwegian documentary filmmaker, Sigve Endresen, is a typical representative of the generation of radical documentarists after *Kampen om Mardøla*, and he started working as a member of a student film collective making the short *Aldri Mer!* (*Never Again!*, 1977)—a film about Neo-Nazism. Like many other Scandinavian filmmakers, he was inspired by Stefan Jarl's films about youth and drugs, and his feature-length *For Harde Livet* (*For Your Life*, 1989) became a huge success. It depicted a treatment programme for young drug addicts. Endresen and his team followed a group of young drug addicts for one-and-a-half years. The film has an open ending, and thus offers no traditional narrative closure. Endresen made a follow-up with *Store gutter gråter ikke* (*Big Boys Don't Cry*, 1995), concentrating on a treatment programme for young drug addicts in jail. Endresen's direct cinema-inspired approach has also been fruitful in his more recent works; *Leve blant løver* (*Living among Lions*, 1998), a portrayal of a group of youths suffering from (and dying of) cancer, and *Vektløs* (*Weightless*, 2002), about a female artist with an eating disorder.

The main representative of the socially concerned documentary in Norway today, besides Endresen, is Margreth Olin. Whether documenting daily life in a senior citizen's home in *Dei mjuke hendene* (*In the House of Angels*, 1998) or discussing how Western society encourages women to develop negative body images in *Kroppen min* (*My Body*, 2002), she makes courageous, personal, and important documentaries.

The personal approach is also an important feature in modern Danish and Swedish documentary. In Denmark, veteran master Jørgen Leth still makes personal portraits of artists, while another veteran, Jon Bang Carlsen, makes provocative self-reflexive documentaries. Sometimes he makes meta-films, such as *How to Invent Reality* (1996), or portraits, such as *Addicted to Solitude* (1999), a portrait of two white women living in an undeveloped and sparsely populated part of South Africa. Carlsen's approach has been criticized, since normally he first observes and then stages the entire film, even writing the lines for the characters who play themselves, but like the earlier *Før gæsterne kommer* (*Before the Guests Arrive*, 1986), his sense of detail and ability to find beauty in any person makes him an important director. Among the younger directors, Sami Saif is one of the most important Danish talents. His *Family* (2001), about the director's search for his father, is a heart-warming and vulnerable, but still analytical, documentary.

In Sweden, Jarl and Troell still make important documentaries, and among the pioneers working with television documentaries one finds Lennart Nilsson, with his fabulous journeys through the human body, or the highly original essayist Eric M. Nilsson, making films about communication (or lack thereof). Younger directors Kristian Petri, PeÅ Holmquist, and Susanna Edwards have also made important contributions to the genre.

Documentary filmmaking is important in Scandinavia. The public subsidizing of documentaries, both from film institutes and the "cassette tax funds," as well as via public service television, guarantees high quality and independence. Factual entertainment and soap documentaries reach increasingly wider audiences on television in Scandinavia, but independently produced documentaries can still be controversial and angry, or essayistic and personal.

GUNNAR IVERSEN

See also **Bang Carlsen, Jon; Jarl, Stefan; Roos, Jörgen**

Further Reading

Birkvad, Søren, *Verden er Leth*, Odense: Odense Universitetsforlag, 1992.

Birkvad, Søren, and Jan Anders Diesen, *Autentiske Inntrykk*, Oslo: Samlaget, 1994.

Brinch, Sara, and Gunnar Iversen, *Virkelighetsbilder*, Oslo: Universitetsforlaget, 2001.

Edström, Mauritz, *Sucksdorff–främlingen i hemmaskogen*, Stockholm: Norstedts 1968.

Furhammar, Leif, *Filmen i Sverige*, Stockholm: Wiken, 1991.

———, *Med TV i verkligheten*, Stockholm, Etermedierna i Sverige, 1995.

Nilsson, Mats, *Rebell i verkligheten–Stefan Jarl och hans filmer*, Göteborg: Filmkonst, 1991.

SCHADT, THOMAS

Coming from a photography background, Thomas Schadt became one of the most active and respected German documentary filmmakers of his generation. He generally develops his projects, produces them with his own company, Odysee-Film, in Berlin, and then acts as cameraman, shooting the footage himself. However, Schadt also values the input of his team. He discusses his concepts and strategies in courses at film schools and universities, and published two books in 2002 on these topics.

The structure of an image has tremendous importance for Schadt, and his goal is to capture the right moment, even if only by coincidence. He also favors strong personalities, displaying people with this characteristic prominently in his work. The camera and sound equipment, whether film or video, is determined based on the topic and the conditions of the production.

One of Schadt's first films was *Das Gefühl des Augenblicks* (*Sensibility of the Moment,* 1989), in which he traced the career of the American photographer Robert Frank. An interview conducted with Frank, which did not go smoothly, communicated the value of authenticity and its importance for documentary. The same aesthetic is evident in *Die vergessene Stadt* (*The Forgotten Town,* 1992), about the town Butte, Montana, which Schadt shot on 35mm film, for theatrical release.

Schadt gained recognition for his television works, such as *Der Autobahnkrieg* (*War on the Highway,* 1991), about the reckless driving on German highways, and *Eiserne Engel* (*Iron Angels,* 1995), about medical rescue teams that use helicopters. He followed Gerhard Schröder on his campaign in 1998 and portrayed him again in 2001, and even Schadt got the impression that it was impossible to get close to the Chancellor of Germany. He also faced difficulties while filming *Wall Street* (1997) because it was difficult to gain access to some locations.

One of his most ambitious projects was *Berlin: Sinfonie einer Großstadt* (*Berlin: Symphony of a City,* 2002), in which he built on Walter Ruttmann's classic *Berlin: Die Sinfonie der Großstadt* (*Berlin: The Symphony of the City,* 1927) to shoot an actual portrayal of Berlin. He did not want to shoot a remake of the montage film, in which Ruttmann presented a futuristic vision of the metropolis, but rather chose to provide a new interpretation. Schadt appropriated the symphonic concept, the aesthetic of black-and-white photography in 35mm, and the narrative structure in his portrayal of the city from early morning to midnight. His images are supported by modern music composed by Helmut Oehring and Iris ter Schipphorst. Over the course of one year, Schadt and his assistant, Thomas Keller, filmed throughout Berlin, capturing typical moments that reflect Berlin today and its history over the last 75 years, since the premiere of Ruttmann's film. They developed a highly abstract concept for the camera movements, which depend on the time of day being filmed. Stills from the film prove the photographic talents of Thomas Schadt.

KAY HOFFMANN

See also **Ruttman, Walter**

Biography

Born 1957 in Nuremberg, Germany. After a high school apprenticeship as a photographer, worked as projectionist, camera assistant, and theater photographer. From 1980 to 1983 studied at the Film and TV Academy (DFFB) in Berlin. Founded his own production company, Odysse-Film, in 1983. Since 1991, has taught at film schools and universities. Professor of documentary film at the film academy Baden-Wuerttemberg in Ludwigsburg since 2000. Cofounded the documentary initiative Der Zweite Blick (The Second View) in 2001.

Selected Films

1982 *Was hab I in Hawaii verloren*: Director, camera, producer
1983 *Für die Ewigkeit*: Director, camera, producer
1986 *Unterwegs nach immer und überall*: Director, camera, producer
1989 *Das Gefühl des Augenblicks*: Director, camera, producer
1989 *Trash-Altenessen*: Director, camera, producer
1990 *Das Magazin der Bilder*: Director, camera, producer
1991 *Der Autobahnkrieg*: Director, camera, producer
1992 *Die vergessene Stadt*: Director, camera, producer
1993 *Elf Freunde müst ihr sein*: Director, camera, producer
1994 *Mordkommission M I/4*: Director, camera, producer
1995 *Eiserne Engel*: Director, camera, producer
1996 *Herr W und Herr W*: Director, camera, producer (together with Gerd Hoffmeister)

1997 *Wall Street*: Director, camera, producer
1997 *Manhattan Stories*: Director, camera, producer
1998 *Augenzeugen*: Director, camera, producer (together with Reiner Holzemer)
1998 *Leben ohne Arbeit*: Director, camera, producer (together with Peter Schmidt)
1998 *Der Kandidat*: Director, camera, producer
1999 *Haupstadtzeitung*: Director, camera, producer
2000 *Demokratie im Schloss*: Director, camera, producer (together with Peter Schmidt)
2001 *My Way—James Last*: Director, camera, producer
2001 *Kanzlerbilder*: Director, camera, producer
2001 *Strasse des ewigen Friedens*: Director, camera, producer
2002 *Berlin: Sinfonie einer Großstadt*: Director, writer, camera, co-producer
2002 *Doppelleben*: Director, camera, co-producer

Further Reading

Fuhr, Eckhard, "Berlin zum Kuscheln," in *Die Welt*, 12.4, 2002.
Gottstein, Björn, "Die Stadt ohne Eigenschaft," in *Die tageszeitung*, 12.4, 2002.
Menden, Alexander, "Leistungssport. Haupstadt-Filmmusik live: 'Berlin: Sinfonie einer Großstadt,'" in *Süddeutsche Zeitung*, 12.4, 2002.
Schadt, Thomas, *Das Gefühl des Augenblicks—Zur Dramaturgie des Dokumentarfilms*, Bergisch-Gladbach: Bastei-Lübbe, 2002.
———, *Berlin: Sinfonie einer Großstadt*, Berlin: Nicolai, 2002.

SCHLESINGER, JOHN

John Richard Schlesinger attended Balliol College, Oxford, where he first became seriously involved with acting and filmmaking. During his days as a student he acted with the Oxford University Dramatic Society, served as president of the local Experimental Theatre Club, and produced his first short film, *Black Legend* (1948).

In 1957 he joined BBC-TV as a second unit director and piloted several episodes of *The Valiant Years* about Winston Churchill and short topical and arts features for *Tonight* and *Monitor* under Huw Wheldon, winning an Edinburgh Festival prize for *The Innocent Eye* (1959). Although recent BBC administrations have usually sought to buy in programmes from freelance production companies, in the 1950s, current affairs shows such as *Monitor* were known for nurturing a diverse range of filmmakers. Subsequently, Schlesinger directed pieces on the Cannes Film Festival, Italian opera, and comparative studies of painters.

Out of this experience, which served as a sound technical foundation for his later work, Schlesinger was offered a 30-minute piece by the veteran documentary maker Edgar Anstey. The British Transport Films sponsored documentary *Terminus* (1961) became the celebrated culmination of his series of BBC-TV documentaries. Set at Waterloo station, in Schlesinger's hands it became far more than a mere observation piece: Substories formed, vanished, and reappeared displaying elements of social realism that foreshadowed his subsequent work. Utilising many different perspectives—close-ups, long shots, and high and low angles—Schlesinger chose on-location sound over narration to show how democratising train travel was. A poignant story of a little boy lost, handcuffed convicts being taken to Dartmoor, discarded flowers meant for an arrival who did not show—these were just some of the many vignetts of everyday life that made up Schlesinger's cinema-vérité portrait of a London railway station. His *Terminus* won Schlesinger a Golden Lion award at the Venice film festival and a British Academy award for Best Short Film.

Schlesinger directed some two dozen documentaries on a vast range of subjects, but he was perhaps best known for his fiction movies, such as *Midnight Cowboy* (1969), for which he won an Academy Award for Best Director, despite the film having an X rating. Schlesinger's oeuvre was characterised by a lifelong preoccupation with gender relations, particularly homosexuality; an interest in analysing and representing subcultures, minorities, and other discriminated social groups; a relatively intellectual middle-class outlook; and a commitment to filmmaking as entertainment rather than politics. Schlesinger also directed theatre and opera and in 1970 he was made CBE (Commander of the British Empire) by Queen Elizabeth II.

D. BRUNO STARRS

Biography

Born February 16, 1926, in London. Attended Balliol College, Oxford. After serving in the army in World War II in England and the Far East, studied English Literature and graduated from Oxford in 1950. Produced his first short film, *Black Legend,* as a student in 1948. Suffered a stroke in 2000 from which he never fully recovered, and died on July 25, 2003, with his companion of many years, the photographer Michael Childers, at his side.

Selected Films

1948 *Black Legend*
1959 *The Innocent Eye*
1961 *Terminus*
1969 *Midnight Cowboy*

Further Reading

BBC Education, *Face to Face: John Schlesinger in Conversation with Jeremy Isaacs.* Date broadcast: February 3, 1993. Date posted: unknown. Date accessed: May17, 2004, www.bbc.co.ulc/education/lzone/movie/schles.htm.
BBC News, *BAFTA to Honour Schlesinger.* Date broadcast: April 26, 2002. Date posted: unknown. Date accessed: 17 May 2004. http://news.bbc.co.uk/1/hi/entertainment/film/1953423.stm.
————. *Your Tributes to John Schlesinger.* Date broadcast: July 29, 2003. Date posted: unknown. Date accessed: May 17, 2004http://news.bbc.co.uk/1/hi/talking_point/3095415.stm.
Brooker, Nancy J., *John Schlesinger: A Guide to References and Resources,* Boston: G. K. Hall, 1978.
Davidson, Ewan, "Terminus (1961)," *Screenonline.* British Film Institute, 2003. Date posted: unknown. Date accessed: May 17, 2004, www.screenonline.org.uk/film.id.520921.
Phillips, Gene D., *John Schlesinger,* Boston: Twayne, 1981.

SCHOEDSACK, ERNEST B.

Ernest Beaumont Schoedsack is best known for bringing a touch of the grand spectacle to the documentary form in the wake of Robert Flaherty's *Nanook of the North* (1922), but his films *Grass: A Nation's Battle for Life* (1925) and *Chang: A Drama of the Wilderness* (1927) did more than merely capitalize on *Nanook*'s unprecedented success. Made in collaboration with his partner, Merian C. Cooper, Schoedsack's travel adventures marked the height of the expeditionary genre. Curiously, neither film is mentioned in André Bazin's famous essay, "Cinema and Exploration," although when Bazin discusses the emergence after World War I of what he calls "travel-films-in-the-grand-manner"—such as Léon Poirier's colonial epic, *La croisiére noire* (1926)—he is describing a genre that Cooper and Schoedsack helped to define (Bazin, 1967). Just as John Ford was credited with the coming of the "sur-western," Cooper and Schoedsack brought an added dimension to the documentary travelog, imbuing the form with a heightened sense of scale and depth; Cooper himself would go on to produce some of Ford's best-known westerns.

Schoedsack's autobiographical accounts of his adventures leading up to the making of *Grass* border on the fantastic. He ran away from home at age 14, working with engineering road gangs and as a surveyor before starting work as a cameraman at the Mack Sennett Keystone Studios. During the First World War he flew combat missions and acted as a photographer for the Army Signal Corps, specializing in images captured while under heavy fire. He sought action even after the Armistice, working as a Red Cross photographer and assisting Polish refugees during the Polish-Russian conflict. Schoedsack drove ambulances, rescued refugees from Russian oil fields, and filmed the destruction of the Dnieper Bridge as the Polish retreated from Kiev. In the midst of this period, in 1918, he first encountered Cooper—a recent prisoner of war—in a Viennese railroad station. In the ensuing years Schoedsack continued to eke out a living doing newsreel camerawork in Europe; in the meantime Cooper was shot down while flying missions for the Polish Army and spent time in a Moscow prison, from which he made a dramatic escape (Schoedsack, 1983).

In 1923, Cooper contacted Schoedsack to join a photographic expedition ship in Djibouti and they traveled throughout the Middle East, spending a brief period with Haile Selassie in Addis Abbaba. The two men's symbiotic relationship was defined from the start: Schoedsack was primarily an action photographer, whereas Cooper was an enthusiastic promoter and showman. They became determined to make a film about nomadic migrations in Iran and Iraq (then known as Persia and British-occupied Mesopotamia, respectively) because it promised the possibility of witnessing skirmishes between Kurds and their neighbors, a prospect they found "alluring" (Schoedsack, 1983). Cooper went to the United States to secure funds, returning with a budget of $10,000 and accompanied by the journalist Marguerite Harrison, who had assisted him in his escape from a Soviet prison. Attempting to economize with their limited film stock, they began in Turkey, shooting travelog and newsreel footage.

Cooper and Harrison began filming the migration of Bakhtiari tribespeople in Persia in April of 1924. The three intended first to follow the tribe's journey from winter to summer grazing grounds, then to capture some intimate scenes of daily life between outward and return migrations, and finally to accompany the group on its journey back. Due to financial constraints, however, the film ended up chronicling a one-way journey, and would ultimately lack the personal details that the filmmakers intended. Barnouw criticizes the film for precisely this, noting that, unlike Flaherty's films, the tribespeople in *Grass* remain strangers, and "no individual portrait emerges from them" (Barnouw, 1983). In place of ethnographic detail, *Grass* sets up the theme of the documentary filmmaker as an adventurer/explorer, a figure who would reappear later in the barely disguised fictional character of Carl Denham, the showman-hero at the center of *King Kong* (1933). Like Denham, Cooper is referred to early on in *Grass* as the impresario behind the spectacle: the "engineer who conceived the idea of recording the migration."

Although for Schoedsack *Grass* would always remain a "great lost opportunity," fragmented and rushed into completion for economic reasons, the film was successful enough to convince Jesse Lasky to fund a second expedition to Siam (now Thailand) to film *Chang* (Schoedsack, 1983). *Chang* follows a more carefully scripted narrative than *Grass*, leading most critics to label it a "semidocumentary." It attempts to focus on the personal and domestic details that were absent in *Grass*, telling the story of a family living on the edge of the jungle

and of their constant encounters with wild animals. It is the animals, and the photographers' heroic efforts to capture them on film, that quickly take center stage, and the film culminates with a dramatic elephant ("chang") stampede.

While the epic scale of Cooper and Schoedsack's early films set them apart from most documentary and travelog work of the day, their talents were quickly (and, apparently, without resistance) appropriated by Hollywood's increasing demand for fictional adventure films grounded in authentic locations. *The Four Feathers* (1929) was typical of this hybrid approach, with scenes shot in the Sudan interspersed with principal work done in a Hollywood studio. At the same time, directors such as W. S. Van Dyke were standardizing the practice of the exotic on-location shoot with films such as *White Shadows in the South Seas* (1928) and *Trader Horn* (1931).

Rango (1931), which takes place in Sumatra, saw Schoedsack's return to the wild animal adventure drama, but his live-action work was now primarily lending authenticity and immediacy to the *mise-en-scéne* of fictional productions. In many ways *King Kong* was the next logical step in this migration from fact to fantasy, and is itself a kind of hybrid film: a fascinating and disturbing allegory of the will of the photographer-adventurer to capture spectacular ethnographic images, and of the public's insatiable demand for them. Cooper and Schoedsack would part ways in the 1930s, Cooper to concentrate on producing, while Schoedsack would continue directing, though he was partially blinded in an aviation accident in the 1940s. They joined forces once more for *Mighty Joe Young* (1949) and another spectacular experiment in actuality filmmaking, *This Is Cinerama* (1952).

JEFFREY GEIGER

See also **Chang; Cooper, Merian C.; Grass**

Biography

Born in Council Bluffs, Iowa, June 8, 1893. Worked on road gangs and as a surveyor, then as cameraman for the Mack Sennett Studios, early 1910s. Aviator and picture correspondent in U.S. Signal Corps during the First World War. Red Cross photographic unit and freelance camerman in Europe, 1918–1922. Joined Merian C. Cooper on photographic correspondence tour, 1923. Produced and directed *Grass* with Cooper and Marguerite Harrison, 1924–1925, distributed by Paramount. Made *Chang* with Cooper in Thailand, funded and released by Paramount in

1927. Married Ruth Rose, screenwriter, 1926. Made a number of features with Cooper and/or Rose, 1928–1935, including *King Kong*. Thereafter worked as feature director in Hollywood. Received permanent eye injury while testing photographic equipment during Second World War. Died December 23, 1979, in Los Angeles, California.

Selected Films

1925 *Grass* (*Grass: A Nation's Battle for Life* / *Grass: The Epic of a Lost Tribe*): Co-director, co-producer, co-photographer
1927 *Chang*: Co-director, co-producer
1929 *The Four Feathers*: Co-producer, co-director
1931 *Rango*: Director, producer
1932 *The Most Dangerous Game* (*The Hounds of Zaroff*): Co-director, co-producer
1933 *King Kong*: Co-director, co-producer
1952 *This Is Cinerama*: Co-director, prologue only

Further Reading

Barnouw, Eric, *Documentary: A History of the Non-Fiction Film*, Oxford: Oxford University Press, 1983.
Bazin, André, *What Is Cinema?* volume 1, edited by Hugh Gray, Berkeley: University of California Press, 1967.
Brownlow, Kevin, *The War, The West and the Wilderness*, New York: Albert A. Knopf, 1979.
Griffith, Richard, "*Grass* and *Chang*," in *The Documentary Tradition*, edited by Lewis Jacobs, New York: W. W. Norton, 1979, 22–24.
Mould, David H., and Gerry Veeder, "The Photographer-Adventurers: Forgotten Heroes of the Silent Screen," in *Journal of Popular Film and Television* 16, Autumn, 1988, 118–129.
Rony, Fatimah Tobing, *The Third Eye: Race, Cinema, and Ethnographic Spectacle*, Durham: Duke University Press, 1996.
Schoedsack, Ernest B., "*Grass*: The Making of an Epic," in *American Cinematographer* 64, February 1983, 40–44, 109–114.

SCHOMBURGK, HANS HERMANN

Schomburgk stands as a pioneer of colonial expedition film. After initial failures, he succeeded with *Treks and Trails in West Africa* (1914). The film, directed in Togo, was first shown in 1914 in London and brought Schomburgk many lecture invitations in the United States, and contracts with the French film company Gaumont. The outbreak of World War I, however, forced him to return to Germany.

Although Schomburgk's primary interest was documentary film, he also produced many feature pictures. Simultaneously with his first expedition film, he produced in Togo several other short films, with Meg Gehrts in the leading role. These films (for example, *The White Goddess of the Wangora*) were small sensations, because Meg Gherts was the first European actress to work in Africa. The stories were trivial and narrated from the perspective of the colonial conquerors and adventurers; they propagated the supposed cultural superiority of the European.

Schomburgk narrated his expedition films and features of the 1920s from a Euro-centered perspective, in accordance with the discourse of that time. Local people are presented in a patronizing or disdainful fashion quite often, and the recourse to the display of physical anomalies is less a matter of ethnography, and more a matter of exotic amusement.

In spite of his colonial position, Schomburgk does show some interest in ethnography, which was unusual for the expedition film of the time. In *Mensch und Tier im Urwald* (1924) a ritual of the Bundu order, a secret bond of the women in Liberia, is shown in its entirety. The dancers were filmed less as an exotic set piece for European voyeurism, and more on their own artistic and cultural terms, deserving of respect.

Schomburgk's interest eventually shifted to African wildlife. *Das letzte Paradies* (1932), which he directed in South Africa with Paul Lieberenz, is a melancholic film about animals, which attempts to discern the soul of Africa through its creatures. Schomburgk detaches himself from any political dimension and ignores the everyday reality in South Africa: the racial segregation and the effect of the colonialism.

Schomburgk's ability to work was limited by the Third Reich. In 1940, he was deemed politically untrustworthy and was persecuted as a "quarter Jew" (he had a Jewish grandmother). His books were censored, and his films were redirected and used for propaganda purposes. He edited what film he retained after World War II under a new title, *Frauen Masken und Dämonen* (1948). He gave lectures and published many adventure and travel books, which sold over two million copies. His last film, *Mein Abschied von Afrika* (1956), which was financed by both German states, is a melancholic farewell to Africa.

GERLINDE WAZ

Biography

Born October 28, 1880, in Hamburg-Bergedorf, Germany. Attended the Realgymnasiums in Hamburg, Lüneburg, and Jena. Sent to South Africa at age 17 by his parents. In 1898, joined the British Natal Mountain Police. In 1901, began service in the German army. From 1902, took part in expeditions to South, East, and West Africa. In 1913/1914, shot his first film in Liberia and Togo (*Treks and Trails in Westafrica*), which premiered at the London Philharmonic Hall (German version: *Im deutschen Sudan*, 1917). Made several expeditions to Africa, including 1923/1924 to Liberia (*Mensch und Tier im Urwald*) and 1931/1932 to South Africa (*Das letzte Paradies*). In 1940, prohibited from making public lectures in Germany. Published seven adventure and travel books (among which are new editions of older titles) from 1947. Died July 26, 1967, in Berlin.

Selected Films (Director)

1913 *Staats-Sekretär Dr. Solf in den Kolonien (Togo im Film)* (Fragment)
1914 *Treks and Trails in Westafrica* [*Im deutschen Sudan, 1917*] (documentary)
1914 *The White Goddess of the Wangora* (fiction)
1917 *Im deutschen Sudan (Neufassung von Treks and Trails in Westafrica)* (documentary)
1919 *Tropengift* (fiction)
1921 *Eine Weisse unter Kannibalen* (fiction)
1921 *Im Kampf um Diamantenfelder* (fiction)
1924 *Mensch und Tier im Urwald* (documentary)
1925 *Verlorenes Land* (compilation)
1932 *Das letzte Paradies* (documentary)
1936 *Die Wildnis stirbt!* (compilation) (co-director; editor Arnold Fanck)

1948 *Frauen, Masken und Dämonen* (compilation)—*Neufassung Mensch und Tier im Urwald*
1958 *Mein Abschied von Afrika* (documentary)

Further Reading

Alexander, Caroline, "Annals of Exploration. The White Goddess of the Wangora," in *The New Yorker*, April 8, 1991, 43–76.

Fuhrmann, Wolfgang, "German Colonial Cinematography in Africa. A Case Study of the History of Early Nonfiction cinema." (Dissertation, University Utrecht, 2003.)

Gehrts, Meg, "A Camera Actress in the Wilds of Togoland. The Adventures, Observations & Experiences of a Cinematograph Actress in West African Forests with an Introduction by Major H. Schomburgk," London: Seeley, Service & Co., Philadelphia: Lippincott 1915 [German Ed.: "Weiße Göttin der Wangora. Eine Filmschauspielerin 1913 in Afrika.", Wuppertal: Peter Hammer, 1999].

Nganang, Alain Patrice, "Koloniale Sehnsuchtsfilme. Vom lieben Afrikaner deutscher Filme der NS-Zeit," in *Welfengarten, Jahrbuch für Essayismus*, 11, 2001, 111–128.

Schomburgk, Hans, "Afrikanische Filmexpeditionen," in *Filmkurier*, 22.06, 1921.

————. "Bwakukama. Fahrten und Forschungen mit Büchse und Film imunbekannten Afrika," Berlin: Deutsch Literarisches Institut, 1922.

————. "35 Jahre Filmarbeit in Afrika," in *Kulturfilm—Almanach*, edited by E. W. M. Lichtwarck, Hamburg: Hermes, 1948, 29–31.

————. "Zelte in Afrika. Fahrten–Forschungen–Abenteuer in sechs Jahrzehnten," Ost-Berlin (GDR): Verlag der Nation, 1960.

Waz, Gerlinde, "Auf der Suche nach dem letzten ParadieSchomburgk Der Afrikaforscher und Regisseur Hans Schomburgk," in *Triviale Tropen. Exotische Reise- und Abenteuerfilme aus Deutschland 1919–1939*, edited by Jörg Schöning, München: edition text + kritik, 1997,95–109.

Zwernemann, J., "Hans Schomburgk: Im Deutschen Sudan," Film D 1221, Publikation des Instituts für den Wissenschaftlichen Film (IWF), Göttingen, Publ. Wiss. Film., Sekt. Ethnol., Ser. 8, Nr. 3/D 1221, 1978.

SCOTLAND

Scotland has made a substantial and distinctive contribution to documentary tradition, culture, theory, and practice. The contribution of Scotland to documentary film is multifaceted, and a subject of dispute. The debate extends beyond questions of form, aesthetics, and subject matter to issues of theory and the conditions and constraints of cultural production.

There are a number of different Scotlands, each discernible to other Scots by a set of signifiers. The

Highlands and the islands are overlapping but distinct, and the Hebrides differ from the Orkneys and Shetlands. What some term the Central Belt contains both Edinburgh and Glasgow, two very opposed cities and cultures. There are three languages spoken in Scotland: English, Scots, and Gaelic. Given these differences, it is inevitable that there are a number of tensions and ambiguities present in the creation, construction, and reception of media texts.

One might expect documentary to reject "tartanry," and to develop a discourse that moves beyond sentimental, stereotypical depictions of Scotland and Scottish life. However, the enduring strengths of the images, meanings, and iconography of tartan, and the romantic nostalgia for a rural elegiac arcadia were and are such that documentary filmmakers have had to operate within the dominant hegemonic ideology that contained strong (albeit not unchallenged) versions of history and national identities.

The problem for critics and radicals, such as Colin McArthur, is that the image and echoes of tartanry was and remains popular with the populace, and that even when a film attempts modernism, as does *Seawards the Great Ships* (Harris, 1961), this is at the very time when what is being recorded is about to disappear into the past and comprise a part of an alternative urban and nostalgic mythology of Clydeside. Nonetheless, documentaries as different as *Children of the City* and *Culloden* ensure that humane, humanist, and socialist values are made available—in the case of these two films, quite explicitly.

A consideration of Scotland and documentary can reasonably begin with John Grierson, often considered the founding father of the British Documentary Movement. The then somewhat austere, Presbyterian, and patriarchal nature of Scottish society and culture likely informed Grierson's ideology, and thus played a distinct role in the shaping of modern documentary film.

First shown at the London Film Society in November 1929, *Drifters* (Grierson, 1929) is perhaps one of the most famous documentaries. Filmed in part in the Shetlands, some scenes were filmed in the North Sea on vessels whose home ports were in England. The film faced technical and logistical difficulties, some of which were impossible to overcome with the cameras and equipment available at that time. The shoals of herring featured in the film, therefore, were filmed in the tank of a marine biological station—and the fish were apparently roach rather than herring. Despite these caveats, this silent film uses montage

and a simple story line to give the viewer an insight into the industrial processes and the human experiences and lives that are required to enable the cook and the shopkeeper to provide a simple and nutritious meal on the family table.

Partly filmed in the fishing village of Footdee in Aberdeen, *Drifters* gives an impressionistic sense of a community; it has its own rituals and rhythms, its own values and truths. It successfully combines a romanticized vision of masculine labor with the articulation of the economic and industrial context. In so doing, and in common with many documentaries of this type, it never quite succeeds in resolving the tensions that are integral to such an endeavor.

Born in Edinburgh, Harry Watt (1906–1987) worked for both the GPO Film Unit and the Crown Unit, and co-directed *Night Mail* (with Basil Wright, 1936) and *London Can Take It* (with Humphrey Jennings, 1940). He directed *North Sea* (1938) and *Target for Tonight* (1941) and later joined Ealing Studios. A competent rather than a brilliant director, his contribution can be exemplified and his inclusion justified not only because of these films but also because of their ethos, best described by Watt himself when speaking of *Target for Tonight* as being "an understated and unemotional account of an average air raid." No better epitaph for the Watt tradition and contribution to documentary can be articulated.

North Sea (1938) is an account of a trawler facing difficulty. It had narrative tension and a happy ending, and can perhaps be criticised on those grounds alone, but there are always dangers in post hoc analysis and in applying and projecting the cultural and ideological ideas from one era onto another or into the past. *North Sea,* like other documentaries, can also be judged by the art of the possible, and by this criterion, it was and remains a significant achievement.

Seawards the Great Ships (1960) was directed by Hilary Harris and made for Films of Scotland. It won the 1961 Oscar for best live action short film, and was the first Scottish-made film to win an Oscar. Based on a treatment by John Grierson, the film celebrates the work of shipbuilders and shipbuilding on the River Clyde at a time when that industry was about to disappear forever. The film is aesthetically distinctive in that it contains a number of abstract and almost surreal shots that use angles and shadows to develop a montage of images and icons that turn machinery and metals into a kind of art in themselves.

Waverley Steps (1947), directed by John Eldridge, presents glimpses of life in Edinburgh, and the activities of individuals visiting or living there over the course of a weekend. *Waverley Steps* was a commercial and critical success. It avoided tartanry and Scottish stereotypes, and realistically conveyed the thoughts and emotions of the citizens of Edinburgh regarding their city. It also managed to capture something of the contemporary reality of the city for a tourist but also for some natives at a time when it had just launched what was to become the biggest arts festival in the world. The film celebrates Edinburgh as a European city—and as an international, as opposed to merely "British," city.

Jenny Gilbertson (nee Brown) is included not because of a prolific output but rather because she is almost unique in being a woman director of documentary during the period in which she worked. Her 1934 film *The Rugged Island—A Shetland Lyric* is an example of a kind of drama documentary and can be said to foreshadow Michael Powell's much better known *The Edge of the World* (1978), which was also filmed in the Shetlands. *The Rugged Island* is an anthropological study of the tension between choosing to stay in poverty or opting for exile. The documentary aspects lie in the photography and the evocation of land, lifestyle, community, and place.

John Gray (1918–) worked with the GPO Film Unit and on films such as *North Sea*. He later moved on to a successful career with the BBC in which he was influential in news and radio. He helped establish and/or organize the Edinburgh Film Festival and later the Television Festivals, and he thus helped to ensure a continuing and vibrant debate and discourse around film as well as media policies and texts. His own work as a filmmaker includes the somewhat elegiac and impressionistic.

West Highland (1960) was one of the last films imbued with the lyrical documentary style dominant in the 1930s. This BBC Scotland documentary was produced and directed by John Gray, who worked in collaboration with Grierson and the GPO Film Unit. *West Highland* follows a day in the life of the railway line from Glasgow Queen Street to Mallaig. It clearly demonstrates the linkages between city and country; urban and rural, and traces a society and lifestyle that has now largely vanished. The story is objective and elegiac and the camerawork benefits from the stunning scenery. The context is Scottish, but the message is universal.

Despite his 1967 Academy Award for *The War Game* (Best Documentary Feature), Peter Watkins remains best known in Scotland for *Culloden*

(1964)—a documentary that can be said to have deconstructed, with savagery and accuracy, the romantic and sentimental mythologising of tartanry and Bonnie Prince Charlie.

Based on the historical book of the same name by John Prebble, Watkins elected to film *Culloden* in newsreel style, with the Battle of Culloden (1746), the last battle to occur on the British mainland, taking place as though cameras were there at the time and reporters were able to ask questions of the combatants. The battle saw the end of the attempts by the exiled Prince to regain power and the throne. It was also the beginning of the end of the clan or tribal lifestyles of the Gaelic ethnic and highland rural minority. Their destruction allowed their culture and symbols to be safely sentimentalised around eighty years later and subsequently through Victorian and early twentieth-century tartanry. Many of the extras and actors in the film were local and native descendants of those who had fought in the battle some 200 years before, and this added to the authenticity and realism of the sometimes shocking scenes.

The residual folk memory of the ruthlessness of the victors of Culloden, the Hanoverians and the Duke of Cumberland, were well shown in the film, but more moving and powerful was the articulation of the hopelessness of the situation of the common man. The inevitability of the defeat due to the incompetence of the Jacobite leaders, and the pain of a civil war in which family members were on opposite sides are powerfully conveyed in the film, as is the horrifying nature of a mid-eighteenth-century battle. Throughout, the narrative is interspersed with interviews with participants; generals and foot soldiers were each allowed their say directly to the camera and the interviewer.

The Edinburgh Film Guild can lay claim to being one of the oldest continuous film societies in the world, as it was founded in 1930. The Guild continues to meet on Sundays in the Filmhouse in Edinburgh and provides opportunities for the viewing of a range of classic and international films that include documentaries. The journal *Cinema Quarterly* (founded 1932) grew out of the Guild.

The Edinburgh International Festival of Documentary Films was founded in August 1947, with a program of approximately 75 films submitted. Although it eventually became the Edinburgh Film Festival, and during the 1950s moved beyond its original focus on documentary, the importance of the festival as a cultural and intellectual event for filmmakers, filmgoers, and film theorists cannot be understated and the stated intention to provide a stage for the documentary idea and practice was achieved.

The Films of Scotland Committee was set up by the Scottish Development Council in the late 1930s in order to ensure that there would be films on modern Scotland for the 1938 Glasgow Empire Exhibition. These films, like many Griersonian documentaries, were a blend of promotion and social comment; of corporate communication and constrained radicalism; of romanticism and modernism. What is significant, however, in the context of the ideological balance of power at the time and since is the fact that as Grierson put it, the committee was a deliberate attempt to use the film for national purposes.

The committee's life began with the need to have available films on contemporary Scotland for the 1938 Glasgow Empire exhibition. The result was four documentaries; *The Face of Scotland, They Made the Land, The Children's Story,* and *Wealth of a Nation.* Inevitably, these films present an optimistic view of the policies of development. Despite this, and their clear subservience to and operation within a contemporary unionist and deferential discourse, the films were excluded, by the British Council from the 1939 New York-based World Fair, on the grounds that they were not complementary to the heritage and royal version of England that was on display.

The Second Films of Scotland Committee operated from 1954 until 1982, and continued some of the traditions of its prewar predecessor. Many of its films were of the travelogue tourism variety, with highland and island landscapes omnipresent. A number were also about Edinburgh's culture, history, and arts, Glasgow's urban redevelopment, and new towns such as East Kilbride and Cumbernauld. Some films about Scottish artists and writers were produced.

The committee acted as a catalyst to persuade other bodies to invest in films and filming. Toward the end of its existence, it became increasingly apparent that although it might be possible to produce, the question of exhibition was becoming ever more problematic given the decline of going to the cinema and the move toward single-feature showings. Television thus became the route and the destination for documentary makers in Scotland and beyond.

ROBERT BEVERIDGE

See also **Culloden**; **Drifters**; **Grierson, John**; **Target for Tonight**; **The War Game**; **Watkins, Peter**; **Watt, Harry**

SDR "Stuttgarter Schule"

There were two different styles in West German television at the end of the 1950s. One was the feature style of Peter von Zahn of NDR (North German Public TV) in Hamburg, which was very much influenced by Anglo-American television reportage and preferred live coverage. The other style was developed by the documentary department at SDR (South German Public TV) in Stuttgart and was strongly influenced on the one hand by radio features and on the other hand by the German news magazine "Der Spiegel," where some of the directors had previously worked. The department wanted to produce something different from the German documentary tradition. In the 1950s, that was typified by the newsreels, which more or less adopted the style of the Nazi newsreel *Die Deutsche Wochenschau* and classical "Kulturfilme." This term refers to the documentary shorts shown before the main program in movie theaters. They often dealt with cultural issues or presented travel reports in an educational way. Both forms tended to be heroic, to exaggerate reality, and to awaken national emotions. The new approach was to produce critical films about West German society with an ironic commentary and powerful camerawork and editing. A very young team, mostly not yet in their thirties, produced the films and SDR gave them some room for experiments.

A report about German Jewish emigrants who fled Nazi Germany and survived German occupation in Paris (*Die Vergessenen / The Forgotten,* 1955) was one of the first films with a new approach, using the camera to present evidence of the poor housing situation. Dieter Ertel's report on a boxing match (*Ein Großkampftag*, 1957) became a prototype for the new series *Zeichen der Zeit / Signs of the Times*. This series became the trademark of the documentary department and 56 films were produced by 1973. Subjects were phenomena of mass culture and entertainment, such as sports, cars, pop music, movies, and surprisingly seldom politics. In 1962, Heinz Huber became head of the new documentary department. He tried to keep his team together and add a new talent every few years. He also published some interesting articles on the theory of documentary filmmaking. Members of his team were Dieter Ertel, Peter Dreesen, Corinne Pulver, Artur Müller, Wilhelm Bittorf, Georg Friedel, Helmut Greulich, and later Roman Brodmann and Elmar Hügler. Peter Nestler produced two of his early films for SDR. In the first ten years, beginning in November 1954, the documentarists produced 210 programs for SDR. Beside *Zeichen der Zeit* there were other documentary formats such as *Augenzeugen berichten / Eyewitnesses Report*, reports on foreign countries, portrait films, and historical programs. SDR was the first German TV station to produce a fourteen-part series on the history of *Das Dritte Reich / The Third Reich* (1960/1961), which brought the station general recognition. Other historical programs were on the American Civil War (1965), the battle of Königrätz (1966), and the German-French War of 1870/1871. The department was influenced by the American direct cinema. Elmar Hügler developed the series *Notizen vom Nachbarn / Notes from the Neighbour*, where events in everyday life—such as birth, dance school, marriages, military recruiting, and death—were shown with original sound only and without any commentary. One of the masterpieces was *Der Polizeitstaaatsbesuch / Visit in a Police State* (1967) by Roman Brodmann. Each director developed his individual style, and a productive rivalry developed, but all of them kept to the critical perspective, essayistic style, and ironic commentary. With the sudden death of Heinz Huber in 1968 and a restructuring of the station, the documentary department lost its independence, and in 1973, most of the documentary filmmakers left the SDR.

KAY HOFFMAN

Further Reading

Gmelin, Otto, *Philosophie des Fernsehens*, Pfullingen, 1967.

Hoffmann, Kay, *Zeichen der Zeit. Zur Geschichte der Stuttgarter Schule*, Munich, 1996.

Müller, Jürgen K., *Zeichen der Zeit. Eine Fernseh-Dokumentationsreihe des Süddeutschen Rundfunks (1957–1973). Sechs Filmanalysen*, M.A. thesis, University of Tübingen, 1991.

Steinmetz, Rüdiger, and Helfried Spitra (eds.), *Dokumentarfilm als "Zeichen der Zeit." Vom Ansehen der Wirklichkeit im Fernsehen*, Munich, 1992.

Zimmermann, Peter (ed.), *Fernseh-Dokumentarismus. Bilanz und Perspektiven*, Munich, 1992.

SECRETS OF NATURE

(UK, Woolfe, 1922–1933)

"Secrets of Nature" is the name of a series of popular science films produced by British Instructional Films that began in 1922 and continued until 1933. H. Bruce Woolfe founded British Instructional shortly after World War I, with a view toward attracting intellectuals to work in the cinema. The company specialized in nonfiction films; in addition to the "Secrets" series, British Instructional focused on documentary reconstructions of episodes from World War I, such as *Zeebrugge* (1924). In the preface to *The Secrets of Nature* (1939), Woolfe recounts how an encounter with Gilbert White's *Natural History of Selborne* (1788/1789) led him to conceive of a series of nature films. White, a curate in Selborne, made detailed studies of the flora and fauna that surrounded his residence. His reliance on field observations makes him a precursor of the field of ethology, which proceeds from the observation of animals in their natural habitats instead of in laboratory settings. Other practitioners of ethology, such as the French entomologist Jean-Henri Fabre, influenced the popular scientific film of the 1910s in France. The "Secrets of Nature" continued this tradition of utilizing the cinema in a manner consistent with ethological principles of observation, although without any explicit claims to the methods of professional science. Indeed, one of the typical approaches used by the films was to anthropomorphize its plant and animal subjects, and this recourse to analogy is something that professional science would reject. The "Secrets" series was consciously and expertly produced for a mass audience, providing an excellent example of how "to administer the powder of instruction in the jam of entertainment."

Renowned for their high-production values and clever, humorous commentary, the films found favor with audiences not only in England but abroad as well, especially in Europe and America. During the series's twelve-year run, 144 one-reel films appeared; some years saw the release of as many as 30 films whereas in other years none were released. This erratic production schedule may result from the occasional changes in leadership and institutional circumstances, and it may also be due to the unpredictable nature of the subjects being filmed (some films were said to have taken as long as four years to complete).

Stoll Picture Productions took over British Instructional in 1924, but Woolfe remained the head of the company. His increasing involvement producing other projects for Stoll, including Anthony Asquith's early films, led him to cede oversight of the "Secrets of Nature" production unit to Mary Field, who began working for British Instructional as a technical advisor on the subject of seventeenth-century fishing in the West Atlantic before she worked her way up through the ranks. One of the only women in the British film industry to figure prominently in the field of production, Field was the main editor of the "Secrets of Nature" and was responsible for directing the majority of zoo films.

Field's principal collaborator was Percy Smith, whose name has become synonymous with the series. Smith's career as a popular scientific filmmaker began in 1907 when Charles Urban, who

was impressed by Smith's photomicrographs of the tongue of a bluebottle fly, employed the young Board of Education clerk. Smith's many films for Urban included Kinemacolour time-lapse studies of blooming flowers (*The Birth of a Flower*, 1910) and studies of insect behavior (*The Balancing Blue-Bottle*, 1908 and *The Strength and Agility of Insects*, 1911). These subjects received extensive and enthusiastic press coverage, and the remarkable ingenuity and humor they displayed would carry over into Smith's work on the "Secrets of Nature." His work for British Instructional consisted of films about insects, plants, underwater creatures, and microscopic subjects. Smith filmed many of his subjects in the laboratory/studio he established in his house in Southgate. An inveterate tinkerer, he engineered sophisticated devices for time-lapse films.

Although Smith's quirky charm perhaps best characterizes the "Secrets of Nature," he was by no means the only individual to make films for the series. In addition to Field's contributions, no less than half a dozen other naturalists provided their expertise to "Secrets." Charles Head shared the insect-film duties with Smith, making one of the series's first films, *The Lair of the Spider* (1922). He also made films about bird life and small mammals. Other prominent contributors included Edgar Chance, who was responsible for *The Cuckoo's Secret* (1922). The first film of the series, *The Cuckoo's Secret,* detailed the life cycle of the cuckoos of Worcestershire and was the product of many years of field observation. H. A. Gilbert and Walter Higham also provided films about birds and small mammals, as did Oliver Pike, who had contributed films about birds to Pathé's popular science catalogue as early as 1912. The bird films underline the affinity the "Secrets" series had with such vernacular scientific activities as bird-watching; in general, the series appealed to a fascination with how scientific observation could transform the everyday world into a fantastic and wonderful place.

The first five years of the series (1922–1926) were characterized by various cameramen and editors, but Woolfe's supervision enabled the finished product to maintain a consistent tone. In 1927, when the company went public, the core staff became more stable, with Field and Smith taking over the primary duties and Head, Pike, Gilbert, and Higham providing additional material.

The series made the switch to sound production in 1930. In 1933, British Instructional was acquired by British International Pictures, which was then in turn taken over by Associated

British Picture Corporation. The head of the latter company was against what he saw as British Instructional's production of "films for the intelligensia." Woolfe resigned his position shortly after the takeover and founded a similar unit, Gaumont British Instructional (GBI), at the Gaumont British Picture Corporation, where Mary Field and Percy Smith also found employment. The "Secrets of Nature" was retitled the "Secrets of Life" in 1934, and it continued to produce educational short films until the death of Percy Smith in March 1945. Many of the "Secrets" films are currently held by British Pathé.

OLIVER GAYCKEN

Further Reading

The Encyclopedia of British Film
Field, Mary, and Percy Smith, *The Secrets of Nature*, London: The Scientific Book Club, 1939.
Gaycken, Oliver, "The Sources of the 'Secrets of Nature': The Popular Science Film at Urban, 1903–11," in *Scene-Stealing: Sources for British Cinema before 1930*, edited by Alan Burton and Laraine Porter, Trowbridge: Flicks Books, 2003, 36–42.
Low, Rachel, *A History of the British Film 1906–1914*, London: Allen & Unwin, 1949.
McKernan, Luke, "'Something More than a Mere Picture Show': Charles Urban and the Early Non-Fiction Film in Great Britain and America, 1897–1925," University of London, Ph.D. thesis, 2004.

SEEING RED

(US, Reichert and Klein, 1983)

Seeing Red (1983) is the last of a series of documentaries co-directed by James Klein and Julia Reichert that address feminist and working-class topics from a socialist perspective using contemporary interviews, archival footage, and popular music. Klein and Reichert's first film together, *Growing Up Female* (1971), is considered the first sustained documentary study of the societal forces in the United States that mold female identities. *Methadone: An American Way of Dealing* (1975) critiques the use of methadone to combat drug addiction. The Oscar-nominated *Union Maids* (1976) collects the oral histories of three women who played roles in the unionization drives in the United States during the 1930s.

In *Seeing Red*, which was nominated for an Oscar, the directors incorporate the direct cinema techniques of their previous films, but they expand the scope of their research and oral interviews. In the early 1980s, Reichert and Klein interviewed 400 of the million people who had been members of the American Communist Party from the 1930s to the 1950s. Of the 400 people interviewed, 16 appear in *Seeing Red*. The co-directors note that people who were angry and dissatisfied with their involvement in the Communist Party declined interviews, so the 16 who appear in the film are generally positive about their experiences in the Communist Party (Shafransky, 1984: 25). The 16 were chosen to give a balanced representation of regions, gender, and race in the United States, although the focus of the film is on the rank and file members of the Communist Party.

Critics have noted that the directors' attempt to address controversial issues, such as the undemocratic structure of the Communist Party, is largely unsuccessful, and that those interviewed often have incomplete or dubious historical interpretations. In interviews, Klein and Reichert defend their approach as an emphasis on personal storytelling rather than history and analysis. Cultivating a sympathetic relationship with the people who will elicit their stories, they claim, precludes a separate, analytic voice (Georgakas, 1984: 27; Shafransky, 1984: 26).

This concern over analytic distance is related to a broader, theoretical controversy over the direct cinema techniques employed in the film. *Seeing Red*, it should be noted, is by no means a pure form of direct cinema: It employs nondiegetic music, there is no immediate drama (it is concerned with past events recalled by those who lived them), it sometimes shows an onscreen questioner during interviews, and it includes archival footage. *Seeing Red* is firmly in a tradition of critical political documentary, pioneered by De Antonio's *In the Year of the Pig* (1969), which draws on direct cinema techniques. In this tradition there are extensive interviews, archival footage, nondiegetic music, and little voice-over narration. Instead of limiting the scope of a film to the immediate representation of a single event in the manner of purer forms of direct cinema, critical political documentary traces broader issues and trends. Films in this subgenre include *With Babies in Banners* (1978), *Word Is Out* (1979), *The Wobblies* (1979), *The Day After Trinity* (1980), and *Lodz Ghetto* (1989). Often such films would include shots of demonstrations or other current political events, but these are precluded by *Seeing Red*'s focus on the past (archival footage can represent some of these past events, but such footage isn't direct cinema in the strict sense).

Because *Seeing Red* employs oral interviews extensively and generally eschews voice-over narration and other modes of objective commentary, the directors are less able to analyze their material or develop the broader context of the topics they explore. Indeed, as noted earlier, instead of attempting to maintain any objective distance from the interviewees during the making of the film, the directors were sympathetic both with them and their politics, and they attempted to edit the film in ways that preserved the narrative, and the convictions, of those interviewed. In this sense, *Seeing Red* can also be categorized as a late example of engaged cinema, not only because of its openly militant stance but also because of its production and distribution. Engaged cinema, which flourished during the 1960s and early 1970s, avoided mainstream media and sought to build alternative collectives to finance and market films. Both Reichert and Klein are founding—and current—members of one such engaged cinema collective, New Day Films, and *Union Maids* is often cited as a prototypical engaged cinema film (Thompson and Bordwell, 1994: 644).

A controversy arose over films in the tradition of critical political cinema and engaged cinema centers on the limited perspective allowed by the direct cinema techniques. *Union Maids* and *Seeing Red*, for example, are criticized for oversimplifying social relations by giving an incomplete, uncontested story primarily through oral interviews of small numbers of like-minded people.

Such an approach can be read as a legitimate form of counter-history, and recent critics have argued for the recuperation of such direct cinema techniques for the creation of counter-histories that dispute conventional representations of authority and give more heteroglossic alternatives (see entry on *Union Maids*). However, other critics have argued that Reichert and Klein tend to present oral histories as independent arguments and not as primary source material in need of a broader explanatory frame—a frame that at the very least would make clear the distinction between conveying the recollection of others and the meta-critical, reflexive attempt to question conventional representations of authority and history. The lack of such a frame, it is claimed, can make films such as *Seeing Red* appear naïve—an endorsement of a partial, self-protective history rather than a meta-critical response to previous histories (Nichols, 1991: 252).

PAUL MILLER

See also **Klein, James; Reichert, Julia;** *Union Maids*

Seeing Red (U.S., Heartland Productions, 1983, 100 mins.). Directed by Julia Reichert and James Klein.

Further Reading

Arthur, Paul, "Jargons of Authenticity (Three American Moments)," in *Theorizing Documentary*, Michael Renov (ed.), New York: Routledge, 1993.
Aufderheide, Pat, "The Good Fight," in *New Challenges for Documentary*, Alan Rosenthal (ed.), Berkeley: University of California Press, 1988.
Boruszkowski, Lilly Ann, "An Interview with Documentary Filmmaker Jim Klein," in *Journal of Film and Video* 46.1, 1994, 34–42.
Georgakas, Dan, "Seeing Red," in *Cineaste*, 13.2, 1984, 27–28.
Kleinhaus, Chuck, "Julia Reichert and Jim Klein, in *Jump Cut*, 5, 1975, 11–12.
Nichols, Bill, *Representing Reality*, Bloomington: Indiana University Press, 1991.
Rosenthal, Alan, "Union Maids," in *Documentary Conscience*, Alan Rosenthal (ed.), Berkeley: University of California Press, 1980.
Rosenthal, Alan (ed.), *New Challenges for Documentary*, Berkeley: University of California Press, 1988.
Rubenstein, Lenny, "Who's Who in Filmmaking: Julia Reichert and James Klein," in *Sightlines*, 20.2, 1986–1987, 22–25.
Shafransky, Renee, "Seeing Red: An Interview with James Klein and Julia Reichert," in *Cineaste*, 13.2, 1984, 24–26.
Thompson, Kristin, and David Bordwell, *Film History*, New York: McGraw-Hill, 1994.
Waldman, Diane, and Janet Walker (eds.), *Feminism and Documentary*, Minneapolis: University of Minnesota Press, 1999.

SEIDL, ULRICH

Stretching the definition of the term *documentary film* to an extreme, Austrian filmmaker Ulrich Seidl has developed a controversial method of documentary realism and the visual imagery of the "authentic" since the late 1980s. Seidl's films are by no means documentaries, although the documentary quality of his *oeuvre* is indisputable. His style is rather a complex blend of various *modi operandi*: Exploiting core values of cinema verité, such as intimacy and immediacy, Seidl's work blurs the boundaries between documentation and fiction, the factual and the poetic, the grotesque and the poignant beyond recognition.

With this unapologetic approach Seidl can confidently be seen as an anticipator of a new generation of documentary filmmakers which has become increasingly popular—not to mention populist—since the late 1990s. The convergence of the documentary toward feature film aesthetics and narrative forms was a widely observed phenomenon during these years, not least due to the international popularity of figures as Errol Morris and Michael Moore. Ulrich Seidl could be fairly credited to this group of filmmakers even if his aesthetics differ from the aforementioned to a considerable extent.

The fashionable hybrid term *docudrame* captures the idea behind Seidl's method best. Seidl himself, rejecting the categorization "documentary" for his work, characterizes the nature of his films as "calculated arrangements." His films are not so much concerned with authentic depictions of social *milieus*, but rather with condensed, dramatic reenactments of a social climate, constantly exploring the relation and tensions between public and private spheres in society. This artistic license enables Seidl to create an austere imagery of social *milieus* that highlights a harsh criticism of contemporary Austrian existential orientations.

As a matter of consequence, his work inevitably touches issues of national identity as Seidl's "semi-documentaries" are engaged in the typology of "the Austrian" as such to a great deal. The remaining influence of Catholicism in society, the slow transformation (and deformation) of the vast middle-class, its underlying xenophobia, and the connection with the legacy of National Socialism resonate throughout his films. The consideration of this cultural environment is a key to the understanding of Seidl's stylistic and aesthetical choices.

Since his work is not influenced by a certain school or "limited" by documentary ethics, Seidl can use his films as demonstrations of a subjective "truths." Dramatization of the largely factual-based material is crucial to his notion of the purposiveness of documentary film: the ability to involve the viewer emotionally by juxtaposing different societal *milieus*. This decision results in a highly stylized visual conception: rather verité-like observations of often redundant actions in long and alienated shots are contrasted with concisely framed *tableaux vivants* that give his images an almost photographic quality.

Seidls's work, largely discussed in the context of the documentary film, is particular interesting for its *laisser faire* attitude toward ethical considerations. It should be noted that Seidl's appreciation for the documentary format was initially a matter of convenience. In the 1980s in Austria documentaries were easier to finance through the public funding system. However, Seidl held fundamental resentments against the "aesthetical double-standard of the form." His notion of the traditional canon of ethical values as obsolete ran parallel with a reconsideration of the documentary codices in other European countries during the 1990s. The acknowledgment of new strategic practices and the increasingly casual exposure to far less "purist" documentary ethics coincided with the rise of the Danish "Dogma" manifesto that aesthetically bore resemblance to Seidl's method.

The growing popularity of the "Dogma" aesthetics during the mid-1990s was clearly an indicator for the necessity for a repositioning of the documentary film as such. "Authenticity" was becoming a quality characteristic the fiction film laid a claim to. The significance of Seidl's work must be understood in the context of this shift of paradigm. His films accompanied, partially even anticipated, this continuous development; at the same time it certainly had a sustainable effect on the reception of his work in terms of its "documentary virtues." Seidl's work exemplifies a new understanding of the documentary film that has abandoned the

SEIDL, ULRICH

paths of traditional thinking. In Seidl's documentary style "subjectivity" is not anymore a discoursive address but simply an assumption.

ANDREAS BUSCHE

Biography

Born in Vienna, Austria, in 1952. Studied publishing, theater studies, and art history. In 1978, he attended the Vienna Film Academy and directed his first short films "Einsvierzig" (1980) and "Der Ball" (1982). Dropped Film Academy in 1982. In 1989, Seidl finished the feature-length documentary *Krieg in Wien,* co-directed with his regular cinematographer Michael Glowegger. His 1990 film, *Good News. Von Kolporteuren, toten Hunden und anderen Wienern,* is widely regarded as Seidl's debut. Since 1984 Seidl has also worked as a freelance filmmaker for Austrian television. In 2001, directed *Hundstage (Dog Days)*, which is generally considered as Seidl's first fiction film although his method hasn't changed in comparison to his previous films.

Selected Films

1990 *Good News. Von Kolporteuren, toten Hunden und anderen Wienern*: director, writer
1993 *Mit Verlust ist zu rechnen*: director, writer
1995 *Tierische Liebe*: director, writer
1997 *Der Busenfreund*: director, writer
1999 *Models*: director, writer
2001 *Hundstage*: director, writer
2003 *Jesus, Du weißt*: director, writer

Further Reading

Dox: Documentary Film Quarterly, No. 10, Winter 1996, 34–37 *Film Comment*, No. 6, November/December 2001, 16–17.
Illetschko, Peter (ed.), *Gegenschuss—16 Regisseure aus Österreich*, Wespennest, Weien, 1995.
Positif, No. 500, October 2002, 192–201.

SELECKIS, IVARS

Ivars Seleckis's documentary films present realistic representations of human society. His documentaries have been noted for their detailed and sophisticated analysis of the social processes. His is a mission to capture the daily struggle for survival in the world, the continuous battle to raise and educate children, to live a decent life in this difficult day and age. Seleckis sees his role of documentary filmmaker as one of rudimentary importance. Through his films the smallest countries and the most insignificant individuals floundering in an ocean of globalization can explore their growing sense of apparent nothingness. In *The Crossroad Street* (1988), Seleckis presents the contemporary people of Riga, a town destined to become the capital of the independent Republic of Latvia. The people will face not only a political crisis but also the more cataclysmic threat of losing their connection to their culture, their language, their people, and ultimately themselves.

Seleckis follows this project with an examination of peasant life in the film *Come Down Pale Moon*. Shot in the Vidzeme region of Latvia in 1993, Seleckis follows the cycle of peasant life from spring through autumn during a critical time in

Latvian political history. These men and women spent the last 50 years living, working, and dying under Soviet rule and Seleckis is there to reveal the jubilation, the fear, and the uncertainty of peasants regaining their land after so many years. His use of documentary as chronicler of political and economic transition creates a biography of the peasant, the unexpected victor over the great Soviet military machine.

Seleckis revisits Riga in *New Times At Crossroad Street* (1998) ten years later. With the Soviet Union in collapse and the creation of the new Latvian Republic, Seleckis chronicles the challenge the people face in preventing themselves from dissolving into a single common primitive mass. The viewer visits inside the evolving world of what by western standards constitutes the insignificant and discovers the universality of human struggle and achievement.

CHRISTINE MARIE HILGER

Biography

Born in 1934 in Riga, Latvia, and graduated from the Academy of Agriculture and the Faculty of Food Technology in Jelgava in 1957, then from the State Institute of Cinematography in 1966. Began work in a Riga film studio in 1958 as an assistant cameraman. In 1968, directed his first film and went on to receive numerous distinctions, including Merrited Master of Arts (1975) and the Three Stars Order, which is the highest reward of the State of Latvia.

Selected Films

1980 *The Widening of the World*, director
1988 *The Crossroad Street*, director
1994 *Come Down, Pale Moon*, director
1998 *New Times at Crossroad Street*, director

Further Reading

Ackerman, Peter, and Jack DuVall, *A Force More Powerful: A Century of Nonviolent Conflict*, New York: St. Martin's Press, 2000.

Aitken, Ian, *European Film Theory and Cinema: A Critical Introduction*, Edinburgh: EUP, 2001.

Corner, John, *Documentary and the Mass Media*, London: Arnold, 1986.

Rotha, Paul, *Documentary Diary*, New York: Hill and Wang, 1973.

SELLING OF THE PENTAGON, THE

(US, Davis, 1971)

The CBS Reports documentary *The Selling of the Pentagon* aired on February 7, 1971. Writer and director Peter Davis and correspondent Roger Mudd based much of their investigation of the Department of Defense's domestic public relations apparatus on Senator J. William Fulbright's book *The Pentagon Propaganda Machine*. *The Selling of the Pentagon* told an estimated 9 million viewers that the Pentagon engaged in a pervasive, persuasive, improper, and expensive propaganda campaign to convince the American people that the United States military and its war in Southeast Asia represented essential and effective checks to the spread of international Communism. Instantly controversial, the film drew condemnations and accusations of distortion from government sources, but ultimately won a congressional confrontation by successfully invoking the applicability of First Amendment protection to broadcast journalism.

In *The Selling of the Pentagon*, director Davis interviews "major taxpayers" impressed with their elaborate tour of military facilities, shows Pentagon speakers extolling military confrontation to international communism, and juxtaposes a segment featuring Green Berets displaying hand-to-hand combat at an Armed Forces day with shots of nearby children mimicking their combat moves. Davis investigates the Pentagon film program, finding a marketing effort crowded with celebrities and expressing an outdated "obsession with mono-

lithic communism." A montage of title cards illustrates the point: "A Day in Vietnam," "The Big Picture," "Why Viet-Nam," "Freedom and You," and "Red Chinese Battle Plan." Davis excerpts segments featuring Robert Stack cleaning a rifle, Chet Huntly standing atop an aircraft carrier, John Wayne discussing revolutionaries with a well-posed group of Marines, and CBS's Walter Cronkite authoritatively intoning that America "must build forces at home" to confront communism. Davis examines several scenes from "Red Nightmare," the Pentagon's imaginative fictional narrative produced with Warner Brothers to illustrate the dangers of a Communist takeover in small-town America.

The Pentagon exalts the virtues of free thought and debate in "Red Nightmare," but *The Selling of the Pentagon* accuses the Pentagon of stifling the free thought and commentary of America's media. Correspondent Roger Mudd describes military sources bombarding local news outlets with thousands of TV and radio tapes and millions of press releases about the military and the war in which "The only news . . . is good news." The *New York Times*'s George Wilson adds that reporters assigned to the Pentagon have no alternative but to "trust big daddy," and shots of daily briefings in Vietnam illustrate their moniker, "Five O'clock Follies." Meanwhile, the Pentagon maintains five teams in Vietnam filming or staging material for television news in what a former Air Force photographer describes as "propagandizing."

The Selling of the Pentagon represented a landmark in the confrontation of U.S. journalists with the Pentagon, reinforcing the schism visually with techniques borrowed from direct cinema. By 1971, most journalists reporting on the Pentagon and the war filed stories adversarial to the Pentagon's positive perspective, and even CBS's staid Walter Cronkite openly broke with the administration in 1968 to advocate a negotiated peace and to warn Americans to no longer place any faith "in the silver linings [American leaders] find in the darkest clouds." Davis illustrated the dichotomy of perspective in *The Selling of the Pentagon* by contrasting CBS's handheld camera shots, tight close-ups, focus racking, and occasional whip pans with the slick images emanating from the Pentagon. Davis augmented this direct cinema camerawork with editing in the same tradition, using juxtaposition, jump cuts, and sequential arrangement to serve as an overt tool of commentary.

Responding to *The Selling of the Pentagon*, The *New York Times* spoke of "integrity" while Vice President Spiro Agnew accused CBS of airing "alleged facts which are untrue." F. Edward Hébert, chairman of the House Armed Service Committee, called the report a "hatchet job" and declared it "un-American." CBS followed a March 23, 1971, rebroadcast with 15 minutes of edited critical comments from Agnew, Hébert, and Secretary of Defense Melvin R. Laird, and a rebuttal by CBS News President Richard S. Salant. An estimated 14 million Americans watched the program, hearing Salant argue that no specific claims had been made against the essential accuracy of the program, only the editing of interviews and one speech within the film. However, the allegations of misleading and misrepresentative editing provided the grounds for another vocal critic, Representative Harley O. Staggers, to mount a congressional investigation.

Staggers, chairman of the House Committee on Interstate and Foreign Commerce, subpoenaed CBS and its president, Frank Stanton, for all materials relating to the production of *The Selling of the Pentagon*. Stanton testified but refused to turn over outtakes and production notes. CBS admitted that it had violated its own operating standards' guidelines relating to attributing answers to questions in taped interviews, but Stanton claimed that congressional oversight of broadcast journalism would have a "chilling effect," and was in violation of the First Amendment's protection of the press.

Staggers countered that "the press" does not include broadcast journalism, and added that as a licensee of public airways, CBS was answerable to Congress. In open debate, representatives widely condemned CBS, but recognized the courts' previous decision that "no rational distinction can be made" between broadcast journalism and print media in terms of First Amendment protection. The House did not act against Stanton and CBS, and it never voted on the "Truth in News Broadcasting Bill," introduced during the floor debates. The bill demanded any "factual reporting," including edited events or interviews, to be "explicitly labeled throughout [the] entire showing."

The congressional battle over First Amendment protection remains the lasting legacy of *The Selling of the Pentagon*, especially in connection with the nearly concurrent Supreme Court case over the Pentagon Papers. CBS continued to defy administration intimidation in 1972, when Walter Cronkite broadcast a two-part investigation of the Watergate scandal on the *CBS Evening News*, becoming the first major media center to support *The Washington Post*'s story. Peter Davis embarked on an independent project that would become the controversial 1974 Vietnam War documentary *Hearts and Minds*. Taking even more from direct cinema, Davis eliminated a narrator and constructed his argument with carefully edited and assembled interviews, location filming, and historical footage. Cronkite's broadcast and Davis's documentary follow the example of *The Selling of the Pentagon*, itself following a decade of increasing conflict between journalism and government in the United States. *The Selling of the Pentagon* represented a major public victory for broadcast journalism both in terms of securing First Amendment protection and demonstrating the potential ability of determined media to inform on political wrongdoing, even in the face of determined official intimidation.

MICHAEL ROBINSON

See also **Hearts and Minds**

The Selling of the Pentagon (US, CBS, 1971, 60 mins.). Produced, written, and directed by Peter Davis, with correspondent Roger Mudd. Executive produced by Perry Wolff. Photographed by William Wagner et al. Edited by Dena Levitt.

Further Reading

Dunham, Corydon B., *Fighting for the First Amendment: Stanton of CBS vs. Congress and the Nixon White House*, Westport, CT: Praeger, 1997.

Fulbright, J. William, *The Pentagon Propaganda Machine*, New York: Liveright, 1970.

Gould, Jack, "The Unselling of the Pentagon" in the *New York Times*, March 7, 1971, D17.

Jowett, Garth S., "'The Selling of the Pentagon': Television Confronts the First Amendment" in *American History, American Television: Interpreting the Video Past*, John E. O'Connor (ed.), New York: Ungar, 1983.

Reeb, Richard H., *Taking Journalism Seriously: "Objectivity" as a Partisan Cause*, Lanham: University Press of America, 1999.

Rogers, Jimmie N., and Theodore Clevenger, Jr., "'The Selling of the Pentagon': Was CBS the Fulbright Propaganda Machine?" in *Quarterly Journal of Speech*, 57, no. 3, 1971, 266–274.

Salant, Richard S., *Salant, CBS, and the Battle for the Soul of Broadcast Journalism: The Memoirs of Richard S. Salant*, Susan and Bill Buzenberg (ed.),, Boulder CO: Westview Press, 1999.

SENSE OF LOSS, A

(France, Ophuls, 1972)

Released between *The Sorrow and the Pity* (Ophuls, 1969) and *The Memory of Justice* (Ophuls, 1976), *A Sense of Loss* is one of Marcel Ophuls's least discussed films. When written about, usually in reviews rather than scholarly texts, the film is often damned with faint praise. Ephraim Katz was able to call it "sensitive" (Katz, 1993); Leonard Maltin has dubbed it "thoughtful" (Maltin, 2002). Peter Biskind was somewhat closer to the mark with his observation that "compassion without commitment leads to the confused, paralysed humanism of Ophuls' *A Sense of Loss*" and he was using the film only as a point of comparison in a review of *Hearts and Minds* (Davis, 1974). The most detailed analysis to date has come from Brian McIlroy (1998), who speaks of it as a "lightning-rod" on which debate may be focused rather than as a fully realised documentary treatment of its subject.

A Sense of Loss was an attempt to explore the "troubles" in Northern Ireland through a series of interviews. The interviews were illustrated with footage shot on location between December 1971 and February 1972. Supplementary scenes and interviews were also filmed in London, Dublin, and New York. Ophuls spoke with people representing nationalist and loyalist traditions, with Protestants and Catholics, with politicians, paramilitaries, and private citizens. An emphasis was given to the experiences of those who had lost relatives during the violence, sometimes by accident, sometimes as a direct result of military or paramilitary activities. Within this framework, Ophuls attempted to provide an overview of the political and social issues at stake in Northern Ireland as seen by those who lived there. By designating it "A film report by Marcel Ophuls," he presumably hoped to sidestep the social and political issues raised by embarking on a more comprehensive "chronicle" such as *The Sorrow and the Pity*.

The film was thematically organised around the idea of human loss, which allowed Ophuls to avoid engaging in active discourse and eliminated the need to come to specific political conclusions. The director's sympathy with the nationalist community was evident, nonetheless, in his selection and juxtaposition of segments, although this partisanship was presented in terms of a liberal-humanist empathy with human tragedy rather than as a political perspective. The film's stated thematic preoccupation with loss raised larger questions about the "loss" of Northern Ireland itself in broader historical terms, which the film did not fully vocalise. Although he presented the stated views of nationalists and loyalists of varying degrees of extremity, Ophuls's questions led his interviewees to use religious designations rather than political ones. This semantic distinction had the effect of portraying the conflict in Northern Ireland as a relatively clear-cut sectarian antagonism that had been instigated by colonial and imperialist Britain imposing its religious values on the native Irish. This provided safe grounds for an empathetic response to the losses represented in the film: loss of family, loss of peace, and loss of innocence.

The film begins and ends with references to the death of children. Its longest and least interrupted interview is with the parents of a baby who was killed in a bomb blast. As the film begins, Ophuls is heard speaking to his mother. The interview in full is not shown until later, but it is used in the opening as part of a montage sequence to sound a note of human tragedy that will inform the film on the whole. The film's conclusion actually intercuts two deaths, one of an IRA volunteer (whose mother also features in the opening montage), the other of a schoolgirl killed in a road accident involving an army patrol vehicle. Although there is a political subtext, emotion once again centres on the tragic randomness of the latter death and on the familial context of the former. The loss of the future is at issue here; the death of a child represents the end of a life not yet lived. It is in this symbolism that we find the film's controlling metaphor. A Sense of Loss is not concerned with the reasons for loss or the context in which loss has occurred, but rather the effect that loss has on people and their hopes for the future.

The film remains reticent about what shape the future might take. It does represent political viewpoints, but Ophuls chooses to do so through his interviewees, which often prompts a response to his presentation of people's personalities rather than of their arguments. The stiff, smug manner of Sir Harry Tuzo, commander of British army forces in Northern Ireland, the fussy, dismissive attitude of anti-Catholic publisher John McKeague, and the characteristic bombast of Reverend Ian Paisley screaming from his pulpit do little to represent a moderate voice for loyalism. Meanwhile, images of nationalist politician Bernadette Devlin walking by the sea, of left-wing activist Gerry O'Hare making breakfast for his children, and of the grieving family of IRA volunteer Gerald McDade give good reason for sympathy for their cause, especially when the film on the whole lacks a representation of the historical context of the struggle itself.

Stylistically, Ophuls confessed, the film was challenged by its subject. He said, "The idea is that you rush around to thirty or forty people in different towns, trying to create epic frescoes on the basis of straight interviewing." (quoted in McIlroy, 1998). Ophuls's devotion to the interview may have provided The Sorrow and the Pity with a powerful centre, but the director's understanding of, and engagement with, his subject was so much more profound in that case that interviews were merely another tool with which he probed the delicate threads of past and present. In the absence of a true understanding of Northern Ireland and its history, Ophuls was ultimately only barely more enlightening on this subject than the dozens of film and TV crews who had, as Marilyn Hyndman put it, "parachuted in for a couple of weeks" and left with footage to be used and reused in news and magazine programmes throughout the world. A Sense of Loss was nonetheless banned from broadcast by the BBC, fearful that the film would contribute to the climate of sectarian bitterness, which it sought to envision in terms of its human costs.

HARVEY O'BRIEN

See also **Ophuls, Marcel;** *Sorrow and the Pity, The*

A Sense of Loss (U.S. Swiss, Cinema X/Sociéte Suisse de Television, 1972, 135 mins.). Produced and directed by Marcel Ophuls. Edited by Marion Kraft. Director of photography: Simon Edelstein. Second unit direction by Edouard Fenwick. Assistant director: Ana Carrigan. Additional photography by Elliott Erwitt. Production manager: William Stitt. Assistant editor: Anne Lewis. Assistant cameraman: Claude Paccaud. Sound engineer: Claude Pellot. Chief electrician: Alain Borga. Chaffeur. Social guide: Robert Moon. Research Assistant: Kathy Keville. Rerecording: Richard Vorisek. Contributing journalist: John Whale of *The Sunday Times*. Executive Producer: Max Palevsky.

Further Reading

Baker, Keith, "Reporting the Conflict," in *Broadcasting in a Divided Community: Seventy Years of the BBC in Northern Ireland*, Martin McLoone (ed.), Belfast: Institute of Irish Studies, The Queen's University of Belfast, 1996.

Buruma, Ian, "Marcel Ophuls," in *Imagining Reality: The Faber Book of Documentary*, Kevin Macdonald and Mark Cousins (eds.), London and Boston: Faber, 1996.

Butler, David, *The Trouble with Reporting Northern Ireland*, Aldershot: Avebury, 1995.

Hyndman, Marilyn, "Resisting Cultural Arrest," in *Film Ireland*, November/December 1992, 16–17.

McIlroy, Brian, *Shooting to Kill: Filmmaking and the Troubles in Northern Ireland*, Wiltshire: Flicks, 1998.

Pryluck, Calvin, "Ultimately We Are All Outsiders: The Ethics of Documentary Filming," in *New Challenges for Documentary*, Alan Rosenthal (ed.), Berkeley, Los Angeles, and London: University of California Press, 1988.

SEPTEMBERWEIZEN

(Germany, Krieg, 1981)

Septemberweizen (September Wheat) is an especially notable film made by the director Peter Krieg. It brought him an international reputation as well as the Adolf-Grimme-Preis, the prestigious German TV award. The film analyses problems of American agriculture, where many farmers have to give up their small farms and even the large farming corporations do not earn enough money and are in an economic crisis. In the United States around 40,000 farmers gave up in 1978, 800 each week. The film shows that farming is closely connected to the capitalist system and is dependent on the agriculture industry, which is continually attempting to create products to streamline farming processes, such as hybrid wheat or a revolutionary fertilizer. The film remains relevant, given its complex and sustained analysis, and the fact that industrial farming remains a controversial issue.

"September wheat" refers to contracts with the wheat exchange in Chicago (harvests are sold in September). The entire American harvest is sold there, 50 percent of it intended for export. Peter Krieg follows the wheat from planning and growth through its sale to the consumer, narrating the tale in seven chapters (the number seven is a reference to the biblical story of Joseph, who saw seven fruitful years and seven years of drought). Krieg's essayistic style avoids an educational commentary, instead concentrating on interviews with people involved, while creating an intriguing montage of images, sounds, and music, which are sometimes used in an ironic way. For example, the crisis of the farmers is accompanied by the song "America, the Beautiful." Or, a montage will contrast expensive homes in the United States with photos of hungry children around the world. Many details and facts are conveyed by short radio reports offscreen, which is an original device.

Krieg succeeds in investigating many of the secrets of this business and analyzing the worldwide food problems and political crises, which are strongly related to wheat production. Only six companies controlled the U.S. market in 1980. They set the prices and decided who received wheat. Producers of seed corn developed new hybrid forms and the farmers became dependent on them. The farmers are then forced to pay high prices, and have to invest in efficient new machinery and fertilizer to obtain the most returns from their investment. However, they receive lower prices at the wheat exchange, because of overproduction. The surplus is exported to so-called Third World countries, influencing the agriculture there and manipulated by the U.S. government as a political tool.

Septemberweizen was released at the time when the environmental movement and Third World groups became influential in Germany. Although the system of industrial production has changed and become even more efficient, *Septemberweizen* is still an interesting case study, an in-depth political analysis free of ideological clichés, which tries to use film as a medium of enlightenment.

KAY HOFFMANN

See also **Krieg, Peter**

Septemberweizen / *September Wheat* (Germany, Teldoc und ZDF / Kleines Fernsehspiel, 1980, 96 mins.). Directed by Peter Krieg. Edited by Peter Krieg. Script by Peter Krieg. Sound by Peter Krieg. Mixing by Thomas Buser. Music by Rolf Riehm. Narration by Ilse Böttcher, Elenor Holder, Rolf Klein, Klaus Krauleidies, Berthold Korner, Peter Loth, and Ullo von Peinen.

Further Reading

Krieg, Peter, *Der Mensch stirbt nicht am Brot allein. Vom Weizen zum Brot zum Hunger*, Frankfurt 1984.

SERBIA AND MONTENEGRO

See **Yugoslavia (former)**

SERIOUS UNDERTAKINGS

(Australia, Helen Grace, 1983)

Serious Undertakings is one of the most complex and influential examples of theoretically informed feminist filmmaking to be produced in Australia in the 1980s. The film was groundbreaking in the way that it successfully combined formal experimentation and radical political problematics in an accessible and specifically Australian manner.

Written and directed by Helen Grace, *Serious Undertakings* was funded by the Women's Film Fund, a body specifically established in order to support less-experienced women filmmakers. The film functions as a densely layered work that references a remarkable number of theoretical and textual traditions. The title, *Serious Undertakings,* is drawn from a quote by feminist philosopher Julia Kristeva, and the five sections of the film allude to the five episodes in Sergei Eisenstein's *Battleship Potemkin* (Hoeben and Moore, 1987), a work that is referenced throughout *Serious Undertakings*. These sections resist a simple chronology and structure a complex treatise that draws together critiques of the production of national identity and history, feminist film theory, and discourses of maternity and child care.

As an experimental mode of documentary, *Serious Undertakings* questions not only phallocentric assumptions but also the tradition of expository filmmaking and the very structures of representation. The film is less concerned with revealing a preexisting reality and more focused on provoking doubts around the reliability of the documentary form. A number of male "academics" are inter-

viewed about issues such as feminism and their own positions as cultural commentators. However, subtitles that query the honesty of the speaker appear on the screen, or they are unexpectedly inserted into scenes of domesticity. One interviewee is speaking while chopping vegetables and a woman vacuuming accompanies another. Eventually the authenticity of the interview is thrown into doubt. Early in the film a voice-over states, "She just wanted to make a film about child care." From this self-reflexive point, *Serious Undertakings* becomes not a document exploring child care, but an examination of the discourses that construct the position of women. This is achieved through a montage of sound and image. Henry Lawson's

Serious Undertakings, 1983.
[*Still courtesy of the British Film Institute*]

colonial short story "The Drover's Wife" and classic images in Australian art are interweaved with representations that rely on the construction of women and children as the embodiment of passivity and innocence, such as *Battleship Potemkin* and reported acts of terrorism.

Although a number of documentaries dealing with issues of gender were produced in the early 1980s in Australia, many, such as *For Love or Money* (1983) and *Bread and Dripping* (1982), remained entrenched in a humanist tradition. These films were often charged with failing to adequately question the representational codes they employed. Although *Serious Undertakings* did attempt to destabilise spectator/text relations, the film has also been critiqued for insufficiently confronting an essentialist feminine image (Hoeben and Moore, 1987). Nevertheless, *Serious Undertakings* firmly established a place for Australia in international feminist avant-garde filmmaking and it can be understood alongside works such as *Thriller* (1980), *Daughter Rite* (1978), and *Riddles of the Sphinx* (1977).

BELINDA SMAILL

See also **For Love or Money**

Serious Undertakings (Australia, Women's Film Fund [AFC], 1983, 28 mins). Distributed by Ronin Films (Aust/NZ) and Circles (UK). Produced by Erika Addis. Written and directed by Helen Grace. Cinematography by Erika Addis. Edited by Sara Bennett. Sound by John Cruthers.

Further Reading

Blonski, Annette, and Freda Freiberg, "Double Trouble: Women's Films" in *The Australian Screen*, Albert Moran and Tom O'Regan (eds.), Melbourne: Penguin Books, 1989, 191–215.
Dermody, Susan, "Not Necessarily a Lead Dress: Thinking Beyond 'Redress' in Women's Films" in *Signs of Independents: Ten Years of the Creative Development Fund*, Megan McMurchy and Jennifer Stott (eds.), Sydney: Australian Film Commission, 1988, 11–15.
Hoeben, Collette, and Catriona Moore, "*Serious Undertakings*: An Inventory of Old Wives' Tales" in *Don't Shoot Darling!: Women's Independent Filmmaking in Australia*, Annette Blonski, Barbara Creed, and Freda Freiberg (eds.), Melbourne: Greenhouse, 1987, 371–379.
Lawson, Sylvia, "Serious Undertakings" in *An Australian Film Reader*, Albert Moran and Tom O'Regan (eds.), Sydney: Currency Press, 1985, 327–332.
Martin, Adrian, "Indefinite Objects: Independent Film and Video" in *The Australian Screen*, Albert Moran and Tom O'Regan (eds.), Melbourne: Penguin Books, 1989, 172–190.
O'Regan, Tom, *Australian National Cinema*, London: Routledge, 1996.

SETA, VITTORIO DE

Sicilian director Vittorio De Seta has been active in the field of documentary film since the 1950s. De Seta's cinema, which may be thought of as poetic anthropology, owes much to Grierson's educational conception of the director's role, and bears a resemblance to Flaherty's work in its attention to nature and the reality of human life, as well as in its ethical ambition of discovering the human story. Even so, De Seta's cinema is utterly original for the creative and narrative function that it assigns to the editing of images and, particularly, of sound, the latter always having a leading role in the construction of rhythm and meaning in his films. De Seta's understanding of southern popular culture is diametrically opposite to mainstream ideological discourse wherein the South is depicted as an irredeemably backward land of poverty, crime, and illiteracy, a burden to the industrialized and progressive North. Following in the footsteps of realist writers such as Giovanni Verga (*I Malavoglia*) and of filmmakers such as Luchino Visconti (*La terra trema / The Earth Trembles*, 1948), De Seta polemically portrays the southern condition as a complex, millennial culture that has died a violent death.

De Seta's work can be roughly divided into four periods: the self-produced 35mm short documentaries made between 1954 and 1959, set in Sicily, Sardinia, and Calabria, a phase concluded by the docufiction *Banditi a Orgosolo* (*Bandits at Orgosolo,* 1961); the fiction, including the highly successful film for television *Diario di un maestro*

(*A Schoomaster's Diary,* 1973); the 16mm documentaries for television, mostly produced by RAI, the Italian public broadcasting service, from 1978 to 1983; and the return to the cinema after ten years of silence with the documentary *In Calabria* (1993).

The 1950s in Italy saw the production of hundreds of documentaries every year, thanks to a law that encouraged a vast production but did not set up criteria for discrimination or quality control. In this context, De Seta's early shorts stand out as innovative and eccentric in their poetic and technical characteristics. Their combination of techniques were widely perceived as conflicting—the "realism" of the subject matter and of the sound, and the "unrealism" of colour and cinemascope—was and were very unusual compared with traditional Italian documentaries. Their subject matter consisted of

> the catching of swordfish in the Strait of Messina, the tuna processing station, the sulphur mine, the sacred representation at Easter, the fishing boats in the Sicilian Channel, the Barbagia shepherds, the peasants harvesting and threshing grain, the 'forgotten people' of a little village in Calabria, are taken away from historical immediacy, from social phenomenology, from political dialectics, and restored to the long, unforgettable time in which those gestures, those rites, that culture were formed and took on a precise identity.
>
> (Consolo, 1995: 37)

Real voices, songs, and sounds were recorded on the set and then mixed in studio—a highly unusual practice at a time when the majority of Italian documentaries adopted the mix of voice-over and studio-recorded music. De Seta's early documentaries, bar the last one of the series, *I dimenticati* (*The Forgotten Ones,* 1959), were instead completely devoid of voice-over, in an attempt to let reality speak for itself. Another way in which De Seta went against mainstream conventions was by using colour at a time when this was seen as an unnecessary luxury for documentaries, and also as an unrealistic device; and by adopting the cinemascope: "It was my impression that the wide screen, together with the colour, helped me in presenting those 'landscapes.' This wideness, this 180-degree look, exalted the realism of the representation, even if it was daring to go and light up the mines and then film them in cinemascope" (De Seta, quoted in Fofi and Volpi, 1999: 14, my translation). It must be said that this innovatory attitude is not accompanied by a revolutionary ideological stance. An "aristocratic" author akin to Visconti, De Seta

does not share the latter's articulation of a Marxist viewpoint in film, and instead frees the narration of any ideological superimposed reading, in an attempt to reach the truth that emerges "naturally" from faces, actions, and sounds.

Whereas the early ten- and eleven-minute shorts were typically constructed around the twelve hours of daylight, from dawn to sunset, *Banditi a Orgosolo* is a black-and-white ninety-eight–minute feature with a story that spans a few days. Shot with a troupe consisting only of himself, his wife and collaborator Vera Gherarducci, cameraman Luciano Tovoli, and casting true Sardinian shepherds, the film is a lucid analysis of the phenomenon of the Sardinian bandits, and of their clash with the alien logic of the State. As in the shorts, it is the silences, the sounds, the gestures, and the environment that take centre stage, making this film a docufiction that impressed the jury and audience of the 1961 Venice Film Festival. *Banditi a Orgosolo* won the prize for the best debut film, and the critic of the *Cahiers du cinéma* described it as the only revelation of the festival (Douchet, 1961). Notable among the documentaries for television produced by RAI is *La Sicilia rivisitata* (*Sicily Revisited,* 1980), which returns to the settings of the early documentaries only to find that the ancient traditions, rites, and work practices have disappeared, leaving behind an incommensurable void.

After ten years of silence, due to the death of his wife and main collaborator, to two operations on his eyes, and to a deep discontent for the direction taken by the Western world, he returned to the cinema with *In Calabria,* a documentary that programmatically highlights the contrast between the sparse surviving areas of an ancient, peaceful culture that functioned in tune with nature, and the questionable "modernization without progress" of this region, with the monsters that it produced—loss of roots and traditions, emigration, environmental degradation, organized crime, and unemployment.

LAURA RASCAROLI

Biography

Born in Palermo (Sicily), October 15, 1923. Studied architecture in Rome, 1941. Joined the Navy, 1943. Arrested by the German Army after September 8, sent to a camp near Salzburg, from which he attempted three times to escape. Returned to Rome after the liberation, 1945. Joined the Italian Communist Party, 1947. Made his debut in the cinema as assistant director of Jean-Paul Le Chanois, 1953. His wife and main collaborator, Vera Gherarducci, died in 1979. Had two eye operations in the 1980s. Moved to a family residence in Sellia Marina, Calabria.

Selected Films

1954 *Pasqua in Sicilia (Easter in Sicily)*: director, photographer, editor, producer
1954 *Lu tempu di li pisci spata (The Swordfish Season)*: director, photographer, editor, producer
1955 *Isole di fuoco (Islands of Fire)*: director, photographer, editor, producer
1955 *Surfarara (Sulphur Mines)*: director, photographer, editor, producer
1959 *I dimenticati (The Forgotten Ones)*: director, photographer, editor, producer
1961 *Banditi a Orgosolo (Bandits at Orgosolo)*: director, photographer, editor, producer
1980 *La Sicilia rivisitata (Sicily Revisited)*: director, photographer, editor
1993 *In Calabria*: director, photographer, editor

Further Reading

Consolo, Vincenzo, "De Seta's Use of the Verga Method," in *Il cinema di Vittorio De Seta/The Films of Vittorio De Seta*, Alessandro Rais (ed.), Palermo: Giuseppe Maimone Editore, 1995.
Douchet, Jean, "Le bandit d'Orgosolo." in *Cahiers du cinéma*, October 1961.
Farassino, Alberto, "De Seta: The 'grand form' of the documentary, in *Il cinema di Vittorio De Seta/The Films of Vittorio De Seta*, Alessandro Rais (ed.), Palermo: Giuseppe Maimone Editore, 1995.
Fofi, Goffredo, and Gianni Volpi, *Vittorio De Seta. Il mondo perduto*, Turin: Lindau, 1999.
Maffettone, Alberto, and Enrico Soci (eds.), *Vittorio De Seta. Una vita d'autore*, Bassano del Grappa: Istituto Paolo Valmarana, 1989.

79 SPRINGTIMES OF HO CHI MINH

(Cuba, Alvarez, 1967)

79 primaveras (79 Springs) is one of a number of films by Alvarez from the 1960s in which the leading documentarist of the Cuban Revolution seems to reinvent the agitprop of Soviet cinema in the 1920s. An incomparably poetic tribute to the Vietnamese leader Ho Chi Minh, the title refers to his age at the time of his death. The film takes the form of a biographical resumé of the principal dates in Ho Chi Minh's political life; decorative titles announce the passing years interspersed among archive footage and other inter-titles inscribed with lines of Ho Chi Minh's poetry.

The opening is beautifully constructed: First come slow-motion shots of flowers opening, then a shot of bombs dropping almost gracefully through the sky. The screen goes blank and we hear the human cry of a singer. After the first credit, a negative image of the young Ho Chi Minh appears, which transforms itself into a positive image and then dissolves into close-ups. These close-ups are refilmed on an optical camera to become somewhat grainy, which at the same time serves to emphasize their material nature and intensify the plasticity of the image. We see Ho Chi Minh aging, the image returns to the negative, the screen turns a brilliant white, and the titles resume. At the end of the credits, we see a close-up of Ho sitting in the open air at his typewriter. A title, "They tied my legs with a rope," is followed by a shot of him washing his feet; another title, "And they tied my arms," is followed by a close-up of his hands rolling a cigarette—a man, the montage says, like any other.

When the biographical resumé reaches the victory of Dien Bien Phu, the film begins to shift gear. The Internationale is heard and we see the faces of international Communist leaders at the funeral. We cut to a popular Cuban performer singing, "The era is giving birth to a heart, it is dying of pain and can stand no more . . ." and her audience of cheerful Vietnamese children. The scene is violently interrupted by bombs and the devastation of napalm. Over horrific images of children's burned faces and bodies the music becomes violent and discordant. A title declares: "They began to kill in order to win." Then, in slow motion, one of the most infamous images of the Vietnam War, a couple of North American soldiers beating a Vietnamese who has collapsed on the ground: We see feet and hands and the rifle butts of his attackers, but not their faces. Then: "And now they kill because they cannot win." No one has ever commented on the Vietnam War with greater economy or dignity.

From here the film moves to shots of anti-war demonstrators in the United States holding placards that unequivocally establish a universal message: "Vietnam, Watts, it's the same struggle," "Avenge Che," and "Fuck the draft." Then another of the most notorious media images of Vietnam—a pair of GIs taking souvenir snapshots of their victims on the battlefield, to which Alvarez attaches another piece of poetry by Ho Chi Minh—and in these lines the film knits its imagery together:

Without the glacial winter, without grief and death,
Who can appreciate your glory, Spring?
The pains which temper my spirit are a crucible
And they forge my heart in pure steel.

At this point, many a filmmaker would have been content to conclude—but not Alvarez, who has the nerve, or the chutzpah, to proceed with more scenes of the funeral, set to the music of Iron Butterfly. This is not simply a grand aesthetic gesture. Since the film was made in a period when sectarians were vocal and Western pop music was banned from Cuban airwaves, Alvarez is making pointed solidarity with popular U.S. protest music.

And then comes the *coup de grâce*. A new title appears: "Don't let disunity in the Socialist camp darken the future." Using animation, the title is torn apart into little pieces that slide off the edges of the frame to leave the screen blank. The music disappears. A gunshot announces a split-screen, multi-image sequence of war footage, freeze frames, scratches, sprocket holes, flashes, guns, planes, bombs, sounds of battle with electric keyboard noises on the sound track, in which brutal reality bursts through the limits of its portrayal on celluloid in an unrelenting and terrifying assault that ends in the annihilation of a freeze frame, which burns up before our eyes, again leaving a blank white screen. And then? The torn pieces of the title reappear and join up again. The

picture cuts to rockets firing, to the accompaniment of energizing music by Bach; bursts of gunfire flash across the screen, the flowers reappear, and a final title appears: "The Yanquis defeated we will construct a Fatherland ten times more beautiful."

If *79 primaveras* is a testimonial of the solidarity that the Cubans felt with the Vietnamese in their struggle against the same enemy, it is also a paradigm of Alvarez's revolutionary aesthetics. Politically an orthodox Marxist-Leninist-Fidelista, artistically Alvarez had a strong anarchistic streak that made him distrustful of conventions, schools, and aesthetic orthodoxy. Instead, he reinvented the newsreel, the compilation film, the travelog, and every other documentary genre he laid hands on in an irrepressible frenzy of filmic bricolage licensed by that supreme act of bricolage—the Cuban Revolution. He learned to raid the archives and incorporate what he found into a pithy, intelligent, didactic montage, in which, abandoning the all-knowing voice of the commentary, he replaced it with something much more playful and open, something that mobilized the cultural gains of the Revolution's literacy campaign: the animation of words on the screen. The result was a dynamic style where deconstruction meets anti-imperialism in a fusion of politics and poetry.

MICHAEL CHANAN

79 Primaveras (79 Springtimes of Ho Chi Minh) (Cuba, ICAIC, 1967, 21 mins.). Directed by Santiago Alvarez. Photography by Iván Nápoles. Special effects by Jorge Pucheux, Pedro Luis Hernández, Pepín Rodríguez, and Santiago Penate. Location recording by Raúl Pérez Ureta. Editing by Norma Torrado. Sound and music editing by Isalberto Gálvez. Sound engineer: Carlos Fernández. Archive material: Hanoi Film Studios, Texts y Ho-Ch-Ming and Jose Martí.

Further Reading

Chanan, Michael, *Cuban Cinema*, Minneapolis: University of Minnesota Press, 2004.
Chanan, Michael (ed.), *Santiago Alvarez*, BFI Dossier No. 2, London: BFI, 1980.
Hess, John, "Santiago Alvarez: Cine-Agitator for the Cuban Revolution and the Third World," in *"Show Us Life," Toward a History and Aesthetics of the Committed Documentary*, Thomas Waugh (ed.), Metuchen, NJ and London: Scarecrow Press, 1984.
Mraz, John, "Santiago Alvarez: From Dramatic Form to Direct Cinema," in *The Social Documentary in Latin America*, Julianne Burton (ed.), Pittsburgh: University of Pittsburgh Press, 1990.

SEYBOLD, KATRIN

Katrin Seybold is one of Germany's most politically engaged documentarists. To date she has made over fifty films that champion the cause of the political outsider, including children, dissidents, Gypsies, and Jews. Her most celebrated cause is the historical persecution of the Roma and Sinti (Gypsies) by the Nazis and the continuing discrimination against this minority. Seybold and Melanie Spitta, a Sinteza who serves as Seybold's consultant and co-director, have produced four films on the Sinti and Roma. The first and second, *Schimpft uns nicht Ziguener* (*Don't Call Us Gypsies*, 1980) and *Wir sind Sinti Kinder und keine Zigeuner* (*We Are Sinti Children and Not Gypsies*, 1981), focus on contemporary Gypsy life and negative attitudes of the general populace toward Gypsy culture. The third and fourth, *Es ging Tag und Nacht, liebes Kind. Zigeuner (Sinti) in Auschwitz* [*It Went on Day and Night, Dear Child: Gypsies (Sinti) in Auschwitz*, 1982] and *Das falsche Wort* (*Calumny*, 1987), focus on the nature of Nazi persecution and its echo in official policies that deny reparations to the Gypsies.

Seybold's films make clear that historical and contemporary attitudes toward Gypsies have two major origins: general ignorance about Gypsy culture and received perceptions that distort their culture. Accordingly, her films inform viewers who may know little or nothing about Gypsies. She includes vignettes of home life to correct the cultural and historical stereotypes that have resulted from centuries of cultural and historical misinformation. Thus her films show Gypsies working, studying, and celebrating family life. Absent are the negative images, first encountered in sixteenth-century literature, of the Gypsy as lazy, sneaky, dirty, and promiscuous. Also absent is the nineteenth-century romantic image of the Gypsy as musically inclined and sensual. Seybold's Gypsies are the same as the German viewer, except they desire to be left alone. That is, they ask that society accept them but not assimilate them.

Seybold's engagement with individuals and groups she feels are left out of the political power structure are the strength and weakness of her style, which is especially apparent in her films on the Sinti and Roma. The rhetoric of the titles reveals from the start that Seybold does not pretend to project objectivity. The films confront viewers with accusations that they turned away from racial genocide, condone the continued use of racial slur, and support government lies. On the one hand, the sympathy she brings to her subjects gives her work an impassioned voice and urgency often missing from the documentary form. On the other hand, her commitment to her subjects has also led to accusations that she "lacks distance." And indeed her films play like broadsides rather than documented reality. Of equal concern is that the lack of objectivity creates its own stereotype—a monolithic, homogeneous world of Gypsies. It is a world that ignores crime, ignores drugs, and for the most part ignores internal dissent. The depiction of Gypsies comes perilously close to the romantic era's noble savage, in particular as it has been manifested in the modern liberal's view of the American Indian or other patronized minorities.

Other Seybold films include *Seit ich weiß, daß ich nicht mehr lange lebe, bin ich Stark. Aidskranke berichten* (*Since I Found Out That I Won't Live Much Longer, I Am Strong. Reports from AIDS Patients*, 1987), a television documentary in the series *Kontakte* (*Contacts*); *Deutsch ist meine Muttersprache. Deutsche Juden errinnern sich an ihre christliche Mitbürger* (*German Is My Native Language. German Jews Remember Their Christian Neighbors*, 1990), a television documentary; *Alle Juden raus! Judenverfolgung in einer deutschen Kleinstadt 1933–1945* (*All Jews Out! The Persecution of the Jews in a Small German Town from 1933–1945*, 1990); and *Nein! Zeugen des Widerstandes in München 1933–1945* (*No! Witnesses of the Resistance in Munich 1933–1945*, 1998).

ROBERT C. REIMER

Biography

Born in 1943. Learned filmmaking with Edgar Reitz, among others. Founded her own production company in 1979. Makes television programs on various social issues. Recognized for her documentary films on the persecution of the Roma and Sinti by the Nazi regime, and the continuing discrimination suffered by this minority.

Selected Films

1980: *Schimpft uns nicht Ziguener (Don't Call Us Gypsies)*
1981: *Wir sind Sinti Kinder und keine Zigeuner (We Are Sinti Children and Not Gypsies)*
1982: *Es ging Tag und Nacht, liebes Kind. Zigeuner (Sinti) in Auschwitz [It Went on Day and Night, Dear Child: Gypsies (Sinti) in Auschwitz]*
1987: *Das falsche Wort (Calumny)*
1987: *Seit ich weiß, daß ich nicht mehr lange lebe, bin ich Stark. Aidskranke berichten (Since I Found Out That I Won't Live Much Longer, I Am Strong. Reports from AIDS Patients)*
1990: *Deutsch ist meine Muttersprache. Deutsche Juden errinnern sich an ihre christliche Mitbürger (German Is My Native Language. German Jews Remember Their Christian Neighbors)*
1990: *Alle Juden raus! Judenverfolgung in einer deutschen Kleinstadt 1933–1945 (All Jews Out! The Persecution of the Jews in a Small German Town from 1933–1945)*
1998: *Nein! Zeugen des Widerstandes in München 1933–1945 (No! Witnesses of the Resistance in Munich 1933–1945)*

Further Reading

"Katrin Seybold—Dokumentarfilm Regisseurin," in *Cine-Graph: Lexikon zum deutschsprachigen Film*, Hans-Michael Bock (ed.), Munich.
Reimer, Robert C., and Carol J. Reimer, *Nazi-retro Film: How German Narrative Cinema Remembers the Past*, Boston: Twayne Publishers, 1992, 165–166.

SHANNON, KATHLEEN

From its inception in 1939, Canada's National Film Board (NFB) had regularly produced documentaries on women's topics. Well into the 1960s these tended to reflect a patriarchal *de haut en bas* approach. However, the burgeoning feminist movement occasioned deep attitudinal changes throughout North American society, and the NFB was not immune. If any one figure came to symbolize a new articulation of the female condition on film, it was producer/director Kathleen Shannon.

Shannon was dismissive of the NFB's professed policy of detached objectivity, regarding it as institutional, fence-sitting blandness. Her attitude toward the director's role was diametrically opposed to that of the increasingly fashionable cult of the auteur. She was adamant that her position as producer be perceived as one of team coordinator, appreciative of the sensitivities of subjects before the camera. She was insistent on personal involvement in the promotion of the finished product through traditional outlets. In this last regard, her thinking ran contrary to that of her superiors. By the mid-1970s, NFB films were finding a larger audience on television than in the time-honoured method of viewing in classrooms and community centres. Her series of ten documentaries on the social and economic demands faced by women reentering the workforce, *Working Mothers* (1974), was not telecast at her insistence. She felt their impact would be dulled by the ambiance of television spectatorship, with its commercial interruptions, focus on ratings, and instant competition from other channels. Attitudes were more likely to be formed, changed, or concentrated when a targeted audience was exposed to the topic in a communal setting without distraction.

The critical and popular success of *Working Mothers* and the Canadian government's decision to give special recognition to International Women's Year, 1975, prompted Shannon to lobby for a production unit devoted almost exclusively to women's and family issues, again with output intended primarily for nontheatrical venues. The idea came to fruition with Studio D. An overwhelmingly female staff, coupled with a self-proclaimed mandate to explore "decades, centuries, millennia of repressed or forgotten history and meanings" gave rise to criticism that the NFB had created a feminist cultural enclave where even sympathetic male filmmakers were less than welcome. Nevertheless, under Shannon's tutelage, it rapidly became the most widely recognized and controversial arm of the NFB. *Not a Love Story* (1981), a scathing condemnation of pornography, gained notoriety by being banned in two provinces. It became, perhaps not coincidentally, the highest grossing film in NFB history. *If You Love This Planet* (1982), a graphically illustrated, pro-nuclear disarmament lecture by activist

Dr. Helen Caldicott, elicited government protest in both Canada and the United States for its perceived special pleading.

While Kathleen Shannon raised the profile of female filmmakers in Canada, her mission to create a truly feminist "counter-cinema" faltered. With contemporary subjects, there tended to be an easy progression in the flow of events that suggested containment and completion, although reality was often far less ordered or coherent. A more theoretically informed approach, especially to historical themes, such as *The Burning Times* (on the persecution of witches), might have placed as much emphasis on the structural and deep-rooted causes of women's oppression as on their effects.

JAMES M. SKINNER

See also **National Film Board of Canada; Studio D**

Biography

Born in Vancouver, Canada, 1935. Music cataloguer for Crawley Films, 1952. Joined the National Film Board of Canada in1956 as sound and music editor. Directed her first film, *Goldwood,* in 1970. Founded Studio D, 1974. Acted as executive producer of Studio D, 1974–1986. Retired from the NFB, 1992. Died 1998.

Further Reading

Evans, Gary, *In The National Interest: A Chronicle of the National Film Board of Canada from 1949 to 1989*, Toronto: University of Toronto Press, 1991.
Gwyn, Richard, and Sandra Gwyn, "The Politics of Peace," *Saturday Night*, May 1984.
Hartt, L., "Working Mothers Series," in *Cinema Canada*, III, no. 15, August–September, 1974.
Macerola, Francois, *Five Year Operational Plan*, Montreal: National Film Board, 1984.

SHEFFIELD FILM CO-OP

The Sheffield Film Co-op was established in 1975 as a women's film cooperative by a small group of women who were involved in the Women's Movement in Sheffield. Founding members were Christine Bellamy, Jenny Woodley, Gill Booth, and Barbara Fowkes. None of them were professional filmmakers. This was a time when a socialist film movement was flourishing in Britain, the most prominent of which was Cinema Action, established as a result of the events in France in May 1968, and Amber Film Collective. None of these socialist groups had a specific women's agenda apart from the short-lived London Women's Film Group (1972–1977), whose members had mostly worked in the film industry and were making feminist films consciously addressing cultural film issues.

The aim of the Sheffield Film Co-op was to make campaigning films and videos that would challenge what the co-op saw as the stereotyped images of women in the media. However, they distanced themselves from the experimentation of the London Women's Film Group. They evolved from a larger group of women who had made a six-part series, *Not Just A Pretty Face,* on women's issues for BBC radio Sheffield. They began with two simple programmes for local cable TV: how child minders needed to be registered and the lack of access for pushchairs in Sheffield. The decision to set up independently as the Sheffield Film Co-op arose because the cable TV station, organised by men, were uncomfortable with their next proposal to make a programme in defense of abortion, at a time when a bill was coming before Parliament to restrict abortion rights.

The group at this time, in keeping with the philosophy of the Women's Movement, worked collectively and shared skills. Their lack of training is evident in *A Woman Like You* (1976), funded by Yorkshire Arts and the British Pregnancy Advisory Service. It is a drama documentary about a pregnant married woman with two children who tries unsuccessfully to get an abortion on the National Health Service; the film takes a clear position on behalf of the woman who is ignored and humiliated. It uses a social realist style and the actors deliver their lines flatly. It follows the woman's visits to two patronising male doctors, one of whom refuses her an abortion while examining her lying prone on a bed. The primary aim of the film was to create discussion and to help train abortion counselors. Like all campaigning films it was seen as having a short life and having a specific function. It was shown in community centres, trade union meetings, and adult education centres. Most centres had a film projector and it was easy to take the film to places where women gathered.

After this success, over the next few years, surviving on small grants, the group made campaigning and educational films, addressing issues such as battered women and the stereotyping of women's jobs. At first resistant to the Independent Filmmakers Association, which was a large umbrella group of independent filmmakers, because of what they saw as their overtheoretical approach, they eventually joined and in 1980 they registered as a workers' cooperative. *A Question of Choice* (1982) begins to establish a more reflexive style. It is a portrait of a group of low-paid women workers—two cleaners, a cook, and a lollipop lady—and a male caretaker in a school in Sheffield. The women do this work because they see their families as their first priority and rely on the man to represent them to improve working conditions. The film was shot without sound or lights and recorded interviews were added later to accompany images of the women at work. This gives it a more intimate, personal feel.

By the mid-1980s, as the group became more experienced and technically proficient, the tensions around cooperative working and the type of films they wanted to make grew. One part of the group wanted to continue making educational films and another wanted to do wider things. Members left and others joined. In 1982 the group became an ACTT Franchised Workshop. (ACTT was the professional film workers' union at the time.) The ACTT operated a closed shop within the industry and the franchise meant that the co-op could now apply for funding and show their films on television. In 1984 they received their first large amount of funding to make a longer film, *Red Skirts On Clydeside*.

The film is about the Glasgow Rent Strike led by women in 1915 during the First World War. It is structured around interviews and photographs documenting the history of the strike, and there is a tentative attempt at reflexivity through the filmmakers' difficulties in researching the women's role in the strike and by using their voices to narrate the film and question the interviewees. It plays a valuable role in excavating women's leadership in an important historical event but the images are burdened with an overly didactic narration.

This was the first film to credit individuals (the directors were Jenny Woodley and Christine Bel-

lamy) but not all the members were happy with the results because of the constraints of cooperative working. However, the group overcame some of the problems of specialism by bringing in professional women crews from outside the group to take on specific roles. This film was used on women's history courses and also shown on Ch4 television; after that, the group began to orientate some of their films toward television.

Diamonds in Brown Paper (1988) returns to the drama documentary format. In social realist style it follows a group of women "buffers" who work polishing cutlery and silver in Sheffield from 1928 to the present day. A series of dramatic episodes shows two workers from their entry into work as young girls, through to their retirement. Intercut is archive footage and popular songs to mark the passing of time. It gives a good insight into changes in work, but the thirty-year time scale prevents it reaching the depths it needs.

The importance of the Sheffield Film Co-operative was its work as women for women. The women took their films directly to women for screening and discussion. They discovered long forgotten women's history and were a group of strong independent women in direct opposition to the mainstream male-dominated film industry. The co-operative continued to make films and videos until 1991 when it was disbanded.

JILL DANIELS

See also **Cinema Action**

Selected Films

1972 *Serve and Obey* (London Women's Film Group)
1972 *Bettshanger '72* (London Women's Film Group)
1974 *Mai* (Amber Films)
1974/1975 *The Miners Film* (Cinema Action)
1975 *The Nightcleaners* (Berwick Street Film Collective)
1976 *A Woman Like You* (Sheffield Film Co-op)
1977 *Class Struggle: Film from the Clyde* (Cinema Action)
1979 *Jobs for the Girls* (Sheffield Film Co-op)
1982 *A Question of Choice* (Sheffield Film Co-op)
1983 *Red Skirts on Clydeside* (Directors: Jenny Woodley, Christine Bellamy, Sheffield Film Co-op)
1985 Bringing It all Back Home (Sheffield Film Co-op)
1988 *Diamonds in Brown Paper* (Director: Gill Booth, Sheffield Film Co-op)
1990 *Thankyou* (Director: Christine Bellamy, Sheffield Film Co-op)
1991 *Running Gay* (Director: Maya Chowdhry, Sheffield Film Co-op)

Further Reading

Dickinson, Margaret, *Rogue Reels, Oppositional Film in Britain, 1945–90*, BFI Publishing, 1999, 41, 53, 289–303.

SHELL FILM UNIT

In 1933 John Grierson, then head of the General Post Office Film Unit (GPO), presented a report on the potential uses of film to the Shell Marketing and Refining Company. The report led to the creation of the Shell Film Unit, which would be highly regarded for its films on scientific and technological subjects. It was the first documentary unit to be formed directly by an industry. Shell's interest in films derived from Jack Beddington, who as assistant general manager and director of publicity for Shell-Mex and British Petroleum (the marketing side of Shell International) was responsible for his company's consistently high publicity standards. (He would become head of the Films Division of the Ministry of Information during World War II.)

At the GPO, Edgar Anstey was moved off the production of *6:30 Collection* early in 1934 to establish the new unit. He planned and equipped the premises, selected staff, and undertook production. In 1936 Anstey was succeeded by Arthur Elton, who maintained a life-long connection with films sponsored by the oil industry. Subsequently, while at Film Centre, he became production consultant and supervisor to the Petroleum Films Bureau and the Shell Film Unit. He developed the latter into what was said to be the best technical film production organization in the world.

Shell Film Unit's first film was *Airport* (Roy Lockwood, 1935) but *Power Unit* (D'Arcy Cartwright, 1937) was its first substantial success. Its success was followed by that of *Transfer of Power* (Geoffrey Bell, 1939), which explains with remarkable clarity and precision the development of the toothed wheel. It and the six-part *How an Aeroplane Flies* (1947), and *The Cornish Engine* (Philip Armitage, 1948), and other outstanding Shell films were all produced by Elton. Francis Rodker's animated diagrams made an important contribution to such Shell films. It was at Shell that Elton demonstrated most fully his "unique gift for presenting a logical, lucid, and, above all, economical account of scientific phenomena and processes," as Anstey put it.

Shell Cinemagazine ran for twenty issues between 1938 and 1952 (interrupted by the war, when the Shell unit, with Anstey again the producer, worked for the Ministry of Information and the Admiralty). Later, the unit's wide range of subjects included the historical compilation *Powered Flight* (1953), *The Rival World* (Bert Haanstra, 1955), on the insect menace, *Song of the Clouds* (John Armstrong, 1956), and *Unseen Enemies* (Michael Clark, 1959), on disease control—all produced by Stuart Legg.

The films carried no advertising and listed Shell's name only in the credit titles. They gained a high reputation, particularly among educators. On Elton's advice, Shell began to distribute its productions nontheatrically through Petroleum Films Bureau in Britain and through Asiatic Petroleum Company in a number of foreign countries. Special versions were prepared in Dutch, French, Hungarian, Italian, German, Portuguese, and Swedish. In the countries covered, libraries of Shell films were established, and the films were loaned in sets to schools and other similar institutions. Film shows were also arranged for various adult agencies. By the 1970s it had eighty-seven film libraries, with every film in thirty languages. Elton thought it the largest single core of films made from a single-minded point of view that there was in the world, excepting the National Film Board of Canada.

JACK C. ELLIS

See also **Anstey, Edgar; Beddington, Jack; Elton, Arthur; Film Centre (UK); Grierson, John; Legg, Stuart**

Selected Films

1935 *Airport* (Roy Lockwood, director)
1937 *Power Unit* (D'Arcy Cartwright, director)
1939 *Transfer of Power* (Geoffrey Bell, director)
1947 *How an Aeroplane Flies*
1948 *The Cornish Engine* (Philip Armitage, director)
1953 *Powered Flight* (Bert Haanstra, director)
1955 *The Rival World* (Bert Haanstra, director)
1956 *Song of the Clouds* (John Armstrong, director)
1959 *Unseen Enemies* (Michael Clark, director)

Further Reading

Sussex, Elizabeth, *The Rise and Fall of British Documentary: The Story of the Film Movement Founded by John Grierson*, Berkeley: University of California Press, 1975.

SHINJUKU BOYS

(Japan, Longinotto, 1995)

Filmed in Shinjuku, Tokyo's queer commercial district, *Shinjuku Boys* focuses on the lives of three *onnabes*, women who live as men and who work as "hosts" for female clients at the New Marilyn Club. The film marks the continued investigation of gender and sexuality in contemporary Japan by the documentary filmmaking team of Kim Longinotto and Jano Williams. Their films are explicitly concerned with women whose lives challenge prevalent assumptions about sex and gender in Japan.

Longinotto and Williams have collaborated on documentaries about Japanese women since *Eat the Kimono*, their 1989 documentary portrait of outspoken feminist and anti-imperial performer Hanayagi Genshu. *Shinjuku Boys* is the second of three films that the duo made in the 1990s about female gender transgression in Japan. *Dream Girls* (1993) explores the world of the Takarazuka Revue, an enormously popular musical theater in which young women play the roles of both sexes. *Gaea Girls* (1999) documents the grueling training regime of aspiring female wrestlers in a camp outside Tokyo.

In all three films, Longinotto and Williams employ a mix of interactive and observational documentary modes, combining interviews with closely observed pro-filmic action. Shot by a low-impact, three-woman crew, Longinotto and Williams's films frequently produce a sense of relaxed intimacy and trust between the filmmakers and their subjects. While *Dream Girls* and *Gaea Girls* furnish their depiction of particular institutions (the Takarazuka theater school and the Gaea training camp) with representative individual portraits of women within them, *Shinjuku Boys* is explicitly presented as a documentary about three particular women, Gaish, Tatsu, and Kazuki. The film's pre-credit sequence introduces its "characters" individually: Gaish is dressing up in front of a mirror, Kazuki is binding his breasts, and Tatsu is at the barber's. At the end of each of these shots, the frame freezes and the subject's name appears across the image.

In a group interview early in the film, the three *onnabes* are asked to characterize each other. They agree that Gaish is the "tough guy," Kazuku, the "cuddly type," and Tatsu, the "good-time guy." While this scene performs a conventional documentary shortcut in distinguishing individual subjects as "character types," *Shinjuku Boys* does not use them for their common documentary function: to facilitate an overarching narrative plot for the film. Rather, these self-characterizations provide the basis on which the film develops its portrayal of the genuine diversity among *onnabes* in terms of their sexual and gender identities. Although *Shinjuku Boys* does use a disembodied female voice-over narration (read in English by Shuko Noguchi), the film restricts it to providing only the most basic expository information. Most of the knowledge the viewer receives about these "Shinjuku boys" comes either from direct address interviews or observed conversations, including one particularly powerful scene in which Kazuki calls up and reconnects with his estranged mother.

Gaish relishes his womanizing role, maintaining several ongoing relationships with clients outside the club. Yet he declares in an interview that he neither wishes to undergo hormone treatment nor identify as a lesbian. His relationship to his clients relies on maintaining the illusion of maleness, which necessitates keeping his clothes on during sex and never letting the client touch him sexually. Both Kazuki and Tatsu are in long-term relationships sustained outside the culture of the New Marilyn Club. Kazuki lives with Kumi, a male-to-female postoperative transsexual, who is a well-known dancer at a local drag bar (one scene is devoted to Kumi's stage performance with Kazuki proudly watching from the bar). Interviewed together in an intimate medium shot, they frankly describe the relationship's blurring of gender roles and its nongenital sexuality. Tatsu has taken male hormones for several years and lives with Tomoe, a nineteen-year-old female student, whom he met at the club. Their interview together is framed in an even more intimate manner by Longinotto's camerawork, which frames only the subject currently speaking, panning whenever the other subject interjects. Tatsu speaks of his desire to know what it feels like to live and have sex as a biological male, while Tomoe adds that if it could happen even for just one day, they would be able to conceive a child together and start a family.

Shinjuku Boys compellingly demonstrates the performativity of gender. The frequent scenes showing the three *onnabes* grooming, dressing up, and generally getting ready for their job emphasize such an understanding of gender as performance. Moreover, the film lends credence to Judith Butler's influential argument that women and queer subjects may achieve agency only through the appropriation and resignification of existing gender norms. The queer reconfiguration of norms performed by *onnabes* consequently generates a proliferation of genders that challenge the hegemony of gendered binaries. Similar to the obsession of teenage girls and housewives with the top "male" Takarazuka stars seen in *Dream Girls*, the heterosexual women who make up the majority of the clients at the New Marilyn Club are attracted to *onnabes* because they see them as "ideal men." Their allure resides in a masculinity "softened" by its female performance. Although both films imply that these institutions (the *onnabe* club and the Takarazuka Revue) provide women (as performers, hosts, spectators, and clients) with vital opportunities to resist the patriarchal hegemony of Japanese society, *Dream Girls* qualifies the suggestion of such resistance by emphasizing how the authoritarian discipline of the Takarazuka school in fact produces "ideal wives" in its performers who are generally pressured to leave the revue in their mid-twenties in order to get married. In its focus on the personal and professional lives of its three principal subjects, *Shinjuku Boys* largely elides questions about the New Marilyn Club, the institution that brings together *onnabes* and their clients.

Consequently, the film's remarkable exploration of gender and sexuality overshadows a consideration of class issues within the *onnabe* scene. Internationally popular at documentary and lesbian and gay film festivals, *Shinjuku Boys* exemplifies the recent surge of documentaries, including *Paris is Burning* (1990), *Transexual Menace* (1996), and *Gendernauts* (1999), which have been concerned with transgender issues.

ROGER HALLAS

See also **Homosexuality: Critical Overview on, and Documentary Film; Longinotto, Kim**

Shinjuku Boys (UK, Twentieth Century Vixen, 1995, color, Japanese with English subtitles, 53 mins.). Distributed by Women Make Movies (USA). Written and directed by Kim Longinotto and Jano Williams. Produced by Kim Longinotto. Cinematography by Kim Longinotto. Music by Nigel Hawks. Editing by John Mister. Sound by Simmy Claire and Rosie Straker. Narrated by Shuko Noguchi. Filmed in Tokyo, Japan.

Further Reading

Brockes, Emma, "Silent Witness," in *The Guardian* (Manchester, UK), February 11, 2000, 8.

Butler, Judith, *Bodies That Matter: On the Discursive Limits of "Sex,"* New York: Routledge, 1993.

Elley, Derek, "Shinjuku Boys," in *Variety*, November 20, 1995, 48–49.

Lunsing, Wim, *Beyond Common Sense: Sexuality and Gender in Contemporary Japan*, London: Kegan Paul, 2001.

Teasley, Sarah, "Interview with Kim Longinotto," in *Documentary Box*, no. 16, December 1, 2000, available from http://www.city.yamagata.yamagata.jp/yidff/docbox/16/box16-2-1-e.html.

SHOAH

(France, Lanzmann, 1985)

Claude Lanzmann's epic film *Shoah* ("wasteland" or "destruction" in Hebrew) is often considered to be one of the most important documentaries ever made. The film's subject is the Holocaust. Yet, the film's scope and its impact on many different dis-

ciplines and fields, from Jewish studies to theories of postmodernism, underscores not only the need for viewers to reflect on the incongruous horror that was and is the Holocaust but also to examine ways in which Lanzmann and his film address issues of historical representation. Over a ten-year period, Lanzmann and his camera crew filmed over 350 hours of interviews from eyewitnesses to the Holocaust; from death camp survivors, Polish farmers, and Nazi guards now in hiding—all gave their testimonies to Lanzmann who, with his editors, Ziva Postec and Anna Ruiz, distilled the film to its running time of nine hours and thirty minutes. While this long-running time may be seen by some as pretentious, it is not; the detailed discussions with the witnesses along with the stark, unsettling nature of many of Lanzmann's exterior shots (such as those from Treblinka) arrest the viewer with their documentation of history.

For the field of documentaries what Lanzmann chooses to show the viewer is of particular importance. For Lanzmann, the decision whether to include archival footage of the Holocaust was an ethical one. Unlike other films whose subject is the Holocaust, such as *Nuit et Brouillard* (*Night and Fog*, 1955) or more recent works such as *The Long Way Home* (1997), *Shoah* contains no trace of archival material. The footage in *Shoah* concerns present-day accounts detailing the events that took place as told by eyewitnesses. Lanzmann himself has stated that if he did come across a piece of archival footage showing the gassing of Jews, he would destroy it. There is also no reconstruction seen in *Shoah*, a device used by documentary as well as other filmmakers of historical subject matter who desire to re-create the past though fabrication. Lanzmann has been critical of such filmmakers who attempt to reconstruct the past through such figurative devices of emplotment, characterization, and external nondiegetic sound, saying that such cinematic techniques by filmmakers trivialize the unique nature of the Holocaust through the directors' transgressions of trying to fictively represent its indescribable horror. In creating a new form, one devoid of archival materials and reconstruction, Lanzmann presents a work of art that, through its content and form, bears witness to what occurred.

As mentioned, the witnesses—the victims, the tormentors, the townspeople who turned a blind eye to the atrocities—all present their unique testimony and commentary on the events. This is where we see the intense human side of the Holocaust, of the people trying to put into words what it was they saw, and at times failing. Simon Srebnik, one of two survivors of the 400,000 men, women, and children killed at Chelmno, tells Lanzmann as they walk through the green field that was the crematorium, "It was terrible. No one can describe it. No one can recreate what happened here. Impossible? No one can understand it. Even I,

Shoah, Henrik Gawkowski, 1985.
[*Courtesy of the Everett Collection*]

here, now . . . I can't believe I'm here." Most of the eyewitness accounts, such as Srebnik's, are spread throughout the film. Each interview then acts as if it were its own small narrative within a much larger narrative framework on which it is commenting. In *Shoah* there is no grand narrative, no overreaching single story that encapsulates the experiences of all those who died in the Holocaust and those who survived. Instead, *Shoah* can be seen as a series of meta-narratives that, though the accounts told, presents a collection of histories that seek to speak for those unable to.

And Lanzmann is very good at getting people to speak, particularly former SS officers who are in "hiding." One such person is Franz Suchomel, a former Nazi guard at Treblinka. Through the use of a hidden camera, Lanzmann is able to get Suchomel to sing a disturbing work song from Treblinka ("No Jew knows that today!" Suchomel exclaims) and to describe, in a very matter-of-fact tone, the detailed process of unloading the trains of Jews and then sending them to the gas chambers. Hannah Arendt's concept of the "banality of evil" is, when viewing the testimonies of the Nazi guards and of the villagers at Chelmno or Treblinka, so very apt; the guards were ordinary men, and those who were in hiding at the time of filming continue to lead very ordinary lives, yet they were responsible for the machinations of the Holocaust.

Shoah is also a film that, through its directness and repetition, steers the viewers into confronting their own perceptions of and feelings toward the genocide that took place. So often in *Shoah* Lanzmann repeats certain images and locations. The stones at Treblinka, the forests around Sobibor, and the trains that led through the countryside to the death camps are some images that are all repeated, and in doing so a great weight is placed on the viewer in witnessing the somber, yet meticulous, method in which Lanzmann has framed each shot. It is no wonder, then, why *Shoah* has become such a touchstone in the field of trauma, for the film presents the testimonies of those who have lived through this traumatic reality and are now, in a sense, confronting it; and the viewers who, through their engagement with the film and its testimonies, may go through a traumatic experience of their own.

The power of *Shoah* is that it disturbs those who watch it. And it should; after all, *Shoah* is a film about death. Lanzmann would return to the subject of the Holocaust with his films *Hotel Terminus: The Life and Times of Klaus Barbie* (1988) and *Sobibor, Oct. 14, 1943, 4 P. M.* (2001), yet *Shoah* remains the film for which he is best known. The final shot of *Shoah*—*that* of a train rolling on into infinity—means that the Holocaust has no end.

ALEXANDER L. KAUFMAN

See also **Lanzmann, Claude**

Shoah (France, Les Films Aleph, 1985, 570 mins.). Distributor: New Yorker Films Video. Directed by Claude Lanzmann. A coproduction by Les Films Aleph and Historia Films with the assistance of the French Ministry of Culture. Production managers: Stella Gregorz-Quef and Séverine Oliver-Lacamp. Production administrator: Raymonde Badé-Mauffroy. Research assistants: Corrina Coulmas, Iréne Steinfeldt-Levi, and Shaimi Bar Mor. Assistants to the director: Corrina Coulmas and Iréne Steinfeldt-Levi. Interpreters: Barbara Janica (Polish), Francine Kaufmann (Hebrew), and Mrs. Apfelbaum (Yiddish). Cameramen: Dominique Chapuis, Jimmy Glasberg, and William Lubchansky. Camera assistants: Caroline Champetier de Ribes, Jean-Yves Escoffier, Slavek Olczyk, and Andrés Silvart. Gaffer: Daniel Bernard. Sound engineers: Bernard Aubouy and Michel Vionnet

Shoah, Simon Srebnik, 1985.
[*Courtesy of the Everett Collection*]

(in Israel). Editors: Ziva Postec and Anna Ruiz (Treblinka sequence). Assistant editors: Genoviéve de Gouvion Saint-Cyr, Bénédicte Mallet, Yael Perlov, and Christine Simonot. Sound editor: Danielle Fillios, Anne-Marie L'Hôte, and Sabine Mamou. Sound editing assistants: Catherine Sabba and Catherine Trouillet. Mixing: Bernard Aubouy. Subtitles: A. Whitelaw and W. Byron. Filmed in Chelmno, Berlin, Munich, Frankfurt, Wannsee, Warsaw, Treblinka, Sobibor, Grabow, Vilna, Wlodawa, Malkinia, Kolo, Auschwitz, Tel Aviv, Ben Shemen, Corfu, Cincinnati, New York City, Washington, DC, and Burlington, Vermont. Awarded the Best Documentary by the New York Film Critics Circle (1985); the Special Award by the Los Angeles Film Critics Association (1985); the Caligari Film Award, the FIPRESCI Prize, and OCIC Award—Honorable Mention by the Berlin International Film Festival (1986); the BSFC Award for Best Documentary by the Boston Society of Film Critics (1986); the IDA Award by the International Documentary Association (1986); the Rotterdam Award for Best Documentary by the Rotterdam International Film Festival (1986); and the Flaherty Documentary Award by the British Academy of Film and Television Arts (1987).

SHOOT TO KILL

(UK, Kosminsky, 1990)

In May 1984, John Stalker was appointed to head the inquiry into the deaths of six republican men shot dead by the Royal Ulster Constabulary's (RUC) antiterrorist unit, E4A, in Northern Ireland in 1982. The docudrama *Shoot to Kill* was based on the "Stalker Inquiry" and followed the RUC and the "shoot to kill" incidents of November and December 1982. The program was broadcast by Yorkshire Television in the UK in May 1990.

On November 11, 1982, three Irish Republican Army (IRA) volunteers were shot a total of 109 times at an RUC roadblock near Lurgan, County Armagh. On November 24, another IRA member was shot dead by RUC members at a hay shed in Lurgan, and on December 12, two more were shot dead by the RUC at Mullacreevie estate, Armagh (IFM, 1987). The program follows Stalker as he apparently gets closer to the truth and his subsequent dismissal.

Director Peter Kosminsky had planned to make a documentary about the Stalker inquiry, but this proved untenable, given that the majority of those he wished to interview were either dead, unavailable, or could not speak because of the Official Secrets Act (Sanderson, 1990). Although Kosminsky recognized the advantage of using drama to reach a wider audience, the focus was that the documentary aspect should have primacy over the dramatic elements: "We strove very hard to not sacrifice reality to the demands of good television" (Stafford-Clarke, 1990: 21).

Kosminsky saw the docudrama as an unproblematic vehicle for the telling of "one of the great untold stories." Others, however, used the label to diminish any claims made by the film. The full committee of the IBA watched the film before it was broadcast, because of the sensitive nature of the subject matter, and agreed to allow the broadcast on the basis that the film would be clearly marked as a docudrama. This was presumably to safeguard viewers who may have been misled into thinking of it as a "true" document of the events. The labeling of the film as a docudrama provided a safeguard for the government, in that any material considered as potentially damaging could be dismissed as fictional.

Shoot to Kill does not mimic or utilise documentary aesthetics, or a "documentary look," in any systematic way. Instead, its referentiality is developed through its use of specific names, places, and dates. The broadcast itself was framed through its use of a voice-over at the beginning, which states that it is based on real events and that actors are used to portray real people. This serves to reinforce the notion that the film uses drama merely to fill in the gaps, and encourages viewers to evaluate it as documentary.

Although the film does not employ documentary codes and conventions systematically, there are instances in which documentary aesthetics are referenced. For example, there is an early scene in which members of the RUC are seen running toward an old farmhouse that has been under surveillance. This is shot from the point of view of the RUC and uses a shaky camcorder style. This serves to suggest the authenticity of the action and heightens the dramatic tension. In another scene, a "fly-on-the-wall" style is used. Members of the RUC are again on surveillance after being given information regarding "suspected" members of the IRA. As the suspects are spotted leaving by car, the surveillance team follows them. A car chase ensues and when the suspects refuse to stop, there is a shooting sequence that ends with the killing of the suspects. The car chase takes place from the RUC point of view. *Shoot to Kill* has a narrative structure that broadly resembles the expositional documentary. The problem has been set up, and the narrative is driven by the desire to collect the facts, analyse them, and present a final solution to the initial question or problem. For example, a key aspect of the investigation is to clarify and confirm the accuracy of RUC officers' accounts of events surrounding the killing of unarmed civilians suspected of terrorist activities. In doing so, Stalker compares officer accounts with the accounts provided by the forensic team in order to establish the truth. However, a final result was never achieved by the Stalker team because as they delved more deeply into the matter, the inquiry was aborted.

After the screening of the film, a televised studio discussion took place. In *Shoot to Kill: The Issues*, Kosminsky, along with representatives from the Conservative party, the Social Democratic Labour party, the Ulster Unionists, and Amnesty International, were invited to discuss the issues raised by the film. Kosminsky was challenged on the basis that the film was misleading and that it had served to encourage the IRA and to discourage the RUC. David Trimble of the Ulster Unionists stated that "film has not told the truth, it has told a lie." He argued that it was misleading because people would be left with the impression that there was a "shoot to kill" policy. He pointed out that neither the Stalker nor the Sampson inquiries had found any evidence of a shoot to kill policy. However, neither inquiry had been published and so it was difficult to use them as evidence. Although there is little chance of ever reaching a definitive account of the events and issues, *Shoot to Kill* aligns itself with the discourses of documentary and factuality, thus making claims to truthfulness and accuracy.

JANE ROSCOE

Shoot to Kill. (UK, Zenith Productions, for Yorkshire Television, 222 mins.). Produced by Yorkshire Television. Directed by Peter Kosminsky. Written by Michael Eaton. Starring Jack Shepherd as John Stalker.

SHUB, ESTHER

Along with Ol'ga Preobrazhanskaya, who worked in conventional narrative film, Shub was one of the most prominent female filmmakers of her generation. Along with Dziga Vertov, the filmmaker with whom she had a close (and frequently stormy) professional relationship, Shub is credited with the creation of the compilation film, a type of documentary constructed almost exclusively of retrieved archival film. While Vertov worked with more contemporary material, Shub recontextualized old newsreel footage to create new films, most notably the trilogy comprising *The Fall of the Romanov Dynasty, The Great Way,* and *The Russia of Nicholas 11 and Lev Tolstoi.* Produced under the auspices of Sovkino, in cooperation with the Museum of the Revolution, the trilogy represents a formidable amount of research; it is estimated that Shub viewed close to three million feet of newsreel footage. This was material shot by multiple, often anonymous, cameramen who had filmed both prerevolutionary and contemporary events. These films are in effect a visual history of Russia from the end of the nineteenth century, through the October revolution, and up to the tenth anniversary of the revolution.

Shub applied to nonfiction film the "montage of attractions" most commonly associated with Sergei Eisenstein (Bruzzi, 2000: 22). But unlike Eisenstein's startling collisions, Shub's films use a subtle method of montage that brings a great deal of ironic play to bear on her material, a technique that radically distinguished her work. The concept she developed for selecting and juxtaposing shots was not schematic but more intuitive and associational. Her ultimate goal was to comment on events by this selection and juxtaposition, while preserving the ontological authenticity of the shots themselves.

This quality was noted with approval by contemporary critics, most notably the Constructivist theorists grouped around the magazine *Novy Lef.* Shub's strength lay in what was considered her mastery of "long sequence" montage, which recreated events while preserving their integral characteristics, and their temporal and spatial reality. At the same time, Shub had a refined and sophisticated conception of the implications and limitations of what she called *podlinnii material* (authentic material). She wrote:

> To assemble a documentary film you only have to think clearly. The spectator has to manage to not only see people and events properly, but to memorise them. Let the lovers of cheap montage effects remember, that to edit simply and with a clear sense is not at all easy, but very difficult.

(Shub, 1971: 18)

Today (1929, released 1930), in which she set up a number of bold oppositions between what she saw as the spiritual as well as economic crisis in the United States and the development of the Soviet Union, was her last compilation film, except for one further venture in 1939. Like a number of her contemporaries, most notably Vertov, Shub had difficulty entering the Stalinist era. She was the victim of Party philistines and ideological prejudice against formal experimentation. Her style changed; she stayed in documentary mode, but as she was dealing with contemporary themes, she began shooting material herself rather than using archive material. Her only exercise in compilation filmmaking thereafter was *Spain* (1939), using film shot by Roman Karmen and Boris Makaseev. Her legacy remains in that form of political documentary cinema where archive material is used dialectically or against the grain as part of a historical argument or debate.

MARINA BURKE

See also **Fall of the Romano Dynasty, The**; **Vertov, Dziga**

Biography

Born in 1894 in the Ukraine into a family of landowners. Studied literature in Moscow a few years before the October revolution. After the revolution, initially worked for the theatrical department of *Narkompros* (the Commisariat of Education), but then in 1922 entered the film profession through the auspices of the newly formed Goskino, where she worked as a re-editor of foreign and prerevolutionary films for Soviet audiences. Between the years 1922 and 1925, re-edited and made new inter-titles for about 200 foreign films and 10 domestic feature films, most famously Fritz Lang's two-part *Dr. Mabuse der Spieler* (1922), on which Eisenstein worked as her assistant. In 1927 and 1928, made her famous film trilogy, which traces the birth of the USSR

SHUB, ESTHER

through to the tenth anniversary of the October revolution. Between 1933 and 1935, supervised the montage class in Eisenstein's workshop in VGIK. In 1935, awarded the title of Most Honoured Artist of the Republic. During the war, edited newsreels and continued to teach montage in VGIK, then transferred to Alma Ata. In 1942, became chief editor of *Novosti Dnya (News of the Day)* in the Central Studio for Documentary Film in Moscow. Wrote *Krupnym planom (In Close-Up)* in 1959, re-issued with additional material as *Zhizn moya–kinematograf (Cinema Is My Life)* in 1971. Died in Moscow in September 1959.

Selected Films

1927 *The Fall of the Romanov Dynasty (Padenie dinastii romanovykh)*
1927 *The Great Road (Velikii put')*
1928 *The Russia of Nicholas 11 and Lev Tolstoi (Rossiya Nikolya 11 i Lev Tolstoi)*
1930 *Today (Segodnya)*
1932 *Komsomol–Leader of Electrification (K-Sh-E)*
1939 *Spain (Ispaniya)*
1942 *The Native Country (Strana rodnaya)*
1946 *On the Other Side of the Araks (Po tu storonu Araksa)*

Further Reading

Bruzzi, Stella, *New Documentary: A Critical Introduction*, London: Routledge, 2000.
Leyda, Jay, *Films Beget Films: A Study of the Compilation Film*, London: Allen and Unwin, 1964.
Petric, Vlada. "Esfir Shub: Cinema Is My Life," *Quarterly Review of Film Studies*, Fall 1978, 429–447.
———. "Esfir Shub's Unrealised Project," *Quarterly Review of Film Studies*, Fall 1978, 448–456.
———, "Esther Shub: Film as a Historical Discourse," in *"Show Us Life!": Towards a History and an Aesthetic of the Committed Documentary*, Thomas Waugh (ed.), Metuchen, NJ: Scarecrow Press, 1984.
Roberts, Graham, *Forward, Soviet! History and Non-fiction Film in the USSR*, London: I.B. Tauris, 1999.
Shub, Esfir, *Zhizn moya–kinematograf Cinema Is My Life)*, Moscow: Isskustvo, 1971.
Yampolsky, Mikhail, "Reality at Second Hand," *Historical Journal of Film, Radio and Television*, 2, no. 2, 1991, 161–171.

SHUKER, GREGORY

Gregory B. Shuker was a journalist, filmmaker, and producer, as well as a core member of Drew Associates, a group of journalists and filmmakers, founded in 1959 and commonly regarded as the originators of the pioneering American Direct Cinema Movement.

Born in Charleston in West Virginia, Gregory Shuker studied at Northwestern University. As editor-in-chief of the student newspaper, he visited Russia in 1954 and on his return had six of his 35mm color slide pictures published by *Life* magazine. Gregory Shuker was later hired as a reporter by *Life*, where he worked on last-minute foreign and domestic news. There he met Robert Drew, who had been working as a correspondent for *Life* since 1946. In 1959 Shuker became one of the first members of Drew Associates, an independent production team founded by Robert Drew that was to play a pivotal role in the 1960s renaissance of American documentary film. The idea behind Drew Associates was to make films that would transport the photojournalism as developed at *Life* magazine into documentary films, in order to move away from the staged, more instructive and illustrative style of documentary filmmaking, and to better represent social realities as they unfold in front of the camera. The most prominent trademark of Drew Associates was the handheld, lightweight 16mm camera and the newly developed synchronous, portable sound, which shaped the style of direct cinema and allowed for a radical rethinking of documentary aesthetics. Other members of Drew Associates alongside Gregory Shuker were Tom Bywaters, Anne Drew, Mike Jackson, Richard Leacock, James Lipscomb, Albert and Davis Maysles, D.A. Pennebaker, and Hope Ryden.

It is often difficult to identify which members of Drew Associates were responsible for what aspects of the work. Since none of these young journalists and filmmakers considered their stories *made* by them, they generally avoided the use of the term *director*. Moreover, since many regularly performed multiple tasks in preproduction, shooting, and postproduction, they simply called themselves "correspondents." By and large, however, Shuker's role was that of a producer. Shuker's central tasks were to "find" stories—stories that did not need narrating, that already contained enough dramatic elements to be able to tell themselves. According to Robert Drew, Shuker's success lay in his ability to operate in ways that did not attract attention—crucially important in a genre that is trying to film people as unself-consciously as possible.

The first documentaries Shuker produced for Drew Associates were *The Children Were Watching*, a documentary about racism and desegregation in New Orleans and *Kenya: Land of the White Ghost* (I) and *Kenya: Land of the Black Ghost* (II), which, in two thirty-minute episodes, documented the outcome of the first election after independence in Kenya, all shot in 1961. These films, with cinematography by Richard Leacock, were produced for the *Close Up* series of the American Broadcasting Company (ABC).

In the years 1961 to 1962 Drew Associates produced a number of television documentaries for *The Living Camera*, a series of ten *direct cinema* films later distributed by Time-Life. These films generally focused on one individual, often public figures such as Jane Fonda and John F. Kennedy. Among the films that Shuker produced for the series are *Nehru*, a fifty-five–minute documentary about the first Indian Prime Minister's last election campaign (in which Shuker breaks the direct cinema "rules" by asking Nehru a question), *Susan Starr*, about a nineteen-year-old concert pianist performing at an important international competition, and *Eddie* (a.k.a. *One the Pole*), about the race driver Eddie Sachs's unpredicted defeat in the Indianapolis 500 race.

Two of Drew Associates' most celebrated films were also produced by Shuker. The first, *The Chair* (1962), a fifty-five–minute film focused on 22-year old Paul Crump who had been sentenced to death by electric chair. Crump had befriended a prison warden and asked the warden to be the man to pull the switch. Shuker "found" this story and entered the prison to film these extraordinary moments. The film was the second to last film of the *Living Camera* Series and won the Special Jury Prize at the Cannes Film Festival.

The second celebrated film was *Crisis: Behind a Presidential Commitment*, a dramatic documentary shot in 1963, which follows the growing crisis between Alabama Governor George Wallace and president John F. Kennedy over Wallace's refusal in 1963 to allow the enrollment of the first black students (after Autherine Lucy in 1956) at the University of Alabama. Shuker was instrumental in persuading Robert Kennedy to allow the camera into the White House. The film moves between John and Robert Kennedy in the Oval Office, Governor Wallace, the students Vivian Malone and James A. Hood and the Deputy Attorney General Nicholas Katzenbach. As Kennedy federalized the National Guards and each party involved weighs the possibilities, the suspense heightens until, finally, Governor Wallace concedes on June 11. When the film was broadcast on ABC four months later it caused a storm of protest over the admission of cameras into the White House and also received harsh criticism by the *New York Times*, which called the access given by the President's office "ill advised" and the film "a peep-show."

Another film produced by Shuker—and the last one of the Kennedy series—is *Faces in November*, made in 1964. The camera quietly observes the funeral of John F. Kennedy by focusing almost exclusively on the faces of the mourners. The film was well received at the Venice Film Festival in the following year.

In 1965 Shuker produced the fifty-minute documentary *Letters from Vietnam*, the first film to use synchronous sound in the depiction of combat. Shuker and cameraman Abbot Mills flew with over sixty missions with a helicopter squadron in Vietnam, and the film was later broadcast by ABC.

In the mid-1960s—long after Pennebaker, Leacock, and the Maysles brothers had left to start their own companies—Gregory Shuker left Drew Associates and went to produce films of his own. He continued making films of a highly political nature. An important example is the fifty-two–minute documentary *Free At Last: His Final Days*, which consists of footage of Martin Luther King, Jr., taken between January and April 1968 during his "Poor People's Campaign" and breaking off with King's death. The film won the Grand Prize in the Venice Film festival and an Emmy Award.

In the following years Shuker worked increasingly on industrial projects and made a range of commercial films, alongside films such as *Life In Outer Space*, sponsored by NASA, and various mini-documentaries for IBM. In 1972 Shuker cofounded *Playback Associates*, which produced industrial training videos and instructional tapes.

Shuker died in New York on March 29, 2000. His career in filmmaking—as a producer, a cameraman, and a finder of stories—was shaped by a commitment to political concerns and a belief in the educational and the history-shaping power of the medium.

JACOBIA DAHM

See also **Drew Associates**

Biography

Born in Charleston, West Virginia. Studied at Northwestern University. Hired as a reporter by *Life* magazine. Met Robert Drew. In 1959, became one of the first members of Drew Associates. Died in New York on March 29, 2000.

Further Reading

Barnouw, Erik, *Documentary: A History of the Non-fiction Film*, Oxford, New York: Oxford University Press, 1993.

Barsam, Richard M., *Nonfiction Film. A Critical History*, Bloomington: Indiana University Press, 1973.

Bluem, A. William, *Documentary in American Television*, New York: Hastings House, 1965.

Breitrose, Henry, "On the Search for the Real Nitty-Gritty: Problems & Possibilities in Cinéma Vérité," in *Film Quarterly*, 17.4, Summer 1964, Berkeley: University of California Press, 1964, 36–40.

Cinema vérité. Defining the Moment (videorecording, 102 min), an NFB film directed by Peter Wintonick, National Film Board of Canada, 1999.

Gould, Jack, "TV: Too Many Cameras; Documentary on the Segregation Crisis Termed Just a Peep Show," the *New York Times*, October 22, 1963, 75.

Lipscomb, James C., "*Cinema-verite,*" *Film Quarterly*, 18, No. 2, Winter 1964, 62–63.

Macdonald, Kevin, and Mark Cousins, *Imagining Reality. The Faber Book of the Documentary*, London, Boston: Faber and Faber, 1996.

New Challenges for Documentary, Allan Rosenthal (ed.), Berkeley, Los Angeles, London: University of California Press, 1988.

O'Connell, P. J, *Robert Drew and the Development of Cinema Verité in America*, Carbondale and Edwardsville: Southern Illinois University Press, 1992.

Watson, Mary Ann, *The Expanding Vista: American Television in the Kennedy Years*, New York: Oxford University Press, 1990; Durham, NC: Duke University Press, 1994.

Young, Colin, "Cinema of Common Sense," *Film Quarterly*, 17, no. 4, Summer 1964, pp. 26–29, 40.

SILENT WORLD, THE

(France, Cousteau, 1956)

Jacques Cousteau's *The Silent World (Le Monde du silence)* is a landmark in wild-life documentary filmmaking. Co-directed with the help of the young Louis Malle, the picture follows the trials and tribulations of the crew of the *Calypso* as they voyage through the Red Sea, the Persian Gulf, and the Indian Ocean. The completed documentary was some two years in the making and is reported to have been founded on more than 1,000 dives. Although sharing its title with an earlier Cousteau publication, *The Silent World* is an original work that served to popularize the previously marginal form of the underwater documentary. Until that film, Cousteau's work had been limited to short reportage-style essays, commercial projects for companies such as British Petroleum, and photographic expeditions associated with publications such as *National Geographic*. After *The Silent World,* Cousteau was able to develop any number of projects in his own right.

The Silent World premiered in Paris on February 7, 1956, at a formal conservative *soirée* attended by the then President of the Republic, René Coty. Subsequently it was a commercial success that was also garlanded with many glittering prizes. Thus, in April 1956 it was awarded the Palme d'Or at Cannes and just one year later was next presented with an Academy Award for Best Documentary. The victory at Cannes was especially impressive since the film was in competition against Henri-Georges Clouzot's *Mystére Picasso* and Ingmar Bergman's *Smiles of a Summer Night*. Remarkably, until the famous victory of Michael Moore's *Fahrenheit 9/11* in 2004, *The Silent World* continued to be the only documentary film to have been awarded the Palme d'Or. Furthermore, it is a fascinating historical coincidence that at the same festival that heralded the arrival of *The Silent World*, the organizers were unprepared to support Alain Resnais's lyrical

The Silent World.
[*Courtesy of the Everett Collection*]

work devoted to the Holocaust, *Nuit et Brouillard*
(*Night and Fog*). In contrast to the triumph of
The Silent World, Resnais's moving piece was
expelled to the fringes of the event, and only
shown "outside competition." In this context it
is important to note that the same Cannes jury
included the disgraced actress, Arletty. Like
Cousteau, she had worked during the Vichy period (1940–1944). Her prominent role at Cannes
1956 therefore marked something of an official
return to the mainstream postwar industry. It
is in this wider sociopolitical context of the collective rewriting of the war and France's role
in the Holocaust that *The Silent World* proved
triumphant and *Night and Fog* was unjustly marginalised. Clearly, Cousteau's work was far
more palatable for audiences who preferred light
entertainment over challenging moral or historical reflection.

Cousteau and Malle's treatment of undersea
wildlife represented a radical advance in cinematography. Genuinely revolutionary underwater
photography was developed in the making of the
documentary. New cameras and diving equipment
filmed sea life at previously unseen depths of the
ocean floor. *The Silent World* created bold iconic
underwater images that have been repeated and
modified around the world in numerous films and
television series. Thus, it is not an exaggeration to
suggest that *The Silent World* almost single-hand-
edly instigated a minor but entertaining subgenre.
More generally speaking, Cousteau and Malle's
work launched the global fashion for amateur diving and photography. The fundamental aesthetic
"look" of the film has probably also influenced
fictional work ranging from Stephen Spielberg's
Jaws (1975) to James Cameron's *The Abyss*

(1989). Rather more amusingly, Cousteau is also
referred to extensively throughout Wes Anderson's
comedy, *Rushmore* (1998). Such postmodern irony
is indicative of the genuine artistic significance of
Cousteau's original work.

In retrospect, significant elements of *The Silent
World* appear to be horribly dated. For example,
the crew's mode of encounter with sea life is predominantly cast through a quasi-Conradian ethic
of man's struggle against the untamed force of the
natural world. Such implicit philosophical underpinnings are closer to the social value system of
the 1890s than to the undercurrents of reform
that were already preparing the way for New
Wave cinema and the freedoms of the 1960s.
Similarly, the film also predates Cousteau's
famous turn to support the ecological movement.
For example, *The Silent World* contains several
passages that would make today's environmentalists wince with discomfort. Thus, Cousteau shows
his sailors' uncontrollable massacre of a shoal of
sharks. Later, the same crew casually hurls dynamite into a coral reef to identify the range of
dead crustaceans and fish that gradually float to
the surface. Any sense of ecologism or environ-
mentalism is limited and it was not until 1960
that Cousteau began to commit himself to that
now more fashionable cause.

The Silent World, Jacques Cousteau, 1956.
[*Courtesy of the Everett Collection*]

The production history of *The Silent World* remains clouded in mystery. Speaking to Philip French in the early 1990s, Louis Malle implied that Cousteau had simply plucked him from the *Institut des Hautes Etudes Cinématographiques* (IDHEC—the Parisian film academy) to work as an intern on the *Calypso*. However, Pierre Billard has suggested that the background to the making of the picture was a more complex commercial affair. For instance, Billard alludes to the fact that Malle not only acted as an assistant director on the film but was also probably influential in obtaining a loan to support part of its production costs. Any investment on the part of the Malle family, who owned the Béghin sugar empire, was richly rewarded, if never explicitly credited. Moreover, the success of the film ensured that the young Malle gained an important profile in the industry. Shortly afterwards, Malle briefly assisted his hero Robert Bresson on *Un condamné à mort s'est échappée* (*A Man Escaped,* 1956) and then produced his own first solo feature, *L'Ascenseur pour l'échafaud* (*Lift to the Scaffold,* 1957). Cousteau's future career was also secured by the triumph. It was on the basis of the global success of *The Silent World* that the Commander resigned his post from the French navy and was appointed to Monaco's oceanographic institute, quickly becoming an international celebrity.

HUGO FREY

See also **Cousteau, Jacques-Yves; Malle, Louis;** *Night and Fog*; **Resnais, Alain**

The Silent World (*Le Monde du Silence*) (Fr, Requins Associés, 1956, 86 mins). Directed Jacques Cousteau and Louis Malle. Cinematography: Edmond Séchan (Technicolor). Photography: J. Cousteau, L. Malle, Frédéric Duma, and Alberto Falco. Music: Yves Baudrier. Editing: Georges Alépée. Special effects: Noël Robert. Commentary: James Dugan (English language edition).

Further Reading

Billard, Pierre, *Louis Malle: le Rebelle solitaire*, Paris: Plon, 2003.
Cousteau, Jacques, and Frédéric Dumas, *The Silent World*, London: Hamnish Hamilton, 1953.
French, Philip (ed.), *Malle on Malle*, London: Faber, 1993.
Frey, Hugo, *Louis Malle*, Manchester: Manchester University Press, 2004.
Madsen, Axel, *Cousteau*, London: Robson Books, 1989.
Violet, Bernard, *Cousteau*, Paris: Plon, 1993.

SINCLAIR, UPTON

Writer and political activist Upton Sinclair was a peripheral figure in film history, but he played a vital role in a misadventure involving a far more significant writer/activist—Sergei Eisenstein. Together they embarked on the debacle that was *Que Viva Mexico!*

By the time Sinclair met Eisenstein he had established a reputation as a leading socialist and the prolific author of muckraking novels. Sinclair's involvement with *Que Viva Mexico!* was not his first contact with the film world. He had long been keen to break into it so that he could extend the message of his books to a new audience, and make enough money to allow himself the freedom to pursue his political activities.

He had appeared as an agitator in the 1914 adaptation of his 1906 novel, *The Jungle*, exposing conditions in the Chicago stockyards, the first pro-labor feature in the United States. Another adaptation, *The Money Changers* (1920), intended as a critical examination of financier J. P. Morgan, became, in Sinclair's view, a melodrama on the Chinatown drug trade. *The Wet Parade* (on Prohibition) was filmed in 1932. Also, Charlie Chaplin's short *The Adventurer* (1917) had been based on a Sinclair story. None of these had been as financially successful as Sinclair had hoped. More lucrative was his 1933 book, *Upton Sinclair Presents William Fox*, charting the rise and fall of a movie mogul. After *Que Viva Mexico!* Sinclair adapted the anti-VD propaganda film *Damaged Goods* (1937).

Eisenstein, together with his assistant Grigori Alexandrov and cinematographer Edouard Tissé, had been invited to the United States in 1930 by Paramount, who wanted to capitalize on his reputation. After failure to agree on a project, and with vocal hostility to his presence in the United States from the right-wing press, Eisenstein's contract was terminated in October. Rather than return to the Soviet Union, he approached Sinclair, through Chaplin, for help in financing his dream to make an independent film in Mexico. Eisenstein had met Robert Flaherty in Hollywood and had discussed an ethnographic approach using amateur actors within the framework of a fictional film.

Sinclair had mixed motives in agreeing; he wanted to participate in a financially successful project but he also felt that Eisenstein had been treated badly in the United States, and wanted him to be able to make at least one film before returning to Moscow. Sinclair and his wife, Craig, raised $25,000 and Eisenstein signed a contract on November 24, 1930, with Craig to make a nonpolitical film in three to four months. The contract was heavily weighted in favor of Craig: There was no reference to Eisenstein editing the film, and crucially everything produced by the Mexican team was to be her property. By signing, Eisenstein showed himself to be naïve in business matters, trusting that the Sinclairs' political leaning would render the terms a formality. Eisenstien's party left for Mexico the following month.

Geduld and Gottesman (1970) provide a chronology of the project by means of the principals' letters, although as it is based on Sinclair's archives it is weighted toward him, with Eisenstein underrepresented. Eisenstein clearly considered the contract to be elastic, and conceived a scheme, involving six separate episodes, that could never be completed within the time-scale and budget specified (Eisenstein later claimed that had they been adhered to the original agreement his efforts "would have merely resulted in a pitiful travelogue").

The modest budget and time-scale were quickly abandoned as Eisenstein's demands increased in line with his ambition. Unable to compromise his artistic vision, he stayed in Mexico for fourteen months and more than doubled the budget. Eventually, Sinclair, who was spending a huge amount of time raising funds and acting as producer, to the detriment of his writing and health, came to feel that he was being blackmailed by Eisenstein, who indicated that unless he received additional funds and film stock there would be no film and the investment would be lost.

Added to the financial difficulties Eisenstein's prolonged stay in Mexico were causing Sinclair, political developments in the Soviet Union were creating a climate inimical to the sense of aesthetic adventure that had prevailed when Eisenstein left in August 1929, and the Mexican film's lyricism ran counter to the emerging doctrine of Socialist Realism. Additionally, Eisenstein had originally been granted permission to travel for only one year and had so far exceeded this period that Sinclair received a telegram from Stalin himself in November 1931 warning that Eisenstein was in danger of being perceived as a deserter at home.

Sinclair, under pressure from his wife, finally called a halt in February 1932, leaving shooting unfinished. He had concluded that Eisenstein had no intention of finishing the project, using it as a pretext to avoid returning to Moscow. Having stopped the filming, Sinclair initially still hoped that Eisenstein would be able to edit the footage but ultimately felt he could not trust him or the Soviet authorities. Instead, producer Sol Lesser was engaged to carve a commercial film from it after Eisenstein had returned home. Sinclair needed a return on the investment—thereby endorsing critics who charged that he was a capitalist at heart.

A campaign against Sinclair was mounted by Eisenstein's supporters, notably Seymour Stern, editor of *Experimental Cinema*, and Sinclair's left-wing credentials were damaged both at home and in the Soviet Union. Given his aspirations, and the problems they had caused, it is ironic that he should have spent such an enormous amount of time and energy struggling to facilitate Eisenstein's relatively nonpolitical film when shortly after, King Vidor wrote and directed the socially aware *Our Daily Bread* (1934), with its vision of working-class solidarity, the dispossessed organizing to create a collective farm.

In order to recoup some of the costs, in addition to the films Lesser produced, footage was sold to Marie Seton, an early biographer of Eisenstein, and more to Bell and Howell to make six educational documentaries. Sinclair presented the remaining material to New York's Museum of Modern Art in 1954, where Jay Leyda assembled a six-hour compilation. In 1973 much of MOMA's holding was sent to Gosfilmofond, where Alexandrov also tried to re-create the spirit of Eisenstein's intentions.

TOM RUFFLES

See also **Que Viva Mexico!**

Biography

Born in Baltimore, Maryland, on September 20, 1878. Attended New York City College, funded by writing for newspapers and magazines. Published first novel in 1901, followed by a steady stream of books and articles on social issues. Achieved fame with *The Jungle* (1906), after which he became known as a muckraking journalist and novelist, exposing institutional corruption. Moved to California in 1915. Active in politics from the age of 24, initially for the Socialist Party, for whom he stood for Congress and Senate and for governorship of California. Switched to the Democrats in 1933. Again ran unsuccessfully for governorship of California on platform "End Poverty in California" (EPIC) in 1934. Wrote over ninety books, fiction and nonfiction. Won Pulitzer Prize in 1943 for novel *Dragon's Teeth*. Moved to Buckeye, Arizona, in 1953. Died in Bound Brook, New Jersey, on November 25, 1968.

Films Produced from Eisenstein's Mexican Footage

1933 *Thunder Over Mexico* (Sol Lesser)
1933 *Death Day* (Sol Lesser)
1933 *S. M. Eisenstein in Mexico* (Sol Lesser)
1939 *Time in the Sun* (Marie Seton)
1942 *Mexican Symphony: Mexico Marches; Conquering Cross; Idol of Hope; Land and Freedom; Spaniard and Indian; Zapotec Village* (Bell and Howell)

1957 *Eisenstein's Mexican Project* (Jay Leyda)
1979 *Que Viva Mexico!* (Grigori Alexandrov)

Further Reading

Amengual, Barthélemy, *Que Viva Eisenstein!*, Lausanne: Éditions L'age d'homme, 1981.
Eisenstein, Sergei, *Que Viva Mexico!*, London, Vision, revised edition 1972.
Foner, Philip S., "Upton Sinclair's 'The Jungle: The Movie," in *Upton Sinclair: Literature and Social Reform,"* Dieter Herms (ed.), Frankfurt: Peter Lang, 1990.
Geduld, Harry M., and Ronald Gottesman (eds.), *Sergei Eisenstein and Upton Sinclair: The Making and Unmaking of Que Viva Mexico!* London: Thames and Hudson, 1970.
Harris, Leon, *Upton Sinclair: American Rebel*, New York: Thomas Y. Crowell, 1975.
Scott, Ivan, *Upton Sinclair, The Forgotten Socialist*, Lewiston, New York: The Edwin Mellen Press, 1997.
Seton, Marie, *Sergei Eisenstein—A Biography*, London: Dennis Dobson, revised edition 1978.
Sinclair, Upton, *The Autobiography of Upton Sinclair*, London: W. H. Allen, revised edition 1963.

SINGAPORE

See **Southeast Asia**

SIODMAK, ROBERT

Robert Siodmak is best known as one of the most talented and prolific directors of film noir from the 1940s. One recalls the masturbatory frenzy of a jazz drummer lusting after a B-girl surrounded by expressionistic shadows in *Phantom Lady* (1944); the placement of killer, potential victim, and avenging angel at different levels on the eponymous structure of *The Spiral Stair-case* (1946); and the hushed resignation of the "Swede" to his own death in *The Killers* (1946). Like other notables making noir (Billy Wilder, Max Ophuls), Siodmak was a Jew who began in Germany, fled after 1933 to France, and immigrated to the United States during World War II. Siodmak's importance to documentary is two-fold: (1) his work on the semidocumentary

Menschen am Sontag / People on Sunday (1930), and (2) his use in noir of documentary stylistics after WWII.

Siodmak and others raised the funds needed to shoot the late silent *Menschen am Sontag*, which he co-directed with Edgar Ulmer. As if teaming these notables were not enough, Fred Zinnemann assisted them; the screenplay was by Wilder, based on reporting by Curt Siodmak (Robert's brother): and Eugene Schufftan did the cinematography. Billed as a "film without actors," featuring people "before the camera for the first time in their lives," the film connects with the city symphonies of Ruttman, Cavalcanti, and Vertov, even if it is less avant garde in focusing on specific characters and featuring a straightforward narrative. The film sketches a Berlin summer day as five performers, charmingly unself-conscious, essentially play themselves. Taxi driver Erwin and his ladies' man friend, Wolfgang, enjoy their day off with record seller Brigitte and film extra Christl. Hurt feelings ensue when Wolfgang flirts with both women, and Erwin returns home to find that his wife, Annie, has slept the day away.

Menschen's freshness surely resulted from the talented neophytes behind the scenes. An early tracking shot of motorcycles and trains links people with the rhythms of the city. The film overflows with documentary moments: shots of street cleaners, field hockey, naked babies, a man dripping water on a caterpillar, and the like. The "story" scenes also feature extraneous moments (e.g., a disorienting shot of a man playing cards). Lengthy plotless scenes commence even before the picnic, as Erwin and Annie deal with an uncooperative door, read the paper, and have a fight. Reflexive in-jokes appear when they discuss Greta Garbo or angrily destroy film postcards. One later finds playfully vertiginous camera angles, with use of natural shadows, as if the future noirs of Siodmak and Ulmer were present in early form. Nonetheless, it is the reportage aspects that proved most influential. Documentary style is foregrounded in a delightful sequence where photographs are taken and the frame freezes for each, while a montage of statues seems more indebted to Soviet editing and the "real" city symphonies. Associative editing keeps the story within persuasive documentary contexts, much as neo-realism would later do. The film's open-air quality and use of nonprofessionals made it a classic, possibly influenced neo-realism

and genuine documentary, and proved a poignant record of a Germany soon to vanish.

Siodmak's French and early Hollywood films reprise little of *Menschen*'s documentary qualities. Nonetheless, for all his Germanic stylizations, documentary creeps into his noir in the deglamorized studio streets, the clinical detailing of crime scenes, and a growing penchant for long takes and deep focus. Overtly documentarian noir really emerges after films like Jules Dassin's *Naked City* (1948); Siodmak's most stunning venture into this realm is the underrated *Cry of the City* (1948), set in New York's Little Italy. Siodmak was reportedly unhappy with the location work and preferred the control possible within the studio, but the final product belies his mastery of combining documentary and expressionistic modes within noir. Before returning to Europe, Siodmak helmed a lesser but even more documentary-style film, *The Whistle at Eaton Falls* (1951), a Capraesque drama about a unionized worker who is named president of a plastics factory. Based on an actual case history, the film strongly bears the mark of *March of Time* producer Louis de Rochemont. Still, de Rochemont had already produced seminal documentary-style noirs like *The House on 92ⁿᵈ Street* (1945) and *Boomerang!* (1947), and the teaming with Siodmak is often successful, as lengthy sequences document mill life in rural New Hampshire.

DAVID M. LUGOWSKI

Biography

Born in Dresden, Saxony, Germany (some sources say Memphis, Tennessee, while his father was on a business trip) August 8, 1900. Attended Marburg University, 1917–1920. Got a job writing subtitles for U.S. films shown in Germany, 1925. Joined UFA, working as a writing scout, film cutter, assistant director, 1927. Left Germany for Paris after the Nazi takeover, 1933. Left for the United States the day before Hitler's army marched into Paris; with brother's aid was signed by Paramount, 1940. Began working for Universal; signed seven-year contract, 1943–1944. Returned to Europe, first France, then Germany, 1952. Died March 10, 1973.

Selected Films

1930 *Menschen am Sontag / People on Sunday*: co-director (with Edgar Ulmer)
1934 *La Crise est Finie / The Crisis Is Over / The Depression Is Over*: director
1939 *Piéges / Snares / Personal Column*: director
1942 *Fly by Night*: director

1944 *Phantom Lady*: director
1944 *Christmas Holiday*: director
1945 *The Strange Affair of Uncle Harry*: director
1946 *The Killers*: director
1946 *The Spiral Staircase*: director
1948 *Cry of the City*: director
1949 *Criss Cross*: director
1951 *The Whistle at Eaton Falls*: director
1952 *The Crimson Pirate*: director
1957 *Nachts, wenn der Teufel kam / The Devil Strikes at Night*: director, producer
1958 *Dorothea Angermann*: director
1967 *Custer of the West*: director

Further Reading

Alpi, Deborah Lazaroff, *Robert Siodmak*, Jefferson, NC: MacFarland, 1998.
Greco, Joseph, *The File on Robert Siodmak in Hollywood, 1941–1951*, Dissertation.com, 1999.
Hirschhorn, Clive, *The Universal Story*, New York: Crown, 1983.
Naremore, James, *More Than Night: Film Noir in Its Contexts*, Berkeley: University of California Press, 1998.
Silver, Alain, and Elizabeth Ward, *Film Noir*, Woodstock, NY: Overlook Press, 1979.

SKLADANOWSKY, MAX

Max Skladanowsky's significance lies with the fact that he was the first individual to project moving images on celluloid band to a paying audience, on November 1, 1895, at the Berlin variety theater Wintergarten. To achieve this, he constructed his own camera (1892) and the double projector "Bioskop" (1895) with which he alternately projected frames from two loops of film in order to achieve the 16fps needed to constitute the illusion of perfect motion. Technically, Skladanowsky's films had to be cut into single frames, which had to be edited alternately into two loops of film, a procedure that limited the length of the moving images considerably. Still, this process had the advantage of exploiting the light better, since the single frames were dissolved into one another without black frames between them. Allegedly this also minimized the flicker of the images.

Skladanowsky's so-called first program consisted of seven short features, only about six seconds each, that were repeated several times to achieve a desirable projection length. The subjects derived from the variety routines of the time: an acrobatic potpourri, an Italian peasant dance, a wrestling bout, a boxing kangaroo, and the like. A second program was set up in 1896—this time projected with a one-lens projector—consisting of street scenes from Berlin. These films, especially *Einfahrt eines Eisenbahnzuges* (1896), clearly proved that, aesthetically, Skladanowsky followed suit in the footsteps of the Lumiére brothers. *Eine kleine Szene aus dem Strassenleben in Stockholm* and *Ein komischer Film, aufgenommen in Tivoli in Stockhold* (both 1896) were shot during Skladanowsky's tour of Sweden and exemplify his interest in narrative films.

After a long pause, in which Skladanowsky concentrated on the production of flip books, he eventually made two feature films: *Eine Fliegenjagd* (1913) and *Die moderne Jungfrau von Orleans* (1914), which were fictional comedies. His flip books routines consisted of features from his earlier films but also of reenactments of royalties and/or prominent politicians: *Seine Majestat Kaiser Wilhelm II* (1896), *Kaiser Friedrich III* (1897?), *Kaiser Franz Joseph, Prince of Wales, Furst Bismarck* (not dated), and *August Bebel* (1896). For these flip books, cinematic films were shot, broken down into single frames, and printed on paper. The personalities depicted in these "films" were impersonated by actors.

Although Skladanowsky's contribution is merely a sideline in the development of the cinema, he became very instrumental in the 1930s in the Nazis' attempt to claim the cinema as a truly German invention.

ULI JUNG

Biography

Born April 30, 1863, in Berlin, Skladanowsky joined his father Carl and his elder brother Emil in 1879 in their magic lantern and mechanical theater tours of central Europe. His Bioskop show in the Wintergarten theater was supposed to be the beginning of yet another tour of Europe. Skladanowsky's appearance in Paris was cancelled after the roaring success of the Cinématographe Lumiére, so Max and Emil Skladanowsky exhibited the invention only in Germany, Scandinavia, and the Netherlands. After a second engagement at the Wintergarten in 1896 Skladanowsky concentrated on the production of flip books, 3-D anaglyphic slides, and albums of 3-D photographs. He also traded in amateur cameras and equipment. Later ventures into the realm of fiction films proofed unsuccessful. He died on November 30, 1939, in Berlin.

Selected Films

November 1 1895 The Wintergarten program
1. *Italienischer Bauerntanz*
2. *Komisches Reck*
3. *Der Jongleur*
4. *Das boxende Känguruh*
5. *Akrobatisches Potpourri*
6. *Kamarinskija*
7. *Ringkampf zwischen Greiner und Sandow*
8. *Die Erfinder des Bioscop (Apotheose)*
1896 *Panoramaaufnahme Berlin Schönhauser Allee/ Pappelallee*
1896 *Alarm der Berliner Feuerwehr*
1896 *Ausfahrt der Berliner Feuerwehr*
1896 *Alexanderplatz in Berlin*
1896 *Einfahrt eines Eisenbahnzuges*
1896 *Die Neue Wache in Berlin*
1896 *Unter den Linden in Berlin*
1896 *Die Wachparade kommt*
1896 *Eine kleine Szene aus dem Strassenleben in Stockholm*
1896 *Ein komischer Film, aufgenommen im Tivoli in Stockholm*
1896 *Apotheose II*
1897 *Am Bollwerk in Stettin*

Further Reading

Castan, Joachim, *Max Skladanowsky oder der Beginn einer deutschen Filmgeschichte*, Stuttgart: Fusslin, 1995.
Lichtenstein, Manfred, "The Brothers Skladanowsky," in *Prima di Caligari: Cinema Tedesco, 1895–1920*, Paolo Cherchi Usai and Lorenzo Codelli (eds.), Pordenone: Giovanni del Cinema Muto, 1990.
Loiperdinger, Martin (ed.), *KINtop 8: Film und Projektionskunst*, Frankfurt/M, Basel: Stroemfeld/Roter Stern, 1999.
Narath, Albert, *Max Skladanowsky*, Berlin: Deutsche Kinemathek, 1970.
Trimborn, Jurgen, *Sammlung Max Skladanowsky: Aus dem nachlab eines Filmpioniers—Ein Bestandsverzeichnis der Theaterwissenschaftlichen Sammlung Universitat zu Koln*, Koln: R Leppin, 1997.
Vogl-Bienek, Ludwig, "Sklasanowsky und die Nebelbilder," in *KINtop 8: Film und Projektionskunst*, Sabine Lenk, Frank Kessler, and Martin Loiperdinger (eds.), Frankfurt/M, Basel: Stroemfeld/Roter Stern, 1999.
Völschow, Undine, *Nachlaß Max Skladanowsky. Bestand N 1435*, Koblenz: Bundesarchiv, 1995—Findbücher zu Beständen des Bundesarchivs, vol. 49.

SLOVAKIA

See **Czech Republic/Slovakia**

SLOVENIA

See **Yugoslavia (former)**

SOKUROV, ALEKSANDR

The Russian director Aleksandr Nikolajevich Sokurov has made about twice as many documentaries as fiction films. One reason for this might be that under the Soviet regime, Sokurov's masterly graduate fiction film *Odinoky Golos Cheloveka / The Lonely Voice of a Man* (1978) for the State Film School (VGIK), was rejected on grounds of what was called "formalism" in state socialism: It was more interested in aesthetics than in ideology—this in itself was regarded as anti-Soviet. Already in this first film, Sokurov rejected aiming at (changing) an outside social or socialist reality in favor of an adaptation of realist literature to initiate a process that starts from an internal perspective—in his documentaries sometimes the literary form of a diary provides the internal voice in response to a filmed reality. Sokurov's insightful critic Mikhail Yampolsky observed: "The mentality of Sokurov's heroes is always limited; they can never comprehend reality as a whole" (Yampolsky, 1994: 114).

The reproach of Sokurov's films being regarded as prerevolutionary was thus predictable. The filmmaker did not make things easy for himself. Consequently, Sokurov graduated one year earlier, but was denied the professional qualification for directing feature films—"feature" generally meaning "fiction" film—and only given official permission to direct documentaries. Supported alone by Andrej Tarkovsky, who, although in exile and regarded as subversive by the Soviet officials, nevertheless got him work at Lenfilm Studios. Sokurov went on to make feature films with Lenfilm, and the Leningrad Studio for Documentary Films continued to fund his documentaries. However, until 1987 all his films remained unscreened. Sokurov frequently had to hide the film rolls to protect his films from being destroyed by the Soviet censors. His films were only approved by the April 1985 Plenary Meeting of the CPDSU Central Committee in the wake of the democratic reforms of perestroika (Stishova, 1995: 260). In 1986, the Soviet Filmmakers Union was appointed a new First Secretary, Elem Klimov, who himself had had several of his films banned and was keen to help other filmmakers who had been subjected to censorship. From 1987 onward, Sokurov's films could be screened publically at home and abroad.

Like his most successful fiction film, *Russkij kovcheg* (2002), Sokurov's documentary *Elegiya iz Rossii* (1992) opens with a black screen. For the first four minutes we hear only the sound of breathing and voices, which seem to indicate that this is the breath of a dying person. After the breathing has stopped, an image emerges from the darkness: only after death, we can finally see. For Sokurov, film is another life (Galetski, 2001: 4). His continuous and original explorations of death have specific implications for documentary. Death cannot be documented; it is a fiction for film as well as for the living. "Documenting" death is a paradox that exceeds comprehension. This is where Sokurov's documentaries go beyond the terrain of conventional subjective documentary about (lived) experience. In many of his documentary elegies (a poetic lament for the dead) as well as in several fiction films, Sokurov explores the subject of death also in terms of movement. His images are often static with barely any motion. Sometimes only the falling of snow, the flying of seagulls, or the moving of light indicate that we are looking at a film and not a photo or a painting. Sokurov's films frequently show people who are only a few movements away from eternal stillness and darkness. In *Elegiya iz Rossii*, an old man is lying immobile on a bed. First we cannot discern whether we see a photo or if he is dead, but then he moves. Sokurov's images evoke uncertainty as to whether their subjects are alive or dead: Is the motionlessness of the image or in the image?

Sokurov has taken Tarkovski's rejection of montage and the embrace of the long take even further. As his films emerge with the seemingly least possible movement, they make the already slow pans of his mentor seem like action films. Sokurov's patience with the long take frequently evokes comparisons to André Bazin.

This neo-realist critic sought the long take with a deep focus for a truer, spiritual understanding of reality manifested in the documentary quality of the images. In contrast to interpretations of Sokurov's long takes as Bazinan (French, 2003) however, this spiritual filmmaker rejects documentary realism and depth-of-field in favor of a flat and opaque painterly look. Unlike the promotion of surface through the long take in Andy Warhol's *Sleep,* however—or Sam Taylor-Wood's video of the sleeping celebrity David Beckham—when Sokurov films a person with his or her eyes closed or sleeping, it suggests a blocking of externality as superficial in favour of an internal reality. And since external reality is usually that which features in documentaries and is in some quarters regarded as the only reality it is possible to document, his subjective documentaries are frequently classified as "semidocumentaries" or not as documentaries at all. Recently, critics have linked Sokurov's deliberate, textual exploration of "blind images" in his work since the late 1970s with the deterioration of Sokurov's own eyesight since the late 1990s (Macnab, 2003).

The rejection of reality as external for Sokurov goes together with a hightened importance of often ambient sound. He thus suggested that the visual film and the sound film "ought to be able to exist apart from one another. If you listen to the sound on the film, it should be enough on its own" (Sokurov in Christie, 1998: 16). The stillness in Sokurov's images is equivalent to the silence on the voice-tracks. In many of his documentaries—for example, *Mariya* (1978/1988)*, Dukhovnyje golosa* (1995), *Hubert Robert. Schastlivaya zhizn* (1996)*, Povinnost* (1998)*, Elegiya dorogi* (2001)—and also in his fiction film *Russkij kovcheg* (2002), the filmmaker narrates in a whisper directly into the microphone as though he were speaking silently to himself. Sometimes his narration describes what we see in the images—often sensual, immediate impressions. In *Dukhovnyje golosa* (1990), for example, we see a landscape clouded in dust to which his voice repeats "Everything is clouded with dust." But the repetition of what we see in his narration does not heighten the immediacy; instead, it manifests the distance between the voice of the documentary subject and what it talks about, which is often what is shown. Thus, paradoxically, the closeness of the filmmaker's voice enhances the distance to its object; intimacy here brings isolation. The reality of the narrator is distinct from the external documentary reality—it is not an objective commentary that uses images illustratively as evidence. Apart from the fact that his father was a professional soldier, Sokurov's frequent observation of soldiers is perhaps also motivated by the fact that they—like their documentary observer—are already in an alien environment. Sokurov even assumes a position of distance with respect to his own past thoughts, by using them like quotes from a literary source, rather than as direct expressions. In *Dukhovnyje golosa,* for instance, he narrates: "Here's another entry from my diary: 'I feel calm and unafraid walking along these paths, following these people. I don't feel excluded by them.' But maybe I'm wrong. Maybe I'm wrong in thinking that I've become one of them." Sokurov's documentaries originally have turned observation into a literary, poetic form. They seldom give their subjects a voice in direct speech and they are not informative. For example *Dukhovnyje golosa,* depicting Russian soldiers at a border post between Afghanistan and Tadjikistan, does not provide any substantial context. Sokurov observes the traces of their existence, not their tasks or their goals. When we finally "see" a soldier shoot, we do not see what he shoots at. We hear the sound and see the ground on which used ammunition casings fall. A pan upwards then shows a soldier from behind. His aim can only be deduced indirectly.

Sokurov's documentaries often manifest disorientation and question understanding. In *Elegiya dorogi,* the off-screen narrating filmmaker is uncertain about what he sees and where he is. In his fiction film *Russkij kovcheg,* the filmmaker too provides the voice of an invisible commentator who wonders where he is. However, whereas in the fiction film the effect of this uncertainty is merely theatrical, in the documentary *Elegiya dorogi* the purported lack of agency of the filmmaker in and over his video has consequences with regard to referentiality. Sokurov's passive narrator's stance pushes the observational attitude of documentary filmmaking to its impossible limits: He denies knowledge and responsibility as a filmmaker and as his own protagonist. The disorientation is not only with respect to his narrative journey in the video but also with regard to the materiality of the medium and the referentiality of the images he sees: He addresses eighteenth-century paintings as though they depicted his recent past, and his own documentary reality as though it was a distant event, directed by someone else. In

Elegiya dorogi, Sokurov's exaggeration of the notion of documentary filmmaking as a passive following of events reverts the orders of before and after, of creation and documentation. Sokurov blocks the viewers' comprehension not only of content but also of the very visual image itself. His images are blurred, soft, dark, and contorted or they take an exceptionally long time to focus. It is often hard to make out what they actually depict. Superimpositions haunt his images like ghosts. The viewer is disorientated by long cross-fades with indiscernible transitions. One does not know what one looks at—or in which medium one looks at it: a photo or a moving image, a painting or reality. As with Wittgenstein's duck-rabbit, one can either switch between the two options or see an altogether new image that does not make sense. Sokurov's images keep us from being able to fully comprehend what we see by making themselves hard to read.

SILKE PANSE

Biography

Born July 14, 1951, in Podorvikha, near Irkutsk, Russia. Tenure as director's assistant for Gorki television and MA in history at Gorky University, 1968–1974. Studied film production in the class of Alexander Zguridi at the State Film School (VGIK) in Moscow with an Eisenstein Scholarship, 1975–1979. Employed by Lenfilm, Leningrad, 1980. Still lives and works in St. Petersburg.

Selected Films

1957–1990 *Leningradskaya retrospektiva (1957–1990) (Leningrad Retrospective (1957–1990)* Partt 1-16

1978/1988 *Mariya/Krestyanskaya elegiya (Maria/Peasant Elegy)*

1979/1989 *Sonata dlya Gitlera (Sonata for Hitler)*

1981 *Altovaya sonata: Dmitrii Shostakovich (Sonata for Viola. Dmitri Shostakovitch)* Co-directed by Semyon Aranovitj

1982/1987 *I nichego bolshe (And Nothing More)*

1984/1987 *Zhertva vechernyaya (Evening Sacrifice)*

1985/1987 *Terpenie trud (Patient Labour)*

1986 *Elegiya (Elegy)*

1986/1988 *Moskovskaya elegiya (Moscow Elegy)*

1989 *Sovetskaya elegiya (Soviet Elegy)*

1990 *Petersburgskaya elegiya (Petersburg Elegy)*

1990 *Leningradskaya kinochronika No. 5 "K Sobytiyam v Zakavkazye" (Leningrad Film Chronicle* Newsreel No. 5, Special Issue *"On the Events in the Transcaucasian Region")*

1990 *Prostaya elegiya (Simple Elegy)*

1991 *Primer intonatsii (An Example of Intonation)*

1992 *Elegiya iz Rossii (Russian Elegy/Sketches for Sleep)*

1995 *Soldatski Son (Soldier's Dream)*

1995 *Dukhovnyje golosa (Spiritual Voices* Part 1-5)

1996 *Vostochnaya elegiya (Oriental Elegy)*

1996 *Robert. Schastlivaya zhizn (Hubert Robert. A Fortunate Life)*

1997 *Smirennaya zhizn (A Humble Life)*

1997 *Petersburgski dnevnik. Otkrytie pamjatnika Dostoevskomu (The St. Petersburg Diary. Inauguration of a Monument to Dostoevsky)*

1998 *Petersburgski dnevnik. Kvartira Kozintseva (The St. Petersburg Diary. Kozintsev's Flat Povinnost / Confession* Part 1-5

1998 *Besedy s Solzhenitsynym (The Dialogues with Solzhenitsyn)*

1999 *Dolce . . . (Tenderly . . .)*

2001 *Elegiya dorogi (Elegy of a Voyage)*

2004 *Peterburgski dnevnik. Motsart Rekviem (The St. Petersburg Diary. Mozart Requiem)*

Further Reading

Christie, Ian (ed.), "Dossier: Aleksandr Sokurov, The Russian Idea," in *Film Studies: An International Review,* no. 1, Spring 1999, 63–77.

Christie, Ian, "The Civilising Russian," in *Sight and Sound,* 13, no. 4, April 2003, 10–11.

French, Phillip, "Take a Chance on a Long Shot," in *The Observer,* 6.4, 2003.

Galetski, Kirill, "The Foundations of Film Art: An Interview with Alexander Sokurov," in *Cineaste,* 26, no. 3, 2001, 4–9.

Halligan, Benjamin, "The Remaining Second World: Sokurov and *Russian Ark,*" in *Senses of Cinema: An Online Film Journal Devoted to the Serious and Eclectic Discussion of Cinema,* no. 25, March–April 2003.

Jameson, Frederick, "On Soviet Magic Realism," in *The Geopolitical Aesthetic: Cinema and Space in the World System,* Frederick Jameson (ed.), Bloomington: Indiana University Press, 1992, 87–113.

Macnab, Geoffrey, "Eyeless in Turin," in *The Guardian,* 19.11, 2003.

Schrader, Paul, "'The History of an Artist's Soul Is a Very Sad History,'" in *Film Comment,* 33, no. 6, 21.11, 1997, 20.

Sokurov, Alexandr, "Sokurov on Sound," Ian Christie (ed.), and "Returning to Zero," in *Sight and Sound,* 8, no.4, April 1998, 4, 14–17.

Sokurov, Aleksandr, "Death, the Banal Leveller (on Tarkovsky)," in *Film Studies: An International Review,* no. 1, Spring 1999, 64.

Stishova, Elena, "Look Who's Here! A New Trend in Soviet Cinema!" in *Re-entering the Sign: Articulating New Russian Culture,* Elle E. Berry and Anesa Miller-Pogacar (eds.), Ann Arbor: University of Michigan Press, 1995, 259–269.

Tuchinskaja, Alexandra, "The Creation," in *The Island of Sokurov. An official Website of Alexander Sokurov,* http://sokurov.spb.ru/island_en/crt.html, 2001.

Yampolsky, Mikhail, "The World as a Mirror for the Other World," in *Russian Critics on the Cinema of Glasnost,* Michael Brashinsky and Andres Horton (eds.), Cambridge: Cambridge University Press, 1994, 114–115.

SONG OF CEYLON, THE

(UK, Wright, 1934–1935)

The Song of Ceylon, a relatively lengthy, intricate, lyrical film directed by Basil Wright, is acclaimed as the crowning achievement of the first phase of the British documentary movement. It clearly displays the shaping influence of modernist aesthetics on early British documentary practice, as well as the more specific influence of documentary pioneer Robert Flaherty. *The Song of Ceylon* won the Prix du Gouvernement Belge at the 1935 Brussels film festival and has long enjoyed a reputation as one of the key texts in the documentary film canon. In recent years critical interest has extended from analysis of the film's aesthetics to interrogation of its relationship to colonial discourse and acknowledgment of its homoerotic representation of Ceylonese bodies.

The Song of Ceylon's genesis lay in the decision by Gervas Huxley at the Ceylon Tea Marketing Board to sponsor a series of public relations films. In doing so he emulated the policy promoted by Stephen Tallents, his former boss at the Empire Marketing Board (EMB). The initial conception was to produce a series of four short films on topics such as Ceylonese agriculture and fisheries. Production began during a period of transition as John Grierson's documentary film unit moved from the EMB to the General Post Office (GPO). Despite these uncertain circumstances Grierson remained fully committed to Wright's project. As the quality of the material became apparent he encouraged Wright to integrate it into a single, more substantial film. Wright's shorts prior to *The Song of Ceylon* had attracted positive critical attention, with some commentators even proclaiming him the first British documentary film "poet." Although Grierson was resistant to any kind of "art for art's sake" stance, having one of his filmmakers regarded in this way enhanced the movement's standing within highbrow British film culture.

Wright always considered *The Song of Ceylon* his best film, partly because he became so immersed in the process of directing it. The contemplative aspects of Buddhism impressed him deeply and he sought to incorporate this feeling into the film. Wright, assisted by John Taylor, was responsible for cinematography as well as direction, and his images represent Ceylon as a domain of calm and beauty, ease and grace. Finely judged camera pans made possible by a tripod with a fluid gyrohead contribute to this impression. Wright had worked with Flaherty earlier in his career and his influence can be detected in camera pans that anticipate subjects' movements. This technique is used to particularly good effect in the sequence featuring marvelously adorned male dancers near to the end of the film.

Several British documentary films of this period, for example *Night Mail* (1936), were influenced by modernist aesthetics. *Night Mail*, however, inaugurated more narrativised forms of British documentary, whereas *The Song of Ceylon*'s structure is indebted to an earlier tradition. It resembles the modernist "city symphony," exemplified by films such as *Rien que les heures* (Alberto Cavalcanti, France, 1926) and *Berlin, Symphony of a Great City* (Walter Ruttmann, Germany, 1927) insofar as it is structured in terms of a geographical demarcation and thematic linkages between shots and sequences (Guynn, 1998). *The Song of Ceylon* is subdivided into four sections, each with its own title: "1. The Buddha," concerned with religious observances; "2. The Virgin Island," traditional handicrafts, house building, harvesting, fishing and the training of dancers; "3. The Voices of Commerce," which represents imperial trade and industrialisation; and "4. The Apparel of a God," which returns to the religious emphasis of the first section.

One important difference between *The Song of Ceylon* and the city symphonies set in Western metropolises is that they often concentrate on diversity and change, whereas Wright's film privileges uniformity and continuity. *The Song of Ceylon* implies that the religious and traditional practices it represents constitute the essence of an

The Song of Ceylon, 1934–1935.
[*Still courtesy of the British Film Institute*]

entire culture rather than a selective record primarily of its rural areas. Urban space and industrial, administrative, and professional work is only briefly represented toward the end of "The Voices of Commerce," and there is no explicit reference to the existence of different ethnic groups, religions other than Buddhism, or secular lifestyles. By referring to the country as a whole rather than just a particular area or aspect of the culture, the title promises comprehensiveness but this is something *The Song of Ceylon* does not actually deliver.

Ceylon also stands largely outside history in this film. As its opening titles explain, the bulk of the voice-over narration consists of extracts drawn from an account of Ceylon written in 1680 by the Scot Robert Knox. Visual images illustrating this account seem to confirm that little has changed in the intervening time. In conventional narrative, film editing dissolves, usually between sequences, denote the passing of a brief period of time, but in *The Song of Ceylon* they are used so frequently within as well as between sequences that time becomes indeterminate. This is particularly the case in "The Buddha," when pilgrims ascend the holy mountain known to Europeans as Adam's Peak. This is as much a spiritual journey as a temporal one. Through such devices the film constructs a representation of the eternal spirit of Ceylon.

Contemporary film historians have argued that early British documentaries adapted modernist techniques to represent unified and harmonious rather than conflictual and contradictory social relationships (Higson, 1986; Nichols, 2001). *The Song of Ceylon* bears this out. Its editing derives from the modernist European montage tradition but generally emphasises correlation rather than radical juxtaposition. One example at the end of the "The Buddha" is a series of exquisite shots of a bird perched on a branch and in flight silhouetted against a lake and sky. These alternate with shots of Buddhist monuments. The abruptness of these transitions and the contrast between static monument and moving bird is tempered by careful matching across shots of the bird's flight, the water's flow, and rapid camera pans along the monument. The cumulative effect of this subtle cross-cutting is to conjure into existence a harmonious realm where Buddhism is part of the natural order rather than a historical or cultural phenomenon that changes and develops over time.

The Song of Ceylon's voice-over narration, spoken by Lionel Wendt, does not conform to the stereotype of a reductive, didactic commentary bludgeoning the listener into submission. It is intermittent and does not attempt to explain everything on the image track. Its quietly meditative tone and unusual accent differentiates it from the confidently authoritative southern English white male middle-class voice heard, for example, in *Housing Problems* (Edgar Anstey and Arthur Elton, 1935). Wendt was a Burgher, an English-speaking descendant of native Ceylonese and early European colonists. His voice-over narration conveys empathy, even reverence, toward the subject matter, rather than a detached assessment or contextualisation of it. This emphasis on feeling and experience as well as explanation includes the recitation of passages from Buddhist religious texts, the delivery of which sometimes approximates a mantra. *The Song of Ceylon*'s unconventional voice-over is comprehensible to white Western listeners but does not provide complete access, except perhaps intuitively, to the alluring non-Western world the film represents.

Tantalising inaccessibility is also rendered visually in Wright's film. Graham Greene, in a perceptive review, noted that *The Song of Ceylon* begins and ends with dark shots of fans of foliage that stand as a natural barrier between the onlooker and the beautiful existence glimpsed in the film. *The Song of Ceylon* constructs Ceylon as a desirable space, different to and separate from the world inhabited by its implied white Western viewers. Wendt's voice-over narration tails off toward the end of "The Apparel of a God"; words are ultimately incapable of providing access to all the sacred mysteries of Ceylonese culture. For this film the

essence of Ceylon is something felt rather than something that can be fully explained through rational exposition. *The Song of Ceylon*'s culminating dance sequence eschews voice-over narration and instead utilises anticipatory camera movements to incorporate the viewer into the rhythms of the dancer's movements.

Experimentation with sound was made possible by the British Visatone system newly acquired for the GPO film unit's premises at Blackheath in London. All of *The Song of Ceylon*'s sound was recorded during postproduction. Wright, Alberto Cavalcanti, and composer Walter Leigh were the main collaborators at this stage. Cavalcanti was the only member of this trio with significant experience of sound film and, like Flaherty earlier in his career, Wright found him a congenial mentor who encouraged him to innovate. While working on the soundtrack, Wright co-authored a manifesto in the highbrow journal *Film Art* endorsing the idea of sound-image counterpoint pioneered in particular by Soviet film maker Sergei Eisenstein in the late 1920s (Macpherson, 1980).

"The Voices of Commerce" is the only one of *The Song of Ceylon*'s sections where a discordant note is struck. An assortment of voices, including Wright's, Cavalcanti's, Grierson's, and Stuart Legg's, conduct business and state commodity prices over images of traditional Ceylonese manual labour (Barnouw, 1983). These voices sound coldly impersonal and indifferent to the spiritual and human dimensions of Ceylonese culture referred to in Wendt's narration and valorised on the image track. Some commentators familiar with the ideas expounded in Wright's manifesto interpreted sound-image counterpoint in "The Voices of Commerce" as a concealed critique of imperialist exploitation (Stollery, 2000).

"The Voices of Commerce" section obliquely hints at possible criticisms of Empire without openly subverting the sponsor's brief. More pervasive in *The Song of Ceylon* is a Romantic conception of non-Western otherness. "The Buddha" opens the film with religious representations and the concluding section "The Apparel of a God" returns to this theme. The film's overarching structure emphasises the timelessness of Ceylon's profoundly traditional culture and the visual style lends beauty to its representation. The extracts from Robert Knox's text narrated by Wendt accentuate Ceylon's otherness for the white Western viewer. The full text of Knox's "An Historical Relation of Ceylon" discusses early Portuguese and Dutch colonisation, but there is no acknowledgment of the long record of Western domination and Ceylonese-European interaction in the quotations used in *The Song of Ceylon*. Apart from what might be gleaned from "The Voices of Commerce," this history is largely absent from the film. Fundamentally, it posits Ceylon as essentially other, a partially accessible space offering a seductive alternative to Western modernity (Stollery, 2000).

One of *The Song of Ceylon*'s most seductive aspects is its focus on Ceylonese male bodies, which seem in tune with nature and at ease with their physicality (Waugh, 1996). The British documentary film movement was committed to the cinematic representation of men at work; *The Song of Ceylon* aestheticises and eroticises this commitment. The buttocks, torsos, and supple limbs of semi-naked men feature prominently in the film. Particularly impressive in this respect is the sequence of a fisherman stripped to the waist standing in water casting his nets in "The Virgin Island." Typically, this eroticisation takes place in the context of documenting traditional labour practices, but more languorous moments, such as a semi-naked lone male worshipper praying in "The Apparel of a God," also carry a similar charge. The experience, which cannot be adequately explained in words, of the dance performed by beautifully adorned men at the end of the film is also a sexual one. Wright's Ceylon is in part the locus for the celebration of a desire that could not be overtly expressed in either fictional or documentary filmmaking at that time.

A Song of Ceylon (Laleen Jayamanne, Australia, 1985) is a nonnarrative film directed by a Sri Lankan-born filmmaker. Like *The Song of Ceylon* it experiments with sound, image, and a voice-over narration quoting extracts from a preexistent anthropological text. Unlike its predecessor *A Song of Ceylon* does not intimate an essential, timeless Ceylon, elusively located outside Western modernity but perhaps fleetingly accessible through intuition and emotion. Its concern is not to record or represent Ceylon/Sri Lanka as such but rather to challenge some of the abiding preoccupations and assumptions of Western colonial discourse (Vigneswaran, 2000).

The crucial difference between the two films is that *A Song of Ceylon* refuses the categorical distinction between the Western and non-Western world on which *The Song of Ceylon* ultimately rests. Instead, it contains utopian moments where unorthodox framing, colour pro-

cessing, and editing collapse visible differences between Western, non-Western, male, and female bodies. For all its aesthetic sophistication, coded critique of imperialism, and genuine admiration for aspects of Ceylonese culture, *The Song of Ceylon* still belongs to a tradition of representing inhabitants of the non-Western world as essentially more vital, primitive, and sexual than the white Western viewers the film is designed to address.

MARTIN STOLLERY

See also **Wright, Basil**

The Song of Ceylon (UK, GPO/New Era, 1934–1935). Produced by John Grierson. Direction by Basil Wright. Cinematography by Basil Wright. Editing by Basil Wright. Assistant John Taylor. Script by John Grierson, Basil Wright, and others. Commentary by Lionel Wendt. Sound recording by E. A. Pawley. Sound supervision by Alberto Cavalcanti. Music by Walter Leigh. Filmed in Ceylon and London.

Further Reading

Aitken, Ian, *The Documentary Film Movement: An Anthology*, Edinburgh: EUP, 1998.

Barnouw, Erik, *Documentary: A History of the Nonfiction Film*, New York: Oxford University Press, 1983.

Guyn, William, "The Art of National Projection: Basil Wright's *The Song of Ceylon*," in *Documenting the Documentary*, Barry Keith Grant and Jeannette Sloniowski (eds.), Detroit: Wayne State University Press, 1998, 83–98.

Higson, Andrew, "'Britain's Outstanding Contribution to the Film': The Documentary-Realist Tradition," in *All Our Yesterdays*, Charles Barr (ed.), London: BFI, 1986, 72–97.

Macpherson, Don (ed.), *Traditions of Independence*, London: BFI, 1980.

Nichols, Bill, "Documentary Film and the Modernist Avant-Garde," *Critical Inquiry*, 27, no. 4, Summer 2001, 580–610.

Starr, Cecile, "*The Song of Ceylon*: An Interview with Basil Wright," in *Imagining Reality: The Faber Book of Documentary*, Kevin Macdonald and Mark Cousins (eds.), London: Faber, 1996, 102–111.

Stollery, Martin, *Alternative Empires: European Modernist Cinemas and Cultures of Imperialism*, Exeter: University of Exeter Press, 2000.

Sussex, Elizabeth, *The Rise and Fall of British Documentary*, Berkeley: UCP, 1975.

Swann, Paul, *The British Documentary Film Movement 1926–1946*, Cambridge: CUP, 1989.

Vigneswaran, Priyadarshini, "Hysteria and the Hybrid Body in Laleen Jayamanne's *A Song of Ceylon*," *Journal of Australian Studies*, June 2000, 173–180.

Waugh, Thomas, *Hard to Imagine: Gay Male Eroticism in Photography and Film from Their Beginnings to Stonewall*, New York: Columbia University Press, 1996.

SORROW AND THE PITY, THE

(France, Ophuls, 1969)

The Sorrow and the Pity is not only the most famous of Marcel Ophuls's films; it is also one of the most controversial documentary films in the history of French cinema. Both its subject and the conditions of its release explain its considerable success in France and abroad. It deals with one of the most contentious periods of contemporary French history—the occupation of France by German troops during the Second World War. The film also raises the issue of artistic independence from the pressures of politics.

The Sorrow and the Pity is an account of life in Clermont-Ferrand during the German occupation, and mainly consists of interviews. As the full title indicates, it is a "Chronicle of a French City under the Occupation." Most of the interviews are with local people from this midsize town in the Auvergne region of France. The choice of Clermont-Ferrand as the setting is significant, given its proximity to Vichy, where the collaborationist government of Maréchal Pétain and Pierre Laval retreated from Paris. It is also in the Auvergne region that the armed Resistance, known as the Maquis, originated in 1943. In its geographical isolation and long history dating back to the Gauls, it is a perfect example of a provincial and insular France, often referred to as "La France profonde." The title of the film is taken from the comment made by one of the town residents when asked what she felt about the occupation. "Sorrow and pity," she replied.

Conducted by Marcel Ophuls and André Harris, the interviews feature several inhabitants of Clermont-Ferrand. Going beyond the local dimension, and avoiding a purely anecdotal version of events, the film also includes interviews with political personalities, among them Pierre Mendés-France; ex-French Prime Minister, Sir Anthony Eden; and Jacques Duclos, a prominent figure in the French Communist Party.

The Sorrow and the Pity portrays a town divided, uncertain how to cope and which side to take. The interviews are interweaved with newsreels dating back to World War II. The film carefully avoids being judgmental or even formulating a specific opinion about these events, giving instead a more balanced view of living conditions during these years. It nevertheless aims to challenge the version of life under German occupation promoted by various regimes since the War, in particular the Gaullist idea of a France united against the occupant, and the glamorization of the Resistance. While the public and most commentators have welcomed this openness about an era largely suppressed until the early 1970s, others criticized its prejudices.

The Sorrow and the Pity is considered a landmark among French documentary films. One of the striking features of the film is the manner of openness with which the interviews are conducted. Marcel Ophuls, who, as a Jew, had to flee France to escape persecution, is often credited with having adopted a humanistic approach to these interviews. He allows for collaborationists as well as resistance fighters, German soldiers, and ordinary French people to talk freely

The Sorrow and the Pity, celebrating the liberation of France, 1971.
[*Courtesy of the Everett Collection*]

about their experience of the war and their role in it. The result is a strikingly blunt account of life during the occupation.

Wartime newsreels are presented in montage, and emphasize that much of the information made available to the French people at the time was propaganda put forth by the Germans or the Vichy regime. *The Sorrow and the Pity* also includes film footage from the BBC, in which De Gaulle is given a low profile. Here again, the public is not provided with any particular interpretation of facts, but a mere account of what it was like to live under German occupation. As such, the newsreels add more depth to the film, giving another dimension to the interviews, and acting as a complement to them.

Marcel Ophuls has frequently explained how he perceives his role as a historian. As a documentary filmmaker, he is not concerned with a history made of great narratives, based on theories and generalisations (a Hegelian vision). He prefers instead to collect stories as told by those who were witnesses, which he then places in the context of the period he is exploring, a pragmatic approach that he developed while working in the United States. The result can be anecdotal, and he has been criticized for a kind of downgrading of events to individual experience, but the use of footage allows him to re-create a wider historical perspective. *The Sorrow and the Pity* is a perfect example of his method, which broke new ground in documentary film at the time of its release, and offered new ways to analyse and present a historical subject.

The Sorrow and the Pity, French collaborators surrendering to gendarmes, 1971.
[*Courtesy of the Everett Collection*]

In *The Sorrow and the Pity*, the subject is not just an account of the everyday struggle of the average person. The film is about how memory of a painful time, like the German occupation, can be easily altered, in favour of that of a glorious nation united against the enemy—a version of events that General de Gaulle and the Resistance were all too keen to promote. The film therefore made very uncomfortable viewing for the generation that experienced the wartime events firsthand, and its emphasis on the collaborationists shattered the official version of events that had been passed on to the next generation.

The conditions of the release of *The Sorrow and the Pity* are highly significant, reflecting the unease of French leaders with the Occupation. Ophuls, who never made a secret of his left-leaning political inclination, belongs to a generation of filmmakers who found themselves in conflict with the Gaullist regime. In the late 1960s, he was working for the ORTF, the French state-owned television company, where he was a segment director of *Zoom,* one of its most popular current-affairs programmes. In 1967, he made *Munich, or Peace in Our Time,* produced by André Harris and Alain de Sédouy, which became a television success. *The Sorrow and the Pity* would have followed, if it had not been for the unrest of May 1968.

Ophuls was among those who openly criticized the attempts of the government to censure the reporting of the unrest that shook France in May 1968. Having left the ORTF, he found funding with Swiss and German television, and after months of filming and editing over sixty hours of interviews, *The Sorrow and the Pity* was released in 1969. It became a huge commercial success abroad, and was nominated for Best Documentary at the Academy Awards. It won the National Society of Film Critics Special award.

In France, *The Sorrow and the Pity* was first screened on April 5, 1971, in a small left-bank cinema in Paris, the Studio Saint Séverin. Due to the enthusiastic response of the public, it was then screened at the Paramount-Elysées, where it remained a feature for a record 87 weeks. Nevertheless, Ophuls had to wait another 10 weeks before his film was shown on French television, for which it was originally intended. Although not censured, as is commonly thought, it was simply either turned down or ignored by French television until 1981, when a leftist administration came into power. The television premiere on FR3 attracted 15 million viewers, confirming the success it had already had in theatres, and providing vindication for Ophuls.

The film is 260 minutes long, divided into two parts. The first part, "The Collapse," lasts 127 minutes, and the second part, "The Choice," runs over 133 minutes. It was shot in black and white using a 16mm Éclair Coutant (NPR) and a Nagra with a budget of 500,000 Deutsche Marks. The editing of sixty hours into four and a half is one of the features that made the film so famous, not only to the aficionados of the documentary film but also to the wider public. While Ophuls or André Harris conducted the interviews, the camera operators were trusted with a large degree of flexibility regarding which techniques to use, the result providing an additional layer of texture to these interviews. The cross-cutting technique used in the editing gives a dynamic to the interviews that sustains the attention of the audience over four and a half hours. The depth of the research into the archives for the footages contributes to the richness of the film.

Ophuls directed *Nuremberg and Vietnam: An American Tragedy* (1976) as a sort of sequel to *The Sorrow and the Pity*. Apart from working for the radio and making a variety of documentaries in France, Germany, and the United States, his three adopted countries, Ophuls's other major work related to the war years is *Hotel Terminus: The Life and Times of Klaus Barbie* (1988).

The Sorrow and the Pity played a key role in the reassessment of the French during the German occupation. Ophuls is often credited as the director who inaugurated what are known as the "retro years" of French cinema. While markedly different as a work of fiction, *Lacombe Lucien*, directed by Louis Malle in 1974, is a similar attempt to demystify these years. Claude Lanzmann's 1985 *Shoah* also attempts to determine the truth of a dark and turbulent time in history.

YVAN TARDY

See also **Ophuls, Marcel;** *Shoah*

The Sorrow and the Pity: Chronicle of a French City under the Occupation / Le Chagrin et la Pitié:- Chronique d'une ville française sous l'Occupation. Distributed by Milestone Film and Video Release, Harrington Park, NJ, USA. Directed by Marcel Ophuls (1969). Produced by André Harris and Alain de Sedouy (Productions Télévision Rencontres S.A. 1969). Production director: Wolfgang Theile, assisted by Claude Vajda. Script and interviews by Marcel Ophuls and André Harris. Photography by André Gazut and Jurgen Thieme. Edited by Claude Vajda assisted by Heidi Endruweit and Wiebke Vogler. Mixing by Wolfgang Schroter. Sound by Bernard Migy. Music by Maurice Chevalier ("Notre Espoir," 1941) and Jean Boyer ("ça fait d'excellent français," 1939). Publications: Francis Day S.A. ("ça sent si bon la France," 1942) and Sam Coslow ("Sweeping the Clouds Away," 1930).

Further Reading

Avisar, Llan, *Screening the Holocaust: Cinema's Images of the Unimaginable,"* Bloomington: University of Indiana Press, 1988.

Canby, Vincent, "A Look Back in 'Sorrow and Pity,'" in the *New York Times*, March 26, 1972.

Cantor, Jay, "Death and the Image," in *TriQuarterly*, 79, Fall 1990, 173–198.

Demby, B. J., "The Sorrow and the Pity, A Sense of Loss. A Discussion with Marcel Ophuls," in *Filmmakers' Newsletter*, Ward Hill, MA: December 1972.

Greene, Naomi, "La Vie en Rose: Images of the Occupation in French Cinema," in *Auschwitz and After: Race, Culture, and 'the Jewish Question' in France*, Lawrence D. Kritzman (ed.), New York: Routledge, 1995, 283–298.

James, Carol Plyley, "Documentary and Allegory: History Moralized in Le Chagrin et la Pitié," *The French Review*, 59, no. 1, October 1985, 84–89.

Kazin, Alfred, "Don't Believe They Didn't Know about Hitler," in the *New York Times*, November 28, 1971.

Knight, Arthur, "Marcel Ophul: 'The Sorrow and the Pity,'" in *The Documentary Tradition*, (2nd ed.), selected, arranged, and introduced by Lewis Jacobs, New York: W. W. Norton, 1979, 521–523.

Lyon, Christopher, *The International Dictionary of Films and Filmmakers, Volume II*, New York: Pedigree Books, 1984.

Porton, Richard, "The Troubles He's Seen: An Interview with Marcel Ophuls," In *Cineaste*, 21, no. 3, 1995, 8–13.

Reilly, C. P., "The Sorrow and the Pity. (Film review)," *Films in Review*, XXIII, no. 4, April 1972, 248.

Reynolds, Sian, "The Sorrow and the Pity Revisited: Or, Be Careful, One Train Can Hide Another," *French Cultural Studies*, 1, no. 2, June 1990, 149–159.

Rubenstein, L., "The Sorrow and the Pity. (Film review)," *Cineaste*, V, no. 1, Winter 1971–1972, 15–18.

Silverman, Michael, "The Sorrow and the Pity. (Film review)," *Film Quarterly*, XXV, no. 4, Summer 1972, 56–59.

Wakeman, John (ed.), *World Film Directors: Volume Two, 1945–1985*, New York: H. W. Wilson Company, 1988.

Wilhelm, Elliot, *VideoHound's World Cinema*, Detroit: Visible Ink Press, 1999.

SOUND

Sound is itself a documentary medium. Recorded sound has evidentiary value and can be edited and arranged to provide commentary or supply illustration. Sound can also be stored for archival purposes and compiled as a component of research. Sound in documentary can be loosely divided into three key elements: speech, music, and noise. Alberto Cavalcanti identified these for practical and analytical purposes in 1939 (Weis and Belton, 1985). There are distinctions to be made between direct and indirect varieties of recorded sounds, between synchronous and nonsynchronous recording methods, and between sounds used for exposition and those used for evidentiary purposes, readings on which can be found in Corner (1996) and Rabiger (1992), among others. Ultimately, sound has been largely underdeveloped as an aesthetic component of documentary film, and many of these distinctions are quite literally academic.

Sound recording was used for documentary purposes on radio well before its application to film, and use of the three key elements of speech, music, and noise had already provided a precise conception of how the soundscape operated. Difficulties arose with the application of the methodologies of aural communication to the visual, which had itself been subject to technological and aesthetic evolution to a point where it was capable of both statement and suggestion through image alone.

The relatively slow introduction of sound to documentary film was the result of a combination of economic and technical factors. Both sound-on-disc and optical sound recording systems were expensive and required specialised personnel. The recording of synchronous sound also required a controlled environment, so much so that camera placement in the fiction films of the late 1920s and early 1930s was frequently determined by the location of the microphone. Human and logistical restrictions such as these were not conducive to efficient documentary production. Producers were unable to raise funds to provide for sound, and many directors, such as Robert Flaherty and Basil Wright, were initially uncertain of its worth. "The use of sound imagistically, the crosscutting of sound and visuals (counterpoint) can undoubtedly be effective, but this does not mean to say that good visuals could not get the same effect more legitimately—in fact I begin to wonder if sound has any advantage at all" (Wright, 1934).

The adoption of sound projection in exhibition venues and continuing public expectation of talking pictures led to increased pressure on documentary filmmakers to embrace the technology regardless of the aesthetic or economic costs. Fox Movietone News used its optical printing process in its popular newsreel service from 1927, taking its formats and subject matter from earlier radio equivalents. Other sound newsreels followed, including the strident editorialising of *The March of Time*, which moved from radio in 1935 under the guidance of Louis De Rochemont. These reportage-based formats were considered unsuitable templates for documentary proper, but they hastened its introduction and influenced its evolution.

The application of sound to documentary was initially tentative. Directors accustomed to ordering their observations through images alone used sound primarily as an ambient element. Asynchronous wild-track sound was added to *Man of Aran* (Flaherty, 1934) to compliment the film's striking images of the sea, for example, and music was grafted onto a range of films regardless of score's relationship with the images. Interviews were first used sparingly because of their association with reportage and journalism, but were employed in *Housing Problems* (Elton, Anstey, 1935) as a means of getting closer to the subject. Voice-over was considered a more fruitful approach to spoken narration, and was quickly (and lazily) added in postproduction to several documentary films in order to increase their marketability.

The integration of the elements of speech, music, and noise into a cinematically coherent whole was evident in *Night Mail* (Watt, Wright, 1935). Editing of both sound and image was crucial: Balance between the two was essential for clarity. Recorded "natural" sounds associated with trains were used throughout, and at the climax, a poem by W. H. Auden was also used in conjunction with an original music score by Benjamin Britten. The rhythms of both sound and image editing were synchronised with the sense of movement associated with train journeys, and the film represented the experience visually and aurally as effectively as it recorded it.

Improved economic conditions for documentary production during the second world war fueled the development and use of sound technology. With increased levels of government and military sponsorship, production units were able to upgrade their equipment and establish more efficient operations. Unfortunately though, the rhetorical mode of address favoured by wartime filmmakers tended to emphasise expository voice-overs and dramatic sound effects (sirens, machine guns, aeroplane engines, explosions). This resulted in a lack of structural and aesthetic innovation, although the quality of recording improved.

The introduction of magnetic tape in the 1950s was a significant technical advance. Coupled with the widespread use of lightweight, portable 16mm cameras, this development allowed for flexibility on lower budgets. Observational documentaries in particular benefited from the ability to synchronise portable sound equipment with the camera by means of a magnetic pulse generated by both camera and tape recorder. Sound could be recorded separately and unobtrusively and either perfectly synched with the image to produce a visual and aural record or used nonsynchronously to create dynamic effects. British filmmakers in particular began to make use of nonsynchronous sound. Voices and noises from Covent Garden Market were used with images taken in different locations around the area in *Every Day Except Christmas* (Anderson, 1958), all of which contributed to a sense of the people and the place that was not tied to the particular images or sounds in any given moment of the film.

Synchronous sound largely prevailed, however, especially with the predominance of direct cinema and *cinema vérité*. The gradual rise of the interview also limited innovation, although some mix of synchronicity and asynchronicity was usual. Eyewitness-based historical documentaries like *Night and Fog* (Resnais, 1955) and *Shoah* (Lanzmann, 1985) benefited from oral testimony, but many interview-based films operated on an informational level that barely required documentary imagery to accompany the sound track. A few filmmakers, such as Emile De Antonio and Errol Morris were able to engage with speech and other sounds to stimulate contrapuntal or counterevidentiary relationships, but on the whole the aims and methods of using sound for informational and expositional purposes inherited from the rhetorical mode of documentary remain dominant.

HARVEY O'BRIEN

See also **Every Day Except Christmas**; **Housing Problems**; **Man of Aran**; **March of Time, The**; **Night Mail**

Further Reading

Corner, John, *The Art of Record*, Manchester: Manchester University Press, 1996.
Konigsberg, Ira, *The Complete Film Dictionary*, London and New York: Meridian, 1989.
Rabiger, Michael, *Directing the Documentary*, Boston and London: Focal Press, 1992.
Salt, Barry, *Film Style and Technology: History and Analysis* (2nd ed.), London: Starword, 1992.
Swann, Paul, *The British Documentary Film Movement, 1926–1946*, Cambridge University Press, 1989.
Weis, Elizabeth, and John Belton (eds.), *Film Sound: Theory and Practice*, New York: Columbia University Press, 1985.

SOUTH

(UK, Hurley, 1919)

South is the best known and most widely shown version of the feature documentary compiled from footage taken by the photographer and filmmaker Frank Hurley (1885–1962), during the 1914–1916 attempt to cross Antarctica undertaken by a team of polar explorers led by the former merchant seaman, Sir Ernest Shackleton (1874–1922). Its restoration by the UK's National Film and Television Archive (NFTVA), completed in 1998, has stimulated renewed interest and research in British polar exploration in general and Shackleton in particular.

The first decade of the twentieth century saw intense interest in polar exploration, focused primarily on the race to reach the South Pole on foot between Shackleton's former colleague Robert Falcon Scott and the Norwegian explorer Roald Amundsen in 1910–1911. The Scott expedition set a precedent that Shackleton's team would follow, in that a celebrity photographer (Herbert Ponting) was hired to accompany the expedition and produce still and moving images for subsequent commercial exploitation. As the opening scenes of the Ealing dramatisation of the Scott expedition, *Scott of the Antarctic* (UK 1948, dir. Charles Frend), point out, fund-raising was always a major problem for the Edwardian polar explorers. Advance sales of exploitation rights for photographs and film had proved to be an important source of revenue for Scott.

Although initially reluctant to do likewise, Shackleton was eventually persuaded to hire the

South, 1919.
[*Still courtesy of the British Film Institute*]

Australian photographer Frank Hurley on the strength of his photographs and film (released in Australia as *Home of the Blizzard*) taken on the 1910–1914 Douglas Mawson expedition. The Imperial Trans-Arctic Film Company was filmed to manage the exploitation rights, and the expedition eventually set off in July 1914.

In terms of its stated objective, the Shackleton expedition was, like Scott's, a complete failure. Their ship, the *Endurance,* became trapped in pack ice some 80 miles from the Antarctic ice shelf, from where it was carried north by tidal currents for nine months before being abandoned on October 27, 1915, and crushed by the pack ice on November 21. The events that then unfolded, however, provided Hurley with some spectacular material that formed the basis of the film as it was eventually released four years later. Footage of the *Endurance*'s gradual destruction by the ice is one such example, and interest in the film was stimulated when details of Shackleton's spectacular rescue operation began to emerge. After abandoning the ship, a group of six crew members sailed a small wooden dinghy seventeen days and 800 miles across the storm-ridden Southern Ocean, eventually reaching the island of South Georgia on May 10, 1916. There then followed a two-day forced march across the island in order to reach its only inhabitants. With help from the Uruguayan and Argentinian navies, Shackleton then organised a fresh expedition to rescue his remaining colleagues, including Hurley.

South is the edited version of Hurley's film as released in 1919, two years after the survivors' return to Britain. It performed moderately well at the box office, but suffered to a certain extent from the fundamental change in political climate that had resulted from the events of World War I. This is clearly demonstrated in the opening intertitles to the film as released, which state that the expedition had set off "one month after Shackleton had offered his ship, stores and all personnel to the cause of the country, only to be told that the authorities desired that the Expedition, which had the full support of the Government, should proceed." Although the rescue operation was universally acknowledged to be an astonishing achievement and a vastly preferable outcome to that of the Scott expedition (which had resulted in several deaths), there was a school of thought that held that Shackleton's abilities might have been more usefully deployed fighting the Kaiser than on yet another polar exploration venture that had failed in all its key objectives. On the back of the release of Ponting's sound version of the Scott footage, *90° South*, a subsequent version of Hurley's footage was shown in 1933 with a synchronised commentary and music. The title says it all—*Endurance: The Story of a Glorious Failure*.

South remained out of circulation for almost 80 years after its initial release until it was restored from a wide range of surviving elements by the NFTVA. The archivists who worked on the project took several years to establish the correct running order of each shot and select the best quality extant elements from which to construct the version used to produce the new preservation master. The NFTVA finally released the film in new tinted and toned 35mm prints and a DVD with extensive contextualising material. The marketing of Caroline Alexander's book on the expedition, published in the same year, was coordinated with that of Hurley's film.

This raises the issue of the role that moving image archives play in mediating our access to moving image heritage, especially in the area of nonfiction film where exposure through other means (e.g., broadcasts and retail video sales) is significantly lower. *South* was an obvious candidate for a major restoration, both from a technical standpoint (i.e., the techniques were available to enable high-quality photochemical duplication from surviving elements, which themselves enabled the complete film to be reconstructed)

and a cultural one. The preexisting, almost mythological status of Captain Scott as established by Ponting's footage and *Scott of the Antarctic* created a public interest in and a market for the polar exploration genre. The details of Shackleton's spectacular rescue mission also ensured the newsworthiness of the restoration of the film, not to mention a revival of interest in Hurley's career as a photographer. But it also illustrates the increasing tendency of national moving image archives to prioritise major projects around a restricted range of films, which some would argue is to the detriment of other titles that are of equal cultural importance but a less attractive marketing proposition.

LEO ENTICKNAP

See also **The Great White Silence**

Further Reading

Alexander, Caroline, *The Endurance: Shackleton's Legendary Antarctic Expedition*, New York: Alfred A. Knopf, 1998.
Bickel, Leonard, *In Search of Frank Hurley*, London: Macmillan, 1980.
Shackleton, Sir Ernest, *South: The Story of Shackleton's 1914–17 Expedition*, London: Heinemann, 1919.
Worsley, Frank, *Endurance*, London: George Allen & Unwin, 1931.

SOUTHEAST ASIA

Geographically speaking, Southeast Asia is made up of Brunei, Cambodia, Indonesia, Laos, Malaysia, Myanmar (Burma), Philippines, Singapore, Thailand, and Vietnam. It is an area covering over 43,000 miles and contains a diverse region of countries, dialects, and religions. It is a region that has experienced war, political upheaval, and economic and social instability. These themes are dominant within the documentary films originating from, and being made within, these southeast Asian nations. A common thread that ties all of these countries together is strong government intervention and censorship, thus documentaries produced and exhibited by citizens of the respective nations are considered to be quite important.

Some countries are yet to rediscover their past through the restoration and rediscovery of documentaries and archives—Laos and Cambodia are prime examples. Decades of war and struggle have resulted in less than favorable conditions for local filmmakers and lack of governmental or private funding in these countries means that most documentaries are produced and distributed overseas, or in neighboring countries. Due to the lack of local education, facilities and services, such as equipment, costs, and bureaucratic red–tape, it is quite the norm to have foreign filmmakers shoot documentaries within the region. Traditionally, "wealthier" countries such as Singapore, Indonesia, the Philippines, and Thailand already had an existing documentary film history (and thus professionally maintained and funded Archives) that contributed to being able to produce and sustain local documentary film, whereas poorer countries, such as Laos and Cambodia, required more funding and local facilities and education. This status quo has continued to the present day, although it is hoped that as countries such as Laos and Cambodia open up to commerce and tourists this may gradually change. Greater economic power should mean increased funding and facilities to promote documentary film.

In Indochina, it was historically the French who brought cinema and thus documentary film and various cinematic techniques to Southeast Asia. The French colonial government had extended influence (as French protectorates) in present-day Burma, Cambodia, Laos, Thailand, and Vietnam, and as such were able to bring in new technology. Burma, Malaysia, and Singapore had access to Indian film markets and technology, whereas the Philippines had both Spanish/European and United States influence and money, thus it also maintains a high level of involvement in all matters of film. It is assumed that documentary filmmaking was introduced into the countries by foreign persons, not by the evolution of an internal film industry, and it appears that trend in foreign film making has continued to the present day.

The majority of contemporary documentaries on Southeast Asia, whether political, economic, socioanthropological, or entertainment, are created and produced either with a fully funded foreign crew or a partially funded local and foreign crew. Singapore, Thailand, Indonesia, Vietnam, and the Philippines are arguably the exceptions, as they seem to have a rich cinematic culture and internal production facilities. However, state censorship is almost always at the forefront of documentary production by domestic producers—especially when dealing with politically sensitive issues.

The Kingdom of Brunei's independent film industry is virtually nonexistent, most locally produced content is passed by government censors as the privately owned press falls under the Sultan's jurisdiction (all family owned with the exception of satellite television). However, the country has made four historically important documentaries under the auspices of the Brunei Information Service (now Information Department). The 1954 documentaries were of the ear-piercing ceremony of the Princess, the birthday of the King, the birthday celebrations of the prophet Mohammad, and the first landing of aircraft to the local airport. They are important, as they map a local history of the Sultan and the introduction of technology to this nation, however, they are difficult to purchase and view.

Burma (formally Myanmar) had a lively film history and was receptive to Indian cinema from across the border. The most famous of Burmese producers are U Nyi Pu and U Ohn Maung, who are believed to be the country's first documentary film directors. On bequest of the Burmese government, they exhibited their commissioned film in London for the 1919 Empire Exhibition—a documentary on the silk, rice, and teak trade in Burma. It was the first Burmese documentary to be exhibited overseas. U Ohn Maung also shot a documentary on the death of a delegate, U Htoon Shein, his funeral procession shown in the Cinema de Paris in Yangon. This was the first documentary shown in Burma made by a Burmese national.

Unfortunately, as the present ruling Junta party and indigenous tribes are technically at war, it is virtually impossible to film documentaries within the country any longer without significant risk. Political documentaries do exist in relation to the ruling Junta party, in particular the political struggles of humanitarian Aung San Suu Kyi. *Aung San Suu Kyi: The Prisoner of Rangoon* (Claude Schauli, 2003) is an example. Major television stations such as the BBC and CNN show documentaries commissioned by themselves, as most are mainly interviews with additional footage of protests dispersed throughout, and are usually dependent on informants within Burma for information or permission to film a specified event for a specified amount of time. With the use of hidden cameras, documentaries are increasingly dealing with the indigenous tribes within Burma and the problems associated with one-party rule. *The Forgotten War* (Frank Smith, 2002) is one such example.

King Norodom Sihanouk has arguably been one of the few Cambodian documentary filmmakers to successfully produce and exhibit his own films. Creating documentaries from the early 1960s to the 1990s, King Sihanouk created a Cambodia in his image, the films usually obscuring or avoiding references to poverty, war, and other hardship that the country has suffered at the hands of Pol Pot and the Khmer Rouge. The most well known documentaries include *Cambodia 1965* (1965), *The Visit of General de Gaulle to the Kingdom of Cambodia* (1966), and *The Pagoda of the Emerald Buddha at Phnom Penh* (1995).

The majority of available Cambodian documentaries are mainly on Pol Pot and the Khmer Rouge. Most documentaries and their producers are not living in Cambodia, as facilities are lacking. The most famous Cambodian documentary producer is Rithy Panh, who is based in France. Panh produced four well-known documentaries that are considered to be Cambodia's finest attempt at addressing the issue of genocide at the hands of the Pol Pot Regime. Panh shot *Around the Borders* (1989), semi-documentary *Bophana, a Cambodian Tragedy* (1996), *The Land of Wandering Souls* (1999), and *S21 The Khmer Rouge Killing Machine* (2003). *S21* was awarded the International Human Rights Film award.

Indonesia has an extensive documentary history. It has a state-run center that produces sanctioned and approved documentaries for television. Documentaries and films must be approved by the Directorate of Film of the Department of Information in Jakarta.

Indonesia covers a vast amount of area and many different religions; thus the range of documentary film on offer is quite astounding. Sociological and anthropological documentaries are common, most focusing on cultural aspects of Indonesian society. *The Three Worlds of Bali* (Ira Abrams, 1979) is especially well known. The Suharto and Sukarno regimes are popular topics; Chris Hilton's *Shadowplay* (2002) is perhaps one of the most famous examples of a film on this topic.

Laos, now a Communist nation, once had a promising cinema and documentary film industry. In 1975 the Communist insurgents overthrew the ruling monarchy and, as a result, few official cinematic representations of the country exists. What did exist had been withheld, or kept in Vietnam at the Vietnam Film Institute until 1998, when it was repatriated to the new Lao National Film Archive and Video center. It was estimated that around 1,192 Lao films were returned; however, it is unknown whether politically sensitive documentaries and footage of the former Royal family were still kept in Vietnam or destroyed. The Lao National Film Archive and Video center now consists of over 2,000 titles and is seen as the official government body in charge of Lao film and video.

The oldest known independently produced documentary film in Laos was shot and produced around 1956 and featured glimpses of the royal family. The majority of documentaries that exist today are shot by either the Communist Lao Patriotic Front Documentary Film Service, which filmed various documentaries about their activities (post- and prewar time), or Lao and Vietnamese soldiers filming incursions into Laos. *Xayxana Ladulaeng* (*Dry Season Victory,* 1970) and *Xaopi*

Haeng Karnpathiwath (*20 Years of the Revolution,* 1965). As both Laos and Vietnam are still considered Communist nations, it remains difficult to gain comprehensive and correct information on documentaries produced within the country, especially when dealing with restoration and "preservation" of important historical records. It is hoped that as the new archive center becomes more autonomous, the Lao will have greater control over visual historical material. Audiovisual material within Laos is also heavily censored.

Documentaries made by non-Lao persons are far more common, however, and receive the most exposure outside of Laos national boundaries. Some interesting Lao-themed documentaries include *The Mekong, A Turbulent River: Laos and Thailand* (1989), *Moving Mountains* (Elaine Velasquez, 1990), and *Blue Collar and Buddha* (Taggart Siegel, 1987). The latter are documentaries that attest to cultural, social, and political upheaval of Lao to the United States, a theme readily explored in the majority of films shot outside of Laos.

In Vietnam, the main topic of documentary interest is the Vietnam War and the postwar era. American involvement in the region and the global consequences of the war have resulted in a higher awareness of the country, and an increased interest in making and showing documentaries. Previously, most readily available (outside of Vietnamese borders) documentary footage shot in Vietnam was shot during the war, with the exception of Vietnamese agents shooting films in neighboring Laos. American GIs and persons stationed in the region to report on the war were avid filmmakers—indeed, quite a lot of documentaries shot in Vietnam are joint productions with U.S. and Vietnamese filmmakers. Domestically, however, Vietnam produces more documentaries than feature films and has had a local history of documentary production. *The Electric Line to the Song Da Construction Site* (Le Manh Thich, 1981) and *Nguyen Ai Quoc-Ho Chi Minh* (Pham Ky Nam) are famous documentaries.

The Vietnam Central Documentary Film Unit has been established in contemporary Vietnam, and one of its employees is Vietnam's best-known contemporary documentary producer. Tran Van Thuy's 1998 documentary, *The Sound of the Violin in My Lai (Tieng Vi Cam O My Lai),* won the 2000 Best Documentary Prize at the Asia Pacific Film Festival. The documentary also won the Golden Dove Prize and the Silver Dove Prize at the Leipzig International Film Festival.

The first set of documentaries thought to have originated from Malaysia were produced by

American Frank Buck in the late 1920s to mid-1930s. The relative success of these meant that a series of wildlife documentaries called *Bring 'Em Back Alive* (Clyde Elliott, 1932), *Wild Cargo* (1934), and *Fang and Claw* (1935) were also shot in Malaysia.

Malaysia has had a solid National Archive since 1957. However, the storing and preserving of film media started to occur only in the late 1970s to early 1980s. The Archives have a standing arrangement with the Malaysian National Film Department and Radio Television section to deposit and store such items. Malaysia also purchased quite a number of documentaries from the United Kingdom and Japan to build on the collection. The Japanese occupation of Malaya also saw documentary newsreels and mini-documentary films produced as propaganda tools. It is believed that the *Bunka Eiga Gekijio* (Government Propaganda Unit) produced and screened over 200 such documentaries, although this was also spread throughout the countries that it occupied.

The Philippines has had a tumultuous film culture, possibly due to the intervention of the Spanish, American, and Filipino interests at particular periods in history. Documentary film is thought that have been introduced to the Philippines by two Swiss businessmen in 1987. They presented a captive audience with a documentary of events and natural disasters taking place in Europe. The first locally produced series of documentaries are thought to have been shot by a local filmmaker, Albert Yearsley. A documentary of the Rizal day celebrations was filmed in 1909 and the ensuring enthusiasm that surrounded it enabled him to film *The Manila Carnival* (1910), *The Eruption of Taal Volcano* (1911), *The Tondo, Paco and Pandacan Fires* (1911), *Igorots to Barcelona* (1912), and *The Cebu Typhoon* (1912). The first Filipino filmmaker was Jose Nepomuceno, who shot a documentary on the funeral of Dona Estefania Velasco Vda. De Osmena (wife to former president). He went on to produce documentaries on the growing Filipino industry sector and social commentary documentaries on U.S. presidential elections.

The first color lab in the Philippines created the first color documentaries and newsreels in 1934 and later evolved into feature films. Filipino cinema is one of the top producers of feature films in the world and thus supports the production of a greater number of documentary films. eKsperimEnto, the Festival of Film, Video and New Media in Manila showcases new local documentaries and has gained quite a global following.

Various documentaries are shown that might not otherwise have an audience.

The nation of Singapore has a thriving documentary community and supports documentary filmmakers more adequately than most southeast Asian nations. The annual Singapore International Documentary Film Festival aims to bring international documentary films and their directors to the nation as well as exposing Singaporean and southeast Asian documentaries to the international community. Sixteen international broadcasting channels have made Singapore their regional base, thus documentaries are readily available and are screened regularly on air. National Geographic Channels International coupled with Singapore Economic Development Board donate from $8 to 10 million U.S. dollars for funding documentaries produced in Singapore. This is considered to be the most allocated funding available within Southeast Asia for documentary film production.

Contemporary Singapore has a strong tertiary emphasis on media, thus despite its totalitarian attitude, it appears to be quite free to make documentaries with the minimal amount of intervention. Arguably the most well known contemporary Singaporean documentary producer is Royston Tan. His cutting edge documentary *15* (2003) was produced with a grant from the Singapore Film Commission and won the NETPAC/FIPRESCI Award at the Singapore International Film Festival and also represented Singapore at the first Paris Asian Film Festival in 2004.

Thailand is often viewed as the entrance to mainland Southeast Asia and has an extensive cinematic history. Thailand, Vietnam, Indonesia, and the Philippines are often seen as the four countries that produce more documentaries than their neighbors. Thailand has a strong filmic culture, and as such has both the funding and facilities to continue its strong presence. Thailand's National Film Archive is said to have over 4,000 documentary films in storage. Most are not considered to fall within the strict confines of "documentary," as they depict everything from celebrations of the Kingdom to simple visual records of areas, and are not filmed with a narrative. They are regarded as such because they provide a visual documentary history of events that may or may not have been publicized outside of the Kingdom. Historically Thai documentary film (film shot within Thailand by Thai nationals) has been somewhat censored with authorities and various official departments controlling content, distribution, and exhibition. The United States Information

Service played a part in producing anti-Communist–themed documentaries within Thailand during the Vietnam War and the showing of such films (and trading of skills and equipment) saw Thailand become accustomed to the dispensation of information visually.

Thailand remains, as most of Southeast Asia, a censored society, and documentaries that depict political and socioeconomical struggles are rare. Thailand experienced two of its bloodiest demonstrations calling for constitutional reforms. The first was on October 14, 1973, and the second period was during May 17–20, 1992. People from different social levels in society attended great public rallies. The brutal government crackdown on the protesters in 1973 resulted in an unknown number of deaths, whereas in 1992 over 52 deaths were recorded. For both incidents all nonofficial visual footage of the event was supposedly censored or confiscated. Thus the independent release of *October 14 (Anuthin 14 Tula)* by Bu Shin Klaipan (1973) is considered to be a very important documentary. Another uncensored independently produced documentary was handed out on the streets of Bangkok. It is called *Bloody May (Phrutsapha Mahawippayok)* and featured actual scenes of the fighting in 1992 and is an unofficial record of events. It, too, is considered to be of high importance to independent documentary film in Thailand.

An equally important and more well known political documentary is *Hara Factory Workers Struggle (Karn Torsu Kong Kammakorn Rongngan Hara)* by Jon Ungpakorn (1975). The documentary deals with the fight to keep factory jobs by garment workers in Nakhon Pathom, to the west of Bangkok. Workers were arrested and subject to harassment, and the poor working conditions were caught on film. This documentary, and its sequel in 1976, are rare, as they illustrate Thailand as a military dictatorship where people could not even approach police or welfare agencies for fear of reprisals.

As the region grows and borders open, documentary film will provide both a visual history of changes as well as a connection to the past that feature films often fail to capture.

SAMARA L. ALLSOP

Selected Films

Burma

Leadingham, Kevin, *A Refugee and Me*
Marty, Irene, *In the Shadows of the Pagodas—The other Burma*, KAIROS-Film GmbH, Zurich, Switzerland
Saunders, David (2001), *Saved*, USA

Cambodia

King Sihanouk and Talabot, Marcel Sos Kem (1995), *Cambodge: Le pays du sourire* (Cambodia: Land of Smiles)
Bruno, Ellen (1989), *Samsara: Death and Rebirth in Cambodia*, Department of Communications, Stanford University, USA
Love, Dean *Guardians of Angkor*, National Geographic Television, Singapore and USA

Indonesia

Hickson, Jill (1999), *Indonesia in Revolt—Democracy or Death*, Australia
Ivens, Joris (1946), *L'Indonésie appelle*

Laos

ABC Australia (2001), *Laos: Closed to Prying Eyes*, Australia
Bouyavong, Douang, Deuane (1991), *From Mulberry Leaves to Silk Textiles*, Vientiane Video Center for the Ministry of Culture, Laos
Kmhmu Apprenticeship Program (1988), *Keeping our Culture Alive*, Kmhmu Apprenticeship Program, Boston, USA

Malaysia

Chauly, Bernice (1995), *Bakun or the Dam*, Malaysia

Thailand

Anderson, Ben and Watthanasuwan, Kritsadarat (1993), *October 14, 1973*, Thailand
Morgan, Susan (1993), *Threads of Life*, Thailand
Children's Foundation of Thailand, under Project for Thai Mercy, *Relatives of May '92 Crackdown*, Thailand

Vietnam

Mason, Michelle (2003), *The Friendship Village*, Cypress Park Productions, USA
Remy, Ada and Yves (1991), *La Memoire et l'oubli*, France 3 TV, France
Tran Van Thuy (1994), *Tolerance for the Dead (Mot Coi Tam Linh)*, Channel 4 Productions, Vietnam

Further Reading

Alexander, William, "Vietnam: An Appropriate Pedagogy," in *Jump Cut*, March 31, 1986, 59–62.
Bayer, William, "Films in Vietnam," in *Film Comment*, 5, no. 2, Spring 1969, 46–80.
Biran, Misbach Yusa, "The History of Indonesian Cinema at a Glance," in *Film in Southeast Asia: Views from the Region*, David Hanan (ed.), Vietnam: SEAPAVAA in Association with the Vietnam Film Institute and the National Screen and Sound Archive of Australia, 2001.
Blum-Reid, *East-West Encounters–Franco-Asian Cinema and Literature*, London: Wallflower Press, 2003.
Boonyaketmala, Boonrak, "The Rise and Fall of the Film Industry in Thailand," *East-West Film Journal*, 6, no. 2, 62–98.
Charlot, John, "Vietnamese Cinema: First Views," in *Colonialism and Nationalism in Asian Cinema*, Wimal

Dissanayake (ed.), Bloomington: Indiana University Press, 1994.

Debrett, Mary, "Reclaiming the Personal as Political: Three Documentaries on East Timor," *Metro Magazine*, Fall 2003.

Hanan, David (ed.), *Film in Southeast Asia: Views from the Region*, Vietnam: SEAPAVAA in Association with the Vietnam Film Institute and the National Screen and Sound Archive of Australia, 2001.

Latif, Baharudin, "A Brief History of Malaysian Film," in *Film in Southeast Asia: Views from the Region*, David Hanan (ed.), Vietnam: SEAPAVAA in Association with the Vietnam Film Institute and the National Screen and Sound Archive of Australia, 2001.

Morgan, Jennyn, *The Film Researcher's Handbook: A Guide to Sources in North America, South America, Asia, Australasia and Africa*, New York: Routledge, 1996.

Phichit, Bounchao, "Lao Cinema," in *Film in Southeast Asia: Views from the Region*, David Hanan (ed.), Vietnam, SEAPAVAA in Association with the Vietnam Film Institute and the National Screen and Sound Archive of Australia, 2001.

Romey, Eliza, "King, Artist, Film-Maker: The Films of Norodom Sihanouk," in *Film in Southeast Asia: Views from the Region*, David Hanan (ed.), Vietnam: SEAPAVAA in Association with the Vietnam Film Institute and the National Screen and Sound Archive of Australia, 2001.

Salumbides, Vicente, *Motion Pictures in the Philippines*, Manila: Vicente Salumbides, 1952.

Sotto, Agustin, "A Brief History of Philippine Cinema," in *Film in Southeast Asia: Views from the Region*, David Hanan (ed.), Vietnam: SEAPAVAA in Association with the Vietnam Film Institute and the National Screen and Sound Archive of Australia, 2001.

Uhde, Jan, and Yvonne Ng Uhde, *Latent Images: Film in Singapore*, Oxford: Oxford University Press, 2000.

SOVIET UNION

See **Russia/Soviet Union**

SPAIN

Spanish documentary film developed at a relatively late stage. In the early days of cinema, Spanish screens were filled with French films and then, from the 1920s, by American films. The political, social, and economic situation influenced filmmaking in Spain. Spain was a constitutional monarchy, with a powerful king and a universal male (vote) controlled by important landlords, a phenomenon known as *caciquismo*, or authoritarianism of local bosses. Some 50 percent of the population was illiterate and 68 percent of the population were rural. Society, dominated by the Catholic church and the military, was preoccupied with colonial ventures in Africa. Employers were continuously confronted with workers' unrest and hired gunmen, and industrial investment depended on foreign capital. In addition, General Primo de Rivera imposed a dictatorship with fascist features in 1923.

The first Spanish images were taken when the Lumiére brothers started selling their equipment. Topical reportage was the most developed genre, since it was cheap and brought relatively easy profit. It became a source of industrial funding for companies (Pérez Perucha, 1995).

At first, Barcelona dominated the film industry. However, Madrid eventually imposed itself as a national filmmaking centre by the 1920s. As of 1925, the banking industry started to invest in the sector—for ideological reasons, however, and not because of economic considerations. The production diversified but without a great take-off: Censorship, foreign competition, and limited exports hindered its expansion. The difficulties caused by the new sound film and the need to invest in new equipment created many problems.

Despite this irregular development, film extended as a popular entertainment. The first cameramen came from different fields, such as photography, optics, theatre, and even cabinetmaking. Some of them studied or worked with large French companies, for example, José Gaspar Serra, Ricardo de Baños, and Segundo de Chomón Ruiz, one of the most creative cameramen. In those days, only small companies existed, which could not survive due to the lack of capital and industrial organization.

Film reportages were repeating topics that ensured success. Images of Alfonso XIII were plentiful; the Spanish audience liked them and they could easily be exported. Reportages were also produced about current events, such as *Semana Trágica de Barcelona (Tragic Week in Barcelona)* (José Gaspar Serra, 1909) and *La Guerra del Rif (The War of the Rif)* (Hispano Films, 1909). Some of them were reconstructions, such as *El asesinato de Canalejas (The Assassination of Canalejas),* created by the journalist and theatre director Adelardo Fernández Arias in 1912. Actors interpreted the moment of the assassination in it. The film also included real images from the funeral of Canalejas, the then Prime Minister of the Spanish government. These films alternated in cinemas with other, everyday-life–type films. However, the most interesting Spanish films were set around bullfighting.

World War I marked the heyday of Spanish filmmaking. The conflict allowed the Spanish film to develop, because the distribution of European films at the time was limited. Twenty-eight production companies produced 242 films, of which 77 were documentaries. When the war was over, however, the foreign production companies returned.

The need for information about WWI led to the creation of the first newsreel in Spain: *Revista Española (Spanish Magazine)* and *Revista Estudio (Studio Magazine,* 1915–1920), produced by Studio Films, under the direction of Solá-Mestres and Fontanals, who edited the first 50 issues. Shortly before closing its studios in 1921, Studio Films shot *España en el Rif (Spain in the Rif),* a report about the African issue, which did not address any unpleasant aspects of the colonial ventures.

After WWI, most nonfiction films covered sports and bullfighting. Some of them made a strong impact on the audience. This, however, was because of the topic, not the quality, as was the case with *Trágica muerte de Joselito (The Tragic Death of Joselito,* 1919). Educational films made by Regia Art Film, whose manager was the expert José Gaspar Serra, also gained a high profile. Many of these films were made in Catalonia and Valencia. They dealt with the small industries typical of these regions, such as bobbin lace making. Their quaint character led to their presentation in U.S. cinemas.

One of the most important reports was *Las Hurdes, País de Leyenda.Viaje de S.M. el Rey Alfonso XIII (Las Hurdes, The Land of the Legend: Travel of His Majesty the King Alfonso XIII,* 1922), created by Armando Pou, a specialist in colonial film and film advertising. It focused on three basic elements: the land, responsible for the social misery; its inhabitants as the victims of the situation; and the royal delegation as their saviours. The king represented hope and change: "His Majesty enters the Alberca being proclaimed redeemer of Las Hurdes." Ten years later, the famous Spanish director Buñuel went on the same trip and, in *Las Hurdes, Tierra sin pan (Las Hurdes, Land without Bread),* proved that nothing had changed.

The Spanish avant-garde did not greatly contribute to the film industry. But a notable avant-garde documentary was *Esencia de verbena (The Essence of Feasts,* 1930) by the writer and politician Ernesto Giménez Caballero. Through popular feasts, it reflected the character and the typical customs of the people of Madrid. It has a remarkable montage based on associating visual ideas, close-ups, and sophisticated techniques.

When the monarchy fell, the Spanish Second Republic was proclaimed. In these times of political agitation and the establishment of a regime that defended civil rights, social conditions of workers' classes improved and the growth of the entertainment industry was encouraged. The contributions of film clubs, which created film audiences, were important. However, the different Republican governments showed little interest in film: Censorship was regulated, national production was protected, and taxes were introduced.

Filmmakers and distributors increasingly responded to informational needs. The Casanova family founded Cifesa (Valencia, 1932), one of the most important production companies of those years. Its political orientation was conservative, Catholic, and anti-Marxist. Spanish newsreels appeared (Spanish Film Information and Spanish Sound News) and, between 1931 and 1936, approximately 95 documentaries were produced. They dealt with different topics—for example, travel and cultural issues that have a strong tradition in Spain. Enrique Guerner, a Jewish refugee, produced the following documentaries for Cifesa in 1935: *Costa Brava, Granada*, and *Valencia*. They stand out because of the camera technique and lighting used. *Un río bien aprovechado (A River Well Used,* 1935) by the Catalan Ramón Biadiu had an original theme: It followed the river Llobregat from its source to its estuary, describing the industries that were lined up alongside it.

Documentaries that focused on formal expression were produced as well. They dealt with literary and artistic themes. They were meant for entertainment purposes, and did not attempt to reflect the social reality. A notable example is *Canto a la emigración (A Hymn to Emigration)* (Antonio Román, 1934).

The most important documentary references of these years are Carlos Velo and Fernando García Mantilla. Carlos Velo was a biologist and a university professor. Collaborating with Fernando García Mantilla, a radio and film critic, he produced many documentaries for Cifesa in 1935, such as *Felipe II y El Escorial (Philip II and El Escorial), Castillos en Castilla (Castles in Castile), Tarraco Augusta, Galicia y Compostela (Galicia and Compostela),* and *La ciudad y el campo (The Town and the Country). Infinitos (The Infinite),* based on an idea of the writer Mauricio Maeterlinck, stands out. It is a scientific and poetic film that, with imagination and artistic ability, re-creates the world of the microbes. But his most important piece was *Almadrabas (Trap-Nets)* about fishing for tuna on the coast of Cadiz. It initiated the tradition of social documentaries in Spain, which was interrupted in 1939. The nets full of tuna firmly caught by the fishermen with harpoons and hauled into the boat, as well as the quartering and preparing the cans, make for expressive scenes. The main story line focuses on the nature of the human labour, analyzed by the camera with an extraordinary functionality, without succumbing to the picturesque.

In 1933 Luis Buñuel produced *Las Hurdes.Tierra sin pan (Las Hurdes. Land without Bread).* This anthropological film showed the causes of the ailments suffered in a region of Extremadura, and served to denounce the political, social, educational, and religious circumstances of the time. The filming team included Eli Lotar, Pierre Unik, and Sánchez Ventura. The means and funds for the shooting were limited. Some scenes were constructed for the camera, such as the shot in which a goat is to be thrown of a cliff. This documentary contains many surrealistic elements. It was drawn up using a dramatic architecture: A problem is presented, hope is raised, and then hope is destroyed.

During the Spanish Civil War (1936–1939), film acquired new momentum: It was used as an instrument of propaganda by both sides. On the Republican side, the initiatives were taken by the central and regional governments, as well as by political parties and trade unions. High-quality newsreels, such as *España al día (Spain Today),* were given great importance.

The anarchists used film for indoctrination and social revolutionary purposes. Their production concentrated on the campaigns of the anarchist leader Durruti: *Aguiluchos de la FAI por tierras de Aragón (Eaglets of the FAI in the Lands of Aragon,* 1936), *Bajo el signo libertario (Under the Libertarian Sign,* 1936), and *En la brecha (In the Division,* 1937).

The Communists regularly produced films, as the production company Film Popular had been created. They distributed Soviet films and produced documentaries and reportages. They cooperated with the Catalan newsreel *España al día (Spain Today),* of which they later created their own issue. Their goal was to defend the "single command" (*Mando único [Single Command]*, 1937) and to show the educated character of the Republic (*Tesoro artístico nacional [National Artistic Treasure]*, 1937).

The Republican government in Madrid used film to obtain a favourable image abroad. *España 1936 (Spain 1936),* created by Buñuel and Le Chanois, is an example of this strategy. Film also served the specific needs of the country, such as the mobilization (*Movilización del campo [Mobilization in the Country]* and *Cuando el soldado es campesino [When Peasants Become Soldiers],* both from 1937), or instructed popular militia how to handle weapons (*El manejo de la ametralladora [Handling a Machine Gun]*, 1937).

The regional government of Catalonia (the Generalitat) created large film campaigns with their production company Laya Films. This company edited the newsreel *Espanya al día (Spain Today)* between March and June 1939 together with Film Popular. It produced numerous documentaries about the war (*Jornadas de victoria: Teruel [Days of Victory, Teruel]*, 1938) and the brutality of the enemy in order to discredit them (*Catalunya mártir [Martyr Catalonia]*, 1938), and about government actions, culture, and work (*Danzas catalanas y aragonesas [Dances from Catalonia and Aragon]*, 1936–1937) to show Catalonia abroad as an educated and hard-working region.

The film production of the Basque government was more limited. It focused on showing the Catholicism of the government (*Semana Santa en Bilbao [Easter in Bilbao]*, 1937), because the Basques were worried about the anticlericalism attributed to the Republic.

In the Nationalist (Franco's) camp, film was treated in a different way. Initially, only military operations were shown, without any propaganda. From October 1936, the *Falange* (a party with its own organization of propaganda) and private production companies (Cifesa) produced documentaries about military successes, such as the series *Para España (For Spain)*. Film was also used to spread awareness of political messages and platforms. When the government of Burgos was created in February 1938, the Francoist Film Services gained power. The entente with Nazi Germany was decisive. Documentaries were created to spread the principles of the new state (*Juventudes de España [Youth of Spain]*, 1938) and to respond to Republican attacks (*Prisioneros de guerra [Prisoners of War]*, 1938). Similarly, the *Noticiario Español (Spanish Newsreel)* was created, which edited news items to reflect the propagandistic needs of the state.

When the conflict ended, a fascist and Catholic dictatorship was established in Spain, with General Franco as the *caudillo*, or leader. His objective was to obtain ideological unity—there were many and different groups that participated in the rebellion—and to justify himself. Propaganda was therefore essential. Filmmaking was marked by this political situation, the postwar economic crisis, and the situation of isolation.

During Franco's rule, professional competition barely existed as a consequence of the exile of many technicians who left the country after the war. Documentary films were considered a subgenre. Distribution mechanisms were lacking, as well as governmental policies to protect and aid this type of film. The film protection norms were established in 1941 and 1944, and showing documentaries became obligatory. In practice, this requirement was met by showing foreign newsreels (by Fox, UFA, and Luce) and, from 1943, NO-DO, the Spanish official newsreel.

In the 1950s, the dictatorship tried to create a more positive image for itself, in the wake of the Allied victory in World War II. Spain became a member of various international organizations and signed, in addition to the Concordat with the Vatican, a bilateral agreement with the United States. Institutions were reorganized and the Ministry of Information and Tourism (July 1951) was put in charge of film production. García Escudero, a man with liberal ideas, was named film director, but lasted in this position only one month.

In 1952, a new Classification and Censorship Board was created to evaluate the moral, political, and social content of films. Financial aid increased; however, it was given based on the "national interest." Films with certain social or political commitment did not receive any subsidies. Nevertheless, the law favoured "Spanish feature films distributed together with Spanish short films." The following prizes and festivals were founded: National Prizes for Short Films; the International Film Festival in San Sebastián (1953), which included prizes for documentaries; and the International Latin American and Philippine Documentary Film Contest (1958), later called Documentary Film Festival of Bilbao. These festivals were to promote Spanish documentaries and to present foreign documentary films in Spain. Financial protection and film rates (quota of screen time) improved, but the main problem remained: The organizers showed little interest in documentaries.

The Spanish newsreel NO-DO (1943–1981) was created as a joint stock company, but with a state subsidy. It enjoyed a monopoly over film-related information. It also controlled documentary production and means of distribution (Tranche and Sánchez-Biosca, 2001). Its main activity was the creation of the newsreel. To make use of news items, the film magazine *Imágenes (Images)* was organized in 1945, offering reportages.

Documentary film production developed sporadically until the 1960s. The usual topics were towns, customs, museums, and geography. The films showed false popular reality, with a timeless appearance. Technically, they were mediocre. Official film, however, gathered great momentum throughout the 1940s and 1950s. Official bodies such as the Ministry of Agriculture, Ministry of Industry, National Trade Union Office, and National Train Network organized their own services to produce documentaries promoting their activities.

Several production companies specializing in documentary film were founded (Hermic, Studio Film, and Filmarte). They encountered many obstacles: a limited range of topics, difficulty in obtaining the licence for filming (which was managed by NO-DO), and censorship. Their financial profits were marginal. Art documentaries were the most interesting contribution. They did not cause political problems and made use of the newly added colour feature. A remarkable documentary series was shot about the black paintings by Goya (*Desastres de la guerra [Disasters of War], La tauromaquia [The Art of Bullfighting]*, and *Los Caprichos [The Caprices]*). With great precision, they reflected the violence and power that Goya applied in his paintings—thanks to a perfect symbiosis between the camera movement and the painting (López Clemente, 1960).

José Val del Omar was an exception in the filmmaking industry of those years. He was an original author who was not understood by his contemporaries. He tried to build a new audiovisual architecture—the so-called pulsating lighting that consisted of changing rhythm, intensity, color, and light location—in order to achieve a more complete vision. He also created the apanoramic overlap technique, based on a double projection of the same still, and the diaphonic sound technique, which contrasted two sound sources.

José Val del Omar produced two documentaries. The first one was *Aguaespejo granadino (Watermirror of Granada)*, shot between 1952 and 1955, which garnered attention at the Berlin Festival in 1956. The second documentary was *Fuego en Castilla (Fire in Castile)*, awarded a prize at the Cannes festival in 1961 for its technical innovations.

In the 1960s, Spanish film was renewed. The so-called Conversations of Salamanca (1955) were an important starting point. This meeting was organized by the film club of the University of Salamanca and directed by Basilio Martín Patino. The participants, film professionals and critics, published a manifesto with the following conclusions: "Our documentary film must acquire a national character by creating films that fulfill a social function and reflect the life of the Spanish people, their conflicts, and their reality in our days." They defended realism against the fascist aesthetics of the regime. Similarly, they demanded the end of the monopoly of NO-DO.

Already at the end of the 1950s, young filmmakers were creating films that were close to the proposals of the Conversations of Salamanca. *Cuenca* (1958) by Carlos Saura is an example. This documentary continued with the tradition set by Buñuel in *Tierra sin pan (Land without Bread)*. It was funded by the city. It is divided into three parts. The first one shows the inhabitants of the place, peasants, shepherds, and woodcutters. The camera focuses on their faces and sweat, caused by their labor. The second part deals with the history of kings and castles. In the last part, current life is the centrepiece displayed through popular feasts: "Cuenca: different, yet always the same."

España 1800 (Spain 1800) (Jesús Fernández Santos, 1958) is also part of this renewal. It recreated eighteen-century Spain through Goya's paintings. *Hombres y Toros (Men and Bulls)* (José Luis Font, 1958) about the feasts of San Fermín, is another exponent of the renewal.

Definitive societal change came in the 1960s. The decade witnessed rapid economic growth, due to the Development Plans launched by the government. Tourism and Spanish emigration favoured openness toward the outside world. In 1966, Franco organized a referendum, which maintained his position as the head of state. In 1970, Franco appointed the then prince Juan Carlos as his successor.

The administration dedicated itself to celebrating the "25 years of peace." The campaign was designed by the Ministry of Information and Tourism. It did not focus on commemorating the end of the Civil War, but rather on emphasizing the "successes" of the regime. Two documentaries supported this endeavour: *Franco, ese hombre (Franco, That Man)* (Sáenz de Heredia, 1964), a hagiography of the dictator, and *Morir en España (To Die in Spain)* (Mariano Ozores, 1965), which was conceived as a reaction to the French documentary *Mourir à Madrid (To Die in Madrid)* (Frédérix Rossif, 1963). No political film existed that would challenge the official line. Thanks to the political changes since 1973, militant filmmaking developed under the auspices of trade unions and community and student associations.

In 1963, a new Censorship Code was approved and García Escudero was named head of the Film Direction again (1962–1969). The Code prevented arbitrariness and was valid until February 1975 (Franco died in November of that year). Work techniques improved with the use of lighter and portable cameras, direct sound, and more sensitive unexposed film. Production costs were lower. New companies, such as Eurofilms, appeared, encouraged by governmental financial aid programmes of 1964. Exhibition space enlarged: Festivals became stronger, film clubs expanded, and, in 1964, the alternative Art and Performance Halls appeared, in which films were shown in their original versions and subtitled. The number of spectators increased, as well as that of the spectators who participated in cultural discussions and read specialized magazines, such as *Nuestro Cinema (Our Film)* and *Film Ideal (Ideal Film)*. Regional filmmaking developed in Catalonia, the Basque Country, and Galicia, due to the recovery of cultural autonomy.

A group of anti-establishment filmmakers, calling themselves New Spanish Film, was established in Madrid and the New School of Barcelona in Barcelona. They came from the Film Research and Experience Institute (1947–1962) and the Official Film School (1962–1976). Their documentaries dealt with the typical Francoist topics (towns, geography, travels, art) but employed a vision that differed from the official perspective.

Juguetes rotos (Broken Toys) (Manuel Summers, 1966) presents the world of boxing, football, and entertainment through pathetic losers who in other times were praised and admired by the great audience. Spectators are shown the "national myths" with criticism. Censorship forced the producers to add a commentary, which was ironic and sharp, with a moralist content repeating that all Spanish people were responsible for forgetting the old national glories. Even without listening to the voice, the images speak for themselves with an overwhelming force through stereotypes, prejudices, and images of black Spain. It was not commercially successful. *Torerillos 61 (Little Bullfighters 61)* (Basilio Martín Patino, 1962) won the first prize at the Documentary Film Festival in Bilbao. It is a chronicle of a Spain that is hungry and lives in poverty. Its reality is shown through the characters of three boys who want to become bullfighters, who wish to escape their world and become famous.

In the 1960s, NO-DO started a new era as a company producing documentaries on travel, art, and sports as a result of the competition with the television. In 1956, Spanish Television (TVE) started to broadcast. Its monopoly lasted until 1983, when the first regional televisions were founded. Private channels were authorized in 1990.

At the beginning, TVE received news, technical means, and staff from NO-DO. It also produced documentary films. This production was educational: Biographies, travel routes, art, and industry were broadcast for educational purposes. Series were created with screenplays written by specialized authors. They were produced by the staff of TVE. Some examples are *Figuras en su mundo (Figures in Their World,* 1966), *Lo que va de siglo (The Century until Now,* 1968), and *La noche de los tiempos (The Night of the Times,* 1971).

Other documentaries responded to the requirements of informative production, such as the series *A toda plana (A Full Page,* 1964), dedicated to important international reportages. Nature documentaries by Dr. Félix Rodríguez de la Fuente were very successful: *Fauna* (1968), *Mi amigo el océano (My Friend the Ocean,* 1970), and the different series of *El Hombre y la Tierra (The Man and the Earth)*.

Several years before Franco died, the dictatorial regime had started to break down. These years of disintegration until the proclamation of the Spanish democratic Constitution in 1978 are known as the Transition. Measures were taken to free up the processes of film production. From 1975, NO-DO lost its monopoly status, and in 1981, it disappeared all together. In 1977, the Ministry of Information and Tourism was renamed the Ministry of Culture and Welfare (later only Culture). The National Entertainment Trade Unions, and the practice of censorship, disappeared as well. A new system of subsidies came into place that favoured artistic and cultural values, cinema ratings, and film distribution. However, the reforms were not able to ward off the effects of the world economic crisis. The number of filmgoers diminished, and the production costs of making films increased.

Two emblematic films of those years were *El desencanto (Disenchantment)* (Jaime Chavarri) and *Canciones para después de una guerra (Songs for after the War)* (Basilio Martín Patino). The first documentary was made in 1971 and the second one in 1975. Both were shown for the first time in 1976. They represented two different documentary forms. *El desencanto* dealt with the present, through interviews in the style of *cinema verité*. *Canciones para después de una guerra* is a montage that re-creates the past. Forty songs—hits of those years—summarize life in Spain in the ten years after the Civil War. The images follow each other in a collage. However, each shot is carefully selected. Music is related to the image in order to achieve specific meanings. The documentary is very powerful and creative. As in *El desencanto*, the lack of objectivity is not disguised.

The political change allowed filmmakers to tackle delicate topics from the past, such as the Civil War and the dictatorship. Documentary film was used to present viewpoints that differed from the official one. *¿Por qué perdimos la guerra? (Why Did We Lose the War?)* (Diego Santillán and Luis Galindo, 1977), for example, delivers an anarchist version of events.

Film also lent a voice to those who had actively participated in the civil war, and whose voices could not be heard in Franco's Spain. *La vieja memoria (Old Memory)* (Jaime Camino, 1977) offers interviews with left-wing politicians, intercut with archival materials. Opinions are compared and organized into dialogues that never existed in reality, such as the statements of Dolores Ibarruri and Federica Montseny about the disagreement between the Communists and the anarchists.

The figure of Franco inspired several documentaries, such as *Caudillo (The Leader)* (Basilio Martín Patino, 1975). Patino gathered diverse material, some of it unpublished. There is no chronological order; themes follow each other in a dynamic montage, full of contrasts. The music, the way of using image and colours (warm tonalities for the Republican camp and cold ones for the Francoists), without commentary, creates a specific analysis of the Civil War, close to the anarchist view. Franco is portrayed as a grotesque dictator who caused devastation and death.

Raza, el espíritu de Franco (Race, Franco's Spirit) (Gonzalo Herralde, 1977) mixes fragments of the film *Raza (Race,* 1942), the screenplay of which was written by Franco himself, with interviews of the main character, the actor Alfredo Mayo, and the general's sister, Pilar Franco. Documentary films that treat the dictatorship period leniently were also produced—for example, *España debe saber (Spain Must Know)* (Eduardo Manzanos, 1976).

The political openness allowed for newsreels and documentaries to become tools of nationalism. In Catalonia, the newsreel *Noticiari de Barcelona (Newsreel of Barcelona,* 1977–1980) was created. It was directed by Joseph María Forn and financed by the city government of Barcelona. In 1981, it was replaced by *Noticiari de Catalunya (Newsreel of Catalonia),* which was less critical and protected by the regional government (*Generalitat*). In the Basque Country, *ikuskas* (1978–1985), reportages focused on nationalist issues, appeared. Documentaries were made with the same objectives. One of the most controversial documentaries of those years was *El proceso de Burgos (The Process of Burgos,* Imanol Uribe, 1979), which recalls the trial of several ETA militants during the dictatorship. It takes the side of the terrorist organization.

Documentary film was able to shed light on topics previously prohibited by censorship. They began to publicize the plight of the mentally ill, homosexuals, and others perceived as living outside mainstream society. Examples include *El asesino de Pedralbes (The Murderer of Pedralbes,* Gonzalo Herralde, 1978) and *Vestida de Azul (Dressed in Blue,* Jiménez Rico, 1983).

The most significant progress was made in television, which gained a large audience. Documen-

taries about nature topics, successfully developed by Rodríguez de la Fuente, were consolidated. Notable reportages, in which the figure of the reporter became very important, also achieved great success (*Otros pueblos [Other Countries]*, *Los marginados [The Down-and-Outs],* and *La ruta de los conquistadores [The Route of the Conquerors]).* Together with these reportages, documentaries about folklore and popular traditions (series *Flamenco, Fiesta [Feast],* directed by Pío Caro Baroja, and *Raíces [Roots]*), and travels were successful.

When the political enthusiasm of the Transition years waned, the documentary film greatly diminished in importance. During the socialist era (1982–1996), with Pilar Miró as General Director of Film, the public subsidies were very high, but the effect of this policy was negative: Nothing was produced without a subsidy. In 1989, Jorge Semprún, the then-Minister of Culture, adjusted the aid to the European model, and full competency was given to autonomous regional administrations to create protection policies for their own film. This legislation was mainly favourable to fiction films. Even the Goya Prizes, awarded by the Academy of Arts and Film Science, neglect the documentary genre; the prize for the best short film was cancelled in 2001.

Nevertheless, the documentary has gained in strength in contemporary Spain, in parallel with developments in Europe. Its main source is the television. Public channels, especially TV 2, broadcast the largest number of documentaries between 1998 and 1999, supported by their own production. Among the private channels, Canal Plus offers the most documentaries; the Spanish documentary films represent the minority, however, the number of coproductions with Spanish private companies has grown recently. Among the regional channels, those in the Basque Country offer a reasonable amount of documentaries. Canal 33 in Catalonia does so as well, favouring European productions.

Despite this progress, the old problems remain. A solid industry dedicated to this type of production is missing, as are specific public subsidies (until 1999 documentaries were not included in the agreements between RTVE, or Spanish Radio and Television, and producers). The same applies to exclusive distributors of documentary films as they exist in other European countries (Català, 2001).

Television channels buy documentary films from international markets because it is less expensive.

However, the Spanish audience increasingly demands Spanish-made films about specifically Spanish topics. Documentary films are increasingly screened in cinemas, as the artistic possibilities of the genre have become more widely recognized.

El sol del membrillo (*The Sun of the Quince Tree,* Víctor Erice, 1992) is a documentary film that follows the work of the painter Antonio López in a very natural manner, depicting the way the artist creates the painting, as well as his moral strength and search for beauty. The camera is involved in the figurative universe of the painter and his memories, as the quince tree he paints is part of his childhood memories. The camera also captures the environment, including the artist's wife, friends, a house that is being built, the surroundings of the town, and the sky. It is a continuous dialogue between film and painting, two artistic forms of visual representation.

In *Sevillas* (1992) and *Flamenco* (1995), Carlos Saura merges film with music, showing different varieties of these genres. In *Sevillas*, which was shot in a studio, dance, dimension, and sense of space, as well as colours and movement, prevail. In *Flamenco*, the best artists in their styles act on different stages. In this case, the singing, the gestures, and the characters are stressed. The camera gets into the heart of the melody in a magical way. These films are not musical catalogues, but rather documentaries that show the history of the art of a nation.

Historical documentaries have become more successful. *Asaltar los cielos* (*Attach the Skies,* Javier Rioyo and López Linares, 1996) reconstructs the life of Ramón Mercader, the assassin of Leon Trotsky. It explains the context and conditions in which Mercader lived, the influence of his mother, and his obsession with the Soviet Union. It involves great research work, including archive images, photographs, documents, and evidence. The range of testimonies of politicians, relatives, friends, and artists is quite varied.

Francicsco Boix, un fotógrafo en el infierno (*Francisco Boix, a Photographer in Hell,* Lorenzo Soler, 2000) narrates the story of the Spanish photographer Francisco Boix, a Republican who, when the Civil War was over, left to fight in France. Taken as a prisoner, he was interned in Mauthausen. In this concentration camp, Boix worked in a photographic laboratory, hiding the pictures that were blaming the Nazi regime of the murders committed. His declarations were decisive in the Nuremberg trials. As the previous documentary, it does not just describe the heroic deeds of this Spaniard, but deals with many other topics, such as the agreement between Franco's and Nazi governments to exterminate the Spanish Republicans.

The Civil War is again the primary inspirational theme for documentaries. They are not about claiming political positions—although all of them are anti-Francoist—but rather about preserving the testimonies of the victims of the conflict: members of the International Brigades and the Spanish Division who fought against the Russians in World War II (*Extranjeros de sí mismos [Foreigners for Themselves]*, Javier Rioyo and López Linares, 2000); children sent to the Soviet Union to save their lives during the conflict (*Los niños de Rusia [The Children of Russia]*, Jaime Camino, 2001); and those who continued fighting against Franco clandestinely—*los maquis*—(*La guerrilla de la memoria [Guerrilla of the Memory]*, Javier Corcuera, 2001).

Social documentaries are important as well. Their goal is to move the spectators' consciences. One of the most striking films is *La espalda del mundo* (*The Back of the World,* Javier Corcuera, 2000). Three stories are intertwined in it, stressing the extreme situation of the characters: a Peruvian eleven-year-old child who works in a quarry, a Turk exiled in Stockholm who lives alone, and a prisoner sentenced to death.

Monos como Becky (*Monkeys Like Becky,* Joaquín Jordá and Nuria Villazán) investigates the life of Egas Moniz, a Nobel Prize winner for medicine in 1949 for his work in neurosurgery. The monkey Becky was the patient on which he performed surgery to eliminate aggressiveness of the mentally ill. It is a complex mixture of archive images, theatrical representation of the ill in a mental hospital, and camera movements that are typical of horror films. The film is a metaphor of the many strategies used by the forces in power to keep under control any kind of behaviour considered as antisocial.

En construcción (*Under Construction,* José Luis Guerin, 2001) found great success at the Festival of San Sebastián. The theme is rather simple: a block of flats being built in a popular neighbourhood in Barcelona. The camera captures all of the events that happen during the construction and the characters that are, in different ways, related to it, such as emigrants, pensioners, children, drug addicts, and prostitutes. It shows how the changing urban landscape also implies a change of the human landscape.

MARÍA ANTONIA PAZ

See also **Fascist Spain;** *Land Without Bread*; **Newsreel series: Spain/Portugal**

Further Reading

Amo, A. del, and M. L. Ibáñez Ferradas, *Catálogo general del cine de la Guerra Civil (General Catalogue: Film of the Spanish Civil War)*, Madrid: Cátedra, 1996.

Bonet, Eugeni, and Manuel Palacio, *Práctica fílmica y vanguardia artística en 1925–1981 (Film Practice and Artistic Avant-Garde 1925–1981)*, Madrid: Universidad Complutense de Madrid, 1983.

Catalá, Joseph María, Josetxo Cerdán, and Casimiro Torreiro (eds.), *Imagen, memoria y fascinación. Notas sobre el documental en España (Image, Memory, and Fascination. Notes about the Documentary Film in Spain)*, Madrid: Ocho y Medio, 2001.

González Ballesteros, Teodoro, *Aspectos jurídicos de la censura cinematográfica en España (Legal Aspects of the Film Censorship in Spain)*, Madrid: Universidad Complutense, 1981.

López Clemente, José, *Cine documental español (Spanish Documentary Film)*, Madrid: Rialp, 1960.

Madrid, Juan Carlos de la, *Primeros tiempos del cinematógrafo en España (The Early Days of Film in Spain)*, Oviedo: Universidad de Oviedo, 1996.

Medina, Pedro, Luis Mariano y Velásquez González, and José Martín (eds.), *Historia del cortometraje español (History of the Spanish Short Film)*, Madrid: Film Festival in Alcalá de Henares, 1996.

Pérez Perucha, Julio, "Narración de un aciago destino (1896–1930)," in *Historia del Cine Español (History of the Spanish Film)*, Roman Gubern, José Enique Monterde, Julio Pérez Perucha, Esteve Riambau, and Casimiro Torreiro (eds.), Madrid: Cátedra, 1995, 19–121.

Sáenz de Buruaga, Gonzalo (ed.), *Ínsula Val del Omar: visiones en su tiempo, descubrimientos actuales (The Isle Called Val del Omar: Visions in His Days, Current Discoveries)*, Madrid: Consejo Superior de Investigaciones Científicas, 1995.

Tranche, Rafael R., and Vicente Sánchez-Biosca, *Nodo. El tiempo y la memoria (Nodo. Time and Memory)*, Madrid: Cátedra, 2001.

Vallés Copeiro del Villar, Antonio, *Historia de la política de fomento del cine español (History of the Policies Supporting the Spanish Film)*, Valencia: Filmoteca de la Generalitat Valenciana, 1992.

SPANISH CIVIL WAR

On July 17, 1936, a military uprising took place in Republican Spain. It failed in crucial regions and gave rise to the Spanish Civil War (1936–1939).

The first documentaries on the Spanish Civil War were essentially propaganda. Later on, the war was depicted based on several influential factors: a desire to reexamine historical memory; the political mood of the time; a wish to warn against the dangers of fascism; and an intent to glorify the work of a specific faction or individual. The productions reflected documentary styles favored in each period. The most noticeable feature is that they contributed to shaping the collective memory of the war.

Chronologically, the documentary production period can be divided into four periods: during the civil war, the 1960s, the transition period, and the period since 1980 (Amo, 1996).

Spanish filmmaking during the Civil War had two goals: to document wartime reality and to convey ideological propaganda. The developments during the war conditioned the filmmaking, which was very different depending on the faction producing the film.

The anarchists, represented by the the National Confederation of Work and the Iberian Anarchist Federation (CNT-FAI), created the first wartime documentary. From 1930, they were in control of the industry through the Single Trade Union of Public Entertainment. *Movimiento Revolucionario en Barcelona (Revolutionary Movement in Barcelona,* Mateo Santos, 1936) is one of the first reportages about the liquidation of the military movement in Barcelona, and is an example of film as propaganda. It combined the need of a social revolution with the fight against Fascism. It intended to indoctrinate and move the masses, not to inform them. It identifies both camps in partisan language—"the guerrillas are libertarian, brave, and magnificent in their anger," meanwhile "the military is treacherous, subversive, without honour, and loyal to the upper classes and the black ravens of the Church." This radical tone and some images—(such as mummies of nuns exposed as evidence of the former tortures of the Church)—discredited the Republican side. Later, they adopted a more moderate approach

(*Aguiluchos de la FAI por las tierras de Aragón* [*Eaglets of the FAI in the Lands of Aragon*], 1936).

The Communist organizations also produced documentaries. The Communist Party defended the unity of the Popular Front as a prime task in order to win the war. It promoted the creation of several centres of production (Sala Noguer, 1993). Again, the result did not benefit the Republic, as it was identified with communism.

The technical quality of the Communist documentaries, however, was better than those of the anarchists. The first productions, *Julio de 1936* (*July 1936,* Fernando G. Mantilla, 1936) and *Soldados campesinos* (*Peasant Soldiers,* Antonio del Amo, 1936), focused on the actions of the Spanish people—workers and peasant—with the slogan "to win the war." When in 1937 the production company Film Popular appeared, documentaries were created to defend the single command line. *Por la unidad hacia la victoria (United towards the Victory)* is a good example of this. It was directed by Fernando García Mantilla, who created excellent documentaries with Carlos Velo before the war.

Por la unidad hacia la victoria shows the congress held by the Communist Party in Valencia in 1937. The montage is creative: Images from the congress alternate with those showing social, political, and military activities. The film tries to show the perfect unity and organization of the party using successive interventions of Spanish and foreign leaders. It identifies the enemy as the fascists and the Trotskyites, and the victims as the peasants, the workers, and the general civilian population of Madrid. It concludes with direct party propaganda: "Confidence in the Communist Party and its firm political line."

Governmental documentary production was mainly geared toward the international community, in order to obtain support and assistance. The best example is *España 1936* (*Spain 1936,* 1937), a film by Luis Buñuel (as producer) and Jean Paul Le Chanois. It was assembled in Paris using the material shot in Spain by Spanish and Soviet cameramen. The documentary emphasizes the legitimacy of the Republican government elected in free elections, and the illegal character of the military coup. It tries to give an objective image, opening with the following: "In 1937 film should follow world events, reproduce and spread them, showing them to the people of all countries. This documentary on the Spanish Civil War is a unique film reportage whose only goal is to serve the cause of History." The commentary intends to provide objective information. However, images and sound are used together to convey the message.

When the Republic is mentioned, images and music emanate joy and enthusiasm. The rebel forces are associated with images of destruction and pain. The support provided by the Italians and Germans to the Nationalist (Francoist) camp is one of the most developed themes. Another one is the resistance of Madrid, converted into "the Verdun of Spain." *España 1936* depicted the defence of Madrid in mythic terms. The images show the civilian population—especially children—as victims of the situation. It ends with close-ups of men and women, to personalize the horrors of war.

The regional government of Catalonia, the Generalitat, used images of the local culture to present a positive image abroad. They showed the working and peaceful character of the Catalans, who, despite the war, continued with their daily lives.

Nationalist filmmaking was more moderate than Republican work. The first production team was organized in Andalusia with the staff of the Cifesa production company, who were filming there when the uprising occurred. They immediately received help from their German and Italian allies. Until 1938, there was no central body of propaganda film production. Then the *Noticiario Español* (*Spanish Newsreel*) was created.

Among the titles produced by Cifesa during the war, a series of documentaries about the occupation of several crucial regions stands out, such as *Asturias para España (Asturias for Spain), Bilbao para España (Bilbao for Spain),* and *Santander para España (Santander for Spain)*. The development of the theme is identical: The city is a prisoner of "the red savagery" and "the Francoist saviours" liberate it. Although passionate and of doubtful veracity (Álvarez, 2000), they were important, since they established rhetorical myths that were often repeated even after the war, such as the ideas of the Reconquest and the Crusade.

Prisioneros de Guerra (*Prisoners of War,* Augusto García Viñolas, 1938) was conceived as a response to the accusations of prisoner mistreatment. Prisoners—members of the International Brigades—are shown in various internment centres and hospitals. They are resting, singing, and reading, being taken care of by nuns and nurses. The commentary states: "Meanwhile the disgraceful propaganda was creating our enemies, Franco was converting them into his men." The footage shows the advantages of these prisons: "Spain offers these men the dignity that they lost . . . Franco gives them fatherland, bread, and justice also to them." The exaltation of Franco intensifies: "The General provides these men—who were but human remains—with peaceful days, learning of useful tasks and regeneration, regeneration by work." The reconstruction labour done by the war prisoners is justified here.

Some sequences are blatant montages, such as a prisoner who converts to Catholicism after looking at a crucifix, or a closed fist that first opens and then changes into the Falangist greeting. Others emphasize visual effects, such as the presence of the Chinese in the Brigades, which should suggest to the audience Communist affiliation.

The foreign audience could see news from both camps. Some filmmakers defended the Republic as their personal antifascist commitment, such as de Malraux and Le Chanois, and Ivor Montagu. The latter created the first foreign film about the Civil War—*The Defence of Madrid* (1936)—and also *Testament of Non Intervention* (1938), which provided evidence of the intervention of German and Italian troops. He interviewed imprisoned officials about their situation, recruitment, type and origin of the weapons used in Spain, as well as about the circumstances of their capture. "They were soldiers and officials. We installed a camera and hid a microphone under the table. . . . They did not know that we were recording the conversations. . . . We took the rolls to Geneva where we hoped to influence the debate . . . the film was not attended by many people and I cannot say that it influenced anything" (Amo, 1996).

Others came to Spain to perform professional work, such as Roman Karmen and Boris Makaseiev, cameramen of the official production company producing Soviet newsreels, who shot most of the films during the war. The great Soviet documentary about the Civil War was called *Ispanija* (*Spain,* August, 1939), directed by Esther Shub. It is dedicated "to the great Spanish nation that fought against Fascism for three years enduring the siege and the blows of the traitors." The commentary is brief and the montage is very emotional. The images of bombing and the presence of children are especially dramatic, as well as the evacuation of Barcelona. At the end, the documentary takes on a fighting tone, full of hope: The Republican flag is vertically waving in the wind. Work of the militiamen and the International Brigades, as well as the Soviet help, are glorified.

In the United States, the media and Hollywood production companies sided with the rebels. However, some groups of progressive intellectuals aligned themselves with the Republic. One of them was Contemporary Historians, a group of antifascist writers who asked Joris Ivens to make a documentary film about the Civil War, which became *The Spanish Earth* (1937). John Dos Passos and Hemingway collaborated in this documentary; the latter wrote the commentary for it. Ivens managed to create a film for the U.S. audience. The armed fight for the Republic is identified with the defence of the poorest: the peasants, traditionally exploited by the upper classes, defended by the authors of the coup.

The Spanish Earth employs fiction and narrative. Julián, a Republican soldier, returns to his village, far from the front, for a short period of time. This story allows Ivens to show the everyday life of the people, who toil the land with energy and courage and who believe in a better future, despite the destruction of war. Ivens offers an image in which the Republican victory was possible. Nevertheless, *The Spanish Earth* was not widely distributed. It was labeled a war documentary and was only distributed by smaller channels.

Frontier Films (1936–1941), with financial help from the North American Committee to Aid Spanish Democracy, made a documentary about a blood bank, attended by the prestigious Canadian doctor Norman Bethune. *Heart of Spain* (1937) by Herbert Kline was a short, twenty-minute film that made efficient use of the emotive side of the war: The disasters of the Spanish War contrast with brotherly and revolutionary solidarity as an element of hope. Kline also shot *Return to Life* (1938) about the rehabilitation of the wounded. Its impact was limited, as was the case with *L'Espagne vivra* (*Spain Will Live,* France, 1939), which asked for solidarity of the French people to stop the Nazi threat in Europe, starting in Spain.

The Nazis used the Civil War to praise their own military force in the documentaries. In *Legión Cóndor* (*Condon Legion; In Kampf Gegen den Weltfeind,* 1939), Karl Ritter created a myth of the invincible German aviation. History was interpreted politically and the Francoist propaganda imitated it; the situation in Spain was critical since it was chosen for the Communist revolution. When the Communists got to power, the war broke out. Franco brought "order and relief to the country." Germany intervened in favour of the Nationalists to "stop the communist advance in Europe." The documentary uses both the brilliant interventions of the German aviation and the image of Franco as a modest official. Fascist Italy used the Spanish war as well, to show its own triumphs.

Film overall established mythical images of the war in the collective memory, such as the defence of Madrid or the liberation of the Alcázar (a castle in Toledo besieged by the Republicans). Later on, other images were used. One of them was Guernica. In 1950, Alain Resnais and Robert Hessens filmed *Guernica,* a montage based on Picasso's works. The Republican discourse is repeated and the bombing of Guernica becomes a symbol of anti-fascism and peace. Later,

Guernica was used in relation with Basque self-government and nationalism (Pablo, 2000).

From the 1960s, the Civil War was approached through political commitment. Frédéric Rossif directed *Mourir à Madrid* (*To Die in Madrid,* 1962) to condemn Fascism that at that time was firmly in power. The film became highly topical, since three days after its premiere, the regime executed Julián Grimau. This documentary is a montage with photographs and images filmed by the best cameramen. It describes the history of Spain with many clichés: the eternal Spain or the two Spains. The approach is overly lyrical and lacking analysis of the conflicts in the Republican camp. The commentaries of the writer Madeleine Chapsal are very dramatic, as is the music by Maurice Jarre. The editing, however, is illustrative and of high quality. The film was a great success and established itself as the most famous film about the Spanish Civil War. It also dealt a severe blow to the international image of Franco's rule in those years.

By that time, the regime had gradually abandoned any references to the war. The propaganda focused on the character of the *caudillo* (*Franco, ese hombre [Franco, That Man]*, José Luis Sáez de Heredia, 1964). However, a reply to Rossif's documentary was necessary. The result was the documentary *Morir en España* (*To Die in Spain,* 1965), which was not widely distributed. The film was directed by Mariano Ozores and the screenplay was written by José María Sánchez Silva and Rafael García Serrano. It was sponsored by the Ministry of Information and Tourism. The commentary is ironic: "The whole world is helping the government of Madrid. . . . Stalin, 'always generous,' is running with his help. . . . All condemn Franco as enemy of peace, as if the Republicans were shooting butter. . . . " Fragments of music of the Spanish composer Falla and popular songs are used. Unpublished audiovisual material is provided.

The image of the Republic presented here is that of "strikes, unemployment, workers who must beg on public roads, hunger, arrests, police charges with searches, fires, and shootings. This is how the Republic keeps its promises."

All of this is very similar to the initial sequences of Capra's *Dividir y Vencer (Divide and Rule).* The war is represented as a fight between chaos and peace: "On July 18, 1936, all Spaniards agreed on one thing: they did not like that particular Spain." Then "the good ones" and "the bad ones" are identified; the rebel's advances are qualified as "land for Spain," meanwhile Republican Spain is in the hands of Communists. The film does not provide arguments; it only appeals to emotions.

After Franco died, it was necessary to recover "other truths" about the war. *Caudillo* (*The Leader,* Basilio Martín Patino, 1977) was an important documentary film. It includes scenes from the beginning of the Civil War until the first victory parade. This documentary was not made by a historian; its author only tried to pass on another vision, silenced by forty years of censorship.

The facts do not follow a chronological order to stress a sensation of irrationality. Neither do the images: They compose a visual puzzle. The montage is dynamic and subjective: Some shots are taken out of context; others alternate with great irony. The important thing for the author is to demystify and ridicule Franco, contrasting the official rhetoric of the winners with wartime reality. The author also exalts the participation of the International Brigades and the fight of the popular militias. He uses very diverse material, such as archive images, photographs, interviews, comics, and music of the period. The audience, however, did not understand it.

Raza, el espíritu de Franco (*Race, Franco's Spirit,* Gonzalo Herralde, 1977) had similar intentions and was accepted similarly. It uses interviews and extracts from the film *Raza (Race),* whose screenplay was written by Franco himself.

¿Por qué perdimos la guerra? (*Why Did We Lose the War?,* Diego Santillán and Luis Galindo, 1977), is a documentary with an anarchist approach that contributes to giving another vision of the war. *La vieja memoria* (*The Old Memory,* Jaime Camino, 1979) interviews alternate with archive images and photographs that provide evidence on the historical context. Different political leaders of the period—Gil Robles, David Jato, Dolores Ibárruri, Federica Montseny, and Tarradellas among others—are interviewed individually. However, the interviews are edited to resemble dialogues. The story thus achieves cohesion, but the audience sees the intentional montage shining through. The statements have little historical value, as they are mainly self-justifying.

Since the mid-1970s, the documentaries about the Civil War, both Spanish and foreign, have focused on specific groups of people. The latest premieres in Spain have dealt with the following topics: children who abandoned Spain during the Civil War (*Los niños de Rusia [Children of Russia]*, Jaime Camino, 2001) and the *maquis*, the guerrillas who fought in the mountains against Franco's dictatorship after the war (*La guerrilla de la memoria [Guerrilla of the Memory]*, Javier Corcuera, 2002). In the first one, the interviewees tell about how the war shattered their families and emotional lives.

The second film describes affectionate, painful, and dramatic situations; in the end, Franco's rule did not destroy the old ideals.

A theme tackled most often is that of the International Brigades: Each country contributed one of them to express their solidarity with the Republic. *A Cause Worth Fighting For* (Michael Rabiger, 1973) is a collection of interviews of former British members of the Brigades who recollect their experience from the Spanish War. *The Last Cause* (Stephen H. Franklin, 1976) pays special attention to Canadian members. *The Good Fight* (Noel Buckner, Mary Dore, and Sam Sills, 1984) is about the Americans who fought in the Lincoln Brigade. Also, *Forever Activists* (Judith Montell, 1990) narrates, through interviews and archive images, the experiences of a group of the Lincoln Brigade veterans, from their participation in the Spanish conflict to their support to Sandinist Nicaragua. In Spain, *Extranjeros de sí mismos* (*Foreigners to Themselves,* Javier Rioyo and López Linares, 2000) presents the memories of Italian volunteers and members of the Brigades, as well as of Spaniards who participated in Franco's Blue Division.

These documentaries generally adapt to the needs of the audiovisual market, targeting large groups of spectators who require emotional stories. Using oral storytelling, they excessively play with nostalgia and emotions. Historical rigor is sacrificed to appealing personal narrations, which are very subjective and imbued with later experiences. On the other hand, few analyse the context in depth. All of that results in simplified accounts of confrontation between "the good ones" and "the bad ones."

María Antonia Paz

See also **Documentary Film: Spain; Fascist Spain; *Heart of Spain*; Ivens, Joris; Malraux, André; Montagu, Ivor; Newsreel Series: Spain/Portugal; Resnais, Alain; Rossif, Frédéric; Shub, Esther; *Testament of Non Intervention; To Die in Madrid***

Further Reading

Aldgate, Anthonuy, *Cinema & History: British Newsreels and the Spanish Civil War*, London: Scolar Press, 1979.

Álvarez, R., and R. Sala, *El cine en la zona nacional, 1936–1939 (Film in the Nationalist Zone, 1936–1939)*, Bilbao: Mensajero, 2000.

Amo, A. del, and M. L. Ibáñez Ferradas, *Catálogo general del cine de la Guerra Civil (General Catalogue: Film of the Spanish Civil War)*, Madrid: Cátedra, 1996.

Gubern, Román, *1936–1939. La Guerra de España en la pantalla (The Spanish Civil War on the Screen)*, Madrid: Filmoteca Española, 1986.

Oms, Marcel, *LaGuerre d'Espagne au Cinéma (The Spanish Civil War in the Cinema)*, París: Les Éditions du Cerf, 1986.

Pablo Contreras, S. de, "¿Símbolo o mito? La memoria cinematográfica del bombardeo de Gernika" (Symbol or Myth? Film Memory of the Bombing of Gernika), in *Ikusgaiak*, 4, 2000, 59–74.

Sala Noguer, Ramón, *El cine en la España republicana durante la Guerra Civil (Film in Republican Spain during the Civil War)*, Bilbao: Mensajero, 1993.

SPANISH EARTH, THE

(UK/Spain, Ivens, 1937)

When Helen van Dongen had edited the film *Spain in Flames* out of newsreel material, a group of film-makers thought it was insufficient to convince the U.S. public of the cause of the Spanish Republican Army. They decided to found Contemporary Historians Inc. in order to produce a documentary, made on the front lines of the people's war against Franco in Spain. Joris Ivens was to make this film, together with Ernest Hemingway and John Dos Passos, who left the production early. Ivens asked his former assistant John Fernhout to come from the Netherlands to Spain to do the camerawork for the film. The aim of the film would be to collect money in order to support the Republican Army by buying ambulances. A detailed script was written beforehand, but once in Spain, Ivens and Hemingway realized that it was impossible to follow the script: "Reality is writing its own script."

Endangering their own lives, they filmed behind and on the front, in trenches, in small villages, and in Madrid. The structure of the film was to come from the two struggles of the Spanish people: one, the resistance and military fight against the Franco fascist armies, and two, the fight of the people for their land and for its exploitation. An irrigation project near the village of Fuentedeña became the thread of the film. One element of the original script was kept: the story of a village boy enrolling the Republican Army to fight on the Madrid front, and his eventual homecoming.

The result of all this is one of the most outstanding documentaries of film history, filmed at the front lines of a war. At the same time it is a hybrid film in which Ivens and Hemingway use a fictional story line as running thread. However, the reality on the ground made them change some plans, making the film slightly unbalanced regarding this story line and the two other main themes of the film: the fight against fascists and the irrigation project. Despite the difficult circumstances Fernhout shot beautiful images of the work on the land and harsh images of the frontline battles. The film bears all the marks of the work of Joris Ivens regarding imagery, style, editing, and narrative, but it should also be considered as a collective effort in which each member of the crew, and most notably Hemingway, Fernhout, van Dongen, and Ivens himself, had a major contribution in the final result.

Initially the commentary, written by Hemingway, was to be spoken by Orson Welles, who was proposed by Archibald MacLeish, one of the founding members of Contemporary Historians. The recordings and the sound editing by Helen van Dongen were finished in June 1937, and a few private screenings were organized in Hollywood and Los Angeles to hear the first reactions to the film. Some collaborators of Contemporary Historians, such as Lillian Hellman, Herman Shumlin, and Dorothy Parker, thought that the voice of Orson Welles was too smooth and slick in relation to the harsh and powerful images. It was decided that Hemingway should speak his own commentary, for he had the direct experience of the front line. According to the critiques, the voice of Hemingway sounded much more sincere and less "polished" than that of Welles. On July 8, Ivens, Hemingway, and Martha Gellhorn were invited to the White House to show the film to President Roosevelt and his wife. They used the Welles-version for this screening, maybe because the sound editing of the Hemingway-version wasn't finished yet. The first public screening was on July 13 that year in the Philharmonic Auditorium of Los Angeles.

KEES BAKKER

See also **Ivens, Joris**

The Spanish Earth (USA, Contemporary Historians, 1937, 52 mins.). Produced by Contemporary Historians Inc. Directed by Joris Ivens. Assistant director: John Fernhout. Cinematography by John Fernhout and Joris Ivens. Edited by Helen van Dongen. Commentary written and spoken by Ernest Hemingway. Music by Marc Blitzstein and Virgil Thomson.

Further Reading

Bakker, Kees (ed.), *Joris Ivens and the Documentary Context*, Amsterdam: Amsterdam University Press, 1999.

Delmar, Rosalind, *Joris Ivens, 50 Years of Film-making*, London: British Film Institute, 1979.

Ivens, Joris, *The Camera and I*, Berlin: Seven Seas Books, 1969.

Ivens, Joris, and Robert Destanque, *Joris Ivens ou la mémoire d'un regard*, Paris: Éditions BFB, 1982.

Schoots, Hans, *Dangerous Life. A Biography of Joris Ivens*, Amsterdam: Amsterdam University Press, 2000.

Waugh, Thomas, *Joris Ivens and the Evolution of the Radical Documentary 1926–1946*, Columbia University, 1981.

ŠPÁTA, JAN

Jan Špáta is among the most prolific and well-known filmmakers in the history of Czech documentary; he is a cameraman-director whose career spanned the series of ideological and political shifts that gripped the Czech nation in the second half of the twentieth century. With his sensitive portraits of individuals and cultures, his interest in philosophical questions of life and death, Špáta pioneered a style of documentary filmmaking that is markedly his own, and that has become a trademark of the Czech documentary tradition.

Špáta graduated from the camera department at FAMU, the Film Faculty of the Academy of Music and Performing Arts in Prague, in 1957, preceding by a few years the filmmakers of the Czech New Wave. At the end of the 1950s, documentary in Czechoslovakia had begun a fundamental shift, moving from the socialist notion of film as the propagator of an idealized image of society— "smiling socialism," as Czech film critic Antonín Navrátil (Navrátil, 2002) has called it—to an interest in authenticity and facts.

This process of change resulted from a combination of internal and external forces in the early 1960s in Czechoslovakia. Internally, as economic and social inequalities in the socialist state became increasingly evident, the notion of reality put forth by the Communist party began to seem false. As politicians began to grapple with new realities, a vanguard of journalists adopted a rational, scientific attitude toward the events they reported, relying on facts rather than ideology to describe events. Simultaneously, international film culture was shifting toward an interest in authenticity. Cinema vérité and cinema direct, aided by technological developments such as portable sound equipment and lighter, handheld film cameras, such as the Éclair, allowed filmmakers to represent the world as they encountered it. Students at FAMU (if not the general public) were exposed to films by John Cassavetes, Shirley Clarke, Richard Leacock, Robert Drew, and others, and graduates in the late 1950s and early 1960s started to integrate cinema vérité techniques into their filmmaking.

It was amidst this trend of rational investigation and renewed interest in authenticity that Špáta began his career. After working as a cameraman for a series of documentary directors (among them Jiří Papoušek, Jaroslav Šikl, and Václav Táborský), in 1962, Špáta met director Evald Schorm, with whom he would have a long collaborative relationship, both as cameraman and co-director. In 1963, the two men co-directed *Proč?* (*Why?*, 1963), an exploration of the declining birth rate in the Czechoslovakia. *Why?* was the first Czechoslovak film to use the man-on-the-street interview, combining methods of sociological investigation with cinema vérité techniques. Špáta revisited this method in later films, including his directorial debut (and the film for which he is best known), 1964's *Nevětší Přání (The Greatest Wish)*, in which he asked young people to describe their greatest wish.

Beyond their interest in people's lives and work, Špáta and Schorm shared a philosophical concern with human attitudes towards life and death, and explored these questions in successive films. Their 1965 vérité film *Zrcadlení (Reflections)*, shot in a hospital, examined the border between life and death, ultimately asking the unanswerable What is the meaning of life? *Reflections*'s combination of poetic vérité images and philosophical voice-over became a trademark of Špáta's style in films such as *Respice Finem*, which he directed after Schorm began to work in fiction filmmaking. In this 1967 film he showed viewers the lives of solitary elderly women in the country—women for whom death is a constant presence. The film ends in a shot taken from within a grave—an existential, poetic vision that is striking in a film whose style is so fundamentally based in objectivity.

Špáta's interest in humanity extended to the lives of people in foreign countries. Between the 1960s and 1990s, he made films in locations as far flung as Cuba, Ireland, and Greece, documenting cultures, livelihoods, and customs. Among the most well-known of his travel films is *Země Svatého Patricka (The Land of St. Patrick)*, shot in Ireland in 1967. It is notable that after August 1968, when the Soviet invasion put an end to the Czechoslovak political thaw and implemented the twenty-year period of so-called Normalization, Špáta was able to continue making films; it is especially notable that he was allowed to travel out of the country. It is perhaps precisely his humanism that allowed Špáta to keep working. His films, especially after 1968, focused on "small" human stories such as that of a doctor whose hobby and passion is the family tradition of making and playing violins, in *Terapie Es Dur (Therapy in E-minor,* 1974). These films were politically innocuous, as were films like *Šumavské Pastorale (Sumava Pastoral,* 1975) and *Molto Cantabile* (1989), practically wordless symphonies of poetic images and music.

Some writers have criticized Špáta as a prisoner of his own style (Brdečková and Hádková, 1990) and have written that his post-1960s films tended toward sentimentality. Regardless, several of the many films Špáta shot or directed between 1968 and 1989 are notable. Music is a great theme in Špáta's work, and several of his films from those years figured musical personalities. Particularly noteworthy is *Etuda o zkoušce (Study of a Rehearsal,* 1976), Špáta's last collaboration with Schorm, this time as a cameraman. The film, a portrait of conductor Václav Neumann preparing Beethoven's Fifth symphony, highlights Špáta's mastery of the camera as an expressive medium, particularly in one unbroken ten-minute shot of Neumann conducting.

After the collapse of the Soviet regime in Czechoslovakia in 1989, Špáta revisited an old theme in *Nevětší Přání II (The Greatest Wish II)*, which he combined with 1968's *Nevětší Přání* to make a feature-length documentary that demonstrates the continuity in human desires and values between moments of social upheaval twenty years apart. In 2001, after the completion of his final films, *Laská, kterou opouštím I & II (The Love I Am Leaving I & II)*, and when he could no longer operate a camera with ease and grace, Špáta decided to end his career in filmmaking.

ALICE LOVEJOY

Biography

Born October 25, 1932, in Náchod, Czechoslovakia. Graduated from the camera department at FAMU, the Film Faculty of the Academy of Music and Performing Arts in Prague, in 1957. Taught at the Hochschule fur Gestaltung in Ulm (NSR) in 1967. Since 1992, has taught in FAMU's documentary department, where he was named professor in 2002. Špáta's films have been honored at numerous festivals.

Selected Films

1963 *Proč? / Why?* (with Evald Schorm) and *Žít svůj život / To Live One's Life* (camera; dir. Schorm)
1964 *Nevětší přání / The Greatest Wish*
1965 *Zrcadlení / Reflections* (with Schorm)
1967 *Respice finem* and *Země svatého Patricka / The Land of Saint Patrick*
1974 *Terapie Es-dur / Therapy in E-minor*
1975 *Šumavské pastorale / Sumava Pastoral*
1976 *Etuda o zkoušce / Study of a Rehearsal* (camera; dir. Schorm)
1980 *Variace na téma Gustava Mahlera / Variations on the Theme of Gustav Mahler*
1989 *Molto Cantabile*
1990 *Nevětší přání II / The Greatest Wish II*
1998 *Laská, kterou opouštím I & II / The Love I Am Leaving I & II*

Further Reading

Brdečková, Tereza, and Jana Hádková, *Jan Špáta Dívej se dolů (Jan Spata: Look Down)*, Prague: Czech Film Institute, 1990, (in Czech).
Buchar, Robert, *Czech New Wave Filmmakers in Interviews*, Jefferson, NC: McFarland, 2004.
Hames, Peter, *The Czechoslovak New Wave*, Berkeley: University of California Press, 1985.
Liehm, Antonín J., and Mira Liehm, *The Most Important Art: Eastern European Film After 1945*, Berkeley: University of California Press, 1977.
Navrátil, Antonín, *Cesty k pravdě či lži: 70 let československého dokumentarního filmu (The Path to Truth or Lies: 70 Years of Czechoslovak Documentary Film)*, Prague: FAMU, 2002, (in Czech).
Slater, Thomas J., "Czechoslovakia," in *Handbook of Soviet and East European Films and Filmmakers*, Thomas J. Slater (ed.), New York: Greenwood Press, 1992.
Štoll, Martin, *Hundred Years of Czech Documentary Film (1898–1998)*, Prague: Malá Skála, 2000.
———, *Okamžiky radosti: Rozhovor Martina Štolla s Janem Špátou (Moments of Joy: Jan Spata Interviewed by Martin Stoll)*, Prague: Malá Skála, 2002 (in Czech).

SPECIAL BROADCASTING SYSTEM (AUSTRALIA)

The Australian Special Broadcasting Service (SBS) promotes itself as "Australia's Multicultural Broadcaster." This multilingual and multicultural national public broadcast system was established under the SBS Act of 1991. As such, it has a mandate to reflect the multicultural nature of Australian society and is overseen by a government-appointed Board of Directors. This act grants overall responsibility for the SBS to the Minister of Communication, Information, Economy, and the Arts; but it also provides, on paper, the SBS editorial independence from government intervention. That said, only 10 percent of SBS's budget comes from sponsors and advertisers. The remaining 90 prcent comes from government appropriations. To critics, this is a troublesome proportion of power.

The SBS was developed as a sister network to Australia's original public broadcasting system, the Australian Broadcast Corporation (ABC). The ABC began in 1932 as the Australian Broadcast Commission with twelve radio channels and changed its name in 1983 during government restructuring of the network. The ABC has faced predictable public broadcasting criticism from various public and private voices since its creation on several issues largely related to government control, program content, and audience aim. Some believe that the ABC is too close to its colonial parent the British Broadcasting Corporation (BBC) and its heavily-governed public broadcasting methodology. Others express concern that the ABC is a class-driven body, with reproaches ranging from the corporation being aimed only at the middle class to it trying to create a middle-class nation. It is likely that the SBS was created to address some of this criticism—to distance Australia's public broadcasting from Britain and to demonstrate a wide cultural and class-relevant aim.

The SBS is designed to reach the ethnic communities of Australia and tell their stories. Although there is controversy regarding the success of this broad goal, the network's numbers show efforts in the right direction. According to the service, the SBS television and radio divisions broadcast in over sixty languages and reach more than 7.8 million Australians weekly across the continent. This is done with subtitles rather than dubbing. The SBS provides both internally created programming with an international bend to externally created programs from an immense range of countries. Their internal production unit is called SBS Independent (SBSI). A great percentage of programming is devoted to non-English speaking news shows. With regard to news, the SBS offers its own news programming featuring stories more focused on international events and issues and less "soft-news" than its other news competitors. They also offer a related channel, SBS World News, whose content consists solely of events from a wide range of countries. The majority of ethnic communities seem to enjoy this service, but it has also caused discord politically for the

SBS. For example, in 2003, four thousand Vietnamese protestors stormed the SBS headquarters demanding that the Hanoi broadcasted news program cease as it propagated a Communist point of view and was not representative. The SBS maintained that it presented balanced opinions—that the protestors did not represent the majority of Australian Vietnamese and refused to stop broadcasting the news program.

The SBS is not solely devoted to news however; other program themes include foreign films, comedy, dramatic programs, and sports. With their films, comedies, and dramas, the network has become known for its open attitudes to sexually explicit programming. Although these international works do represent the stations charter to provide multicultural and multilingual programming to the various ethnic communities of Australia, the nature of these shows are also becoming part of increasing controversy surrounding the direction of the SBS.

Critical discussions of the SBS center around the direction of network programming and the inclusion of commercial advertisements on the service. Many believe that the high cultural aims of the SBS have been lost in favor of low-brow, crass entertainment. Some viewers and media pundits express concern that the aims of the charter have been sacrificed for cheap viewership. Others outcry about the presence of the five minutes per hour of advertisements inserted at the beginnings and end of programs. There has been talk of possible future mid-program promotional insertion, but thus far SBS programs remain uninterrupted.

JUSTINE NAGAN

Further Reading

Australia *Australian Broadcast Corporation Act* Commonwealth of Australia 1992.

Breen, Marcus, "Australia: Broadcasting, Policy and Information Technology," in *Public Broadcasting for the 21st Century*, Marc RaBoy (ed.). Luton, Bedfordshire, UK: University of Luton Press, 1995.

Cunningham, Stuart, *The Media in Australia: Industries, Texts, Audiences*, Sydney: Allen and Unwin, 1993.

Jacka, L., *Remapping the Australian Television System*, CIRCIT Working Paper, no 2, June 1993.

Molnar, Helen, "Remote Aboriginal Community Broadcasting: Australia," in *Alternative Media: Linking Global and Local*, Peter Lewis (ed.), Paris: UNESCO: 1993.

O'Regan, T., *Australian Television Culture*, Sydney: Allen and Unwin, 1993.

SPELLBOUND

(US, Blitz, 2003)

Producer/Director Jeff Blitz's Academy-Award nominated debut documentary *Spellbound* examines regional spelling bee competitions and the 1999 Scripps Howard National Spelling Bee in which they culminate. The film begins by introducing eight of 250 National Spelling Bee contestants: Angela, a second-generation Mexican immigrant in rural Texas; Nupur, a middle-class girl of Indian descent in Miami; Ted, an aloof loner in a lower-class Missouri town; Emily, an upper-class daughter of academic parents in Connecticut; Ashley, an African-American teen living with her mother and sister in a Washington, DC apartment; Neil, an affluent Indian-American living in a beach house in California; Amber, a working-class daughter of a bartender in a small, industrial hub of Pennsylvania; and Harry, the son of an office worker in New Jersey. The action intensifies when the eight converge in Washington, DC for the actual spelling bee and the film climaxes in a duel between the last two spellers.

Blitz masterfully constructs a narrative arc that is at once comedic, dramatic, and suspenseful. The children, at times overzealous in their desire to succeed, and the parents, supportive, indulgent, and proud, provide comic relief. The personal narratives of each family make the film enthralling and socially relevant. And ongoing competition at the regional and culminating spelling bees builds an uneasy sense of competition and conflict that propels the film out of its steady state.

Blitz provides no narration of his own, but sews together interviews from the spelling bee participants, their family members and mentors, and former spelling bee contestants. This technique adds to the authentic, intimate, and seemingly objective nature of the film, yet, it does not remove Blitz from the film; instead, his presence is often detectable and never far from the lens of the camera. Blitz uses interstitial slates and consistent music to orient the viewer, introduce the participants, and buttress the narrative.

Although the narrative is structured around the children's preparation for and participation in spelling bees, Blitz uses the spelling bee as an exemplar for the value of education and the opportunity that it

holds for Americans. By selecting children from various ethnic and socioeconomic groups, Blitz shows a plurality of children working diligently to better themselves through America's educational system.

Blitz emphasizes the distinctively American roots of spelling bees, and, by extension, education in general, by engaging images, sounds, and commentary that provoke a sense of Americana and patriotism. A former spelling bee champion comments, "It's just a great American tradition that has filtered out to the world." Blitz peppers the film with shots of the American Flag, Washington Monument, and a parade, as well as Harry strumming the *American Anthem* on his guitar. *Spellbound* suggests that, despite one's race or social class, anyone can advance economically in America, given enough fortitude. Ashley is shown ascending an escalator much as she hopes to rise in the world, with the frame freezing as she is about to step off at the top. In another sequence, while Ashley comments "as I go higher my goals go higher, too...I just keep on reaching," images of the Washington Monument are shown, reminiscent of both American ideals and the March on Washington.

This message is articulated more directly by the spelling bee announcer, who says, "In America back in the eighteenth century, people had this sense of opportunity, you could leap out of one social class, you could move up, and I think they understood education was a basic part of that." Other interviews serve to reinforce the assertion. An Indian mother remarks, "You don't get second chances in India the way you do in America." Another Indian émigré, father of Neil, comments, "There's no way you can fail in this country...if you work hard you will make it...that's nonexistent in other parts of the world."

On the surface, the subtext in *Spellbound* is valid: Education is a fundamental means of advancing one's economic class in America regardless of one's racial background or economic status; however, the finer nuances of this assertion go unexamined. Using primarily pathos, *Spellbound* puts little substantial evidence, by way of sociologists, historians, and statistics, behind its assertions. *Spellbound* implies that, through hard work and perseverance, members of any race or class can achieve success in America. Unfortunately, this optimistic portrait of American life fails to impart the burdens that racism, prejudice, and poverty truly place on American minorities, immigrants, and lower classes.

Rather, the film's emphasis on diversity within such a small sample, and with a necessarily superficial treatment of its eight subjects, runs the risk of perpetuating race- and class-based stereotypes. For instance, Ashley, the only African-American individual in the film, has two uncles who are incarcerated; Ted and his brother, who live in rural Missouri, like to "shoot guns"; Emily, an only child whose parents have a large colonial home in New Haven, speaks of the "au pair" as though they are her possessions; and Angela, the only Mexican-American, is the daughter of parents who tried to cross the border illegally. By attempting to achieve diversity with such a small group of students, Blitz ultimately may have presented his subjects as little more than stereotypical caricatures. Moreover, although the children are from disparate backgrounds, they may not be as dissimilar as they seem. In fact, they share some critical commonalities that transcend race and class. They all have supportive, involved parents; teachers or tutors who provide sustained mentorship; and determination, self-motivation, and high cognitive skills.

Ultimately, *Spellbound* is entertainment, and the characters are perhaps more entertaining than widely representative. On her uphill walk home from school, Ashley hints that this might be the case; she says, "My life is like a movie...I go through different trials and tribulations and then I finally overcome." In *Spellbound*, we see the trials and tribulations, but we do not quite see any of them overcome. Herein lies the false promise of *Spellbound*: in America, just like elsewhere, there is no guarantee of who will get the last word.

JEFF BERGIN

Spellbound (US, THINKFilms, 2003, 97 min) Distributed by HBO/Cinemax. Produced by Jeffrey Blitz and Sean Welch. Directed by Jeffrey Blitz. Edited by Yama Gorskaya. Musical score composed by Daniel Hulsizer. Graphics by Adam Byrne. Additional Producer: Ronnie Eisen. Rerecording Mixer: Peter Brown. Sound FX Editor: Joe Dzuban.

Further Reading

Bruzzi, Stella, *New Documentary: A Critical Introduction*, New York: Routledge, 2000.
Howard, Maureen, "You Are There," in *Beyond Document: Essays on Nonfiction Film*, Edited by Charles Warren, Hanover: University Press of New England, 1996.
Nichols, Bill, *Introduction to Documentary*, Bloomington: Indiana University Press, 2001.
Plantinga, Carl R., *Rhetoric and Representation in Nonfiction Film*, Cambridge: Cambridge University Press, 1997.
Shapiro, Arnold, "Ten Golden Rules," *The Search for Reality: The Art of Documentary Filmmaking*, edited by Michael Tobias, Studio City: Michael Wiese Productions, 1998.
Sherman, Sharon R., *Documenting Ourselves: Film, Video, and Culture*, Lexington: University Press of Kentucky, 1998.

SPOKEN COMMENTARY ("VOICE OF GOD")

Given the widespread use of spoken commentary in documentary, and the variety of its many applications, prejudice against this common device has been a curiously persistent feature of documentary criticism. Critics have objected to the didactic quality to "voice-over" commentary and its capacity to control or limit the process by which knowledge is construed from documentary images and sounds. Compounded by the acoustic "spacelessness" of a close-miked studio recording, this presumption of authority also has given rise to the ironic if not derisive notion of the documentary "Voice of God," with the strident male voice of *The March of Time* newsreel series of the 1930s and 1940s often advanced as a prime example. Beyond matters of tone and taste, moreover, ethical questions about spoken commentary have been raised. For some verité or direct cinema filmmakers and their advocates in the 1960s and 1970s, an opposition to postsynchronized commentary became an axiom, founded on a professed concern for the integrity and complexity of the documented event or subject, and a reluctance to unduly influence the spectator's judgment or response.

These criticisms often betray a naïve faith in the power of documentary films to transcend the interpretive constraints of any compositional practice, with or without spoken commentary, and overlook the rich and varied tradition of vocal address in documentary, the possibilities of which are no means exhausted by the notion of an overbearing, all-knowing voice. Vocal commentary serves what linguists refer to as *phatic* function, establishing terms of contact between commentator and viewer above and beyond the content of the remarks. A commenting voice also can refine, extend, counterpoint, or contradict the implications of images and other sounds it accompanies. Spoken commentary often complicates the temporality of depicted action, opening up images to retrospective and prospective thinking, a strategy conspicuously in evidence in works seeking to explain historical change or reconstruct a troubling or contested past.

Inspired in part by experiments in radio drama, early innovators in social documentary—including Alberto Cavalcanti, Joris Ivens, Humphrey Jennings, and Pare Lorentz—exploited the affective dimension of spoken language, collaborating with writers and composers in the orchestration of poetic or dramatized voices precisely timed to the images. In early travelog "talkies," moreover, on-screen appearances by the adventurer-filmmaker signaled the commentator's corporeal presence and participation in the affairs of the world, a practice still routinely used by television journalists and likewise evident in personal, essayistic documentaries by Agnés Varda and Ross McIwee,

among others, and in investigative works by partisan political filmmakers such as Michael Moore. Experiments with spoken commentary also have returned with new force in many post-verité documentaries. In works by Chris Marker, Trinh T. Minh-ha, Raoul Ruiz, and Su Friedrich, for example, commentary is fragmentary, self-interrogating, oblique, or circuitous, rather than fully explanatory or unifying and foregrounds the relation of voiced language to gender, ethnic, national, or exilic identity. Clearly our ability to assess the sources, functions, and effects of such commentary requires a more subtle and precise vocabulary than conventional terms such as *voice-over* or *Voice-of-God* provide.

CHARLES WOLFE

Further Reading

Bonitzer, Pascal, "Les Silences de la voix," *Cahiers du Cinéma* No. 256 (February/March, 1975); reprinted as "The Silences of the Voice," in Philip Rosen (ed.), *Narrative, Apparatus, Ideology: A Film Reader*, New York: Columbia University Press, 1986.

Bruzzi, Stella, *New Documentary: A Critical Introduction*, London and New York: Routledge, 2000.

Cavalcanti, Alberto, "Sound in Films," in *Films*, 1, 1, November 1939, 25–39; reprinted in John Belton and Elisbeth Weis, *Film Sound: Theory and Practice*, New York: Columbia University Press, 1985.

Doane, Mary Anne, "The Voice in Cinema: The Articulation of Body in Space," in *Yale French Studies* 60, 1980, 33–50; reprinted in John Belton and Elisbeth Weis, *Film Sound: Theory and Practice*, New York: Columbia University Press, 1985.

Green, J. Ronald, "The Illustrated Lecture," in *Quarterly Review of Film & Video*, 15, 2, 1994, 1–23.

Nichols, Bill, *Ideology and the Image*, Bloomington, Indiana: Indiana University Press, 1981.

Plantinga, Carl, *Rhetoric and Representation in Nonfiction Film*, Cambridge, UK: Cambridge University Press, 1997.

Rouff, Jeffrey K., "Conventions of Sound in Documentary," in *Sound Theory/Sound Practice*, edited by Rick Altman, American Film Institute Film Readers Series, New York, London: Routledge, 1992.

Wolfe, Charles, "Historicizing the 'Voice of God': The Place of Vocal Narration in Classical Documentary," in *Film History*, 9, 2, 1997, 149–167.

Youdelman, Jeffrey, "Narration, Invention and History: A Documentary Dilemma," in *Cineaste*, 12, 2, 1982; reprinted in Alan Rosenthal (ed.), *New Challenges for Documentary*, Berkeley: University of California Press, 1988.

SPORTS

In the first half of the twentieth century, sports remained a signifier of class: cricket and rugby union for the middle classes, football and rugby league for the working classes, and boxing as a route out of the slums. Films of the time uncritically endorse the distinction between players and gentlemen, enshrining amateur ideals in those sports whose players could finance themselves. By the end of the century, the democratisation of culture and the commodification of sport had largely eradicated those divisions, save for boxing, perhaps more accurately redefined as a route out of the ghetto. The returns in both cash and public adulation have transformed sport and its media of exploitation, yet surprisingly few documentaries contrive to context its compelling drama in the lives of those who both play and support it.

One shining exception is *Hoop Dreams* (US, 1994), Steve James's epic 170-minute film following two African-American boys in Chicago through their four years in high school basketball. Introducing them at the time that the talent scout captures them from the housing projects to boost the suburban St Joseph High, the film charts their often painful adolescent ups and downs until they both scrape through graduation and take sports scholarships to college. Although the basketball games, frequently with knife-edge conclusions in the hands of our heroes, are featured throughout, it is the support, love, and pride of their respective families that leave the strongest impression. It is a universal tale of growing up with aspiration, with a sly take on the competitive forces that encircle young talent like vultures. At a Nike-sponsored summer camp at Princeton, college scouts frankly admit that it is a meat market, with them as dead meat if they don't select wisely. A visiting speech from film director Spike Lee drives the point home:

> Nobody cares about you. You're black; you're a young male. All you're supposed to do is deal drugs and mug women. The only reason why you're here is you can make their team win. If their team wins, the school gets lots of money. This whole thing is revolving around money.

Nike hired Spike Lee to direct the famous commercials featuring basketball legend Michael Jordan that cemented their market lead in the 1990s, making Jordan the richest sportsman on earth. By 1998, Jordan had made $130 million from the relationship; Nike had made $2.6 billion. Astronomical sums are tied up in sports, originally as television networks, particularly in the United States, bid up the price of major sports coverage rights, then as sponsorship deals helped produce these gigantic multinational business returns. In this world, the documentarian, normally a poorly resourced individual or small company attempting a novel insight to this world, fares no better than a dinghy in the path of an ocean-going tanker. The television stations that pay millions for sports rights and the companies that own them face a conflict of interest, with investigations that may undermine the celebrities and take the shine off the contests that pull their punters and ensure their profits.

Before television, filmed newsreel was the main means of transmitting the excitement of matches most missed. The largest production company in Britain between 1898 and 1910 was the Warwick Trading Co., and among the military subjects and travel shoots they specialized in were odd sporting moments. *Jack's Game of Cricket on Board H.M.S. Gibraltar* (UK, 1900) is the oddest of these titles, though typically English in its conflation of cricket, ships, and eccentricity, and the *English Cup Final: Barnsley v. Newcastle United* (UK, 1910) the most predictable. Winning 2-0 on the replay and making the following year's Cup Final, too, Newcastle features regularly in the football clips that the U.K. National Film and Television Archive holds from the early years of film. One minute (forty feet) of Lumiére's shots of an unidentified French team at practice is the earliest surviving football film; *Blackburn Rovers v. West Bromwich* (1898) is the oldest extant footage of a game, which Blackburn won 4-nil. The 1901 replay between Tottenham Hotspur and Sheffield United is the earliest surviving F.A. Cup Final footage.

The first boxing match to be filmed was "Gentleman" Jim Corbett's fight with Peter Courtney in America in 1894, with two-minute rounds to accommodate the reloading of Edison's Kinetoscope

SPORTS

cameras. Corbett's knock-out in the fourteenth round of his world heavyweight championship bout with Bob Fitzsimmons in 1897 is also amongst the earliest surviving sequences. But the most influential of early bouts to be captured on film was the 1910 heavyweight championship fight in Reno, Nevada, when the reigning champion Jack Johnson knocked the white Jim Jefferies through the ropes in the fifteenth round. This result was blamed for inciting racial unrest and so, in 1912, the U.S. federal government banned the interstate transportation of film of "any prize fight or encounter of pugilists, under whatever name, or any record or account of betting on the same."

The ban was not repealed until 1940, and only then under pressure from television, but the racial and national significance of major bouts ensured that many were filmed and widely seen. Notable films include white boxer Jess Willard's seizure of Johnson's seven-year crown in round twenty-six of a mammoth forty-five-round bout in Havana, Cuba, and the much-promoted "Battle of the Century" between Jack Dempsey and French challenger George Carpentier in 1921. The half-million dollar purse and the vast open-air stadium built especially for this fight indicate how lucrative boxing had become. The storm clouds that gathered over Europe meant that a rather different complexion was put on the Joe Louis/Max Schmeling bout in 1936, which the German won, and the rematch in 1938, with its first-round knock out and Louis's world heavyweight title in contention that time. Barak Goodman's *The Fight* (US, 2004) revisits the political implications of this encounter.

Schmeling was no Nazi, but Hitler's government had already seen the value of sports as the iconic means of trumpeting Aryan racial mastery. Their staging of the Berlin Olympics and Leni Riefanstahl's monumental film of it, *Olympia* (Germany, 1936), was a pledge of what was in store for Europe. The Olympics were magnificently staged and the film is a ground-breaking work of exciting and innovative cinematography and editing, particularly in its marriage of image and sound. Its first part, *Fest Der Völker / Festival of the People*, sets the context within the history of the early Olympics. The second part, *Fest Der Schönheit / Festival of Beauty*, invokes the Nazi fetishisation of gilded youth; but the inclusion of the achievements on track and field of other nations' athletes, notably the four gold medals won by black American sprinter Jesse Owens, arguably makes *Olympia* a more balanced and classic sports documentary than a nationalist tract. Riefenstahl always denied that her film was Nazi propaganda but, coming after

The Triumph of the Will (Germany, 1934) about Hitler's Nuremburg rallies, and, like that film, financed by the National Socialist Party Minister of Propaganda, Joseph Goebbels, it served the Nazi purpose well enough.

Mussolini and Franco also recognised the value of sports as a medium for their message, as a recent BBC documentary, *Football and Fascism* (UK, 2004), records. Using archive film from the time and contemporary historical analysis, it covers Mussolini's alleged fixing of the 1934 World Cup, Hitler's use of the Berlin Olympics and the 1938 World Cup, and Franco's exploitation of Real Madrid to cement his dictatorship. Politics and sport would never be fully divorced, but the aestheticisation of the body was not exclusively a fascist phenomenon.

The second of the four films that Jean Vigo made before his death at age 29 from tuberculosis was a documentary short about French swimming champion Jean Taris, *Taris, le roi d'eau* aka *Taris, champion de notation / Taris, Swimming Champion* (France 1931). This film is best known for its playful subversion of filmic convention, progressing from beautiful, heroic, black-and-white shots of Taris diving and swimming toward camera to slow motion, underwater cavorting for the camera, and reversed film that has him apparently jump backward out of the pool three times, before mixing to him fully dressed, doffing his hat, and walking away from camera through overlaid waves. It is a surreal piece with a homoerotic delight in the swimmer's body.

The narcissistic in sport and its filmic expression largely disappeared during World War II and the age of austerity that followed through the 1950s. It reappeared with a bang in the 1960s, as sport joined music in offering the main two trajectories through which the aspiring young could find their "fifteen minutes of fame," as Warhol coined it.

One of the more extraordinary career paths was introduced to the world by George Butler and Robert Fiore's *Pumping Iron* (US, 1977). In this, we meet the Austrian five-times Mr. Olympia, Arnold Schwarznegger, defending his title in the 1975 body-building season. Some other contestants featured are the young Lou Ferrigno (who went on to be TV's *The Incredible Hulk*), and the Sardinian Franco Colombu lifting his car into a tight parking place (and who went on to play alongside Arnie in *Conan the Barbarian* and *The Terminator*). But it is Schwarznegger who became a film phenomenon and completed the ultimate sporting apotheosis by being elected

Governor of his adopted California, a bizarre tale told in Alex Cooke's *Arnold Schwarznegger: The Governator* (UK, 2003).

George Butler returned to the well-oiled territory in *Pumping Iron II: The Women* (US, 1985), which features the female bodybuilder Bev Francis training in her native Australia before heading for the United States for the 1983 Caesar's Cup in Las Vegas. Her whipcord, masculine body and her revealing swimsuit confront the double standards of the International Female Bodybuilding Association head on, occasioning comments like "There is a point beyond which women cannot go" and Bev "does not represent what women want to look like." They eventually dock her points and place her last. Some discover a light feminist text here, but the shots of nude contestants soaping in the shower and relaxing in the pool together do contrive to suggest a more male imperative. In a series of occasional documentaries under the rubric "Sports in the 20th Century," HBO also produced Dan Klein's *Playing the Field: Sports and Sex in America* (US, 2000), which further explores the sexploitation of women in sports and the general development of sex appeal as a sales tool in every sport from the still fiercely male American football to women's World Cup soccer.

The history of what the rest of the world calls football reflects its transformation from a field of chaps in baggy shorts to a game of glamour and global marketing. In 2003, a long-forgotten film made by the young John Boorman in 1963 was discovered in the BBC archives. Made in the year that the British Professional Footballers' Association finally won the battle to remove the maximum wage, *Six Days to Saturday* follows a week in the lives of the struggling Swindon Town team and its manager. Repackaged in 2004 with a contemporary commentary, it explains a long-lost world before multimillion pound deals and commercial sponsorship. In the interim, icons have appeared that have attracted media adulation, then documentary revision when their stars have fallen from the firmament, a particular feature of UK Channel 4's series *Football Stories*, which the channel claims is one of its most successful returning documentary series.

George Best was a fabulously gifted centre forward for Manchester United when he turned professional at age 17 in 1963. *George Best's Body* (UK, 2000) was a biographical x-ray of Best's decaying physique and its ravages from alcoholism, after he was rushed to hospital in 2000, yellow from liver failure. Paul Gascoigne was another talented footballer who initially sprang to prominence with his hometown Newcastle United in the 1980s, before going on to Spurs and England, giving rise to "Gazza-mania," notably after the Italia 1990 World Cup. *Inside the Mind of Paul Gascoigne* (UK, 2003) deploys psychiatrists, journalists, and other footballers to suggest several psychiatric conditions that might have led to Gazza's depression, drinking, and downfall. England captain David Beckham's even greater fame and emergence as a global brand has spawned a string of documentaries that sell around the world. These include traditional biopics like *Something About Beckham* (UK, 2001), "fly-on-the-wall" ITV documentaries such as *The "Real" Beckhams* (UK, 2003), and premature obituaries like *David Beckham: ByeBye Becks* (UK, 2004). His ultimate immortalization occurred in 2004, when leading British artist Sam Taylor-Wood revealed her latest video art installation: sixty-seven minutes of Beckham sleeping, simply named, like Michelangelo's young hero, *David*.

For the most part, these documentaries explore the points of recognition that fans seek in comparing their lives to those of their heroes. It is part of the price that sports stars pay for their celebrity and high earnings, and contradicts sports commissioners' oft-repeated, but disingenuous, view that audiences only want their sports live and unmediated. There is also a growing production line of archive-driven documentaries, partly stimulated by the success of the BBC's *Bodyline: It's Just Not Cricket* (UK, 1984). This film, about England's infamous 1932–1933 Test cricket tour of Australia, retells the story of England captain Douglas Jardine organizing pace bowlers Harold Larwood and Bill Voce to bowl aggressively and directly at batsmen, destabilizing the reign of batsman Don Bradman. It was deemed so unsporting that it caused diplomatic repercussions in Canberra and Whitehall. Trying to do justice to both the sport and the context can also lead to long films. American filmmaker Ken Burns's monumental series on the 150-year history of *Baseball* (US, 1994) runs eighteen hours and manages to pack in much about the racial segregation of the early game and its many labour disputes. Online fan reviews complain about all the teams and series he has omitted.

Sport in the Sixties: A TV revolution (UK, 2004) affectionately charts a decade in which technological evolution allowed sports coverage to come of age, with the first live satellite transmissions, notably of the then Cassius Clay's surprise victory over Sonny Liston and of the Tokyo Olympics in 1964. The first day of the All-England Tennis Championships at Wimbledon in 1967 was the first colour transmission in Europe; the previous year's World

Cup football in England was transmitted in black and white. *Goal! The World Cup* (UK, 1966), directed by Ross Devenish and Abidine Dino, was shot on 35mm Technicolour as a theatre feature, capturing England's finest footballing hour, as well as some of the all-time greats, such as Brazil's Pele and Garrincha. Their archived genius is also the subject of French sports documentarist Jean-Christophe Rosé's *Gods of Brazil* (France, 2002), with Garrincha being credited as the real genius behind the 1960s transformation of Brazilian football, despite Pele going on to greatness while Garrincha died at age 49, alcoholic, broken, and forgotten.

One of the most extraordinary stories from the 1966 World Cup is that of the unrated North Koreans, who defied expectations to knock the highly favoured Italian team out, a story retold in *The Game of Their Lives* (UK, 2002). British documentarist Daniel Gordon had been fascinated by this story since a child and achieved the equally improbable task of gaining access to this notoriously closed communist society.

> The Korean authorities were quite curious and pleased that someone wanted to do something fairly neutral about the country. The players were really delighted because they thought they'd been forgotten by the rest of the world. The first thing that one of the players said to us was, "Is the Mayor of Middlesbrough still alive?" The fact that they were underdogs obviously appeals to the English. Middlesbrough is an underdog itself. Their team had been relegated; they also played in red, so there were a lot of things that made them empathise with the North Koreans.

This sympathetic dialogue led to the producers bringing the survivors of the team on an emotional return to the northeastern English town of Middlesbrough. The popularity of *The Game of Their Lives* on North Korea's only television channel also enabled them to return there to make a second documentary, about two young gymnasts' preparation for the Mass Games. These games are the biggest and most spectacular event of their kind on earth, and *A State of Mind* (UK, 2004) shows them, while offering another rare insight into the minds and lives of this largely hidden society.

The nature of the West's sporting links with Asia are also explored in Ferne Pearlstein and Robert Edwards' *Sumo: East and West* (US, 2003), a film that records the intervention of American wrestlers on the sumo stage. In 1993, Hawaiian Chad Rowan became the first non-Japanese to become *yokozunu*, grand champion, and Americans have taken to mounting glitzy, homogenised versions of this ancient Shinto ritual sport in places like Las Vegas and Atlantic City. The film explores the clash between Japanese purists and modernists whose push to gain sumo Olympic status involves concessions, such as the use of a nondirt sumo ring, the acceptance of bicycle-style Lycra shorts under the sumo belt, and, most radically, the introduction of sumo competition for women.

The fear is that an ancient and honourable tradition will be taken down the road wrestling took, where the entertainment imperatives would now make the sport unrecognizable to its Greek originators. The stand-off between the commercial interests of the wrestling fraternity and the outside world came to a head in a CBS *20/20* report on February 1, 1985, when reporter John Stossel went out to prove that wrestling was all one elaborate fake. Pressing an obviously hostile David "Dr. D." Schultz on this point outside the ring, he receives a double ear slap and a kicking when he falls to the ground, as Schultz rams the point home. *20/20* anchor Barbara Walters had to assure the audience that this was not faked and Stossel was indeed injured. The rules may have changed, but this sport was still an arena of gladiatorial combat.

As the pursuit of the money has increasingly dominated sports, there has been a countervailing search for the elemental, with sports that pit man (and woman) against nature. By definition, these only reach the public eye through the medium of the camera. An early and extreme example of the form is *The Man Who Skied Down Everest* (US, 1970), Bruce Myznick's Oscar-winning documentary about Yuchiro Miura's death-defying feat skiing 8,000 feet down the precipitous glacier of the South Col on the world's tallest mountain, having first climbed it. The narration is supplied by the diary Miura kept on the trip, but the cinematography is what perfectly matches the grandeur of the landscape with the epic nature of the ambition. A third of a century on, another mountaineering film found the form to match failed ambition, albeit celebrating the indomitable courage with which Joe Simpson crawled away from death. Kevin Macdonald's *Touching the Void* (UK, 2003) re-creates the climbing accident in the Andes when Simpson's partner had to cut his rope, leaving him apparently to fall to his death in a crevasse. Watching these men recount to camera what they had been through, as well as seeing it compellingly reenacted, enables the audience to share something of the visceral appeal of these extreme sports.

A similar buzz was captured on 16mm film by the surfing beach bums who inhabited Hawaii's North Shore during the 1950s and 1960s. This is collected and lovingly packaged, along with interviews with surviving surf legends like Greg Noll, by Stacy Peralta in *Riding Giants* (US, 2004). The film brings the story up-to-date, with off-shore tow-surfing, but it is the early material that captures the essence. Peralta told the English *Guardian* newspaper (August 13, 2004):

> They were adamant about shooting it, and surfing's such a beautiful aesthetic, it's tailor-made for amateurs. You don't need to know too much to get a great shot. After they'd acquired a lot of footage, they realized there was a market out there for it. They started hiring high school auditoriums and showing it with live, on-the-spot commentary. And typically the commentator would be the filmmaker himself, like Greg.

Before this, Peralta's favourite surf documentary was Bruce Brown's *Endless Summer* (US, 1966), which followed surfers Michael Hynson and Robert August all over the world in search of the perfect wave. In this film, spectacular footage from America, Africa, Asia, and Australia underlines the heroic nature of the quest. In the 1970s, Stacy Peralta was a skateboard champion and his previous documentary, *Dogtown and the Z-Boys* (US, 2001), is an exploration of this land-based, poor boys' version of surfing, "where the debris meets the sea," as one of them says, from the pioneering Zephyr Team of the 1970s to the multimillion dollar revival of skateboarding in the 1990s. It brought mainstream recognition to a form that had spawned a thousand videos documenting the "grabs" and "grinds" of this urban ballet, circulating among skaters themselves and through specialist skate shops.

Britain's oldest sport of survival is its own duel with the sea, but this was the subject of few early documentaries. Even the epic exploits of round-the-world solo sailors Sir Francis Chichester in 1966–1967 and Robin Knox-Johnston in 1968–1969, the latter being the first nonstop circumnavigation, were recorded only by on-shore news crews. In the 1980s, specialist companies started filming the growing taste for these "against-the-elements" contests, such as the first BOC Around the World yacht race in 1982–1983, captured in *Universal Challenge* (US, 1984) and narrated by Robin Knox-Johnston. It was only with the arrival of lightweight DV cameras and satellite communications that viewers at home could vicariously share the perils at sea more immediately. Ellen MacArthur captured the hearts and minds of not just her own country, but much of Europe, in her solo transatlantic races and particularly in her lonely 100-day Vendée Globe Challenge to the South Pole in 2000. *Ellen MacArthur: Sailing Through Heaven and Hell* (UK, 2001) was told with the help of four fixed cameras on board Ellen's boat *Kingfisher*, plus two waterproof handheld ones and one fixed to her waterproof helmet. Trained in their use, 24-year old Ellen pours out the agony and ecstasy of her extraordinary experience in what serves as an electronic confessional. The producer Steve Robinson agrees it is an autobiographical documentary:

> This is Ellen MacArthur's film. The pressure on a lone sailor, particularly in a race, is immense, and yet Ellen was able to give a lot of consideration to the camera angles and sequences. Before she went up the mast, for example, to repair or adjust some ropes, she would set up the camera and ensure it got the best pictures.

The video diary form was pioneered by the BBC in the 1980s and travel challenges featured from the start; but a new use was explored in the 1990s, getting Olympic athletes to chart their training for the 1996 Olympics in Atlanta. *Olympic Diaries* (UK, 1996) is more of an inward voyage, revealing unique insights into the pains and pressures of athletes in training. Middle distance runner Kelly Holmes, hurdler Tony Jarrett, sailor Shirley Robertson, show jumper Karen Dixon, rowers Steve Redgrave and Matthew Pinsent, and gymnast Annika Reeder share their families and friends, their marital discords and nagging doubts as they face the successive trials of qualifying events, selection, and arrival at the ultimate contest. In the end, only the rowers won medals. Series producers Sue Davidson and Karen Hamilton bring to bear the human interests of documentarians rather than the enthusiasms of sports producers, whose approach they feel is rarely critical:

> It is hard for these sports personalities to open up and admit to doubts, fears, failings, as they are programmed to be positive and deliver fighting talk at all times. Sports interviewers also tend to be reverential, as they are often in awe of the celebrity status of the sportsmen and women, which was never an issue for us as neither had an appetite for sport and couldn't give a toss.

This makes clear the distinction between the excellence and originality of technical cover, which distinguishes and drives sports on television, and the complexity and contradictions of the humans behind the endeavour, which is the eternal concern of documentary. Davidson and Hamilton cared enough for what they did, and the original techniques involved in getting sportsmen to think in film terms, to return to the field and follow the Olympic rowers for another four years for *Gold*

Fever (UK, 2000). This follows the rowers contending to form the coxless four that eventually delivered Steve Redgrave his fifth successive gold in Sydney. This film reveals depressed men putting on smiling performances for visiting sports journalists and delves even deeper into the minds and motivation of men putting themselves through years of pain, injury, and disappointment to achieve those momentary highs. Matthew Pinsent put this well in his earlier *Olympic Diary*:

> Part of the pleasure of winning at the Olympics is that you win through all that. You are so nervous that you feel you just can't go on. Through that pressure and that cauldron of emotions you come through and you win. And that makes it enjoyable. You may not enjoy it at the time. In fact, it's very unlikely that an hour before the race you're enjoying it. Maybe during the race you're not enjoying it. But, standing on the podium, getting the medal around your neck, hearing the national anthem and then—yeah, that's enjoyable.

Just as the Olympics represents the ultimate test for so many sports and athletes, so it is for the constantly evolving form of sports documentary. Its aesthetic high points remain Riefenstahl's *Olympia*, Kon Ichikawa's *Tokyo Olympiad* (Japan, 1965), and the portfolio piece *Visions of Eight* (US, 1973), made about the Munich Olympics in 1972. Where Ichikawa's film is a more formal structure of forty chapters encapsulating the Tokyo Olympics from opening to closing ceremony, the 1973 film takes a more expressionist approach through the eyes of eight of the world's top feature directors, each choosing a theme. The USSR's Juri Ozerov takes the moment of waiting; Sweden's Mai Zetterling films the weightlifters; American Arthur Penn covers pole-vaulting; Germany's Michael Pfleghar celebrates the greatest ever number of women contestants; Japan's Kon Ichikawa shoots the 100-metre sprint; Czechoslovakia's Milos Forman frames the decathlon; France's Claude Lelouch watches the losers; and Britain's John Schlesinger documents the marathon.

Visions of Eight is presented "In memory of the eleven slain Israeli athletes, tragic victims of the violence of our times," but does not cover the events of the kidnap and bungled rescue that led to those deaths. That had to wait for Kevin Macdonald's *One Day in September* (US, 2000), which retells the story with the help of survivors and computer graphics. It is not a sports documentary, but it raises the question of how sports can continue to act in isolation of the harsher realities

around, just as the IOC tried to continue the Munich games even as the siege continued. Allegations of corruption in the process for awarding the multibillion dollar prize of staging the games have dogged the Olympics in television reports, at least since the award to Salt Lake City of the 2002 Winter Games. The BBC's *Panorama: Buying the Games* (UK, 2004) unearths new allegations with regard to the sale of 2012 votes on the eve of the Athens Olympics, while the UK's Channel 4 was running a long documentary on *Cheating at Athens: Is It Worth It?* (UK, 2004). This puts twenty-four athletes through a six-month training programme as part of a scientific test in which some were given performance-enhancing drugs. It proves that relatively small amounts of anabolic steroids do make a significant difference to performance, but also raises the widespread academic belief that they are no more eradicable than any other path to perfection. Ellis Cashmore, Professor of Culture, Media and Sport at Staffordshire University, articulates the argument succinctly in this film: "Athletes will always stay ahead of the game . . . they are risk-takers and they will always take dope."

This is similar to the line taken by *Ben Johnson: Drugs and the Quest for Gold* (Canada 2004), in which Johnson admits to long-term drug abuse, but not to the use of Stanazol that had his gold medal disallowed for the 100 metres at the Seoul Olympics in 1988. He asserts that everyone, not just the bulked-up East Europeans, were taking drugs. It seems more than a lifetime since sports documentaries were more about the heroic battles against adversity that define Johnson's namesake in Mel Stuart's *The Rafer Johnson Story* (US, 1961). This black-and-white film chronicles the struggles and injuries overcome by the great decathlon champion Rafer Johnson, the first black Olympic flag bearer and team captain at the Rome Olympics in 1960. At that Olympics, the greatest ever amateur basketball team won gold for the United States, and a young Cassius Clay took the light heavyweight boxing title.

Then they were all amateurs; now the Olympics has reluctantly had to give way to the professionals, save (ironically, given its history) for boxing. But the career of that young boxer, who became Muhammed Ali, is an image of the revolution sports has undergone since 1960. That image has been captured in two of the best sports documentaries, both featuring Ali's regaining his world title in the famous "Rumble in the Jungle" with

George Foreman. Photojournalist William Klein's *Muhammed Ali: The Greatest* (US, 1974) and Leon Gast's *When We Were Kings* (US, 1996) take complementary approaches to that extraordinary bout in Zaire, with its metaphorical essence of heroic combat and epic endeavour, albeit for a $10 million purse put up by the dictatorial President Mobutu. But the symbolic meaning that Ali sought, as an African-American ambassador, speaks out beyond the title fight to a world still hungry to hear the messages that documentaries find on sports' fields of dreams.

PETER LEE-WRIGHT

See also **Burns, Ken;** *Hoop Dreams; Olympia; Pumping Iron; Tokyo Olympiad; Triumph of the Will; Visions of Eight; When We Were Kings*

Further Reading

Allison, Lincoln, and Mangan, J. A., *Amateurism in Sport: An Analysis and a Defence*, London: Frank Cass, 2001.

Barnett, Steven, *Games and Sets: The Changing Face of Sport on Television*, London: BFI, 1990.

Barthes, Roland, *The World of Wrestling*, in *Mythologies* translated by Annette Lavers, New York, 1972.

Cashmore, Ellis, *Making Sense of Sports* (3rd ed.), London: Routledge, 2000.

———, *Sports Culture: An A-Z Guide*, London: Routledge, 2002.

Davidson, Judith (ed.) and Adler, Daryl (comp.), *Sport on Film and Video: The North American Society for Sport History Guide*, Lanham: Scarecrow Press, 1993.

Gavora, Jessica, *Tilting the Playing Field: Schools, Sports, Sex and Title IX*, San Francisco: Encounter Books, 2002.

Goldlust, John, *Playing for Keeps: Sport, the Media and Society*, Melbourne: Longman Cheshire, 1988.

Hargreaves, Jennifer, *Sport, Culture and Ideology*, London: Routledge, 1982.

———, *Sporting Females: Critical Issues in the History and Sociology of Women's Sports*, London: Routledge, 1994.

Hargreaves, John: *Sport, Power and Culture: A Social & Historical Analysis of Popular Sport*, Oxford: Polity Press, 1986.

Houlihan, Barrie (ed.), *Sport and Society: A Student Introduction*, London: Sage Publications, 2003.

King, Anthony, *The End of the Terraces: The Transformation of English Football in the 1990s* (revised ed.), Leicester: Leicester University Press, 2002.

Mandell, Richard, *Sport: A Cultural History*, New York: Columbia University Press, 1984.

Mazer, Sharon, *Professional Wrestling: Sport and Spectacle*, Jackson: University Press of Mississippi, 1998.

Whannel, Garry, *Fields in Vision: Television, Sport & Cultural Transformation*, London: Routledge, 1992.

SPOTTISWOODE, RAYMOND

As a student at Oxford University, Raymond Spottiswoode had written *A Grammar of the Film: An Analysis of Film Technique*, published in 1935. Though in it his approach is resolutely aesthetic and mainly devoted to the fictional feature film, he gives what must have been considered an inordinate amount of attention to the early documentary film, beginning with the statement that: "England's only solid contribution to the cinema lies in her documentary groups, and in particular the G.P.O. Film Unit."

He proceeds to offer one of the most adequate definitions of documentary, as it was being made in the 1930s, at any rate: "The documentary film is in subject and approach a dramatized presentation of man's relation to his institutional life, whether industrial, social or political; and in technique a subordination of form to content." However, Spottiswoode does not acknowledge as part of documentary the filmmakers' social purposes or their concern with the effects of their films on audiences.

Spottiswoode was subsequently hired at the General Post Office Film Unit by John Grierson, who had read that important book of theory and classification (had reviewed it severely, in fact) and ordained, as a result, that Spottiswoode should begin his training as a tea boy. After six months, Grierson thought Spottiswoode still was not humble enough, according to a popular anecdote, anyway. Grierson regarded the purposes and effects of films of ultimate importance.

After Grierson became founding head of the National Film Board of Canada in 1939, he brought Spottiswoode, then at Metro-Goldwyn-Mayer in Hollywood, to Canada, along with other veterans of British documentary. By this time a trained technician and producer, Spottiswoode was made co-producer with Stuart Legg on a Film Board production about the Commonwealth Air Training Plan entitled *Wings of Youth*. After producing some other films, along with teaching NFB apprentices, he became supervisor of technical services for the Board, writing a valuable summary of "Developments at the National Film Board of Canada, 1939–44," published in the *Journal of the Society of Motion Picture Engineers* (of which he was a Fellow).

When Grierson left the Film Board after the war to set up the short-lived The World Today in New York City, Spottiswoode went with him. He produced the most successful by far of its few films, *Round Trip: U.S.A. in World Trade* (1947). Directed by Roger Barlow (who had also directed *Wings of Youth*), it was sponsored by the Twentieth-Century Fund, a foundation that sought to promote liberal economic policy, including lowering or total removal of tariff barriers. Spottiswoode also produced a film for the Motion Picture Association of America on new techniques for teaching classroom subjects. Subsequently he became particularly interested in stereoscopic film, returned to England during the Festival of Britain in 1951, and was technical director of the stereoscopic film program at the Telekinema in London.

Spottiswoode also became a writer on film of considerable distinction, particularly regarding technical subjects. In 1950, the University of California Press republished his *A Grammar of Film* and, in 1951, his *Film and Its Techniques*. In the 1950s he was engaged in thorough research into the potential development of 3-D systems of cinematography and co-authored the book, *Theory of Stereoscopic Transmission* (1953). Among other publications was his general editorship of *The Focal Encyclopedia of Film & Television Techniques*, a monumental work begun in 1964 and published in 1969.

JACK C. ELLIS

See also **General Post Office Film Unit; National Film Board of Canada**

Biography

Born 1913 in London. Oxford University, M.A., circa 1933. General Post Office Film Unit, circa 1935–1937. Metro-Goldwyn-Mayer, circa 1937–1939. National Film Board of Canada, producer and then technical supervisor, circa 1940–1945. The World Today, New York City, 1946–1948. Technical director of the stereoscopic film programs shown at the Telekinema during the Festival of Britain, 1951. His principal books are *A Grammar of the Film*, 1935; *Film and Its Techniques*, 1951, and *The Theory of Stereoscopic Transmission* (with Nigel Spottiswoode), 1953. Died 1970.

Further Reading

Ellis, Jack C., *John Grierson: Life, Contributions, Influence*, Carbondale: Southern Illinois University Press, 2000.
Hardy, Forsyth, *John Grierson: A Documentary Biography*, London: Faber and Faber, 1979.

STAROWICZ, MARK

Mark Starowicz was one of the most celebrated figures in contemporary Canadian broadcasting. His entire career trajectory, although it comprises both radio and television work, has been associated with innovative programming in the nonfiction or documentary arenas.

His early career began with positions in the print and radio media, and he rose to prominence at the Canadian Broadcasting Corporation (CBC) in the early 1970s for his major role in the creation of the innovative and long-running programs *As It Happens* and *Sunday Morning*. The former, still running, attracts large audiences with its combination of serious and timely telephone interviews with the major newsmakers of the moment, on the one hand, and its cheeky interest in and attention to news stories from around the world, which fall somewhere under the umbrella of "human interest" and bizarre, or at the least, off-beat, on the other.

Because of his prominent role in the revitalization of CBC radio broadcasting, it is unsurprising that he should have been asked to be part of the team that radically reorganized the network's flagship television news program in the early 1980s. The result was the creation of a one-hour program broadcast at 10 PM (earlier than the customary 11 PM newscast hour) composed of the nightly newscast (called *The National*) followed by a documentary/current affairs program (*The Journal*). The new format proved enormously successful, and *The Journal*, particularly, made an important contribution to the history of documentary in Canada, producing and broadcasting thousands of documentaries, many of them celebrated internationally, to significant audiences.

After ten years with *The Journal*, Starowicz was appointed to the newly-created position of Executive Producer for Documentaries in 1992, the position he holds to this day. In this capacity, he overseas documentary production at large at CBC television, films that are broadcast on a handful of documentary programs including the biographical *Life and Times*, the nationally specific *The Canadian Experience*, and the long-running *Witness*, among others, in addition to one-off special documentaries not produced for a specific series.

Starowicz's major contribution to documentary filmmaking, however, comes with his participation as a driving force behind the monumental series *Canada: A People's History*, a fully bilingual seventeen-part documentary on Canadian history from the prehistoric to the contemporary periods. The series was produced at a cost of $25 million (Canadian) and broadcast in French and English versions simultaneously on the CBC, and its French-language arm *Société Radio-Canada* (SRC) in one nine-part and one eight-part series. The first part began in autumn 2000 and the second the following autumn. Broadcast on Sunday nights and rebroadcast on the CBC's Newsworld channel, more than half of the nation's citizens (some fifteen million) watched all or part of one or more of the first nine episodes, with average viewership in the neighborhood of 2.2 million per episode. These are extraordinary numbers, more the kind of audiences generated for an important hockey match than for a CBC-produced history documentary.

Starowicz's reputation as an influential broadcaster and the catalyst behind many innovative documentary initiatives have earned him a central place in the Canadian documentary tradition, especially insofar as documentary, as a practice, remains so important to the state-funded broadcast media of the CBC.

PETER URQUHART

See also **Canadian Broadcasting Corporation**

Biography

Born September 8, 1946 in Worksop, UK. Earned a BA from McGill University, 1968. Worked as the producer of the CBC Radio series, 1970–1979. Executive producer of *The Journal*, 1982–1992. Has been executive documentary producer at the CBC since 1992. Has won the following awards: Canadian Broadcasting League's Cybil Award, 1973; Ohio State Documentary Award, 1973; Anik Award, 1987; Gemini Award, 1987.

STERN, BERT

Bert Stern stands as an unusual case in documentary history, for he entered and left in a whirlwind that closely resembles his career as a photographer. Stern has made only one film, *Jazz on a Summer's Day* (1960), but it exists as perhaps one of the greatest concert films ever made, and certainly the most well-known film about the jazz experience.

Stern began his career as an art director, but his ambition and skill quickly made him a preferred artist in freelance photography. His sharpness and artistry vaulted him into high commodity status with his work on various advertisement campaigns, and eventually his unique style brought him world fame through fashion photography and the images he created of Marilyn Monroe. Stern's photographs have appeared in *Vogue, Esquire, Life, Glamour,* and many other magazines. It is apparent that his career as a photographer and designer prepared him well for his single cinematic effort. Stern's desire to find new angles on his subjects makes *Jazz on a Summer's Day* a celebratory experience and less a traditional documentary, once again putting him outside the mainstream, while at the same time making his work highly distinct.

Stern's first experiences with filmmaking and photography came as part of the U.S. Army's Motion Picture Division from 1951 to 1953. Self-taught, he advanced quickly from mailroom clerk to art director of *Mayfair Magazine*. From there he went on as a freelance photographer in the mid-1950s. His unique vision, often brash and irreverent, proved to be a success in Stern's commercial work. This led to clients as diverse as IBM, Pepsi, Volkswagen, Smirnoff, U.S. Steel, DuPont, and others. Stern was able to break away from the standard photographic experience because he was able to recognize and capture both artistry and effectiveness in his commercial photography, and later, in his fashion and profile work. He was capable of selling ideas, products, people, lifestyles, and visions without commercial crassness. Stern's style has strictly adhered to the "less is more" concept, and his use of lighting and composition replaced the cluttered and contrived photographs that inundated the commercial market before his arrival.

Perhaps Stern's greatest breakthrough and legacy is his photographic essay on Marilyn Monroe titled *The Last Sitting*. Stern's two-day shoot of Monroe was her last before her death, and the photographs are as passionate as they are revealing, both externally and internally of the movie star.

Much of his passionate technique and irreverence transferred to his only attempt at filmmaking as well in 1958 at The Newport Jazz Festival. *Jazz on a Summer's Day* remains an engaging and elegant film, though its place in the history of documentary is murky. The reason lies somewhere between its experimental format and singularity. *Jazz on a Summer's Day* is shot as Stern would have photographed one of his beautiful models or objects. It is highly stylized and dramatically executed. Stern designed the festival's stage lighting and chose all the film's camera movement and placement. Stern fashioned still photographic long lenses to his film cameras so that he could invade spaces unnoticed. In technique and film mechanics, he was an innovator.

He was not afraid to get in his subject's face. He often used extreme close-ups, where performers would be-bop in and out of frame. He manages to use extremely static shots but still convey the passion and urgency of the performance. Stern, filming within an audience of hundreds, was able to provide a separate and unique intimate experience for his film audience. It is the result of the relationship that is obtained between artist and subject and artist and audience.

Jazz on a Summer's Day flows gracefully. Stern's editing is a stream of fluid cross-cuts between the festival and the concurrent World's Cup Race. He uses images of water, boats, and birds as matching visuals to the festival's swaying beats.

Stern is as interested in the audience as much as in the performing artists. The woman in the red sweater, the man in the little hat, the dancing, drinking coed, the interracial couple all become as important to the film as the musicians. The film celebrates a musical form and a cultural movement.

Jazz on a Summer's Day began as a single passion for Stern. A life goal of the artist was to make a film by the time he was thirty. The project was almost abandoned on several occasions, but Stern credits his final decision to a conversation he had with another passenger on a plane. On returning from a scouting trip of the grounds, Stern wrote off the location as uninteresting and unmanageable. The gentleman he was sitting next to on the plane, after hearing about the reason for Stern's trip, insisted that Stern must make the film. Coming out of that experience Stern was finally convinced that the film should be made.

At the start of production, the film went through many trials and changes. It began as a hybrid documentary/fictionalized narrative. Stern and his team devised scripts, and even shot rehearsals for an improvisational love story. The idea felt stale and unbelievable when it came time for actual filming and Stern dropped the contrived story lines. In an interview in 1999, included on the DVD release, Stern discussed the film's development. "We tried to devise a story, but I wasn't equipped to produce a story . . . so I stuck to the festival and to the music, and interpreted that with my camera."

Some controversy hovers over the making of the film. Stern's producing partners still claim more stake in the films creation than Stern has given them. While others claim directorial credit, Stern writes it off as his vision created entirely by himself. He sums the argument up in the 1999 interview by saying, "I don't know if you want to call the movie directed. It's more of a happening . . . *Jazz on a Summer's Day* is not directed. It was produced and filmed."

Jazz on a Summer's Day does not adhere to traditional investigative or exploratory documentary formulas. The film exists as a celebratory film documenting a people, place, and event. Stern brings glamour to an open field in Rhode Island and brings "jazz into the sun," as he describes

STERN, BERT

it. Stern achieves what most concert films hope to with the experimentalism and newness of the form it documents: a lasting image of a singular moment in musical history.

ROBERT A. EMMONS, JR.

See also Jazz on a Summer's Day

Biography

Born in Brooklyn, New York, October 3, 1929. U.S. Army 1951–1953. Freelance photographer with L.C. Gumbiner Agency, New York, NY, 1953–1971, Freelance commercial and magazine photographer 1959–. Founder and President of Libra Productions, a television commercial production company, New York, NY, 1961–1971. Has exhibited his photographs around the world from New York to France, Germany, and Switzerland. Author of several books, publishing his own library of work as well as texts on photographic process and technique. Received the Documentary Film Award, Venice Film Festival for his only film, *Jazz on a Summer's Day*, 1960 as well as several Art Directors Club Awards from 1964–1971.

Selected Films

1960 *Jazz on a Summer's Day*: producer, writer, director, editor

Further Reading

Silverman, Harold, Gilbert Simon, Bert Stern, and Milton Glaser, *The Pill Book*, New York: Bantam Books, 1980.
Stern, Bert, *The Photo Illustration*, New York: Crowell, 1974.
Stern, Bert, *The Last Sitting*, New York: William Morrow & Co., 1982.
Stern, Bert, and Robert A. Sobieszek, *Bert Stern: Adventures*, Boston: Bantam Books, 1998.

STERN, HORST

In the 1970s, the television series *Sterns Stunde* (Stern's Hour) broke new ground in exposing and examining the relation of society to nature and animals. Horst Stern eschewed traditional filmmaking in his approach to his chosen topic. To Stern, an examination of our relationship to nature was important because it taught us about ourselves and our society.

Twenty-six episodes of *Sterns Stunde* were produced between 1969 and 1979. The topics covered included animals as a food source, animals as pets, and animals in scientific experiments. He also devoted episodes to single species and creatures, such as spiders, butterflies, and hedgehogs. He always spoke the commentary with his hoarse and rough voice. His style was sharp, provocative, ironic, sometimes even polemic. His approach was marked by a scientific and educational, as opposed to entertaining, tone. His programs were always meticulously researched.

Stern did not refrain from airing his opinions. On Christmas Day in 1971, his program *Bemerkungen über den Rothirsch / Remarks on the Red Deer* was broadcast, in which he criticized German hunters for not hunting and killing enough deer. Other episodes attacked industrialized agriculture, which submits chickens and cows to miserable, mass production conditions. Other episodes discussed the use of animals in sports and the circus. The 1978 three-part program on animal experimentation in the pharmaceutical industry generated much discussion and controversy

Beside these political statements, he and his cameramen, especially Kurt Hirschel, produced cinematographic masterpieces, for which they developed new techniques to shoot animals such as spiders and bees. One of his theses was that the best way to respect animals in nature is to simply leave them alone.

Horst Stern was under the impression that all his efforts to change society were not as successful as he had hoped. Therefore he stopped shooting films and started a print magazine in 1980. In the mid-1980s, he resigned and started to write literature. In his novel *Klint*, he describes a journalist who despairs over his love for unblemished nature and his sorrow about the destruction of the environment.

KAY HOFFMANN

Biography

Born in Stettin, Germany, October 24, 1922. Did an apprenticeship at a bank. Served in World War II. Worked as a court reporter for a Stuttgart newspaper in 1947. Worked as a consultant for the publisher Delius Claasing in Bielefeld. Became Editor-in-Chief for various leisure magazines. In the 1960s, wrote more than fifty radio programs on animals for the school program of Süddeutscher Rundfunk (SDR), the public broadcaster for southwest Germany. From 1969 on, directed the ecological television series, *Sterns Stunde* for the SDR. In 1972, founded the Gruppe Ökologie (Ecology group) with Konrad Lorenz, Irenäus Eibl-Eibesfeldt, Bernhard Grzimek, and Heinz Sielmann. In 1974, awarded an honorary doctorate from the University of Stuttgart-Hohenheim. In 1980, started the magazine *Natur*. Publisher and Editor-in-Chief until 1984. Published three novels, which were quite successful in Germany. In 1993, moved to Ireland. Currently resides in Germany.

Selected Films

1970 *Bemerkungen über das Pferd*: director, writer
1970 *Bemerkungen über die Biene*: director, writer
1970 *Bemerkungen über das Rind*: director, writer
1971 *Bemerkungen über das Huhn*: director, writer
1971 *Bemerkungen über den Rothirsch*: director, writer
1973 *Bemerkungen über das Tier im Handel*: director, writer
1973 *Bemerkungen über den Storch*: director, writer
1975 *Bemerkungen über die Spinne*: director, writer
1976 *Bemerkungen über den Hund als Ware*: director, writer
1978 *Die Stellvertreter — Tiere in der Pharmaforschung*: director, writer
1979 *Bemerkungen über Gemse*: director, writer
1997 *Sterns Bemerkungen über einen sterbenden Wald*: director, writer

Further Reading

Grefe, Christiane, "Horst Stern — Das Vertrauen ins Fernsehen ist verloren," in *Dokumentarisches Fernsehen*, edited by Cornelia Bolesch, Munich: List, 1990, 76–80.
"Horst Stern," in catalogue 16. Internationales Dokumentarfilmfestival München, Munich, 2001.
Stern, Horst, *Sterns Bemerkungen über das Pferd, . . . die Biene, . . . die Hunde*, Munich: Kindler, 1971.
———, *Tierversuche in der Pharmaforschung*, Munich: Kindler, 1979.
———, *Jagdnovelle*, Munich: Kindler, 1989.
———, *Klint. Stationen einer Verwirrung*, Munich: Knaus, 1993.

STEWART, CHARLES

Although not a household name, cameraman and director Charles Stewart has played a crucial part in the development of television documentary from the 1960s to the present day. He is probably best known for his work with Roger Graef, for whom he has shot a number of programs. He also co-directed *Police* (BBC 1980–1981) with him. He thus played a central role in the dissemination of direct cinema techniques within British television during the 1960s and, most prominently, the 1970s (when the "fly on the wall" documentary began to become an established part of British television). He has also worked in other forms, such as television drama, feature films, and anthropological documentaries.

Stewart became an early innovator in the use of handheld, synch-sound camera work. He quickly became adept at using the Éclair NPR and, as lightweight cameras became increasingly taken up within television, his services were in increasing demand. Using the NPR, he could handhold the camera and thus capture a large range of different events in many different spaces. Free from the restrictions of lighting set ups and camera repositioning, Stewart could work faster and create a fluid sense of action, breaking down the distance between action and camera.

It was unsurprising that Stewart began to work for Alan King Associates, which became a kind of centre for young, innovative filmmakers working with new, lightweight equipment. Stewart first worked with Graef when making a film under the aegis of AKA: *The Life and Times of John Huston Esq.* (BBC, 1967) was a Graef-directed documentary on the film director that mixed verité techniques with some dramatic, symbolic sequences. This programme led to the creation of a twelve-part series on artists that mixed verité techniques with occasional experimental sequences: *Who Is?* (BBC, 1968) was an attempt to break new ground in arts documentaries and was the first series to be co-produced by four different television companies from around the world (the BBC, the Canadian Broadcasting Corporation, National Education Television [United States], and Bayerischer Rundfunk [Germany]). In between the Huston programme and the *Who Is?* series, Stewart had worked on the Mike Hodges-produced series *New Tempo* (ABC, 1967), an extremely experimental, montage-based arts series.

Toward the end of the 1960s, in line with the growing confluence of documentary and drama in many areas, Stewart shot many documentary-influenced television dramas and feature films. These included work with directors such as Ken Loach and Jean-Luc Godard, who represented the "realistic" and "experimental" sides of lightweight camera use, both of which Stewart was associated with. Perhaps the most controversial documentary-influenced drama that Stewart shot in this period was Roy Battersby's *Some Women* (BBC, 1968), a film covering interviews with women who had been in prison. Based on extensive research, the film used actresses to reenact original interviews and was not transmitted until 1969 because of the manner in which it was seen to confuse the boundaries between fact and fiction. Stewart shot the film in an intimate, still manner, diverting from the more roving manner associated with lightweight equipment.

In the 1970s, Stewart undertook work with Graef on a number of "fly on the wall" documentaries, most often documenting a number of decision-making processes. The first of these was *The Space Between Words* (BBC, 1972), a five-part series that filmed a series of incidents that reflected communication problems within different environments (such as in a family, at work, and at school). This documentary marked a new stage of verité within Britain, a much more austere and painstaking detailing of words, movements, and gestures. This called for Stewart to observe a whole set of details at quick speed, so that he could shift his focus appropriately. The series was shot on a relatively high ration of 30:1, which allowed the crew to amass a wealth of film and thus select what they thought were the most interesting sequences for transmission. Graef continued this style for a number of documentaries made for Granada, including *State of the Nation: A Law in the Making* (Granada, 1973) and *Decision* (Granada, 1976). In 1981 Graef and Stewart made the now famous *Police* (transmitted 1982) for the BBC, a thirteen-part, minutely focused portrait of the Thames Valley police force, which attracted more than ten million viewers, an enormous amount for a documentary.

Stewart is most famous for his work with Graef, but he has also worked in many other fields, and has often worked as sole director. His first directorial assignment was an ATV documentary on a road-widening scheme, *Could Your Street Be Next?* (ATV, 1972). In the late 1970s, he made two television dramas, both of which evidence a realistic tone: *Speech Day* (Thames, 1977) and *Billy* (BBC, 1979). In the 1980s, Stewart began to work on programmes that documented environmental and political aspects of Ethiopia in *Seeds of Despair* (Central, 1984) and *Seeds of Hope* (Central, 1985). These programmes (the second of which was a six-part series) evidenced influences of both vérité and anthropological television that had developed in the 1970s and that Stewart was involved with. Stewart shot some episodes of Granada's popular anthropological series *Disappearing World* (Granada, 1970–1991), as well as Adrian Cowell's well-received, experimentally tinged anthropology programme *The Tribe That Hides from Man* (ATV, 1970).

Although Stewart's work was varied, it was also marked by certain thematic and stylistic preoccupations: capturing "authentic," minimally mediated action; detailing events often "hidden" or ignored by the media; plus a sensitivity to detail and an ability to capture the minutiae of human interaction, such as facial expressions or significant body gestures. He was, along with Dick Fontaine, among the most innovative camera stylists working with lightweight equipment in British television during the 1960s, helping to break down the boundaries between drama and documentary in the late 1960s and early 1970s, and was involved in the new wave of politically sensitive anthropological documentaries in the 1970s and 1980s.

JAMIE SEXTON

See also **Graef, Roger**

Biography

Born in Newcastle-upon-Tyne, 1937. Two years national service in the navy from 1956. In 1958 went to Regent Street Polytechnic to study photography. Moved to London in 1961 and started to work as a fashion photographer. Started Document film production in 1964. In 1965, began working with AKA, and first met Roger Graef.

Selected Films

As Photographer

1967 *New Tempo* (ABC, series, various directors)
1968 *The Life and Times of John Huston Esq.* (BBC, Graef,)

1968 *Who Is* (BBC, series, various directors)
1969 *Some Women* (BBC, Battersby)
1970 *The Tribe that Hides from Man* (ATV, Cowell)
1970 *The Important Thing Is Love* (ATV, Kitts)
1971 *Rank and File* (BBC, Loach)
1972 *The Space Between Words* (BBC, series, Graef)
1973 *The State of the Nation—A Law in the Making* (Granada, Graef)
1974 *Disappearing World: Masai Women* (Granada, Curling)
1974 *Disappearing World: Masai Manhood* (Granada, Curling)
1975 *The State of the Nation: Inside Brussels HQ* (Granada, Graef)
1976 *Decision* (Granada, series, Graef)
1977 *Disappearing World: The Rendille* (Granada, Curling)
1978 *Decision: British Communism* (Granada, Graef)

As Director and Producer*

1972 *Could Your Street Be Next* (ATV)
1974 *Retirement: End or Beginning?* (ATV)
1979 *Billy* (BBC)
1982 **Police* (BBC, series co-directed and produced with Roger Graef)

1984 *Seeds of Despair* (Central)
1985 *Seeds of Hope* (Central)
1991 *Cutting Edge: Plague in Your Own Home* (Channel 4)
1992 **Town Hall* (BBC, series)
1995 *Witness: Mecca on the Thames* (Channel 4)
1996 **True Stories: Inside Sellafield* (Channel 4)
1996 **Red Base One Four* (Channel 4)

Further Reading

Orbanz, Eva (ed.), *Journey to a Legend and Back: The British Realistic Film*, translated by Stuart Hood, Berlin: Edition Volker Spiess, 1977.
Petley, Julian, "The Good Stewart," in *Broadcast*, July, 19, 1985.
Swallow, Norman, "Television, the Integrity of Fact and Fiction," in *Sight and Sound*, 45, 3, Summer 1976.
Winston, Brian, *Claiming the Real: The Griersonian Documentary and its Legitimations*, London: BFI, 1995.
Wyver, John (ed.), *Nothing But the Truth: Cinéma Vérité and the Films of the Roger Graef Team*, London: ICA/BFI, 1982.
———, "Police Taped," in *Framework*, 18, 1982.

STONEY, GEORGE

George Stoney is a leading figure in the American documentary film movement, having made more than fifty documentaries and founded a movement of community-based media producers in the 1960s and 1970s in North America. He has played a major agenda setting role in debates about documentary, its forms, its ethics, and its social function. Stoney began his career working in 16mm as a socially aware documentary filmmaker using aspects of direct cinema and later switched to video format in the 1970s as it was ideal for the mobility and ease needed for the informal community-based media he produced or oversaw production of. In addition to using video as a means of making media more democratically available to nonprofessionals, he also was responsible for leading the creation of public access cable, a designated community "free speech" zone negotiated for with cable operators. Stoney also provided the pedagogy and philosophy to underpin the production of this new genre of video documentary. As the cofounder of the influential Alternative Media Center in 1970, which became a training ground for the first generation of producers, Stoney played a major role in influencing the content of this programming. Besides working in television, Stoney has collaborated on numerous films around the world, including those by his many former students, which share a common commitment to social change media in their production, content, and distribution.

From his first documentary *All My Babies* in 1953, a training film for the Georgia Department of Public Health a dramatic reenactment of a black midwife's work from her perspective, he has been committed to producing films and videos that show life from the perspective of people who have been disenfranchised or excluded from mainstream media. He uses narrative as a strategy, preferring to tell a story or cover an event than letting the camera be a "fly on the wall." This extends to letting participants in the film take the microphone, use direct address and other surprising rule-breaking moments in the films, and video productions that have, as their goal, social change and education rather than aesthetic purity.

Stoney's filmmaking practice and philosophy challenges the auteurship that defined direct cinema. A former student of Basil Wright and an educator for the FSA using Pare Lorentz's films, his filmmaking practice comes with an awareness of the history and practices that inform his work. His interest in the history of documentary film culminated in his intensive study of documentary pioneer Robert Flaherty in *How the Myth Was Made* (1978). This acclaimed film critically explored the early roots of documentary practice. Indeed, despite his critical approach, all of Stoney's films are informed by fundamental attributes of cinema verité such as direct address, natural lighting, and ambient sound but always with a question of the morality of filmmaking, an issue that some direct cinema directors eschewed. Thus, Stoney's interest in who and how the story is being told—its fidelity to truth—is more than an aesthetic but an ethical working out of the film-maker/subject relationship, a debate that shaped the direct cinema movement.

His respect for the subject's perspective extends to letting them shape the final cut, a process that few directors would ever allow. This active engagement with the subjects allows them to retain authorial control. He established this practice early on, and it has stayed with him throughout his career. It was his concern with retaining the subjectivity of the participants in documentary that led him to take a job as an executive producer of an experimental project at the Canadian Nation Film Board in 1968. One of his first films, *You Are on Indian Land*, involved an Indian film crew that was trained by the NFBC and covered a border dispute from an Indian perspective, countering the view of the television news. It was used also as a tool of understanding and shown to Royal Canadian Mounted Police and the local police.

It was while at Challenge for Change that Stoney recognized the importance of the newly developed lightweight video portapak in community production. It enabled filmmakers to make documentary films in the field, cheaply and without expert training, making it an ideal medium for social activists who could now gain the authority of media producers without the cost or technical expertise of film. A documentary of the use of this early video tool was *VTR ST. JACQUES*. Shot on 16mm, it chronicles the first use of ½-inch consumer grade black-and-white video as a tool for community building and people empowerment. In 1970, when he returned

from the Challenge for Change program, he took the next step toward creating a democratized distribution to match the style and content of the video's community-based productions when he cofounded the Alternative Media Center at NYU. In this effort, he is fundamentally concerned with the documentaries/audience relationship, which owes its concern to political activism and the pedagogical strategies of Paulo Frerie. Stoney uses media in situations that would encourage dialogue and understanding and lead to political change. This meant creating other groundbreaking forums for viewing in and out of the public sphere, as in public access's carving out of a space for community media in a medium surrounded by mainstream productions and also in other ways, such in the screenings of films in unusual places or to facilitate dialogue among groups.

DANIELLE SCHWARTZ

See also **Wright, Basil**

Biography

Born in 1916, studied journalism at the University of North Carolina and at New York University. Worked as free-lance journalist, an information officer for the Farm Security Administration and a photo intelligence officer in World War II. Joined the Southern Educational Film Service as a writer and a director in 1946. In 1948, he received a Rosenwald Fellowship. Appointed the first executive director of the Canadian Film Board's Challenge for Change Program 1968. In 1972, with Red Burns, he cofounded the Alternate Media Center at New York University. In 1976, he was founder of the National Federation of Local Cable Programmers. Stoney is currently Paulette Goddard Professor in Film, Tisch School of the Arts, Department of Film and Television.

Selected Films

1953 *All My Babies*
1965 *The Mask*
1972 *First Transmissions of ACTV*
1978 *Shepherd of the Night Flock* (with James Brown)
1978 *How the Myth Was Made* (1978)
VTR ST. JACQUES
1989 *We Shall Overcome* (1989)
1995 *The Uprising of '34*: co-directed with Judith Helfand

Further Reading

Barnouw, Eric, *Documentary: A History of the Non-Fiction Film*, New York: Oxford University Press, 1993.
Mertes, Cara, "Toasts and Tributes," in *Wide Angle*, 21, 2, March 1999, 137–165.

Rapport, Leonard, "George Stoney, Writer: The Early Years," in *Wide Angle*, 21, 2, March 1999, 19–25.

Stoney, George, "The Mirror Machine," in *Sight and Sound (London)*, 41, 1, winter 1971–1972, 9–11.

———, "The Future of Documentary," in *Sightlines*, fall–winter, 1983–1984.

Sturken, Marita, "An Interview with George Stoney," in *Afterimage*, January 1984.

Watson, Patricia, "Challenge for Change," in *Art Canada*, 142–143, 1970.

Wide Angle, 21, 2, 1999, Special Issue devoted to George Stoney.

Winston, Brian, "Documentary: How the Myth Was Deconstructed," in *Wide Angle*, 21, 2, March 1999, 71–86.

STORCK, HENRI

Having made more than seventy films, comprising for the most part documentaries and shorts combined with a few medium and feature-length films, Henri Storck is undoubtedly the leading figure of Belgian cinema. Throughout his varied career, he dealt to a greater or lesser degree with such practices as formalism, impressionism, social and political concerns, and ethnography. He generally worked in an ordered fashion, gained a certain reputation with art critique films, but never fulfilled his Hollywood dreams. He fought relentlessly for a national cinema, sometimes displayed ideological flexibility, never abandoned his life's passions and remained a genuinely modest individual.

His first attempts at film, shot on 9.5mm and subsequently on 35mm, focused on his immediate surroundings, and combined formal research, an acute study of social behaviour and a surrealist sense of rebellion. *Films d'Amateur sur Ostende/ Amateur Films upon Ostende* (1928) and *Images d'Ostende/Images of Ostende* (1929), with their poetic mood and rhythmic feeling, recall the early works of Joris Ivens. In 1930, *Trains de Plaisir/Trains of Pleasure*, *Les Fêtes du Centenaire/Feasts of the Centenary*, *Ostende Reine des Plages/Ostende Queen of the Beaches* all display an aptitude for observing rituals and feasts. Storck had in fact been declared "the official cinematographer of the city of Ostende."

Images d'Ostende, *Trains de Plaisir*, and *Une Pêche aux Harengs* (1930) (Herring Fishing) were shown at the 2nd International Congress of Independent Cinema, held in Brussels between November 27 and December 1, 1930. Storck's work met with acclaim. During the Congress Storck met Joris Ivens, with whom he would later collaborate on "Borinage," Boris Kaufman, Jean Painlevé, and Jean Vigo, who was to become his close friend. In 1931, he moved to Paris and became involved with *Zéro de Conduite* in which he had a small role, that of a priest. By the end of 1933, however, Storck had moved back to Brussels.

In 1932, Storck directed two films: *Sur les Bords de la Caméra/On the Edge of the Camera* and *Histoire du Soldat Inconnu/History of the Unknown Soldier*. These two short films, made on commission (Storck had to edit sequences of athletics taken from news images), exploit a surrealist and often satirical vein reminiscent of René Clair's *Entr'acte* (1924) or Vigo's *A Propos de Nice* (1930). *Histoire du Soldat Inconnu* is, in addition, a pacifist manifesto denouncing the illusions of the Briand-Kellog Pact (1928), the rise of fascism, and the impotence of the League of Nations.

In 1933, at the behest of the Screen Club of Brussels (Club de l'Ecran de Bruxelles), Storck began the *Borinage* project (*Misére au Borinage*). Contacted by the leaders of this leftist cine club, known for its projection of avant-garde and political films, Storck took on the project and requested the collaboration of Joris Ivens, who accepted immediately. The film, largely based on a study into the wretched living conditions of the mining community, written by a doctor and published by Workers Aid International (Secours Ouvrier International), depicts the strike movement and the confrontations with the law enforcement. It is a testimony to the consciousness of filmmakers and left-wing intellectuals with regard to the subject. The film ends with a direct call for the dictatorship of the proletariat. The film was made with little money; there is no sound track and it is filmed largely with lightweight cameras that are, above all, hidden from the authorities.

To depict the episodes concerning the strikers' conflict, however, the two directors were faced with the problem of reconstruction. They needed to show, for example, the tactic implemented by the community to avoid eviction (other miners would arrive and strategically sit on the furniture to prevent the bailiff from seizing it). The directors had no other choice than to "produce an honest and direct imitation" (Ivens), and for this they needed to hire two police uniforms and find two miners willing to act the part of policemen. The other important scene that had to be reconstructed was that of the demonstration that appears at the end of the film and that had taken place to commemorate the fiftieth anniversary of the death of Karl Marx. The directors asked the miners to proceed as normal. The portrait of Marx, held by two men, leads the march, followed by small groups of men, each group separated by about ten paces from the next, thus rendering them an impossible target and facilitating escape in the event of police intervention. According to Ivens, the miners forgot that they were participating in the making of a film, and the scene became a genuine demonstration, hence the arrival and intervention of the police and the urgent need to hide the camera.

In 1934, Henri Storck, along with René-Ghislain Levaux, created the organisation Cinéma-Edition-Production (CEP), which would later fulfill numerous commissions. *Les Maisons de la Misére/Houses of Poverty* (1937), made for The National Society for Low Cost Housing (Société Nationale des Habitations à Bon Marché), is reminiscent of both *Housing Problems* (Anstey and Elton, 1935), which Storck had viewed, and certain scenes of *Borinage*. One of the two cameramen was Eli Lotar, who worked for Buñuel on *Las Hurdes* and would subsequently direct *Aubervilliers*. Whereas *Borinage* used the real protagonists and adhered to a documentary structure, the production of *Les Maisons de la Misére* opted for professional stage actors.

La Belgique Nouvelle/New Belgium (1937) is essentially a film of election propaganda for the Prime Minister Van Zeeland, and it is entirely a product of its context, that of the front against fascism. *Le Patron est Mort/The Boss Is Dead* (1938) retraces the funeral procession of Socialist leader Emile Vandervelde (nicknamed "le patron," "the boss"). The particular attention paid to the behaviour of the largely working-class crowds during this ritual prefigures the ethnographic approach of his later works.

In the period leading up to World War II, Storck devoted much energy to a historical production about the colonisation of the Congo, *Bula Matari*. His associate, Le Vaux, from the CEP, spent a long period between 1939 and 1940 in Hollywood, trying to secure the interest of the majors. He seemed to be on the verge of success when the war broke out. The project was relaunched in 1950 with Alexander Korda, only to fall through once again.

In the middle of World War II, from 1942 to 1944, Storck devoted himself to *Symphonie Paysanne/Peasant Symphony*, a feature-length documentary in five parts (the four seasons plus a rural wedding celebration, which serves as a conclusion). Aesthetically speaking, this film is probably Storck's chef-d'oeuvre; however, from an ideological and symbolic perspective, the film is somewhat surprising. This chronicle of rural farm life in Brabant, which omits any reference to the current world conflict, seems to glorify the values of "a return to the land," "back to nature," and "national cohesion," values greatly extolled by the occupying forces. The semi-ethnographic approach is also completely a-historical, and the continual insistence on the timeless rural rituals and the cyclical concept of time immemorial are in total opposition to any progressive vision.

After the war Storck mainly focused on films about art. In 1945, the innovative short film *Le Monde de Paul Delvaux/The World of Paul Delvaux* broke new ground in its seeming ability to penetrate the interior of the art works. Storck would later return to this subject in 1970 with *Paul Delvaux ou les Femmes Défendues/Paul Delvaux or Forbidden Women*. *Rubens* (1948), made in collaboration with the critic Paul Haesaerts, anticipated an analytical approach that would become widespread many years later. The use of split screen, cross-cutting, extreme close-ups, and the superimposition of geometric lines on the artwork, all produced on 35mm black-and-white film, prefigured the video effects which made the French series *Palettes* (Alain Jaubert) so successful in the 1990s.

In this postwar period, Storck also worked on one of his rare fiction films, *Le Banquet des Fraudeurs/The Smuggler's Banquet* (1951), which deals with the creation of Bénélux in the context of the Marshall Plan. This humorous chronicle of a village with three borders, two of which are going to disappear, paradoxically goes to great lengths to appeal to a wide European audience.

Without interrupting his numerous and diverse commissions such as *Au Carrefour de la Vie/At the Crossroad of Life* (1949), commissioned by the United Nations on the subject of the rehabilitation of young offenders, Storck increasingly turned to films about Belgian society, history, and traditions. *Fêtes de Belgique ou l'Effusion Collective/Feasts of Belgium or Collective Effusion* (1970–1971), a series of ten short films on 35mm, provided a perfect ethnographic example of the country's folk traditions.

Storck's career drew to a close in 1985 with a feature-length biopic on the painter Permeke. Toward the end of his life, Storck, anxious to pass on his experiences and documents, agreed to participate in various interviews by filmmakers and researchers. Such examples include *Henri Storck, Cinéaste/Henri Storck Filmmaker* (1986) by Robbe De Hert and *Mes Entretiens Filmés/My Conversations on Film* (1998) by Boris Lehman.

Storck was always motivated by his love of the cinema. He initiated many projects. He was co-founder of the Cinématheque Royale de Belgique (1938), he created the Audiovisual Centre in Brussels (Centre de l'Audiovisuel [CBA]), and the Centre for Films on Art (Centre du Film sur l'Art). In 1950, he carried out a study for UNESCO into the recreational film for the child spectator. In 1959, he produced *Les Seigneurs de la Forêt/Masters of the Congo Jungle* (Heinz Sielmann and Henri Brandt) and in 1967, Luc de Heusch's *Jeudi On Chantera Comme Dimanche/Thursday We Shall Sing Like Sunday*. In 1975, he appeared in Chantal Ackerman's film *Jeanne Dielman*.

In terms of Storck's ideas, he was not devoid from certain surprising contradictions: a poetic filmmaker who admired John Ford, a modest director who dreamed of making Hollywood blockbusters, a staunch socialist who sometimes accepted astonishing political concessions, a quiet man who was also a determined rebel. In the famous May 1968 revolt in Paris, despite being a teacher at the renowned National School of Cinema (IAD, Ecole Nationale de Cinéma), he took the side of the students, a decision that cost him his teaching post.

Storck was acquainted with many highly esteemed directors and lived through the leading cinematic trends of the twentieth century. The imprints left by this father figure of Belgian cinema are still visible today. A formal invention, an openness to international subjects, and a commitment to social concerns—which today epitomize the Belgian documentary movement—are all inherent in Storck's varied work.

JEAN-LUC LIOULT

See also **Ivens, Joris**

Biography

Born September 5, 1907 to shoe shop owners. Graduated with a degree in physics from the Université Libre de Bruxelles. Died September 23, 1999.

Selected Films

1928 *Films d'amateur sur Ostende/Amateur Films upon Ostende*: cinematographer, director
1929 *Images d'Ostende/Images of Ostende*: cinematographer, director
1930 *Une pêche au hareng/Herring Fishing*: cinematographer, director
1932 *Histoire du soldat inconnu/History of the Unknown Soldier*: cinematographer, director, editor
1933 *Borinage*: co-cinematographer, co-director, writer
1936 *Les Maisons de la misére/Houses of Poverty*: director
1944 *Symphonie paysanne/Peasant Symphony*: cinematographer, director, writer, editor, producer
1949 *Rubens*: director, writer, editor, producer
1971 *Paul Delvaux ou les femmes défendues/Paul Delvaux or Forbidden Women*: director
1973 *Les Fêtes de Belgique/Feasts of Belgium*: director
1998 *Mes entretiens filmés/My Conversations on Film* (Lehman): actor

Further Reading

Aubenas, Jacqueline (dir.), *Dic Doc, Le Dictionnaire du Documentaire—191 réalisateurs*, Bruxelles: Communauté Française de Belgique Wallonie-Bruxelles, 1999.

Le Borinage : "la gréve des mineurs de 1932 et le film de Joris Ivens et Henri Storck," *Revue belge du Cinéma*, 6–7, 1983–1984, Bruxelles: A.P.E.C.

Geens, Vincent, *Bula Matari: Un rêve d'Henri Storck*, Crisnée: Fonds Henri Storck/Yellow Now Côté cinéma, 2000.

Lioult, Jean-Luc, "Autour du *Rubens* de Storck et du *Van Gogh* de Resnais: quels films sur l'art?" in *Le Film sur l'Art et ses Frontiéres*, Aix-en-Provence: Publications de l'Université de Provence & Institut de l'Image, 1998, 45–60.

Vichi, Laura, *Henri Storck—De l'avant-garde au documentaire social*, Crisnée: Yellow Now Côté cinéma, 2002.

STRAND, PAUL

Paul Strand is one of the most important figures in the development of modern American photography, as well as contributing to a series of groundbreaking documentary films between the 1920s and early 1940s. A pioneer of photographic abstraction in the 1910s, Strand dealt with subject matter that ranged from urban scenes and landscapes to found objects and intensely personal close-ups. He was particularly interested in the purity of simple images and geometric patterns and composed his photographs to capture what in 1917 he called "a formal conception born of the emotions, the intellect, or of both." He was a modernist in his belief that the camera gives access to the truth of objects, and the photograph brings to life a hidden potentiality often overlooked in daily life. Alan Trachtenberg has argued that, although Strand was interested in documenting the factual world, he developed a romantic version of modernism in searching for organic properties within hard forms, heightening perceptions and illuminating hidden depths.

Born into a Jewish family on the Upper West Side of New York City, Strand was educated at the Ethical Culture School in New York from 1904–1909. His teacher, the social reformer Lewis W. Hime, taught Strand how to use a camera to document working-class life and introduced him to art exhibitions in 1907. After graduation and a short trip to Europe, Strand joined the Camera Club of New York and worked briefly as a commercial portrait photographer. He began working in pictorialist and impressionist modes, but in the mid-1910s became very interested in "straight photographs," in which he achieved a high measure of objectivity by reverting to a sharp focus lens and refusing to tamper with the negative. The purity of Strand's work caught the interest of the photographic innovator and art exhibitor Alfred Stieglitz in 1915. Stieglitz held Strand in high esteem; he was the only photographer Stieglitz would exhibit in the late 1910s; and in a June 1917 issue of *Camera Work*, Stieglitz praised him for his "brutal directness" and for resisting trickery for his visual effect.

Toward the end of his career, in 1971, Strand spoke about three roads that opened for him after he saw Stieglitz's Armory Show of 1913: first, "to understand the new developments in painting"; second, "a desire to express certain feelings I had about New York"; and, third, a desire to "photograph people without their being aware of the camera." Strand followed Stieglitz's preference for a handheld camera to take instantaneous pictures, which enabled events to come together by chance, rather than viewing composition in a fixed, unmoving way. He discussed ideas with artists that Stieglitz exhibited in his 291 Gallery on Fifth Avenue, including Morgan Russell, Marcel Duchamp, and Francis Picabia. But where Duchamp and Picabia's art explored the chaos of modernity, Strand sought a heightened objectivity that was epitomised by the modernity of Manhattan. Sometimes he appeared to celebrate urban designs through his sharply focused images and his interest in light, line, and volume, whereas at others (such as a 1922 essay in *Broom*), he set his work against the destructive force of mechanization. Just as Stieglitz was interested in the relationship between industry and nature, so Strand was keen to rescue a sense of organicism from inanimate forms.

In the mid-1910s and early 1920s (on either side of serving in the U.S. Army Medical Corps as a x-ray technician), Strand spent most of his energy putting into effect his "brutal directness" to document New York City life. His photograph of "Wall Street" (1915), for example, on one level portrays just another day in the life of the financial district. But the photograph depicts a group of figures reduced to little more than silhouettes: no facial features are discernible, and they walk mechanically and in isolation from each other. Long shadows are cast by a restricted light source located outside the frame, and the sombre mood of the photograph is exacerbated by a sequence of gigantic dark windows of Wall Street that loom over the figures. Other photographs from this time are more conventional and lighter in tone, replicating Stieglitz's interest in the interaction between urban and natural forces (such as "City Hall Park," 1915), but with much closer attention to the abstract shapes conjured up by the developing city. Although Strand photographed nonurban images (such as "Abstraction, Porch Shadows" and the almost cubist "Still Life, Pear and Bowls" in a 1916 trip to Twin Lakes, Connecticut), he was deeply engaged with the variety of city life, where European impulses fused with native experiences. Although he spent time photographing working Manhattan, he was also interested in the poor immigrants living in areas such as the Bowery. One of his most haunting images is "Blind Woman" (1916), depicting an ageing woman with a "blind" placard around her neck who stares away from the camera without recognition. In a different context, this could be seen as an exploitative image, but Strand had deep respect for his subjects and he spoke of the blind woman's "absolutely unforgettable and noble face."

Many of the still images of New York, including "Wall Street" and "City Hall Park," were reused in Strand's seven-minute documentary collaboration *Manhatta* with the painter Charles Sheeler (1921). *Manhatta* pioneered the vogue for city symphonies, leading to documentaries on Berlin, Amsterdam, and Moscow in the 1920s. Strand and Sheeler used Walt Whitman's poetry as a lyrical contrast to the multiple perspectives they deployed to depict a working day in downtown Manhattan. Just as Strand's written statements shift between fascination with the modern city and a critique of new forms of alienation created by urban development, so *Manhatta* can be read either as a paean to, or a critique of, city life. The plumes of smoke pumped out by boats in the Hudson Bay contrast ironically with the still image of the celestial city that frames Whitman's celebratory lyrics (see *Manhatta* entry). This interest in textuality resurfaced later in Strand's mid-1940s' collaboration with Nancy Newhall, *Time in New England* (1950), in which written texts were juxtaposed with ninety-four images of New England to create "a portrait more dynamic than either medium could present alone" (although Strand was not altogether pleased with the result).

From the mid-1920s, Strand moved away from New York City as his primary location, taking his "brutal directness" to other North American scenes, particularly New England, Canada, and the Southwest. He shared an interest with Mexico and the Southwest with Stieglitz's partner Georgia O'Keeffe, but Strand offered a different perspective from O'Keeffe's painterly exuberance. He visited the Southwest regularly between 1930 and 1932, developing location and portrait photographs that retain a directness born out of his urban sensibility, together with a respect for the peoples of the region. Strand also became more radical in the early 1930s, advising the Group Theatre, visiting the Soviet Union (where he met Sergei Eisenstein), and collaborating on the documentary *The Plow*

That Broke the Plains (1935), the first publicly shown federal government documentary that focused on the creation of the Dust Bowl as a result of over-ploughing and the drought of 1929. He shared the photographic credits for the film with Ralph Steiner and Leo Hurwitz under Pare Lorentz's direction. Lorentz had been inspired by Dorothea Lange's photographs of the effects of the Depression and had been commissioned by the Resettlement Administration to document the plight of workers in the Great Plains region. Strand and Hurwitz favoured a script that would cast blame on greedy capitalists, but Lorentz was more moderate in his politics and argued that this would undermine the emphasis on the drought and the "melodrama of nature." Strand and Hurwitz spent much of their time taking location shots of dust-storms, with Lorentz working closely with Ralph Steiner on the narrative sections. Although Strand thought that "the guts had been taken out" of the film, his influence can be seen in the montage of still images (skull, disused machinery, cracked earth, desolate landscape) that heighten the impact of the disaster.

Strand's work on *The Plow That Broke the Plains* had been preceded by his work on *The Wave* (*Redes*) sponsored by the Mexican government, completed in 1934 but not shown in the United States until 1936. *The Wave* explored the economic problems faced by a fishing village near Vera Cruz, developing Strand's interest in working Mexican life, emphasizing the meagre wage that fishermen receive for a long day's work and the united action of workers. Strand was the chief architect of the film, even though it was directed by Fred Zinnemann. William Alexander argues that one of Strand's photographic signatures is used to great effect in *The Wave*: a technique in which shots "begin with a single, posed figure in close-up or medium close-up; movement in the shot then consists of a single movement of the head." This aesthetic mode was developed in *Heart of Spain* in 1937, co-edited by Leo Hurwitz, which dealt with the Loyalist fight against Franco. The central focus of *Heart of Spain* is on the relationship between Spanish peasants and the land, which creates a romantic-poetic drama rather than a narrative-based documentary.

Strand's most important film project was the prolabor film *Native Land* in 1942. Once again Strand collaborated with Hurwitz, this time as co-directors, under the label of Frontier Films, which had been formed in 1936 as a development of the Group Theatre project. Frontier Films was "an independent, nonprofit motion picture organization devoted to the production of realistic depictions of American life" set against Hollywood's emphasis on individualism and sentimentality. The influence of Eisenstein and Dovzhenko is apparent in *Native Land*, which is filmed in a Soviet documentary style to expose pernicious right-wing forces in America. It was scripted by Ben Maddow and uses Paul Robeson's narrative voice against a panoply of stark images to highlight the perversion of American ideals, the deep-rooted corruption of exploitative capitalists, and the fascism of the Ku Klux Klan. The film is deeply prolabor and anti-fascist, as emphasized at the end of Robeson's spoken epilogue: "With the united power of field and factory and arms, we will deliver the blows to crush fascism. For only absolute victory over Hitler and Japan can safeguard our democratic gains and preserve the independence of America."

Through his film projects, Strand retained his interest in photographic montage, but *Native Land* is much more impressionistic than Strand's "straight photography" of the 1910s and 1920s. This shifting style demonstrated that he did not wish to be pigeonholed as an artist who could only work within a single aesthetic mode. His work was much more politicized in the 1930s and 1940s; his involvement in the left-wing film projects of Frontier Films actually led to un-American accusations being levelled against him and the blacklisting of the Photo League in 1947. Strand stood firmly along with photographers, such as Ansel Adams, against the blacklisting, and when the Photo League called a special meeting in December 1947 to discuss what action should be taken, Strand commented defiantly: "although artists have not in the past wanted to mix art with politics the politicians have already mixed politics in art. So we are now in politics, very much so." Strand was active in the late 1940s in defending the blacklisted Hollywood Ten, and he joined with the playwright Clifford Odets in June 1949 in calling for a Bill of Rights conference to protest "the police state methods of certain Army and FBI officials." The charges against him and the blacklisting of Leo Hurwitz were the main reason why Strand moved to France at the beginning of the 1950s, but these statements on the intermingling of art and politics are a gauge of how far his art had progressed since the 1910s.

Strand turned away from filmmaking after World War II (partly for financial reasons), settling in Orgeval near Paris in 1951 and spending time travelling and photographing in Europe and Africa. The first full Paul Strand exhibition was held in the Museum of Modern Art, New York City in 1945, which was followed by a Strand retrospective at the Philadelphia Museum of Art in 1971, and exhibitions at the New York Metropolitan Museum of Art and the Los Angles Country Museum in 1973.

MARTIN HALLIWELL

See also **Heart of Spain; Manhatta; Native Land; Plow That Broke the Plains, The**

Biography

Born in New York City, October 16, 1890 to middle-class Jewish parents. Attended the private Ethical Culture School from 1904–1909 where he was introduced to photography by Lewis W. Hime. First photographs published in 1911. Began correspondence with Alfred Stieglitz in the 1910s; started to visit the 291 Gallery in Manhattan. Began abstract phase of photography in 1916 and was published in Stieglitz's *Camera Work*. From September 1918 to July 1919 served in the U.S. Army Medical Corps as x-ray technician. Experimented with a movie camera owned by Charles Sheeler and released *Manhatta* as *New York the Magnificent* in 1921. Married Rebecca Salsbury in 1922; worked on news and sports coverage and experimented with machine photographs. Freelance work dried up when film industry moved to California and first marriage broke down in 1931; spent time in the Southwest and Mexico 1930–1934; visits the Soviet Union in 1935. Worked on documentary films and photography through the 1930s and early 1940s. Married Virginia Stevens in 1935–1948 and then Hazel Kingsbury in 1951. Settled in Orgeval, near Paris, in 1951. Frequently exhibited in Europe and America and travelled to Africa in 1960s. Stopped working due to cataracts in 1970s; died at home in Orgeval in 1976.

Selected Films

1921 *Manhatta*: co-director and photographer (with Charles Sheeler)
1935 *The Plow That Broke the Plains*: photographer (with Ralph Steiner and Leo Hurwitz)
1936 *The Wave* (*Redes*): director, producer and photographer (with Augustine V. Chávez, Henwar Rodakiewicz and Fred Zinnemann)
1937 *Heart of Spain* (edited by Paul Strand and Leo Hurwitz)
1942 *Native Land*: co-director and photographer (with Leo Hurwitz)
1944 *Tomorrow We Fly*: photographer

Further Reading

Alexander, William, *Film on the Left: American Documentary Film from 1931 to 1942*, Princeton, NJ: Princeton University Press, 1981.
Busselle, Rebecca, and Trudy Wilmer Stack (eds.), *Paul Strand Southwest*, New York: Aperture, 2004.
Crowther, Bosley, "*Native Land*, Impassioned and Dramatic Documentary Film on American Civil Liberties," *New York Times*, May 12, 1942, 16.

Hammen, Scott, "Sheeler and Strand's 'Manhatta': A Neglected Masterpiece," *Afterimage*, 6, 6, January 1979, 6–7.

Homer, William Innes, *Alfred Stieglitz and the American Avant-Garde*, Boston: New York Graphic Society, 1977.

Horak, Jan-Christopher (ed.), *Lovers of Cinema: The First American Film Avant-Garde, 1919-1945*, Madison: University of Wisconsin Press, 1995.

MacCann, Richard Dyer, *The People's Films: A Political History of U. S. Government Motion Pictures*, New York: Hastings House, 1973.

Newhall, Nancy, *Strand: Photographs 1915-1945*, New York: The Museum of Modern Art, 1945.

Rosenblum, Naomi, *Paul Strand: The Stieglitz Years at 291 (1915-1917)*, New York: Zabriskie Gallery, 1983.

Strand, Paul, "Photography," in *Seven Arts*, 2, August 1917, 524–525; reprinted in *Camera Work*, 49–50, June 1917, 3–4-and in *Classic Essays on Photography*, edited by Alan Trachtenberg, New Haven: Leete's Island Books, 1980, 141–144.

———, *Time in New England*, edited by Nancy Newhall, New York: Oxford University Press, 1950; reprinted New York: Aperture, 1980.

———, *Paul Strand: Sixty Years of Photographs*, New York: Aperture, 1976.

———, *Essays on his Life and Work*, Maren Stange (ed.), New York: Aperture, 1990.

Whelan, Richard (ed.), *Stieglitz on Photography: His Selected Essays and Notes*, New York: Aperture, 2000.

STRICK, JOSEPH

During World War II, Strick was a cameraman with the U.S. Army Air Force. After the war he worked with Irving Lerner, jack-of-all-film-crafts, to learn how to make movies, while serving as copyboy at the *Los Angeles Times*. Together they created the short *Muscle Beach* (1948), candid impressions of muscle-builders beside the Pacific Ocean in Venice, California. Later Strick became a wealthy businessman, owning a controlling interest in several large electronic corporations, and was able to form a new collaboration that led to *The Savage Eye* (1959), which he initiated. It was worked on part-time for four or five years, mostly on weekends. Strick's first feature, the most important of his few documentaries, it was an anomaly in many ways.

Made mostly by people who had been on the political left, *The Savage Eye* attempted to combine a scathing view of current social ills and disorders with the new emphasis in American documentaries on individuals, narrative, and characterization. The film is credited as being "by" Ben Maddow, Sidney Meyers, and Joseph Strick. Cinematographers are listed as Jack Couffer, Helen Levitt, and Haskell Wexler. The last of these would subsequently become a highly valued Hollywood cameraman (with Academy Awards for *Who's Afraid of Virginia Woolf?* [1966] and *Bound for Glory* [1976]), and also sometime director (*Medium Cool* [1969]). Two others are listed as "contributing photogra-

phers," but it was said that Strick was responsible for about half the camera work, though he took no cinematography credit. Music is by Leonard Rosenman. Irving Lerner is credited as technical consultant.

The visuals are made up largely of unstaged scenes of the seamier side of Los Angeles: sleazy bars, beauty and massage parlors, wrestling matches, traffic jams, animal cemeteries, addicts and transvestites, strippers and faith healers. All this is seen through the eyes of a recently divorced, alienated, and angry woman (played by Barbara Baxley); hers is "the savage eye." As she wanders through these urban settings, she carries on a dialogue with a subjective interlocutor, "the poet" (voice of Gary Merrill), who introduces himself to her as her "vile dreamer, conscience, ghost."

Initially *The Savage Eye* received a great deal of attention, including several international festival awards. At the Edinburgh International Film Festival, instead of being shown once, as scheduled, it had to be shown eight times to accommodate all those who wanted to see it. Reviewing it in the *New York Post* (June 7, 1960), Archer Winston concluded: "*The Savage Eye* is all of one piece, masterfully, artfully wrought by its three makers, a work that must be recognized as great no matter how unlikable, a film that will be seen for many a year no matter who rejects it now."

The contrary proved to be the case. It soon fell into virtual obscurity, remembered chiefly as a precursor of cinema verité, which was about to begin. Today we are more likely to agree with another critical reaction at the time: "The fragments of documentary film in themselves are bitterly sure-footed. They show us clearly the irresolute and pernicious side of modern American life. Personally, I would like very much to see this footage combined into another form, without the contrived story and dialogue" (Benjamin T. Jackson, *Film Quarterly*, Summer 1960).

In the 1960s, Strick turned away from documentary to a succession of literary adaptations including his controversial version of James Joyces's *Ulysses* (1967). The only noteworthy exception was *Interviews with My Lai Veterans* (1970), which he wrote, produced, and directed. It received an Oscar for best documentary short.

JACK C. ELLIS

Biography

Born 1923, in Pittsburgh. Attended University of California at Los Angeles, circa 1941–1943, until military service, as cameraman in the U.S. Army Air Force, circa 1943–1945. Worked on the *Los Angeles Times* and then television. Documentaries are *Muscle Beach* (1948), *Jour de Fête* (1949), *The Big Break* (1953), *The Savage Eye* (1959), and *Interviews with My Lai Veterans* (1970).

STUDIO D

Studio D was the women's film unit within the National Film Board of Canada, operating between 1974 and 1996 in the basement of the NFB headquarters in Montreal. It was the first ever publicly funded women's film production unit.

The formation of a separate film unit materialized after many years of tireless lobbying, by women within the organization, for a distinctive voice within the male dominated hierarchy, as well as within the tradition of Canadian documentary filmmaking as a whole. At the time, women commonly worked in the world of documentary film as assistants, editors, and producers, but not as directors. Kathleen Shannon became the first female executive producer when she was appointed to head the Unit.

The desire for a prominent, collective female voice came out of the feminist movement of the 1960s, when a wave of media arts/activist organizations were set up, which eventually led to film festivals and forums. Their mission was to raise the visibility of women within the filmmaking community, fulfilling the hunger for films made by women, about women for women.

Working as a sound editor in 1956, Shannon was outspoken about the need for female representation on both sides of the camera. It was Studio D's remit to correct the imbalance of Canadian cinematic and historical tradition. The Studio sought to achieve this by training women to produce their own images, so that they could develop and express their creativity in a collective environment. This female perspective through film would promote a social, political, and personal awareness.

Shannon's vision came under scrutiny even though the Unit was winning international awards, including Academy Awards for *I'll Find a Way* (Shaffer) in 1977 and *If You Love This Planet* (Nash) in 1982. Many women's groups felt excluded and saw Studio D's sociopolitical ideology as being too narrowly focused and deeply rooted in white middle class culture. In addition, the filmmakers in the Unit were permanent staff members, which may have led to some degree of complacency. Shannon resigned and in 1987 Rina Fraticelli took over the position. Her main focus was to promote more innovated filmmaking both within and beyond the studio through many initiatives and programs aimed at aboriginal women and women of colour.

By 1996, the NFB suffered severe cutbacks in its funding, and the organisation was realigned and then shut down. During the course of its approximately twenty-year existence, the Unit had always had a precarious position within the

NFB. Nevertheless, the formation of Studio D was a pivotal moment in women's history. The Unit had a tremendous influence on feminist filmmaking, and many of its aims were achieved. Most important, it let women become film-makers in their own right.

MELISSA BROMLEY

Selected Films

1975 *My Friends Call Me Tony* from *Children of Canada* series (Shaffer)
1977 *The Lady from Grey County* (Brown)
1977 *Some American Feminists* (Brossard, Guilbeault, Wescott)
1979 *Prairie Album* (James)
1981 *Not a Love Story* (Sherr Klein)
1984 *Behind the Veil: Nuns* (Westcott)
1989 *Older Wiser Stronger* (Prieto)
1991 *Wisecracks* (Singer)
1992 *Making Perfect Babies* (Basen)

Further Reading

Anderson, Elizabeth, *Studio D's Imagined Community: From Development (1974) to Realignment (1986–1990)* in *Gendering the Nation: Canadian Women's Cinema*, Kay Armatage, Kass Banning, Brenda Longfellow, and Janine Marchessault (eds.), Toronto: University Press, 1999.

Gittings, Christopher E., *Canadian National Cinema*, London: Routledge, 2002.

Grierson, John, *A Film Policy for Canada (1944)* from *Documents in Canadian Film*, Douglas Fetherling (ed.), Peterborough: Broadview Press, 1988.

Jones, D. B., "Assessing the National Film Board, Crediting Grierson," in *Historical Journal of Film, Radio and Television*, 3, 1989, 301–307.

Jones, D. B., "Brave New Film World," in *North of Everything English-Canadian Cinema Since 1980*, edited by William Beard and Jerry White (eds.), Edmonton: University of Alberta Press, 2002.

Sherbarth, Chris, *Studio D, the Women's Unit of the NFB*, in *Cinema Canada*, 139, March 1987, 9–13.

SUBJUNCTIVE DOCUMENTARY

Following the use of "subjunctive" as a grammatical tense, "subjunctive documentary" is a form of documentary that documents what could be, would be, or might have been, through speculation, extrapolation, and the use of reconstruction or simulation based on factual data and theories.

Subjunctive documentary involves simulated appearances, simulated events, or both, constructed from indexical data linked to the referent being depicted. Although some simulations can be achieved through traditional means (such as the reconstruction of a crime based on evidence and eyewitness accounts, images of what dinosaurs supposedly looked like, a police sketch made from descriptions of a suspect, or the re-creation of historical events through photographs, writings, and artifacts), today many simulations are done with the aid of computer technology, which allows for the collecting, integrating, and imaging of large numbers of data. Appearances are simulated when computer imaging is used to create images of objects that are different than what the human eye would see or are invisible to the human eye because they are too large, too small, or involve wavelengths outside the spectrum of visible light. Examples of simulated appearances include the false colorings found in histology, medical imaging technologies (such as computerized axial tomography [CAT] scans, positron emission tomography [PET] scans, magnetic resonance imaging [MRI], and ultrasound), and computer-generated graphical displays of subatomic events in particle physics. Even black-and-white film could be said to be simulating how things would look if our eyes were sensitive to tone but not color.

Similarly, computer simulations of events attempt to reproduce conditions, situations, and behavior based on factual data, theory, and extrapolation based on probabilities and known facts. These include simulations of molecular and chemical reactions, flight simulators used for pilot training, architectural walkthroughs, product design and testing, and reconstructions of crimes, airplane crashes, and architectural ruins. Such simulations are relied on by science, industry, courts of law, medicine, and the government, where they are often given the same weight as real events. In this way, their truth claim is similar to, and at least as great as, that of documentary film and video (which are also subjunctive to some degree, insofar as they reconstruct events to varying degrees through existing objects, documents, and personal recollections). Through the use of computer technology, a wide variety of different kinds of data (including practically any kind of physical measurement or property) can be correlated, integrated, and combined together into a visualization depicting aspects of the events in question. Photography, then, is just one of many ways of creating an image from data that have an indexical link to a physical referent.

Subjunctive documentary attempts to construct a coherent whole from disparate or even incomplete data. Instead of merely recording a perceptual appearance, subjunctive documentary documents the invisible, imperceptible, and conceptual, by translating them into visual analogs. By acknowledging that a certain degree of speculation or extrapolation is present, the term *subjunctive* *documentary* suggests that there is a difference between what is called "documentary film" and "nonfiction film."

MARK J. P. WOLF

See also **Computer Imaging; Computer Simulation; Indexicality**

Further Reading

Crary, Jonathan, *Techniques of the Observer*, London and Cambridge, Massachusetts: MIT, 1990.
Ihde, Don, *Instrumental Realism: The Interface between Philosophy of Science and Philosophy of Technology*, Bloomington and Indianapolis: Indiana University Press, 1991.
Wolf, Mark J. P., "Subjunctive Documentary: Computer Imaging and Simulation" in *Collecting Visible Evidence*, Michael Renov and Jane Gaines (eds.), Minneapolis: University of Minnesota Press, 1999.
———, *Abstracting Reality: Art, Communication, and Cognition in the Digital Age*, New York, Oxford, and Lanham, MA: University Press of America, 2000.

SWALLOW, NORMAN

Norman Swallow was a pioneer of British documentary television and a leading producer at both the BBC and independent companies. He helped determine a specific identity for documentary television, which initially was in the thrall of the critically praised traditions in film and radio, developing a more journalistic approach while maintaining the reformist character of the earlier forms. This was evident in his first great achievement, the current affairs series *Special Enquiry* (1952–1956), which each month addressed national problems such as immigration, illiteracy, and slum housing. Swallow was determined to make the programme accessible, "to be doing the programme from the point of view of the audience, not from the top down, but from the bottom up. We were not the Establishment. We were not the BBC telling the people what they should think" (Quoted in Bell, 1986: 78).

His contribution to current affairs programming continued at the BBC, where he served as assistant editor on the acclaimed *Panorama* series. In 1963, he joined the thrusting commercial channel Granada, based in Manchester, where he produced the influential *A Wedding on Saturday* (1964). The film was an observational treatment of this family occasion occurring in a Yorkshire mining village. It used the minimum of intervening narration or commentary and won the Prix Italia for its pioneering use of video to record unobtrusively a natural and ordinary event.

Norman Swallow made significant contributions to Arts television in Britain, being Editor of the celebrated *Omnibus* series at the BBC in the late 1960s, and acting as head of arts programmes for BBC TV between 1971 and 1974. His status in television documentary was evident in his participation in international co-productions like *Ten Days That Shook the World* (1967), made with Grigori Alexandrov to mark the fiftieth anniversary of the Soviet Revolution, Lorna Pegram's and Robert Hughes's acclaimed *Shock of the New*

(1980), and ambitious series like *Television*, a detailed history of the medium made for Granada in 1985. He was awarded BAFTA's Desmond Davis Award for his "outstanding creative contribution to television."

ALAN BURTON

Biography

The son of a headmaster born in Eccles, Lancashire in 1921, educated at the Manchester Grammar School, and awarded a scholarship to Oxford where he read History and Moral Philosophy. Served in the Duke of Cornwall's Light Infantry during the war and later in Palestine as an intelligence officer. Joined the BBC in Manchester in 1946 as a radio features producer, transferred to the BBC TV Service at Alexandria Palace in 1950 and was Assistant Head of Films 1957–1960. In 1963, moved to Granada TV, but later in the 1960s was back at the BBC working primarily in Arts programming. Produced several prestigious series for Granada in the 1970s and 1980s. Died in London on December 5, 2000.

Further Reading

Bell, Elaine, "The Origins of British Television Documentary: The BBC 1946-55," in *Documentary and the Mass Media*, John Corner (ed.), London: Edward Arnold, 1986.

Swallow, Norman, "Documentary TV Journalism," in *Television in the Making*, Paul Rotha (ed.), London: Focal Press, 1956.

———, *Factual Television*, London: Focal Press, 1966.

SWITZERLAND

Switzerland is one of the few countries in the world where documentary feature films are regularly released in theaters and find an audience. A cinephile country where almost one third of a total of roughly 600 screens are located in arthouse theaters, Switzerland has also been a fertile ground for documentary production for several decades, with theatrical films being shown on television after their initial release and television production of documentaries feeding back into the theatrical market in important ways. Because of the constraints of a domestic market of only seven million divided into three language groups and the reluctance of the country's famous, and sometimes infamous, financial service industries to invest in a business as unsafe as film production, fiction film production in Switzerland has always been relatively weak, despite occasional peak periods in the war and postwar years, when a domestic popular cinema with its own set of stars and patriotic themes flourished briefly, and in the 1970s and 1980s, when directors such as Alain Tanner, Claude Goretta, and Fredi M. Murer put the Swiss auteur film on the map of the art cinema world.

By contrast, documentary production has been characterized by an impressive continuity both in terms of the quantity and the quality of output. Nonfiction films account for the majority of films produced before the 1960s, and nonfiction film production has served as both the economic backbone of film production in general and as a fertile training ground for both fiction and documentary filmmakers and technicians throughout the decades. Until fairly recently, critics considered documentary as the domain of Swiss German filmmakers, and the fiction film was considered to be the domain of their Swiss French colleagues, a notion, however, that was always rather dubious. Culturally, the strength of the Swiss documentary may also be rooted in the country's strong tradition in pedagogy (Johann Heinrich Pestalozzi, one of the founders of modern pedagogy, was a Swiss school teacher) and in Switzerland's predominantly protestant urban culture, which tends to favor art forms with pedagogical and other useful side effects over those that merely aim to please and entertain.

Although many of the directors working in nonfiction film before the 1960s remain virtually unknown even inside the country—their work has been researched only in recent years—avant-garde filmmakers such as Hans Richter found work in Switzerland directing public service films for state authorities and private companies in the 1930s and

1940s. In the early 1960s, the federal government started funding for film production, joining a trend toward similar programs in other European countries. State funding was initially limited to documentary films, a restriction that proved to be productive in the sense that it contributed to the emergence of an auteurist documentary cinema, a tradition of *documentaire de création*, to cite the French term generally used in the French part of Switzerland that has continued to this day. In fact, conventional film histories suggest that the New Swiss cinema of the 1960s and 1970s began with a series of documentary films produced by such notable figures as Henry Brandt in connection with the Swiss national exhibition in Lausanne in 1964, and with the work of documentarists Walter Marti and Reni Mertens who, after a number of short films, attracted particular notice with *Ursula oder das unwerte Leben* (1966), a portrait of a handicapped woman.

The year 1964, the same time as the Swiss national exhibition, also saw the production of *Siamo Italiani / We Are Italians*, directed by Alexander J. Seiler, June Kovach, and Rob Gnant, the first feature-length "auteur" documentary in Swiss cinema. *Siamo Italiani* focused on the daily lives of Italian immigrant workers in Switzerland and awakened the Swiss public to the presence and the plight of an important migrant workforce in their midst, a migrant workforce that had remained mostly invisible despite its substantial contribution to the country's postwar economic boom. Financed in part with money from the Swiss government, *Siamo* was a social documentary in a kind of direct cinema style that signaled a departure for, as well as a departure from, a commercial film production in crisis. But if state funding laid part of the groundwork for documentary feature production in Switzerland and the emergence of the New Swiss film, television also played an important role. The contribution of television is particularly evident in the early work of Swiss French filmmakers such as Alain Tanner and Claude Goretta. Formed in the creative climate of 1950s' British cinema, where they attracted critical attention with their experimental short *Nice Time* in 1957, Tanner and Goretta joined Swiss French television TSR on their return to Switzerland in the 1960s to work as documentary filmmakers. In the late 1960s, Tanner, Goretta, and a number of their television-trained colleagues, such as Michel Soutter, moved into fiction films and emerged among the figureheads of the New Swiss cinema in the 1970s. The respective careers of Alexander J. Seiler and Alain Tanner are quite typical for the trajectories of Swiss direc-

tors in and through the field of documentary. Seiler devoted his entire career to the documentary genre, but Tanner used the documentary as a stepping stone to the feature film and only once returned to the genre after his move into fiction in 1969 with *Charles mort ou vif,* with *Les hommes du port,* a documentary about port workers in Genoa harbor from 1995. Like Tanner, other important fiction film directors, such as Fredi M. Murer and Daniel Schmid, made a passage through documentary cinema at one point in their careers. The country's most important experimental filmmaker in the 1960s, Fredi M. Murer, shot *Wir Bergler in den Bergen . . .*, a documentary about three small alpine valleys in his native canton of Uri in 1974. He later developed the material into his fiction film *Alpine Fire* from 1985, a story of an incestuous relationship between a mute peasant's son and his sister and arguably the most artistically accomplished film ever to come out of Switzerland. Daniel Schmid, a friend and sometime collaborator of German director Rainer Werner Fassbinder in the 1970s, went back and forth between fiction and documentary throughout his career. After a series of fiction films, Schmid turned to documentary in 1984 with *Il Bacio di Tosca*, a film about a retirement home for opera singers in Milan, and in 1995 he traveled to Japan for the production of *The Written Face*, a documentary portrait of a male Kabuki actor who specializes in female roles. Both *Il Bacio di Tosca* and *The Written Face* count among Schmid's strongest works.

Although Daniel Schmid has remained an occasional documentarist, his two films about artists are quite representative of one of the four main strands of documentary filmmaking in Switzerland, the artist documentary. Apart from films about art and artists, the four major strands include a strong tradition of ethnographic documentaries, a continuous output of political documentaries, particularly of films focusing on state authorities and institutions and their procedures, and a more recent, but very strong tradition of filmmaking about migration and the blurring of ethnic and geographical boundaries.

The two major representatives of ethnographic filmmaking in Switzerland are Jacqueline Veuve, a documentary auteur of the first generation and a creator of an important body of work on rural handicraft, and Erich Langjahr, whose films and particularly his peasant trilogy *Sennenballade* (1996), *Bauernkrieg* (1998), and *Hirtenreise ins dritte Jahrtausend* (2002) chronicle the rapid transformation of rural life in Switzerland over the last twenty-five years. If ethnographic filmmaking in Switzerland focuses on the country's alpine interior rather than on more traditionally "exotic" (foreign) subjects, this may be read as an indication of the important symbolic charge rural life carries in Swiss society, despite the fact that farmers now make up only 2 percent of the working population. Not least under the influence of Jean-Jacques Rousseau, a Swiss native, modern Switzerland has defined itself as a democracy historically rooted in rural self-governance, even at a time when it was the most industrialized country on the continent. According to this somewhat delusional self-definition, what happens to the peasant happens to the country. In addition, in the 1970s, and again in the spirit of Rousseau, critical documentary filmmakers chose rural life as one of the privileged sites where to locate alternatives to the rampant capitalism of the urban and industrialized parts of the country. Thus many filmmakers sought the remedy to capitalist alienation on the green pastures of the Alps, only to find there more evidence of the destructive forces of capitalism at work. Apart from the films of Jacqueline Veuve and Erich Langjahr, this logic informs, in varying degrees of consciousness, Fredi M. Murer's *Wir Bergler in den Bergen . . .* and another one of the key works of the filmed ethnography of rural life in Switzerland, Beatrice Michel's and Hans Stuerm's *Gossliwil* (1985), a monumental long-term study of one peasant village in the Swiss Mittelland.

Whereas Jacqueline Veuve and Erich Langjahr have stayed true to the ethnographic documentary throughout their careers, few filmmakers have limited themselves to the field of documentaries about artists and art with such consistency. The major example is perhaps Felix Kappeler, whose portraits of artists such as the popular singer-songwriter Mani Matter (2002) have sometimes reached audiences as large as those of Hollywood mainstream films. A number of filmmakers have been active in both documentaries about artists and the political documentary. Hans-Ulrich Schlumpf started out with a portrait of Armand Schulthess (*Armand Schulthess — j'ai le telephone*, 1974), a key figure of "art brut" in the 1970s and later went on to make *Kongress der Pinguine* in 1993, an ecologist manifesto about the life of penguins in the Arctic that was one of the major box office successes for Swiss cinema in the 1990s. Richard Dindo, perhaps the best-known documentary filmmaker of his generation outside of Switzerland, has combined political issues with an interest in art and particularly the literary genre of the autobiography in his films, often using literature and painting as a means to

approach political topics such as the Holocaust (*Charlotte — vie ou theater*, 1992, a film about a French Jewish painter who disappeared in the Nazi concentration camps), the Middle East conflict (*Genet à Chatila*, 1999), or the violent police crackdown on rebellious youths in Switzerland in the 1980s (*Dani, Michi, Renato und Max*, 1987). Feminist filmmakers have made an important, albeit critically somewhat neglected contribution to the political documentary in Switzerland, with key works such as Gertrud Pinkus *Il valore della donna è il suo silenzio* (1980) often blurring the boundaries between fiction and nonfiction filmmaking. Working at the crossroads of ethnographic and political documentary, one of the most interesting filmmakers of the 1990s, Thomas Imbach, explored the professional world of bank employees in *Well Done* in 1994 and the private lives of suburban youths in *Ghetto* in 1997. Using a distinctly innovative style of serial montage of dialogue and action fragments, the films of Imbach, who has moved on to experimental fiction films since, broke new ground both in terms of documentary aesthetics and subject matter in Swiss documentary and beyond.

Although political documentaries have always formed an important part of documentary production in Switzerland, a number of strongly political films have been among the most important films released in theaters in recent years. Although reflecting a worldwide surge in interest in nonfiction formats and critical documentary films, as witnessed in the global successes of Michael Moore, this trend can also be explained by the emergence of a new generation of documentary filmmakers who replace the dour didacticism of much earlier work in political documentary with a new kind of critical stance that is both penetrating and humorous. Key figures are Sabine Gisiger and Marcel Zwingli, who chronicle the adventures of a group of Swiss would-be terrorist from the 1970s in *Do It* (2000), and Jean-Stéphane Bron, who casts an ironic look at the Swiss secret service in *Connu de nos services*, (1997) and paints a highly engaging and dramatic portrait of a parliamentary commission at work on a new law on genetic engineering *Le génie helvétique* (2003). Continuing a long tradition of documentaries dealing with state authorities and institutions at work, Bron's films found a wide audience, and *Le génie helvétique* was even picked up by the Swiss foreign ministry to explain the Swiss political system to audiences in emerging democracies (a backhanded compliment of sorts).

Finally, films about migration and the crossing and blurring of ethnic, as well as other boundaries, have formed a major part of Swiss documentary filmmaking in the 1990s. Swiss-Canadian filmmaker Peter Mettler insistently and inspiringly explores geographically and socially marginal spaces in such films such as *Picture of Light* (1994) and *Gambling, Gods and LSD* (2002); Andrea Staka, a Swiss-born filmmaker of Bosnian origin, reflects on her condition as an artist in exile in *Yugodivas* (2000), a group portrait of female artists from former Yugoslavia living in New York; Samir Jamal Aldin, a Zurich film director and producer, traces his Iraqi family origins in *Forget Bagdad* (2002); and finally, Gabrielle Baur ventures into world of drag kings in *Venus Boyz* (2002), a documentary exploration of the boundaries of gender and geography that covers the nightclub scenes of London, New York, and other cities.

If there is anything distinctly Swiss about these films and filmmakers, it is perhaps their shared sensibility for the live of cultural differences, a sensibility that is easily gained and lost in a society that is in itself composed of a multitude of language groups and cultures.

VINZENZ HEDIGER AND ALEXANDRA SCHNEIDER

Further Reading

Blöchlinger, Brigitte et al. (eds.), *Cut: Film- und Videomacherinnen Schweiz von den Anfängen bis 1994: eine Bestandesaufnahme*, in collaboration with: Claudine von Niederhäusern, Ursula Ganz-Blättler, Erika Keil, Basel etc.: Stroemfeld, © 1995, *Nexus*, 11.

Buache, Freddy, *Trente ans de cinéma suisse: 1965–1995*, Paris: Centre Georges Pompidou, 1995

Film in der Schweiz with contributions by Bernhard Giger et al., München etc.: Hanser, 1978.

Giger, Bernhard, and Theres Scherer (eds.), *1957–1976 - von Nice Time bis Früchte der Arbeit: Materialien zur Entwicklung des Dokumentarfilms in der Schweiz/Kellerkino Bern*; Bern: Kellerkino, 1977.

Roth, Wilhelm, *DerDokumentarfilm seit 1960*, München etc.: Bucher, 1982.

Schlappner, Martin, and Schaub, Martin, *Vergangenheit und Gegenwart des Schweizer Films (1896 bis 1987): eine kritische Wertung*, Zürich: Schweizerisches Filmzentrum, 1987.

For further information and documentation see also www.swissfilms.ch.

SYMPHONY OF THE DON BASIN

See **Enthusiasm**

T

TALLENTS, STEPHEN

Stephen Tallents's first connection with documentary film was as Secretary of the Empire Marketing Board (EMB). Established in 1926, the EMB was intended to promote the marketing of products of the British Empire and to encourage research and development among the member states. The broader purpose implicit from the outset was to substitute for the decaying military and political ties of empire the economic ones of a commonwealth of nations. Tallents saw that the motion picture might be a valuable tool in this new and unique governmental public relations endeavor.

The first EMB film production misfired, however. It was a sort of fantasy of empire suggested by Rudyard Kipling and executed by Walter Creighton entitled *One Family* and subtitled *A Dream of Real Things*. Begun in 1926, it was not released until 1930 and generated little enthusiasm.

The EMB's true start on film production, and what would become the documentary film movement, began in 1927 when Tallents interviewed John Grierson, just returned to Britain from a four-year sojourn in the United States. Much taken with Grierson's ideas about the use of film communication by governments to their citizens, Tallents hired him in an unofficial advisory capacity.

After Grierson's research into film activities of other governments and EMB screenings of relevant films, Tallents succeeded in talking the Department of Treasury into backing production of a film by the EMB. *Drifters* (1929) was the result. As a result of its success, in 1930 the EMB Film Unit was established, a collective filmmaking enterprise, a sort of workshop and schoolhouse, with Grierson as its head. Out of it the British documentary movement would emerge.

In 1933, at the depth of the Depression, the EMB was terminated on grounds of necessary government economy. Tallents moved to the General Post Office as its first public relations officer on condition that he could bring the EMB Film Unit and the Empire Film Library with him. Thus the EMB Film Unit became the GPO Film Unit.

Tallents left the General Post Office in 1935 to become public relations controller for the British Broadcasting Corporation Overseas Service. Though he maintained contact with members of the documentary group and was, on several occasions and in various ways, honored by them, his last formal assistance to the documentary movement occurred at the end of the 1930s. Tallents was on the Imperial Relations Trust set up by the British government in 1937. When the Trust created a film subcommittee, Film Centre, which Grierson had helped form, was made its film adviser. The Canadian government had long been interested in the use of films for promotion, and when the question of the production of Canadian documentaries was raised, Grierson was invited to undertake an investigation into that possibility. This led to his drafting the legislation that established the National Film Board (NFB) of Canada and to his being appointed first Film Commissioner.

The legislation creating the NFB decreed its principal mandate that of helping "Canadians in all parts of Canada to understand the ways of living and the problems of Canadians in other parts." This was the same function conceived at the EMB ten years earlier by Tallents and Grierson in their credo of showing one part of the Empire to the rest. So it can be said that if Grierson took a leading role in setting the direction for the growth of documentary, Tallents was the enabler who arranged for it to happen in its early stages and provided some of the energy to push it along.

JACK C. ELLIS

See also **Drifters**; **Grierson, John; General Post Office Film Unit; Ministry of Information**

Biography

Born 1884, in London. Educated at Harrow and Balliol College, Oxford University. 1909, appointed to Board of Trade; 1915, to Ministry of Munitions; 1918, Principal Assistant Secretary, Ministry of Food, and member of Food Council. 1926–1933, Secretary, Empire Marketing Board. 1933–1935, Public Relations Director, General Post Office. 1935–, Public Relations Controller, BBC Overseas Service; 1935–1938, Director-General Designate, Ministry of Information. Died, 1958.

Further Reading

Ellis, Jack C., *John Grierson: Life, Contributions, Influence*, Carbondale: Southern Illinois University Press, 2000.

Hardy, Forsyth, *John Grierson: A Documentary Biography*, London: Faber and Faber, 1979.

Rotha, Paul, *Documentary Diary: An Informal History of the British Documentary Film, 1928–1939*, New York: Hill and Wang, 1973.

TARGET FOR TONIGHT

(UK, Watt, 1941)

In *Target for Tonight,* documentary approach and technique was applied for the first time to a feature-length war film. The result was the most commercially successful documentary film of the time.

Unlike *Britain Can Take It, Target for Tonight* is, in Watt's words, a "hitting back film." And unlike the *Why We Fight* series, it is primarily concerned with people, not battles, and focuses on small groups in operation rather than a vast struggle between right and wrong. Like other British war films, it exalts the sense of mission, not destiny. Undeniably aimed to propagandize, its approach in human terms is congruent with Humphrey Jennings's notion of "propaganda for the human race."

An account of a night bombing raid on Germany, *Target for Tonight* describes the operation as an apparently easy, if carefully planned, procedure. Out of real individuals, it creates an anonymous collective hero of unshakeable optimism.

Harry Watt had been previously assigned to direct another RAF film, *Squadron 992* (1939), about the work of a balloon squadron, which he found boring. For *Target for Tonight*, he went through two or three thousand reports of bombing raids. He came to an agreement with the RAF Bomber Command on a script he considered "utterly straightforward, just the choice of a new small target, the selection of a squadron to bomb it, and the adventures of one bomber, 'F for Freddie', during the raid." The Mildenhall RAF bomber station (renamed 'Millerton' in the film) had been chosen as the operations base.

Watt greatly valued the use on nonprofessional actors, and he insisted on using the airmen themselves, casting every single one in his own role, from gunners to pilots to officers, up to the Commander-in-Chief. These amateurs proved to be so good that *Variety* could not believe that they were not actors. Watt also carefully struck a balance of the men's origins: one half of F-for-Freddie's crew appears to be English; the other three men can be identified as one Scot, one Australian, and one Canadian. Conversely, only two women—of the WAAF—come into view.

The script reproduces the airmen's idiomatic language, with a good amount of humour. The pilot suggests to "go down and smell the breath" of a little German city "famous for its breweries" or asserts "the natives appear hostile" as Flak fires burst around the aircraft.

Shooting on location at Mildenhall started on the second week in April, and the film delivery deadline was mid-summer. Watt and his crew were able to gather documentary footage of the N 149 Squadron and its two-engined Vickers-Armstrong Wellington aircraft. But procuring good images of bombing turned out almost impossible because of the lack of film stock sensibility; however, some dramatic shots of F-Freddie flying against the clouds were obtained.

Every interior sequence was made in the studio. The airmen's changing room was reconstructed at Elstree Studios. A sound stage at Denham Studios was converted into a replica of the Operations Room. To convey a sense of action on board the aircraft, the camera and lights had to be placed in a split-up Wellington fuselage. The shots of anti-

Target for Tonight, RAF bombardier, documentary, 1941.
[*Courtesy of the Everett Collection*]

aircraft guns operated by men in German helmets were provided by the Army Film Unit. And twelve feet of German newsreel material appear in reel four.

Target for Tonight had its premiere in London on July 24 at the Empire Theatre. As early as August 18, two councillors of the Ministry of Information in film distribution, Sidney Bernstein and Arthur Jarratt, left for the United States, carrying a copy of the film. Bernstein came to an agreement with Warner Brothers for its commercial distribution, which turned out to be an enormous success. Fifty million people overall viewed *Target for Tonight* in the United States. The film made a profit of over £73,000 for the Ministry during the war.

JEAN-LUC LIOULT

See also **Crown Film Unit; Ministry of Information; Watt, Harry**

Target for Tonight (UK, Watt, 1941, 48 min.). Distributed by Wanr Bros. Produced by Crown Film Unit and Ministry of Information. Directed by Harry Watt (uncredited). Written by Harry Watt (uncredited). Cinematography by Teddy Catford and Jonah Jones. Edited by Alfred Hitchcock and Stewart McAllister.

Target for Tonight, RAF reconnaissance officers plan air strike, documentary, 1941.
[*Courtesy of the Everett Collection*]

Further Reading

Aitken, Ian, "The Crown Film Unit, 1941–1952," in *The Documentary Film Movement, An Anthology*, Edinburgh: Edinburgh University Press, 1998.

Barsam, Richard M., "British Films for World War II," in *Non-Fiction Film, A Critical History* (revised and expanded), Bloomington and Indianapolis: Indiana University Press, 1992.

Lioult, Jean-Luc, "Autour de *Passage to Marseille*: du mythique au politique, et retour," in *Cinéma et politique*, colloque de la Sercia, Bordeaux: forthcoming.

Short, K.R.M, "RAF Bomber Command's *Target for Tonight* (1941)," in *Historical Journal of Film, Radio and Television*, 17, 2, 1997, 181–218.

Swann, Paul, "The Documentary Movement during the War, 1939–1945," in *The British Documentary Film Movement, 1926–1946*, Cambridge: Cambridge University Press, 1989.

TAYLOR, JOHN

John Taylor's work in documentary was firmly tied to that of John Grierson, leader of the British documentary movement. To begin with, he was Grierson's brother-in-law, younger brother of Grierson's wife, Margaret. He joined the Empire Marketing Board Film Unit in 1930, shortly after it was formed, at the age of 16. His first noteworthy assignment was in 1931, accompanying and assisting Robert Flaherty in the production of *Industrial Britain*. After that he was loaned to Flaherty in 1932 to assist on *Man of Aran*; it was said (by Harry Watt, who was also assisting) that Taylor shot more than a little of the footage. After that, in 1933, he went with Basil Wright to serve as his assistant on *The Song of Ceylon*. While with the General Post Office Film Unit, Taylor served as cameraman on *Housing Problems* (1935), made for the British Commercial Gas Association, and on four films Alberto Cavalcanti made in Switzerland for the GPO and Pro Telephon, Zürich.

When Grierson left the GPO in 1937, Wright also left to form the Realist Film Unit and Taylor joined it shortly thereafter. For Realist he directed *The Smoke Menace* (1937). The next year Wright left Realist to join Film Centre, a promotional body Grierson had helped to set up, and Taylor ran Realist from that time on through the war. Realist's most ambitious prewar production was *The Londoners* (1939), which Taylor wrote and directed.

During the war the government was the sole sponsor of documentary films in Britain, and the Ministry of Information assigned hundreds of nonfiction films on all sorts of subjects to the independent documentary units. For example, *Cameramen at War* (1943), *Atlantic Trawler* (1944), and *Plastic Surgery in Wartime* (1944) were among the forty-seven films assigned to Realist, one of the busiest of the units. Taylor seems to have been credited as producer on all of these. Though he directed a few films of value, his real strengths appear to have been as cinematographer in the early part of his career and producer in the latter part; a steady contributor rather than a star.

After the war Taylor became producer in charge at the Crown Film Unit (in January 1947) and remained in that position until 1949. After Grierson's return to Britain to become head of the Films Division of the Central Office of Information (peacetime equivalent of the Ministry of Information), which Crown Film Unit came under, Taylor was moved to the Colonial Film Unit. After a year he returned to private documentary production. This included involvement with Countryman Films and its biggest success, *The Conquest of Everest* (1953), most of the profits of which, curiously, went to the government-funded Group 3, which Grierson by then co-headed.

Although these postwar events strained their relationship, Taylor remained close to Grierson. At the time of his death, Taylor and his wife, Barbara Mullen, a popular actress (and daughter of Flaherty's cicerone on Aran, Pat Mullen), were the only persons other than his wife Margaret whom Grierson would see in his last days.

JACK C. ELLIS

See also **Flaherty, Robert; General Post Office Film Unit; Grierson, John; *Housing Problems*; *Industrial Britain*; *Man of Aran*; *Song of Ceylon*; Wright, Basil**

Biography

Born 1914, London. Employed: Empire Marketing Board Film Unit, 1930–1933; General Post Office Film Unit, 1933–1937; Realist Film Unit, 1937–1947; Crown Film Unit and Colonial Film Unit, 1947–1949; private documentary production units, 1949– . Most significant productions: assistant on *Industrial Britain, Man of Aran, Song of Ceylon*; cinematographer on *Pett and Pott, Housing Problems*; director on *Smoke Menace, The Londoners*.

Further Reading

Ellis, Jack C., *John Grierson: Life, Contributions, Influence*, Carbondale: Southern Illinois University Press, 2000.

Hardy, Forsyth, *John Grierson: A Documentary Biography*, London: Faber and Faber, 1979.

Rotha, Paul, *Documentary Diary: An Informal History of the British Documentary Film, 1928–1939*, New York: Hill and Wang, 1973.

———. *Robert J. Flaherty: A Biography*, Philadelphia: University of Pennsylvania Press, 1983.

TELEVISION DOCUMENTARY: OVERVIEW

The documentary has been a constituent ingredient of television from the technology's very inception. To this day, despite prohibitive costs and relatively low audience share, the format remains a prestigious aspect of broadcasting, attracting kudos for its programme-makers and regularly receiving the critical attentions of the press and other media. Nevertheless, any attempt at a comprehensive overview of television documentary is bound to be incomplete because television is only recently beginning to enjoy the kind of serious, theoretical, and analytical attention that film has long received (Newcomb, 2000; Corner, 1999). But more obviously, the incomplete review is due to the prolific and ephemeral nature of television itself. There are, of course, various long-standing documentary programme formats covering a wide range of topics including science, nature, crime, and current affairs. Each has been able to boast an avid audience, as well as contribute to broader public debates. There are also numerous canonical documentary series, including, for example, David Attenborough's *Life on Earth* (BBC, 1979–1980), Jeremy Isaacs's *The Cold War* (BBC/CNN, 1999), and Channel Four's *The Dying Rooms* (1996). The last, a documentary of scandal in Chinese orphanages, reached a purported 100 million viewers across thirty-seven countries. There are also countless examples of one-off programmes and lesser known series, however, that go to make up the general diet of television's non-fiction output, most of which attracting only minority audiences. This makes it difficult for a general history of the form to be told. Also, not only are television documentaries typically made to reflect the issues of the day they are also largely culturally specific. Exceptions to this include documentaries of an international scope, which, on occasion, result in collaboration between international partners. Another strategy to cater to overseas markets is to produce cheap "versioning" of programmes. This is done by reediting and re-voicing a mixture of footage from networks and freelancers around the world (Tunstall, 1993: 42–44). Generally, however, television documentaries are not exported to a more global audience in the way, for example, that has long been the case with television films, dramas, soap operas, and situation-comedies.

In the early period of the development of the medium, factual television drew substantially on the surrounding media output of cinema newsreels, radio news and documentary, educational film, and photojournalism. In terms of format and style, however, the television documentary was most directly influenced by the work of the pioneering filmmakers of the late 1920s and early 1930s (operating in Britain, Germany, the Soviet Union, and the United States). In particular, John Grierson's influence on the documentary film movement in Britain had a profound effect, both in terms of a mode of production and belief in documentary's role for social comment and analysis. Nevertheless, the television documentary has developed its own styles and values, the television medium itself becoming the main outlet for factual film. Nichols (1991) described the development of four main modes of documentary representation: the expository, observational, interactive, and reflexive modes, each offering their own conventions of production and systems of meaning. Although these forms can all be said to exist alongside each other (and to combine in hybrid forms), it is also suggested that they belong to a dialectical process, "in which new forms arise from the limitations and constraints of previous forms and in which the credibility of the impression of documentary reality changes historically" (Nichols, 32). Thus as awareness of the norms and conventions of each mode overrides an ability to offer a fresh perspective on reality, a new mode is established.

A key component of the expository mode is its direct address to the audience. Because of the technical limitations of the early filmmaking practice, it was far easier to dub on a voice-over, resulting in a disembodied narrator often referred to as the "voice-of-God." Although television production overcame these technical restrictions, it continued to rely on the authority of a single narrator's voice as a means of presenting a clear argument or story, eliminating any ambiguities of the visual material. Thus in the expository mode, images are edited in accordance to the narrator's script, providing visual evidence to what is generally considered an expert and objective commentary. Because many documentaries are made retrospectively of events, it is not uncommon for elements to be reconstructed specifically for the camera. And even when filming is conducted contemporary to events, it is often the case that some of the action will be restaged several times to shoot from multiple angles. Later in editing this helps broaden visual interest but equally aids the logic of meaning in a narrative. So for example, close-ups are inserted into a sequence to draw the viewer's attention to a specific item. Editing in this fashion generally works to maintain rhetorical continuity more than spatial or temporal continuity. Overall, the expository documentary aims to present a specific message, to expound on an idea or topic, while turning attention away from the structures of mediation. The natural history programme, a staple of television documentary, is an obvious and very successful example of the expository format. In these productions, an array of complicated filming techniques are used, often under difficult conditions, over a long time (including, for example, time-lapse photography). Yet the final result is the calm and expert chronological account of subject matter.

The clarity and directness of the expository mode lend themselves well to television programming, as the concern has always been to maintain the attentions of the viewer against the various distractions of the domestic setting. A long-standing criticism, however, is that to achieve a supposedly objective and knowledgeable account expository documentary tends to *manufacture* coherence out of what in "reality" is often more ambiguous. A particular concern is that the restaging of events and the dominance of script can lead to a reliance on visual stereotypes and false contrasts. Additional props and visual aids are frequently introduced into filming to simply move the narrative along more effectively. One much reiterated visual cliché, for example, is to position a subject by a desk or in front of a bookcase to help denote a learned, expert character. A more general problem is the adverse impact and intrusion that the technology of filmmaking can have on the recording of events. Nevertheless, as technology has advanced, these concerns have lessened and television in particular has been quick to make use of the more sophisticated and experimental technologies as they have come along. In the 1980s, television was quick to embrace video as a serious means of documentary production; more recently the use of digital 3D modelling software and cheap, disposable cameras have begun to radically alter the very "landscape" into which television documentarists can venture.

As a reaction against the expository mode, an observational style gained favour. In this case events are filmed as they unfold and typically with narrative led by sync dialogue rather than voice-over. Overall, observational documentary relies less heavily on the editing and packaging of the programme as is the case with expository documentary. When newly emerging, this format represented a new generation of programme makers who wanted to remove the distance that an expository mode held over its subjects, gain direct access to events and participants (away from the studio environment), whilst also wishing to refrain from restaging events. The new style also came as a response to the changing economic and political context. Governments in the postwar period no longer relied so much on the kind of social "propaganda" that, for example, in Britain, the grierisonian approach had offered. The needs of corporate sponsors had also altered. The economic conditions for releasing films had been changing on both sides of the Atlantic, making it less viable to show serious documentaries in the cinema. In contrast, television's growing popularity and relatively cheap production enabled it to become the principal backer and outlet of documentary programme making. As a developing medium, television was able to offer a different context and set of possibilities within which programmes could be made. In contrast to a cinematic experience, the uniqueness of television's "small screen," which enables pictures to be brought directly into the living room, fostered a more intimate and quotidian kind of enquiry

(Ellis, 1992; Fiske, 1987). Of importance, the new aesthetic of observational documentary was very much aided by technological advancements. Lightweight cameras and faster film stocks provided ever-greater flexibility, whilst portable and improved sound equipment meant for the first time it was feasible to synchronise sound with image regardless of action, allowing, for example, participants to speak for themselves in shot and thus potentially affording a very different role to the individual subject.

There are two main influences on television's observational documentary: North American direct cinema and the French cinema verité (the latter evolving as interactive documentary). In direct cinema the viewer is supposedly afforded the opportunity to witness the lives of others without interruption or intervention. The emphasis is on close and unmediated access to the world. Typically, in aiding the sense of direct connection with events, a small film crew remain off camera, invisible to the viewer who is presented with a "fly-on-the-wall" perspective of events. In most cases there is no staging or special lighting, and the camera follows events supposedly unaware of when and how points of interest will arise. Awkward moments can result when a participant acknowledges the camera, and an aversion to the use of commentary (considered a distancing device) means that difficulties can arise in maintaining the narrative. Television's ability to bring together footage from a range of sources (including its own news output), however, has enabled this form of observational documentary to have developed a screen language all of its own. An omnipresent narrator, for example, can be substituted by including archive footage from press conferences, news reports, or interviews unaffiliated with the film itself. These elements can help foreground specific issues or individuals, making them convenient forms of hidden narration. Direct cinema-styled television also portrays a distinct rhythm. In addition to key action events, scenes are often intercut, which show relatively mundane, routine activities, seemingly bearing little narrative significance. As Nichols notes, the portrayal of this "dead," or "empty" time serves, in contrast to the expository mode, to "sustain the spatial and temporal continuity of observation rather than the logical continuity of an argument or case" (1991: 40).

The camera in observational documentary testifies to an immediate engagement with the historical world, and it is not uncommon for the privileges of an ideal spectator's view to be lost temporarily as people perhaps walk in front of the lens, or the main subjects walk out of view. Nevertheless, pre-

production is an important aspect of observational documentary, for whilst the subject has ultimate control of any given situation, it is often the case that filming only occurs when it is believed something significant is likely to happen. Furthermore, choice of subject is crucial. Observational documentaries tend to foreground the individual or small groups. As a result the subject is often chosen for contemporary symbolic value, they may be famous or represent a constituent social role or value. Examples of the latter include public servants such as teachers and police officers, or members of a specific professional community such as miners, environmentalists, or scientists. One of the earliest examples of the direct cinema approach is *Primary* (Time-Life Broadcasting, 1960), a "fly-on-the-wall" style programme, which followed John F. Kennedy and Hubert Humphrey as they fought to become presidential candidates. Such topicality and personality remain a constant with observational documentary. Many years later, for example, the same production team of *Primary* used a similar format for *The War Room* (BBC2, 1993), this time charting the ups and downs of Bill Clinton's presidential campaign.

In contrast to direct cinema, in which the documentarist remains outside the frame, in cinema verité an active role is encouraged, prompting what is regarded a more interactive mode of documentary making; the camera and crew, for example, often being recognised by those being filmed, and even incorporated into the action. Preexisting televisual journalistic practices of engaging directly with interviewees helped normalise such an interactive format, which might typically incorporate on-camera testimonies from the subject. Thus, whereas the viewer in direct documentary is only privy to information witnessed during filming, interaction with the subject allows a discursive account of the action, which in turn can potentially influence subsequent events. This renews the need for logical continuity to be maintained, as opposed to the temporal/spatial concerns of direct documentary. And crucially the editing of images to voice-tracks (whether reflexive testimonials, or direct sync speech) can be utilised to powerful effect to either support or undermine what participants intend. Editorially, filmmakers can appear close and involved with their subject, or they may seem impartial. Alternatively, they can assert a more hostile relationship, prompting a challenging response. Such circumstance can inevitably lead to tensions and controversy, which often gets picked up by the press and other media. As a result, influential observational documentaries such as Paul Waston's *The*

Family (BBC, 1974) and later his *Sylvania Walters* (1993)—in which it was suggested scenes were deliberately chosen to emphasis the family's rowdiness and racism—can be seen to court the insatiable desire of schedulers to entertain the audience. Observational documentaries can be considered as precursors to a popular wave of a hybrid genre referred to as "docusoap," which appeared in abundance in the mid- to late 1990s. Following the same episodic form of soap opera, these programmes interweave over a period of weeks several plot lines, each developed by following specific individuals chosen for their idiosyncratic, but nonetheless entertaining behaviour. Typically, filming centres on a particular institution or profession, with, for example, programmes having been made about airports, hospitals, police stations, and holiday resorts. Generally, little intrusion is made by the film crew, although the cameras are openly acknowledged by the "characters" involved. Holland (2000: 148) suggested this style of documentary presents contemporary subjects as no longer prepared simply to be observed, but to have some stake in the making of the programme. It is a logic seemingly taken to its limits with the ironically voyeuristic show *The Osbournes* (MTV, 2002). This series, which offered twenty-four-hour surveillance of the dysfunctional domestic life of rock-star Ozzy Osbourne, combines an overt (and increasingly common) interest in the notion of celebrity with immediate access and self-interrogation.

Despite the obvious differences between expository, observational, and interactive modes of documentary, it is frequently the case that television mixes these modes leading to hybrid documentary styles. Whilst in big screen documentary such an approach might disrupt the overall mood of a work, in television hybridisation is more common. Raymond Williams (2003) defined television in terms of continuous flow, the experience of which we tend to describe as "watching television," rather than to say we have watched a specific programme "on television." Such an appraisal has had the effect of demoting television to that of a homogenous, low art form, but equally it describes an important facet of its particular aesthetic. Television is an unending and changeable form. It is also a medium that generates discussion and reflection about itself and its output. Programmes often refer to other programmes due on air; the news, for example, might inform the viewer of a forthcoming documentary that deals with a particular news story in more depth. And programme scheduling is occasionally arranged thematically, perhaps relating to an anniversary or cultural event, during which times, documentaries might be paired with drama programmes, even perhaps a special episode of a soap opera. As Ellis (1999) has argued, television programmes are open-ended, usually made as a series and frequently inviting, albeit limited, audience participation. Likening it to the psychoanalytical process of "working-through," he describes television overall as "a vast mechanism for processing the raw data of news reality into more narrativised, explained forms" (55). Thus, like its own soap operas, television would seem to come to no firm conclusions. Instead, as a medium able to reach a wide public audience, it provides a complex, vibrant context for the showing of documentary programmes. It is a medium open to ongoing public debate and the innovation and experimentation of formats.

One particular trend in the changing form of documentary has been an increase in what can be termed reflexive documentary. Whilst the roots of such programme-making lies with the films of Vertov and Eisenstein, as well as a generation of European political filmmaking of the 1960s and 1970s, television's reflexive mode is perhaps rather more prosaic. Nonetheless, popular programmes such as *Crimewatch UK* (BBC, 1984–), a regular documentary staging public appeals for help in solving real, ongoing police investigations, use deliberate techniques to engender critical reflection and public response. In this case, not unlike brechtian theatre, actors are used to reconstruct events with the intent not to entertain its audience as such, but instead to prompt analytical engagement. And whilst dramatisation has long been a method used in documentary to great effect, it is also now the case that the same high standards of documentary have become equally important to fictional drama programmes, too. In effect blurring the boundaries between fictional and nonfictional genres. This is particularly the case for dramas set against a professional context such as medical, police, or legal series. The highly successful medical drama *ER* (NBC, 1994–) is a good example. Devised by an ex-medic and filmed in a former hospital building, this show goes to great lengths to faithfully represent the nature of a busy emergency care unit (even to the point of sacrificing visual coherence usually associated with television narrative drama). Increasingly, dramas programmes are assuming a role equivalent to more traditional documentaries in bringing hard-hitting social and political issues to the viewing public.

In the late 1980s and early 1990s, broadcast television experienced a seismic change. As regulations were relaxed and new technologies came on stream, a swathe of satellite and cable channels quickly established subjecting the terrestrial channels to the full force of commercialism. Not only did this radically alter national trends in the broadcast sector, it also brought about a new internationalisation of the medium, notably with the rise of twenty-hour-news channels (which frequently make slots for documentary programmes as supplement to the daily reporting of events). It also ushered in specialist commercial channels, such as *Discovery*, *The History Channel*, and *National Geographic*. The future of documentary programme-making, however, was not necessarily felt to be buoyant. In fact, fears continue to grow over waning financial support from the main television companies, along with concerns of a perceived trivialisation of the format. Many new programmes are now considered to be rather bland, with too much concentration on wildlife and lifestyle documentaries at the expense of programmes of a more politically challenging nature. Arguably, the majority of television documentary output today is dominated by what Tunstall (1993) refers to as "edinfotainment," referring to a light, formulaic, and informal documentary style epitomised by programmes on cookery, travel, home improvement, antiques, and gardening.

Nevertheless, one particular success story of a fragmented television industry has been the rise of regional and community-based programming, which has certainly taken economic advantage of video, and then later digital technology. The BBC, for example, in the mid-1990s, established its own Community Programme Unit, which has since enabled many members of the public to make their own documentaries, giving rise to a whole new genre of "video diaries." Typically, in the first-person and using less professional equipment to make films of anything between two minutes to an hour, these programmes range widely in terms of content and representation, undoubtedly giving voice to a wider spectrum of people and ideas. Criticism of the video dairy has been its tendency to trade documentary's founding dictate of objectivity for subjectivity (with, for example, imagination often overriding observation). Nevertheless, community-based programming initiatives continue to flourish. And with cheaper and ever more versatile technologies coming onto the market, the role and significance of a long tradition of independent and even amateur filmmaking would seem set to grow in importance.

Finally, stemming from the late 1990s, the most significant new development in television (one generally unique to the medium) has been the popular rise in "Reality Television." In varying guises this format has reached wide audiences, whether directly through the viewing public or indirectly from sustained interest in the popular press and a wider cultural discourse. It is a format that has genuinely been able to export to a global market, making it an important addition to a network's portfolio. Furthermore, in its early stages reality television attracted a great deal of critical and academic interest (Jermyn and Holmes, 2003; Kilborn, 2003). In shows such as *Big Brother* (Endemol, 1999–) and *Survivor* (CBS, 2000–) members of the public are segregated from the outside world, placed into a controlled environment under permanent surveillance. "Highlights" are packaged for discrete programmes on major channels, whilst on subsidiary digital channels and via Internet streaming live footage is provided on a twenty-four-hour basis; the results are a combination of the mundane and the extreme. An important difference with these programmes, in contrast to traditional documentary forms, is the role of the viewer in "voting" on the outcome of the show week by week. Thus, not only are these shows concerned with the observational recording of the specific participants, there is also direct relationship with a "reality" beyond the show.

Potentially more game-show than documentary, reality television has signalled for many a clear decline in "serious" television documentary production. Nicholls (1994: 46–48), for example, picking up on Grierson's concept of the documentary, has argued that reality shows stand in marked contrast to the documentary's espoused purpose and responsibility in engaging in the world. Yet, as an extreme form of observation documentary (combined with resident experts offering cultural, social, and psychological commentary), reality television has provided a fresh "window on the world," which, whilst ostensibly itself contributing to the reshaping of our culture, has undoubtedly offered a noteworthy comment on many of the desires and attitudes of contemporary society. Of note, however, is that the very success and flexibility of this format have prompted a seemingly perpetual quest to devise ever more extreme and artificial situations in which to film its subjects. As the authors of *Shooting People* (Brenton and Cohen, 2003) argue, the "rash of car-crash TV" has developed into a rather ruthless business, willing to take advantage of its "contestants" and inculcating a nefarious psychologism. In general, by being anterior to a historical context and with an intense focus on individuality, reality television would seem symptomatic of a postmodern, anti-political culture.

Despite the current ubiquity of reality television, however, it is still apparent that traditional television documentary formats continue to enjoy wide popularity and in some cases increased prestige. Furthermore, intellectual discourse has greatly consolidated with a growth in publications, specialist conferences and international documentary festivals around the world. Of course, given that the economics of media production are unlikely to get any less competitive, it is sure to remain the case that the light, informal documentary formats will continue to dominant the television airwaves. Nevertheless, over the years television has certainly proved to be a particularly flexible medium for the production of both traditional and hybrid documentary forms. It would seem fair to expect there will always be room for a wide variety of documentary styles, covering an ever greater array of subject matter. The future of television as a traditional *broadcast* medium, however, is perhaps a little less certain. In light of the developments of digital television (enabling viewers to pick and choose programmes at will) and other competing means of dissemination (most notably the Internet), it is highly likely that in the mid- to long-term the face of television will be quite different. This will hardly put an end to the spirit of documentary filmmaking in itself, but it will inevitably have a direct impact on both the kinds of factual programmes being made and the audience who might be watching them.

SUNIL MANGHANI

See also **Reality Television**

Further Reading

Barnouw, Erik, *Tube of Plenty: Evolution of American Television*, Oxford: Oxford University Press, 1992.

Brenton, Sam, and Reuben Cohen, *Shooting People: Adventures in Reality TV*, London: Verso Books, 2003.

Corner, John, *The Art of Record: A Critical Introduction to Documentary*, Manchester: Manchester University Press, 1996.

———, *Critical Ideas in Television Studies*, Oxford: Oxford University Press, 1999.

Ellis, John, *Visible Fictions: Cinema, Television, Video*, London: Routledge, 1992.

———, "Television as Working-Through," in *Television and Common Knowledge*, edited by Jostein Gripsurd, London: Routledge, 1999.

Fiske, John, *Television Culture*, London: Routledge, 1987.

Holland, Patricia, *The Television Handbook*, 2nd edition, London: Routledge, 2000.

Jermyn, Deborah, and Su Holmes, *Understanding Reality Television*, London: Routledge, 2003.

Kilborn, Richard, and John Izod, *An Introduction to Television Documentary: Confronting Reality*, Manchester: Manchester University Press, 1997.

———. (eds.), *From Grierson to the Docu-Soap*, Luton: University of Luton Press, 2000.

Kilborn, Richard, *Staging the Real: Factual TV Programming in the Age of "Big Brother,"* Manchester: Manchester University Press, 2003.

Morley, David, *Television, Audiences and Cultural Studies*, London: Routledge, 1992.

Morley, David, and Charlotte Brunsdon, *The Nationwide Television Studies*, London: Routledge, 1999.

Newcomb, Horace (ed.), *Television: The Critical View*, New York: Oxford University Press, 2000.

Nichols, Bill, *Representing Reality*, Bloomington: Indiana University Press, 1991.

———, *Blurred Boundaries: Questions of Meaning in Contemporary Culture*, Bloomington: Indiana University Press, 1994.

Rabinowitz, Paula, *They Must be Represented*, London: Verso, 1994.

Tunstall, Jeremy, *Television Producers*, London: Routledge, 1993.

Williams, Raymond, *Television*, London: Routledge, 2003 [1974].

TESTIMONY ON NON-INTERVENTION

(UK/Spain, Montagu, 1938)

Testimony on Non-Intervention is one of several films produced by the British left in response to the Spanish civil war, urging their fellows to protest against it and to support the Popular Front, Spain's democratically elected government, as a buttress against fascism. Though the subject was covered by filmmakers from several countries, in Britain this flurry of films was in large part driven by the communist aristocrat Ivor Montagu. Montagu had been involved with several left-wing film organisations and in March 1935 helped set up the Progressive Film Institute (PFI), which began as a distribution company before moving into production, making several films on the Spanish civil war. The best known of these is *The Defence of Madrid* (1936), which Montagu directed, but there were also social documentaries such as *Spanish ABC,* directed by Sidney Cole and Thorold Dickinson (1938) and dealing with the literacy campaign. Other countries also joined in, and Joris Ivens's *Spanish Earth* (1936) is particularly famous, perhaps for the participation of Ernest Hemingway. *Testimony on Non-Intervention's* severe aesthetic, however, has prevented it from becoming popular or even relatively well known, and it fell under the shadow of these other films.

In January 1938, producer/director Montagu arrived in Barcelona with his small PFI crew: cameramen Arthur Graham and Alan Lawson, assistants Philip Leacock and Ray Pitt, and editors Sidney Cole and Thorold Dickinson. They intended to make three films on a range of subjects, but conditions were such that they completed only *Spanish ABC* though they did shoot material towards several other projects.

Germany and Italy were among the countries that had agreed not to become involved in the Spanish civil war, but it was clear that troops from both nations were supporting Franco. To show this participation to a wider public, Montagu filmed Italian and German prisoners of war relating their experiences, and back in London used these to make the short *Prisoners Prove Intervention in Spain*. At the time, and to make the same point, they made *Behind the Spanish Lines*. Despite its dryness, *Prisoners Prove Intervention in Spain* was popular and useful in raising funds for Spanish relief, and Montagu returned to the footage almost immediately, drawing on it much more extensively, and within three months released the seven-times longer *Testimony on Non-Intervention*.

The content of the forty-minute *Testimony on Non-Intervention* can be easily described: Four soldiers (three Italians and a German) are interviewed about their involvement in the Spanish civil war. Questions include how they came to take part and the degree of their nations' involvement. The static camera looks over the questioner's shoulder and edits within the interviews are minimal. Each interview begins with the soldier giving his name and rank, before going on to explain how he came to go to Spain.

The interviews show that rank and file soldiers entered the conflict unwillingly if not in ignorance. One was told that he would be a trainer in an unspecified foreign country, while another reports having volunteered. When the interviewer expresses surprise at this, the prisoner says that "nonvolunteers" would have been punished. Some Italians were diverted from Africa implying that intervention in Spain was seen as more important than their own conflict in Abyssinia. They continued to think of themselves as Italian and not Spanish soldiers despite being paid by both Italy and Spain, showing the home country's collaboration and underlining the soldiers' uncertain position, as they did not know when they were to be sent home. While Spain is made complicit, Spaniards themselves were used only in menial, nonfighting positions.

Both Germany and Italy provided and exclusively used their own weaponry and transport, though the German prisoner exposes the underhand measures by revealing that the markings on armaments were removed to conceal their provenance. He further says that both "armies," composed exclusively of men from their respective countries, and they were kept completely apart, knowing nothing of each others' activities but then, as he notes: "I'm a nobody." Despite this, the German thinks that his compatriots are clearly the better fliers.

Testimony of Non-Intervention's anti-fascist message is particularly pointed by its use of soldiers from Germany and Italy, the other two centres of European fascism, and Franco's natural allies. Unfortunately in doing this it massively simplifies the situation, ignoring splits within "right" and "left" and the role of the Catholic church.

The film clearly attempts to persuade the viewer of its objectivity, with its unblinking camera and catechism of questions; but even before that, the title, with its echoes of legal process, implies that this is a cinematic court, investigating all the circumstances, a proposal strengthened by the lack of any credits that could remind the viewer of the makers' presence. Yet the title's "Non-Intervention" is obviously an ironic comment, the film's only moment of lightness, counterbalancing *Testimony*'s "objectivity." The format had worked well for *Prisoners Prove Intervention* but *Testimony*'s attempts to persuade the viewer of its objectivity quickly becomes boring: The shorter, first film had made the point more concisely. For the monoglot English viewer, the film is made even more difficult by the number of exchanges that are completely untranslated, and this must have affected its popularity and effectiveness, if not making people suspect that only those sequences that were politically acceptable were translated.

In 1939, Britain recognised Franco's government and as the wider world situation darkened, British left-wing film circles turned to the wider threat and the home front. Having thoroughly documented the civil war, the PFI moved on, though quickly fell into abeyance.

JOHN RILEY

See also **Montagu, Ivor; Progressive Film Institute**

Testimony on Non-Intervention (Progressive Film Institute, 1936, 40 min.). Director Ivor Montagu.

Further Reading

Dickinson, Thorold, "Experiences in the Spanish Civil War," in *Historical Journal of Film Radio and Television*, 4, 2, 1984, 189–194.
Hogenkamp, Bert, *Deadly Parallels: Film and the Left in Britain 1929–39*, London: Lawrence and Wishart, 1986.
Jones, Stephen. G., *The British Labour Movement and Film, 1918–1939*, London: Routledge and Kegan Paul, 1987.

THAILAND

See **Southeast Asia**

THAMES TELEVISION

Begun in 1968, Thames Television was one of the most recognizable of Britain's ITV companies for a number of decades. From its start until 1992, Thames provided London with its weekday scheduling (handing over to London Weekend Television on Friday nights) and produced some of the most popular programming on British television. Shows such as *The Sweeney* (1975–1978), *Minder* (1979–1994), and *The Bill* (1983–) established Thames as a production company that could compete with the BBC for audiences and, to a lesser degree, institutional significance. Although Thames still produces programming under its very familiar name, it lost the London ITV rights in 1992

to Carlton and was purchased by Pearson Television in 1993.

Thames did not only produce popular entertainment. The company generated hours of factual programming and documentary. Documentaries produced by Thames include *Auschwitz—The Final Solution* (1975); *Botanic Man* (1976), which launched the popular career of naturalist David Bellamy and arguably did much to cement the conventions of the nature documentary on television; *Destination America* (1976); and 1983's *Unknown Chaplin*.

The last is one of Thames's most successful documentaries. Made by Kevin Brownlow and David Gill, the three-part series has proved popular in both Britain and America. Many critics argue that the importance and appeal of the documentary lies as much in what it reveals about Chaplin's behind the camera strategies as it does in the restoration to viewers of deleted scenes from Chaplin's films. The series also features excerpts from Chaplin's home movies and interviews with family members and colleagues.

By far Thames's most significant contribution to documentary, however, is *The World at War*, the twenty-six-part series on the human and military drama of World War II. The series, widely recognized as one of the most important documentaries made for television, continues to be screened around the world and deserves a disproportionately extended study in any account of Thames's output. The production values, the questioning intelligence of the series, and its colossal scope make it an unparalleled project. As Nick Cohen puts it, *The World at War* is remembered as "a summit of public service broadcasting that can never be climbed again . . . Competition in a medium stuffed with channels has downsized budgets. The need to catch and hold attention with any trick, however meretricious, has undermined respect for the viewers' intelligence" (*The Guardian*, April 22, 2001).

The series took approximately three years to make, starting in April 1971, and six months to screen, beginning in October 1973. Each episode has a focus, telling, as the series' producer Jeremy Isaacs notes, a single "good story." Some of the episodes tell the story of a military battle or campaign, and others focus on the political and social contexts of the war. Regardless of whether the documentary is considering a battle, or, say, the attempts of Jews to evade German concentration camps, the focus is always on the human rather than the grandly historical nature of the moment. We hear, for example, the farmer's daughter give her account of a Hitler rally and his effect on her as he moved through the crowd. But equally the film gives us the member of Parliament as he recalls the House of Commons debate that led to the downfall of Neville Chamberlain. It is the close proximity of this firsthand perspective, whether it comes from within or without the circles of power, that generates the film's astonishingly intimate power. Perhaps, moreover, as the years pass by and a generation of viewers who know the war only as a historical phenomenon arrive, the poignancy of these interviews will grow greater still.

The film's haunting emphasis on the meeting between ordinary people and places and the extraordinary violence of war is established in the opening scene before the first title sequence. An aerial camera swoops across a deserted and abandoned French village, ruined by war and left uninhabited in the decades after. *The World at War* chooses to establish itself not with a grand monument in London or Berlin, or a montage of the great and the good, but with an eerie testimony to the suffering of the millions of everyday people who rarely find a voice in history.

Certainly the filmmakers wanted these voices to be unambiguously central to the documentary, not only at the level of content but also of form. Isaacs tells us that it was a certain and deliberate choice, for example, to have no "presenter" or "authority" speaking to the camera. There is narration, by Laurence Olivier, but it is unobtrusive in spirit. The narrative thrust is instead provided primarily by the intercutting of interviews with the film's historical images, reams of authentic footage, from newsreels to personal archive materials.

The result is rare: a documentary as much or more watched than it is talked about. *The World at War*, then, may likely prove to be Thames's most far-reaching and long-lived production. But if it is the crowning achievement of the company, it is also more. The film shows that television, a medium much maligned and too often with justification, is capable of producing not just distraction but meaningful and profound accomplishments. If documentary at the time of writing is experiencing something of a revival, it is hoped that growth in documentary making spreads once again into television production. If a cinematic release can likely reach for no longer than three hours of running time, *The World at War*, with a total running time of over a day, reveals how television documentary may be one of the very best arenas we have for sustained and intricately detailed analysis of historic or contemporary phenomena.

PAUL GLEED

See also **World at War, The**

Further Reading

Crisell, Andrew, *An Introductory History of British Broadcasting*, London: Routledge, 1997.
Scott, Peter Graham, *British Television: An Insider's History*, London: McFarland and Company, 1999.
World at War web site, http://www.theworldatwar.com.

THIN BLUE LINE, THE

(US, Morris, 1988)

The title of Errol Morris's third film is taken from Doug Mulder's closing arguments in the 1977 capital murder trial of Randall Adams, a "drifter" accused of shooting Dallas police officer Robert Wood. Mulder referred to law enforcement personnel as the "thin blue line" protecting law-abiding citizens and ordered society from chaos and crime. This compelling metaphor also serves as the thesis of Morris's self-described "nonfiction *Twilight Zone* episode," a piece that marked a simultaneously emerging investment and investigation into reflexivity and performativity within documentary film (and photography) in the late 1980s.

The Thin Blue Line opens with the story of how a chance meeting between two men—28-year-old Ohio native Randall Adams and 16-year-old Texas teenager David Harris,—on November 27, 1976, resulted in both the death of a police officer and the conviction of an innocent man. Morris spends the majority of the film dissecting the multiple players in this crime drama, directing the viewer's attention to they ways in which individuals construct events according to their beliefs and obligations. In an effort to enhance both the contradictory and fragmentary nature of testimony, Morris focuses on three surprise witnesses from the original trial who, under the camera lights, reveal personal stakes in the case that significantly undermine their credibility. It is here that Morris's investment as "director-detective" appears most clearly on screen, even as his physical presence does not. There is no attempt to disguise the theatrical nature of the interview; the subjects are *staged* for the camera by the director. "That unblinking eye in some strange way makes people willing to talk," Morris asserts. It is this staging and its artificiality, argues Morris, that lures the informants into revealing themselves with a kind of complicated honesty that is too often lost in documentary's use of "natural" surroundings: "What I do has absolutely nothing to do with cinema verité. [. . .] We go in with a lot of equipment, the camera is on a tripod, and the person who speaks to the camera is perfectly aware of what is going on. In some sense, he is performing for the camera" (Dieckmann, 1988).

Each eyewitness account is accompanied by a dramatic reenactment. These staples of fictional storytelling appear in this documentary, however, to undermine the veracity of the witnesses without conceding the factuality of the investigation. The original score by Philip Glass pulses underneath the film with an unrelenting theme, punctuated by slight but significant variations in tone or pitch to match the film noir elements (lighting and camera angle specifically) of the reenactments without forfeiting their surrealist qualities to melodramatic emotionalism. Tight close-ups on the neon clock and popcorn popper at a drive-in concession stand, the slow-motion catapult of a chocolate milkshake to the ground, a partial view of the words of a police report, iconic images of the tools of the crime— these details do not culminate, at least not *on screen*, into a climatic reversal of fortune for the story's hero, Adams. Instead, they are parts of a puzzle whose final image changes depending on who selects and connects them. Slowly, inexorably, the drama that unfolds in *The Thin Blue Line* exposes how many of the puzzle pieces were reformed

The Thin Blue Line, director Errol Morris, 1988, ©Miramax Films. [*Courtesy of the Everett Collection*]

The Thin Blue Line, 1988.
[*Courtesy of the Everett Collection*]

during Adams's investigation and trial and forced fit into a predetermined portrait, one created and controlled by the police and prosecutors in their rush to justice for a heinous crime.

The Thin Blue Line straddles multiple narrative categories, a hybridity not lost on critics who struggled with genre-specific language available to them on the film's debut. Morris engages an uncanny mix of styles, because, as the filmmaker himself asserts, the film is *not* just an investigation of a murder mystery, it *is* a murder investigation. In light of the evidence he uncovers, Morris himself describes the film as a "non-fiction feature" in the tradition of Truman Capote's *In Cold Blood*. For Morris, this documentary pushes the envelope, with its generic expectation of objectivity, focusing instead on the possible rhetorical and aesthetic value of the form. He argues: "There's no reason why documentaries can't be as personal as fiction filmmaking and bear the imprint of those who made them. Truth isn't guaranteed by style or expression. It isn't guaranteed by anything" (Bates, 1989).

Perhaps in response to definitions of the "postmodern" emerging in cultural theory in the late 1980s as nihilist, anarchist, and apolitical, Morris maintains that his intention, unlike Akira Kirosawa's in *Rashamon*, a film to which *The Thin Blue Line* is often compared, was to expose the "*fact* of what happened [. . .] We have access to the world out there. We aren't just prisoners of our own fantasies and dreams. I wanted to make a movie about how truth is difficult to know, not how it's *impossible* to know" (O'Connor, 1989). Morris's very personal and political document engages and embraces the idea that subjectivity, historicity, and cultural predispositions imbue our perception without ceding that this particular form of investigation could uncover *a* truth capable of "combating the pernicious scapegoating fictions that can put the wrong man on death row" (Williams, 1998).

Many critics assumed that Morris's highly praised film would garner the 1988 Academy Award for Best Documentary, but the film was not even nominated. Writers have speculated that this exclusion was due to any number of factors, including the employment of Morris's footage in Adams's appeals process, his own assessment of the piece as a "non-fiction feature," the use of stylized reenactments, and subsequent charges of manipulation by informants. Nonetheless, this omission would serve to fuel subsequent debates over documentary film's form, focus, and function. In the year surrounding the release of *The Thin Blue Line*, other films that extended the boundaries of foundational documentary film principles would appear (for example, *Roger and Me*, *Who Killed Vincent Chin*, *Tongues Untied*, and *Surname Viet Given Name Nam*), some even gaining both mainstream box office success and Academy Award nominations, reflecting the growing incursion of postmodernist perspectives, politics, and innovations on the "real" and its documentation.

JULES ODENDAHL-JAMES

See also **Morris, Errol**

The Thin Blue Line (USA, Third Floor Productions, 1988, 101 min.). Distributed by Miramax Films. Produced by Mark Lipson, Lindsay Law, and Brad Fuller in association with Channel 4 (UK), The Program Development Company and American Playhouse. Directed by Errol Morris. Original score by Philip Glass. Cinematography by Robert Chappell and Stefan Czapsky. Editing by Paul Barnes. Production design by Ted Bafoloukos. Interviews filmed in Dallas, Huntsville, and Vidor, Texas. Reenactments filmed in locations in New York City and New Jersey with Randall Adams played by Adam Goldfine, David Harris played by Derek Horton,

Officer Robert Wood played by Ron Thornhill, Officer Teresa Turko played by Marianne Leone. Received following awards: Best Movie of 1988, *Washington Post* Film Critics Survey; Best Documentary, New York Film Critics Circle, 1988; Best Documentary, National Board of Review, 1988; Best Documentary, International Documentary Association, 1988; Best Documentary, National Society of Film Critics, 1988; Best Documentary, Kansas City Film Critics, 1988; Best Foreign Film, Taiwan International Film Festival, 1988; Best Motion Picture, Edgar Allan Poe Award, 1989; #95 on *Premiere* magazine's list of "100 Most Daring Films Ever Made," 1998; selected for National Film Registry by National Film Preservation Foundation, 2001

Further Reading

Barnouw, Dagmar, "Seeing and Believing: The Thin Blue Line of Documentary Objectivity," in *Common Knowledge* 4, 1, 1995, 129–143.

Bates, Peter, "Truth Not Guaranteed: An Interview with Errol Morris," in *Cineaste*, 17, 1, 1989, 16–17.

Dieckmann, Katherine, "Private Eye," in *American Film*, 8, 4, January/February 1988, 32–38.

McIllroy, Brian, "Observing and Walking the Thinnest of Lines: Phenomenology, Documentary Film and Errol Morris," in *Recherches-Sémiotiques/Semiotic-Inquiry*, 13, 1–2, 1993, 285–299.

Michaels, Lloyd, "*The Thin Blue Line* and the Limits of Documentary," in *Post Script: Essays in Film and the Humanities*, 13, 2, 1994, 44–50.

Nichols, Bill, "'Getting to Know You . . . ': Knowledge, Power, and the Body," in *Theorizing Documentary*, edited by Michael Renov, New York, Routledge, 1993, 174–192.

O'Connor, John, "The Film That Challenged 'Dr. Death,'" in *The New York Times*, May 24, 1989, C22

Plantinga, Carl R., *Rhetoric and Representation in Nonfiction Film*, Cambridge: Cambridge University Press, 1997.

Sherwin, Richard K., "Law Frames: Historical Truth and Narrative Necessity in a Criminal Case," in *Stanford Law Review*, 47, 1994, 39–83.

Williams, Linda, "Mirrors without Memories: Truth, History, and the New Documentary," in *Documenting the Documentary: Close Readings of Documentary Film and Video*, edited by Barry Keith Grant, and Jeannette Sloniowski, Detroit: Wayne State University Press, 1998, 379–396.

THIRD CINEMA

The term *Third Cinema* is somewhat ambiguous, although it is certainly associated with "Third World," although not all films and filmmakers considered representative of the ideals of Third Cinema are located in the nations once categorized as Third World.

Third Cinema has been associated equally with both fiction and documentary film. Third Cinema documentaries support and explore Paulo Freire's concepts of pedagogy, critical consciousness, and perceptions of contradictions, while synthesizing social reality and its political significance.

A variety of approaches are taken in Third Cinema conceptualization, analysis, and production. The often complex theoretical implications behind Third Cinema productions include:

Anti-model dependence (as opposed to the conventions of establishment cinema)
Active audiences (as opposed to the passive and illusionary inscribed audiences)
Committed authorship (as opposed to an uncritical realist cinema)

Ultimately many Third Cinema documentaries came to entrench the importance of process and dialectical relationships rather than the final product. This was a critical divergence from traditional filmmaking practices. Fernando Solanas, an Argentinian filmmaker and key developer of Third Cinema, said: "We realised that the most important thing was not the film and the information in it so much as the way this information was debated. One of the aims of such films is to provide the occasion for people to find themselves and speak of about their own problems" ("Cinéma d'auteur ou cinéma d'intervention?":60).

With its central proponents and theoreticians coming first from Latin America, Third Cinema provoked a reconsideration of how viewers translate media information about other countries, and how documentaries convey social relations in general. Indeed, documentaries by early Latin American filmmakers (proponents of Third Cinema) argue for the advantage of the insider's eye, as well as the contradictions found in the relations evoked in front of the camera when the film producers are *from* the culture they are representing.

In her *Towards a "Third" and "Imperfect" Cinema: A Theoretical and Historical Study of Filmmaking in Latin America* (1989) Ana Lopez argues:

> . . .[Third Cinema] sought to bring to light that which was kept in darkness and silenced by the socio-political and economic mechanisms of underdevelopment. And this light would also be shined onto the process of representation itself, questioning the filmmakers' own position in the filmmaking process, their engagement with their subject, their position as social actors in the universe being recorded. . . . This cinema ought also to provide the spectators with different consciousness of their worlds . . . which would breakdown rationalisations and preconceived ideas.

In Africa and Latin America, the Third Cinema documentary took the position of both fictionalising history and documenting history. Although the principal driving forces behind African documentaries have been education and historical recording, there is also a tradition of blending the fictional with the documented. Films such as Garcia Espinosa's *Las Aventuras de Juan Quin Quin* (1967), *Memorias del Subdesarrolo* (1968), and *El Chacal* (1969) (by Miguel Littin), or Sembene Usmane's *Camp de Thiaroye* (1987) highlight the historical as a fictionalised document, which the fictions (the films themselves) interrogate. In these films there is a demonstration of the process of fictionalising history and an attempt at documenting it through the making of a film. For these filmmakers documentary materials are not simply proof of authenticity or reality of history; rather, the films themselves are the documents that will enter history to prove a new reading of history.

Moreover, documentary-like materials were appearing in fictional texts to underline historicity exemplified by the use of authentic locations, and at times even characters. Films such as *Come Back Africa* (1960, Lionel Rogosin) or *Last Grave at Dimbaza* (1973, Nana Mahamo), and Jorge Sanjines's *Ukamau* (1966) and *Yawar Malku* (1969) are good examples of those type of films.

Alternatively, other films in the Third Cinema mode began to reveal an ideological rejection of formal conventions. Jean Marie Teno's films, including *Africa, I Will Pluck You* (1993) or Chaz Maviyane's *After the Wax* (1992) reasserted the argumentative and therefore educational base of Third Cinema documentaries by creating hybrid styles that would not only inform and educate, but also take a determined ideological stance. These films juxtaposed personal points of view with history, thus deconstructing the conventional filmic vision of Africa.

An interesting experiment that took place in Mozambique during the 1970s and 1980s highlighted the place of the spectator as participant, which is an aesthetic highly developed in African theatre and other spectator arts. The making of the film *Mueda, Memoria e Massacre* (1980) by Ruy Guerra emphasized the crossover between lived and living history, which later became a major theme of Third Cinema documentaries all over the world in the 1980s. A good example was the Kuxa Kanema experiment.

Kuxa Kanema's importance as a cultural experience lies in its role in creating a path to theoretical foundations of revolutionary cinema in Mozambique. Theoretically, the project wished to create conditions for the equal participation of the viewer and the producer in creating messages coming out of the screen. To do this a complex production and distribution situation was developed. Most of the productions were limited to short news excerpts that were bound together in a ten-minute reel. The reel was shot, edited, and released within a week or two at most.

From these audience-based experiments came the Participatory Video productions of the 1980s and 1990s, which further reveal the deconstructive nature of Third Cinema documentaries. These video-based documentaries became statements of freedom, rejecting the formally structured and market-oriented documentaries suggesting rather the need for filmmaking to be part of the development processes taking place in African societies.

Other films went further in contesting the mythic and imperialistic telling of African histories. One such good example is *The Life and Times of Sarah Baartman* (1998, Zola Maseko). In many ways, although not necessarily reactive to the portrayals of African on the big and silver screens, the filmmaker offers a contrasting view of history and drives what one could call a humanistic vein into the narrativising of history. See, too, a good example in Jakub Barua's *Shades of Poland* (2000) or Safi Faye's *Letter from My Village (* 1975), which work toward enhancing that humanistic approach to reveal the considerable strength of culture as an important front for liberation and knowledge.

Acknowledged theorists of Third Cinema include Fernando Solanas, Octavio Getino, Jullianne

Burton, Gabriel Teshome, Coco Fusco, Isaac Julien, Mercer Kobena, Julio Garcia-Espinosa, Robert Stam, Clyde Taylor, Roy Armes, Mbye Cham, Imruh Bakari, and Jim Pines.

MARTIN MHANDO

See also Activist Filmmaking; Africa; Underground/ Activist Documentary: Chile

Further Reading

Bakari, Imruh, and Mbye, Cham (eds.), African Experiences of Cinema, London: British Film Institute, 1996.
Burton, Julianne (ed.), Cinema and Social Change in Latin America: Conversations with Filmmakers, Austin: University of Texas Press, 1986.
———, The Social Documentary in Latin America, Pittsburgh: University of Pittsburgh, 1990.
"Cinéma d'auteur ou cinéma d'intervention?" Table Ronde avec Fernando Solanas et al., in CinémAction I, Paris, 1978, 60.
Espinosa, Julio Garcia, "For an Imperfect Cinema," Afterimage 3, 1971, 54–67.
Freire, Paulo, Pedagogy of the Oppressed, London: Penguin Books, 1990.
Fusco, Coco, "Fantasies of Oppositionality," in Screen, 29, 4, autumn, 1988.
Guneratne, Anthony R., and Wimal Dissanayake (eds.), Rethinking Third Cinema, New York: Routledge, 2003.
Julien, Isaac, and Mercer Kobena, "De Centre and De Margin," in Screen, 29, 4, autumn, 1988.
Lesage, Julia, "Women Make Media: Three Modes of Production," in The Social Documentary in Latin America, edited by Julianne Burton, Pittsburgh: University of Pittsburgh Press, 1990.
Lopez, Ana M., Towards a "Third" and "Imperfect Cinema: A Theoretical and Historical Study of Filmaking in Latin America, UMI Dissertation Information Service, 1989.
Pines, Jim, and Paul Willemen (eds.), Questions of Third Cinema, edited by Publisher, London: BFI Pub., 1989.
Stam, Robert, "The Hour of the Furnaces and the Two Avant-Gardes," in The Social Documentary in Latin America, edited by Julianne Burton, Pittsburgh: University of Pittsburgh Press, 1990.
Wayne, Mike, Political Film: The Dialectics of Third Cinema, Pluto Press, 2001.

THOMAS, ANTONY

Antony (sometimes Anthony) Thomas's documentaries films have made a significant contribution to British and American public television broadcasting since the late 1970s. His documentaries are predominantly news-style films produced for television. In the style of public television and investigative documentary filmmaking, his documentaries are characterized by in-depth research, numerous interviews, and a narrator. His films have a Rashomon-esque quality, presenting varying subjective perspectives; he juxtaposes interviews, paces sequences, and includes voice-over narration to create a cohesive argument that reveals his own perspectives through cinematic and editorial techniques. Although his films address a range of topics over several decades, they share one commonality; they deal exclusively with social or political topics contentious at the time of their release. His views on certain issues have changed over time, particularly those on apartheid and South African politics as expressed in The Anatomy of Apartheid (1964), The South

African Experience (1977), and the feature film Rhodes; the Life & Legend of Cecil Rhodes (1997). His biases, particularly in his later films, are intentionally transparent, making them best understood within the cultural context of their production. His contribution to documentary film, particularly in the realm of public television, has been to challenge public opinion on controversial topics through his own occasionally contentious stances.

Not shy of debate, his films espouse positions on issues as diverse as celibacy in the Catholic Church, animal rights, issues of genetic predisposition in biology and psychology, and the role of fundamentalism in politics, whether American or Saudi. His 2002–2004 film Celibacy presents celibacy as a late Medieval amendment to Catholic doctrine that assures priestly wealth revert to the Church on death, and the film explores the potential relationship of repressed sexuality to the contemporary abuse scandals of the Catholic Church. Fat (1997–1998) explores cultural and medical views on obesity that submit to cultural aesthetics and disregard genetic diversity when diagnosing clinical obesity. *Twins: The Divided Self* (1997), which won eight international awards, probes genetic predispositions for character and intelligence. Winning six prestigious awards, *To Love or Kill: Man vs. Animal* (1995), reveals human animal relationships as both loving and gory. *Thy Kingdom Come; Thy Will Be Done* (1987) links the Christian Right and American politics. Thomas won the U.S. Emmy for *Frank Terpil: Portrait of a Dangerous Man* (1982), for which he interviewed the ex-CIA agent who was living in hiding, at the time. David Fanning produced this film; he also co-wrote and produced the docudrama *Death of a Princess* (1979–1980), which aired to one of the highest ratings in PBS broadcast history, won The Gold Award at the New York International Festival, and disrupted British-Saudi diplomatic relations. The film reenacts Thomas's investigation of the public execution of a Saudi princess and her lover. The subject matter and docudrama style both provoked debate and criticism; however, the genre choice made it feasible to present explosive subject matter without compromising the safety of Thomas's sources by revealing their identities.

By 1980, Antony Thomas had already demonstrated his affinity for politically transgressive topics. *The South African Experience* (1977) had exposed the Apartheid regime, and earned him both the British Academy Award and prohibition from his home-country, South Africa. The publicity scandal surrounding *Death of a Princess*, however, irrevocably established both Antony Thomas and co-writer/producer David Fanning as provocative documentary filmmakers. It also established a long-term relationship between Antony Thomas and *Frontline*, for which Fanning is the co-founder and executive producer. In the vein of public television, the framework within which the majority of his films have been created, Antony Thomas's documentaries are story-driven and pointedly controversial, stimulating debate on and adding liberal nuance to mainstream media representations.

SHEENA WILSON

See also **Death of a Princess**

Biography

Born Calcutta, India in 1940. Lived in South Africa between 1946 and 1967. At age 27, moved to England. Later banned from South Africa because of political views expressed in *The South African Apart-heid Experience* (1977 trilogy). Continued to reside in Britain. Has won prestigious awards including the George Foster Peabody Award for *Twins: The Divided Self* (1997), the Grierson Award for Best British Documentary for *Man and Animal* (1995), a U.S. Emmy for *Frank Terpil—Portrait of a Dangerous Man* (1982), and the British Academy Award for his trilogy *The South African Experience* (1977). Since the 1994 fall of apartheid, has been able to return to South Africa, which provided a rich backdrop for the six part historical feature film *Rhodes: The Life & Legend of Cecil Rhodes* (1997), and the two-part documentary *The Real Olympics* (2002–2004). Continues to write, direct, and produce TV documentaries that are aired internationally on PBS, HBO (United States), ITV, BBC, CBC (Britain & Canada), Televisio Valencia (Spain), Odeseia (Spain & Portugal), Yes TV (Israel), ATV (Hong Kong), and SABC (South Africa). His portfolio also includes non-documentary films and he is the author of *Rhodes* (1996) and co-author of *The Arab Experience* (1975).

Selected Films (credited as writer, producer, director)

1964 *The Anatomy of Apartheid*
1970 *A Touch of Churchill, A Touch of Hitler* (The Life of Cecil Rhodes); director
1977 *The South African Experience* (Trilogy)
1979–1980 *Death of a Princess*; writer, director
1982 *Frank Terpil: Portrait of a Dangerous Man*
1987 *Thy Kingdom Come; Thy Will be Done* (Two part)
1990 *Never Say Die: The Pursuit of Eternal Youth* (U.K. Title: *Heaven Must Wait*)
1994 *By Satan Possessed; The Search for the Devil* (U.K. Title: *In Satan's Name*)
1995 *To Love or Kill: Man vs. Animal* (U.K. Title: *Man & Animal*)
1996 *Between Life and Death*
1997 *Twins: The Divided Self*
1997–1998 *Fat* (Six part series)
1999–2000 *A Question of Miracle* (U.K. Title: *Miracles*)
2002–2004 *The Real Olympics* (U.K. Title: *The Ancient Greek Olympics*) (Two part)
2004 *Celibacy* (U.K. Title: *Flesh and the Devil*)

Further Reading

Bullert, B. J., *Public Television Politics and the Battle Over Documentary Film*, New Brunswick, NJ: Rutgers University Press, 1997.

Burns, James, "Biopics and Politics: The Making and the Unmaking of the Rhodes Movies," in *Biography*, 23, 1, 2000, 108–126.

Hees, Edwin, "'Truly, the Ways of the White Man Are Strange': Tribal Utopianism in Two South African Propaganda Films," in *South African Theatre Journal*: *SATJ*, 5, 1, 1991, 74–97.

Pfaff, Françoise, *Focus on African Films*, Bloomington: Indiana University Press, 2004.

Rosenthal, Alan (ed.), *Why Docudrama? Fact-Fiction on Film and TV*. Carbondale, IL: Southern Illinois University Press, 1999.

THOMSON, MARGARET

Margaret Thomson's prolific instructional film-making career, like many of her female contemporaries in the nonfiction sector, has been neglected in most histories of documentary film. Thomson worked more or less continuously in instructional filmmaking for more than forty years. Arriving in Britain from New Zealand in 1934, with a degree in zoology, she started her film career at Bruce Woolfe's Gaumont-British Instructional. After a year in the library shot listing films, she was offered a series of her own, and from 1936–1937, she directed six educational films examining different ecosystems in Britain. These films were in the tradition of the *Secrets of Nature* series using animation, diagrams, and macro-photography as well as actuality footage and proved an excellent training ground for Thomson; however the film industry slump in 1938 found Thomson out of work. For the next three years she did a variety of jobs both in and out of the film industry including editing for various documentary units, making travelogs with Marion Grierson for the Trade and Industrial Development Association, teaching English in Spain, and beginning to retrain as an electrician.

In 1941, Thomson found regular work at the Realist Film Unit making instructional films as part of the wartime Home Front propaganda campaign, mainly for nontheatrical distribution. Her first six films, made for the Dig for Victory campaign, illustrate the basic skills required to work an allotment, and store, produce, and maintain gardening tools. Later films were made for specialised audiences such as the farming community and introduced new farming methods, showcased traditional crafts, and exemplified ways of increasing yields. Thomson also made four films about anaesthesia for medical undergraduates. Considering the diversity of the subject matter, all of the films are characterised by their visual simplicity, clear instruction, and ability to relay complex information to the audience in a clear nonpatronising way.

After the war, Thomson produced two children's hygiene films, but she returned to directing to make two recruitment films for the Ministry of Education, *Children Learning by Experience* (1946) and *Children Growing Up with Other People* (1947). She filmed children playing on London's bomb sites and in parks and said that she tried not to intrude on the children's environment, allowing shots to run longer than normal to consider the significance of the children's behaviour. She believed this to be an early example of the cinema verité style. In 1948, she returned to New Zealand where she directed several cinemagazines for the New Zealand Film Unit before coming back to work for the Crown Film Unit in Britain in 1950. In 1953, she made a fiction film for children, *Child's Play*, which was funded by the government backed feature unit Group 3. After several years as a children's acting coach at Pinewood Studios, she returned to nonfiction filmmaking, directing industrial and government-sponsored medical films, including several for the Coal Board, until she retired in 1977.

SARAH EASEN

Biography

Born Australia, 1910 and educated in New Zealand. Emigrated to Britain in 1934. Film librarian, Gaumont-British Instructional 1938. Director, Gaumont-British Instructional 1936–1937. Freelance cutter, 1938. Director, editor, and producer, Travel and Industrial Development Association; New Zealand Trade and Industrial Development Association 1939. Director, Realist Film Unit, 1941–1947. Director, New Zealand Film Unit, 1948–1949. Director, Crown Film Unit, 1950–1951. Director, Group 3, 1954. Children's acting coach, Pinewood Studios, 1954. Director, various production companies, 1955–1977.

Selected films

1936–1937 *Chalk Downlands, Meadowlands, Moorlands, Oakwoods, Salt Marshes, Healthlands*
1941 *Cultivation; Storing Vegetables Indoors; Storing Vegetables Outdoors*
1942 *Clamping Potatoes, Hedging, Ditching, Making a Compost Heap, Garden Tools*
1943 *Clean Milk, Making Good Hay, Making Grass Silage, Re-seeding for Better Grass, Save Your Own Seeds*
1944 *The Technique of Anaesthesia* series: director of four of the eleven films in the series
1945 *Your Children's Ears, Your Children's Eyes, Your Children's Teeth*: producer
1946–1947 *Children Learning by Experience, Children Growing Up with Other People*
1948–1949 Cinemagazines for the New Zealand Film Unit

1950–1951 *A Family Affair, Cross-infection in Children's Wards No 1* and *No 2*
1954 *Friend of the Family*
1955–1956 *Continuous Observation of a Depressed Patient, Understanding Aggression*

1957 *Yorkshire Imperial on Thames, Yorkshire Imperial Way With Water*
1960s Medical training films for the nursing profession
1967–1977 Coal Board filmstrips, *TB-The Forgotten Disease, Margin of Safety*

THREE SONGS ABOUT LENIN

(USSR, Vertov, 1933–1934)

Contemporary Western film scholars typically consider Soviet director Dziga Vertov's *Tri pesni o Lenine/Three Songs about Lenin* less important than his reflexive masterpiece *Chelovek s kinoapparatom/Man with a Movie Camera* (1929). In the Soviet Union, however, *Three Songs about Lenin* represented the more acceptable face of Vertov's work, even though the director himself continued to be regarded with suspicion by the cinema authorities because of his modernist leanings. Although hampered by considerable difficulties during its production and initial distribution, *Three Songs about Lenin* earned Vertov the Order of the Red Star and was endorsed by film industry chief Boris Shumyatksy as an improvement on his earlier work. The film was reedited in 1938 to include additional material favouring Stalin. The hundredth anniversary of Lenin's birth in 1970 saw a version closer to the original print restored by Vertov's editor, Elizaveta Svilova. Whatever its aesthetic value, *Three Songs about Lenin* was more central to Soviet cultural history than *Man with a Movie Camera*.

Three Songs about Lenin, produced to mark the tenth anniversary of Lenin's death, documents his funeral and includes shots of him working, meeting people, and giving speeches. In an attempt to document how Leninism has enabled the country to progress in the intervening ten years, the film represents the liberation of Soviet Asian women and industrial achievements of the First Five Year Plan in diverse parts of the Soviet Union. There is, of course, no indication of the scale of coercion and sacrifice involved. Footage from the civil war is also included to remind viewers of the momentous struggle to secure the revolution.

Like *Shestaya chast' mira/One Sixth of the Earth*, Dziga Vertov (1926), *Three Songs about Lenin* was an ambitious undertaking, combining library footage with new material shot across a vast geographical area. *Three Songs about Lenin*'s cinematography is less distinguished than *Man with a Movie Camera*'s; the earlier film's outstanding cameraman Mikhail Kaufman had left Vertov's group to direct his own documentaries. Svilova painstakingly trawled archives and collated fragments of newsreel film of Lenin to construct a fuller cinematic record of the revered leader's public activities than had previously been possible. Similarly, sound engineer Shtro reconstructed part of a Lenin speech for the film. According to Vertov's diaries, this arduous work was constantly disrupted by lack of support and resources during production and attacks from opponents critical of his conception of documentary film. Finally, there were difficulties getting the completed film distributed.

Contemporary Western film scholars tend to dismiss *Three Songs about Lenin* not only on aesthetic grounds but also because they see it as a wholesale capitulation to Stalinism and the pseudo-religious Lenin cult (Michelson, 1992). These retrospective judgments need to be carefully contextualised. From a Stalinist perspective, one of the film's shortcomings was the initial lack of prominence it gave to Stalin. Also problematic is the stridency of the Lenin speech heard midway through the film and reiterated on revolving inter-titles near the end. "The landowners and capitalists, destroyed in Russia, will be defeated throughout the world" was inconsistent with mid-1930s Soviet foreign policy as it moved toward its more conciliatory Popular

Three Songs about Lenin, 1933–1934.
[*Still courtesy of the British Film Institute*]

Front phase (Roberts, 1999). *Three Songs about Lenin* highlights how there was some scope within the Lenin cult for emphasising different aspects of his political legacy. Equally, a limited range of different perspectives on Lenin himself was possible. This film stresses Lenin's exemplary humanity, industriousness, and unpretentiousness—his status as a role model for good Soviet citizens—rather than just his deification.

Vertov saw *Three Songs about Lenin* as a continuation of his ongoing kino-eye and, after the coming of sound, radio-eye experiment to develop an international film language. It can be seen and listened to as one of the last examples of early European film modernism. Vertov wanted to develop a film practice that would facilitate communication between workers in geographically disparate locations. *Three Songs about Lenin* represents their unity and, according

to Vertov, the film's combination of sounds and images achieved a "crystalline" purity of universal accessibility (Michelson, 1984). Thus, even if the spoken language of the industrial and collective farm workers and engineer who address the camera directly toward the end of the film is not translated, their gestures and facial expressions enable them to be understood within its overall context.

As the film's title suggests, it is primarily structured around various types of music rather than interviews or voice-over narration. Folk songs sung by Soviet Asian women subdivide the film, moving gradually from lamenting their oppression in the first song, to sorrow at Lenin's death in the second, to optimism in the third. Two other types of music also feature significantly; nineteenth century classical at Lenin's funeral, and Yuri Shaporin's modern Soviet *The*

March of the Shock Workers, written specially for the film. Shaporin's composition dominates the soundtrack whenever intense productive activity is represented, particularly the final section's images of coal transportation, steel works, and newly constructed factories, canals, and dams. Ultimately, Shaporin's music is the sound of the future in *Three Songs about Lenin*.

Three Songs about Lenin was quite well received by Soviet and Western audiences in the 1930s, gaining plaudits from luminaries as diverse as Walter Benjamin and Cecil B de Mille. The documentary *Turksib* (Viktor Turin, USSR, 1929) scored a similar success several years earlier. What the two films share is a basic ideological contrast between progressive modernity and the backward East that cuts across Soviet-Western differences. In its representation of primitive, stagnant Islamic cultures and veiled women *Three Songs about Lenin* taps into a fund of imagery familiar to other European imperial cultures (Stollery, 2000). Revealingly, the film's most blatant transgressions of Vertov's commitment to filming "life caught unawares" occur in shots underwriting the notion that Soviet power in Central Asia constitutes liberation and not domination. Early in the film women unveil and smile at the camera. Later on close-ups of their eyes signify sadness at Lenin's death and the new Leninist vision they have attained. These are carefully lit, manifestly staged images rather than any kind of documentary record of reality.

MARTIN STOLLERY

See also **Vertov, Dziga**

Three Songs about Lenin (USSR, Mezhrabpomfilm, 1933–1934). Direction and scenario by Dziga Vertov. Edited by Elizaveta Svilova. Assisted by Ilya Kopalin, Semiramida Pumpyanskaya. Cinematography by Mark Magidson, Bentsion Monastyrsky, Dmitri Surensky. Sound by Pyotr Shtro. Music by Yuri Shaporin. Filmed in Turkmenistan, Uzbekistan, Azerbaijan, and elsewhere in the Soviet Union.

Further Reading

"Intertitles to *Three Songs of Lenin*," in *October*, 52, 1990, 40–51.
Leyda, Jay, *Kino: A History of the Russian and Soviet Film*, London: George Allen and Unwin, 1983.
Michelson, Annette, "The Kinetic Icon in the Work of Mourning," in *The Red Screen*, edited by Anna Lawton, London: Routledge, 1992, 113–131.
———, (ed.), *Kino-Eye: The Writings of Dziga Vertov*, London: Pluto Press, 1984.
Petric, Vlada, "Vertov, Lenin and Perestroika: The Cinematic Transposition of Reality," in *Beyond Documents: Essays on the Non-fiction Film*, edited by Charles Warren, New Hampshire: University Press of New England, 1996, 271–294.
Roberts, Graham, *Forward Soviet! History and Non-fiction Film in the USSR*, London: I. B. Tauris, 1999.
Stollery, Martin, *Alternative Empires: European Modernist Cinemas and Cultures of Imperialism*, Exeter: University of Exeter Press, 2000.
Taylor, Richard, and Ian Christie, (eds.), *The Film Factory: Russian and Soviet Cinema in Documents 1896–1939*, London: Routledge, 1988.
Taylor, Richard, *Film Propaganda: Soviet Russia and Nazi Germany*, London: I. B. Tauris, 1998.
Tumarkin, Nina, *Lenin Lives!: The Cult of Lenin in Soviet Russia*, Cambridge, MA: Harvard University Press, 1997.
Youngblood, Denise, *Soviet Cinema in the Silent Era, 1918–35*, Austin: University of Texas Press, 1991.

TIME MAGAZINE

Time Magazine is a weekly magazine published by Time Inc. that has an estimated readership of around 22 million per publication. Co-founded in 1923 by Henry R. Luce and Briton Haddon, the magazine has grown to include regional representations such as *Time Asia*, *Time Canada*, *Time Europe*, and *Time Pacific*. It also includes a dedicated web site where subscribers have access to dynamic content not offered by the print magazine. The first issue of the magazine was published on the March 3, 1923, and aimed, in part, at a majority readership of Graduands (which has continued into the present time). It has evolved into a highly popular magazine that presents an essentially light mixture of popular culture, politics, social commentary, and opinion pieces about important people, situations, and events that shape and reshape the world.

Historically, being a weekly publication of news and other reports of interest, *Time Magazine* has frequently reviewed various documentary films and directors. These have often been films that are widely circulated and are thought to have a direct political, social, or economic value attached to them, thus making them a point of interest to the readers of the magazine. There have also been reviews and pieces written about documentaries for the pure spectatorship that they use such as Jacques Cluzaud *Le Peuple migrateur/Winged Migration* (2001) and Joe Berlinger and Bruce Sinofsky's *Metallica: Some Kind of Monster* (2004). Reviews such as these tend to be of less substance than documentary reviews on historically important events or people. Most of the articles that appear within the publication are therefore placed in the entertainment section of the magazine unless substantial public interest surrounds the release of a documentary, or high interest in a director is shown as was seen with the appearance of Michael Moore on the July 12, 2004 cover.

Time has arguably been somewhat instrumental in bringing documentaries and documentary film-makers and directors to the attention of the American (and global) public and promoting discussion and reviews on them. The magazine was perhaps one of the first and therefore one of the few mainstream running publications that has taken an interest in documentary film, and continues to sporadically publish articles on them. Overall, *Time* does not appear to specifically aim at presenting only documentaries that fall within certain genres and, indeed, seems to cover a wide range of both documentary film and directors throughout its printing years. Wide coverage of important historical events (such as the Vietnam War) or issues have no doubt influenced the appearance of reviews concerning documentaries that deal with such issues and also influences the amount of space devoted to the writing within the magazine.

Time Magazine is an accessible weekly news magazine that will, because of its very nature in providing snippets from various social, economic, and cultural news items, include reviews of popular documentaries and directors. However, it most often seeks to review those that either endeavour to make a direct statement on current or historically driven events or situations, or those that are seen as being popular and accessible to its readers. *Time* does not often provide in-depth readings and reviews of documentaries and directors; however, it does attempt (in reviews mainly) to cover the most accessible and popular ones.

SAMARA L. ALLSOP

Further Reading

Baughman, James, "Henry R. Luce and the Rise of the American News Media," in Twayne's 20th Century American Biography Series, No 5, Gale Group, November 1, 1987.

Corliss, Richard, "The World According to Michael," in *TIME Magazine*, 164, 27, July 12, 2004.

Elson, Robert, "*Time Inc: The Intimate History of a Publishing Enterprise, 1923–1941*," Scribner, November 1985.

Morrow, Lance, "The Tap . . . Tap Tap of Courage," in *TIME Magazine*, 154, 3, July 19, 1999.

Schickel, Richard, "The Alternate Realities of Hot Documentaries," in *TIME Magazine*, 162, 2, July 14, 2003.

Tyrangiel, Josh, "Some Kind of Movie," in *TIME Magazine*, 164, 2, July 12, 2004.

TIMES OF HARVEY MILK, THE

(US, Epstein, 1984)

On November 27, 1978, Dan White climbed through a window into San Francisco City Hall and shot to death Supervisor Harvey Milk and Mayor George Moscone. White fired eight times at Moscone, reloaded his gun, and then went down a hallway and emptied it again into Harvey Milk. The deaths shocked the city and its gay community. With the killing, Milk had become the modern gay movement's first martyr (Benson, 1984: 1).

Dan White was an embittered ex-supervisor who had resigned and then wanted his job back. Moscone, backed by Milk, refused to have him reinstated. The rejection precipitated the murders. White had resigned because of the defeat of Proposition 6, an amendment that barred gays and lesbians from employment in California public schools.

The planned documentary was originally to focus on White. However, director and co-producer Robert Epstein found White uninteresting. "The more we got into the story," Epstein said, "the more rich it became as to what it represented—which was trying to better humanity. Harvey Milk was really trying to do something positive" (Smith, 1985: 1). This shift in focus resulted in *The Times of Harvey Milk*, a ninety-minute portrait of San Francisco's first openly gay elected official. Shot in 16mm, the documentary took six years and cost $300,000 to make.

Narrated by Harvey Fierstein, the documentary opens with news footage. Included are the gurneys carrying the bodies of Milk and Moscone, the attempt to capture Dan White, and the tearful press announcement by supervisor (now senator) Diane Feinstein of the murders. The footage was on-the-scene coverage, as the story unfolded, adding to its drama.

The film then turns to the years leading up to the murders. While some of Milk's youth is disclosed, the filmmakers focus on his emergence as a political leader. The viewer sees Milk transformed from a quirky, ex-hippy into a savvy, polished politician who advocated for gay and minority rights, senior citizen rights, and rent control. One of his first political challenges came after California State Senator John Briggs introduced Proposition 6 onto the State ballot. It was intended to ban all openly gay people from working in the public

The Times of Harvey Milk, 1984.
[*Courtesy of the Everett Collection*]

The Times of Harvey Milk, George Moscone, 1984.
[*Courtesy of the Everett Collection*]

school system, playing on parents' fears that their children might hold up gay people as role models or be molested by them. Milk debated Briggs and is credited with helping to defeat the measure, which for a time seemed certain to pass. Milk's stature and reputation grew.

The film's closing scenes are powerful. The filmmakers recorded a silent candlelight walk by 40,000 people held on the evening of Milk and Moscone's deaths. The film then moves ahead six months when White is found guilty, not of murder, but of the lesser charge of involuntary manslaughter. His defense attorney argued that White had become deranged by eating too much junk food, which became known as the "Twinkie defense." The verdict caused a riot in San Francisco. City Hall was stormed, and six police cars were burned.

White served 5 1/2 years of his 7-year sentence. He received no psychiatric treatment. In October 1985, nearly two years after his release, White committed suicide.

The film's structure includes segments focusing on eight San Francisco men and women, both heterosexual and homosexual, who each talk about how Harvey Milk affected their lives. One of the more poignant remarks of the eight is spoken by Jim Elliot, a machinist and secretary of a local union. When he first met Milk, and heard he was gay, Elliot wondered how he was "gonna go back to these guys at the union and tell them that we're supporting a fruit?" Then Elliot goes on to say, "But as I listened to him, you realized that he wasn't only for gay rights. He was for anything that affected little people."

The film does not examine Dan White's character or trial in any depth. Some critics considered this one of the film's few weaknesses. Other than this, the film's critics were nearly unanimous in their praise for this "extraordinarily wise and sensitive" film (Mathews, 1984).

Although eloquently partisan, the film is much more than a "gay" film. It is a positive story about one man who made a difference in the lives of others. The film is a triumph of democratic hope. As many have said, the story is not about gay rights, but human rights.

LOU BUTTINO

The Times of Harvey Milk (US, Black Sand Productions/ Pacific Arts, 1984, 90 min.). Distributed by New Yorker Films and TC Films International. Directed by Rob Epstein. Written by Judith Coburn and Carter Wilson. Academy Award Winner: Best Feature. New York Film Critics Circle Award: Best Documentary. Three National Emmy Awards.

Further Reading

Benson, Shiela, "The Times of Harvey Milk," *Los Angeles Times*, November 2, 1984, 1.
Galbraith, Stuart IV, "The Times of Harvey Milk," www. dvdtalk.com/reviews/read, 2.
Mathews, Jack, "Hollywood," *USA Today*, October 16, 1984.
Smith, Lynn, "Harvey Milk Film-Pride, Sorrow UCI Presentation of Honored Picture Triggers Emotions [Orange County Edition], *Los Angeles Times*, October 31, 1985, 1.
"The Times of Harvey Milk," *The New York Times*, October 28, 1984.

TIRE DIÉ

(Argentina, Birri, 1956, 1959)

Tire dié/Throw Me a Dime is considered the most important documentary short in Latin America. It was made collaboratively between Argentine filmmaker Fernando Birri and his students at the Documentary School of Santa Fe at the University of Litoral (Santa Fe, Argentina), the first school of its kind in Latin America. *Tire dié* is a thirty-three-minute document of poor children in Santa Fe, (a city in a northern province of Argentina) where a mode of survival is for the children to await passing trains, balance precariously on the elevated tracks, and to run alongside the trains, begging for small change by shouting "Tire dié! Tire dié!" (Throw me a dime).

On its release in 1958, the film marked the entrance of an Italian neorealist-inspired political filmmaking that was to indelibly mark the landscape of Latin American film production from the late 1950s to the 1970s. Dubbed the New Latin American Cinema movement, these films documented and exposed the economic, social, and political disparities in Latin America, often made absent in the studio-made films from the 1940s and 1950s. Fernando Birri was trained at the prestigious film school, the Centro Sperimentale in Rome, where he worked as an assistant to Zavattini and De Sica. There he was inspired by neorealism, or what he described as "the tenderness of the Italian films that in a simple manner document the everyday" (Sendros, 1994). On returning to Argentina and seeing the lack of infrastructure for filmmaking, coupled with the harsh reality of poverty, Birri resolved to make what he dubbed a "cinema of underdevelopment." He condemned apolitical cinema in a manifesto by stating that "one must place oneself face to face with the reality with a camera and document it, document underdevelopment. . . . Cinema which makes itself an accomplice of that underdevelopment is subcinema" (Birri, 1987).

Tire dié is a landmark film because of the direct, honest, and gritty portrayal of its subject matter, but it was also important in terms of the production process. Birri worked with two borrowed film cameras and nonprofessional sound recording devices. Birri's aim was to make films despite the lack of infrastructure and financing, because he felt that social problems were important to make visible vis-à-vis the cinema. His philosophy of making films under difficult circumstances and not for

Tire Dié, 1956, 1959.
[*Still courtesy of the British Film Institute*]

to a traditional documentary (for example, geographic location, population). As Julianne Burton observes:

> As conventional descriptive data give way to the less conventional (statistics concerning the number of streetlamps and hairdressers) the parodistic becomes clear. As the houses give way to shanties, the narrator declares, "Upon reaching the edge of the city proper, statistics become uncertain. This is where, between four and five in the afternoon during 1956, 1957, and 1958, the following social survey film was shot"
>
> (Burton, 2000).

Birri and his students first spent time documenting the children and their families with a still camera and a tape recorder and then later transformed the photo documentary into a film. The film project was first cut as a sixty-minute version. During the premiere of the film in Santa Fe, a cross-section of the population numbering four thousand in total filled the university theatre. Present were the subjects of the film along with the filmmakers, the children of the slums and their parents, along with the student filmmakers. In addition, university and city officials and film critics were in attendance. The film met with an enthusiastic crowd and was replayed three times that evening for the same audience. After the screening, hundreds of questionnaires were given out, and consultations were done with the film subjects about which parts were effective, and why. Through this collaboration to some extent the film advocated for the problems of the poor in Santa Fe. Moreover, it served as a model of collaborative filmmaking, one in which subjects determined, to some extent, how they were being represented.

The result was a more concise, thirty-three-minute version replete with a new voice track. Two revered film actors of the time, Francisco Petrone and Maria Rosa Gallo were asked to speak over the voices in the film that were poorly recorded. According to Birri and his student filmmakers, the point was not to dub over what people were saying, but rather to have the actors additional vocal support for the subjects. Some critics have charged that this voice-over approach ultimately undermined the original intent of the film's democratic agenda. Although this may have altered the objective of having a marginalized community speak for itself, it worked on a practical level to vastly improve the sound quality of the original film. Inadvertently, it provided increased opportunities for the film to be screened outside of local settings.

commercial profit would not be labeled until the late 1960s with the term an *imperfect cinema* (*un cine imperfecto*) coined by Cuban filmmaker Julio García Espinosa.

Birri's class of eighty students was split up into various groups to spend time with the subjects in a riverside squatters' community. Birri described the making of the film: "*Tire dié* was the product of constant, ongoing discussion. During that two year period [the film took to complete], we went almost every afternoon to the river flats to film. We went to observe and understand and exchange ideas with the people who lived there, but we ended up sharing their lives. The film became secondary to the interpersonal relationships that developed between us" (Burton, 1986).

The film opens with an aerial shot of Santa Fe. The voice-over narration that accompanies these shots of the city describes in a matter-of-fact manner the typical information one would ascribe

TIRE DIÉ

The film was shown at film festivals in Argentina and Uruguay, and it circulated throughout the provinces of Argentina via a rudimentary mobile cinema van that provided a no-cost viewing opportunity for poor residents. This was especially important in areas with an absence of movie theatres.

Tire dié is a groundbreaking film and has significant historical importance in the annals of Latin American film scholarship. Despite its great influence, however, the film is practically impossible to see, Latin America included. As Julianne Burton points out, "most viewers know only the fragment presented in Fernando Solanas and Octavio Getino's three-part documentary on Argentine politics, *The Hour of the Furnaces* (*La hora de los hornos*) (1969) . . . " (Burton, 2000). Nonetheless, *Tire dié* epitomized and served as a template for the continent-wide movement of political filmmaking in Latin America through the late 1970s.

TAMARA L. FALICOV

See also **Birri, Fernando;** *Hour of the Furnaces*

(First version)

Tire dié (Argentina, 1956, 60 min.). Produced by the Institute of Cinema of the National University of the Litoral. Directed by Fernando Birri and students Hugo Abad, Blanca C. de Brasco, Eduardo Ates, Elena de Azcuenaga, Cesar Caprio, Manuel Horacio Gimenez, Rodolfo Neder, Juan Oliva, Carlos Pais, Ninfa Pajon, Eduardo Pallero, Jose M. Paolantonio, Jorge Planas, Viader y Enrique Urteaga. Script, Birri and above-mentioned students. Narrator, Alfredo Daniel Carrio, Editor, Antonio Ripoll, Sound, Leopoldo Orlazi, Film stock, black and white 16mm film developed at Alex Laboratories. Shot in Santa Fe, Argentina.

(Second and more widely released version)

Tire dié (Argentina, 1959, 33 min.). Distributed by Argentina Sono Film. Produced by the Institute of Cinema of the National University of the Litoral. Produced, Scripted and Directed by the above-mentioned people. Voices, Francisco Petrone, Maria Rosa Gallo. Narrator, Guillermo Cervantes Luro. Assistant Director, Manuel Horacio Gimenez, Sound, Mario Fezia, Rerecording, Argentina Sono Film, Film stock, transferred to black and white 35mm. Shot in Santa Fe, Argentina. Awarded the following: Grand Prize for the Best Short Film. SODRE festival, Montevideo, Uruguay (1956); Grand Prize for the Special Jury Selection. 4th International Documentary and Experimental Film Festival of Montevideo, Uruguay (1956); Special Prize at the Educational Film Festival in the Province of Buenos Aires (1962).

Further Reading

Birri, Fernando, *La escuela documental de Santa Fe*, Santa Fe: Editorial Documento del Instituto de Cinematografía de la U.N.L, 1964.
———, *Pionero y peregrino*, Buenos Aires: Editorial Contrapunto, 1987.
Burton, Julianne, *Cinema and Social Change: Conversations with Filmmakers*, Austin: University of Texas Press, 1986.
———, *The Social Documentary in Latin America*, Pittsburgh: University of Pittsburgh Press, 1990.
———, "Tire dié," in *International Dictionary of Films and Filmmakers*, Vol. 1, edited by Sara, and Tom Pendergast, Detroit: St. James Press, 2000, 215–217.
Pick, Zuzana, *The New Latin American Cinema: A Continental Project*, Austin: University of Texas Press, 1993.
Sendros, Paraná, *Fernando Birri*, Buenos Aires: Centro Editor de America Latina con el Instituto Nacional de Cinematografia, 1994.

TITICUT FOLLIES

(US, Wiseman, 1967)

Filmed from April to June 1966, over twenty-nine days and culled from forty hours of material, *Titicut Follies* would lay the foundation for Frederick Wiseman's vision of documentary film, with its observational shooting style and exclusion of voice-over narration. Wiseman and co-director James Marshall captured the day-to-day routine of the patients, guards, and care staff at the Massachusetts Correctional Institution at Bridgewater. The facility, designed to hold both criminal offenders and nonthreatening psychiatric patients admitted for observation, was selected by Wiseman because of his familiarity with Bridgewater and its superintendent, Charles Gaughan, after visits made by the filmmaker as part of summer seminars during his time as a law instructor at Boston University during the late 1950s. An indictment of the practices captured on film at Bridgewater is never explicitly stated, but it is clear that the filmmakers take issue with the treatment of the patients.

Titicut Follies will likely be remembered as much for its content as the stories surrounding both its production and its troubled release. With his portrait of the patients at the MCI Bridgewater, first-time filmmaker Wiseman presented audiences with a controversial glimpse inside the state-funded facility and was met with both harsh criticism and praise. The film was banned in the Commonwealth of Massachusetts for twenty-four years for reasons pertaining to the issue of informed consent with regard to the patients and their appearance in the film and, secondarily, the right of the state to approve of the finished film. Commercial screenings did occur outside of the Commonwealth after several other state Supreme Courts refused to ban the film; *Titicut Follies*' first public showing occurred at the 1967 New York Film Festival. All screenings within Massachusetts during that period, however, were required to meet strict regulations related to the nature of the viewing audiences. Only students and professionals in fields related to the concerns of the film were permitted to view *Titicut Follies*, and the screenings were not open to the general public. Its first national television broadcast did not occur until 1993. As the only film ever censored in the United States for reasons other than national security or obscenity, the legacy of *Titicut Follies* and its status as a canonical nonfiction film is tied to these issues of censorship and documentary ethics.

From daily cell inspections that reveal the startling conditions of the facility to conversations between guards and patients that reveal the human side of Bridgewater (particularly senior correction guard Edward Pacheco who figures prominently throughout the film), the lives of the men at the institution are observed with a cool detachment rarely inflected by a humanist concern. That is not to suggest that *Titicut Follies* should be considered an attempt to objectively present life at the institution; the creative rendering of events at Bridgewater through Wiseman's editing confirms the constructed nature of the film's central narrative, thus fracturing any notion of a strictly observa-

Titicut Follies, inmates at Bridgewater State Hospital, documentary by Frederick Wiseman, 1967.
[*Courtesy of the Everett Collection*]

tional positioning. Sequences spotlighting specific patients seem designed to promote sympathy and identification with the men, a viewer position presumably shared by Wiseman.

The sequence for which *Titicut Follies* is best remembered is the most stylized of the film and illustrates Wiseman's subjective construction of the text. It involves the tubefeeding of an aged and starving patient and offers one of Wiseman's most direct attacks on the senior staff at Bridgewater. Repeated scans of the patient's body as the chief medical officer inserts a rubber tube into his nostril are cross-cut with images of a mortician prepping a corpse for embalming. The intensity of these inserts increases during the feeding until the corpse, dressed and placed behind the steel door of a morgue storage compartment, is positively identified as the force-fed man. Throughout *Titicut Follies*, Wiseman casts particular members of Bridgewater's senior staff in a suspect light while patients appear as victims; in this case, it is with the inclusion of footage clearly detailing the doctor's disregard for the patient as he carelessly inserts the feeding tube well beyond the safety threshold indicated by a white marker. The doctor, smoking a cigarette with its ash dangling over the patient's head, notices his error only after an assisting guard points it out to him. It is this type of parallel editing system that would be further developed in Wiseman's subsequent work and operates as a virtual commentary guiding the viewer through the narrative, absent in its conventional documentary form of voice-over commentary.

That James Marshall acted as director of photography while Wiseman handled the synch-sound recording equipment not only indicates the magnitude of the role Marshall played in the production, but also suggests the importance of sound in Wiseman's representation of life at Bridgewater. All through *Titicut Follies*, Wiseman bridges distinct segments of the film with a lapse in the synchronous soundtrack. The result not only suggests a temporal and spatial linearity of the presentation, but comments on the manic sonic environment of the facility. This privileging of the sonic space of the profilmic location greatly informs Wiseman's representation of reality.

Described by some as a film that created one set of social problems as it sought to alleviate another, the production of *Titicut Follies*, its exhibition, and its trials raise crucial issues about the relation of social documentary to its subjects and audiences (Anderson and Benson, 1991). As is the case with all of his films, Wiseman is the sole distributor of the film through his own company, Zipporah Films. In spite of the legal issues that marred the original release of *Titicut Follies* and restricted its audience for decades, the film remains a critical text with regards to issues of consent, participation, and representation within nonfiction film.

MICHAEL B. BAKER

See also **Wiseman, Frederick**

Titicut Follies (USA, Bridgewater Film Company, Inc., 1967, 84 min.). Distributed by Zipporah Films. Directed and produced by Frederick Wiseman. Co-directed and photographed by James Marshall. Editing by Frederick Wiseman. Associate editor, Alyne Model. Associate producer, David Eames.

Further Reading

Anderson, Carolyn, and Thomas W. Benson, *Documentary Dilemmas: Frederick Wiseman's Titicut Follies*, Carbondale: Southern Illinois University Press, 1991.

Armstrong, Dan, "Wiseman's Realm of Transgression: *Titicut Follies*, the Symbolic Father, and the Spectacle of Confinement," in *Cinema Journal*, 29, 1989.

Atkins, Thomas R. (ed.), *Frederick Wiseman*, New York: Monarch Press, 1976.

Ellsworth, Liz, *Frederick Wiseman: A Guide to References and Resources*, Boston: G. K. Hall, 1979.

Grant, Barry K., "Ethnography in the First Person: Frederick Wiseman's *Titicut Follies*," in *Documenting the Documentary: Close Readings of Documentary Film and Video*, edited by Barry Keith Grant, and Jeannette Sloniowski, Detroit: Wayne State University Press, 1998.

———, *Voyages of Discovery: The Cinema of Frederick Wiseman*, Urbana: University of Illinois Press, 1992.

Levin, G. Roy, *Documentary Explorations: 15 Interviews with Filmmakers*, New York: Doubleday, 1971.

Stevenson, Jack, "Interview with Frederick Wiseman," in *Pandemonium*, 3, 1989.

TO DIE IN MADRID

(France, Rossif, 1962)

On March 26, 1962, French producer Nicole Stéphane asked the Spanish government for permission to shoot in Spain some scenes needed for a TV documentary entitled *Espagne éternelle/Eternal Spain*, to be directed by the prestigious filmmaker Frédéric Rossif. The Francoist officials were uncertain and surprised, because the proposed script dealt with the most crude clichés about Spain: gypsies, flamenco music, bullfights, and Catholicism, for example. The production was supported by Marcelin Defourneaux, then cultural attaché to the French Embassy in Madrid and representative of Unifrance Film, who assured the administration that the image of contemporary Spain presented in

the film would be absolutely positive. Subsequently permission to film was granted, as was the unconditional cooperation of the local authorities involved in the five weeks of shooting.

Some months later, in an interview to the weekly magazine *Candide*, Rossif discussed the *Espagne éternelle* affair, stating that his intention was not to make a film on contemporary Spain, but only to find images to complement the archive footage he had selected for a full-length documentary on the Spanish civil war to be titled *Mourir à Madrid/To Die in Madrid*. Since the approach was to be anti-Franco, the images captured in 1962 Spain were clearly appointed to

To Die in Madrid, 1962.
[*Still courtesy of the British Film Institute*]

give the audience the impression that Franco's victory had been disastrous for Spain.

The film was premiered in Cannes during the Festival—but not *in* the Festival, due to its documentary condition—and received unanimous critical acclaim, mainly for its proloyalist, anti-Franco bias, but also for its technical skill in the editing of the great amount of old footage taken from various film archives around the world. The contemporary shots defined Rossif's message: the foggy, somber Castilian landscape, inhabited by long-suffering, impoverished peasants, was a symbol of Franco's victory and his subsequent reign of terror.

Nevertheless, some objections to the film were raised. Conservative Roman Catholics reacted angrily against the film for its attack on the right-wing side of the Spanish civil war. According to the traditionalist interpretation, the *Alzamiento* was a crusade against the enemies of Spain and the religion. But there was also criticism from the Left. The prominent Catalan anarchist and former minister in the days of the Popular Front, Frederica Montseny, accused Rossif's film of being communist propaganda that deliberately ignored the contribution of the Libertarian movement to the Revolution in Spain. In fact, this was partly true. Rossif centers its interpretation in the defense of Madrid, defining very well the enemy, that is, the "evil ones"—the Army, the Church, the Falange, the Italians, and the Germans—but is somewhat imprecise in the depiction of the "good" Republicans. The viewer learns little about the Republican ideology. One curious example is that the gigantic posters with the faces of Lenin and Stalin, which decorated the streets and places of Madrid during all the war years are never shown on screen. Spanish Republicans are seen only as innocent victims of savage bombardments and sadistic repression, through such events as the Guernica massacre, or the murder of García Lorca. On the other hand, the role of the International Brigades is overemphasized. Another objection was addressed to the "aestheticist" treatment of some episodes, heavily supported by a solemn (especially in the French soundtrack) spoken commentary. It is curious to note that Rossif's only concession to "impartiality" is his approbation of one of the classic myths of Francoist propaganda: the siege of the Toledo Alcázar.

The reaction of Spanish authorities to the critical and commercial success of *Mourir à Madrid* was a blend of impotence and anger. They were unable to forbid its release abroad, but did try, via diplomacy, to curb its reception in "friendly" countries, with some degree of success. The Spanish government also sponsored two full-length documentaries intended to refute Rossif's thesis. *Morir en España/ To Die in Spain* (1965, director, Mariano Ozores) made relatively imaginative use of some interesting archive shots, but *¿Por qué morir en Madrid?/Why To Die in Madrid?* (1966, director, Eduardo Manzanos) was considered ineffective, and the film was never released. The original *Mourir à Madrid* was premiered in Spain in May 1978.

RAFAEL DE ESPANA

See also **Rossif, Frédéric; Spanish Civil War**

Mourir à Madrid/To Die in Madrid (France, Rossif, 1962, 83 min.). An Ancinex production. Written and directed by Frédéric Rossif. Narrated by Madeleine Chapsal. Voices: Suzanne Flon, Germaine Montero, Roger Mollion, Pierre Vaneck, and Jean Vilar. English adaptation: Helen Scott, with the voices of John Gielgud, Irene Worth, William Hutt, and George Gonneau.

Further Reading

del Amo, Alfonso (ed.), *Catálogo general del cine de la Guerra Civil*, Madrid: Cátedra/Filmoteca Española, 1996, 637–639, 765–766.

Crusells, Magí, *La Guerra Civil española: cine y propaganda*, Barcelona: Ariel, 2003, 107–132.

Cuenca, Carlos Fernández, *La Guerra de España y el cine*, Madrid: Editora Nacional, vol I, 1972, 427–441.

de España, Rafael, "Images of the Spanish Civil War in Spanish Feature Films, 1939–1985," *Historical Journal of Film, Radio and Television*, 6, 2, 1986, 223–236.

Furhammar, Leif, and Folke Isaksson, *Politics and Film*, London: Studio Vista, 1971, 54–55.

Gubern, Román, 1936–1939. *La Guerra de España en la pantalla*, Madrid: Filmoteca Española, 1986, 132–134.

Rossif, Frédéric, and Madeleine Chapsal, *Mourir à Madrid*, Paris: Seghers, 1963.

TOKYO ORINPIKKU

(Tokyo Olympiad, 1965)

Tokyo Olympiad is generally recognized, along with Leni Reifenstahl's *Olympia* (1938), as one of the finest documentaries on the Olympics. The film was originally to be directed by Kurosawa Akira. In the course of preproduction, however, it became evident that Kurosawa desired an unprecedented degree of creative control that spilled out into the events themselves. He demanded, for example, the right to design and choreograph the Opening Ceremony himself in order to lend the event to cinematography. Kurosawa was summarily replaced by Ichikawa Kon, who was known both for his cinematic craftsmanship and also for reliably rescuing troubled films in mid-production. Ichikawa was also famous for his adaptations of previous texts, which also may have been a factor in his selection; unlike Kurosawa, he was not interested in tampering with the original text of the Olympics.

The year 1964 was a crucial time in Japanese history. The government was intent on using the Olympics to signal Japan's reemergence on the world stage after its devastating defeat in World War II. They had renewed their security relationship with the United States, and their economy was entering a phase of high growth. Tokyo, which had been leveled to dust during the war, was transformed into a bustling modern landscape of paved roads and a newly modernized environment, something Ichikawa gestures to at the beginning with images of prewar buildings being torn down with a wrecking ball. He also seems to inject the film with the faint stench of Japanese nationalism with stylized images of the rising sun, stunningly shot by the renown documentary cameraman Hayashida Shigeo.

The finished film, however, was roundly criticized by both the conservative government and the Communist Party, which we can probably take as a measure of Ichikawa's achievement. Before the film was even finished, it ran into severe problems with the government ministry that was overseeing the production. A preview was staged for Hirohito, and rumors flew in the popular media that the emperor was displeased. Numerous government officials publicly attacked Ichikawa, baffled by his aestheticization of the games and calling for a new version that was "record centric" (*kirokuchushin*) and not "artistic" (*geijutsuteki*). Ironically, a similar debate over the nature of documentary aesthetics took place in 1930s Japan and was resolved in favor of artfulness by the immensely popular reception of Reifenstahl's *Olympia*. Ichikawa basically prevailed and completed a 154-minute film that became the highest grossing film in Japanese history in 1965. The film has recently been restored to Ichikawa's original 169-minute cut. There are countless regionalized versions, however, as local distributors typically cut out what they felt was unimportant; for example, the initial U.S. version was thirty minutes of gold medal victories by American athletes.

It seems one cannot discuss the film without mentioning a slew of statistics that indicate its unusual scale: 164 cameramen, 100 cameras, 250 lenses, 57 sound recordists, 165,000 feet of audio tape, and 70 hours of film exposed. The film was made "under the sign of gigantism," as Jacques Demeure so aptly put it (Quandt et al.;315). Seen in today's era, when the Olympics are an exclusively televisual

Tokyo Olympiad, 1964.
[*Still courtesy of the British Film Institute*]

event, the film is truly a wonder to behold. Ichikawa shot in CinemaScope and stereo sound, with enough access and control to set his cameras where he wished and light scenes with the polish of his feature films. The director's eye for abstract pattern and spectacular splashes of color found ample material in the pageantry of the Olympics. Although he certainly knew he was expected to produce a document of national pride, Ichikawa managed to undercut the political nature of the games with his patent irony, a wry attention paid to the banal margins adjacent to the spectacle of Olympian feats of bodily strength, and an unusual emphasis on the athletes' pain and suffering in their quest for gold. For every predictable, if unforgettable, image of Olympic spectacle, there is a sequence so ambiguous or perplexing that it infuses the film with contradiction that simultaneously invites and frustrates interpretation. The film is often singled out to represent the best of Japanese documentary, but it is really quite anomalous. (Other Tokyo Olympics films by Noda Shinkichi and Kuroki Kazuo are far more typical, especially in their political charge.) Ichikawa's film is best seen as a great Olympics film, perhaps the last

great one now that we have entered the age of global live television, to which it stands in such striking and admirable contrast.

ABÉ MARK NORNES

Tokyo orinpikku (*Tokyo Olympiad*) (Japan, 1965) Produced by Taguchi Suketaru. Directed by Ichikawa Kon. Written by Ichikawa Kon, Shirasaka Yoshio, Tanikawa Shuntaro, Wada Natto. Cinematography by Miyagawa Kazuo, Murata Shigeo, Nagano Shigeichi, Nakamura Kenji, Tanaka Tadashi. Music by Mayuzumi Toshiro. Sound Recording by Inoue Toshihiko. Editing by Ehara Yoshio, Nakashizu Tatsuji. Art Direction by Kamekura Yusaku. Narration (Japanese version) by Mikuni Ichiro.

Further Reading

Cazdyn, Eric, A. M. Nornes, James Quant, Catherine Russell, and Mitsuhiro Yoshimoto, "*Tokyo Olympiad:* A Symposium," in *Ichikawa Kon*, edited by James Quant, Toronto: Cinemateque Ontario, 2001, 315–336. Reprinted as liner notes for Criterion Collection's DVD of *Tokyo Olympiad*, 2002.

Vaughn, Dai, "Tokyo versus Berlin," in *Documentary: Twelve Essays*, Berkeley: University of California Press, 1999, 90–110.

TOSCANO, SALVADOR

Toscano's career began at the end of nineteenth century, shortly after Lumière's representatives brought the cinematograph to Mexico, and ended around 1920, when Hollywood fiction films practically put an end to the commercial exhibition of documentaries. Unfortunately, most of Toscano's works have not survived as they were originally edited—silent and with titles—but many fragments were reedited in *Memorias de un mexicano* (Carmen Toscano, 1950), a fiction film made by his daughter.

In his first years as a filmmaker, Toscano shot city monuments, landscapes, theater numbers, popular festivals, parades, bull fights, and the results of catastrophic events such as floods and earthquakes. Thematically similar to their French models, most of these documentaries were only a few minutes long and composed of conservative shots, with no camera movement or outstanding emplace-

ments. They simply recorded, from a fixed point of view, selected events from reality. Toscano, like other filmmakers and the Mexican public in general at that time, shared the assumption that documentaries had an informative or recreational purpose similar to that of the press. In any case, they satisfied communicative needs in an almost totally illiterate country.

By 1906, the development of film narrative allowed Toscano to make longer and more complex films, such as *Fiestas presidenciales en Mérida* (1906), *Inauguración del tráfico internacional en el istmo de Tehuantepec* (1907), and his first feature, *Fiestas del centenario de la Independencia* (1910). Their character was again journalistic, but at the same time they were in a sense propaganda films, because they invariably presented a fairly positive image of dictator Porfirio Díaz and the material achievements of his administration. As far as we can see in the surviving fragments, the style of these films was still based on a very discreet use of the camera, although there is some innovation in shots.

Fiestas del centenario de la Independencia, which registered the one-month celebrations held to commemorate the centenary of the beginning of the war of independence against Spain, was a popular film, but its success was far surpassed by the 1911 documentaries, which showed episodes related to Francisco I. Madero's military rebellion against President Díaz. Toscano's main work about that event was *La toma de Ciudad Juárez y el viaje del héroe de la revolución don Francisco I. Madero* (1911), a long film that combined information and propaganda. Until then, the image of Porfirio Díaz had been emphasized in documentaries about his trips and the high points of his government. Now, there was also a trip, but in this case it was enhanced by a much more important element for the construction of a charismatic image—that of military victory.

Madero defeated Díaz and became the new president of the country, but was attacked and put to death by his own army. After that, there was another revolution, which lasted for about five years. Many documentary makers of this period showed Pancho Villa, Álvaro Obregón, Venustiano Carranza, Emiliano Zapata, or some other *caudillo* defeating their enemies in battles or cities under siege. These films almost always presented the perspective of the winner and ended with the victory of one group, as in Toscano's *Historia completa de la revolución de 1910 a 1915* (1915). They were propaganda films intentionally covered up with the objective aura of informative reportage: partial victories were presented as definite, local processes as national, and so on. The effect produced by their sensational contents guaranteed their success, although their form was still conservative. They were structured in chronological order, their "clear" shots aimed basically at fulfilling the minimum requirements needed to make the events represented intelligible for any public. In a sense, this lack of aesthetic or narrative risks is what characterizes Toscano's style and that of most Mexican revolution documentary makers. Another central characteristic is that almost none of them resorted to using recreated scenes, studio shots, or other inauthentic documentary material.

Toscano went beyond combining information and propaganda, however. In his long career as a filmmaker, he collected scenes of different political regimes, and this in turn became the source of a panoramic historical film first entitled *Historia de la revolución de 1910 a 1920* (1920), and finally, with the addition of excerpts filmed by other documentary makers, *Historia completa de la revolución mexicana, 1900-1927* (1927). In this last 35-reel long film, there were no value judgments about the actions of the protagonists or about the traumatic social process that occurred during that period. That is, the film gave equal legitimacy to all its main characters, both on the side of the government and of the rebels. Other Mexican documentary makers, like Jesús H. Abitia, also intended to give an encompassing, historical overview of the same period, but their pictures inevitably revealed their sympathies for one *caudillo* or another. Only Toscano, who never fully embraced a political cause, managed to give a detached version of that turbulent episode.

The Mexican revolution ended in 1917. That same year, a crucial transformation of documentaries occurred when war films came to an end. Filmmakers became involved with the new government and redirected their production. Toscano was commissioned to film *Las riquezas de Quintana Roo* (1917) so as to promote inversion in, and migration to, that abandoned region; a few years later, he was again contacted to make the official film of the festivals held to commemorate the centenary of the consummation of independence: *Las fiestas del centenario* (1921). Although this was in fact his last documentary, he never stopped adding scenes, filmed by others, to his great work-in-progress, *Historia de la revolución mexicana.*

ÁNGEL MIQUEL

See also **Mexico**

Biography

Born in Guadalajara, Jalisco, Mexico, March 24, 1872. Graduated as an engineer from Universidad Nacional de México, 1897. Up to 1921, combined his career with filmmaking and exhibition; afterwards, worked mainly in highway construction. Collected films, stereographic photographs, and early film posters which now form part of one of Mexico's main private historical archives. Died April 14, 1947 in Mexico City.

Selected Films

1906 *Fiestas presidenciales en Mérida*
1907 *Inauguración del tráfico internacional en el istmo de Tehuantepe*
1910 *Fiestas del centenario de la Independencia*
1911 *La toma de Ciudad Juárez y el viaje del héroe de la revolución don Francisco I. Madero*
1915 *Historia completa de la revolución de 1910 a 1915*
1920 *Historia de la revolución de 1910 a 1920*
1921 *Las fiestas del centenario*
1927 *Historia completa de la revolución mexicana, 1900-1927*

Further Reading

De los Reyes, Aurelio, *Vivir de sueños*, vol. I of *Cine y sociedad en México 1896-1930*, Mexico City: UNAM, 1983.

Miquel, Ángel, *Salvador Toscano*, Mexico City: Filmoteca de la UNAM, Universidad de Guadalajara, Universidad Veracruzana, Secretaría de Cultura del Estado de Puebla, 1997.

Ramírez, Gabriel, *Crónica del cine mudo mexicano*, Mexico City: Cineteca Nacional, 1989.

Toscano, Carmen, *Memorias de un mexicano*, Mexico City: Fundación Carmen Toscano, 1996.

Vaidovits, Guillermo, *El cine mudo en Guadalajara*, Guadalajara: Universidad de Guadalajara, 1989.

TRADE UNIONS AND LABOUR/ WORKERS MOVEMENTS

Workers and their workplaces have been subjects of fascination to filmmakers since the very first "movie," the Lumière brothers' *La sortie des usines Lumière/Workers Leaving the Factory* (1895), and the evolution of their representation affords a useful insight to the disparate uses and abuses of documentary film. Those Lumière images were necessarily silent, and it was only with the emergence of sound was there any possibility that the worker's voice would form a persuasive part of the filmmaker's art. Before that, the visual possibilities of the workplace continued to inspire cinematographic development, as in the classic 1906 film made in Bermondsey, south London, *A Visit to the Peek Frean and Co.'s Biscuit Works*, with its compelling scenes of men and boys cutting and baking biscuits and women packing them. At thirty-two minutes, this is a substantial piece of work for its time, with most documentary film then being shot as shorts and packaged as newsreel.

In a more radicalised America, a working-class film movement flourished in the silent era, between 1907 and 1930, and worker filmmakers repeatedly clashed with censors, cinema owners, and federal agencies over the images and perspectives people should be allowed to see. Movies from *A Martyr to His Cause* (1911) to *The Gastonia Textile Strike* (1929) depicted a unified working class using strikes, unions, and socialism to transform a nation. J. Edgar Hoover considered these class-conscious productions so dangerous that he assigned secret agents to spy on worker filmmakers, but it was the commercial clout of Hollywood that finally put an end to this movement.

In Europe, what filmmakers chose to film in the early years reflects contemporary priorities and national perspectives, with Britain concentrating on troop movements to and from the Boer War, and events featuring the Royal family, while French filmmakers were more concerned with Parisian landmarks and artistic celebrities, such as Colette and Gide, Renoir and Rodin. The confluence of those two cultures, with the establishment of British Pathé in 1902 and their bi-weekly newsreel by 1910, had a powerful impact on defining public views, not least of the evolving labour movement. Strong footage of police bearing down on striking dockers and railway workers in 1911 was entitled: *Civil War: Liverpool and London under Mob Law*, and that threatening image of organised labour persisted in British film coverage up to the 1984 miners' strike, when Mrs. Thatcher memorably cast men fighting for their livelihood as "the enemy within."

In that year, television coverage of this bitter dispute tended to reflect the Tory government views of this as a last stand of entrenched trade unionism against the forces of corporate modernisation. Footage was routinely shot from behind police lines, favouring the minority of miners still trying to work, and focusing on violence perpetrated by the flying pickets. Yet BBC News was surprised to report that: "Anger was turned against the media and our camera was sent flying" (BBC TV News March 12, 1984). It was only some weeks into the dispute, when a documentary unit from the BBC's Community Programme Unit access series *Open Space* was sent to cover the story from the miners' support groups' perspective, that the union side was articulated and the partiality of news cover called into question. Their filming came to a head at the a British Steel coking plant at the village of Orgreave in South Yorkshire on June 14, 1984, when mounted riot police charged a crowd of miners, provoking a violent battle. The resultant furore about news bias resulted in a subtle shift of news coverage back toward the middle ground it always claimed. The miners were proved right when most pits were closed and more than 95 percent of them lost their jobs. *The Battle of Orgreave* entered into folk history, being revisited as a documentary of that name by the same producer, Yvette Vanson, for Channel 4 in 1986, and restaged for a drama documentary, also for Channel 4, by Mike Figgis in 2001. Both give pride of place to the spoken memories of miners who were there.

That voice was not always to be heard, even though the mines afforded documentarists some of the most elemental images for the nobility of work, a key theme during the heyday of the 1930s. In 1935, Grierson's Film Unit at the General Post Office made an intriguing short film called *Coalface*, which the uncredited Alberto Cavalcanti claims as his own conception and edit, and as "an experiment for *Night Mail*" (Aitken, 1998). Drawing on sequences shot by Watt, Jennings, and Flaherty, it uses montage and effects the first marriage of W. H. Auden's poetry and Benjamin Britten's music. They express the romantic nature of the piece:

> O lurcher-loving collier, black as night,Follow your love across the smokeless hill.

Arguably the best sequence is one where the miners march to work past the camera, stating their names and jobs, orchestrated with Britten's music. It gives us a brief glimpse of the voices from whom today's audience would want to hear more, but that was not the dominant view of the time, nor of those whose money commissioned the films. In the case of *Coalface*, it was not even clear whose objectives the film served. *Sight and Sound* critic Anthony Vesselo called it "incoherent in conception and ineffectual in execution," and expressed a preference for *The Mine*, a 1936 two-reeler made by Gaumont-British with the Safety in Mines Research Board, one of several such no-nonsense documentaries (*Sight and Sound* No. 18, 1936). In 1937, John

Grierson was still able to write: "The thought of making work an honoured theme, and a workman, of whatever kind, an honourable figure, is still liable to the charge of subversion" (Grierson, 1979).

An earlier attempt by workers to grasp some alternative control of the news agenda had faltered after just three editions of the *Workers' Topical News*. These leftwing newsreels, issued by the Federation of Workers' Film Societies, ironically focus their ire on the then Labour Government of Ramsay MacDonald. Issue No 1 features Unemployment Day on March 6, 1930, a march from Tower Hill to the Mansion House, and the Workers' International Food Kitchen. Issue No. 2 in May 1930 covers the National Hunger March, with 900 men from all over Britain marching on London. Their banners speak eloquently for the silent sea of cloth caps: one reading "UNDER-CLAD, UNDERFED, UNDER THE LABOUR GOVERNMENT" leads the procession. The banners speak of international solidarity with Irish and Indian freedom fighters, and with the communists of Soviet Russia. In 1933, the Workers' Film and Photo League took on the making of "News-reels from the working-class point of view," documenting the hunger marches including Ellen Wilkinson leading the Jarrow Crusaders, the International Anti-Fascist Sports League in Paris, the Wrexham colliery disaster and opposition to the British Union of Fascists' March through Cable Street in London's East End. The outbreak of war put an end to this idealistic strain of socialist movie-making. It would be thirty years until the same kind of collective spirit took to the London streets again and the opportunity to express such passion in film was made available to organised labour in Britain.

Fellow workers of the world fared no better in getting their voices heard. Even in Soviet Russia, where film was the medium of choice for the politburo to commend its people to ever more heroic acts of communal toil, film used workers as emblems, not individuals. All the great public engineering works were lovingly recorded on film, with the armies of volunteer communist youth, the Komsomol, braving all weathers in their canvas cities to realise these epic dreams, but the microphones (when they arrived) were reserved for the encouragements of their political leaders. Even the generally well-regarded *Turksib*, Victor Turin's 1929 film about the building of the Trans-Siberian Railroad branch line into Turkistan, managed to evade both the personal and the political. At the time, both Grierson and Paul

Rotha commended it, Rotha writing originally in 1935 (Rotha, 1966):

> Turin's Turksib alone defined the line of Soviet approach to pure documentary . . . Turksib marked the beginning of a new documentary method and has probably had more influence on later developments than any other picture.

Ian Aitken has argued that this influence was greater on Grierson than *Battleship Potemkin*, with which his own film about the herring fleet, *Drifters*, was premiered at a meeting of the London Film Society in 1929 (Aitken, 1998). Agreeing, Brian Winston has suggested that this was because both filmmakers, in their differently didactic societies, were equally keen to evade the political, preferring to preserve their aesthetic freedom at all costs, "running away from social meaning," as he puts it, echoing Rotha (Winston, 1995).

In the United States, Pare Lorentz fills a similar role to Grierson, championing the big projects of the New Deal Democrats through films like *The Plow That Broke the Plains* (1936) and *The River* (1937). But while the canvas of the first film is the same as that of the Farm Security Association project that sponsored Walker Evans's famous Dust Bowl photographs, the humanity of those photographs is missing, featuring great landscapes with tractors more than people, and an overly rhetorical commentary. The dust storms that are displacing 50,000 souls a month are written off as an act of God: "The sun and wind wrote the most tragic chapter in American agriculture," and the faceless poor are uncomplainingly resettled on smallholdings on the edge of industrial cities. A more critical, political script was suggested by the film's cinematographers, Leo Hurwitz and Paul Strand, but rejected in favour of Lorentz's. His script for *The River* is more robust in its criticism of poor land management leading to the sorry condition of the Mississippi:

> We've planted and ploughed with no regard for the future. And four million tons of topsoil, four million tons of our most valuable natural resource, have been washed into the Gulf of Mexico every year. . . . Today, two out of five farmers in the valley are tenant farmers, ten per cent of them sharecroppers living in a state of squalor unknown to the poorest peasant in Europe.

We do see some examples of this dirt and poverty, but we don't hear from them. We learn that, thanks to the film's sponsors, the Tennessee Valley Authority, "we have the power to put it together again." This New Deal optimism is very American, and later infuses Joris Ivens's *The Power and the Land* (1940), made to promote the Rural Electrification Administration. At least this features a classic farm family, the Parkinsons, exploring their working lives in loving detail and charting the benefits they receive from introducing electricity, but still without granting them the benefit of speech.

Joris Ivens was a Dutchman who had made such a hit with his early, impressionist films *De Brug/The Bridge* (1928) and *Regan/The Rain* (1929), and then making a two-hour film for the twenty-fifth anniversary of the Dutch Building Workers' Union—*Wij Bouwen/We Are Building* (1929)—that he was the first Western filmmaker to be invited to make a film in the Soviet Union. *Pesn o Gorojach/Komsomol or Song of Heroes* (1931) is about a band of young communist workers building a blast furnace at Magnitogorsk in the Urals. He builds the story round one character, Afanaseyev, who signs on for work at the building site; and he also built the set of the employment office in a Moscow studio and reenacted the scene, allowing the use of lip synchronisation. On return from Russia, Ivens was invited to Belgium to make a film about the revolutionary miners' strike that had taken place in the Borinage in 1932. Winning the trust of the miners and involving them in reenactment, filming by oil-light in their homes without electricity and hiding from the police, who had been alerted by the mine management, Ivens arrived at a new level of political engagement in *Misére au Borinage/Borinage* (1933). His Belgian co-director, Henri Storck, wrote (Storck, 1979):

> Our film did not lie, and nor did it exaggerate. From that reality we chose the aspects with the most meaning. Above all, we wanted to shout our indignation by using the starkest images possible, images of an abominable reality we had seen and lived through with the miners and their families.

Returning to the Netherlands, and to a pet project started with his building union chums on the *Zuiderzee* in 1930, Ivens completed his film on reclaiming the sea to make a new Holland in *Nieuwe Gronden/New Earth* in 1934. This effective, dynamic story of an engineering triumph calls to mind the Soviet collectivist documentary more than the human saga of *Borinage*. The human face comes back into dramatic focus in Ivens's brave Spanish War epic, *Spanish Earth* (1937), Ivens's first American-produced, English-language film, with a commentary written and read by Ernest Hemingway:

> This Spanish earth is dry and hard—and the faces of the men that work this land are hard and dry from the sun . . .

> This is the true face of men going into action. It is a little different from any other face that you will see . . . . Men cannot act before the camera in the presence of death.

Even in the heat of battle, shots are carefully framed and exposed, often making beautiful use of the harsh contrasts in light and landscape. The film intercuts extraordinary footage of the bombardment of Madrid and battles for control of the vital Valencia supply road with a village near the front line, where Republican peasants are fighting to irrigate the land and produce food for the people. This is heroic work in a common cause, and the character of one young villager, Julian, who fights and comes home on leave, unites the two elements. There is some synch-dialogue, not least from the President of the Republic:

> We, the people of Spain, obtained the land and the right to cultivate it by democratic elections—but fascist landlords try to take our land away. Now we are forced to fight for the defence of the Spanish earth.

While the civil war consumed Spain, attracting some of the most politically active men and women of their generation, gentler advances were taking place in Britain. It is perhaps telling that the introduction of direct speech, recorded on location— what Grierson called "the greatest advance of all" (Aitken, 1998)—was accorded to people more dependent, less heroic than soldiers, miners or railroad men. Both released in 1935, Arthur Elton's *Workers and Jobs* featured the unemployed men and officials of Poplar Labour Exchange, and Edgar Anstey's *Housing Problems* showed men and women wanting to escape London slums. Their personal pleas, however poorly performed and recorded, capture a moment when working people were beginning to have a say in society, which, through the crucible of World War II, would eventually emerge as the landslide Labour government of 1945 with the attendant benefits of the welfare state.

Before that, socialist ideas had begun to emerge in response to the Depression, engaging workers in self-help projects, and filmmakers were keen to record these. Donald Alexander's *Eastern Valley* (1937), its opening caption tells us, is "The story of a social experiment in one of the mining valleys of South Wales." It sets the scene in a once rural valley built over by mine workings and long streets of poor housing that are now home to mass unemployment. The film charts the cooperative society that has sprung up, employing men on a farm, in food distribution and allied trades, that provide for their needs and keep them proudly occupied. It doesn't oversell the scheme's benefits,

and an older miner delivers this summary in the co-op shop:

> I reckon what you get out of it doesn't come to much. The main point is: you have an interest in it, and you're keeping fit for a job that may come along, and you're helping others . . . There's a lot of mistakes, but we are showing this can be done.

Ruby Grierson made two films for the National Council of Social Service, about their grants and work for helping rebuild disadvantaged communities. The first, *Today and Tomorrow* (1936), details various initiatives in Villages, Distressed Areas, Land Settlement, New Housing Estates, and Youth Movements. A miner, a blacksmith, and a lorry-driver are all "brought to the camera and the microphone," but so are a list of establishment names, including a halting and embarrassing performance by the Duke of Kent. The best of them is Sir William Deedes, who manages to find the right words to describe the community centres that the NCSS are helping build:

> These centres are not just buildings. They are the hub of a small universe, the heart and the brain of the community, a visible expression of a democracy in action; in a word—a new England in the making.

Some of this material was fleshed out the following year in a film produced by Paul Rotha for theatrical distribution, *Today We Live*. This intercuts two narratives: an unemployed Rhondda miner gets up a group to build an occupational social centre, and a Gloucestershire village woman raises the interest to turn a disused barn into a village hall. The empowerment that is being promoted is apparent in the roles the people play in the film, including the airing of dissenting opinions. The payoff commentary is equally phlegmatic:

> Social services cannot do everything. There are fundamental problems that strike at the very root of our existence. Only by working together, with unsparing energy, can we hope to solve them.

This is quietly radical film, inadvertently part of a process that was equipping the British people with the communal spirit for war. In the United States, Willard Van Dyke, the young cameraman who had contributed the cotton sequences to *The River*, was also building a reputation for himself as a social documentarian, working for agency sponsors. *The City* (1939) was commissioned by the American Institute of Planners, who had professional answers to the questions the film posed about the slums. *Valley Town* was made the next year for the Sloan Foundation and announces at the start: "The people in this are not actors. They are the men and women of an American town." They do, however, act for Van Dyke's camera, creating an opera of depression in this steel town, where a new rolling mill has thrown 3,000 out of work. The anti-hero narrator is the Mayor, walking home through this decaying town to a miserable wife who sings a song of longing for a place "far away from here." The chorus of unemployed watch silently as the smokestacks of their former workplace are felled. The faces are effective, but the commentary's rhetorical question—"Why should these men be thrown away as if they were obsolete, as if they were broken machines?"—remains unanswered.

In later life, Willard Van Dyke said that *Valley Town* is "more my film than any other," (Rothschild, 1980) and regrets that he could not return to making social documentaries again. Like documentarists on both sides of the Atlantic, he unashamedly turned to propaganda during the War, but prevailing conditions in the 1950s, particularly with McCarthy, made taking up critical filmmaking again impossible. "For a long time I prostituted, or forgot, the qualities I had as an artist" (Rothschild, 1980). There are those who argue that it was precisely the qualities of the artist that had short-changed the most needy, proletarian subjects of documentary, aestheticising their pain and romanticising their problems. It was only with the development of television as the prime documentary vehicle, and the reemergence of liberal thinking in the postwar period, that documentary featuring the working viewpoint got its second wind. This tended to take a campaigning journalistic, rather than an artistic, approach, archetypally in the CBS series *See It Now* (1951–1958), produced by Fred Friendly and fronted by Ed Murrow, and most famous for helping bring down Senator Joseph P. McCarthy.

The CBS Reports special Ed Murrow presented from a Florida field was one such piece. *Harvest of Shame* (1960) followed the migrant trails up through the United States, where near-destitute families took piece work for minimal rates, living in appalling conditions. It starts with the early morning market for the day's field work.

> These are citizens of the United States in 1960 . . . . This is the way that people that harvest the food for the best fed people in the world get hired . . . . We used to own our slaves. Now we just rent them.

The film caused a scandal as families revealed the conditions of their lives, at work on the road, and in their winter quarters in Belle Glade, Florida. A BBC film crew returned twenty-eight years later, for *Child Slaves* (1989), a documentary about the industrialisation of child labour around the world. The only significant difference is that this was filmed in colour. There had been new federal legislation on safety and welfare, but children still followed their families into the fields and trekked up the migrant trails for much of the year, at cost to their health and education. Pay rates were relatively worse than in 1960, in part kept down by the influx of migrants from Salvador, Guatemala, and Haiti. Belle Glade had meanwhile acquired one of the highest rates of HIV infection in the country. The harvest was the same, the shame somewhat dissipated. Ed Murrow went on to head President John F. Kennedy's U.S. Information Agency in 1961, and as such tried, unsuccessfully, to suppress that year's BBC's repeat broadcast of *Harvest of Shame*.

In Britain, the Manchester-based regional ITV broadcaster Granada was the home to the longest-running documentary current affairs strand, *World in Action*. Between 1963 and 1998, this series not only produced some of the most consistently hard-hitting journalism but made many films that reflected the true voices and interests of working people. Among a roster of filmmaking talent too long to list, there are names such as Michael Grigsby, whose quiet style typically allowed airtime to people not naturally given to speak for themselves, such as the lowly paid agricultural workers in *Working the Land* (1976). Grigsby says (Petley, 1997):

> It is important that one really tries to let people be what they are, and to come across in the way they want to come across. People are perfectly capable of talking in their own terms and we should allow them to do so.

At the BBC, the most radical opening occurred rather improbably when BBC-2's *Late Night Line-Up* was casting around for a way of introducing the 1972 Autumn programme schedules. In the event they went down to the nearby Guinness factory in Park Royal to seek the workers' views. They were taken aback to be treated to a sustained critique of BBC attitudes, elitist programmes, and class assumptions. This so affronted the liberal sensibilities of some quite radical programme-makers that they managed to secure funding for a new Community Programme Unit. This was to enshrine the spirit of access television for the next twenty-five years, a place to which people who felt their ideas and experience were being ignored elsewhere could turn to make original programmes. Among many claims on their limited airtime and resources were trade unions, largely ignored elsewhere except as news-making strikers. Early in the first series, *Open Door, Tribunal* (1974) helped one group of wronged workers to reenact the industrial relations tribunal in which they had triumphed against established odds. In another, *Fit as a Fiddle* (1980) the Trade Union Research Unit at the workers' Ruskin College, Oxford explored three cases of fatal industrial disease affecting different workplaces. Flying in the face of a then rigorous demand that BBC programmes should be balanced and impartial, these low budget documentaries were avowedly partial and effectively made under the editorial control of their subjects.

During the 1980s, this series morphed into *Open Space* and continued to offer trade unionists and other activists a platform. Often at that time, these were from industries such as coal mining that were fighting last-ditch stands against their ultimate demise, from railway engineering workers and lighthouse keepers, to steelworkers and shipwrights. In the late 1960s and 1970s, a film and video workshop movement in Britain had also given expression to a range of such views. The Amber Film Collective, founded in the northeast of England in 1969, is one that survived, making a string of powerful films about working lives. Murray Martin's *Launch* (1973), about the construction and launch of a tanker at the Wallsend shipyards, follows in the honourable tradition of documenting ships and shipbuilding that stretches back to films like Paul Rotha's *Shipyard* (1935). Martin's *Tyne Lives* (1979) more discursively reflects on the gathering threats to their way of life, giving considerable time to an articulate shop steward, Jim Murray:

> Here on Tyneside we have the closures [of shipyards, mines, &c.] . . . . Unless we have a strong trade union movement for socialist ideals, we can't solve people's everyday problems—environment, education and health . . . I always find it ironic when people talk about unions being powerful and strong, whereas, during the Scotswood campaign, I felt impotent.

In many other parts of the world, workers' movements and trade unions were filmed in bitter confrontation with increasingly remote corporate powers. Barbara Kopple's *Harlan County, U.S.A.* (1976) is a particularly fine example of a Kentucky mineworkers' long fight for union recognition in the face of increasingly violent intimidation. It reflects the plastic virtues of lighter cameras, faster stock, and the willingness of filmmakers to spend long, uncomfortable periods with their subjects capturing everyday life as it happens.

Latin America was in political foment and filmmaking exploded there between the 1960s and the 1980s, with a cornucopia from auteurist filmmakers to indigenous video groups.

Each developing nation was making its own myths from its own struggles. In Colombia, Marta Rodriguez and Jorge Silva spent six years painstakingly documenting the life of the Castañeda family as the parents and their twelve children toil in the mud and toxin-belching kiln as *Brickmakers* (1972). In the Honduran *Elvia: The Fight for Land and Liberty* (1988), Rick Tejada Flores and Laura Rodriguez tell the story of the epic fight of one woman to enforce an agrarian law reform enacted back in 1972, in the face of external U.S. commercial and aid pressures. And in Brazil, one story alone—the murder of the Amazon Rubbertappers' union president by the son of a landowner—spawned several documentaries, including English filmmaker Adrian Cowell's *The Killing of Chico Mendes* (1990) and Raquel Couto and Edilson Martins's *Chico Mendes* (1994).

Since the early 1990s, digital technology has made cameras and editing available to a much wider constituency, and British television for one has seized the opportunity to make more personal and less expensive documentaries. These rarely feature issues or group perspectives. That field has been left to a new breed of video collective that has grown around the environmental and antiglobalisation movements. Operating on a shoestring, few survive their first burst of enthusiasm. Exceptionally, *Undercurrents* celebrated its tenth anniversary in 2004, producing "alternative news" and documentary reports for distribution on tape and, latterly, online. By often being at the heart of action, both nationally and internationally, *Undercurrents* has frequently shot exclusive footage that has earned the occasional showing on terrestrial television, and they retain a central organising and training role in the video activist movement.

As documentary filmmakers across the developing world have found—from Iraq to India, Nigeria to the Philippines—the global market that supplies new technology has also imported the transnational television product that makes it hard for indigenous documentary to compete with. The commodification of the form may have momentarily helped revive the documentary as a theatrical form in the United States and United Kingdom, but it has also displaced it from its poll position at the heart of British television. Just as trade unions have lost jobs and power, so the workers' voice and collective strength has given way to individual aspiration and so-called "reality television." As

Hollywood and Hoover managed to defeat the American workers' film movement in 1930, Sky and what Francis Fukiyama infamously hailed as "the end of history" have globalised a mass media and rid it of mass movements.

PETER LEE-WRIGHT

See also **Bridge, The**; **Grierson, John**; **Ivens, Joris**; **Lorentz, Pare**; ***Plow That Broke the Plains, The***; ***Rain, The; River, The;*** **Turin, Victor**; ***Turksib***

Further Reading

Aitken, Ian (ed.), *The Documentary Film Movement*, Edinburgh: Edinburgh University Press, 1998.
Burton, Julianne (ed.), *Cinema and Social Change in Latin America: Conversations with Filmmakers*, Austin: University of Texas Press, 1986.
———, *The Social Documentary in Latin American Cinema*, Pittsburgh: Pittsburgh University Press, 1990.
Delmar, Rosalind, *Joris Ivens: 50 Years of film-making*, London: BFI, 1979.
Dickinson, Margaret, *Rogue Reels: Oppositional Film in Britain 1945-90*, London: BFI, 1999.
Grierson, John, *Grierson on Documentary*, edited by Forsyth Hardy, London: Faber, 1979.
Johnson, Randal, and Stam, Robert, *Brazilian Cinema*, Columbia University Press, 1995.
Lee-Wright, Peter, *Child Slaves*, London: Earthscan, 1990.
Low, Rachel, *The History of the British Film 1929–39: Documentary and Educational Films of the 1930s*, London: Allen & Unwin, 1979.
Petley, Julian, "Free Cinema—Mike Grigsby," *Monthly Film Bulletin*, London, June 1987.
Rabinowitz, Paula, *They Must Be Represented: The Politics of Documentary*, London: Verso, 1994.
Ross, Steven J., *Working-Class Hollywood: Silent Film and the Shaping of Class in America*, Princeton: Princeton University Press, 1998.
Rotha, Paul, *Documentary Film*, 3rd edition, London: Faber, 1966.
Storck, Henri, *Joris Ivens, 50 ans de cinéma*, Paris: Jean-Loup Passek, 1979.
Winston, Brian, *Claiming the Real: The Documentary Film Revisited*, London: BFI 1995.

TRANSPORT FILMS

See **British Transport Films**

TRINH T. MINH-HA

The filmmaker, writer, composer, and cultural critic Trinh T. Minh-ha radically redefines cinematic conventions through films that attempt to challenge the structures of oppression and domination in commercial cinema and in Western society as a whole. A key figure among contemporary postcolonialist feminists, Trinh uses innovative forms such as poetic language, disruptions of linear time, negative space and silences, multiple voices, repetition and recontextuality, and cultural repositioning in her films and writing to critique patriarchal fixed meanings and notions of Otherness.

Trinh has been influenced by the work of influential postmodern thinkers including Jacques Derrida, Michel Foucault, Roland Barthes, Jean-François Lyotard, and Hélène Cixous. Like them, Trinh questions the viability of scientific objectivity and linguistic certainty. Trinh's work also shares the commitment to reclaiming marginalized subjectivities with feminists such as Gloria Anzaldua and

TRINH T. MINH-HA

Audre Lorde. A filmmaker of the Asian diaspora, Trinh is part of an intellectual movement of women of color whose work has been particularly affected by the shift from colonialism to a global capitalist economy, which has fostered migrations, the dominance of Western mass media, and the commodification of "native" cultures. Trinh has written extensively about cinematic theory, and her films serve to put those theories into practice. She has also gone to great lengths to share her own "readings" of her films through numerous interviews and uessays.

Trinh's films aim at deliberately blurring the boundaries of genre. Her documentaries such as *Reassemblage* (1982) on Senegal, *Naked Spaces–Living Is Round* (1985) on rural West Africa, *Surname Viet Given Name Nam* (1989) on Vietnamese female subjectivity, *Shoot for the Contents* (1991) on culture and politics in China, and *The Fourth Dimension* (2001), a digital video on Japanese culture, all incorporate narrative and poetic language, carefully manipulated visuals, and experimental sounds and music. Moreover, her films use nonlinear structure, silences, abrupt jump cuts, repetition of images and sounds, and unsynched rhythms. She also uses almost random panning to, in her words, avoid moving from one captured object to another, and to expose the limits of a camera eye that purports to present the viewer with a unified, "objective" package. In all her films, Trinh repeats diverse images and sounds with slight changes in an effort to displace viewers and to avoid the certainty and closure of traditional documentaries.

Trinh questions the motives and methods of commercial filmmaking through her own departures from mainstream conventions, which serve to foreground and interrogate these practices. For example, instead of speaking for or speaking about her subjects, Trinh describes her position as "speaking nearby." None of her works use a traditional, objective, male voice-over concerned with informing spectators about "other" cultures. An example of her method is provided by *Reassemblage*, a montage of images and sounds of the everyday life of women and children in Senegal. This film features Trinh's own voice, which, according to interviewer Berenice Reynaud, proves "unsettling," since the narrative is "unmistakably feminine, unmistakably foreign, hesitant yet resolute, ironical yet poetic" (Trinh Minh-ha, 1999). *Naked Spaces*, on life in Senegal, Mauritania, Mali, Burkina Faso, Benin, and Togo, also departs from the omniscient voice-over with three female narrators from different yet nonconflicting stances.

Trinh's departure from traditional documentary practice is most evident in *Surname Viet Given Name Nam*. The film includes staged reenactments of interviews with Vietnamese women, although the viewer is never informed that the interviews are inauthentic. *Surname* also confronts viewers with a barrage of voices, in the form of simultaneous voice-overs, written text, and speech in both English and Vietnamese. *Shoot for the Contents*, Trinh's film about Chinese culture, features narration by two Chinese-American women, a series of interviews, and Trinh's own voice. Again, not all of the language is translated, drawing attention to the notion, as Trinh has pointed out, that documentaries constitutes a form of translation on both the part of the filmmaker or speaker, and the spectators.

Trinh's films feature both difference and similarity within differences. The appearance of a different albino child in her two films about Africa, the use of Vietnamese-Americans in the staged interviews of women in *Surname*, and the appearance of an African-American interviewee speaking on Chinese culture in *Shoot* all function as subtle reminders of the unfixed boundaries of subjectivity. As Trinh has noted, most documentaries use scholars or other "experts" on a culture to push the filmmaker's message. Her practice of featuring nonexperts or unexpected voices of authority calls that into question and asserts the mobility of marginalized peoples across boundaries. Trinh's own relationship to Africa, Vietnam, China, and Japan in her documentaries underscores the shifting quality of insider/outsider status. Although she is an outsider filming these peoples, as a Vietnamese-American she shares their marginalization by Western culture.

In recent years, Trinh has incorporated more narrative into her work. *The Fourth Dimension* (1991) is a visual essay on time and ritual. *A Tale of Love* (1995), a story about a Vietnamese-American model who investigates a traditional Vietnamese love poem, and *Night Passage* (2004), on a spiritual journey undertaken by two Asian women and a little boy, are both feature-length narratives.

SHARON SHELTON-COLANGELO

Biography

Born in Hanoi, Viet Nam, in 1952. Graduated from Wilmington College in Ohio in 1972 with a BA in French literature and music. Received MA in French literature in 1973, MFA in music composition in 1976, and PhD in French literature in 1977 from the University of Illinois. Taught at the National Conservatory of Music in Dakar, Senegal, and in U.S. universities including San Francisco

State, Cornell, and Harvard. Currently teaches in the Departments of Women's Studies and Rhetoric at the University of California at Berkeley. Winner of numerous awards including the 1991 AFI National Independent Filmmaker Maya Deren Award, the 1992 Sundance Film Festival Jury's Best Cinematography Award, the 1992 Athens International Film Festival Best Experimental Feature Documentary, the 1990 American Film and Video Festival's first-prize Blue Ribbon Award for Best Film as Art Feature, the 1990 Society for the Encouragement of Contemporary Art's first-prize Film as Art Award, the 1990 Bombay International Film Festival's Merit Award, the 1987 American Film and Video Festival's first-prize Blue Ribbon Award for Best Experimental Feature, the 1986 Athens International Film Festival's Golden Athena Award for Best Feature Documentary, the 1984 Hong Kong International Film Festival's Certificate of Recognition, and the 1982 Humboldt State Film Festival's Honorable Mention Award.

Selected Films

1982 *Reassemblage*
1985 *Naked Spaces–Living Is Round*
1989 *Surname Viet Given Name Nam*

1991 *Shoot for the Contents*
2001 *The Fourth Dimension*

Further Reading

Feng, Peter X, *Identities in Motion: Asian American Film and Video*, Durham: Duke University Press, 2002.

Foster, Gwendolyn Audrey, *Women Filmmakers of the African and Asian Diaspora: Decolonizing the Gaze, Locating Subjectivity*, Carbondale: Southern Illinois Press, 1977.

MacDonald, Scott, *Avant-Garde Film: Motion Studies*, New York: Cambridge University Press, 1993.

Meskimmon, Marsha, *Women Making Art: History, Subjectivity, Aesthetics*, New York: Routledge, 2003.

Peckham, Linda, "Surname Viet Given Name Nam: Spreading Rumors & Ex/Changing Histories," in *Screening Asian-Americans*, edited by Peter X. Feng, New Brunswick: Rutgers University Press, 2002.

Trinh T. Minh-ha. *Women, Native, Other: Writing Postcoloniality and Feminism*, Bloomington: Indiana University Press, 1989.

———. When *the Moon Waxes Red: Representation, Gender and Cultural Politics*, New York: Routledge, 1991.

———. *Framer Framed*, New York: Routledge, 1992.

———. *Cinema Interval*, New York: Routledge, 1999.

TRIUMPH OF THE WILL

(Germany, Riefenstahl, 1935)

Triumph of the Will/Triumpf des Willens is a documentary—some have even called it a staged documentary—of the Nationalist Socialist Party rally held in Nuremberg in 1934. One of the best-known documentaries ever made and certainly the best-known German documentary, *Triumph des Willens* brought its director Leni Riefenstahl both fame and infamy that continued to follow her throughout her life. The controversy surrounding the filmmaker and her film focused on three major issues: the extent to which the Ministry of Propaganda, under the control of Joseph Goebbels, was involved in the project; the degree to which the film is an authentic document of history; and the genuineness of Riefenstahl's claim that she did not make the film because of any belief in or support for the ideology of National Socialism.

The genesis of the making of a documentary film of the 1934 National Socialist Party Congress in Nuremberg contributes to doubts that Riefenstahl worked independently of National Socialist control on *Triumph des Willens*. One year earlier the director had completed a film on the 1933 Party Congress, *Sieg des Glaubens/Victory of Faith* (1933). The film was short, according to accounts, either because Riefenstahl had not been informed by Joseph Goebbels that she was to make the film and thus, with only three cameramen to assist her, hurried it into production only a few days before the Congress was to begin (Hinton, 1978: 28) or because Goebbels placed so many obstacles in her path during production that she could not get enough footage. Her difficulties with Goebbels, whether preproduction or during production, reportedly moved

Hitler to offer her a chance to direct a film of the 1934 Nuremberg Congress, which she at first declined (Infield, 1976:62).

Riefenstahl initially turned down directorial duties for *Triumph des Willens* to work on a narrative feature film *Tiefland/Lowlands* (1940–1953). She turned the project over to Walther Ruttmann, director of *Berlin: Die Synfonie der Großstadt/Berlin: Symphony of a Great City* (1927), who completed the opening credit sequence before Riefenstahl, at Hitler's insistence, took over directorial duties. Perhaps because Hitler was intent on having Riefenstahl make the movie (Berg-Pan, 1980: 98), the director insisted on three conditions: the film had to be made by her production company, neither Hitler nor Goebbels could see the film before completed, and Hitler would never ask her to make another film (Hinton, 1978: 30). Yet even if her production company made the movie, evidence indicates that the main source of financing came from the Nazi Party. Moreover the Party's cooperation before and during filming suggests that even if Riefenstahl had artistic control, the film nonetheless suggests outside involvement.

Persistent allegations that *Triumph des Willens* is not a genuine documentary, but that the events of the party congress were staged for the film, can be traced back to Siegfried Kracauer's comments in his book *From Caligari to Hitler*. Kracauer insists that "the Convention was planned not only as a spectacular mass meeting, but also as spectacular film propaganda" (301). Susan

Triumph of the Will, Adolf Hitler (ctr), Rudolf Hess, 1934.
[*Courtesy of the Everett Collection*]

Sontag in her essay "Fascinating Fascism" likewise claims that Riefenstahl's film "was from the beginning, conceived as the set of a film spectacle" (24), backing up her accusation with a quote from a book Riefenstahl published in 1935 in which the director wrote that "the ceremonies and precise plans of the parades, marches, processions, the architecture of the halls and stadium were designed for the convenience of the cameras" (25). On the other hand, that the rally accommodated Riefenstahl's crews does not prove that the film rally was staged for the documentary. David Hinton asks: "is it really logical to presume that the Rally, and the architecture designed for it, would have been any different without the presence of Riefenstahl and her camera crews?" (55).

Riefenstahl's commitment to Nazi ideology, as related to *Triumph des Willens*, is unambiguous for most critics. Berg-Pan summarizes the film's reception in her book on Riefenstahl, concluding herself that "there is little doubt, however, that no director or producer could have made a film such as *Triumph of the Will* without having an avid interest in the subject: Hitler and the Nazi Party." Riefenstahl herself, however, maintained that the film was simply the result of accepting a commission to document history: "A commission was proposed to me. Good. I accepted. Good. I agreed, like so many others, to make a film. . . . It is history. A pure historical film. . . . It reflects the truth as it was then" (quoted in Berg-Pan, 1980: 127). As late as 1997, when Riefenstahl was interviewed by Ray Mueller for a documentary on the filmmaker, Riefenstahl maintained that she was not political and neither was her film.

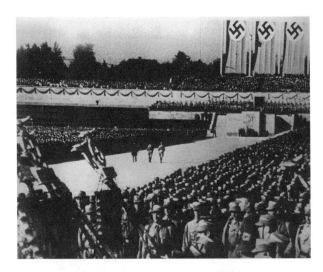

Triumph of the Will, Leni Riefenstahl pro-Hitler documentary on Nazi Germany, 1934.
[*Courtesy of the Everett Collection*]

Critics may disagree about the extent of Nazi participation in the planning and producing of the film, the integrity of the film as a document of a genuinely historical rally, and Riefenstahl's commitment to the Nazi cause. Yet, they are unanimous in their belief that the film is a powerful work of Nazi propaganda, owing to Leni Riefenstahl's insistence on artistic perfection. The director's skill for creating emotional response in viewers through editing, image content, and soundtrack is indeed astonishing, although the incessant marching scenes and speechifying might lessen the impact on nonsympathetic viewers. That is, removed from the historical context, audiences, whether German or non-German, could easily find the film tedious.

That contemporary audiences were moved by the film traces to Riefenstahl's love of movement. The film differs from the newsreels or documentaries of the time in that the film is never static, and because of the flow of images, the film can eschew conventional narration. Riefenstahl attributed the movie's power as follows: "It's a feeling for links between images, a connection between one picture and the next . . . or from one visual colour-range, say from grey tones, to another. It's like a musical composition. It's very important to put a climax at the right point in a film . . . so that there's a continuous build-up."

A close analysis of any of the twelve to sixteen sequences (depending on how one divides the segments) reveals that Riefenstahl did indeed score the film's images like a musical composition, beginning with quiet images, for example, a plane flying through the clouds (opening sequence showing Hitler's arrival in Nuremberg), a glimpse of church towers in the morning dawn (third sequence introducing labor's role in Nazi Germany), and a roll call of workers (fifth sequence, relating labor's role to the military). She intensified the scenes, building excitement through faster and faster editing (opening sequence), a series of segments displaying an escalating degree of fun among the camp participants (third sequence), and increasing emotional content (fifth sequence). She ended each of these sequences with a crescendo, crowds along a parade route shouting "Heil Hitler" (first sequence), participants being tossed high in the air in a blanket (third sequence), and flags that had been lowered being suddenly lifted into the air (fifth sequence). Scenes of dramatic intensity are interspersed with ones of tranquility. Thus sequence two shows a crowd outside Hitler's window at night. The screen reveals points of light in an otherwise dark landscape. The camera slowly glides over underlit images finding rest on the words "Heil Hitler," which are flanked by Nazi flags. Sequence four presents the Nazi leadership, each speaker iterating the theme of Hitler's contribution of work and peace to the nation. In these sequences and throughout the film, the motion and rest seem paramount, as Riefenstahl emphasized what she viewed as the movie's main themes, employment and peace, and underscores the idea that Germany was improving because of Hitler.

If *Triumph des Willens* emphasizes the themes of work and peace, it does so, as many film historians and critics have pointed out, to present, or even sell, Hitler and the Nazis first to the German people and then to the rest of the world. Although the Party had been in existence since the early 1920s, and Adolf Hitler had gained notoriety through the Munich Putsch (1924) and was known to Germans as the head of the National Socialist Party and as a member of Parliament, he and his party had been in power only nineteen months, as the film proclaims in its prologue. The footage of *Victory of Faith*, Riefenstahl's attempt at filming the Nazi Rally of 1933, shows a more chaotic meeting. More important, the footage suggests a less central role for its leader, who appears as part of the Nazi leadership, rather than above and apart from it. For example, during one speech, SA leader Ernst Rohm appears next to and on the same level as Hitler. By the time of the 1934 Rally, Hitler's clique in the Party was beginning to solidify its power, having assassinated Ernst Rohm and other SA members a few months early in a violent purge known as the "Night of Long Knives."

Viewed from this historical context, *Triumph des Willens* becomes more than a movie to sell Hitler and the Nazis to the public. It becomes one of the first films of the Nazi era to legitimize him and the Party, to place National Socialism into German history, indeed into world history. The opening credits, for example, imprinted in Gothic script and styled like woodcarvings, create a link to Nuremberg, the city of emperors and also the city of the great artist Albrecht Dürer. The text further relates Nazi Germany to the Germany of Kaiser Wilhelm, lamenting Germany's defeat in World War I and proclaiming its rebirth, thus jumping over and essentially discounting the intervening years of the Weimar Republic. The opening scene of Hitler's arrival continues the fusion of past and present, as Hitler deplanes to cheering crowds as a returning Roman leader might have marched triumphant in earlier times. The soundtrack in this scene intones Herbert Windt's score, which here approaches the grandeur of Wagnerian opera, followed by the strains of the Nazi anthem, "Die Fahne hoch." In sequence four Windt's soundtrack continues, weaving a thread between past and present, as a melody from Wagner's *Meistersinger von Nürnberg* underscores a visual of Nuremberg's cathedral towers in the dawn. The subsequent sequence varies the theme, showing how universally German the Nazi movement is, presenting workers individually and in unison from every part of Germany, united under Hitler. But even a connection is made to the past, as the workers take part in a ceremony honoring the fallen heroes of World War I. The scene is meant to once again connect pre-1918 Germany to Nazi Germany and remind viewers at the same time of the ignominy forced on the country by the intervening and now past years of the Weimar Republic, whose books had been burned in a sequence preceding this one. Throughout the film Riefenstahl makes connections between Germany past (pre-1918) to Germany present, German regionalism to Germany united, German youth to German leadership.

Triumph des Willens is much more than Riefenstahl's interpretation of a simple documentation of Hitler and what he meant to the German populace. It is also more than a propaganda document meant to introduce Hitler and more than a love feast meant to impress and scare with its scenes of unity and militaristic power. Feature films of the Third Reich were generally not political in theme. But their content was certainly political in that they were concerned with German classics, historical leaders, and great men of letters, hoping the viewer would make the association between Nazi Germany and past German greatness. In similar fashion, Riefenstahl's film is also not political, or not just political. It is a narrative playing to the emotions of a public wanting answers to problems but also wanting to connect to a more heroic German past.

Although we cannot answer definitively whether the Nuremberg Rally was genuine, whether the Nazis or Riefenstahl produced the movie, and whether Riefenstahl supported Nazi ideology, it is clear that the overly controlled nature of the film's style produces the effect of something that was staged. Furthermore, there is no doubt that the Nazis benefited from the film, whether or not they were involved in its making. Finally, whether or not Riefenstahl supported Nazi ideology, her film clearly does. The movie is an undeniably powerful piece of propaganda filmmaking, glorifying the political and military power of the Nazis. Riefenstahl uses the human form as architectural building blocks, elevates military marching into a religious ritual, and encloses and opens space with banners, flags, and columns.

Whether one sees the film as serving the art of documentary filmmaking or the evils of National Socialism, however, there is no denying its effect as propaganda and its influence on filmmakers. Erwin Leiser uses several scenes from the film, including the well-known sequence of the Nazi labor corps (earlier discussed as sequence five) in his documentary *Mein Kampf* (1960). Directors of entertainment films have also referenced Riefenstahl, including George Lukas in *Star Wars* (1977), Lewis Teague in *Jewel of the Nile* (1985), Jim Sharman in *The Rocky Horror Picture Show* (1975), and Paul Verhoeven in *Starship Troopers* (1997).

ROBERT C. REIMER

See also **Mein Kampf**; **Riefenstahl, Leni**

Triumph of the Will/ Triumpf des Willens (Germany, Riefenstahl, 1935, 114 min.). Produced by Leni Riefenstahl-Produktion and NSDAP Reichsleitung. Directed by Leni Riefenstahl. Written by Leni Riefenstahl and Walter Ruttmann.

Further Reading

Berg-Pan, Renata, *Leni Riefenstahl*, Boston: Twayne Publishers, 1980.

Hinton, David B., *The Films of Leni Riefenstahl*, Metuchen, NJ: Scarecrow Press, 1978.

Hull, David Stewart, *Film in the Third Reich: A Study of the German Cinema 1933-1945*, Berkeley and Los Angeles: University of California Press, 1969.

Infield, Glenn B., *Leni Riefenstahl: The Fallen Film Goddess*, New York: Thomas Y. Crowell, 1976.

Kracauer, Siegfried, *From Caligari to Hitler: A Psychological Study of the German Film*, Princeton, NJ: Princeton University Press, 1947.

"Leni Riefenstahl - Regisseurin, Schauspielerin," in *Cine-Graph: Lexikon zum deutschsprachigen Film*, edited by Hans-Michael Bock, Munich.

Schwartzman, Roy J., "Racial Theory and Propaganda in *Triumph of the Will*," in *Authority and Transgression in Literature and Film*, edited by Bonnie Braendlin, and Hans Braendlin, Gainesville, FL: University Press of Florida, 1996, 136–151.

Sontag, Susan, "Fascinating Fascism," *The New York Review of Books*, February 6, 1975, 23–25.

TROELLER, GORDIAN

Gordian Troeller's oeuvre would not have been possible outside the German public television system. There he found the room to maneuver in the field of highly controversial approaches to the living conditions of the underprivileged peoples of the so-called Third World. Early on, his leftist convictions led him to understand that underdevelopment is something brought about by colonialism and imperialism. He found ample evidence, that the Third World peoples lived in a state he called "pre-underdevelopment"; that is, they lived, if not in riches, then at least in stable social conditions where anybody's needs were being catered to. Only when Western colonialists attempted to "elevate" these peoples to Western economic standards, the traditional structures collapsed and left the people in utter impoverishment. This is the main idea behind most of Troeller's documentary features he made from 1963 onwards and which he exemplified in a series of films, *Im Namen des Fortschritts* (1974–1984). Later, he realized that suppression was not only an issue in the Third World but rather in the so-called Developed World as well, at least as far as women and children are concerned. This led him to yet another two series of films, *Frauen der Welt* (1979–1983) and *Kinder der Welt* (1984–), respectively.

Troeller, who started out as a writing journalist, shoots his film without a preconceived script. He rather prefers to spend as much time as possible with the people he is covering, trying to get as much footage as possible. He uses a light, handheld 16mm camera and a direct sound system that he can handle with a small team. He never lights the set, nor does he ever ask people to repeat actions which he missed to cover on film. His aim is to achieve as authentic an image as possible. Critics accuse Troeller's films to be too "wordy." His films, they say, do not make their points with the images, but rather state their arguments in an in-depth off-commentary. This, critics maintain, Troeller does even at the cost of a considerable discrepancy between the images and the commentary. They accuse Troeller's approach of being overly didactic.

ULI JUNG

Biography

Born March 3, 1917, in Pierrevillers, Luxembourg (he always refuses to state his date of birth, in protest against ageism). Took part in the Spanish civil war and subsequently went to Portugal where he helped refugees from German occupied territories. After World War II, founded a leftist journal, *L'indépandant*, in Luxembourg, which annoyed the government. After the journal's bankruptcy, became a correspondent for various European newspapers. With his wife (until 1974) and work-companion (until her death in 1984), Marie-Claude Deffarge, he traveled through many Arabian countries, writing reports for various journals, predominantly the prestigious German journal *Der Stern*. In 1958, published their first book together: *Persien ohne Maske*. Made their first film in Yemen: *Une Française chez les guerries au Yemen*. Filmmaking became Troeller's foremost medium of work. After working freelance for several years, found a constant assignment with the German public television station Radio Bremen who produced his long running film series *Im Namen des Fortschritts, Frauen der Welt und Kinder der Welt*. While his films every now and then caused political trouble (especially when he attacked official Israeli policies), he established himself as one of the most noted TV documentarists in Germany who was awarded numerous awards. After Marie-Claude Deffarge's death, teamed up with Ingrid Becker-Ross, who he married in 1986. Died March 22, 2002, in Hamburg, Germany.

Selected Films

1963 *Ein Kriegsbericht aus dem Mittelalter*
1964 *Durchs blutige Kurdistan*
1967 *Ein vergessener Völkermord*
1967 *Im belagerten Sanaa*
1969 *Die Revolte der Sklaven*
1969 *Ein Jahr nach der Revolution*
1969 *Die revolutionäre Kirche in Lateinamerika*
1970 *Das Mittelalter will nicht sterben*
1970 *Juden im Nordjemen*
1970 *Südsudan – Noch ein Biafra?* (1970)
1971 *Im Land der 1001 Bohrtürme*
1971 *Das Zeitalter der Söldner*
1971 *Das Sultanat Oman*
1972 *Südjemen, das Kuba der arabischen Welt*
1972 *Algier, Hauptstadt der Revolutionäre*
1973 *Kommunisten seit 1000 Jahren*
1973 *Die Revolution der kleinen Leute*
1973 *Der Zorn der Korsen*
1974–1984 *Series: Im Namen des Fortschritts*: 22 installments
1979–1983 *Series: Frauen der Welt*: 12 installments
1984– *Series: Kinder der Welt*: 26 installments

Further Reading

Adick, Christel, and Stuke Franz R. (eds.), *Ferne Länder—fremde Sitten: Analysen zum Filmwerk von Gordian Troeller*, Frankfurt/M.: IKO Verlag für Interkulturelle Kommunikation, 1996.

Deffarge, Marie-Claude, and Gordian Troeller, *Die Herren: Ein Pamphlet gegen Männerherrschaft*, Frankfurt/M.: Zweitausendeins, 1985.

———, *Frauen der Welt*, Frankfurt/M.: Zweitausendeins, 1984.

Gordian Troeller und Marie-Claude Deffarge im Gespräch. Bremen: CON-Film, 1988.

Paschen, Joachim, Ulrich Spies, and Detlef Ziegert (eds.), *Kein Respekt vor großen Tieren: Gordian Troeller und seine Filme*. Bremen: Edition CON, 1992.

TROUBLES WE'VE SEEN, THE

(France, Ophuls, 1994)

Although the primary topic of the film is the war in Bosnia and its journalistic coverage, *Veillees d'armes; le journalisme en temps de guerre, 1er et 2eme voyages/The Troubles We've Seen: A History of Journalism in Wartime, 1st and 2nd Journeys*, Ophuls's postmodern documentary collage, is dedicated to a wider investigation into Western reporting on conflict and its underlying motives. To Ophuls, concern for others is only an extension of a self-centered interest, hence the variety of inherent ethical tensions found in international news production.

Troubles was produced by the director's friend Bertrand Tavernier, who secured most of the financing (Jacobsen, 1996). Contributions to the budget were made by the BBC (quoted at £ 80, 000, circa $130,000) and by the French subsidy system. The plan was to make a three-part documentary, but by 1994, only two parts were completed and shown. Ophuls has said on various occasions that *Troubles* should be regarded as a work-in-progress. There have been indications that in the late 1990s, he was still thinking of completing it, but no third part has been released as of 2005.

The first two parts of what was supposed to be a trilogy, *First Journey* (92 min.) and *Second Journey* (139 min.), were screened at the closing day of Cannes Film Festival in 1994, with little preliminary information released. Later, the film screened at the festivals in Toronto and New York and was broadcast by the BBC in September 1995. As it is regarded as an unfinished work, however, the director has been reluctant to have it released theatrically and on video; thus *Troubles* is largely unavailable and is considered an esoteric piece of work.

Ophuls's central concern is the effect of the media's instant and continuous live reporting on Western perceptions and reactions to conflicts abroad. He looks into a wide spectrum of journalistic behaviour by placing it into the framework of morality in war reporting. Even though the focus is on Bosnia, there are numerous references to media coverage and construction of past conflicts, mostly the Gulf War, but also the Vietnam War, World War II, and the Spanish civil war. In an interview, Ophuls hinted that it was

The Troubles We've Seen (a.k.a. Veillees d'armes) Director Marcel Ophuls (r) with a German war correspondent in Sarajevo 1994.
[*Courtesy of the Everett Collection*]

the distinction between legitimate show business and "perverted show business" that sustained his interest to news production and international conflict coverage (to Jacobsen, 1996).

The two parts of the film are structured loosely around two journeys to Bosnia, with the first part concentrated mostly on the logistics and the morals of reporting from the war zone and the second on war reporting at the recipient end and its function within the Western (mainly French) public discourse. Even though the filmed interviews are cut and presented in a mosaic fashion, one can distinguish two main spheres of investigation. In Bosnia, Ophuls talks to numerous Western journalists based in Sarajevo (the *New York Times*'s John F. Burns, the BBC's John Simpson, France Presse's Remi Oudran, TF1's Isabelle Ballancourt), uses footage of reporters such as Christiane Amanpour (CNN) and Martin Bell (BBC), and enters street dialogues with some ordinary inhabitants of the city and visiting Westerners (such as like film director Romain Goupil). The investigation in this part looks mostly into the inherent ethical tensions of the trade and the journalist's special attitudes to danger, courage, and moral responsibility.

The second part explores the coverage of conflict as seen at the recipient's end, in Western Europe, and mostly in France. Ophuls uses his friend Philippe Noiret to deliver some biting commentary on the indifference of French politicians and their evasive PR strategy over Bosnia. He features interviews with intellectual critic Alain Finkielkraut and with self-proclaimed humanitarian Bernard Kouchner. No one is spared, from General Philippe Morillon to Simone Veil and François Mitterand; all are shown making compromising statements. Ophuls also challenges the superficial approach of French TV star-anchor Patrick Poivre D'Arvoir, dispatched into Sarajevo on a twenty-four-hour parachute-style visit.

In this film Ophuls is particularly sensitive to the "rhetorical potency of Eisensteinian montage" (Lopate, 1994). He cuts back and forth between seemingly unconnected footage, to impose his own political associations on the viewer and build the argument. From a Serb priest blessing a house, he cuts to an archival newsreel of a Nazi cleric blessing the troops. He exposes the evasiveness of the UN by featuring embarrassing press conference moments of officials such as Jose Maria Mendiluce and Boutros Boutros-Gali. He adds scenes of President Clinton's jogging routine, President Mitterand's interview with the wife of one of his own ministers, and footage of public statements made by Chancellor Kohl and Prime Minister John Major. In addition, the film cross-references a range of well-known Hollywood pictures—from the Marx brothers' *Duck Soup* (1933) and Max Ophuls's *De Mayerling à Sarajevo* (1940), to Mark Sandrich's *Holiday Inn* (1942) and Fellini's *8 1/2* (1963)—to sharpen the contrast between a self-obsessed West and a forsaken Bosnia. A frequently used ironic device, for example, is Bing Crosby's song from the film *Holiday Inn*, hummed by the war correspondents stationed at the infamous "Holiday Inn" hotel in Sarajevo. Another sequence of the film shows a woman and child running through a snowy square in Sarajevo to escape sniper fire. The background music is the song "White Christmas," again from *Holiday Inn*.

Yet another line of referencing is the inclusion of staged episodes from everyday life routines in the West, once again asserting the indifferent attitude of ordinary Westerners to conflict between faraway peoples. These include footage from Venice; for example, like Sarajevo, it is a dying city as well, yet one that is absorbed by its self-importance. Ophuls does not spare himself either, and extends the sarcasm by including a set-up scene showing him in a Viennese hotel room, shortly after he has left Sarajevo, discussing the Bosnian project on the phone, while in the background a naked woman sips champagne, waiting for him in bed. It is a clear statement of self-criticism: as a Westerner he is, by default, complicit in the attitudes he exposes.

As far as the Bosnian dimension of the film is concerned, Ophuls never becomes too involved, even though he has declared his official commitment to the plight of Bosnian Muslims. During his Northern Ireland investigation in *Sense of Loss* (1972) he talked extensively to the ordinary victims of terror, but in Sarajevo his discussions with local people are restricted to occasional street interviews. Although present throughout the film, the experiences of ordinary Bosnians remain outside the main narrative and do not integrate into the investigation, which remains preoccupied with Western journalists' coverage of the conflict.

As a legendary filmmaker, Ophuls enjoys privileged treatment and is granted exclusive interviews with some of the main players in the conflict, including Nikola Koljević, Radovan Karadzić, and Slobodan Milošević. Because his investigative focus lies elsewhere, however, he does not make much use of this rare material and only includes occasional sound bites from these conversations. Pursuing his own line of inquiry, he takes this particular conflict as a backdrop for the moral investigation that evolves around Western coverage.

Ophuls neglects important statements made by the Yugoslav and Bosnian players and fails to analyse the rhetoric of blaming Western media coverage, widely practised by these politicians. Many of the issues discussed in *The Troubles We've Seen* make sense only in the wider context of themes such as history, remembrance, and morality, which have been the focus of Ophuls's work throughout his career. It is a context in which Bosnia's function is of a case study, a background against which he develops his views.

The main line of inquiry in Marcel Ophuls's work has always been a moralistic one, from dissecting the reasons why ordinary people turn a blind eye to historical horrors such as the deportation of Jews in occupied France (*The Sorrow and the Pity*, 1971; *The Memory of Justice*, 1976; *Hotel Terminus*, 1988) through exposing the tragic consequences of the mismanaged dialogue in Northern Ireland (*A Sense of Loss,* 1972), to dealing with the side effects of the German reunification (*November Days*, 1992). Ophuls's mature brand of investigative sarcasm sets the tone also in *Troubles*, where he once again looks into the question why knowledge of injustice and atrocities does not change the outcome of conflicts and why Western politics is once again inoperative when confronted with abundant evidence of the ethnic cleansing and terror. Opening with evidence of uninformed shallowness in war reporting, he explores whether the superficiality in reporting is due to intrinsic media patterns or to the deeply ingrained smugness of institutionalised consumer culture. He remains sceptical about the possibility of adequately conveying information across borders and cultures. Some critics read his pessimism as a general "radical scepticism about the moral decency of any image-making" (Lopate, 1994, 74), whereas others found that the turns of his investigation were taking "rambling, frequently surprising ways" and were excessively subjective (Maslin, 1994). Yet, given the fact that officially sanctioned injustice was Ophuls's lifelong topic and that the métier of the director was exposing complicity in all its subtle forms, according to others, *Troubles* was to be seen as a logical continuation in his earlier investigations (Jacobsen, 1996).

As with most of Ophuls's other films, the reception of *Troubles* was a mixture of admiration and reservation over the ponderous and long-winded format that causes "bafflement and irritation" (Dunkley, 1995). Once again, critics noted, it was a profoundly subjective piece of work, which never pretends otherwise. Even though the film was seen as "too elliptical" (Dunkley, 1995), critics noted with satisfaction that Ophuls had managed to, once again, successfully sustain his obstinate role as a "thorn in the side of all authorities" (Jacobsen, 1996) and that it was "tremendously valuable to have one person ignoring the perpetual straining after balance and objectivity to go instead for ultra subjectivity" (Dunkley, 1995). Many critics questioned the associative choices made by the director, but all were unanimous that if one is ready to trust Ophuls and follow his investigation, many answers become clear at the end.

In an international political climate marked by a continuous range of armed conflicts and civil wars, the theme of *The Troubles We Have Seen* remains persistently important. The film became topical, once again, with the 2002 resignation of the Dutch government over revelations of the 1995 inaction of its soldiers in the Bosnian safe heaven in Srebrenitza, which resulted in the deaths of more than 7,000 Bosnian men. Alongside academic investigations on the workings of media in covering armed clashes (by authors such as Daniel Hallin, Philip Taylor, Tim Allen, Jean Seaton, Susan Carruthers, and others), *Troubles* could be considered a classical work on issues of media and international coverage. Even in its unfinished format, the film should be made available to wider audiences.

DINA IORDANOVA

See also **Ophuls, Marcel;** *The Sorrow and the Pity*

The Troubles We Have Seen: A History of Journalism in Wartime (1st and 2nd Journeys). Veillees d'armes; le journalisme en temps de guerre (1er et 2eme voyages). (France/UK/Germany, Little Bear Productions (Paris). Premiere (Germany), with the participation of Canal+, BBC 199, 231 min.). Produced by Bertrand Tavernier and Frederic Bourboulon. Directed and written by Marcel Ophuls. Cinematography by Pierre Boffrey, Pierre Milon. Assistant direction by Dominiki Moll, Laurent Cantet. Editing by Sophie Brunet. Sound by Michel Faure and Eric Devulder. Sound editing by Ariane Doublet. Filmed in Sarajevo, Zagreb, Vienna, Paris. Dialogue in English, French, German, Serbian and Croatian.

Further Reading

Dunkley, Christopher, "War from a Different Perspective," in *Financial Times*, September 2, 1995, XII.

Iordanova, Dina, *Cinema of Flames: Balkan Film, Culture and the Media*, London: BFI, 2001, 153–155.

Jacobsen, Kurt, "Memories of Injustice: Marcel Ophuls's Cinema of Conscience," in *Film Comment*, 32, 4, July 1996, 61–71 (includes an interview with Ophuls).

Johnson, William, "A Short Take on Long Films, Very Long Films," in *Film Comment*, 31, 5, September 1995, 78.

Lopate, Phillip, "New York Film Festival," in *Film Comment*, 30, 6, November 1994, 72–77.

Maslin, Janet, "A Report on Reporters in the World's Hot Spots," in *The New York Times*, October 6, 1994, Section C, 17.

Nesselson, Lisa, "*The Troubles We Have Seen*," *Variety*, June 19, 1994.

TRUE GLORY, THE

(UK, Carol Reed, 1945)

The last film in the "victory series"—which included *Desert Victory* (1943), *Tunisian Victory* (1944), and *Burma Victory* (1945)—*The True Glory* covers the period from the preparations for the D-day landings in Normandy through the fall of Berlin to the establishing of contact between the Western Allies and Soviet troops at the Elbe River. Made from 5.5 million feet of combat footage shot by 500 American, British, and other Allied cameramen, it is a vast panorama, yet intensely human, even intimate at moments.

Emotional involvement is gained largely through the experimental use of commentary. Alternating with blank verse choruses are multiple voices representing soldiers involved with the particular action being shown. The words are complementary to the images, sometimes in humorous or ironic counterpoint to them. The general's version, spoken by Dwight D. Eisenhower himself, supreme commander of Allied forces in Europe, is irreverently interrupted by enlisted men who were there: New York cab driver, cockney Londoner, member of the French Maquis, and others. One marvelous moment occurs when a black American MP directing military traffic at a crossroads explains that the situation is tough, that the invasion forces are bottled up in the Caen Pennisula. "Then we heard that the Third Army was taking off," he says. "They'd pulled a rabbit out of a hat—and what a rabbit! A rabbit with pearl-handled revolvers." As he says this a tank bearing an erect General George S. Patton roars by.

The True Glory was the triumphant record and hymn to Allied victory in Europe. The occasion permitted a kind of boasting and self-congratulation without it appearing to be so. Pride is expressed in the massiveness and efficiency of the military machine and in its democratic nature. The participation of many nations is indirectly reiterated without explicit statement being required. The Allied attitude toward war is presented as being purposeful and matter-of-fact, its violence accepted as part of a job to be done, as in the British semi-documentaries (*Target for Tonight*, 1941; *Fires Were Started*, 1943; *Western Approaches*, 1944). Unlike the semi-documentaries, however, dislike and distrust of the German enemy are strongly stated. The horrors of what the advancing forces found at the Belsen concentration camp are included. An American GI, talking about guarding German prisoners of war, says: "I just kept 'em covered. . . . It wasn't my job to figure 'em out. . . . But, brother, I never gave 'em more than the Geneva

The True Glory, 1945.
[*Still courtesy of the British Film Institute*]

convention, and that was all." Finally, though, it is the positive corollary of the GI's attitude that receives the strongest emphasis. What *The True Glory* is saying mostly is that this was a just and necessary war and that on the Allied side we can all feel proud of our part in winning it. Like *Desert Victory* before it, it was awarded an Oscar by the Academy of Motion Picture Arts and Sciences as "the most Outstanding Documentary Feature of 1945."

JACK C. ELLIS

See also **Desert Victory; Ministry of Information**

The True Glory (US/UK, British Army Film and Photographic Unit and American and Allied Film Services, 1945, 87 min.). Distributed by Office of War Information and Ministry of Information. Produced and directed by Carol Reed and Garson Kanin. Screenplay by Eric Maschwitz, Arthur Macrae, Jenny Nicholson, Gerald Kersh, Guy Trosper. Music by William Alwyn. Cinematography by British Army Film Unit and American Army Pictorial Service. Editing supervision by Robert Verrell; editing by Leiberwitz, Bob Farrell, Jerry Cowen, Bob Carrick, Bob Clarke. Commentary read by Robert Harris.

TRUJILLO, MARISOL

See **Prayer**

TRUE STORY OF LILI MARLENE, THE

(UK, Jennings, 1943)

The True Story of Lili Marlene raises important questions relating not only to the films of Humphrey Jennings but to the entire British documentary film movement, and indeed to any canonical hierarchy selected from a more general range of expression and discussion. The films that we write about and remember contribute much to our critical attitudes and our historical understanding. A closer look at the films that we have not remembered reminds us of how arbitrary the processes of selection and validation can be.

Discussions about the work of Humphrey Jennings have often proceeded in terms of masterpieces and also-rans, with the latter quickly disappearing from view. Contemporary reports suggest that this division is rooted in the initial reactions to the various films. The acknowledged masterpieces *Listen to Britain, I Was a Fireman/*

Fires Were Started, and *A Diary for Timothy* were much remarked upon and generally, though not universally, appreciated from the start. Some of the other films, less effective, or perhaps more elusive, also elicited immediate responses, which seem for the most part to have been quite a bit cooler.

The hardening of this division into a kind of received wisdom probably begins with Lindsay Anderson's celebrated appreciation of Jennings's work, which first appeared in *Sight and Sound* in1954. This critical eulogy, entitled "Only Connect," is a superb piece of sympathetic criticism that is largely evaluative. This is to say that Anderson is speaking of good films and bad films, and that his judgments are based on criteria that are more personal than they are textual or historical. The result is a critical position that is quite defensible without being quite comprehensive.

The True Story of Lili Marlene, 1943.
[*Still courtesy of the British Film Institute*]

The Humphrey Jennings in Anderson's portrait is an intellectual and a propagandist, who in his finest work avoids by his great humanity the pitfalls of these parts, the elitist inaccessibility and the hectoring coercion to which intellectuals and propagandists are prone. This is certainly a true likeness, or at least part of one, and through its continued inclusion (Jacobs, 1975; MacDonald and Cousins, 1996) or reflection (Barnouw, Ellis, Barsam) in the most popular documentary anthologies and histories, it has become a matter of record.

In a survey sense this is as it should be, but connected to all this enthusiasm there has emerged a consistent and connected idea that appears even in the more specialized studies of Jennings's work. This idea is that the other, more complicated elements of Jennings's personal and aesthetic makeup—the scholarly complexity, the intellectual's irony, the surrealist's awareness of the indeterminate—are not as easy to contain or to comprehend. It is suggested that the films that are reflective of these less tractable qualities are less coherent, less representative, and, finally, less useful.

The True Story of Lili Marlene is one of these films, and if its almost universal dismissal needs reconsidering, then its undoubted difficulties also need to be accounted for. Both its subject and treatment are unlikely. It traces the permutations of a sentimental German song, "Lili Marlene," from its first appearance in the 1920s, through its appropriation as part of the Nazi propaganda machine, to its final "capture" and recouping by the victorious Allies. Its careful juxtapositions and its telling use of music are typical of Jennings's work, but the lack of a real protagonist, single or collective, and the lack of a clearly unifying mood or message or even through line separate it from the best known and, most would say, the best of his films.

The record suggests that Jennings himself was frustrated during the film's production and not fully satisfied with the final result. It is not coincidental that this frustration, the mixed feelings and lack of focus, would become the explicit subject of Jennings's next film and last unequivocal success, *A Diary for Timothy*. With regard to finding a place for *Lili Marlene*, it could at the very least be argued that its production provided a refining space in which Jennings confronted and came to terms with his own confusions, the better to counsel with and console his countrymen in their own.

But *Lili Marlene* has merit beyond its contribution to more acclaimed works. As with Jennings's similarly underconsidered *Eighty Days* and *The Silent Village* (both 1943), in this film we see the intellectual emerging from beneath his propagandist's banner. If the results are uncertain then it is at least partly because Jennings is exploring new ground, both in representing the war and in critically questioning the documentary film's place in that representation.

Lili Marlene reveals much about the conflict during late 1943 and early 1944, as well as the state of the nation and its citizens. With the tide having turned and victory becoming a real possibility, the need for unambiguously reassuring propaganda gave way and made room for admissions of doubt and vulnerability, for searching and questioning. If *Eighty Days* hints at how bewildered and broken the victims of German bombings must have been, even in the days when London was proclaiming how well it could take it, then *Lili Marlene* reaffirms the common ground—humanity, sentimentality and sentiment, susceptibility to suggestion—that all of the combatants shared.

But it is particularly in exploring that susceptibility, in turning its gaze on its own workings, that *Lili Marlene* marks an advance, however tentative, in the history and maturing of the documentary film, most particularly in Britain. The elusiveness of its story suggests that story is only the ostensible subject, a means to investigate the rhetorical and ideological underpinnings of our unquestioned communications. Its formal and narrative strategies and its much criticized unconventionality and artificiality all inhibit conventional illusion and identification, allowing for and even demanding a deeper intellectual engagement. This is not a propaganda film, so much as it is a film about propaganda.

The True Story of Lili Marlene raises the possibility that there is a substantial neutrality in the songs, stories, ideas, and representations that we take to heart and take for granted. It is no wonder, then, that a wartime film about propaganda's neutral nature, and its susceptibility to tone and context, a film that exposes the workings of narrativity by tracing the history of a not-so-Nazi air did not quite motivate the masses like the standard words for battle. These many years later such notions are familiar and just as disconcerting. Jennings's neglected film deserves credit and attention for its contribution to this current and always relevant discussion.

DEAN DUNCAN

See also **Diary for Timothy, A; Fires Were Started; Jennings, Humphrey; Listen to Britain**

The True Story of Lili Marlene (UK, Crown Film Unit, 30 min.). Produced by J.B. Holmes. Direction and Script by Humphrey Jennings. Narration by Marius Goring. Cinematography by Henry "Chick" Fowle. Music by Dennis Blood, directed by Muir Mathieson. Editing by Sid Stone. Sound by Ken Cameron.

Further Reading

Brecht, Bertolt, "The Modern Theatre Is the Epic Theatre," in *Brecht on Theatre*, translated and edited by John Willett, New York: Hill and Wang, 1957.
Hodgkinson, Anthony W., and Sheratsky, Rodney E., Humphrey Jennings: *More than a Maker of Films*, Hanover: University Press of New England, 1982.
Jackson, Kevin (ed.), *The Humphrey Jennings Film Reader*, Manchester: Carcanet Press, 1993.
Jacobs, Lewis (ed.), *The Documentary Tradition*, New York: Hopkinson and Blake, 197
Jennings, Mary-Lou (ed.), *Humphrey Jennings: Film-Maker, Painter, Poet*, London: British Film Institute, 1982.
MacDonald, Kevin, and Mark Cousins, *Imagining Reality: The Faber Book of Documentary*, London: Faber, 1996.
Swann, Paul, *The British Documentary Film Movement*, Cambridge: Cambridge University Press, 1989.
Sussex, Elizabeth, *The Rise and Fall of British Documentary*, Berkeley: University of California Press, 1975.
Winston, Brian, *Claiming the Real*, London: British Film Institute, 1995.

TUNISIAN VICTORY

(US and UK, Capra and Stewart, 1944)

Jointly produced by the British and U.S. army film units during 1943–1944, *Tunisian Victory* was designed to provide domestic audiences in both countries with a vivid pictorial account of the Allied victory in North Africa and put a positive face on Anglo-American cooperation in the conduct of the war. The making of the film, however, also revealed the challenges and limitations of coordinating international efforts in the production of wartime propaganda in light of national divisions that the rhetoric of Allied unity inevitably masked.

Work on *Tunisian Victory* originated in separate British and American projects: *Africa Freed*, a follow-up to *Desert Victory* (1943), the British army and air force film units' acclaimed account of the expulsion of Rommel's African Korps from Libya and Egypt; and *Operation Torch*, undertaken by Frank Capra's newly formed U.S. Signal Corps Special Coverage Unit (with John Huston, Anthony Veiller, and George Stevens) in an effort to give greater visibility to the participation of U.S. forces in the North African campaign. Under pressure to promote the trans-Atlantic partnership, and hoping to reap the benefits of pooled combat footage, officials at the British Ministry of Information and the U.S. Office of War Information decided to merge the projects in the summer of 1943. Capra joined Hugh Stewart in London as co-producer/director, and writing duties were divided between Veiller and J. H. Hodson, the latter the author of *Desert Victory*'s spoken commentary. By all accounts collaboration was tense and work proceeded slowly, in part because of what Capra later described as "sticky high policy decisions involving dual command and national pride and prejudices" (*The Name above the Title*, 352). Capra and Stewart oversaw postproduction in Los Angeles in the winter of 1943–1944, with Stewart using the opportunity to encourage stronger ties between the British and American film industries. At its commercial release in March 1944, the completed documentary received high praise from the Hollywood trade press but mixed reviews from U.S. critics and still less favorable ones in Great Britain.

Like *Desert Victory*, *Tunisian Victory* outlines military strategy in North Africa, links battle preparation to events at home, and uses voice-over commentary to provide an overarching narrative of the unfolding campaign. During combat passages, camera jolts, rapid montages, and percussive sound effects register the impact of explosions and artillery fire. Even *Tunisian Victory*'s controversial fabrication of two night battles—the British crossing of Wadi Zig-Zauo (shot at Pinewood studios) and the American assault on Tunisia's Hill 609 (staged by Capra and Huston in the Mojave Desert for *Operation Torch*)—have precedent in combat scenes reconstructed at Pinewood for *Desert Victory*.

But *Tunisian Victory*'s strenuous even-handedness—evident in the patterned alternation between U.S. and British convoys, camps, and combat sites—makes for a knottier story, as does its tentative effort to incorporate French forces into the story. The complicated logistics are clarified in part through the use of slick animated diagrams and extensive commentary by Veiller and his British vocal counterpart, Leo Glenn. In a bid to personalize the drama, *Tunisian Victory* also adds into the mix the voices of a fictional British Tommy (Bernard Miles) and a fictional American GI (Burgess Meredith) who convey the thoughts of soldiers in their respective camps, then enter into a colloquy at the close. Both praised and criticized at the time,

Tunisian Victory, documentary by Frank Capra and John Huston, 1944.
[*Courtesy of the Everett Collection*]

this last device provides the occasion for the film to consider the prospects for postwar renewal, as an array of Germans POWs, North African refugees, and Allied soldiers from many nations that appear on screen. Here *Tunisian Victory* trades the immediacy of a combat record—victory in Tunis, after all, was by now a full year past—for a longer view in which the fate of postwar international alliances must be considered.

CHARLES WOLFE

Further Reading

Aldgate, Anthony, "Creative Tension: *Desert Victory*, the Army Film Unit and Anglo-American Rivalry, 1943–5," in *Britain and the Cinema in the Second World War*, edited by Philip M. Taylor, London: Macmillan, 1988.

———. "Mr Capra Goes to War: Frank Capra, the British Army Film Unit, and Anglo-American Travails in the Production of 'Tunisian Victory,'" in *Historical Journal of Film, Radio and Television*, 11, 1, 1991, 21–39; reprinted as "National Pride and Prejudices: *Tunisian Victory*," in *Britain Can Take It: The British Cinema in the Second World War*, 2nd edition, edited by Anthony Aldgate, and Jeffrey Richards, Edinburgh: Edinburgh University Press, 1994.

Capra, Frank, *The Name above the Title: An Autobiography*, New York: Macmillan, 1971.

Chapman, James, *The British at War: Cinema, State and Propaganda, 1939–1945*, London: New York: I. B. Tauris, 1998.

Coultass, Clive, "*Tunisian Victory*—a film too late?," in *Imperial War Museum Review*, 1, 1986, 64–73.

———. *Images for Battle: British Film and the Second World War, 1939–1945*, Newark: University of Delaware Press, 1989.

Huston, John, *An Open Book*, New York: Alfred A. Knopf, 1980.

Krome, Frederic, "'Tunisian Victory' and Anglo-American Film Propaganda in World War II," in *The Historian*, 58, 3, spring 1996, 517–530.

McBride, Joseph, *Frank Capra: The Catastrophe of Success*, New York: Simon and Schuster, 1992.

Tunisian Victory, documentary by Frank Capra and John Huston, 1944.
[*Courtesy of the Everett Collection*]

TURIN, VIKTOR

Viktor A. Turin was a Russian director who lived in America and trained in Hollywood before the Russian Revolution. His best-known film, *Turksib* (1929), is a documentary on the construction of the Turkestano-Siberian railroad, one of Stalin's projects for industrializing the Soviet Union. An argument for efficient transportation and trade between regions of the country, the film best illustrates Turin's ideas about what the documentary should accomplish. Although it makes a dry economic argument comprehensible, it also tells a story and rouses an emotional response. Soviet cinema made a distinction between "played" (or fiction) and "unplayed" (or documentary) films, but Turin was willing to blur that distinction to make the film's message more effective. This included staging scenes to make a point that was valuable in the film's larger argument. Turin's philosophy of the documentary, then, is at the intersection of communism and Hollywood: A film should appeal to the masses, but it should also teach them something.

Turin began working on *Turksib* at a time when the Soviet culture-film (a didactic documentary) had fallen out of favor. Most of the films were so poorly or cheaply done that bad filmmaking turned the audiences away from ideologically good ideas. Turin felt that documentary films could present complex ideas to mass audiences, but only if they were presented in an exciting (and often staged) narrative that made the ideas worthy of attention. His ideas about the making of documentary film differed dramatically from those of Dziga Vertov, the most important Soviet documentarian of the era. Vertov was opposed to fiction films and staged scenes, arguing instead for films that showed "life caught unawares" and presented unfiltered reality. In contrast, Viktor Turin used his Hollywood training to plan for and construct *Turksib* in a way that was remarkably similar to a fiction film. Viktor Shlovkii wrote a scenario for the film (though much of it was abandoned in production), and Turin expressed regret at several "good shots" that he missed. This position resulted in many elements of the film that seem more allegorical or stereotypical than realistic. The characters are very broadly drawn and easily understood "types" like the noble savage and the heroic engineer, for example, and the film's economic argument is thematized in anecdotal scenes like the race between native horse and modern automobile.

Turin adhered to a more constructed version of the documentary because he felt that structure and story was necessary to make complex ideas palatable to the average viewer. He spoke to a worker's club on the obligation of filmmakers to come into contact with and speak to the working classes; the lack of culture-film's lack of recent success was, he felt, a result of its inability to connect with the masses through a clear and compelling story. In this respect, Turin believed a film's successful communication of an argument can be judged only by its reception:

> The greatest defect in most of the culture-films produced up to now seems to be the absence of a precisely articulated theme. . . . The usual result is a tiresome hodge-podge of shots spliced together with merely mechanical links . . . This makes even the sharpest facts grow dull on the screen and leaves the spectator unmoved.
>
> (Leyda, 1960)

The director and editor have the responsibility to plan the story and shape the shots' relationship to one another so that the film presents not mere reality but a precisely articulated argument that can change the spectators' minds, both through facts and through emotions. The first section of *Turksib*, for example, tells spectators the facts about Turkish production of cotton; it also affects spectators by cutting from worried faces to wilting fields to a panting dog, links that are emotional rather than merely mechanical. Also, the film's editing begins at a leisurely pace when it lays out the background information for its argument, but it speeds up at the end to create excitement in the audience as the film concludes. Most critics feels that the film's success was due to the clarity of its argument and the simplicity of its structure, one that combined the comprehensibility of the fiction film and the articulacy of the culture-film.

The need for both emotional impact and a clear argument leads to a disjunction between two important elements of Turin's style. Although his characterizations and anecdotes within the film are often stereotypical, the film is consistently shot in a style that was much more direct, similar to a newsreel in its graininess and focus. Jay Leyda, for example, marvels at the fact that a Hollywood-trained director would make such an "anti-pretty" film, particularly because he made *Turksib* at a time when even documentaries had a more glossy style and used a cameraman accustomed to shooting fiction films (Leyda, 1960). This choice of style may have been Turin's way of maintaining a visual authenticity that gave credence to his argument—another way of creating an emotional connection with the audience by giving them the sense that this problem is an immediate and real one.

Turin's gritty style shared important characteristics with those of other filmmakers working in the same era. The newsreel was one of the most important documentary forms during and after the Russian Revolution, and other filmmakers used newsreel footage in larger documentary work (like Esfir Shub) or imitated its style (like Sergei Eisenstein) communicate immediacy and realism. Like these other filmmakers, Turin used "newsreel" realism as a style with a specific and intentional emotional result, an aesthetic choice rather than a direct or unproblematic way of representing the real world.

This combination of fiction and reality is one of Turin's most important contributions to the theory of the documentary in Soviet Russia. In addition, his emphasis on the residents of Turkestan as exotic and Eastern led to an interest in orientalism in films such as Vertov's *Tri pesni o Lenine/Three Songs about Lenin* (1934). Critics disagree about the effects of *Turksib* on Turin's career, but all agree that his union of Hollywood and communism—the live and the staged, the East and the West—was unique and influential in Soviet documentary history.

SUNNY STALTER

See also **Turksib**

Biography

Born c. 1895 in Leningrad, Russia. Died 1945.

Selected Films

1929 *Turksib*
1938 *Bakintsy*

Further Reading

Leyda, Jay, *Kino: A History of the Russian and Soviet Film*, New York: Macmillan, 1960.

Payne, Matthew, "Viktor Turin's *Turksib* (1929) and Soviet Orientalism," in *Historical Journal of Film, Radio, and Television*, 21, 1, 2001, 37–62.

Roberts, Graham, *Forward Soviet!: History and Non-fiction Film in the USSR*, London and New York: I. B. Tauris, 1999.

Shlapentokh, Dmitry, and Vladimir Shlapentokh, *Soviet Cinematography 1918–1991: Ideological Conflict and Social Reality*, New York: Aldine de Gruyter, 1993.

Taylor, Richard, and Ian Christie (eds.), *The Film Factory: Russian and Soviet Cinema In Documents 1896–1939*, London and New York: Routledge, 1988.

Youngblood, Denise. *Soviet Cinema in the Silent Era, 1918–1935*, Ann Arbor: UMI Research Press, 1985.

TURKSIB

(USSR, Turin, 1929)

Turksib is a Soviet culture-film (a didactic documentary) about the Turkestano-Siberian railway. The film was directed by Viktor A. Turin and released by Vostok-Kino, a studio mandated to make films for the eastern areas of the Soviet Union. Acclaimed at home for its comprehensible argument and compelling story, it was also critically lauded in Europe and America for its modernist techniques and exotic subject. In spite of its initial critical and popular reception, *Turksib* was banned in the mid-1930s. The film was thought not to give enough credit to Stalin for the railway plan, it did not deal with communist ideals like class-consciousness, and some Russian critics found fault in the film's combination of documentary and fiction film techniques. Today, the film is best understood both in the tradition of Soviet orient-alism and the communist belief in technology's power to conquer nature, as well as in the wider context of modernist meditations on the primitive and the machine.

Documentary film had an important role as propaganda in the Soviet Union from the time of the Russian Revolution. The Soviet film industry in the 1920s, however, moved away from overtly didactic films. One of the key reasons for this shift was that documentaries were often so poorly made that they alienated their audiences and worked against their own ideological purposes. Turin believed the failure of the culture-film in the 1920s was based on its failure to articulate its theme, something he tried to accomplish through a combination of logical structure and exciting storytelling (Payne, 2001).

The interest in storytelling was what led to later suspicion and criticism of the film. The background of those involved and Turin's intentions in making the film place *Turksib* squarely in opposition to the philosophy of documentary film espoused by Dziga Vertov. The most important Soviet documentarian of the 1920s, Vertov harshly criticized all fiction film and even staged documentaries, famously stating that film should display "life caught unawares." Turin had spent ten years working in Hollywood, and the rest of his crew had similar experience in the world of fiction. The scenario was written by Viktor Shlovskii, a noted literary critic, and his camera-man, Evgeni Slavinksky, had worked on fiction films since before the Revolution.

Turksib is perhaps closest to the films of Sergei Eisenstein in its combination of staged scenes and gritty visual aesthetic. Turin's film uses the techniques of fiction film to tell what would otherwise be

Turksib, 1929.
[*Still courtesy of the British Film Institute*]

a dry economic argument about the need for efficient transportation and trade between different regions of the Soviet Union. The first section, called "Cotton," shows Turkestani farmers laboring in hot fields. Because of their limited supply of water, they are forced to choose between irrigating the cotton they could trade with the rest of the Soviet states and the wheat they need to survive. These problems are all presented rapidly, in an abbreviated and impressionistic style. The heat is suggested by panting dogs, concern over the crops by cuts between close-ups of worried faces and wilting fields.

The film's second section, called "The Way of the Road," deals with movement as the underlying cause of the economic impediments in regions like Turkistan and Siberia. Transportation's inefficient progress is subject to the whims of the natural world. In the best-known sequence illustrating this conflict, the Turks' camel caravan, while attempting to trade the cotton and wool, is halted in the desert by a sandstorm. This scene has a surreal quality, reveling in the sculptural beauty of the sand dunes but juxtaposing this with an inter-title describing the scene as "a burial ground for travelers and their cargoes."

This chaos contrasts dramatically with the abilities of the planners introduced in the third section, "Here Come the Engineer-Surveyors." Not only can they move efficiently through and above the Kazakh steppes in their car and airplane, but they can also rationalize movement through this area with their maps and plans for railroad construction. This section moves from a direct illustration of the region's problems to an imagined solution. In a scene indebted to avant-garde art styles like such as constructivism and Russian futurism, stop-motion, animated blueprints, charts, and numbers dance around the screen; an animated train draws its path across a map, showing the distance between the regions it will be connecting.

This section of the film has the most obviously staged sequences, including a race between the engineers' car and a Kazakh nomad on a horse. This scene makes clear the film's intentions in equating the Eastern with the primitive and the Western with the technologically advanced or modern. Some critics think that *Turksib* avoided conventional communist issues of this era, such as class conflict, to emphasize the clear distinction between East and West, a distinction that may have led to the film's popularity elsewhere (Payne, 2001).

Primitivism places the film within the modernist colonialist tradition. The audience is meant to be fascinated by and desire to subjugate cultural others. In addition, the film's belief in the conquering power of the machine over nature is both part of Marxist theories of collectivization and the American theories of Taylorist efficiency. The railroad workers' labor is naturalized through cross-cutting with the work of reapers, but the construction of the railroad is meant to rationalize nature by taming it. The cutting speeds up as the film moves back and forth between the mechanized movements of workers and the humanized movements of machines. The film ends with the exhortation to finish the railway line by 1936, but Turin's combination of logic and emotional appeal make the construction seem inevitable.

Western film critics have dismissed the film in the recent past, characterizing it as unsuccessful or not truly documentary; however, even more recent assessments of *Turksib* ignore genre arguments to address its historical and cultural complexity. The film's stylistic and ideological impurity both lead to unevenness in technique between different sections of the film, but it has an overall emotional and intellectual coherence that is quite powerful. *Turksib* is an underrated Soviet documentary, one that uses modernist film techniques in a powerfully populist way.

SUNNY STALTER

See also **Russia/Soviet Union; Turin, Viktor; Vertov, Dziga**

Turksib (USSR, Vostokkino, 1929, 57 min.). Distributed by Amkino Corporation and Kino International Corp. Directed by Viktor A. Turin. Written by Yakov Aron and Viktor Shklovsky. Cinematography by Boris Frantsisson and Yevgeni Slavinsky.

Further Reading

Leyda, Jay, *Kino: A History of the Russian and Soviet Film*, New York: Macmillan, 1960.

Payne, Matthew, "Viktor Turin's *Turksib* (1929) and Soviet Orientalism," in *Historical Journal of Film, Radio, and Television*, 21, 1, 2001, 37–62.

Roberts, Graham, *Forward Soviet!: History and Non-fiction Film in the USSR*, London and New York: I. B. Tauris, 1999.

Shlapentokh, Dmitry, and Vladimir Shlapentokh, *Soviet Cinematography 1918–1991: Ideological Conflict and Social Reality*, New York: Aldine de Gruyter, 1993.

Taylor, Richard, and Ian Christie (eds.), *The Film Factory: Russian and Soviet Cinema In Documents 1896–1939*, London and New York: Routledge, 1988.

Youngblood, Denise, *Soviet Cinema in the Silent Era, 1918–1935*, Ann Arbor: UMI Research Press, 1985.

TYNESIDE STORY

(UK, Gunn, 1944)

Tyneside Story was one of the wartime films of social purpose that has led some critics to believe that British documentary cinema contributed to the radicalisation of the public during the "People's War" and ushered in the postwar Labour government with the mandate to win the "People's Peace." Numerous shorts and documentaries distributed by the Ministry of Information, films like *Dawn Guard* (1941), *New Towns for Old* (1942), *World of Plenty* (1943), and *The Plan and the People* (1945), articulated a set of peace aims about reconstruction and postwar planning. These helped determine an outlook that firmly rejected the bankrupt prewar social and political framework and raised expectations about a planned and managed economy predicated on state welfare.

The film commences with a documentary sequence concerning the history and tradition of shipbuilding in Newcastle, which had declined as a result of depression. The great Eldon Yard is now closed, but we are reminded of its proud tradition. It built the first oil tanker, and it once launched three iron steamships in a single day. In the wartime emergency the yard is being made good again, brought back to life through orders from the Admiralty. The Ministry of Labour tackles the problem of a shortage of skilled workers and seeks out former employees to re-recruit them. Some are keen to return and reignite their skills, but Fred is less sure. He now works on a building site and does not want to uproot only to get thrown out again at some future date. Within a short time British craftsmen are active again building ships and a vessel is launched. Skilled men are in short supply, however, and to confront the problem are being instructed at a government training centre where they are told that there are "hundreds of jobs in the yards that can be done by women as well, or better than, men." There are carefully presented scenes of women being trained as welders and other essential skills of shipbuilding, and viewers are informed that one operative, Betty, "is as good as any man in the yard."

The wartime policy is a success and the resurrected industry on Tyneside now builds cargo ships, tankers, submarines, and aircraft carriers. As the narrator patriotically declares: "As long as Britain calls for ships, the call will be answered by the ring of steel on steel in the shipyards of the Tyne." Finally, Fred returns as the voice of scepticism and declares direct to camera: "Aye, but wait a minute. Tyneside's busy enough today, old uns and young uns hard at work makin' good ships, but just remember what the yards looked like five years ago: idle, empty, some of 'em derelict, and the skilled men that worked in them scattered and forgotten. Will it be the same again five years from now? That's what we on Tyneside want to know."

Tyneside Story, 1944.
[*Still courtesy of the British Film Institute*]

The presentation of peace aims was officially avoided during the war, and attention was concentrated on the difficult job of winning the conflict. It has been argued, however, that "by the close of World War II, significant sections of the British people had been treated to visions of a grandiose post-war Utopia which exceeded anything promised during World War I" (Pronay, 1983). Paradoxically, this propaganda emanated from the Films Division of the Ministry of Information (MOI), which commissioned huge numbers of documentary films during the war and distributed them nontheatrically to vast audiences. The progressive nature of some of these films derived from the left-leaning members of the documentary film movement who contributed 74 percent of the titles produced or commissioned by the MOI. Basil Wright and Paul Rotha were perhaps the most outspoken advocates of the "world revolution," but New Jerusalem ideals found their way into significant numbers of documentaries. Gilbert Gunn and Michael Hankinson at Spectator Films preceded *Tyneside Story* with *Birth of a Tank* (1942) and *Women Away From Home* (1942), two people's war titles documenting wartime social changes and the home front's contribution to the war effort. Gunn followed it with *Housing in Scotland* (1945), a significant example of the later wartime emphasis on planning and reconstruction. Taken together these films were typical presentations of the loosely articulated peace aims that circulated through wartime documentary cinema.

Tyneside Story was a classic example of this wartime progressive documentary cinema. The cast was drawn from the local socialist drama collective, the People's Theatre Company, and its message conformed to the characteristic "Never Again" idealism of the time and its rejection of the boom and bust polarities of unregulated private enterprise and the newly acknowledged potential of the fully planned economy. The wartime emergency had produced the will to resurrect the idle yards; the will now had to be carried forward into the peace and the commitment to maintain jobs and to draw on workers' skills.

ALAN BURTON

See also **Rotha, Paul; Wright, Basil;** *World of Plenty*

Tyneside Story (UK, 1944, 14 min.). Produced by Spectator Films for the M.O.I. Directed by Gilbert Gunn and produced by Michael Hankinson. Story by Jack Common. Photography by A. H. Luff. Edited by Ralph Kemplen. Sound by W. S. Bland. Music by Ken Hughes.

Featuring Alf Simpson, Alan Thompson, W. Crabtree, John Bell, G. G. Whitingham, Sal Sturgeon and F. R. Gibson.

Further Reading

Addison, Paul, *The Road to 1945*, London: Jonathan Cape, 1975.

Burton, Alan, "Projecting the New Jerusalem: The Workers' Film Association, 1938–1946," in *War Culture. Social Change and Changing Experience in World War Two*, edited by Pat Kirkham, and David Thoms, London: Lawrence and Wishart, 1995.

Forman, Helen, "The Non-theatrical Distribution of Films by the Ministry of Information," in *Propaganda, Politics and Film, 1918–45*, edited by N. Pronay and D.W. Spring, London: Macmillan, 1982.

Pronay, Nicholas, "'The Land of Promise:' The Projection of Peace Aims in Britain," in *Film & Radio Propaganda in World War II*, edited by K. R. M. Short, London & Canberra: Croom Helm, 1983.

Swann, Paul, *The British Documentary Film Movement, 1926–1946*, Cambridge: CUP, 1989.

Thorpe, Frances, and Nicholas Pronay, *British Official Films in the Second World War*, Oxford: Clio Press, 1980.

The Arts Enquiry. The Factual Film, London: PEP, 1947.

U

UNDERGROUND/ACTIVIST DOCUMENTARY: AUSTRALASIA/ OCEANIA

Activism has more often shaped non-mainstream documentary making within Australasia/Oceania than have underground influences. Activist documentaries may be informed by radical motives based on "grassroots" issues; anger or frustration with prevailing hegemonies; a committed belief in social change through action and consciousness; and/or a godardian sense of not only making political films, but making films politically (the politics of form, production, and distribution are as important as the politics of content).

Integral to the activist tradition has been the Trade Union strand of documentaries. Cecil Holmes directed *Fighting Back* (1949) after his suspension for Communist Party membership from the government-run National Film Unit (NFU). The documentary was publicized by the Carpenter's Union as "the first on-the-spot film of an industrial dispute ever recorded in the Southern Hemisphere." *Fighting Back* enabled Holmes to break out of the mould of Weekly Review items and experiment more with dramatic reenactments, as well as articulate his political views indepen-

dently of an institution. In 1949, Holmes left for Australia to continue making films "his way."

Themes of workers dissatisfied with union officials and their ties to the state are echoed within a number of documentaries made during the early 1980s. *Wildcat* (1981) was the first documentary made by Vanguard Films (Alister Barry, Russell Campbell, and Rod Prosser). The longest-running documentary collective in New Zealand, if not Oceania, Vanguard Films is still producing work. *Wildcat*, about the Timberworkers' fight for a democratic union structure, is notable for its approach to collective interviewing techniques, the insertion of montage commentaries that work to elicit both affective and critical identification, and the use of sound in counterpoint to the visual track.

MerGer Productions's *The Bridge: A Story of Men in Dispute*, was also finished in 1981. Directors Gerd Pohlmann and Merata Mita had made a number of documentaries together about struggles for *Maaoritanga* (Maaori culture) and trade union movements. The Carpenter's Union appears again in this film, but the inclusion of excerpts from

Fighting Back has an ironic function. This time the union secretary is seen by members of the rank-and-file to be part of the problem. The voice-over of Zac Wallace, a protagonist-worker, gives narrative cohesion to a ranging story. It is also a story with layers, and his ambivalence can be read as the ambivalence of a Maaori perspective toward union structures.

Alister Barry's 1996 documentary *Someone Else's Country* (SEC) examined the effects of neo-liberal restructuring and its implications for democracy in Aotearoa. Commentary about the erosion of unions and dissipation of worker solidarity is tied to an analysis of the incursions of transnational corporations and global capital into the New Zealand economy. Despite having an obvious point of view, the uncomplicated expositional narrative (distinct from *Wildcat*'s dialectical structure) invites an analogy with current affairs documentary. The documentary was narrowcast on community television stations around the country; video copies were distributed through Vanguard Films and a bookstore chain with shops nationwide (thousands of copies were sold for domestic and community-group viewing). There were town hall screenings, and the left-oriented Alliance Party endorsed the documentary as part of its preelection publicity campaign. The stylistic choices made were strategic, and this, together with historical conjuncture (the documentary was released a few months before the 1996 general election), contributed to the unprecedented scale of audience reception for a non-broadcast documentary.

Merata Mita directed *Patu!* (1983) and co-directed *Bastion Point: Day 507* (1980) alongside Leon Narbey and Gerd Pohlmann. Both documentaries are crucial for the traditions of Maaori and indigenous filmmaking and share many formal characteristics: observational-style handheld camera, expressively textured sound tracks, ironic or associative juxtaposition in editing (sound-image/image-image), borrowed and resurrected film stock, sequences of photographic montage, inclusion of radio commentary, and the sparing use of Mita's voice-over narration. Differences between the documentaries lie in *Bastion Point* focusing on the struggle over land rights for *Ngati Whatua o Orakei* (the Auckland tribal group leading the occupation), and *Patu!* needing to accommodate a range of community interests involved in national and indigenous struggles over identity. In the case of the former, Mita could readily locate herself as a Maaori woman making a documentary about Maaori issues, whereas *Patu!* focused on the anti-

Springbok Tour protests of 1981 and was made with the principal intention of holding a mirror up to race relations and state governance in New Zealand society. One overriding irony not lost on the documentary was that it took protest against apartheid in South Africa to act as a catalyst for anti-racist protest within Aotearoa.

Other important strands of activist documentary include the feminist films of the 1970s and 1980s that worked to emphasize women-in-community and consciousness-raising (see Shepard, 2000). *Some of My Best Friends Are Women* (1975), *I Want to Be Joan* (1978), and *Even Dogs Are Given Bones: Women Workers Fight Back, Rixen NZ* (1981) give some indication of the range of work produced during this time, from personal growth narratives to the power of collective action. In the manner of situationist bricolage, gay filmmaker Stewart Main's *Captive State* (1986) offers a provocative set of associations between the Indonesian oppression of East Timor, the silence of New Zealand government and media, and the obliviousness of New Zealanders held in the thrall of consumerism. A subtextual element of the film associates the oppression of the Timorese with the more subtle forms of oppression operating within a homophobic society, insensitive to difference.

GERALDENE PETERS

Articles published in New Zealand film magazines *Illusions* (Wellington, 1986–) and *Alternative Cinema* (Auckland, 1973–1986) provide useful information about production and critical contexts for the documentaries discussed in this article.

Selected Films

1949 *Fighting Back* (Cecil Holmes, director)
1975 *Some of My Best Friends Are Women* (Deidre McCartin, director)
1978 *I Want to Be Joan* (Stephanie Robinson, director)
1980 *Bastion Point: Day 507* (Merata Mita, Leon Narbey and Gerd Pohlmann)
1981 *Even Dogs Are Given Bones: Women Workers Fight Back, Rixen NZ* (Carole Stewart, director)
1981 *Wildcat* (Alister Barry, Russell Campbell, and Rod Prosser, directors)
1981 *The Bridge: A Story of Men in Dispute* (Gerd Pohlmann and Merata Mita, directors)
1983 *Patu!* (Merata Mita, director), and co-director.
1986 *Captive State* (Stewart Main, director).
1996 *Someone Else's Country* (Alister Barry)

Further Reading

Campbell, Russell, "The Discourse of Documentary: Narrational Strategies in *Bastion Point Day 507*, *Wildcat*, *The Bridge*, and *Patu!*," in *Illusions*, 4, Summer 1987, 10–17.

———, "Plain Hard Hazardous Work: Cecil Holmes at the NFU," in *Illusions*, 7, 1988, 4–13.

Horrocks, Roger, and Karl Mutch, "Political Films in New Zealand: From 'Liberal' to 'Radical,'" in *Alternative Cinema* 10, 1–2, Autumn–Winter, 1982, 6–12.

Parker, Dean, "Scoundrel Times at the Film Unit," in *Illusions*, 7, 1988, 4–8.

Peters, Geraldene, "Lives of Their Own: Films by Merata Mita," in *New Zealand Film Makers*, Ian Conrich and Stuart Murray (eds.), Michigan: Wayne State University Press, forthcoming.

Shepard, Deborah, *Reframing Women: A History of New Zealand Film*, Auckland: HarperCollins, 2000

UNDERGROUND/ACTIVIST DOCUMENTARY: CHILE

During the twentieth century, Latin American countries developed an activist and underground documentary movement that has been recognized increasingly as a vital and notable historical development. Chile developed these underground films, parallel to the official production of documentaries, as a consequence of the restrictive atmosphere perpetrated by the government of General Augusto Pinochet.

Pinochet was head of the military government from 1973 until 1990. He came to power in a violent coup that deposed Salvador Allende, the first socialist to be elected president of Chile. Once in power, Pinochet and his government suppressed any opposition. Constitutional civil liberties and human rights were curtailed. Censorship was the norm. Thousands of people died as a result of the practices of the Pinochet regime.

Many Chilean directors began their careers during the Allende administration, and they had to emigrate during the Pinochet era. As a result, numerous notable underground documentaries were filmed partially in Chile and partially abroad. These filmmakers continued to develop their work while in exile. Most of these films were overtly political and were made with limited resources. Sometimes filmmakers secretly returned to Chile to film and then left again to do postproduction abroad.

Between 1973 and 1983, approximately ninety underground Chilean documentaries were produced. Generally made with small budgets and modest production values, they focus on the repressive political climate and the suffering of the Chilean people. A list of the most notable of these films appears at the end of this entry.

In 1980, the opposition of the Chilean people to the Pinochet administration, as well as the pressures of the international community, forced the Chilean government to developed a new constitution that called for a single-candidate presidential plebiscite in 1988. Pinochet lost the plebiscite, and Chile had a presidential election in 1989. Pinochet transferred power to his successor, Patricio Aylwin, in 1990, but retained his post as commander-in-chief of the army until 1998, when he assumed a lifelong seat in the Chilean senate, a position he had to abandon four years later because of health concerns.

A new era began in media and the arts, although many censorship regulations remained in place for a long time. Many Chilean directors, such as Patricio Guzmán, recognized the importance of this period and the value of the underground documentaries. Guzmán's *El caso Pinochet*, a new version of his first documentary, *La batalla de Chile*, was presented at the Cannes Festival in 2001.

Some of the most important directors of underground and activist documentaries are Raul Ruiz, Patricio Guzmán, Miguel Littín, Claudio Sapiain, Sergio Bravo, Valeria Sarmiento, Pedro Chaskel, and Leuten Rojas.

CATALINA CERON

See also **Battle of Chile, The**; **Guzmán, Patricio**

Underground and Activist Chilean Films, 1973 to 1983

1973 *La Primera Página* (Sebastián Alarcón, 35mm)
1975 *Los puños frente al cañón* (Gaston Ancelovic and Orlando Lubert, 16mm)
1975 *Nombre de Guerra* (Miguel, Henriquez, 35mm)

1975 *La Batalla de Chile, primera parte: La insurrección de la Burguesía* (Patricio Guzmán, 16mm)

1975 *La historia es nuestra y la hacen los Pueblos* (Alvaro Ramirez, 16mm)

1975 *Yo recuerdo también* (Letuen Rojas, 16mm)

1975 *El cuerpo repartido y el mundo al revés* (Raul Ruiz, 16mm)

1975 *La Canción No Muere, generales* (Claudio Sapiain, 16mm)

1975 *La dueña de casa* (Valeria Sarmiento, 16mm)

1975 *Dos años en Finlandia* (Angelina Vasquez, 16mm)

1975 *Yo vendo, usted elige* (Luis Roberto Vera, 16mm)

1976 *Los tres Pablos* (Sebastian Alarcón, 35mm)

1976 *Roja como Camila* (Sergio Castilla, 16mm)

1976 *La batalla de Chile, sugunda parte: El golpe de estado* (Patricio Guzmán, 35 and 16mm)

1976 *Crónica de Tlacotalpan* (Miguel Littín, Jorge Perelman, Jorge Sanchez, 16mm)

1976 *Sotelo* (Raul Ruiz, 16mm)

1976 *He venido a llevarme una semilla* (Luis Vera, 16mm)

1977 *Margarita* (José Echeverría, 16mm)

1977 *Las cámaras también* (Federico Elton, 35mm)

1977 *Lamento de una rima* (Leo Mendoza, 16mm).

1978 *Testimonio* (Rafael Guzmán, 16mm)

1978 *El evangelio en Solentiname* (Marilu Mallet, 16mm)

1978 *Los Chilenos* (Jorge Montesi, 16mm)

1978 *Las divisions de la naturaleza* (Raul Ruiz, 16mm)

1978 *Victor Jara vive* (Claudio Sapiain, 16mm)

1979 *Eramos una vez* (Leonardo De La Barra, 16mm)

1979 *Exilio 79* (Leonardo De La Barra, 16mm)

1981 *Inti-Illimani, una experiencia de vida* (Gustavo Francia, 16mm)

1982 *From the strings of my guitar* (Leuten Rojas, 16mm)

1983 *Chile, no invoco tu nombre en vano* (Cine-ojo Colectivo, 16mm)

1983 *Después de 10 años* (Jorge Lubbert, 16mm)

1983 *Chile, donde comienza el dolor* (Jorge Lubbert, 16mm)

1983 *El regreso de Amateurs en bibliotecas* (Raul Ruiz, video 14')

Further Reading

Cine Chileno en el exilio, Cuadernos Hispanoamericanos No. 482–483, 1990.

Filmografía del Cine Chileno en el exilio, Cinemateca Chilena en el Exilio, Paris, Francia, 1983.

Hojas de Cine, Testimonios y Documentos del Nuevo Cine Latinoamericano, Volume I and III, Colección Serie Universitaria, Fundación Mexicana de Cineastas, 1988.

Periódico El Tiempo, Colombia, Mayo 13, 2004.

Pick, Zuzana M, *Cronologia del Cine Chileno en el Exilio 1973–1983*, Hojas de Cine, Testimonios y Documentos del Nuevo Cine Latinoamericano, Volumen I, Colección Serie Universitaria, Fundación Mexicana de Cineastas, 1988.

Sadoul, G., *Historia del Cine Mundial*, Siglo XXI, 1991.

UNION MAIDS

(US, Reichert and others, 1976)

Union Maids is one of a number of films that emerged out of the growth of the women's movement in the United States at the end of the 1960s. As women began to move into documentary filmmaking in increasing numbers, a number of films in which women and their environments were made visible in a new way appeared. This was frequently done through the use of archival film material and contemporary interviews, an aesthetic derived in many cases from Emile de Antonio's prototype *In the Year of the Pig* (1969). *Union Maids*, made by the team of Julia Reichert, James Klein, and Miles Mogulescu in 1976, was one such project of historical excavation.

The film is a collective portrait of three women labour organisers in the late 1920s and 1930s, who were part of a community of working class Chicago socialists. Using a compilation structure that mixed archive footage and direct interview, the filmmakers attempt to reconstruct a history of women's involvement in labour organising. The women, Kate Hyndman, Stella Nowicki, and Sylvia Woods, tell their stories in the course of three separate interviews, which are intercut with each other and with period newsreel footage. In a partial retreat from direct cinema aesthetics, these interviews are conducted by audible and sometimes visible interviewers, a technique that adds to the personal and strongly narrative thrust of the documentary. The interviewees recount their experiences of organising to counteract exploitation in the workforce from a strongly radical perspective. They also tell a tale of sexism on the job, as well as within the unions and among leftist men. The one black woman, Sylvia, speaks of racial discrimination and her own conversion to interracial class unity by evidence of white class solidarity.

Union Maids works best as a tale of three working-class heroines in a period of great working-class power. The film is full of stirring stories of the women's militancy and bravery. Sylvia Woods describes how in the laundry where she first worked the women conducted what she believes may have been the first sit-down strike of the 1930s. Stella Nowicki recounts how often the packinghouse workers would stop the line, shutting down production. Kate Hyndman, the most obviously radical of the women, was laid off after writing an article for the *Daily Worker*. The use of three exceptional women, however, means that the film denies the larger reality of women's working lives, which were concentrated in mainly non-unionised clerical and service work. The film also skirts somewhat coyly around the question of the women's likely affiliations with the Communist Party, a strategy that ultimately serves to weaken both the film's documentary stance and radical underpinnings.

On a formal level, critical reception of *Union Maids* was initially informed by the 1970s critique of realism that affected both nonfiction and fiction film studies. A number of feminist film critics objected to the use of direct cinema techniques in the presentation of history. It was felt that the privileged film subjects of the interview format could become problematic if a film relied on them as the primary informants. The accounts of oral history subjects could be partial, fragmentary, idiosyncratic, and possibly misleading (Michel, 1981). In the context of a perceived need to construct a cinema that could both present individuals within the context of a complex social structure and simultaneously critique the film process itself, *Union Maids* was viewed as a flawed text.

The film was seen by several contemporary critics as deriving its central importance as an organising tool for women's and worker's organisations. Its importance as a potential catalyst was thus considered to render it immune from ideological analysis (McCormick, 1977; Nichols, 1991). The problem is one of unaccustomed "against the grain" readings of leftist texts, texts that may contain a number of ideological contradictions. In the case of *Union Maids*, these devices could be said to be the interview format itself and the intersection of discourses of biography, autobiography, and popular narrative history. For Noel King, these discourses coalesce to present a pro-

blematic humanist-historicist, populist mode, particularly evident in the interview format used in the film. In this reading *Union Maids* tells its story of past events through an uncontested re-presentation of the memories of the three women, suppressing any awkward questions on the social construction of these women themselves. Bill Nichols has also drawn attention to the epistemological problems presented by the use of archival footage as a confirmation for commentary, which normalises the footage as authentic (in Renov, 1993).

More recently, a critical recuperation of the realistic strategies used in *Union Maids* and similar historical documentaries has underlined its status as a feminist counterhistory. While recognising the dangers of an uncritical acceptance of documentary's realist illusions, several writers have pointed out that the same formal attributes of interviews, photographs, or voice-over narration can serve different functions in different films (Waldman and Walker, 1999). Recognition of past struggles of working-class women, such as those depicted in *Union Maids*, can illuminate the extent to which individual volition and equal opportunity can be illusory or at least conditional.

MARINA BURKE

See also **In the Year of the Pig; Reichert, Julia**

Union Maids (U.S., New Day Films, 1976, 54 min.). Produced and directed by James Klein, Miles Mogulesco, and Julia Reichert. Edited by James Klein and Julia Reichert. Cinematography by Sherry Novick and Tony Heriza. Archival Film and Photographic Research by Julia Reichert with Barbara Tuss and Sherry Novick.

Further Reading

Erens, Patricia, "Women's Documentary Filmmaking: The Personal Is Political," in *New Challenges for Documentary*, Alan Rosenthal, (ed.), Berkeley: University of California Press, 1988.

Gordon, Lynda, "Union Maids: Working Class Heroines," in *Jump Cut: Hollywood, Politics and Counter-Cinema*, Peter Steven (ed.), Toronto: Between the Lines, 1985.

Kaplan, E. Ann, "Theories and Strategies of the Feminist Documentary," in *New Challenges for Documentary*, Alan Rosenthal (ed.), Berkeley: University of California Press, 1988.

King, Noel, "Notes on 'Union Maids' and 'Harlan County USA'," in *Screen*, 22, 2, 1981, 7–18.

Lesage, Julia, "The Political Aesthetics of the Feminist Documentary Film," in *Quarterly Review of Film Studies*, Fall 1978, 506–523.

McCormick, Ruth, "Union Maids," in *Cineaste*, 8, 1, Summer 1997.

UNION MAIDS

Nichols, Bill, *Representing Reality*, Bloomington and Indianapolis: Indiana University Press, 1991.
Renov, Michael (ed.), *Theorising Documentary*, London: Routledge, 1993.

Waldman, Diane, and Walker, Janet (eds.), *Feminism and Documentary*, Minneapolis: University of Minnesota Press, 1999.
Winston, Brian, *Claiming the Real*, London: British Film Institute, 1995.

UNIT B

Unit B was one of a varying number of production units into which the National Film Board (NFB) of Canada was organized near the end of World War II. In the 1950s, the Unit evolved into a distinctive, remarkably creative entity that became almost as well known among the film community as the NFB itself. It pioneered documentary technique, technology, and style, yielding several enduring classics and influencing the NFB documentary overall.

Headed by Tom Daly, Unit B functioned collaboratively and, compared with other units at the NFB, with little hierarchy. Its key filmmakers were Colin Low, Roman Kroitor, Wolf Koenig, the writer Stanley Jackson, and Daly himself, who not only produced the films but often edited them. Their best films combined meticulous attention to the details of craft with an intense interest in structure. The films were innovative in one way or another, and usually involved the breaking of rules and opposition to convention. *Corral* (1954) was shot with a handheld 35mm camera. *City of Gold* (1957) was made with a specially invented camera-tracking device that enabled its still photographs to be filmed with full three-dimensional movements. *Universe* (1960), which took years to complete, inspired NASA and Stanley Kubrick, who used the narrator for the voice of Hal in *2001: A Space Odyssey*. The Candid Eye series (1958–1961) pioneered direct-cinema style, and it was the first time at the NFB that cameramen were included as part of the production team. *Lonely Boy* (1961) set a standard for the structuring of unscripted material, as well as unpretentious reflexivity. *Circle of the Sun* (1961) melded imagery, narration, and story into a compelling representation of Blood Indian mythology.

Unit B came to an end in 1964, when the unit system was dismantled and replaced by an arrangement that freed NFB filmmakers from fixed hierarchical structures. Unit B's influence on documentary film and the Film Board continued. Donald Brittain, a major agitator against the unit system, was inspired by Unit B's craftsmanship and wanted opportunities to make films of comparable worth. French-Canadian filmmakers such as Michel Brault and Gilles Groulx were encouraged and inspired by their early work on Candid Eye. Filmmakers who joined the NFB after Unit B's demise found themselves influenced by both its films and its filmmakers. Low took his expertise to the new, activist Challenge for Change program; Koenig headed Animation for a time. Daly became a producer for young anglophone filmmakers.

Unit B's body of work has been criticized for a lack of strong interest in social or political issues. Its key members saw life in an optimistic light, shaded by mystic overtones. But their attitude toward the craft and their almost messianic perfectionism, profoundly affected more politically minded filmmakers, enabling the latter to make films on political subjects but transcending the topical, such as Brittain's *Memorandum* (1966) or Michael Rubbo's *Sad Song of Yellow Skin* (1970).

D.B. JONES

See also **Brault, Michel;** *City of Gold***; Daly, Tom; Grierson, John; Koenig, Wolf; Kroiter, Roman;** *Lonely Boy***; Low, Colin; Macartney-Filgate, Terrence;** *Memorandum***; National Film Board of Canada;** *Sad Song of Yellow Skin*

Further Reading

Feldman, Seth (ed.), *Take Two*, Toronto: Irwin Publishing, 1984.
Feldman, Seth, and Joyce Nelson (eds.), *The Canadian Film Reader*, Toronto: Peter Martin, 1984.
Harcourt, Peter, "The Innocent Eye," in *Sight and Sound*, Winter 1964–1965, 19–23.

Jones, D.B., *Movies and Memoranda*, Ottawa: Deneau, 1982.
————, *The Best Butler in the Business: Tom Daly of the National Film Board of Canada*, Toronto: University of Toronto Press, 1996.

Pâquet, André (ed.), *How to Make or Not to Make a Canadian Film*, Montreal: La Cinémathèque canadienne, 1967.

UNITED KINGDOM

The emergence of documentary filmmaking in Britain may be traced back to footage shot by amateur and professional cameramen that chronicled various expeditions during the early years of the twentieth century. Although such footage hardly resembles documentaries in the sense the term is commonly used today, these films used the cinematic medium to document "realistic" elements that later would be exhibited for public audiences. Such visual records include the wildlife films of Cherry Kearton (which began production as far back as 1908) and the long running *Secrets of Nature* series (1919–1933), produced by Harry Bruce Woolfe and Percy Smith. After World War I, filmmakers such as Woolfe, Walter Summers, and Geoffrey Barkas produced films (including *Armageddon* [Woolfe, 1923], *The Battle of the Falkland and Coronel Islands* [Summers, 1927], and *Q Ships* [Barkas, 1928]), which combine authentic combat footage with reconstructed sequences. Although Britain was not the first to document elements outside the realm of fiction, such works were foundational in using film for educational and instructional purposes. Films such as these may be considered logical predecessors to what would become the British documentary film movement of the 1930s, arguably Britain's greatest contribution to the development of cinema.

After World War I, the outlook of domestic politics changed in Britain. The nature of the British government began to transform from the limited hierarchical undertakings of the nineteenth century to one that embraced a more active public interaction. The state began to feel an obligation to become involved in how its citizens were informed about various policies via publicity. The Empire Marketing Board (EMB) was set up in May 1926 by a Conservative government to administer the newly created Empire Marketing Fund to improve trade. Although the majority of the EMB's budget was spent on research, the Board became most recognized for its publicity activities.

The EMB's approach toward publicity was greatly influenced by public relation policies practiced in the United States. Such policies stressed the importance of education as the foundation for public relations initiated by government departments. Developments in media such as the use of film for publicity had effectively been used in the United States during World War I, and it soon became clear to the EMB that any official department would logically use film as a means to instruct and educate citizens. The secretary of the EMB was Stephen Tallents (1884–1958), an instrumental figure in the formation of the British documentary film movement. It was Tallents who would meet and collaborate with John Grierson and, in the process, initiate the assemblage of filmmakers who would compose the movement.

John Grierson (1898–1972) was born in Scotland and graduated from Glasgow University with a M.A. degree in English and moral philosophy in 1923. The next year he traveled to the United States on a Rockefeller research fellowship in social science. It was while studying in America that he became interested with how mass media (the popular press and eventually the cinema) could be used to propagandistic ends. During the late 1920s, Grierson became influenced by the work of American author Walter Lippmann, whose views on education made quite an impression on him. Lippmann's *Public Opinion* (1922) is widely credited for inspiring Grierson to consider American propaganda expertise to develop films that would serve as educational tools. Grierson believed "that because the citizen, under modern conditions, could not know everything about everything all the time, democratic citizenship was therefore impossible" (Grierson, 1946). Considering that motion pictures are a form of expression that target a mass audience, Grierson became dedicated to developing films that would inform citizens of social concerns they perhaps weren't familiar with, ideally contributing to the formation of citizens who could make informed decisions based on democratic ideals.

Grierson believed that documentary films (or all films constructed from natural material, as he describes) were better suited to portray the reality of social issues in Britain than the dramatic conventions of fiction. Hollywood's motivation was purely commercial by his assessment, completely devoid of qualities he believed to be moral or artistic. Early cinematic influences on Grierson were the films of Robert Flaherty (1884–1951) and Soviet cinema of the 1920s; both provided an alternative to Hollywood through their tendency to dramatize fiction. Grierson himself familiarized the term *documentary* when he used it in a review of Flaherty's *Moana* (1926), describing it as "a poetic record of Polynesian tribal life which had 'documentary value.'" Grierson's insistence that documentary film was the most effective means to educate the public is reiterated in his three principles of "documentary proper." First, "Documentary would photograph the living scene and the living story" (Grierson, 1946). Grierson believed that studio films largely ignored the potential for film to open up the screen to reality and instead relied on artificiality to communicate to an audience. Second is "(the belief) that the original (or native) actor, and the original (or native) scene, are better guides to a screen interpretation of the modern world" (Grierson, 1946). Finally Grierson subscribed to "(the belief) that the materials and the stories thus taken from the raw can be finer (more real in the philosophic sense) than the acted article" (Grierson, 1946).

Grierson returned to Britain from the United States in 1927 and met Stephen Tallents, who at the time was developing a feature film suggested by Rudyard Kipling for the EMB entitled *One Family*. Tallents had appointed Walter Creighton, a man who knew little of filmmaking, as director of the project at the suggestion of Kipling. On meeting Grierson, Tallents was impressed with his ideas but had already appointed Creighton as the EMB's first Film Officer. Unwilling to lose Grierson as a collaborator, Tallents asked him to write a series of reports on film production for the EMB Film Committee. The first report (which dealt with the two issues most valuable to the Committee: how to use film as propaganda and how to compete with

the American film industry) was titled "Notes for English Producers." In it, Grierson stated his interest in establishing a permanent film unit within the EMB. Grierson's second report dealt with the topic of film distribution and explained the possibilities of nontheatrical distribution as a means to circulate the films he envisioned the EMB producing. He also began to organize a series of screenings at the Imperial Institute where he screened various films such as British Instructional's *Secrets of Nature* series and various Russian films from the early 1920s.

In early 1928, Grierson proposed the production of two films to the Film Committee to be made from newly shot footage. One of the films was to concern the herring industry, a topic that interested Financial Secretary to the Treasury Arthur Samuel (who contributed in approving the decision to begin film work) because of his position as Britain's authority on herring. On approval, Grierson set out to direct his first film *Drifters* in the summer of 1928.

The EMB entered into a contract with New Era Films in order to finance and distribute *Drifters*, as production of Creighton's feature film *One Family* had secured a generous amount of the Board's funding without any tangible results. The film was shot quickly and for the sum of nearly 3,000 pounds. Running 50 minutes, the film depicts fishermen as they pursue herring shoals along the east coast of Britain. Shot by professional cameraman Basil Emmott, *Drifters* is obviously influenced by the silent Soviet filmic style, which Grierson was familiar with and admired. The film is among the first attempts at national cinema to stray from the Hollywood style of illusionism and to make use of montage to locate melodramatic effects in realistic material. It also portrays the working class in a romantic manner, a thematic development Grierson's productions would repeatedly return to.

Drifters was finished in the summer of 1929. It premiered in a noncommercial setting on a bill with Eisenstein's *Battleship Potemkin* in front of the London Film Society, where it was well received. The film enjoyed commercial success as well, practically recouping its production costs after one year of distribution. The major triumph of *Drifters* was that it suggested that an alternate method of obtaining finance for filmmaking was possible that existed largely (although not entirely) outside commercial concerns. Its success aided Grierson in convincing the EMB of setting up its own film unit in January 1930.

After officially being appointed Assistant Film Officer of the EMB Film Unit in 1930, John Grierson began to assemble a crew of collaborators who would produce many of Britain's most important early documentary works. Among Grierson's first recruits for the EMB Film Unit was Basil Wright (1907–1987), who began work in December 1929. Under Grierson, Wright assembled *Conquest* in 1930, a compilation film designed for schools about the wilderness of North America and the effects of technology, which pulls a portion its source material from footage of American westerns such as *The Covered Wagon* (James Cruze, 1923). In addition to Wright, those filmmakers who would become the first generation of the documentary film movement in Britain included Arthur Elton, Edgar Anstey, Stuart Legg, J.N.G. Davidson, John Taylor, Paul Rotha, Donald Taylor, Grierson's sisters, Marion and Ruby, Evelyn Spice, and Margaret Taylor, who would become Grierson's wife. The EMB Film Unit was also among the few units who would employ women behind the camera during this period. The majority of the recruits were middle class and had a public school and university (Oxbridge) education. Of these new recruits, only Davidson, Elton, and Rotha had previous significant filmmaking experience.

Nearly all of Grierson's collaborators spent the early part of their time with the unit assembling films out of existing footage, as budget limitations prevented excessive shooting of new footage. These films found their source material from large stocks of film available from various parts of the Empire, primarily Canada where a large number of travel films were available. The unit also produced "poster" films, which were loops of film intended for use on projectors at EMB exhibitions and in shop windows. These early predecessors to the television commercial typically involved promoting Empire products such as Scottish tomatoes, Empire timber, wool, and butter.

By the 1920s, American film industries had managed to dominate 95 percent of the film market in Britain, which led to the establishment of the Cinematograph Films Act in 1927. The purpose of the act was to introduce a system of quotas that would increase the number of British films shown in the country, but in reality it had little effect. Although the British film industry did recover somewhat in the 1930s, American films still made up for more than 70 percent of films shown in Britain after the drafting of the act. In addition, many of the films that were produced to meet the quota were made cheaply and shown to empty cinemas. Documentary films typically did not count in meeting the demands of the quota. It was not until the Cinematograph Films Act of 1938, when a separate standard of quotas were introduced for short films, that documentary films became eligible. The failure of documentary films to be incredibly successful in commercial release would lead Grierson and his collaborators to look toward nontheatrical distribution for the films they were producing.

In January 1931, Grierson wanted to expand the production of the unit by producing a series of films that would be intended purely for nontheatrical distribution, including distribution to schools. He and the unit began to produce films that were slightly more advanced than previous efforts. Arthur Elton (1906–1973) produced *An Experiment in the Welsh Hills* (1931), which documents a professor's experiments to obtain grasses and increase the suitability of sheep rearing in the Welsh mountain region. Elton also made *Upstream* (1931), which concerns salmon fishing in Scotland and makes use of impressive visuals, including a sequence of salmon leaping from waterfalls. Basil Wright made a one-reel film called *Lumber* (1931), which compiles footage from Canada about lumberjacking and also shot *The Country Comes to Town* (1931), which draws connections between the countryside and the food industry. Wright also made his first truly personal film in 1932 with *O'er Hill and Dale*, a film about a border shepherd in lambing season. Documentary pioneer Robert Flaherty collaborated with Wright on *The Country Comes to Town* and became loosely associated with the unit in 1931. Grierson decided to spend nearly 2,500 pounds to allow Flaherty to produce a film for the unit on craftsmanship in industry. Flaherty set out to film the steel bridge at Saltash, but the result was footage that began to come back to London without a concrete script. The EMB could not afford to continue the project, so the collaboration ended. *Industrial Britain* was later produced, however, combining the Flaherty footage with footage of waterways shot by Basil Wright and footage of coal mining shot by Arthur Elton. The film was released in 1933 under a combined production credit of Grierson and Flaherty. The necessity to maintain films for use in schools and other nontheatrical venues led to the creation of the Empire Film Library in October 1931. By 1936, the Empire Film Library was the largest film distributor to schools in Britain.

The incorporation of sound into motion pictures made it more difficult for the EMB Film

Unit to get their films commercially released. The unit possessed no resources for recording sound, and all of the films made by the unit were silent, with some manner of musical accompaniment produced during exhibition. By 1932, it was difficult for silent films to obtain commercial distribution at all. Grierson, realizing the potential for the unit's films to obtain commercial distribution if sound were to be incorporated, asked the Film Committee in December 1931 for additional funds to create a sound studio. Although the Committee denied his request, both Tallents and Grierson began to negotiate with Gaumont-British Distributors in 1932 for the sale of six EMB films for commercial release. The films that were purchased—*Shadow on the Mountain* (Elton, 1933), *King Log* (Wright, 1932), *The Country Comes to Town*, *Industrial Britain*, *Upstream*, and *O'er Hill and Dale*—were given commentaries and musical scores by Andrew Buchanan (a leading short film director and producer) and packaged as the *Imperial Six* in 1933. *Shadow on the Mountain* and *King Log* were actually Elton's *An Experiment in the Welsh Hills* and Wright's *Lumber*, but were retitled and slightly edited when synchronized sound was added to them. Unfortunately, the films of the *Imperial Six* compromised Grierson's original vision. The commentaries and musical scores proved to be quite contradictory from the films themselves, and the *Imperial Six* proved to be the only films the EMB Film Unit would get into commercial release.

Grierson soon realized that industrial sponsorship could provide additional resources to finance films. Individual members of the unit were successful in obtaining sponsorship from industry and Arthur Elton made *Voice of the World* for His Master's Voice Gramophone Company in 1932, the first film to be made for an outside body by the unit. By this time Grierson's abilities as a producer were known outside of the confines of the unit, and he advised government agencies such as the Travel and Industrial Association and the Ministry of Labour on the unit's film activity. Such films produced as a result included Donald Taylor's *Lancashire at Work and Play* (1933) and *Spring Comes to England* (1934), as well as travel films such as *So This Is London* (1933) and *For All Eternity* (1934) by Marion Grierson. Edgar Anstey (1907–1987) emerged with his first two solo efforts *Eskimo Village* and *Uncharted Waters* in 1932, while *Aero Engine* established Arthur Elton as a skilled filmmaker in 1934. Another film financed outside the central government was Stuart Legg's *The New Genera-*

tion, completed for the Chesterfield Education Authority in 1932.

By 1932, an earlier decision by the Select Committee on Estimates to abolish the EMB had begun to reveal its consequences. It had become increasingly difficult for Grierson to maintain funding for the unit, and he had begun to keep Tallents and many his collaborators in the dark about financial and production concerns. Around this period, Tallents had been appointed the first public relations officer of the Post Office and ensured that the film unit would be among those organizations saved from the dissolvement of the Board. Tallents believed in Grierson's vision that film had the potential to play perhaps the most important role in public information services, and, in September 1933, he and the unit moved under the authority of the Post Office.

The commercial film trade industry began to become hostile toward the newly christened General Post Office (GPO) Film Unit after its transition from the EMB. The Gaumont-British group of film companies entered into the field of educational films in late 1933 and believed that the unit's intention to produce films for agencies outside the GPO would provide unfair competition. Even the Accountant General's Department within the GPO felt that the unit's current home perhaps was not the best agency for a film unit to take on work for other departments and semipublic bodies. Despite the protests, the Treasury authorized the transfer of the unit to the Post Office for a trial period of six months.

The unit's transfer to the GPO provided the acquisition of sound recording equipment, although what was provided was not competitive with the equipment used by the Hollywood studios of the era. Nevertheless, the ability to record sound allowed the unit to become potentially more competitive in securing regular commercial distribution for their films. Grierson and his collaborators continued to operate much in the same manner they did when the unit was part of the EMB. Grierson ensured that only himself and his office manager Stanley Fletcher were on the GPO's official payroll. The others members of the unit were employed by New Era Films, which by then no longer operated as a commercial company and largely participated solely in carrying out work for the GPO. Grierson used the employment of his unit by New Era to deter any accusations by the commercial film trade of using public resources to enter into competition with private enterprise. Grierson claimed that the unit was actually employing a commercial contractor in hiring New Era, and thereby satisfied requests by the film trade for the unit to exclusively hire outside contractors for their film work. The Treasury eventually realized what the unit was up to and ruled that the unit had to directly employ its staff and would not be allowed to produce work for other governmental departments and outside bodies.

Grierson then reorganized the unit according to the Treasury's requirements while largely ignoring the other restrictions it implemented. He continued production as he saw fit by maintaining that staff members not on the official payroll would continue to produce films for outside bodies, but those films already in production could be completed by staff members on the payroll. One of the most interesting films began while the unit was still under the EMB was *Granton Trawler* (1934), a companion piece to *Drifters* that chronicles dragnet fishing off the Scottish Coast. Although John Grierson has claimed that he produced the film himself, various records list J.D. Davidson as cameraman and Edgar Anstey as editor. Other significant films beginning their production while the unit was still under the EMB included *Song of Ceylon* (Basil Wright, 1934), *BBC: Voice of Britain* (Stuart Legg, 1934), and *Workers and Jobs* (Arthur Elton, 1935).

The Empire Tea Marketing Expansion Board had requested four one-reel films of Ceylon in 1933 and Basil Wright traveled there to shoot them after completing footage for *Cargo from Jamaica*, *Liner Cruising South*, and *Windmill in Barbados* shortly beforehand the same year. He returned to cut *Song of Ceylon* in 1934 and a sound track was subsequently added. The film, a combination of the four one-reelers, juxtaposes its sound track (including a seventeenth-century description of Ceylon and the modern echoes of radio broadcasts and phone conversations) with a beautiful visual depiction of the practices and rituals of Ceylon's inhabitants. The result draws attention to a contrast between the effect the sound track provides and the stability of traditional practices in Ceylon. *The Song of Ceylon* is widely considered to be one of the most important documentaries to be produced by the movement and received first prize in the documentary class at the International Film Festival in Brussels. The film signified a renewed level of artistic achievement for the films of the British documentary movement.

The GPO Film Unit received 7,500 pounds from the British Broadcasting Corporation in 1932 to produce *BBC: The Voice of Britain*. Like *Song of Ceylon*, the film is a collaborative effort under the primary guidance of one filmmaker, in this case Stuart Legg. The film was the longest and most expensive venture the movement had undertaken up to that point, and even Grierson expressed some doubt that it would be completed efficiently. *BBC: The Voice of Britain* chronicles one day of broadcasting in Britain, which served to assist the BBC in showing the public a glimpse behind the scenes of its operations and a view of its new building. The film was widely shown in cinemas and was regarded as a triumph by the public and the film trade. While working for the GPO Film Unit, Arthur Elton produced *Workers and Jobs* for the Ministry of Labour in 1935. Elton wasn't officially on the payroll and thus was able to complete the work in accordance with the Treasury's requests. The film is about the work of Labour Exchanges and is revolutionary in its pioneering use of direct speech recording on location. The film resembles a newsreel and predates technically similar television reports by several years.

A major addition to the GPO Film Unit to come from the commercial film industry was Brazilian filmmaker Alberto Cavalcanti (1897–1983) in 1933. Cavalcanti had previously been a director in France and perhaps saw the GPO Film Unit as a way to break into the British feature film industry. He initially contributed to *Song of Ceylon* by suggesting various experiments to Basil Wright, and he directed the films *The Glorious Sixth of June* and *Pett and Pott* for the GPO film unit in 1934. Cavalcanti's contribution to the film *Coal Face* (1935) is particularly notable. Although there is some dispute about the screen credits for *Coal Face*, it generally is regarded as Cavalcanti's film. It portrays an informative account of Britain's coal industry and emphasizes the tragedies of mining labour. The film features the collaboration of W.H. Auden and Benjamin Britten on the film's script and musical score respectively, and "(foregrounds) the use of music and sound in a non-naturalistic way, so that natural sounds, dialogue, speech, music, and choral singing (are) integrated into a dramatic unity" (Aitken, 1990). Although the film was not widely praised on its release, it received a medal of honor at Brussels. Grierson labeled the film "Empo," a term he used to label films he thought were experimental.

The British Commercial Gas Association and the Gas Light and Coke Company commissioned Arthur Elton and Edgar Anstey early in 1935 to produce a number of films, two of which would prove to be significant: *Housing Problems* (1935) and *Enough to Eat* (1936). Elton and Anstey had begun to allow subjects they were filming to speak directly for themselves on the sound track while filming. *Housing Problems* was significant in that it was among the first films to make use of interviews in this manner (predating the *March of Time* style of interviewing, which was typically manipulated in the studio) and to be sponsored by an industry in which no direct promotion of that industry or its products are mentioned in the film. The film introduces slum dwellers who in their own words explain their living conditions. For the first time, underprivileged people spoke freely about the condition of their lives, a radically different portrayal of citizens compared to the romantic image of the working class in many other films produced by Grierson. In 1936, Anstey wrote and directed *Enough to Eat*, a film based on the work of Sir John Boyd Orr, which draws parallels between malnutrition and social class in Britain. The direct interviews in the film were of "experts" commenting on the film's subject, an innovation that would set the standard for thousands of informative documentary films.

Also in 1936 came *Night Mail*, directed by Basil Wright and Harry Watt (1906–1987). Watt began working for Grierson in 1931 as general assistant at the EMB. The film portrays a postal express train traveling from Euston to Glasgow, collecting and distributing mail. It contains little commentary and sound for the film was shot on location. One scene depicting letters being sorted in a railway carriage was actually recreated in a studio. Films such as *Night Mail* "were not, significantly, of the straightforward pedagogical type of film, but were much more humanistic, and most important perhaps, employed narrative devices such as scripted dialogue, studio sets, and conventional dramatic development and resolution, which engaged viewers like regular commercial motion pictures" (Swann, 1989). Paul Rotha mildly criticized Grierson for the use of overt romanticism toward the end of *Night Mail*, speculating that its inclusion may have been prompted by an attempt for box-office appeal (Rotha, 1973). Regardless, the film proved to be one of the most popular documentaries turned out by the movement, achieving wide critical success and enjoying a modest theatrical run in commercial cinemas.

Paul Rotha (1907–1984) was among the first of Grierson's collaborators to venture away permanently from the unit. Rotha wanted to make what he believed to be more personal films, an ambition that was not possible working with Grierson's unit. Having previously made short trailers for the unit, Rotha produced *Contact* in 1933, a film that was financed by Shell-Mex and British Petroleum for 2,500 pounds. The film demonstrates how air routes and planes are assembled and concludes with a journey by air. Rotha would receive commercial backing from British Instructional over the next several years and would produce films such as *Roadwards* (1933), *Rising Tide* (1934), and *Great Cargoes* (1935). For Vickers Armstrong and the Orient Shipping Line, Rotha made *Shipyard*, a project shot over a period of months in 1934–1935. The film documents the building of an Orient liner called the *Orion* and communicates the notion that, on completion of the ship, thousands of workers will face unemployment. Another significant film directed by Rotha is *The Face of Britain* (1935), which was sponsored by Hugh Quigley of the Central Electricity Board and deals with the use of electricity to organize a more efficient Britain. Rotha would eventually join an independent company producing sponsored documentary films to be shown in commercial cinemas called the Strand Film Unit as Director of Productions in 1935.

Eventually, the restrictions placed on the GPO Film Unit and the desire to work elsewhere led to a number of significant departures. Arthur Elton left to make films for the Ministry of Labour and later would create the Shell Film Unit. Edgar Anstey departed to work for Shell and then ran the American *March of Time* series British film unit. Stuart Legg left to work for the Strand Film Company and Basil Wright parted ways to establish the Realist Film Unit. Finally, John Grierson left the unit in June 1937 to create Film Centre, an organization whose intent was to take over the functions of Associated Realist Film Producers, which included the organization of sponsors and filmmakers.

Grierson's departure from the GPO Film Unit was met with the promotion of A.G. Highet to the position of Controller of Publicity and J.B. Holms to the post of Production Supervisor. Alberto Cavalcanti and Harry Watt both stayed on with the unit and brought a significant change to the kind of films the unit would produce. Cavalcanti and Watt led the GPO Film Unit away from the type of filmmaking the unit was previously known for and toward films that used narrative techniques commonly associated with commercial cinema. Harry Watt made one of the first of these types of films while Grierson was still at the GPO Film Unit called *The Saving of Bill Blewiit* (1936). The film makes use of scripted dialogue and studio sets and is based around a fictitious story. The film also is largely shot on location and uses nonprofessionals actors. It proposes that the Post Office Savings

Bank is the solution to the small businessman's problems. Harry Watt was to continue to produce these types of story documentaries on a much larger scale with *North Sea* (1938), a film he made for presentation at the Empire Exhibition in Glasgow. Based on true events, the film dramatizes a series of reports Watt read involving ships caught in winter storms. The film was the most widely distributed film of all films produced by the GPO Film Unit, even receiving commercial distribution overseas.

The GPO Film Unit also produced a series of films dealing with international communications, including *We Live in Two Worlds* (1937) and *Line to Tcherva Hut* (1937), both directed by Alberto Cavalcanti. In addition to *North Sea*, other films produced for the Empire Exhibition included *Mony a Pickle* (1938) and *The Tocher* (1938). Another film the unit produced for the Ministry of Health was *Health for the Nation* (John Monck, 1939), which was a social document film directly about its sponsor. The unit also produced a series of films for display in the British Pavilion at the 1939 New York World's Fair dealing with British workers including *Men in Danger* (Pat Jackson, 1939), *British Made* (George Pearson, 1939), and *Spare Time* (1939) directed by Humphrey Jennings (1907–1950), one of the most significant directors of the British documentary movement. *Spare Time* is based on Jennings's connection with Mass Observation, a movement that attempted to apply ethnography to British society. The film shifts among portrayals of a brass band in the steel industry, the marching of a carnival band in the cotton industry, and the singing of a coal miners' choir. It contains hardly any commentary and tends to place its emphasis on the individuals in the various industries. The film paints a sympathetic, yet hardly romanticized, depiction of working class leisure activities, later leading John Grierson to criticize the film. It would be the beginning of an artistically impressive output of production from Jennings during World War II.

The GPO Film Unit became the Crown Film Unit early in 1941, after the relocation of the unit's activity to the newly created Ministry of Information. The Crown Film Unit continued to produce documentaries that possessed a style similar to commercial films, a trend that had been occurring more frequently toward the end of the 1930s. The result was a steady output of films that were readily embraced by commercial audiences. Harry Watt's *Target for Tonight* (1941), which portrays a day in the life of a bomber squadron,

became the most commercially successful documentary produced during World War II. Pat Jackson's *Western Approaches* (1944) was cast entirely from merchant seamen and depicts the aftermath of a torpedo attack on a convoy. *Desert Victory* (Roy Boulting, 1943) won the Academy Award for best feature-length documentary. By this point the unit had access to increased budgets and elaborate studio sets, factors that would distinctly separate their films from other documentaries of the time. The films they produced were also now regularly rented commercially.

The films of Humphrey Jennings during this period have been especially praised for their contribution to film art. His short film, *Listen to Britain* (1941), depicts a day in the life of Britain during wartime, presenting such imagery as factory workers juxtaposed with leisure activities taking place in a dance hall. Jennings's *Fires Were Started* (1943) documents a unit of the Auxiliary Fire Service and uses actual firemen as performers, and *A Diary for Timothy* (1944–1945) combines the four stories of a farmer, an RAF pilot, a miner, and a railway engineer with the tale of a baby named Timothy. The contribution of Jennings' poetic marriage of sound and visual image remains a focus of critical attention on the documentaries produced by the Crown Film Unit.

The development of documentaries for television in Britain had begun as early as 1934 when the Selsdon Committee was formed to consider the medium's development. The British Broadcasting Corporation (BBC) had established itself as a major sound broadcasting organization and was reluctant to invest their attention in television initially. By 1939, television in Britain had become a modest success, although during World War II, the BBC would close down its operations and not reinstate them until 1946. By 1953, the BBC had began to prioritize television's development and appointed former Grierson collaborator Paul Rotha as Head of Documentaries. Rotha saw the potential for television documentary and was committed to developing the new medium to socially inform Britain's citizens.

The television unit at the BBC during these early years was characterized by members who came from a multitude of backgrounds including Steve McCormack (theatre), Robert Barr and Norman Swallow (journalism), Caryl Doncaster (education), and Denis Mitchell (radio features). Three categories of programs that fell under the identification of "documentary" were the dramatized documentary, the actuality documentary, and the magazine documentary (Bell, 1986).

The dramatized documentary was a scripted, live production that featured professional actors. Locations were typically reproduced in the studio if possible, and the content of the stories for these films was taken from true life situations. Various subjects these films engaged included "hooliganism, borstal, drugs, working women, children in care, problems of youth, marriage and old age, prostitution, industrial relations, declining industries" (Bell, 1986). These programs were met with immediate popularity, but the cost of their production was significant. These dramatized documentaries re-created situations that caused controversy among those purists who were used to the documentation of real life events or "actualities" in documentary film. Rotha defended these dramatized films through his assessment that realism within subject material was the true nature of documentary, regardless of how films are constructed.

Both the magazine and the actuality documentaries possessed content that was more journalistic than the dramatized documentary. Both used "actualities" rather than scripted acting and interviews. One such notable actuality documentary production was the monthly series *Special Enquiry* (1952–1957), which involved such national dilemmas as racial discrimination, illiteracy, slums, and international problems such as refugees, malaria, and soil erosion (Bell, 1986). *Special Enquiry* was the first television program to speak from the point of view of the audience. It began to invite a consideration of documentary as a form of reporting (Corner, 1991). Each episode was forty-five minutes long, consisting of an introduction from a studio presenter and concluding with a discussion with a studio guest following a filmed location report. The series was influential to the structure of British television journalism through its presentation of nonofficial speakers and presented a documentary type that moved beyond the sole portrayal of filmed or photojournalistic depiction.

The magazine documentary was far less serious in its intentions. Among the most popular television documentaries to be developed at the time, the magazine documentary resembled "highly skillful travelogues with less scenery and more people" (Bell, 1986). Within this form, represented by series such as *London Town* and *About Britain*, the first unscripted interviews in television documentary were used. The Documentary Department at the BBC was dissolved with the arrival of commercial television in 1955, with Rotha and its staff moving on to other projects.

Beginning in 1956, a screenings at the National Film Theatre were organized in London. The films screened were organized by a group of young filmmakers and exhibited under the banner of Free Cinema. Those organizing the screenings (including Lindsay Anderson, best known as a critic at the time, and Karel Reisz, who had been programme planner of the National Film Theatre) exhibited a variety of films, including documentary films they had produced. "In the broadest terms, Free Cinema had two objectives: to show what it valued in the cinema, with the emphasis on the work of young contemporary filmmakers; and (to show) films to encourage other films to be made" (Lovell and Hillier, 1972). The Free Cinema programmes were committed to demonstrating the relationship between society and art, and the documentaries screened were assumed by the young organizers to portray this notion.

The films shown in the Free Cinema programmes were generally free from the formal constraints placed on many commercial documentaries of the era. Their subject material, including a candid study of a jazz club in *Momma Don't Allow* (Karel Reisz and Tony Richardson, 1956) and an examination of popular culture through the people and exhibits of an amusement park in *O Dreamland* (Lindsay Anderson, 1953), were far different than many conventional documentary topics. Lindsay Anderson's *Every Day Except Christmas* (1957) offers a celebratory portrayal of British working class people and owes much of its formal technique to the wartime films of Humphrey Jennings. Such films made use of new, lightweight equipment that brought a renewed level of intimacy to documentary. The films were more ambiguous than previous documentary efforts and brought the viewer into places that were previously restricted. Lorenza Mazzetti's *Together* (1953) stands apart from other Free Cinema offerings because of its unique composition. The film uses long takes and slow editing rhythms to portray two oppositional communities, one of deaf mutes and the other of traditional working class people. Although most all of the documentaries screened at the Free Cinema programmes may be described simply as portrayals of British society in the 1950s, they approached their representations from a contemporary perspective that had not been experienced before. The Free Cinema showings lasted nearly three years and included a total of six programmes. Its organizers would shortly thereafter venture into the realm of feature filmmaking, producing films that would make use of many of the techniques of the Free Cinema documentaries. Such notable examples include *Look Back in Anger* (Tony Richardson, 1959), *The Entertainer* (Tony

Richardson, 1960), *A Taste of Honey* (Tony Richardson, 1961), and *Saturday Night and Sunday Morning* (Karel Reisz, 1960).

In the early 1960s, the nature of programming at the BBC began to change. New possibilities were offered from technological advances (such as the use of videotape), allowing broadcasts to depart from transmitting live dramatic performances. The boundary between fiction and documentary subsequently began to blur in broadcasts known as documentary dramas, programs that took advantage of the opportunities offered by the advances such as editing and the incorporation of nonprofessional actors into productions. Among the most influential directors of such works is Ken Loach (1936–), who along with socialist playwright Jim Allen (1926–1999), would produce some of the most important documentary dramas of the era

Loach's career at the BBC began as director of three episodes of *Z Cars* (1962–1978) in 1964 and soon led him to direct three episodes of the six-part series *Diary of a Young Man* in late 1964. These early works, however, were not representative of the stylistic blurring of documentary and drama that Loach would eventually use in his later films. In 1965, he began to direct the first of ten plays he would produce for *The Wednesday Play* series. Three of these plays, *Up the Junction* (1965), *Cathy Come Home* (1966), and *In Two Minds* (1967), would establish Loach as a politically minded visionary whose films combine social and political dilemmas as a commentary on the contemporary climate of Britain.

Up the Junction's realistic depiction of abortion was viewed by more than 10 million people during its first transmission. More than 400 complaints were expressed to the BBC after its broadcast, most concerning the film's use of language and portrayal of abortion. The film uses documentary elements including an interview with a doctor who suggests the revision of laws preventing legalized abortions. Many viewers were confused as to whether they were watching a news broadcast or a fictionalized drama when the film originally aired, as it was shown directly after the evening news. Loach claimed that "(he) was very anxious for (his) plays (to) not be considered dramas but as continuations of the news." *Up the Junction* makes use of 1960s pop music and uses a fragmentary narrative structure similar to its source novel, written by Nell Dunn.

Cathy Come Home's portrayal of homelessness and poverty has reached iconic status in Britain since its original broadcast in 1966. The film's blending of documentary elements with fiction rea-listically portrays the tragedies that befall a working-class family after an accident, eventually resulting in the family's destruction. In one particularly memorable scene, Social Services removes Cathy's (Carol White) children from her after her separation from husband Reg (Ray Brooks). The film favors location shooting, and its formal techniques owe much to the stylistic influence of the Free Cinema documentaries. *Cathy Come Home* also prompted political outrage from its audience after its original broadcast, so much so that its reairing a few months later revealed several omissions from the version originally broadcast. The reaction from the film's audience eventually led to the establishment of Shelter, a homelessness charity.

In Two Minds involves the story of Kate Winter (Anna Cropper), a young woman who eventually is driven to madness by her familial environment. Loach would remake the film in 1971 as *Family Life*, but not before controversy would surround the original. *In Two Minds* prompted concern from critics such as James Thomas in the *Daily Express* who believed that its intense style was too realistic not to carry announcements before and after broadcasts explaining the film's fictional nature. The film also received criticism from the psychiatric community who judged its portrayal of schizophrenia and of medical workers who assist Kate as inaccurate.

Loach's collaborations with Jim Allen are arguably his most politically important works produced for television. Having previously written scripts for the British soap opera *Coronation Street* in 1964, Allen was commissioned to write *The Lump* for *Wednesday Play* in 1967. His first collaboration with Loach, *The Big Flame* (1969), recounts the story of the occupation of a port in Liverpool by dock workers. Widely considered to be among Loach's most political films, *The Big Flame* "dealt head-on with fundamental questions of ownership, class conflict, the role of the state, and political organization and mobilization" (Petley, 1997). The dock workers form a port workers' council and attempt to run the dock themselves. Eventually they are defeated by forces that include the trade union movement and the Labour Party. "Here appears the key theme which will dominate much of Loach's subsequent work, whether in dramas such as *The Rank and File* (1971) and *Days of Hope* (1975), or ill-fated documentaries, such as *Questions of Leadership* (1983): namely, that Labour politicians and trade union leaders are terrified of mass action by the militant working class, since it threatens the very structures on which their own power and position are based" (Petley, 1997).

Loach and Allen would again work together on the film *The Rank and File*, based on the Pilkington's glass workers' strike of 1970. The film was followed by yet another collaboration, the ambitious four-part *Days of Hope* in 1975, a film that traces the upheavals of the British Labour movement from 1916 to the General Strike in 1926. The film (Loach's first historical piece) unveils its narrative through the lives of three characters. It is strongly influenced by the politics of 1970s Britain and was condemned by Conservative politicians for its harsh portrayal of the government. The film's style continues Loach's naturalistic visual approach and breaks the conventional expectations of television drama through the use of a technique with spoken dialogue that seems improvisational and unorganized. Ultimately, Allen was accused of mixing fact and fiction and of distorting the facts of history to deliver a political message, and some critics began to suspect that the BBC was adopting a left-wing philosophy. Loach would move toward directing feature films in the years after working for the BBC including *Poor Cow* (1967), *Land and Freedom* (1995), *Carla's Song* (1996), *My Name is Joe* (1998), and *The Navigators* (2001).

Another important figure who produced ground-breaking documentary dramas for the BBC is Peter Watkins (1935–). After receiving his education at Cambridge, Watkins became an amateur documentary filmmaker producing short works such as *The Diary of an Unknown Soldier* (1959), in which a World War I soldier narrates his last days of being alive, and *The Forgotten Faces* (1961), a film concerning a revolt in Hungary. In 1964, Watkins was hired by the BBC and produced his first notable work, *Culloden*. The film showcases Watkins's trademark style, which combines drama with handheld camerawork and faux "newsreel" interview footage of nonprofessional actors who were instructed to acknowledge the camera. *Culloden* follows a television crew as they cover the 1746 Battle of Culloden and contains realistic battle footage as Watkins places the viewer "on location" with the news crew, complete with jarring camerawork and a sound track that allows the viewer to hear the horrors of war without actually viewing them. The film not only challenges the notion of how history has traditionally been recorded but also makes evident the fallacies of historical fiction.

Watkins's next film was *The War Game* (1966), which again uses his distinctive style to portray the atrocities of nuclear war. The film features interviews with "survivors" of a nuclear strike on Brit-

ain and is convincing through its use of documents, scientific studies, charts, and face-to-face interviews. The BBC originally banned the film from being broadcast in 1966 because of its intensely graphic nature and the chance that it could convince its viewers into believing its authenticity. The film was eventually transmitted on television nearly twenty years later in 1985. *The War Game* did receive a small theatrical run shortly after its completion, winning the Oscar for Best Documentary Feature in 1967. Watkins later would direct his only feature film, the science fiction failure *Privilege*, with funding from Universal in 1966 and subsequently worked primarily in Scandinavia after leaving the United Kingdom. *Punishment Park* (1971), a pseudo-documentary that follows a group of soldiers as they escort liberals across a desert and *Edvard Munch* (1974), a biography of the Norwegian artist later followed.

In 1963, Britain's Granada Television began what would become the longest running documentary series in visual history with the production of *7 Up* (Paul Almond), a film that interviews a group of British children from various backgrounds about a variety of subjects, including their outlook on life and prospects for the future. Michael Apted (who was an assistant on the film) revisited the same children seven years later and directed *7 Plus Seven* in 1970. Apted would revisit the children in seven-year intervals after *7 Plus Seven*, resulting in the films *21 Up* (1977), *28 Up* (1984), *35 Up* (1992), and *42 Up* (1999). The films provide an interesting chronology of the social progression of Britain and contemporary culture at large, as various participants become poverty stricken while others appear to find fulfillment in their lives.

One of Britain's most recognizable documentary filmmakers, Nick Broomfield (1948–), is also one of documentary film's most innovative. His insistence on placing himself within the context and frame of those subjects and situations he documents has become characteristic of what Stella Bruzzi calls "performative" documentary filmmaking. Broomfield's presence within his films draws attention to the construction of nonfiction filmmaking as one type of representation, as opposed to a portrayal of unmediated reality (Bruzzi, 2000).

Broomfield was born in London and made his first film *Who Cares?* (1971), a study of a working-class community in Liverpool, with financial assistance from the British Film Institute. After studying law at Essex University, he joined the National Film School at Beaconsfield and produced *Proud to Be British* in 1973. The film is a series of opportunities for various citizens to explain what it means to them to be English. *Behind the Rent Strike* was completed in 1974 and features people from *Who Cares?* as a companion piece to the earlier film. Beginning in 1976, Broomfield made the first of several films with American filmmaker Joan Churchhill and began to apply a style more aligned with the observational cinema of Fredrick Wiseman. *Juvenile Liaison* (1976) follows two police officers and their dealings with youth. The film documents incredibly harsh treatment of the youth at the hands of the police and was later withdrawn from distribution after pressure from the authorities. Broomfield would later revisit the subject in 1990 with *Juvenile Liaison 2* (1990).

After temporarily dissolving his partnership with Churchill, Broomfield began to more readily exhibit the confrontational, participatory documentary style that has characterized his career, with 1988's *Driving Me Crazy*. The film, about the making of a film of a black stage musical, begins to take an unfortunate turn, and Broomfield soon places himself within the film's frame. The result is what Broomfield believes to be a more honest approach to filmmaking, allowing the viewer to make decisions based on the interaction between interviewer and interviewee instead of the former hiding behind the scenes.

Broomfield uses the same stylistic approach in his film *The Leader, His Driver and the Driver's Wife* (1991) a documentation of Eugene Terreblanche, the leader of the neo-Nazi Afrikaner Resistance Movement (the AWB) in South Africa. *Tracking Down Maggie* (1994) continues to use the same participatory approach through its attempt to document Margret Thatcher, with little success, as does many of Broomfield's more recent and financially successful documentaries including: *Aileen Wuornos: The Selling of a Serial Killer* (1992), *Heidi Fleiss: Hollywood Madam* (1995), *Kurt and Courtney* (1998), and *Biggie and Tupac* (2002).

Filmmaker Molly Dineen similarly uses herself as an active participant in her films. Instead of becoming actively visible like the stylistic approach of Broomfield, however, Dineen uses her voice behind the camera not only to communicate with on-screen interviewees but also to constantly remind the viewer of the constructedness of documentary. Her earlier work includes *Home from the Hill* (1985), a film made while she was attending the National Film and Television School that documents a retired soldier and safari operator returning from Kenya to England and *My African Farm* (1988), a portrait of Colonel Sylvia Richardson and her servants on a farm in Kenya over Christmas. A

documentary about people working at the Angel Underground Station, 1989's *Heart of the Angel* characterizes Dineen's early style in that it refuses explanatory voice over narration in an exchange for Dineen's personal encounters with her subjects. "As with many 1960s direct cinema films such as *Salesman*, *Heart of the Angel* is reliant upon the subjects' performances for and to the camera" (Bruzzi, 2000).

Dineen's 1993 BBC effort, *The Ark* is a series of four, one-hour films about the London Zoo during six months of crisis. Facing financial ruin, the zoo exports more than 1,300 animals (about one third of the entire zoo's collection) and 26 keepers. The film clearly continues the observational style of Dineen's previous efforts, with scenes extending for minutes without any commentary from the director. Critics drew parallels between the situation presented in the film and growing turmoil within official bodies such as the Labour Party, The Church of England, and the BBC itself. The film never really sentimentalizes the subject material and instead offers the observation of stunning visuals to communicate to its audience. Dineen's later work includes *In the Company of Men* (1995), a series of three, one-hour films with "The Prince of Wales" company of the Welsh Guards on a tour of duty in Northern Ireland, *Tony Blair* (1997), a ten-minute portrait of Tony Blair broadcast before the 1997 election campaign, and *Geri* 1999), a ninety-minute documentary that follows Geri Halliwell (Ginger Spice) in the three months after her departure from the pop group, The Spice Girls. In 2002, Molly Dineen produced *The Lord's Tale*, a film for Channel 4, about the reform of the House of Lords.

Another notable filmmaker hailing from Britain who helped destroy the conventions associated with documentary is Nicholas Barker. Barker's television series, *Signs of the Times* (BBC, 1992) consists of a series of interviews with individuals about good and bad taste. The approach to the series "is minimalist, stylized and possesses a stylistic uniformity that gives it a clear identity and lends it a fetishistic intensity, mesmerized by superficialities, appearance and detail" (Bruzzi, 2000). Stella Bruzzi argues that because *Signs of the Times* is self-conscious in its style, it reflects its subjectivity and authorship and thereby becomes performative by challenging notions of fixed identity and truth. The characters on the show "are performative on two counts: they are performing their words by being the embodiments of their identified tastes and attitudes, and they perform their interviews in such a way as to raise questions about spontaneity and documentary authenticity" (Bruzzi, 2000).

Barker's film *Unmade Beds* (1997) expands on this notion through setting up a premise that calls attention to the authenticating procedures of documentary. Barker, deciding to make a film about the personals scene in New York City, began interviewing more than 400 candidates before eventually deciding on the four individuals used in the film. Working from the actors' own versions of their life's stories, Barker produced a script that the actors followed while shooting the film. The result is a fictional documentation based on real-life events and acted out by the people on whom those events are based. Questions of authenticity are problematic in the film and in the process raises important questions about the possibility of truthful representation. *Unmade Beds* demonstrates that perhaps all representations contain elements of both fiction and nonfiction, and that the attempt to capture "reality" in visual media is indeed an impossible pursuit.

KEVIN SHERMAN

See also **Anderson, Lindsay; Anstey, Edgar;** *BBC: Voice of Britain;* **Broomfield, Nick;** *Cathy Come Home;* **Cavalcanti, Alberto;** *Coal Face;* **Culloden;** *Desert Victory;* **Drifters; Elton, Arthur; Empire Marketing Board Film Unit;** *Enough to Eat; Every Day Except Christmas;* **General Post Office Film Unit;** *Granton Trawler;* **Grierson, John;** *Housing Problems;* **Industrial Britain; Legg, Stuart;** *Line to Tcherva Hut;* **Loach, Ken;** *Momma Don't Allow; Night Mail;* **Reisz, Karel; Rotha, Paul;** *Song of Ceylon;* **Tallents, Stephen;** *Target for Tonight; War Game, The;* **Watkins, Peter; Watt, Harry;** *We Live in Two Worlds;* **Wright, Basil**

Further Reading

Aitken, Ian, *Film and Reform: John Grierson and the Documentary Film Movement*, London; New York: Routledge, 1990.
Bell, Elaine, "The Origins of British Television Documentary: The BBC 1946–1955," in *Documentary and the Mass Media*, John Corner (ed.), London: Edward Arnold, 1986.
Bruzzi, Stella, *New Documentary: A Critical Introduction*, London; New York: Routledge, 2000.
Corner, John, "Documentary Voices," in *Popular Television in Britain: Studies in Cultural History*, John Corner (ed.), London: British Film Institute, 1991.
Grierson, John, *Grierson on Documentary*, Forsyth Hardy (ed.), London: Faber & Faber, 1979.
Hillier, Jim, and Alan, Lovell, *Studies in Documentary*, London: Secker & Warburg, 1972.
Izod, John, Richard, Kilborn, and Matthew, Hibberd (eds.), *From Grierson to the Docu-Soap: Breaking the Boundaries*, Luton: University of Luton Press, 2000.
Laing, Stuart, "Ken Loach: Histories and Contexts," in *Agent of Challenge and Defiance: The Films of Ken Loach*, George McKnight (ed.), Westport, CT: Praeger Publishers, 1997.
Low, Rachael, *Documentary and Educational Films of the 1930s*, London: Allen & Unwin, 1979.
Orbanz, Eva, *Journey to a Legend and Back: The British Realistic Film*, translated by Stuart Hood, Berlin: Volker Speiss, 1977.
Petley, Julian, "Factual Fictions and Fictional Fallacies: Ken Loach's Documentary Dramas," in *Agent of Challenge and Defiance: The Films of Ken Loach*, George McKnight (ed.), Westport, CT: Praeger Publishers, 1997.
Rotha, Paul, *Documentary Diary*, New York: Hill & Wang, 1973.
Sussex, Elizabeth, *The Rise and Fall of British Documentary*, Berkeley: University of California Press, 1975.
Swann, Paul, *The British Documentary Film Movement 1926–1946*, Cambridge: Cambridge University Press, 1989.

UNITED KINGDOM: DOCUMENTARY DRAMA

The use of drama in documentary has a long history in British film and television. The technical deficiencies under which the early documentary filmmakers of Grierson's Empire Marketing and GPO Film Units laboured in the 1930s ensured that a certain amount of reenacted and rehearsed material would have to be used. Tripod-mounted cameras were not only cumbersome, they also needed good light and plenty of time between set-ups. In addition, synchronized sound was not possible and the available microphone technology performed better under controlled conditions in the studio. Partly because of these restrictions, the founding father of British documentary, John Grierson, had argued for the "creative treatment" of real-world material, thereby seeking theoretical legitimization of practices that were pragmatically indispensable.

As a result, the makers of celebrated films like *Night Mail* (1936) were constrained to produce sequences that were essentially illustrative fictions. For example, any activity on the train was re-created in the studio. The movement of the sorting carriage, open on one side, was simulated and the Post Office workers were given lines to say. Such sequences could be rather laboured (as this one is), but they could equally offer opportunities to the filmmaker. For example, the sequence involving the despatching and picking up of mailbags from the speeding train develops a rhythm and urgency through its artful montage of actuality and reenactment. During World War II, these same filmmakers (now working for the Ministry of Information as the Crown Film Unit) routinely dramatised scenes in the studio and on location for films such as *Western Approaches* (1944). The judicious mixing of library footage from agencies and rehearsed action filmed in the studio (plus an audience eager for and ready to believe in information) made for a powerful genre in a difficult historical era.

Film technology gradually increased its capacity to document directly in the period after the war, and the representational possibilities of documentary film increased accordingly. By the 1960s, the camera and microphone were present more and more often at real world events. The fledgling television industry, however, faced electronic restrictions in the decade after 1945 not dissimilar to the photographic limitations of the prewar film industry. Essentially, a good deal of television was restricted to studio production. Electronic cameras could manage sporting events and public occasions, but benefited from being in relatively fixed positions in a studio for speech-based programmes. Sound technology in television and film only began to acquire the flexibility to keep up with human interaction in the real world in the late 1950s. Even on British radio, the patient recreation of real-world speech, its systematic "cleaning up" for broadcast, had been a given of the so-called "Features" department from the time of the first mobile recording studios in the 1930s. Many of the personnel for the TV "story documentary" of the 1950s started their careers in radio. Television drama was live, with poor quality telecine offering the only possibility of recorded location inserts. As late as 1963, Arthur Swinson, a TV writer of the period, could define the difference between film and TV in terms of television being a live and film a recorded medium.

Early BBC television documentary therefore used considerable reenactment and invented speech to fulfill its public information remit. The story documentary perfected immediately after World War II ensured high levels of documentary content within an essentially invented programme. In a variant, real world protagonists were persuaded to act out simulated situations (in, for example, programmes about the new post-war public services). Cutaways to documentary film sequences could always reinforce the material by referencing actuality, but the factual information conveyed in dialogue and voice-over constituted the principal means of informing the audience. One entirely acted story documentary, *It's Your Money They're After* (1948) was even described as part of the "first ever [television] 'documentary series'" by the TV documentary producer Norman Swallow. Its maker, Robert Barr, believed TV documentary could only exist with dramatic reconstruction. In television, as John Caughie (2002) has remarked, the literate has always struck a balance with the visual (more so than in fiction film, for example). Nowhere was this more the case than in the information-laden BBC story documentaries of the 1940s and 1950s.

The situation in which documentaries were written more than found was the dominant practice until lightweight, synch-sound film equipment became widely available in the early 1960s. Thereafter, unprecedented levels of immediacy were available to documentary and reinforced a more sophisticated audience's belief in the camera's power by demonstrably "being there" at the pro-filmic action. The makers of both film and television drama seized the opportunity to import into their fictions the raw edge of reality so much a part of the documentary films of American practitioners like Robert Drew, Richard Leacock, and Frederick Wiseman. A wish to take cameras into areas of social life previously denied to film representation defines the thrust of much drama, as well as documentary in this post-1960 period. When the Canadian executive Sydney Newman took over the BBC's flagship television drama series *The Wednesday Play*, he introduced a policy he called "agitational contemporaneity." He wanted to shift BBC drama into a new contemporary relevance and produce plays that provoked debate about postwar society in Britain. Newman's policy was broadly similar to the cultural revolution that had occurred throughout the arts in Britain in the late 1950s, after the 1956 production of John Osborne's *Look Back in Anger* at London's Royal Court Theatre.

The most controversial of the plays for which Newman was responsible used documentary styles based on the new technology. The form of the documentary drama was also linked to a radical politics that sought to interrogate the break-up of the old British class system. This was the force that energized Ken Loach and Tony Garnett's 1964 *Up the Junction* and the same team's 1966 *Cathy Come Home*, both examples of the best of the Newman regime. They dealt with pressing social problems in Britain (sexuality, poverty, homelessness) and illuminated tensions within a working–class breaking up under the strains of a new world. The plays convinced partly through a visual presentation heavily dependent on actuality (or quasi-actuality) filming and dialogue that appeared to be improvised rather than written. *Cathy Come Home* achieved two repeat showings within the first year of its original transmission and occasioned active debate about the postwar housing problem within the wider society (even if it did not trigger long-lasting change).

If these films caused some controversy with their hard-hitting social comment, Peter Watkins' 1965 *The War Game* (about surviving nuclear war) went even further in testing the boundaries of the possible in documentary drama. The film provocatively took British government preparations for nuclear war (enshrined in Civil Defence booklets like the infamous *Protect and Survive*) and played it out as an invented scenario in the conditional tense. If there were a nuclear strike on London, the film asked, what would be the effects in a small town in Kent, according to the government's own (and other) experts? The production team utilised a mixture of news and documentary styles and amateur performers and real individuals to demonstrate the difficulties that a new kind of war would occasion. The film drew pessimistic conclusions, and BBC management came under some governmental pressure (exerted through the BBC Governing Board) to withdraw it. In deciding not to screen the film, they effectively banned it. Thus the BBC deferred to the government of the day's fear of the consequences of a mass medium exposé of the realities of nuclear war. The resultant storm of protest ensured that *The War Game* became a famous film and a key marker of the difference between film and television censorship; historically, policy makers have more often interfered with television.

The film was given a kind of controlled release (mainly to film societies), but was not shown on British television until the 1980s, by which time the nuclear threat had become less of an issue.

By the mid-1960s, documentary drama was established as an important and potentially controversial subgenre of British television drama and documentary/current affairs. In the 1970s, the mixed form was used extensively by Granada TV's magazine programme *World in Action*, to the extent that a special production unit was formed at the end of the decade. The investigations in which *World in Action* became involved often needed this "last resort" format. Whenever events had passed without cameras having been present, whenever witnesses were dead or had to remain silent, producers like Leslie Woodhead used their research to anchor filmed dramatizations. It was about this time that the distinction between "documentary drama" and "drama documentary" began to be part of debates around the mixed form. These terms have continued to be problematical both to the industry and the academy, but the personnel of the Granada unit saw themselves as documentary makers first and makers of drama second. Indeed, they did not think of themselves as makers of fiction at all, staking their claim to documentary authenticity on a rigorous research methodology that demanded the warrant of primary research before material could be dramatised. In two films transmitted in 1980 (*Strike*, about the contemporary Polish "Solidarity" movement; and *Invasion*, about the 1968 Russian invasion of Czechoslovakia), there is a painstaking attempt in a lengthy credits sequences to establish documentary credentials as primary before any dramatization begins. Unlike ATV's 1980 *Death of a Princess*, which caused great difficulties with the Arab world, these films were seen as part of West's ongoing campaign for democracy in the Communist Bloc.

Throughout the 1980s and 1990s, drama documentaries (broadly, those films made by current affairs departments) and documentary dramas (those made mainly by drama departments) continued to play a vital but occasional role in the schedules. The most important of these were attempts to depict key social and political events of the period. Such films as *Who Bombed Birmingham?* (about the 1974 IRA pub bombings), *Shoot to Kill* (about covert British policies in Ireland), *Why Lockerbie?* (about the downing of Pan-Am 103 by Libyan-backed terrorists), and *Hillsborough* (about the 1989 football stadium disaster) were arguably the heirs to the *Cathy Come Home* tradition, animating public debate. But the key shift in this later period was toward American culture. At the "low concept" end of the spectrum, this meant that British documentary drama makers became increasingly involved in the sensational and tabloid similar to American television. (American academic Jane Feuer calls such docudramas "trauma dramas.") These films frequently place a single individual protagonist at their centre, and use this individual to personalize any issues raised. The individual can be famous, but notoriety is equally acceptable (so sensational murders and deadly diseases are popular subjects). At this end of the market, the emergence of "Reality TV" has ensured a great deal of "reenactment" in popular programmes such as *Crimewatch UK* (which began in 1984).

At the "high concept" end, co-productions like the Granada films mentioned previously tackled issues of fundamental, indeed international, importance. The American cable company Home Box Office struck deals for films with Granada, the BBC, and other British production companies during this phase, ensuring wide audience reach, as well as occasionally impressive grasp of issues. The end result of the move into international co-production has undoubtedly been an enhancement of dramatic values at the expense of the documentary impulse. The tendency toward genre hybridization has ensured that the vast majority of TV dramas now seek recognisable generic templates whether they are "pure fiction" or "documentary drama." This coincided with an increase in Hollywood's own use of real world material for films

from *Schindler's List* (1993) to *A Beautiful Mind* (2002). Like the literary adaptation and the "biopic," the docudrama is endemic in commercial fiction film culture, as well as in broadcast television production.

DEREK PAGET

See also **Drew, Robert; Empire Marketing Board Film Unit; General Post Office Film Unit; Grierson, John; Leacock, Richard; Ministry of Information; *Night Mail;* Wiseman, Frederick**

Further Reading

Caughie, John, *Television Drama: Realism, Modernism and British Culture*, Oxford: Oxford University Press, 2002.

Corner, John (ed.), *Documentary and the Mass Media*, London: Edward Arnold, 1986.

Feuer, Jane, *Seeing Through the Eighties: Television and Reaganism*, London: British Film Institute, 1995.

Goodwin, Andrew, and Paul Kerr, *BFI Dossier 19: Drama-documentary*, London: British Film Institute, 1983.

Lipkin, Steven N., *Real Emotional Logic: Film and Television Docudrama as Persuasive Practice*, Carbondale: Southern Illinois University Press, 2002.

Paget, Derek, *No Other Way To Tell It: Dramadoc/Docudrama on Television*, Manchester: Manchester University Press, 1998.

Rosenthal, Alan (ed.), *New Challenges for Documentary*, Berkeley: University of California Press, 1988.

Swallow, Norman, *Factual Television*, London: Focal Press, 1966.

Swinson, Arthur, *Writing for Television*, London: Adam and Charles Black, 1955.

Winston, Brian, *Claiming the Real: The Documentary Film Revisited*, London: British Film Institute, 1995.

URBAN, CHARLES

Charles Urban is arguably the leading pioneer of the nonfiction film. Others, such as the Lumières, Léon Gaumont, Charles Pathé, and George Kleine, may have worked in similar fields, but none spoke as loudly or covered so wide a range as Urban. His ambitions were laid out in his 1907 booklet, *The Cinematograph in Science, Education and Matters of State*, which expounded his belief in the instructional role that film had to take in society (as well as having what is probably the first use in English

of the word *documentary* in a filmic sense). Urban's career is distinctive not only for its idealistic espousal of nonfiction film, but because he tried to marry this mission with the fields of salesmanship and showmanship in which his career was grounded. His career demonstrates both the exciting range of options for the producer that the early cinema period seemed to promise and the narrowing of those options in reality as the cinema programme became established along specific lines.

Urban's rise and fall can be traced through five distinctive phases, each illustrative of the options open to the producer of nonfiction film in the first years of cinema. The first phase, to 1903, was that of the American salesman galvanising the complacent early British film business. Urban's first thirty years were spent in America, where he started out as a high-class book salesman, moving through the systems of automation and production found in office stores to market phonographs, Kinetoscopes, Vitascopes, and finally his own film projector, the Bioscope. It was with this practical device that he came to Britain in 1897, turning an American off-shoot company into the dynamic Warwick Trading Company. As producer, distributor, and equipment supplier, Urban made an indelible stamp on the British film business and laid the groundwork for what seemed like a native aptitude for film of reality.

The second phase saw Urban as owner of his own company, the Charles Urban Trading Company (founded 1903). Here Urban opened up the range of nonfiction films as fiction films themselves began to grow in length and range of forms. For Urban, his films of science, travel, sport, exploration, and medicine were every bit as entertaining as the fiction film, with the added value of social usefulness. "To amuse and entertain is good" ran one of his slogans; "to do both and instruct is better." Urban employed skillful scientific filmmakers with a populist bent, such as F. Martin Duncan and Percy Smith, French surgeon Eugène-Louis Doyen, mountaineer F. Ormiston-Smith and war cameraman Joseph Rosenthal, all of whom could contribute to Urban's proudest slogan, "We Put the World Before You." At a time when 50 percent of all British film production was nonfiction, at least 50 percent of all British nonfiction film was produced by Urban. He established Britain's national cinematic picture of itself.

In 1908, Urban launched Kinemacolor (first named 1909), a natural colour process using red and green filters, which seemed to promise cinema's greatest fidelity to real life yet. Urban's Kinemacolor productions caused a sensation in the period 1909–1913, for the dazzling nature of the colour (inadequate as it now seems to modern eyes), for its theatrical presentation and consequent high prices, for the unprecedented length of its programmes, and particularly for its emphasis on royal spectacle. Urban's greatest Kinemacolor triumph came with *With Our King and Queen Through India* (1912), which ran for 2½ hours and featured the spectacular Delhi Durbar ceremonies.

Kinemacolor fiction films were made as well, but Urban had little aptitude for drama, and the result were notably poor. Urban sold exclusive Kinemacolor licences to international territories and seemed to have made his fortune, but a court case from a rival colour system in 1913 led to the invalidation of the patent.

World War I saw Urban faced with the reality of putting his motion pictures at the service of the state. What Urban had advocated urgently, in practice proved far more problematic. He produced a documentary feature for the covert War Propaganda Bureau, *Britain Prepared*, and was directed to take it to America in 1916. Urban battled equally against hostile American exhibitors and British propagandists unsympathetic toward his showman's sensibilities. Urban edited the outstanding documentary feature, *The Battle of the Somme*, but found this no easier to get onto American scenes, blundering badly when he tried to get a distribution deal with the anti-British Hearst's International Film Service. America's entry into the war made Urban's task suddenly much easier, and he proved an effective editor and distributor of British official films in America for the remainder of the war.

The British film business now in ruins, Urban decided to settle once more in America and, in the final phase of his career, to establish himself as an educational filmmaker. Urban had always viewed himself in this light, producing the world's first educational film catalogue in 1908, even if the specific educational utility of his films was never made clear. In postwar America, the Visual Education movement was encouraging greater use of moving pictures in the classroom, and Urban was one among many producers fighting for this new market. Urban became over-ambitious, creating the grandiose Urban Institute building in Irvington, NY, and pouring thousands into a filmless disk viewer called the Spirograph; however, all that Urban had to support this activity were two minor cinemagazines and some imaginative documentary features made with the naturalist Raymond Ditmars. His business collapsed in 1924. Ironically, 16mm film and a fully fledged nontheatrical film circuit now emerged, just as Urban—who had so long advocated for film to reach out to where specific audiences needed it—was forced to bow out of the scene.

Urban was the preeminent advocate of the full function of cinema at just that time when the options for exhibiting films were at their narrowest. As the cinema programme evolved, the nonfiction film came to occupy an increasingly small portion of what was shown on the screen. Exasperated by the inexorable rise of the fiction film, Urban was ultimately a prophet for the nontheatrical film who never made it himself to the promised land.

LUKE MCKERNAN

See also **Battle of the Somme**

Biography

Born Cincinnati, Ohio, April 15, 1867. Settled in Detroit in 1889, opening Phonograph parlour, 1893. Expanded business to include Kinetoscopes, 1895. Obtained Michigan agency for Vitascope projector, before developing own projector, the Bioscope, 1896. Moved to Britain as manager of London branch of Maguire & Baucus, 1897, which became Warwick Trading Company, 1898. Formed own film business, Charles Urban Trading Company, 1903. Launched two-colour natural colour film system, later called Kinemacolor, 1908. Natural Color Kinematograph Company forced into liquidation, 1914. Produced documentary feature *Britain Prepared* for War Propaganda Bureau, 1915. Marketed British official war films in America, 1916–1918. Formed Urban Motion Picture Industries, based in Irvington, NY, 1920. Urban Motion Picture Industries bankrupt, 1924. Returned to Britain by end of 1920s and retired from film business. Died in Brighton, August 29, 1942.

Selected Films

1902 *Le Sacre d'Edouard* (Méliès): producer
1907 *Torpedo Attack on HMS Dreadnought*: producer
1908 *The Balancing Bluebottle*: producer
1910 *A Day in the Life of a Coal Miner*: producer
1910 *S.S. Olympic*: producer
1911 *The Coronation of King George V and Queen Mary*: producer
1912 *With Our King and Queen Through India*: producer.
1915 *Britain Prepared*: producer
1916 *The Battle of the Somme* (McDowell, Malins): editor
1921 *The Four Seasons* (Ditmars): producer
1921 *Permanent Peace*: producer
1923 *Evolution* (Ditmars): producer

Further Reading

McKernan, Luke, "Putting the World Before You: The Charles Urban Story," in Andrew Higson (ed.), *Young and Innocent? The Cinema in Britain, 1896–1930*, Exeter: University of Exeter Press, 2002.
Urban, Charles, *A Yank in Britain: The Lost Memoirs of Charles Urban, Film Pioneer*, Luke McKernan (ed.), Hastings: The Projection Box, 1999.

V

VACHEK, KAREL

From his cinema verité films of the 1960s through his "film novels" of the 1990s, maverick Czech filmmaker Karel Vachek has been known for his outspoken refusal to conform to aesthetic or political trends and for pioneering a new visual and narrative style for social documentary. A 1963 graduate of FAMU, the Film Faculty of the Academy of Music and Performing Arts in Prague, Vachek has been called the *enfant terrible* of the Czechoslovak New Wave (Navrátil, 1992), a group of artists whose formal and conceptual experimentation gained international recognition in the 1960s. This reputation was born with his FAMU thesis film, *Moravská Hellas/Moravian Hellas* (1963). The thirty-three-minute documentary, filmed at the Strážnice folk festival, satirized communist perversion of folk culture, using a hybrid style that combined elements of cinema verité with staged interviews. The film was so controversial that after its release, Vachek was banned from filmmaking until 1968, when the reforms of Alexander Dubcek's "socialism with a human face" eliminated censorship and lessened restrictions on personal and creative expression. That year, Vachek produced the cinema verité film *Spřižnění volbou/Elective Affinities* (1968).

Shot on a handheld 16mm Éclair camera, the film chronicles the events and climate surrounding Antonín Novotný's fall from power and the beginning of Ludvík Svobodá's presidency. Less than 6 months later, Warsaw Pact armies invaded Czechoslovakia, marking the end of the Prague Spring and heralding the beginning of more than twenty years of Soviet rule. With censorship and restrictions on artists more stringent than ever, Vachek, like many other intellectuals and artists, was unable to make films. After a five-year period of exile in France and the United States, and a number of years working outside of the film industry in Czechoslovakia, Vachek returned to his profession in 1989.

Vachek's films of the 1990s mark a shift in his style and approach, although his new work retains characteristics of his cinema verité heritage. The four parts of the "Little Capitalist Tetralogy," each between three and four hours long, are *Nový Hyperion aneb Rovnost volnost bratrsví/New Hyperion or Equality Liberty Brotherhood* (1992), which traces the presidential elections of 1990 in Czechoslovakia; *Co Dělat? Cesta z Prahy do Českého Krumlova aneb Jak jsem sestavoval novou vladu/ What Is to Be Done? A Journey from Prague to*

Cesky Krumlov or How I Formed a New Government (1996), which follows a group of artists and intellectuals on a bus trip between the two cities, capturing their debates and arguments alongside the mystical history of Cesky Krumlov; *Bohemia Docta aneb Labyrint světa a lusthauz srdce (Božská Komedie)/Bohemia Docta or Labyrinth of the World and Paradise of the Heart (Divine Comedy)* (2000), a commentary on the state of the intellectual in the Czech Republic; and *Dalibor: Kdo bude hlídat hlídače aneb Klíč k chaloupce strýčka Toma/Dalibor: Who's Gonna Watch the Watchman? or The Key to Uncle Tom's Cabin* (2003), a probing of the state of the nation at the end of the millennium, set during a piano rehearsal of Bedřich Smetana's opera *Dalibor*. Taken collectively, the films comprise a dialogic history of the political and social changes that gripped the Czech lands between 1990 and the end of the millennium.

The films of the Tetralogy develop their narratives with a mixture of verité moments, staged sections, and long on-screen conversations between the director and a series of subjects, set in aesthetically interesting or connotative locations. Most of the men and women who populate the films, many of them recurring figures, were generally dissidents or outsiders under the Soviet regime and remain on the fringes of post-1989 society. They are artists and professors, writers and political activists. Vachek guides these subjects through philosophical or political debates in circuitous, frequently comical paths toward a poetic vision of the state and the individual in the modern world. Although politics are central to these films, Vachek is primarily concerned with the philosophical aspects of politics. His perspective is that of an exile, guided by a conviction that social and political change can originate only in the periphery of society.

Although the Tetralogy draw its characters and themes from the era in which it was created, the films resist strict categorization as documentary, moving instead between reportage and fictionalization, performance and poetic reflection. The director, in fact, objects to his films' classification as documentaries, preferring to call them "film novels." Their titles, indeed, are derived from literature—*New Hyperion*, for example, from Holderlein, and *What Is to Be Done?* from Chernishevsky. Further distinguishing his work from traditional documentary, Vachek uses aesthetics borrowed from fiction films. He shoots with cumbersome, expensive 35mm film instead of video or 16mm film; his sequences and shots are highly planned; and, alongside documentary moments, Vachek inserts staged scenes. Although Vachek's films have been criticized as hermetic or provocative, his work has nonetheless proved a central influence on a successive generation of documentary filmmakers in the Czech Republic, among them Jan Gogola Jr. and Vít Janeček, and has found a pedagogical home in the documentary department of FAMU, where Vachek has taught since 1993.

ALICE LOVEJOY

Biography

Born August 4, 1940 in Tišnov, Czechoslovakia. Attended FAMU, the Film Faculty of the Academy of Music and Performing Arts in Prague, from 1958–1963, where he studied directing under Elmar Klos. Worked in the Czechoslovak Army Film Unit 1965–1965. Banned from filmmaking after the release of *Moravian Hellas* in 1963, and again after the release of *Elective Affinities* in 1968. Emigrated in 1979, first to France, and then to the United States. Returned to Czechoslovakia in 1984. Awarded the Berlinale Camera award in 1990. Since 1993, has taught documentary at FAMU; since 2002, chair of FAMU's documentary department.

Selected Films

1963 *Moravská Hellas / Moravian Hellas*
1968 *Spřižnění volbou / Elective Affinities*
1992 *New Hyperion or Equality Liberty Brotherhood*
1996 *Co Dělat? Cesta z Prahy do Českého Krumlova aneb Jak jsem sestavoval novou vladu/What Is to Be Done? A Journey from Prague to Cesky Krumlov or How I Formed a New Government*
2000 *Bohemia Docta aneb Labyrint Světa a Lusthauz Srdce (Božská Komedie) / Bohemia Docta or Labyrinth of the World and Paradise of the Heart (Divine Comedy)*
2003 *Dalibor: Kdo bude hlídat hlídače aneb Klíč k chaloupce strýčka Toma / Dalibor: Who's Gonna Watch the Watchman or The Key to Uncle Tom's Cabin*

Further Reading

Buchar, Robert, *Czech New Wave Filmmakers in Interviews*, Jefferson, NC: McFarland & Company, Inc., 2004.

Camhi, Leslie, "Spring Forward," in *The Village Voice*, February 13–19, 2002.

Hames, Peter, *The Czechoslovak New Wave*, Berkeley: University of California Press, 1985.

Liehm, Antonín J., and Mira Liehm, *The Most Important Art: Eastern European Film After 1945*, Berkeley: University of California Press, 1977.

Navrátil, Antonín, "Nejdelší Český Film," in *Lidové Noviny*, April 16, 1992 (in Czech).

Slater, Thomas J., "Czechoslovakia," in *Handbook of Soviet and East European Films and Filmmakers*, edited by Thomas J. Slater, New York: Greenwood Press, 1992.

Štoll, Martin, *Hundred Years of Czech Documentary Film (1898–1998)*, Prague: Malá Skála, 2000.

VARDA, AGNÈS

Agnès Varda is often referred to as the "grandmother" of the French New Wave. Varda is the only woman strongly connected to this avant-garde film movement of the 1950s and 1960s, and her work is both technically innovative and politically motivated as she uses the camera as a tool for social investigation. Varda's interest in the construction of gender and the inherent codification of gender via popular representation is seen throughout her body of work. Her *La Pointe Courte* (1956) is often cited as the first New Wave feature. Sandy Flitterman-Lewis argues for this association as she describes the aesthetics of the film, noting its "concern with temporality, the interfacing of subjective realities, the articulation of discursive modes, the pervasive 'sense of place,' the aspect of research, both sociological and linguistic, the interest in permutations of the narrative form, the techniques of distancing and cultural critique, the redefinition of spectatorship, the self-reflexivity about cinematic meaning, and the challenge to establish forms of cinematic story-telling..." (Flitterman-Lewis, 260). The film explores the struggles of people in a small Mediterranean fishing village. Her *L'Opéra-Mouffe* (1958) displays her evolving documentary technique, as it shows scenes from a market without the intervention of reportage or other narration.

As her work continued, Varda made both documentary and fictional narratives, using each to engage in social commentary. Her films deal with personal expression, the differences between people and the way they behave, and the social and culture contexts that shape us. After a few well-received feature narratives, Varda made two documentaries in the United States in the late 1960s. Her *Uncle Yanco* (1967) deals with the "discovery" of Varda's uncle living in San Francisco, California. This was followed by her 1968 documentary, *Black Panthers*, a piece that showed this politically active group as an integral part of the shifting culture in the United States. The work shows the experience of a rally to free Panther Huey Newton from jail. Panthers Stokely Carmichel, Bobby Seale, and H. Rap Brown are also shown.

Daguerreotypes (1975) looks at the use of the still image within a motion picture. There are close-ups of objects and shopkeepers in Rue Daguerre. As the film continues, objects are shown in different contexts, and the ways in which this causes the image to change is paramount. At the end of the film, the human subjects shown each turn to face the camera for several seconds, a live, in-motion, still moment. The interplay between the filmed image and the photographed still is contemplated as the piece ends. Varda's documentary works began to look at the idea of memory and the passage of time as an element of our culture in the late 1970s and into the 1980s.

Jacquot de Nantes (1990), Varda's tribute to the life and work of her late husband, uses black-and-white images for tales from Demy's childhood in the 1930s and 1940s and color images of Demy in the 1980s. These are edited into this charming work along with clips from Demy's films to show the ways in which his work reflected his life and interests.

Varda's *The Gleaners and I/Les Glaneurs et la Glaneuse* (2000) was shot entirely on digital video. The work looks at people who harvest the castoff belongings of others and survive from their "hunting" in gutters, trash bins, and other such places where useful but unwanted things are found. This is a vision of recycling and reusing in a grand sense. Varda's film explores this notion in an art-making context as well; she sees herself as a collector of images, a gleaner in both the gathering of material and the assemblage of it. Varda spoke of her approach to this work"

> I think that documentary means "real," that you have to meet these real people, and let them express what they feel about the subject. The more I met them, the more I could see I had nothing to make as a statement. They make the statement; they explain the subject better than anybody. So it's not like having an idea about a subject and "lets illustrate it." It's meeting real people and discovering with them what they express about the subject, building the subject through real people. So it is a documentary, but the shape that I gave to it—including the original score and the editing—is really for me a narrative film. Not that

documentary is "not good" and narrative is "good." But I really work as a filmmaker, I would say, to give a specific shape to that subject. And so far, it's worked, because whether people are cinephiles or not, they like the film. They like the people they meet in the film.

(Anderson, 2001: 25–26)

When Varda received the 2003 Inaugural Eisenstein Award from University of Southern California's School of Cinema-Television, University Provost Lloyd Armstrong described Varda as an artist "whose work challenges the artificial constructs that separate people and ideas." (*In Motion*, 2004: 10). The award honors filmmakers with international stature for their visionary work and distinguished contributions to the cinematic arts. Varda continues to work in documentary film and to explore cultural diversity in ways that delve into the experience of being human.

TAMMY A. KINSEY

Biography

Born May 1928, Brussels, Belgium. Trained in art history and photography. Worked as official photographer for Jean Vilar's Theatre National Populaire. Married to filmmaker Jacques Demy from 1962 until his death in 1990. Commissioned to make two short films for French National Tourist Office, late 1950s. Won Cesar Award for Best Documentary Short for *Ulysse*, 1982. Museum of Modern Art Retrospective show, 1997. Awarded Melies Prize for Best French Film of 2000 by French Union of Film Critics for *The Gleaners and I*.

Selected Films

1958 *L'Opera-Mouffe*
1958 *Du cote de la Cote*
1959 *La Cocette d'Azur*
1960 *Champagne France/Italy*
1963 *Salut les Cubains/Salute to Cuba*
1964 *Les Enfants du musee*/Episode of television series "Chroniques de France"
1967 *Loin du Vietnam/Long Metrage Collectif*
1968 *The Black Panthers*
1975 *Daguerreotypes*
1980 *Murs Murs/Murals, Murals*
1984 *Les Dites Caryatides*
1993 *Les Demoiselles ont eu 25 ans/The Young Girls Turn 25*
1995 *L'Univers de Jacques Demy/The World of Jacques Demy*

Further Reading

Anderson, Melissa, "The Modest Gesture of the Filmmaker: An Interview with Agnès Varda," in *Cineaste*, 26, 4, fall 2001, 24–27.
Anthony, Elizabeth, "From Fauna to Flora in Agnès Varda's *Cleo de 5 a 7*," in *Film Quarterly*, 26, , 1998, 88–96.
Darke, Chris, "Refuseniks," in *Sight and Sound*, 11, 1, Jan. 2001, 30–33.
Flitterman-Lewis, Sandy, *To Desire Differently: Feminism and the French Cinema*, Urbanna: Illinois University Press, 1990.
In Motion, winter 2004, USC School of Cinema-Television.

VAS, ROBERT

Hungarian exile Robert Vas went from being a marginal figure on the periphery of Free Cinema to one of the most highly regarded documentary film directors working at the BBC in the 1960s and 1970s. During those years he made thirty films before his tragically early death at the age of 47. Essentially an autodidact strongly influenced by the work of Humphrey Jennings, Vas is less concerned with political ideology than with liberal humanist consciousness.

The personal sensibility that marks Vas's best work cannot be grasped without reference to his experiences as a refugee living in exile. Although his family survived the Holocaust in the Budapest ghetto by acquiring Swedish passports, his mother committed suicide after the war and his father abandoned the family, emigrating to Australia. Military service as an army projectionist was terminated by a nervous breakdown and a spell in a psychiatric hospital. Unable to acquire a formal education, Vas did, however, attend lectures at the Academy of Dramatic Arts and later worked as a trainee script editor at the National Theatre in Budapest. The failure of the 1956 Hungarian Uprising led him to leave the country, crossing the border into Austria with his wife and child and making his way to London shortly afterward.

Initially working in menial cleaning jobs, he soon found a niche in the Information Department at the British Film Institute where he gained an encyclopaedic knowledge of world cinema, as well as a passion for the films of Humphrey Jennings. Contact with Lindsay Anderson and Karel Reisz led to his first film, funded by the newly formed BFI Experimental Film Fund. *Refuge England* combined documentary observation with acted scenes to tell the story of a refugee's first day in London. This was screened in the final Free Cinema programme in March 1959 alongside Reisz's *We Are the Lambeth Boys*. Vas's next project, *The Vanishing Street* (1962), about a Jewish community in the East End was followed by his first film for the BBC, the autobiographical *The Frontier* shot on the Austro-Hungarian border.

During the next fourteen years, Vas consolidated his work as a freelancer, straddling different departments at the Corporation and making films for strands such as Omnibus and Horizon. Subjects included popular culture in *The Golden Years of Alexander Korda* (1968) and *Cuckoo—A Celebration of Laurel and Hardy* (1974); science and society in films on Arthur Koestler (*Koestler on Creativity*, 1967) and Claude Lévi-Strauss (*The Savage Mind*, 1970); portraits of artists (*Miklos Radnoti*, 1969) and directors Miklos Jansco (*The Quiet Hungarian*, 1967) and Humphrey Jennings (*Heart of Britain*, 1970); and the world of music in *Bartok* (1970) and the Austrian conductor *Bruno Walter* (1972).

It was in a series of historical films that Vas made his mark, in some cases even causing political controversy. *The Issue Should Be Avoided* (1971), an investigation into the 1941 Katyn Forest massacre where more than 4,000 captive Polish officers were murdered by the Soviet NKVD, was later to be complemented by the magisterial 2 ½-hour *Stalin* in 1973. *Nine Days in '26* (1974), exploring untold accounts of the 1926 General Strike from the miners' point of view, was deemed to be sufficiently sensitive to be unofficially shelved by the BBC for several months, much to Vas's dismay. *To Die—To Live* (1975) dealt with the legacy of Hiroshima; *Orders from Above* (1975) examined the forcible repatriation of Russian prisoners-of-war by Allied troops between 1945–1947. Based on *The Last Secret* by Nicholas Bethell, the film triggered extensive debate.

Vas's filmmaking methods were eclectic and varied. He used actors to portray historical figures on location and in the studio and combined eyewitness reports with archive, poetry, and commentary to create work that, although not overly marked by formal experiment, was multilayered and complex in its range. *My Homeland* (1976) arguably his finest film, was both an elegy on the twentieth anniversary of the Hungarian Revolution and a deeply subjective meditation on memory and loss in the poetic tradition he so admired in Jennings. Very much an authored essay, the film stands out in its use of counterpoint, juxtaposing banal colour travel films of the 1970s with starkly contrasting black-and-white stills of the uprising. Often taking over at the editing table himself, Vas could be single-minded to the point of obstinacy, but his visionary passion also engendered fierce loyalty amongst his collaborators.

Robert Vas saw his artistic mission as being to remind and warn, primarily of the abuses of power. Regarding himself as a victim of both totalitarian ideologies of the twentieth century, he avoided making explicit political judgments other than putting forward a broad liberal humanism, but he defined his task according to a strict moral imperative, untrammelled by relativism. Likewise, although his Judaism was secular rather than religious, he could never forget that 90 percent of Budapest's Jews did not survive the Holocaust.

Cas's death in 1978 came as a shock to friends and colleagues who held him in highest regard. Ironically, after a lifetime's insecurity, he had only just signed a staff contract at the BBC. Years later the circumstances and cause of his death still raise strong and contradictory passions. The drug overdose and weeks of ensuing coma and death on April 10, 1978 is regarded by some as suicide and by others as a tragic accident. Perhaps also lost with him was the tradition of the subjective, poetic vision that he had made his signature as a filmmaker.

JOHN BURGAN

See also **Anderson, Lindsay; BBC; British Film Institute; Jennings, Humphrey; Reisz, Karel**

Biography

Born in Budapest, Hungary, March 3, 1931. Survived the Holocaust in the ghetto. Military service interrupted by a spell in psychiatric hospital. Fled for the West after the failure of the 1956 Hungarian revolution, arriving in London as a refugee. Worked in the Information Department of the British Film Institute and wrote criticism for Sight and Sound and Monthly

Film Bulletin. First film made in 1959 for the British Film Institute's newly formed Experimental Film Fund. Worked as a film editor in the early 1960s, then as producer/director for the BBC 1964–1978. Died in London on April 10, 1978 after a drug overdose and lengthy coma.

Selected Films

1959 *Refuge England*: writer, director
1964 *The Frontier:* director
1968 *The Golden Years of Alexander Korda*: writer, producer
1970 *Heart of Britain*: writer, director
1971 *The Issue Should Be Avoided*: writer, director
1973 *Stalin*: writer, producer
1974 *Nine Days in '26*: producer
1975 *Orders from Above*: producer
1976 *My Homeland*: writer, director

Further Reading

Lovell, Alan, and Hillier, Jim, *Studies in Documentary*, London: Secker and Warburg, 1972.
Rosenthal, Ian, *The Documentary Conscience: A Casebook in Film Making*, Berkeley: University of California Press, 1980.

VEIEL, ANDRES

With his analytical and in some way political films on German society, Andres Veiel succeeded in becoming one of the most important German documentary filmmakers of the younger generation. He has not produced many films, but with them he built up his reputation and was successful even in the cinemas. His films are moving and often strike the Zeitgeist. They make public the conflicts of an era and its generation. With his films he often search the limits of existence.

During his studies of psychology and the humanities, it became clear to him that he did not want to work in this profession. He became aware that there is a difference between his patients and what it is said about them in their papers. On the other hand, he learned how to handle conflicts and not to take verbal attacks too personally. He wrote a theatrical piece about a prison, which premiered in 1987 in Berlin with the prisoners as actors. His first two films also portrayed acting in special situations. An 83-year-old actress is in the center of *Winternachtstraum/ Winternightsdream* (1991–1992). She is staging *Marat* by Peter Weiss with her companions in a home for elderly people. Her dream come true.

Much more political and topical even today is his film *Balagan/Balagan* (1993), in which Veiel showed a theatre group in Israelian Acco, which not only presented a provocative piece on the Holocaust, but the group itself also represents different parts of Israeli society. One actor has his roots as a European Jew, one came from an Islamic country, and one is Palestinian. Their theatre work reflects questions of identity and solidarity, as does *Balagan.* The film polarized and started fruitful discussions; it won various prizes like the Peace Prize at the Berlin International Film Festival and the German Film Prize in Silver, which enabled him to produce the next film.

Die Überlebenden/The Survivors (1995–1996) is Veiel's most personal film. Because three of his classmates committed suicide, he started in-depth research about their reasons and the general feelings of his generation, which found themselves in an "in-between" situation. It came too late for the political fight and was too early for economic revolution of the 1990s. In his fanatic chase for truth, his study helps solve the problem that, on the one hand, he was very close to his protagonists and, on the other hand, that he is also a filmmaker and the confessions will become public with the film. He is quite aware of his responsibility and avoided becoming voyeuristic. This edge is very small of course. The film uses all kind of material including personal amateur footage, newsreels, film, and video to develop a feeling for that time and the reasons for their suicides. Using a similar approach, in 1997 he started his long-term observation of a class of actors from the first audition to their appearance on stage and their development after school. *Die Spielwütigen/Furious for Acting* (2003) will be a film about the growing-up of the next generation.

But his masterpiece is *Black Box BRD* (2001), where he contrast the lives of Alfred Herrhausen, managing director of Deutsche Bank, with the RAF terrorist Wolfgang Grams, who the police blamed for participating in the assault on Herrhausen and who was shot by the police. Andres Veiel won the European Documentary Prize in 2001 and German Film Prize 2002 for *Black Box BRD*.

KAY HOFFMANN

See also **Black Box BRD**

Biography

Born in Stuttgart, Germany, on October 16, 1959. Studied psychology in Berlin from 1982 to 1988 and participated from 1985 to 1989 at a course for directing and dramaturgy in the international director seminars at Künstlerhaus Bethanien in Berlin. Much influenced by Polish director Krzysztof Kieslowski. Since then, productions of films and scripts and work in the theatre. Since 1996, also teaching, for example, at the Free University Berlin. Member of the European Film Academy.

Selected Films

1991–1992 *Winternachtstraum:* director, writer
1993 *Balagan:* director, writer
1995–1996 *Die Überlebenden:* director, writer
1997 *Drei von Tausend:* director, writer
2001 *Black Box BRD:* director, writer
1997–2002 *Die Spielwütigen:* director, writer (in preparation)

Further Reading

Dockhorn, Katharina, "Focus auf zwei Lebensläufe," in *Filmecho/Filmwoche*, 19, 2001, 37.
Klingenmaier, Thomas, "Niemand soll sprachlos aus dem Kino gehen," in *Stuttgarter Zeitung*, 22,12, 2001, 46.
Veiel, Andres, *Black Box BRD—Alfred Herrhausen, die Deutsche Bank, die RAF und Wolfgang Grams*, Munich: DVA, 2002.

VERTOV, DZIGA

The Soviet Russian director Dziga Vertov was instrumental in transforming actuality and newsreel filmmaking into what became known as documentary. Extending Russian and communist traditions of interpretive political journalism to cinema, Vertov's films used the inherent evidential power of documentary footage rhetorically, not simply to illustrate and record, but overwhelmingly for political persuasion, revealing film's immense capacity for the visual presentation of an argument. At the same time, Vertov's enduring commitment to formal experimentation meant that his greatest films combined this rhetorical force with poetry's heightened expressive freedom and associative combination of images. This example exerted a powerful influence not only on documentary filmmaking from Grierson to Marker and beyond, but also on the style of 1920s Soviet Montage films, particularly those of Sergei Eisenstein. His expansive style of filmmaking jarred with the tight control of cinema in 1930s Soviet Union and led to his marginalisation for unacceptably formalist tendencies.

Although Vertov's theoretical writings bear the heavy imprint of an age of iconoclastic modernist manifestos, he nevertheless makes a seminal attempt to defend and define what was dubbed documentary film. Vertov drew a fundamental distinction between unstaged (*neigrovye*) films such as his and staged, acted, films. Not content simply to dispense with the use of actors, he advocated the method of "life caught unawares" (*zhizn' vrasplokh*) aimed at ensuring the subjects photographed are not posing. He attempt to achieve this by a wide variety of means including telephoto lenses, as well as hidden and decoy cameras. Yet probably the most characteristic aspect of Vertov's concept of filmmaking is the stress on the "organisation" of this ontologically authentic material through editing so as to show "life as it is" (*zhizn' kak ona est'*). This misleading notion does not imply a striving to be impartial or objective. On the contrary, the material is to be analysed and arranged so as to persuade the spectator of the communist perspective. Characteristic of this method was his groundbreaking newsreel series, *Kino-Truth*, named by analogy with the Soviet Communist Party daily newspaper, *Pravda* (meaning truth). In place of the long takes recording official visits, portraits of dignitaries, sports events, and train crashes that were the staple of newsreels of the time, *Kino-Truth* strove to use editing to combine images in a dynamic and highly tendentious manner, as, for example his coverage of the famine on the Volga in *Kino-Truth* No.1 (1922), which begins with the slogan "Save the Starving Children" as an inter-title. Shots of children starving are then intercut with pictures of the destruction of icons for their valuables. The sequence ends with an image of children being fed soup accompanied by the inter-title "Every pearl saves a starving child."

Vertov called his approach to filmmaking *Kino-Eye*, and dubbed his collaborators and followers *kinoki*, a neologism combining the Russian words for cinema and for eye. The *kinoki* were conceived as a grassroots international organisation of filmmakers and would be filmmakers, dedicated to rescuing cinema from entertainment and commerce and turning it to the rational political analysis of everyday life. Films were to develop from observation, rather than from an already written screenplay. The term *kinok* also symbolizes Vertov's determination that the technology of film should be used to enable a step change in perception and thought. The camera for Vertov was associated with the enhanced power of scientific optical tools such as the microscope and the telescope. Whereas the microscope enabled the human eye to see natural phenomena invisible to the naked eye, Vertov thought that by means of techniques such as superimposition, reverse motion, and editing the camera could enable people to see the meaning underlying the misleading chaos of the world as it appears to unassisted human vision. A typical example of this approach is his treatment of Lenin's death in *Kino-Truth* Nos. 21 and 22 (1925), whereby the slogan "Lenin is dead but his cause lives on" is illustrated by superimposition of the image of Lenin on the mausoleum in Red Square. Similarly, *Kino-Eye* (1924) uses reverse motion to resurrect grazing cattle from the butcher's slab so as to prove that meat bought in a cooperative comes directly from the countryside. This kind of sequence attracted criticism as unwarranted stylistic exuberance in a film, the main purpose of which should be to inform. This commitment to formal experiment grew stronger in films such as *Forward, Soviet!* and *One Sixth of the World*. In the latter the organisation of much of the film has

been shown to resemble that of the poetry of Walt Whitman (Singer, 1987). The culmination of this drive to innovate was the film for which he is most celebrated outside Russia, *The Man with the Movie Camera* (1929), a silent film made without inter-titles, "directed toward the creation of a genuine, international purely cinematic language" (Feldman, 1979). Variously described as celebration of the city (Roberts, 2000), meta-cinema (Mayne, 1975), and the first database film (Monovich, 1999), this dazzling display of cinema's expressive power is at the same time demythification of that power and an extended enquiry into the nature of film and the place of cinema in society.

In his lifelong hostility to films made with actors, Vertov was articulating a view influential in the 1920s Soviet avant-garde. In particular productivists and constructivists argued that art, and especially fiction, was conceived by bourgeois societies to distract people from their essential dissatisfaction with the capitalist world. Art under communism should not divert people from real life, but rather be a reworking of real material, a remaking of life, using tools and techniques derived from art. It is this perspective that informs Vertov's striving not only to use documentary footage for the purposes of political persuasion, but also to seek to experiment formally, to expand the borders of cinematic expression. Vertov's practice, however, was not always as rigorous as his programmatic statements might lead us to believe. Even his most experimental films, *Kino-Eye* and *The Man with the Movie Camera* included obviously staged footage, notably in the latter of a man holding a camera.

Although, like many other Soviet Montage filmmakers, he found it increasingly difficult to work in the 1930s, unlike them, Vertov immediately welcomed the coming of sound cinema as affording new opportunities. Indeed, Vertov had anticipated sound cinema as early as 1925 with his theory of Radio-Eye, an audio concept of documentary equivalent to Kino-Eye. Indeed *Enthusiam* (1930) was the name of his first sound film, a celebration of the industrial transformation of the first five-year plan, which incorporated a wide variety of source sound, recorded on location in the Donbass region. This is a bold experiment in which the sounds of heavy industry, church bells, and military bands interact symbolically, not simply illustrating the image with which they are combined. Vertov's other major film of the talking era was *Three Songs about Lenin* (1934). This film revisited a theme treated with much success by Vertov in the 1920s, but this time he drew on popular conceptions of Lenin in the folk songs of Azerbaijan, Turkmenistan, and Uzbekistan. Made in physically demanding circumstances in a critical climate increasingly hostile to Vertov's approach to documentary film, this film nevertheless retains much of the engaging visual style, creative use of sound, and poetic qualities of his earlier films. After considerable delays and wrangles it eventually reached the public and won Vertov critical and official recognition, but all was not as it seemed. *Three Songs about Lenin* broke the unwritten laws of the Lenin cult film of the time by failing to show Stalin to have been his right-hand man and faithful disciple. It was withdrawn soon after its release and later reedited so as to foreground the role of the Soviet leader (Feldman, 1979). The point was not lost on Vertov. When next given an opportunity to make a feature-length documentary, *Lullaby* (1937), he made sure it included the requisite lengthy standing ovation to Stalin. Yet, in this film little remains of the stylistic élan of his earlier works, and it is barely distinguishable from the run-of-the-mill products of the Soviet Newsreel Studio. The years of administrative obstruction and hostility began to take a toll on his creative powers as well as his health, and by the end of World War II, Vertov gradually ceased even to produce new projects. The last decade of his life was spent editing newsreels of the kind he had long abhorred.

JEREMY HICKS

See also **Man with a Movie Camera, The; Three Songs about Lenin**

Biography

Born David Abelovich (later Denis Arkadievich) Kaufman in Bialystok, then Russia, now Poland, on January 2, 1896. Mobilised by Russian Imperial army during World War I and sent to Military-Musical College in Chuguev, Ukraine, before being decommissioned on grounds of ill health. Enrolled in St Petersburg Psycho-neurological Institute. After February revolution of 1917 came to Moscow, where in early 1918 he became secretary of newsreel department of Moscow Cinema Committee (later the All-Russian Photo-Cinema Department or VFKO). Changing his name to Dziga Vertov (meaning something like "spinning gypsy") directed group of newsreel filmmakers 1918–1919 making *Kino-nedelia/Cine Weekly*, ran cinema section of agit-trains and ships, 1920, and made propaganda shorts about Russian Civil War (1918–1921). From 1922 initiated *Kino Truth* newsreel series, as well as making Goskino's newsreel series *Goskinokalendar* from 1923 to 1925. Also employed from 1924 by Kultkino, a educational or documentary films department of Goskino

(later Sovkino) until his sacking in 1926. Worked for the rival Ukrainian Film Directorate (VUFKU) from 1927 to 1932. Visited Western Europe in 1929 and 1931 to promote his films and views of film. Made *Three Songs about Lenin* at Mezhrabpom Films from 1932, for which he was awarded The Order of Red Star in 1935. Taken on by Soviet Newsreel Films (Soiuzkinokhronika) in 1935. Here, with the exception of a short spell at the Soviet Children's Film Studio (Soiuzdetfilm) between 1939 and 1941, he continued to work editing *Novosti dnia/News of the Day* newsreel compilations until his death, in Moscow, February 12, 1954.

Selected Films

1922–1925 *Kino-Pravda/Kino-Truth*, (23 editions): writer, director
1924 *Kino-Glaz/Kino-Eye*: writer, director
1926 *Shagai, Sovet!/Forward, Soviet!*: writer, director
1926 *Shestaia chast' mira/One Sixth of the World*: writer, director
1928 *Odinnadtsatyi/The Eleventh Year*: writer, director
1929 *Chelovek s kinoapparatom/The Man with the Movie Camera*: writer, director
1930 *Simfoniia Donbassa (Entuziazm)/Enthusiasm, Or the Symphony of the Donbass*: writer, director
1934 *Tri pesni o Lenine/Three Songs about Lenin*: writer, director
1937 *Kolybel'naia/Lullaby*: writer, director

Further Reading

Feldman, Seth, *Evolution of Style in the Early Work of Dziga Vertov*, New York: Arno Press, 1975.
———, *Dziga Vertov: A Guide to References and Resources*, Boston: G.K. Hall, 1979.
Mayne, Judith, "Ideologies of Metacinema," unpublished PhD thesis, State University of New York at Buffalo, 1975.
Monovich, Lev, "Database as Symbolic Form," in *Millenium Film Journal*, 34, fall 1999, 24–43.
Petric, Vlada, *Constructivism in Film: The Man with the Movie Camera: A Cinematic Analysis*, Cambridge: Cambridge University Press, 1993.
———, "Vertov's Cinematic Transposition of Reality," in *Beyond Document: Essays in Nonfiction Film*, edited by Charles Warren, Hanover NH and London: Wesleyan University Press, 1996.
Roberts, Graham, *Forward Soviet!*, London and New York: I.B. Tauris, 1999.
———, *The Man with a Movie Camera*, London and New York: I.B.Tauris, 2000.
Roshal, Lev, *Dziga Vertov*, Moscow: Iskusstvo, 1982.
Singer, Ben, "Conoisseurs of Chaos: Whitman, Vertov and the 'Poetic Survey,'" in *Literature/Film Quarterly*, 15, 4, 1987, 247–258.
Stollery, Martin, *Alternative Empires: European Modernist Cinemas and Cultures of Imperialism*, Exeter: Exeter University Press, 2000.
Vertov, Dziga, *Dziga Vertov: stat'i, dnevniki, zamysly*, edited by Sergei Drobashenko, Moscow: Iskusstvo, 1966.
———, *Kino-Eye: The Writings of Dziga Vertov*, edited by Annette Michelson, translated by Kevin O'Brian, Berkeley: University of California Press, 1984.

VICTORY AT SEA

(US, Salomon and Kleinerman, 1952–1953)

This epic-length television documentary concerning naval operations during World War II combined wartime footage with narration and music to present an emotional view of combat history. Produced during the Korean conflict of the Cold War, the compilation film series, as its title implies, focused on the strength and ultimate triumph of Allied forces (particularly American forces) during wartime. One of the most ambitious documentaries produced by network television, the twenty-six episode series originally aired on NBC (National Broadcast Corporation) from October 1952 to April 1953 on Sunday afternoons from 3 to 3:30 PM. Critically acclaimed during its time, the series won more than thirteen industry awards, including a George Peabody Award and a special Emmy for Best Public Affairs Program. The series demonstrated that an historical compilation documentary was a viable television format and led to the production of several others in the genre, particularly *The Twentieth Century* (CBS, 1957–1969).

Victory at Sea was the brainchild of World War II veteran and naval historian Henry Salomon and his former college classmate, Robert Sarnoff, the son of RCA/NBC patriarch David Sarnoff. Robert Sarnoff was then an executive at NBC-Television. In the early days of television, film projects had distinct practical advantages over live television shows, particularly the idea for residual incomes through syndication. The half-hour series relied on archival footage obtained from many sources including the U.S. Signal Corps, the U.S. Navy and newsreels, and European and Japanese archives. The archival footage obtained amounted to approximately 11,000 miles of film, which was then reduced to 62,000 feet. The editor for the series, Isaac Kleinerman, relied on an indexing system of 60,000 note cards so as to organize the quantity of film for the compilation series. The addition of composer Richard Rodgers name to the credits added further prestige to the project. It also allowed NBC to gain additional revenues through the marketing of LP recordings of the series musical score. The Richard Rodgers score was sold in several record versions by RCA-Victor. By 1963, the album had grossed $4 million, and one tune from the score, "No Other Love," earned additional sales as a single.

Unlike many wartime propaganda films, *Victory at Sea* presented a narrative of more historical sweep encompassing as it did both the Eastern and Western hemispheres. The series, however, was not without bias toward the victors. Produced at a time when the world was in the depths of the Cold War struggle between the United States and the Soviet Union, the series had an organizing theme—the triumph of democracy and freedom over totalitarianism. The active role of the United States in international affairs is constantly invoked, as is the determination to bring "freedom" to those parts of the world under the yoke of military despotism. Its ethnocentric viewpoint was constantly expressed using the rhetoric of liberation and military strength by reinforcing the historical conflict as a lesson of history, a rhetoric that continued to grow into the polarity of Cold War era politics and diplomacy.

RONALD WILSON

Victory at Sea (USA, NBC Television, 1952–1953, 26 episodes). Produced by Henry Salomon. Written by Henry Salomon with Richard Hanser, based on the multivolume *History of the United States Naval Operations in*

Victory at Sea, 1954, World War II navel ship.
[*Courtesy of the Everett Collection*]

Victory at Sea, 1954, airplane on fire.
[Courtesy of the Everett Collection]

World War II by Samuel Eliot Morison. Directed by M. Clay Adams. Music by Richard Rodgers. Musical arrangement by Robert Russell Bennett conducting the NBC Symphony Orchestra. Narrated by Leonard Graves. Edited by Isaac Kleinerman. Technical Advisor Captain Walter Karig, U.S.N. Film research by Daniel Jones and Douglas Wood. Television co-coordinator Robert M. Sarnoff.

Further Reading

Bartone, Richard C., "Victory at Sea: A Case Study in Official Telehistory," in *Film and History*, XXI, 4, December 1991.

Kepley, Vance, Jr., "The Origins of NBC's Project XX in Compilation Documentaries," in *Journalism Quarterly*, 61, 1–2, 1984.

———, "*Victory at Sea*," in *Encyclopedia of Television*, edited by Horace Newcomb, Chicago: Fitzroy Dearborn Publications, 1997.

Leyda, Jay, *Films Beget Films*, New York: Hill and Wang, 1964.

Morison, Samuel Eliot, *History of United States Naval Operations in World War II*. 15 volumes. Boston: Little, Brown and Company, 1947–1962.

Rollins, Peter C., "*Victory at Sea*: Cold War Epic," in *Journal of Popular Culture*, VI, spring, 1973.

VIDEO

The term *video* (from the Latin *videre*, "to see") refers to the means of electronically recording and reproducing the signals that can be reproduced as the images and sounds on a television display. Attempts to develop these technologies go back as far as television itself. The earliest example known to have been successfully demonstrated was the "Phonovision" system. Developed by the British engineer John Logie Baird in the 1930s, this used modified audio recording technology to capture the broadcast signal from his electromechanical TV system as grooves in a record. It was only used experimentally, and there is no evidence that any recorded material was ever broadcast or captured live off-air.

Regular television broadcasts began in 1941 in the United States and in 1946 in the United Kingdom, following their suspension during World War II. Throughout the 1940s and 1950s, the principal medium used for transmitting recorded material and for recording live broadcasts was 16mm film, which has been used extensively as an offline medium throughout the history of the television industry. The first "telecine" devices consisted of modified film projectors fitted with a cathode ray tube camera to capture the image for broadcast, while the "telerecording" (or "kinescope" in U.S. English) process exposed images onto film from a high definition monitor.

Magnetic tape had been developed and used extensively for audio recording and broadcasting by the Nazis since the 1930s, and this technology was subsequently developed and mass-manufactured in the United States in the immediate aftermath of the war. The tape consisted of a thin, flexible base (initially the same cellulose acetate as was used in photographic film, but subsequently polyester) onto which was coated a layer of iron oxide particles. When subjected to an electromagnetic force, the particles could be magnetised or demagnetised to represent a pattern of modulation. This could then be reproduced by passing the tape over a second "head," which generated a modulating electrical current in response to the signal on the tape. Given the vastly greater signal bandwidth needed to store the video information, the development of magnetic video recording into a commercially viable technology happened almost a decade later than with audio.

One of the first successfully demonstrated prototypes was developed for the American singer and comedian Bing Crosby, who commissioned engineers to develop equipment to prerecord his performances to reduce the number of live broadcasts needed for different time zones. The Radio Corporation of America (RCA) produced a modified version some years later; the British Broadcasting Corporation (BBC) developed its own prototype videotape recorder, the Visual Electronic Recording Apparatus (VERA) in 1957. The first internationally adopted videotape format was launched by the American Ampex corporation in the previous year. It used open-reel tape two inches wide that passed a static head at a speed of thirty inches per second.

This first generation of mass-manufactured videotape technology was used on a significant scale only as a "time shifting" device by television studios. Initially, videotape had two crucial advantages over film: A recording could be replayed instantaneously, and the tapes themselves could be erased and re-recorded without practical limit (tragically, this perceived advantage inadvertently resulted in a significant proportion of the world's television heritage from the 1960s and 1970s being permanently lost). There were also some drawbacks. Initially, tapes could be played back only on the machine that recorded them, and editing was difficult and cumbersome.

For these reasons videotape was not used on any significant scale for documentary production until the advent of the videocassette in the 1970s. The Umatic format, introduced by Sony in 1971, was the first to enter mainstream use among broadcasters and programme-makers. Portable and rugged recorders became available that did not require extensive technical expertise to operate. This development marked the beginning of "electronic news gathering" within the television industry, a process that would ultimately cause the decline of 16mm film as an origination medium in television news and documentary production. This process was further accelerated by the advent of the "camcorder," a television camera and videocassette recorder housed within a single, compact, battery-powered unit. These were originally sold from 1984 for amateur use as a replacement for Super 8mm film, but as their versatility and ease of use became apparent, broadcast standard camcorders became an established technology within the television industry.

The emergence of digital videotape in the early 1990s further increased the versatility and image quality offered by the medium. Editing was now possible without any loss of signal quality (with videotape, editing is carried out by selectively copying content from one tape to another, hence the generational signal loss with analog). The increased

definition offered by the higher end digital formats has made video a genuine alternative to small-gauge film in situations where large quantities of footage need to be shot on a limited budget, even for documentaries intended for theatrical release on film prints. Examples include *East Side Story* (Germany, 1998, directed by Dana Ranga & Andrew Horn) and *Buena Vista Social Club* (Germany/Cuba/US, 1999, directed by Wim Wenders), for which original footage was shot using the Digital Betacam format, and *Bowling for Columbine* (US 2002, directed by Michael Moore), which incorporated footage shot both on 16mm and digital video.

Even lower definition video formats and those intended for consumer and industrial use have had a significant impact on the role of nonfiction in film and television culture. The broadcast of surreptitiously taken amateur footage shot on VHS, showing a racially motivated attack by Los Angeles policemen in 1991, is believed to have been a major cause of riots that took place shortly afterward. The use of miniature cameras designed for CCTV and surveillance use is now routine practice by investigative journalists, with such footage being broadcast almost daily. There are many who believe that video and other electronic moving image technologies will never match the quality of film, but its lower cost and comparative versatility have made video the medium of choice for the majority of documentary production, a situation that is likely to continue for the foreseeable future.

LEO ENTICKNAP

Further Reading

Abramson, Albert, *Electronic Motion Pictures: History of the Television Camera*, New York: Arno Press, 1976.

Fisher, David E., and Marshall, Jon Fisher, *Tube—The Invention of Television*, San Diego: Harcourt Brace and Company, 1996.

Fullerton, John, and Soderbergh-Wilding, Astrid (eds.), *Moving Images, from Edison to Web Cam*, Eastleigh: John Libbey Publishing, 2000.

Kallenberger, Richard H., and Cvjetnicanin, George D., *Film into Video: A Guide to Merging the Technologies*, Boston & London: Focal Press, 1994.

Kirk, David K., *25 Years of Video Tape Recording*, Bracknell: 3M Corporation, 1981.

Pawley, Edward, *BBC Engineering, 1922–1972*, London: BBC Publications, 1972.

Petrie, Duncan, "British Low-budget Production and Digital Technology," in *Journal of Popular British Cinema*, 5, 2002, 64–76.

Sexton, Jamie, "Televerite Hits Britain: Documentary, Drama and the Growth of 16mm Filmmaking in British Television," in *Screen*, 44, 4, winter 2003, 429–444.

Winston, Brian, *Media, Technology and Society*, London: Routledge, 1998.

VIDEO DIARIES

(UK, BBC, 1990–2001)

The *Video Diaries* series was a product of the BBC's Community Programme Unit (CPU) developed by unit head Jeremy Gibson and series producer Bob Long. First broadcast on Saturday evenings on BBC2 in the summer of 1990, the series proved an immediate success with audiences and critics. Exceptionally for BBC access programming, it regularly received up to a million and half viewers and won a number of awards for both the series and individual programs.

Video Diaries was a radical extension of the CPU's remit to provide members of the public with access to television broadcasting. It built on the department's previous access programming strands *Open Door* and *Open Space*, where selected individuals and groups who approached the Unit worked alongside professional crews to produce programmes on specific topics of concern. The innovative approach taken by *Video Diaries* involved training chosen applicants in the use of domestic video camcorders, enabling them to record their own material themselves. This experiment was both an attempt by the CPU to engage with the newly emerging camcorder culture, and a genuine attempt to redefine the parameters of access television. Allowing individual subjects to control their own representation was directly aimed at circumventing the mediating influence of professional filmmakers, with their often highly developed personal or institutional methodologies.

Selected *Video Diaries* applicants received training in the basics of film grammar and use of S-VHS or Hi-8 camcorders. Diarists gathered their own footage and later edited this in collaboration with the CPU postproduction team. Throughout the process there was both support and monitoring from CPU staff who oversaw the development of the project. Although the aim was to give the individual as much control as possible, the unit always exerted a corrective influence, steering the project through in an attempt to ensure that the structure of the programme was both intelligible to audiences and communicated the diarists' intentions in the most efficient way. The early series of *Video Diaries*

were also notable for having programmes of variable length. Within a range that spanned between one to two hours, programme-makers were allowed to find the duration that best suited the requirements of the project. In 1993, the CPU introduced *Teenage Diaries*, which followed a similar approach but were produced by diarists under 18 years of age.

The degree of control exerted by the CPU over the outcome has been an area of critical debate. Although the CPU has been seen as providing a constraining influence on the diarists' intuitive approach to their subject, it could equally be said that they often challenged diarists to step outside the normative approaches to documentary practice as absorbed via their own television viewing. It was this dynamic between the diarists, who underwent a demanding developmental experience as they sought to tell their stories, and the guiding hand of the experienced CPU staff that produced a blend of formally inventive programmes, which, if sometimes demanding of their audience, were nonetheless coherent. The diarist, as well as offering insights into their specific areas of concern, also provided, via piece-to-camera or voice-over, a diary of the production process. Thus, elements usually excluded in mainstream documentary filmmaking, were often a central part of the diary's developing narrative, as the diarists sought to find their own voice, while negotiating the video technology and developing a working methodology. The often crude technique and undisguised subjectivity of the diarist seem to give *Video Diaries* an honesty and an emotional impact that was regarded by many as a welcome revitalisation of the television documentary form. If technical naivety in itself is no guarantee of "authenticity," the particular production context of the CPU did provide an ethical framework that mitigated against the "amateurish" technique becoming just a stylistic device (Keighron, 1993).

Video Diaries covered a wide range of subjects, from light-hearted offerings such as Steve Feltham's monster-quest *Desperately Seeking Nessie* (1990), to the Bafta-winning *The Man Who Loved Gary Lineker* (1992), Ylli Hasani's account of his life as an Albanian doctor and refugee. One of the most challenging programmes in the first series was Willa Woolston's *My Demons* (1990). In this program the diarist returned to her hometown to confront the personal legacy of systematic abuse she had suffered from her stepmother as a child. This high level of introspection was regarded by some as an uncomfortable precedent, pushing television documentary into the realms of personal therapy. It could be debated that the relative success of this series encouraged the shift toward a more populist, character-centred documentary programming, a widely observed trend in the more competitive multichannel environment of contemporary British television. However, *My Demons* provoked a significant response from viewers who had also suffered abusive family situations, and led to the establishment of a support network for sufferers. By often dealing with significant situation and issues, the diaries, although based on intensely personal stories and subjective viewpoints, could also be seen as a continuation of the more overtly social campaigning work of the CPU.

Video Diaries was undoubtedly important institutionally for challenging barriers to broadcast television access that had been long-maintained through rigid standards of professional practice and an insistence on the use of expensive video or film formats as guarantors of image quality. Although these distinctions have, to a certain extent, been rendered obsolete by the high quality images now afforded by digital camcorders, *Video Diaries* was influential in opening up British television screens to a much wider range of video material from nonprofessional sources.

The video diary form has become an integral part of many other documentary and television genres such as travel programmes and "reality" television. Despite the ubiquity of the approach and the less serious ends to which it is now often used, the series' innovative force should not be underestimated. *Video Diaries* represented a significant widening of the BBC's Public Service remit and extended democratisation of the broadcast documentary. It also encouraged many more people outside television to realise the potential of domestic camcorders for personal exploration and social activism.

DAVID CHAPMAN

Video Diaries (UK, BBC Community Programme Unit, 11 series between 1991 and 2001) CPU Head, Jeremy Gibson. Series producer/CPU Head Bob Long. Producers/ Series Producers, Rachel Foster and Steve Sklair.

Further Reading

Barker, Paul, "The Rise of Camcorder Culture," in *The Times*, July 27, 1992, reprinted in MacDonald, Kevin and Cousins, Mark, *Imagining Reality*, London, Faber & Faber 1998.

Dovey, Jon, "Old Dogs and New Tricks; Access Television in the UK, in *Channels of Resistance*, edited by Tony Dowment: London: BFI 1993.

Humm, Peter, "Real TV: Camcorders, Access and Authenticity," in *The Television Studies Book*, edited by Christine Geraghty & David Lusted, London: Arnold 1998.

Keighron, Peter, and Wayne, Mike, "Video Diaries" in *Independent Media*, 101–102, July–August 1990, 8–9.

Keighron, Peter, "Video Diaries: What's up Doc?" in *Sight and Sound*, 3, 10, 1993, 24–25.

Kilborn, Richard and Izod, John, *An Introduction to Television Documentary*, Manchester: Manchester University Press, 1997.

VIDEOTAPE

The term *video* is multivalent, referring to a practice of media production defined in opposition to film and television, to a set of technological devices used in that practice (recorder, monitor, editing deck, cassette, or disc), and to an electromagnetic or digital image. Because videotape is a substrate that records and plays audiovisual signals on a monitor, its images can be difficult to distinguish from a live television broadcast without such clues

as faulty playback, evidence of editing, or postproduction effects. The first videotape recorder was, in fact, invented to preserve early live television programs, and thus video has been intimately embroiled in television's history at the same time that it has staked out its own identity.

Given the medium's association with television's live broadcast and simultaneous transmission to a constellation of viewers, video, even when prerecorded on tape or disc, has been coded with an ideology of immediacy. Because this ideology dovetailed with the goals of direct cinema, which favored a naturalistic approach to its subject matter, video enhanced this predominant mode of documentary practice by presenting events as though they were instantaneous, a slice of "raw" reality directly available to the viewer in real time, literal and unmanipulated, and thus closer to the truth. Although video's heightened capacity for truth has been questioned for almost forty years, its ideology of immediacy remains pervasive.

The history of video documentary in the United States typically begins in 1965, when Sony released its "Portapak" into the American market. As the technology matured over the next several decades, video's technical capabilities that encouraged documentary production would include its light-weight mobility, synchronous sound and image recording, reusable substrate, long takes without the need to change reels, clear image reproduction in low light levels, immediate playback of footage, multi-camera switching from a central control panel, the capacity for live exhibition, computerized editing, and multiple forms of distribution, including network broadcast, cable systems, and satellite signals.

By 1975, when portable video cameras, recorders, and editing decks switched from reel-to-reel tape to video cassettes, television journalists began recording news events electronically, particularly in overseas coverage of the Vietnam War. Given the name "electronic news gathering," or "ENG," broadcast journalism eventually abandoned film for video, which today remains the medium of choice of network news. In the decade before the diffusion of ENG, however, the Sony Portapak's technology was limited to a black-and-white image track and a single synchronous sound track that were difficult to edit together. Moreover, the FCC deemed the Portapak's image quality "substandard," unable to meet broadcast engineering standards, and thus unavailable for commercial television broadcast.

For these reasons, the first video documentaries in the 1960s and early 1970s were produced by independent filmmakers and cooperatives, most often in direct opposition to the professional style and ideological content of commercial television. The emphasis of these early works was to create a grass-roots network of video activists who would promote the medium as an agent of social change that would foster alternative states of consciousness, communities, and political structures. Video's ability to seize the moment with instantaneous feedback and real-time monitoring of events often stressed the process of making documentaries more than the documentary product itself. Referred to as "process video," this nonfiction media practice celebrated collaboration and access to as many participants as possible. Another popular genre of the period, "street tapes," such as Les Levine's *Bum* (1965), which documented the homeless on New York's skid row, capitalized on video's lightweight mobility that allowed video-makers to move intimately among the inhabitants of various subcultures.

As video's popularity increased, underground collectives formed to support a burgeoning nationwide video network. The most important groups included Videofreex, which specialized in innovative production techniques; People's Video Theater, which exhibited live and taped feedback of embattled community groups as a catalyst for social change; Global Village, which initiated the first closed-circuit video theater to exhibit underground works; and Raindance, which published the journal *Radical Software*, the video underground's chief source of information and networking tool. In 1971, Michael Shamberg, the director of Raindance, published *Guerilla Television*, which outlined a plan to decentralize the power of the commercial broadcast networks. The title of his book has since become an umbrella term covering a wide variety of socially activist video documentaries negating the political ideologies and corporate structures of mainstream television.

With improvements to video's technology, such as color, electronic editing, and a time base corrector, guerilla programming in the 1970s looked increasingly to public television and cable access as the chief venues for exhibition. For example, in 1972, Top Value Television (TVTV) produced "Four More Years," two hour-long video documentaries on the Democratic and Republican National Conventions. Like direct cinema of the 1960s, these ground-breaking tapes challenged the objectivity of professional journalism to provide an unconventional, radical perspective on the political proceedings.

As television news adopted ENG units, corporate television absorbed many of guerilla television's techniques, depoliticized its countercultural agendas, and hired many of its video-makers as network producers, in effect terminating the promise of a utopian era of democratic media exchange through broadcasting. Independent video documentaries returned to local communities as a means to organizing multicultural special-interest groups, such as women, gays, blacks, Latinos, Asians, and Native Americans. Community media centers developed nationwide, including the

Alternate Media Center in New York, Urban Planning in Boston, and Videopolis in Chicago. Although some groups continued to seek broadcast outlets for their videotapes, most exhibited unedited tapes to citizens in their homes, community centers, and other closed-circuit environments.

By the 1980s, as consumer video technologies pervaded the retail marketplace, video documentaries diversified into multiple practices moving beyond strategies to negate television, subvert professional journalism, and create community. Much provocative and innovative work has been accomplished on the independent front, but channels for video documentaries and funding by private and government agencies have diminished. Revised FCC rulings over the last thirty years have undermined public access programming by deregulating cable television. Although organizations such as Deep Dish TV have achieved limited success distributing public access series via satellite to participating cable systems and public TV stations, most video guerillas at the turn of the century seeking large public audiences have had to work either within commercial institutions or find space within established art museums showcasing single-channel videotapes.

JAMES M. MORAN

Further Reading

Armes, Roy, *On Video*, New York: Routledge, 1988.
Boyle, Deirdre, *Subject to Change: Guerilla Television Revisited*, New York: Oxford University Press, 1997.
Cubitt, Sean, *Timeshift: On Video Culture*, New York: Routledge, 1991.
———, *Videography: Video Media as Art and Culture*, New York: St. Martin's Press, 1993.
Hall, Doug, and Fifer, Sally Jo (eds.), *Illuminating Video: An Essential Guide to Video Art*, New York: Aperture, 1990.
Hanhardt, John (ed.), *Video Culture: An Investigation*, Visual Studies Workshop Press, 1986.
London, Barbara, "Video: A Brief History and Selected Chronology," in *Transmission*, edited by Peter D'Agostino, New York: Tanam, 1985.
Marshall, Stuart, "Video: From Art to Independence. A Short History of a New Technology," in *Screen*, 26, 2, March–April 1985, 66–71.
———, "Video: Technology and Practice," in *Screen*, 20, 1, 1979, 109–119.
Moran, James M., *There's No Place Like Home Video*, Minneapolis: University of Minnesota Press, 2002.
Renov, Michael, and Suderburg, Erika (eds.), *Resolutions: Contemporary Video Practices*, Minneapolis: University of Minnesota Press, 1996.
"The Great Face Off: Video vs. Film: Two Experts Exchange Fire!" in *Video Review*, 5, 11, February 1985, 28–30.

VIETNAM

See **Southeast Asia**

VIETNAM WAR

The Vietnam War was the first to be comprehensively covered by cameramen in the field; it was likewise the first to be widely interpreted, debated, protested, and critically reflected upon through documentary. Unlike World War II, in which films made or sponsored by governments and military agencies—designed to direct the popular imagination toward the shared causes of war and nationalism—dominated documentary representations, the Vietnam War was documented by many groups and individuals who used film to communicate their views about this divisive war, its political causes, and cultural effects.

American interest in Vietnam began with the Geneva agreement of 1954, subsequent to the defeat of Indochina's French colonisers. This agreement would have guaranteed a free election in Vietnam, which Ho Chi Minh would have won according to U.S. intelligence reports of the time. Roman Karmen's film *Vietnam* (a.k.a. *Peace Comes to Vietnam,* USSR, 1955) celebrated the resilience of Ho Chi Minh's followers by intercutting images of war's devastation with images of Vietnam rebuilding itself in the jungle—its schools, industries, culture—and preparing for peace.

American efforts to prevent the success of Ho Chi Minh over the next two decades escalated into a conflict that, although never officially declared as a war, was, from the U.S. bombing of the North in 1964 and the deployment of ground troops in 1965, consistently represented as such. American commercial television initially aligned itself with the government's position and President Johnson closely monitored its coverage. Despite moments of violence at odds with the government's representation of its role in Vietnam—such as Morley Safer's 1965 report on CBS that showed Marines lighting the thatched roofs of Cam Ne with Zippo lighters, primetime television took over what had been the role of government documentary in previous wars. In that role, U.S. television coverage would be the focus of critique by political documentary both at home and abroad.

Television's key role did not entirely supersede U.S. government-produced documentaries, however. The first of these was the Defense Department's *Why Vietnam?* (1965). Its title was a deliberate echo of Frank Capra's *Why We Fight* series of World War II (1943–1945) as was much of its documentary technique. Unlike subsequent government documentaries, *Why Vietnam?* was shown to civilians as well as to GIs. Like Capra's films, it endeavoured to condense the causes of the conflict into a simple opposition of good and evil and to establish a common moral ground between film and viewer. To this end it used direct-address narration punctuated by emotionally charged orchestration as it forged rhetorical links between the conflict in Vietnam and earlier wars. It opened with catastrophic images of World War II and represented Ho Chi Minh as an analog to Hitler. A surface plausibility produced by emotional appeals and extended comparisons between Vietnam and previous wars hid its distortions of history, which in 1967 were criticised publicly and in 1971 were exposed as deliberately fraudulent by *The Pentagon Papers*.

Although the basic tenets of *Why Vietnam?*—that the Vietnam War was a defensive one and that America had a moral obligation to aid South Vietnam—persisted, subsequent U.S. government productions were more evasive in their rhetoric, particularly when dealing with the causes of the war and the nature of America's enemy. Films intended to educate and motivate GIs, such as *The Unique War* (USDD, 1966) *A Nation Builds Under Fire* (USDD, 1967), and *Vietnamese Village Reborn* (USDD, 1967), no longer attempted to present Vietnam as an analog to World War II, but termed it "different," "strange," and "unique." These films favoured ethnographic techniques—long takes framed by authoritative commentary—to show with apparent objectivity the South Vietnamese as childlike, simple, primitive, and innocent. At the same time Americans were described as pious, freedom-loving, and noble. By virtue of their nature, the South Vietnamese were in need of aid from the more sophisticated and technologically superior Americans, and they were worthy to receive it. Narrations by Jack Webb, Glenn Ford, Charlton Heston, and John Wayne in these and other government films voiced the role of the United States and provided a site for identification laden with connotations of reliability and paternalistic strength.

While government documentary worked to engage its audience with the cause of South Vietnam, the North Vietnamese and National Liberation Front (NLF)/Viet Cong were rarely represented. The enemy was more generally referred to as "communists" or "insurgents." An exception was the film *Know Your Enemy—the Vietcong* (USDD, 1966), that used the Capra-esque technique of reframing enemy film. Although government films emphasised the transparency of their images of the South Vietnamese, these representations of the NLF were couched in qualification. The narrator, shown surrounded by reels of film and projection devices, was himself a visual reminder that these NLF films were fabrications; and, his narration worked to distance the viewer, warning that they were merely "the Viet Cong as the Viet Cong would like to see themselves."

As protests against the war grew (a 1967 poll showed that a majority of Americans considered the war was a "mistake"), it became increasingly difficult to sustain the representation of America's foreign policy as benign. This difficulty culminated in the U.S. Information Agency (USIA) documentary *Vietnam! Vietnam!* (1968–1971). At a quarter of a million dollars, it was the most expensive film ever made by the USIA. Planned in 1966 as a full-colour feature-length effort to win over the world to the nobility of the American cause, the film had legendary Hollywood director John Ford as its executive producer. Fordian pastoral images of the South Vietnamese culture were placed in stark opposition to explicit images of atrocities attributed to the Viet Cong. The particulars of historical context and combat excised, the film was entirely directed towar dramatising the evils of communism as aggressive, destructive, and alien, in contrast to the American ideology of freedom. By its release in 1971, it was deemed inappropriate for screening in most of the USIA's 112 foreign outposts; there was no longer an audience for this version of the Vietnam War.

While the U.S. government struggled to find a documentary representation sufficient to support its cause, the North Vietnamese and the NLF also used documentary film to inform and inspire. *Chu Tich Nguyen Hun Tho Noi Chuyen Voi Nhan Dan My/Hun Tho Speaks to the American People,* NLF (1965) was one of the first of these, an illustrated political speech. Other documentaries presented inspirational images of collectivity, the everyday life of soldiers and civilians. *Duong Ra Phia Truoc/The Way to the Front,* NLF (1969) showed the camaraderie, humour, and determination of a group ferrying supplies across country; *Mat trân dân tôc giai phóng mi'ên nam Viêt Nam/Struggle for Life: Medicine and Public Health in Vietnam* (NLF, 1968) showed doctors working in concealed tunnels and setting up mobile medical centres. In *Nghê thuât cua tuôi tho/Young Puppeteers of Vietnam* (NLF, 1969), teenagers in NLF-controlled/liberated areas of South Vietnam made puppets from the remains of downed U.S. planes and performed theatricals for village children as American planes flew overhead. North Vietnamese documentary also showed the toll taken by war in Vietnam. *Vai Toibac Cua De Quoc My/Some Evidence* (1969) gave a detailed visual and statistical account of American weaponry including antipersonnel weapons, pellet bombs, and napalm, and its effects on Vietnam's people, animals, and homes and villages.

The NLF used silent film strips that were narrated by a lecturer who tailored commentary to the local audience and situation. In addition, these films circulated in both communist and noncommunist countries. This guerrilla cinema was influential for political filmmakers worldwide, including the New Left and Newsreel movement in America, where distribution of these films was limited and clandestine. Their significance extended beyond the parameters of the antiwar movement, as the Vietnam War came to be viewed as a master metaphor for anti-imperialist struggles across the globe.

In addition to U.S. and Vietnamese productions, responses to the Vietnam War came from many countries. A few years before North Vietnam's *Some Evidence,* a Japanese series produced for television, entitled *Minami betonamu Kaiheidaitai Senki/With a South Vietnamese Marine Battalion* (Junichi Ushiyama, 1965), was one of the first to document the war's atrocities. Cameramen followed a search-and-destroy mission that went from village to village looking for Vietcong. When one "suspect" was beheaded in the second of three films, the series was cancelled.

Less controversial in its representation of the war was *The Anderson Platoon* (France, Pierre Schoendoerffer, 1966) made by a three-man crew from the French television service. Their ground-level view of the war, through the eyes of a U.S. platoon, won an Oscar for best Documentary Feature in 1967. Like Eugene S. Jones's *A Face of War* (US, 1966–1968), it focused on soldiers' everyday experiences of discomfort and hardship, as well as the long stretches of boredom interrupted by violence. Both Schoendoerffer's and Jones's verité accounts of the war deliberately downplayed political issues and contexts in favour of a detailed rendering of the everyday experience of soldiers, who were thus located as the main site for understanding the war. This manner of representing Vietnam with its valorisation of the eyewitness perspective would be influential on later documentaries, as well as on Hollywood treatments of the war in the 1980s.

Joris Ivens's *17e Paralléle/The 17th Parallel* (France, 1967) was likewise a verité account that focused on the daily routine of war, but looked at the experiences of the North Vietnamese under attack. *Sad Song of Yellow Skin* (Canada, Michael Rubbo, 1970) similarly represented the Vietnamese experience of war; it was different in its focus not on combat situations, but on the urban culture of Saigon. *Sad Song* shows the impact of years devoted to servicing the appetites of an occupying army through interviews with Americans who lived with and aided those street children working as dealers, pimps, and prostitutes.

An omnibus film, *Loin du Vietnam/Far from Vietnam* (France, S.L.O.N., 1967) commented on the war through a bricolage aesthetic that offered multiple perspectives on the war. In its use of television footage and other media images, it adopted the guerrilla tactic of recycling enemy technologies. Similar in this guerrilla aesthetic was the caustic *Napalm* (Syria Nabil Malech, 1970), a two-minute film that "advertised" napalm "as though it were a beauty aid or patent medicine" (Barnouw, 1993). In its send-up of American commercial television, it criticized both the war and the media culture that promoted and profited from it.

Cuban filmmaker Santiago Alvarez made a number of films on the war, all of which likewise used this method of bricolage. They compiled disparate elements to engage the viewer emotionally and intellectually in the cause of the North Vietnamese. *Hanoi Martes Trece/Hanoi Tuesday the 13th* (Cuba, Santiago Alvarez, 1967) commemorated the day when President Johnson authorised the bombing of the North. The film was both lyrical and critical in its use of stock footage, still images, music, and the occasional didactic inter-title. Using similar techniques, Alvarez's *79 Primaveras/ 79 Springtimes* (Cuba,1969) was a poetic homage to the life of Ho Chi Minh and the birth of a new nation, metaphorically represented through the motif of bombs exploding and flowers opening.

Political films like those of Alvarez and the S.L. O.N. collective had limited circulation in the United States, but despite this and despite bans by the State Department on travel to North Vietnam that kept journalists and filmmakers at home, alternative visions of the war made it to screen in the United States as well. A number of these focussed on alternative views of the war, from civilians and veterans. Felix Greene travelled to Vietnam and shot on his own, without a crew, *Inside North Vietnam: A Personal Report* (1967–1969). Initially sponsored by CBS, the film showed the effects of routine bombing on civilians living in the smaller cities and villages of Vietnam. It was deemed inappropriate for broadcast by the network but was later aired by public television. In *No Vietnamese Ever Called Me Nigger* (1968), David Loeb Weiss used interviews with black veterans to explore the relation between black America's struggle for civil rights and the Vietnamese struggle against foreign powers. The film focused on the alienation of Harlem residents from the government's pursuit of war and black veterans' memories of racist treatment by the military. Joseph Strick's short film, *Interviews with Mai Lai Veterans* (US, 1971), sought witness testimony from the five veterans who had, under the command of Lt. Calley, destroyed the village of Mai Lai in 1968. What emerged was less a factual representation or confession than a symptomatic portrait of the psychological damage inflicted by war and the dehumanising effect of war crimes on perpetrators as well as victims. It won an Oscar for best short documentary in 1971.

Other U.S. documentaries offered alternative histories of the war, specifically directed toward a critique of the U.S. government and media's role. *In the Year of the Pig* (USA de Antonio, 1969) was a compilation documentary that used witness testimony and archival footage as a form of historical reconstruction and politically-charged historiographic inquiry. It was different from previous documentaries in the way that it endeavoured to cover in a critical manner the entire history of the Vietnam War, filling in gaps left by media coverage even as it exposed its falsity. But perhaps the most significant documentary in this respect was *The Selling of the Pentagon* (Peter Davis, 1971). It did not protest the war directly, but showed how the Pentagon had promoted it through its films and its manipulation of the media. Broadcast in primetime, it garnered wide response from viewers and marked a definitive break between television coverage and the government stance on the war. Peter Davis's next film, released the year after the withdrawal of U.S. troops was *Hearts and Minds* (1974). Like *In the Year of the Pig*, it combined archival materials and interviews but unlike de Antonio's film, it organised them thematically to the end of exciting emotional responses in the viewer, both against the war and against those who promoted and supported it. It was widely distributed in the United States and won an Academy Award in 1974.

It would be a decade after the end of the war before documentaries would be made that fully contextualised it historically. *Vietnam: A Television History* (1983) was a collaborative project between the United States, Britain, and France that covered the war from Vietnam's precolonial history through its independence. It was broadcast on television as a thirteen-part series. The product of international research, with footage drawn from many countries, it endeavoured to present the conflict from all sides and used testimony from soldiers and civilians, political leaders and decision makers, with the objective of encouraging reconciliation and understanding.

Documentary treatment of the Vietnam War continued in films that directed attention to the scope of war's effects in both Vietnam and the United States. *Where War Has Passed* (Vietnam, Vu Le My and Luong Duc Won, 1998) recounted the horrific and ongoing effects of Agent Orange. Originally a piece of advocacy journalism designed to support a call for benefits from the Vietnamese government to Agent Orange's victims, it was circulated widely and won awards in German and Japanese film festivals. *Tieng Vi O My Lai/The Sound of the Violin in My Lai* (Vietnam, Tran Van Thuy,1998) produced by the Viet

Nam Documentary Film Unit with the cooperation of CBS, returned to My Lai (Son My) on the occasion of the opening of the My Lai Peace Park, a project organised by a U.S. veteran. Intercutting between the past and present, it focused on My Lai as an emotional symbol for both Americans and the Vietnamese. *Gao Rang/Riz Grillé/Grilled Rice* (France, Claude Grunspan, 2000) told the story of North Vietnamese and NLF combat cinematographers. Acknowledging the importance of eyewitness perspectives of the war and the limitations of its official representations, these cameramen expressed regret that they had not recorded more of everyday life under combat. In *Daughter from Danang* (US, Gail Dolgin and Vicente Franco, 2002), a reunion between an Amerasian woman, removed from Danang by "Operation Babylift" in 1975, and her Vietnamese mother dramatised the wide-ranging and long-lasting effects of war on noncombatant populations.

Evident in this survey as a dominant trope in Vietnam War documentary is an historiographic consciousness, a concern with what constitutes knowledge of the war and thus a concern with what types of representations might be adequate to understand it. Compilation films in their densely textured combination of archival materials and oral histories are homologous to the complexity of war's causes and effects and an explicit corrective to the limited perspectives of the media soundbite. Verité accounts of the war appear in binary opposition to such films, insofar as they constrict the scope of query to a singular perspective and often privilege emotional identification over intellectual understanding; but they were also a response to the limitations of the official representations of war. Recent documentaries tend to combine these approaches. As historical and cultural contexts of the Vietnam War are more completely explored, a multiplicity of personal perspectives are documented, bearing witness to the scope and longevity of war's effects on those who fight and those who live with its legacies.

Amanda Howell

See also **Alvarez, Santiago;** *Far from Vietnam*

Further Reading

Barnouw, Eric, *Documentary: A History of the Non-Fiction Film*, 2nd edition, Oxford: Oxford University Press, 1993.

Barsam, Richard M., *Nonfiction Film: A Critical History*, Bloomington: Indiana University Press, 1992.

Commager, Henry Steele, "On the Way to 1984," in *The Saturday Review*, April 15, 1967.

James, David E., "Film and the War: Representing Vietnam," in *Allegories of Cinema: American Film in the Sixties*, Princeton: Princeton UP, 1989, 195–213.

Kaplan, Fred, "*Vietnam! Vietnam!*" An exclusive report on John Ford's Propaganda Documentary for the USIA," *Cineaste*, 7, 3, 1976, 20–23.

Lichty, Lawrence, "*Vietnam: A Television History*" in *New Challenges for Documentary*, edited by Alan Rosenthal, Berkeley: University of California Press, 1988, 495–505.

McBride, Joseph, "Drums Along the Mekong," in *Sight and Sound*, 41, 4, 1972, 213–216.

Nichols, Bill, *Representing Reality: Issues and Concepts in Documentary*, Bloomington: Indiana University Press, 1991.

Renov, Michael, "Imaging the Other: Representations of Vietnam in Sixties Political Documentary," in *From Hanoi to Hollywood: The Vietnam War in American Film*, edited by Linda Dittmar and Gene Michaud New Brunswick: Rutgers University Press, 1990, 255–268.

Rowe, John Carlos, "Eyewitness: Documentary Styles in the American Representations of Vietnam," in *The Vietnam War and American Culture*, edited by John Carlos Rowe and Rick Berg, New York: Columbia University Press, 1991, 148–174.

Springer, Claudia, "Propaganda: Defense Department Films" in *The Vietnam War and American Culture*, edited by John Carlos Row and Rick Berg, New York: Columbia University Press, 1991, 95–114.

VIGO, JEAN

Jean Vigo, an avant-garde filmmaker of the 1930s, helped shape the development of surrealistic and French New Wave films during a career that was cut tragically short. Producing only four films, two of which were documentaries, his works reflect a poetic realism while sharing the aim of upsetting the status quo and celebrating the working class. Vigo's poverty-stricken life, the lingering influence of the revolutionary Paris Commune, and the injustice of the murder of his famous anarchist father combine to give his films a sharp social edge. His documentary theories were shaped by anger at societal inequities and his cinematic technique owes much to the Russian Bolshevik filmmakers of the 1920s, particularly Sergei Eisenstein and Dziga Vertov. Best known as a genius who created intense films with a magical mode of representation, Vigo's legacy is a witty style that leaves the viewer disoriented and shocked.

Although Vigo was neither an anarchist nor a communist, he was sympathetic to both philsophies and his interest lay in bettering the situation of the working class. He had an air of hostile disdain toward anything that represented authority or the established social order, and his films, with the exception of the eleven-minute *Taris: Champion de Natation*, reflect this antagonistic attitude. *A Propos de Nice: Point De Vue Documentee*, Vigo's first film, is a forty-two minute anarchistic manifesto that exposes the corrupt bourgeois values of the city while demanding a revolt of the unappreciated workers. Both of the documentaries celebrate the individual imagination, one of Vigo's favorite themes.

A Propos de Nice, so named because the film aimed to affect the world beyond Nice, was an attempt to use satire to pillory a rich and decadent society. Nice is a city famed for its gambling and tourism. The shots that Vigo selected emphasized the decadence of the bourgeois while celebrating the workers as the unacknowledged and unrewarded foundation of the city. Typical of the style of city films, *A Propos* opens with scenes of the empty metropolis, then proceeds to show a bustling urban center at the height of day. In the early morning, workers wash down the street to prepare for the day while another man paints the nose of a huge carnival doll. At midday, holiday-makers are shown in fancy dress on the Promenade as they uselessly pass the time. Images of one woman are intercut with footage of an ostrich. A series of dissolves on a young woman seated in the sun at the beach portray her in the attire of different seasons and then without any attire at all. Her nudity mocks the ostentations of the tourists. Vigo next turns to the scruffy poor quarter and a deformed child, then back to the wealthy as they dance in splendid gowns. Additional shots of a military parade, the local cemetery, the dancers again, and warships link indulgence and excess to war and death. The film concludes with images of the workers, as Vigo calls his class to arms.

The image relationships in *A Propos* are as often based on formal similarities and contrast such as direction of movement and similarity of shape or texture as on thematic relationships. Vigo did not plan to make extensive use of montage, a characteristic of Soviet filmmaking of the 1920s, but had to adapt to the unexpected disparity of the usable film. He linked the fragments together so that they would enrich each other by creating a series of associations. This juxtaposition of diverse and unrelated materials creates a new meaning. The film is also marked by a high degree of spatial disorientation effected by the use of several photographic strategies, including radical shooting angles and the use of a handheld camera, that violate the canons of three-dimensional perspective. Vigo shoots from a low angle and from overhead, as well as tilting the camera to show a hotel at a ninety-degree angle to its actual position.

Vigo made his next film, *Taris*, not because of any great interest in athletics but because he needed the money offered by the producer. It is his first sound film, although he preferred silent filmmaking; and, in it, Vigo demonstrates the strategy of discomfort and spatial disorientation that was becoming his trademark. After the swimming champion, Jean Taris, explained the sport to Vigo, the filmmaker spent two days preparing a shooting script of fifty-six shots. Most of the shooting took place at the swimming pool of the Automobile Club de France, including a humorous sequence that follows the sound of a megaphone into the funnel to the speaker's lips. Most of the film shows Taris racing, practicing, or talking about swimming. The race, which includes underwater photography, is in accelerated motion interspersed with three brief inserted shots of Taris in normal speed. The action in the images is always the same—swimming—and Vigo cuts off the sound of splashing but not its image when the champion is narrating. Although Vigo had once argued that the value of documentaries could only be maintained by taking the characters in a film unaware, *Taris* is far from ignorant of the camera. On several occasions he looks directly at the camera, thereby calling attention to its presence. At the end, Taris emerges out of the water backward in reverse motion and dissolves to appear next fully dressed complete with a derby hat. He then walks off over the surface of the pool, through the magic of superimposition. The short reflects the avant-garde effects of slow and fast motion, reverse motion, dissolves and superimpositions, as well as photography through material, specifically glass.

A radical and passionate filmmaker unafraid of courting controversy, Vigo died in poverty long before any of his films enjoyed popular success. The fantastical images and sounds that mark him as one of the most innovative of the 1930s directors also make him into one of the most significant influences on subsequent documentarians.

CARYN E. NEUMANN

Biography

Born April 26, 1905 in Paris to Eugéne Bonaventure de Vigo (alias Miguel Almereyda) and Emily Cléro. Visited his political prisoner father often in jail, 1905–1917. After his father's 1917 murder, took an assumed name to hide their connection, and attended school in Millau. Attended the Sorbonne under his real name for a certificate in ethics, sociology, and psychology but did not graduate. Failed his physical for the military because of tuberculosis and spent the rest of his life in perennially poor health, 1925. Patient at tuberculosis clinic, 1926–1928. Worked as an assistant at the Victorine studio in Nice, 1928. Married Elizabeth ("Lydou") Lozinska, 1929. Daughter Luce born June 30, 1931. Elected to the Comité Directeur of the Fédération Française de Ciné-Clubs. Filmed, 1932–1933. Died October 5, 1934 of septicemia in Paris.

Selected Films

1928 *Vénus*: fourth assistant to director Léone-Henri Burel
1930 *A Propos de Nice:* director, writer, editor
1931 *Taris*: director, writer, editor
1933 *Zéro de Conduite*: director, writer, editor
1934 *L'Atalante*: director and co-writer.

Further Reading

Salles-Gomes, Paulo Emilio, *Jean Vigo*, Berkeley: University of California Press, 1971.
Simon, William G., *The Films of Jean Vigo*, Ann Arbor, MI: UMI Research Press, 1981.
Smith, John M., *Jean Vigo*, New York: Praeger, 1972.
Weinberg, Herman G. (ed.), *Jean Vigo*, London: British Film Institute, 1951.

VISIONS OF EIGHT

(US/West Germany, various directors, 1973)

Leni Riefenstahl's poetic record of the 1936 Berlin games, *Olympische Spiele/Olympia* (1938), is often singled out as a sensual celebration of the human form in flight and—despite its links to the Nazi Party—is generally thought to be "the definitive cinematic treatment of the Games." Nevertheless, it falls short of the pyrotechnics on display in what is perhaps the most unusual of Olympic documentaries, *Visions of Eight/München 1972—8 berühmte Regisseure sehen die Spiele der XX Olympiade.*

On the surface, this multi-director episode film produced by legendary documentarian David L. Wolper and Stan Margulies (then-vice-president of Wolper Productions) appears curiously "empty" insofar as it captures only fleeting, impressionistic glimpses of the festival held in Munich (from August 26 to September 11, 1972) and furthermore only begrudgingly alludes to the deadly act of terrorism that capped the Olympics that year. Nevertheless, as an omnibus film composed of eight discrete yet connected sections, each averaging ten minutes, *Visions of Eight* is in fact a very "full" evocation of the Olympic experience, for it manages to convey both the personal and collective aspirations of the participants involved (athletes as well as filmmakers) through a narrative form naturally amenable to political allegory and the theme of competition.

Ironically, it was Wolper's interest in the ostensibly apolitical world of sports-based entertainment (he had already made *October Madness: The World Series* [1965] and *Pro Football: Mayhem on a Sunday Afternoon* [1965]) that gave him a decided advantage in the race to make the official film about the 1972 Summer Olympics. This event that would become mired in political debate when, on September 5, eight Palestinian guerrilla fighters known as "Black September" climbed the cyclone fence surrounding Olympic Village and took eleven

Visions of Eight, Claude Lelouch, co-director of documentary of 1972 Olympics in Munich, 1973.
[*Courtesy of the Everett Collection*]

members of the Israeli wrestling team hostage before killing them. Dedicated to the memory of the martyred athletes, *Visions of Eight* actually makes only passing reference to the actions of the terrorists, who easily circumvented the minimum-security measures that fateful day in Munich and put all of Germany—a nation eager to dissociate itself from Hitler's Berlin Games—on high alert. That the film at first appears so uncommitted in its political aspirations, that it seems so disinterested in the ideological implications of the Olympics, can be partly attributed to the fact that ninety percent of its principal photography had been completed by the time the terrorists took their hostages. Wolper, who had no intention of extending the schedule to include footage of an event that would already be telecast around the world before the film's theatrical debut the next year, left the task of footnoting the tragic occurrence to the one filmmaker who had not yet completed his contribution to *Visions of Eight*, John Schlesinger.

Although the making of any documentary is rife with potential problems, filming the Olympics proves to be particularly challenging, even for those producers like Wolper who are experienced in the fine art of on-location shooting, crowd-control, juggling simultaneous events, deploying large numbers of crew members, and maintaining a balance between proximity and distance. Given the vast nature of the event, just choosing what to shoot can be a vexing and time-consuming endeavor. Fortunately, Wolper had hit on the novel idea of apportioning those choices to a handful of the world's top directors—Juri Ozerov, Mai Zetterling, Arthur Penn, Michael Pfleghar, Kon Ichikawa, Claude Lelouch, Milos Forman, and John Schlesinger.

Fittingly, the film kicks off with "The Beginning," Ozerov's tension-filled depiction of athletic preparation. Through powerful yet whimsically juxtaposed images that foreshadow the yawning judge in Forman's "Decathlon" episode, Ozerov captures the pre-performance jitters and boredom faced by the world's greatest athletes—men and women fluttering between patience and nerve-jangling anticipation. A Soviet filmmaker who would later direct the feature-length account of the Olympic Games held in Moscow, *O Sport, Ty-Mir* (1980), Ozerov—an outspoken communist—draws on the theories of dialectical and poetic montage launched by his cinematic predecessors (Eisenstein, Vertov, Pudovkin) and turns the clash between individuality and community, between secular and spiritual comforts, into a profound (if all-too-brief) meditation on the underlying ideals of Western culture.

Following Ozerov's episode is Mai Zetterling's contribution to *Visions of Eight*, a look at the men's weightlifting competition entitled "The Strongest." Although initially attracted to the idea of filming the women athletes in Munich, Zetterling instead set her sights on what she described as the most "sensual" and "obsessive" of Olympic events. As a result, this pioneering feminist filmmaker (who admits in the episode's introduction to not being interested in sports) expanded her already diverse repertoire of key themes—sexual awakening, personal isolation, and the various forms of violence perpetrated against women—to accommodate these mutually impacting images of masculine hegemony and physical prowess. "The Highest," Arthur Penn's contribution, comes next—a decidedly apolitical and poetic vision of pole-vaulters reaching for the heavens.

Visions of Eight, documentary of 1972 Olympics in Munich, 1973.
[*Courtesy of the Everett Collection*]

With little-to-no sound to accompany the balletic movements of the vaulters' bodies rising and falling in midair, this sequence is the most abstract and impressionistic of the film, capturing in slow motion (96 to 600 frames/second) and soft-focus shots the sense of transcendence and freedom only a select few experience in their struggle against gravity to clear the fragile bar.

After witnessing these men plant their poles in the ground and push themselves upward, the viewer—perhaps struck by the conflation of sexual and spiritual aims implicit in such imagery—can be excused for feeling disappointed when literally brought back to earth in the fourth episode. Entitled "The Women," this episode finds German filmmaker Michael Pfleghar casting a decidedly male gaze at female athletes. Among the cinematically fetishized bodies are fifteen-year-old Australian swimmer Shane Gould, Russian gymnast Ludmilla Tourischeva, and West German pentathlete Heidi Rosendahl (world record-holder in the long jump) whose accomplishments in Munich and capacity for liberating mobility and agency are undercut by Pfleghar's leering close-ups and fragmented editing. Putting as much emphasis on their hairdressers as on the finish lines, this episode nevertheless says less about women than men—its reliance on film's traditional visual paradigm (masculine viewing subject and feminine object of desire) unwittingly underscoring an engrained facet of Western culture, which continues to perpetuate gender stereotypes through ocularcentric fictions.

Thankfully, this low point in the film is followed by one of its most effective and self-reflexive sequences: Kon Ichikawa's "The Fastest." Armed with a battalion of thirty-four over-cranked cameras, Ichikawa and his cinematographers filmed the men's 100-meter dash as it had never been filmed, effectively transforming this most accelerated of sports into a decelerated evocation of the dedication and training that goes into the Olympics. By stretching a ten-second race into a grueling, eleven-minute mini-marathon of facial contortions and wobbling muscles, Ichikawa not only conveys a Muybridge-like fascination with human physiognomy and locomotion, but also taps into the very technological preconditions behind their cinematic recording (the medium's ontological grounding in photographic realism plus the various apparati that confer the illusion of movement onto still images). This reflexive gesture is compounded by the director's decision to show all eight sprinters in a line, head-on, their individual yet contiguous lanes connoting the eight separate yet linked episodes of the film. A voice-over draws the spectator's attention to the runners' expressions, their eyes focused and full of yearning. After the gunshot is fired, one of the runners falls behind and gives up. These small details, in addition to Ichikawa's decision to show with 600mm telephoto lens each runner individually before capturing the entirety of the event in wide-shot, evokes the sense of humanity that comes, ironically, from selfhood—a theme for which the filmmaker has become famous.

Like Ichikawa, who had earlier made *Tokyo Olympiad* (1965), Claude Lelouch was no stranger to the Olympics. Four years before *Visions of Eight*, the French director had teamed up with François Reichenbach to chronicle the 1968 Winter Olympics held in Grenoble. Titled *Treize jours en France/Thirteen Days in France* (1968), this documentary gave international audiences a taste of the joy of victory, juxtaposing images of such heroic gold-medallists as skater Peggy Fleming and skier Jean-Claude Killy with political figures like President Charles DeGaulle. In Munich, however, Lelouch was drawn not to the Flemings and Killys of the world, not to the record-setting swimmer Mark Spitz (the famous Californian who in 1972 took home seven gold medals), but rather to the nearly 7,000 "nameless" men and women who—like the runner who gives up mid-race in Ichikawa's episode—know the bitter taste of defeat and sudden loneliness. These imbricated themes inform "The Losers," which segues from a boxer throwing a "hissy-fit," to an injured bicyclist, to weeping women athletes, to equestrian collisions, to dejected swimmers, to injured yet persistent wrestlers.

Of interest, "The Losers" comes in sixth, not last, among the eight episodes, immediately preceding Milos Forman's humorous interlude "The Decathlon." Ostensibly concerned with the most demanding and drawn-out of the disciplines (ten different events performed over two days), Forman's episode opts for a satiric critique of Olympic officialdom and spectatorship itself, a mode of dispassionate engagement personified by a green-suited judge who struggles to stay awake in the stands during the decathlon. Departing periodically from the games to explore the city's various manifestations of local color (yodeling, bell-ringing, Bavarian folk-dancing, and the Munich Symphony Orchestra's performance of "Ode to Joy" from Beethoven's Ninth), Forman manages to convey yet another aspect of Olympic spectatorship, which is pulled in several directions by cultural and sporting events and therefore dispersed or discursive in a way that resonates with both the multievent decathlon and episodic film spectatorship (a mode of engagement that can be literally wrenching insofar as viewers are habitually yanked from one story, setting, or group of characters to a completely different one).

If Forman's comic juxtapositions undercut the grandeur of the Olympics, this irreverence seems downright irrelevant in light of the tragedy that befell the "Games of Peace and Joy." As mentioned earlier, the only episode that references the act of terrorism is the final one, John Schlesinger's "The Longest." Like runners with tunnel vision, the first seven contributing directors focus exclusively on the nonpolitical aspects of the Olympics. Ironically, the concept of tunnel vision is personified by British runner Ron Hill, the ostensible subject of Schlesinger's episode whose utter refusal to see beyond his personal goal and whose outward indifference toward the incident disquieted the politically committed filmmaker. Although Schlesinger was as unprepared for the shocking news at Munich as the rest of Wolper's crew, he was the most prepared insofar as he had done extensive filming back in England. Having set up camp in the Lancashire countryside where Hill did his rigorous training (running approximately 130 miles a week outside his Manchester home), the director was able to interview his subject about the upcoming marathon, a twenty-six-mile race that he and his forty-five camera units would eventually cover with sixty-five cameras. In a sense, Schlesinger had been preparing for this moment his entire career, which stretches back to the mid-1950s, when he was first drawn to the documentary form during his prep school days at Uppingham. (There he shot *Sunday in the Park* [1956], eventually cutting his teeth making dozens of short nonfiction films for *Tonight* and

Monitor, two BBC series enjoying popularity during the 1950s.)

Images of the last runner finally trickling into the stadium in the rain are intercut with a shot of Olympic official Avery Brundage declaring the Games officially ended. The flame is extinguished, and shots of the Olympic flag at half-mast and the Israeli flag provide sobering reminders that, behind the joyful façade, several lives have been wasted. A sign reading "Montreal 1976" is visible in these final images, which bring closure to *Visions of Eight* and gesture toward the next Olympics.

DAVID DIFFRIENT

See also **Ichikawa, Kon; Lelouch, Claude; Schlesinger, John; Zetterling, Mai**

Visions of Eight (*München 1972—8 berühmte Regisseure sehen die Spiele der XX Olympiade*) (US and West Germany, Wolper Productions, 1972, 109 mins.). Distributed by Cinema 5 Distributing and EuroVideo. Directed by Juri Ozerov, Mai Zetterling, Arthur Penn, Michael Pfleghar, Kon Ichikawa, Claude Lelouch, Milos Forman, and John Schlesinger.

Further Reading:

Guttmann, Allen, *The Erotic in Sports*, New York: Columbia University Press, 1996.
———, *The Olympics: A History of Modern Games*, Urbana: University of Illinois Press, 2002.
Phillips, Gene D., *John Schlesinger*, Boston: Twayne Publishers, 1981.
Plimpton, George, "Olympic 'Visions of Eight,'" in *Sports Illustrated*, 39, August 27, 1973, 30–35.
Quand, James (ed.), *Kon Ichikawa*, Bloomington: Indiana University Press, 2001.
Wolper, David L., *Producer: A Memoir*, New York: Scribner, 2003.
Young, David C., *The Modern Olympics: A Struggle for Revival*, Baltimore: Johns Hopkins University Press, 2003.

VOIGT, ANDREAS

Voigt's participation in *Leipzig im Herbst/Leipzig in Autumn*, the documentation of the protests in Leipzig in October and November 1989, established his international reputation. He became one of the most important younger directors to document the political changes in East Germany

after unification. Particularly his five films on the city of Leipzig function as a sensitive seismograph of the feelings of the people. Voigt started his career as director quite late. His diploma film *Alfred* (1987), in which he portrayed a worker who was expelled from the party, had already gotten him into political trouble with the Communist Party. The film could be seen only at restricted screenings, because it indirectly criticized the economic system of the GDR, when a group of workers sit together to complain about their working conditions. "The fact that Voigt was given a contract as a director of the DEFA-Studios für Dokumentarfilme is categorical proof that times were changing. During the early and mid-eighties barely any filmmakers had been given full contracts" (Hughes, 1999: 288).

The protests against the GDR government began on October 7, 1989, but the documentary studio did not begin shooting until October 16, after the filmmakers met at the film festival in Brandenburg and realized that they could sit together and discuss the issues, but the real changes were taking place on the streets. Therefore, they decided to document these events in different towns. The DEFA team, with its heavy 35mm camera and additional lighting, was welcomed warmly by the protesters, a sequence that opens the film *Leipzig im Herbst*. In the interviews, they openly demand more freedom, free elections and travelling, and the right to express their political opinions. In contrast, the state officials were thinking only of how best to control the situation. The aesthetic style is typical for the DEFA, with an interesting cadrage in black and white, long takes, and patient interviews with the protesters to get the essence of what was happening. The camera actively participates in getting an impression of the atmosphere at this demonstration. There are also ironic situations, as for example when the street cleaners remove protest banners from the streets, but at the same time agree that their demands are totally correct. The film, collectively made by Andreas Voigt, Gerd Kroske, and cameraman Sebastian Richter, was shown at the Leipzig Documentary Festival, the most important documentary festival in the GDR, and won the Jury Prize there in 1989.

His next film, *Letztes Jahr Titanic/Last Year Titanic* (1991) follows a journalist, a worker, a left-wing skinhead, a teenager, and a pub owner between December 1989 and 1990, the last year of the GDR and the first one in reunified Germany. This film centers not on political opinions but on actual situations, developments, and personal feelings. Of course, in the beginning of the shoot, reunification could not have been predicted. So the film is an important document about the time of change, the social and economic insecurity, but it also has some ironic

and even absurd moments and uses the metaphor of the last dance. Voigt's fourth Leipzig film, *Glaube Liebe Hoffnung/Faith Love Hope* (1994), portrays a group of skinheads, some politically left wing, others extremely right wing. One feels the cold atmosphere of the society. The film was controversial. It was praised by some for its insight into the skinhead scene, but attacked by others for giving these radicals a platform for their arguments. Even more confusing were the images in its brilliant black-and-white cinematography. The last film in his Leipzig cycle is *Grosse Weite Welt/Big Wide World* (1997). It addresses the statements of the protagonists of his other Leipzig films by showing their development and how their lives have changed. His most recent film, *Invisible—Illegal in Europe* (2004) follows five people, who are either illegal refugees or trying to enter Europe, over a one-year period. It is a film about hopes and dreams, about the search for luck, and the despair of a system that did not allow existence under humane conditions. The wall has fallen, but Europe is still protecting its borders.

KAY HOFFMANN

Biography

Born August 25, 1953 in Eisleben, Germany. Grew up in Dessau. Studied physics for one year in Kraków, then political economy and economic history in Berlin from 1973 to 1978. From 1978 on, Voigt worked as a dramaturgist at the DEFA documentary studio and shot children's programs as a director. 1984–1987 external study at the film school in Potsdam Babelsberg. 1987–1990 director and author at the DEFA documentary studio. 1988–1990 member of directory of the Federation of Film and TV Creators of the GDR. After 1991 independent documentary filmmaker, author and producer for cinema and television, Voigt won many prices at national and international film festivals (for example, Adolf-Grimme-Preis, Silver Wolf Amsterdam, Taube Leipzig Festival, Grand Prix Strasbourg).

Selected Films

1987 *Alfred*: director
1988 *Leute mit Landschaft/People with Landscape*: director
1989 *Leipzig im Herbst/Leipzig in Autumn*: director with Gerd Kroske, co-script
1991 *Letztes Jahr Titanic/Last Year Titanic*: director, co-sprist
1992 *Grenzland eine Reise/Frontierland, a Journey*: director, script
1994 *Glaube Liebe Hoffnung/Faith, Love, Hope*: director, script
1995 *Ostpreussenland/Land of East Prussia*: director, script
1995 *Mr. Behrmann Leben Traum Tod/Mr. Behrmann Life Dream Death*: director, script

1995 *Begegnung mit Krystof Kieslowski/Meeting with Krystof Kieslowski*: director, script
1996 *Neues Leben/New Life*: director, script
1997 *Grosse Weite Welt/Big Wide World*: director
1999 *Trouble Spots*: director
2001 *David@New York*: director, script
2004 *Invisible—Illegal in Europe:* director, script

Further Reading

Hauke, Lutz, *Deutschland, Deutschland. Wertewandel im Prozeß der Wiedervereinigung im Blickfeld Berliner Dokumentarfilmer (1988–1991)*, in *Deutschlandbilder Ost. Dokumentarfilme der DEFA von der Nachkriegszeit bis zur Wiedervereinigung*, edited by Peter Zimmermann, Konstanz, 1995, 201–215.

Hecht, Heidemarie, *Der letzte Akt. 1989 bis 1992*, in *Schwarzweiß und Farbe. DEFA-Dokumentarfilme 1946–92*, edited by Günter Jordan and Ralf Schenk (eds.), Berlin, 1996, 235–267.

Hughes, Helen, *Documenting the Wende: The Films of Andreas Voigt*, in *DEFA. East German Cinema, 1946–1992*, edited by Séan Allan and John Sanford New York/Oxford, 1999, 283–301.

VOYAGE AU CONGO

(France, Allégret and Gide, 1926)

Voyage au Congo at first appears to be a simple travelog of Marc Allégret's journey with his uncle, André Gide, through what was then known as French Equatorial Africa. Gide, sensing his age and seeking renewed inspiration for his writing, sold his collection of presentation copies in 1925 and set sail with Allégret for the Congo, hoping to retrace the steps of Joseph Conrad's *Heart of Darkness*. Working from an itinerary determined by Allégret, the pair wound their way up the Congo River and beyond, passing through what is now the Congo, Central African Republic, Chad, and Cameroon. The trip would yield the 25-year-old Allégret's first motion picture, initiating an illustrious career in the French film industry. Gide himself remained largely detached from the filming process, absorbed in writing the journals that would later be published successively as *Voyage au Congo* (1927) and *Le retour du Tchad* (1928).

In spite of opening titles that proclaim, "rapportées par André Gide et Marc Allégret," the film is almost wholly Allégret's, with participation from Gide that mainly extended to the inter-titles. Allégret performed the essential geographical, ethnographic, and medical research for the journey; and it was Allégret's idea, in the summer of 1924, to further validate his role by including still photography and, soon after, a motion picture camera (Allégret, 1987). What resulted was neither a simple travelog, nor an ethnographic study, nor a documentary, but an experimental mixture of approaches loosely organized around the theme of the journey. It includes images of travel; staged reenactments of indigenous daily life; actuality scenes of local performances, games, and customs; as well as brief shots of landscapes and exotic flora and fauna. At times the film's episodic structure seems to follow the example of Robert Flaherty, whose *Nanook of the North* (1922) was much admired in France. Daniel Durosay, however, argues that Allégret consciously went against these tendencies, deliberately suppressing in the film any visual impression of effort, risk, or adventure (Allégret, 1987). In this sense, the principles behind *Voyage au Congo* could be seen as more closely aligned to Flaherty's second film, *Moana* (1926). Subtitled "a romance of the Golden Age," *Moana* focused more on domestic daily activities, physical sensuality, and bodily movement. A little more than a month after returning from his African trip, Gide wrote of seeing the "voluptuous" *Moana* in Paris, though it is unknown whether the film had an influence on Allégret's final cut (Geiger, 2000).

Allégret's fantasy of the primitive shares with Flaherty a tendency toward romantic idealism and fails to acknowledge the colonial framework within which it operates and the effects of that colonial system. Allégret was hardly shielded from the fact of colonialism; on the contrary, as Gide's journals attest, French commercial interests and the exploitation of African labour were everywhere in evidence, and even prevented the pair from finding the ideal, unspoiled Africa they were seeking. Yet the film also suggests contemporary trends in ethnographic surrealism as practiced by Paul Rivet, Lucien Lévy-Bruhl, and Marcel Mauss, who were establishing the Institut d'Ethnologie in Paris during the same year as Allégret and Gide's travels. The primitivist fantastic would take on other forms in Allégret's later work, particularly in such projects as the Josephine Baker film *Zou Zou* (1934), which portrayed Baker as a bird in a golden cage.

The content and style of *Voyage au Congo* gesture to various modes of documentary practice, but as a whole it does not comfortably fit into any single category. Opening with scenes on the deck of the Asie off the coast of the Canary Islands, the film sets itself up as a spectacular travel narrative seen through Western eyes. The viewer is at first positioned with the traveler, as the camera shows a woman playfully taking a pair of binoculars and looking through them in the direction of the camera. Soon afterward the viewer follows the route of the Matadi-Kinshassa colonial railroad, with the camera perched on a moving train. Assisted by maps marking the route, the traveler is encouraged to identify with the camera as a journeying eye. One of the first glimpses of a native, near Bangui, takes on overtones of romanticized first contact, as out on the river a young man standing in a canoe glides across the water toward the camera, arriving like a guide who embodies primitive life harmoniously at one with nature.

Allégret includes some visually powerful images, such as the falls at M'Bali and a dance presented by the Dakpas near Bambari. These fragments lead to the core of the film, which is made up of episodes structured around five indigenous groups. Each sequence incorporates a distinct style and theme, always with an emphasis on display and performance. The Bayas are shown at work, as men hunt and women dig for tubers, suggesting a self-sustaining world at harmony with nature. The film then moves to the Saras where Allégret, in perhaps the film's most striking episode, inserts an intricately staged tale of a marriage negotiation between two young lovers, Kaddé and Djimta. The film's underlying voyeurism and primitivism is suggested in the shot introducing Kaddé, which

tightly pans along her torso to her breasts, then moves across her body to reveal her face, where a small disc is fixed to her upper lip. The image recalls an earlier shot of Sara's girls: their bodies are examined in a slow left-to-right pan while the inter-titles explain that they "in turn prove their value."

The Kaddé and Djimta interlude is followed by further travelog sequences. The Massas are featured for their striking architecture, and the scenes among the Moundangs are almost wholly given over to an extravagant dance. The final episode shows a ceremony filmed at Reï-Bouba, offering a glimpse of local hierarchies, games, and the equestrian displays that Gide also describes with admiration in his journals. Though the film rarely achieves the sort of sensitivity to the colonial setting found in Gide's writings, or in Conrad's novel, it is a remarkable feature-length work, full of the rich aesthetic sensibilities also on display in Allégret's still photographs. Though it resists argument or instruction, its final moments do begin to incorporate a sense of ambiguity. After scenes at Reï-Bouba, images of "la civilisation" flash across the screen: a protestant mission school, schoolchildren playing in uncomfortable-looking Western clothing, the endless transit of boats arriving and leaving at the port of Douala, and finally the sky over the sea, fading to black.

JEFFREY GEIGER

See also **Allégret, Marc; France**

Voyage au Congo (France, 1927, 100 min. approx.). Produced, directed, written, photographed and edited by Marc Allégret. Titles by Allégret and André Gide. Filmed in Congo, Central African Republic, Chad, and Cameroon.

Further Reading

Allégret, Marc, *Carnets du Congo: Voyage avec Gide*, Introduction and notes by Daniel Durosay, Paris: Presses du C.N.R.S., 1987.

Durosay, Daniel, "Analyse synoptique du *Voyage au Congo* de Marc Allégret avec l'intégralité des inter-titres," in *Bulletin des Amis d'André Gide*, January 22, 1994, 71–85.

———, "Les 'cartons' retrouvés du *Voyage au Congo*," in *Bulletin des Amis d'André Gide*, January, 22, 1994, 65–70.

Geiger, Jeffrey, "Sightseeing: *Voyage au Congo* and the Ethnographic Spectacle," in André Gide's *Politics*, edited by Tom Conner, New York: Palgrave, 2000, 111–130.

Gide, André, *Travels in the Congo* [*Voyage au Congo*/Le retour du Tchad], translated by Dorothy Bussy, Hopewell, NJ: Ecco Press, 1994.

WAITING FOR FIDEL

(Canada, Rubbo, 1974)

Waiting for Fidel is the film in which Australian-born National Film Board of Canada director Michael Rubbo consolidated his inimitable style of personal filmmaking. The film meshes three elements tentatively present in his earlier documentary, *Sad Song of Yellow Skin* (1970), and that here, in full-bodied combination, make Rubbo's style distinctive to him. These elements are his participation in the on-screen action, his generosity toward his subjects, and a recognition of the superficiality and unreliability of documentary truth.

The film begins with three men in an airplane on its way to Cuba to film a promised interview with Fidel Castro. Geoff Stirling, a hip, capitalist media mogul, is making the film in co-production with the National Film Board. Rubbo is the director. Joining them is the former Prime Minister of Newfoundland and the man who brought the province into confederation with Canada, the socialist Joey Smallwood. Different as their personalities are, at a certain level of generality the three share the hope that the interview with Cas-

tro will promote understanding between Cuba and the capitalist West.

As hinted in the film's title, the interview never happens. The film team bides its time in comparative luxury, waiting and hoping for the phone call summoning them to Castro. The focus of the film becomes the interaction among the three characters and their responses to Cuba. It is through this interplay among characters and between them and Cuba that the film rewards the audience with entertainment and insight.

The most famous scene in the film occurs late, when the three men have become frustrated at the stonewalling their quest for a promised interview has met. Rubbo has been filming their dinners, their recreations, and their controlled visits that their Cuban liaison man set up for them at such sites as a housing project, two schools, a chicken farm, and the Bay of Pigs. Stirling, who has put up the outside money for the project, gets into a heated argument with Rubbo over his shooting ratio. Rubbo has been filming at roughly a 25:1 clip. Stirling insists that a 3:1 clip would be more than sufficient. He berates Rubbo for his profligacy and calls him incompetent. Rubbo defends his way, and the Film Board's way, of making documentaries. During their argument, they curse a lot, their cuss words bleeped out on the sound track. It is funny and revealing, but its charm also lies in Rubbo's involvement as an actor, not just an observer, and his willingness to allow his own foolishness to remain on screen. Few directors who appear in their films are as willing to be as harsh on themselves as they are on others.

Rubbo's generosity toward his characters is remarkable. Stirling could have been made to look merely ridiculous and unsavory. He seems incapable of acknowledging anything positive in the Cuban system, railing against fact that schoolchildren have to spend part of their day working in a factory and complaining that a broadcaster like him would not be allowed on the air in Cuba. Smallwood, who is in his seventies, could have been portrayed as tiresome and dotty, but he comes off as admirable in his low-key but stubborn determination to think the best of Cuba and to do his best to ensure that the film contributes positively to international understanding. Interspersed throughout the film are brief scenes of Smallwood preparing his questions for Castro. The film's Cuban liaison comes off as a likeable, unofficious human being, somewhat bemused by the antics of his Canadian charges. And Rubbo's willingness to see himself as one of the characters, with foibles and blind spots of his own, saves the film from the kind of condescension or sanctimony that so often detracts from films featuring the filmmaker as the documentary protagonist.

Ostensibly the film may appear to offer a vision of Cuba in lieu of the hoped-for scoop with Castro. In the state-sponsored location scenes, we get some interesting, off-the-cuff interaction with Cubans speaking without script. A pair of university students set the visitors straight on finer points of Marxism. An inmate of a mental hospital suggests that Rubbo, not her, may be the crazy one. A lyrically shot scene of a pick-up baseball game seems to capture a certain innocence in the Cuban personality. But these encounters are superficial, and Rubbo knows it. What matters is not what they reveal about Cuba, because they reveal very little. Far more interesting is what they reveal about Stirling, Smallwood, and Rubbo. They interpret the encounters so that they fit in with their existing ideological concerns. For Stirling, nothing he sees

is good; only a restoration of capitalism can save Cuba. Smallwood is impressed by the progress Cuba has made and thinks it is headed in the right direction. Rubbo is ambivalent, wanting to be impressed. What the film finally demonstrates has little to do with Cuba and everything to do with how our mindsets shape the way we perceive and interpret new experiences.

It is now quite common for documentary filmmakers to assume an on-screen role of provocateur. What remains rare, however, is the willingness to keep one's on-screen role roughly equal in dramatic force to other characters. And Rubbo's awareness of the limitations of documentary, while widely shared, is rarely expressed in such a natural way, organic to the story, but instead is typically announced or stated in a way external to the narrative.

D.B. JONES

See also **Rubbo, Michael;** *Sad Song of Yellow Skin*

Waiting for Fidel (Canada, National Film Board, 1974, 58 min). Distributed by the National Film Board of Canada. Produced by Tom Daly and Michael Rubbo. Directed and edited by Michael Rubbo. Cinematography by Douglas Kiefer. Sound by Jacques Chevigny.

Further Reading

Denby, David, "How to Make a Castro Movie Without Castro," in *New York Times*, November 16, 1975.

Dobi, Steve, "Michael Rubbo" (interview), *Sightlines*, Fall, 1975, 17–20.

Handling, Piers, "The Diary Films of Mike Rubbo," in *Take Two*, Seth Feldman (ed.), Toronto: Irwin Publishing, 1984.

Hughes, John, "Michael Rubbo: Hiding Behind the 'I'" (interview), in *Cinema Papers*, January–February 1981, 41–45, 89.

Jones, D.B., *Movies and Memoranda*, Ottawa: Deneau, 1982.

———, *The Best Butler in the Business: Tom Daly of the National Film Board of Canada*, Toronto, University of Toronto Press, 1996.

Knelman, Martin, "*Waiting for Fidel*," *Toronto Globe & Mail*, July 24, 1976.

Rosenthal, Alan, "*Sad Song of Yellow Skin* and *Waiting for Fidel*" (interview with Michael Rubbo), in *The Documentary Conscience: A Casebook in Film Making*, Berkeley: University of California Press, 1980.

Sloniowski, Jeannette, "Questioning the Master Narratives: Michael Rubbo's *Waiting for Fidel*," in *Candid Eyes: A Canadian Documentary Reader*, James Leach, and Jeannette Sloniowski (eds.), Toronto: University of Toronto Press, forthcoming.

WAR

See **Falklands War; Vietnam War; World War I; World War II**

WAR GAME, THE

(UK, Watkins, 1965)

Peter Watkins's meticulously researched vision of a "limited" nuclear attack on England, *The War Game*, was officially banned from television screens worldwide for twenty years. It was produced for BBC Television in 1965, released for cinema in 1967, but not shown on television until 1985. The extent of its suppression and the political controversy that hounded it are perhaps unparalleled in UK television history. Watkins believed that there was a conspiracy of silence on the subject of nuclear warfare. Certainly this film touched such a raw nerve that the BBC, the government, and the right wing press (which dubbed it propaganda for the Campaign for Nuclear Disarmament) all conspired to suppress it. But it had its champions as well as denigrators, and the debate about whether to shelve it raged for over a year.

Watkins's film is a tour de force of cinematic techniques, using a fluid, handheld camera style that he had developed since his amateur days. He subverts the forms of documentary and newsreel to deliberately disorientate the viewer, engaging them emotionally, intellectually, and actively. In this way the film has been compared somewhat to Orson Welles's radio broadcast of *The War of the Worlds* (1938). *The War Game* is a drama shot to *look* like a documentary, a film with an inner logic that immediately suspends disbelief and invites the viewer to question the morality of nuclear weapons and the state's civil defence policy. As its narrative

unfolds, the consequences of nuclear war at a very human level are explored, creating a reaction that is overpowering in its intensity.

Brechtian detachment techniques are deployed at times to create emotional distancing, such as the cameos to camera of some of the "experts" attempting to reassure us of the "wisdom" of nuclear weapons. But the effect is one of ironic counterpoint to the dramatic newsreel-like action on the screen. The contrast between these scenes is like attending a lecture on thermonuclear weapons and being there when one explodes. Occasionally Watkins breaks the narrative to question the cast

The War Game, 1965.
[*Courtesy of the Everett Collection*]

The War Game, 1965 Documentary Drama by Peter Watkins. [*Courtesy of the Everett Collection*]

directly about their knowledge of nuclear weapons, civil defence, and the Cold War. *The War Game* was shot on 16mm black and white to add to its illusory documentary/newsreel feel. This effect was further enhanced by a deliberate increase in tonal contrast at the processing stage to give the scenes after the bomb had dropped a stark, nightmare quality. *The War Game* used an amateur cast, as is Watkins's preference. He has been criticised for the occasional "stiffness" of their performances, but feels that new faces and actors free from the traditional conventions of film acting are important additions to his conception of film realism. The stunning special effects of *The War Games* (such as the battlefield combat scene using "tactical" nuclear weapons in Europe and the hellish firestorm depicted in England) all owe much to the crew's inventiveness rather than a big budget.

The film achieved notoriety even before it was screened. The co-founder of the "Clean-up Television" campaign, Mary Whitehouse, wrote on September 5, 1965 to Hugh Carleton Greene, the Director General of the BBC, and Prime Minister Harold Wilson that nuclear war was not a subject for "entertainment." She added, ominously that, "the Home Office, not the BBC" should decide whether or not to show it. The letter was quoted in *The Guardian* (1965) and other sources. The decision to ban *The War Game* was raised at 10 Downing Street, discussed in the Cabinet, and debated in Parliament. A salvo of communication passed between the Home Office (the government department responsible for broadcasting *and* civil defence) and the BBC. It should not be forgotten that *The War Game* exposed, for the first time on film, the rudimentary "protect and survive" methods that were promoted by the government against nuclear attack.

The Guardian (1999) reported that Prime Minister Churchill personally intervened in 1955 when the BBC proposed to make a film about the newly developed hydrogen bomb. These new weapons were thousands of times more deadly than the atomic bombs used on Japan in 1945. Churchill's edict to the BBC declared that any plans for a film on the H-bomb should be discussed in advance. The BBC "at once accepted—very willingly" his order. Cold War tension was the underlining factor here, but also the curious relationship between the BBC and the British government, which only grants the BBC a licence to broadcast for a period of usually up to ten years at any one time. In 1965, the protocol was that the Home Office could instruct the BBC via the Post Master General to ban any programme it considered "not in the National interest." The BBC Chair of Governors in 1965 was Lord Normanbrook, whose previous posts included Secretary to the Cabinet and Head of the Civil Service, and was reputedly one of Churchill's most trusted advisors (Colville, 1985). In 1954, he headed a top-secret committee to advise on civil defence and war strategy in the event of a nuclear attack, a role well documented in Hennessy (2003).

Retired Member of Parliament and ex-Cabinet Minister Tony Benn was the Post Master General in 1965. He told me personally and in writing (2003) that he was instructed by the Home Office to officially ban *The War Game*: "My recollection is that the Home Secretary—[Frank] Soskice—decided to ban *The War Game* and, as PMG [Post Master General] and Minister for the BBC, I was told to transmit the instruction to them."

The film was eventually granted a licence for cinema release but only after public protest, led by Watkins himself. It was shown in church halls, municipal buildings, and independent cinemas and immediately galvanised support. Cultural icons, such as Lennon and Ono, Paul McCartney, and the Beatles's manager Brian Epstein, all supported Watkins's film. The respected theatre and film critic, Kenneth Tynan, wrote in the *Observer*: "It may be the most important film ever made. We are always being told that works of art cannot change the course of history. Given wide enough dissemination, I believe this one can." John Lennon, in *Rolling Stone* (1970) said that seeing the film and corresponding with Watkins "was like getting your call up papers for peace" This impact on Lennon and Ono's "give peace a chance" activities is elaborated in Coleman (1995).

The War Game further embarrassed the BBC by winning the Academy Award in 1967 for the Best

Documentary Feature of 1966. Typically, Watkins declined to attend. Kenneth Adam, the Director of BBC Television, was sent to represent him, although one of the BBC's explanations for "its" decision not to show the film was that it was "less than a masterpiece" and a failed "experiment" (Gomez, 1979). But Watkins sent a telegram insisting that Adam was not to accept the Oscar if he won and the BBC was denied this opportunistic moment of reflected glory.

As a child Watkins lived in London and experienced the Blitz, the VI flying bomb, and the even more terrifying V2 rocket. After the war he was conscripted for military service, and his abhorrence of war found expression in most of his subsequent work.

Tynan (Lahr, 2001) wrote that Watkins is "the finest auteur we have" responsible for "three masterpieces, more than any other living English director" [*Culloden*,1964; *The War Game,* 1965; and *Edvard Munch*, 1973].

PATRICK MURPHY AND JOHN COOK

See also **Watkins, Peter**

The War Game (UK, BBC Television, 1965, 47 min.). Distributed by The British Film Institute, London, on VHS or DVD with voice-over commentary and audio essay by Patrick Murphy. Written, produced and directed by Peter Watkins. Photography Peter Bartlett. Editor Mike Bradsell; Art direction Tony Cornell and Anne Davey. Action sequences Derek Ware. Sound Derek Williams, Lou Hanks, and Stanley Morcom. Costumes Vanessa Clarke. Make up Lilias Munro; Production assistant Peter Norton. Commentaries Dick Graham and Michael Aspel. Filmed in Kent, England.

Further Reading

Anon, "Letter to PM on TV Film," in *The Guardian*, UK, September 7, 1965, 5.
——, in *Rolling Stone*, U.S./UK, February 7, 1970.
The BBC Handbook, London, published annually by the BBC.
Coleman, R., "Peace," in *Lennon: The Definitive Biography*, London: Pan Books, 1995, revised edition.
Colville, J., *The Fringes of Power*, London: Hodder and Stroughton Ltd., 1985.
Cook, J., and P. Murphy, "After the Bomb Dropped: The Cinema Half-Life of the War Game," in *The Journal of Popular British Cinema*, 3, 2000, 129–132, London, Flicks Books.
Ferris, P., "The War Game," in *Sir Huge: the Life of Huw Wheldon*, London: Michael Joseph, 1990.
Gomez, J., *Peter Watkins*, Boston: Twayne Publishers, 1979.
Hennessy, P., *The Secret State*, London: Allen Lane, The Penguin Press, 2002.
Murphy, P., "Let Them Watch Strindberg," in *The Times Higher Education Supplement*, London, February 7, 1997.
——, "The Film the BBC Tried to Bury," *The New Statesman*, London, August 24, 1997, 22–24.
——, "*The War Game*—The Controversy, Sweden, in *Film International*, 3, 2003, 25–28.
Rosenthal, A., "*The War Game*," in *The New Documentary in Action*, California: University of California Press, 1971.
Travis, A., "Churchill gagged BBC on H-bomb," in *The Guardian*, UK, August 20, 1999, 6.
Tynan, K., "A Warning Masterpiece," in *Observer*, London, February 13, 1966.
Watkins, P., *The War Game*, London: Sphere Books/Andre Deutsch, 1967.
Welsh, J.M., *Peter Watkins—A Guide to References and Resources*, Boston: G.K. Hall & Co., 1986.

WAR ROOM, THE

(US, Pennebaker and Hegedus, 1993)

The War Room (1993) follows two documentary traditions pioneered with *Primary* (1960): cinema verité and the insider's view on U.S. presidential election campaigns. Like *Primary*, *The War Room* observes events on the campaign trail, but instead of limiting itself to one state, the film follows Bill Clinton's 1992 odyssey through the New Hampshire primary, the Democratic Party nomination and bus tour, the debates, and the election night victory. The film also addresses the monkey wrenches thrown into the works, including Gennifer Flowers's allegations, draft-dodging accusations, and other mud-slinging on platform issues. In all, filmmakers D.A. Pennebaker (who worked on *Primary*) and Chris Hegedus spent almost thirty-five hours inside the war room, Clinton's moniker for his campaign headquarters in Little Rock, Arkansas.

The film does show some moments with Clinton (one features him wearing a ball cap, an Arkansas Razorbacks T-shirt, a digital watch, and running shoes as he talks to a reporter on the phone), but *The War Room* is more about his image and his image-makers than Clinton himself. As such, the focus is more on campaign manager James Carville and communications director George Stephanopoulos. The two are polar opposites, yet both are dedicated to seeing their candidate win. With his Southern affectations, quick mind, and dazzling one-liners, "Ragin' Cajun" Carville brings his passionate spirit to meetings, press conferences, and even radio talk shows. George Stephanopoulos plays the straight man to Carville's one-man act, though he brings no less dedication to the efforts.

Pennebaker and Hegedus also incorporate television clips and shots of newspaper headlines to fill in some gaps in their timeline. In doing so, they provide an additional perspective on events, that of the mass media. Television footage reveals the dings in the candidate's reputation. One early segment juxtaposes Flowers's press conference ("Did Governor Clinton use a condom?" asks one reporter) and her revelation of their affair with shots of reporters asking Clinton for comments on the accusations. Newspaper headlines chart Clinton's rise and fall at both primary and public opinion polls.

The filmmakers played the cinema verité waiting game in making *The War Room*, but Carville

The War Room, George Stephanopoulos, James Carville, 1993. © October Films.
[*Courtesy of the Everett Collection*]

delivers an emotional climax. During a staff meeting, Stephanopoulos calmly introduces Carville with a thank you. Carville gets up to give a final rally cry for the troops, but a close-up reveals his chin quivering as he speaks. A tear emerges and he wipes it away, fighting the wash of tears coming on.

The filmmakers also risked Clinton losing the election. If he had lost, according to Hegedus, "the value of a film about a losing campaign staff wasn't going to be too salable for us. There is a risk in any story where you're following real life and you don't know what's going to happen" (Stubbs, 2002: 46). Voters elected Clinton by a "landslide," in Stephanopoulos's word.

The film shows how an unconventional candidate needs an unconventional team. By mixing observed footage with television clips and newspaper headlines, Hegedus and Pennebaker create a forum in which to showcase Carville, Stephanopoulos, and the rest of Clinton's staff.

HEATHER MCINTOSH

The War Room, George Stephanopoulos, James Carville, 1993. © October Films.
[*Courtesy of the Everett Collection*]

1418

The War Room (US, Pennebaker Associates, 1993, 96 min). Distributed by October Films. Directed by Chris Hegedus and D.A. Pennebaker. Produced by R.J. Cutler, Wendy Ettinger, and Frazer Pennebaker. Cinematography by Nick Doob, D.A. Pennebaker, and Kevin Rafferty. Film Editing by Chris Hegedus, Erez Laufer, and D.A. Pennebaker.

Further Reading

Pennebaker Hegedus Films, http://www.phfilms.com/index. php.
Stubbs, Liz, "D.A. Pennebaker and Chris Hegedus: Engineering Nonfiction Cinema," in *Documentary Filmmakers Speak*, New York: Allworth, 2002, 41–68.

WARHOL, ANDY

Pop artist Andy Warhol made many films in the 1960s in his New York studio, the well-known "Factory." Warhol began working with 16mm film around 1963 and continued to produce great numbers of cinematic works for several years. These films are among the most noted of the 1960s avant-garde and are counted among the canon of experimental film, as they challenged narrative convention and explored daily life in exciting new ways. This movement into filmmaking was a natural progression for Warhol, whose work as a painter and illustrator was already revered. The pop icon was always interested in new ways to replicate the events and people of the world around him, and the film camera provided a direct and seemingly truthful means of capturing this. As Warhol evolved as a filmmaker, his works became less clearly documentary and more fictional in their content. So, too, the formal aspects seen in Warhol's early films changed as the decade continued, an apparently organic aesthetic response to the times.

The first Warhol films recall the simple constructions of the Lumiére's actualities from the 1890s. These works are far more complex, however, and may be seen as a perfect representation of the prevailing attitudes and concerns of their time. *Sleep* (1963), the first Warhol film shown publicly, is a record of John Giorno in bed sleeping. The film is in real time, so it lasts more than five hours and is a complete document of a man sleeping. The impact of showing such an event in real time cannot be underestimated. Viewers are often disturbed by this technique, and they may become agitated or angry, perhaps even verbally abusive to the screen itself. Warhol continued his investigation of real time with such works as the trio of *Haircut* films (1963), *Empire* (1964), and *Eat* (1964). Each of these titles refers rather directly to the content of

the film. In the *Haircut* works, numbered consecutively in order of creation, we witness various men having haircuts. In *Eat*, we watch painter Robert Indiana slowly consume a mushroom, an experience that lasts nearly forty minutes. Warhol's notorious *Empire* is an eight-hour study of the Empire State Building. The camera is unmoving, and only a full viewing of the film can show that there is much movement indeed, as sunlight shifts and falls, clouds drift by, and electrical lights are switched on and off in the building.

This cinematic experimentation evolved in several different ways. These very early films investigated time in a meditative way, but other "real time" works moved less slowly in the same period. *Kiss* (1963–1964) is a series of short works that cleverly defies the viewer-viewed comfort zone. Warhol was interested in voyeurism and sought to play with this concept in his film work. *Kiss* also exploits the single spool (100' reel) of home movies and independent filmmaking. Each set of people seen in the *Kiss* works engages in kissing for nearly three minutes, the length of one reel of 16mm film. The couples are diverse (same sex, opposite sex, questionable gender, etc.) as are the styles of kissing seen (from very passionate to softly tender). What is undeniable here is the atypical experience of watching anyone kiss for more than the usual thirty seconds or less seen in typical movies. *Blow Job* (1964) is of the same time period, and it also strongly deals with the nature of voyeurism and the viewer's experience. In this film, a man leans against a brick wall as fellatio is performed on him. The framing of this scene is paramount, as the shot shows the man's head, shoulders, and torso, but nothing below his midsection. The viewer is left to ponder the unseen person kneeling in front of the subject, and as the film lasts more than thirty minutes, the act of watching the subject's face is clearly the point of the exercise.

One of the most fascinating projects seen in the Warhol film archive is that of the *Screen Tests* (1964–1966), which also exploited the 100' reel of 16mm film as a time element. There are more than 500 known *Screen Tests* (The Andy Warhol Museum is in the process of identifying and cataloging all of the works that have surfaced in Warhol's belongings), each a three-minute study of a person's face. With the camera mounted on a tripod, turned on, and left to create a record, each subject reacted differently. Facing a camera is a difficult task for some, a chance to perform for others, but each *Screen Test* shows a change in the subject's face as the minutes of this confrontation pass. These works are beautiful in their formal simplicity and extremely intriguing as complex explorations of individuals.

These types of investigations continued throughout the 1960s and into the early 1970s, as Warhol turned his camera onto the people who hung around the Factory. Documentary studies were still the bulk of the films made, but they became more elaborate studies of the artists, musicians, junkies, and superstars who were a part of the Warhol scene. *Chelsea Girls* (1967) is a double-projected film (two reels shown side-by-side and simultaneously) that is more than three hours long. It moves from room to room in the Chelsea Hotel, pausing for various periods of time to reveal these people in various scenarios in largely unscripted scenes. The "actors" play themselves here, and the film is a document of these people in this time doing the strange things they did. Other works were made with this same kind of curiosity and honesty as these lives were memorialized in hundreds of films.

TAMMY A. KINSEY

*See also **The Chelsea Girls***

Biography

Born near Pittsburgh, PA, 1928. Attended Carnegie Institute of Technology (now Carnegie Mellon University). Moved to New York City, 1949. Began working in commercial art as an illustrator. First exhibition, Ferus Gallery, 1962. Included in group show at the Guggenheim Museum, 1963. Received Independent Film Award from *Film Culture*, 1964. Film installation exhibited in New York Film Festival, 1964. Produced Exploding Plastic Inevitable, multimedia events that included performances by the Velvet Underground, 1966. Produced first rock and roll album by Velvet Underground and Nico, 1966. Shot and seriously wounded by Valerie Solanas, former Factory dweller, 1968. First retrospective show, Europe, 1968. First issue of *Interview* magazine published 1969. Major retrospective show, United States and Europe, 1970. Produced short segments, "Andy Warhol's TV" for use on *Saturday Night Live*, 1981. Directed music video for the Cars, 1984. Hosted *Andy Warhol's Fifteen Minutes*, regular program on MTV, 1985–1987. Died from complications following routine gallbladder surgery, 1987.

Selected Films

1964 *Couch*
1965 *Horse*
1966 *Suicide*
1968 *Blue Movie*

Further Reading

Koch, Stephen, *Stargazer*, New York: Marion Boyars, 1973.
O'Pray, Michael (ed.), *Andy Warhol: Film Factory*, London: British Film Institute, 1989.
Warhol, Andy, and Hackett, Pat, *POPism: The Warhol 60's*, New York: Harper & Row, 1980.
Wolf, Reva, Andy *Warhol, Poetry, and Gossip in the 1960s*, Chicago and London: University of Chicago Press, 1997.

WATKINS, PETER

In 2000, Peter Watkins completed a 345-minute documentary commissioned by La Sept ARTE, the French-German TV network. *La Commune de Paris 1871* was produced with a cast of more than 200, recruited from newspaper adverts, who researched and improvised together the story of the uprising. Told through the eyes of two fictional TV stations, the actors, in and out of character and in and out of period, debate the issues of the Commune, but also the role of the media in 1871 and at the end of the millennium. La Sept ARTE first tried to reedit, then scheduled the program for the graveyard shift. Distributed on video by supporters, the film has done the round of festivals to considerable acclaim and some controversy. It has also been effectively kept off the television screens for which it was designed and on which it comments so directly. It is, as far as there is such a thing, a typical Watkins project.

In his online account of the film, Watkins's comments of TV that "The medium has become a thoroughly mean-spirited profession, ruthlessly resisting all dialogue for change, completely devoid of respect, and allied without reservation to the development of globalization in its most centralizing and brutal forms." The bitter tone is all too familiar and only too understandable. A prize-winning amateur filmmaker, Watkins clearly relished the inventive, improvisational character of nonprofessional documentary and continues to draw on it in his most recent work. With *Culloden* (1964), he achieved star status, bringing his verité camera, direct address, voice-over, and volunteer cast aesthetic to the network public and critical esteem. His follow-up, *The War Game* (1965), despite its Best Documentary Oscar, was banned from British broadcasting for twenty years. Characterised by the same gritty montage of dramatisation, recitations of fact, and precise naming of protagonists that characterised his earliest films, *The War Game*'s depiction of the likely effects of a nuclear strike on Kent, England, made the fatal error of tying its horrors not just to Vietnam, as he had done in *Culloden*, but to the fire-bombing of Dresden, subject of at least two other documentaries banned on British television.

Forays into speculation as a mode of political commentary followed (1966's *Privilege*, 1969's *The Gladiators [The Peace Game]*, 1971's *Punishment Park*), beginning Watkins's peripatetic career outside a United Kingdom that remained closed to him and largely closed to his films. In 1974, he completed *Edvard Munch* for Norwegian television, a vivid historical reconstruction of the decaying society and personal tragedies of the celebrated painter. Far removed from the norms of costume drama, this drama-doc uses a cold palette dominated by greens and blues to communicate the tubercular world of its protagonist, and in what seems a deeply personal statement, covers the artist's family and professional life as a series of brechtian "gestus," marked by incomprehension, refusal, and despair.

There followed a series of low-budget experiments, mainly with Scandinavian companies, exploring with increasing fascination the powers of the long take and mobile camerawork to reveal with increasing intensity the emotional life of his characters. In 1987, the various strands of Watkins career came together in an extraordinary project, released as *The Journey*. More than 14 hours long, shot in more than a dozen countries, always with scraps of money, short-ends, volunteer craft and cast, *The Journey* documents not so much the international effects of nuclear war, its ostensible subject, as its own process. Actors move in and out of character to debate the rights and wrongs of their actions, and Watkins's theatrical investment in revealing his sets as sets moves toward making explicit the produced nature of the documentary, while at the same time assaulting the network wisdom that an hour is forty-three minutes punctuated by adverts. The duration of the piece derives from its internal logic, not that of broadcast sales, two reasons for its lack of distribution.

The Freethinker (1994) returns to the territory of *Munch* in its dramatisation of the life of Strindberg. Shot on video with cast and crew derived from a film school where Watkins was working, the film also resembles *Munch* in its portrait of a reviled creator. But like *The Journey, The Freethinker* expends much of its energy investigating the conditions of its making, a self-conscious essay on the potential of documentary to inform drama; to engage its performers' knowledge, opinions, and passion into the script; to foreground the medium by intrusive anachronisms, especially direct "TV" interviews of characters; and the willingness to allow viewers time to watch, listen, and decide about the actions presented. *The Freethinker* is also characterised by a complex spiral structure interweaving five distinct times in Strindberg's life, not just contesting chronological biography, but allowing complex rhymes and analogies between phases of a life to emerge into the light.

The bulk of critical writing on Watkins concentrates on earlier work, largely because *The War Game* and *Culloden* remain the easiest of his films to find. The disastrous relationship with La Sept ARTE means that his most significant achievement to date, *La Commune*, is scarcely beginning to have the impact it deserves. The film draws together previous technical developments in his oeuvre but also develops a powerful use of wide-angle lenses and hand-held mobile camera takes of up to ten minutes to assert the complexity of understanding a history made by crowds rather than by individuals or even types. As the amateur cast debate the action and its relation to contemporary events in France, Watkins draws racism, gender, and colonialism into the history of the Commune. All the while, the stories are conveyed by two contrasting TV stations, using, as in *The War Game*, inter-titles to add information and draw parallels. Characters and actors alike disagree with the film's thesis, apologising for the massacre of the communards, appealing for the past to be forgotten. None of this is excluded, though the direction frequently allows an expression of opinion to be interrupted by new narrative action, and vice versa. Still committed to a pedagogical documentary form, still at war with the "monoform" standards of broadcast media, Watkins can easily be portrayed as a dinosaur. His work, however, is increasingly relevant to any claim that documentary has a public role in a postmodern mediascape.

SEAN CUBITT

See also **Culloden; War Game, The**

WATSON, PATRICK

Patrick Watson's influence on Canadian television is profound. Affected by Marshall McLuhan's ideas of electronic media producing a global village, Watson has stridently challenged the medium of television as a tool for mass communication and thought-provoking work.

To develop these ideas, Watson initially delved into the political realm of Parliament Hill, producing and presenting news and current affairs programs such as *Close-Up* (1959) and *Inquiry* (1960). Dissatisfied, Watson wanted to produce a cutting-edge current affairs program that could combine McLuhan's philosophy, approach controversial topics, and have entertainment value. The satirical *This Hour Has Seven Days* (1964–1966) fulfilled his ideas for merging political and current affairs to the general television public. It was the most watched program in Canada and caused a furor of complaints and compliments—exactly what Watson had wanted.

After the cancellation of *This Hour*, Watson, with his newly formed independent production company, started to produce and direct a wider range of television programming, including such examples as *Steeltown* (1966), *Undersea World of Jacques Cousteau* (1968), *Witness to Yesterday* (1970) *51st State* (1970), and *Question of Television Violence* (1972). Most of these documentaries try to understand the world we live in, and with this information, encourage the public to ask questions about that world.

The 1970s and 1980s saw more of Watson's penchant for Canadian history and politics with an array of programs such as *The Watson Report* (1975–1981) and *The Canadian Establishment* (1980). Reaching viewers beyond Canada, he wrote, produced, and presented the highly acclaimed series *The Chinese* (1983) and *The Struggle for Democracy* (1989).

The Struggle for Democracy would become his crowning achievement. To explore the idea of democracy, this series would be five years in the making and take him to thirty countries. It was an ideal project that brought together all of Watson's talents as a presenter, researcher, philosopher, and historian. It was the first documentary series to be transmitted simultaneously in French and English on the CBC in January 1989. This series cemented Watson's status as an auteur.

Watson's thirty-year career with the CBC came to a climax in 1989, when he became chairman, with the mandate to strengthen the CBC and help turn it into a world class broadcasting organization. Watson soon found this challenge frustrating, as the board of directors was rife with Conservative patronage appointments, which in turn fuelled the on-going debate over privatization. Most frustrating of all was the public's high and unrealistic expectations of Watson, in an ineffectual role, as savior of the CBC. Watson resigned in 1991, four months before his tenure expired.

Patrick Watson saw the potential of television as a limitless device for communicating and provoking discussion. He made Canadians aware of social and political issues, as well as their global environment. Long before his 1989 mandate to strengthen the CBC as a world broadcaster, Watson wanted the Corporation to be at the forefront of this media revolution, constantly pushing them to have more ingenuity with programming ideas. He saw the general television public as people with a thirst for knowledge, which is why as a documentarian, Watson is so successful and popular; he connects high ideals with popular communication.

MELISSA BROMLEY

See also **Canadian Broadcasting Corporation**

Biography

Born Toronto, Ontario, Canada, December 23, 1929. Graduated from University of Toronto, M.A., D.Litt. Companion in the Order of Canada (2002). Radio actor 1943, producer, writer at the CBC from 1955 to 1966. Became independent producer, director, and presenter founder of Patrick Watson Enterprises 1966. Co-founder of Immedia 1967. Chair of the CBC 1989–1994; first North American filmmaker to film in the People's Republic of China; recipient of ACTRA Outstanding Achievement to Canadian Broadcasting; creative director of the CRB Foundation's Heritage Project and commissioning editor, documentaries, for History Television.

Further Reading

Barber, Benjamin, and Watson, Patrick, *The Struggle for Democracy*, Toronto: Key Porter Books, revised edition, 2002.

Lee, Rohama, "The Struggle for Democracy," in *Sightlines*, 4, 1989, 32–33.

Manera, Tony, *A Dream Betrayed: The Battle for the CBC*, Toronto: Stoddart Publishing Co. Limited, 1996.

McLuhan, Marshall, and Fiore, Quentin, *The Medium Is the Message*, Corte Madera, CA: Gingko Press, 2001.

McLuhan, Marshall, *Understanding Media*, London: Routledge, Classics edition, 2001.

Nash, Knowlton, *The Microphone Wars: A History of Triumph and Betrayal at the CBC*, Toronto: McClelland & Stewart Inc, 1994.

Watson, Patrick, *The Canadians: Biographies of a Nation, Volume III*, Toronto: McArthur and Co., 2002.

WATT, HARRY

Harry Watt was a key figure in the rapprochement between British documentary and realist feature film production during World War II. In a career spanning the documentary movement of the 1930s and early 1940s, and Michael Balcon's regime at Ealing studios in the 1940s and 1950s, he successfully directed both types of film. He came into his own as a filmmaker in the latter part of the 1930s at the GPO (General Post Office) film unit, having joined its previous incarnation, the EMB (Empire Marketing Board) film unit, after studying at Edinburgh University and working at various jobs including sailor and shop worker. In this respect he differed from other recruits to the British documentary movement, for example Basil Wright, who joined immediately after university. Watt shared a middle-class background with his colleagues, but his down-to-earth manner and personal experience of some of the occupations represented in the movement's films partly account for his ability to coax credible performances from nonactors in documentaries such as *North Sea* (1938) and *Target for Tonight* (1941).

BBC-Droitwich (1935), one of the earliest documentaries Watt directed, benefited from a concluding experimental sound montage of radio transmissions devised by Alberto Cavalcanti. Temperamentally, Watt found Cavalcanti's professional yet Catholic approach to filmmaking more congenial than John Grierson's. Watt's career as a director with an emerging style of his own flourished after Cavalcanti succeeded Grierson as head of the GPO film unit in 1937. Subsequent developments in Watt's filmmaking emphasised previously neglected or subordinate aspects of the documentary project. One ambition Watt and Cavalcanti shared, which Grierson gave less emphasis to in the later 1930s, was to get documentaries screened in mainstream theatrical circuit cinemas. *North Sea*, a narrative documentary reconstructing an actual incident in which a fishing trawler caught in a storm was guided home by a radio station, was specifically designed with this in mind.

Rudimentary narrative structures and reconstruction of events that had happened or would typically happen existed within British documentary before Watt's work (Winston, 1995). *Drifters* (John Grierson, 1929), like *North Sea*, used the basic journey structure of a trawler's fishing expedition and incorporated footage shot on a specially constructed set to represent the interior of the trawler's cabin. From the outset rudimentary narrative structures and reconstructions were taken for granted as a standard part of documentary practice, but what generated support from critics and endowed the documentary movement with cultural legitimacy during its earlier phase was modernist experimentation in, for example, *Drifters*, *Song of Ceylon* (Basil Wright 1934–1935), and even *BBC-Droitwich* (Stollery, 2000). Watt's innovation in documentaries such as *North Sea* was to explicitly prioritise narrative and characterisation and attract attention and praise for doing so.

Night Mail (1936) is Watt's transitional film. It uses a mlultifunctional voice-over, and its cinematography and editing are indebted to the modernist experimentation of the documentary movement's earlier phase (Guynn, 1990; Aitken, 1998). At the same time, the synch-sound equipment, which had been available only to the GPO film unit for a couple of years, enabled Watt to direct sequences featuring actual postal workers conversing in a set built to resemble the interior of a sorting carriage. The scripted dialogue they speak nominally individualises their characters, advances the narrative, and conveys information about the mail sorting process. Combined with the narrative momentum of the train's journey and the use of diegetic sound, this gives a particular sense of realism to the actions represented. These broad similarities to feature film technique partly account for *Night Mail*'s relative success in mainstream cinema exhibition.

In *The Saving of Bill Blewitt* (1937), a robust Cornish fisherman saves money with the Post Office and in the latter part of the narrative works to a deadline to achieve his goal of buying a new boat. The film largely eschews voice-over commentary and uses an attenuated version of continuity editing favouring long and medium shots to draw the spectator into its narrative while locating its protagonist within a social context. *North Sea* (1938) is more sophisticated. Its narrative structure and editing strategies are similar to, yet more complex than, Watt's

previous film (Higson, 1986). Suspense is engendered by alternating between a worried community and radio operators on land, and endangered men at sea. The storm provides modestly spectacular action recorded in overexposed footage, giving the film a compellingly raw texture. Editing links the actions of different crew members and radio operators to construct a visceral impression of integrated team work. Voice-over commentary is used briefly at the end to generalise the incident by referring to the numerous Post Office radio stations guarding Britain's ships.

North Sea was a commercial success, heralded as a minor breakthrough by reviewers and the trade press. Nonetheless certain British documentary filmmakers closer to Grierson felt Watt's approach to narrative made the film less informative about work processes than it should have been (Aitken, 1998). Unlike some of his colleagues, Watt was not inclined to theoretical debate, but in an article written to accompany *North Sea*'s release, he argued that what gave the film credibility was its narrative restraint. For him the absence of the dramatic embellishment that a fictionalised treatment would have brought to the narrative guaranteed its documentary authenticity (Vaughan, 1983). Watt further refined the template he established in *North Sea* in *Target for Tonight*, a classic wartime documentary about an RAF bombing raid (Short, 1997).

The influence of *North Sea* and *Target for Tonight* is evident in prestigious Crown Film Unit documentary productions for the MOI (Ministry of Information) such as *Western Approaches* (1944), directed toward the end of the war by Watt's former assistant Pat Jackson (Jackson, 1999). Watt's activities during World War II included recording and reconstructing some of the earliest iconic documentary images associated with this period in *The First Days* (Watt, Humphrey Jennings, Pat Jackson, 1939). Subsequent films, *London Can Take It* (Watt, Jennings, 1940) and *Christmas Under Fire* (1941), narrated by American journalist Quentin Reynolds, were designed to build American support for Britain's war effort.

In 1942, Watt followed Cavalcanti to Ealing Studios to direct his first feature, *Nine Men* (1943) (Barr, 1999). This was a logical extension of the direction his documentaries had taken. Other Ealing films such as *The Foreman Went to France* (Charles Frend, 1942) and certain British wartime features beyond Ealing registered the influence of what critic Dilys Powell described as Watt's "semi-fictional documentaries" (Short,

1997). In retrospect, the films in this category directed by Watt have been criticised, along with other strands of 1930s and 1940s British documentary, for ignoring controversial social, political, and economic issues because of institutional constraints. Watt himself concedes this criticism in his candid memoirs (Watt, 1974). Yet his most notable documentaries played a historically significant role, contributing to an emerging tendency within wartime and postwar British cinema toward a new type of realist representation.

MARTIN STOLLERY

See also **Night Mail; Target for Tonight**

Biography

Born in Glasgow, Scotland, October 18, 1906. Attended Edinburgh University. Joined Empire Marketing Board (EMB) film unit in 1931–1932. Assisted Robert Flaherty during the production of *Man of Aran* (1934). Co-directed his first film, *Six-Thirty Collection*, with Edgar Anstey in 1934. Moved with the film unit to the General Post Office (GPO) in 1934, stayed on when it became the Crown Film Unit in 1939, and also worked for the Army Film Unit between 1939 and 1942. Contributed items to *The March of Time* 1936–1937. Directed second unit on *Jamaica Inn* (Alfred Hitchcock, 1939). Directed numerous documentaries including *North Sea* (1938) and *Target for Tonight* (1941). Joined Ealing studios in 1942 and directed seven features there including *The Overlanders* (1946) on location in Australia and *Where No Vultures Fly* (1951) in Africa. Worked as a producer at Granada Television in 1955. Published his memoirs *Don't Look at the Camera* in 1974. Died April 2, 1987.

Selected Films

1935 *BBC-Droitwich*: director
1936 *Night Mail*: director
1937 *The Saving of Bill Blewitt*: director
1938 *North Sea*: director
1939 *The First Days*: director, with Humphrey Jennings and Pat Jackson
1940 *London Can Take It*: director, with Humphrey Jennings (both uncredited)
1941 *Christmas Under Fire*: director, with Charles Hasse
1941 *Target for Tonight*: director and writer (uncredited)
1943 *Nine Men*: director

Further Reading

Aitken, Ian, *The Documentary Film Movement: An Anthology*, Edinburgh: EUP, 1998.

Barr, Charles, *Ealing Studios* (3rd ed.), Moffat: Cameron and Hollis, 1999.

Guynn, William, *A Cinema of Nonfiction*, London: Associated University Press, 1990.

Higson, Andrew, "Britain's Outstanding Contribution to the Film: The Documentary-Realist Tradition," in *All Our Yesterdays*, Charles Barr (ed.), London: BFI, 1986, 72–97.

Jackson, Pat, *A Retake Please! Night Mail to Western Approaches*, Liverpool: Liverpool University Press, 1999.

Short, K.R.M., "RAF Bomber Command's *Target for Tonight* (1941)," in *Historical Journal of Film, Radio and Television*, 17, 2, June 1997, 181–218.

Stollery, Martin, *Alternative Empires: European Modernist Cinemas and Cultures of Imperialism*, Exeter: University of Exeter Press, 2000.

Vaughan, Dai, *Portrait of an Invisible Man*, London: BFI, 1983.

Watt, Harry, *Don't Look at the Camera*, London: Elek, 1974.

Winston, Brian, *Claiming the Real*, London: BFI, 1995.

WAVE, THE

(US, Strand and Zinnemann, 1934–1935)

The Wave (alternatively titled *Redes*, literally, "Nets," or *Pescados,* meaning "Fish") marks Mexico's participation in revolutionary, sociopolitical filmmaking, in the tradition of Sergei Eisenstein's films of the 1920s and 1930s. Like many of Eisenstein's films, *The Wave* often escapes strict categorization as a documentary. Rather, many critics and scholars have qualified *The Wave* (*Redes/Pescados*) as a "quasi-documentary" or "documentary fiction." Shot on location in Veracruz, Mexico, *The Wave* follows the lives of local fishermen as they struggle to unionize and combat labor inequality. Despite shooting on location and using real fishermen, the sociopolitical narrative in the film has prevented critics and scholars from labeling *The Wave* a documentary.

The producer and cinematographer of the film, Paul Strand, is credited as the brainchild of *The Wave*. Strand was a well-established, still-life photographer—and would become one of the most important twentieth century American photographers—before turning to film in the mid-1930s. His interest in cinema reportedly occurred after the photographer traveled to the Soviet Union and met film director Sergei Eisenstein. When Strand returned to the states, he began to make social-commentary documentaries and traveled to Mexico on that mission almost immediately.

While in Mexico, Strand began discussions with Carlos Chavez, a composer, conductor, and the head of the Mexican Department of Fine Arts, about making a film that would portray the life of fishermen. Chavez and Strand wanted to restore a sense of social consciousness to a Mexican audience and considered the plight of the poor fishermen to be a neglected and potentially powerful subject. The Mexican minister of education gave the filmmakers money to get their project off of the ground. When Chavez was replaced by Silvestre Revueltas as the head of the Mexican Department of Fine Arts, Revueltas took over Chavez's duties on *The Wave* as well. Although Chavez is still credited as one of several writers who worked on the film, Revueltas created the haunting and evocative musical score for *The Wave*. Despite the quality of the score, however, records show that it was absent from the initial screenings of *The Wave* in the United States. Fortunately, the original score was eventually restored, and it continues to be performed by orchestras around the world during Revueltas festivals and Mexican music festivals.

Initially, Strand asked Henwar Rodakiewicz to direct the film, but Rodakiewicz had a conflict that would interfere with the shooting schedule and recommended Fred Zinnemann as his replacement. Although Rodakiewicz reportedly shot two sequences in the film and retained credit as one of the film's writers, *The Wave* became Zinnemann's first feature film. Although the credits of the film list Emilio Gómez Muriel as a co-director, Zinnemann has stated for the record that he was the primary director on the film, and that Muriel only fulfilled the duties of an assistant director.

At the time of *The Wave*, Zinnemann had established himself within the filmmaking community as a filmmaker interested in social documentaries.

He had garnered this reputation by assisting the venerable documentarian Robert Flaherty before making *The Waves*. Flaherty and Zinnemann had been working on a Russian documentary project that was eventually abandoned. Zinnemann often called the experience of working with Flaherty one of the most significant experiences in his life, and the impetus behind his humanistic interest in social documentary.

The Wave exhibits Zinnemann's social concerns, namely his sympathy for the average worker who is willing to fight for what he believes to be right. Zinnemann, however, did not continue making documentaries for long after shooting *The Waves*. Although initially he secured a position in MGM's Shorts Department, after showing the head of the department, Jack Chertok, two sample reels from *The Wave*, he went on to become a "Features director" for MGM. Zinnemann gained fame and a number of Academy awards for directing such films as *High Noon* (1952), *From Here to Eternity* (1953), *The Nun's Story* (1959), and *A Man for All Seasons* (1966). As a documentary filmmaker, Zinnemann is perhaps best remembered by the Oscar he won for the Best Short Film of 1938. The film was *That Mothers Might Live,* and it chronicled the work of Dr. Ignaz Philipp Semmelweis, a Hungarian obstetrician who explored the use of antiseptics in his practice.

Several elements of *The Wave* contribute to its ongoing critical significance: Fred Zinnemann's direction, Paul Strand's cinematography, Gunther von Fritsch's editing, and Silvestre Revueltas' score. Zinnemann was responsible for shooting the "narrative" sections of the film, and toward that end, he worked primarily with the principal actors. He brought to the film his thematic interest in the portrayal of human dignity and his aesthetic preference for realism. Paul Strand shot the non-narrative parts of the film, including many still, tableau shots, and numerous scenes of the local fisherman at work and at play. Von Fritsch edited Strand's cinematography in the style of Soviet montage, highlighting the film's use of metaphorical imagery. Fishing nets (the literal translation of the Spanish title, *Redes*) are featured throughout the film, evoking the fishermen's confinement under the current labor structure. Elsewhere, shots of twisted rope correlate to the fishermen's muscular arms.

Eisenstein's influence on Strand and Zinnemann is obvious. Poetic, metaphoric imagery, used intentionally to communicate a sociopolitical message, can be found in numerous Eisenstein films, including *Strike* (1925), *Battleship Potemkin* (1925), *October* (1927), and *The General*

Line (1929). Like these films, *The Wave* contains sequences of shots in conflict with each other. These shots, or "cells" as Eisenstein called them, create a Marxist dialectic and encourage the spectator to form meaning from the synthesis of the images. In addition, the film conforms to Eisenstein's use of typage in its choice of actors, both professional and nonprofessional. Zinnemann and Strand chose people who looked like the type of weathered, earthy, world-weary Mexican fishermen they were trying to portray.

Although *The Wave* seldom receives recognition as a particularly unique or radical achievement in the history of documentary film, it remains an important achievement in the careers of three major artists—Fred Zinnemann, Paul Strand, and Silvestre Revueltas—and it represents an important piece of social commentary in the portrayal of Mexican life.

STARR MARCELLO

See also **Strand, Paul**

The Wave/Redes/Pescados (Mexico, Azteca Films & Secretaría de Educación Pública, 1936, 65 min.). Distributed by Garrison Film Distributors Inc (US, 1937). Produced by Paul Strand. Directed by Fred Zinnemann, additional direction by Emilio Gómez Muriel. Written by Emilio Gómez Muiel, Henwar Rodakiewicz, Paul Strand, Agustín Velázquez Chávez, and Fred Zinnemann. Cinematography by Paul Strand. Original music by Silvestre Revueltas. Editing by Emilio Gómez Muriel and Gunther von Fritsch. Filmed in Papdoapan and Tacotalpan, Veracruz, Mexico.

Further Reading

Maddow, Ben, "A View from below: Paul Strand's Monumental Presence," in *American Art*, 5, 3, Summer 1991, 48–67.

Nolletti, Arthur, Jr., *The Films of Fred Zinnemann: Critical Perspectives*, New York: State University of New York Press, 1999.

Sinyard, Neil, *Fred Zinnemann: Films of Character and Conscience*, North Carolina: McFarland & Company, Inc., 2003.

Tomkins, Calvin, *Paul Strand: Sixty Years of Photographs: Excerpts from Correspondence, Interviews, and Other Documents*, New York: Aperture, 1976.

Zinnemann, Fred, John Houseman, Irvin Kershner, Kent MacKenzie, Pauline Kael, Colin Young, "Personal Creation in Hollywood: Can It Be Done?" in *Film Quarterly*, 15, 3, Spring 1962, 16–34.

WE ARE THE LAMBETH BOYS

(UK, Reisz, 1959)

We Are the Lambeth Boys was the main film in "The Last Free Cinema" program shown at the National Film Theatre in March 1959 and was the second (and last) in the Ford-sponsored "Look at Britain" series (of which Lindsay Anderson's *Every Day Except Christmas* was the first). The film is linked in several ways with *Every Day Except Christmas*: Both were part of the Free Cinema movement, and Reisz was co-producer of Anderson's film. At least one of the youths in *We Are the Lambeth Boys* worked in Covent Garden market, where Anderson's film was shot; *Every Day Except Christmas* looked at work, while *We Are the Lambeth Boys* looks at leisure time, documenting the activities of the Alford House youth club in Lambeth. That the film was explicitly about working-class young people links it strongly to the so-called British New Wave of fictional features, of which Reisz's *Saturday Night and Sunday Morning* (1960) was a key film.

Like *Every Day Except Christmas*, *We Are the Lambeth Boys* was photographed by Walter Lassally and recorded and edited by the often overlooked John Fletcher, but the years between the two films were marked by important changes in technology. Whereas *Every Day Except Christmas* appears to have little or no direct sound—though efforts are made to fake it from time to time—some major sequences in *We Are the Lambeth Boys* make important use of it (as well as of more mobile cameras). The discussion about murder and the death penalty, for example, and the late night chip shop sequence—both relatively controlled situations—rely on it. Indeed, near the start of the film, when the boys are in the cricket nets and the girls are chatting in groups, and they begin to tease each other, the film seems to *celebrate* its ability to use direct sound recorded on location.

Elsewhere, however, sound is used in the same "creative" way that it was used in *Every Day Except Christmas*, and the same way it was used in most 1930s and wartime British documentary films. Having shown us the end of a club evening, and larking about in the chip shop and street, the film fades to black then fades in on: morning, deserted block of council flats, one boy leaves on his own on his bicycle, sound of a train (atmospheric, though no train is visible); voice-over: "Being young in the morning is different from being young at night..." This is followed by a sequence of two younger boys arriving at school and singing a hymn ("The King of love my shepherd is") in school assembly, which is continued over a sequence of shots of other young people at work—seamstress, office worker, post office boy, butcher's apprentice, assembly line pie-maker, all later put into context—learning a trade, waiting to get married, and so on—by the voice-over.

Although it is undoubtedly true that Free Cinema films, and perhaps *We Are the Lambeth Boys* in particular, offered relatively new, fresh images (and sounds) of British society and especially of youth culture—images in which we could at last, however partially,

We Are the Lambeth Boys, 1959.
[*Still courtesy of the British Film Institute*]

recognise ourselves—such a sequence raises large questions about the way the film uses voice-over commentary and music, and about the film's use of "we" in its title. Though the subjects of the film—aside from those (barely glimpsed) who run the club and the Mill Hill School boys (who seem really only a foil for the Lambeth boys)—are working class, the filmmakers are conscious that they are not. The heated club discussion about capital punishment, for example, is both introduced by the middle-class voice-over and crucially framed by it.

It is less likely that the filmmakers were conscious of the implications of their choice of music—orchestrated jazz composed by Johnny Dankworth. The music is generally effective at setting the tone of the film (and for punctuating it at certain points), but why jazz? Remembering *Momma Don't Allow* (one of the first Free Cinema films, directed by Tony Richardson and Reisz, 1955), about a traditional jazz club, and even the Happy Wanderers street jazz band in *Every Day Except Christmas*, jazz seems to be one of the popular culture credentials of the middle-class filmmakers, whereas, as the film makes clear, what the young people themselves like is rock 'n' roll and "skiffle." The jazzy score, then, functions as another, unspoken, judgment or commentary, implying that jazz is a superior popular form, just as the voice-over implies that the boys' political or moral judgments are defective or underdeveloped (though it could be argued that the film's critique is directed at the education system).

Overall, the class aspects of the film are quite difficult to discern, partly because the film sometimes suggests a critique but then withdraws from elaboration into easier conclusions. Having raised questions about the adequacy of the boys' judgments in the capital punishment discussion, for example, the voice-over retreats with: "Not that they're worried. They're good at making the most of everyday, and just talking about things, like this, is a beginning. And it's good for a giggle."

The extended sequence that follows, of the boys' trip to Mill Hill School for the annual cricket match, and an occasion allowing the overt juxtaposition of the working class boys and the public school class, is more difficult to read. The boys' initial exuberance is replaced by what may be sullen passivity or jealousy, or just

reflection, as they see the sumptuous facilities of the school. The return to Lambeth is marked by the boys' apparently wanting to leave their noisy mark on Central London as they pass through, but the film wants us to believe that, on crossing Westminster Bridge, the boys fall silent and, again, reflective or even morose. Why? Are we to feel that the boys are conscious of their class disadvantages, of their more limited opportunities? This is not made at all clear or explicit, and the film ends on a less uncomfortable note: Saturday night dancing at the club and the commentary's conclusion that "a good evening for young people is much as it has always been, it's for being together with friends, and shouting when you feel like it—things we'd all like to do" (although the close of the film, with its nocturnal views of council flats, perhaps strikes a darker note).

JIM HILLIER

See also **Every Day Except Christmas**; **Reisz, Karel**

We Are the Lambeth Boys (UK, Graphic Films for the Ford Motor Company Ltd, 1959, 52 min) (second film in series "Look at Britain"). Distributed by the British Film Institute. Produced by Leon Clore. Directed by Karel Reisz. Cinematography by Walter Lassally. Music composed by Johnny Dankworth, played by members of the Johnny Dankworth Orchestra. Editing by John Fletcher. Commentary spoken by Jon Rollason. Assistants Louis Wolfers and Raoul Sobel. Filmed in London.

Further Reading

Anderson, Lindsay, "Free Cinema," in *Universities and Left Review*, 2, Summer 1957, reprinted in Barsam, Richard Meran (eds.), *Nonfiction Film Theory and Criticism*, New York: E.P. Dutton, 1976.

Ellis, Jack, *The Documentary Idea*, Englewood Cliffs, NJ and London: Prentice-Hall, 1989.

Gaston, Georg, *Karel Reisz*, Boston: Twayne Publishers, 1980.

Hoggart, Richard, "We Are the Lambeth Boys," in *Sight & Sound*, 28, Summer–Autumn, 1959.

Lambert, Gavin, "Free Cinema," in *Sight & Sound*, 25, Spring 1956.

Lovell, Alan, and Hillier, Jim, *Studies in Documentary*, London: Secker & Warburg/New York: Viking, 1972.

Reisz, Karel, "A Use for Documentary," *Universities and Left Review*, 3, Winter 1957.

Sussex, Elizabeth, *The Rise and Fall of British Documentary*, Berkeley, Los Angeles, and London: University of California Press, 1975.

WE LIVE IN TWO WORLDS

(UK, Cavalcanti, 1937)

We Live in Two Worlds (1937) was the second of the seven films that Alberto Cavalcanti directed for the Swiss telephone company Pro-Telephone Zurich between 1936 and 1939. The seven films are *Line to Tcherva Hut*, *We Live in Two Worlds* (1937), *Who Writes to Switzerland?* (1937), *Message from Geneva* (1937), *Four Barriers* (1937), *Alice au pays romand* (1938), and *Men of the Alps* (1939). *We Live in Two Worlds* is also the best known of these films, principally because of the involvement of the novelist and public figure, J.B. Priestley. Paul Rotha thought the film to be the best GPO Film Unit film, alongside Harry Watt's *The Saving of Bill Blewitt*, to emerge in 1937. Forsyth Hardy, John Grierson's biographer, also thought *We Live in Two Worlds* to be particularly successful. However, Cavalcanti himself believed that another of the Swiss films, the less well-known *Line to Tcherva Hut* (1936) was a better film than *We Live in Two Worlds*.

The origins of *We Live in Two Worlds* lay in John Grierson's wish to utilise the footage left over from the making of *Line to Tcherva Hut*. Such a practice of reusing stock footage to make new films was common within the documentary film movement. To achieve this goal in this particular film, Grierson asked J.B. Priestley to compose an appropriate "film talk," which could then be illustrated by the leftover footage. Priestley then constructed the narrative around the footage. Priestley called this process of "turning a series of photographs into a narrative" "creating a film backwards," and he went on to "concoct a little talk about nationalism and the new internationalism of transport and communication." (Aitken, 2001: 86–87).

Priestley had been associated with the documentary film movement for a few years before the making of *We Live in Two Worlds*. His book *English Journey* (1934) had directly inspired Paul Rotha's *The Face of Britain* (1935), and he had also published several articles in *World Film News*, one of the house journals of the documentary film movement. In books such as *Angel Pavement* (1930) and *English Journey*, Priestley focused on problems of corruption, unemployment, and poverty in Britain, and he was also active in the antifascist movement of the late 1930s. All this made him sympathetic to the general aims of the documentary film movement and eager to participate in the making of *We Live in Two Worlds*.

In *We Live in Two Worlds*, a distinction is made between the two worlds that characterise modern society: the world of separate nation states, and the "growing international world." The film begins by depicting traditional Swiss folk and labour practices. Then, the film shifts to the theme of the modernisation of Switzerland, and, in particular, to the role played by mass communication in creating links with Switzerland's neighbors. In contrast, the growth of nationalism and militarism in neighboring Germany is explicitly criticised and contrasted with Swiss internationalism.

We Live in Two Worlds could be regarded as a griersonian documentary because of its emphasis on international communications and the relationship between labour and institutional structures, and this, in turn, may explain why griersonians, such as Paul Rotha and Forsyth Hardy, thought so highly of it. The truth is, however, that *We Live in Two Worlds* is a rather mediocre film, whilst Priestley's commentary, which is full of pompous, vernacular Yorkshire gravitas, is often predictable and rudimentary.

Cavalcanti's influence on *We Live in Two Worlds* can be found mainly in the film's use of sound and in the music track, which was composed by Cavalcanti's old acquaintance, Maurice Jaubert. That influence can also be seen most clearly in the final sequences of the film, in which Priestley's pedestrian didacticism gives way to an idealistic proclamation concerning the way in which the natural world transcends artificial nationalistic demarcations. These final sequences are almost abstract in quality as, for example, when superimposed images of ships at sea fade into a shot of the earth against Priestley's rhetorical claim that "rain and sea and air serve all men." The final shots of the film re-create abstract patterns of rain drops, and this leads on to the end titles of the film.

These final sequences, with their innovative and impressionistic use of sound and image are reminiscent of other Cavalcanti films, from the mid-1920s to the late-1950s. They can be clearly associated with Cavalcanti in *We Live in Two Worlds*, and it is this aspect of the film, rather than Priestley's commentary, that makes the film still worth watching today.

IAN AITKEN

See also **Cavalcanti, Alberto**

We Live in Two Worlds (1937). Directed and edited by Alberto Cavalcanti. Music by Maurice Jaubert. Produced by John Grierson and Alberto Cavalcanti. Commentary by J.B. Priestley.

Further Reading

Aitken, Ian, *Film and Reform*, London: Routledge, 1990.
————, *The Documentary Film Movement, An Anthology*, Edinburgh: Edinburgh University Press, 1998.
————, *Alberto Cavalcanti, Realism, Surealism and National Cinemas*, London: Flicks Books, 2001.
Cavalcanti, Alberto, *Filme e Realidade*, Rio de Janeiro: Editora Artenova, in collaboration with Empresa Brasiliera de Filmes—Embrafilme, 1977.
Rotha, Paul, *Documentary Film*, London: Faber & Faber, 1939.
Sussex, Elizabeth, "Cavalcanti in England," *Sight and Sound*, 44, 4, Autumn, 1975.

WEIMAR: LEFTIST DOCUMENTARY

A skeptical attitude toward modernization, and a mistrust of new media technologies, are a longstanding tradition among German leftists. A suspicious attitude toward film, which developed in the prewar era, marked the first years of the Weimar republic as well. This attitude was modified only on the arrival of short Russian documentary films, which began appearing in Germany in 1922. Import and distribution of these films were organized by the Internationale Arbeiter Hilfe (IAH) (the International Workers Help). They awakened a desire to make not only films, specifically for workers, but to make German films in general.

Willi Münzenberg, a talented publicist and a forecaster of Communist media politics, called in 1925 for a rapid German development of media and film. He founded Prometheus-Film Ltd., a key producer of proletarian film until 1932, which produced both feature films and documentaries. Kartell Weltfilm, established at the end of 1927, produced thirty-three documentaries. The success of Sergei Eisenstein's *Bronenosets Potemkin/Battleship Potemkin*, 1925 convinced skeptics of the financial and propagandistic possibilities of film. In 1926, the social democrats established an individual company for distribution and production, the Film-und Lichtbilddienst.

Through the 1920s, the documentary productions of the leftists depict mainly deployments, conventions, and self-portrayals of their organizations. Only the organized side of the worker movement (with parades, flags, and mass appearances) was considered notable and valuable. Structurally, these films differ little from industry and contract films. Few films fall defied convention, including Phil Jutzi's *Hunderttausend unter roten Fahnen* (1930) and the social democratic convention film *Streiter heraus! Kämpfer hervor!* (1931).

Films depicting workers taking part in organized sport were a notable subgenre. Fifty-five such films were made during the Weimar Republic. Several film companies and unions specialized in films on youth at work, another popular topic.

Communist filmmakers often focused on the compilation film. These films, usually edited from Soviet and German newsreel recordings, have as their subject the Weimar period, Russian history from 1905 to 1917, and World War I. The film department of the Piscator stage production company became a workshop for cadres of montage specialists, of whom Albrecht Viktor Blum, J. A. Hübler-Kahla, Alex Strasser, and Leo Lania also later worked with Prometheus and Weltfilm.

Compilation films were popular among filmmakers associated with the workers' movement. They realized that existing films could be reappraised via montage. Lively contrast montages are to be found in the election film *Die Rote Kamera* (1928, J. A. Hübler-Kahla), in the manifesto films *Eröffnungsfilm des Volks-Film-Verbandes* (1928, Blum, Béla Balázs), and *Zeitbericht—Zeitgesicht* (1928, Blum, Ernst Angel), as well as in the newspaper promotional film *Tatsachen* (1930, Blum). Carl Junghans produced several compilations for the communists with his own production company. *Der Weg zum Sieg* (1927–1928) treats the ascent of the communist movement in Russia. *Weltwende* (1928) looks at recent history, from 1912.

From 1929, Soviet documentaries emphasizing social commitment and artistic representation, such as those made by Dziga Vertov and Viktor Turin, became increasingly influential. At the same time, some German filmmakers appeared, including Blum, Jutzi, and Hochbaum. For the first time, topics like workers' leisure time, private and vocational life circumstances, and protests against poor residential and work situations appeared in films such as Jutzi's and Lania's *Ums tägliche Brot/Hunger in Waldenburg* (1929), Jutzi's *Blutmai 1929* (1929) and *Die Todeszeche* (1930), Blum's *Im Schatten der Weltstadt* (1930), and Slatan Dudow's *Zeitprobleme: Wie der Arbeiter wohnt* (1930). The social democrats had success with intelligent election publicity: Ernö Metzner's *Dein Schicksal!* (1928) and Werner Hochbaum's *Zwei Welten* (1930) place the election proposals of competing parties briefly and summarily in scenes and dismantles them satirically and ironically.

The film avant-garde increasingly turned its attention to the socially engaged documentary. More than the political films, they relied observation and discovery. These films include the astounding subview recordings in Alex Strasser's *Impressionen einer Großstadt* (1929) and the bird's-eye view of the week market that fills up with stands, horse vehicles, and carts in Wilfried Basse's *Market in Berlin* (1929). The process of perception is emphasized in Hans Richter's early film essays *Inflation* (1928) and *Rennsymphonie* (1928). In Heinrich Hauser's *Weltstadt in Flegeljahren* (1931), the unemployed eke out a life at the foot of pompous monuments or drift in the streets as alcoholics.

Ella Bergmann-Michel's subjects radicalize themselves continuously. *Erwerbslose kochen für Erwerbslose* (1932) portrays a program in which the unemployed assist one another without pity or a patronizing attitude. *Letzte Wahl* (1932) records soberly the increasing aggression on election day between the political camps in Frankfurt.

THOMAS TODE

See also **Basse, Wilfred; Junghans, Carl; Turin, Viktor; Vertov, Dziga**

Further Reading

Kinter, Jürgen, *Arbeiterbewegung und Film (1895-1933)*, Hamburg: Medienpädagogik-Zentrum, 1985.

Film und revolutionäre Arbeiterbewegung in Deutschland 1918–1932, edited by Gertraude Kühn, Karl Tümmler, and Walter Wimmer, Berlin (East): Henschel, 1978.

Münzenberg, Willi, *Erobert den Film!*, Berlin: Neuer Deutscher Verlag, 1925.

Murray, Bruce, *Film and the German Left in the Weimar Republic*, Austin: University of Texas Press, 1990.

Tode, Thomas, Dosiertes Muskelspiel. Die linke Filmkultur der Weimarer Republik, in *Geschichte und Ästhetik des dokumentarischen Films in Deutschland 1895–1945*, vol 2: 1918–1933 (Weimarer Republik), Antje Ehmann, Jean-paul Goergen, and Klaus Kreimeier (eds.), Stuttgart: Reclam, 2005 (in preparation).

Voigt, Hans-Gunter, Filmdokumente zur Geschichte der deutschen Arbeiterbewegung 1911–1933, Koblenz / Berlin: Bundesarchiv-Filmarchiv, 1991.

Weber, Richard (ed.), *Arbeiterbühne und Film*, Reprint, Köln: Gaehme Henke, 1974.

———, *Film und Volk*, Reprint, Köln: Prometh, 1978.

WEISS, ANDREA

Independent documentary filmmaker Andrea Weiss engages a complex terrain of simultaneous roles. Weiss is a director, author, educator, archival researcher, producer, and historian. In 1984, Weiss and her partner Greta Schiller co-founded the nonprofit film company Jezebel Productions. Weiss's successful negotiation of her numerous roles has resulted in a rich array of projects that bespeak her commitment to pedagogy, representational ethics, and creative ingenuity.

Weiss has made or participated in making films about a range of provocative subjects, including: the U.S. election process (*Recall Florida*); the lives of Thomas Mann's oldest children during Hitler's ascendancy (*Escape to Life*); a Hungarian girl's life during the Holocaust (*Seed of Sarah*); the stereotyping of gay characters by the mainstream British film industry since World War II (*A Bit of Scarlet*); the role of women in the literary and art world of the Parisian Left Bank during the early twentieth century (*Paris Was a Woman*); a multi-racial all-women jazz and swing band of the 1940s (*International Sweethearts of Rhythm*); the long-term relationship of African-American lesbian jazz musicians Tiny Davis and Ruby Lucas (*Tiny & Ruby: Hell Divin' Women*); and the history of the gay and lesbian community in the United States before the onset of the modern LGBT liberation movement (*Before Stonewall*).

During the introductory voice-over to Paris Was a Woman, the audience is told, "Neither mistress nor muse, Paris became a haven for a new kind of woman." This "new kind of woman" not only indexes the independently minded (and often bourgeois) intellectual women who moved from the United States to Paris at the beginning of the twentieth century to make a "new life," but implicitly refers to the largely open orientation toward lesbianism and other homosocial alliances between women in Paris at that time.

In *Paris*, Janet Flanner describes cubism as "what you cannot see rendered visible." This remark could also be made regarding the film's treatment of lesbian relationships in early twentieth-century Paris.

Flanner's statement likewise announces the film's stance and Weiss's perspective as a filmmaker: There is value in uncovering "silenced" voices and "missing" texts, and it is crucial to critique oversimplified and often romanticized revisionist histories by presenting the crucial contributions of multidimensional people who speak on their own behalf in the films and books that represent and describe them. By speaking with and through her films' images and by sensitively promoting her narrators' voices, Weiss points out that, as African-American lesbian musician "Ruby" puts it, "[the past] wasn't quite as open as it is now" (*Tiny & Ruby*). Weiss's work teaches viewers about racism, homophobia, classism, and sexism, and promotes social justice.

In her discussion of minority-produced feminist documentaries, Alexandra Juhasz notes that "'rea-list' footage ends up recording people reflexively discussing the meaning, reinterpretation, and importance of their own identity" (1999: 208). Juhasz asserts that this is especially important "[b]ecause so much of feminist and other 'identity' video movements are specifically about constructing our own identities in a society that has usually done this for minorities" (Ibid., original emphasis). Thus, the formal elements of "realism" in these kinds of films may be used to forward a specialized feminist cultural critique, a visualizable social constructionism.

According to Juhasz, feminist documentaries have the potential to engage anti-essentialist notions of identity for political ends, because they can "[provide] a space in culture where political women with limited access to cultural production can partake in 'radical postmodernism'" (1999: 212). Explaining "radical postmodernism" (as borrowed from bell hooks), Juhasz states, "the political instance of access to media production allows us to speak our needs, define our agenda, counter irresponsible depictions of our lives, and recognize our similarities and differences" (Ibid.). As vehicles for marginalized narrators, both living and as depicted posthumously, Weiss's films are instances of "radical postmodernism."

Escape to Life is described on the Jezebel Productions website as a "remarkable pairing between fiction and nonfiction." Using a "postmodernist" orientation to blur the boundaries between reality/fantasy and truth/fiction, *Escape* frames the relationship between Erika and Klaus Mann. In its meta-narrative form and content, the film may be read as doubly postmodern, because Erika and Klaus Mann enacted their own fusion of fiction and nonfiction in order to survive. Using an approach that today might be called "passing," they pretended to be identical twins when they were different genders and more than a year apart in age.

Weiss's films consistently show how those who have social dominance wield power and how disempowered individuals strategically engage their subject positions. During a portion of *Tiny & Ruby*, the narrators discuss the racially segregated lesbian house parties of the 1940s through 1960s. Feminist scholars Kennedy and Davis (1994) argue that these parties played a crucial part in setting a tone for the American lesbian and gay liberation movement in the decades preceding Stonewall. At one point, Tiny looks directly at the camera and asserts that if one wants to "do something" and "has the power," then one can "do it." Tiny's advice, a note of appreciation for having the opportunity to tell her story on film and a commentary on her identity, relays to both the audience members and the filmmakers her awareness of her power as compared with the power of the filmmakers who re-present her story.

As part of a supplement on film and history, Weiss was recently asked by the editors of *Cineaste* magazine to respond to a documentary filmmaker questionnaire. She remarks, "I'm searching for something too through these women's lives and through the stories of all the people in my entire collection of films—I'm searching for clues for how to live my own life, a life lived by my own wits, in several different countries, a life without conventional forms or models to follow" (2004: 60). Weiss, an out Jewish lesbian who lives in England and the United States, is a role model for those who negotiate a variety of complicated borders and boundaries in order to function within and critique late capitalism.

DIANE R. WIENER

Biography

Born in New York City, 1956. Ph.D. Cultural History, Rutgers University, 1991. Won a 1987 Emmy award for Best Historical Research for her work on *Before Stonewall*, which also won an Emmy for Best Historical and Cultural Program. Won a 1989 Teddy Award for Best Documentary Film for *Tiny & Ruby* at the Berlin International Film Festival. Won "Best of the Fest" award for *A Bit of Scarlet* at Edinburgh Film Festival in 1996, and also won Best Documentary at the Creteil women's film festival, Festival de Films de Femmes. Was artist-in-residence at the Banff Centre for the Arts in Canada in 1998, where she produced the short experimental video *Seed of Sarah* (a revisiting of the longer film made three years earlier), which premiered in the Marseilles Documentary Festival, Vue Sur les Docs. *Escape to Life*, which premiered at the 2001 Rotterdam International Film Festival and was a special festival program at Berlin, was chosen as the closing night event of the New German Film Series at the Museum of Modern Art in New York and won the "Award for Excellence" for Best Documentary at the 2001 Seattle Lesbian and Gay Film Festival. Co-author (with Greta Schiller) of *Before Stonewall: The Making of a Gay and Lesbian Community* (1988). Author of *Vampires and Violets* (originally published 1992), *Paris Was a Woman: Portraits from the Left Bank* (published 1995, won a Lambda Literary Award in 1996), and *Flucht ins Leben: Die Erika und Klaus Mann Story* (2000), soon to be available in American print edition as *Escape to Life: The Erika and Klaus Mann Story*. Currently resides in London with partner and collaborator Greta Schiller.

Selected Films

1985 *Before Stonewall: The Making of a Gay and Lesbian Community*: archive research director
1986 *International Sweethearts of Rhythm*: co-director and co-producer
1988 *Tiny & Ruby: Hell Divin' Women*: co-director and co-producer
1995 *Paris Was a Woman*: writer, researcher, co-producer
1995 *Seed of Sarah*: director, editor, co-producer
1997 *A Bit of Scarlet*: director and editor
2000 *Die Erika und Klaus Mann Story* also known as *Escape to Life: The Erika and Klaus Mann Story*: co-writer and co-director
2003 *Recall Florida*: writer, editor, co-producer

Further Reading

Edelman, Rob, "Greta Schiller," in *The St. James Women Filmmakers Encyclopedia: Women on the Other Side of the Camera*, Amy L. Unterburger (ed.), Detroit: Visible Ink Press, 1999, 370–372.
"Film and History: Questions to Filmmakers and Historians," in *Cineaste*, 29, 2, Spring 2004, 55–68.
Gross, Larry, *Up From Invisibility: Lesbians, Gay Men, and the Media in America*, New York: Columbia University Press, 2001.
Holmlund, Chris, and Fuchs, Cynthia (eds.), in *Between the Sheets, in the Streets: Queer, Lesbian, Gay Documentary*, Minneapolis: University of Minnesota Press, 1997.
Hooks, Bell, *Yearning: Race, Gender, and Cultural Politics*, Boston: South End Press, 1990.
Hunn, Deborah, "Andrea Weiss," in *GLBTQ: An Encyclopedia of Gay, Lesbian, Bisexual, Transgender, and Queer Culture*, http://www.glbtq.com/arts/weiss_a.html.
Jezebel Productions website, http://www.jezebel.org/.
Juhasz, Alexandra, "They Said We Were Trying to Show Reality—All I Want to Show Is My Video: The Politics of the Realist Feminist Documentary," in *Collecting Visible Evidence*, Jane M. Gaines, and Michael Renov (eds.), Minneapolis and London: University of Minnesota Press, 1999, 190–215.
Kennedy, Elizabeth Lapovsky, and Madeline D. Davis, *Boots of Leather, Slippers of Gold: The History of a Lesbian Community*, New York: Penguin Books, 1994.
Murray, Raymond, "Greta Schiller," in *Images in the Dark: An Encyclopedia of Gay and Lesbian Film and Video*. New York: Plume (Penguin Books), 1996, 118–119.
Weiss, Andrea, *Flucht ins Leben: Die Erika und Klaus Mann Story*, 2000. This text is available in Germany and Sweden, and according to the Jezebel Productions website, the American print edition (*Escape to Life: The Erika and Klaus Mann Story*) is forthcoming.
———, *Paris Was a Woman: Portraits from the Left Bank*, San Francisco: Harper San Francisco, 1995.
———, *Vampires and Violets: Lesbians in Film*, New York: Penguin Books, 1993.
Weiss, Andrea, and Greta Schiller, *Before Stonewall: The Making of a Gay and Lesbian Community*, Tallahassee: Naiad Press, 1988.

WELFARE

(US, Wiseman, 1975)

In *Welfare*, American filmmaker Frederick Wiseman, whose films tend to focus on institutions and their operations, one New York City Welfare Office where the film was shot is presented as the closed system *par excellence*, a nightmare vision of institutional bureaucracy out of control. It is no accident that, chronologically, *Welfare* comes between *Primate* (1974) and *Meat* (1976), for the titles of these two films express how far, for Wiseman, living has become objectified and commodified.

The film, like the welfare center itself, is swamped with various kinds of forms. We see or hear about application forms; referral slips; notarized, registered, and certified letters; verifications of pregnancy; marriage licenses and driver's licenses; bills and receipts; change of address forms and prenatal forms; written budgets and pay stubs; food stamps; Medicaid cards and social security cards; housing deeds, disability checks and pro-ration checks; carbon copies and photocopies; time clock cards; computers; and printouts. One client complains that she has to "get a notarized letter for this, a notarized letter for that." Another client, standing aimlessly against a post, launches into a monologue about the "rigamarole of forms" he must fill out; "Papers, papers, papers," he says, finally dropping them on the floor and leaving in frustration.

In the film, the camera leaves the building just once—at the beginning. After this we remain confined within, unlike most of Wiseman's films, which at the least offer periodic exterior shots as rhythmic punctuation. Here, though, our physical point of view remains claustrophobically confined within the harsh walls of this one welfare office, an absurd *huis clos* where we as spectators must dwell along with the system's needy clients. The first thing we hear in the film, a receptionist's "Please have a seat," is not only a self-reflexive acknowledgment to the viewer that the film is now beginning, but also an ironic invitation to sit through a long ordeal, as the applicants themselves must. *Welfare*'s lengthy running time of just under three

hours is itself an expression of the labyrinthine and involved system of procedures and paperwork through which welfare applicants must navigate.

Consistent with the film's sense of enclosure and entrapment, Wiseman structures the film through a motif of circles. Clients are frequently trapped in a variety of Catch-22 situations, the victims of circular logic. One client, for example, wants to move but cannot, because there is no record of housing violations, but she is unable to get a buildings inspector to come and formally record the necessary violations; another client becomes ineligible for benefits because he missed his appointment at the welfare office while attending his hearing required by welfare procedures. Toward the beginning of the film, a man seeking immediate help says that he is getting a "run around." The phrase is echoed periodically by several other clients, and yet again toward the end by the woman who, speaking for her mother, angrily complains that she is caught in a never-ending "vicious cycle." The first couple interviewed in the film are shown again at the end, waiting, suggesting that they have hardly progressed in their application.

In *Welfare,* social and economic relations are reduced to a seemingly interminable series of exchanges between welfare workers and clients, the clients seeking the money that the workers have the power to dispense. *Welfare* foregrounds the economic disparity shown in some of Wiseman's other films, as everyone seeking help from the welfare system is penniless, many seeming on the verge of starvation, and they must prove their poverty. As Mr. Hirsch, the final client shown in the film, says, "There's no middle class any more. There's just the rich and the poor."

Like a pressure cooker, this enclosed world of *Welfare* inevitably reaches the boiling point. So after watching a parade of clients being frustrated in every possible way for two hours, we are not surprised when two of them are unable to restrain themselves any longer and tempers flare. The welfare worker Elaine also loses her temper in turn. ("Get a job," she snaps unhelpfully at one of the clients.) The evident anger and frustration of both worker and clients in this climactic scene are the understandable result of everything that has come before. The institutional workers at the welfare center, as in many other Wiseman films, have become inured to the pain and misfortune of the clients in order to cope with the burdens of administering an overloaded public system. In one problematic case, the supervisor instructs the worker to reject or accept the client, "either one," not wanting to become involved any further.

The institution's regulations and procedures have overwhelmed the human element in the welfare office. The welfare workers speak of "re-entertaining applications" and "financial servicing" for the clients, their language like the euphemistic discourse of military indoctrination in *Basic Training* and of nuclear holocaust in *Missile*. "Void this 913," says one worker, using a kind of newspeak to avoid the harsh reality of the client's fate. Like the split between morality and technology in *High School*, one client complains that in the welfare office "You give me technicality. I'm telling you about a condition."

In keeping with its depressing depiction of the welfare system, the film ends on a bleak and ironic note. One of the clients, Mr. Hirsch, who has been made to sit and wait alone on a bench, looks up and addresses the neon firmament and an absent God, saying he will wait as long as He deems it necessary.

BARRY KEITH GRANT

See also **High School**; **Meat**; **Wiseman, Frederick**

Welfare (US., 1975, 167 min). Distributed by Zipporah Films. Produced, edited, and directed by Frederick Wiseman. Cinematography by William Brayne. Sound recorded by Frederick Wiseman.

Further Reading

Atkins, Thomas R. (ed.), *Frederick Wiseman*. New York: Monarch Press, 1976.

Benson, Thomas W., and Caroline Anderson, *Reality Fictions: The Films of Frederick Wiseman*. Carbondale: Southern Illinois University Press, 1989.

Grant, Barry Keith, *Voyages of Discovery: The Cinema of Frederick Wiseman*, Urbana and Chicago: University of Illinois Press, 1992.

Mamber, Stephen, *Cinema Verite in America: Studies in Uncontrolled Documentary*. Cambridge, MA: MIT Press, 1974.

Nichols, Bill, *Ideology and the Image*. Bloomington: Indiana University Press, 1981.

WEST INDIES AND CARIBBEAN

Historically, documentary films in the Caribbean, like films in the Caribbean generally, make up a broad array of productions, the diversity of which on one level is defined by language (including the work of Anglophone Caribbean, Francophone Caribbean, Hispanic Caribbean, and Dutch Caribbean producers) (Cham, 1992). Consideration of some key documentary productions from the Caribbean region, however, reveals common themes, styles of productions, and similar experiences shared by the documentary filmmakers of this ethnically, historically, culturally, and linguistically diverse region. Documentary films of the Caribbean are a heterogeneous body of work representing a culturally complex region, but there are many Caribbean productions that deserve to be included in the broader canon of documentary film. This article provides introductions to key producers of Caribbean documentary film, the cultural significance of Caribbean documentary, and the economic and political issues dealt with by Caribbean documentary filmmakers.

The local development of film industries and documentary film production has been a concern for both independent producers and Caribbean governments alike to varying degrees for more than fifty years. State-authored manifestations of these concerns include Jamaica's 1948 *Motion Picture Industry* (*Encouragement*) *Law* (Lent, 1977), Martinique's 1977 *Service Municipal d'Action Culturelle* (Cham, 1992) and Trinidad and Tobago's 2003 *Master Plan for the Strategic Development of the Trinidad and Tobago Film Industry* (Tourism and Industrial Development Company of Trinidad and Tobago, 2003). Documentaries from and about this region reflect the significant social and political struggles of the constituent countries as they emerged from colonial domination, through social revolution to cultural revitalization. Christian Lara's definition of Caribbean or Antillean film provides a basis on which Caribbean documentary film can be defined. Caribbean documentary is used here to include productions whose directors are from the Caribbean, with subject matter focusing on the Caribbean, featuring Caribbean lead actors, using Creole, and produced by a Caribbean production unit (Cham, 1992). Although these criteria provide useful guidelines for attempting to represent a canon of Caribbean documentary film, there are also films whose place in such a canon is significant even though they may not fulfill one or two of the outlined criteria.

In the Caribbean from the 1970s to the early 2000s, nongovernmental documentaries were produced as a result of Caribbean filmmakers' struggles for recognition within local media cultures in which prepackaged, imported programs were readily received and broadcast for economic reasons (Lent, 1977; Brown, 1987). During this period, television stations across the Caribbean justified the high percentages of imported (usually North American or European) programs, including documentaries, by citing the lower costs associated with importing programs against the higher costs of producing local programs. Station-originated television documentaries were thus a low priority in the management of television stations across the Caribbean (Lent, 1977). Further, after the advent of television in the 1960s and color in the 1970s, television stations placed emphasis on investigative reports on contemporary issues, while local documentary film production was ignored (St. Juste, 2004).

In the preindependent Caribbean, documentaries were also produced by colonial governments, tracing the stories of peoples of the then-colonies and the development of the Caribbean from colonial rule to independence (Warner, 2000). Spanning the 1950s and 1960s, these colonial documentaries provided valuable insights into colonial rule. In the preindependence era, the Colonial Office in England sent documentaries to the colonies for viewing. In later colonial times, however the Colonial Film Unit was closed down, as it became more cost effective to train people in the colonies in documentary filmmaking. These documentaries were produced in black-and-white, 35mm film and usually dealt with population and health issues (St. Juste, 1992).

This archive of preindependence Caribbean documentaries included: a film intended to motivate Jamaican teachers in the face of adversity (*Builders of the Nation*) (Warner, 2000); coverage of prerevolutionary Cuba (*Cuba Collection,* 1950s); *Marketing What We Grow* (1963), a documentary about farming practices in Jamaica; *This Is Ska,* (1964), a two-part production on the origins of Ska music by the Jamaican Film Unit; *The Lion of Judah* (1966), a documentary account of the state visit of Ethiopian Emperor Haile Selassie to Jamaica; *The Royal Tour of the Caribbean* (1966), and a film produced by the Colonial Office about the Queen's 1966 visit to British Guiana, Trinidad and Tobago, Grenada, St. Vincent, Barbados, St. Lucia, Dominica, Montserrat, Antigua, St. Kitts-Nevis, Tortola, Grand Turk, the Caicos, the Bahamas, and Jamaica (CASBAH, 2002). Outside the realm of colonial pasts, historically there has been significant interest by international producers, researchers, and scholars to use film to document different aspects of culture, geography, and history of the Caribbean region (Found, 2003–2004).

After Caribbean nations gained their independence, documentary film, like other media, became an outlet for the expression of emerging national identities and a medium for the exploration of regional development. Documentary film, against the broader backdrop of the visual mass media, became sensitive to building and maintaining cultural sovereignty within the Caribbean (Brown, 1987). In the Caribbean in the 1970s, significant social and cultural development included the rise in popularity of Caribbean music, struggles for political or economic independence, and the increasing empowerment of the previously disempowered. Further along this path of evolution, in the 1980s, 1990s, and early twenty-first century, Caribbean filmmakers (and documentary filmmakers) placed emphasis on and explored themes of postcolonial nationalism and concerns for cultural imperialism resulting from foreign investment and ownership (Brown, 1987; Cham, 1992; Warner, 2000).

Several significant documentary films exemplify this Caribbean focus on themes of postcolonialism, national identity, and the effects of globalization and tourism in the countries that make up this geographical region. Three such films are *And the Dish Ran Away with the Spoon* (1992), *Los Hijos de Baragua / My Footsteps in Baragua* (1996), and *Life and Debt* (2001). *And the Dish Ran Away with the Spoon*, originally produced to address regional environmental problems, took the unique approach of exploring the dominance of North American programming in the Caribbean region as an environmental issue (Laird, 2004). *Los Hijos de Baragua /*

My Footsteps in Baragua explores the cultural history of Anglophone West Indians in Cuba and the sociopolitical reasons for their migration. In *Life and Debt,* documentary filmmaker Stephanie Black explored aspects of Jamaican everyday existence that are affected by economic agendas of such entities as the World Bank, the Inter-American Development Bank, and the International Monetary Fund. This documentary reveals the contradictions of Jamaican life most often not seen by visiting tourists (Black, 2001–2002). These three Caribbean documentaries explore identity and culture, the Caribbean diaspora, postcolonialism, and the search for cultural and political sovereignty.

One series of documentaries, *Caribbean Eye*, was produced in 1992 by Banyan, a video production house based in Trinidad and Tobago, whose contributions across the Caribbean included co-productions and the training of video units throughout the region (Banyan, 2004). Key players in the founding and development of Banyan included Bruce Paddington, Christopher Laird, and Anthony Hall. Thirteen one-hour episodes made up the full series of *Caribbean Eye*, with each episode focused on a different aspect of Caribbean culture, including dance, theatre, festivals, indigenous peoples, music, oral traditions, women, leaders, games, and film. The *Caribbean Eye* series was recognized for excellence in documentary production and won numerous awards including the Caribbean Publishers and Broadcasters Association award for "Best Caribbean Television Series" and the Caricom Prize "for fostering regional integration" (Banyan, 2004). One episode of *Caribbean Eye*, titled *Film Caribbean*, explored factors influencing regional production, featuring the works of filmmakers from the Dutch-, French-, Spanish-, and English-speaking Caribbean, noting that Cuba is the only Caribbean territory in which there had been significant production up to the date of production for that episode (Banyan, 2004).

Banyan produced *And the Dish Ran Away With the Spoon* in 1992, the same year as the *Caribbean Eye* series. This documentary, which was part of the BBC/TVE Developing World series, focused on the domination in the Caribbean of television programs from the North, primarily the United States. *And the Dish Ran Away With the Spoon* illustrates the wider project of Banyan and its producers, "to produce a uniquely Caribbean approach" to television and documentary production. This unique Caribbean approach positions this documentary as both reflexive and performative (Hight and Roscoe, 2001). Through juxtaposition of interviews, poetry, music, performance, and excerpts of imported and indigenous television programs, the producers explored the question, "What happens when people have to dream other people's dreams?" *And the Dish Ran Way with the Spoon* was not simply an account of a trend in Caribbean media, it was also an indictment of the North American practice of jamming signals from Cuban broadcasting houses, in response to Cuba's policy to restrict programming to local, or at least regional (and non-North American), content. *"Dish"* and the *Caribbean Eye* series crystallized the talents of Caribbean documentary producers and showcased the wealth of documentary material in the Caribbean, and the ability of local filmmakers to produce high quality, regionally significant films using local production resources and talent.

The documentaries of Cuban filmmaker Gloria Rolando provide important windows into Afrocuban culture and serve the strategy of Rolando's desire to "rescue and preserve afrocuban (sic) cultural expressions" (Rolando, 2004). Themes of transcending borders take on multiple forms in Rolando's documentaries, including *Nosotros y el Jazz/Us and Jazz*, which spotlights the common cultural history of Afrocubans and African Americans, and *El Acaran/The Scorpion*, which celebrates the music and dance styles of Congo origin that are popular in Cuban carnivals (Rolando, 2004). *Los Hijos de Baraguå/My Footsteps in Baragua* (1996) is a feature documentary by Rolando, about the presence of English-speaking West Indians settled in Cuba. Rolando's documentaries have advanced themes of diaspora, exploring cultural artifacts and texts that survived through migration. In *Los Hijos de Baraguå*, Rolando revealed the stories of Caribbean men and women who traveled throughout the Caribbean seeking work and opportunity in the early twentieth century. Like *And the Dish Ran Away with the Spoon* and *Life and Debt*, *Los Hijos* explored themes of imperialism, colonialism, exploitation, identity, and culture. In *Los Hijos de Baraguå*, these themes are traced by following the stories of West Indians in Cuba, who preserved their traditions and cultural pride through music and dance, despite their existence in segregated towns culturally dominated by North American companies.

From the mid-twentieth century to the early twenty-first century, documentary filmmaking in the Caribbean required resourcefulness and dedication on the part of producers and directors. Financial collaboration and other support frequently came from institutions both within and outside the Caribbean (UNESCO, TVE, and the BBC in the case of Banyan; PBS in the case of Stephanie Black's *Life and Debt*; and ICAIC, the Cuban national film institute in earlier Rolando productions). In her later productions (including those documentaries produced under her own organization, "Images del Caribe" or Images of the Caribbean), Gloria Rolando relied on the unpaid work of friends and family. Like many independent documentary filmmakers in the Caribbean, Rolando often began her documentary projects without the means to finish them, but with a desire to share the documented stories of Caribbean people and Caribbean life through film (Morris, 1998).

North American documentary filmmaker Stephanie Black produced *Life and Debt* in 2001. Black had previously produced *H-2 Worker*, a documentary about the abuses of Caribbean farm workers in the sugarcane fields of Florida (Black, 2001–2002). According to Lara's definition of Caribbean film, Black's films could be excluded from the canon of Caribbean documentary films, because she is not a Caribbean filmmaker. However, *Life and Debt* becomes a significant inclusion, as the film spent many weeks in Jamaican cinemas, playing to audiences eager to see Jamaica represented on screen (Popplewell, 2003), demonstrating the film's significance to the local audience. *Life and Debt* also underscored issues that are key to the Caribbean experience, including economic and political subjugation by external forces. This documentary was successful in achieving acclaim and exhibition success both in Jamaica and internationally, which to many Caribbean critics became further indicative of cultural imperialism at work and raised the question of why documentaries by native Jamaicans or Caribbean filmmakers were not received with equal local and international interest.

Life and Debt received international critical acclaim (winning the Paris Human Rights Film Festival Special Jury Prize and the 2002 One World Prague Human Rights Film Festival Audience Award for Best Film of the Festival), but it also became the focus of debate regarding Jamaican emphasis on tourism and development and the severe costs that were paid in the struggle toward development as tradition and modernity collided (Black 2001–2002). Discourse in the Jamaican context surrounding the release of *Life and Debt* was divided along the lines of prodevelopment versus pronationalism, the former represented by Jamaicans who argued the importance of tourism and foreign investment in Jamaica's economy, and the latter asserted by those who believed that Jamaican everyday life was negatively affected by the mounting billion-dollar debt under which Jamaica,

according to Black's film, had become enslaved to the IMF, the IADB, and the World Bank.

The style of *Life and Debt* was similar in significant ways to that of *And the Dish Ran Away with the Spoon*. *Life and Debt* mixed interviews, poetry, music, and narration in its exploration. The genesis of this documentary was, in fact, the nonfiction text *A Small Place* by Antiguan writer Jamaica Kincaid, whose voice provides narrator bridges throughout the film (Black, 2001–2002). Using this hybrid style, director Stephanie Black delved into the complexity of Jamaican sovereignty against the backdrop forces of globalization, tourism, and industrial development. *Life and Debt* thus represented the voices of the Jamaican government, the workers whose lives were changed by the coming and going of multinational corporations, the Jamaican farmers whose crops went unsold, the executives within the IMF and the World Bank, and the American tourists. The result of this approach was a documentary that manifests as a polyvocal ethnography, consisting of partial truths and fragments of discourse that provide the viewer with a handle for entering the world of others through the stories of ethnographers (Clifford 1986; Tyler, 1986) and, in this case, the stories told by the documentary filmmaker.

Life and Debt captured the widespread recognition in Jamaican society of the implications of Jamaica's ties to the IMF and the World Bank. Black interviewed farmers who asserted their views on the role that these institutions play in Jamaican policy making and in everyday life. Jamaican audience reception of this documentary also illustrated the widespread relevance and concern that these issues held in Jamaican society at the time of this film's release. When *Life and Debt* was shown in Jamaican cinemas, audiences turned out to fill the cinemas, a fact that confirmed the dual significance of this film (Popplewell, 2003–2004). The first significance was that Jamaican (and wider Caribbean) audiences were drawn to images and representations of themselves on large and small screens. The second significance of audience reception of *Life and Debt* was that a documentary dealing with sober sociopolitical issues had significant appeal to a broad cross-section of Jamaican society.

In the English-speaking Caribbean, The University of the West Indies has played an important role in the training of emerging visual artists, filmmakers, and documentary producers (Brown, 1987). At the Mona campus in Jamaica, the Caribbean Institute of Mass Communication (CARIMAC) offers an undergraduate program in Broadcast Journalism, with an emphasis in television. This program provides students with "a variety of creative experiences in the conceptualization (sic), development and production phases of film and television" (UWI Mona, 2004). In Trinidad and Tobago, at the St. Augustine Campus, the Centre for Creative and Festival Arts offered a Bachelor of Arts degree in Visual Arts, including courses in Film and Video production (UWI St. Augustine, 2002). By 2004, students of this Visual Arts program had produced more than sixty short films, including documentaries. One such film, shown at the 2004 end-of-year exhibition, looked at basic infrastructure in a developing country and explored the problems with pipe-borne water in Trinidad and Tobago (Holder, 2004). Modules in the St. Augustine program were taught by scholar/producer/director and one of the original founders of Banyan, Bruce Paddington, and Yao Ramesar, a prominent contemporary Caribbean filmmaker who refers to his production aesthetic as "Caribbeing" (UWI, 2003). The focus in this program at St. Augustine was on helping filmmakers to develop a unique Caribbean and local aesthetic, and an understanding of local, small budget filmmaking (Gibbons, 2004). The philosophical emphases of Paddington and Ramesar, as well as of Rawle Gibbons (the Head of the Centre for Creative and Festival Arts) have been geared notably toward the development of local voices and local visual aesthetics (Gibbons, 2004).

Caribbean documentary films also feature narratives that focus on musicians and dancers of the region or that use music and dance in their telling. *Chutney in Yuh Soca* (1996) is one such film, which explored the fusion of Afro-Caribbean and Indo-Caribbean culture. *Calypso Dreams* (2002) explored the stories and music of key calypsonians from Trinidad and Tobago, celebrating the history and evolution of calypso as an art form. Horace Ové's *Reggae* (1970) also built on the centrality of music to Caribbean culture and documented the significance of the 1970 London Reggae Festival at Wembley through interviews, songs, and the narration of Caribbean author Andrew Salkey. In 1988, Christopher Laird produced a musical documentary titled *Crossing Over*, the narrative of which follows a Trinidadian calypso musician to Ghana to explore Ghanaian highlife music and then follows a Ghanaian musician to Trinidad where Trinidadian musicians and practitioners of West African Orisha embrace him (Banyan, 2004). As outlined earlier, the work of Cuban filmmaker Gloria Rolando also uses music to trace Caribbean migrations and cultural influences.

Caribbean filmmakers have produced documentaries despite the often-lacking incentives to produce local features. The focus on the importance of localizing visual culture through television and cinema continued to increase through the early twenty-first century. In Trinidad and Tobago, a new community-based television station was born of the production house Banyan. Launched in 2004, Gayelle the Channel promised 90 percent local content, and used its archive of shorts, series, features, and documentaries, as a source of programming. With such changes taking place in the first few years of the new millennium, scholars, filmmakers, and other media practitioners were optimistic that the media landscape would change toward increasing localization, including increases in the numbers of Caribbean documentary films produced. With the popularization of digital technologies, productions budgets for documentaries decreased, as did the training required, thereby increasing access of a wider cross-section of producers and directors to the equipment used for documentary production. In the late 1990s and early 2000s, digital video technology became significant to increased activity in and the localization of production (Laird, 2004) and specifically to increased activity in the production of Caribbean documentary films.

SUSAN MCFARLANE-ALVAREZ

Selected Films

1992 *And the Dish Ran Away with the Spoon*: Banyan Limited/BBC, 49 min; directed by Christopher Laird and Anthony Hall
1996 *Los Hijos de Baraguá/My Footsteps in Baraguá*: Images Caribes, 53 min; directed by Gloria Rolando
2001 *Life and Debt*: Tuff Gong Pictures, 80 min; produced and directed by Stephanie Black

Further Reading

Banyan. "Inside the People TV," website, http://www.pancaribbean.com/banyan/banyan.htm. 2004.
Black, Stephanie. *Life and Debt: A Film by Stephanie Black*. Official website of the film, http://www.lifeanddebt.org. Kingston: Tuff Gong Productions, 2001–2002.
Brown, Aggrey, and Roderick Sanatan, *Talking with Whom? A Report on the State of the Media in the Caribbean*. Mona: CARIMAC, University of the West Indies Printery, 1987.
Caribbean Studies Black Asian History (CASBAH). website, www.casbah.a.uk/cats/print/224/OFTP00001.htm. "Overseas Film and Television Centre Collection Description" hosted by The Institute of Commonwealth Studies. London, 2002.
Cham, Mbye, "Introduction: Shape and Shaping of Caribbean Cinema" in *Ex-iles: Essays on Caribbean Cinema*, Mbye Cham (eds.), Trenton, NJ: Africa World Press, 1992.
Clifford, J., Introduction: Partial Truths, in *Writing Culture: the Poetics and Politics of Ethnography*, J. Clifford

and G. Marcus (eds.), Berkeley, and Los Angeles: University of California Press, 1986.

Found, William, "Documentary Films on Caribbean Islands" on York University website, http://www.arts.yorku.ca/geog/wfound/video/ 2003–2004.

Gibbons, Rawle, Head/Theatre Arts Coordinator, Centre for Creative and Festival Arts, The University of the West Indies. Personal interview, January 2004.

Hight, Craig, and Jane Roscoe, *Faking It: Mock Documentary and the Subversion of Factuality*, Manchester: Manchester University Press, 2001.

Holder, Zia, "Films with Local Flavour: UWI Students Exhibit 12 Pieces" in *Trinidad Express Newspaper*, May 13, 2004, 27.

Laird, Christopher, Personal Interview. Trinidad and Tobago, January 2004.

Lent, John, *Third World Mass Media and Their Search for Modernity: The Case of the Commonwealth Caribbean 1917-1976*, Lewisburg: Bucknell University Press, 1977.

Morris, Holly, "Winging It on Lots of Dream" on www.abcnews.com, 1998.

Popplewell, Georgia, "Picture This," in *Business Trinidad and Tobago*, 2003–2004 edition.

Rolando, Gloria, Personal website of Gloria Rolando, http://www.gloriarolando.com, Havana, Cuba, Site visited June 2, 2004.

St. Juste, Franklyn, Interview in *Ex-iles: Essays on Caribbean Cinema*, Mbye Cham (ed.), Trenton, NJ: Africa World Press, 1992.

———, Telephone and e-mail interviews. Jamaica-Atlanta, May to June 2004.

Tourism and Industrial Development Company of Trinidad and Tobago, *A Master Plan for the Strategic Development of The Trinidad and Tobago Film Industry*. 2003.

Tyler, S., "Post-modern Ethnography: From Document of the Occult to Occult Document," in *Writing Culture*, J. Clifford and G. Marcus (eds.), Berkeley and Los Angeles: University of California Press, 1986.

The University of the West Indies at St. Augustine. (UWI St. Augustine), "Centre for Festival and Creative Arts," website, http://www.festival.uwi.tt/courses5.htm, 2002.

The University of the West Indies (UWI), "Second Festival of African and Caribbean Film," website, http://humanities.uwichill.edu.bb/filmfestival/2003/, Cave Hill, Barbados: UWI, 2003.

The University of the West Indies at Mona (UWI Mona), "CARIMAC" website, http://www.mona.uwi.edu/carimac/Pubjt.html, 2004.

Warner, Keith, *On Location: Cinema and Film in the Anglophone Caribbean*, London and Oxford: Macmillan Education, 2000.

WHEN THE DOG BITES

(UK, Woolcock, 1988)

Throughout the 1970s, the loosely affiliated independent film sector in Britain maintained a difficult relationship with the industry trade union, the Association of Cinematograph and Television Technicians. One particular contention concerned the status of independent filmmakers working unpaid or supported by small grants, an important framework for radical cinema practice. A degree of rapprochement was achieved at the end of the decade with the Workshop Agreement, "an extraordinary innovation which gave formal recognition to the principles of workshop practice and opened up the possibility of extending them as a basis for fully professional participation in the industry" (Dickinson, 1999: 58–59). This new policy endorsed a number of workshops around the country managed by the workers and operating on a nonprofit basis. Trade Films in Gates-head was established on this format and immediately set about the task of documenting the stark economic and social prospects of the North East in the Thatcher period.

When the Dog Bites (WTDB, 1988) is an unconventional documentary that deals with the town of Consett in County Durham in the years after the closure of the principal industry, the steel works. It draws on a plethora of documentary techniques to assess the impact of economic restructuring on the town, the resulting frustration and nostalgia engendered in the community, and efforts to establish alternative forms of employment. By using juxtaposing interviews (sometimes in strikingly unexpected settings), observational techniques, stylistic allusions to canonical fictional films, dramatic enactments, and a degree of self-parody, the film displaces the conventional evidential foundation of verité and traditional journalistic modes with a more associational and playful approach. Director Penny Woolcock, recently having worked on Trade Films' *Northern Newsreels*, had felt constrained thematically and formally by the predictable framework of current affairs programming and purposely set out to create "an element of fantasy and desire, a more dreamy quality" (Corner, 1996: 151).

The formal inventiveness of WTDB arguably undermined the film's accessibility, and, although acceptable in a radical independent work, was untypical of a film destined for national television broadcast. Aired on Channel Four's *Eleventh Hour* slot, a showcase for new approaches and experimentation, WTDB proved controversial in Consett where the film was deemed too arty and audiences were unready for self-conscious directorial stylisation. In addition, local officials and representatives thought the film was irresponsible and had por- trayed the area negatively; some of the people in the film thought they had been treated dishonestly. The film now stands as a fascinating imaginative response to acute social change and once again raises the time-honoured problem of balance between form and purpose, so central to the doc- umentary project.

ALAN BURTON

When the Dog Bites (UK, Trade Films, 1988). Directed by Penny Woolcock. Produced by Belinda Williams and Ingrid Sinclair. Cast includes Lisa Sanderson and Art Davies.

Further Reading

Corner, John, *The Art of Record. A Critical Introduction to Documentary*, Manchester: MUP, 1996.
Dickinson, Margaret, *Rogue Reels. Oppositional Film in Britain, 1945–90*, London: BFI Publishing, 1999.

WHEN WE WERE KINGS

(US, Gast, 1996)

When We Were Kings portrays the 1974 match between heavyweight boxing champion George Foreman and underdog Muhammad Ali, which promoter Don King staged in Zaire (now the Democratic Republic of Congo). The film high- lights Ali's mix of boxing prowess, black politics, and comic bravado, all of which strives to link African Americans and their ancestral home. A chronicle of press conferences, training, travel, and especially a black music festival precedes the fight and builds the expectation that Foreman, a heavy favorite, will annihilate Ali. The audience is well prepared for the stirring upset and the aftermath pays homage to Ali's courage and determination.

The film is a hybrid of documentary trends, blend- ing sports, biography, music, and cultural history into a heroic political anthem. *When We Were Kings* combines observational filming of the 1974 events, compilation materials that develop historical per- spective, and contemporary interviews reflecting on Ali's mix of self-promotion, physical ability, and social concern. Its extraordinary emotional impact arises from its graceful design and harmo- nious synthesis of elements.

The subject evolves out of the history of its production. *When We Were Kings* was initially planned as a concert film. Leon Gast, a New York filmmaker and still photographer, was com- missioned to shoot the three-day music festival that was to precede the 1974 bout and produce an African-American Woodstock in the "direct cinema" style. Gast had already made *Hell's Angels Forever* and two music films, *The Dead*, on the San Francisco rock band The Grateful Dead, and *Salsa*, featuring the Panamanian singer Ruben Blades. Four days before the title fight, however, George Foreman received a cut over his eye that required the bout to be delayed for six weeks.

The concert went ahead as scheduled, but the tie- in with the fight was aborted and the audience inconsequential. Nonetheless, Gast remained in Zaire after the concert, filming the scene as

When We Were Kings, Muhammad Ali giving boxing training to young kids, in Zaire, 1974 (documentary released in 1996).
[*Courtesy of the Everett Collection*]

everyone lingered. More than 300,000 feet of film was shot, but financing for the movie dried up. Gast nursed plans to complete the project for twenty-two years. In 1989, David Sonenberg, a talent manager in the music business, raised money and over the next six years, he and Gast put together eight different versions. Eventually they decided to shift the focus onto Muhammad Ali and acquired additional fight footage and archival material to frame the story around the boxing champion. In addition to the nine concert numbers, Sonenberg added two new songs at the close of the film, "When We Were Kings" and "Rumble in the Jungle." The music track functions as a rhythmic foundation thoroughly integrated into the unfolding montage of events and underlining the film's politics.

In 1995, Taylor Hackford joined the team and convinced them to include contemporary interviews. The commentators included Norman Mailer, George Plimpton, and Malik Bowens, each of whom witnessed the bout more than twenty years

before and remembered it vividly. A screening at the Sundance Film Festival drew seventeen offers to distribute the motion picture. Its successful theatrical run culminated in its winning the Academy Award for "Best Documentary Feature" in 1997. Over the years, *When We Were Kings* evolved from a concert film into an homage to a boxing legend. In doing so, it had taken on a historical perspective that turned out to be essential to its impact.

Leon Gast constructs his documentary like a heroic legend that unfolds in four movements. The first movement focuses on Ali's background as a fighter and the announcement of the forthcoming title bout in Zaire. Episodes from Ali's early career are associated with the Civil Rights struggle and further matched with images from the anti-colonial rebellion in the Democratic Republic of Congo. The film treats Ali as a political leader working to reunite black America and black Africa. The film's second movement follows the Americans to Africa, and, as they prepare for the bout, Ali meets his brethren in Zaire, serenaded by songs from the black music festival such as "Say It Loud, I'm Black and I'm Proud." The former champion ties himself so closely to the destiny of the black community that the Africans express surprise when the champion arrives and they discover that he is black, too. George Foreman, meanwhile, displays an underdeveloped social consciousness. Ali ties his quest to awakening black America from the political apathy personified by Foreman. The third movement begins with the injury to Foreman, which delays the fight and allows the alliance between Ali and the Africans to grow. The movement culminates in the bout and Ali's victory, which becomes a triumph for a renewed American-African brotherhood. The closing act

When We Were Kings, Muhammad Ali in Zaire, 1974 (documentary released in 1996).
[*Courtesy of the Everett Collection*]

1443

meditates on the meaning of Ali as a historical hero and suggests a reunification of black and white America in their mutual recognition of, and admiration for, the heroic boxer. The film embraces Ali as a crusader whose courage and determination evokes a time "when we were kings," when heroism raised common men and women to majesty.

When We Were Kings attempts to revive African-American solidarity in the 1990s through a quest for racial identity. The film highlights the connection between blacks in America and Africa, but finally the quest focuses on the black athlete as a community hero. History and memory link the racial politics of 1974 to the need for revival in 1996. The crossing between continents parallels the crossing back through time to embrace the heritage embodied in Muhammad Ali.

In addition to promoting the Ali legend, *When We Were Kings* celebrates the optimism, fortitude, and determination necessary to command one's destiny. The hero in *When We Were Kings* emerges as a crusader for social justice whose identity is drawn from his racial community. The closing "When We Were Kings" montage does not simply valorize Ali, but inspires the audience to acknowledge the prospects for heroic action that combines physical excellence with social leadership, fervent conviction, self-sacrifice, and a commitment to others. *When We Were Kings* imparts a feeling of renewed possibility and the suggestion of the potential for heroism in everyday life.

LEGER GRINDON

When We Were Kings (U.S.,1996, 87 min) a Gramercy Pictures release, a DAS Films presentation. Directed by Leon Gast. Produced by David Sonenberg, Leon Gast, and Taylor Hackford. Edited by Leon Gast, Taylor Hackford, Jeffrey Levy-Hinte, and Keith Robinson. Cinematography by Maryse Alberti, Paul Goldsmith, Kevin Keating, Albert Maysles, and Roderick Young. Cast features: Muhammad Ali, George Foreman, Don King, James Brown, B.B. King, Mobutu Sese Seko, Spike Lee, Norman Mailer, George Plimpton, Thomas Hauser, Malik Bowens, Lloyd Price, The Spinners, the Crusaders, and Miriam Makeba. Music Credits: "Am Am Pondo" (written by Miriam Makeba, performed by Miriam Makeba), "Say It Loud, I'm Black and I'm Proud (written by James Brown and Alfred James Ellis, performed by James Brown), "Young Rabbits" (written by Wayne Henderson, performed by The Crusaders), "Musical Interlude" (written by Tabu Ley Rochereau and Seigneur Rochereau, performed by L'Orchestre Afrisa International), "I'm Coming Home" (written by Thom Bell and Linda Creed, performed by The Spinners), "Sweet Sixteen" (written by B. B. King and Joe Josea, performed by B. B. King), "In a Cold Sweat" (written by James Brown and Alfred James Ellis, performed by James Brown), "Gonna Have a Funky Good Time" (written by James Brown, performed by James Brown), "African Chant" (written by Franco Luongo, performed by OK Jazz), "When We Were Kings" (written by Andy Marvel, Amy Powers, and Arnie Roman, performed by Brian McKnight and Diana King), "Rumble in the Jungle" (written by Wyclef Jean, Prakazrel Michel, Lauryn Hill, Benny Anderson, Bjorn Ulvaes, Stig Anderson, Chip Taylor, Kamaal Fareed, Malik Taylor, Trevor Smith, and John Forte, performed by The Fugees).

Further Reading

Corliss, Richard, "*When We Were Kings*," in *Time*, 49, 7, February 17, 1997, 83.

Denby, David, "*When We Were Kings*" in *New York*, 47, 7, February 24, 1997, 123.

Early, Gerald, "Ali's rumble," in *Sight and Sound*, 7, 5, May 1997, 10–12.

Gelder, Lawrence Van, "In Africa with Ali and the Rope-a-Dope," in *New York Times*, Friday October 25, 1996: C26–27.

Macdonald, Kevin, "*When We Were Kings*," in *Sight and Sound*, 7, 5, May 1997, 56.

Mailer, Norman, *The Fight*, Boston: Little, Brown, 1975.

McCarthy, Todd, "*When We Were Kings*," in *Variety*, 362, 2, February 12, 1996, 82–83.

O'Brien, Richard, "*When We Were Kings*," in *Sports Illustrated*, 85, 19, November 4, 1996, 20.

Ryan, Susan, "*When We Were Kings*," in *Cineaste*, 22, 4, Fall 1996, 54–55.

WHITEHEAD, PETER

Peter Whitehead is renowned as the consummate documentarist of the 1960s counterculture. In a series of films made between 1965 and 1969, he not only captured the events, places, people, and attitudes that defined the decade, but succeeded in tapping deep into its shifting zeitgeist. Whitehead's knack for being in the right place at the right time (and switching the camera on at the right moment) has certainly contributed amply to the compulsive mythography of the "swinging sixties," but his films also offer a sophisticated analysis and critique of the procedures by which such legends are created. They register and extend the wider preoccupations of an era when the role of media representations in shaping, controlling, and potentially transforming human experience was at the forefront of radical artistic, intellectual, and political concerns.

Whitehead's early films show his fascination with the immediacy and involvement of American cinema verité. In later works verité shooting methods are fused with the visual lexicon of underground cinema and the self-reflexive, brechtian strategies developed by Jean-Luc Godard. This stylistic amalgam points to Whitehead's distinctive authorship of his work, a fact materially underlined by his artisanal working methods as director, producer, editor, and cameraman of his own films. From the outset Whitehead approached verité filming as a subjective process, openly acknowledging that his works register personal choices, opinions, and reactions to circumstances, and refusing the shibboleth of objectivity that has tended (unjustly) to dominate responses to American verité work.

The film that first made Whitehead's reputation was *Wholly Communion* (1965), a record of the International Poetry Incarnation that took place at the Royal Albert Hall on June 11, 1965. Whitehead borrowed an NPR Éclair 16mm camera to film the proceedings with minimal disturbance and took in 45 minutes' worth of film stock. For an event scheduled to last more than three hours, this meant that he was compelled from the outset to be highly selective in what he chose to shoot. The resulting thirty-three-minute film clearly registers Whitehead's personal interpretations and reactions to the occasion, as the trademark zooms, pans, and sweeps of verité filming are used to shift focus between performers and audience, and to frame the poets differently according to the tone, delivery, and reception of their readings (Sargeant, 1997). Gregory Corso's introspection is conveyed by initially framing the seated poet between two chatting spectators, and then holding his face in a tight close-up. In contrast, the public gravitas of Adrian Mitchell reading his cathartic Vietnam poem *To Whom It May Concern* is carried by using a medium close-up of the poet and cutaways to rapt faces in the audience. Whitehead's focus on the collective experience of the event in the interaction of performers and listeners anticipates the subsequent view of the Albert Hall reading as less about individual performers and their work than as a defining moment in the self-awareness and public visibility of the counterculture.

On the strength of *Wholly Communion*, Whitehead was approached by The Rolling Stones' manager Andrew Oldham and invited to film the band. *Charlie Is My Darling* (1965), a film diary of the Stones' 1965 tour of Ireland, predates better known rock documentaries like D. A. Pennebaker's *Don't Look Back* (1967) in minting the trademark verité iconography of the mundane routines of touring, and probing the enigmatic contrast between on-stage and offstage performance. Unlike Pennebaker's film, which follows many verité documentaries in avoiding direct interaction with its subject by filming press interviews, *Charlie Is My Darling* includes sequences in which Whitehead interviews the band members, his articulate voice on the sound track probing and questioning them in a manner that occasionally—notably when targeting a diffident Charlie Watts—ruptures the verité protocol of invisible observation and feels painfully intrusive. Whitehead's use of the same technique when pressing a group of fans about why exactly they like the band and getting only vague and unconvincing replies has the disquieting effect of making the Stones' undeniable talent and power as performers seem suddenly fragile and insubstantial, which perhaps explains the frequent assessment of the film as melancholy and elegaic.

For *Benefit of the Doubt* (1966), Whitehead filmed a performance of Peter Brook's Royal Shakespeare Company production of the anti-Vietnam War play *U.S.*, and conducted a series of interviews with Brook and his cast members including Glenda Jackson. The treatment of the performance recalls *Wholly Communion* in attending as much to the audience as to the actors, but the film also anticipates Whitehead's later film, *The Fall*, in its ultimate scepticism toward the political efficacy of radical theatre.

Whitehead's involvement with the Rolling Stones led him into filming other bands and making pop promos for *Top of the Pops*. His position at the center of the London counterculture led him to undertake a wider exploration of the scene, galvanized by the media spectre of "Swinging London" launched by *Time* magazine in 1966. *Tonite Let's All Make Love in London* (1967), billed by Whitehead as "a Pop concerto for Film," remains an unparalleled celebration and dissection of the mystique of the 1960s. It features stage and studio footage of rock bands, including the Animals and the Rolling Stones (material reused from *Charlie Is My Darling*), and impressionistic sequences shot in London's streets and nightclubs, some processed in slow motion or edited to create lyrical stop-motion effects. Interviews, both relatively formal encounters with celebrities like Michael Caine, Julie Christie, Mick Jagger, and David Hockney, and spontaneous vox-pops with anonymous "dolly birds" sound out the moral temper of the times. Whitehead again proves willing to press his subjects hard from behind the camera about their opinions and values, situating himself as a detached observer as much as a participant and bringing out both conviction and flimsiness in contemporary attitudes. The critical stance toward the poses and values of "Swinging London" is enhanced by the brechtian (godardian) division of the film into chapters, and the ambitious early montage of the media images and articles that spawned the phenomenon, which is reminiscent of the ironic all-out visual assaults found in the underground films of Bruce Conner.

The Fall (1969), Whitehead's most searching and accomplished film and his final contemporary meditation on the iconic images and realities of the 1960s, may have started out as "Tonite Let's All Make Love in New York," but quickly mutated under subjective and external pressures into something very different. The film is divided into three sections: "Image," "Word," and "Word + Image." The first two explore shooting and editing as stages in the production of filmed images, and all three together reconstruct Whitehead's attempt to document political and underground activity in New York (while conducting an affair with a fashion model), his increasing loss of faith in the ability of media images to have any significant impact in a revolutionary situation, and finally his discovery of a solution in direct political action, when he joins and films the student occupation of Columbia University and its eventual violent liquidation by police in the spring of 1968. *The Fall* is a landmark of counter-cinema in its reflexive interrogation of personal commitment, media imagery, and the possibility of direct political intervention, but it also retains tremendous documentary significance as a work that captured and gave form to the rapidly shifting temper and fortunes of the counterculture as the 1960s drew to a close, when protest was abandoned in favour of direct action, and the response of the authorities escalated to the use of extreme violence.

Although *The Fall* was not Whitehead's last film, the journey out from under the weight of media representations that it records was to prove prophetic. In 1973, Whitehead abandoned filmmaking for falconry, judging that the verité camera that he had believed connected him to the world was in fact keeping him apart from it.

CATHERINE LUPTON

Biography

Born 1937, Liverpool. Degree in Philosophy of Science and Crystallography from Cambridge, 1961. Scholarship to Slade School of Art, 1963. News cameraman for Italian television in London, 1964. Made scientific documentary *Perception of Life* for the Nuffield Foundation, 1964. *Wholly Communion* won the Gold Medal at the Mannheim Documentary Film Festival, 1965. Published English translations of thirty-two classic film scripts under the Lorrimer imprint, 1966–1971. Took up falconry in 1972. Directed two further films, *Daddy* (1974, with Niki de St. Phalle) and *Fire in the Water* (1977). Ran falcon breeding centre for Prince Khalid Al Faisal in Saudi Arabia, 1982–1990. From 1990 published novels: *Nora and . . .* (1990), *The Risen: A Holographic Novel* (1994), *Pulp Election: The Booker Prize Fix* (1996, under the pseudonym Carmen St Keeldare), *Brontëgate* (1997), *Girl on the Train* (1998), *Tonite Let's All Make Love in London* (1999). Interactive novel *Nohzone* (2000).

Selected Films

1965 *Wholly Communion*
1965 *Charlie Is My Darling*
1966 *Benefit of the Doubt*
1967 *Tonite Let's All Make Love in London*
1969 *The Fall*
1994 *Pink Floyd, London: 1966–1967*

Further Reading

Crofts, Stephen, "Peter Whitehead Talks about His New Film—*The Fall*" in *Cinema*, December 1968, 18–21.

Drummond, Phillip, "Peter Whitehead and *The Fall*," in *Isis*, 21, May 1969.

Durgnat, Raymond, "Tonite Let's All Make Love in London," in *Films and Filming*, 14, 5, February 1968, 22–23.

———, "The Falconer: Three Lives of Peter Whitehead," in *Entropy*, 1, 1, 1997, 10–21.

Paul, R. F., "The Inadvertent Agent," in *Mondo, 2000*, 46–59.

Sargeant, Jack, "A Few Poets Trying to Be Natural," in *Naked Lens: Beat Cinema*, London: Creation Books, 1997.

Whitehead, Peter (ed.), *Wholly Communion*, London: Lorrimer Films Ltd., 1965.

WHO BOMBED BIRMINGHAM?

(UK, Granada, 1990)

During the 1990s, there were a number of drama documentaries produced in the United Kingdom based on the Troubles in Northern Ireland, and 1990 stands out as a particularly fruitful year with the production of *Shoot to Kill* (Yorkshire TV), *The Treaty* (Thames/RTE), and the controversial *Who Bombed Birmingham?* (Granada) also known in the United States as *Investigation: Inside a Terrorist Bombing*.

Drama-documentary has been produced with relative frequency on British television and is a hybrid genre based on journalistic research and evidence, in a similar mode as the traditional documentary, but that also uses the aesthetic codes of drama to mediate the real world. There have been a number of drama documentaries produced in the United Kingdom that have dealt with the cases of innocent people charged by the state and wrongly convicted for crimes they did not commit.

One of the most eminent in the genre is *Who Bombed Birmingham?*, which recounts the British Labour MP Chris Mullen's campaign to free the Birmingham Six and which also led to public pressure to free the men wrongfully convicted of the IRA terror attack on a pub in Guildford fifteen years earlier.

The programme recounts how Mullen challenged the convictions and eventually ascertained that the Six were never members of the IRA, that their confessions emerged after suffering assaults by the police, that the forensic evidence was seriously flawed, and that the police were aware of the identity of the actual bombers. The programme is based on Mullen's journey to establish who planted the bombs and on the reconstruction of the night of November 21, 1974, when five Irish immigrants with families in Birmingham were arrested as they prepared to return to Northern Ireland. The five men were travelling back to Belfast for the funeral of an IRA man, James McDaid killed by his own bomb in the West Midlands city of Coventry.

The programme recounts the journey as the group made their way to catch the ferry back to Belfast, and as the IRA detonated two bombs in two pubs, the Mulberry Bush and the Tavern killing twenty-one people and injuring more than 160 in Birmingham city centre. All five were arrested and later a sixth man was also arrested. Confessions were extracted from some members of the group by West Midlands Police after their arrests.

Indeed, there was widespread revulsion at the attack and the men received heavy sentences despite withdrawing their confessions and claiming police brutality at their trial. After a campaign by the men's families, investigative journalists, human rights activists and politicians, however, many began to believe the six were in fact innocent. What the programme also uncovered was a police file that detailed the interrogation of an alleged IRA informer in December 1975. The programme makers claimed that this exonerated the Six and identified the perpetrators.

Questions were subsequently raised about the tactics deployed by the West Midlands Police to gain the confessions, with widespread allegations of police brutality and dubious forensic evidence. The case also had particularly sensitive aftereffects for the British legal system after an unsuccessful appeal and allegations that the judiciary did not want to admit to a miscarriage of justice.

The imminent broadcasting of *Who Bombed Birmingham?* provoked widespread discussion within the various authorities involved, and the British Home Office, the Chief Constable of Birmingham Police, and the British Prime Minister were in complete agreement in their claim that no new evidence would emerge and therefore nothing would change. Indeed, *Who Bombed Birmingham?* undeniably brought the appeal cases of the Birmingham Six to the attention of huge television audiences and a prebroadcast furor in Parliament saw Conservative ministers having to answer difficult questions and Prime Minister Margaret Thatcher claim that no television programme would alter any decisions concerning the case.

Programme makers, Granada Television's current affairs programme "*World in Action*," had declared that they were about to reveal the identities of the people they believed to be responsible for the Birmingham bombs. The programme was by now highly controversial and the ethics of this decision were widely discussed in the British press in the days before the broadcast, which ensured a massive build-up in publicity and virtually guaranteed large viewing figures. The programme was finally broadcast on various ITV channels and also on RTE on a Wednesday evening in March 1990.

Despite the staunch position in Parliament, the programme did indeed reveal evidence to suggest that the Six were wrongly imprisoned, and the police and government were forced to investigate the case once more. A year later, the sentences of the Birmingham Six were quashed.

The programme was undeniably powerful in its aims and managed to successfully portray realistic depictions of an investigative reporting programme, as the team interviews various people and tries to disprove the tests through the use of flashbacks and follows the current affairs team's attempts to prove the men's innocence by querying the reliability of the forensic evidence.

The three lead actors, John Hurt as Mullen, Roger Allam as *World in Action* journalist Charles Tremayne, and Martin Shaw as his producer Ian McBride, give commanding performances; and the six, played by Ciaran Hinds, Niall Tobin, Brendan Laird, Niall O'Brien, Vincent Murphy, and Brendan Cauldwell, in turn offer heartbreaking performances with the occasional poignant comic interplay. Bob Peck, Terence Rigby, and John Woodvine provide fascinating portrayals of different faces of the law and most notably, John Kavanagh's depiction of the IRA gang's bomb maker, Donal McCann's indignant republican, and Sean McGinley's tormented terrorist.

Despite the eventual triumph of *Who Bombed Birmingham?* the programme raises a number of critical concerns about the hybrid nature of drama-documentary as a form. The method of casting well-known charismatic actors such as John Hurt in the roles that the programme makers endorse and often unknown performers to portray the opposition, which, coupled with the visual grammar of television journalism designed to portray the truth, makes a potent combination that more than any other genre leaves the viewer hopelessly dependent on the good faith of the director.

Yet *Who Bombed Birmingham?* is without doubt a powerful television programme that has since set the standard for subsequent British TV docudramas based on real events including Jimmy McGovern's "Hillsborough," Paul Greengrass's "Bloody Sunday," and the recent "Omagh."

KIRSTY FAIRCLOUGH

Who Bombed Birmingham? (UK, Granada Television, 1990 105 min). Directed by Mike Beckham. Written by Rob Ritchie. Produced by Mike Beckham. Original Music by Shaun Davey. Cinematography by Ken Morgan. Sound by Nick Steer. Cast: Roger Allam, Andy Bradford, Brendan Cauldwell, Ciarán Hinds, John Hurt, John Kavanagh, Brendan Laird, Robert Lang, Patrick Malahide, Donal McCann, Gerard McSorley, Vincent Murphy, Niall O'Brien, Bob Peck, Terence Rigby, David Ryall Martin Shaw, Niall Toibin, and John Woodvine.

Further Reading:

Paget, D., *No Other Way to Tell It: Dramadoc/Docudrama on Television*, Manchester: Manchester University Press, 1998.

Pettitt, L. *Screening Ireland: Film and Television Representation*, Manchester: Manchester University Press, 2000.

Rosenthal, Alan (ed.), *Why Docudrama?: Fact-fiction on Film and TV*, Illinois: Southern Illinois University Press, 1998.

WHY WE FIGHT

(US, Capra, 1942–1945)

Why We Fight was the most widely circulating North American propaganda documentary series about World War II, both inside and outside the United States. The producer, Frank Capra, made this series between 1942 and 1945, directing a large team of Hollywood volunteers—script writers, editors, directors, music composers, commentators, and so on—among whom were, most noticeably, Anthony Veiller, Anatole Litvak, Walter Huston, William Hornbeck, Carl Foreman, Lloyd Nolan,

Dimitri Tiomkim, Eric Knight, and several others. Although Ivens and Flaherty participated in the project on a temporary basis, their contributions were not significant to the final result. What was significant was the collaboration of the Disney studios in producing the geographical animations. The series consists of seven episodes: *Prelude to War* (1942), *The Nazis Strike* (1942), *Divide and Conquer* (1943), *The Battle of Britain* (1943), *The Battle of Russia* (1943), *The Battle of China* (1944), and *War Comes to America* (1945).

Why We Fight was produced to motivate North American recruits who were mobilized for the war. Before the attack on Pearl Harbor, the majority of North Americans viewed the war in Europe as something remote and rather strange. Pearl Harbor marked a radical change in this perception and mobilized the entire country. The production was subject to strict control measures. The initial content of the series was defined by the Army's Bureau of Public Relations in fifteen texts, slightly before Pearl Harbor. A team of script writers made the first adaptation, and Capra started to screen any type of filmed material, including Nazi, Italian, and Soviet material such as documentaries and newsreels. In May 1942, the final setup of the chapters and their basic features were determined. September 1942 already saw the first rough-cut editing of the first parts. In November 1942, the first film of the series, *Prelude to War*, was released. Each phase of the production process was meticulously revised by the military.

In *Why We Fight*, Capra opted for persuasive arguments and emotive techniques. His messages were simple, clear, and repetitive. First of all,

Why We Fight: Prelude to War, Chiang Kai-Shek, 1943.
[*Courtesy of the Everett Collection*]

the war was necessary; survival so dictated it. Refraining from engaging in it was equivalent to choosing slavery under the Japanese, German, and Italian enemies. The enemy was represented as cruel and treacherous; the message was to beat them first and then talk. The Allied countries were defended, especially Great Britain and the Soviet Union. The corresponding explanations did not leave the audience with any doubts either: France had fallen into German hands through inside treason, as had Danmark, Sweden, and Norway; Great Britain and the Soviet Union had resisted surrender by their own efforts and had fought until the end like heroes. There were no sociological analyses or ideological explanations. The one-front policy that the state propaganda proclaimed required straightforward explanations that were easy to understand. Capra and his team converted the series into the concise and all-understanding history that the recruits needed to be able to face their enemies.

For the editing of *Why We Fight*, Capra used a large variety of filmed material. This obviously included newsreels and documentaries from both the Allied Forces and the enemy, blended, however, with footage from feature films. The series reminded one of *The March of Time*; however, the typical hints of humor, sentiment, human feeling, decision, and determination were Capra's, who followed the final cuts from a close distance.

In *Why We Fight*, everything was subjected to efficiency in terms of propaganda. It is impossible to prove the persuasive argument of the series; however, the results of the questionnaires

Why We Fight: Prelude to War, Schoolchildren in Nazi Germany, 1943.
[*Courtesy of the Everett Collection*]

completed by soldiers gave the semblance of a major success. Not all of the chapters were equally successful. The first four chapters were appreciated the most. Their impact surpassed any expectations. In the United States, the series won an Oscar, which facilitated its way to commercial cinemas, apart from being obligatory material in the military training for North American recruits. It was also released in Allied and neutral countries, as copies were distributed in various languages. For obvious reasons, *The Battle of Britain* was shown in Great Britain, on direct instruction by Churchill, and *The Battle of Russia* was released in the Soviet Union, ordered expressly by Stalin. No real information is available, however, about the audience at the time. In the year 2000, the National Film Preservation Board decided to include *Why We Fight* into the National Film Registry.

JULIO MONTERO

See also **Capra, Frank**

Why We Fight series:

Prelude to War (U.S. Army Special Service Division; U.S. War Department. Animation: Walt Disney Productions; Research Aid: Academy of Motion Picture Arts and Sciences; Photography: Consolidated Film Industries [CFI], 1942). Distributed by 20th Century Fox Film Corporation; LS Video; Office of War Information, Bureau of Motion Pictures; War Activities Committee; Questar Video Inc. Produced by Frank Capra (uncredited) and Anatole Litvak (uncredited). Writing credits: Julius J. Epstein, Phillip G. Epstein, Robert Heller (uncredited), Eric Knight (uncredited) and Anthony Veiller (uncredited). Original music by Hugo Friedhofer (uncredited), Leigh Harline (uncredited), Arthur Lange (uncredited), Cyril J. Mockridge (uncredited), and David Raksin (uncredited). Cinematography by Robert Flaherty (uncredited). Film editing by William Hornbeck (uncredited). Narrators (uncredited): Walter Huston and Anthony Veiller

The Nazis Strike (U.S. Army Special Service Division; U.S. War Department Distributed by Office of War Information, Bureau of Motion Pictures; War Activities Committee; Questar Video Inc., 1942). Produced by Frank Capra. Directed by Frank Capra and Anatole Litvak. Writing credits: Julius J. Epstein and Phillip G. Epstein. Original music by Anthony Collins (uncredited), Louis Gruenberg (uncredited), Leigh Harline (uncredited), Dimitri Tiomkim (uncredited), and Roy Webb (uncredited). Film editing by William Hornbeck (uncredited). Narrator (uncredited): Walter Huston.

Divide and Conquer (U.S. Army Special Service Division; U.S. War Department. Animation: Walt Disney Productions. Distributed by Office of War Information, Bureau of Motion Pictures; War Activities Committee; Questar Video Inc., 1943). Produced by Frank Capra (uncredited). Directed by Frank Capra and Anatole Litvak (uncredited). Writing credits: Julius J. Epstein and Phillip G. Epstein. Original music by Dimitri Tiomkim. Film editing by William Hornbeck (uncredited). Narrators (uncredited): Walter Huston and Anthony Veiller.

The Battle of Britain (U.S. Army Special Service Division; U.S. War Departament. Animation: Walt Disney Productions. Distributed by Office of War Information, Bureau of Motion Pictures; War Activities Committee; Questar Video Inc. 1943). Produced by Frank Capra (uncredited). Directed by Frank Capra and Anthony Veiller (uncredited). Writing credits: Julius J. Epstein and Phillip G. Epstein. Original music by Dimitri Tiomkim (uncredited), Howard Jackson (uncredited), William Lava (uncredited), and Max Steiner (uncredited). Film editing by William Hornbeck (uncredited). Narrators (uncredited): Walter Huston and Anthony Veiller.

The Battle of Russia (U.S. Army Special Service Division; U.S. War Department, 1943. Distributed by 20th Century Fox film Corporation; Office of War Information, Bureau of Motion Pictures; War Activities Committee; Questar Video Inc.). Produced by Frank Capra (uncredited). Directed by Frank Capra and Anatole Litvak. Writing credits: Julius J. Epstein, Phillip G. Epstein, Anatole Litvak, Anthony Veiller, and Robert Heller. Original music by Dimitri Tiomkim. Film editing by William Hornbeck (uncredited). Narrators (uncredited): Walter Huston and Anthony Veiller.

The Battle of China (U.S. Army Special Service Division; U.S. War Departament, 1944. Distributed by Office of War Information, Bureau of Motion Pictures; War Activities Committee; Questar Video Inc. and MPI Home Video). Produced by Anatole Litvak (uncredited). Directed by Frank Capra and Anatole Litvak (uncredited). Writing credits: Julius J. Epstein and Phillip G. Epstein. Original music by Dimitri Tiomkim (uncredited). Film editing by William Hornbeck (uncredited). Narrators (uncredited): Walter Huston and Anthony Veiller.

War Comes to America (U.S. Army Pictorial Services, 1945. Distributed by MPI Home Video; Questar Video Inc.; RKO; War Activities Committee of the Motion Pictures Industry). Produced by Frank Capra. Directed by Frank Capra and Anatole Litvak. Writing credits: Julius J. Epstein, Phillip G. Epstein, Anatole Litvak, and Anthony Veiller. Original music by Dimitri Tiomkim (uncredited). Film editing by William Hornbeck. Narrators (uncredited): Lloyd Nolan and Walter Huston.

Further Reading

Bohn, Thomas W., *An Historical and Descriptive Analysis of the "Why We Fight" Series*, with a new Introduction, New York: Arno Press, 1977.

Capra, Frank, *The Name above the Title: An Autobiography*, New York: Da Capo Press, 1997.

Culbert, David, "'Why We Fight': Social Engineering for a Democratic Society at War," in *Film & Radio Propaganda in World War II*, K.R.M. Short (ed.), London & Canberra: Croom Helm, 1983.

Murphy, William, "The Method of Why We Fight," in *Journal of Popular Film*, I, 1972, 185–196.

WILD, NETTIE

A former actor and radio journalist, Wild is known for four feature-length documentaries made since 1988. The films, direct cinema studies of complex political and social confrontations, are driven by what Wild refers to as her "sense of cinematic drama."

Her first feature, *A Rustling of Leaves: Inside the Philippine Revolution.* placed her and her crew within a guerrilla war waged against the government of Corazon Aquino and right wing paramilitary squads. Throughout the documentary, the filmmakers negotiate their vulnerability, first with members of the heavy-handed Filipino army and death squads and later, when traveling with the guerrilla New People's Army, against the hazards of the war itself. The film's most shocking moment is a firefight between the rebels and government forces in which Wild's soundman is shot and killed.

Wild's second film, *Blockade*, focuses on the struggle between the Gitksan first nation in British Columbia and non-native logging families to determine who controls the forests around them. The Gitksan block the Canadian Pacific Railway tracks, leading to a confrontation with the Royal Canadian Mounted Police. Wild, although sympathetic to the Gitksan, recognizes that the non-native loggers, many of whom have worked in the woods for generations, are being placed in an equally precarious situation.

In her most ambitious film to date, *A Place Called Chiapas*, Wild studies the aftermath of the 1994 Zapatista revolution. The film is not only a study of the peasant rebellion itself but also of the role of an outside observer. In one sequence, the enigmatic Subcommandante Marcos invites sympathizers from North America and Europe to visit his "postmodern revolution." Wild films the political tourists with various degrees of bemusement but also with a growing realization that she herself is just another visitor. When she finally is granted her interview with Marcos, the resulting footage says as much about the awkwardness of the encounter as it does about the nature of the revolution.

It is with this same sense of nondetached irony that Wild filmed a small revolution in her own city. *Fix: The Story of an Addicted City* documents the personalities around efforts to build North America's first legal safe drug injection site in Vancouver's notorious Downtown Eastside. For two years, Wild followed the charismatic Dean Wilson, a heroin addict and president of the Vancouver Area Network of Drug Users and his equally dedicated partner, Ann Livingston, a faith-based organizer and nonuser. Opening the injection site in the face of opposition from the nearby community, Dean and Livingston also work with Vancouver's conservative mayor, Phillip Owen in an effort to establish a humane and realistic policy toward the city's addicts (an effort that would later cost Owen his own party's support for reelection).

As was the case with her other films, Wild and her company, Canada Wild Productions, used *Fix* as an organizing tool. The film has played mainstream cinemas in more than forty Canadian cities. Each screening has been followed by a community forum with local drug users, health care professionals, activists, politicians, and police.

SETH FELDMAN

Biography

Born in New York City in 1952 and educated at the University of British Columbia. Beginning her career as an actor, she cofounded and performed with Touchstone Theatre and Headlines Theatre (where she produced, wrote, as well as acted in various productions). Wild worked as a broadcast journalist for the Canadian Broadcasting Corporation, producing documentaries for several radio programs as well CBC's national news. Wild's first independent documentary was a video based on the Headlines Theatre production of *Buy, Buy, Vancouver*. The documentary, about the disappearance of affordable housing, was the first video invited to the Grierson Documentary Seminar where it attracted the attention and support of Santiago Alvarez. Her subsequent films have been widely recognized. *A Rustling of Leaves* won The People's Choice Award at the 1989 Berlin Film Festival (Forum of New Cinema), the *Prix du Public* at the National Film Board's Salute to the Documentary, and the Grand Prize at the Houston Film Festival. In 1993, *Blockade* shared honors as Most Popular Canadian Feature at the Vancouver International Film Festival, won the Red Ribbon at the American Film and Video Festival, and the Silver Award at the Houston International Film Festival. In 1998, *A Place Called Chiapas* won the Audience Award for Best Documentary at the AFI-Los Angeles Film Festival, Best Feature Documentary from the International Documentary Association, and a Genie Award for best Canadian Feature Documentary. In 2003, *Fix* won Wild's second Genie for Best Canadian Documentary. That same year, her work was the subject of a retrospective at the Hot Docs documentary film festival in Toronto.

Selected Films

1988 *A Rustling of Leaves: Inside the Philippine Revolution*: director, producer, writer
1993 *Blockade*: director, producer, second camera
1999 *A Place Called Chiapas*: director, producer, writer, co-camera
2002 *Addicted City*: director, producer, co-camera

Further Reading

Hoover Travis, "Nettie Wild: The Documentarian Becomes the Documented," in *Film Freak Central* [online journal], http://www.filmfreakcentral.net/hotdocs/hotdocsnettiewild.htm.
Posner, Michael, "Hanging onto the Horses: *A Rustling of Leaves: Inside the Philippine Revolution*," in *Canadian Dreams: The Making and Marketing of Independent Films*. Vancouver: Donglas & McIntyre, 1993, 51–78.
Wild, Nettie, "*Just Some Lady with a Camera*: Canadian National Railroad versus Filmmaker Nettie Wild," in *Point of View*, fall, 1993. 6–8.
————, "*In Search of Light on the Road to Jolnixti.e*" *Brick*, 63, Fall, 1999, 8–17.
————, "Nettie Wild," in *Point of View*, 39, 2000, 11.
————, Interview. University of Calgary *Gauntlet*, March 25, 2004, http://gauntlet.ucalgary.ca/story/3746.
Wintonick, Peter, "Time, Trust and Money," in *Cinema Canada*, 160, 1989, 13–16.

WILDENHAHN, KLAUS

Klaus Wildenhahn's career ran parallel to the development of television documentary in postwar Germany. Wildenhahn came to television two years after the six regional stations in Western Germany had been merged into the federal umbrella organization ARD (Arbeitsgemeinschaft der öffentlich-rechtlichen Rundfunkanstalten). His first assignment, to the political magazine programme *Panorama* in 1961, occurred when the administrative structure of public service television was still a work in progress. Wildenhahn profited from the fact that, in these formative years, editorial responsibilities and limits had yet to be established. This freedom enabled him to experiment with new journalistic formats.

The political situation at that time provided an important background for Wildenhahn's professional career, as well as for his ideas on the ethics of documentary filmmaking. During the 1950s, Germany had experienced a radical turn toward political and cultural conservatism as a result of the decade-long governance of the Christian-Democratic Party (CDU) under chancellor Konrad Adenauer. Wildenhahn's early setting must be understood in this context. Against the historical backdrop of the Third Reich, the first German postwar government had established a rigorous political agenda based on the denial of moral guilt for the Holocaust and the subordination of civic needs to the state's requirements in favour of public welfare. By the mid-1950s, the "Wirtschaftswunder" (economy miracle) had led to a social climate of exclusion and economic sedation. The rise of the television medium became strongly interwoven with the idea of national identity, not least owing to the victory of the German soccer team at the World Championship in 1954, the first major televised event of postwar Germany.

Wildenhahn's ideas of the purposiveness of documentary films were shaped in these particular years of rapid social changes. Claiming the necessity of an ethical bias toward misrepresented milieus and social groups in documentary film, Wildenhahn considered television as an important mouthpiece for the "unheard voices" (Wildenhahn, 1992) in society. In retrospect it can be said that the urgency of his demand was underlined by the fact that throughout the 1960s, in which Wildenhahn realized two documentaries a year, the Adenauer government was succeeded by two other conservative governments. Wildenhahn's description of his style as an "aesthetic of resistance" in reference to the German culture critic Peter Weiss must be seen in this political context.

Wildenhahn's work was almost exclusively concerned with subjects of social justice and public life. In his second documentary for "Panorama," "Der Tod kam wie bestellt" (1962), Wildenhahn examined the murder of Patrice Lumumba and the involvement of the UNO. His leftist biography earned him the reputation of a controversial figure, and typically this judgement did not change when the Social-Democratic Party came into power in 1969. By the mid-1960s, the seeming liberalism during the first years of public service television had turned out to be nothing more than an early misconception that was corrected with a few personnel changes. That Wildenhahn was able to work within the structure of the ARD until his retirement in 1995, however, underlines his pivotal role in the development of the documentary film and television journalism in Western Germany.

Wildenhahn repeatedly criticized the authoritative top-down configuration of public service journalism. In opposition to this intellectual elitism cultivated by the political class, he claimed that the documentary content itself should determine its form. For Wildenhahn, the virtues of documentary film were not defined aesthetically, but solely by ethical and political nature: through the intimacy between the filmmaker and the filmed person, thorough long-term observations, long shots, and the renunciation of external comments or "synthetic" inserts. This documentary altruism affected a whole generation of German filmmakers and became the main characteristic of Wildenhahn's distinctive style.

In the late 1970s, this influence led to the controversy between Wildenhahn and the media critic Klaus Kreimeier about partiality in the documentary film and "the filmmaker's deliberate subordination under the reality of the camera" (Kreimeier). Their disagreement provoked an influential debate about the political and social responsibility of the documentary film as a part of the media public. In his 1980 essay "Industrielandschaft mit Einzelhändlern"("Industrial Landscape with Retail Sellers") Wildenhahn responded to Kreimeier's criticism with the argument that "the documented" themselves should take over the author's role, as the filmmaker only provides the technical framework for their story.

Wildenhahn was not so naïve to believe that his documentary method would automatically reveal an absolute truth or an accurate representation of social reality. He had become familiar with the work of D. A. Pennebaker, Albert Maysles, and Richard Leacock in 1963 while working on a TV feature about the beginnings of direct cinema. The impact of their work was already noticeable in Wildenhahn's first "on location" documentary *Parteitag '64* (1964) about the national convention of the Social-Democratic Party. Wildenhahn was the first German filmmaker who adopted the methods of the direct cinema movement, but he remained sceptical about its effect on filmic realism, the new immediacy of the documentary experience, as a sheer consequence of smaller and therefore more mobile film equipment. He considered an ideological discourse primarily based on a technological premise as equally problematic as the hierarchical practice he tried to overcome. Wildenhahn evaded this dilemma by turning toward a highly political position. Because the documentary filmmaker can never obtain absolute objectivity, he or she has no other choice but to endorse this partiality.

Wildenhahn's output of "worker films" remained the strongest indication of this ethical bias. According to Wildenhahn the working-class milieu was the scene where the slow transformation of the government's social paradigm became most evident. He continuously returned to close observations of workplaces and documentations of worker strikes until the early 1990s. The strong position films, such as *Emden goes to USA* (1975–1976) or *Rheinhausen. Herbst '88* (1988), adopted between the factions of workers and the union emphasized the social-democratic values maintained in the body of Wildenhahn's work. His conviction that only a unified position would help to defy the forces of free market made his films a rare example of social- and class-conscious documentary filmmaking in German television.

Constancy characterizes Wildenhahn's oeuvre. He consistently articulated his social policy, even in his late films. His final documentary for the ARD in 1995 was the only one not shot on 16mm.

ANDREAS BUSCHE

See also **Leacock, Richard; Maysles, Albert; Pennebaker, D.A.**

Biography

Born in Bonn, Germany, June 19, 1930. Studied sociology, publishing and political science at the Free University

Hamburg. Left the university in 1953 and moved to London, where he worked in an insane asylum. Returned to Hamburg in 1959. Produced commercials on 35mm for the National Lottery. Between 1960 and 1964, "visual realizer" for journalistic television programmes at the ARD. 1964–1975, editor at the department "teleplay" at the NDR/ARD. 1968–1972, scholar at the German Film-und Fernsehakademie (Film and Television Academy) in Berlin. 1969, first documentary, "Institussommer," with the newly founded filmmaker collective "Gruppe Wochenschau." In 1975, laid off at the NDR/ARD for his controversial documentary "Emden geht nach USA." 1976, "Emden geht nach USA" wins Golden Grimme Award. 1975, freelance editor at the radio of the WDR/ARD. 1977/1979/1980, jury member of the documentary film festival Duisburger Filmwoche. 1975–1995, freelance editor for the departments "education," "philosophy, history, education," "religion and history," "feature, documentary, history," and "society and education" at the NDR/ARD and freelance contributor for the WDR/ARD. Retired in 1995.

Selected Films

1964 *Parteitag 1964*: director, concept, writer

1967 *In der Fremde:* director, writer
1971 *Der Hamburger Aufstand Oktober 1923*: director, concept, co-writer
1975–1976 *Emden geht nach USA*: director, concept, co-writer
1988 *Rheinhausen. Herbst '88*: director, narrator,
1992 *Freier Fall: Johanna K.*: director, concept
1994–1995 *Reise nach Mostar*: director, concept

Further Reading

Biedermann, Werner, and Angela, Haardt (eds.), *Beiträge aus der Wirklichkeit*, Duisburg: Filmforum der Volkshochschule, 1981.

Berg, Jan, "Die Fiktion des Nichtfiktionalen. Zur Abbildtheorie von Klaus Wildenhahn," in *Filme*, 4, August 1980.

Kluge, Alexander, *Debatte über den Dokumentarfilm*, in *Ulmer Dramaturgien. Reibungsverluste*, Klaus Eder and Alexander Kluge (eds.), München: Carl Hanser Verlag, 1980.

Schröder, Nicolaus (ed.), *Klaus Wildenhahn, Dokumentarist*, Berlin: Freunde der Deutschen Kinemathek, 2000.

Wildenhahn, Klaus, *Teilstücke*, in *Fernsehdokumentarismus. Bilanz und Perspektiven*, Peter Zimmermann (eds.), Stuttgart: Europäisches Medienforum, 1992.

WINTONICK, PETER

With roots in fiction filmmaking during a period of the late 1970s and early 1980s, Canadian Peter Wintonick turned his interests to documentaries after honing his skills as an editor on a series of feature-length productions. *The New Cinema* (1984), a feature video documentary about independent film, marked Wintonick's directorial debut and hinted at his future as a filmmaker interested in the social ramifications of the form and its ties with fiction. The use of both fiction and nonfiction film language and techniques under the rubric of documentary filmmaking is a recurrent feature of Wintonick's highly constructed work, resulting in texts that touch but do not quite blur the line between the two practices.

Wintonick's films are pragmatic in nature, his exploration of subject matter satisfying both his personal search for knowledge and his desire to share that information with an audience. Much of his body of work could be classified as committed filmmaking insofar as his socioideological position

behind the camera is rarely concealed. Although Wintonick's personal politics are not necessarily on display, his perspective is echoed in the particular discourse presented onscreen.

Wintonick is best known for *Manufacturing Consent: Noam Chomsky and the Media* (1992), an epic feature-length documentary detailing activist-academic Noam Chomsky's critique of corporate news gathering and the vested interests that lie behind media coverage. Co-directed with Mark Achbar, the film is a complex system of compilation footage, interviews, and staged elements. According to the National Film Board of Canada, it is the most successful documentary in Canadian history. It has played theatrically in 200 cities around the world, won twenty-two awards, appeared in more than fifty international film festivals, has been broadcast in thirty markets, and has been translated into a dozen languages. It marked the first production from Necessary Illusions, a company founded by Wintonick, Achbar, and Francis Miquet devoted to the development, production, and distribution of media on sociocultural issues. Preceded by a number of smaller productions prepared for television broadcast, *Cinema Vérité: Defining the Moment* (1999), was Wintonick's next major achievement. It continued his examination of media, filmmaking, and journalism through his own filmmaking while attempting to delineate the major currents that spawned the vérité movement and established its profile within the documentary world. A hybrid of documentary styles, the film is notable for its first-person interviews with the luminaries of the movement, including Robert Drew, Richard Leacock, Jean Rouch, and Michel Brault.

Wintonick's interest in the virtual forum of information exchange offered by the Internet led to his development of The Virtual Film Festival. Founded in 1996, the site functioned as a point of convergence for documentary filmmakers to showcase their independently produced digital works and exchange ideas with other documentarians from around the world. Issues related to funding ultimately saw the closing of the site, but Wintonick's interest in multimedia as a vital link between both filmmakers and audiences alike continues to inform his ongoing role as a post-production consultant and executive producer for independent productions.

MICHAEL B. BAKER

See also **Manufacturing Consent**

Biography

Born in Trenton, Ontario, June 10, 1953. Attended Carelton University in Ottawa with an interest in journalism, theatre, film, photography, 1972. Graduated from the Algonquin College Film Production Centre in Ottawa, 1973. Editor at the International Cinemedia Centre Ltd.,

1972–1977. Editor and associate producer for Ron Mann's *Poetry in Motion*, a theatrical documentary about the history and art of performance poetry. Produced and directed first documentary, *The New Cinema*, winner of the Blue Ribbon Award at the American Film Festival, 1984. Formed Necessary Illusions with Mark Achbar and Francis Miquet, 1988. Associate Professor at Concordia University in the Department of Film Studies, 1988–1989. Completed *Manufacturing Consent: Noam Chomsky and the Media*, a coproduction of Necessary Illusions and the National Film Board of Canada, 1992. Co-producer and co-director of web-based Virtual Film Festival (now archived on CD-ROM), 1994–1996. Cofounder/chair of the Banff New Media Institute's *Digidocs* programme, 1995. Programmer for Canadian International Documentary Festival (Toronto), Visions on the Real (Adelaide), and Amsterdam International Documentary Festival.

Selected Films

1982 *Poetry in Motion* (Mann): associate producer, editor
1984 *The New Cinema*: director, producer, editor
1985 *The Journey* (Watkins): co-producer, co-editor (Canadian unit)
1987 *A Rustling of Leaves: Inside the Philippine Revolution* (Wild): editor, associate producer
1992 *Manufacturing Consent: Noam Chomsky and the Media* (Achbar): co-director, co-producer, editor
1999 *Cinema Vérité: Defining the Moment*: director, co-editor
2002 *Seeing Is Believing: Handicams, Human Rights and the News* (Cizek): co-director, co-producer

Further Reading

Achbar, Mark, and Peter Wintonick, "Manufacturing Dissent," in *Cineaste*, 3, 1993.
Enright, Robert, "Vérité, Vérité, All Is Vérité," in *Border Crossings*, 3, 2000.
Glassman, Marc, "Mediating Noam Chomsky; *Manufacturing Consent: Noam Chomsky and the Media*," in *Take One*, 2, Winter 1993.

WISEMAN, FREDERICK

Frederick Wiseman is a verité documentary film-maker with a long record of achievement. He chose a "fly on the wall" approach to filmmaking and continued with this method throughout his career. Wiseman lets the camera roll for long periods and does not use interviews, music, titles, or narration.

Editing is where the film's structure is born. He has been called a "pioneer" of verité, along with D. A. Pennebaker and the Maysles brothers (Poppy, 2000), and is considered "one of the most influential and prolific figures in documentary filmmaking" (Aftab and Weltz, 1).

Trained in law, Wiseman was teaching at Boston University's Institute of Law and Medicine when he turned his attention to the conditions at a nearby Massachusetts mental hospital. He was an amateur filmmaker and uninterested in the abstractions of the law. The result, in 1967, was his eighty-four-minute film *Titicut Follies*. It is considered by many to be a documentary classic. Because of its importance to Wiseman's career and documentary filmmaking, it is worth focusing on.

The story takes its name from a musical revue put on by the guards and mental patients at the Bridgewater State Hospital for the Criminally Insane. The black-and-white footage heightens the drama and terror; the unfolding story blurs the lines between sanity and insanity. So controversial was the film that the Massachusetts Supreme Court banned it from being shown. It ruled that the film was both obscene and exploitive, and had invaded inmate privacy. But supporters of the film argued that the public's right to know what happens at public institutions outweighs privacy issues. Wiseman himself has argued that if an institution receives public tax support, citizens are entitled to observe its operation.

Though a masterpiece to many, *Titicut Follies* was not without its critics. A *Time* magazine reviewer said the film was "a raw poorly edited report" that offered no solutions ("Cinema: Festival Action, Side Show Action, Titicut Follies"). A critic for *America* maintained that the privacy issue was bogus and that the real question was whether the film was an "objective documentary" or a "propaganda stunt" ("Cinema: Festival Action, Side Show Action, Titicut Follies"). Accused of filming with hidden cameras, Wiseman denied the charge. Additionally, the film raised questions as to whether or not it was art. In 1993, after twenty-four years, the film aired on public television.

Titicut Follies helped launch a career that included more than thirty documentaries. PBS nationally broadcast Wiseman's *Law and Order*, *Hospital*, *Juvenile Court*, *Essene*, *Basic Training*, *Primate*, *Welfare*, *Meat*, *Canal Zone*, and *Sinai Field Mission* among others. Additional broadcasts of his work have taken place in Sweden, The Netherlands, Japan, Italy, Norway, and Denmark.

Wiseman's films have won numerous awards, including the New York Film Festival, San Francisco International Film Festival, Spoleto Film Festival, London Film Festival, Athens International Film Festival, American Film Festival, and the Melbourne and Sydney Festivals. He has earned Emmys, Dupont Awards, and the Personal Achievement Gabriel Award, presented by the Catholic Broadcasters' Association. Retrospective screenings of his work have occurred at the Chicago Film Festival, London Film Festival, and Paris Film Cinematheque, among other venues.

Wiseman has remained steadfast in his convictions regarding documentary filmmaking. To the annoyance of some, he refuses to comment about what his films are about and what should be done in terms of what he has exposed. He believes this information is in the film and viewers have to make up their own mind. His films have also been criticized for being overly long.

Though often considered the "dean" of "cinema verité," Wiseman himself says it is "just a pompous French term that has absolutely no meaning as far as I'm concerned. The effort is to be selective about your observations and organize them into a dramatic structure" (Aftab, 2).

Wiseman's long and somewhat controversial career has provided the United States and the world with some of the most poignant examinations of institutions and life in America. He continues to see America as a largely unexplored country cinematically. Although primarily a documentary filmmaker, he has made two fiction films (*The Stunt Man*, 1980, and *Seraphita's Diary*, 1982).

LOU BUTTINO

Frederick Wiseman (Director).
[*Courtesy of the Everett Collection*]

See also **Basic Training**; **High School**; **Hospital**; **Law and Order**; **Meat**; **Titicut Follies**

Biography

Born in Boston, Massachusetts, January 1, 1930. B.A., Williams College, Williamstown, M.A., 1951. L.L.B., Yale University. Initially practiced and taught law before taking up documentary filmmaking in 1967.

Films

1967 *Titicut Follies*
1969 *High School*
1969 *Law and Order*
1970 *Hospital*
1971 *Basic Training*
1972 *Essene*
1973 *Juvenile Court*
1974 *Primate*
1975 *Welfare*
1976 *Meat*
1977 *Canal Zone*
1978 *Sinai Field Mission*
1980 *Model*
1983 *The Store*
1985 *Racetrack*
1986 *Multi-handicapped*
1986 *Adjustment & Work*
1987 *Deaf*
1987 *Missile*
1989 *Near Death*
1991 *Aspen*
1993 *Zoo*
1994 *High School II*
1995 *Ballet*
1996 *La Comedie Francaise*
1997 *Public Housing*
1999 *Belfast, Maine*
2001 *Domestic Violence I*
2002 *Domestic Violence II*

Further Reading

Aftab, Kaleem, and Alexandra Weltz, "Fred Wiseman," www.iol.ie/galfilm/filmwest, 1.

Anon, "The Talk of the Town: New Producer," in *The New Yorker*, 39, September 14, 1963, 33–35.

———, "Cinema: Festival Action, Side Show Action, Titicut Follies," *Time*, 90, 13, September 29, 1967.

———, "Tempest in a Snake Pit," In *Newsweek*, 70, November 11, 1967, 539.

Arlen, Michael J., *The Camera Age: Essays on Television*, New York: Penguin, 1982.

Barnouw, Erik, *Documentary: A History of Non-fiction Film*, New York: Oxford University Press, 1974.

Benson, Thomas W., Documentary Dilemmas: Frederick Wiseman's "Titicut Follies," Southern Illinois Press, 1991.

Eames, David, "Watching Wiseman Watch," in *the New York Times Magazine*, October 2, 96–102, 108.

Edelstein, David, "Frederick Wiseman," in *the New York Times*, March 16, 2003.

Ellsworth, Liz, *Frederick Wiseman: A Guide to References and Resources*, Boston: G.K. Hall & Co., 1979.

Fenton, John H., "Film Stirs Furor in Mass., Legislators See *Follies* Made at Memorial Hospital," in *the New York Times*, October 18, 1967, 40.

Gill, Brendan, "The Current Cinema," in *The New Yorker*, 43, October 28, 1967, 166–167.

Houston, Bobby, "Titicut Follies," in *Documentary*, December 2003.

Nichols, Bill, "Fred Wiseman's Documentaries: Theory and Structure," *Film Quarterly*, 31, 3, Spring, 15–28.

O'Connor, John, "Wiseman's Latest Film Is Another 'Reality Fiction,'" in *the New York Times*, November 7, 27.

Poppy, Nick, "Frederick Wiseman," Salon.com.2002/01/30.

Rosenthal, Alan (ed.), *New Challenges in Documentary*, Berkeley: University of California Press, 1988.

Schickel, Richard, "Sorriest Spectacle: The Titicut Follies," in *Life*, 63, December 1, 1967, 12.

Walker, Jess, "*The Cool World*," in *Film Comment*, 2, 1964, 51–52.

WOMEN, AMERICAN: EARLY FILMMAKERS

The names of Lee Burgess Dick, Helen Gayson, and Erica Anderson rarely appear in film histories or reference books, even in those devoted entirely to women filmmakers. Yet they were among the first professional female directors of documentaries in the United States, in the period 1930s to the late 1950s. Before them, Osa Johnson, Frances Flaherty, and the anthropologist Margaret Mead had noteworthy careers, as their husbands' partners, before documentary had been recognized as an independent motion picture genre. Even Helen Van Dongen and Helen Levitt, who are widely lauded for their work in film editing and still photography, are rarely remembered for their achievements as documentary filmmakers.

Why have these women been so consistently overlooked? Mainly because in the first half of the twentieth century, filmmaking in America was essentially the province of males. The few females who sidled into documentary film work in the early decades were either too modest or not modest enough to win the support and recognition of their male colleagues. Prints of many of the films made by pioneering women had limited distribution at the start. Since then, some have entirely vanished, making them unavailable to the critical eyes of later scholars and historians; but their viewpoints, experiences, and contributions as documentary filmmakers were as fulfilling and worthwhile as those of their male counterparts.

Lee Burgess Dick deserves recognition as the first American woman to make a full-fledged documentary film. That film, entitled *School*, produced in 1939 by her own company, Lee Dick, Inc., ran twenty-two minutes and was sponsored by the Progressive Education Association and the American Film, *Oenter* (the latter funded by the Rockefeller Foundation).

Helen Grayson's first documentary film, *The Cummington Story* (1944–1945), has been signaled out by her contemporaries and later filmmakers and writers, as one of the best productions of the U.S. government's Office of War Information (OWI). Before them, between 1917 and 1937, Osa Johnson, Frances Flaherty, and Margaret Mead all began their film work as their husband's partners in faraway areas of the South Pacific—the Solomon Islands, Samoa, and Bali, respectively.

During World War II, Helen Van Dongen directed and edited an Artkino compilation film entitled *Russians at War* and an OWl "News Review" filmed by official combat cameramen around the world. At the same time, still photographer Helen Levitt, an assistant editor at the OWI, was out on the streets with friends on holidays and weekends, filming material that would ultimately become one of the most important American documentaries of all time. Erica Anderson, also a still photographer, learned movie-making and at war's end began making low-budget art films at prestigious New York museums on French tapestries and sculptor Henry Moore, the first to be filmed in the United States in 16mm color.

Most of these women were based in New York City, when they were not travelling far and wide, and some of them certainly knew each other. Lee Burgess and Helen Grayson, for example, were the only two female members of the Screen Directors Guild some years after its founding. In 1951, they served on the Guild's 14-member committee honoring Robert Flaherty for his lifetime achievements, at a series of programs at New York's Museum of Modern Art. At the opening event, Frances Flaherty was introduced and applauded from her seat in the auditorium.

But nobody thought about the full meaning of her extraordinary credits on the films that were shown by Robert Flaherty in association with Frances Hubbard Flaherty. Interestingly enough, Frances Hubbard, Helen Gayson, and Lee Burgess were all graduates of the same college, Bryn Mawr in Pennsylvania—Frances in 1906, Helen in 1926, and Lee in 1930. Bryn Mawr was the East Coast's elite college for bright young women of means with primary interests in the arts.

Therefore it is not surprising that Lee Burgess, aspiring actress, founded a small theater group in Cape Cod (Massachusetts) before marrying wealthy photographer/poet Sheldon Dick. Helen Grayson worked as an actress with Maria Ouspenskaya before moving into costume and dress design for the theater and artist friends. In 1922, Frances Flaherty had a piano shipped to Samoa so that she could play duets with husband Bob (on violin) during the production of their *Moana*.

While there she took nearly 1,500 still photographs used to select cast and settings for the film. Many are now considered works of art in their own right. (See *Picturing Paradise* for samples of her work.) Margaret Mead, who arrived in Samoa a year after the Flahertyls had left, decorated her walls there with the *Moana* photos she had found in Asia Magazine, illustrating a series of articles written by Frances. Mead also took a few photos herself, used later in her many books and articles, beginning with *Coming of Age in Samoa* (1928), which made her world famous. In Bali and New Guinea (1936–1938), with Gregory Bateson (her third husband), Mead took meticulous notes that became the basis for the commentaries she wrote and narrated on the finished films (released between 1950 and 1954).

Although she lacked a college education, Osa Johnson wrote many books and articles about her travels and adventures. She had met Martin Johnson when she was still a Kansas high school girl and married him soon after graduating.

Helen Levitt left school in Brooklyn even before finishing, and had her first one-person exhibition in 1943 at New York's new Museum of Modern Art, which subsequently published her first book of photographs, with written introduction by her friend James Agee. Erica Anderson's highly successful films about Anna Mary studied to earn Moses, known to the art world as the celebrated Grandma Moses, and about Albert Schweitzer, famed organist and medical missionary, both made in collaboration with Jerome Hill—place her among the leading motion picture biographers of artists of that time.

As different as they were in background, temperament, and talent, these eight women had in common this one overriding fact: they were de facto members of what Virginia Wolff identified (in *Three Guineas*, 1938) as "the Society of Outsiders." Most were dependent on husbands to provide their opportunities to work in film. And most were innovators, who are almost always outsiders, whether male or female.

As outsiders they had a good share of disappointments. In the 1950s, Helen Grayson, for example, would have loved to make documentaries on her own, particularly one on the up-and-coming New York City Ballet and one on Benjamin Franklin in France, but financing was not available to her from government or foundation sources. Frances Flaherty wanted to perpetuate what she called "the Flaherty way" of filmmaking in the Flaherty Seminars, which she founded after her husband's death. The seminars became a major attraction for filmmakers and students, but her goal and even Frances herself were soon circumvented, and only the magical Flaherty name remained.

Being Albert Schweitzer's occasional chauffeur and secretary was perhaps more important to Erica Anderson than was having her feature-length film about him win an Academy Award, although she was certainly disappointed that only her partner, Jerome Hill, attended the ceremonies. But these women had support from many of their colleagues and friends. Grayson, for example, was said to be the only American ever invited to Jean-Paul Sartre's Sunday salon in Paris.

Anderson, in the course of establishing an Albert Schweitzer Center in America, won the enthusiastic affection of novelist Kurt Vonnegut. Osa Johnson became a particular favorite of Kodak's George Eastman, who visited the Johnsons at their safari headquarters in Africa, as did England's Prince of Wales. Margaret Mead was known to famous people in the film world. She has been memorialized in The American Museum of Natural History by many professions all over the world through the museum's annual Margaret Mead Film Festival. Helen Levitt may have noticed that James Agee's name sometimes was listed before hers in reviews of her now classic documentary film, *In the Street*, but their long friendship was much more important to her than any credits or reviews.

Any number of critics agreed with Helen Van Dongen that her strengths as a film and sound editor had covered up many of Robert Flaherty's weaknesses in his last two films. Only Lee Burgess left few traces of her career in film, but Leo Hurwitz remembered her as bright and energetic in her days at Frontier Films many decades earlier. Not every colleague was pleased to see these women become filmmakers on their own. Their full stories are not likely ever to be known, but scholarly attention eventually will reveal much more about them than is known right now. What we do know, and can say for sure, is that they loved film and the lives they led as documentary filmmakers.

CECILE STARR

Biography: Erica Anderson

Born in Vienna, Austria, August 8, 1914. After high school, worked as assistant to portrait photographer while attending photography school at night. Worked in art gallery in London, 1936–1940. Brief marriage to Dr. Lawrence Anderson, 1940. Came to New York and studied motion picture photography at the New York School of Photography, 1940. Became American citizen, 1945. Worked freelance for United Specialists, Inc., Hartley Productions and others as camera operator, researcher, writer, editor, director, 1940–1947. Chief filmmaker of art films for Falcon Films, 1947–1950. Academy Award nomination for best short documentary for *Grandma Moses*, 1950. Academy Award for best feature-length documentary for *Albert Schweitzer*, 1957. (Both films were made in collaboration with artist/filmmaker Jerome Hill.) Founded The Albert Schweitzer Friendship House in Great Barrington, Massachusetts, 1966. Died in Great Barrington, Massachusetts, September 1976.

Selected Films

1947 *Henry Moore*
1948 *French Tapestries Visit America*
1950 *Grandma Moses*: co-director with Jerome Hill
1957 *Albert Schweitzer* (co-director with Jerome Hill)
1958 *No Man Is a Stranger*
1965 *The Living Work of Albert Schweitzer*

Biography: Lee Burgess

Nothing is known about Margaret Lee Burgess's early life. Graduated from Bryn Mawr College, Bryn Mawr, Pennsylvania, 1930. Married photographer/poet Sheldon Dick, 1933. Unpaid assistant on various projects for Frontier Films in New York City and on *The City* (Van Dyke and Steiner), mid- to late 1930s. Produced and directed *The School* for her own company, Lee Dick, Inc., 1939. Cofounder with Mary Losey of Association of Documentary Film Producers, 1939. Produced and directed *Day After Day* for a second company she headed, 1940. Co-produced and directed sound track for *Men and Dust*, photographed, co-produced, and co-directed by Sheldon Dick, 1940. Married writer/producer Frank Beckwith after divorce from Sheldon Dick, 1945. Worked as editor for

Willard Pictures for many years; also directed a series of films on nursing and a State Department film called *Rural Nursing.* None of the films Burgess directed is known to exist. Died in Florida, 1970.

Selected Films

1939 *School*: producer
1940 *Men and Dust*: co-producer (with Seldon Dick, sound director)
1940 *Day After Day*: producer

Biography: Frances Hubbard Flaherty

Born in Cambridge, Massachusetts, December 5, 1883. Graduated from Bryn Mawr College in 1905. Engaged to Robert Flaherty in 1908, married in 1914. Three daughters: Barbara, born 1916; Frances, born 1917; Monica, born 1920. Collaborated with Robert Flaherty in the making of the films for which he is best known, 1923–1948. After Robert's death in 1951, Frances founded the Robert J. Flaherty Foundation to honor his memory and his works. Organized and directed (with help from Robert's brother, David) the first Flaherty Seminar held at the Flaherty farm in Vermont, to disseminate what she called "the Flaherty way" of non-preconceived filmmaking, 1955. Remained an important attraction at the Seminars throughout her life, although less and less attention was paid to her, as she grew older and as younger men (notably Willard Van Dyke and Erik Barnouw) took over the Seminars under auspice of the nonprofit International Film Seminars, Inc., 1960 onwards. Died in Dummerston, Vermont, June 22, 1972.

Selected Films

1925 *Moana of the South Seas*: collaborator
1934 *Man of Aran*: collaborator
1948 *Louisiana Story*: collaborator

Biography: Helen Grayson

Born in Philadelphia, Pennsylvania, October 31, 1902. Privately tutored in France where she lived with her artist father, her mother, and her younger brother, 1905–1919. Graduated from Bryn Mawr College (Pennsylvania) in 1926. Studied acting and designed clothes and costumes for the theater and for artist friends, leading to close associations with actress Maria Ouspenskaya, scholar Jay Leyda, and filmmaker Irving Jacoby, from late 1920s to early 1940s. Assistant film editor to John Ferno at the Office of War Information (OWI) Overseas Branch, 1943. Special consultant on OWI's Salute to France, 1943. Director of two Owl productions, and six or more freelance documentaries, 1945–1953. Member of the Screen Directors Guild in New York City, 1946–1962. Unofficial goodwill ambassador, selecting and promoting American films for festivals in France and the United Kingdom, 1955–1959. Died in New York City, May 5, 1962.

Selected Films

1945 *The Cummington Story Starting Line*
1947 *Bryn Mawr College*

1947 *The House in Sea Cliff*
1948 *Wings to Hawaii*
1951 *The New World*
1953 *To Freedom*

Biography: Osa (Leighty) Johnson

Born in Chanute, Kansas, March 14, 1894. Eloped at age 16 with Martin Johnson, ten years her senior, 1910. Toured the United States, Canada, and London, England, singing on stage in a fake Hawaiian costume, while Martin showed silent movies and still photographs taken on his earlier expedition to the South Seas with Jack London, 1910–1917. Expedition to the Solomon Islands and New Hebrides, followed by release of their first film, *Cannibals of the South Seas*, 1917–1918. First of many expeditions to Africa, resulting in a series of popular motion pictures widely praised for their spectacular animal sequences but condemned for their ridicule of the native people, 1923–1935. Honorary New York's Explorers Club, 1923. Flight over membership for Osa in Africa from Cape Town to Kenya in their newly acquired airplanes, Osa's Ark and The Spirit of Africa, 1933. Return to the South Seas, 1935–1936. Martin killed in California plane crash; Osa seriously hurt, but survived, 1937. Release of Columbia Pictures' *I Married Adventure* (based on her best-selling ghostwritten book of that name), in which Osa played herself, 1940. Honorary Doctor of Science degree from Rollins College in Florida, 1940. Second marriage to business manager Clark Getts, 1941; divorce 1941. Died in New York City, January 7, 1953.

Selected Films

(collaborator, with husband Martin Johnson)
1918 *Cannibals of the South Seas*
1923 *Trailing African Wild Animals*
1928 *Simba*
1932 *Congorilla*
1935 *Baboona*
1937 *Borneo*
1940 *I Married Adventure*, produced by Columbia pictures using extensive Johnson footage (Martin and Osa Johnson Safari Museum, Chanute, Kansas) opened 1961

Biography: Helen Levitt

Born in Brooklyn, New York. First still photography exhibition at New York's Museum of Modern Art, 1943. Assistant film editor at the Office of Inter-American Affairs, 1943. Producer-editor of stock footage film, *Here Is China*, 1943. Assistant film editor at the Office of War Information Overseas Branch in New York City, 1944–1945. Filming movie footage in East Harlem with friends Janice Loeb and James Agee, 1945–1946. Co-producer (with Janice Loeb) and some camera work on *The Quiet One*, 1946–1947. Awards for *The Quiet One* at film festivals in Edinburgh and Venice, 1948. Producer, *Steps of Age*, for Mental Health Film Board, 1951. Editor, *In The Street* (using footage she shot earlier with Loeb and Agee), 1952. Director, *Another Light*, for U.S. Public Health Service, 1953. Honorary Doctor of Fine Arts degree from Pratt Institute, Brooklyn, New York, 1995.

Selected Films

1945 *In the Street*: co-photographer
1952 *In the Street*: editor

Biography: Margaret Mead

Born in Philadelphia, Pennsylvania, December 16, 1901. Graduated from Barnard College in New York City, in 1923. Received M.A. (1924) and Ph.D. degree in anthropology (1929) from Columbia University, under the guidance of Franz Boas and Ruth Benedict. Married three times: to Luther Cressman (1923, divorced 1926), to Reo Fortune (1928, divorced 1935), to Gregory Bateson (1935, divorced 1943). Fieldwork in Taue, American Samoa, 1925–1926, resulting publication of her book, *Coming of Age in Samoa*, 1928. Assistant curator of ethnology at the American Museum of Natural History, 1926–1942; associate curator, 1942–1969; curator emeritus, 1969–1978. Fieldwork in Bali and New Guinea, in collaboration with Gregory Bateson, her third husband, who took some 22,000 feet of 16mm film, plus 25,000 still pictures, 1936–1938. Filming of birth of Mary Catherine Bateson, Mead's only child, and of the succeeding stages of her infancy and childhood, 1939 onwards. Editing and release of the Bali and New Guinea films, using Mead's detailed notes as guides for scripts and commentaries, 1950–1954. Return trip to New Guinea to make *Margaret Mead's New Guinea Journal* with producer Craig Gilbert for public television, 1967. Hosted, narrated, and consulted on so many documentaries and television programs that one of her younger colleagues nicknamed her "Margaret Media." Died November 15, 1978.

Selected Films (with Gregory Bateson, filmed 1936–1938; edited and released 1950–1954)

Karba's First Year
Dance and Trance in Bali
The Balinese Family
First Days in the Life of a New Guinea Baby Childhood Rivalry in Bali and New Guinea Bathing Babies in Three Cultures

Biography: Helen Van Dongen

Born in Amsterdam, January 5, 1909. Assisted Joris Ivens on his earliest films, 1928–1931. Studied and observed at studios in Berlin and Paris and at The Academy of Cinematography in Moscow, 1930–1934. In America, edited films directed by Ivens and by Robert Flaherty, 1937–1942. Abortive projects as editor for the Office of Inter-American Affairs and for the Netherland East Indies Film Commission, 1940–1943. Producer and editor of compilation films for Artkino and for The Office of War Information Overseas Branch, 1943–1945. Associate producer and supervising editor of Flaherty's

last film, *Louisiana Story*. Producer, director, and editor of *Human Rights* for the United Nations, 1950. Married Kenneth Durant, and retired from filmmaking, 1951. Author of numerous articles on her work with Flaherty, especially on *Louisiana Story,* 1951 onward. Died in Vermont.

Selected Films

1928 *The Bridge* (Ivens): general assistant
1930 *Zuiderzee* (Ivens), camera assistant: editor
1934 *Daily Life* (Richter): editor
1937 *The Spanish Earth* (Ivens): editor
1939 *The 400 Million* (Ivens): editor
1940 *Power and the Land* (Ivens): editor
1941 *The Land* (Flaherty): editor
1942 *Russians at War*: producer, editor
1948 *Louisiana Story* (Flaherty): associate producer, supervising editor

Further Reading

Anderson, Erica, *Albert Schweitzer's Gift of Friendship*, New York: Harper & Row, 1964.
Barnouw, Erik, *Documentary, A History of the Non-Fiction Film*, New York: Oxford University Press, 1974.
Flaherty, Frances Hubbard, "The Bryn Mawr Film," in *Bryn Mawr Alumnae Bulletin*, April 1948, 12.
———, "The Flaherty Way," in *The Saturday Review*, September 13, 1952, 50–52.
Grieco, D. Marie, *Frances Hubbard Flaherty, A True Seer*, New York: International Film Seminars, 1972.
Griffith, Richard, *The World of Robert Flaherty*, New York: Duell, Sloan and Parce, 1953.
Howard, Jane, *Margaret Mead, A Life*, New York; Simon and Schuster, 1984.
Imperator, Pascal James, and Eleanor M., *They Married Adventure*, Rutgers: Rutgers University Press, 1992. (Subtitled, *The Wandering Lives of Martin and Osa Johnson*).
Jacknis, I., "Margaret Mead and Gregory Bateson in Bali: Their Use of Photography and Film," in *Cultural Anthropology* 3, 1988, 160–177, cited in Bowman-Kruhon, Mary, *Margaret Mead, A Biography*, Westport and London: Greenwood Press, 2003.
Johnson, Martin, "In Borneo with the Martin Johnsons," in *Natural History*, 39, 1937, 3–18.
Johnson, Osa, *I Married Adventure*, Garden City: Garden City Publishing, 1940. (Subtitled, *The Lives and Adventures of Martin and Osa Johnson*).
———, *Four Years in Paradise*, Philadelphia and New York: J.B. Lippincott, 1941.
Kelman, Ken, "The Quintessential Documentary," in *The Essential Cinema: Essays on the Films in the Collection of Anthology*.
Leacock, Ricky, "Remembering Frances Flaherty," in *Film Comment*, November–December, 1973, 30.
Melton, Hollis, "Frances Flaherty: Hidden and Seeking," in *Film Library Quarterly*, 48–49.
Nornes, Abe Mark, "Interview with Helen van Dongen," in *Doc Box*, 17, 2–14.
Rotha, Paul, *Robert J. Flaherty: A Biography*, Jay Ruby (ed.), Philadelphia: University of Pennsylvania Press, 1983.

Starr, Cecile, "Helen Grayson, Documentary Film Director," in *Sightlines*, Summer 1976.
———, "Forgotten Trailblazer, Documentarian Erica Anderson," in *Sightlines*, Fall/Winter, 1984–1985.
———, "Women on the Verge," in *International Documentary*, Fall 1990, 15–19.
———, "Distaff Documentarians: Three American Pioneers," in *Documentary*, July/August 1995.

———, "Recollections of Frances Flaherty and the Early Flaherty Seminars," in *Wide Angle*, 17, 1–4, 1995, 167–172.
A Tribute to Erica Anderson, Reverence No.4, Great Barrington: The Albert Schweitzer Center, December 1981.
Van Dongen, Helen, "Robert Flaherty, 1884-1951," in *Film Quarterly*, Summer 1965, 2–14.

WOODSTOCK: THREE DAYS OF PEACE AND MUSIC

(US, Wadleigh, 1970)

Michael Wadleigh's epic documentary of the three-day Woodstock Music and Art Fair, which took place on August 15–17, 1969 at Max Yasgur's farm outside Woodstock, in upstate New York, represents one of the most vivid accounts of the 1960s American counterculture. The Woodstock Festival built on the success of the International Pop Festival at Monterey, California in June 1967 and the free concert in Hyde Park, London (Stones in the Park) in June 1969, attracting an audience of 400,00 over the three days. Filmed by D. A. Pennebaker as Monterey Pop (1968), the Monterey Festival was the first to bill a plethora of West Coast rock bands such as Country Joe & The Fish, Canned Heat, Jefferson Airplane, and Big Brother & The Holding Company, with The Who and Jimi Hendrix headlining. The Woodstock Festival also concentrated on folk, blues, and rock, featuring many of the bands that played at Monterey, together with Joan Baez, Joe Cocker, Crosby, Stills & Nash, Arlo Guthrie, and Richie Havens, all of whom feature in the film, as well as Ravi Shankar, The Grateful Dead, and The Band, who were not included. The original director's cut of 225 minutes was made from more than 120 hours of footage of the Festival, but edited to 185 minutes for the film's release in 1970. The director's cut has been available since 1994, with eight further segments on the widescreen DVD released by Warner in 2000.

Wadleigh's film won Best Documentary Feature at the Academy Awards in 1971 (as well as being nominated for Editing and Sound awards), and it is treated by many as the best concert film ever made. Shot on 16mm film, Woodstock combines a vivid account of many of the artists and bands that played over the three days, with attention given to the audience (listening, dancing, talking, tripping on drugs, bathing, getting soaked) as well as interviews with the organisers and the reaction of locals. Wadleigh intended to depict the Festival as a contemporary version of *The Canterbury Tales*: a pilgrimage for hippies seeking communal expression of music and love. The film begins with images of the bucolic setting, symbolic of the ideal lifestyle the Festival attempted to embody. In the early scenes the camera cuts between pastoral images and the building of the enormous concert stage, switching from ground-level angles to helicopter-eye views of events. The visual style derives from the editing work of Thelma Schoonmaker and a young Martin Scorsese (whose music documentary of The Band, *The Last Waltz*, 1978, shows the influence of *Woodstock*), particularly the liberal use of split screens that are deployed partly to incorporate extra footage, partly to emphasise the massive scale of the event, and partly to juxtapose images of the crowd, the musicians, and the construction of the stage.

Although individual performances stand out in the film—notably, those of Joan Baez, The Who, and Jimi Hendrix—the gathering of so many people suggests, as Sheila Whiteley argues, that the triumph of the Festival was to engender "participation rather than passivity" in the audience. Given that there was not enough stock to film all the acts, Wadleigh was more interested in documenting antiwar and political songs than ballads. This political edge is most evident when Joan Baez calls for the release of the labor union organiser Joe Hill, with Country Joe McDonald singing the quintessential anti-Vietnam anthem "I-Feel-Like-I'm-Fixin'-to-Die-Rag." Three tracks from Jimi Hendrix's set ("Voodoo Chile," "The Star Spangled Banner," and "Purple Haze") played at 6:30 AM on the Monday, close the film in electrifying fashion.

Although Woodstock is commonly seen as the apotheosis of the counterculture and peace movement, Wadleigh's film also hints at the commercial side of the Festival, as it provided a forum for the promoters and organisers to target the crowds as consumers. The Festival promoters Joel Rosenman and John Roberts make a case for the commercial integrity of the event in *Young Men with Unlimited Capital*, but the fact that the audience was vastly greater than expected meant that it was impossible to control tickets and many avoided paying. Wadleigh's film and the album were part of the $1,500,000 package that offset the $3,400,000 spent on or after the Festival (leaving only a loss of $100,000 a year on). Wadleigh's film does not detail these figures, but does provide glimpses of the tensions between the free festival that Woodstock became

Woodstock, 1970.
[*Courtesy of the Everett Collection*]

and the economics of running the event. This commercial undercurrent affected many of the rock festivals in the late 1960s and early 1970s, particularly the three Isle of Wight Festivals held in August 1968, 1969, and 1970. The documentary *Message to Love: The Isle of White Festival* (Murray Lerner, 1995) conveys the almost complete organisational breakdown of the third Festival in 1970, revealing a discontented audience, many of whom refused to pay the entrance fee. Both documentaries offset the musical exuberance of the bands by exposing some of the logistical problems of running such massive scale events, with muddy roads, congested campsites, lack of adequate facilities, and electrical problems hampering filming. Problems also surfaced in the production of *Woodstock*, most notably when the music producer David Geffen exerted control over the film, arguing that Wadleigh could not use the concert footage of Crosby, Stills & Nash unless he included their version of Joni Mitchell's "Woodstock" as the closing song (a track inspired by the Festival).

MARTIN HALLIWELL

See also **Monterey Pop**

Woodstock (US, Warner Bros, 1970, 216 min). Distributed by Warner Bros. Produced by Bob Maurice. Directed by Michael Wadleigh. Cinematography by Michael Wadleigh, David Myers, Richard Pearce, Don Lenzer, and Al Wertheimer. Music by Joan Baez, Canned Heat, Joe Cocker & The Grease Band, Country Joe McDonald, Country Joe & The Fish, Crosby, Stills & Nash, Arlo Guthrie, Richie Havens, Jimi Hendrix, Jefferson Airplane, Janis Joplin, Santana, John Sebastian, Sha-na-na, Sly & The Family Stone, Ten Years After, and The Who. Editing by Thelma Shoonmaker and Martin

Woodstock, 1970.
[*Courtesy of the Everett Collection*]

Scorsese. Sound direction by Larry Johnson. Filmed at White Lake, Bethel, New York, August 1969.

Further Reading

Hinton, Brian, *Message to Love: The Isle of Wight Festival 1968–1969–1970*, Chessington: Castle Communications, 1995.

Makower, Joel, *Woodstock: The Oral History*, New York: Doubleday, 1989.

Palmer, Robert, *Rock & Roll: An Unruly History*, New York: Harmony Books, 1995.

Rosenman, Joel, *Young Men with Unlimited Capital: The Story of Woodstock*, New York: Harcourt Brace Jovanovich, 1974; Houston, TX: Scriveny Press, 1999.

Santelli, Robert, *Aquarius Rising: The Rock Festival Years*, New York: Dell, 1980.

Spitz, Robert Stephen, *Barefoot in Babylon: The Creation of the Woodstock Music Festival 1969*, New York: Viking, 1979.

Whiteley, Sheila, *Women and Popular Music: Sexuality, Identity and Subjectivity*, London: Routledge, 2000.

Young, Jean, *Woodstock Festival Remembered*, New York: Ballatine Books, 1979.

WOOLCOCK, PENNY

See **When the Dog Bites**

WOOLFE, H. BRUCE

H. Bruce Woolfe entered the British film trade around 1910 and was active in film sales and exhibition. After war service, he registered British Instructional Films (BIF) with a capital of £3,000. The company operated in a former army hut at the old Neptune studios at Elstree and produced distinctive reconstructions of Great War battles. The series commenced with *The Battle of Jutland* (1921), both a critical and commercial success. Other titles appeared across the 1920s and included *Armageddon* (1924), retelling Allenby's campaign in Palestine and made with War Office assistance, *Mons* (1926), and *The Battles of the Coronel and Falkland Islands* (1927) made with ships lent by the Admiralty.

Equally distinctive and popular were the short nature films collectively known as *Secrets of Nature*, a series that commenced in 1922. More than a hundred of these films were produced by the end of the 1920s and worked on by such well-known nature cinematographers as Percy Smith, Oliver Pike, Captain H. A. Gilbert, and Walter Higham. Woolfe increasingly assumed a supervisory role at the company and left the actual filmmaking to producers like Mary Field who had headed the company's Educational Dept. Since its inception in 1925, one of a number of talented young individuals coming into British film from university around that time.

Woolfe's success in factual filmmaking in the 1920s was remarkable. Film production in general in Britain was in crisis and numerous producers of entertainment films were failing. However, British Instructional was kept going, despite the absence of a developed nontheatrical market for documentary films. For one eminent film historian, the intelligent *Secrets of Nature* series "added a small but precious glow to the reputation of British film making" at the moment of its nadir. The battle reconstruction films have faired less well with critics, their overt patriotism often getting in the way of their pedagogical virtues. While admired in the trade and popular press, a contemporary reviewer for the intellectual film journal *Close-Up* dismissed *Mons* as "disappointing from every point of view . . . badly photographed . . . [and] full of the kind of sentimentality that makes one shudder." While preferring *The Battles of the Coronel and Falkland Islands*, the reviewer strongly criticised its view of war as "an elaborate and permissible [boys'] adventure."

The World War I films had increasingly used dramatic reconstruction, and toward the end of the 1920s, British Instructional Films (BIF) turned to fictional features with the first to deal with the Gallipoli campaign. However, *Tell England*, commenced in 1928, was not released until 1931 because of protracted problems for BIF converting to sound. The company was incorporated into the larger British International Pictures around that time and as a consequence was led to work almost exclusively on educational and documentary films. The market for such films was growing steadily with improved demand from schools and other nontheatrical users. Commissions were accepted from numerous clients, such as the British Social Hygiene Council who toured public awareness films on venereal diseases in mobile cinemas. In 1932, BIF in association with the large A.B.C. circuit, launched a series of Saturday morning picture shows for children and so extended its long involvement in educational films for young people and schools. Such films would increasingly become a staple of BIF's production and continued after World War II with a regular programme of what were termed "classroom films." A wildlife series with such individual titles as *Cape Buffaloes* (1947) and *The Dog Family* (1947) harked back to the formative *Secrets of Nature* films of the 1920s.

The factual films of H. Bruce Woolfe were a significant precursor to the Documentary Film Movement in Britain. His productions displayed none of the poetic qualities that informed some of the later acclaimed documentaries but were, alternatively, characterised by a rather functional aesthetic and instrumental purpose. This possibly matched his personality, which has been reported as cautious and humourless, although he was highly regarded for his integrity and achievements. Somewhat out of character, he provided practical support to the Film Society, the haven of intellectual film culture in Britain in the 1920s, and he drew around him some of the bright young talent of the time, notably Anthony Asquith and Mary Field. In the troubled context of British cinema in the 1920s, Woolfe has been assessed as an original contributor to the national film.

ALAN BURTON

See also **British Instructional Films;** *Secrets of Nature*

Biography

Born Harry Bruce Woolfe in Marylebone, London, April 4, 1880. Served in the army during World War I. Founded British Instructional Films in 1919, overseeing important war documentaries and the famed *Secrets of Nature* series. Served on numerous committees and bodies, becoming the first Film Producers' Representative on the Board of Trade Advisory Committee, a member of the Film Production Committee on its formation in 1944, trade member on the Ministry of Education Committee for the Preparation and Production of Visual Aids, honorary president of the Association of Specialised Film Producers, member of the British Film Academy, and represented the Federation of British Industry on the Educational and Cultural Films Commission, which resulted in the formation of the British Film Institute. Became an honorary member of this latter body in 1950 and was made a Commander of the British Empire for his outstanding service to British cinema. Died December 6, 1965 in Brighton, Sussex.

Further Reading

Field, Mary, and Percy Smith, *Secrets of Nature*, London: The Scientific Book Club, 1939.
Kelly, Andrew, *Cinema and the Great War*, London: Routledge, 1997.
Low, Rachael, *The History of the British Film 1918–1929*, London: Allen and Unwin, 1971.
———, *Documentary and Educational Films of the 1930s*, London: Allen and Unwin, 1979.
———, *Films of Comment and Persuasion of the 1930s*, London: Allen and Unwin, 1979.
———, *Film Making in 1930s Britain*, London: Allen and Unwin, 1985.
Paris, Michael, "Enduring Heroes: British Feature Films and the First World War, 1919–1997," in *The First World War and Popular Cinema. 1914 to the Present*, Michael Paris (ed.), Edinburgh: EUP, 1999.

WORKERS LEAVING THE LUMIÈRE FACTORY AND OTHER LUMIÈRE SHORTS

(France, Lumière, 1895)

The technical contributions of the Lumière brothers, Auguste and Louis, to the development of the motion picture have received much deserved recognition in most histories of the cinema. The reputation of the films they produced between 1895 and the turn of the century has fared less well. More than one commentator has dubbed them "primitive cinema" in the most pejorative sense, devoid of any form, artistry, or purpose beyond that of recording movement. Their approach has been likened to that of today's rank amateur with a video camera, eager to record scenery, family life, and action but sadly deficient in terms of cinematic literacy, resulting in fifty-foot home movies running for a minute or less. Theirs, it is charged, was simply the recording of an unadjusted, unmodified reality. Thus it happened that these Frenchmen, with their images of daily life (*actualités*, or unbiased records of observation), unwittingly established that nonfictional genre of the cinema, the documentary, which may be some compensation for the alleged lack of structure in their considerable output.

This unflattering depiction of two artless, naïve pioneers requires revision. A useful starting point is their extraordinarily successful careers as owners of a photographic plate manufacturing business in Lyons, already well established by the time they encountered motion pictures. Like Thomas Alva Edison, they viewed their invention, the *cinématographe,* as a potentially profitable expansion of an existing enterprise. It is surely not accidental that two of their earliest public screenings, in June 1895, of *Disembarcation of Congress Members at Neuville-sur-Saône/ Arrivée des Congressistes à Neuville-sur-Saône* and of the eminent physicist, *Pierre-Jules-César Janssen in Conversation*, were presented within twenty-four hours of their creation, to the subjects of the film. This group was a technically knowledgeable audience of scientists and photographers whose interest, presumably, would be in the practical and financial possibilities of the new medium rather than in the entertainment value of the vaudeville turns of Edison's Kinetoscope, their competitor. In a sense, these *actualités* were publicity projects designed to flatter and impress potential customers with the capabilities of their camera-printer-projector. It is illuminating to note that this movie demonstration, in Lyons, and subsequently at the Brussels Exposition that same summer, was only part of the programme. The remainder was devoted to another of their commercial ventures, Autochromie, a colour photographic process, also designed to reproduce life more realistically. Obeying one of the most important tenets of business, they waited until they had shot a sufficient number of movie items to satisfy demand before staging their much-publicized exhibition in Paris on December 28. Significantly, it opened with what can be regarded as an industrial "commercial" for their centre of production, *Workers Leaving the Lumière Factory/Sortie d'usine*. So many prints had to be made that the original negative wore out, necessitating the shooting of an identically staged version in 1896, the movies first remake! The same business acumen is observable in their initial foray into Russia in May of that same year. The subject, *Coronation of Tsar Nicholas II*, was carefully chosen for its potential appeal to the tens of millions throughout his empire. Its success was not lost on the tsar himself, who ordered the appointment of two movie photographers to film future state occasions. Naturally they used equipment rented from the Lumières.

Of course entrepreneurial skill is not necessarily synonymous with artistic ability. It must be admitted that the sheer volume of titles produced in the first two years—in the many hundreds—include numerous examples of the "unmediated representation of reality" charge levelled at them by critics. This was, perhaps, inevitable given that the Lumières had limited control over their scores of cameramen operating on four continents. Trains enter and leave stations with much of a sameness; what could be interchangeable crowds promenade around race courses from Melbourne to Madrid; and there are multiple episodes of cavalry galloping to and from the camera. That said, we may discern a definite pattern in those items that were the work of the brothers themselves. First, they conform to fundamental narrative conventions, with beginnings, centres, and conclusions. Second, their expertise as still photographers is diligently transferred to the new medium with due attention paid to compositional framing, balance, and perspective. Consider, again, *Workers Leaving the Lumière Factory*. The audience sits, as if in a live theatre facing a proscenium arch, the screen. As the film begins, the two factory doors are closed. Then, continuing the theatrical analogy, they swing open for the camera as if the curtain is being raised. Men and women stream out into the street. Unlike the conventioneers disembarking at Neuville sur Saône, who acknowledge Louis Lumière by smiling or doffing their hats to the camera, these workers are totally oblivious to its objectivity as they move out of range to the left and right, at the same time giving the scene its symmetry. Once all have exited, the left-hand door begins to swing shut. After all movement has stopped, the camera ceases operation signifying the end of the episode. Because it is rooted to the spot throughout, the opening and closing images are virtually identical to the extent that they could be spliced together and the entire incident shown in a never-ending loop.

This concern with beginnings and ends, features usually associated with the narrative mode, is observable in many of their very early works. *Destruction of a Wall/Démolition d'un Mûr* opens with a group of workmen contemplating the task at hand after which one of them applies a winch to the free-standing edifice. While a second labourer delivers a series of blows to weaken the foundation, a third looks on, ready to assist him. The supervisor orders more pressure to be applied by the winch at which point the wall falls over. In a cloud of dust all three labourers begin to smash the debris into smaller pieces. There is a comprehensiveness in this "how to" film that is surely at odds with its categorisation as a formless vignette. Similarly, *Carmaux: Bringing Out the Coke/Carmaux: défournage du coke* is a step-by-step account of dealing with one component of iron production. A long slab of red-hot coke emerges from its oven and is set on by a worker wielding a hose of cold water. Others join him with long metal rods and proceed to prod at the mass to reduce it to useable chunks.

On the negative side, it must be admitted that the Lumières, at least in the earliest years, were prisoners of their own limited technique and technology. A camera that remained rigidly anchored, moving neither to the left nor right, and a magazine's capacity to hold, effectively, no more than one minute's running time of film were singly or in combination responsible for certain shortcomings, not the least of which are inconclusive endings to a number of their films. *Arrival of a Train at the Station/Arrivée d'un train en gare à La Ciotât*, one of the works included in the Paris exhibition, opens with an angle shot of the platform and waiting passengers. An engine, pulling eleven carriages, steams into the foreground and comes to a stop as the doors open and a few disembark. Those waiting prepare to board at which point the film comes to an end. Though we have been privileged to see one step in the process of passenger movement, it would have made for more satisfactory viewing had the process of embarkation been complete, but that would have entailed a running time at least half as long again. The limitation imposed by the amount of film in the camera is more dramatically illustrated in *Boat Leaving the Port/Barque sortant du port*. Two men row an open boat toward the open sea while a third sits in the stern. Their actions are observed from the edge of a breakwater by two women with small children. As the craft passes the jetty, one of the women acknowledges them. Both females then prepare for departure. At this point, a large wave hits the craft, turning it at right angles to its intended direction, and forces it dangerously near the breakwater. Filming ceases at this juncture, and so we are denied what might well have been a dramatic reaction by those spectators to the rowers' plight.

The lack of fluidity imposed by the Lumières' immobile camera is illustrated in what is probably their most famous work from this early period, *The Gardener and the Bad Boy/ L'Arroseur arrosé*. A humorous anecdote, it contains the seeds of what was to become a staple of the silent screen for the next three decades: slapstick comedy. Again careful symmetrical construction of the scene is observable in the opening frames where, left of centre, a gardener is busily watering a flowerbed. A boy enters from the right and steps on the hose located centre. The flow of water stops and the gardener, puzzled at what has happened, turns the nozzle toward his face to investigate. The boy then releases his foot and the water gushes out with so much force that it knocks the gardener's cap from his head. Enraged, he drops the hose and runs after the perpetrator. At this juncture both individuals disappear left of frame, and one wishes the camera would make a slight pan in their direction. Instead, the victim of the prank has to drag the boy into view before administering a spanking, after which the youngster exits right. The story ends as it had begun with the gardener returning to his watering chore. Despite the technical shortcoming, this film lends itself to reflection on at least two levels. It may be regarded as a simple morality tale: Interfere with the work of a diligent labourer and one must pay the consequence, although the spectator can find enjoyment both in the naughty deed and in the miscreant's punishment. As a precursor of silent screen comedy, it embodies a number of classic elements. The participants are mere moving objects, lacking any character trait that might detract from enjoyment of the joke. The gardener is an innocent victim of circumstance; the spanking he administers is a mild one, otherwise the audience would be uneasy. And, in the end, after comic disruption has upset the status quo, moral equilibrium is restored.

The films of the Lumière brothers constitute a milestone in the representation of the real. In the innumerable scenes of life on city streets that predominate in their catalogue listings, we are witnessing a mode of representation first made available in the picture postcard. That, in turn, was made possible with the appearance of high-speed emulsion, as distinct from the collodion wet plate process. The latter had permitted the reproduction of static rural vistas; but the newer one enabled filmmakers to capture the fin de siècle urban landscape in all its unscripted, unpredictable hustle and bustle. The Lumières and their cameramen chose a framing to catch moments of reality, known in outline only, and

filmed them without attempting to manipulate the subjects before their lens. The results, for all the shortcomings, fascinated audiences of the day, and have continued to do so for more than a century.

JAMES M. SKINNER

See also **Lumière Brothers**

Selected Films

The Lumière catalogue lists more than 2,000 entries made by the company between 1895 and 1904 when production ceased. These are accessible to the public only in compilation form. The most complete of these is *The Lumière Brothers' First Films (1895–97/ 1996)*, made in collaboration with the Institut and containing eighty-three titles, with narration by Bernard Tavernier. *The Movies Begin: Volume II, The European Pioneers,* produced by Kino Video and utilizing British Film Institute archival material contains examples personally directed by Louis Lumière. These include, *La Sortie des usines* (1895)/*Exiting the Factory, Démolition d'un mûr* (1895)/*Demolition of a wall, Querelle enfantine* (1895) / *Childish Quarrel, Carmaux, défournage du coke* (1896)/*Carmaux: Drawing out the Coke* and several examples of assistants' work in the U.S. in 1896. Granada Television's *Early Photography: Camera & Moving Pictures, Vol. 8,* includes *L'arroseur arosé* (1895)/*The Gardener and the Bad Boy, Partie d'écarte* (1895) / *Card game, Barque sortant du port* (1895)/*Barque Leaving harbor, Arrivée d'un train à La Ciotât* (1895) / *Arrival of a Train at La Ciotât* and films made abroad, including examples from Russia (*Couronnement du Tsar* (1895)/ *Crowning of Tsar Nicholas II*), Switzerland (*Cortège arabe (1896)/Arab Cortege, Geneva*), Australia and Egypt.

Further Reading

Barsam, Richard M., *Non-Fiction Film: A Critical History*, Bloomington: Indiana University Press, 1963.

Burch, Noel, *Life to these Shadows*, London: BFI, 1990.

Elsaesser, Thomas (ed.), *Early Cinema: Space-Frame-Narrative*, London: BFI, 1990.

Fell, John L. (ed.), *Film Before Griffith*, Berkeley and Los Angeles: University of California Press, 1983.

———, *Film and the Narrative Tradition*, Berkeley and Los Angeles: University of California Press, 1986.

Mitry, Jean, *Histoire du cinema, art et industrie, 1895–1914*, T.1, Paris: Editions Universitaires, 1967.

North, Joseph H., *The Early Development of the Motion Picture, 1887–1900*, New York: Arno, 1973.

Pinèl, Vincent, Lumiere:, *Anthologie du cinéma No. 78*. Supplement to *L'avant-scène cinéma, No. 147*, May, 1974.

Sadoul, Georges, *Louis Lumière*, Paris: Seghers, 1964.

WORKERS' FILM AND PHOTO LEAGUE

The Workers' Film and Photo League (WFPL) is one of the most important instances of radical newsreel production in the history of the United States. In its seven-year lifespan (1930–1937), the organization produced countless newsreels as a response to the conspicuous absence of working class issues in *The March of Times* and other mainstream newsreels. Motivated by the desire to erase this representational deficit, the WFPL sought to situate the production of still and moving images in the thick of the social upheaval that prevailed during the Great Depression. The first chapter of the WFPL was founded in New York, and subsequent chapters eventually surfaced in Detroit, Chicago, and Los Angeles.

The WFPL was one of many cultural ventures that had been nurtured by the *Internationale Arbeiterhilfe* or Workers International Relief (WIR), a worldwide communist relief organization based in Berlin. Established in 1921 with the full support and encouragement of Lenin, the WIR's primary aim was to offer material support to workers in Russia, Germany, Japan, and the United States. Whether the workers were suffering from famine or a strike, the WIR set out to provide essentials such as food and clothing. Eventually the WIR began to supplement its relief efforts with cultural actions. The recognition in the United States that the arts could serve a radicalizing function was manifested in the Workers Laboratory Theatre and the Red Dancers. After mainstream commercial newsreels had consistently demonstrated an aversion to covering protests, deliberations were initiated in New York to consider the feasibility of establishing a workers newsreel production company that would not only cover events that were otherwise ignored by the capitalist press but also represent them from a working-class point of view. On December 11, 1930, the Workers Film and Photo League was formed through an expansion of the preexisting Workers' Camera League, a coalition of leftist photographers. The organization (known as the "Film and Photo League" after 1933) began producing newsreels that covered strikes, rallies, and hunger marches and, in turn, exhibited them in a variety of public spaces (such as union halls and churches).

Early members of the New York-based WFPL who were central to the chapter's operations included Sam Brody, Lester Balog, and Robert Del Duca while later members consisted of Leo Seltzer, Tom Brandon, Leo Hurwitz, David Platt, Jay Leyda, Irving Lerner, and Ralph Steiner (Campbell, 1977). Running the WFPL necessitated a precarious balancing of financial, theoretical, and political issues as well as the coordination of the production, distribution, and exhibition of the newsreels. Additionally, the League organized photo exhibits, sponsored classes on film and photography, published essays (in publications like *Filmfront*), and presented lectures as well as panel discussions. Much of the newsreels were hastily edited and exhibited, but most footage was recycled and arranged into longer documentaries dealing with labor strife and poverty. Examples of films produced by the WFPL include *The Strike Against Starvation* (1931), *Bonus March* (1932), *Hunger 1932* (1933), *Marine* (1934), *Taxi* (1935), *The Birth of New China* (1936), *The Scottsboro Boys* (1937), and *Sheriffed* (1937).

Toward the end of 1934, some members of the League began to feel inhibited by a strict adherence to the newsreel format. Hurwitz, in particular, had expressed his desire to develop an enclave within the League that could be dedicated to the production of "documentary-dramatic revolutionary films." Such films would aim to integrate more traditional forms of narrative into the newsreel. The initiative aroused a great deal of controversy among the League's members. Although the central issues in this debate revolved around finances rather than aesthetics, the rift eventually led to the departure of Hurwitz, Steiner, and Lerner who proceeded to establish a new leftist filmmaking body, "Nykino" (an abbreviation for "New York Kino").

Subsequent to this split, the League came under heavy criticism for failing to produce films that matched the impact of Soviet cinema, as well as for adhering too stringently to the genre of the newsreel. In 1935, the League suffered a near fatal blow when the WIR collapsed in both Germany and Russia. The organization struggled to maintain its operations but eventually, in 1937, it collapsed under financial and bureaucratic strain that was, in part, the result of the League's loss of the WIR support network. In addition, the photographers in the League splintered into their own organization—the Photo League—dedicated exclusively to a socially conscious photography.

An intense pragmatism and urgency wholly informed the production methods of the Workers Film and Photo League during its years of operation. As a result, technical proficiency mattered little. Indicative of this was the League's tendency toward a democratic cinematography in which "anybody who breathed became a cameraman" (quotation from an interview with Leo Seltzer on April 23, 1998). Moreover, the urgency with which these films were shot emerged out of the fact that the films themselves were part of the very movement they sought to record. Many of the camerapeople shot from *within* the marches and rallies. Often the spaces presented in the League's films are characterized by an intimate interiorization, as rallies and marches are depicted from the inside rather than from "objective" long shots. The "average newsreel was two blocks away," but most WFPL cinematographers were "in there" and up close (Seltzer, 1998).

This close relationship between the League and the events it covered is evident at the level of exhibition as well. Presented in civic spaces such as churches and union halls, the films, according to Leo Seltzer, frequently sought to legitimize the actions of their audiences rather than simply teach. Speaking about the audiences, Seltzer himself noted:

> These were people who were already motivated and concerned. . . . Very often we showed these films to pickets who had been on the picket line two days before and now they saw themselves on film. And you have to understand that, in those days, if a thing were projected on the movie screen it must be important. And what they were doing then became important.

(Seltzer, 1998)

STEPHEN CHARBONNEAU

Selected Films

1931 *The Strike Against Starvation* (photographed by Joseph Hudyma, Tom Brandon, Lewis Jacobs)

1931 *Workers' Newsreel—Unemployment Special* (photographed by Robert Del Duca and Leo Seltzer; edited by Leo Seltzer)

1932 *Bonus March* (photographed by Leo Seltzer; edited by Leo Seltzer, Lester Balog)

1933 *Hunger 1932* (photographed by Leo Seltzer, Leo T. Hurwitz, Robert Del Duca, Sam Brody, C.O. Nelson, William Kruck, Irving Lerner, and Alfredo Valente; edited by Leo T. Hurwitz, Robert Del Duca, Leo Seltzer, and Norman Warren)

1934 *Marine* (directed by Edward Kern; photographed by Leo Seltzer and Julian Roffman; edited by Leo Seltzer)

1935 *Taxi* (directed by Nancy Naumburg and James Guy)

1936 *The Birth of New China* (edited by Julian Roffman)

1937 *The Scottsboro Boys* (directed by Leo T. Hurwitz; photographed by Lewis Jacobs, Leo T. Hurwitz, and Leo Seltzer; edited by Leo T. Hurwitz)

1937 *Sheriffed* (directed by Nancy Naumburg and James Guy; photographed by Nancy Naumburg)

Further Reading

Alexander, William, *Film on the Left: American Documentary from 1931 to 1942*, Princeton: Princeton University Press, 1981.

Barnouw, Erik, *Documentary: A History of the Non-Fiction Film*, Oxford: Oxford University Press, 1993.

Campbell, Russell, "Introduction/Film and Photo League/Radical Cinema in the 30s," in *Jump Cut*, 14, 1977, 23–25.

——, *Cinema Strikes Back: Radical Filmmaking in the United States, 1930–1942*, Ann Arbor, MI: UMI Research Press, 1982.

Hurwitz, Leo T., "One Man's Voyage: Ideas and Films in the 1930s," in *Cinema Journal*, 15, Fall, 1975, 1–15.

Stott, William, *Documentary Expression and Thirties America*, New York: Oxford University, 1974.

Sweet, Fred, Eugen Rosow, and Allan Francovich, "Pioneers: An Interview with Tom Brandon," in *Film Quarterly*, 27, Fall, 1973, 12–24.

Waugh, Thomas (ed.), *Show Us Life: Toward a History and Aesthetics of the Committed Documentary*, London: The Scarecrow Press, Inc., 1984.

WORKERS' FILM ASSOCIATION

The Workers' Film Association (WFA) was formed in Britain in the autumn of 1938 to provide a film service for the three democratic labour organisations: the Labour Party, the trades unions, and the Co-operative Movement. Of these groups only Co-operators had a tradition of cinema propaganda, having used film for nearly four decades in educational and publicity work. The initial stimulus to the formation of the association was the film activity of the National

Association of Co-operative Education Committees (NACECS), an "unofficial" body in the Co-operative Movement that had developed a network of film societies to distribute and exhibit progressive films to members and workers. The guiding force of the cinema work at the NACECS was Joseph Reeves, who had first come to support film propaganda as education secretary at the Royal Arsenal Co-operative Society (RACS) in southeast London. The success of the NACECS film society was enough to bring the formerly tentative Labour Party and the Trades Union Congress into the new Association, but the official Co-operative Movement, most significantly in the form of the influential Co-operative Union and the Co-operative Wholesale Society (CWS), refused to commit to it. The powerful CWS already had a substantial investment in publicity film work and saw no need to divert resources elsewhere, but the Co-operative Union had long been annoyed by what it considered to be a usurpation of its responsibilities in the field of cooperative education by the NACECS.

Reeves assumed the post of Secretary-Organiser of the new Workers' Film Association in November 1938 and immediately set about making the labour movement "film conscious." Initially, he built on the groundwork of the National Co-operative Film Society and extended the network of 16mm film exhibition out into the broader labour movement. More important, he brought into the orbit of the WFA a scheme he had formerly developed among the London cooperative societies to fund a programme of film production. In 1937, the combined London societies had agreed to a "Five Year Film Plan" of labour films. These were to be budgeted at a substantial £1,000 each, and commenced with *Advance Democracy* (1938), a film promoting the Popular Front against fascism. The series was extended the following year with *The Voice of the People* (1939), whose general treatment of "the struggles of the workers to obtain their present important place in the state" was reflective of Reeves's intention to embrace the broader labour movement in film propaganda work. Both films were innovative in their blending of documentary and dramatic reconstruction and achieved a polish rare for worker's films in the period.

The Five Year Film Plan was halted by the outbreak of war in September 1939 and Reeves's ambitions for the WFA were seriously affected. At a trade union conference in 1938, in an attempt to stimulate film production, he had encouraged delegates to "provide an annual film appropriation for the purpose of producing documentary films on

subjects of interest to their members." However, the Association attracted only modest commissions, such as those from the Amalgamated Union of Building Trade Workers, the National Society of Operative Printers and Assistants, the children's organisation the Woodcraft Folk, and Reeves's former society, RACS.

Although Reeves was lost for a period to the Ministry of Information, he and his small team were able to keep the Association going. Its main activity was in film distribution and a library of progressive documentary films was maintained and developed throughout the war years. Principal among these were Soviet films, for which the WFA had exclusive distribution rights for the substandard 16mm format, as well as British documentaries promoting social reconstruction. Where possible film shows were organised thematically, so users were offered programmes reflective of Educational Advance, Housing and Town Planning, and the Nation's Health. In this respect, the WFA was part of that pronounced war time trend for social change and encapsulated in the democratic epithet of "the people's war." Its film schools attracted sympathetic speakers from the commercial film industry such as Michael Balcon, Bernard Miles, Basil Dearden, and Roy Boulting, as well as labour people such as George Elvin of the film workers' trade union and Joe Reeves.

Gradually, the official Co-operative bodies were drawn into the work of the WFA, with only the Co-operative Union remaining intransigent throughout the war period. The CWS had relented in the winter of 1941–1942, and its newly formed film unit assumed responsibility for production on the standard 35mm gauge, while the film unit of the London Co-operative Society handled commissions for the Association on the substandard format. In view of the circumstances, only a few films were produced, and these were entirely for cooperative bodies. The most significant of these was *Two Good Fairies* (1943) for the Scottish Co-operative Wholesale Society, a film promoting the recently published *Beveridge Report* and its aims for postwar social insurance.

In the summer of 1945, Britain elected its first ever majority Labour Government. The war had substantially altered the social outlook of voters and "never again" did they want to return to the harsh realities endured by many in the interwar years. During the election the WFA provided numerous meetings with public address equipment, enabling Labour candidates to get across their message more effectively. Of importance, throughout the war years the Association distributed and exhibited thousands of progressive documentary films and promoted advanced discussion of "peace aims" at a time when the official attitude was to be vague about the postwar world and to concentrate attention on winning the war. In 1946, the National Film Association replaced the WFA, but this group also struggled to bring labour and trades union groups to film work. It was disbanded in 1953.

ALAN BURTON

See also **Balcon, Michael; Boulting, Roy; Reeves, Joseph**

Further Reading

Burton, Alan, "Projecting the New Jerusalem: The Workers' Film Association, 1938–1946," in Pat Kirkham and David Thoms, *War Culture. Social Change and Changing Experience in World War Two*, London: Lawrence and Wishart, 1995.

———, *The British Consumer Co-operative Movement and Film, 1890s–1960s*, Manchester: MUP, 2005.

Hogenkamp, Bert, *Deadly Parallels: Film and the Left in Britain 1929–1939*, London: Lawrence and Wishart, 1986.

Jones, Stephen G., *The British Labour Movement and Film, 1918–1939*, London: RKP, 1987.

WORLD AT WAR, THE

(UK, Thames Television, 1974–1975)

The World at War is one of the most ambitious and comprehensive documentaries on World War II. It consists of a series of twenty-six episodes, each lasting almost one hour, produced by Jeremy Isaacs for Thames Television. The first episode, "A New Germany," was broadcasted on BBC on October 31, 1973. Three years later, six new episodes were added, for a total running time of almost thirty-two hours. Broadcast in many countries around the world, *The World at War* won several awards, including an International Emmy and the George Polk Memorial Award. It is regularly used as an educational aid in British secondary schools.

The team that produced the programme included fourteen writers and ten producers, with Dr. Noble Frankland DFC as Chief Historical Adviser. The popular voice of Sir Laurence Olivier provided continuity to the firsts twenty-six episodes. Work on the documentary began in 1971, with research carried out in the archives of many countries. *The World at War* presents excerpts from an array of original audiovisual materials, including newsreels, original raw rushes from war cameramen, filmed testimonies and interviews, propaganda films, photographs taken by soldiers on the battlefront, and fragments of radio transmissions, documentaries, songs, and music from the war years. The final result is a montage of thousands of images and clips, which convey the chronological progression of the events, as well as give account of a multiplicity of points of view. Despite this sweeping kaleidoscope of materials, the documentary presents a strong narrative continuity, being divided into episodes that are coherent both in spatial and chronological terms. *The World at War*, which is clearly aimed at eliciting the empathy of the spectator, includes many testimonies that intertwine with and comment on the original documents. There is no academic commentary; much space is given instead to interviews, including with ordinary people, veterans, and survivors. Among the better-known interviewees are Karl Wolff (Himmler's adjutant); Traudi Junge (Hitler's secretary); John Colville (Parliamentary Private Secretary to Winston Churchill); and actor James Stewart, former USAAF bomber pilot.

The original twenty-six-episode series opens with "A new Germany," dedicated to Hitler's rise to power in Germany; this is followed by twenty-four episodes that give account of the involvement of the various countries in the war and analyze the most important battles. The last episode, "Remember," is entirely devoted to the testimonies of survivors and to official celebrations and yearly gatherings of veterans. The structure of the programme is partly reminiscent of Frank Capra's series of films, *Why We Fight*.

The organization of each episode is similar: an analysis of the domestic political situation and of the foreign agenda of each country is followed by a study of the military tactics and of the reality of the war front. Attention is always devoted to the preparations for war, both in terms of the protection of civilians (construction of bunkers, distribution of gas masks) and in terms of the race to arms and to technological innovations in weaponry. The breaking of the war into the daily life of the various cities targeted by air raids is documented, as well as the international reactions to the bombings.

The various episodes are connected through the use of animation maps and of contemporary images of the sites of the great battles. Images of the two fronts alternate, in the attempt to recreate the battle step-by-step; the involvement of the spectator is encouraged by a series of questions and answers: What will be the right move? Why did the Maginot Line not hold? The advancements of the troops are recreated by a forward movement of the camera, conveying a subjective vision. Spectators are invited to being entirely involved in the flow of images and music; rarely are they informed about their sources. Oliver's persuasive voice is simultaneously the strong and the weak point of the documentary. Because it is easily recognisable, it functions as a real bond between the different episodes; on the other hand, the actor's at times subdued, at times emphatic tones seek to elicit the audience's emotional response, almost undervaluing the force of the images.

After the first few episodes, which follow a predominately chronological development ending with the entrance of the United States in the war, *The World at War* presents a series of episodes devoted to the great battles and to the crucial moments of the war. We travel to Africa with "Desert—The War in North Africa"; to Russia with "Stalingrad" and "Red Star—The Soviet Union"; to Italy for the march of the Allies with "Tough Old Gut"; and to Asia for the British defeat with "It's a Lovely Day Tomorrow." Special episodes are devoted to the atomic catastrophe ("The Bomb") and to the holocaust ("Genocide"). "Britain Alone" is devoted to the situation in Great Britain after the capitulation of France and before the American intervention, to the heroic resistance to the Nazi air raids, to the preparation of the cities and coastal lines against the feared German landing. In line with documentary films such as *Listen to Britain* (Jeggins, 1942), "Britain Alone" places emphasis on the characteristic British understatement and reserve: We see the population carrying out the normal working activities in a London destroyed by the bombs. Many of the episodes devoted to Britain, in fact, look like the products of the Crown Film Unit. The most spectacular and dramatic episode is doubtlessly "Morning," devoted to the D-Day invasion. It presents a succession of sequences from the two fronts, in which the preparations of the German defence alternate with those for the American landing. We are shown the training of the American soldiers, the generals' speeches, the long preparations, and the departure for Normandy. The landing is shot with a subjective camera, and we are not spared the most gruesome images of the dead and injured on the Omaha beach.

The six episodes added in 1976—"Secretary to Hitler," "Who Won World War II?" "Warrior," "Hitler's Germany," "The Two Deaths of Adolf Hitler," and "The Final Solution—Auschwitz" are a sort of appendix to the documentary. They further examine some of the topics of the previous series, and in particular Nazism, the concentration camps, and the figure of Hitler. "Hitler's Germany" investigates the German history before the material covered by the first series, including the Weimar Republic and the ascent of Hitler to power. The last six episodes are no longer narrated by Laurence Olivier, but by Eric Porter. Among the new episodes, "Warrior" is an examination of the memories of veterans of all factions focusing on their traumas and problems, somehow suggesting the communal destiny of all the fighters of World War II.

STEFANO BASCHIERA

See also **Thames Television**

The World at War (UK, Thames Television, 1973–1976, almost 32 hours). Distributed by Thames Television. Series Producer: Jeremy Isaacs. Unit Production Manager: Liz Sutherland. Writers: Laurence Thompson, Peter Batty, Jerome Kuehl, JPW Mallalieu, Neal Ascherson, Charles Douglas-Home, David Wheeler, John Williams, Angus Calder, Charles Bloomberg, Stuart Hood, Courtney Browne, David Elstein, and Jeremy Isaacs. Producers: David Elstein, Peter Batty, Ted Childs, Martin Smith, Ben Shephard, John Pett, Phillip Whitehead, Michael Darlow, Hugh Raggett, and Jermome Kuehl. Chief Historical Adviser: Dr. Noble Frankland DFC. Music: Carl Davis. Narrated by Sir Laurence Olivier and Eric Porter.

WORLD IN ACTION

(Canada, NFB of Canada, 1941–1953)

Shortly after it was founded, and with the outbreak of World War II, the National Film Board of Canada began two monthly theatrical series of twenty-minute news magazines modeled on the highly successful American *The March of Time*. The first was *Canada Carries On*, intended to depict Canada's part in the war to its own people and to others. It was produced by Stuart Legg, veteran English documentarian whom John Grierson, head of the NFB, had brought over to assist in the work of the new institution. Once the first series was underway (the first issue was April 1940), Legg began to develop the second, *The World in Action* (*WIA*), which became his project. With some exceptions he wrote and directed every issue. United Artists distributed the series.

This Is Blitz (January 1942) was the first of the *WIA*. It used captured newsreel footage to reveal the devastation German aggression had caused. The second part dealt with Allied counter-strategy. Many of the issues concerned noncombative but important wartime topics. Its treatment of economic/social/political issues became one of its special distinctions. *Food—Weapon of Conquest* (March 1942) was the second *WIA* release. *Time* magazine called it "a blueprint of how to make an involved, dull, major aspect of World War II understandable and acceptable to moviegoers." *Inside Fighting Russia* (April 1942) was composed mostly of footage obtained from the Soviets. As the Russians tended to be secretive, this represented quite a coup. *War for Men's Minds* (June 1943) concerned psychological warfare. The most ambitious and intellectual of the *WIA* films, it was also the first of the Canadian films to look ahead to peace.

The two series were noteworthy for their departures from usual wartime propaganda strategy; they contain little hatred or violence. There are two recurrent emphases. One is that we Canadians are doing our part (in a distinctive Canadian way). The other is that Canada is an important part of the world. These themes would seem to follow from Canada's uncertainty about its national character and its sense of geographical isolation, from its newness as a nation and lack of recognition as a world power. The divisive issue of differences between French-speaking Canada (which did not fully support the war) and English-speaking Canada (which did) was avoided.

World in Action emphasis shifted from matters of immediate wartime concerns to those that would concern the postwar world. The international view and steady look ahead to peace were quite exceptional during wartime. Examples of internationalism would be *Labour Front* (October 1943) and especially *Global Air Routes* (April 1944). Grierson took satisfaction in turning the globe upside down, as he put it, in the NFB films: putting Canada at the center rather than the periphery of the world. *When Asia Speaks* (June 1944) was so accurate and farseeing in its analysis that it was still in active nontheatrical distribution long after the war. *Now—The Peace* (May 1945) dealt with the new United Nations organization.

If *Canada Carries On* paid *The March of Time* the compliment of imitation, *World in Action* began to compete with it in the world market, including the United States. By the end of the war *WIA* was reaching a monthly audience of thirty million in twenty-one countries. Although *Canada Carries On* lasted until April 1951 (the same year MOT ended), however, *World in Action* appeared only irregularly after 1946. One can assume that at least part of the reason for this was because Grierson and Legg had left Canada. It remains a memorable achievement in the history of the National Film Board.

JACK C. ELLIS

***See also* Grierson, John; Legg, Stuart; National Film Board of Canada**

World in Action (Canada, National Film Board, 1942–1946, 20 min each monthly issue). Distributed by United Artists. Written, produced, and directed by Stuart

Legg. Usual collaborators: assistant editor Tom Daly; music composed by Lucio Agostini; commentary read by Lorne Greene; animated maps by Evelyn Lambart.

Further Reading

Ellis, Jack C., *John Grierson: Life, Contributions, Influence*, Carbondale: Southern Illinois University Press, 2000.

Evans, Gary, *John Grierson and the National Film Board: The Politics of Wartime Propaganda*, Toronto: University of Toronto Press, 1984.

Grierson Project, McGill University, The John, *John Grierson and the NFB*, Toronto: ECW Press, 1984.

Hardy, Forsyth, *John Grierson: A Documentary Biography*, London: Faber and Faber, 1979.

Jones, D.B., *Movies and Memoranda: An Interpretive History of the National Film Board of Canada*, Ottawa: Canadian Film Institute and Deneau Publishers, 1981.

McKay, Marjorie, *History of the National Film Board of Canada*, Montreal: National Film Board, 1964.

Nelson, Joyce, *The Colonized Eye: Rethinking the Grierson Legend*, Toronto: Between the Lines, 1988.

WORLD UNION OF DOCUMENTARY

The World Union of Documentary (WUD) was founded in June 1947 in Brussels. Meeting at the fringe of the glamorous Brussels International Film Festival, a dozen documentary filmmakers discussed the situation of their genre. The group included several notable filmmakers: Joris Ivens, just returned to Europe from Australia; the French scientific filmmaker Jean Painlevé; the Belgian Henri Storck; the Czech avant-garde filmmaker and photographer Jiri Lehovec; the future film historian Jerzy Toeplitz from Poland; and a British delegation of John Grierson, Paul Rotha, Ralph Bond, Edgar Anstey, and Basil Wright.

The meeting reflected the confidence that the documentarists had gained during World War II. They were convinced that their film genre had not only made an indispensable contribution to the Allied cause, but an impact too on feature films that were becoming more "realist." They adopted the so-called Brussels declaration, stating confidently that "the documentary film has established itself as a form of film art" and appealed to "the responsibility of every documentary worker to master the technical and artistic potentialities of the documentary so that art and technique are fused with the social purpose of documentary."

The "International Association of Friends of the Documentary Film," founded in April 1946 in Paris by Georges Franju and film archivist Henri Langlois, made way for the WUD. Prague was chosen as the location of the Union's first congress. A preparatory committee was elected. With the financial support of Czechoslovak State Film, the congress was held from July 17 to 21, 1948 in the spa town of Marianske Lazne, coinciding with the international film festival. It was attended by eighteen delegates and six observers, only six of whom had been present in Brussels. The absence of Soviet documentarists was conspicuous, although Michael Romm and Ivan Pyriev, guests of the international film festival, made a brief appearance as observers. The two British delegates, Donald Alexander and Basil Wright, were the only officially elected representatives of a national section. British Documentary, counting more than a hundred members, had been founded after the Brussels meeting with the purpose of representing the interests of British documentary production. The documentary credentials of some delegates were somewhat suspect. Of the two Brazilians Carlos Scliar was a painter and Jorge Amado a writer, while the Belgian Gaston Vernaillen had made a name in political theatre.

Despite increasing international tensions (Communist coup in Prague in February 1948, Stalin's fallout with Tito), few problems of a political nature surfaced at the congress itself. The personalities of Ivens, open-minded and with a sense of humour, and Toeplitz, calm and erudite, helped a great deal. After long deliberations a common definition was agreed upon: "By 'documentary' is meant the business of recording on celluloid any aspects of reality, interpreted either by factual shooting or by sincere and justifiable reconstruction, so as to appeal either to reason for emotion, for the purposes of stimulating the desire for and the widening of human knowledge and understanding, and of truthfully posing problems and their solutions in the sphere of economics, culture and human relations." A constitution was drawn up, laying down that only national sections could join. Elections were held, with each country present having one vote. Elected on the executive committee were Wright (president), Ivens and the Czech Elmar Klos (vice-presidents), Toeplitz (secretary general), and the absent Brazilian Ruy Santos (treasurer). The British delegation offered to organise the next congress in September 1949 to coincide with the Edinburgh Film Festival.

After their return to the United Kingdom, Alexander and Wright submitted an account of their trip to the trade paper *Kinematograph Weekly*. It painted a rosy picture of the health of the nationalised film industries in the Socialist countries. One remark in particular did not go down well with Grierson, now Controller of Films at the Central Office of Information:

> As for official government films, we learned that in most countries the pattern for nationalisation of production was much nearer to our own BBC or National Coal Board than to the Central Office of Information. [. . .] We saw . . . many imaginative and experimental films, which no power on earth could have persuaded some of our more stodgy Government departments to sponsor.

Grierson reacted immediately by sending in a lengthy and provocative retort, stating that creative problems could not be solved by "government dictat" and inferring that Alexander and Wright were dupes of Communist propaganda. At the next meeting of British Documentary in September, an organised opposition, mobilised by Grierson, voiced its objections to the ratification of the WUD constitution and to Warsaw as the location of its headquarters. Although a compromise was reached, it was the beginning of the end for both British Documentary and the WUD.

As WUD president, Wright attended a few executive meetings in Warsaw and Prague, but despite desperate pleas from Toeplitz, he was unable to give shape to the promise of holding the next congress in the United Kingdom. But it was the executive's decision that the WUD would attend the Paris Peace Congress in April 1949 that really closed the door. Wright, not present at the meeting, appealed in vain against adoption of the resolution as "this made it impossible for British Documentary to appeal to the Government and authorities for financial support for the organisation of the congress." The authorities in the West saw the Paris Peace Congress as an ideological litmus test, considering those taking part to side with the "enemy," that is, the Communists. The Dansk Filmforbund then agreed to look into the possibilities of organising the event in Copenhagen. As the Danes had modelled their documentary movement on the British, Copenhagen was considered the next best venue after Edinburgh. A date for the congress was even announced—November 1949, but in the end nothing came of it. By 1950, WUD secretary Toeplitz had no other option but to close the files on the organisation.

BERT HOGENKAMP

See also **Alexander, Donald; Grierson, John; Wright, Basil**

WORLD WAR I

It has been claimed that World War I was the crucible in which modern-style propagandist methods were formed. Although world war demanded global resources, most importantly met by the cinema, methods of mass persuasion began with the first mass medium, the pulpit. With the challenge of print, and the Church's failure to command it, Rome's dominance of Western Europe ended.

During the Boer War, the economist J.A. Hobson argued that the strife had been engendered by a knot of businessmen and politicians, through "the simple device of securing all important avenues of intelligence." Avenues controlled by press barons and purveyors of popular entertainment were unequalled in fostering a "national hysteria" masquerading as patriotism; and Hobson foresaw that it would not be long before vested interests were again "subserved by a war conducted at the expense of the British public." He had no power to avert that; and while some were alerted to the danger of newspaper government, by 1918 press barons Beaverbrook and Northcliffe were controlling virtually all official propaganda. But Hobson's influence shows in that concern to separate Boer War-style jingoism from genuine patriotism. The restrained titling in official wartime films is in line with this, like those measured interventions in the *Bryce Report*, which reassures that horror stories have been carefully sifted by a wise authority.

The adoption of a fairly austere tone was complementary to the extravagance of press and popular entertainment; it was an integrated whole reflecting those interactions of wealth and power, of which Westminster forms but one part. This and other contextual factors are important to any assessment of the effectiveness of wartime documentary. Thus Walter de Marney's "films from the seat of war in Belgium" were accompanied at the Philharmonic Hall in October 1914 by that of Scott's expedition, bespeaking British heroism in another sphere. Marney had been commissioned by the Philharmonic, but an official film might equally well be bracketed by Chaplin and a drama depicting "all the horrors of invasion; women and children murdered and tortured and their houses burnt." Impassioned rhetoric also contributed, as exemplified at the Scala, one of London's largest and most prestigious theatres, which during the war confined itself almost entirely to showing war documentaries. In early 1915, St. John Hamund described "pictures actually taken from the decks of the HMS Invincible during the battle off the Falkland Islands," while on another occasion audiences heard from Lord Derby, whose War Office colleagues had suggested that he supply "the prefatory remarks *needed* for the pictures." In January 1916, Sir J.D. Rees protested in Parliament at the Scala's showing of German documentaries, but was reassured by the Under-Secretary for War that "a lecturer explains exactly what they are. I am informed that he forgets nothing." When the Department of Information sent ten cinemotors around various parts of the country to illustrate what the war really meant, a lecturer accompanied each lorry. It was a two-way process. In 1918, the Ministry of Information supplied films to concretize verbal abstraction, showing "what 'No Man's Land' looks like through the periscope, what a 'barrage' really is, [or] what the earth looks like from a height of 8,000 feet." At the same time "they would lose much of their force and effect without the accompanying 'talk.'" Commentary was widespread enough to draw complaint from the *Saturday Review* in September 1916. This "intervention of lecturers" was impertinent at the screening of films able to "show, without concealment or senti-

mentalism, or loads of adjectives," the British army's extremities of sacrifice and endurance.

Britain, world leader until 1914, had to hand over a discourse refined for more than 40 years, which identified Britain's political ascendancy with moral stature and its enemies as the ungodly. This meant that Britain could easily match German war preparedness in the sphere of propaganda. Although the authorities had long recognized the power and imaginative scope of film (an early 1914 recruiting picture used Royal Flying Corps footage shot "from the airship Beta"), however, opening of hostilities made the War Office wary of a medium that might expose military activity to an enemy or to unwelcome scrutiny at home. (That this worry about public scrutiny was shared by the government shows in the mind-change over release of the 1916 Cabinet films, though even Hepworth's filmed interviews—Asquith fidgeted, Bonar Law exuded confidence, and Lloyd George was at his best— were alleged to have helped in bringing Asquith down.) At the outbreak of hostilities, music-hall tycoons engaged "all the leading film producers to give a constant supply of war films"; but within two months cameramen were banned from the western war zone . Activities at home were likewise restricted: In early 1915, a Tyneside cinema operator, who "took a film of a war vessel," was fined and had the film confiscated. By contrast, the German government sought to integrate film into its war programme from the outset. A neutral wrote to *The Times* in August 1915, setting the extensive coverage on German screens against his experience at one of Britain's largest cinemas: "The only sign of war was that some of your generals were thrown on the screen," and they aroused little interest compared with Chaplin. By the end of 1914, the Copenhagen-based Nordisk Company was given facilities to film German troops in action, although by early 1917, chauvinism had replaced it with a number of frontline film units controlled jointly by German War Ministry and Foreign Office. The results were shown in Turkey, and every neutral country was targeted: Mid-1918 saw a flurry of Foreign Office correspondence over German documentaries in Java.

The United States, however, was the great prize. Seven weeks into war *The Times* reported that "a consignment of German war films depicting the humane perfection of the German military machine" was sent there, and later deplored the demand for these films in the United States. One inducement was that they were being "offered at cost price" (Bioscope). In 1916, Harry Brittain found American cinemas filled with "pictures of the German Army under every conceivable condition of work and play and rest and fight"; yet "nothing worth looking at . . . of our troops." Essanay's publicity chief, Langford Reed, in Cassell's Saturday Journal (October 1916), described how official German film was used at home to assure the public of neutrals' sympathy, and in America to persuade that Zeppelin raids were battering the heart out of London and its inhabitants. At America's entry into the war, the *Weekly Dispatch* attributed her delay largely to the 200 documentaries "shown to America's millions picturing the German Kaiser, his Army, and his people in a kindly light." The Boche, wrote Sefton Delmer in August 1917 (*Times*), appears "now standing with bowed head in some ruined church, and anon feeding a Belgian baby from a bottle." But the "grim realism" of the Möwe film allegedly backfired even with German audiences, who gloomily muttered "*Schrecklich*" as they began to understand the meaning of unrestricted war against merchantmen.

When the French authorized "four large cinematograph firms to send operators to the front" in April 1915, the prime concern was to combat German propaganda in neutral countries. It spurred an arrangement between Britain's War Office and the country's seven leading newsreel and documentary filmmakers, one that lasted until December 1916, when the War Office Cinematograph Committee was established. This WOCC became part of the newly formed Ministry of Information in March 1918. Only two or three cameramen filmed on the western front at any one time, the first two being Geoffrey Malins and Teddy Tong. Malins had been filming the Belgian army in that 1914 phase when anyone with a camera was liable to be shot as a spy. But now, like padres, they wore officers' uniforms, at first without badges of rank but rated as lieutenants, which tied them firmly to the army establishment despite receiving commercial salaries. Considering the danger faced, they were poorly paid, though a pound a day would have seemed a princely sum to the bob-a-day soldier who ran rather graver risks. The first result was six series of shorts released between January and June 1916. January also saw the release of pictures from the Dardanelles taken by newsman Ellis Ashmead-Bartlett. This, the only film shot of the Gallipoli campaign, included the Suvla landing and repulsion of a Turkish trench assault. In contrast, the western front footage was disappointing: "When shall we see real war films?" (*Film Censor*). *Cinema* witheringly dubbed the first installment "a string of photographic platitudes." Press criticism tended to blame censorship and restriction, even

the relatively positive *Times* comparing one batch unfavourably with a German series taken "for the edification of neutral countries."

More promising had been *Britain Prepared*, launched in December 1915 by the Wellington House Cinema Committee. Designed to convey "the message of our national might," it showed munitions-work and shipbuilding, creation of the New Army, and naval sequences with guns in action, which gave the film fresh appeal after Jutland. This was Britain's first feature-length documentary, and although Wellington House never followed it up, it inspired the highly successful Somme film and a further string of feature-length documentaries: *The King Meets His Armies in the Great Advance* (October 1916), *The Battle of the Ancre* and the *Advance of the Tanks, Sons of Our Empire* (released in five weekly parts), and *The German Retreat* and the *Battle of Arras* (all 1917). Both royal and Tanks films had their own appeal, arousing enormous interest in the provinces after opening in more than 80 and 112 Greater London cinemas, respectively. The royal film emphasized a wise and humane leadership, reaffirmed in *The Life of Lloyd George* (1918), which was overtaken by events and never shown. The Tanks film worked differently. If the Italian official film *On the Road to Gorizia* pictured an army battling not only against Austrians but against harsh Alpine conditions, so the Tanks film showed the British bogged down in mud. Theme and aesthetics are beautifully married in a picture of artillery horsemen carrying shells to the gun positions panier-fashion, as the roads are impassable to wheeled traffic. As they move picturesquely along the skyline, a soldier in the foreground, trying to skirt the quagmire they have just paddled through, sinks up to the calf in ooze. Then there were the tanks, scorning mud and other obstacles. Malins and soldier-companions, seeing them for the first time, "were doubled up with mirth [over] the acrobatic antics of this mechanical marvel"; and pictures promised fans that they provided "some of the comic relief in this vivid picture of war." But they also represented hope that at last the deadlock would be broken; and audiences were reported to have "stood up and cheered" at their appearance on screen. Reviewers watched with the eye of faith, one writing: "Preceded by the 'tanks,' which amble over the wire defences, the troops leap forward and waves of men are poured into the German position." More accurately, R.C. Buchanan, presiding at a branch meeting of the Cinematograph Exhibitors' Association, complained that the film was "shorn of every incident of actual warfare." He also noted that, while it had been a big success generally (realizing £35,000 over the first three months), undifferentiated charges meant that this and other "official battle films have resulted in a substantial loss" to small exhibitors "constrained to take them out of patriotism."

Buchanan's complaint registers the WOCC's sense that to follow the Somme film in portraying violence and death would be counterproductive in the 1917 atmosphere of war weariness. From Malins's account of what he shot for the Tanks film, it seems that both the best of the tank footage and that in devastated villages was cut because it included corpses. Despite lacking the tanks novelty, *The German Retreat* was well patronized, although Charles Urban found that it "achieved far greater success in America than in England."

The WOCC next concentrated on newsreel, having taken over the Topical Film Company's *Budget* in May 1917 and acquiring it outright in November. This alarmed the trade, W.G. Barker, deeply involved in actuality film, seeking assurance that the takeover was purely a wartime measure. He need not have worried: state control of industry was relinquished with indecent haste at the Armistice. *Topical Budget* continued central when the Ministry of Information, established in February 1918 under Beaverbrook, assumed responsibility for the bulk of official propaganda. *Budget*'s official status prompted Stoll to screen it at all his music-halls, and facilitated a reciprocal arrangement with the French government to handle *Annales de la Guerre*. But the contribution of Gaumont and Pathé's newsreels remained unabated. Malins had secured some impressive Belgian footage for Gaumont in 1914, and it was also at the forefront in documenting the Russian Revolution. In 1914, Pathé was filming the Russians in action, and the following November *Bioscope* credited it with obtaining the first picture of an actual air raid (Russian bombing of a Turkish coastal town). In March 1917, *Pictures* readers were invited to communicate why they liked *Pathé Gazette*, one writing: "It shows us all the frightfulness of the war and the good morale of the soldiers in these circumstances. The strong and well-armed positions of our Allies which these pictures show give us the assurance of a certain victory." Another reader liked the opportunity for spotting someone she recognized in khaki. This was also catered for by the WOCC's series of regimental shorts, playing to local pride, and pioneered well before the advent of official documentary. A Swansea paper publicized one early 1915 instance, the Carlton Cinema showing *Swansea Troops in Training*, which it had commissioned from the Williamson Kinematograph Company. Pictures of local war heroes often figured, and at a Manchester showing of *With the Empire's Fighters*, made by H.D. Girdwood in early 1915 but not released for over a year, "Private Stringer, Manchester's first native-born V.C., . . . recognised himself in a platoon of Manchesters returning from the trenches through a cornfield." Girdwood's patter alluded to "a man who travelled all the way from London to see the picture of his son, since killed, marching merry and bright, on La Bassée Road in the ranks of a London Territorial Regiment."

The year 1915 had found *The Times* calling for more realism, even for footage of war's "more tragic side." But the Somme film was the only attempt to meet this demand. Thereafter officialdom had returned to playing safe, faced with growing war weariness and working-class resentment at government policies. A *Weekly Dispatch* leader discovered a significant subtext in the Tanks film: Besides astonishing technical developments the film revealed "the sublime chivalry and monumental patience" of Britain's citizen army. Its achievements, "created by the first real unity England has ever known," promised an end to the old class antagonisms. But this ignores the point made in Lawrence Cowen's *It Is for England* (a patriotic novel, which in 1916 spawned a £40,000, ten-reel movie) that capital as well as labour must foot the bill for national unity. One scene had St. George in Parliament, arguing that the blood sacrifice required a corresponding wealth sacrifice, MPs voting away their salaries "with a cheerfulness that would not be quite so pronounced had the incident been real." Topicals could throw 1917 inequalities into relief: "During the last few days there has been shown on practically every cinema screen throughout the country the opening of the Law Courts in London." Many judges, "each in a coach drawn by two stout well-fed horses, that would have been better employed in agricultural pursuits," are each attended by four men looking fit enough for military service. Juxtaposed are pictures "exhorting the poor people to 'eat less bread'" (slogan of Food Controller Lord Devonport, desperate to stave off rationing). Even *The Times* objected that bread was the poor's "staple food"; and the most notable film on the subject, *Everybody's Business*, was vitiated by showing class unanimity in an upstairs-downstairs context. This was one of a number of documentary-flavoured fiction films emerging in 1917–1918 when every state department was competing for the cinema's services. Another, *Motherhood*, written by actor Henry Irving's wife for showing in 1917's Baby Week, sought to appease those resenting their husbands' wartime absence with the prospect of postwar homes fit for heroes.

Another technique was to submerge growing discontent in a revival of Hun-baiting, his image as incendiary and infanticide also serving as disincentive to resuming postwar trade relations. Thus the Ministry of Information short, *Leopard's Spots*, as well as Griffith's *Hearts of the World*, where a newsreel prologue of Griffith filming in the trenches and meeting Lloyd George in Downing Street sought to turn sensational fiction into documentary drama. E. Codd (*Pictures*, July 13, 1918) contrasts the success of Griffith's film with "the hopelessness of bringing this war home to people by a pageant of War's modern Frankensteins, tanks, poison-gas and long-range guns." E.T.H. (*Kinematograph Weekly*, September 27, 1917) likewise reflects the trade's commitment to narrative fiction as the most profitable film mode, identifying documentary's weakness as "lack of human interest and want of cohesion." Narrative coherence had only recently come to dominate the screen, and being an aesthetic bound up with prose fiction, it might have appeared less binding on, perhaps even a disadvantage to, what professed to be nonfiction. But editorial shaping was inescapable, a *Times* reviewer (August 30, 1917) observing that while two minutes' worth of "newly-captured German prisoners on the march" might be cheering, "ten minutes of them become merely stupefying." However, it was difficult to distinguish between creative editing and outright fakery. WOCC claims to authenticity were continually endorsed by the press in contrast to German fabrication. A November 1916 leader in *Screen* noted that, as trickery was inherent in the moviemaking process, scepticism had been aroused over more sensational moments even in the Somme film. The healthiness of such scepticism is affirmed by footage of the 1914 Lord Mayor's Show, which, "by an ingenious change of title," was imposed on Parisians "as the triumphant departure of the British troops from London on their way to the front."

GORDON WILLIAMS

See also **Battle of the Somme**; **Urban, Charles**

Further Reading

Brownlow, Kevin, *The War, the West and the Wilderness*, London: Secker and Warburg, 1979.

Dibbets, Karl, and Bert Hogenkamp, (eds.), *Film and the First World War*, Amsterdam: Amsterdam University Press, 1995.

Hiley, Nicholas P., "'The British Army Film', 'You!' and 'For the Empire': Reconstructed Propaganda Films, 1914–1916", in *Historical Journal of Film, Radio and Television* 5, 1985, 165–182.

Hobson, J.A., *The Psychology of Jingoism*, London: Grant Richards, 1901.

Low, Rachael, *The History of the British Film 1914–1918*, London: Allen and Unwin, 1973.

Malins, Geoffrey, *How I Filmed the War*, rept. London: Imperial War Museum/Nashville: Battery Press, 1993.

McKernan, Luke, *Topical Budget*, London: BFI, 1992.

Musser, Charles, "Film Propaganda and World War I: Images of War in the United States during the First Months of Neutrality," in *Cinéma sans frontières 1896–1918 Images Across Borders*, Roland Cosandey, and François Albera (eds.), Lausanne: Editions Payot/Quebec: Nuit Blanche Editeur, 1995, 261–271.

Reeves, Nicholas, *Official British Film Propaganda During the First World War*, London: Croom Helm, 1986.

Sanders, M. L., "British Film Propaganda in Russia, 1916–1918," in *Historical Journal of Film Radio and Television* 3, 1983, 117–129.

Smither, Roger (ed.), *The Battles of the Somme and Ancre*, London: Imperial War Museum/DD Video, 1993.

Taylor, Philip M., and Kelly Andrew Kelly (eds.), "Britain and the Cinema in the First World War," in special issue of *Historical Journal of Film, Radio and Television*, 13, 2, 1993.

Van Dopperen, Ron, "Shooting the Great War. Albert Dawson and the American Correspondent Film Company, 1914–1918," in *Film History*, 4, 1990, 123–129.

Ward, Larry Wayne, *The Motion Picture Goes to War. The U.S. Government Film Effort during World War I*, Ann Arbor: University of Michigan Research Press, 1985.

WORLD WAR II

World War II (1939–1945), the last major international military conflict before the commercial breakthrough of television, gave newsreels and documentaries a special momentum. Their information appeal was so high that there have probably never been as many cinemas worldwide that showed only newsreels and documentaries as during World War II. The propagandistic importance attached to newsreels and documentaries was high as well, which resulted in vast amounts of money and personnel being invested in their production and distribution. Although each of the warring nations considered film propaganda of great value, probably none dedicated as much attention to the subject as Nazi Germany, where the highest authorities, such as Führer Adolf Hitler and his propaganda minister Joseph Goebbels, were personally involved in the production of many newsreel issues and of some documentaries, such as the infamous *Der ewige Jude/The Wandering Jew* (often mistranslated as *The Eternal Jew*) (1940). The mobilizing power of such documentaries and newsreels, as well as their ability to change attitudes, was and is often overrated. Their history is nevertheless fascinating, for it contributes, among other things, to a better assessment of both the power and limitations of film propaganda (Reeves, 1999) and the dynamic ways in which each of the warring nations tried to inform or influence public opinion. Experiences gained with World War II newsreels and documentaries also influenced the way in which states have since attempted to use audiovisual media for different purposes, from the use of nonfiction films in the reeducation of de-nazified Germany to the installment of "embedded journalists" in the Second Gulf War. World War II documentary and newsreel footage have also found an afterlife in cinema and television documentaries about the military conflict and related subjects such as the Holocaust.

During the first years of World War II, German propaganda minister Joseph Goebbels seized the opportunities offered by the military successes of the German Wehrmacht and started orientating the European film sector toward Berlin. In that process, Goebbels paid particular attention to establishing a German newsreel empire (Vande Winkel, 2004). From the 1933 foundation of his Reich Ministry for Popular Enlightenment and Propaganda (*Reichsministerium für Volksaufklärung und Propaganda*) onwards, Goebbels and his collaborators increasingly strengthened their control over all newsreels produced and screened in Germany. After the 1935 rearmament of the German army and the 1936 occupation of the demilitarized Rhineland, newsreels, like all other German communication media, slowly started to prepare the German nation for the outbreak of war and helped to justify German actions such as the occupation of Sudetenland and the rest of Czechoslovakia. The compulsory showing of a newsreel at every film screening, promulgated in November 1938, underlines the importance attached to newsreel propaganda in that context.

In September 1939, as the German invasion of Poland required tight control over all military press coverage, the four existing German newsreels were "temporarily" (until the final victory had been achieved) merged into one, identical version. The newsreels initially kept their own opening titles but, from June 1940, carried the same title: the *Deutsche Wochenschau* or *German Weekly Newsreel* (DW). A newsreel centre working directly for the German propaganda ministry strictly controlled the German Weekly Newsreel and was eventually transformed into a separate organization: the *Deutsche Wochenschau GmbH* or German Newsreel Company. Although legally speaking the company was a subsidiary of the state-owned Ufa film company, all its members were directly subordinate to the ministry. Goebbels often personally supervised or acted as chief editor of DW issues. Hitler did so, too, until the military situation started to look less and less bright.

The German Newsreel Company not only produced a domestic newsreel that was shown all over the Reich (including annexed territories such as the Grand Duchy of Luxembourg) but also made the *Auslandstonwoche* or *Foreign Weekly Newsreel* (ATW), specifically produced to be screened abroad. The difference between the DW and the ATW is—although historians regularly mistake the latter for a mere foreign version of the former—of crucial importance. Being the only German export newsreel, the ATW played an important role in the propaganda ministry's foreign policies. As a rule, each ATW combined German items with a selection of international subjects. At first only one ATW version was edited, which means that newsreels exported abroad only differed in terms of language. No later than August 1940, but possibly earlier, this one-size-fits-all policy was dropped, and newsreels sent to a particular destination were edited with the specific target audience in mind. From then on, ATW versions distributed in different countries or regions still carried the same serial number, but they often featured different items. These differences became wider and wider as the German Newsreel Company started in autumn 1940 to establish foreign branches: editorial offices that were to produce a customized local ATW version. The distribution of these ATW versions was—wherever possible—carried out by local Ufa subsidiaries. The ATW, which in 1943 was distributed in thirty-six languages, claimed in 1941 to be distributed on nearly 2,000 prints.

The military footage that ended up in the DW and ATW was filmed by cameramen belonging to the so-called propaganda units (*Propaganda-Kompanien*). These units were appointed by the propaganda ministry but operated at the front under the command of the operational headquarters they had been assigned to. It was also the (propaganda service of) the military supreme command that censored the images before handing them over to the ministry of propaganda. The stylistic quality of the battle footage and in particular the feel of reality conveyed by those images, often shot with handheld 35mm Ariflex cameras or even lighter Siemens D 16mm cameras, was praised by friend and foe. German newsreels were also outstandingly well edited and stylistically influenced the newsreels of befriended and neutral nations, as well as of adversaries, such as the British Army Film and Photographic Unit (AFPU), which had ATW issues secretly duped and smuggled to Great Britain (Gladstone, 1987) to improve its own combat filming. The German newsreel editors felt of course free to manipulate the footage at will. In 1943, they did not even refrain from including old footage of the war ship Thor that (unknown to the Allies) had gone lost a year before and pretending (Vande Winkel, 2004) that it was still roaming the seas, hunting for Allied trade vessels.

The activities of the German Newsreel Company, which attempted to present the world with a national-socialist view of the world while taking into account the need for numerous languages and local concerns, formed part of a sophisticated multinational newsreel program, comparable to the ministry's attempt to influence foreign print, press, and radio as much as possible. It must be emphasized that the German Newsreel Company was not always successful in that matter. First, the newsreels, which were obligatory screening in German cinemas as well as in many occupied countries, were received with mixed feelings by cinemagoers. In Germany, the population initially flocked to theaters to see its Wehrmacht conquer Europe. As soon as the tide turned, however, enthusiasm dropped as well. Reports of the secret services leave no doubt that, especially after the debacle of Stalingrad (1934), few Germans people shared positive feelings about the newsreels (and likewise deceptive other media). In the occupied regions, too, German newsreels were met with hostility or indifference and never managed to have long-term influence on the local population.

Further, the arrival of the ATW often caused friction with local authorities or collaborationists. In many Nazi-occupied states, local power groups, both local and German, were eager to obtain control over local propaganda matters themselves and therefore reluctant to give the ATW access to all cinemas, let alone a newsreel monopoly. In the occupied Netherlands, where Reich Commissioner Seyss-Inquart had a propaganda agenda of his own, it took the propaganda ministry until late 1944 to succeed in exercising a newsreel monopoly. In France, where German occupation authorities were cautious not to offend the collaborationist Vichy government too strongly, the ATW was even replaced by another newsreel, in which the German Newsreel Company held only a minority stake. Axis-satellites such as Romania also held on to their national newsreel. In several neutral states (Sweden, Switzerland and, before they were invaded, Belgium and the Netherlands), the ATW also regularly met with official resistance, often resulting in censorship of certain scenes or of complete ATW issues. Germany did its utmost to protest against such measures. In Sweden, the German efforts apparently paid off and resulted in the establishment of an ATW editorial board in Stockholm.

Ironically, Germany was more successful in distributing ATW in neutral states than in gaining access to its main Axis partners, Italy and Japan. The Italian-state newsreel Luce, reportedly the only part of the film program that Benito Mussolini really liked, had been created on behalf of the Duce in 1926 and was shown in every theatre. The Luce Institution and the German Newsreel Company regularly exchanged items but did not allow each other's newsreels on their territories or spheres of influence. Likewise, Japan exchanged items without importing complete ATW issues. German war items, in particular a state-of-the-art report on the audacious airborne taking of Crete, were a major influence (Okumara, 2000) on the photography and editing of the Japanese Nihon Nyūsu newsreel. The latter, which first appeared in June 1940, replaced all four newsreels that previously existed (Daniels, 1981).

Unlike the authoritarian regimes of their foes (Nazi Germany, Japan, and Italy) and (temporary) friend (Soviet-Union), the democratic governments of Great Britain and the United States did not decide to centralize newsreel production and distribution. Obviously, that did not mean that the British and Americans were not concerned with newsreels at all. In Great Britain, newsreels fell, like other communication media, under the competence of the Ministry of Information (MOI). The MOI was initially ill-prepared for its task and caused so much criticism during the first year of its existence that it could never shake off its negative public image. Nevertheless, it worked quite efficiently for most of the war (Chapman, 1998). The MOI made the initial mistake (1939) of censoring newsreels too heavily and not even giving them access to battle footage. This made the homefront think it was being kept in the dark. It also made British newsreels shown in neutral cinemas territory look rather pale in comparison to German newsreels. In the MOI's defense, the lack of adequate combat footage was also due to the armed services' initial lack of proper film units. In the summer of 1940, when the so-called Phony War had come to an end, this was corrected by the establishment of the Army Film Unit, which in October 1941 was restyled into the Army Film and Photographic Unit (AFPU). The MOI became instrumental in supplying the newsreel companies with AFPU footage (as mentioned previously, AFPU cameramen had carefully studied intercepted German newsreels) that had already been censored by the military forces. Newsreels, which were given first priority in the allocation of raw film stock, were, as before the war, produced by private companies (*Gaumont-British News*, *British Movietone*, *British Paramount*, *Universal*, and *Pathé*) and subject to security censorship by the MOI's press and censorship division. The relationship among all parties, largely based on mutual cooperation, was relatively good and resulted in British audiences getting a visual report on the war that, although certainly not always complete or entirely correct, was far closer to the truth than most newsreels produced by other warring parties. Incidentally, this did not make them any more popular with cinema audiences until the closing months of the war (Reeves, 1999).

In the United States (Fielding, 1972), the American entry into the war urged the Department of War to impose a pool-coverage system on the five big civilian newsreel-producing companies: Paramount, Fox Movietone, Warner-Pathé (part of RKO), Universal, and MGM (which distributed a newsreel owned by the Hearst Corporation). Within this system, each newsreel company provided the War Department with two camera teams that were subsequently assigned to several theatres of operation. The images shot by those teams were shared by all the companies, regardless of whose team had actually filmed them. Most of the combat footage that ended up in the newsreels, however, was not filmed by the civilian cameramen, but by members of the United States Signal Corps and by navy cameramen. (Admittedly, many of those had received their training as military combat training man in one of the schools set up by newsreel companies such as Fox Movietone.)

All materials shot by civilian and military cameramen were developed and censored by the War Department (Office of War Information) before being transmitted to all newsreel companies. Censorship was strict, especially in the first years of the war. Newsreel footage of the Japanese attack on Pearl Harbor was for instance only released a year after the event. As a matter of fact, pre-censorship of the military footage, as well as the government monitoring of the newsreel production process, was so tightly coordinated that finalized newsreel issues were not even submitted to formal censorship. This policy, resulting in most "competing" newsreels featuring identical war footage, was carried on until the end of the war. By the end of the war, when dealing with footage that was gruesome but not directly related to American citizens or civilians, the censors were less strict and allowed for instance horrible scenes filmed in the Nazi camps of Dachau and Buchenwald.

The U.S. government did not produce a newsreel of its own for domestic use, but, as the American answer to the German *Auslandstonwoche*, also produced a nonprofit newsreel that was exported to befriended and neutral regions. This *United Newsreel*, established in 1942 by the five commercial majors in association with the American Office of War Information, was reportedly even dropped in German-language versions behind the enemy lines.

In the Soviet Union, newsreel production had in comparison to documentary film been treated in an unfeelingly way since the mid-1920s. After the German invasion, however, newsreel production rapidly expanded. Between June 1941 and September 1945 (Pronay and Spring, 1982), 435 newsreel issues were released on an irregular basis, varying from two or more issues per week (1941), to one per week (1943), to one per fortnight (1945). *Soyuzkinozhurnal/Union Film Journal*, the main journal until mid-1944, was produced by the Central Newsreel Studio (also known as the Union Newsreel Studio), which in mid-1944 became the Central Studio for Documentary Film (also known as the Union Documentary Studio). The organizational changeover resulted from a special statement "on the production of newsreels and documentary films," which the Central Committee of the Communist Party launched in May 1944. The committee criticized newsreels and some documentaries for their lack of ideological educative value and, more important, because they failed to portray the "growing power of technical competence of the Soviet army," which had crossed the Soviet borders and entered into Eastern Europe.

Also as a result of the organizational changes instigated by the committee, the *Union Film Journal* vanished. Its place was, on the one hand, taken by *Special Front Issues*, newsreel-like war reports that per issue dealt with one single phase of campaign, and on the other hand by *Novosti Dyna/News of the Day*, a newsreel that had existed before and did not deal with military events. Although Soviet producers received foreign footage through international exchange (mainly with Great Britain) and sometimes inserted foreign items in their newsreels, most newsreel issues focused entirely on the Soviet Union.

During World War II, Nazi Germany yielded remarkably few full-length documentaries. Their production was by and large outnumbered by the many *Kulturfilme* or documentary shorts that formed an obligatory part of any film screening in the Third Reich. The few feature-length documentaries that were produced, however, belong to the most famous examples of twentieth-century film propaganda and have until recently received far greater scholarly attention (Zimmerman and Hoffmann, 2005). Although often translated as "cultural shorts," Kulturfilme (the term was coined in 1919) did not treat cultural subjects only. On the contrary, their subjects ranged from a variety of cultural or educational areas: biology, medicine, technology, art, literature, ethnology, geography, etc. (Hoffmann, 1996: 1196). Its educational component had been widely accepted since the era of silent cinema, so it was manifestly logical that Nazi propagandists showed an interest in the Kulturfilm. In 1934, it was made obligatory to have every feature film screening accompanied by a Kulturfilm. Four years later, by making the screening of a newsreel also obligatory, the ministry established a compulsory "cinematic trinity" of newsreel, Kulturfilm and feature film that during World War II was enforced on many European countries as well.

During World War II, although (like feature cinema) never entirely orientated toward direct propaganda purposes, the Kultur film sector produced many war-related films. Walter Ruttmann, who started his career as a leftist documentarist but in 1933 quickly adapted to the new regime, directed *Deutsche Panzer/German Tanks* (1940), which celebrated Germany's military strength. Other war-influenced Kulturfilme, some of them produced by the already mentioned German Newsreel Company, were Hans Weidemann's *Soldaten von Morgen/Soldiers of Tomorrow* (1941), Wolf Art's *Rüstungsarbeiter/Armaments Workers* (1943), and Arnold Fanck's *Atlantikwall/Atlantic Wall* (1944).

Mention should also be made of *Im Wald von Katyn / In Katyn Forest* (1943), which put the exhumation of Polish soldiers executed by Soviet forces to use as anti-Soviet horror propaganda. Incidentally, this film, like the newsreel items that previously reported on these mass graves (Vande Winkel, 2004), was shown only outside Germany, so as not to fuel domestic public fears about relatives fighting at the Eastern front or held in Soviet captivity.

Just like German newsreels and feature films, Kulturfilme such as *Rund um die Freiheitsstatue/ Round the Statue of Liberty* (1941)—released before Germany declared war on the United States— *Herr Roosevelt plaudert/Mr. Roosevelt Chats* (1943), and *Roter Nebel/Red Fog* (1943) occasionally used anti-Semitic elements to vilify the American and Soviet enemy states. In general, however, anti-Semitism was not an issue dealt with extensively in German cinema. The exception to the previously mentioned rule is, apart from Veit Harlan's *Jud Süss/Jew Süss* (1940) and some other feature films with minor anti-Semitic tendencies, a feature-length documentary already cited in the introduction to this entry. *The Wandering Jew* (1940), produced before the Nazi leadership decided to exterminate all Jews but imbued with the racist ideas that would lead toward that path, featured a semi-historical warning against the "danger" imposed by the "world Jewry." Pretending to offer "documentary proof of the Jewish threat," the film actually remains proof of the vicious anti-Semitism that characterized the Nazi regime. *The Wandering Jew*, which compares Jews to rats and warns for "civilized" Jews whose "inferiority" and "perfidiousness" is less easily recognizable than those of "uncivilized" Jews living in ghettos, was officially directed by Fritz Hippler, one of Goebbels' closest collaborators. Hippler was indeed heavily involved in the production of this film. He personally organized the filming of scenes involving Polish Jews in the Warsaw ghetto and coordinated the entire production process. Goebbels, collaborators such as Eberhard Taubert, and Hitler himself designed the concept of the film (Hornshøj-Møller, 1995) and closely monitored the production. As a propaganda weapon, *The Wandering Jew* was rather ineffective. The film was badly received by German audiences and quickly withdrawn from commercial distribution (Culbert, 2002).

In 1944–1945, another "documentary" related to the so-called Jewish question was produced in occupied Czechoslovakia (Margry, 1992). *Theresienstadt—EinDokumentarfilm aus dem Jüdischen*

Siedlungsgebiet/Theresienstadt—A Documentary Film from the Jewish Settlement Area portrayed the Theresienstadt ghetto camp as a holiday resort. The film, commissioned by the Gestapo Central Jewish Office in Prague, was produced without any collaboration from the propaganda ministry and intended to be screened abroad to neutral countries and organizations such as the Red Cross. A full copy of *Theresienstadt*, which was not finished until March 1945, is not available, but some scenes have emerged in film archives. Because of the lack of a complete print, *Theresienstadt* has become the subject of many misconceptions. One includes the widespread use of an apocryphal title (*Der Führer schenkt den Juden eine Stadt/The Führer Donates a Town to the Jews*), which the film never bore.

Probably the only feature-length documentaries truly popular with German audiences, if only for a limited time, were the campaign films that documented the first eighteen months of World War II (Sakmyster, 1996). The German invasion of Poland in September 1939 was registered by many military cameramen, which formed part of the propaganda units. The battle footage they shot for the newsreels proved powerful and so successful that the newsreel editorial board (led by Fritz Hippler) compiled a full-length documentary. This film, *Feldzug in Polen/Campaign in Poland* (1940), was received enthusiastically by German officials, as well as by the general public. Its success inspired Reich marshal Hermann Göring and his German *Luftwaffe*, rather unhappy that *Campaign in Poland* focused so much on the land forces, to produce a documentary on the accomplishments of the Air Force. The result, *Feuertaufe/Baptism of Fire* (1940) was also well received by audiences, who flocked to cinemas to see how their soldiers and aviators conquered Europe. Both films, as other German media before, blamed the war entirely on Poland, which had forced the Germans to "shoot back" and to "counterattack." The same public approval was awarded to *Sieg im Westen/Victory in the West* (1941), which covered the successful conquering of Western Europe. As German victories waned, so did public interest in related footage. A feature-length war documentary on the Eastern front was never released.

Nazi Germany's most famous documentary director, Leni Riefenstahl, worked during the war years on various film projects, only one of which (*Tiefland*, 1954) was completed many years later. Sixty years after the end of the war, research (Rother, 2002; Trimborn, 2002) revealed that she, too, had followed the *Wehrmacht* into Poland in 1939. Everything indicates that Riefenstahl and her collaborators prepared a documentary on the campaign. It was probably the mishandling and execution of Polish civilians in the Polish city of Konskie, which Riefenstahl witnessed and protested against in vain, that made her give up the war reporting. Several of her cameramen, joining the propaganda units, kept on recording the war in images that eventually ended up in *Campaign in Poland*.

In Italy, the fascist state and *El Duce*, Benito Mussolini, backed the rebirth of cinema but, unlike other totalitarian regimes, left the actual production of films almost entirely in private hands (Sorlin, 1985). During World War II (which for the fascist regime ended in 1943), the Italian film industry produced, apart from the *Luce* newsreels, no nonfiction titles worth mentioning. Incidentally, footage of those newsreels was reedited by Roberto Cavalcanti in 1940, who ridiculed Mussolini in his British GPO Film Unit production *Yellow Caesar*.

In France, a demarcation line separated the northern German-occupied zone from the southern unoccupied zone. The latter, also known as Vichy France, was headed by an authoritarian government and symbolized by marshal Pétain, around whom a leader cult was established. During World War II, approximately 400 documentaries (Bertin-Maghit, 2004) were produced by French film services, 178 of which have been currently restored, while at least 50 others have survived, too. Some of these films were adapted from German documentaries. *Le péril Juif/The Jewish Peril* was, for example, a French version of *The Wandering Jew*, in which footage of French Jews had been inserted. Most of the documentaries, however, were of French origin. Whereas films produced in occupied France were orientated toward Nazi-Germany and supported French collaboration to the "new European order," documentaries produced in Vichy France (for instance: *Pétain et la France*, 1941) tried to keep their distance from the Nazi-government, avoided the subject of French-German collaboration and strived instead to assert the independence of the new state and its marshal. One of the most famous documentaries produced in this era, *La tragédie de Mers-el-Kébir/The Tragedy at Mers-el-Kebir* (1940), attacked Great Britain for having destroyed the French war fleet after the French capitulation in the summer of 1940 (Bowles, 2004).

In Japan (Nornes, 2003) wartime cinema was, much more than its European or American counterparts, marked by a strong blending of documentary and fiction, with fiction films incorporating long documentary sequences (footage of military trainings and campaigns) and documentaries incorporating several elements of melodramas and other fictional devices. The Japanese government, which since its renewed war on China (1936), showed an increased interest in film propaganda, favored nonfiction films in general and *bunka eiga* (cultural shorts, comparable to German Kulturfilme), in particular above fiction productions. This government interest led on the one hand to a period of great productivity and experimentation for Japanese documentary cinema, but on the other to heavy censorship. The leftist Proletarian Film League (Prokino) was outlawed and the government, which in 1939 remodeled its film legislation after the German example, granted film direction exclusively to those licensed. Fumio Kamei, one of Japan's most talented directors, had his license withdrawn and was even imprisoned while his *Tatakau Heitai/Fighting Soldiers* (1939), now considered one of the best Japanese films of the twentieth century, angered military officials so much that it was banned.

In Great Britain, war film production and its propagandistic use was one of the many responsibilities of the Ministry of Information (MOI). As mentioned previously, the MOI and its film division were initially harshly criticized for lack of competence and of a coordinated propaganda policy, but gained experience during the Phony War (September 1939–April 1940) and ended up doing a fairly good job for most of the war (Chapman, 1998). The documentary film movement, which under the influence of John Grierson's GPO Film Unit had since the 1930s seen its role as an educational and informative one, played a far bigger role in the British propaganda campaign than the government, which initially favored feature film, had anticipated. That the GPO Film Unit was initially entirely ignored by the MOI, however, is a myth. Grierson, who had left for Canada in 1939 to set up the National Film Board, played no personal role in this process, but indirectly he left his mark on the work of many "griersonian" documentarists, the most famous of which was Humphrey Jennings.

All in all, the MOI distributed some 1,400 nonfiction shorts during the war years, most of them five- or fifteen-minutes films, shown alongside features in the commercial circuit or in nontheatrical screenings. The films, commissioned by the MOI, were produced by newsreel companies, commercial studios, independent producers, and the GPO Film Unit. In late 1940, the GPO Film Unit, which had been transferred to the MOI and was around that time renamed into the Crown Film Unit, released a documentary short that received public and critic acclaim. *Britain Can Take It!* (1940), a shortened version of a documentary (*London Can Take It!*) originally destined for the neutral United States only, propagated the calmness with which Great Britain endured the German bombardments. *Britain Can Take It!* was directed by Humphrey Jennings, who went on to make several more acclaimed short documentaries (*Listen to Britain* 1942; *The Eighty Days*, 1945), as well as feature-length documentaries (*Fires Were Started*, 1943) for the Crown Film Unit. What made Jennings films so powerful was their modest and defensive tone. Unlike many other, rather offensive war documentaries and newsreels (British or foreign), there were neither hate-propaganda campaigns launched against the enemy nor extreme outbursts of patriotism. In tune with the spirit of the moment, Jennings showed British and foreign audiences how Great Britain and its population carried on. As Erik Barnouw (1997) remarked, it is this quality that makes *Listen to Britain* or *Fires Were Started* films that decades later can still be watched without embarrassment.

Obviously, more offensive productions and war documentaries were produced. This was in particular true for feature and short-feature documentaries produced by, or in collaboration with, Service Units of the armed forces. Some of these films, and particularly those produced by the Army Film and Photographic Unit (AFPU), became successful and cause for competition with other players such as the Crown Film Unit, with whom the AFPU regularly collaborated. The RAF Film Production Unit also contributed to the production of combat documentaries. An early example is Harry Watt's *Target for Tonight* (1941), showing RAF bombers raiding German cities. David MacDonald's *Desert Victory* (1943), a feature on the defeat of German Marshal Erwin Rommel and his Africa Corps, was so successful that several more feature-length campaign films were released, demonstrating British military strength and celebrating victorious campaigns. Among the most popular productions were *Tunisian Victory* (1944), *Burma Victory* (1944), and *The True Glory* (1945). Directed by Garson Kanin and Carol Reed, *The True Glory* was a British-American coproduction. Narrated by the voice-over of General Eisenhower, the film celebrated the individual and joint effort of the Allied forces from the invasion of Normandy to the occupation of Germany.

In the Soviet Union (Barnouw, 1993; Kenez, 2001), the importance attached to nonfiction film as a propagandistic weapon is perfectly illustrated by the fact that, when all fiction film studios were evacuated from Moscow in autumn 1941, documentary and newsreel production activities remained in the capital. Working under most difficult circumstances, Soviet directors and editors turned the footage, delivered by hundreds of cameramen, into a long series of newsreels, but also in documentaries. The first feature-length documentary produced after the German invasion was *Nasha Moskva/Our Moscow* (autumn 1941), for which director Mikhail Slutskii received a Stalin Prize. Under the difficult circumstances imposed by war, Slutskii and the directors after him were almost never involved in the actual filming process and saw their creative role limited to editing the available combat footage as well as possible. *Our Moscow* was followed by *Razgrom Nemetzkikh voisk pod Moskvoi/Defeat of the German Armies near Moscow* (1942), produced by Leonid Varlamov and Ilya Kopalin. The film attracted huge audiences and was exported to the United States. Retitled *Moscow Strikes Back*, showing American audiences images of German prisoners of war being led to Moscow, the film created much sympathy for America's former enemy and new ally. In 1943, *Moscow Strikes Back* even won an Academy Award. Other Soviet documentaries, too, were exported to the United States (and Great Britain), which underlines that their propagandistic function was not limited to the homefront.

Varlamov's next feature documentary, *Stalingrad* (1943), celebrated the German defeat and contained newsreel footage of German Field Marshal Friedrich Paulus, who according to German propaganda, had died together with his entire Sixth army, surrendering to Soviet military officers. The German defeat at Stalingrad was such a major turning point, from a military as well as from a propagandistic point of view, that it became the subject of several other documentaries, such as Lydia Stepanova's and Sergei Gurov's *Komsomolsk* (1943). Another remarkable film was produced under supervision of Mikhail Slutskii. *Den'voiny/A Day of War* (1942) compiled footage of 200 cameramen, reportedly all shot on June 13 of the same year. The example set by Slutskii, Varlamov, Kopalin, and other documentarists, such as Roman Karmen (*Leningrad v Borbe/Leningrad at War*, 1942), was followed by directors who had previously mainly been making fiction films. Several of these productions have become classics, especially Yuil Raizman's *Berlin* (1945)—an

incredibly powerful report on the Soviet capture of the German capital—and Alexander Dovzhenko's *Bytva za nashu radiansku Ukrainu/The Battle for Our Soviet Ukraine* (1943) and *Pobeda na Provoberezhnoi Ukrainu/Victory in the Ukraine* (1945).

The United States, the last superpower to enter the war, produced not only the largest and most consistent, but according to specialist scholars (Barsam, 1992) also the best body of nonfiction film made in World War II. As civilians from all occupational groups were drafted into military service, so were the Hollywood professionals. In 1941–1945, Hollywood, represented by the War Activities Committee of the Motion Picture Industry, produced in collaboration with various government departments an innumerable amount of fiction and nonfiction films for many purposes. Various well-known film directors temporarily stepped away from fiction film and dedicated their time and talent to the production of documentaries. To carry out their jobs while functioning normally within the military structure and hierarchy, most of them were assigned a provisional rank without meeting the usual military requirements in terms of training and so forth. Frank Capra, for example, was given the rank of army major, and John Ford found himself lieutenant-commander with the navy.

Of all American nonfiction films produced during World War II, best known is the *Why We Fight* series of United States Army training films produced by Frank Capra. As its title indicates, *Why We Fight* aimed to motivate young recruits, many of whom, before the Japanese attack on Pearl Harbor, had shown little interest in a war fought across distant waters. The *Why We Fight* series included seven documentaries, each about fifty minutes long: *Prelude to War* (1941), *The Nazis Strike* (1941), *Divide and Conquer* (1942), *The Battle of Britain* (1942), *Battle of Russia* (1942), *Battle of China* (1942) and *War Comes to America* (1943). An eighth title, *War Comes to America, Part II*, was never finished. The films compiled newsreel and documentary footage from various sources (Nazi and Soviet newsreels, Riefenstahl documentaries, fiction films, animated maps provided by the Disney studios, etc.) to give their public a crash course in international politics and history. Their emotional and rough tone, which was shared (copied) by many other American war nonfiction productions, rather imitated Nazi examples than the more sophisticated style Humphrey Jennings displayed in his British documentaries. Officials were so pleased with *Why We Fight* that some of the films were also released to the general public at home and abroad. Capra's unit, which temporarily included internationally renowned documentarists such as Robert Flaherty and Joris Ivens, produced also various other nonfiction series (*Know Your Allies—Know Your Enemy*, *The Army-Navy Screen Magazine*) and individual titles, the best known of which is probably *The Negro Soldier* (1944), a documentary with good intentions that nevertheless typecasts African Americans in 1940s stereotypes that would not be accepted today.

The first American military successes created an immediate need for documentaries celebrating those campaigns and victories. In 1944–1945, when the Japanese power in the Pacific collapsed and the Allied invasion of Normandy had opened a second front in Europe, the demand for victorious documentaries heightened. Again, the most famous titles were produced by directors who had gained name and fame in fiction film. John Ford directed the famous documentary short, *The Battle of Midway* (1942), and coordinated a unit that produced many other titles of strategic (*How to Operate between Enemy Lines*) or other (*Sex Hygiene*) importance. William Wyler made *Memphis Belle* (1944), the story of an American bomber raiding Germany, stylistically resembling the already mentioned British production *Target for Tonight* (1941). John Huston, who had debuted in the documentary genre with *Reports from the Aleutians* (1942), made two other impressive documentaries, the anti-militaristic undertone of which was quite obvious. *The Battle of San Pietro* (1945), released only when the war was virtually over, is an authentic document on the war in Italy and features scenes (soldiers being killed, bodies being put in bags) rarely shown in any military production. *Let There Be Light* (1946) was meant to convince the American public in general and employers in particular that people who returned from the front with shellshock or other nervous damages were ill, not crazy. *Let There Be Light* urged society to accept and support such people to help them heal as quickly as possible. Huston's observations of mentally ill recruits were so strong, however, that the film was banned from public screening.

Among the many other American documentaries produced during World War II, mention should also be made of the work of the United States Office of War Information, which (apart from coordinating the newsreel production) had films produced for the homefront (for instance *Japanese Relocation*, which in 1943 attempted to the justify the imprisonment of civilians of Japanese origin, many of whom were American citizens) as well as for overseas audiences (for instance *The Cumming-*

ton Story, 1945), which had to be presented with positive and romantic views of the United States.

World War II and, by extension, the history of Nazi Germany and all subjects related to the war have proven an object of interest and fascination for many generations. As such, they remain a rewarding subject for documentary producers (Leyda, 1964; Barsam, 1992; Barnouw, 1993). The great amount of battle footage (authentic or to some extent staged) filmed during the war years, as well as the many other newsreel and documentary images have often been used for several decades, and probably for many more to come, to produce documentaries and all kinds of television programs about World War II. Whereas most producers and directors chose to make extensive use of archive materials, some rejected this practice and only included filmed testimonies of eyewitnesses. The most famous example of this practice is Claude Lanzmann's *Shoah* (1985), a monumental documentary on the Holocaust, using nothing but in-depth interviews with eyewitnesses, victims, and perpetrators.

In the first postwar years, every of the triumphing states yielded documentaries that celebrated the end of the war. Many productions, like the previously mentioned documentaries *Berlin* (Soviet Union, 1945) and *The True Glory* (Great Britain, 1945) looked back on the military campaigns that had lead to the final victory. Some documentaries focused on the work of the very combat cameramen that had made such compilation films possible. One of the most self-reflexive of these postwar documentaries can be found in the Soviet production *Frontovoj Kinooperator/A Cameraman at the Front* (1946), in which Maria Slavinskaya commemorates the work of Vladimir Sushinsky by compiling his battle footage. The film became famous for including images Sushinsky was filming when he was suddenly hit by a deadly bullet, as well as the footage a colleague filmed of Sushinsky being shot.

Shortly after the liberation of formerly Nazi-occupied territories and the discovery of Nazi concentration and extermination camps that had been established there, documentary films started indicting the defeated oppressors and their collaborators. *Majdanek* (Poland, 1944) and *Jasenovac* (Yugoslavia, 1945), emotional productions featuring gruesome footage, were among the first documentaries dedicated to the concentration camps. Many others would follow, one of most impressive documentaries produced in this tradition is *Requiem dla 500.000* (*Requiem for the 500,000*, Poland, 1963). Other examples can be found in *Wreszien September 1939* (1961), also a Polish production, and Soviet films such as *Sud naradnov/Judgment of the*

Nations (1946), and *Obyknovennyi Faschism/Ordinary Fascism* (1965). German documentarists, too, dug up Third Reich archive materials and turned them into powerful compilation films, for instance Erwin Leiser's *Mein Kampf* (1960), produced with Swedish money and originally titled *Den Blodiga Tiden* or *Bloody Times* and Paul Rotha's *Das Leben Adolf Hitlers/The Life of Adolf Hitler* (1961). In East Germany, Andrew and Annelie Thorndike specialized into the production of compilation films dealing with Germany's fascist past, such as *Du und mancher Kamerad/You and Many Comrades* (1955) and *Unternehmen Teutonenschwert/Operation Teutonic Sword* (1958).

Several of the most famous documentaries about World War II were produced by French documentarists. Alain Resnais's *Nuit et Brouillard/Night and Fog* (1955), which ten years after the end of the war mediated about life in the Nazi extermination camps, met public and critic approval and is in the eyes of many still the ultimate documentary made about this subject. Marcel Ophüls's *Le Chagrin et la Pitié/The Sorrow and the Pity* (1971) mixed authentic newsreel and documentary footage with contemporary interviews to reconstruct life in a provincial French town, and by extension in France, under the Nazi occupation. The film, which indicated that the role of the French resistance was much smaller than popular myth propagated, was received with mixed feelings and for ten years banned from French public television. To some degree, the film could be compared to another, older but equally famous film about life under the Nazi occupation: Roberto Rosselini's *Roma, città aperta/Rome, Open City* (1946). Seventeen years later, Ophüls finished the Oscar-winning masterpiece *Hotel Terminus* (1988) about the life and trial of the Nazi war criminal Klaus Barbie.

One can produce a book listing all feature films and television miniseries in which Hitler is portrayed (Mitchell, 2002), but it would be impossible to draw up an inventory of all film and television documentaries focusing on some aspect of World War II. Television especially played a vital role in the nonstop production of World War II documentaries. Already in 1952–1953, the American Public Broadcasting Company produced a twenty-six part chronicle series (*Victory at Sea*) on naval warfare in the war. The series were so successful that television stations all over the world started similar projects in the 1950s and 1960s. Although military aspects of the World War II remained a favorable subject, a great many documentaries focused on related topics: life in Nazi Germany and the countries it occupied, histories of local resistance or collaboration movements, the lives and times of Nazi officials, the Nazi persecution of Jews and other minority groups, and others.

It must be emphasized that not all documentaries about aspects of World War II focus on the involvement of Nazi Germany solely or exclusively. The involvement of other countries and parties also received attention from national or international productions. Nevertheless, it cannot be denied that documentaries dealing with the past of Nazi Germany are more likely to attract international audiences that series on contemporaries such as Benito Mussolini or Josef Stalin and are therefore more often produced.

In the 1990s and in the beginning of the twenty-first century, the internationally most successful series about World War II were probably the BBC production *The Nazis: A Warning from History* (1997)—historically advised by Ian Kershaw, who went on to write an acclaimed two-volume biography of Adolf Hitler—and several series that, under the auspices of Guido Knopp, were produced for German broadcaster ZDF: *Hitlers Helfer/Hitler's Helpers* (1996), *Hitler's Krieger/Hitler's Warriors* (1998), *Hitlers Kinder/Hitler's Children* (2000), *Holokaust/Holocaust* (2000), *Hitlers Frauen/Hitler's Women* (2001), and *Stalingrad* (2002). In 2004–2005, the sixtieth anniversary of the end of the World War II was commemorated worldwide with the launch of new documentaries (and fiction films).

With a few exceptions, like the German news magazine *Panorama* that was produced in 1944–1945 (Stamm, 1999) and some American military instruction films, all newsreels and documentaries shot during World War II were recorded on black-and-white film. Documentaries about the war were therefore almost always exclusively using black-and-white archive footage. At the end of the twentieth century, however, film historians and footage researchers (Binns and Wood, 1999) rediscovered unique archive footage in color. Some of these color films were originally produced by military forces, but most of the retrieved material was amateur footage shot on Gasparcolor (introduced by the German Agfa company in 1931) or on Kodachrome (launched in the American market by Eastman Kodak in 1935). Many of these film records had been saved for over half a century in the private collections of those who originally filmed it or of their families. Television series such as *The Second World War in Color* (1999), which gratefully seized the opportunity to show a formerly unknown (and unseen) aspect of the war, were internationally successful. The success even inspired commercial firms without scruples to hastily throw digitally colored black-and-white images on the market, deliberately causing confusion with the authentic color materials.

Only a couple of years later new trends suggest that in the near future, it will become increasingly less important whether or not archive footage of a particular event has survived. It was only a matter of time before computer-generated imagery (CGI)—originally used to create special effects and fantasy worlds for big-budget fiction films, but after some time also used to revive dinosaurs and other extinct creatures for "historical documentaries"—would be applied to the more recent past. It was also to be expected that any such experiment, still a very expensive undertaking, would focus on what seems to be the most popular historical period. In late 2004, the "virtual history" production, *The Secret Plot to Kill Hitler*, was released. For this production, the content of which was based on historically documented events that originally had not been filmed, Hitler, Churchill, Roosevelt, and Stalin were brought to life using physically similar actors, which with the help of computerized "face wrapping" techniques were given the real, fully animated faces of their historical characters. The final result, which from a technical viewpoint is very convincing (the image is "scratched," noise layers are added to the soundtrack), could in the eyes of the general public easily pass for genuine archive footage and raises several ethical questions for future documentary producers and their audiences.

ROEL VANDE WINKEL

See also **Fires Were Started**; **Hitler and National Socialist Party**; *Listen to Britain*; *London Can Take It*; **Ministry of Information: World War II**; **Newsreel Series:** *Night and Fog*; *Why We Fight*

Further Reading

Bertin-Maghit, Jean-Pierre, *Les documenteurs des années noires: les documentaires de propagande, France 1940–1944*, Paris: Nouveau Monde, 2004.

Binns, Stewart, and Adrian Wood, *The Second World War in Color*, Pavilion Books Limited, 1999.

Bowles, Brett C., "'La tragédie de Mers-el-Kébir' and the politics of filmed news in France, 1940–1944," in *Journal of Modern History*, 2, 2004, 347–388.

Chapman, James, *The British at War: Cinema, State and Propaganda, 1939–1945*, London, New York: IB Tauris, 1998.

Culbert, David (ed.), *Film and Propaganda in America: A Documentary History*, volumes 2 and 3: World War II, Westport: Greenwood Press, 1990.

———, "The Impact of Anti-Semitic Film Propaganda on German Audiences: Jew Süss and the Wandering Jew (1940)," in *Art, Culture and Media under the Third Reich*, Richard A. Etlin (ed.), Chicago, London: University of Chicago Press, 2002.

Fielding, Raymond, *The American Newsreel 1911–1967*, Norman: University of Oklahoma Press, 1972.

Gladstone, Kay, "British Interception of German Export Newsreels, and the Development of British Combat Filming, 1939–1942," in *Imperial War Museum Review*, 2, 1987, 27–55.

Hoffmann, Hilmar, *The Triumph of Propaganda. Film and National Socialism 1933–1945*, Providence, Oxford: Berghahn Books, 1996.

Hornshøj-Møller, Stig, *Der ewige Jude. Quellenkritische Analyse eines antisemitischen Propagandafilms*, Göttingen: Institut für den Wissenschaftlichen Film, 1995.

Kenez, Peter, *Cinema and Soviet Society: From the Revolution to the Death of Stalin*, London, New York: I.B. Tauris, 2001.

Leyda, Jay, *Films Beget Films. A Study of The Compilation Film*, New York: Hill and Wang, 1964.

Margry, Karel, "'Theresienstadt' (1944–1945): The Nazi Propaganda Film Depicting the Concentration Camp as Paradise," in *Historical Journal of Film, Radio and Television*, 2, 1992, 145–162.

Mitchell, Charles P., *The Hitler Filmography: Worldwide Feature Film and Television Miniseries Portrayals, 1940 through 2000*, Jefferson, NC, London: McFarland & Company Inc., 2002.

Moeller, Felix, *The Film Minister. Goebbels and the Cinema in the 'Third Reich'*, Stuttgart, London: Edition Axel Menges, 2000.

Nornes, Abe Mark, *Japanese Documentary Film: The Meiji Era Through Hiroshima*, Minneapolis: University of Minnesota Press, 2003.

Okumura, Masaru, "Uber den Einfluss der Deutschen Wochenschau auf die Japanischen Nihon Nyusu während des zweiten Weltkrieges," in *Iconics*, 5, 2000, 27–55.

Pronay, Nicholas, and D.W. Spring (eds.), *Propaganda, Politics and Film, 1918–1945*, London, Basingstoke: MacMillan Press, 1982.

Reeves, Nicholas, *The Power of Film Propaganda. Myth or Reality?*, London, New York: Cassell, 1999.

Rother, Rainer, *Leni Riefenstahl: The Seduction of Genius*, London, New York: The Continuum, 2002.

Sakmyster, Thomas, "Nazi documentaries of intimidation: 'Feldzug in Polen' (1940), 'Feurtaufe' (1940) and 'Sieg im Westen' (1941)," in *Historical Journal of Film, Radio and Television*, 4, 1996, 27–55.

Short, K. R. M., and Stephan Dolezel (eds.), *Hitler's Fall. The Newsreel Witness*, New York: Croom Helm, 1988.

Sorlin, Pierre, "Italian cinema's rebirth, 1937–1943: A Paradox of Fascism," in *Historical Journal of Film, Radio and Television*, 1, 1994, 3–14.

Stamm, Karl, "Panorama. Farbige Auslands-Filmpropaganda 1944/45," in *Filmblatt*, 12, 1999, 27–55.

Tranche, Rafael R., and Vicente Sánchez-Biosca, *No-Do: El tiempo y la Memoria*, Madrid: Cátedra/Filmoteca Española, 2002.

Trimborn, Jürgen, *Riefenstahl-Eine deutsche Karriere*, Berlin: Aufbau-Verlag, 2002.

Trimmel, Gerhard, "Gefilmte Lügen": Der Theresienstadt-Propagandafilm von 1944, Krems, 2003.

Vande Winkel, Roel. "The Auxiliary Cruiser Thor's Death and Transfiguration: A Case Study in Nazi Wartime Newsreel Propaganda," in *Historical Journal of Film, Radio and Television*, 3, 2003, 27–55.

Vande Winkel, Roel, "Nazi Newsreels in Europe, 1939–1945: The Many Faces of Ufa's Foreign Weekly Newsreel (Auslandstonwoche) versus the German Weekly Newsreel (Deutsche Wochenschau)," in *Historical Journal of Film, Radio and Television* [*Special issue: Nazi Newsreels in German-occupied Europe*], 1939–1945], 1, 2004, 27–55.

Welch, David, *Propaganda and the German cinema 1933–1945*, Oxford: Clarendon Press, 2001, revised.

Zimmerman, Peter, and Kay Hoffman (eds.), *Geschichte und Ästhetik des dokumentarischen Films in Deutschland. Band 3: Drittes Reich*, Stuttgart: Reclam, 2005.

WRESTLING

(Canada, Brault, Carrière, Fournier, and Jutra, 1961)

Made under the auspices of the French Unit at the National Film Board (NFB) of Canada, *La lutte* (1961) / *Wrestling* occupies a central place in the Canadian documentary tradition. The film is a key example of *cinema direct*, a style practiced by a group of young Québécois filmmakers in the late 1950s and early 1960s. Influenced by the films of Jean Rouch, they sought to avoid the didacticism and sentimentalism they felt characterized the griersonian tradition dominant within the NFB. Yet, the *cinema direct* filmmakers did not want to succumb to a coolly dispassionate, observational stance they associated with the new wave of English-Canadian productions within the NFB known as "Candid Eye" films. Instead, they wanted cinema to bear the mark of the filmmaker's passionate engagement with his or her subject while retaining a measure of critical distance. *La lutte* negotiates this difficult path. The film follows the action of an evening of professional wrestling at the Montréal Forum. Its focus is split between the drama unfolding within the ring and the reaction of the crowd to the epic battles staged for their pleasure. The film recognizes that the clashes are more theatrical than real, but does not dwell on the phoniness of the sport. Instead, using irony and humour, the film examines the mechanics of modern-day ritual.

Like several of the early *cinema direct* films, *La lutte* was directed collaboratively. Michel Brault, Marcel Carrière, Claude Fournier, and Claude Jutra all contributed to its production. Fournier is usually credited with the original idea, the accomplished cinematographer Brault with its distinct look, and sound engineer Carrière with its innovations in location sound recording. Jutra's contribution cannot be as specifically identified. A formidable thinker, Jutra had been in France during the emergence of the *nouvelle vague* and had travelled to Africa with legendary documentarian Rouch. This experience perhaps contributed to the conceptual sophistication of *La lutte*. The montage of the film owes something to the jump cuts made popular by the young generation of French filmmakers, but more important it shares the autoethnographic impulse of Rouch and Edgar Morin's *Chronique d'été / Chronicle of a Summer* (1961).

Jutra's experience with Rouch (documented in a series of three articles published in *Cahiers du Cinéma*) was not the only connection between this young group of filmmakers and the French master. Brault had screened a film he had co-directed with Gilles Groulx, *Les raquetteurs/The Snowshoers* (1958), for Rouch at the Flaherty Seminar in 1959 and was subsequently invited to collaborate with Rouch and Morin on *Chronique d'été*. *Les raquetteurs* anticipates *La lutte* in its focus on the rituals that bind a community together. Shot on location at a winter festival in small-town Québec, the film captures the anarchy of the event, but refuses to sentimentalize it as folklore or to condemn it as outmoded. As such, it paves the way for *La lutte*'s consideration of the transformation of Québécois society and the persistence of ritual in a culture in the throes of modernization.

The film's nuanced understanding of modern ritual was influenced by Roland Barthes, whose "The World of Wrestling," published in *Mythologies* (1957), offered an interpretation of wrestling as spectacle. Although Barthes did not directly participate in the making of the film, he is acknowledged in the credits for his "assistance." Barthes recognized in wrestling the same "exhaustion of the content by the form" that characterizes classical art (Barthes, 1972: 19). The script by which the events in the ring unfold may be known to all, but the force of the spectacle resides in the performance. The camera in *La lutte* is perfectly attuned to these spectacular moments. From ringside it captures the images of pain and suffering the hero endures, as well as the grandiloquent gestures of the villain. At the same time, it turns the camera on the spectators who react with indignation when the villain pulls a dirty trick and with joy when the hero recovers and lands the blow that will lead to victory. Wrestling is represented as a modern form of classical theatre, capable of triggering catharsis in its audience, for whom the event is expressive of deep collective desires.

The narrative of the film is classical in its construction and presents the wrestling ring as a stage on which the age-old battle between good and evil is fought. It begins with a prologue that visits aspiring wrestlers training in the gym, but quickly proceeds to the preparations of the arena for the big event and the arrival of the crowd. Before the competition begins, a striking shot shows the empty ring bathed in light. In Catholic Québec, such an image is resonant, as it suggests that the spectacles of mass entertainment, especially sport, have the allure to displace religion as the focal point of community identification. The preliminary matches see the crowd grow increasingly enthusiastic. In an audacious montage sequence, shots of the struggle within the ring, including several close-ups of wrestlers' faces showing agony or arrogance, are interspersed with images of the faces in the crowd, alternately rapturous and outraged. The sequence is scored with the Allegro from the Concerto in G by Bach-Vivaldi, a juxtaposition of refinement and brutality that renders iconic the images of suffering and bodily punishment and transforms the images of the spectators' passion into signs of an almost religious devotion.

The climax of the film is the main event on the wrestling card, a tag-team battle featuring local hero Edouard Carpentier against the Russian Kalimnakov. This lengthy sequence follows the ebb and flow of the match, using radio commentary to describe the action. Although Carpentier was from France and not Québec, his eventual victory is celebrated as the triumph of the hometown champion. As well, in the era of the cold war, the win holds a certain geopolitical significance. The film underscores this

in the epilogue, which visits the combatants in their respective dressing rooms. Carpentier graciously signs autographs for his fans, while Kalimnakov and his tag-team partner condemn the referee and vow revenge on Carpentier. The Russian speaks in English, but the film subtitles him in Russian, thereby emphasizing the difference that marks him as a villain in the world of wrestling.

Given its subject matter and its occasionally ironic tone, there is the danger that *La lutte* can be dismissed as a formal exercise by four filmmakers who would go on to make more serious films. However, *La lutte* exemplifies the philosophical and political principles that underlie the *cinema direct* movement. The film is driven by a desire to document the transformation of postwar Québécois society. Wrestling offers an opportunity to observe the passions of ordinary people invested in a spectacle that is at once part of a modern, capitalist entertainment industry but evokes much older forms of communal gathering. As such, it is a fitting subject to measure the transformation of Québec in the early years of what is usually termed the Quiet Revolution, a period in which Québecois society was secularized, its economy modernized, and its claims to nationhood more openly and compellingly expressed.

ANDREW BURKE

See also **Brault, Michel; National Film Board of Canada; Rouch, Jean**

La lutte/Wrestling (Canada, National Film Board, 1961, 28 min.). Directed by Michel Brault, Marcel Carrière, Claude Fournier, and Claude Jutra. Made with the assistance of Roland Barthes, Maurice de Ernsted, Léo Ewaschuck, Bernard Gosselin, Stanley Jackson, Wolf Koenig, Roger Lamoureux, Guy Lescouflair, Arthur Lipsett, Don Owen, and Claude Pelletier. Allegro from the Concerto in G by Bach-Vivaldi performed by Kelsey Jones. Produced by Jacques Bobet.

Further Reading

Barthes, Roland, *Mythologies*, 1957, Translated by Annette Lavers, London: Jonathan Cape, 1972.

Clandfield, David, *Canadian Film*. Toronto: Oxford University Press, 1987.

Coloumbe, Michel (ed.), *Le Dictionnaire du cinema québécois*, (4th ed.), Montréal: Boreal, 1999.

Evans, Gary, *In the National Interest: A Chronicle of the National Film Board of Canada from 1949 to 1989*, Toronto: University of Toronto Press, 1991.

Leach, Jim, *Claude Jutra: Filmmaker*, Montreal and Kingston: McGill-Queen's University Press, 1999.

Mackenzie, Scott, "The Missing Mythology: Barthes in Québec," in *Canadian Journal of Film Studies*, 6, 2, 1998 65–74.

Marsolais, Gilles, *L'aventure du cinema direct revisitée*, Laval: Les 400 coups, 1997.

WRIGHT, BASIL

Basil Wright developed an interest in film aesthetics and made some student films at Cambridge. He became the first young filmmaker inducted into the British documentary film movement by its founder, his lifelong mentor John Grierson. Wright joined the movement shortly after being hugely impressed by the famous November 1929 London Film Society double bill of *Drifters* (John Grierson, 1929) and *Battleship Potemkin* (Sergei Eisenstein, USSR, 1926). Wright's landmark achievement *Song of Ceylon* (1934–1935) demonstrated that the movement was capable of producing outstanding work. It established Wright as a noted documentary filmmaker but has somewhat overshadowed his other films and his contributions as a producer, writer, and conscientious documentary activist.

Wright was the first British documentary movement filmmaker to have the adjective "poetic" applied his work. He was accompanied during the shooting of his first full-fledged directorial assignment, *The Country Comes to Town* (1931) by Robert Flaherty, renowned director of *Nanook of the North* (1920–1921). Wright credited Flaherty with showing him how to immerse himself in the environment being filmed, and with making him aware of the value of recording serendipitous events. Flaherty also demonstrated how to frame shots with sensitivity and, through careful observation, anticipate subjects' movements. Wright returned the favour by contributing strong material to *Industrial Britain* (Robert Flaherty, 1931), an important early documentary produced in the collaborative manner typical of the movement during this period (Calder-Marshall, 1963). Later, Wright played a key role in the similarly collaborative *Night Mail* (1936).

Wright consolidated his personal style and attracted serious critical attention with the direction of *Liner Cruising South* (1933), *Cargo from Jamaica* (1933), and *Windmill in Barbados* (1933–1934), filmed en route to and in the Caribbean. Far removed from the other documentary movement filmmakers, he exercised considerable autonomy shooting these films. Grierson encouraged the maturation of Wright's individual poetic talent, offering creative input and imposing control during postproduction. Wright's modest trilogy, characterised by graceful camera pans, an eye for human and natural beauty, and a slightly elliptical tone, was praised by modernist critics writing for the influential journals *Close-Up* and *Film Art*, as well as by Grierson (Stollery, 2000). The consequences for film art of the coming of sound was a live issue at this time. Alberto Cavalcanti's collaboration with Wright as *Windmill in Barbados'* "sound supervisor" presaged their more extensive experimental work on *Song of Ceylon*.

After Wright's early years at the Empire Marketing Board (EMB) and General Post Office (GPO) Film Units the documentary movement diversified. He moved into more senior roles as an organiser and producer, founding the Realist Film Unit and working with Grierson at Film Centre to supply documentaries for a range of sponsors. Wright directed *Children at School* (1937), on good and bad practices and conditions in state education. This was part of the series of documentaries, including *Housing Problems* (Edgar Anstey and Arthur Elton, 1935), commissioned to promote the gas industry while simultaneously addressing social problems. *The Face of Scotland* (1938) reunited Wright with *Song of Ceylon*'s composer Walter Leigh and displayed some similarities to their earlier collaboration.

Wright's wartime commissions for the Ministry of Information (MOI) provided less scope for innovation. Harry Watt continued experimenting with narrativised forms of documentary in films such as *Target for Tonight* (1941) before directing features at Ealing, but Wright remained faithful to a more purist conception of the aesthetic and social role of documentary. However it was Humphrey Jennings and Stewart McAllister, for example in *Listen to Britain* (1942), who advanced the development of poetic documentary during World War II. As a senior figure, Wright's major contribution was advisory and supervisory. He worked intermittently with Grierson in Canada, then in 1945 briefly took over as producer in charge of the Crown Film Unit.

An underexplored dimension of Wright's work is its representations of the world beyond Britain. Internationalism was a central preoccupation of Grierson's that Wright revisited in a number of different contexts. Some of Wright's earliest published writing criticised conventional travelogs, a genre he sought to elevate through modernist aesthetics in his Caribbean films and in *Song of Ceylon* (Low, 1979). Wright's films differed from other British documentary movement Empire films, such as *Contact* (Paul Rotha, 1933), which tended to celebrate modernisation, Western technology, and progress. Wright's early Empire films take a more individualistic approach. They romanticise non-Western cultures as appealing yet tantalisingly inaccessible repositories of sensuality and traditional wisdom (Stollery, 2000).

In the 1930s, liberal internationalism overlapped with enlightened imperialism; different emphases arose from different combinations of collaborators and sponsors. *Modern Orphans of the Storm* (Basil Wright and Ian Dalrymple, 1937), was a campaign film responding immediately to the plight of child refugees displaced by the Spanish civil war. *Men of Africa* (Alex Shaw, 1940), written and produced by Wright for the Colonial Office, can be seen as a hybrid between orthodox British documentary perspectives on Empire and Wright's more Romantic view of native cultures. It lauds the benevolence of British rule in East Africa, representing apparently progressive developments in various fields of endeavour, but also celebrates the vibrant sights and sounds of African cultures.

After the war an optimistic, progressive internationalism prevailed within the documentary movement, and Wright began working with Grierson for UNESCO. Along with others in the movement, Wright argued, for example in his 1947 essay "Documentary Today," that documentary production must arrive at a new equilibrium between national and international concerns (Aitken, 1998). *World Without End* (Basil Wright, Paul Rotha, 1953) integrates Wright's delicately poetic approach with the urgent internationalism of *The World Is Rich* (1947), Rotha's earlier film about world food. In *World Without End* material shot by Wright in Thailand is intercut with material shot by Rotha in Mexico, outlining the need for global solutions to global problems.

Grierson's status as British documentary's leading proponent, with Rotha a close second, has led to Wright's publications being overlooked. Yet in a quieter way he, too, was constantly active as a proselytiser for the movement, writing for all the documentary movement journals and becoming *The Spectator*'s film critic in 1938. In 1936, when the movement's diversification required a new London-based publication to keep its various constitu-

ents and sponsors in touch with each other, Wright's family's money helped establish *World Film News* (Low, 1997). Later in his career, he wrote books and began teaching. Wright's most illuminating reflections occur in articles or interviews where he discusses his individual creative processes, his collaborations, and specific technicalities of filmmaking. In this respect he is the most intimate of the early British documentary theorist-practitioners. He lived in an era and belonged to a tradition, however, that precluded any public recognition of the gay sensibility informing some of his more poetic, personal work.

MARTIN STOLLERY

See also **Night Mail; Song of Ceylon.**

Biography

Born London, June 12, 1907. Graduated Corpus Christi College, Cambridge, reading classics and economics in 1929. Met John Grierson and joined Empire Marketing Board (EMB) film unit in 1930, directed first film 1931. Directed his most acclaimed film, *Song of Ceylon*, 1934–1935. Moved with the film unit to the General Post Office (GPO) in 1934. Moved into producing, cofounded the Realist Film Unit and joined Grierson at Film Centre in 1937. Made films for the Ministry of Information during World War II and advised Grierson on National Film Board policy in Canada. Appointed producer in charge of the Crown Film Unit 1945. Worked at UNESCO with Grierson and Julian Huxley in the immediate postwar period. Lectured on film making at the University of California in the 1960s. Published a critical history of film, *The Long View*, in 1974. Died October 14, 1987, in London.

Further Reading

Aitken, Ian, *The Documentary Film Movement: An Anthology*, Edinburgh: EUP, 1998.
Calder-Marshall, Arthur, *The Innocent Eye: The Life of Robert J. Flaherty*, London: W.H. Allen, 1963.
Hardy, Forsyth H. (ed.), *Grierson on Documentary*, London: Faber, 1946.
Hardy, Forsyth H., *John Grierson: A Documentary Biography*, London: Faber, 1979.
Low, Rachael, *Films of Comment and Persuasion of the 1930s*, London: George Allen and Unwin, 1979.
Low, Rachael, *Documentary and Educational Films of the 1930s*, London: Routledge, 1997.
Stollery, Martin, *Alternative Empires: European Modernist Cinemas and Cultures of Imperialism*, Exeter: University of Exeter Press, 2000.
Sussex, Elizabeth, *The Rise and Fall of British Documentary*, Berkeley: UCP, 1975.
Swann, Paul, *The British Documentary Film Movement 1926–1946*, Cambridge: CUP, 1989.
Wright, Basil, *Use of the Film*, London: Bodley Head, 1948.
———, *The Long View*, London: Secker and Warburg, 1974.

YUGOSLAVIA (FORMER)

The first documentary films in the territory of the former Yugoslavia were made by Dr. Karel Grossman in Slovenia (1903) and by Milton Manaki who was filming local rituals and folk dances of Macedonia (1905). *The Arrival of the Sultan Reshad the Fifth in Solun and Bitolj* was one of the first important documentaries by Manaki, an amazing film enthusiast after whom, during the 1990s, the Camera Film Festival in Bitola was named. Another man holding a special place in history is the Croat Josip Karaman for using film media to express his patriotic feelings, using the Croatian language instead of Italian, which was predominant at that time in Dalmatia (1910).

During the time of the Kingdom of Yugoslavia, between the two World Wars, documentary production was very lively. In Croatia the School of National Health made popular and scientific films, and The State Film Centre in Belgrade managed the production and distribution of the whole country. World War II made the country unable to indulge in film activities, except for Croatia, where under the occupation of Nazi Germany, the puppet nationalistic regime NDH (Independent State of Croatia) erected the Film Company Hrvatski Slikopis. Besides the militant propaganda

films, NDH produced romantic patriotic documentaries that emphasised "national values." At the same time, a partisan resistance movement, led by the Communist Party, became aware of the importance and power of moving images. The committee decided to register on-camera some of the important war battles, and, in 1943, the first film team was formed.

More importance was accorded to film the next year, when Marshall Tito, the leader of the Communist resistance, ordained the founding of The Film Association as a part of the National Liberation Struggle. Two years later, when the war was over, the Federate Republic of Yugoslavia started its first National Film Committee. Cinema was considered to be a powerful means of mass propaganda. Film became a "must" in a new society that was enthusiastically creating "people's culture" and had also to deal with illiteracy. The very first films were documentaries that reflected on the tragedy of the war that just ended. Films like *Jasenovac* by Gustav Gavrin and Kosta Hlavaty, on the horror of the biggest concentration camp in Yugoslavia, or *Belgrade* by Nikola Popovic, *Steps of Freedom* by Rados Novakovic, and *Istra* by Branko Marjanovic, were all made in 1945, the year of the liberation.

The first two postwar years were a period of documentary making that acted as film education, which officially did not exist at the time. A huge number of filmmakers entered the business either by order or by recommendation of the Communist Party; they schooled themselves through practice. Later, many of them went into feature fiction production (Marjanovic, Popovic, Novakovic).

The newsreel monthlies *Filmski Mjesecnik* were the first regular documentaries produced by the state in socialist Yugoslavia. They captured the relevant issues regarding spreading the communist political doctrine, enthusiasm in rebuilding the country, agrarian reforms, and important political and cultural events. They were screened on a regular basis in cinemas before the feature films. In the beginning, after World War II, cinema production and distribution from Slovenia to Macedonia were managed by The State Film Company of Yugoslavia (Drzavno Filmsko Poduzece Jugoslavije). But soon thereafter, according to the governments' intentions to decentralise film production, new companies came into being in each republic and autonomous territory. Some of them specialised in producing documentaries and shorts (Dunav film, Zastava , Bosna, Duga, Kinoteka 16, Zagreb, Studio film).

Because films were produced, distributed, and owned by the state, censorship was an obligatory aspect of the film business. Nevertheless, it was far less rigid than in other countries of Eastern Europe. A certain degree of freedom regarding the choice of the film theme, and especially regarding the style, was always present. The authors were exposed to cinema from the West, and some of them followed new trends such as cinema-verité and direct film styles. The filmmakers travelled with their works to Western and Eastern European festivals and were in touch with new cultural movements.

After making "politically correct" films in the 1950s that glorified the revolutionary struggle and the working class and denouncing the bourgeoisie, most of the filmmakers switched in the 1960s to visually strong and poetic documentary miniatures or analytical essays that were critical of society. Most of these short pieces were visually powerful and verbally ascetic, fitting perfectly in regular screenings as a prefilm in the theatres. No wonder Yugoslavian spectators held the documentary genre in high esteem.

A remarkable opus was created by filmmakers Rudolf Sremec, Krsto Skanata, Stjepan Zaninovic, and Zika Ristic. The cinema approach of Croatian director Sremec was characterised by a "friendly"

camera style. With his almost hundred films, he showed an enormous ability to penetrate invisibly into the lives of the people he filmed. His moving documentary *Time of Silence/Vrijeme sutnje* (1971) unveiled the shocking custom in a Slavonian village of "storing" old people in houses on the edge of the forest and leaving them alone to die. This devoted documentary maker was known abroad by his *People on Wheels/Ljudi na tockovima* (1963), in which he vividly portrayed people who travel everyday from the rural area to the cities for work. Krsto Skanata and Stjepan Zaninovic marked the early documentary production in Serbia and became known by challenging the themes that concern the consequences of World War II. Krsto Skanata approached his subjects in the style of direct cinema. He tried to follow the path of the truth and make films that would reveal the essence of the problem. At the same time, he was smart enough to nuance his approach in such a way that censors would accept and approve the film. One of his first films, *In the shadow of magic/U senci magije* (1955) uncovers the deep backwardness in socialist Yugoslavia. His film *First case—a man* (*Prvi padez—covek* (1964) addresses the human dignity of a miner who loses his arm and has to struggle on his own. *Soldier, at ease!/Ratnice, voljno!* (1966) focuses on the tragedy of a soldier who fought in the war and believed in a certain ideology that he later realized was false. Skanata's style was straightforward and analytical. Stylistically, the films were often done in a traditional manner. His reputation allowed him to challenge all sort of subjects, those that were pro regime as well as those that were questioning the justice of it. The films *Terrorists/Teroristi* (1970) and *12 Months of Winter/12 Meseci zime* (released 1983, shot 1971) were in certain parts of Yugoslavia forbidden for public screenings and only later on released.

Another author who dealt with revolution and the indebtedness of those who survived toward those who fell for freedom is Sjepan Zaninovic. His first big success was the film *Messages/Poruke* (1960), which revived the ideals of people who inscribed graffiti on the walls of the war prisons during World War II. His film *The Dialogue of Comrades on a War Photo/Dijalog drugova sa ratnog fotosa* (1968) portrayed the destinies of freedom fighters and of those who disappeared after the war in the post-revolutionary madness. Zika Ristic from Bosnia and Herzegovina produced remarkable documentaries both in quantity and quality. The best ones are *The Barge-Steerers of* the Drina/Splavari na Drini (1951), an exciting ode on humanity's struggle against nature; Yet – a City/ Ipak jedan grad (1966), a satirical commentary on bureaucracy; and Helmets/Sljemovi (1967), an engaged essay on war and peace. In the embrace of Bosna Film, later on Sutjeska, many documentary enthusiasts gathered in Sarajevo and created dozens of inspiring films (see entry Sarajevos' School of Documentary Filmmaking).

In Croatia, a director who introduced a new approach in treating small, everyday subjects was Kreso Golik. His film From 3 to 22/Od 3 do 22 (1966) follows a working mother at her exhausting daily activities. Through the destiny of an individual, Golik portrays the socialist society in many of its dark shades. This sharp and visually strong documentary is even today one of the most powerful ones ever made in Yugoslavia.

A director from the younger generation, Krsto Papic mastered portraying the mentality of the tough people from the robust area of Herzegovina. When My Knife Strikes You/Kad te moja cakija ubode (1968) deals powerfully with murderers who confess their crimes that were often triggered by trivial reasons. Following the cinema verité style, Papic treats every issue quite critically, giving a profound analysis of the social milieu. Special Trains/Specijalni vlakovi (1972) is a socially and politically engaged film that observes the consequences of the huge workers' emigration that took place in Yugoslavia during the 1960s and 1970s when hundreds of thousands of people went to work in West Germany.

One of the most profound documentary makers in Croatia is Petar Krelja who devoted his whole opus to people at the margin of society, uncovering the daily lives of those who seem to be merely a statistic in social research (see the entry Petar Krelja).

During the movement in the early 1970s known as Croatian Spring, a short period of liberalisation, Krelja dared to make some documentaries that went beyond the Communist Party norms, and three of his films were banned. This was the time of national "awakening," with attempts to political and cultural decentralisation toward the different Republics of Yugoslavia. It was the struggle for a more liberal socialism—the "socialism with a human face."

As a reaction to these tendencies, the existing political establishment forbade many filmmakers to continue with their projects. President Tito reacted severely, and many film authors had a hard time returning to their previous positions.

The Serbian director Želimir Žilnik suffered a similar fate. His June Turmoil/Lipanjaska gibanja (1969), which depicted student demonstrations, was banned. Žilnik, who took an active part in a cultural movement in fiction film called Black Wave, was considered by the authorities as a dangerous, provocative political rebel; and many of his films were banned; but he was highly appreciated for his directness and visually expressive film language by the film critics at home and abroad. The film The Unemployed/Nezaposleni ljudi (1968) received the Grand Prix at the Oberhausen Festival but was criticised at home on ideological grounds at home, along with Freedom or Cartoons/Sloboda ili strip (1972) which was banned.

At the same time, a younger generation of filmmakers became influenced by film trends from the West and started to be more intrigued by film aesthetics than political issues. Zoran Tadic made sophisticated documentaries about human solitude. His films Last post station Donji Dolac/ Zadnja posta Donji Dolac (1971), Friends/Druge (1972), Plaits/Pletenice (1974), and Festivity/Dernek (1975) were done with an ascetic constraint and minimalism, but emphasised the intimacy of the human stories. His profoundly composed visual miniatures were odes to the values of a simple lifestyle.

Nikola Babic became known for his visually powerful analysis of human nature. His films Sije (1970), Vox Populi (1970), Bino, oko galebovo/Bino, seagal's eye (1973) were cinematically intriguing studies of peoples' mentalities.

Meanwhile, in Serbia, apart from Skanata, Zaninovic, J. Zivanovic, and M. Strbac, a group of film enthusiasts gathered around Dunav Film and started to make more exciting and fresher documentaries. Italian film critics in 1966 named the style of the new authors Sarajevo's Documentary Film School. Most of these directors later went into fiction film; but at that time, Aleksandar Petrovic, Purisa Djordjevic, Dusan Makavajev, and later Petar Lalovic and Aleksandar Ilic introduced a contemplative, philosophical, and cinematically thrilling approach in treating reality. Filmmakers tried to avoid the traditional narrative structure and followed an unconventional way of storytelling characterised by poetic, rather surrealist, inputs. Some of them, such as Makavejev, were able to perform intriguing twists in treating politically and socially sensitive issues. The Parade/Parada (1962) portrays one of the socialist populist marches with humour and hidden sarcasm.

Two directors who gained a special place in the documentary scene are Vlatko Gilic and Zivko

Nikolic. Both were born in Monte Negro, lived in Belgrade, and were often concerned with aspects of life in their home country such as rigid traditionalism, suppression of women, and the tough life in the hilly deserted areas. What made their work special was a strong personal imprint in crossing borders of film genres and mixing the real and surreal. Their contemplative films, characterised by specific moods and atmospheres, were transforming the documentary starting point to the metaphorical level. In Gilics' film *In continuo* (1971), the focus is on a slaughterhouse, transmitting the metaphor of human destiny toward killing and bloodshed. In his *Love*Ljubav (1973), there is an ordinary meeting of a wife and husband during a lunch break that gets elevated to an ode of pure love. During the 1980s, Zivko Nikolic was even more radical in breaking the conventions of fiction and documentary. He would recreate a whole mysterious world out of a small documentary element. With few words and minimalist sound track, Nikolics's visuals, carefully created in many layers, invoke a philosophical discourse on life. *Ane* (1980) portrays the world of a woman who is patiently waiting for her husband, a sailor. *The Builder/Graditelj* (1980) speaks of a man who builds houses for others but does not have one himself. *Marko Perov* (1975) creates the world of an old dying man who observes life around him. *A Stamp/Biljeg* (1981) is a powerful ironic work of the society in which a hydrocentral is erected in an area where there is no water.

In Macedonia the most remarkable documentary maker was Stole Popov, whose films *Australia, Australia* (1976) and *Dae* (1979) spoke eloquently about the pain and nostalgia of Macedonians abroad and of the Gypsy minority at home, respectively. In Slovenia, the most intriguing author was Dusan Povh whose film *Three monuments/Trije spomeniki* (1958) evokes poetically memories of World War II. Milan Ljubic, Filip Robar Dorin, and Frantisek Cap also made films that ged political and social ideas.

The years after the death of President Tito (1980) brought a certain degree of disobedience and rebelliousness. Some political issues were more directly addressed; others, not being previously touched at all, were now courageously depicted. Zaninovic stirred the public with the documentary *The Case of Dr. Milos Zanko/Slucaj dr. Milosa Zanka* (1987) in which he anticipated the decay of Yugoslavia. Some politically radical directors appeared again on the documentary scene, such as Želimir Žilnik, Lordan Zafranovic, Joca Jovanovic, Petar Ljubojev, and, from the younger generation, Nikola

Lorencin, Nenad Puhovski, Selamu Taraku, Mirjana Zoranovic, Želimir Gvardiol, Miroslav Mandic, Vuk Janic, Vladimir Perovic, Momir Matovic, and Milan Knezevic. Their films dealt with social and political changes, emigration, injustice, and peoples' dissatisfaction.

In 1991 and 1992, peaking conflicts led to war and the final split of Yugoslavia into five independent states. Although the cinema industry was heavily hit both by the transitional structural socioeconomic processes and by poverty cause by war, documentary filmmaking was still alive and very vivid. Each of the new states focused on making documentaries in favour of their national policy, justifying the deeds of military and political authorities. But apart from more or less hidden propaganda films done during the period of war (1991–1995) and the time of transitional crises (1991–1999), some valuable documentary pieces were created as well.

Because with the fall of the country only Serbia and Montenegro kept the name Yugoslavia, the following sections do not concern the newly erected independent states of Croatia, Slovenia, Bosnia and Herzegovina, and Macedonia, but only documentary production done in the new Yugoslavia.

In Serbia, production was mostly television orientated, with many attempts of small producers to create relevant works. Dozens of new companies appeared, but only a few made an impact and survived. One of the most ambitious ones is Film Focus, led by Miroslav Bata Petrovic who made interesting, often humorous comments on the turbulent reality, as well as giving others a chance to make these kinds of films. The independent media group *B 92,* besides having radio and television production, indulged itself in the production of meaningful documentaries. *Belgrade Follies* (1997), directed by feature film director Goran Markovic, is a shocking and disturbing documentary about people's anger toward Milosevic's regime. His next feature-length autobiographical documentary *Serbia, Year Zero/Srbija, godine nulte* (2001) is a rather moving self-analysis of the responsibility of those who witnessed the tragedy of Yugoslavia, done in a personal and quite humorous style. Goran Radovanovic is one of the Belgrade-based authors who found support abroad and managed to make several daring and intriguing films. Both *My Country-For Internal Use Only/Moja domovina-za unutrasnju upotrebu* (2000) and *Otpor! The Fight to Save Serbia/ Otpor! Borba za opstanak Srbije* (2001) were critical toward the regime of that time. His last feature-length documentary, *Casting!* (2003), speaks of the devaluation of moral values among youngsters in today's Serbia.

In Monte Negro, one of the rare directors who continued from the 1980s on is Momir Matovic. He stayed faithful to his personal, special style of non-narrative, nonverbal documentary impressions of life. *The Last Cinema Screening/Posljednja bioskopska predstava* (1993) portrays a cinema freak who walks dozens of kilometres every day to go to the cinema. *The String of Life/Zica zivota* (1996) depicts the sober, ascetic lifestyle of villagers far from civilisation. Similar in approach is another Monte Negro-born director working in Serbia, Vladimir Perovic, who often, like Matovic, expresses political criticism in a hidden way. His films *The Guard/Cuvar* (2002) and *Vanishing/Nestajanje* (2003) are done without words. They focus on people who lead lonely lives in an absurd society, guarding a factory that does not work or going to a school that has only one student.

After the fall of the former Yugoslavia, the five new states that used to logistically depend on each other before the war had to learn how to survive on their own in the film world. The political conflict created an atmosphere of noncollaboration and hostility that started to diminish only around the year 2000. Economical crises in all of the new states caused lack of money for independent productions, and the possible solution lies in cooperation with Western European funds, as well as in the reconstruction of the previous cultural liaisons between the different states of the former Yugoslavia.

RADA SESIC

See also **Bosnian Documentary Movement; Zilnik, Zelimir**

YUGOSLAVIA: DEATH OF A NATION

(UK, MacQueen and Mitchell, 1995)

More than 200 documentaries have been made on the topic of Yugoslavia's break-up in the 1990s. Among those, *Yugoslavia: Death of a Nation* (1995) remains probably the best known, commonly perceived as a film in which "the facts are allowed to speak for themselves, and responsibilities are made clear" (Cohen, 1995).

The international television co-production was realised by the London-based Brian Lapping Associates, a production company specialising in current affairs, including documentaries on the Falklands War, the Gulf War, South Africa, as well as the acclaimed series on the end of the Soviet Union, *The Second Russian Revolution* (1992). Producer Norma Percy has to her credit a number of documentaries dealing with controversy and conflict, ranging from the U.S. Watergate scandal to the Israeli-Arab troubles, and including works on Algeria, China, and Northern Ireland.

Death of a Nation was completed in 1995 and broadcast in the United Kingdom and Europe in the autumn (after the Srebrenica massacre had taken place) and in the United States (Discovery Channel) during Christmas week. It also played in the former Yugoslav republics. An accompanying book, by journalists Laura Silber (who had acted as a consultant) and Allan Little, was also published, to make for a complete study pack. Lesson plans, containing clips from the film and excerpts from the book, are available on the Internet study web sites supported by The Guardian and by the Discovery Channel.

The film tells the story through well-selected footage and features numerous interviews with various parties in the conflict. It follows a chronological approach, tackling the crisis by beginning with the early Kosovo troubles, and structuring the story around the 1987 rise of Milosevic to political leadership. From this narrative point of view, it then gives accounts on the break-up of Slovenia, Croatia, and Bosnia. In five hourly segments ("The Cracks Appear," "Descent into War," "The Collapse of Unity," "The Gates of Hell," "No Escape"), it attempts to present a systematic account of the reasons and responsibilities for the country's violent break-up. It makes use of a large variety of documentary sources and features interviews with most of the main Yugoslav players. Even though issues of the Western involvement in the conflict are not addressed explicitly, a number of Western diplomats are also interviewed. The result is a convincing account of the claims, misunderstandings, and reactions of the main actors, presented within an absorbing narrative revealing how the recent tensions mounted. Although historians questioned some of the choices, the overall recognition was that the book and the documentary had granted to all sides the opportunity to speak, thus making the bias negligible and remaining an "accessible guide to the immediate causes and the detailed course of the wars" (Stokes, Lampe and Rusinow, 1996, 147).

Producer Percy has stated that, above all, she is interested in "how big decisions are made." A leading principle in her approach is to stress the role individuals play in the story by securing interviews with key players, aiming to have them experience a "catharsis on camera." "Things are generally dictated by a few people or one man," she said. "So we try to speak to everyone involved, which is a very good research technique, in that you check statements against each other" (quoted in Cohen, 1995). In the preproduction period, a series of informal interviews were carried out, allowing identification of the major themes that were also to be researched. Later, the filmmakers returned for filmed interviews, during which the same question was often put to the interviewees, particularly to those who were known to have been involved in a key situation. For example, both Milosevic and Tudjman were questioned about their alleged 1991 meeting over the division of Bosnia between Serbia and Croatia, both presenting twisted and evasive accounts.

Background researchers looked through hundreds of hours of archival material; Michael Simkin's discovery of a forgotten reportage showing Milosevic's notorious visit to Kosovo in 1987 became one of the best-known images related to Yugoslavia's break-up. A wealth of videotaped events was made available to the filmmakers in all republics (for example, unused footage of atrocities in the town of Zvornik by Arkan's paramilitary Tigers, was found in Reuters' Belgrade office). According to director Paul Mitchell, the warring parties filmed most events "because they believed they would thus be able to show who had allowed Yugoslavia to be destroyed" (quoted in Cohen).

The film enjoyed wide international acclaim. However, it also became the subject of criticism, raising questions of a wider theoretical nature regarding the function of documentary film as historical record.

Talking of the film, political scientist Susan Woodward (1997) identified three problematic consequences of what she described as "journalistic dominance" and its "insidious influence for historical scholarship": first, the leading "role of narrative in shaping perceptions of the war"; second, "the ahistorical character of these narratives that, ironically, seem almost obsessed with identifying these conflicts as historical"; and third, the use of a "personalized 'source' as primary evidence." In *Death of a Nation*, she noted, facts that did not fit the narrative had been frequently ignored, and similar events had been recorded with different sympathies in different parts of the country. These seemingly minor inaccuracies, Woodward argued, were accountable for the most serious troubles. She criticized the film for taking nationalism out of its concrete politicoeconomic context, for misunderstanding and misreporting the blanked-labelled "Titoist period" and its immediate aftermath, and for selectively paying attention to nationalist tendencies and outcomes. The causes of nationalism, she claimed, could never be correctly identified if they were only explained by referencing to incidents of "rising nationalism" (as seen in the use of the Milosevic's visit to Kosovo as a key historical event taken out of socioeconomic context). While putting together an absorbing narrative, the filmmakers had failed to trace the roots of nationalism in the changes of domestic economic powers of the republics, in the controversial policies of the International Monetary Fund, and in the adverse impact that economic reforms had on employment and redistribution during the 1980s. Leaving those issues out meant that the film failed to identify the real factors behind the rise of nationalism, Woodward insisted.

As a current affairs documentary, *Death of a Nation* inevitably catered to the explanatory needs of the day. It explained the violence by referencing to select events and thus asserting certain causal links that brought most elements together in a plausible narrative. Deciding which images and events to use and which ones to lay to rest depended on the preferred narrative on Yugoslavia's break-up adopted by the filmmakers. The approach was premised on a belief that there is a direct causal link between the present-day state of things and concrete past events. But which events precisely? In their interpretative endeavors, the filmmakers were compelled to highlight events that fell in line with the chosen explanatory framework, thus walking a dangerous tightrope between reconstruction and manipulation. And while claiming that "social sweep and history are not really our focus" (Percy quoted in Cohen), the authors of the film extensively adjusted the complex picture of the past to fit the prevailing media interpretation of current events (see Iordanova, 2001).

The credibility of *Death of a Nation* was seriously questioned on at least one occasion. During the first trial at the International Tribunal for War Crimes in Yugoslavia at the Hague in 1996, British political scientist James Gow, who had acted as one of the film's consultants, was called in by the prosecution as expert witness. In his testimony, Gow used excerpts of the film. In cross-examination, defense attorney Fons Orie questioned examples of incorrect translation of statements made during interviews (some by Milosevic), and asked Gow to elaborate on his views of the difference between translation and interpretation. In response, Gow explained that the translations were a matter "of the choice of a particular word which in this case, I think, made no substantive difference to the sense" [....] "it is important for the translator to interpret the sense which is intended to be conveyed by the speaker" (Gow in Tadic-Transcripts, 577–578).

Using *Death of a Nation* as evidence set a precedent that was continued at the Hague with the use of other documentaries. In 2002, during opening statements at his trial, Slobodan Milosevic screened excerpts of the BBC documentary *Moral Combat* (2000, Alan Little) and the entire German film *Es began min einer Lüge/It Began with a Lie* (Jo Angerer and Mathias Werth, 2002). This use of documentaries (as works that inevitably contain significant interpretative element) as evidence raises a range of further questions.

The troubles in Yugoslavia continued beyond 1995, and the country was in the news headlines on a continuous basis. The well-known visuals of the Bosnian war and of Milosevic's visit to Kosovo were continuously recycled by broadcasters. At the time of the Kosovo war in 1999, *Death of a Nation* was edited and played in a shorter version on BBC, the narrative respectively adjusted to stress more on the Kosovo aspects, making a well-suited background introduction to the continued hostilities. The book and the film remain the most popular background material on the Yugoslav wars, thus making the chosen narrative line shape all further perceptions about the region.

DINA IORDANOVA

See also **Krelja, Petar; Sarajevo School of Documentary Filmmaking**

Yugoslavia: Death of a Nation. (USA/UK/France, BBC (UK), Canal+ (France), Discovery USA, ORF (Austria), VRPO (The Netherlands), RTBF (Belgium), SVT2 (Sweden), NRK (Norway), Danmarks Radio (Denmark), and ABC (Australia), 1995, 250 min.). Produced by Brian Lapping Associates (Norma Percy), London. Directed by Angus McQueen and Paul Mitchell. Narrated by Robin Ellis. Consultant Laura Silber.

Further Reading

Cohen, Roger, "Covering All Sides in the Balkan War," in *The New York Times*, December 24, 1995, Section 2, 37.

Gow, James, Paterson, Richard, and Preston, Alison (eds.), *Bosnia by Television*, London: British Film Institute, 1996.

Gow, James, "Testimony at Dusko Tadic Trial," Tadic-Transcripts, *International Criminal Tribunal for the Former Yugoslavia*, Available: http://www.un.org/icty/inde.htm, May 13, 1996, 534–578.

Iordanova, Dina, *Cinema of Flames: Balkan Film, Culture and the Media*, London: BFI, 2001, 71–89.

Silber, Laura and Little, Allan, *The Death of Yugoslavia*, London: Penguin Books/BBC Books; New York: Penguin Books, 1995.

Stokes, Gale, Lampe, John, and Rusinow, Dennison Rusinow, with Julie Mostov, "Instant History: Understanding the Wars of Yugoslav Succession," in *Slavic Review*, 55, 1, Spring 1996, 147.

Woodward, Susan L., "It Depends on When You Start the Story: Narratives as Camouflage and the Political Use of Scholarship on the Yugoslav Wars, 1991–1996," Paper presented at the workshop on "Doing History in the Shadow of the Balkan Wars" Working Group on Southeast European Studies. University of Michigan, Ann Arbor, January 17–18, 1997.

Z

ZAHN, PETER VON

Having made more than 1,000 films for television, Peter von Zahn is one of the legends of German TV history. He was one of the pioneers of the first trial operations of radio and television in Hamburg (NWDR), and he became the head of the text department as early as July 1945. His characteristic reportage style was very much influenced by Anglo-American journalism. He was sent to the United States by the NWDR as a result of conflicts with Chancellor Konrad Adenauer about his independent radio commentaries. There he started with his TV reports, *Berichte aus der neuen Welt/Reports from the New World* in 1955. He reported with his typical, high-pressured voice about daily life and his family's experiences in this modern society. These stories set standards for reportage and documentary in early German television. His style was a mixture of the features that he had made for radio and the American style of reporting represented by Edward R. Murrow, Fred Firendly, and others. This style was primarily oriented to text and content and then looked for the images needed to illustrate it. It stands in sharp contrast to the newsreels and the cultural films of the Third Reich period, which concentrated strongly on the image and dynamic editing. His personal features, which were broadcast once a month, shaped the image of the United States in postwar Germany.

Beside the series *Berichte aus der neuen Welt*, von Zahn also created a series called *Bilder aus der farbigen Welt/Images from the Colourful World*, where he presented political topics from Africa, South America, and Asia and showed the clash between modern industrialization and traditional cultures. He built a wordwide network of journalists working for his own Washington-based company, Documentary Programs Inc. The idea was to report on the same topic from different countries and thus provide a deeper perspective. In October 1961, he started the weekly series *Reporter der Windrose/Reporter of the Wind Rose* and reported from different regions in the world to bring them into German homes. The idea was for audiences to learn about and see something from the countries and cultures outside of Europe. It was the first attempt at a regular broadcast on foreign affairs subjects. The goal was to analyze the structure of the societies in the modern world and to compare developments. The first program had the title *People on the Move* and presented case studies of people moving to the huge cities and political emigrants, as well as economic migration and holidays in sunny places. After 104 programs and two years of intensive work, the stations decided to terminate the series and begin using their own foreign correspondents in different countries. Peter von Zahn also produced portraits of important statesman like Ben Gurion, which brought him the Grimme Prize in 1964.

Besides shaping the documentary work of the SDR (Stuttgarter Schule), Peter von Zahn successfully established another journalistic style in German television, which was influenced by the radio essays and Anglo-American school of reporting. He produced many more films until 1993, when at 80 years of age, he decided to withdraw from active filmmaking but still published columns as a journalist and wrote his memoirs. He is seen as one of the pioneers and legends of German television.

KAY HOFFMANN

Biography

Born January 29, 1913, in Chemnitz; grew up in Dresden. After working as voluntary worker in a publishing house, began to study jurisprudence, history, and philosophy in Vienna, Jena, and Freiburg in 1931. 1939–1945 soldier in World War II. After the war, worked for the British military station "Radio Hamburg" and became one of the pioneers of the Northwest German Radio (NWDR). 1948–1951 head of the Düsseldorf studio of NWDR. 1951–1960 American correspondent for the NWDR, first only in radio, then from 1955 on for TV as well. Founded own company, Documentary Programs Inc., in Washington. Back in Germany, founded own production company, Windrose Film- und Fernsehproduktion GmbH in 1960 and Anatol AV und Filmproduktion GmbH in 1976; worked as director, author, and producer until 1996. Died July 26, 2001 in Hamburg.

Selected Films

1955 *Bilder aus der Neuen Welt / Images from the New World*: director, script
1961 *Bericht aus der farbigen Welt / Images from the Colourful World*: director
1961 *Reporter der Windrose/Reporter of the Wind Rose*: producer, director
1963 *Windrose der Zeit/Wind Rose of Time*: director
1970 *Die Kuba-Krise 1962/The Cuba Crisis 1962*: director
1974 *Die geheimen Papiere des Pentagon / The Secret Papers of Pentagon*: director
1976 *Fünf Prüfungen des Oberbürgermeisters—Konrad Adenauer / Five Examinations of the Mayor—Konrad Adenauer*: script
1993 *Shalom Dresden*: director
1996 *Beobachtungen im Ruhrgebiet I + II/Observations in the Ruhr Area I + II*: script, director

Further Reading

Zahn, Peter von, *Stimme der ersten Stunde. Erinnerungen 1913–1951*, Stuttgart, 1991.
———, *Reporter der Windrose. Erinnerungen 1951–1964*, Stuttgart, 1994.
———, "Reporter der Windrose," in *Blicke in die Welt. Reportagen und Magazine des nordwestdeutschen Fernsehens in den 50er und 60er Jahren*, Heinz B. Heller and Peter Zimmermann (eds.), Konstanz, 1995, 117–125.
———, *Bilder aus der farbigen Welt*, in *Strategie der Blicke. Zur Modellierung von Wirklichkeit in Dokumentarfilm und Reportage*, Dieter Ertel and Peter Zimmermann (eds.), Konstanz, 1996, 177–182.
Zimmermann, Peter, *Beruf Reporter. Ein Interview mit Peter von Zahn*, in *Blicke in die Welt. Reportagen und Magazine des nordwestdeutschen Fernsehens in den 50er und 60er Jahren*, Heinz B. Heller and Peter Zimmermann (eds.), Konstanz, 1995, 127–140.

ZETTERLING, MAI

A pioneering feminist filmmaker noted for her social consciousness, Mai Zetterling made psychologically complex films in the latter half of her career that challenge various orthodoxies (religious, sexual, ideological) and exhibit a pessimistic, sometimes bleak, worldview familiar to fans of her more famous compatriot, Ingmar Bergman. Although a product of the same industrial/artistic complex in which Bergman and earlier luminaries of Swedish cinema (such as Victor Sjöström, Mauritz Stiller, and Gösta Werner) came into being, Zetterling evinces in her work a more modern take on heterosexual relationships and institutionalized forms of injustice.

This can be partly attributed to her exposure, both direct and indirect, to a wide variety of cultures and lifestyles throughout the world before the actress's mid-career makeover as a writer-director. Indeed, it was during her years spent abroad as an actress working primarily in British and American film that she first came to inhabit the worlds of spiritually dispossessed and emotionally estranged women—roles that would prove substantive for her own controversial forays into Freudian-Marxist territory. Any attempt to sort through the major themes of Zetterling's work behind the camera should therefore take into account her many onscreen appearances across a range of internationally diverse productions, from her countrymen's angst-ridden social dramas of the 1940s to the English-language potboilers she starred in during the 1950s. While critics often remarked on the actress's charm and beauty (her blue eyes and blonde hair were apparently made for Technicolor), these stereotypically Swedish traits were matched by a rigorous intelligence and devotion to philosophical inquiry, key elements of her stark black-and-white films.

After training at Stockholm's Royal Dramatic Theater and starring in such plays as Ella Wilcke's "En sommar på egen hand" (1941), the 16-year-old Swede made her screen debut in the swashbuckler *Lasse-Maja* (1942). Her most famous early starring role was Bertha, the teenage girlfriend of a school pupil in Alf Sjöberg's *Hets/ Torment* (1944). With a plot that sounds reminiscent of those peppering Zetterling's own oeuvre, the film explores Bertha and Jan-Erick's titular feelings of anguish, which spring from the latter's sadistic teacher (whose own torment drives him to rape and murder the young girl).

After winning international acclaim for her role in *Hets*, which gave the 19-year-old actress the opportunity to betray a mature understanding of the cruelties people inflict on others, Zetterling continued acting in Swedish films (including Gustaf Molander's domestically successful *Nu Borjar Livet/We Live Now* [1948] and Ingmar Bergman's *Musik i mörker/Night Is My Future* [1948]), making the occasional trip to London to appear in such films as Basil Dearden's *Frieda* (1947). This latter film, which concerns an immigrant woman residing in England during the postwar period, contains autobiographical elements impossible to ignore; for by this time in her career Zetterling was oscillating not only between stage and screen but also between two countries, with England becoming her temporary residence after she signed on with the Rank Organisation. This British film company was intent on molding her into an international star, although the spate of melodramas and crime thrillers in which she appeared did little to further this goal. Throughout the 1950s, a period of economic uncertainty and upheaval for the British film industry, many of Zetterling's star-vehicles were box-office failures; but, in tackling a multitude of roles in low-budget films, and by eventually gravitating away from Rank, she was able to expand her acting repertoire to accommodate different ethnicities and cultural backgrounds (playing everything from a French exchange student in Edmond T. Greville's *The Romantic Age* [1949] and an exploited prima ballerina in Val Guest's *Dance Little Lady* [1954] to a murder suspect in Marc Allégret's *Blackmailed* [1951]). Significantly, she played numerous German roles throughout this period, from the frowned-upon war-bride of a British RAF officer in *Frieda* to Hildegarde, the amnesiac object of a German professor's fatherly desire in *Portrait from Life* (1948). Whether in these British films or in such Hollywood fare as *A Prize of Gold* (1955), a drama about a war refugee dedicated to saving a group of German orphans, Teutonic themes and iconography frequently congealed around the Swedish actress as cross-cultural signifiers of her uncanny "otherness."

By the early 1960s, Zetterling had become increasingly dissatisfied with her acting career and was seeking opportunities to step behind the cameras. Given the green light by Roger Moorfoot of the BBC, she directed numerous shorts for television, including *The Polite Invasion* (1960), concerning Swedish immigration; *Lords of Little Egypt* (1961), about the gypsies at St. Maries-de-la-Mer; *The Prosperity Race* (1962), which delves into the emerging sense of affluence and entitlement among the Swedish middle-class; and *Do-It-Yourself Democracy* (1963), her look at social and political concerns unique to Iceland. Among this BBC batch, her antiwar short, *The War Game* (1961), stands out not only because it garnered the Golden Lion award at the 1963 Venice Film Festival, but, more important because of its satirical take on the way violence (here represented by a toy gun) snakes surreptitiously into childhood.

Five years after her divorce from dance choreographer Tutte Lemkow, Zetterling wed director and screenwriter David Hughes. Their marriage, which lasted from 1958 to 1979, was mutually nourishing as a source of cinematic inspiration and collaboration. The two co-directed a half-dozen films, beginning with the flashback-laden literary adaptation *Älskande par / Loving Couples* (1964) and ending with a ten-minute episode for the omnibus feature *Visions of Eight* (1972–1973) entitled "The Strongest." These two films bookend an extremely fertile period in Zetterling's career, one that witnessed not only a stylistic maturation but also a developing sense of the struggles historically faced by women from various social and cultural backgrounds. Fed into her introspective narratives are images of loneliness and obsession—themes that, as biographer Louise Heck-Rabi argues, permeate her filmography and filter into the director's vested interests in feminism. Although these motifs are primarily reserved for her nondocumentary work—most notably *Doktor Glas* (1968), the pessimistic story of a physician driven to murder by his insatiable desire for a pastor's nonreciprocating wife; and *Nattlek/Night Games* (1966), a notoriously provocative examination of what polite society deems sexually perverse (incest, orgies, masturbation) and corporeally abject (vomiting, childbirth)—one can detect analogous themes percolating throughout her nonfiction films as well. For instance, *Vincent the Dutchman*, her 1971 color documentary about Vincent Van Gogh, pivots on isolation and obsession, customary states of mind for the notoriously tormented and introspective painter.

After making *Vincent the Dutchman* for British television, Zetterling was approached by producer David Wolper and asked to contribute an episode to the multi-director documentary *Visions of Eight*. Appropriately entitled "The Strongest," this segment—which playfully deconstructs the men's weightlifting competition at the 1972 Olympic Games in Munich and provides yet another glimpse of the filmmaker's interest in man's peculiar fixations—finds her tapping into her own strengths as a satirist, as well as a technical virtuoso attuned to the short-film format. In the wake of *Visions of Eight* came even more documentary shorts. These run the gamut from a tour of the city of Stockholm to a hagiographic piece on tennis legend Stan Smith. Zetterling's frequent forays into nonfiction filmmaking throughout the 1970s suggest that she, like the narrator of her 1976 novel *Bird of Passage*, was becoming "a creature of habit," sensitive not only to each day's "particular rhythm" (Zetterling, 1976: 102) but also to the guiding spirit of documentary investigation—its purported pursuit of truth and ontological grounding in reality.

With the publication of *Bird of Passage*, Zetterling had already begun making a name for herself as an accomplished novelist and essayist, pursuits she had begun a decade earlier when her book, *Night Games*, was unleashed on an unsuspecting public. A passage from that 1966 novel— "One concentrates on one's perversions to get rid of that greasy film of boredom that has begun to form on everything and everyone one knows" (Zetterling, 1966: 30)—might just as well have been included in her 1985 autobiography, *All Those Tomorrows*, so indicative is it of Zetterling's own *modus operandi*. That she became even more focused on the "perversions" of modern life during the 1980s, that she continued to zero in on the tormented psyches of women in such films as *Scrubbers* (1982), a reform-school/prison drama, and *Amorosa* (1986), a documentary-like biopic concerning the short, scandal-ridden life of Swedish novelist Agnes von Krusenstjana (the author on whose work Zetterling's first feature, *Älskande par*, was based), is a testament of her lifelong dedication to feminist concerns. By the time she succumbed to cancer in London on March 17, 1994, Zetterling had amassed a staggering body of work whose legacy and longevity secure her a pivotal place in film history.

DAVID DIFFRIENT

See also **Visions of Eight**

Biography

Born Mai Elizabeth Zetterling in Västerås, Sweden on May 24, 1925. Lived with her mother and stepfather in Australia from 1929 to 1932 before returning home and beginning a career in stage acting. After training at Stockholm's Royal Dramatic Theater and starring in such plays as Ella Wilcke's "En sommar på egen hand" (1941), made her screen debut in *Lasse-Maja* (1942). Continued acting in Swedish films throughout the 1940s and 1950s. Began directing shorts for television in the early 1960s. Married and divorced the dance choreographer Tutte Lemkow. Married director and screenwriter David Hughes in 1958. Divorced from Hughes in 1979. Died in London March 17, 1994.

Selected Films

1960 *The Polite Invasion*: director
1961 *Lords of Little Egypt*: director
1961 *The War Game*: director, producer
1962 *The Prosperity Race*: director
1963 *Do-It-Yourself Democracy*: director
1971 *Vincent the Dutchman*: co-director (with David Hughes), producer
1973 "The Strongest"(episode in *Visions of Eight*): co-director (with David Hughes)
1978 *The Rain's Hat*: director, editor

Further Reading

De Beauvoir, Simone, *The Second Sex*, New York: Vintage, 1989 reissue.

Gilbert, Harriet (ed.), *The Sexual Imagination: A Feminist Companion*, London: Jonathon Cape, 1993.

Heck-Rabi, Louise, "Zetterling, Mai," in *The St. James Encyclopedia of Women Filmmakers*, Amy L. Unterburdger (ed.), Farmington Hills, MI: Visible Ink Press, 1999.

Kaplan, E. Ann (ed.), *Feminism and Film*, Oxford: Oxford University Press, 2000.

McGregor, C., "Mai Is Behind the Camera Now," in *New York Times*, April 30, 1972.

Meyer, Donald B., *Sex and Power: The Rise of Women in America, Russia, Sweden, and Italy*, Middletown, CT: Wesleyan University Press, 1987.

Waldman, Diane and Janet Walker (eds.), *Feminism and Documentary*, Minneapolis: University of Minnesota Press, 1999.

Zetterling, Mai, *Night Games*, New York: Coward-McCann, Inc., 1966.

——, *Shadow of the Sun*, New York: Vintage, 1975.

——, *Bird of Passage*, New York: Vintage, 1976.

——, *All Those Tomorrows*, Grove Press, 1986.

ZIELKE, WILLY

Willy Zielke is one of few German filmmakers notable for having done avant-garde work during the National Socialist, or Nazi, era in Germany. His work is exemplary for many. After a visionary start in the 1920s, his career stagnated under national socialism, and he enjoyed only modest success in the new Federal Republic.

Zielke originally worked as a photographer. In 1929, he presented a series of studies at the pioneering film and photography exhibition (FiFo) in Stuttgart, which established photography as a serious art form worthy of respect and brought attention to Zielke's concern with objectivity.

In 1931, Zielke experimented with film. Critics praised the original camera tricks and the unusual settings of his unfortunately forgotten first silent films: *Bubi träumt,* (1931), *München. Willy Zielke zeigt eine Stadt* (1931), and *Anton Nicklas, ein Münchner Original* (1932).

In 1932, Zielke shot his first contracted work (without pay), a socially engaged short film with the title *Arbeitslos—Das Schicksal von Millionen/ Unemployed—The Destiny of Millions*. Most of the actors were found at an unemployment office, and production costs were covered by donations from Munich factories. The film, which was influenced by the aesthetics of Brecht's proletarian theater, denounced unemployment as a hopeless, demoralized state of being. Assembled images and symbolic characters showed the influence of Zielke's photographic work, as well as the Constructivists, known for their cutting technique. After its debut performance on April 3, 1933, in the Atlantic Cinema in Munich, the film disappeared from public view.

In 1943, Zielke agreed to direct a longer, funded version of *Arbeitslos—Das Schicksal von Millionen,* changing the name of the film to *Die Wahrheit/The Truth*. The dominant figure in the newer version of the film is the idealized worker, who replaces the realistic portrait of the unemployed found in the first *Arbeitslos*. The workers enter empty factory halls in marching formation to the song *Deutschland erwache* ("Germany Awake"). The passage from the Weimar Republic to the National Socialist regime is presented as the solution to the world economic crisis.

Until 1934, Zielke taught at the Bayerischen Staatslehranstalt. He left his academic position to devote himself entirely to filmmaking. He married Elfriede Weissberger and lived in Munich.

In July 1934, Zielke was asked to create a film with sound to mark the hundredth anniversary of the German railway system. He wrote, directed, and did camera work for *Das Stahltier/The Steel Animal,* a title he chose himself. He did not follow the conventional pattern of such films by enumerating the steps of development. Rather, he mixed elements from feature films, documentaries, and experimental films to present his theme from multiple perspectives. *Das Stahltier/The Steel Anaimal,* defies established aesthetic and generic conventions. This film is also influenced by the Russian constructivist, as well as Brechtian theater.

Technical modernization is presented in the film as the superior means of modern social development. In the plot, a prospective engineer overcomes the initial suspicion and distrust of the workers, gaining their respect and trust. Zilke used railway workers, rather than actors, to play the roles of the workers. Close-ups of their expressive faces and gestures are reminders of Zielke's photographic background. Some scenes, which show the men working half-naked or wrestling, suggest a homoerotic element, at least when viewed today.

The financial backers of *Das Stahltier* were not pleased with the results, as the film was intended to promote train travel and use the opportunity of the hundredth anniversary as an occasion for propaganda and advertisement. *Das Stahltier* was not approved for public screening. The film was shown at Walter Frentz's seminar for cinematic film at the Lessing faculty, the only public screening during the National Socialist regime.

Leni Riefenstahl attended the seminar and was impressed by *Das Stahltier*. She hired Zielke as a cameraman for her production company. Their first project together was made in 1935, and was called *Tag der Freiheit!—Unsere Wehrmacht!/Freedom day! Our Army!,* a film that was supposed to document Germany's military power on the occasion of the reintroduction of the armed forces.

Riefensthal's Olympia Film GmbH asked Zielke to make the prologue to a film on the 1936 Olympic Games. Riefenstahl used the material shot by Zielke, but she cut a new prologue to the film, which he rejected. The cooperative relationship ended in a quarrel.

In February 1937, Zielke was admitted into the University Hospital in Munich, with a diagnosis of schizophrenia. He spent the next five years in several psychiatric institutions and in the labor camp Herzogsägmühle in Bavaria. His diagnosis had drastic consequences, as his disease and prognosis were classified as "genetically transmitted with no recovery" and, on the basis of this judgment, he was sterilized. Zielke's suffered harsh treatment in numerous mental hospitals under the Nazi regime.

In 1942, Leni Riefenstahl arranged for Zielke's release. From 1944 until the end of the war in 1945, Zielke shot for Riefenstahl's *Tiefland* in Kitzbühel (Bavaria) and later in Prague. Riefenstahl, however, claimed she was unable to use the footage. She stated that she could not find any use for Zielke's material. During this period, Zielke married his second wife, Ilse Fischer.

Zielke suffered though a long period of sickness on his release from the mental hospitals, as a result of his treatment there. After working for Riefenstahl on *Tiefland,* he stopped working until 1952. He made a fresh start, under the name Viktor Valet, with a short film about the landscapes of Niederrhein, *Verzauberter Niederrhein/Magic Niederhein*. The expressionist, structured imagery is highly reminiscent of the German silent film tradition.

Despite several small contracts with the innovative production company Gesellschaft für bildende Filme (GbF) in Munich, Zielke could barely support himself. He was consigned to do some takes for *Schöpfung ohne Ende/Neverending Creation*, a film by GbF produced for the Bavaria factories. He ignored schedules production specifications, and was considered difficult and uncooperative by his colleagues and assistants on the film.

Das Stahltier, long considered lost, resurfaced in France in 1953. The legal owner of the film, the now-called Deutsche Bahn AG, agreed to a public representation after some of the more experimental scenes were edited out. Zielke saw this as a destructive infringement on his rights as a filmmaker. Nevertheless, in February 1954, the edited version was shown in Frankfurt am Main.

In 1956, Zielke made *Verlorene Freiheit/Lost Freedom*. The plot, which centers on a little blind girl's failed attempts to set a bird free, suggests a parallel with Zielke's situation and his sense of frustration at the restrictions placed on his creativity. *Aluminium—Porträt eines Metalles/Aluminum—Portrait of a Metal*, which appeared in 1957, was the last Zielke film to receive a public screening. The picture, produced by the GfB, traced the development of aluminum. The filmmaker's innovative use of color, light, and montage illustrate that, even at this late stage in his career, Zilke remained a creative artist.

In the 1960s, Zielke accepted sporadic German/Russian translation projects, mostly under the name Viktor Valet. In 1962, he patented one of his technical shooting processes, the *jalousie system* (sun drape system).

During the last ten years of his life, Zielke enjoyed a renewed interest in his photography. He had an exhibition of his photography in Arles, France in 1982.

THOMAS TODE

See also **Riefenstahl, Leni**

Biography

Born in Lodz, Poland, September 18, 1902. Relocated to Munich, 1921. Student at the *Bayrischen Staatslehranstalt für Fotografie* in Munich until 1926. Assistant in the portrait studio of Franz Grainer, Munich and Minya Dietz-Dührkoop, Hamburg, 1927. Member between 1928 and 1934 of the *Gesellschaft Deutscher Lichtbildner* (GDL). Assistant Professor at the *Bayrischen Staatslehranstalt für Fotografie*. Admitted to the Schwabing hospital because of a nervous breakdown, February 1937. Two months later, transferred to the psychiatric hospital Eglfing Haar (München), with a diagnosis of schizophrenia. In October, sent to the Wanderhof Herzogsägmühle work camp. Initiated a hunger strike and was committed to the Eglfing Haar psychiatric hospital from 1939 to 1942. Upon release, moved in with mother and uncle, and met Ilse Will, whom he later married. Resided in Berlin from 1961. Moved to Lichtenberg. 1969. Died September 16, 1989, Hannover, Lower Saxony, West Germany.

Selected Films

1931 *Bubi träumt*
1931 *München. Willy Zielke zeigt eine Stadt*
1932 *Anton Nicklas, ein Münchner Original*
1933 *Arbeitslos—Das Schicksal von Millionen*
1934 *Die Wahrheit*
1935 *Das Stahltier*
1953 *Verzauberter Niederrhein*
1956 *Verlorene Freiheit*
1957 *Aluminium—Porträt eines Metalles*

Further Reading

Cozarinsky, Edgardo, *Resistance des images, tilages, saur-egarde et restaurations dans la collection films de la Cine-mateque francaise, Ed*, Paris: Cinemateque francaise, 1996.

Elsaesser, Thomas, *Das Weimarer Kino–aufgeklärt und doppelbödig*, Berlin, 1999.

Graham, Cooper C., *Leni Riefenstahl and Olympia*, New York, 1986.

Riefenstahl, Leni, *Memoiren*, Frankfurt/Main: Ullstein Verlag, 1996.

Rother, Rainer, *Leni Riefenstahl—Die Verführung des Talents*, Berlin, 2000.

Sch öppe, Wilhelm Sch (Hg), *Meister der Kamera erzählen*, Halle/Saale, 1935.

Wetzel, Kraft, and Peter Hagemann, *Zensur. Verbotene deutsche Filme. 1933–1945*, Berlin, 1978.

Zielke, Willy, *Technik des Bromöl-Umdruckes, Enzyklopädie der Photographie und Kinematographie, Heft 116*, Halle Saale, 1931.

———, (n)akt–Einführung in die Aktfofografie

ŽILNIK, ŽELIMIR

Žilnik's highly original works—mostly docudramas, reenacted documentaries, and provocative features—have cemented his reputation as the Yugoslav master of subversive filmmaking. His consistently daring explorations of social taboos are informed by a serious commitment to radicalism and liberalism. Challenging the conventions of the documentary genre has helped Žilnik to examine and expose some popular myths of Yugoslavia's historical destiny.

Žilnik's critical approach and gritty visuals were first appreciated internationally in the late 1960s. His documentary on the homeless *Nezaposleni ljudi/The Unemployed* (1968) won at Oberhausen, and his experimental feature *Rani radovi/Early Works* (1969) won the Grand Prix at the Berlin Film Festival. Named after the highly contested Hegelian writings of Marx, *Early Works* is considered a prime example of the Yugoslav Black Wave, made at a period when the influence of the neo-Marxist Praxis group was at its height in Yugoslavia. Tito's personal disapproval of Žilnik's work, however, led to the ban of *Lipanjska gibanja/June Turmoil* (1969), a documentary on the awkward subject of student dissent, as well as of *Early Works* and *Sloboda ili strip/Freedom or Cartoons* (1972).

In interviews given around this time, Žilnik said he particularly appreciated feature films that mixed documentary parts, as long fiction and documentary were clearly distinguishable. "In the final analysis," he said, "if you are using film as a tool, as a means of communication that, hopefully, will change people, then I think the documentary film is always stronger. I think a documentary film will live longer" (Van Dyke, 1970).

In the 1970s, Žilnik worked in exile in Germany, making independent leftist documentaries on Gastarbeiters and anarcho-terrorism and was censored once again, this time by the Germans. Back in Yugoslavia, Žilnik deployed his trademark sarcasm in a number of made-for-TV documentaries on socially sensitive topics. His black comedy *Tako se kalio čelik/How the Steel Was Tempered* (1988) revealed the disastrous state of the underground personal economies flourishing within the mismanaged system of state socialism.

In the 1990s, Žilnik became an outspoken critic of nationalism and worked on subversive satires realised for Belgrade's dissident *Studio B 92*. His internationally acclaimed "mockumentary" *Tito po drugi put medju srbima/Tito Among the Serbs for a Second Time* (1993) questioned the cult to Tito's personality and effectively weakened the overwhelming referencing to Tito as the source of all Yugoslav troubles. In this film, Žilnik lets a well-known Tito impersonator spend a few hours on the sidewalks of Milošević's Belgrade pretending that Tito has been resurrected and has come to confront (and rebuff) the spontaneous opinions of ordinary people on the streets. The footage of this improvisation is intercut with archival footage, thus producing a powerful statement on the past and present iconic quality of Tito's personality.

In his docudrama *Dupe Od Mramora/Marble Ass* (1995), Zilnik attacks the Serbian brand of "machismo" by featuring a male prostitute who claims that by enduring the sometimes excessive passions of his lovers, he in fact absorbs the violence that plights society at large. The film is yet another example where a fictional narrative evolves from reenacting the protagonist's real-life experiences.

In the late 1990s, Žilnik's interest was focused mostly on the issue of European-wide migrations. *Kud plovi ovaj brod/Wanderlust* (1998) critically examines the movements of East block nationals during the first decade of post-communism. *Tvrdjnava Evropa/Fortress Europe* (2000), yet another reenacted documentary shot on digital video in Slovenia and Italy, mixes the litanies of Russian émigré Artjom and his daughter Katja with shattering footage of interviews with detainees in the asylum seekers camps in Italy and Austria.

DINA IORDANOVA

See also **Makavejev, Dušan**

Biography

Born in 1942, in Niš, Yugoslavia (Serbia). Studied law and entered filmmaking as an amateur. Has more

than sixty shorts, documentaries, and features to his credit. Suffered censorship in Yugoslavia and migrated to Germany in the 1970s in search of artistic freedom, but was soon disillusioned and returned. Worked in theatre and television through the 1980s. In the 1990s associated with the anti-nationalist critical intelligentsia in Serbia. Winner of numerous awards at international feature and documentary festivals.

Selected Films

1967 *Žurnal o omladini na selu zimi/Newsreel on Village Youth in Winter* (Yugoslavia): writer, director
1967 *Pioniri maleni, mi samo vojska prava, svakog dana nicemo ko zelena trava/Little Pioneers* (Yugoslavia): writer, director
1968 *Nezaposledni ljudi/The Unemployed* (Yugoslavia): writer, director
1969 *Rani radovi/Early Works* (Yugoslavia): writer, director
1969 *Lipanjska gibanja/June Turmoil* (Yugoslavia): writer, director
1970 *Crni film/Black Film* (Yugoslavia): director
1972 *Sloboda ili strip/Freedom or Cartoons*, (Yugoslavia): director
1972 *Žene dolaze/The Women are Coming*, (Yugoslavia): director
1972 *Ustanak u Jasku/The Uprising in Jazak* (Yugoslavia): director
1972 *Öffentliche Hinrichtung/Public Execution* (Germany): director
1972 *Unter Denkmalschutz/Protected Heritage* (Germany): director
1988 *Tako se kalio čelik/How the Steel Was Tempered* (Yugoslavia): writer, director
1993 *Tito po drugi put medju srbima/Tito Among the Serbs for a Second Time* (Yugoslavia): writer, director
1995 *Dupe od mramora/Marble Ass* (Yugoslavia): writer, director
1998 *Kud plovi ovaj brod/Wanderlust* (Yugoslavia): writer, director
2000 *Tvrdjnava Evropa/Fortress Europe* (Slovenia/Italy): writer, director

Further Reading

Iordanova, Dina, *Cinema of Flames: Balkan Film, Culture and the Media*, London: British Film Institute, 2001, 96–99.
Miltojevic, Branislav, *Rani Radovi Želimira Žilnika*, Nis: Sirus, 1992.
Zelimir Zilnik Website. Available: http://www.geocities.com/zilnik_zelimir (April 4, 2002).
Steinberg, Stefan, and Anders, Ernst, Interview with the filmmaker Zelimir Zilnik. *World Socialist Web Site*. June 29, 2001. Available: http://www.wsws.org/articles/2001/jun2001/bint-j29.shtml (April 4, 2002).
Van Dyke, Willard, "Early Works: An Interview with Zelimir Zilnik," in *Grove Press International Film Festival Book*, 1970. Available: http://www.geocities.com/zilnik_zelimir (April 4, 2002).

ZONE, LA

(France, Lacombe, 1927)

La Zone. Au pays des chiffonniers/The Zone. The Rag-pickers' Country is a twenty-eight-minute documentary film about the rag-pickers and second-hand dealers of Paris. This historic trade allowed poor people to earn a meager living in the urban wasteland on the outskirts of the capital. *La Zone* belongs to the cluster of poetic documentaries with a social awareness made during the late 1920s, a dynamic period of filmmaking just before the arrival of sound film. It blends together different strands of French avant-garde, modernism, naturalism, and impressionism.

The film opens with chain mixes that set the scene and atmosphere about the "unknown places" in our midst that the viewer is about to discover. An animated map of Paris demarcates the old fortifications surrounding the city. Beyond that point is a no-man's land, a material and psychological frontier between the city and its suburbs, an uncertain zone between two worlds that is as alien to the ordinary inner city Parisian as a foreign land with unusual inhabitants. Its narrowness is visually conveyed by the opening's long shots of alleyways. What there is to discover here is the appalling living conditions of the poor in a shantytown only a stone's throw away from the last stop on the metro.

The narrative structure of *La Zone* uses the time frame of one day in the city, which is also found in other films of the period, including *Rien que les heures* (Alberto Cavalcanti, 1926) and *Berlin. Die Sinfonie der Großstadt/Berlin. Symphony of a Great City* (Walther Ruttmann, 1927). The final fade-out signals the end of the day, not the end of the story. The people who live in *La Zone* create a familiar social structure in their particular urban environment: working families, children playing, dogs and cats in alleyways, a lunch break on the job, neighbors chatting, street musicians and vendors, and the flea market, the "commercial center" of *La Zone*. What underpins this recognizable setting is a realization of how some of them make a precarious living; they recycle what richer people throw away.

The film story follows the work day of a team, a woman and two men, as they begin their collection route in the early hours of morning before the garbage trucks pick up what still has some value: glass, paper, clothes, bread. It is an efficient working team, moving rapidly along the streets, foraging in the rubbish with their bare hands, and taking away what they find in a wheeled cart. They sell what can be recycled. There is also a "lower caste" in the world of the *chiffonniers*—those who work the huge garbage piles and try to salvage what may have been missed once the trucks reach the city incinerator.

Georges Lacombe depicted a harsh reality of urban society that many would prefer to ignore altogether. He did so with empathy, the *chiffonniers* do useful work. There are also other people living in this parallel city, people who have lost everything. One is the former music hall singer, La Goulue, who has only memories to share, but who found shelter in *La Zone*.

The 1920s were a time of profound turmoil in European life and social conditions that were a consequence of years of war and revolution. It was also a time when new technologies were becoming facts of everyday life for the increasing urban masses—the radio, the automobile, the refrigerator. Despite this new way of life, old social problems and barriers persisted, aggravated by economic uncertainties and postwar migration. Poor immigrants, fleeing devastated Eastern Europe, arrived in Western Europe. Some were skilled workers, like the Polish miners who restarted the coal mines of northeastern France; but many were unskilled, and some ended up joining the small army of social outcasts living and working, surviving at the geographical and social periphery of rich Parisian *arrondissements*.

Film audiences of the 1920s were increasingly attracted to exploration and ethnographic films. The camera could renew the discovery of the world and its peoples. These films were diverse; they could introduce traditional societies, as did *Nanook of the North* (Robert Flaherty, 1923), or

La Zone, 1927.
[*Still courtesy of the British Film Institute*]

present some technological challenge and travel adventure such as *La Croisière noire* (Léon Poirier, 1926), the Citroën expedition across Africa. Some films praised the colonial empire; others introduced a documentary point of view—*Voyage au Congo* (Marc Allégret, 1927)—at a time when reporter Albert Londres published his powerful indictment of colonialism. The subtitle of *La Zone—Au pays des chiffonniers*, introduces some "foreign" locale, another "country" subtly playing on words and depicting a disquieting world of its own.

Georges Lacombe (1902–1990) was assistant director to René Clair. Like several filmmakers of his generation, he started with a short film, using basic equipment and taking advantage of his immediate urban surroundings. He looked at it with a curious and open mind. *La Zone* was his first and most accomplished essay in short documentary film, and it caught the attention of the cinematographic avant garde of the 1920s.

Other films would later explore this universe on the margins of society and often include a subtext defending those who have been abandoned or humiliated (*Aubervilliers*, Eli Lotar, 1945). *La Zone* was not a militant film but a statement of fact revealing social implications, and Lacombe benefited from the specialized infrastructure—theaters, periodicals, and ciné-clubs—put in place during the 1920s to support avant garde films.

La Zone. Au pays des chiffonniers has become a classic of the era and continues to be regularly scheduled in film retrospectives around the world. Its topic, its critical and social perspective, and its formal quality beautifully blending its realist content and impressionist images all contribute to its relevance in documentary film history, as well as in social history.

SUZANNE LANGLOIS

See also **Lacombe, Georges**

La Zone. Au pays des chiffonniers (France, 1928, 35mm, 28 min). Produced by La Société des films Charles Dullin. Directed by Georges Lacombe. Photography: Georges Périnal and D. Pierson. Filmed in Paris and its surroundings, along the city limits of the old fortifications, the municipal incinerator at Ivry, and the flea market at the Porte de Clignancourt.

Further Reading

100 Années Lumière, Paris: AFAA Intermedia, 1989.

Abel, Richard, *French Cinema: The First Wave 1915–1929*, Princeton, NJ: Princeton University Press, 1984.

Aitken, Ian, *European Film Theory and Cinema. A Critical Introduction*, Bloomington: Indiana University Press, 2001.

Bordwell, David, *French Impressionist Cinema: Film Culture, Film Theory and Film Style*, New York: Arno Press, 1980.

Dictionnaire du cinéma français des années vingt, François Albera and Jean A. Gili (eds.), in *1895 Revue de l'Association française de recherche sur l'histoire du cinéma*, 33, June 2001.

Ghali, Noureddine, *L' Avant-Garde cinématographique en France dans les années vingt*, Paris: Éditions Paris Expérimental, 1995.

INDEX

A

Aadel, Shahaboddin, 620
Abbott, Jennifer, 163
ABC. *See* American Broadcasting Company (ABC); Australian
   Broadcasting Corporation (ABC)
A.BC. Africa, 702–704
ABC of Ethnocide/ABC del Etnocidio, 759
ABC of the Strike, The/ABC da Greve, 214
Abdes-Salam, Shadi, 945
Abel Gance: The Charm of Dynamite, 2
Abel Gance: Yesterday and Tomorrow, 1, 2
Abitia, Jesùs, 876, 877
aborigines. *See* indigenous people
About Britain, 1360
About the Learning Human Being/Vom lernenden Menschen, 683
above-the-line costs, 1063
Abrahão, Benjamin, 132
Abrego, Eugenio, 207
absolute film, 110, 111
Absolute Majority/Maioria Absoluta, 133, 213
abstraction, realism and, 1084, 1085
Abyssinian Flames/Fiamme abissine, 634
Académie du Cinéma, 430
Acadia/Acadia?!?/L'Acadie/l'Acadie?!?, 131, 930, 931, 1026
Acción Chicano, 195, 197
Accordion Dreams, 442
Aces/Asse, 447
Achbar, Mark, 163, 843, 844, 1440, 1441
Achilleas, 500
Acin, Ramon, 744
Ackerman, Chantal, 68
Across the Border/Cruzando Fronteras, 196
Across the Interior of Iceland/Yfir Kjöl, 597
ACT Films Ltd., 120
acting, 4–6
Acting: Lee Strasberg and the Actors Studio, 714
activist filmmaking, 6–9
   Angela: Portrait of a Revolutionary, 40–42
   anti-pornography, 382
   Barclay, 78–80
   Bond, 119–121
   Cinema Action, 209, 210
   Film and Photo League, 394, 395
   Goldson, 479, 480
   Guzman, 515, 516
   Hell Unlimited, 539–541
   Hiroshima-Nagasaki-August 1945, 550–552
   Makavejev, 824–826
   Marxism and, 856, 857
   The Mills of the Gods, 883, 884

Mita, 887, 888
Moore, 911, 912
Near/Middle East, 942, 943
Obamsawin, 993, 994
Ogawa Productions, 997, 998
Rotha, 1134, 1135
Zilnik, 1495, 1496
Act of God, 2–4
Actualidades de Angola, 267
Actualidades de Moçambique, 267
Actualidades Militares, 267, 268
Actualidades NO-DO para Brasil, 968
Actualidades Portuguesas, 267, 268
Actualités françaises, 975
Actualités Ufa/Ufa Wereldnieuws, 961
actualities, 927–928
   Lumière, 1452–1454
   Near/Middle East, 941
   newsreels, 971
   Scandinavia, 1168
   United Kingdom, 1360
   Vertov, 1377
Adair, John, 347
Adalil, 541
Adam, Fritz, 484
Adam, Kenneth, 1403
Adamopoulos, Theodoros, 500
Adams, Ansel, 1276
Adams, Randall, 1298
Adams, Sam, 186
Adamson, Margaret Ann, 157
Addicted to Solitude, 77, 1171
Adenauer, Konrad, 1489
Adio Kerida, 794
Adolescents, The (A.K.A. That Tender Age), 6–9
Adriatic Shipyards/I cantieri dell'Adriatico, 633
Advance, Democracy!, 120, 1093, 1457
Advance of the Tanks, 1464
Adventurer, The (Sinclair), 1212
Adventures on the New Frontier, 766
advertising films, 610
Aenigma Est, 502
Aero Engine, 1356
aesthetics and documentary film: poetics, 12, 13
   Benoit-Lévy on, 109
   Grierson on, 509–512
   Heynowski and Scheumann, 547
   Junge and, 683, 684
   modernism and, 897, 898
   narration and, 929
   New Earth, 952, 953

C

INDEX

INDEX

London Video Arts, 815
London Weekend Television, 301
London Women's Film Co-Op, 392
London Women's Film Group, 403
London Workers' Film Society, 119, 1107
Lonely Boy, 261, 733, 747, 748, 816–818
   cinema verité in, 158
   reflexivity in, 1366
   scriptless film and, 948
Lonely Boys, Los, 456
Lonely Men/Uomini soli, 650
Lonely Night, The, 666
Lonely Voice of a Man, The/Odinoky Golos Cheloveka, 1232
Long, Bob, 1397
Long Distance Runner, The/Hosszú futásodra mindig számithatunk, 463
Long Goodbye, The, 1088
Longinotto, Kim, 820, 821, 1216, 1217
Long Night's Journey into Day, 597, 598–600
long takes, 1232, 1233
Long Tan: The True Story, 818, 819
Look at Life, 216, 984
Look at This City/Schaut auf diese Stadt, 461
Look Back in Anger, 916, 1374, 1380
Look Back in Anger (Osborne), 366
Looking at a Painting, 1142
Looking for Langston, 694, 695, 821–823
Looking for Love, 399
Look into This City/Schaut auf dises Stadt, 471
Loon's Necklace, The, 156
Lopes, Fernando, 1065
Lopez, Ana, 1315
López, Leobardo, 891
Lopez, M. Georges, 363
Lord, Kate, 756
Lord, Russell, 756
Lorde, Audre, 400
L'or des mers, 351, 352
Lord of the Bush, 59
Lords of Little Egypt, 1505
Lord's Tale, The, 1377
Lorentz, Pare, 823–826
   The City, 227
   Dyke and, 316
   Flaherty and, 424
   influence of, 1048, 1049
   The Land, 756
   The Plow That Broke the Plains, 1048–1051
   poetics and, 13
   The River, 1129–1131
   spoken commentary and, 1269
   workers movements and, 1335
Loreto Square/Piazzale Loreto, 651
Loridan, Marcelline, 376, 656, 657
Lorraine Steel Heart/Lorraine coeur d'acier, 440
Losev, 737
Losey, Joseph, 664
Los Olvidados, 760
Lost, Lost, Lost, 1114
Lost Boundaries, 1134
Lost Continent/Continento perduto, 650
Lost Freedom/Verlorene Freiheit, 1508
Lost Horizon (Hilton), 797
Lost in La Mancha, 145
Lost Patrol, The, 1144

Lost Tribe, The, 602
Lotar, Eli, 55, 56, 437, 758, 760, 1286
Loud, Lance, 34, 576, 577
Loud, Pat, 34
Loud family, 33–35, 576, 577
Louis, Joe, 1271
Louisiana Story, 326, 424, 779, 826–828, 1016
Lounsbury, Ruth Ozeki, 69
Lourdes et ses Miracles, 1156
Love, 1498
Love, Women and Flowers/Amor, Mujeres Y Flores, 1135
*Love Affair or the Case of the Missing Switchboard Operator/
   Ljubavni slucaj ili tragedija sluzbenice PTT*, 838, 839
Love and Kisses from Bangkok/Bons baisers de Bangkok, 842
Love at Twenty, 10
Love Exists. See L'Amour Existe
Love I Am Leaving I & II, The/Laská, kterou opoustím I & II, 1265
Love Is a Funny Thing/Un homme qui me plaît, 786, 787
Love/Laska, 257
Lovely May, The. See Joli Mai, Le
Love Meetings/Comizi d'amore, 652
Loves of a Blonde/Lasky Jedne Plavovlasky, 256
Love Tapes, The, 1114
Loving Couples/Älskande par, 1506
Low, Colin, 828, 829
   Challenge for Change, 159
   City of Gold, 229–231
   Daly and, 261
   Labyrinth pavilion, 159
   Transitions, 602
   Unit B, 158
   Unit B and, 1366
Low, Stephen, 163
Lowe, David, 229
Lower the Sails/Les voiles bas et en travers, 1040
Lowlands/Tiefland, 1342
Loyalties, 950
Lozinski, Marcel, 829, 830, 1058, 1059
Lucanian Magic/Magia lucana, 649
Lucas, George, 319
Lucasfilm, Ltd., 319
LUCE. *See* L'Unione Cinematografica Educativa (LUCE)
Luce, Henry, 859, 1321
Luchian, 1142
Lucic, Karen, 854
Lucky to Be Born in Russia/Povezlo roditsia v Rossii, 491
Ludwig van Beethoven, 470
Ludwig Wittgenstein, 64
Lukacs, Georg, 189, 191
Lukas, George, 1344
Lullaby, 1393
Lulu in Berlin, 781
Lumber, 1369
Lumière and Company, 832
Lumière brothers, 830–833
   acting and, 4
   in Canada, 154
   ethnography and, 66
   in French film, 435
   in Ireland, 636
   Langlois and, 764
   Near/Middle East films, 955
   newsreels, 985
   in Romania, 1140
   shorts by, 1466–1468

INDEX